Historical Statistics OF Black America

Historical Statistics O̲F̲ Black America

Agriculture t̲o̲ *Labor & Employment*

Compiled & Edited by

Jessie Carney Smith • *Fisk University*

and

Carrell Peterson Horton • *Fisk University*

Gale Research Inc.

An International Thomson Publishing Company

I(T)P

NEW YORK • LONDON • BONN • BOSTON • DETROIT • MADRID
MELBOURNE • MEXICO CITY • PARIS • SINGAPORE • TOKYO
TORONTO • WASHINGTON • ALBANY NY • BELMONT CA • CINCINNATI OH

Jessie Carney Smith and Carrell Peterson Horton, *Editors*

Gale Research Inc. Staff
Mary Beth Trimper, *Production Director*
Mary Kelley, *Production Assistant*

Cynthia Baldwin, *Product Design Manager*
Sherrell Hobbs, *Desktop Publisher*
Pamela Galbreath, *Cover Design*

Editorial Code and Data Inc. Staff
Nancy Ratliff, Sherae Carroll, *Data Entry*
Gary Alampi, *Data Processing*

Library of Congress Cataloging-in-Publication Data

Historical statistics of black america: compiled and edited by Jessie Carney Smith and
Carrell Peterson Horton.
    p.   cm.
    Includes bibliographical references (p.) and index.
    ISBN 0-8103-8542-2 : $125.00. -- ISBN 0-8103-9391-3 (v. 1). --
ISBN 0-8103-9392-1 (v. 2)
    1. Afro-Americans--History--Statistics.   I. Smith, Jessie Carney.
II. Horton, Carrell.
E185.H543   1995
973'.0496073'021--dc20   94-29718
                                                                CIP

∞ This book is printed on acid-free paper that meets the minimum requirements of American National Standard for Information
Sciences—Permanence Paper for Printed Library Materials, ANSI Z39.48-1984.

Library of Congress Catalog Card Number 94-29718
ISBN 0-8103-8542-2
Vol 1 ISBN 0-8103-9391-3

Printed in the United States of America
Published simultaneously in the United Kingdom
by Gale Research International Limited
(An affiliated company of Gale Research Inc.)

I(T)P™   Gale Research Inc., an International Thomson Publishing Company.
          ITP logo is a trademark under license.

10 9 8 7 6 5 4 3 2 1

TABLE OF CONTENTS

CHAPTER 1 - AGRICULTURE continued:

CHAPTER 1 - AGRICULTURE continued:

CHAPTER 1 - AGRICULTURE continued:

CHAPTER 1 - AGRICULTURE continued:

CHAPTER 1 - AGRICULTURE continued:

CHAPTER 1 - AGRICULTURE continued:

CHAPTER 1 - AGRICULTURE continued:

CHAPTER 1 - AGRICULTURE continued:

CHAPTER 2 - BUSINESS AND ECONOMICS continued:

CHAPTER 2 - BUSINESS AND ECONOMICS continued:

CHAPTER 3 - CRIME, LAW ENFORCEMENT, AND LEGAL JUSTICE continued:

CHAPTER 3 - CRIME, LAW ENFORCEMENT, AND LEGAL JUSTICE continued:

CHAPTER 4 - EDUCATION continued:

CHAPTER 4 - EDUCATION continued:

CHAPTER 4 - EDUCATION continued:

CHAPTER 4 - EDUCATION continued:

CHAPTER 4 - EDUCATION continued:

CHAPTER 4 - EDUCATION continued:

CHAPTER 4 - EDUCATION continued:

CHAPTER 4 - EDUCATION continued:

CHAPTER 4 - EDUCATION continued:

CHAPTER 4 - EDUCATION continued:

CHAPTER 4 - EDUCATION continued:

CHAPTER 5 - THE FAMILY continued:

CHAPTER 5 - THE FAMILY continued:

CHAPTER 5 - THE FAMILY continued:

CHAPTER 7 - HOUSING continued:

CHAPTER 9 - LABOR AND EMPLOYMENT continued:

CHAPTER 9 - LABOR AND EMPLOYMENT continued:

CHAPTER 9 - LABOR AND EMPLOYMENT continued:

CHAPTER 14 - POPULATION continued:

CHAPTER 14 - POPULATION continued:

CHAPTER 14 - POPULATION continued:

CHAPTER 14 - POPULATION continued:

CHAPTER 14 - POPULATION continued:

CHAPTER 14 - POPULATION continued:

CHAPTER 14 - POPULATION continued:

CHAPTER 16 - RELIGION continued:

CHAPTER 16 - RELIGION continued:

CHAPTER 19 - VITAL STATISTICS continued:

CHAPTER 19 - VITAL STATISTICS continued:

INTRODUCTION

Historical Statistics of Black America is a work that should have enormous value as a practical resource for those who seek a chronology of the condition, status, and experiences of African Americans. Tables and text reports in this volume begin with information recorded in the eighteenth century and extend through 1975. Although some of the tables in the *Statistical Record of Black America* companion series contain historical information, the majority of the material included here represents a uniquely different presentation than those works. This volume also is somewhat different in the areas that are included and in the quantity of information available in the various areas. It was, for example, necessary to add a separate chapter on agriculture, reflecting the importance of agricultural pursuits to African Americans in earlier times. In contrast, there is less recorded information on African-American business or African Americans in sports, and even somewhat less information on the health of AfricanAmericans. The careful user can thus compare the contents of this volume with those in the *Statistical Record of Black America* and gain insight and understanding of the general context of African-American life from the time of slavery to the present.

Beyond its usefulness as a chronological record, *Historical Statistics of Black America* can be a revelation. It is one thing to know that slavery existed, was abolished, and led to new and different challenges, problems, and opportunities for African Americans and for society. It is quite another to note the social context in which all of this occurred. The reader may be surprised at what tables on lynchings reveal about its frequency over the years and the "reasons" for which it occurred. The reader who pays attention to the tables as they were titled in the original sources can follow along various designations given to the subjects of this volume, from "colored" to "Negro" to "black" to today's "African-American."

One particularly interesting aspect of assembling material for this volume was related to the sources of the material. Much of the information came, as has been the case with the *Statistical Record of Black America* series, from U.S. government publications, but a significant amount of material came from publications originating at African-American institutions or from African-American authors. The amount of information obtained from *The Negro Year Book* (initially published at Tuskegee Institute) and *The Negro Handbook* (edited by Florence Murray) is quite astounding. In many instances, these publications used U.S. government data as their starting point and then added new analyses which greatly increased the usefulness of the information. In addition, they often collected data on aspects of African-American life and issues confronting African Americans that other publications had not yet begun to consider. In material available to the editors, for example, the earliest record of African-American achievements in sports was found in issues of *The Negro Handbook.*

Interpreting the Data

There is an inherent risk in compiling any historical record. Unless there have been periodic compilations at previous intervals, the age of original source documents will in some cases lead researchers to very fragile documents. Such was the case here. Volumes published originally in the 1800s clearly showed their age in the fragility of their pages and in some instances in the figures they presented. This volume presents such material as it was found.

We have made every effort to assure that figures presented are accurate and that there is consistency between column and row categories and totals. There are still, however, a few instances in which inconsistencies could not be resolved and in which row or column figures do not sum to the exact total that is printed. Percent totals may also fail to sum to exactly 100 because of rounding procedures used in original sources. The differences are in all instances minor.

Acknowledgments

The editors are deeply appreciative of the cooperation of those individuals and organizations that gave us access to this vast store of information and permission to reproduce it here. Our gratitude is also extended to those who helped us compile, assemble, and organize a volume that we hope will be as useful and interesting to readers as it has been to us. For their assistance in photocopying massive amounts of materials, we give thanks to Vallie Pursley of Tennessee State University and her family, Tobey and Yolanda Pursley. To our colleagues at Fisk University we thank library staff members Jackie London for helping to locate information and Dixie Jernigan and Sharon Williams for copying tables. We also wish to thank Robert L. Johns of the Fisk faculty for recommending sources. President Henry Ponder of Fisk University continued his support of our research and publication, and we express our kind appreciation to him. For their guidance, patience, support, and magnificent layout of the tables we thank our Gale editors James E. Person, Jr., Sandra C. Davis, and Kathryn Horste.

Carrell Peterson Horton

Jessie Carney Smith

Historical
Statistics
OF Black
America

Chapter 1
AGRICULTURE

Agricultural Training

★ 1 ★

Organizations: New Farmers of America, 1951

"A national system of awards for outstanding achievement in farming is made possible by the future farmers of America Foundation, which receives its funds by grants from business and industrial firms. In 1951, the NFA had $9,196.68 available for farming awards to worthy Negro farm boys."

Source: [Untitled text], *1952 Negro Year Book: A Review of Events Affecting Negro Life.* 1952, p. 112. Primary source: Guzman, Jessie Parkhurst (Ed.), *1952 Negro Year Book: A Review of Events Affecting Negro Life.* New York. Wm. H. Wise & Co., Inc., 1952.

★ 2 ★

Agricultural Training

Schools: Summary Characteristics of Agricultural Schools, c. 1916 - I

School groups	Number of schools	Pupils		Teachers		Acres of land	
		Total	Above elementary grade	Total	Of agriculture	Owned	Cultivated
Total	85	21,462	6,232	1,838	115	23,940	10,929
Schools supported largely by public funds	29	7,988	3,614	619	49	5,974	2,675
Land-grant schools	16[1]	5,175	2,298	400	39	4,812	1,981
State schools	13	2,813	1,316	219	10	1,162	694
Schools supported largely by private funds	56	13,474	2,618	1,219	66	17,966	8,254
Large schools offering 4-year courses in agriculture	2	2,100	716	394	30	3,270	1,636
Smaller schools offering some class theory and farm practice	22	4,380	572	376	25	8,695	2,970
Schools offering class theory but farming on commercial basis	18	4,807	795	298	11	4,111	2,115
Schools giving no instruction, but farming on a commercial basis	14	2,187	535	151	...	1,890	1,533

Source: "Summary of Agricultural Schools," *Negro Education: A Study of the Private and Higher Schools for Colored People in the United States,* vol. 1. Bulletin, 1916, No. 38, 1917, pp. 103-104. Primary source: U.S. Office of Education. *Negro Education: A Study of the Private and Higher Schools for Colored People in the United States,* vol. I. Bulletin, 1916, No. 38. Washington, D.C.: Government Printing Office, 1917. *Note:* 1. Hampton is grouped with the private institutions below.

★ 3 ★

Agricultural Training

Schools: Summary Characteristics of Agricultural Schools, c. 1916 - II

School groups	Value of agricultural plant			Total income
	Total	Land	Buildings, equipment, and live stock	
Total	$1,766,557	$1,431,967	$334,590	$2,013,155
Schools supported largely by public funds	542,093	409,950	132,143	828,073
Land-grant schools[1]	395,660	290,350	105,310	543,623
State schools	146,433	119,600	26,833	284,450
Schools supported largely by private funds	1,224,464	1,022,017	202,447	1,185,082
Large schools offering 4-year courses in agriculture	364,979	215,000	149,979	557,444
Smaller schools offering some class theory and farm practice	221,343	168,875	52,468	304,669
Schools offering class theory but farming on commercial basis	260,292	260,292	...	229,161
Schools giving no instruction, but farming on a commercial basis	377,850	377,850	...	93,808

Source: "Summary of Agricultural Schools," *Negro Education: A Study of the Private and Higher Schools for Colored People in the United States,* vol. 1. Bulletin, 1916, No. 38, 1917, pp. 103-104. Primary source: U.S. Office of Education. *Negro Education: A Study of the Private and Higher Schools for Colored People in the United States,* vol. I. Bulletin, 1916, No. 38. Washington, D.C.: Government Printing Office, 1917. *Note:* 1. Hampton is grouped with the private institutions below.

Crops/Livestock/Animals

★ 4 ★

Animals: Dairy Cows, Work Horses, and Work Mules on Southern Farms by Owner Status, 1910

TENURE	Colored	White	Percentage distribution by tenure		Average per 100 farms (All farms)	
			Colored	White	Colored	White
DAIRY COWS						
Total	929,883	4,758,485	100.0	100.0	104	216
Owners, free	211,318	2,315,071	22.7	48.7	164	255
Owners, mortgaged	79,950	659,945	8.6	13.9	171	268
Part owners	62,962	417,127	6.8	8.8	146	243
Cash tenants[1]	308,757	416,294	33.2	8.7	108	181
Share tenants[2]	264,089	885,859	28.4	18.6	69	139
Managers	2,807	64,189	0.3	1.3	234	426

[Continued]

★ 4 ★

Animals: Dairy Cows, Work Horses, and Work Mules on Southern Farms by Owner Status, 1910

[Continued]

TENURE	Colored	White	Percentage distribution by tenure		Average per 100 farms (All farms)	
			Colored	White	Colored	White
WORK HORSES						
Total	509,087	3,564,855	100.0	100.0	57	161
Owners, free	130,102	1,528,189	25.6	42.9	101	168
Owners, mortgaged	46,272	546,570	9.1	15.3	99	222
Part owners	41,715	368,390	8.2	10.3	97	214
Cash tenants[1]	141,798	301,721	27.9	8.5	50	131
Share tenants[2]	146,815	747,712	28.8	21.0	38	117
Managers	2,385	72,273	0.5	2.0	199	479
WORK MULES						
Total	645,320	2,188,166	100.0	100.0	72	99
Owners, free	82,998	855,973	12.9	39.1	65	94
Owners, mortgaged	44,446	296,726	6.9	13.6	95	121
Part owners	37,307	205,911	5.8	9.4	86	120
Cash tenants[1]	246,934	216,728	38.3	9.9	86	94
Share tenants[2]	231,263	547,085	35.8	25.0	60	86
Managers	2,372	65,743	0.4	3.0	198	436

Source: "Number of Animals on Farms in the South: 1910," *Negro Population, 1790- 1915,* 1918, p. 580. Primary source: U.S. Bureau of the Census. *Negroes in the United States, 1790-1915.* Washington, D.C.: U.S. Government Printing Office, 1918. *Notes:* "Colored" may include persons other than Black. 1. Includes not specified tenure. 2. Includes share-cash tenants.

★ 5 ★

Crops/Livestock/Animals

Animals: Domestic Animals on Farms – Value by Region, 1910

CLASS OF ANIMAL	Aggregate			Average per farm		Of total, percentage on colored farms
	Total	Colored farms	White farms	Colored farms	White farms	
UNITED STATES						
Total	$4,760,060,093	$199,095,103	$4,560,964,990	$216.20	$838.32	4.2
Neat cattle	1,499,523,607	39,475,839	1,460,047,768	42.87	268.36	2.6
Horses	2,083,588,195	58,190,838	2,025,397,357	63.19	372.27	2.8
Mules	525,391,863	85,128,116	440,263,747	92.44	80.92	16.2
Sheep	232,841,585	2,545,227	230,296,358	2.76	42.33	1.1
Swine	399,338,308	13,152,267	386,186,041	14.28	70.98	3.3
Asses and burros	13,200,112	228,630	12,971,482	0.25	2.38	1.7
Goats	6,176,423	374,186	5,802,237	0.41	1.07	6.1

[Continued]

★ 5 ★

Animals: Domestic Animals on Farms – Value by Region, 1910
[Continued]

CLASS OF ANIMAL	Aggregate			Average per farm		Of total, percentage on colored farms
	Total	Colored farms	White farms	Colored farms	White farms	
THE SOUTH						
Total	$1,284,298,714	$177,461,964	$1,106,836,750	$199.36	$501.42	13.8
Neat cattle	368,180,311	33,028,881	335,151,430	37.11	151.83	9.0
Horses	422,048,624	47,537,525	374,511,099	53.40	169.66	11.3
Mules	378,258,226	84,127,172	294,131,054	94.51	133.25	22.2
Sheep	25,611,834	200,128	25,411,706	0.22	11.51	0.8
Swine	81,017,335	12,331,574	68,685,761	13.85	31.12	15.2
Asses and burros	5,963,005	176,400	5,786,605	0.20	2.62	3.0
Goats	3,219,379	60,284	3,159,095	0.07	1.43	1.9
THE NORTH AND WEST						
Total	$3,475,761,379	$21,633,139	$3,454,128,240	$703.70	$1,068.33	0.6
Neat cattle	1,131,343,296	6,446,958	1,124,896,338	209.71	347.92	0.6
Horses	1,661,539,571	10,653,313	1,650,886,258	346.54	510.60	0.6
Mules	147,133,637	1,000,944	146,132,693	43.56	45.20	0.7
Sheep	207,229,751	2,345,099	204,884,652	76.28	63.37	1.1
Swine	318,320,973	820,693	317,500,280	26.70	98.20	0.3
Asses and burros	7,237,107	52,230	7,184,877	1.70	2.22	0.7
Goats	2,957,044	313,902	2,643,142	10.21	0.82	10.6

Source: "Value of Domestic Animals on Farms: 1910," *Negro Population, 1790-1915*, 1918, p. 563. Primary source: U.S. Bureau of the Census. *Negro Population, 1790-1915.* Washington, D.C.: Government Printing Office, 1918. *Note:* "Colored" may include persons other than Black.

★ 6 ★

Crops/Livestock/Animals

Animals: Farms with and without Specified Animals by Region, 1900 and 1910

CLASS OF ANIMAL	Colored farms				White farms: 1910	
	Reporting		Not reporting		Reporting	Not reporting
	1910	1900	1910	1900		
UNITED STATES						
Neat cattle	570,068	412,201	350,815	355,563	4,714,848	725,771
Dairy cows	524,535	348,857	396,348	418,907	4,616,334	824,285
Horses	360,708	360,557	560,175	407,207	4,332,106	1,108,513
Mules	444,877	350,567	476,006	417,197	1,424,128	4,016,491
Sheep	6,743	6,802	914,140	760,962	604,151	4,836,468
Swine	612,069	521,207	308,814	246,557	3,739,682	1,700,937

[Continued]

★ 6 ★

Animals: Farms with and without Specified Animals by Region, 1900 and 1910
[Continued]

CLASS OF ANIMAL	Colored farms				White farms: 1910	
	Reporting		Not reporting			
	1910	1900	1910	1900	Reporting	Not reporting
THE SOUTH						
Neat cattle	551,940	397,314	338,201	343,356	1,874,362	333,044
Dairy cows	512,242	337,870	377,899	402,800	1,822,363	385,043
Horses	334,537	337,129	555,604	403,541	1,427,122	770,284
Mules	441,178	346,771	448,963	393,899	1,037,204	1,170,202
Sheep	3,386	5,365	886,755	735,305	180,908	2,026,498
Swine	602,090	509,495	288,051	231,175	1,628,751	578,655
THE NORTH AND WEST						
Neat cattle	18,128	14,887	12,614	12,207	2,840,486	392,727
Dairy cows	12,293	10,987	18,449	16,107	2,793,971	439,242
Horses	26,171	23,428	4,571	3,666	2,894,984	338,229
Mules	3,669	3,796	27,043	23,298	386,924	2,846,289
Sheep	3,357	1,437	27,385	25,657	423,243	2,809,970
Swine	9,979	11,712	20,763	15,382	2,110,931	1,122,282

Source: "Farms Reporting and Not Reporting Animals of Class Specified," *Negro Population, 1790-1915*, 1918, p. 562. Primary source: U.S. Bureau of the Census. *Negro Population, 1790-1915*. Washington, D.C.: Government Printing Office, 1918. *Note:* "Colored" may include persons other than Black.

★ 7 ★

Crops/Livestock/Animals

Animals: Horses and Mules on Black Farms – Value by Farm Location, 1930

[Colored farmers include Negroes, Indians, Chinese, Japanese, and all other nonwhite races].

DIVISION AND STATE	Total number of horses and mules	NUMBER		VALUE		AVERAGE VALUE PER HEAD	
		Horses	Mules	Horses	Mules	Horses	Mules
The South	1,247,749	320,750	926,999	$19,032,769	$81,306,636	$59,34	$87.71
SOUTH ATLANTIC	371,389	79,813	291,576	6,437,466	30,602,643	80.66	104.96
Delaware	1,832	1,201	631	114,683	75,670	95.49	119.92
Maryland	10,397	7,739	2,658	788,759	326,456	101.92	122.82
District of Columbia	7	7	...	753	...	107.61	...
Virginia	51,517	28,120	23,397	2,335,085	2,596,833	83.04	110.90
West Virginia	589	534	55	48,055	5,101	89.99	92.74
North Carolina	94,909	14,691	80,218	1,185,270	9,255,553	80.68	115.38
South Carolina	85,167	13,450	71,717	966,114	7,293,619	71.83	101.70
Georgia	114,584	9,009	105,575	612,972	10,272,448	68.04	97.30
Florida	12,387	5,062	7,325	385,775	776,963	76.21	106.07
EAST SOUTH CENTRAL	394,730	93,721	301,009	5,980,369	27,718,619	63.81	92.09
Kentucky	12,509	6,239	6,270	423,940	543,546	67.95	86.69
Tennessee	52,289	17,702	34,587	1,154,347	3,123,898	65.21	90.32
Alabama	123,699	22,584	101,115	1,521,710	9,858,713	67.38	97.50

[Continued]

★ 7 ★

Animals: Horses and Mules on Black Farms – Value by Farm Location, 1930

[Continued]

DIVISION AND STATE	Total number of horses and mules	NUMBER		VALUE		AVERAGE VALUE PER HEAD	
		Horses	Mules	Horses	Mules	Horses	Mules
Mississippi	206,233	47,196	159,037	2,880,372	14,192,462	61.03	89.24
WEST SOUTH CENTRAL	481,630	147,216	334,414	6,614,934	22,985,374	44.93	68.73
Arkansas	118,474	19,825	98,649	870,912	6,782,119	43.93	68.75
Louisiana	111,167	39,229	71,938	2,092,475	5,534,910	53.34	76.94
Oklahoma	69,531	36,727	32,804	1,449,615	1,866,220	39.47	56.89
Texas	182,458	51,435	131,023	2,201,932	8,802,125	42.81	67.18
SELECTED NORTHERN STATES[1]	21,631	12,517	9,114	891,368	709,509	71.21	77.85
New Jersey	663	584	79	68,211	9,531	116.80	120.65
Pennsylvania	705	592	113	68,483	14,571	115.68	128.95
Ohio	2,585	2,383	202	244,258	21,283	102.50	105.36
Indiana	1,043	764	279	61,105	24,515	79.98	87.87
Illinois	2,274	1,121	1,153	83,055	100,461	74.09	87.13
Missouri	10,343	3,985	6,358	219,175	478,948	55.00	75.33
Kansas	4,018	3,088	930	147,081	60,169	47.63	64.73

Source: "Number and Value of Horses and Mules on Farms of Colored Operators, by Southern Divisions, and States, and Selected Northern States: 1930," *Negroes in the United States, 1920-1932*, 1935, p. 590. Primary source: U.S. Bureau of the Census. *Negroes in the United States, 1920-1932.* Washington, D.C.: U.S. Government Printing Office, 1935. *Notes:* "Colored" may include persons other than Black. 1. States having 200 or more Negro farmers who constitute 90 percent or more of the colored farmers in the State.

★ 8 ★

Crops/Livestock/Animals

Animals: Number "Mature" Animals on Farms by Region, 1910

CLASS OF ANIMAL	Number of animals		Value of animals		Value per head		
	Colored farms	White farms	Colored farms	White farms	Colored farms	White farms	White excess
UNITED STATES							
Dairy cows	969,685	19,655,747	$22,240,132	$683,996,175	$22.94	$34.80	$11.86
Work horses	649,907	16,780,511	54,942,151	1,903,612,666	84.54	113.44	28.90
Work mules	653,576	3,133,740	84,451,579	413,530,751	129.21	131.96	2.75
Sheep	751,068	38,892,978	2,141,579	201,374,565	2.85	5.18	2.33
Hogs	2,184,943	32,949,154	11,090,162	341,067,796	5.08	10.35	5.27
THE SOUTH							
Dairy cows	929,893	4,758,485	$20,803,304	$130,043,230	$22.37	$27.33	$4.96
Work horses	509,091	3,564,855	45,880,457	350,100,726	90.12	98.21	8.09
Work mules	645,321	2,188,166	83,514,577	282,108,899	129.42	128.92	0.50[1]
Sheep	45,867	4,683,109	146,398	19,131,062	3.19	4.09	0.90
Hogs	2,117,916	10,266,535	10,376,574	59,389,940	4.90	5.78	0.88
THE NORTH AND WEST							
Dairy cows	39,792	14,897,262	$1,436,828	$553,952,946	$36.11	$37.18	$1.07

[Continued]

★ 8 ★

Animals: Number "Mature" Animals on Farms by Region, 1910

[Continued]

CLASS OF ANIMAL	Number of animals		Value of animals		Value per head		
	Colored farms	White farms	Colored farms	White farms	Colored farms	White farms	White excess
Work horses	140,816	13,215,656	9,061,694	1,553,511,940	64.35	117.55	53.20
Work mules	8,255	945,574	937,602	131,421,852	113.51	138.99	25.48
Sheep	705,201	34,209,869	1,995,181	182,243,503	2.83	5.33	2.50
Hogs	67,027	22,682,619	713,588	281,677,856	10.65	12.42	1.77

Source: "Mature Animals on Farms: 1910," *Negro Population, 1790-1915*, 1918, p. 563. Primary source: U.S. Bureau of the Census. *Negro Population, 1790-1915*. Washington, D.C.: Government Printing Office, 1918. *Notes:* "Colored" may include persons other than Black. 1. Colored excess.

★ 9 ★

Crops/Livestock/Animals

Animals: Percentage Distribution of Animals on Black Farms by Region, 1900 and 1910

CLASS OF ANIMAL	The South			The North and West		
	Of colored farms		Of white farms:	Of colored farms		Of white farms:
	1910	1900	1910	1910	1900	1910
Neat cattle	62.0	53.6	84.9	59.0	54.9	87.9
Dairy cows	57.5	45.6	82.6	40.0	40.6	86.4
Horses	37.6	45.5	65.1	85.1	86.5	89.5
Mules	49.6	46.8	47.0	12.0	14.0	12.0
Sheep	0.4	0.7	8.2	10.9	5.3	13.1
Swine	67.6	68.8	73.8	32.5	43.2	65.3

Source: "Percentage Reporting Animals of Class Specified," *Negro Population, 1790-1915*, 1918, p. 562. Primary source: U.S. Bureau of the Census. *Negro Population, 1790-1915*. Washington, D.C.: Government Printing Office, 1918. *Note:* "Colored" may include persons other than Black.

★ 10 ★

Crops/Livestock/Animals

Animals: Total (and per 100 Farms) Specified Animals on Black Farms by Region, 1910

DIVISION AND CLASS OF ANIMAL	Number of farms	Reporting specified class of animal				Number not reporting specified class of animal
		Number of farms	Animals reported			
			Aggregate	Per 100 farms	Per 100 farms reporting	
The South	890,141	...	...	...	...	...
Dairy cows	...	512,242	929,883	104	182	377,899
Work horses	...	332,370	509,087	57	153	557,771
Work mules	...	436,398	645,320	72	148	453,743
South Atlantic	355,862	...	...	...	...	...
Dairy cows	...	189,758	285,141	80	150	166,104
Work horses	...	108,252	140,394	39	130	247,610
Work mules	...	166,050	221,694	62	134	189,812
East South Central	325,218	...	...	...	...	...
Dairy cows	...	203,679	358,406	110	176	121,539
Work horses	...	113,134	158,346	49	140	212,084
Work mules	...	170,094	248,161	76	146	155,124
West South Central	209,061	...	...	...	...	...
Dairy cows	...	118,805	286,336	137	241	90,256
Work horses	...	110,984	210,347	101	190	98,077
Work mules	...	100,254	175,465	84	175	108,807

Source: "Farms Operated by Colored Farmers: 1910," *Negro Population, 1790-1915,* 1918, p. 564. Primary source: U.S. Bureau of the Census. *Negro Population, 1790-1915.* Washington, D.C.: Government Printing Office, 1918. *Note:* "Colored" may include persons other than Black.

★ 11 ★

Crops/Livestock/Animals

Crops: Acreage Crop Yield and Value on Black Southern Farms, 1909

CROP	Unit of measure	Average yield of crop		Average value of crop	
		Per farm reporting	Per acre planted	Per farm reporting	Per acre planted
Cotton	Bales	5.9	0.3	$394.13	$22.31
Corn	Bushels	127.4	12.9	103.32	10.43
Cottonseed	Tons	3.0	0.2	68.74	3.89
Tobacco	Pounds	2,576.7	645.4	231.06	57.87
Sweet potatoes	Bushels	40.7	72.5	25.32	45.11
Hay and forage	Tons	[1]	1.0	[1]	10.68
Peanuts	Bushels	65.0	21.5	61.51	20.31
Oats	Bushels	53.3	13.5	33.32	8.47

[Continued]

★ 11 ★

Crops: Acreage Crop Yield and Value on Black Southern Farms, 1909

[Continued]

CROP	Unit of measure	Average yield of crop		Average value of crop	
		Per farm reporting	Per acre planted	Per farm reporting	Per acre planted
Potatoes	Bushels	35.1	67.8	24.62	47.56
Wheat	Bushels	50.1	9.0	53.07	9.49
Dry peas	Bushels	14.2	3.6	23.81	6.10
Rice	Bushels	179.0	30.4	136.41	23.18
Alfalfa	Tons	10.2	1.8	146.62	25.99
Rye	Bushels	24.9	7.3	22.73	6.69
Dry edible beans	Bushels	7.7	5.9	12.89	9.93
Kraft corn	Bushels	68.2	11.9	39.36	6.86
Soy beans	Bushels	55.7	10.0	70.70	12.72
Broom corn	Pounds	671.2	238.0	39.19	13.89
Buckwheat	Bushels	41.4	11.1	25.80	6.94
Barley	Bushels	40.4	20.5	29.49	14.97

Source: "Colored Farms in the South: 1909," *Negro Population, 1790-1915,* 1918, p. 566. Primary source: U.S. Bureau of the Census. *Negroes in the United States, 1790-1915.* Washington, D.C.: U.S. Government Printing Office, 1918. *Notes:* "Colored" may include persons other than Black. 1. Data not available.

★ 12 ★

Crops/Livestock/Animals

Crops: Acreage in Selected Crops on Southern Black Farms by Division and State, 1899 and 1909, Part 1

DIVISION AND STATE	ACRES IN SPECIFIED CROPS ON FARMS OF COLORED FARMER									
	CORN		COTTON		HAY AND FORAGE		OATS		POTATOES	
	1909	1899	1909	1899	1909	1899	1909	1899	1909	1899
THE SOUTH	7,377,221	6,993,999	12,096,638	9,656,262	468,581	316,528	321,960	261,982	50,680	30,308
South Atlantic	3,066,496	2,855,482	4,442,773	3,005,870	189,680	105,189	213,778	152,717	29,508	15,839
East South Central	2,309,639	2,387,838	4,614,109	3,870,339	137,315	68,645	69,132	53,774	9,077	7,314
West South Central	2,001,086	1,750,679	3,039,526	2,780,283	141,586	142,694	39,050	55,491	12,095	7,155
South Atlantic:										
Delaware	12,636	11,055	...	...	2,621	2,237	81	98	491	264
Maryland	52,139	54,476	...	...	8,799	6,675	822	1,093	1,865	1,223
District of Columbia	2	16	...	...	...	20	...	3	4	9
Virginia	338,378	327,566	13,362	11,937	36,027	28,928	18,021	26,492	16,501	6,535
West Virginia	4,421	5,103	...	...	1,804	1,883	287	365	98	150
North Carolina	535,037	537,044	474,889	321,654	48,915	16,170	22,761	25,864	3,401	2,094
South Carolina	653,856	688,000	1,364,375	1,021,700	45,055	29,217	80,443	44,458	2,424	2,669
Georgia	1,278,627	1,051,877	2,468,242	1,544,897	39,375	17,139	82,401	49,545	3,197	1,960
Florida	191,400	180,345	121,905	105,682	7,084	2,920	8,962	4,799	1,527	935
East South Central:										
Kentucky	104,055	108,911	2,937	135	11,703	12,492	3,024	5,818	905	655
Tennessee	354,996	365,264	387,527	308,333	43,900	26,884	12,891	7,351	2,490	1,874

[Continued]

★ 12 ★

Crops: Acreage in Selected Crops on Southern Black Farms by Division and State, 1899 and 1909, Part I
[Continued]

DIVISION AND STATE	ACRES IN SPECIFIED CROPS ON FARMS OF COLORED FARMER									
	CORN		COTTON		HAY AND FORAGE		OATS		POTATOES	
	1909	1899	1909	1899	1909	1899	1909	1899	1909	1899
Alabama	818,175	854,877	1,960,709	1,644,079	35,593	12,621	37,648	27,452	2,830	2,501
Mississippi	1,032,413	1,058,786	2,263,166	1,917,562	46,119	16,648	15,569	13,153	2,852	2,284
West South Central:										
Arkansas	386,913	359,981	949,734	700,351	16,456	10,710	6,699	12,135	2,678	2,263
Louisiana	505,431	450,501	514,352	784,216	14,077	6,646	3,235	3,952	3,586	1,600
Oklahoma[1]	369,818	254,095	217,231	90,262	92,610	108,414	20,105	20,418	3,267	1,497
Texas	738,924	686,102	1,358,209	1,205,454	18,443	16,924	9,011	18,986	2,564	1,795

Source: "Acreage in Selected Crops on Colored Farms of the South, by Divisions and States: 1909 and 1899," *Negro Population, 1790-1915*, 1918, p. 601. Primary source: U.S. Bureau of the Census. *Negroes in the United States, 1790-1915*. Washington, D.C.: U.S. Government Printing Office, 1918. *Note:* 1. Includes Indian Territory for 1899.

★ 13 ★

Crops/Livestock/Animals

Crops: Acreage in Selected Crops on Southern Black Farms by Division and State, 1899 and 1909, Part II

DIVISION AND STATE	ACRES IN SPECIFIED CROPS ON FARMS OF COLORED FARMERS							
	RICE		SWEET POTATOES		TOBACCO		WHEAT	
	1909	1899	1909	1899	1909	1899	1909	1899
THE SOUTH	29,235	48,980	166,072	132,891	169,568	142,145	294,387	435,036
South Atlantic	7,836	38,246	88,459	75,262	131,019	104,801	152,828	253,516
East South Central	76	977	48,086	37,918	38,425	37,052	37,876	99,886
West South Central	21,323	9,757	29,527	19,711	124	292	13,683	81,634
South Atlantic:								
Delaware	...	...	408	133	...	...	3,679	3,579
Maryland	...	...	840	623	7,055	11,208	16,479	20,594
District of Columbia	...	...	11	9	...	...	...	...
Virginia	...	17	13,094	10,171	59,051	47,383	38,293	61,876
West Virginia	...	...	3	15	15	31	1,448	2,773
North Carolina	195	5,418	17,488	13,146	56,471	41,296	45,747	69,837
South Carolina	5,401	26,243	23,399	24,440	7,884	4,247	11,586	49,300
Georgia	2,088	5,521	27,327	19,724	95	165	15,594	45,542
Florida	152	1,047	5,889	7,001	448	471	2	15
East South Central:								
Kentucky	...	...	222	269	26,298	27,122	14,185	32,162
Tennessee	...	...	2,664	2,044	12,087	9,823	22,070	54,245
Alabama	15	442	23,418	20,235	22	59	1,518	12,774
Mississippi	61	535	21,752	15,370	18	48	103	705

[Continued]

★ 13 ★

Crops: Acreage in Selected Crops on Southern Black Farms by Division and State, 1899 and 1909, Part II

[Continued]

DIVISION AND STATE	ACRES IN SPECIFIED CROPS ON FARMS OF COLORED FARMERS							
	RICE		SWEET POTATOES		TOBACCO		WHEAT	
	1909	1899	1909	1899	1909	1899	1909	1899
West South Central:								
Arkansas	68	5	5,589	3,411	50	104	743	8,223
Louisiana	13,894	9,748	16,490	7,937	37	48	...	24
Oklahoma[1]	...	...	825	549	17	57	11,777	61,890
Texas	7,361	4	6,623	7,814	20	83	1,163	11,487

Source: "Acreage in Selected Crops on Colored Farms of the South, by Divisions and States: 1909 and 1899," *Negro Population, 1790-1915*, 1918, p. 601. Primary source: U.S. Bureau of the Census. *Negroes in the United States, 1790-1915*. Washington, D.C.: U.S. Government Printing Office, 1918. *Notes:* "Colored" may include persons other than Black. 1. Includes Indian Territory for 1899.

★ 14 ★

Crops/Livestock/Animals

Crops: Acreage, Yield, and Value on Black Southern Farms, 1909

CROP	Number of farms			Acres in crop			Yield of crop			Value of crop		
	Total	Colored farms		Total	Colored farms		Total	Colored farms		Total	Colored farms	
		Number	Percent		Acres	Percent		Yield	Percent		Value	Percent
Cotton	1,706,767	684,721	40.1	31,946,142	12,096,638	52.7	Bales 10,594,360	Bales 4,065,978	38.4	$700,199,244	$269,868,346	32.4
Corn	2,571,566	744,458	28.9	37,627,319	7,377,221	19.6	Bushels 623,068,626	Bushels 94,876,350	15.2	443,460,455	76,918,106	17.3
Cotton seed	1,706,767	684,721	40.1	31,946,142	12,096,638	52.7	Tons 5,297,182	Tons 2,032,991	38.4	122,521,349	47,068,246	38.4
Tobacco	260,287	42,470	16.3	1,049,617	169,568	16.2	Pounds 802,618,483	Pounds 109,433,038	13.6	78,506,324	9,813,199	12.5
Sweet potatoes	1,015,019	295,854	29.1	538,042	166,072	28.5	Bushels 52,227,661	Bushels 12,047,068	23.1	31,528,482	7,491,817	23.8
Hay and forage	1	1	1	8,620,243	468,581	5.4	Tons 8,866,596	Tons 468,394	5.2	97,264,658	5,003,872	5.1
Peanuts	217,379	77,984	35.9	869,176	236,139	27.2	Bushels 19,400,338	Bushels 5,069,004	26.1	18,253,270	4,797,046	26.3
Oats	495,381	81,831	16.5	3,516,128	321,960	9.2	60,126,382	4,358,927	7.2	32,688,105	2,736,848	8.3
Potatoes	847,863	97,875	11.5	477,064	50,680	10.6	39,332,677	3,438,024	8.7	25,472,023	2,410,099	9.5
Wheat	331,069	36,553	11.0	5,112,675	204,387	4.0	59,121,317	1,829,742	3.0	61,854,632	1,930,790	3.1
Dry peas	209,064	72,989	34.9	1,009,836	284,854	28.2	3,803,461	1,028,529	27.3	6,461,667	1,737,609	26.9
Rice	13,706	4,967	36.2	610,163	29,235	4.8	21,838,520	889,103	4.1	16,019,567	677,542	4.2
Alfalfa	32,754	1,172	3.6	340,651	6,611	1.9	Tons 574,149	Tons 11,901	2.1	6,654,473	171,836	2.6
Rye	40,769	1,941	4.8	213,563	6,597	3.1	Bushels 1,772,326	Bushels 48,279	2.7	1,484,934	44,111	3.0
Dry edible beans	47,549	2,881	6.1	47,808	3,742	7.8	301,927	22,083	7.3	527,201	37,143	7.0
Kraft corn	54,193	593	1.1	1,018,129	3,402	0.3	10,546,626	40,430	0.4	6,338,581	23,343	0.4
Soy beans	2,055	252	12.3	14,029	1,401	9.9	169,379	14,042	8.3	225,512	17,817	7.9
Broom corn	16,172	245	1.5	228,569	691	0.3	Pounds 46,005,312	Pounds 164,447	0.4	2,774,354	9,601	0.3
Buckwheat	22,798	268	1.2	89,757	997	1.1	Bushels 1,269,120	Bushels 11,089	1.0	829,668	6,915	0.8
Barley	5,291	98	1.9	35,202	193	0.5	710,883	3,960	0.6	463,987	2,890	0.6

Source: "Farms Reporting Specified Crop, Acreage, Yield, and Value of Crop: 1910," *Negro Population, 1790-1915*, 1918, p. 564. Primary source: U.S. Bureau of the Census. *Negroes in the United States, 1790-1915*. Washington, D.C.: U.S. Government Printing Office, 1918. *Notes:* "Colored" may include persons other than Black. 1. Data not available.

★ 15 ★
Crops/Livestock/Animals

Crops: Acres of Selected Crops in the East South Central Division, 1899 and 1909

CROP	ACRES IN SPECIFIED CROPS AND OTHER IMPROVED ACRES						Percentage in colored farms		Increase: 1899-1909[1]			
	1909			1899					Acres		Per cent	
	Total	Colored farms	White farms	Total	Colored farms	White farms	1909	1899	Colored farms	White farms	Colored farms	White farms
EAST SOUTH CENTRAL DIVISION												
Total improved	33,946,846	9,556,529	34,390,317	40,237,337	8,191,628	32,045,709	28.2	20.4	1,364,901	2,344,608	16.7	7.3
Corn	11,328,268	2,309,639	9,018,629	11,713,504	2,387,838	9,325,666	20.4	20.4	-78,199	-307,037	-3.3	-3.3
Cotton	7,926,019	4,614,339	3,311,680	6,725,588	3,870,109	2,855,479	57.5	58.2	744,230	456,201	19.2	16.0
Hay and forage	2,487,554	137,315	2,350,239	1,513,371	68,645	1,444,726	5.5	4.5	68,670	905,513	100.0	62.7
Oats	870,672	69,132	801,630	855,842	53,774	802,068	7.9	6.3	15,358	-438	28.6	-0.1
Potatoes	119,541	9,077	110,464	80,138	7,314	72,314	7.6	9.1	1,763	37,640	24.1	51.7
Rice	560	76	484	4,424	977	3,447	13.6	22.1	-901	-2,063	-92.2	-86.0
Sweet potatoes	160,756	48,086	112,670	126,586	37,918	88,668	29.9	30.0	10,168	24,002	26.8	27.1
Tobacco	560,523	38,425	522,098	457,998	37,052	420,946	6.9	8.1	1,373	101,152	3.7	24.0
Wheat	1,315,243	37,876	1,277,367	2,987,483	99,886	2,887,597	2.9	3.3	-62,010	-1,610,250	62.1	-55.8
Other improved	9,177,620	2,292,564	16,885,056	15,772,403	1,628,115	14,144,288	25.0	10.3	664,449	2,740,768	40.8	19.4

Source: "Colored and White Acreage in Specified Crops, with Decennial Increase, by Southern Divisions: 1910 and 1900," *Negro Population, 1790-1915*, 1918, p. 566. Primary source: U.S. Bureau of the Census. *Negroes in the United States, 1790-1915.* Washington, D.C.: U.S. Government Printing Office, 1918. *Notes:* "Colored" may include persons other than Black. 1. A minus sign (-) denotes decrease.

★ 16 ★
Crops/Livestock/Animals

Crops: Acres of Selected Crops in the South Atlantic Division, 1899 and 1909

CROP	ACRES IN SPECIFIED CROPS AND OTHER IMPROVED ACRES						Percentage in colored farms		Increase: 1899-1909[1]			
	1909			1899					Acres		Per cent	
	Total	Colored farms	White farms	Total	Colored farms	White farms	1909	1899	Colored farms	White farms	Colored farms	White farms
SOUTH ATLANTIC DIVISION												
Total improved	48,479,733	10,990,069	37,489,664	42,100,226	8,895,862	33,204,364	22.7	21.1	2,094,207	4,285,300	23.5	12.9
Corn	11,386,984	3,066,496	8,320,488	12,024,742	2,855,482	9,169,260	26.9	23.7	210,310	-848,772	7.4	-9.3
Cotton	9,002,776	4,442,773	4,560,003	6,842,489	3,005,870	3,836,619	49.3	43.9	1,436,903	723,384	47.8	18.9
Hay and forage	2,856,398	189,680	2,668,718	2,161,201	105,189	2,056,012	6.6	4.9	84,491	610,706	80.3	29.7
Oats	1,368,832	213,778	1,155,054	1,268,081	152,717	1,115,364	15.6	12.0	61,061	39,690	40.0	3.6
Potatoes	239,762	29,508	210,254	157,481	15,839	141,642	12.3	10.1	13,069	68,612	86.3	48.4
Rice	27,080	7,836	19,244	127,369	38,246	89,123	28.9	30.0	-30,410	-69,879	-79.5	-78.4
Sweet potatoes	295,879	88,459	207,420	263,925	75,262	188,663	29.9	28.5	13,197	18,757	17.5	9.9
Tobacco	487,411	131,019	356,392	465,754	104,801	360,953	26.9	22.5	26,218	-4,561	25.0	-1.3
Wheat	2,241,345	152,828	2,088,517	3,368,872	253,516	3,115,356	6.8	7.5	-100,683	-1,026,839	-39.7	-33.0
Other improved	20,573,266	2,667,692	17,905,574	15,420,312	2,288,940	13,131,372	13.0	14.8	379,456	4,774,202	16.6	36.4

Source: "Colored and White Acreage in Specified Crops, with Decennial Increase, by Southern Divisions: 1910 and 1900," *Negro Population, 1790-1915*, 1918, p. 566. Primary source: U.S. Bureau of the Census. *Negroes in the United States, 1790-1915.* Washington, D.C.: U.S. Government Printing Office, 1918. *Notes:* "Colored" may include persons other than Black. 1. A minus sign (-) denotes decrease.

★ 17 ★

Crops/Livestock/Animals

Crops: Acres of Selected Crops in the South, 1899 and 1909

CROP	ACRES IN SPECIFIED CROPS AND OTHER IMPROVED ACRES											
	1909			1899			Percentage in colored farms		Increase: 1899-1909[1]			
									Acres		Per cent	
	Total	Colored farms	White farms	Total	Colored farms	White farms	1909	1899	Colored farms	White farms	Colored farms	White farms
					THE SOUTH							
Total improved	140,690,852	27,735,743	122,955,109	126,108,093	23,214,607	102,893,486	19.7	18.4	4,521,136	20,061,623	19.5	19.5
Corn	37,627,319	7,377,221	30,250,098	34,919,379	6,993,999	27,925,380	19.6	20.0	382,518	2,324,718	5.5	8.3
Cotton	31,946,142	12,096,638	19,849,504	24,229,296	9,656,262	14,573,034	37.9	39.9	2,440,376	5,276,470	25.3	36.2
Hay and forage	8,620,243	468,581	8,151,662	6,044,864	316,528	5,728,336	5.4	5.2	152,053	2,423,326	48.0	42.3
Oats	3,516,128	321,960	3,194,168	2,596,372	261,982	3,334,390	9.2	7.3	59,978	-140,222	22.9	-4.2
Potatoes	477,064	50,680	426,384	310,495	30,308	280,187	10.6	9.8	20,372	146,197	67.2	52.2
Rice	610,163	29,235	580,928	342,214	48,980	293,234	4.8	14.3	-19,745	287,694	-40.3	98.1
Sweet potatoes	583,042	166,072	416,970	478,291	132,891	345,400	28.5	27.8	33,181	71,570	25.0	20.7
Tobacco	1,049,617	169,568	880,049	927,609	142,145	785,464	16.2	15.3	27,423	94,585	19.3	12.0
Wheat	5,112,675	204,387	4,908,288	9,291,042	435,036	8,856,006	4.0	4.7	-230,649	-3,947,718	-53.0	-44.6
Other improved	51,148,459	6,851,401	54,297,058	45,968,531	5,196,476	40,772,055	13.4	11.3	1,655,629	13,525,003	31.9	33.2

Source: "Colored and White Acreage in Specified Crops, with Decennial Increase, by Southern Divisions: 1910 and 1900," *Negro Population, 1790-1915*, 1918, p. 566. Primary source: U.S. Bureau of the Census. *Negroes in the United States, 1790-1915*. Washington, D.C.: U.S. Government Printing Office, 1918. *Notes:* "Colored" may include persons other than Black. 1. A minus sign (-) denotes decrease.

★ 18 ★

Crops/Livestock/Animals

Crops: Acres of Selected Crops in the West South Central Division, 1899 and 1909

CROP	ACRES IN SPECIFIED CROPS AND OTHER IMPROVED ACRES											
	1909			1899			Percentage in colored farms		Increase: 1899-1909[1]			
									Acres		Per cent	
	Total	Colored farms	White farms	Total	Colored farms	White farms	1909	1899	Colored farms	White farms	Colored farms	White farms
				WEST SOUTH CENTRAL DIVISION								
Total improved	58,264,273	7,189,145	51,075,128	39,770,530	6,127,117	33,643,413	12.3	15.4	1,062,028	17,431,715	17.3	51.8
Corn	14,912,067	2,001,086	12,910,981	11,181,133	1,750,679	9,430,454	13.4	15.7	250,407	3,480,527	14.3	36.9
Cotton	15,017,347	3,039,526	11,977,821	10,661,219	2,780,283	7,880,936	20.2	26.0	259,243	4,096,885	9.3	52.0
Hay and forage	3,276,291	141,586	3,134,705	2,370,292	142,694	2,227,598	4.3	6.0	-1,108	907,107	-0.8	40.7
Oats	1,276,534	39,050	1,237,484	1,472,449	55,491	1,416,958	3.1	3.3	-16,441	-179,474	-29.6	-12.7
Potatoes	117,761	12,095	105,666	72,876	7,155	65,721	10.3	9.8	4,940	39,945	69.9	60.8
Rice	582,523	21,323	561,200	210,421	9,757	200,664	3.7	4.6	11,566	360,536	118.5	179.7
Sweet potatoes	126,407	29,527	96,880	87,780	19,711	68,069	23.4	22.5	9,816	28,811	49.8	42.3
Tobacco	1,683	124	1,559	3,857	292	3,565	7.4	8.0	-168	-2,096	-57.5	-56.3
Wheat	1,556,087	13,683	1,542,404	2,934,687	81,634	2,853,053	0.9	2.8	-67,951	-1,310,649	-84.2	-45.9
Other improved	21,397,573	1,891,145	19,506,428	19,775,816	1,279,421	9,496,395	8.8	11.9	611,724	10,010,033	47.8	105.4

Source: "Colored and White Acreage in Specified Crops, with Decennial Increase, by Southern Divisions: 1910 and 1900," *Negro Population, 1790-1915*, 1918, p. 566. Primary source: U.S. Bureau of the Census. *Negroes in the United States, 1790-1915*. Washington, D.C.: U.S. Government Printing Office, 1918. *Notes:* "Colored" may include persons other than Black. 1. A minus sign (-) denotes decrease.

★ 19 ★
Crops/Livestock/Animals

Crops: Alfalfa Produced on Farms by Southern Division and State, 1909

DIVISION AND STATE	CROPS IN 1909											
	Number of farms reporting crop			Acreage in crop			Yield of crop			Value of crop		
	Total	Colored farms		All farms	Colored farms		All farms	Colored farms		All farms	Colored farms	
		Number	Percent		Number	Percent		Amount	Percent		Amount	Percent
ALFALFA												
							Tons	Tons				
THE SOUTH	32,754	1,172	3.6	340,651	6,611	1.9	574,149	11,901	2.1	$6,654,473	$171,836	2.6
South Atlantic	2,362	134	5.7	8,710	298	3.4	18,967	453	2.4	291,294	6,361	2.2
East South Central	5,878	357	6.1	41,784	1,541	3.7	74,194	2,304	3.1	973,044	36,898	3.8
West South Central	24,516	681	2.8	290,157	4,772	1.6	480,988	9,144	1.9	5,390,135	108,577	2.0
South Atlantic:												
Delaware	70	4	5.7	205	10	4.9	580	16	2.8	7,927	208	2.6
Maryland	789	14	1.8	3,188	64	2.0	6,806	144	2.1	104,633	1,812	1.7
District of Columbia	1	...	...	28	...	...	108	...	...	1,620	...	...
Virginia	796	69	8.7	3,126	122	3.9	7,203	180	2.5	109,409	2,543	2.3
West Virginia	179	...	...	696	...	...	1,406	...	...	17,932	...	...
North Carolina	272	22	8.1	735	54	7.3	1,394	59	4.2	22,276	770	3.5
South Carolina	65	2	3.1	138	1	0.7	328	1	0.3	6,835	21	0.3
Georgia	182	23	12.6	545	47	8.6	1,079	53	4.9	19,758	1,007	5.1
Florida	8	...	...	49	...	...	63	...	...	886	...	...
East South Central:												
Kentucky	3,676	18	0.5	20,229	57	0.3	37,978	83	0.2	426,879	940	0.2
Tennessee	945	36	3.8	5,323	168	3.2	10,600	206	1.9	138,525	2,720	2.0
Alabama	416	89	21.4	6,987	598	8.6	8,906	799	9.0	137,970	14,165	10.3
Mississippi	841	214	25.4	9,245	718	7.8	16,710	1,211	7.2	269,670	19,073	7.1
West South Central:												
Arkansas	2,363	207	8.8	15,929	853	5.4	33,231	1,600	4.8	443,875	23,138	5.2
Louisiana	685	143	20.9	12,073	939	7.8	28,146	1,999	7.1	376,562	27,062	7.2
Oklahoma	17,467	249	1.4	206,823	2,512	1.2	321,675	4,966	1.5	3,230,384	50,051	1.5
Texas	4,001	82	2.0	55,332	468	0.8	97,936	579	0.6	1,339,314	8,326	0.6

Source: "Crops in 1909 on Farms in the South—Farms Reporting, Acreage, Yield, and Value of Specified Crops on All Farms and on Colored Farms, by Divisions and States," *Negro Population, 1790-1915,* 1918, p. 598. Primary source: U.S. Bureau of the Census. *Negro Population, 1790-1915.* Washington, D.C.: Government Printing Office, 1918. *Note:* "Colored" may include persons other than Black.

★ 20 ★
Crops/Livestock/Animals

Crops: Average Acreage and Yield of Corn on Black Farms in the South, 1909 - I

DIVISION AND STATE	COLORED FARMERS REPORTING CORN: 1909						
	Total	Owners, free	Owners, mortgaged	Part owners	Cash not specified tenants	Share and sharecash tenants	Managers
AVERAGE ACRES IN CORN PER FARM REPORTING CORN							
THE SOUTH							
Total	9.9	10.4	11.7	12.9	9.4	9.6	20.9
South Atlantic	9.8	8.2	10.2	10.5	10.6	9.8	20.3

[Continued]

★ 20 ★

Crops: Average Acreage and Yield of Corn on Black Farms in the South, 1909 - I
[Continued]

DIVISION AND STATE	COLORED FARMERS REPORTING CORN: 1909						
	Total	Owners, free	Owners, mortgaged	Part owners	Cash not specified tenants	Share and sharecash tenants	Managers
East South Central	8.7	10.0	10.8	11.4	8.3	8.1	27.4
West South Central	11.9	14.6	15.2	16.3	9.3	11.0	17.9

Source: "Acres in Crops Specified on Farms in the South: 1909," *Negro Population, 1790-1915*, 1918, pp. 583-584. Primary source: U.S. Bureau of the Census. *Negro Population, 1790-1915.* Washington, D.C.: Government Printing Office, 1918.

★ 21 ★

Crops/Livestock/Animals

Crops: Average Acreage and Yield of Corn on Black Farms in the South, 1909 - II

DIVISION AND STATE	COLORED FARMERS REPORTING CORN: 1909						
	Total	Owners, free	Owners, mortgaged	Part owners	Cash not specified tenants	Share and sharecash tenants	Managers
AVERAGE YIELD IN BUSHELS PER ACRE PLANTED							
Total	12.9	13.2	12.2	13.5	11.5	18.7	20.2
South Atlantic	11.2	12.5	11.1	11.8	8.8	11.8	20.0
East South Central	13.0	13.1	11.4	15.0	12.0	14.2	19.7
West South Central	15.2	14.0	13.9	14.7	16.5	15.7	21.1

Source: "Acres in Crops Specified on Farms in the South: 1909," *Negro Population, 1790-1915*, 1918, pp. 583-584. Primary source: U.S. Bureau of the Census. *Negro Population, 1790-1915.* Washington, D.C.; Government Printing Office, 1918.

★ 22 ★

Crops/Livestock/Animals

Crops: Average Acreage and Yield of Cotton on Black Farms in the South, 1909 - I

DIVISION AND STATE	COLORED FARMERS REPORTING COTTON: 1909						
	Total	Owners, free	Owners, mortgaged	Part owners	Cash not specified tenants	Share and sharecash tenants	Managers
AVERAGE ACRES IN COTTON PER FARM REPORTING COTTON							
THE SOUTH							
Total	17.7	13.8	18.2	17.4	19.2	17.3	33.6
South Atlantic	17.5	11.3	16.5	13.6	19.3	18.0	26.0

[Continued]

★ 22 ★

Crops: Average Acreage and Yield of Cotton on Black Farms in the South, 1909 - I

[Continued]

DIVISION AND STATE	COLORED FARMERS REPORTING COTTON: 1909						
	Total	Owners, free	Owners, mortgaged	Part owners	Cash not specified tenants	Share and sharecash tenants	Managers
East South Central	17.3	14.9	17.9	18.2	19.2	15.3	46.9
West South Central	18.4	15.8	20.1	22.0	18.6	18.6	32.9

Source: "Acres in Crops Specified on Farms in the South: 1909," *Negro Population, 1790-1915*, 1918, pp. 583-584. Primary source: U.S. Bureau of the Census. *Negro Population, 1790-1915*. Washington, D.C.: Government Printing Office, 1918.

★ 23 ★

Crops/Livestock/Animals

Crops: Average Acreage and Yield of Cotton on Black Farms in the South, 1909 - II

DIVISION AND STATE	COLORED FARMERS REPORTING COTTON: 1909						
	Total	Owners, free	Owners, mortgaged	Part owners	Cash not specified tenants	Share and sharecash tenants	Managers
AVERAGE ACRES IN BALES PER FARM REPORTING COTTON							
THE SOUTH							
Total	5.9	4.4	5.3	5.5	6.2	6.2	12.5
South Atlantic	7.1	4.7	6.3	5.6	7.2	7.9	15.1
East South Central	5.1	4.4	4.9	5.1	5.4	4.9	10.0
West South Central	5.5	4.2	5.0	5.7	6.5	5.5	10.5

Source: "Acres in Crops Specified on Farms in the South: 1909," *Negro Population, 1790-1915*, 1918, pp. 583-584. Primary source: U.S. Bureau of the Census. *Negro Population, 1790-1915*. Washington, D.C.: Government Printing Office, 1918.

★ 24 ★

Crops/Livestock/Animals

Crops: Barley Raised on Farms by Southern Division and State, 1909

DIVISION AND STATE	CROPS IN 1909											
	Number of farms reporting crop			Acreage in crop			Yield of crop			Value of crop		
	Total	Colored farms		All farms	Colored farms		All farms	Colored farms		All farms	Colored farms	
		Number	Percent		Number	Percent		Amount	Percent		Amount	Percent
BARLEY												
THE SOUTH	5,291	98	1.9	35,202	193	0.5	Bushels 710,883	Bushels 3,960	0.6	$463,987	$2,890	0.6
South Atlantic	3,775	83	2.2	15,561	94	0.6	409,615	2,120	0.5	276,981	1,684	0.6
East South Central	442	8	1.8	5,388	69	1.3	119,922	1,220	1.0	79,171	696	0.9

[Continued]

★ 24 ★

Crops: Barley Raised on Farms by Southern Division and State, 1909

[Continued]

DIVISION AND STATE	CROPS IN 1909											
	Number of farms reporting crop			Acreage in crop			Yield of crop			Value of crop		
	Total	Colored farms		All farms	Colored farms		All farms	Colored farms		All farms	Colored farms	
		Number	Percent		Number	Percent		Amount	Percent		Amount	Percent
West South Central	1,074	7	0.7	14,253	30	0.2	181,346	620	0.3	107,835	510	0.5
South Atlantic:												
Delaware	8	1	12.5	31	...	...	422	10	2.4	258	5	1.7
Maryland	1,215	7	0.6	4,494	20	0.4	135,454	698	0.5	79,231	314	0.4
District of Columbia	...	...	...	...	...	...	...	...	...	...	...	...
Virginia	2,057	10	0.5	9,890	40	0.4	253,649	872	0.3	179,712	642	0.4
West Virginia	119	...	...	408	...	...	8,407	...	...	3,640	...	...
North Carolina	149	2	1.3	504	3	0.6	7,535	21	0.3	6,863	18	0.3
South Carolina	190	57	30.0	189	26	13.8	3,483	440	12.6	4,297	604	14.1
Georgia	36	6	16.6	44	5	11.4	655	79	12.1	942	101	10.7
Florida	1	...	...	1	...	...	10	...	...	8	...	...
East South Central:												
Kentucky	175	1	0.6	2,738	15	0.5	65,596	300	0.5	42,929	150	0.3
Tennessee	248	7	2.8	2,567	54	2.1	53,201	920	1.7	35,363	546	1.5
Alabama	14	...	...	41	...	...	372	...	...	336	...	...
Mississippi	5	...	...	42	...	...	753	...	...	543	...	...
West South Central:												
Arkansas	41	2	4.9	82	11	13.4	1,267	260	20.5	1,136	265	23.3
Louisiana	...	...	...	...	...	...	...	...	...	...	...	...
Oklahoma	834	4	0.5	10,283	9	0.1	127,641	160	0.1	75,059	95	0.1
Texas	199	1	0.5	3,888	10	0.3	52,438	200	0.4	31,640	150	0.5

Source: "Crops in 1909 on Farms in the South—Farms Reporting, Acreage, Yield, and Value of Specified Crops on All Farms and on Colored Farms, by Divisions and States," *Negro Population, 1790-1915,* 1918, p. 600. Primary source: U.S. Bureau of the Census. *Negro Population, 1790-1915.* Washington, D.C.: Government Printing Office, 1918. *Note:* "Colored" may include persons other than Black.

★ 25 ★

Crops/Livestock/Animals

Crops: Broom Corn Raised on Farms by Southern Division and State, 1909

DIVISION AND STATE	CROPS IN 1909											
	Number of farms reporting crop			Acreage in crop			Yield of crop			Value of crop		
	Total	Colored farms		All farms	Colored farms		All farms	Colored farms		All farms	Colored farms	
		Number	Percent		Number	Percent		Amount	Percent		Amount	Percent
							BROOM CORN					
							Pounds	Pounds				
THE SOUTH	16,172	245	1.5	228,569	691	0.3	46,005,312	164,447	0.4	$2,774,354	$9,601	0.3
South Atlantic	1,514	41	2.7	223	29	13.0	113,479	10,588	9.3	10,619	911	8.6
East South Central	3,419	99	2.9	1,886	102	5.4	582,834	23,879	4.1	48,484	1,654	3.4
West South Central	11,239	105	0.9	226,450	560	0.2	45,308,999	129,980	0.3	2,715,251	7,036	0.3
South Atlantic:												
Delaware	21	2	9.5	13	...	...	4,198	65	1.5	492	10	2.0 [1]
Maryland	291	1	0.3	19	...	...	18,599	60	0.3	2,006	2	
District of Columbia	...	...	...	...	...	...	...	...	...	...	...	...
Virginia	666	26	3.9	107	5	4.7	46,016	2,996	6.5	3,586	180	5.2
West Virginia	397	...	...	45	...	...	30,456	...	...	3,229	...	...
North Carolina	128	8	6.3	15	3	20.0	6,493	1,242	19.1	549	98	17.9
South Carolina	3	1	33.3	2	...	...	650	100	15.4	63	10	15.9
Georgia	8	3	37.5	22	21	95.5	7,067	6,125	86.7	694	611	88.0
Florida	...	...	...	...	...	...	...	...	...	...	...	...
East South Central:												
Kentucky	1,041	12	1.2	342	5	1.5	157,286	3,193	2.0	13,641	169	1.2
Tennessee	2,220	76	3.4	1,348	68	5.0	347,064	15,851	4.6	27,733	1,172	4.2
Alabama	115	5	4.3	52	3	5.8	17,910	445	2.5	1,562	30	1.9
Mississippi	43	6	14.0	154	26	16.9	60,574	4,390	7.2	5,548	283	5.1

[Continued]

★ 25 ★

Crops: Broom Corn Raised on Farms by Southern Division and State, 1909

[Continued]

DIVISION AND STATE	CROPS IN 1909											
	Number of farms reporting crop			Acreage in crop			Yield of crop			Value of crop		
	Total	Colored farms		All farms	Colored farms		All farms	Colored farms		All farms	Colored farms	
		Number	Percent		Number	Percent		Amount	Percent		Amount	Percent
West South Central:												
Arkansas	294	6	2.0	332	5	1.5	106,576	1,467	1.4	8,198	87	1.1
Louisiana	263	57	21.7	320	35	10.9	92,208	10,653	11.6	7,285	949	13.0
Oklahoma	10,151	38	0.4	216,350	494	0.2	42,741,725	113,310	0.3	2,559,235	5,737	0.2
Texas	531	4	0.8	9,448	26	0.3	2,368,490	4,550	0.2	140,533	264	0.2

Source: "Crops in 1909 on Farms in the South—Farms Reporting, Acreage, Yield, and Value of Specified Crops on All Farms and on Colored Farms, by Divisions and States," *Negro Population, 1790-1915*, 1918, p. 599. Primary source: U.S. Bureau of the Census. *Negro Population, 1790-1915*. Washington, D.C.: Government Printing Office, 1918. *Notes:* "Colored" may include persons other than Black. 1. Less than one-tenth of 1 per cent.

★ 26 ★

Crops/Livestock/Animals

Crops: Buckwheat Raised on Farms by Southern Division and State, 1909

DIVISION AND STATE	CROPS IN 1909											
	Number of farms reporting crop			Acreage in crop			Yield of crop			Value of crop		
	Total	Colored farms		All farms	Colored farms		All farms	Colored farms		All farms	Colored farms	
		Number	Percent		Number	Percent		Amount	Percent		Amount	Percent
BUCKWHEAT												
							Bushels	Bushels				
THE SOUTH	22,793	268	1.2	89,757	997	1.1	1,269,120	11,089	1.0	$829,668	$6,915	0.8
South Atlantic	21,466	263	1.2	84,864	975	1.1	1,216,608	10,873	0.9	791,546	6,796	0.9
East South Central	1,296	4	0.3	4,772	20	0.4	51,525	136	0.3	37,268	79	0.2
West South Central	31	1	3.2	121	2	1.7	987	80	8.1	854	40	4.7
South Atlantic:												
Delaware	743	54	7.3	4,002	227	5.6	43,903	2,268	4.2	30,839	1,203	3.9
Maryland	2,411	38	1.6	10,388	205	2.2	152,216	2,961	1.9	99,216	1,651	1.7
District of Columbia	...	...	...	...	...	...	...	...	...	...	...	...
Virginia	5,954	83	1.4	25,481	317	1.2	332,222	3,200	1.0	196,196	1,920	1.0
West Virginia	9,028	2	1	33,323	2	1	533,670	58	1	351,171	33	1
North Carolina	3,304	75	2.3	11,606	202	1.7	144,186	2,167	1.5	113,577	1,708	1.5
South Carolina	6	3	50.0	9	5	55.5	84	53	63.0	101	65	64.4
Georgia	20	8	40.0	55	17	30.9	327	166	50.8	446	216	48.4
Florida	...	...	...	...	...	...	...	...	...	...	...	...
East South Central:												
Kentucky	452	3	0.7	1,887	19	1.0	18,074	116	0.6	12,028	65	0.5
Tennessee	831	1	0.1	2,867	1	1	33,249	20	1	25,078	14	1
Alabama	13	...	...	18	...	1	202	...	1	162	...	1
Mississippi	...	...	...	...	...	...	...	...	...	...	...	...
West South Central:												
Arkansas	13	...	...	20	...	1	123	...	1	133	...	...
Louisiana	1	...	...	1	...	1	16	...	...	16	...	...
Oklahoma	12	1	8.3	43	2	4.6	375	80	21.0	370	40	10.8
Texas	5	...	...	57	...	1	473	...	...	335	...	...

Source: "Crops in 1909 on Farms in the South—Farms Reporting, Acreage, Yield, and Value of Specified Crops on All Farms and on Colored Farms, by Divisions and States," *Negro Population, 1790-1915*, 1918, p. 600. Primary source: U.S. Bureau of the Census. *Negro Population, 1790-1915*. Washington, D.C.: Government Printing Office, 1918. *Notes:* "Colored" may include persons other than Black. 1. Less than one-tenth of 1 per cent.

★ 27 ★

Crops/Livestock/Animals

Crops: Corn Raised on Farms by Southern Division and State, 1909

DIVISION AND STATE	Number of farms reporting crop			Acreage in crop			Yield of crop			Value of crop		
	Total	Colored farms		All farms	Colored farms		All farms	Colored farms		All farms	Colored farms	
		Number	Percent		Acres	Percent		Amount	Percent		Amount	Percent

CROPS IN 1909

CORN

							Bushels	Bushels				
THE SOUTH	2,571,566	744,458	28.9	37,627,319	7,377,221	19.6	623,068,626	94,876,350	15.2	$443,460,455	$76,918,406	17.3
South Atlantic	974,833	311,725	32.0	11,386,984	3,066,496	26.9	179,511,702	34,442,488	19.2	149,449,304	31,149,841	20.8
East South Central	882,737	265,078	30.0	11,328,268	2,309,639	20.4	210,154,917	30,038,296	14.3	150,975,613	25,377,730	16.8
West South Central	713,996	167,655	23.5	14,912,067	2,001,086	13.4	233,402,007	30,395,566	13.0	143,035,538	20,390,835	14.3
South Atlantic:												
Delaware	9,923	836	8.4	188,755	12,636	6.7	4,839,548	252,478	5.2	2,903,442	146,047	5.0
Maryland	42,084	5,269	12.5	647,012	52,139	8.1	17,911,436	985,310	5.5	11,015,298	601,694	5.5
District of Columbia	68	1	1.5	426	2	0.5	12,667	50	0.4	9,535	40	0.4
Virginia	163,680	43,401	26.5	1,860,359	338,378	18.2	38,295,141	4,966,904	13.0	28,885,944	4,011,144	13.9
West Virginia	83,028	500	0.6	676,311	4,421	0.5	17,119,097	105,814	0.6	11,907,261	62,943	0.5
North Carolina	228,322	57,911	25.4	2,459,457	533,037	21.8	34,063,531	5,876,253	17.3	31,286,102	5,482,779	17.5
South Carolina	156,589	84,744	54.1	1,565,832	653,856	41.8	20,871,946	7,309,064	35.0	20,682,632	7,237,073	35.0
Georgia	253,410	106,426	42.0	3,383,061	1,278,627	37.8	39,374,569	12,881,533	32.7	37,079,981	12,049,851	32.5
Florida	37,729	12,637	33.5	605,771	191,400	31.6	7,021,767	2,065,082	29.4	5,709,009	1,558,270	27.3
East South Central:												
Kentucky	216,224	8,184	3.8	3,436,340	104,055	3.0	83,348,024	2,442,054	2.9	50,449,112	1,445,369	2.9
Tennessee	211,119	32,779	15.5	3,146,348	354,996	11.3	67,682,489	6,331,010	9.4	45,819,093	4,616,979	10.1
Alabama	229,113	93,839	41.0	2,572,968	818,175	31.8	30,695,737	8,557,923	27.9	28,677,032	7,912,376	27.6
Mississippi	226,281	130,276	57.6	2,172,612	1,032,413	47.5	28,428,667	12,707,309	44.7	26,030,376	11,403,006	43.8
West South Central:												
Arkansas	176,106	48,120	27.3	2,277,116	386,913	17.0	37,609,544	6,107,452	16.2	27,910,044	5,103,515	18.3
Louisiana	100,943	45,790	45.4	1,590,830	505,431	31.1	26,010,361	7,432,322	28.6	16,480,322	4,623,633	28.0
Oklahoma	148,590	15,643	10.5	5,914,069	369,818	6.3	94,283,407	5,949,363	6.3	48,080,554	3,019,702	6.3
Texas	288,357	58,102	20.1	5,130,052	738,924	14.4	75,498,695	10,906,429	14.4	50,564,618	7,643,984	15.1

Source: "Crops in 1909 on Farms in the South—Farms Reporting, Acreage, Yield, and Value of Specified Crops on All Farms and on Colored Farms, by Divisions and States," *Negro Population, 1790-1915,* 1918, p. 594 Primary source: U.S. Bureau of the Census. *Negro Population, 1790-1915.* Washington, D.C.: Government Printing Office, 1918.

★ 28 ★

Crops/Livestock/Animals

Crops: Corn and Cotton – Acreage on Farms in the South by Owner Status, 1909

TENURE	ACRES IN CROP SPECIFIED ON FARMS IN THE SOUTH: 1909					
	Total	On colored farms	On white farms	Percentage distribution by tenure		Percentage on colored farms
				Colored	White	

CORN

Total	37,627,319	7,377,221	30,250,098	100.0	100.0	19.6
Owners, free	12,942,116	1,197,845	11,744,271	16.2	38.8	9.3
Owners, mortgaged	4,276,426	505,239	3,771,187	6.8	12.5	11.8
Part owners	3,413,758	476,709	2,937,049	6.5	9.7	14.0
Cash tenants[1]	5,417,421	2,314,540	3,102,881	31.4	10.3	42.7
Share tenants[2]	11,094,179	2,861,607	8,232,572	38.8	27.2	25.8
Managers	483,419	21,281	462,138	0.3	1.5	4.4

[Continued]

★ 28 ★

Crops: Corn and Cotton – Acreage on Farms in the South by Owner Status, 1909

[Continued]

TENURE	ACRES IN CROP SPECIFIED ON FARMS IN THE SOUTH: 1909					
	Total	On colored farms	On white farms	Percentage distribution by tenure		Percentage on colored farms
				Colored	White	
COTTON						
Total	31,946,142	12,096,638	19,849,504	100.0	100.0	37.9
Owners, free	6,541,507	1,019,469	5,522,038	8.4	27.8	15.6
Owners, mortgaged	3,335,997	627,287	2,708,710	5.2	13.6	18.8
Part owners	1,976,747	499,841	1,476,906	4.1	7.4	25.3
Cash tenants[1]	7,216,231	4,829,018	2,387,213	39.9	12.0	66.9
Share tenants[2]	12,586,510	5,104,042	7,482,468	42.2	37.7	40.6
Managers	289,150	16,981	272,169	0.1	1.4	5.7

Source: "Acres in Crop Specified on Farms in the South: 1909," *Negro Population, 1790-1915*, 1918, p. 583. Primary source: U.S. Bureau of the Census. *Negro Population, 1790-1915*. Washington, D.C.: Government Printing Office, 1918. *Notes:* "Colored" may include persons other than Black. 1. Includes not specified tenure. 2. Includes share-cash tenants.

★ 29 ★

Crops/Livestock/Animals

Crops: Cotton Raised on Farms by Southern Division and State, 1909

DIVISION AND STATE	CROPS IN 1909											
	Number of farms reporting crop			Acreage in crop			Yield of crop			Value of crop		
	Total	Colored farms		All farms	Colored farms		All farms	Colored farms		All farms	Colored farms	
		Number	Percent		Number	Percent		Amount	Percent		Amount	Percent
COTTON												
							Bales	Bales				
THE SOUTH	1,706,767	684,721	40.1	31,946,142	12,096,638	52.7	10,594,360	4,065,978	38.4	$700,199,244	$269,868,346	32.4
South Atlantic	556,504	253,286	45.5	9,002,776	4,442,773	49.3	4,012,942	1,806,026	45.0	254,636,958	113,311,266	44.5
East South Central	522,735	266,450	51.0	7,926,019	4,614,339	58.2	2,524,714	1,356,813	53.7	175,543,582	95,717,387	54.5
West South Central	627,528	164,985	26.3	15,017,347	3,039,526	20.2	4,056,704	903,139	22.3	270,618,704	60,839,693	22.5
South Atlantic:												
Delaware	...	...	...	...	...	...	...	...	...	...	...	...
Maryland	...	...	...	...	...	...	...	...	...	...	...	...
District of Columbia	...	...	...	...	...	...	...	...	...	...	...	...
Virginia	5,283	3,102	58.7	25,147	13,362	53.1	10,480	5,051	48.2	695,721	334,465	48.0
West Virginia	...	...	...	...	...	...	...	...	...	...	...	...
North Carolina	129,704	44,256	34.1	1,274,404	474,889	37.3	665,132	232,536	35.0	42,066,099	14,551,099	34.6
South Carolina	158,167	88,904	56.2	2,556,467	1,364,275	53.4	1,279,866	612,953	47.9	80,337,945	38,248,916	47.6
Georgia	242,673	108,115	44.6	4,883,304	2,468,242	50.5	1,992,408	927,162	46.5	126,695,612	58,195,483	45.9
Florida	20,677	8,909	43.1	263,454	121,905	46.3	65,056	28,324	43.5	4,841,581	1,981,303	40.9
East South Central:												
Kentucky	504	155	30.8	7,811	2,937	37.6	3,469	1,478	42.6	223,024	96,247	43.1
Tennessee	67,663	24,740	36.6	787,516	387,527	49.2	264,562	116,874	44.2	17,966,517	8,062,110	44.9
Alabama	224,871	100,506	44.7	3,730,482	1,960,709	5.6	1,129,527	510,465	45.2	74,205,236	33,261,538	44.8
Mississippi	229,697	141,049	61.4	3,400,210	2,263,166	66.6	1,127,156	727,996	64.6	83,148,805	54,297,492	65.3
West South Central:												
Arkansas	148,311	54,296	36.6	2,153,222	949,734	44.1	776,879	348,635	44.9	54,559,503	25,262,870	46.3
Louisiana	74,373	40,607	54.6	957,011	514,352	53.7	268,909	141,882	52.8	17,324,804	9,203,157	53.1
Oklahoma	88,140	11,270	12.8	1,976,935	217,231	11.0	555,742	70,738	12.7	35,399,356	4,314,200	12.2
Texas	316,704	58,812	18.6	9,930,179	1,358,209	13.7	2,455,174	341,884	13.9	162,735,041	22,059,466	13.5

Source: "Crops in 1909 on Farms in the South—Farms Reporting, Acreage, Yield, and Value of Specified Crops on All Farms and on Colored Farms, by Divisions and States," *Negro Population, 1790-1915*, 1918, p. 594. Primary source: U.S. Bureau of the Census. *Negro Population, 1790-1915*. Washington, D.C.: Government Printing Office, 1918. *Notes:* "Colored" may include persons other than Black. 1. A small percentage of the crop in Oklahoma was produced by Indians, who are included with Negroes in the census classification "colored."

★ 30 ★
Crops/Livestock/Animals

Crops: Cotton Seed Produced on Farms by Southern Division and State, 1909

Estimated yield and value based on cotton crop.

DIVISION AND STATE	CROPS IN 1909					
	Yield of crop			Value of crop		
	All farms	Colored farms		All farms	Colored farms	
		Amount	Percent		Amount	Percent
	COTTON SEED					
	Tons	Tons				
THE SOUTH	5,297,182	2,032,991	38.4	$122,521,349	$47,068,246	38.4
South Atlantic	2,006,471	903,014	45.0	50,501,177	21,781,036	43.1
East South Central	1,262,358	678,407	53.7	28,747,084	15,514,367	54.0
West South Central	2,028,353	451,570	22.3	43,273,088	9,762,843	22.6
South Atlantic:						
Delaware	...	...	...	...	...	...
Maryland	...	...	...	...	...	...
District of Columbia	...	...	...	...	...	...
Virginia	5,240	2,526	48.2	126,546	61,903	48.2
West Virginia	...	...	...	...	...	...
North Carolina	322,566	116,268	35.0	8,417,246	2,942,743	35.0
South Carolina	639,933	364,477	47.9	16,043,122	7,683,378	47.9
Georgia	996,204	463,581	46.5	23,241,446	10,815,345	46.5
Florida	32,528	14,162	43.5	639,826	278,567	43.5
East South Central:						
Kentucky	1,735	739	42.6	23,590	10,050	42.6
Tennessee	132,281	58,437	44.2	2,715,670	1,190,712	44.2
Alabama	564,764	255,233	45.2	12,803,196	5,786,132	45.2
Mississippi	563,578	363,998	64.6	13,204,628	8,528,473	64.6
West South Central:						
Arkansas	388,440	174,318	44.9	8,596,180	3,857,657	44.9
Louisiana	134,455	70,941	52.8	2,949,943	1,556,446	52.8
Oklahoma	277,871	35,369	12.7	5,788,052	736,736	12.7
Texas	1,227,587	170,942	13.9	25,938,913	3,612,004	13.9

Source: "Crops in 1909 on Farms in the South—Farms Reporting, Acreage, Yield, and Value of Specified Crops on All Farms and on Colored Farms, by Divisions and States," *Negro Population, 1790-1915*, 1918, p. 594. Primary source: U.S. Bureau of the Census. *Negroes in the United States, 1790-1915*. Washington, D.C.: U.S. Government Printing Office, 1918. *Notes:* "Colored" may include persons other than Black. .

★ 31 ★

Crops/Livestock/Animals

Crops: Cotton and Cottonseed Produced by State, 1929

[Colored farmers included Negroes, Indians, Chinese, Japanese, and all other nonwhite races]

| STATE | ALL FARM OPERATORS REPORTING- | | COLORED FARM OPERATORS REPORTING- | | | |
| | Lint cotton (bales) | Cotton-seed (tons) | Lint cotton (bales) | Cotton-seed (tons) | Percent of total | |
					Lint cotton (bales)	Cotton seed (tons)
Total	14,080,231	6,672,232	4,535,323	2,175,484	32.2	33.6
Virginia	52,442	25,266	25,791	12,371	49.2	49.0
North Carolina	764,328	354,164	297,838	137,679	39.0	38.9
South Carolina	835,963	381,260	390,999	177,807	46.8	46.6
Georgia	1,344,488	625,735	479,031	223,884	35.6	35.8
Florida	34,426	17,093	7,726	3,846	22.4	22.5
Kentucky	8,955	4,465	3,893	1,942	43.5	43.5
Tennessee	503,816	240,613	163,440	78,648	32.4	32.7
Alabama	1,312,963	629,410	423,198	203,214	32.2	32.3
Mississippi	1,875,108	914,893	1,234,841	606,612	65.9	66.3
Arkansas	1,398,475	685,902	540,522	267,657	38.7	39.0
Louisiana	798,828	385,476	425,386	204,952	53.3	53.2
Oklahoma	1,130,415	534,123	88,017	43,021	7.8	8.1
Texas	3,793,392	1,762,736	412,125	193,023	10.9	11.0
Illinois	826	419	544	284	65.9	67.8
Missouri	225,351	110,449	41,619	20,317	18.5	18.4
Kansas	455	228	353	177	77.6	77.6

Source: "Production of Cotton and Cottonseed, by Selected States: 1929," *Negroes in the United States, 1920-1932,* 1935, p. 588. Primary source: U.S. Bureau of the Census. *Negroes in the United States, 1920-1932.* Washington, D.C.: U.S. Government Printing Office, 1935.

★ 32 ★

Crops/Livestock/Animals

Crops: Dry Edible Beans Raised on Farms by Southern Division and State, 1909

DIVISION AND STATE	CROPS IN 1909											
	Number of farms reporting crop			Acreage in crop			Yield of crop			Value of crop		
	Total	Colored farms		All farms	Colored farms		All farms	Colored farms		All farms	Colored farms	
		Number	Percent		Number	Percent		Amount	Percent		Amount	Percent
							DRY EDIBLE BEANS					
THE SOUTH	47,549	2,881	6.1	47,808	3,742	7.8	Bushels 301,927	Bushels 22,083	7.3	$527,201	$37,143	7.0
South Atlantic	25,544	2,202	8.6	25,776	2,497	9.7	162,853	16,333	10.0	291,885	28,029	9.6
East South Central	20,558	476	2.3	18,481	628	3.4	114,022	3,270	2.9	189,599	5,680	3.0
West South Central	1,447	203	14.0	3,551	617	17.4	25,052	2,480	9.5	45,717	3,434	7.5
South Atlantic:												
Delaware	102	12	11.8	55	1[1]	1.8	648	32	4.9	1,387	77	5.6
Maryland	312	26	8.3	196	11	5.6	1,833	122	6.7	3,342	247	7.4
District of Columbia	...	...	...	...	...	...	...	...	...	...	...	...
Virginia	7,660	1,131	14.8	4,777	498	10.4	29,435	3,525	12.0	61,864	7,877	12.7

[Continued]

★ 32 ★

Crops: Dry Edible Beans Raised on Farms by Southern Division and State, 1909

[Continued]

DIVISION AND STATE	Number of farms reporting crop			Acreage in crop			Yield of crop			Value of crop		
		Colored farms			Colored farms			Colored farms			Colored farms	
	Total	Number	Percent	All farms	Number	Percent	All farms	Amount	Percent	All farms	Amount	Percent
West Virginia	8,626	...	...	8,111	...	...	39,794	...	...	81,049	...	...
North Carolina	6,574	529	8.0	5,521	623	11.3	35,937	4,704	13.1	57,528	6,839	11.8
South Carolina	517	242	46.8	1,528	628	41.1	6,825	2,937	43.0	12,778	5,324	41.6
Georgia	1,329	197	14.8	2,947	553	18.8	16,546	2,729	16.5	30,018	4,322	14.4
Florida	424	65	15.3	2,641	183	6.9	31,835	2,284	7.2	43,919	3,343	7.6
East South Central:												
Kentucky	14,248	123	0.9	12,434	117	0.9	70,557	530	0.8	105,309	741	0.7
Tennessee	5,312	116	2.2	3,398	114	3.3	19,526	477	2.4	40,966	1,067	2.6
Alabama	647	159	24.6	1,557	240	15.4	15,212	1,615	10.6	19,887	2,534	12.7
Mississippi	351	78	22.2	1,092	157	14.4	8,727	648	7.4	23,647	1,338	5.7
West South Central:												
Arkansas	538	122	22.7	819	401	50.0	4,080	1,639	40.2	6,588	2,197	33.3
Louisiana	78	6	7.7	311	9	2.9	5,557	40	0.7	6,982	55	0.8
Oklahoma	224	20	8.9	575	13	2.3	2,529	85	3.4	5,942	124	2.1
Texas	607	55	9.1	1,846	194	10.5	12,895	716	5.6	26,205	1,058	4.0

Source: "Crops in 1909 on Farms in the South—Farms Reporting, Acreage, Yield, and Value of Specified Crops on All Farms and on Colored Farms, by Divisions and States," *Negro Population, 1790-1915,* 1918, p. 598. Primary source: U.S. Bureau of the Census. *Negro Population, 1790-1915.* Washington, D.C.: Government Printing Office, 1918. *Notes:* "Colored" may include persons other than Black. 1. Acreage of farms less than 1 acre not included.

★ 33 ★

Crops/Livestock/Animals

Crops: Dry Peas Raised on Farms by Southern Division and State, 1909

DIVISION AND STATE	Number of farms reporting crop			Acreage in crop			Yield of crop			Value of crop		
		Colored farms			Colored farms			Colored farms			Colored farms	
	Total	Number	Percent	All farms	Number	Percent	All farms	Amount	Percent	All farms	Amount	Percent
							Bushels	Bushels				
THE SOUTH	209,064	72,989	34.9	1,009,836	284,854	28.2	3,803,461	1,038,529	27.3	$6,461,667	$1,737,609	26.9
South Atlantic	118,172	45,297	38.3	667,705	216,842	32.6	2,242,244	687,987	30.9	3,806,792	1,165,660	30.6
East South Central	58,833	19,984	34.0	203,229	47,706	23.5	882,471	229,529	26.0	1,560,726	387,563	24.8
West South Central	32,059	7,708	24.0	138,902	20,306	14.6	678,746	121,013	17.8	1,095,149	184,386	16.8
South Atlantic:												
Delaware	523	29	5.5	1,615	50	3.1	12,521	366	2.9	25,278	738	2.9
Maryland	350	32	9.1	742	44	5.9	5,603	660	11.8	11,143	1,284	11.5
District of Columbia	...	...	...	...	...	...	...	...	...	...	...	...
Virginia	4,462	1,587	35.6	12,091	2,624	21.7	66,468	15,445	23.2	127,211	29,944	23.5
West Virginia	93	...	...	232	...	...	1,490	...	...	3,312	...	...
North Carolina	39,726	8,349	21.0	169,934	33,262	19.6	651,567	102,470	15.7	1,024,228	160,362	15.6
South Carolina	35,660	18,997	53.3	265,632	103,257	38.9	711,853	301,354	43.2	1,311,454	543,123	41.4
Georgia	34,716	15,133	43.6	210,315	75,312	35.8	736,009	248,350	33.7	1,204,783	398,171	33.0
Florida	2,642	1,170	44.3	7,144	2,293	32.1	56,713	19,342	34.1	98,383	32,038	32.6
East South Central:												
Kentucky	1,732	39	2.3	8,465	193	2.3	44,772	764	1.7	84,514	1,286	1.5
Tennessee	10,175	1,402	13.8	36,640	3,515	9.6	133,924	12,084	9.0	245,434	22,819	9.3
Alabama	26,905	10,988	4.8	85,034	24,592	28.9	418,007	138,733	33.2	660,270	209,719	31.8
Mississippi	20,021	7,555	37.7	73,090	19,406	26.6	285,768	77,948	27.3	570,508	153,739	26.9
West South Central:												
Arkansas	13,821	2,995	21.7	52,730	7,325	14.0	229,444	42,640	18.6	376,076	67,271	17.9
Louisiana	6,330	1,974	31.2	33,150	5,240	15.8	161,659	43,421	20.6	252,362	45,067	17.9

[Continued]

★ 33 ★

Crops: Dry Peas Raised on Farms by Southern Division and State, 1909

[Continued]

DIVISION AND STATE	CROPS IN 1909											
	Number of farms reporting crop			Acreage in crop			Yield of crop			Value of crop		
	Total	Colored farms		All farms	Colored farms		All farms	Colored farms		All farms	Colored farms	
		Number	Percent		Number	Percent		Amount	Percent		Amount	Percent
Oklahoma	1,612	290	18.0	6,245	489	7.8	33,282	3,836	11.6	63,857	7,605	11.9
Texas	10,296	2,449	23.8	46,777	7,252	15.5	254,361	42,116	16.6	402,854	64,443	16.0

Source: "Crops in 1909 on Farms in the South—Farms Reporting, Acreage, Yield, and Value of Specified Crops on All Farms and on Colored Farms, by Divisions and States," *Negro Population, 1790-1915*, 1918, p. 597. Primary source: U.S. Bureau of the Census. *Negro Population, 1790-1915*. Washington, D.C.: Government Printing Office, 1918. *Note:* "Colored" may include persons other than Black.

★ 34 ★

Crops/Livestock/Animals

Crops: Hay and Forage Raised on Farms by Southern Division and State, 1909

DIVISION AND STATE	CROPS IN 1909											
	Number of farms reporting crop			Acreage in crop			Yield of crop			Value of crop		
	Total	Colored farms		All farms	Colored farms		All farms	Colored farms		All farms	Colored farms	
		Number	Percent		Acres	Percent		Amount	Percent		Amount	Percent
HAY AND FORAGE												
							Tons	Tons				
THE SOUTH	...	...	...	8,620,243	468,581	5.4	8,866,596	468,394	5.2	$97,264,658	$5,008,872	5.1
South Atlantic	...	...	...	2,856,398	189,680	6.6	2,917,870	174,793	6.0	37,836,676	2,177,069	5.8
East South Central	...	...	...	2,487,554	137,315	5.5	2,565,716	137,957	5.4	29,644,661	1,634,059	5.5
West South Central	...	...	...	2,276,291	141,586	4.3	3,383,010	155,644	4.6	29,783,321	1,192,804	4.0
South Atlantic:												
Delaware	...	...	...	80,669	2,621	3.2	103,575	3,430	3.3	1,174,478	33,448	2.8
Maryland	...	...	...	398,842	8,799	2.2	477,564	9,734	2.0	6,011,749	119,921	2.0
District of Columbia	...	...	...	962	...	...	2,148	...	...	25,633	...	...
Virginia	...	...	...	773,577	36,027	4.7	823,383	34,609	4.2	10,256,998	469,902	4.6
West Virginia	...	...	...	708,900	1,804	0.3	639,104	1,728	0.3	7,492,747	21,767	0.3
North Carolina	...	...	...	375,795	48,915	13.0	369,382	48,748	13.2	4,781,562	290,232	6.1
South Carolina	...	...	...	209,767	45,055	21.5	186,131	34,173	18.4	3,189,122	585,679	18.4
Georgia	...	...	...	253,157	39,375	15.6	261,333	36,326	13.9	4,056,907	569,275	14.0
Florida	...	...	...	54,729	7,084	12.9	55,300	6,045	10.9	847,485	86,791	10.2
East South Central:												
Kentucky	...	...	...	966,377	11,703	1.2	957,241	10,943	1.1	10,306,344	118,581	1.2
Tennessee	...	...	...	1,052,816	43,900	4.2	1,077,836	40,399	0.4	12,617,538	493,424	3.9
Alabama	...	...	...	238,656	35,593	14.9	251,403	35,738	14.2	3,357,132	439,366	13.1
Mississippi	...	...	...	229,705	46,119	20.1	279,236	50,877	18.2	3,363,647	582,688	17.3
West South Central:												
Arkansas	...	...	...	435,915	16,456	3.8	461,817	19,233	4.2	4,887,139	239,774	4.9
Louisiana	...	...	...	180,811	14,077	7.7	245,815	19,162	7.8	2,433,101	178,054	7.3
Oklahoma	...	...	...	1,347,508	92,610	6.9	1,417,533	93,942	6.6	9,638,648	517,174	5.4
Texas	...	...	...	1,311,967	18,443	1.4	1,257,845	23,307	1.9	12,824,433	257,802	2.0

Source: "Crops in 1909 on Farms in the South—Farms Reporting, Acreage, Yield, and Value of Specified Crops on All Farms and on Colored Farms, by Divisions and States," *Negro Population, 1790-1915*, 1918, p. 595. Primary source: U.S. Bureau of the Census. *Negroes Population, 1790-1915*. Washington, D.C.: U.S. Government Printing Office, 1918. *Note:* "Colored" may include persons other than Black.

★ 35 ★

Crops/Livestock/Animals

Crops: Kafir Corn Raised on Farms by Southern Division and State, 1909

DIVISION AND STATE	CROPS IN 1909											
	Number of farms reporting crop			Acreage in crop			Yield of crop			Value of crop		
	Total	Colored farms		All farms	Colored farms		All farms	Colored farms		All farms	Colored farms	
		Number	Percent		Number	Percent		Amount	Percent		Amount	Percent
KAFIR CORN												
							Bushels	Bushels				
THE SOUTH	54,193	593	1.1	1,108,129	3,402	0.3	10,546,626	40,430	0.4	$6,338,581	$23,343	0.4
South Atlantic	125	13	10.4	230	18	7.8	3,561	214	6.0	2,918	201	6.9
East South Central	215	4	1.9	493	5	1.0	6,453	121	1.9	4,998	117	2.3
West South Central	53,853	576	1.1	1,107,406	3,379	0.3	10,536,612	40,095	0.4	6,330,665	23,025	0.4
South Atlantic:												
Delaware	2	...	...	1	...	...	25	...	...	25	...	...
Maryland	9	1	11.1	19	...	...	238	10	4.2	173	5	2.9
District of Columbia	...	...	...	...	...	...	...	...	...	...	...	...
Virginia	33	5	15.1	80	5	6.2	1,438	41	2.9	1,032	38	3.7
West Virginia	16	...	...	26	...	...	467	...	...	326	...	...
North Carolina	32	1	3.1	65	4	6.1	599	20	3.3	537	20	3.7
South Carolina	7	4	57.1	8	7	87.5	135	116	85.9	132	111	84.1
Georgia	14	1	7.1	15	1	6.6	237	15	6.3	258	12	4.7
Florida	12	1	8.3	16	1	6.2	422	12	2.8	435	15	3.4
East South Central:												
Kentucky	87	1	1.1	190	1	0.5	2,404	10	0.4	1,588	6	0.4
Tennessee	45	...	...	119	...	...	1,539	...	...	1,093	...	...
Alabama	51	1	2.0	140	1	0.7	1,716	80	4.7	1,611	80	5.0
Mississippi	32	2	6.2	44	3	6.8	794	31	3.9	706	31	4.4
West South Central:												
Arkansas	530	7	1.3	1,294	10	0.8	15,284	192	1.3	12,074	202	1.7
Louisiana	32	2	6.2	213	1	0.5	2,132	27	1.3	2,092	22	1.1
Oklahoma	29,660	541	1.8	532,215	3,202	0.6	4,658,752	38,468	0.8	2,531,036	21,700	0.9
Texas	23,631	26	0.1	573,384	166	[1]	5,860,444	1,408	[1]	3,785,463	1,101	[1]

Source: "Crops in 1909 on Farms in the South—Farms Reporting, Acreage, Yield, and Value of Specified Crops on All Farms and on Colored Farms, by Divisions and States," *Negro Population, 1790-1915*, 1918, p. 599. Primary source: U.S. Bureau of the Census. *Negro Population, 1790-1915*, Washington, D.C.: Government Printing Office, 1918. *Note:* "Colored" may include persons other than Black.

★ 36 ★

Crops/Livestock/Animals

Crops: Main Crops Produced by Black Farmers, c. 1913

Crop	Quantity Produced		Per cent of Total Crop raised in United States
	Unit of measure	Total	
Cotton	Bales	4,000,000	39.0
Corn	Bushels	100,000,000	3.5
Oats	Bushels	4,500,000	0.4
Wheat	Bushels	4,000,000	0.5
Rice	Pounds	20,000,000	9.0
White Potatoes	Bushels	4,000,000	1.0
Sweet Potatoes	Bushels	12,000,000	21.0

[Continued]

★ 36 ★

Crops: Main Crops Produced by Black Farmers, c. 1913
[Continued]

| Crop | Quantity Produced | | Per cent of Total Crop raised in United States |
	Unit of measure	Total	
Tobacco	Pounds	90,000,000	10.0
Hay and Forage	Tons	500,000	0.5

Source: "Amount Principal Crops Raised by Negro Farmers," *Negro Year Book and Annual Encyclopedia of the Negro,* 1913, p. 290. Primary source: Work, Monroe N. (Ed.) *Negro Year Book and Annual Encyclopedia of the Negro.* Tuskegee Institute, AL: Negro Year Book Co., 1913. Published by permission.

★ 37 ★

Crops/Livestock/Animals

Crops: Oats Produced on Farms by Southern Division and State, 1909

DIVISION AND STATE	CROPS IN 1909											
	Number of farms reporting crop			Acreage in crop			Yield of crop			Value of crop		
	Total	Colored farms		All farms	Colored farms		All farms	Colored farms		All farms	Colored farms	
		Number	Percent		Acres	Percent		Amount	Percent		Amount	Percent
							OATS					
							Bushels	Bushels				
THE SOUTH	495,381	81,831	16.5	3,516,128	321,960	9.2	60,126,382	4,358,927	7.2	$32,688,105	$2,726,848	8.3
South Atlantic	251,129	57,463	22.9	1,368,832	213,778	15.6	21,206,000	2,758,384	13.0	13,388,578	1,842,629	13.8
East South Central	144,577	18,105	12.5	870,762	69,132	7.9	11,646,687	840,120	7.2	6,535,286	521,697	8.0
West South Central	99,675	6,263	6.3	1,276,534	39,050	3.1	27,273,695	760,423	2.8	12,764,241	362,522	2.8
South Atlantic:												
Delaware	698	19	2.7	4,226	81	1.9	98,239	794	0.8	51,022	396	0.8
Maryland	8,831	212	2.4	49,210	822	1.7	1,160,663	14,065	1.2	584,395	7,031	1.2
District of Columbia	2	...	...	13	...	...	375	...	...	165	...	...
Virginia	36,306	5,340	14.7	204,455	18,021	8.8	2,884,495	192,882	6.7	1,609,973	118,527	7.4
West Virginia	22,412	81	0.4	103,758	287	0.3	1,728,806	4,192	0.2	912,388	2,437	0.3
North Carolina	48,958	6,619	13.5	228,120	22,761	10.0	2,782,508	246,857	8.9	1,741,561	156,174	9.0
South Carolina	57,398	22,610	39.4	324,180	80,443	24.8	5,745,291	1,150,309	20.0	3,809,345	763,909	20.1
Georgia	70,379	20,728	29.5	411,664	82,401	20.0	6,199,243	1,033,728	16.7	4,236,625	705,315	16.6
Florida	6,145	1,854	30.2	43,206	8,962	20.7	606,380	115,557	19.1	443,104	88,840	20.0
East South Central:												
Kentucky	25,548	489	1.9	174,315	3,024	1.7	2,406,064	44,601	1.9	1,216,187	22,414	1.8
Tennessee	44,432	2,434	5.5	342,086	12,891	3.8	4,720,692	172,714	3.7	2,378,464	87,724	3.7
Alabama	51,857	10,247	19.8	257,276	37,648	14.6	3,251,146	443,387	13.6	2,117,703	293,505	13.9
Mississippi	22,740	4,395	21.7	97,085	15,569	16.0	1,268,785	179,418	14.1	822,932	118,054	14.3
West South Central:												
Arkansas	31,836	2,078	6.5	197,449	6,699	3.4	3,212,801	79,038	2.5	1,641,752	48,244	2.9
Louisiana	4,579	841	18.4	29,711	3,235	10.9	420,033	34,546	8.2	250,598	21,473	8.6
Oklahoma	33,002	1,630	4.9	609,373	20,105	3.3	16,606,154	504,053	3.0	7,172,267	213,779	3.0
Texas	30,258	1,714	5.7	440,001	9,011	2.0	7,034,617	142,786	2.0	3,699,634	79,026	2.1

Source: "Crops in 1909 on Farms in the South—Farms Reporting, Acreage, Yield, and Value of Specified Crops on All Farms and on Colored Farms, by Divisions and States," *Negro Population, 1790-1915,* 1918, p. 596. Primary source: U.S. Bureau of the Census. *Negroes Population, 1790-1915.* Washington, D.C.: U.S. Government Printing Office, 1918. *Note:* "Colored" may include persons other than Black.

★ 38 ★

Crops/Livestock/Animals

Crops: Peanuts Produced on Farms by Southern Division and State, 1909

DIVISION AND STATE	CROPS IN 1909											
	Number of farms reporting crop			Acreage in crop			Yield of crop			Value of crop		
	Total	Colored farms		All farms	Colored farms		All farms	Colored farms		All farms	Colored farms	
		Number	Percent		Acres	Percent		Amount	Percent		Amount	Percent
PEANUTS												
							Bushels	Bushels				
THE SOUTH	217,379	77,984	35.9	869,176	236,139	27.2	19,400,338	5,069,004	26.1	$18,253,270	$4,797,046	26.3
South Atlantic	102,128	39,405	38.6	634,436	199,518	31.4	15,305,253	4,470,237	29.2	14,341,058	4,190,919	29.2
East South Central	64,960	25,491	39.2	133,637	22,751	17.0	2,407,562	371,777	15.4	2,196,522	370,621	16.9
West South Central	50,291	13,088	26.0	101,103	13,870	13.7	1,687,523	226,990	13.5	1,715,690	235,506	13.7
South Atlantic:												
Delaware	10	1	10.0	25	7	28.0	202	160	79.2	196	132	67.3
Maryland	12	1	8.3	1	...	...	30	2	6.7	37	7	18.9
District of Columbia	...	...	...	...	...	...	...	...	...	...	...	...
Virginia	12,927	6,227	48.2	145,213	55,134	38.0	4,284,340	1,404,523	32.8	4,239,832	1,390,104	32.8
West Virginia	21	...	...	...	...	...	64	...	...	168	...	...
North Carolina	31,503	11,972	38.0	195,134	76,264	39.1	5,980,919	2,000,778	33.5	5,368,826	1,813,564	33.8
South Carolina	5,846	2,487	42.5	7,596	2,081	27.4	154,822	36,925	23.8	114,211	34,293	23.8
Georgia	32,590	11,891	36.5	160,317	39,230	24.5	2,569,787	585,432	22.8	2,440,926	540,806	22.2
Florida	19,219	6,826	35.5	126,150	26,802	21.2	2,315,089	442,417	19.1	2,146,862	412,013	19.2
East South Central:												
Kentucky	140	6	4.3	79	...	...	1,735	8	0.5	1,867	13	0.7
Tennessee	3,947	213	5.4	18,952	608	3.2	547,240	15,157	2.7	386,765	10,382	2.7
Alabama	37,702	14,547	38.6	100,609	17,818	17.7	1,573,796	272,786	17.3	1,490,654	264,630	17.7
Mississippi	23,171	10,725	46.3	13,997	4,325	30.9	284,791	83,826	29.4	317,236	95,596	30.1
West South Central:												
Arkansas	10,025	2,777	27.7	10,192	2,196	21.5	168,608	35,435	21.0	183,364	40,068	21.8
Louisiana	14,492	4,932	34.0	25,020	4,612	18.4	412,037	77,705	18.9	422,232	77,574	18.4
Oklahoma	1,299	203	15.6	1,564	150	9.6	31,880	2,526	7.9	34,984	3,504	10.0
Texas	24,475	5,176	21.1	64,327	6,912	10.7	1,074,998	111,324	10.4	1,075,110	114,360	10.6

Source: "Crops in 1909 on Farms in the South—Farms Reporting, Acreage, Yield, and Value of Specified Crops on All Farms and on Colored Farms, by Divisions and States," *Negro Population, 1790-1915*, 1918, p. 596. Primary source: U.S. Bureau of the Census. *Negroes Population, 1790-1915*. Washington, D.C.: U.S. Government Printing Office, 1918. *Note:* "Colored" may include persons other than Black.

★ 39 ★

Crops/Livestock/Animals

Crops: Percentage Distribution of Main Crops Produced by Black Farmers, c. 1913

Crop	Per Cent
Cotton	37.0
Corn	20.0
Potatoes	16.0
Hay and Forage	15.0
Oats	7.0
Tobacco	3.0
Wheat	2.0
Rice	0.05

[Continued]

★ 39 ★

Crops: Percentage Distribution of Main Crops
Produced by Black Farmers, c. 1913
[Continued]

Crop	Per Cent
Miscellaneous	0.05
Total	100.00

Source: "Principal Crops Raised by Negro Farmers Distributed on a Percentage Basis," *Negro Year Book and Annual Encyclopedia of the Negro*, 1913, p. 290. Primary source: Work, Monroe N. (Ed.) *Negro Year Book and Annual Encyclopedia of the Negro*. Tuskegee Institute, AL: Negro Year Book Co., 1913. Published by permission.

★ 40 ★

Crops/Livestock/Animals

Crops: Potatoes Raised on Farms by Southern Division and State, 1909

DIVISION AND STATE	CROPS IN 1909											
	Number of farms reporting crop			Acreage in crop			Yield of crop			Value of crop		
	Total	Colored farms		All farms	Colored farms		All farms	Colored farms		All farms	Colored farms	
		Number	Percent		Number	Percent		Amount	Percent		Amount	Percent
POTATOES												
							Bushels	Bushels				
THE SOUTH	847,963	97,875	11.5	477,064	50,680	10.6	39,332,677	3,138,024	8.7	$25,472,023	$2,140,099	9.5
South Atlantic	350,428	48,128	13.7	239,762	29,508	12.4	22,102,630	2,179,583	9.9	14,091,735	1,179,417	10.5
East South Central	307,436	28,778	9.4	119,541	9,077	7.6	9,816,160	560,753	5.8	5,910,784	429,879	7.2
West South Central	189,999	20,969	11.0	117,761	12,095	10.3	7,413,887	688,688	9.3	5,439,504	500,803	9.2
South Atlantic:												
Delaware	7,641	565	7.4	9,703	491	5.1	880,360	10,187	4.6	453,400	18,669	4.1
Maryland	34,870	3,054	8.8	39,299	1,865	4.7	3,444,311	133,434	3.9	1,782,954	66,515	3.7
District of Columbia	91	6	6.6	226	4	1.8	32,028	490	1.5	20,231	303	1.5
Virginia	106,499	22,471	21.1	86,927	16,501	19.0	8,770,778	1,318,800	15.0	5,667,557	895,815	15.8
West Virginia	81,297	261	0.3	42,621	98	0.2	4,077,086	9,427	0.2	2,278,638	5,410	2.4
North Carolina	77,421	9,282	12.0	31,990	3,401	10.6	2,372,280	226,454	9.5	1,755,413	167,934	9.6
South Carolina	13,656	4,999	36.6	8,610	2,424	28.2	782,430	146,139	18.7	609,424	102,532	16.8
Georgia	23,861	5,919	24.8	11,877	3,197	26.9	886,430	196,042	22.1	684,427	135,659	19.8
Florida	5,092	1,571	30.9	8,509	1,527	17.9	856,967	108,610	12.7	839,691	86,580	10.3
East South Central:												
Kentucky	130,076	2,860	2.1	55,750	905	1.6	5,120,141	76,871	1.5	2,724,043	42,992	1.6
Tennessee	111,967	8,333	7.4	40,963	2,490	6.1	2,922,713	145,028	5.0	1,790,233	93,276	5.2
Alabama	37,374	6,694	17.9	14,486	2,830	19.5	1,128,564	162,593	14.4	884,497	130,256	14.7
Mississippi	28,019	10,891	38.9	8,342	2,852	34.2	644,742	185,261	28.7	542,011	163,355	30.1
West South Central:												
Arkansas	79,127	9,304	11.8	29,719	2,678	9.0	2,096,893	158,093	7.5	1,439,991	125,367	8.7
Louisiana	18,230	4,159	22.8	19,655	3,566	18.2	1,183,525	196,119	16.1	924,311	143,804	10.6
Oklahoma	45,369	3,320	7.3	32,295	3,267	10.1	1,897,486	189,627	10.0	1,250,052	115,081	9.2
Texas	47,273	4,186	8.9	36,092	2,564	7.1	2,235,983	144,839	6.5	1,825,150	116,551	6.4

Source: "Crops in 1909 on Farms in the South—Farms Reporting, Acreage, Yield, and Value of Specified Crops on All Farms and on Colored Farms, by Divisions and States," *Negro Population, 1790-1915*, 1918, p. 596. Primary source: U.S. Bureau of the Census. *Negro Population, 1790-1915*. Washington, D.C.: Government Printing Office, 1918. *Note:* "Colored" may include persons other than Black.

★ 41 ★

Crops/Livestock/Animals

Crops: Rice Produced on Farms by Southern Division and State, 1909

DIVISION AND STATE	CROPS IN 1909											
	Number of farms reporting crop			Acreage in crop			Yield of crop			Value of crop		
	Total	Colored farms		All farms	Colored farms		All farms	Colored farms		All farms	Colored farms	
		Number	Percent		Number	Percent		Amount	Percent		Amount	Percent
RICE												
							Bushels	Bushels				
THE SOUTH	13,706	4,967	36.2	610,163	29,235	4.8	21,838,520	889,103	4.1	$16,019,567	$677,542	4.2
South Atlantic	5,527	3,843	69.5	27,080	7,836	28.9	713,966	166,119	23.3	691,372	157,887	22.8
East South Central	596	156	26.2	560	76	13.6	10,006	1,318	13.2	10,547	1,618	15.3
West South Central	7,583	968	12.8	582,523	21,323	3.7	21,114,548	721,666	3.4	15,317,648	518,037	3.4
South Atlantic:												
Delaware	...	...	...	...	...	...	...	...	...	...	...	...
Maryland	...	...	...	...	...	...	...	...	...	...	...	...
District of Columbia	...	...	...	...	...	...	...	...	...	...	...	...
Virginia	...	...	...	...	...	...	...	...	...	...	...	...
West Virginia	...	...	...	...	...	...	...	...	...	...	...	...
North Carolina	161	64	39.8	521	195	37.4	11,357	4,042	35.6	10,269	4,056	39.5
South Carolina	3,017	2,379	78.9	19,491	5,401	27.7	541,570	110,188	20.3	520,000	100,977	19.4
Georgia	1,740	1,241	71.3	6,445	2,088	32.4	148,698	49,534	33.3	145,813	50,124	34.4
Florida	609	159	26.2	623	152	24.4	12,341	2,355	19.1	15,290	2,730	17.9
East South Central:												
Kentucky	...	...	...	...	...	...	...	...	...	...	...	...
Tennessee	...	...	...	...	...	...	...	...	...	...	...	...
Alabama	238	50	21.0	279	15	5.4	5,170	402	7.8	5,179	564	10.9
Mississippi	358	106	29.6	281	61	21.7	4,836	916	18.9	5,368	1,054	19.6
West South Central:												
Arkansas	290	5	1.7	27,419	68	0.2	1,282,830	4,352	0.3	1,156,103	3,091	0.3
Louisiana	6,138	932	15.2	317,518	13,894	4.4	10,839,973	390,359	3.6	8,053,222	314,096	3.9
Oklahoma	...	...	...	...	...	...	...	...	...	...	...	...
Texas	1,155	31	2.7	237,586	7,361	3.1	8,991,745	326,955	3.6	6,106,323	200,850	3.3

Source: "Crops in 1909 on Farms in the South—Farms Reporting, Acreage, Yield, and Value of Specified Crops on All Farms and on Colored Farms, by Divisions and States," *Negro Population, 1790-1915*, 1918, p. 597. Primary source: U.S. Bureau of the Census. *Negro Population, 1790-1915.* Washington, D.C.: Government Printing Office, 1918. *Note:* "Colored" may include persons other than Black.

★ 42 ★

Crops/Livestock/Animals

Crops: Rye Produced on Farms by Southern Division and State, 1909

DIVISION AND STATE	CROPS IN 1909											
	Number of farms reporting crop			Acreage in crop			Yield of crop			Value of crop		
	Total	Colored farms		All farms	Colored farms		All farms	Colored farms		All farms	Colored farms	
		Number	Percent		Number	Percent		Amount	Percent		Amount	Percent
RYE												
							Bushels	Bushels				
THE SOUTH	40,769	1,941	4.8	213,563	6,597	3.1	1,772,320	48,279	2.7	$1,484,934	$44,111	3.0
South Atlantic	32,982	1,773	5.4	157,546	5,469	3.5	1,322,474	39,044	2.9	1,106,617	36,179	3.3
East South Central	6,940	145	2.1	50,091	996	2.0	400,709	7,847	2.0	337,152	6,836	2.0
West South Central	847	23	2.7	5,926	132	2.2	49,137	1,388	2.8	41,165	1,096	2.7
South Atlantic:												
Delaware	210	13	6.2	1,017	39	3.8	11,423	389	3.4	8,169	272	3.3
Maryland	5,181	215	4.1	28,093	929	3.3	357,562	9,174	2.6	252,691	6,581	2.6
District of Columbia	2	...	...	13	...	...	190	...	...	135	...	...
Virginia	8,509	524	6.2	47,890	1,728	3.6	438,345	13,994	3.2	344,241	11,080	3.2

[Continued]

★ 42 ★

Crops: Rye Produced on Farms by Southern Division and State, 1909
[Continued]

DIVISION AND STATE	CROPS IN 1909											
	Number of farms reporting crop			Acreage in crop			Yield of crop			Value of crop		
	Total	Colored farms		All farms	Colored farms		All farms	Colored farms		All farms	Colored farms	
		Number	Percent		Number	Percent		Amount	Percent		Amount	Percent
West Virginia	2,774	1	[1]	15,679	7	[1]	148,676	70	[1]	122,258	56	[1]
North Carolina	12,830	706	5.5	48,685	1,957	4.0	280,431	10,033	3.6	269,566	9,981	3.7
South Carolina	1,043	141	13.5	2,958	368	12.1	20,631	2,151	10.4	32,197	3,651	11.3
Georgia	2,340	154	6.6	12,352	307	2.5	59,937	2,182	3.6	69,365	3,102	4.5
Florida	93	19	20.4	859	144	16.8	5,279	1,051	19.9	7,995	1,456	18.2
East South Central:												
Kentucky	3,488	43	1.2	26,813	357	1.3	255,532	3,561	1.4	202,534	3,085	1.5
Tennessee	3,166	86	2.7	22,798	615	2.7	140,925	3,980	2.8	129,845	3,464	2.7
Alabama	267	15	5.6	437	24	5.5	3,736	304	8.1	4,314	286	6.6
Mississippi	19	1	5.3	43	...	...	516	2	0.4	459	1	0.2
West South Central:												
Arkansas	303	12	4.0	1,080	27	2.5	7,354	389	5.3	6,834	268	3.1
Louisiana	9	...	...	19	...	...	193	...	...	236	...	...
Oklahoma	396	9	2.3	4,291	88	2.1	37,240	881	2.4	30,364	706	2.3
Texas	139	2	1.4	536	17	3.2	4,350	118	2.7	3,731	122	3.3

Source: "Crops in 1909 on Farms in the South—Farms Reporting, Acreage, Yield, and Value of Specified Crops on All Farms and on Colored Farms, by Divisions and States," *Negro Population, 1790-1915,* 1918, p. 598. Primary source: U.S. Bureau of the Census. *Negro Population, 1790-1915.* Washington, D.C.: Government Printing Office, 1918. *Notes:* "Colored" may include persons other than Black. 1. Less than one-tenth of 1 per cent.

★ 43 ★

Crops/Livestock/Animals

Crops: Soy Beans Raised on Farms by Southern Division and State, 1909

DIVISION AND STATE	CROPS IN 1909											
	Number of farms reporting crop			Acreage in crop			Yield of crop			Value of crop		
	Total	Colored farms		All farms	Colored farms		All farms	Colored farms		All farms	Colored farms	
		Number	Percent		Number	Percent		Amount	Percent		Amount	Percent
SOY BEANS												
							Bushels	Bushels				
THE SOUTH	2,055	252	12.3	14,029	1,401	9.9	169,379	14,042	8.3	$225,512	$17,817	7.9
South Atlantic	1,397	203	14.5	10,079	1,166	11.6	132,408	12,339	9.3	175,963	15,361	8.7
East South Central	655	48	7.3	3,946	234	5.9	36,833	1,698	4.6	49,211	2,451	5.0
West South Central	3	1	33.3	4	1	25.0	138	5	3.6	388	5	1.5
South Atlantic:												
Delaware	...	...	...	...	...	...	...	...	...	...	...	...
Maryland	...	...	...	...	...	...	...	...	...	...	...	...
District of Columbia	...	...	...	...	...	...	...	...	...	...	...	...
Virginia	6	1	16.7	29	5	17.2	415	100	24.1	695	100	14.4
West Virginia	...	...	...	...	...	...	...	...	...	...	...	...
North Carolina	264	46	17.4	1,249	188	15.1	13,313	1,953	14.7	14,141	1,980	14.0
South Carolina	1	...	...	1	...	...	12	...	...	36	...	4.9
Georgia	66[1]	2	3.0	437	12	2.7	4,264	190	4.5	8,612	420	4.9
Florida	1,060	154	14.5	8,363	961	11.5	114,404	10,096	8.8	152,479	12,861	8.4
East South Central:												
Kentucky	6	...	...	8	...	...	27	...	...	53	...	...
Tennessee	41	2	4.9	256	...	...	2,037	4	0.2	3,387	8	0.2
Alabama	602	45	7.5	3,667	234	6.4	34,617	1,689	4.9	45,393	2,431	5.4
Mississippi	6	1	16.7	15	...	...	152	5	3.3	378	12	3.2
West South Central:												
Arkansas	...	...	...	...	...	...	...	...	...	...	...	...
Louisiana	2	...	...	3	...	...	133	...	...	333	...	...

[Continued]

★ 43 ★

Crops: Soy Beans Raised on Farms by Southern Division and State, 1909
[Continued]

DIVISION AND STATE	CROPS IN 1909											
	Number of farms reporting crop			Acreage in crop			Yield of crop			Value of crop		
	Total	Colored farms		All farms	Colored farms		All farms	Colored farms		All farms	Colored farms	
		Number	Percent		Number	Percent		Amount	Percent		Amount	Percent
Oklahoma	...	...	...	...	...	...	...	...	...	...	...	...
Texas	1	1	100.0	1	1	100.0	5	5	100.0	5	5	100.0

Source: "Crops in 1909 on Farms in the South—Farms Reporting, Acreage, Yield, and Value of Specified Crops on All Farms and on Colored Farms, by Divisions and States," *Negro Population, 1790-1915*, 1918, p. 599. Primary source: U.S. Bureau of the Census. *Negro Population, 1790-1915*. Washington, D.C.: Government Printing Office, 1918. *Notes:* "Colored" may include persons other than Black. 1. Includes velvet beans.

★ 44 ★

Crops/Livestock/Animals

Crops: Sweet Potato and Yam Production in States with High Sweet Potato/Yam-Producing (10,000 Bushels or More) Black Farmers, 1929
[Colored farmers include Negroes, Indians, Chinese, Japanese, and all other nonwhite races]

STATE	ALL FARM OPERATORS REPORTING-		COLORED FARM OPERATORS REPORTING-			
	Acreage	Production (pounds)	Acreage	Production (pounds)	Percent of total	
					Acreage	Production
Total	618,356	61,979,860	166,520	14,998,766	26.9	24.2
Alabama	68,105	6,601,508	27,533	2,361,303	40.4	35.8
Mississippi	53,412	6,141,197	20,881	2,135,310	39.1	34.8
Georgia	84,855	7,889,447	24,440	2,127,760	28.8	27.0
South Carolina	46,776	5,011,099	21,473	1,968,343	45.9	39.3
Virginia	35,720	5,042,596	11,617	1,545,236	32.5	30.6
Louisiana	66,579	4,953,138	20,952	1,443,584	31.5	29.1
North Carolina	60,352	6,716,596	13,132	1,292,998	21.8	19.3
Texas	44,652	3,392,764	8,237	563,153	18.4	16.6
Tennessee	53,842	5,498,467	5,072	445,664	9.4	8.1
Florida	19,753	1,796,764	4,888	362,281	24.7	20.2
Arkansas	22,235	1,863,240	4,174	315,324	18.8	16.9
Maryland	8,984	1,629,673	996	173,956	11.1	10.7
Oklahoma	15,998	1,334,798	1,864	124,672	11.7	9.3
Delaware	6,106	884,527	484	61,178	7.9	6.9
Kentucky	14,076	1,266,724	392	37,004	2.8	2.9
New Jersey	12,147	1,498,709	242	28,850	2.0	1.9
Illinois	4,764	458,523	143	12,150	3.0	2.6

Source: "Sweetpotatoes and Yams—Acreage and Production, by States Reporting 10,000 Bushels or More Produced by Colored Farmers: 1929," *Negroes in the United States, 1920-1932*, 1935, p. 588. Primary source: U.S. Bureau of the Census. *Negroes in the United States, 1920-1932*. Washington, D.C.: U.S. Government Printing Office, 1935.

★ 45 ★

Crops/Livestock/Animals

Crops: Sweet Potatoes Raised on Farms by Southern Division and State, 1909

DIVISION AND STATE	CROPS IN 1909											
	Number of farms reporting crop			Acreage in crop			Yield of crop			Value of crop		
	Total	Colored farms		All farms	Colored farms		All farms	Colored farms		All farms	Colored farms	
		Number	Percent		Acres	Percent		Amount	Percent		Amount	Percent
							SWEET POTATOES					
							Bushels	Bushels				
THE SOUTH	1,015,019	295,854	29.1	583,042	166,072	28.5	52,277,661	12,047,068	23.1	$31,528,482	$7,491,817	23.8
South Atlantic	484,044	156,436	32.3	295,879	88,459	29.9	29,628,153	6,898,014	23.3	16,146,222	3,876,236	24.0
East South Central	368,122	96,052	26.1	160,756	48,086	29.9	13,573,580	3,173,155	23.4	9,116,510	2,308,140	25.3
West South Central	162,853	43,366	27.2	126,407	29,527	23.4	9,025,928	1,975,899	21.9	6,255,750	1,307,441	20.9
South Atlantic:												
Delaware	4,566	388	8.5	5,229	408	7.8	733,746	51,841	7.1	276,679	18,718	6.8
Maryland	11,175	1,610	14.4	7,956	840	10.6	1,065,956	84,232	7.9	483,751	38,168	7.9
District of Columbia	53	3	5.7	126	11	8.7	19,662	185	0.9	13,287	122	0.9
Virginia	67,506	22,480	33.3	40,838	13,094	32.1	5,270,202	1,409,041	26.7	2,681,472	721,405	26.9
West Virginia	15,632	11	0.1	2,079	3	0.1	215,582	262	0.1	170,086	237	0.1
North Carolina	142,238	32,559	22.9	84,740	17,488	20.6	8,403,283	1,375,050	16.2	4,333,297	720,809	16.6
South Carolina	88,340	44,801	50.7	48,878	23,399	47.9	4,319,926	1,610,248	37.3	2,606,606	967,968	37.1
Georgia	131,458	48,035	36.5	84,038	27,327	32.5	7,426,131	1,984,022	26.7	4,349,806	1,184,965	27.2
Florida	23,076	6,459	28.4	21,995	5,889	26.8	2,083,665	383,133	18.4	1,231,238	223,844	18.2
East South Central:												
Kentucky	63,646	1,380	2.2	11,882	222	1.9	1,326,245	22,443	1.7	839,454	14,733	1.8
Tennessee	89,361	8,369	9.4	26,216	2,604	10.3	2,504,490	212,990	8.5	1,625,056	146,599	9.0
Alabama	117,522	41,840	35.6	66,613	23,418	35.2	5,314,857	1,418,179	26.7	3,578,710	1,003,800	28.0
Mississippi	97,593	44,463	45.6	56,045	21,752	38.8	4,427,988	1,519,543	34.3	3,073,290	1,143,008	37.2
West South Central:												
Arkansas	53,297	13,252	24.9	22,388	5,589	25.0	1,685,308	404,891	24.0	1,359,669	339,212	24.9
Louisiana	52,074	18,775	36.1	56,953	16,490	29.0	4,251,086	1,118,549	26.3	2,357,729	605,152	25.7
Oklahoma	9,480	1,596	16.8	5,056	825	16.3	359,451	49,822	13.9	350,553	49,737	14.2
Texas	48,002	9,743	20.3	42,010	6,623	15.8	2,730,083	402,637	14.7	2,197,799	313,340	14.3

Source: "Crops in 1909 on Farms in the South—Farms Reporting, Acreage, Yield, and Value of Specified Crops on All Farms and on Colored Farms, by Divisions and States," *Negro Population, 1790-1915*, 1918, p. 595. Primary source: U.S. Bureau of the Census. *Negroes Population, 1790-1915*. Washington, D.C.: U.S. Government Printing Office, 1918. *Note:* "Colored" may include persons other than Black.

★ 46 ★

Crops/Livestock/Animals

Crops: Tobacco Produced on Farms by Southern Division and State, 1909

DIVISION AND STATE	CROPS IN 1909											
	Number of farms reporting crop			Acreage in crop			Yield of crop			Value of crop		
	Total	Colored farms		All farms	Colored farms		All farms	Colored farms		All farms	Colored farms	
		Number	Percent		Acres	Percent		Amount	Percent		Amount	Percent
							Pounds	Pounds				
THE SOUTH	260,287	42,470	16.3	1,049,617	169,568	16.2	802,618,483	109,433,038	13.6	$78,506,324	$9,813,199	12.5
South Atlantic	120,731	33,717	27.9	487,411	131,019	26.9	334,569,496	80,767,734	24.1	32,843,156	7,319,700	22.3
East South Central	135,360	8,300	6.1	560,523	38,425	6.8	467,348,072	28,620,776	6.1	45,548,716	2,485,182	14.5
West South Central	4,196	453	10.8	1,683	124	7.4	700,915	44,528	6.4	114,452	8,317	7.3
South Atlantic:												
Delaware	...	...	...	...	...	...	...	...	...	...	...	...
Maryland	4,392	1,303	29.7	26,072	7,055	27.1	17,845,699	4,010,587	22.5	1,457,112	325,267	22.3
District of Columbia	...	...	...	...	...	...	...	...	...	...	...	...
Virginia	44,472	16,705	37.6	185,427	59,051	31.8	132,979,390	37,568,274	28.2	12,169,086	3,274,760	26.9

[Continued]

★ 46 ★

Crops: Tobacco Produced on Farms by Southern Division and State, 1909
[Continued]

DIVISION AND STATE	CROPS IN 1909											
	Number of farms reporting crop			Acreage in crop			Yield of crop			Value of crop		
	Total	Colored farms		All farms	Colored farms		All farms	Colored farms		All farms	Colored farms	
		Number	Percent		Acres	Percent		Amount	Percent		Amount	Percent
West Virginia	9,229	7	0.1	17,928	15	0.1	14,356,400	8,461	0.1	1,923,180	906	1
North Carolina	51,926	12,701	24.5	221,890	56,471	25.4	138,813,163	32,783,801	23.6	13,847,559	3,171,381	22.9
South Carolina	8,166	2,700	33.1	30,082	7,884	26.2	25,583,049	6,005,630	23.5	2,123,576	478,428	22.8
Georgia	1,760	88	5.0	2,025	95	4.7	1,485,994	60,260	4.1	297,167	7,508	2.5
Florida	716	213	29.7	3,987	448	11.2	3,505,801	330,721	9.4	1,025,476	55,450	5.4
East South Central:												
Kentucky	108,050	5,388	5.0	469,795	26,298	5.6	398,482,301	19,670,377	4.9	39,868,753	1,749,790	4.4
Tennessee	25,637	2,608	10.2	90,468	12,087	13.4	68,756,599	8,933,339	13.0	5,661,681	732,721	12.9
Alabama	1,267	117	9.2	211	22	10.4	90,572	8,595	9.5	14,892	1,204	8.1
Mississippi	406	187	46.0	49	18	36.7	18,600	8,465	45.5	3,390	1,467	43.0
West South Central:												
Arkansas	3,329	325	9.8	758	50	6.6	316,418	18,733	5.9	40,489	2,925	7.2
Louisiana	208	37	17.8	519	37	7.1	172,418	12,311	7.1	42,617	3,520	9.3
Oklahoma	207	39	18.8	82	17	20.7	50,546	6,316	12.5	5,312	694	13.1
Texas	452	52	11.5	221	20	6.0	161,333	7,188	4.4	26,034	1,178	4.5

Source: "Crops in 1909 on Farms in the South—Farms Reporting, Acreage, Yield, and Value of Specified Crops on All Farms and on Colored Farms, by Divisions and States," *Negro Population, 1790-1915,* 1918, p. 595. Primary source: U.S. Bureau of the Census. *Negroes in the United States, 1790-1915.* Washington, D.C.: U.S. Government Printing Office, 1918. *Notes:* "Colored" may include persons other than Black. 1. Less than one-tenth of 1 per cent.

★ 47 ★

Crops/Livestock/Animals

Crops: Tobacco Production in States with High Tobacco-Producing (10,000 Pounds or More) Black Farmers, 1929

[Colored farmers include Negroes, Indians, Chinese, Japanese, and all other nonwhite races]

STATE	ALL FARM OPERATORS REPORTING-		COLORED FARM OPERATORS REPORTING-			
	Acreage	Production (pounds)	Acreage	Production (pounds)	Percent of total	
					Acreage	Production
Total	1,814,170	1,366,693,200	365,798	239,049,788	20.2	17.5
North Carolina	685,074	454,222,610	212,144	132,096,917	31.0	29.1
Virginia	172,134	115,825,610	52,501	32,073,630	30.5	27.7
South Carolina	112,852	83,302,706	39,190	26,767,233	34.7	32.1
Kentucky	466,118	376,648,533	25,420	20,389,130	5.5	5.4
Tennessee	129,973	112,236,961	13,359	10,611,826	10.3	9.5
Georgia	90,170	82,363,722	11,572	9,910,692	12.8	12.0
Maryland	32,974	21,624,127	9,400	5,326,232	28.5	24.6
Florida	10,302	9,248,190	1,618	1,410,717	15.7	15.3
Ohio	49,575	39,828,515	303	277,580	.6	.6
Indiana	19,372	15,901,768	184	141,414	.9	.9
Alabama	547	357,093	64	51,820	11.7	14.5

[Continued]

★ 47 ★

Crops: Tobacco Production in States with High Tobacco-Producing (10,000 Pounds or More) Black Farmers, 1929

[Continued]

STATE	ALL FARM OPERATORS REPORTING-		COLORED FARM OPERATORS REPORTING-			
	Acreage	Production (pounds)	Acreage	Production (pounds)	Percent of total	
					Acreage	Production
Pennsylvania	40,040	50,584,276	21	25,630	.1	.1
Missouri	5,039	4,549,089	22	16,967	.4	.4

Source: "Tobacco—Acreage and Production, by States Reporting 10,000 Pounds or More Produced by Colored Farmers: 1929," *Negroes in the United States, 1920-1932,* 1935, p. 588. Primary source: U.S. Bureau of the Census. *Negroes in the United States, 1920-1932.* Washington, D.C.: U.S. Government Printing Office, 1935.

★ 48 ★

Crops/Livestock/Animals

Crops: Wheat Raised on Farms by Southern Division and State, 1909

DIVISION AND STATE	CROPS IN 1909											
	Number of farms reporting crop			Acreage in crop			Yield of crop			Value of crop		
	Total	Colored farms		All farms	Colored farms		All farms	Colored farms		All farms	Colored farms	
		Number	Percent		Number	Percent		Amount	Percent		Amount	Percent
WHEAT												
							Bushels	Bushels				
THE SOUTH	331,069	36,553	11.0	5,112,675	204,387	4.0	59,121,317	1,829,742	3.0	$61,854,632	$1,939,790	3.1
South Atlantic	212,246	32,717	15.4	2,241,345	152,828	6.8	26,650,768	1,262,466	4.7	28,725,004	1,360,487	4.7
East South Central	83,775	3,290	3.9	1,315,243	37,876	2.9	15,374,422	409,673	2.7	15,851,025	419,715	2.6
West South Central	35,048	546	1.6	1,556,087	13,683	0.9	17,096,127	157,603	0.9	17,278,603	159,588	0.9
South Atlantic:												
Delaware	4,827	215	4.5	111,215	3,679	3.3	1,643,572	45,429	2.8	1,697,539	46,543	2.7
Maryland	23,358	1,305	5.6	589,893	16,479	2.8	9,463,457	189,012	2.0	9,876,480	194,072	2.0
District of Columbia	...	...	...	...	...	...	...	...	...	...	...	...
Virginia	63,405	13,462	21.2	692,907	58,293	8.4	8,076,989	509,787	6.3	8,776,061	526,592	6.0
West Virginia	22,344	125	0.6	209,315	1,448	0.7	2,575,996	20,693	0.8	2,697,141	21,278	0.8
North Carolina	65,124	8,652	13.3	501,912	45,747	9.1	3,827,145	311,842	8.1	4,420,322	347,806	7.9
South Carolina	11,356	3,946	34.7	43,028	11,586	29.6	310,614	73,416	23.6	385,835	91,782	23.8
Georgia	21,827	5,010	23.0	93,065	15,594	16.8	752,858	112,265	14.9	871,494	132,397	15.2
Florida	5	2	40.0	10	2	20.0	137	22	16.0	132	17	12.9
East South Central:												
Kentucky	37,164	988	2.7	681,323	14,185	2.0	8,739,260	166,781	1.9	8,812,469	166,868	1.9
Tennessee	44,013	1,896	4.3	619,861	22,070	3.6	6,516,539	229,190	3.5	6,913,335	239,025	3.5
Alabama	2,463	355	14.4	13,665	1,518	11.1	113,953	12,625	11.1	120,873	13,000	10.8
Mississippi	135	51	37.8	394	103	26.1	4,670	1,077	28.1	4,348	822	18.9
West South Central:												
Arkansas	5,197	133	2.6	60,426	743	1.2	526,414	3,305	0.6	532,712	3,356	0.6
Louisiana	23	...	...	65	...	...	488	...	...	508	...	...
Oklahoma	23,003	362	1.6	1,169,420	11,777	1.0	14,008,334	143,400	1.0	13,854,322	142,969	1.0
Texas	6,825	51	0.7	326,176	1,163	0.4	2,560,891	10,898	0.4	2,891,061	13,263	0.5

Source: "Crops in 1909 on Farms in the South—Farms Reporting, Acreage, Yield, and Value of Specified Crops on All Farms and on Colored Farms, by Divisions and States," *Negro Population, 1790-1915,* 1918, p. 597. Primary source: U.S. Bureau of the Census. *Negro Population, 1790-1915.* Washington, D.C.: Government Printing Office, 1918. *Note:* "Colored" may include persons other than Black.

★ 49 ★

Crops/Livestock/Animals

Livestock: Black Farms with and without Livestock by Region, 1900 and 1910

SECTION AND YEAR	Total	Domestic animals		Poultry		Bees	
		Farms reporting	Farms not reporting	Farms reporting	Farms not reporting	Farms reporting	Farms not reporting
NUMBER OF FARMS							
United States:							
1910	920,883	833,374	87,509	730,055	190,828	20,943	899,940
1900	767,764	710,118	57,646	623,649	144,115	29,252	738,512
The South:							
1910	890,141	804,994	85,147	714,043	176,098	20,342	869,799
1900	740,670	684,571	56,099	606,991	133,679	28,514	712,156
The North and West:							
1910	30,742	28,380	2,362	16,012	14,730	601	30,141
1900	27,094	25,547	1,547	16,038	10,436	738	26,356
PERCENTAGE OF TOTAL							
United States:							
1910	100.0	90.5	9.5	79.3	20.7	2.3	97.7
1900	100.0	92.5	7.5	81.2	18.8	3.8	96.2
The South:							
1910	100.0	90.4	9.6	80.2	19.8	2.3	97.7
1900	100.0	92.4	7.6	82.0	18.0	3.8	96.2
The North and West:							
1910	100.0	92.3	7.7	52.1	47.9	2.0	98.0
1900	100.0	94.3	5.7	61.5	38.5	2.7	97.3
INCREASE IN NUMBER OF FARMS: 1900-1910[1]							
United States	153,119	123,256	29,863	106,406	46,713	-8,309	161,428
The South	149,471	120,423	29,048	107,052	42,419	-8,172	157,643
The North and West	3,648	2,833	815	-646	4,294	-137	3,785

Source: "Colored Farms Reporting and Not Reporting Live Stock," *Negro Population, 1790-1915*, 1918, p. 561. Primary source: U.S. Bureau of the Census. *Negro Population, 1790-1915*. Washington, D.C.: Government Printing Office, 1918. *Note:* 1. A minus sing (-) denotes decrease.

★ 50 ★

Crops/Livestock/Animals

Livestock: Livestock on Black Farms by Farm Location, 1930

[Colored farmers include Negroes, Indians, Chinese, Japanese, and all other nonwhite races]

SECTION, DIVISION, AND STATE	Total colored farm operators	HORSES AND (OR) MULES		CATTLE		SWINE	
		Farms reporting	Percent	Farms reporting	Percent	Farms reporting	Percent
The South	881,687	651,750	73.9	415,172	47.1	510,016	57.8
SOUTH ATLANTIC	881,687	651,750	73.9	415,172	47.1	510,016	57.80
Delaware	807	718	89.0	394	48.8	539	66.8
Maryland	5,267	4,247	80.6	2,441	46.3	2,788	52.9
District of Columbia	11	7	63.6	3	27.3	3	27.3
Virginia	39,673	30,265	76.3	23,006	58.0	27,619	69.6
West Virginia	491	315	64.2	342	69.7	315	64.2
North Carolina	76,873	59,012	76.8	27,212	35.4	45,552	59.3
South Carolina	77,425	57,346	74.1	37,073	47.9	45,425	58.7
Georgia	86,789	74,684	86.1	41,999	48.4	55,476	63.9
Florida	11,043	8,468	76.7	5,089	46.1	7,344	66.5
EAST SOUTH CENTRAL	320,959	210,410	65.6	165,602	51.6	187,388	58.4
Kentucky	9,104	5,258	57.8	4,964	54.5	4,219	46.3
Tennessee	35,138	22,990	65.4	19,652	55.9	20,411	58.1
Alabama	93,829	73,410	78.2	58,579	62.4	63,971	68.2
Mississippi	182,888	108,752	59.5	82,407	45.1	98,787	54.0
WEST SOUTH CENTRAL	262,349	206,278	78.6	112,011	42.7	137,567	52.4
Arkansas	79,579	65,059	81.8	28,853	36.3	39,011	49.0
Louisiana	73,770	54,196	73.5	31,210	42.3	40,866	55.4
Oklahoma	22,937	19,165	83.6	12,446	54.3	13,029	56.8
Texas	86,063	67,858	78.8	39,502	45.9	44,661	51.9
SELECTED NORTHERN STATES[1]	10,250	6,951	67.8	4,651	45.4	5,051	49.3
New Jersey	384	263	68.5	164	42.7	153	39.8
Pennsylvania	363	264	72.7	230	63.4	149	41.0
Ohio	1,237	941	76.1	904	73.1	729	58.9
Indiana	475	353	74.3	291	61.3	269	56.6
Illinois	894	765	85.6	479	53.6	535	59.8
Missouri	5,861	3,511	59.9	1,880	32.1	2,597	44.3
Kansas	1,036	854	82.4	703	67.9	619	59.7

Source: "Colored Farm Operators Reporting Specified Classes of Livestock, by Sections, Divisions, and States: 1930," *Negroes in the United States, 1920- 1932*, 1935, p. 589. Primary source: U.S. Bureau of the Census. *Negroes in the United States, 1920-1932.* Washington, D.C.: U.S. Government Printing Office, 1935. *Notes:* 1. States having 200 or more Negro farmers who constitute 90 percent or more of the colored farm operators in the State.

★ 51 ★

Crops/Livestock/Animals

Livestock: Value of Domestic Animals, Poultry, and Bees on Farms by Region, 1900 and 1910

SECTION AND CLASS OF FARM	1910	1900	Increase:[1] 1900-1910	Percentage distribution	
				1910	1900
DOMESTIC ANIMALS					
United States	$4,760,060,093	$2,979,197,586	$1,780,862,507	100.0	100.0
Colored farms	199,095,103	95,470,177	103,624,926	4.2	3.2
White farms	4,560,964,990	2,883,727,409	1,677,237,581	95.8	96.8
The South	1,284,298,714	782,407,960	501,890,754	100.0	100.0
Colored farms	177,461,964	85,216,337	92,245,627	13.8	10.9
White farms	1,106,836,750	697,191,623	409,645,127	86.2	89.1
The North and West	3,475,761,379	2,196,789,626	1,278,971,753	100.0	100.0
Colored farms	21,633,139	10,253,840	11,379,299	0.6	0.5
White farms	3,454,128,240	2,186,535,786	1,267,592,454	99.4	99.5
POULTRY					
United States	$154,663,220	$85,807,818	$68,855,402	100.0	100.0
Colored farms	5,505,445	4,019,577	1,485,868	3.6	4.7
White farms	149,157,775	81,788,241	67,369,534	96.4	95.3
The South	37,415,336	24,222,562	13,192,774	100.0	100.0
Colored farms	5,121,775	3,788,792	1,332,983	13.7	15.6
White farms	32,293,561	20,433,770	11,859,791	86.3	84.4
The North and West	117,247,884	61,585,256	55,662,628	100.0	100.0
Colored farms	383,670	230,785	152,885	0.3	0.4
White farms	116,864,214	61,354,471	55,509,743	99.7	99.6
BEES					
United States	$10,373,615	$10,178,087	$195,528	100.0	100.0
Colored farms	158,148	185,086	-26,938	1.5	1.8
White farms	10,215,467	9,993,001	222,466	98.5	98.2
The South	3,680,547	4,178,033	-488,486	100.0	100.0
Colored farms	148,385	176,914	-28,529	4.0	4.2
White farms	3,541,162	4,001,119	-459,957	96.0	95.8
The North and West	6,684,068	6,000,054	684,014	100.0	100.0
Colored farms	9,763	8,172	1,591	0.1	0.1
White farms	6,674,305	5,991,882	682,423	99.9	99.9

Source: "Value Reported," *Negro Population, 1790-1915*, 1918, p. 562. Primary source: U.S. Bureau of the Census. *Negro Population, 1790-1915*. Washington, D.C.: Government Printing Office, 1918. *Note:* 1. A minus sing (-) denotes decrease.

★ 52 ★

Crops/Livestock/Animals

Livestock: Value of Livestock on Black Farms by Region, 1900 and 1910

SECTION AND DIVISION	VALUE OF PROPERTY OF FARMS OPERATED BY NEGROES					
	Aggregate			Average per farm		
	1910	1900	Increase: 1910-1900	1910	1900	Increase: 1910-1900
	LIVE STOCK					
United States	$184,896,771	$84,936,215	$99,960,556	$207	$114	$93
The South	177,320,650	81,286,858	96,033,792	201	111	90
South Atlantic	62,659,295	24,052,600	38,606,695	177	84	93
East South Central	66,394,408	32,769,692	33,624,716	204	122	82
West South Central	48,266,947	24,464,566	23,802,381	240	138	102
The North	6,894,468	3,464,631	3,429,837	572	247	325
New England	99,930	45,709	54,221	322	173	149
Middle Atlantic	574,248	393,541	180,707	438	263	175
East North Central	2,144,969	1,212,893	932,076	443	234	209
West North Central	4,075,321	1,812,488	2,262,833	729	256	473
The West	681,653	184,726	496,927	1,414	548	866
Mountain	406,491	84,731	321,760	1,856	637	1,219
Pacific	275,162	99,995	175,167	1,046	490	556

Source: "Value of Property on Farms Operated by Negroes," *Negro Population, 1790-1915*, 1918, p. 561. Primary source: U.S. Bureau of the Census. *Negro Population, 1790-1915*. Washington, D.C.: Government Printing Office, 1918.

★ 53 ★

Crops/Livestock/Animals

Relationships: Percentage Distribution of Corn Acreage on Southern Farms by Owner Status and Southern Division and State, 1910 - I

DIVISION AND STATE	FARMS OPERATED BY COLORED FARMERS: 1910						
	Total	Owners and part owners			Tenants		Managers
		Owners		Part owners	Cash, and not specified	Share and share cash	
		Free	Mortgaged				
THE SOUTH							
Total	100.0	16.2	6.8	6.5	31.4	38.8	0.3
South Atlantic	100.0	15.5	5.3	6.7	34.9	37.3	0.4
East South Central	100.0	11.2	7.5	5.5	41.6	34.0	0.2
West South Central	100.0	23.3	8.5	7.1	14.3	46.5	0.2

[Continued]

★ 53 ★

Relationships: Percentage Distribution of Corn Acreage on Southern Farms by Owner Status and Southern Division and State, 1910 - I

[Continued]

DIVISION AND STATE	FARMS OPERATED BY COLORED FARMERS: 1910						
	Total	Owners and part owners			Tenants		Managers
		Owners		Part owners	Cash, and not specified	Share and share cash	
		Free	Mortgaged				
SOUTH ATLANTIC							
Delaware	100.0	12.1	9.7	5.9	6.0	62.9	3.4
Maryland	100.0	17.1	11.3	10.5	8.8	49.7	2.5
District of Columbia	100.0	...	...	100.0	...	...	...
Virginia	100.0	38.0	9.3	15.9	9.3	26.9	0.7
West Virginia	100.0	46.5	10.9	11.0	8.8	21.8	1.1
North Carolina	100.0	15.4	6.0	11.4	17.5	49.5	0.2
South Carolina	100.0	12.8	4.7	5.5	12.1	34.6	0.3
Georgia	100.0	8.6	3.4	2.7	45.8	39.3	0.2
Florida	100.0	30.3	8.0	8.2	40.4	12.5	0.6
EAST SOUTH CENTRAL							
Kentucky	100.0	26.2	9.0	15.8	6.6	41.6	0.8
Tennessee	100.0	14.2	5.6	9.9	31.2	38.7	0.4
Alabama	100.0	8.7	6.2	4.8	54.4	25.8	0.1
Mississippi	100.0	10.5	9.1	3.5	38.5	38.2	0.2
WEST SOUTH CENTRAL							
Arkansas	100.0	19.6	10.2	7.2	30.0	32.9	0.2
Louisiana	100.0	16.2	5.9	3.3	15.8	58.3	0.4
Oklahoma	100.0	40.0	14.4	10.0	8.0	27.4	0.2
Texas	100.0	21.6	6.5	8.2	8.2	55.2	0.2

Source: "Number of Acres in Corn on Colored and White Farms, Classified by Tenure, by Southern Divisions and States: 1910," *Negro Population, 1790-1915*, 1918, p. 623. Primary source: U.S. Bureau of the Census. *Negro Population, 1790-1915*. Washington, D.C.: Government Printing Office, 1918. *Note:* "Colored" may include persons other than Black.

★ 54 ★
Crops/Livestock/Animals

Relationships: Percentage Distribution of Corn Acreage on Southern Farms by Owner Status and Southern Division and State, 1910 - II

DIVISION AND STATE	Total	FARMS OPERATED BY WHITE FARMERS: 1910					
		Owners and part owners			Tenants		Managers
		Owners		Part owners	Cash, and not specified	Share and share cash	
		Free	Mortgaged				
THE SOUTH							
Total	100.0	38.8	12.5	9.7	10.3	27.2	1.5
South Atlantic	100.0	48.3	11.2	7.1	10.6	20.7	2.1
East South Central	100.0	47.1	12.0	9.6	8.8	21.5	1.1
West South Central	100.0	26.9	13.6	11.5	11.1	35.4	1.5
SOUTH ATLANTIC							
Delaware	100.0	30.7	15.4	2.6	5.4	44.6	1.4
Maryland	100.0	31.6	20.4	4.1	7.2	33.7	3.0
District of Columbia	100.0	30.2	8.0	2.8	40.8	1.2	17.0
Virginia	100.0	54.3	11.8	8.2	6.4	16.8	2.6
West Virginia	100.0	59.7	8.9	9.3	7.7	13.2	1.1
North Carolina	100.0	49.5	9.6	9.8	6.5	23.2	1.3
South Carolina	100.0	44.3	13.8	6.8	16.1	16.5	2.6
Georgia	100.0	43.8	9.0	4.7	17.5	22.7	2.3
Florida	100.0	64.7	10.4	5.9	9.8	6.3	2.9
EAST SOUTH CENTRAL							
Kentucky	100.0	50.5	12.6	9.3	5.9	21.0	0.9
Tennessee	100.0	46.4	9.1	12.1	7.8	23.8	0.7
Alabama	100.0	42.2	12.2	8.8	14.1	21.6	1.0
Mississippi	100.0	46.5	16.7	5.4	11.6	16.9	2.8
WEST SOUTH CENTRAL							
Arkansas	100.0	45.0	9.7	12.1	8.6	23.6	1.0
Louisiana	100.0	46.1	13.1	6.0	9.3	16.7	8.9
Oklahoma	100.0	14.1	14.5	14.7	17.6	38.6	0.5
Texas	100.0	30.7	14.4	8.5	4.3	41.1	1.0

Source: "Number of Acres in Corn on Colored and White Farms, Classified by Tenure, by Southern Divisions and States: 1910," *Negro Population, 1790-1915*, 1918, p. 623. Primary source: U.S. Bureau of the Census. *Negro Population, 1790-1915*. Washington, D.C.: Government Printing Office, 1918.

★ 55 ★

Crops/Livestock/Animals

Relationships: Animals and Livestock on Black Farms in the South by Owner Status and Southern Division, 1910 - I

DIVISION AND STATE	FARMS OPERATED BY COLORED FARMERS: 1910					
	Total		Owners		Part owners	
	Reporting	Not reporting	Reporting	Not reporting	Reporting	Not reporting
DAIRY COWS						
THE SOUTH						
Total	512,242	377,899	126,999	48,291	31,102	12,075
South Atlantic	189,758	166,104	49,921	30,993	13,040	8,007
East South Central	203,679	121,539	38,300	8,020	10,158	2,259
West South Central	118,805	90,256	38,778	9,278	7,904	1,809
WORK HORSES						
THE SOUTH						
Total	332,370	557,771	101,570	73,720	24,975	18,202
South Atlantic	108,252	247,610	39,869	41,045	10,716	10,331
East South Central	113,134	212,084	26,464	19,856	7,165	5,252
West South Central	110,984	98,077	35,237	12,819	7,094	2,619
WORK MULES						
THE SOUTH						
Total	436,398	453,743	73,319	101,971	21,472	21,705
South Atlantic	166,050	189,812	22,947	57,967	8,110	12,937
East South Central	170,094	155,124	25,472	20,848	7,380	5,037
West South Central	100,254	108,807	24,900	23,156	5,982	3,731

Source: "Colored Farms Reporting and Not Reporting Dairy Cows, Work Horses, and Work Mules, by Tenure Classes, by Southern States: 1910," *Negro Population, 1790-1915,* 1918, pp. 581-582. Primary source: U.S. Bureau of the Census. *Negro Population, 1790-1915.* Washington, D.C.: Government Printing Office, 1918. *Note:* "Colored" may include persons other than Black.

★ 56 ★
Crops/Livestock/Animals

Relationships: Animals and Livestock on Black Farms in the South by Owner Status and Southern Division, 1910 - II

DIVISION AND STATE	FARMS OPERATED BY COLORED FARMERS: 1910					
	Cash tenants		Share tenants		Managers	
	Reporting	Not reporting	Reporting	Not reporting	Reporting	Not reporting
DAIRY COWS						
THE SOUTH						
Total	180,459	105,491	172,996	211,528	686	514
South Atlantic	64,340	48,857	62,067	77,917	390	330
East South Central	93,414	41,509	61,640	66,579	167	82
West South Central	22,705	15,035	49,289	64,032	129	102
WORK HORSES						
THE SOUTH						
Total	103,409	182,541	101,727	282,797	689	511
South Atlantic	31,916	81,281	25,359	114,625	392	328
East South Central	50,772	84,241	28,590	102,629	143	106
West South Central	20,721	17,019	47,778	65,543	154	77
WORK MULES						
THE SOUTH						
Total	168,599	117,351	172,411	212,113	597	603
South Atlantic	65,076	48,121	69,603	70,381	314	406
East South Central	83,083	51,930	54,007	77,212	152	97
West South Central	20,440	17,300	48,801	64,520	131	100

Source: "Colored Farms Reporting and Not Reporting Dairy Cows, Work Horses, and Work Mules, by Tenure Classes, by Southern States: 1910," *Negro Population, 1790-1915,* 1918, pp. 581-582. Primary source: U.S. Bureau of the Census. *Negro Population, 1790-1915.* Washington, D.C.: Government Printing Office, 1918. *Note:* "Colored" may include persons other than Black.

★ 57 ★

Crops/Livestock/Animals

Relationships: Average and Total Number of Black Farms with Dairy Cows, Work Horses, and Work Mules by Owner Status and Southern Division, 1910

DIVISION AND CLASS OF ANIMAL	Total	Owners free	Owners mortgaged	Part owners	Cash tenants[1]	Share tenants[2]	Managers
NUMBER OF FARMS REPORTING							
The South:							
Dairy cows	512,242	91,048	35,951	31,102	180,459	172,996	686
Work horses	332,370	74,420	27,150	24,975	103,409	101,727	689
Work mules	436,398	48,219	25,100	21,472	168,599	172,411	597
South Atlantic:							
Dairy cows	189,758	39,010	10,911	13,040	64,340	62,067	390
Work horses	108,252	31,077	8,792	10,716	31,916	25,359	392
Work mules	166,050	16,066	6,881	8,110	65,076	69,603	314
East South Central:							
Dairy cows	203,679	23,395	14,905	10,158	93,414	61,640	167
Work horses	113,134	16,698	9,766	7,165	50,772	28,590	143
Work mules	170,094	14,396	11,076	7,380	83,083	54,007	152
West South Central:							
Dairy cows	118,805	28,643	10,135	7,904	22,705	49,289	129
Work horses	110,984	26,645	8,592	7,094	20,721	47,778	154
Work mules	100,254	17,757	7,143	5,982	20,440	48,801	131
NUMBER OF ANIMALS REPORTED							
The South:							
Dairy cows	929,883	211,318	79,950	62,962	308,757	264,089	2,807
Work horses	509,087	130,102	46,272	41,715	141,798	146,815	2,385
Work mules	645,320	82,998	44,446	37,307	246,934	231,263	2,372
South Atlantic:							
Dairy cows	285,141	69,990	18,488	20,277	93,407	81,645	1,384
Work horses	140,394	41,792	12,177	14,483	38,026	32,891	1,025
Work mules	221,694	23,611	10,900	11,859	89,617	84,708	999
East South Central:							
Dairy cows	358,406	49,925	31,732	19,825	165,573	90,575	776
Work horses	158,346	25,960	14,933	11,213	69,390	36,264	586
Work mules	248,161	24,630	19,125	13,020	122,436	68,209	741
West South Central:							
Dairy cows:	286,336	91,403	29,730	22,910	49,777	91,869	647
Work horses	210,347	62,350	19,162	16,019	34,382	77,660	774
Work mules	175,465	34,757	14,421	12,428	34,881	78,346	632
AVERAGE NUMBER OF ANIMALS PER 100 FARMS (ALL FARMS)							
The South:							
Dairy cows	104	164	171	146	108	60	234
Work horses	57	101	99	97	50	38	199
Work mules	72	65	95	86	86	60	198

[Continued]

★ 57 ★

Relationships: Average and Total Number of Black Farms with Dairy Cows, Work Horses, and Work Mules by Owner Status and Southern Division, 1910

[Continued]

DIVISION AND CLASS OF ANIMAL	Total	Owners free	Owners mortgaged	Part owners	Cash tenants[1]	Share tenants[2]	Managers
South Atlantic:							
Dairy cows	80	110	107	96	83	58	192
Work horses	39	66	71	69	34	23	142
Work mules	62	37	63	56	79	61	139
East South Central:							
Dairy cows	110	173	182	160	123	69	312
Work horses	49	90	86	90	51	28	235
Work mules	76	85	110	105	91	52	298
West South Central:							
Dairy cows	137	254	246	236	132	81	280
Work horses	101	713	158	165	91	69	335
Work mules	84	97	119	128	92	69	274

Source: "Colored Farm Operators Dairy Cows, Work Horses, and Work Mules, by Tenure Classes for Southern Divisions: 1910," *Negro Population, 1790-1915,* 1918, p. 581. Primary source: U.S. Bureau of the Census. *Negro Population, 1790-1915.* Washington, D.C.: Government Printing Office, 1918. *Notes:* 1. Includes not specified tenure. 2. Includes share-cash tenants.

★ 58 ★

Crops/Livestock/Animals

Relationships: Corn Acreage on Southern Farms by Owner Status and Southern Division and State, 1910 - I

DIVISION AND STATE	FARMS OPERATED BY COLORED FARMERS: 1910						
	Total	Owners and part owners			Tenants		Managers
		Owners		Part owners	Cash, and not specified	Share and share cash	
		Free	Mortgaged				
THE SOUTH							
Total	7,377,221	1,197,845	505,239	476,709	2,314,540	2,861,607	21,281
South Atlantic	3,066,496	474,580	161,109	206,686	1,068,857	1,143,861	11,403
East South Central	2,309,639	257,804	173,461	127,320	959,744	786,379	4,931
West South Central	2,001,086	465,461	170,669	142,703	285,939	931,367	4,947
SOUTH ATLANTIC							
Delaware	12,636	1,532	1,232	746	754	7,943	429
Maryland	52,139	8,937	5,901	5,459	4,607	25,915	1,320
District of Columbia	2	...	...	2	...	...	...
Virginia	338,378	128,589	31,343	53,650	31,322	91,026	2,448
West Virginia	4,421	2,054	482	487	387	963	48
North Carolina	535,037	82,350	32,021	60,963	93,554	264,909	1,240
South Carolina	653,856	83,749	30,930	35,746	275,023	226,480	1,928

[Continued]

★ 58 ★

Relationships: Corn Acreage on Southern Farms by Owner Status and Southern Division and State, 1910 - I
[Continued]

DIVISION AND STATE	FARMS OPERATED BY COLORED FARMERS: 1910						
	Total	Owners and part owners			Tenants		Managers
		Owners		Part owners	Cash, and not specified	Share and share cash	
		Free	Mortgaged				
Georgia	1,278,627	109,368	43,827	34,028	585,814	502,728	2,862
Florida	191,400	58,001	15,373	15,605	77,396	23,897	1,128
EAST SOUTH CENTRAL							
Kentucky	104,055	27,302	9,349	16,415	6,899	43,291	799
Tennessee	354,996	50,490	19,850	35,148	110,677	137,501	1,330
Alabama	818,175	71,442	50,565	39,573	444,842	210,752	1,001
Mississippi	1,032,413	108,570	93,697	36,184	397,326	394,835	1,801
WEST SOUTH CENTRAL							
Arkansas	386,913	75,729	39,434	28,018	115,962	127,121	649
Louisiana	505,431	82,092	29,631	16,865	79,709	294,888	2,248
Oklahoma	369,818	148,033	53,367	37,132	29,417	101,283	586
Texas	738,924	159,609	48,237	60,688	60,851	408,075	1,464

Source: "Number of Acres in Corn on Colored and White Farms, Classified by Tenure, by Southern Divisions and States: 1910," *Negro Population, 1790- 1915,* 1918, p. 623. Primary source: U.S. Bureau of the Census. *Negro Population, 1790-1915.* Washington, D.C.: Government Printing Office, 1918.

★ 59 ★

Crops/Livestock/Animals

Relationships: Corn Acreage on Southern Farms by Owner Status and Southern Division and State, 1910 - II

DIVISION AND STATE	FARMS OPERATED BY WHITE FARMERS: 1910						
	Total	Owners and part owners			Tenants		Managers
		Owners		Part owners	Cash, and not specified	Share and share cash	
		Free	Mortgaged				
THE SOUTH							
Total	30,250,098	11,744,271	3,771,187	2,937,049	3,102,881	8,232,572	462,138
South Atlantic	8,320,488	4,018,322	930,806	589,655	881,696	1,724,573	175,436
East South Central	9,018,629	4,247,513	1,078,513	862,826	794,199	1,936,710	98,868
West South Central	12,910,981	3,478,436	1,761,868	1,484,568	1,426,986	4,571,289	187,834
SOUTH ATLANTIC							
Delaware	176,119	54,114	27,104	4,534	9,434	78,513	2,420
Maryland	594,873	188,052	121,553	24,633	42,555	200,261	17,819

[Continued]

★ 59 ★

Relationships: Corn Acreage on Southern Farms by Owner Status and Southern Division and State, 1910 - II

[Continued]

DIVISION AND STATE	FARMS OPERATED BY WHITE FARMERS: 1910						
	Total	Owners and part owners			Tenants		Managers
		Owners		Part owners	Cash, and not specified	Share and share cash	
		Free	Mortgaged				
District of Columbia	424	128	34	12	173	5	72
Virginia	1,521,981	826,907	179,336	124,101	96,686	255,703	39,248
West Virginia	671,890	401,391	60,101	62,671	52,008	88,505	7,214
North Carolina	1,924,420	953,537	184,362	188,670	125,902	446,200	25,749
South Carolina	911,976	403,807	125,420	62,300	146,564	150,555	23,330
Georgia	2,104,434	922,304	189,741	98,378	367,840	478,617	47,554
Florida	414,371	268,082	43,155	24,356	40,534	26,214	12,030
EAST SOUTH CENTRAL							
Kentucky	3,332,285	1,681,396	418,692	308,841	195,549	698,730	29,077
Tennessee	2,791,352	1,295,368	254,568	337,399	218,205	655,728	20,084
Alabama	1,754,793	740,379	214,430	154,596	248,236	379,715	17,437
Mississippi	1,140,199	530,370	190,823	61,990	132,209	192,537	32,270
WEST SOUTH CENTRAL							
Arkansas	1,890,203	850,184	182,757	229,554	163,124	446,210	18,374
Louisiana	1,085,399	500,329	141,652	64,800	101,116	181,035	96,467
Oklahoma	5,544,251	780,866	806,444	816,245	974,855	2,137,714	28,127
Texas	4,391,128	1,347,057	631,015	373,969	187,891	1,806,330	44,866

Source: "Number of Acres in Corn on Colored and White Farms, Classified by Tenure, by Southern Divisions and States: 1910," *Negro Population, 1790- 1915,* 1918, p. 623. Primary source: U.S. Bureau of the Census. *Negro Population, 1790-1915.* Washington, D.C.: Government Printing Office, 1918.

★ 60 ★

Crops/Livestock/Animals

Relationships: Dairy Products on Black Farms in the South by Owner Status and Farm Location, 1930

[Colored farmers include Negroes, Indians, Chinese, Japanese, and all other nonwhite farmers]

DIVISION AND STATE	DAIRY PRODUCTS, 1929					
	Milk		Cream		Butter	
			Cream sold as butterfat	Cream sold not as butterfat		
	Produced (gallons)	Sold (gallons)	(pounds)	(gallons)	Churned (pounds)	Sold (pounds)
The South	175,986,295	8,935,810	2,460,815	75,451	38,768,185	2,891,252
South Atlantic	53,736,001	2,250,590	362,821	25,803	12,962,046	1,432,716
East South Central	72,024,992	4,993,715	1,212,908	27,124	15,716,615	847,823

[Continued]

★ 60 ★

Relationships: Dairy Products on Black Farms in the South by Owner Status and Farm Location, 1930

[Continued]

DIVISION AND STATE	DAIRY PRODUCTS, 1929					
	Milk		Cream		Butter	
			Cream sold as butterfat	Cream sold not as butterfat		
	Produced (gallons)	Sold (gallons)	(pounds)	(gallons)	Churned (pounds)	Sold (pounds)
West South Central	50,225,302	1,709,505	885,086	22,524	10,089,524	610,713
Selected Northern States[1]	5,311,005	1,814,444	443,600	3,781	329,860	73,606

Source: "Number and Value of Cattle on Farms of Colored Operators, by Tenure of Farmer, 1930, with Specified Dairy Products Produced and Sold, 1929," *Negroes in the United States, 1920-1932,* 1935, p. 625. Primary source: U.S. Bureau of the Census. *Negroes in the United States, 1920-1932.* Washington, D.C.: U.S. Government Printing Office, 1935. *Notes:* "Colored" may include persons other than Black. 1. States having 200 or more Negro farmers who constitute 90 percent or more of the colored farmers in the State.

★ 61 ★

Crops/Livestock/Animals

Relationships: Number Dairy Cows on Farms by Owner Status and Southern Division and State, 1910 - I

DIVISION AND STATE	FARMS OPERATED BY COLORED FARMERS: 1910						
	Total	Owners and part owners			Tenants		Managers
		Owners		Part owners	Cash and not specified	Share and share cash	
		Free	Mortgaged				
THE SOUTH							
Total	929,883	211,318	79,950	62,962	308,757	264,089	2,807
South Atlantic	285,141	69,990	18,488	20,277	93,407	81,645	1,384
East South Central	358,406	49,925	31,732	19,825	165,573	90,575	776
West South Central	286,336	91,403	29,730	22,910	49,777	91,869	647
SOUTH ATLANTIC							
Delaware	1,077	148	139	42	69	615	64
Maryland	6,339	1,554	906	492	522	2,611	254
District of Columbia	11	8	...	1	2	...	...
Virginia	42,242	21,264	4,154	5,434	2,900	8,042	448
West Virginia	1,111	637	125	119	75	135	20
North Carolina	42,637	9,448	3,289	5,022	7,972	16,740	166
South Carolina	70,886	13,211	3,659	4,073	29,241	20,531	171
Georgia	104,966	16,342	4,869	3,791	47,808	31,950	206
Florida	15,872	7,378	1,347	1,253	4,818	1,021	55

NUMBER OF DAIRY COWS

[Continued]

★ 61 ★

Relationships: Number Dairy Cows on Farms by Owner Status and Southern Division and State, 1910 - I
[Continued]

DIVISION AND STATE	FARMS OPERATED BY COLORED FARMERS: 1910						
	Total	Owners and part owners			Tenants		Managers
		Owners		Part owners	Cash and not specified	Share and share cash	
		Free	Mortgaged				
EAST SOUTH CENTRAL							
Kentucky	9,882	8,595	1,045	1,451	531	3,155	105
Tennessee	42,522	8,010	2,868	3,963	16,079	11,454	148
Alabama	126,570	13,821	8,420	6,922	75,410	21,741	256
Mississippi	179,432	24,499	19,399	7,489	73,553	54,225	267
WEST SOUTH CENTRAL							
Arkansas	81,122	19,793	9,563	6,410	26,655	18,590	111
Louisiana	64,204	17,928	5,152	2,158	12,117	26,613	236
Oklahoma	40,874	21,191	5,699	3,550	2,836	7,566	32
Texas	100,136	32,491	9,316	10,792	8,169	39,100	268

Source: "Number of Dairy Cows on Colored and White Farms, Classified by Tenure, by Southern Divisions and States: 1910," *Negro Population, 1790-1915,* 1918, p. 620. Primary source: U.S. Bureau of the Census. *Negro Population, 1790-1915.* Washington, D.C.: Government Printing Office, 1918. *Note:* "Colored" may include persons other than Black.

★ 62 ★

Crops/Livestock/Animals

Relationships: Number Dairy Cows on Farms by Owner Status and Southern Division and State, 1910 - II

DIVISION AND STATE	FARMS OPERATED BY WHITE FARMERS: 1910						
	Total	Owners and part owners			Tenants		Managers
		Owners		Part owners	Cash and not specified	Share and share cash	
		Free	Mortgaged				
NUMBER OF DAIRY COWS							
THE SOUTH							
Total	4,758,485	2,315,071	659,945	417,127	416,294	885,859	64,189
South Atlantic	1,525,613	851,121	182,191	100,789	128,025	234,349	29,138
East South Central	1,269,655	666,386	161,287	110,589	115,008	202,113	14,272
West South Central	1,963,217	797,564	316,467	205,749	173,261	449,397	20,779

[Continued]

★ 62 ★

Relationships: Number Dairy Cows on Farms by Owner Status and Southern Division and State, 1910 - II

[Continued]

DIVISION AND STATE	FARMS OPERATED BY WHITE FARMERS: 1910						
		Owners and part owners			Tenants		
	Total	Owners		Part owners	Cash and not specified	Share and share cash	Managers
		Free	Mortgaged				
SOUTH ATLANTIC							
Delaware	34,631	8,763	6,437	442	3,586	14,420	983
Maryland	160,520	54,827	36,715	5,705	12,279	45,754	5,240
District of Columbia	846	133	8	1	285	1	418
Virginia	314,042	191,317	36,795	25,054	16,190	36,881	7,805
West Virginia	238,428	159,848	21,110	20,625	16,333	17,814	2,698
North Carolina	266,277	151,862	26,568	24,777	14,017	45,678	3,375
South Carolina	109,956	53,522	15,708	6,546	15,437	16,180	2,563
Georgia	300,744	155,049	29,740	13,423	43,531	54,342	4,659
Florida	100,169	75,800	9,110	4,216	6,367	3,279	1,397
EAST SOUTH CENTRAL							
Kentucky	399,952	219,284	50,109	34,842	22,275	69,620	3,822
Tennessee	354,582	187,684	33,096	38,717	29,292	62,047	3,746
Alabama	264,966	125,626	35,242	23,396	35,992	41,451	3,259
Mississippi	250,155	133,792	42,840	13,634	27,449	28,995	3,445
WEST SOUTH CENTRAL							
Arkansas	344,671	180,403	37,690	39,597	28,602	56,540	1,839
Louisiana	214,893	131,840	25,404	10,358	18,246	24,349	4,696
Oklahoma	489,922	101,263	87,594	79,804	77,547	141,646	2,068
Texas	913,731	384,058	165,779	75,990	48,866	226,862	12,176

Source: "Number of Dairy Cows on Colored and White Farms, Classified by Tenure, by Southern Divisions and States: 1910," *Negro Population, 1790-1915,* 1918, p. 620. Primary source: U.S. Bureau of the Census. *Negro Population, 1790-1915.* Washington, D.C.: Government Printing Office, 1918.

★ 63 ★
Crops/Livestock/Animals

Relationships: Number Work Horses on Farms by Owner Status and Southern Division and State, 1910 - I

DIVISION AND STATE	FARMS OPERATED BY COLORED FARMERS: 1910						
	Total	Owners and part owners			Tenants		Managers
		Owners		Part owners	Cash and not specified	Share and share cash	
		Free	Mortgaged				

NUMBER OF WORK HORSES

DIVISION AND STATE	Total	Free	Mortgaged	Part owners	Cash and not specified	Share and share cash	Managers
THE SOUTH							
Total	590,087	130,102	46,272	41,715	141,798	146,815	2,385
South Atlantic	140,394	41,792	12,177	14,483	38,026	32,891	1,025
East South Central	₃8,346	25,960	14,933	11,213	69,390	36,264	586
West South Central	210,347	62,350	19,162	16,019	34,382	77,660	774
SOUTH ATLANTIC							
Delaware	1,529	276	238	99	105	750	61
Maryland	9,169	2,387	1,402	941	856	3,297	286
District of Columbia	18	4	2	8	3	...	1
Virginia	38,905	18,290	4,120	5,621	3,123	7,401	350
West Virginia	888	472	96	90	59	149	22
North Carolina	24,926	5,073	2,315	3,241	5,249	8,985	63
South Carolina	27,075	6,135	1,556	2,062	12,106	5,132	84
Georgia	28,090	4,864	1,595	1,454	13,617	6,458	102
Florida	9,794	4,291	853	967	2,908	719	56
EAST SOUTH CENTRAL							
Kentucky	10,362	3,545	1,146	1,736	587	3,120	228
Tennessee	30,097	6,009	2,165	3,342	11,354	7,117	110
Alabama	35,816	4,673	2,665	2,503	21,292	4,603	80
Mississippi	82,071	11,733	8,957	3,632	36,157	21,424	168
WEST SOUTH CENTRAL							
Arkansas	36,948	7,920	3,719	2,808	13,987	8,469	45
Louisiana	47,589	9,923	3,027	1,569	9,113	23,824	133
Oklahoma	51,953	25,645	6,641	4,535	3,846	11,181	105
Texas	73,857	18,862	5,775	7,107	7,436	34,186	491

Source: "Number of Work Horses on Colored and White Farms, Classified by Tenure, by Southern Divisions and States: 1910," *Negro Population, 1790-1915*, 1918, p. 621. Primary source: U.S. Bureau of the Census. *Negro Population, 1790-1915*. Washington, D.C.: Government Printing Office, 1918. *Note:* "Colored" may include persons other than Black.

★ 64 ★

Crops/Livestock/Animals

Relationships: Number Work Horses on Farms by Owner Status and Southern Division and State, 1910 - II

DIVISION AND STATE	FARMS OPERATED BY WHITE FARMERS: 1910						
	Total	Owners and part owners			Tenants		Managers
		Owners		Part owners	Cash and not specified	Share and share cash	
		Free	Mortgaged				
		NUMBER OF WORK HORSES					
THE SOUTH							
Total	3,564,855	1,528,189	546,570	368,390	301,721	747,712	72,273
South Atlantic	866,091	469,365	114,181	62,260	67,705	133,572	19,008
East South Central	851,449	449,358	111,556	82,090	67,773	131,282	9,390
West South Central	1,847,315	609,466	320,833	224,040	166,243	482,858	43,875
SOUTH ATLANTIC							
Delaware	28,103	8,235	5,391	510	2,160	11,279	528
Maryland	128,109	44,161	28,187	5,212	9,143	36,798	4,308
District of Columbia	545	183	29	13	184	6	130
Virginia	249,954	148,604	31,260	20,269	12,871	30,528	6,422
West Virginia	158,669	103,611	15,138	15,203	8,978	13,405	2,334
North Carolina	131,023	72,765	14,523	11,708	8,358	21,781	1,888
South Carolina	49,896	24,410	7,607	3,337	8,556	5,070	916
Georgia	86,571	43,581	8,785	4,346	14,914	13,318	1,627
Florida	33,221	23,515	3,261	1,662	2,541	1,387	855
EAST SOUTH CENTRAL							
Kentucky	377,433	203,470	52,269	36,127	18,546	63,186	3,835
Tennessee	270,230	145,686	27,833	30,839	21,275	42,364	2,233
Alabama	89,448	42,615	11,682	8,445	13,126	12,279	1,301
Mississippi	114,338	57,587	19,772	6,679	14,826	13,453	2,021
WEST SOUTH CENTRAL							
Arkansas	191,531	91,282	21,979	21,835	17,637	37,011	1,787
Louisiana	117,015	61,270	13,502	6,974	10,292	21,329	3,648
Oklahoma	591,465	119,711	103,152	100,834	86,955	176,639	4,174
Texas	947,304	337,203	182,200	94,397	51,359	247,879	34,266

Source: "Number of Work Horses on Colored and White Farms, Classified by Tenure, by Southern Divisions and States: 1910," *Negro Population, 1790-1915,* 1918, p. 621. Primary source: U.S. Bureau of the Census. *Negro Population, 1790-1915.* Washington, D.C.: Government Printing Office, 1918.

★ 65 ★

Crops/Livestock/Animals

Relationships: Percentage Distribution of Dairy Cows on Farms by Owner Status and Southern Division and State, 1910 - I

DIVISION AND STATE	Total	FARMS OPERATED BY COLORED FARMERS: 1910					
		Owners and part owners			Tenants		
		Owners		Part owners	Cash and not specified	Share and share cash	Managers
		Free	Mortgaged				

PERCENTAGE DISTRIBUTION OF DAIRY COWS, BY TENURE

DIVISION AND STATE	Total	Free	Mortgaged	Part owners	Cash and not specified	Share and share cash	Managers
THE SOUTH							
Total	100.0	22.7	8.6	6.8	33.2	28.4	0.3
South Atlantic	100.0	24.5	6.5	7.1	32.8	28.6	0.5
East South Central	100.0	13.9	8.9	5.5	46.2	25.3	0.2
West South Central	100.0	31.9	10.4	8.0	17.4	32.1	0.2
SOUTH ATLANTIC							
Delaware	100.0	13.7	12.9	3.9	6.4	57.1	6.0
Maryland	100.0	24.5	14.3	7.8	8.2	41.2	4.0
District of Columbia	100.0	72.7	...	9.1	18.2	...	...
Virginia	100.0	50.3	9.8	12.9	6.9	19.0	1.1
West Virginia	100.0	57.3	11.3	10.7	6.8	12.2	1.8
North Carolina	100.0	22.2	7.7	11.8	18.7	39.3	0.4
South Carolina	100.0	18.6	5.2	5.7	41.3	29.0	0.2
Georgia	100.0	15.6	4.6	3.6	45.5	30.4	0.2
Florida	100.0	46.5	8.5	7.9	30.4	6.4	0.3
EAST SOUTH CENTRAL							
Kentucky	100.0	36.4	10.6	14.7	5.4	31.9	1.1
Tennessee	100.0	18.8	6.7	9.3	37.8	26.9	0.3
Alabama	100.0	10.9	6.7	5.5	59.6	17.2	0.2
Mississippi	100.0	13.7	10.8	4.2	41.0	30.2	0.1
WEST SOUTH CENTRAL							
Arkansas	100.0	24.4	11.8	7.9	32.9	22.9	0.1
Louisiana	100.0	27.9	8.0	3.4	18.9	41.5	0.4
Oklahoma	100.0	51.8	13.9	8.7	6.9	18.5	0.1
Texas	100.0	32.4	9.3	10.8	8.2	39.0	0.3

Source: "Number of Dairy Cows on Colored and White Farms, Classified by Tenure, by Southern Divisions and States: 1910," *Negro Population, 1790-1915,* 1918, p. 620. Primary source: U.S. Bureau of the Census. *Negro Population, 1790-1915.* Washington, D.C.: Government Printing Office, 1918. *Notes:* "Colored" may include persons other than Black. 1. Less than one-tenth of 1 per cent.

★ 66 ★
Crops/Livestock/Animals

Relationships: Percentage Distribution of Dairy Cows on Farms by Owner Status and Southern Division and State, 1910 - II

DIVISION AND STATE	FARMS OPERATED BY WHITE FARMERS: 1910						
	Total	Owners and part owners			Tenants		Managers
		Owners		Part owners	Cash and not specified	Share and share cash	
		Free	Mortgaged				
PERCENTAGE DISTRIBUTION OF DAIRY COWS, BY TENURE							
THE SOUTH							
Total	100.0	48.7	13.9	8.8	8.7	18.6	1.3
South Atlantic	100.0	55.8	11.9	6.6	8.4	15.4	1.9
East South Central	100.0	52.5	12.7	8.7	9.1	15.9	1.1
West South Central	100.0	40.6	16.1	10.5	8.8	22.9	1.1
SOUTH ATLANTIC							
Delaware	100.0	25.3	18.6	1.3	10.4	41.6	2.8
Maryland	100.0	34.2	22.9	3.6	7.6	28.5	3.3
District of Columbia	100.0	15.7	0.9	1	33.7	1	49.4
Virginia	100.0	60.9	11.7	8.0	5.2	11.7	2.5
West Virginia	100.0	67.0	8.9	8.7	6.9	7.5	1.1
North Carolina	100.0	57.0	10.0	9.3	5.3	17.2	1.3
South Carolina	100.0	48.7	14.3	6.0	14.0	14.7	2.3
Georgia	100.0	51.6	9.9	4.5	14.5	18.1	1.5
Florida	100.0	75.7	9.1	4.2	6.4	3.3	1.4
EAST SOUTH CENTRAL							
Kentucky	100.0	54.8	12.5	8.7	5.6	17.4	1.0
Tennessee	100.0	52.9	9.3	10.9	8.3	17.5	1.1
Alabama	100.0	47.4	13.3	8.8	13.6	15.6	1.2
Mississippi	100.0	53.5	17.1	5.5	11.0	11.6	1.4
WEST SOUTH CENTRAL							
Arkansas	100.0	52.3	10.9	11.5	8.3	16.4	0.5
Louisiana	100.0	61.4	11.8	4.8	8.5	11.3	2.2
Oklahoma	100.0	20.7	17.9	16.3	15.8	28.9	0.4
Texas	100.0	42.0	18.1	8.3	5.3	24.8	1.3

Source: "Number of Dairy Cows on Colored and White Farms, Classified by Tenure, by Southern Divisions and States: 1910," *Negro Population, 1790-1915,* 1918, p. 620. Primary source: U.S. Bureau of the Census. *Negro Population, 1790-1915.* Washington, D.C.: Government Printing Office, 1918. *Note:* 1. Less than one-tenth of 1 per cent.

★ 67 ★
Crops/Livestock/Animals

Relationships: Percentage Distribution of Work Horses on Farms by Owner Status and Southern Division and State, 1910 - I

DIVISION AND STATE	FARMS OPERATED BY COLORED FARMERS: 1910						
	Total	Owners and part owners			Tenants		Managers
		Owners		Part owners	Cash and not specified	Share and share cash	
		Free	Mortgaged				

PERCENTAGE DISTRIBUTION OF WORK HORSES, BY TENURE

DIVISION AND STATE	Total	Free	Mortgaged	Part owners	Cash and not specified	Share and share cash	Managers
THE SOUTH							
Total	100.0	25.6	9.1	8.2	27.9	28.8	0.5
South Atlantic	100.0	29.8	8.7	10.3	27.1	23.4	0.7
East South Central	100.0	16.4	9.4	7.1	43.8	22.9	0.4
West South Central	100.0	29.6	9.1	7.6	16.3	36.9	0.4
SOUTH ATLANTIC							
Delaware	100.0	18.1	15.6	6.5	6.9	49.1	4.0
Maryland	100.0	26.0	15.3	10.3	9.3	36.0	3.1
District of Columbia	100.0	22.2	11.1	44.4	16.7	...	5.6
Virginia	100.0	47.0	10.6	14.4	8.0	19.0	0.9
West Virginia	100.0	53.2	10.8	10.1	6.6	16.8	2.5
North Carolina	100.0	20.4	9.3	13.0	21.1	36.0	0.3
South Carolina	100.0	22.7	5.7	7.6	44.7	19.0	0.3
Georgia	100.0	17.3	5.7	5.2	48.5	23.0	0.4
Florida	100.0	43.8	8.7	9.9	29.7	7.3	0.6
EAST SOUTH CENTRAL							
Kentucky	100.0	34.2	11.1	16.8	5.7	30.1	2.2
Tennessee	100.0	20.0	7.2	11.1	37.7	23.6	0.4
Alabama	100.0	13.0	7.4	7.0	59.4	12.9	0.2
Mississippi	100.0	14.3	10.9	4.4	44.1	26.1	0.2
WEST SOUTH CENTRAL							
Arkansas	100.0	21.4	10.1	7.6	37.9	22.9	0.1
Louisiana	100.0	20.9	6.4	3.3	19.1	50.1	0.3
Oklahoma	100.0	49.4	12.8	8.7	7.4	21.5	0.2
Texas	100.0	25.5	7.8	9.6	10.1	46.3	0.7

Source: "Number of Work Horses on Colored and White Farms, Classified by Tenure, by Southern Divisions and States: 1910," *Negro Population, 1790-1915*, 1918, p. 621. Primary source: U.S. Bureau of the Census. *Negro Population, 1790-1915.* Washington, D.C.: Government Printing Office, 1918. *Note:* "Colored" may include persons other than Black.

★ 68 ★

Crops/Livestock/Animals

Relationships: Percentage Distribution of Work Horses on Farms by Owner Status and Southern Division and State, 1910 - II

DIVISION AND STATE	FARMS OPERATED BY WHITE FARMERS: 1910						
	Total	Owners and part owners			Tenants		Managers
		Owners		Part owners	Cash and not specified	Share and share cash	
		Free	Mortgaged				

PERCENTAGE DISTRIBUTION OF WORK HORSES, BY TENURE

DIVISION AND STATE	Total	Free	Mortgaged	Part owners	Cash and not specified	Share and share cash	Managers
THE SOUTH							
Total	100.0	42.9	15.3	10.3	8.5	21.0	2.0
South Atlantic	100.0	54.2	13.2	7.2	7.8	15.4	2.2
East South Central	100.0	52.8	13.1	9.6	8.0	15.4	1.1
West South Central	100.0	33.0	17.4	12.1	9.0	26.1	2.4
SOUTH ATLANTIC							
Delaware	100.0	29.3	19.2	1.8	7.7	40.1	1.9
Maryland	100.0	34.7	22.0	4.1	7.1	28.7	3.4
District of Columbia	100.0	33.6	5.3	2.4	33.8	1.1	23.9
Virginia	100.0	59.5	12.5	8.1	5.1	12.2	2.6
West Virginia	100.0	65.3	9.5	9.6	5.7	8.4	1.5
North Carolina	100.0	55.5	11.1	8.9	6.4	16.6	1.4
South Carolina	100.0	48.9	15.2	6.7	17.1	10.2	1.8
Georgia	100.0	50.3	10.1	5.0	17.2	15.4	1.9
Florida	100.0	70.8	9.8	5.0	7.6	4.2	2.6
EAST SOUTH CENTRAL							
Kentucky	100.0	53.9	13.8	9.6	4.9	16.7	1.0
Tennessee	100.0	53.9	10.3	11.4	7.9	15.7	0.8
Alabama	100.0	47.6	13.1	9.4	14.7	13.7	1.5
Mississippi	100.0	50.4	17.3	5.8	13.0	11.8	1.8
WEST SOUTH CENTRAL							
Arkansas	100.0	47.7	11.5	11.4	9.2	19.3	0.9
Louisiana	100.0	52.4	11.5	6.0	8.8	18.2	3.1
Oklahoma	100.0	20.2	17.4	17.0	14.7	30.0	7.1
Texas	100.0	35.6	19.2	10.0	5.4	26.2	3.6

Source: "Number of Work Horses on Colored and White Farms, Classified by Tenure, by Southern Divisions and States: 1910," *Negro Population, 1790-1915*, 1918, p. 621. Primary source: U.S. Bureau of the Census. *Negro Population, 1790-1915*. Washington, D.C.: Government Printing Office, 1918.

★ 69 ★

Crops/Livestock/Animals

Relationships: Percentage Distribution of Work Mules on Southern Farms by Owner Status and Southern Division and State, 1910 - I

DIVISION AND STATE	FARMS OPERATED BY COLORED FARMERS: 1910						
	Total	Owners and part owners			Tenants		Managers
		Owners		Part owners	Cash, and not specified	Share and share cash	
		Free	Mortgaged				
PERCENTAGE DISTRIBUTION OF WORK MULES, BY TENURE							
THE SOUTH							
Total	100.0	12.9	6.9	5.8	38.3	35.8	0.4
South Atlantic	100.0	10.7	4.9	5.3	40.4	38.2	0.5
East South Central	100.0	9.9	7.7	5.2	49.3	27.5	0.3
West South Central	100.0	19.8	8.2	7.1	19.9	44.7	0.4
SOUTH ATLANTIC							
Delaware	100.0	15.2	10.0	3.4	4.6	61.0	5.7
Maryland	100.0	15.5	11.1	7.4	9.8	44.2	12.0
District of Columbia	100.0	...	...	...	100.0	...	...
Virginia	100.0	38.2	10.7	14.4	9.5	25.4	1.8
West Virginia	100.0	55.6	8.6	9.9	11.1	14.8	...
North Carolina	100.0	14.6	6.4	11.0	19.0	48.5	0.3
South Carolina	100.0	9.2	5.3	5.2	43.5	36.5	0.3
Georgia	100.0	7.2	3.5	2.8	48.3	37.9	0.3
Florida	100.0	26.2	9.3	8.3	40.8	14.7	0.8
EAST SOUTH CENTRAL							
Kentucky	100.0	30.7	12.7	16.6	8.4	30.6	1.1
Tennessee	100.0	15.7	7.2	10.6	40.7	25.1	0.6
Alabama	100.0	7.5	6.0	5.0	60.5	20.7	0.2
Mississippi	100.0	9.3	8.8	3.7	45.6	32.5	0.2
WEST SOUTH CENTRAL							
Arkansas	100.0	16.4	9.3	6.6	39.3	28.3	0.2
Louisiana	100.0	16.8	6.3	3.9	18.3	54.2	0.6
Oklahoma	100.0	35.1	12.3	8.5	10.9	33.0	0.1
Texas	100.0	20.1	7.3	8.7	8.2	55.3	0.4

Source: "Number of Work Mules on Colored and White Farms, Classified by Tenure, by Southern Divisions and States: 1910," *Negro Population, 1790-1915,* 1918, p. 622. Primary source: U.S. Bureau of the Census. *Negro Population, 1790-1915.* Washington, D.C.: Government Printing Office, 1918. *Note:* "Colored" may include persons other than Black.

★ 70 ★
Crops/Livestock/Animals

Relationships: Percentage Distribution of Work Mules on Southern Farms by Owner Status and Southern Division and State, 1910 - II

DIVISION AND STATE	FARMS OPERATED BY WHITE FARMERS: 1910						
	Total	Owners and part owners			Tenants		Managers
		Owners		Part owners	Cash, and not specified	Share and share cash	
		Free	Mortgaged				
	PERCENTAGE DISTRIBUTION OF WORK MULES, BY TENURE						
THE SOUTH							
Total	100.0	39.1	13.6	9.4	9.9	25.0	3.0
South Atlantic	100.0	46.9	11.7	7.1	12.4	18.6	3.3
East South Central	100.0	47.4	13.1	9.9	9.9	17.7	2.0
West South Central	100.0	29.5	14.8	10.2	8.6	33.3	3.5
SOUTH ATLANTIC							
Delaware	100.0	38.8	16.0	2.5	3.6	36.8	2.4
Maryland	100.0	31.8	22.3	4.3	7.5	27.9	6.3
District of Columbia	100.0	9.6	...	28.8	15.4	5.8	40.4
Virginia	100.0	57.0	11.8	7.3	6.4	12.8	4.6
West Virginia	100.0	63.3	7.4	9.0	8.9	8.7	2.8
North Carolina	100.0	51.0	10.6	10.1	6.6	19.7	2.1
South Carolina	100.0	42.9	15.2	7.3	15.9	15.0	3.6
Georgia	100.0	42.8	9.8	5.1	17.8	21.5	3.0
Florida	100.0	60.0	11.8	7.0	8.3	5.7	7.2
EAST SOUTH CENTRAL							
Kentucky	100.0	52.6	13.6	9.6	5.7	16.9	1.6
Tennessee	100.0	47.8	9.8	12.8	8.9	19.7	1.1
Alabama	100.0	41.5	13.4	9.4	14.7	19.2	1.8
Mississippi	100.0	46.2	17.6	6.0	12.2	13.4	4.7
WEST SOUTH CENTRAL							
Arkansas	100.0	43.6	9.8	12.0	11.8	20.2	2.6
Louisiana	100.0	38.0	14.4	7.2	10.6	12.4	17.4
Oklahoma	100.0	16.0	13.8	15.2	16.4	37.8	0.8
Texas	100.0	29.1	16.7	8.4	4.5	38.8	2.4

Source: "Number of Work Mules on Colored and White Farms, Classified by Tenure, by Southern Divisions and States: 1910," *Negro Population, 1790-1915*, 1918, p. 622. Primary source: U.S. Bureau of the Census. *Negro Population, 1790-1915.* Washington, D.C.: Government Printing Office, 1918.

★ 71 ★

Crops/Livestock/Animals

Relationships: Products Sold, Traded, or Used by Black Farm Operators – Value by Farm Location and Owner Status, 1929

[Colored farmers included Negroes, Indians, Chinese, Japanese, and all other nonwhite races]

DIVISION AND STATE	VALUE OF PRODUCTS REPORTED BY-						
	Total	Owners	Tenants	Managers	Percent distribution		
					Owners	Tenants	Managers
The South	$646,641,216	$119,415,311	$524,974,053	$2,251,852	18.5	81.2	0.3
SOUTH ATLANTIC	222,454,239	49,111,473	172,103,916	1,239,150	22.1	77.4	.6
Delaware	764,973	288,057	431,807	45,109	37.7	56.4	5.9
Maryland	4,791,394	1,937,047	2,574,103	280,244	40.4	53.7	5.8
District of Columbia	11,460	3,720	1,850	5,890	32.5	16.1	51.4
Virginia	27,130,851	13,462,260	13,435,870	232,721	49.6	49.5	.9
West Virginia	267,361	193,621	66,517	7,223	72.4	24.9	2.7
North Carolina	67,810,383	14,107,815	53,623,883	78,685	20.8	79.1	.1
South Carolina	52,240,775	8,823,166	43,276,542	141,067	16.9	82.8	.3
Georgia	63,489,255	7,370,780	55,910,339	208,136	11.6	88.1	.3
Florida	5,948,087	2,925,007	2,783,005	240,075	9.2	46.8	4.0
EAST SOUTH CENTRAL	239,301,592	35,025,231	203,868,996	407,365	14.6	85.2	.2
Kentucky	6,195,476	2,616,064	3,553,811	25,601	42.2	57.4	.4
Tennessee	25,147,620	4,990,850	20,081,668	75,102	19.8	79.9	.3
Alabama	57,954,853	10,670,736	47,149,048	135,069	18.4	81.4	.2
Mississippi	150,003,643	16,747,581	133,084,469	171,593	11.2	88.7	.1
WEST SOUTH CENTRAL	184,885,085	35,278,607	149,001,141	605,337	19.1	80.6	.3
Arkansas	61,721,444	8,479,772	53,182,042	59,630	13.7	86.2	.1
Louisiana	54,729,926	7,440,862	47,181,923	107,141	13.6	86.2	.2
Oklahoma	16,068,774	6,457,086	9,377,480	234,208	40.2	58.4	1.5
Texas	52,364,941	12,900,887	39,259,696	204,358	24.6	75.0	.4
SELECTED NORTHERN STATES[1]	9,225,358	3,090,587	5,896,362	238,409	33.5	63.9	2.6
New Jersey	692,808	342,050	276,034	74,719	49.4	39.8	10.8
Pennsylvania	391,810	203,648	157,293	30,869	52.0	40.1	7.9
Ohio	1,017,640	542,097	451,735	23,808	53.3	44.4	2.3
Indiana	365,305	183,459	174,589	7,257	50.2	47.8	2.0
Illinois	665,389	323,620	327,782	13,987	48.6	49.3	2.1
Missouri	4,992,925	844,463	4,076,005	72,457	16.9	81.6	1.5
Kansas	1,099,486	651,250	432,924	15,312	59.2	39.4	1.4

Source: "Value of Farm Products Sold, Traded, or Used by the Family of Colored Operators, by Tenure, by Southern Divisions, and States, and Selected Northern States: 1929," *Negroes in the United States, 1920-1932,* 1935, p. 588. Primary source: U.S. Bureau of the Census. *Negro Population, 1790-1915.* Washington, D.C.: U.S. Government Printing Office, 1935. *Notes:* 1. States having 200 or more Negro farmers who constitute 90 percent or more of the colored farmers in the State.

★ 72 ★

Crops/Livestock/Animals

Relationships: Southern Farms with and without Goats and Kids, Poultry and Bees, and Value of Livestock by Owner Status, 1910

| | LIVE STOCK ON FARMS | | | | | | | |
| | Domestic animals Goats and kids | | | Poultry | | | Bees | |
	Farms reporting	Farms not reporting	Value	Farms reporting	Farms not reporting	Value	Farms reporting	Value
THE SOUTH								
Colored farmers	7,531	882,610	$60,284	714,043	176,098	$5,121,77⋅	20,342	$138,385
Owners, free	2,216	126,341	24,630	113,450	15,107	1,133,308	6,223	55,890
Owners, mortgaged	922	45,811	8,090	42,903	3,830	408,464	2,451	19,594
Part owners	698	42,479	5,515	39,834	3,343	365,686	2,201	15,683
Cash tenants	2,280	283,670	12,044	234,661	51,289	1,525,526	5,215	33,121
Share tenants	1,384	383,140	9,117	282,360	102,164	1,668,246	4,215	23,539
Managers	31	1,169	888	835	365	20,545	37	558
White farmers	44,487[1]	2,162,919	3,159,095	1,963,127	244,279	32,293,561	278,301	3,541,162
Owners, free	25,720	882,491	1,109,230	839,767	68,444	15,188,015	167,950	2,268,679
Owners, mortgaged	6,610	239,279	695,615	229,836	16,053	4,528,058	34,407	458,878
Part owners	3,979	167,965	757,348	162,397	9,547	2,898,234	26,249	292,976
Cash tenants	3,446	226,015	300,098	192,389	37,012	2,695,858	14,930	187,630
Share tenants	4,098	632,719	118,209	527,839	108,978	6,559,556	33,475	305,782
Managers	634	14,450	178,595	10,899	4,185	383,840	1,290	27,217

Source: "Number of Farms Reporting and Not Reporting Live Stock, and Value of Each Class of Live Stock Reported, by Tenure of Farmer, for Colored and White Farmers, for Southern States: 1910," *Negro Population, 1790-1915,* 1918, pp. 628-637. Primary source: U.S. Bureau of the Census. *Negro Population, 1790-1915.* Washington, D.C.: Government Printing Office, 1918. *Notes:* "Colored" may include persons other than Black. 1. By correction of errors the number of farms reporting goats and kids is reduced, as compared with figures previously published for Georgia, by 5 and for Texas by 1, and is increased for Louisiana by 3; giving a net reduction of 3 for the South as a whole.

★ 73 ★

Crops/Livestock/Animals

Relationships: Southern Farms with and without Hogs and Pigs, Sheep and Lambs, and Asses and Burros, and Value of Livestock by Owner Status, 1910

| | LIVE STOCK ON FARMS Domestic animals | | | | | | | | |
| | Hogs and pigs | | | Sheep and lambs | | | Asses and burros | | |
	Farms reporting	Farms not reporting	Value	Farms reporting	Farms not reporting	Value	Farms reporting	Farms not reporting	Value
THE SOUTH									
Colored farmers	602,090	288,051	$12,331,574	3,386	868,755	$200,128	1,353	888,788	$176,400
Owners, free	96,503	32,054	2,665,627	1,676	126,881	81,119	481	128,076	66,129
Owners, mortgaged	37,446	9,287	1,009,994	475	46,258	22,194	214	46,519	26,196

[Continued]

★ 73 ★

Relationships: Southern Farms with and without Hogs and Pigs, Sheep and Lambs, and Asses and Burros, and Value of Livestock by Owner Status, 1910

[Continued]

| | LIVE STOCK ON FARMS Domestic animals | | | | | | | | |
| | Hogs and pigs | | | Sheep and lambs | | | Asses and burros | | |
	Farms reporting	Farms not reporting	Value	Farms reporting	Farms not reporting	Value	Farms reporting	Farms not reporting	Value
Part owners	34,596	8,581	835,855	346	42,831	20,107	154	43,023	20,638
Cash tenants	206,102	79,848	3,906,120	257	285,693	8,960	201	285,749	27,478
Share tenants	226,737	157,787	3,842,172	561	383,963	51,897	297	384,227	34,674
Managers	706	494	71,806	71	1,129	15,851	6	1,194	1,285
White farmers	1,628,751	578,655	68,685,761	180,908	2,026,498	25,411,706	21,757	2,185,649	5,786,605
Owners, free	718,419	189,792	31,927,943	119,380	788,831	14,272,126	10,249	897,962	2,836,373
Owners, mortgaged	193,818	51,071	10,352,014	19,869	226,020	3,733,403	4,086	241,803	1,156,624
Part owners	140,610	31,334	6,967,678	16,226	155,718	2,930,855	2,671	169,273	762,697
Cash tenants	157,812	71,649	6,076,371	6,617	222,844	1,406,927	1,371	228,090	352,262
Share tenants	408,589	228,228	11,940,838	17,148	619,669	1,982,884	2,970	633,847	499,801
Managers	9,503	5,581	1,420,917	1,668	13,416	1,085,511	410	14,674	178,848

Source: "Number of Farms Reporting and Not Reporting Live Stock, and Value of Each Class of Live Stock Reported, by Tenure of Farmer, for Colored and White Farmers, for Southern States: 1910," *Negro Population, 1790-1915*, 1918, pp. 628-637. Primary source: U.S. Bureau of the Census. *Negro Population, 1790-1915*. Washington, D.C.: Government Printing Office, 1918. *Note:* "Colored" may include persons other than Black.

★ 74 ★

Crops/Livestock/Animals

Relationships: Southern Farms with and without Horses, Neat Cattle and Mules, and Value of Livestock by Owner Status, 1910

| DIVISION, COLOR OF FARMER, AND TENURE CLASS | LIVE STOCK OF FARMS Domestic animals | | | | | |
| | Neat cattle | | | Mules | | |
	Farms reporting	Farms not reporting	Value	Farms reporting	Farms not reporting	Value
THE SOUTH						
Colored farmers	551,940	338,201	$33,028,831	441,178	448,963	$84,127,172
Owners, free	99,180	29,377	8,461,971	49,174	79,383	9,958,968
Owners, mortgaged	38,032	8,701	2,893,798	25,465	21,268	5,424,462
Part owners	33,632	9,545	2,624,308	21,817	21,360	4,620,451
Cash tenants	195,128	90,822	10,160,831	170,569	115,381	32,945,564
Share tenants	185,216	199,308	8,616,588	173,546	210,978	30,788,483
Managers	752[1]	448	271,385	607	593	390,244
White farmers	1,874,362	333,044	335,151,430[2]	1,037,204	1,170,202	294,131,054
Owners, free	829,439	78,772	144,399,038	410,409	497,802	115,476,367
Owners, mortgaged	223,767	22,122	48,762,402	127,732	118,157	40,021,654
Part owners	158,115	13,829	39,703,373	92,245	79,699	28,129,531
Cash tenants	178,383	51,078	32,600,988	110,285	119,176	29,784,731

[Continued]

★ 74 ★

Relationships: Southern Farms with and without Horses, Neat Cattle and Mules, and Value of Livestock by Owner Status, 1910

[Continued]

DIVISION, COLOR OF FARMER, AND TENURE CLASS	LIVE STOCK OF FARMS Domestic animals					
	Neat cattle			Mules		
	Farms reporting	Farms not reporting	Value	Farms reporting	Farms not reporting	Value
Share tenants	473,169	163,648	40,597,993	288,209	348,608	70,841,951
Managers	11,489	3,595	29,087,636	8,324	6,760	9,876,820

Source: "Number of Farms Reporting and Not Reporting Live Stock, and Value of Each Class of Live Stock Reported, by Tenure of Farmer, for Colored and White Farmers, for Southern States: 1910," *Negro Population, 1790-1915*, 1918, pp. 628-637. Primary source: U.S. Bureau of the Census. *Negro Population, 1790-1915*. Washington, D.C.: Government Printing Office, 1918. *Notes:* "Colored" may include persons other than Black. 1. Correction of an error in West Virginia has reduced the number of managers by 1, as compared with figures previously published. 2. The total for the white farmers of the South includes $2,240 not distributed by tenure, which represents value of animals (Belgian hares, ostriches, etc.) not shown separately in this table. Of this total $10 are included in the total for the South Atlantic division, $300 in the total for the East South Central division, and $1,930 in the total for the West South Central division.

★ 75 ★

Crops/Livestock/Animals

Relationships: Southern Farms with and without Horses, and Value of Livestock by Owner Status, 1910

DIVISION, COLOR OF FARMER, AND TENURE CLASS	Number of farms	LIVE STOCK OF FARMS Domestic animals					
		Total			Horses		
		Farms reporting	Farms not reporting	Value	Farms reporting	Farms not reporting	Value
THE SOUTH							
Colored farmers	890,141	804,994[1]	85,147	$177,461,964	334,537	555,604	$47,537,525
Owners, free	128,557	121,856	6,701	32,921,123	74,930	53,627	11,664,679
Owners, mortgaged	46,733	45,393	1,340	13,641,333	27,310	19,423	4,256,599
Part owners	43,177	42,058	1,119	12,038,689	25,098	18,079	3,911,815
Cash tenants	285,950	267,869	18,081	61,459,567	104,112	181,838	14,397,570
Share tenants	384,524	326,748	57,776	56,043,805	102,389	282,135	12,700,874
Managers	1,200	1,070[1]	130	1,357,447	698	502	605,988
White farmers	2,207,406	2,118,896	88,510	1,106,838,990[2]	1,437,122	770,284	374,511,099
Owners, free	908,211	884,823	23,388	474,921,450	639,427	268,784	164,900,373
Owners, mortgaged	245,889	241,481	4,408	162,241,548	184,735	61,154	57,519,836
Part owners	171,944	169,926	2,018	117,791,944	123,585	48,359	38,540,462
Cash tenants	229,461	218,111	11,350	101,745,745	134,501	94,960	31,224,368
Share tenants	636,817	591,200	45,617	199,924,868	344,222	292,595	73,943,192
Managers	15,084	13,355	1,729	50,211,195	10,652	4,432	8,382,868

Source: "Number of Farms Reporting and Not Reporting Live Stock, and Value of Each Class of Live Stock Reported, by Tenure of Farmer, for Colored and White Farmers, for Southern States: 1910," *Negro Population, 1790-1915*, 1918, pp. 628-637. Primary source: U.S. Bureau of the Census. *Negro Population, 1790-1915*. Washington, D.C.: Government Printing Office, 1918. *Notes:* "Colored" may include persons other than Black. 1. Correction of an error in West Virginia has reduced the number of managers by 1, as compared with figures previously published. 2. The total for the white farmers of the South includes $2,240 not distributed by tenure, which represents value of animals (Belgian hares, ostriches, etc.) not shown separately in this table. Of this total $10 are included in the total for the South Atlantic division, $300 in the total for the East South Central division, and $1,930 in the total for the West South Central division.

★ 76 ★

Crops/Livestock/Animals

Relationships: Swine on Black Farms by Owner Status and Farm Location, 1930

[Colored farmers include Negroes, Indians, Chinese, Japanese, and all other nonwhite races]

| DIVISION AND STATE | Total | SWINE REPORTED BY- | | | | | |
| | | Owners | | Tenants | | Managers | |
		Number	Percent	Number	Percent	Number	Percent
The South	2,152,882	660,865	30.7	1,481,563	68.8	10,454	0.5
SOUTH ATLANTIC	789,273	271,882	34.4	512,293	64.9	5,098	.6
Delaware	1,942	758	39.0	1,079	55.6	105	5.4
Maryland	11,851	5,449	46.0	5,500	46.4	902	7.6
District of Columbia	6	6	100.0	...	...	...	...
Virginia	100,892	61,859	61.3	38,018	37.7	1,015	1.0
West Virginia	1,881	930	49.4	851	45.2	100	5.3
North Carolina	166,725	54,428	32.6	111,863	67..1	434	.3
South Carolina	152,173	49,999	32.9	101,734	66.9	440	.3
Georgia	282,131	58,937	20.9	221,967	78.7	1,227	.4
Florida	71,672	39,516	55.1	31,281	43.6	875	1.2
EAST SOUTH CENTRAL	732,165	173,346	23.7	556,372	76.0	2,447	.3
Kentucky	23,534	12,686	53.9	10,650	45.3	198	.8
Tennessee	78,880	24,924	31.6	53,307	67.6	649	.8
Alabama	273,970	61,977	22.6	211,080	77.0	913	.3
Mississippi	355,781	73,759	20.7	281,355	79.1	687	.2
WEST SOUTH CENTRAL	631,444	215,637	34.1	412,898	65.4	2,909	.5
Arkansas	154,192	43,588	28.3	110,347	71.6	257	.2
Louisiana	202,896	47,554	23.4	154,895	76.3	447	.2
Oklahoma	89,416	49,114	54.9	38,875	43.5	1,427	1.6
Texas	184,940	75,381	40.8	108,781	58.8	778	.4
SELECTED NORTHERN STATES[1]	52,011	24,649	47.4	25,294	48.6	2,068	4.0
New Jersey	2,242	1,331	59.4	865	38.6	46	2.1
Pennsylvania	1,027	405	39.4	468	45.6	154	15.0
Ohio	10,353	4,453	43.0	5,704	55.1	196	1.9
Indiana	4,194	1,860	44.3	2,253	53.7	81	1.9
Illinois	4,870	2,382	48.9	2,372	48.7	116	2.4
Missouri	21,681	9,412	43.4	11,349	52.3	920	4.2
Kansas	7,644	4,806	62.9	2,283	29.9	555	7.3

Source: "Number of Swine on Farms of Colored Operators, by Tenure of Farmer, by Southern Divisions, and States, and Selected Northern States: 1930," *Negroes in the United States, 1920-1932,* 1935, p. 589. Primary source: U.S. Bureau of the Census. *Negroes in the United States, 1920-1932.* Washington, D.C.: U.S. Government Printing Office, 1935. *Notes:* 1. States having 200 or more Negro farmers who constitute 90 percent or more of the colored farmers in the State.

★ 77 ★

Crops/Livestock/Animals

Relationships: Value of Cattle on Black Farms in the South by Owner Status and Farm Location, 1930

[Colored farmers include Negroes, Indians, Chinese, Japanese, and all other nonwhite farmers]

| DIVISION AND STATE | CATTLE ON FARMS, 1930 | | | | | | | |
| | Total | | Owners | | Tenants | | Managers | |
	Number	Value	Number	Value	Number	Value	Number	Value
The South	1,298,821	$54,322,234	503,816	$21,634,400	777,277	$31,868,718	17,728	$829,516
South Atlantic	307,764	13,864,958	124,614	5,818,662	179,566	7,842,450	3,584	203,846
East South Central	539,744	21,406,087	168,037	6,738,385	369,099	14,557,463	2,608	110,239
West South Central	451,313	19,061,189	211,165	9,076,953	228,612	9,468,805	11,536	515,431
Selected Northern States[1]	25,101	1,568,755	14,119	862,542	9,726	621,169	1,256	85,044

Source: "Number and Value of Cattle on Farms of Colored Operators, by Tenure of Farmer, 1930, with Specified Dairy Products Produced and Sold, 1929," *Negroes in the United States, 1920-1932,* 1935, p. 625. Primary source: U.S. Bureau of the Census. *Negroes in the United States, 1920-1932.* Washington, D.C.: U.S. Government Printing Office, 1935. *Notes:* "Colored" may include persons other than Black. 1. States having 200 or more Negro farmers who constitute 90 percent or more of the colored farmers in the State.

★ 78 ★

Crops/Livestock/Animals

Relationships: Work Mules on Southern Farms by Owner Status, and Southern Division and State, 1910 - I

DIVISION AND STATE	FARMS OPERATED BY COLORED FARMERS: 1910						
	Total	Owners and part owners			Tenants		Managers
		Owners		Part owners	Cash, and not specified	Share and share cash	
		Free	Mortgaged				
THE SOUTH							
Total	645,320	82,998	44,446	37,307	246,934	231,263	2,372
South Atlantic	221,694	23,611	10,900	11,859	89,617	84,708	999
East South Central	248,161	24,630	19,125	13,020	122,436	68,209	741
West South Central	175,465	34,757	14,421	12,428	34,881	78,346	632
SOUTH ATLANTIC							
Delaware	349	53	35	12	16	213	20
Maryland	1,178	183	131	87	115	521	141
District of Columbia	1	...	...	...	1	...	...
Virginia	8,783	3,351	938	1,269	835	2,234	156
West Virginia	81	45	7	8	9	12	...
North Carolina	34,532	5,058	2,233	3,795	6,577	16,765	114
South Carolina	61,761	5,659	3,265	3,242	26,864	22,539	192
Georgia	109,983	7,947	3,836	3,028	53,151	41,687	334

[Continued]

★ 78 ★

Relationships: Work Mules on Southern Farms by Owner Status, and Southern Division and State, 1910 - I

[Continued]

DIVISION AND STATE	FARMS OPERATED BY COLORED FARMERS: 1910						
	Total	Owners and part owners			Tenants		Managers
		Owners		Part owners	Cash, and not specified	Share and share cash	
		Free	Mortgaged				
Florida	5,026	1,315	465	418	2,049	737	42
EAST SOUTH CENTRAL							
Kentucky	6,157	1,888	781	1,021	516	1,883	68
Tennessee	28,526	4,485	2,035	3,026	11,619	7,173	188
Alabama	87,172	6,552	5,236	4,345	52,780	18,073	186
Mississippi	126,306	11,705	11,073	4,628	57,521	41,080	299
WEST SOUTH CENTRAL							
Arkansas	52,772	8,633	4,917	3,464	20,717	14,920	121
Louisiana	35,760	5,992	2,240	1,396	6,548	19,370	214
Oklahoma	17,854	6,772	2,205	1,526	1,942	5,887	22
Texas	69,079	13,860	5,059	6,042	5,674	38,169	275

Source: "Number of Work Mules on Colored and White Farms, Classified by Tenure, by Southern Divisions and States: 1910," *Negro Population, 1790-1915,* 1918, p. 622. Primary source: U.S. Bureau of the Census. *Negro Population, 1790-1915.* Washington, D.C.: Government Printing Office, 1918. *Note:* "Colored" may include persons other than Black.

★ 79 ★

Crops/Livestock/Animals

Relationships: Work Mules on Southern Farms by Owner Status, and Southern Division and State, 1910 - II

DIVISION AND STATE	FARMS OPERATED BY WHITE FARMERS: 1910						
	Total	Owners and part owners			Tenants		Managers
		Owners		Part owners	Cash, and not specified	Share and share cash	
		Free	Mortgaged				
THE SOUTH							
Total	2,188,166	855,973	296,726	205,911	216,728	547,085	65,743
South Atlantic	514,649	241,170	60,455	36,638	63,639	95,892	16,855
East South Central	676,717	320,691	88,427	67,159	67,083	119,538	13,819
West South Central	996,800	294,112	147,844	102,114	86,006	331,655	35,069
SOUTH ATLANTIC							
Delaware	5,327	2,067	850	133	193	1,958	126
Maryland	20,320	6,464	4,522	880	1,519	5,661	1,274

[Continued]

★ 79 ★

Relationships: Work Mules on Southern Farms by Owner Status, and Southern Division and State, 1910 - II

[Continued]

DIVISION AND STATE	FARMS OPERATED BY WHITE FARMERS: 1910						
	Total	Owners and part owners			Tenants		Managers
		Owners		Part owners	Cash, and not specified	Share and share cash	
		Free	Mortgaged				
District of Columbia	52	5	...	15	8	3	21
Virginia	47,233	26,927	5,590	3,449	3,038	6,042	2,187
West Virginia	10,719	6,786	792	961	955	930	295
North Carolina	138,603	69,692	14,420	13,812	8,974	26,902	2,803
South Carolina	93,045	39,959	14,183	6,762	14,813	13,962	3,366
Georgia	183,248	78,415	17,959	9,362	32,639	39,402	5,471
Florida	18,102	10,855	2,139	1,264	1,500	1,032	1,312
EAST SOUTH CENTRAL							
Kentucky	189,518	99,632	25,722	18,283	10,811	32,052	3,018
Tennessee	211,756	101,139	20,717	27,107	18,833	41,638	2,322
Alabama	155,113	64,379	20,823	14,550	22,791	29,732	2,838
Mississippi	120,330	55,541	21,165	7,219	14,648	18,116	5,641
WEST SOUTH CENTRAL							
Arkansas	153,680	67,032	15,089	18,443	18,203	30,977	3,936
Louisiana	92,907	35,296	13,357	6,721	9,813	11,565	16,155
Oklahoma	202,136	32,255	27,816	30,748	33,174	76,443	1,700
Texas	548,077	159,529	91,582	46,202	24,816	212,670	13,278

Source: "Number of Work Mules on Colored and White Farms, Classified by Tenure, by Southern Divisions and States: 1910," *Negro Population, 1790-1915*, 1918, p. 622. Primary source: U.S. Bureau of the Census. *Negro Population, 1790-1915*. Washington, D.C.: Government Printing Office, 1918.

★ 80 ★

Crops/Livestock/Animals

Value: Products Sold, Traded, or Used by Black Farmers – Value by Farm Location, 1929

[Colored farmers include Negroes, Indians, Chinese, Japanese, and all other nonwhite races]

DIVISION AND STATE	Total value of farm products	CROPS SOLD OR TRADED		LIVESTOCK OR TRADED		LIVESTOCK PRODUCTS SOLD OR TRADED		FOREST PRODUCTS SOLD		PRODUCTS USED BY FAMILY	
		Value	Percent	Value	Percent	Value	Percent	Value	Percent	Value	Percent
The South	$646,641,216	$509,171,918	78.7	$10,429,511	1.6	$15,618,421	2.4	$3,809,793	0.6	$107,611,573	16.6
SOUTH ATLANTIC	222,454,539	168,121,953	75.6	2,831,544	1.3	6,823,015	3.1	1,825,566	0.8	42,852,461	19.3
Delaware	764,973	408,129	53.4	18,816	2.5	140,739	18.4	3,233	0.4	194,056	25.4
Maryland	4,791,394	3,069,474	64.1	159,176	3.3	485,263	10.1	67,478	1.4	1,010,003	21.1
District of Columbia	11,460	5,095	44.5	...	...	3,935	34.3	190	1.7	2,240	19.5
Virginia	27,130,851	15,278,648	56.3	719,922	2.7	1,950,272	7.2	512,724	1.9	8,669,285	32.0
West Virginia	267,361	37,771	14.1	29,997	11.2	47,615	17.8	8,982	3.4	142,996	53.5
North Carolina	67,810,383	54,366,347	80.2	433,890	0.6	1,389,758	2.0	370,044	0.5	11,250,344	16.6
South Carolina	52,240,775	41,432,909	79.3	455,310	0.9	1,109,133	2.1	327,119	0.6	8,916,304	17.1
Georgia	63,489,255	49,906,288	78.6	762,588	1.2	1,272,578	2.0	484,710	0.8	11,063,091	17.4
Florida	5,948,087	3,617,292	60.8	251,845	4.2	423,722	7.1	51,086	0.9	1,604,142	27.0
EAST SOUTH CENTRAL	239,301,592	192,358,242	80.4	3,311,494	1.4	4,942,579	2.1	912,162	0.4	37,777,115	15.8
Kentucky	6,195,476	3,806,127	61.4	469,632	7.6	481,015	7.8	22,581	0.4	1,416,121	22.9
Tennessee	25,147,620	18,331,716	72.9	660,292	2.6	1,001,564	4.0	75,598	0.3	5,078,450	20.2
Alabama	57,954,853	42,444,023	73.2	1,076,382	1.9	1,540,167	2.7	353,290	0.6	12,543,991	21.6

[Continued]

★ 80 ★

Value: Products Sold, Traded, or Used by Black Farmers – Value by Farm Location, 1929

[Continued]

DIVISION AND STATE	Total value of farm products	CROPS SOLD OR TRADED		LIVESTOCK OR TRADED		LIVESTOCK PRODUCTS SOLD OR TRADED		FOREST PRODUCTS SOLD		PRODUCTS USED BY FAMILY	
		Value	Percent	Value	Percent	Value	Percent	Value	Percent	Value	Percent
Mississippi	150,003,643	127,779,376	85.2	1,105,188	0.7	1,919,833	1.3	460,693	0.3	18,738,553	12.5
WEST SOUTH CENTRAL	184,885,085	148,691,723	80.4	4,286,473	2.3	3,852,827	2.1	1,072,065	0.6	26,981,997	14.6
Arkansas	61,721,444	53,832,645	87.2	393,267	0.6	467,868	0.8	246,133	0.4	6,781,531	11.0
Louisiana	54,729,926	45,319,226	82.8	593,580	1.1	854,217	1.6	194,735	0.4	7,768,168	14.2
Oklahoma	16,068,774	9,110,311	56.7	2,062,307	12.8	1,143,154	7.1	196,330	1.2	3,556,672	22.1
Texas	52,364,941	40,429,541	77.2	1,237,319	2.4	1,387,588	2.6	434,867	0.8	8,875,626	16.9
SELECTED NORTHERN STATES[1]	9,225,358	5,426,178	58.8	1,257,911	13.6	1,167,248	12.7	48,974	0.5	1,325,047	14.3
New Jersey	692,803	405,826	58.6	25,371	3.7	186,714	27.0	1,127	0.2	73,765	10.6
Pennsylvania	391,810	96,935	24.7	49,287	12.6	160,004	40.8	5,716	1.5	79,868	20.4
Ohio	1,017,640	288,313	28.3	257,257	25.3	232,572	22.9	9,867	1.0	229,631	22.6
Indiana	365,305	115,815	31.7	92,984	25.5	86,499	23.7	1,897	0.5	68,110	18.6
Illinois	665,389	283,282	42.6	144,791	21.8	89,874	13.5	11,697	1.8	135,745	20.4
Missouri	4,992,925	3,666,920	73.4	490,269	9.8	262,140	5.3	15,036	0.3	558,560	11.2
Kansas	1,099,486	569,087	51.8	197,952	18.0	149,445	13.6	3,634	0.3	179,368	16.3

Source: "Value of Farm Products Sold, Traded, or Used by the Family of Colored Operator's Family by Southern Divisions, and States, and Selected Northern States: 1929," *Negroes in the United States, 1920-1932,* 1935, p. 590. Primary source: U.S. Bureau of the Census. *Negro Population, 1790-1915.* Washington, D.C.: U.S. Government Printing Office, 1935. *Notes:* 1. States having 200 or more Negro farmers who constitute 90 percent or more of the colored farmers in the State.

Extension Work and Workers

★ 81 ★

Number/Percent: Increase/Decrease in Southern Extension Workers by Program Type, 1925, 1937, and 1941 - I

Type of Program	Year	Number of agents			Percent of total
		Total	White	Negro	
All Types	1925	2,072	1,772	300	15
	1937	3,734	3,286	448	12
	1941	4,149	3,600	549	13
Farm Demonstration	1925	1,246	1,073	173	14
	1937	2,297	2,045	252	11
	1941	2,427	2,134	293	12

[Continued]

★ 81 ★

Number/Percent: Increase/Decrease in Southern Extension Workers by Program Type, 1925, 1937, and 1941 - I

[Continued]

Type of Program	Year	Number of agents			Percent of total
		Total	White	Negro	
Home Demonstration	1925	766	651	115	12
	1937	1,363	1,174	189	14
	1941	1,632	1,386	246	15
Boy-Girl Club Work	1925	60	48	12	29
	1937	74	67	7	9
	1941	89	80	9	10

Source: "Number and Percentage Increase of Extension Agents in 16 Southern States, by Type of Program and Race: 1925 (December 31), 1937 (February 28), and 1941 (June 30), *Negro Year Book: A Review of Events Affecting Negro Life, 1941-1946,* 1947, p. 170. Primary source: Cooperative Extension Service. Published by permission. *Notes:* Data supplied by the Cooperative Extension Service. (It will be noted that data are for different months and seasons in the three years involved. This fact, however, should in no way tend to invalidate racial comparisons). Table cited from study by Doxey Wilkerson, Howard University, 1942, by permission of author. 1. Decrease.

★ 82 ★

Extension Work and Workers

Number/Percent: Increase/Decrease in Southern Extension Workers by Program Type, 1925, 1937, and 1941 - II

Type of Program	Number increase over 1925			Number increase over 1937			Per cent increase over 1925			Per cent increase over 1937		
	Total	White	Negro	Total	White	Negro	Total	White	Negro	Total	White	Negro
All Types	...	...	...	...	...	...	...	...	...	...	...	...
	1,662	1,514	148	...	...	...	80	81	50	...	...	...
	2,077	1,828	249	415	134	101	100	103	83	11	10	21
Farm Demonstration	...	...	...	...	...	...	...	...	...	...	...	...
	1,051	972	79	...	...	...	81	91	46	...	...	...
	1,181	1,061	120	130	89	41	94	98	69	6	4	16
Home Demonstration	...	...	...	...	...	...	...	...	...	...	...	...
	597	523	...	...	...	...	78	80	64	...	...	...
	866	735	131	269	212	57	88	88	87	20	18	30
Boy-Girl Club Work	...	...	...	...	...	...	...	...	...	...	...	...
	14	19	-5[1]	...	...	...	23	40	-42[1]	...	...	...
	29	32	-3[1]	15	13	2	48	66	-25[1]	20	19	29

Source: "Number and Percentage Increase of Extension Agents in 16 Southern States, by Type of Program and Race: 1925 (December 31), 1937 (February 28), and 1941 (June 30), *Negro Year Book: A Review of Events Affecting Negro Life, 1941-1946,* 1947, p. 170. Primary source: Cooperative Extension Service. Published by permission. *Notes:* Data supplied by the Cooperative Extension Service. The States Represented are those listed in Table 8. (It will be noted that data are for different months and seasons in the three years involved. This fact, however, should in no way tend to invalidate racial comparisons). Table cited from study by Doxey Wilkerson, Howard University, 1942, by permission of author. 1. Decrease.

★ 83 ★

Extension Work and Workers

Number/Percent: Southern Extension Agents by States and Program Type, 1941

STATES	All Agents		Percent	Farm Agents		Home Agents		Boy-Girl Agents	
	Total	Negro	Negro	Total	Negro	Total	Negro	Total	Negro
Alabama	366	72	21	202	36	129	34	5	2
Arkansas	215	33	15	106	14	107	18	1	0
Florida	132	19	14	76	10	54	9	2	0
Georgia	339	52	15	208	25	126	25	5	2
Kentucky	251	7	3	175	5	67	2	9	0
Louisiana	206	20	10	115	12	88	7	3	1
Maryland	64	6	9	32	2	29	4	8	0
Mississippi	299	76	25	164	34	127	40	3	2
Missouri	239	1	[1]	141	0	91	1	7	0
North Carolina	379	58	15	234	36	143	22	2	0
Oklahoma	206	20	10	103	10	99	10	4	0
South Carolina	171	38	22	89	20	78	18	7	0
Tennessee	308	20	7	200	11	105	9	3	0
Texas	615	85	14	344	48	268	37	3	0
Virginia	253	37	15	173	28	77	9	3	0
West Virginia	136	5	4	65	2	44	1	27	2
TOTAL	4,149	549	13	2,427	293	1,632	246	89	9

Source: "Number of Extension Agents ("Total and Number of Negro) in 16 Southern States, by States and Type of Programs, September 30, 1941," *Negro Year Book: A Review of Events Affecting Negro Life, 1941-1946*, 1947, p. 168. Primary source: Data from Cooperative Extension Service. (Adapted from study by Doxey Wilkerson, Howard University, 1942, by permission of author). Published by permission. *Note:* 1. Less than .5 per cent.

★ 84 ★

Extension Work and Workers

Number/Percent: Southern Extension Workers by States and Program Type, 1951

States	County Agent Work				Home Demonstration Work				4-H Club	
	Supervisors[1]		Agents[2]		Supervisors		Agents[2]		Leaders	
	Negro	White	Negro	White	Negro	White	Negro	White	Negro	White
Alabama	3	6	36	182	2	5	36	127	2	2
Arkansas	2	4	24	126	2	5	28	94	1	2
Delaware	0	1	0	5	0	1	1	3	0	5
Florida	1	3	10	97	1	4	11	63	0	4
Georgia	2	6	44	224	1	7	32	149	2	5
Kentucky	1	7	3	172	0	7	6	108	0	12
Louisiana	1	6	19	134	1	5	21	107	1	4

[Continued]

★ 84 ★

Number/Percent: Southern Extension Workers by States and Program Type, 1951
[Continued]

| States | County Agent Work | | | | Home Demonstration Work | | | | 4-H Club | |
| | Supervisors[1] | | Agents[2] | | Supervisors | | Agents[2] | | Leaders | |
	Negro	White	Negro	White	Negro	White	Negro	White	Negro	White
Maryland	1	1	7	41	0	2	5	36	0	4
Mississippi	2	4	43	172	2	7	61	110	2	5
Missouri	0	6	0	202	0	6	4	109	0	7
North Carolina[3]	4	6	54	238	3	8	53	177	2	7
Oklahoma	1	4	13	145	1	6	14	111	0	4
South Carolina	2	3	31	97	2	5	28	78	0	5
Tennessee	2	6	13	190	1	5	12	126	0	4
Texas	4	15	56	352	3	17	46	233	1	4
Virginia	2	6	30	152	1	7	31	109	0	5
West Virginia	1	2	2	58	1	3	8	38	4	43
Totals	29	86	385	2587	21	100	397	1742	15	122

Source: "Number of Extension Workers in South by States and Race, June 1951," *1952 Negro Year Book: A Review of Events Affecting Negro Life,* 1952, p. 107. Primary source: USDA Extension Service Report on Number of Extension Workers, June 30, 1951. Published by permission. *Notes:* 1. The 41 white directors and assistant directors are not included. 2. Assistant agents are included. 3. North Carolina has four Negro subject matter specialists, not included in totals.

★ 85 ★

Extension Work and Workers

Relationships: Southern Black Extension Workers in Relation to Number Needed by States, 1941

STATE	Per cent Negro of Rural Population 1940	Number of Negroes Required for Equity	Actual Number of Negro Agents	Difference Between Actual No. and Equitable No.	Per cent Actual No. is of Equitable No.
Alabama	35.6	120	72	-48	60
Arkansas	26.5	57	32	-24	58
Florida	31.3	41	19	-22	46
Georgia	37.5	127	52	-75	41
Kentucky	6.0	14	7	-7	50
Louisiana	40.9	84	20	-64	24
Maryland	17.8	11	6	-5	55
Mississippi	53.4	157	76	-61	49
Missouri	3.0	7	1	+6	14
North Carolina	28.5	108	58	-50	54
Oklahoma	6.6	14	20	-6	143
South Carolina	47.9	52	38	-14	73
Tennessee	13.8	44	20	-24	46

[Continued]

★ 85 ★

Relationships: Southern Black Extension Workers in Relation to Number Needed by States, 1941

[Continued]

STATE	Per cent Negro of Rural Population 1940	Number of Negroes Required for Equity	Actual Number of Negro Agents	Difference Between Actual No. and Equitable No.	Per cent Actual No. is of Equitable No.
Texas	15.3	94	85	-9	91
Virginia	26.7	69	37	-32	54
West Virginia	6.8	9	5	-4	56
TOTAL	24.1	1,000	549	451	55

Source: "Actual Number of Negro Extension Agents in Relation to the Number Required for Equity, by States, September 30, 1941," *Negro Year Book: A Review of Events Affecting Negro Life, 1941-1946*, 1947, p. 169. Primary source: Adapted from study by Doxey Wilkerson, Howard University, 1942. Published by permission.

★ 86 ★

Extension Work and Workers

Relationships: Southern Expenditures for Black Extension Work in Relation to Black Rural/ Farm Population, 1925, 1936, and 1941

State	1925		1936		1941		Percent Negro of total			Percent Negro of Rural Population 1930	Rural-farm Population 1930
	Total	Negro	Total	Negro	Total	Negro	1925	1936	1941		
Alabama	$485,177	$46,810	$834,906	$131,402	$975,503	$154,589	9.7	15.6	15.8	36	37
Arkansas	435,951	45,246	774,575	34,540	913,949	73,345	10.4	4.5	8.0	27	29
Florida	253,116	16,886	410,992	31,434	552,406	32,544	6.6	7.6	5.9	31	27
Georgia	562,882	34,480	998,037	64,733	1,075,369	68,460	6.1	6.5	6.4	38	39
Kentucky	445,909	4,500	802,948	4,690	931,147	11,152	1.0	.6	1.2	6	4
Louisiana	362,919	21,773	655,534	37,550	751,867	40,486	6.0	5.7	5.4	41	45
Maryland	264,493	1,475	370,921	5,398	389,771	9,464	.5	1.5	2.4	18	19
Mississippi	516,549	55,292	892,121	87,284	1,043,660	111,864	10.8	9.8	10.6	52	56
Missouri	475,775	2,200	746,120	...	922,275	2,400	.5	...	2.6	3	3
North Carolina	623,735	36,548	1,019,519	73,408	1,233,234	111,692	5.9	7.3	9.0	29	31
Oklahoma	500,280	29,141	723,564	34,658	889,575	35,310	5.8	4.8	4.0	7	8
South Carolina	416,217	16,233	603,319	42,052	703,398	61,602	3.9	7.0	8.7	48	55
Tennessee	413,287	6,800	809,110	25,500	922,684	43,685	1.6	3.2	4.7	14	14
Texas	980,050	63,624	1,714,749	112,227	2,044,190	158,524	6.5	6.6	7.7	15	18
Virginia	508,653	44,759	802,010	52,998	930,695	64,619	8.8	6.6	6.9	27	27
West Virginia	368,807	5,735	464,767	3,695	515,545	8,130	1.6	.8	1.6	7	9
Total	$7,613,801	$431,502	$12,623,200	$741,660	$14,795,258	$987,836	5.7	5.9	6.7	24	27

Source: "Expenditures for Total and Negro Extension Work in 16 Southern States, 1925, 1936, and 1941: Per Cent Negro of Total Expenditures and of Rural and Farm Population,: *Negro Year Book: A Review of Events Affecting Negro Life, 1941-1946*, 1947, p. 173. Primary source: Expenditure data from Cooperative Extension Service; population data from Negroes in the United States: 1920-32, pp. 52-3. Table edited from study by Doxey Wilkerson, Howard University, 1942 by permission of author.

★ 87 ★

Extension Work and Workers

Salaries: Southern Extension Workers' Annual Average Salaries by State, 1950

States	County Agent Negro	County Agent White	Asst. Agents White	Home Agents Negro	Home Agents White	Asst. Agents White
Alabama	$2,752	$5,011	$3,683	$2,288	$3,560	$3009
Arkansas	4,713	4,259	3,050	2,563	3,602	2,687
Delaware	-	-	-	3,300	3,500	-
Florida	2,604	4,368	3,669	2,604	3,533	3,087
Georgia	2,298	3,508	2,950	2,049	2,821	2,446
Kentucky	2,860	4,254	3,262	2,808	3,605	2,950
Louisiana	2,980	4,879	3,455	2,668	3,973	2,722
Maryland	3,214	5,197	3,422	2,973	3,825	3,100
Mississippi	2,782	4,333	3,366	2,327	3,557	2,758
Missouri	-	-	-	2,477	3,059	-
North Carolina	3,732	5,202	3,841	3,221	3,910	3,071
Oklahoma	2,943	4,436	3,466	2,547	2,737	2,967
South Carolina	2,791	4,297	3,263	2,323	3,067	2,445
Tennessee	2,745	4,046	3,403	2,510	3,300	2,935
Texas	3,079	4,481	3,427	2,684	3842	3,312
Virginia	3,152	4,401	3,100	2,951	3,784	2,744
West Virginia		(no report)			(no report)	

Source: "Average Annual Salaries of Extension Workers in South by States and Race, October 1950," *1952 Negro Year Book: A Review of Events Affecting Negro Life*, 1952, p. 107. Primary source: USDA Extension Service Report on Average Annual Salaries, No. 1033 (10-50). Published by permission. *Note:* White County and Home Agents have assistants; Negro Agents do not.

★ 88 ★

Extension Work and Workers

Support: Allotment Sources for Black Southern Extension Work by State, 1935-1936 - I

	ALLOTMENTS				OTHER ALLOTMENTS			
	Smith-Lever	Capper-Ketcham	Additional Cooperative	U.S.D.A	State and Colleges	County	Other	Total
J.B. Pierce, Field agent for:								
Arkansas	$21,490.00	$4,800.00	$2,260.00	$600.00	-	$5,390.00	-	$34,540.00
Kentucky	900.00	-	900.00	-	2,890.00	-	-	4,690.00
Maryland	2,314.00	-	-	-	2,784.00	300.00	-	5,398.00
North Carolina	38,560.00	-	-	100.0	19,130.00	13,678.50	2,030.00	73,498.50
South Carolina	10,125.00	925.00	2,000.00	1,076.25	22,303.57	5,622.00	-	42,051.82
Tennessee	23,000.00	-	1,400.00	600.00	500.00	-	-	25,500.00
Virginia	46,169.00	-	-	-	-	6,630.00	199.00	52,998.00
West Virginia	3,620.00	32.37	-	-	43.03	-	-	3,695.40
Total	146,178.00	5,757.37	6,560.00	2,376.25	47,650.60	31,620.50	2,229.00	242,371.72

[Continued]

★ 88 ★

Support: Allotment Sources for Black Southern Extension Work by State, 1935-1936 - I
[Continued]

| | ALLOTMENTS | | | | OTHER ALLOTMENTS | | | |
	Smith-Lever	Capper-Ketcham	Additional Cooperative	U.S.D.A	State and Colleges	County	Other	Total
T.M. Campbell Field agent for:								
Alabama	104,035.00	16,000.000	10,850.00	516.66	-	-	-	131,401.66
Florida	14,054.00	8,700.00	4,000.00		3,180.00	1,500.00	-	31,434.00
Georgia	52,533.47	-	7,500.00	1,700.00	3,000.00	-	-	64,733.47
Louisiana	18,204.00	5,808.00	2,140.00	1,020.00	9,556.00	822.00	-	37,550.00
Mississippi	27,670.42	35,462.93	404.18	50.00	1,800.00	15,596.00	6,300.00	87,283.53
Oklahoma	28,658.33	6,000.00	-	-	-	-	-	34,658.33
Texas	79,849.41	-	-	600.00	11,503.00	19.400.88	874.00	112,287.29
Total	325,004.63	71,970.93	24,894.18	3,886.66	29,039.00	37,318.88	7,174.00	499.288.28
Grand Total	471,182.63	77,728.30	31,454.18	6,262.91	76,689.60	68,939.38	9,403.00	741,660.00

Source: "Sources of Allotments for Negro Extension Work 1935-1936," *Negro Year Book: An Annual Encyclopedia of the Negro, 1937-1938*, 1937, p. 44. Primary source: Work, Monroe N. (Ed.), *Negro Year Book: An Annual Encyclopedia of the Negro, 1937-1938.* Tuskegee Institute, AL: The Negro Year Book Pub. Co., 1937. Published by permission.

★ 89 ★

Extension Work and Workers

Support: Allotment Sources for Black Southern Extension Work by State, 1935-1936 - II

	County Agents	Home Demonstration	Club Work	Total
J.B. Pierce, Field agent for:				
Arkansas	$15,150.00	$19,390.00	-	$34,540.00
Kentucky	4,960.00	-	-	4,690.00
Maryland	2,084.00	3,314.00	-	5,398.00
North Carolina	56,821.00	16,677.50	-	73,498.50
South Carolina	26,754.82	15,297.00	-	42.051.82
Tennessee	9,600.00	15,900.00	-	25,500.00
Virginia	41,548.00	11,450.00	-	52,998.00
West Virginia	-	-	3,695.40	3,695.40
Total	156,647.82	82,028.50	3,695.40	242,371.72
T.M. Campbell Field agent for:				
Alabama	73,811.66	54,970.00	2,620.00	131,401.66
Florida	14,322.00	17,112.00	-	31,434.00
Georgia	39,453.47	22,480.00	2,800.00	64,733.47
Louisiana	23,425.00	14,125.00	-	37,550.00
Mississippi	42,850.86	39,582.67	4,850.00	87,283.53
Oklahoma	21,750.00	13,483.33	-	34,658.33
Texas	65,947.62	46,279.67	-	112,227.29

[Continued]

★ 89 ★

Support: Allotment Sources for Black Southern Extension Work by State, 1935-1936 - II

[Continued]

	County Agents	Home Demonstration	Club Work	Total
Total	280,985.61	208,032.67	10,270.00	499,288.28
Grand Total	437,633.43	290,061.17	13,965.40	741,660.00

Source: "Sources of Allotments for Negro Extension Work 1935-1936," *Negro Year Book: An Annual Encyclopedia of the Negro, 1937-1938*, 1937, p. 44. Primary source: Work, Monroe N. (Ed.), *Negro Year Book: An Annual Encyclopedia of the Negro, 1937-1938*. Tuskegee Institute, AL: The Negro Year Book Pub. Co., 1937. Published by permission.

★ 90 ★

Extension Work and Workers

Support: Allotments for Black Southern Extension Work by State, 1942 and 1947 - I

STATES	1942		
	Funds	Percent of Funds	Extension Workers
Alabama	$156,708.80	20.1	71
Arkansas	68,388.75	8.9	33
Florida	35,450.00	9.2	18
Georgia	64,515.00	6.9	51
Kentucky	11,352.00	1.5	7
Louisiana	41,890.00	6.8	19
Maryland	9,684.00	4.0	5
Mississippi	117,054.00	13.8	77
North Carolina	138,744.00	13.1	55
Oklahoma	41,560.00	5.9	20
South Carolina	62,038.00	12.6	37
Tennessee	43,060.00	5.4	20
Texas	171,726.26	9.5	84
Virginia	62,018.00	8.3	37
West Virginia	12,480.00	2.8	5
TOTALS	$1,036,668.81	9.1	539

Source: "Allotment of Funds for Extension Work Among Negro Farmers: the Number of Negro Extension Agents and Supervisors in 15 Southern States for Fiscal Years 1942 and 1937," *Negro Year Book: A Review of Events Affecting Negro Life, 1941-1946*, 1947, p. 175. Primary source: United States Department of Agriculture, Special Report, January 13, 1947. Published by permission.

★ 91 ★

Extension Work and Workers

Support: Allotments for Black Southern Extension Work by State, 1942 and 1947 - II

| STATES | 1947 | | | |
	Funds	Percent of Funds	Percent of Increase	Workers
Alabama	$239,133.00	16.2	52.6	86
Arkansas	154,604.33	14.5	126.1	51
Florida	62,853.82	10.4	77.3	29
Georgia	147,636.82	9.5	128.8	85
Kentucky	24,675.00	2.1	117.4	10
Louisiana	126,230.00	10.6	201.3	47
Maryland	19,260.00	5.3	98.8	8
Mississippi	226,069.00	16.4	93.1	107
North Carolina	473,506.00	23.5	241.3	99
Oklahoma	64,701.20	5.7	55.7	29
South Carolina	140,185.65	17.1	126.0	59
Tennessee	81,730.00	6.7	80.8	28
Texas	256,343.59	10.3	49.3	106
Virginia	161,922.20	13.1	161.1	56
West Virginia	39,358.85	6.4	215.4	17
TOTALS	$2,218,209.46	12.1	114.0	817

Source: "Allotment of Funds for Extension Work Among Negro Farmers: the Number of Negro Extension Agents and Supervisors in 15 Southern States for Fiscal Years 1942 and 1937," *Negro Year Book: A Review of Events Affecting Negro Life, 1941-1946*, 1947, p. 175. Primary source: United States Department of Agriculture, Special Report, January 13, 1947. Published by permission.

★ 92 ★

Extension Work and Workers

Support: Allotments for Southern Extension Work by State, 1950-51 - I

| States | County Extension Work | | Home Demonstration Work | |
	White and Negro	Negro	White and Negro	Negro
Alabama	$1,260,962.07	$148,060.00	$755,802.70	$120,340.03
Arkansas	776,780.00	98,790.00	608,897.18	110,898.18
Delaware	-	-	22,820.71	2,340.71
Florida	566,394.39	38,230.00	381,737.41	39,330.00
Georgia	1,151,950.20	115,820.00	642,635.00	66,880.00
Kentucky	919,515.04	14,982.00	515,340.00	21,530.00
Louisiana	1,000,432.72	90,386.22	602,862.51	96,820.53
Maryland	283,822.00	35,713.50	218,693.71	27,023.00
Mississippi	1,058,158.47	159,302.00	745,082.56	177,495.00
Missouri	1,004,188.34	-	587,106.26	10,210.00

[Continued]

★ 92 ★

Support: Allotments for Southern Extension Work by State, 1950-51 - I

[Continued]

States	County Extension Work		Home Demonstration Work	
	White and Negro	Negro	White and Negro	Negro
North Carolina	1,947,508.00	337,149.00	1,085,805.62	222,126.00
Oklahoma	778,110.22	51,703.88	607,525.38	42,437.84
South Carolina	685,439.67	121,500.00	437,332.10	92,091.00
Tennessee	881,996.18	56,326.36	661,657.09	45,400.00
Texas	2,123,824.66	221,177.40	1,282,065.02	160,662.23
Virginia	1,038,523.41	133,565.00	653,113.95	116,277.00
West Virginia	357,586.67	15,850.00	200,713.71	26,557.00
TOTALS	$15,835,192.04	$1,638,555.36	$10,009,190.91	$1,378,418.52

Source: "Allotments for County Extension Work (Including Supervision) and Specialists from All Sources for Fiscal Year 1950-51," *1952 Negro Year Book: A Review of Events Affecting Negro Life,* 1952, p. 108. Primary source: Division of Business Administration, Extension Service, U.S. Dept. of Agriculture, 10-5-51. Published by permission.

★ 93 ★

Extension Work and Workers

Support: Allotments for Southern Extension Work by State, 1950-51 - II

States	Club Work		Specialists	
	White and Negro	Negro	White and Negro	Negro
Alabama	$24,580.00	$8,560.00	$302,200.00	$4,120.00
Arkansas	16,980.00	4,000.00	242,168.30	-
Delaware	23,409.29	2,159.29	69,755.00	-
Florida	65,434.00	-	195,110.00	-
Georgia	45,518.00	4,203.00	320,924.40	-
Kentucky	78,520.00	-	267,149.17	-
Louisiana	36,890.00	4,700.00	313,466.00	-
Maryland	88,013.00	-	448,551.50	-
Mississippi	52,960.00	10,800.00	394,432.59	-
Missouri	47,177.50	-	289.714.12	-
North Carolina	70,709.00	10,500.00	568,477.20	22,816.00
Oklahoma	44,540.00	-	379,164.08	-
South Carolina	18,150.00	-	346.110.00	-
Tennessee	39,460.70	-	399,490.00	-
Texas	31,678.30	-	428,002.53	-
Virginia	39,798.00	-	462,493,84	-

[Continued]

★ 93 ★

Support: Allotments for Southern Extension Work by State, 1950-51 - II

[Continued]

States	Club Work		Specialists	
	White and Negro	Negro	White and Negro	Negro
West Virginia	239,031.33	10,393.00	180,370.00	-
TOTALS	$962,849.12	$55,315.29	$5,607,548.73	$26,936.00

Source: "Allotments for County Extension Work (Including Supervision) and Specialists from All Sources for Fiscal Year 1950-51," *1952 Negro Year Book: A Review of Events Affecting Negro Life,* 1952, p. 108. Primary source: Division of Business Administration, Extension Service, U.S. Dept. of Agriculture, 10-5-51. Published by permission.

★ 94 ★

Extension Work and Workers

Support: Allotments for Southern Extension Work, 1925-1941

Year Ending June 30	Funds Allotted for Extension Work			Expenditure for Work Among Negroes		Per cent of 1942 Amount	
	Total	Federal	State and Local[1]	Amount	Per Cent Of Total	Total	Negro
1925	$7,613,801	$3,322,751	$4,291,050	$431,502	5.7	48.5	43.0
1929	9,002,117	4,098,060	4,903,148	509,574	5.7	59.6	50.9
1931	10,244,467	4,515,944	5,728,523	560,134	5.5	66.6	55.9
1932	10,153,309	4,528,149	5,625,161	561,785	5.5	66.5	56.0
1933	9,278,684	4,493,785	4,784,899	534,473	5.8	61.3	53.2
1935	8,096,113	4,134,894	3,961,219	509,995	6.3	53.7	50.8
1936	12,623,200	8,329,186	4,294,114	741,660	5.9	83.5	74.0
1937	13,044,284	8,538,740	4,505,544	804,657	6.2	86.1	80.0
1938	13,533,706	8,719,280	4,814,426	809,665	6.0	89.4	80.6
1939	14,089,409	8,995,294	5,094,115	911,892	6.1	92.9	91.0
1940	14,492,183	9,393,461	5,098,722	962,807	6.7	95.5	96.0
1941	14,795,257	9,382,953	5,412,304	987,836	6.7	97.6	98.1
1942	15,137,175	9,543,509	5,593,666	1,042,155[2]	6.7	100.0	100.0

Source: "Total, Federal, and State, and Local Funds Allotted for Extension Work in 16 Southern States: Amounts and Percentages for Negroes, by Fiscal Years: 1925 to 1941," *Negro Year Book: A Review of Events Affecting Negro Life, 1941-1946,* 1947, p. 171. Primary source: Data supplied by Extension Service, United States Department of Agriculture. (Cited from study by Doxey Wilkerson, Howard University, 1942; by permission of author). Published by permission. *Notes:* 1. Includes State and College Funds, County Funds, Farmers organizations, etc. 2. Allotment.

Farms and Farmers

★ 95 ★

Acreage/Square Miles: Acreage of Black Farms by Location of Farm 1910 and 1930, and Change for 1910-1930

SECTION AND DIVISION	LAND IN FARMS (ACRES)			
	1930	1910	Increase or decrease (-) 1910-30	
			Number	Percent
United States	37,597,132	42,279,510	-4,682,378	-11.1
The North	720,872	868,630	-147,758	-17.0
The South	36,758,484	41,284,471	-4,525,987	-11.0
The West	117,776	126,409	-8,633	-6.8
New England	9,397	14,759	-5,362	-36.3
Middle Atlantic	55,808	74,849	-19,041	-25.4
East North Central	214,596	287,513	-72,917	-25.4
West North Central	441,071	491,509	-50,438	-10.3
South Atlantic	14,550,451	17,605,488	-3,055,037	-17.4
East South Central	11,918,057	13,573,980	-1,655,923	-12.2
West South Central	10,289,976	10,105,003	184,973	1.8
Mountain	77,228	62,807	14,421	23.0
Pacific	40,548	63,602	-23,054	-36.2

Source: "Farms Operated by Negroes—Number, Farm Acreage, and Value of Land and Buildings, Sections, Divisions, and States: 1930 and 1910," *Negroes in the United States, 1920-1932*, 1935, p. 601. Primary source: U.S. Bureau of the Census. *Negroes In the United States, 1920-1933.* Washington, D.C.. Government Printing Office, 1935.

★ 96 ★

Farms and Farmers

Acreage/Square Miles: Acreage on Black Tenant Farms by Farm Location, 1910 - I

TENURE	United States	The South				The North	The West
		Total	South Atlantic division	East South Central division	West South Central division		
NUMBER OF ACRES							
All tenants	27,129,953	26,567,802	11,883,633	8,979,405	5,704,764	339,657	222,494
Cash	11,898,533	11,705,291	5,394,424	5,037,289	1,273,578	81,491	111,751
Share	13,358,580	13,074,769	5,660,907	3,453,809	3,960,053	200,678	83,133

[Continued]

★ 96 ★

Acreage/Square Miles: Acreage on Black Tenant Farms by Farm Location, 1910 - I
[Continued]

| TENURE | United States | The South | | | | The North | The West |
		Total	South Atlantic division	East South Central division	West South Central division		
Share-cash	655,093	616,725	240,823	177,296	198,606	29,340	9,028
Unspecified	1,217,747	1,171,017	587,479	311,011	272,527	28,148	18,582

Source: "Acreage of Colored Tenant Farms, by Tenant Tenures, by Sections and Southern Divisions: 1910," *Negro Population, 1790-1915*, 1918, p. 575. Primary source: U.S. Bureau of the Census. *Negroes in the United States, 1790-1915*. Washington, D.C.: U.S. Government Printing Office, 1918. *Note:* "Colored" may include persons other than black.

★ 97 ★

Farms and Farmers

Acreage/Square Miles: Acreage on Black Tenant Farms by Farm Location, 1910 - II

| TENURE | United States | The South | | | | The North | The West |
		Total	South Atlantic division	East South Central division	West South Central division		

PERCENTAGE DISTRIBUTION BY TENURE

	United States	Total	South Atlantic division	East South Central division	West South Central division	The North	The West
All tenants	100.0	100.0	100.0	100.0	100.0	100.0	100.0
Cash	43.9	44.1	45.4	56.1	22.3	24.0	50.2
Share	49.2	49.2	47.6	38.5	69.4	59.1	37.4
Share-cash	2.4	2.3	2.0	2.0	3.5	8.6	4.1
Unspecified	4.5	4.4	4.9	3.5	4.8	8.3	8.4

Source: "Acreage of Colored Tenant Farms, by Tenant Tenures, by Sections and Southern Divisions: 1910," *Negro Population, 1790-1915*, 1918, p. 575. Primary source: U.S. Bureau of the Census. *Negroes in the United States, 1790-1915*. Washington, D.C.: U.S. Government Printing Office, 1918. *Note:* "Colored" may include persons other than black.

★ 98 ★

Farms and Farmers

Acreage/Square Miles: Acreage on Farms by Location of Farm, 1920 and 1930

SECTION AND DIVISION	LAND IN FARMS (ACRES)		INCREASE OR DECREASE (-)		PERCENT DISTRIBUTION	
	1930	1920	Acres	Percent	1930	1920
			TOTAL			
United States	986,771,016	955,883,715	30,887,301	3.2	100.0	100.0
THE SOUTH	343,086,418	350,121,833	-7,035,415	-2.0	34.8	36.6
South Atlantic	86,362,715	97,775,243	-11,412,528	-11.7	8.8	10.2
East South Central	72,817,357	78,897,463	-6,080,106	-7.7	7.4	8.3
West South Central	183,906,346	173,449,127	10,457,219	6.0	18.6	18.1
THE NORTH	425,709,428	432,271,951	-6,562,523	-1.5	43.1	45.2
THE WEST	217,975,170	173,489,931	44,485,239	25.6	22.1	18.1
			NEGRO			
United States	37,597,132	41,432,182	-3,835,050	-9.3	100.0	100.0
THE SOUTH	36,758,484	40,544,241	-3,785,757	-9.3	97.8	97.9
South Atlantic	14,550,451	18,151,071	-3,600,620	-19.8	38.7	43.8
East South Central	11,918,057	12,104,977	-186,920	-1.5	31.7	29.2
West South Central	10,289,976	10,288,193	1,783	[1]	27.4	24.8
THE NORTH	720,872	767,953	-47,081	-6.1	1.9	1.9
THE WEST	117,776	119,988	-2,212	-1.8	.3	.3

Source: "All Land in Farms, by Sections and Southern Divisions: 1930 and 1920," *Negroes in the United States, 1920-1932,* 1935, p. 576. Primary source: U.S. Bureau of the Census. *Negroes in the United States, 1920-1932.* Washington, D.C.: U.S. Government Printing Office, 1935. *Note:* 1. Less than 1/10 of 1 percent.

★ 99 ★

Farms and Farmers

Acreage/Square Miles: Average Farm Acreage by Farm Location in 1900 and 1910, and Change 1900-1910

[Colored farmers include Negroes, Indians, Chinese, Japanese, and all other nonwhite races]

DIVISION AND STATE	1910		1900		Decrease: 1900-1910[1]	
	Negro farms	White farms	Negro farms	White farms	Negro farms	White farms
United States	47.3	153.0	51.2	160.3	3.9	7.3
The South	46.9	141.3	50.9	172.1	4.0	30.8
South Atlantic	49.7	113.9	54.1	131.7	4.4	17.8
East South Central	41.8	94.7	47.1	108.0	5.3	13.3
West South Central	50.2	215.0	51.5	291.0	1.3	76.0
The North	72.1	143.0	62.2	133.3	+9.9	+9.7

[Continued]

★ 99 ★

Acreage/Square Miles: Average Farm Acreage by Farm Location in 1900 and 1910, and Change 1900-1910

[Continued]

DIVISION AND STATE	1910		1900		Decrease: 1900-1910[1]	
	Negro farms	White farms	Negro farms	White farms	Negro farms	White farms
The West	262.3	303.8	225.5	395.8	+36.8	92.0
THE SOUTH						
South Atlantic:						
Delaware	61.8	99.0	64.3	114.3	2.5	15.3
Maryland	56.3	110.4	64.1	119.4	7.8	9.0
District of Columbia	7.9	29.1	18.1	32.5	10.2	3.4
Virginia	46.5	127.0	49.7	143.7	1.2	16.7
West Virginia	48.8	104.1	56.0	115.2	7.2	11.1
North Carolina	48.4	102.4	53.6	116.6	5.2	14.2
South Carolina	40.7	120.2	44.4	145.7	3.7	25.5
Georgia	57.9	117.9	66.1	147.4	8.2	29.5
Florida	52.3	127.1	53.0	133.6	0.7	6.5
East South Central:						
Kentucky	37.5	87.9	39.8	96.4	2.3	8.5
Tennessee	41.9	88.8	45.7	98.5	3.8	9.7
Alabama	46.1	102.6	50.2	123.6	4.1	21.0
Mississippi	39.2	110.4	45.9	133.9	6.7	23.5
West South Central:						
Arkansas	41.7	97.7	49.0	108.8	7.3	11.1
Louisiana	38.7	126.6	40.3	150.7	1.6	24.1
Oklahoma	80.8	156.8	98.9	222.9	18.1	66.1
Texas	61.1	310.9	58.9	425.5	+2.5	114.6

Source: "Average Number of Acres Per Farm," *Negro Population, 1790-1915*, 1918, p. 557. Primary source: U.S. Bureau of the Census. *Negro Population, 1790-1915*. Washington, D.C.: U.S. Government Printing Office, 1918.
Note: 1. A plus sign (+) denotes increase.

★ 100 ★

Farms and Farmers

Acreage/Square Miles: Average Farm Acreage by Location of Farm, 1920 and 1930

SECTION, DIVISION, AND STATE	AVERAGE ACREAGE PER FARM OPERATED BY-					
	Negroes			White[1]		
	1930	1920	Increase or decrease (-)	1930	1920	Increase or decrease (-)
United States	42.6	44.8	-2.2	176.0	165.7	10.3
THE SOUTH	42.2	44.3	-2.1	130.3	135.2	-4.9
South Atlantic	49.2	47.5	1.7	94.3	102.6	-8.3

[Continued]

★ 100 ★

Acreage/Square Miles: Average Farm Acreage by Location of Farm, 1920 and 1930
[Continued]

| SECTION, DIVISION, AND STATE | AVERAGE ACREAGE PER FARM OPERATED BY- | | | | | |
| | Negroes | | | White[1] | | |
	1930	1920	Increase or decrease (-)	1930	1920	Increase or decrease (-)
East South Central	37.2	39.4	-2.2	82.1	89.7	-7.6
West South Central	40.4	45.5	-5.1	205.4	212.6	-7.2
THE NORTH	64.9	81.9	-17.0	166.5	156.5	10.0
THE WEST	145.4	163.7	-18.3	446.6	369.8	76.8
THE SOUTH						
SOUTH ATLANTIC:						
Delaware	67.9	62.9	5.0	95.1	96.0	-0.9
Maryland	65.6	56.6	9.0	106.2	105.7	.5
District of Columbia	8.6	14.4	-5.8	32.0	29.2	2.8
Virginia	51.5	47.3	4.2	112.1	117.7	-5.6
West Virginia	57.2	54.7	2.5	106.8	110.0	-3.2
North Carolina	44.2	45.0	-.8	72.3	85.7	-13.4
South Carolina	41.0	40.2	.8	89.7	96.2	-6.5
Georgia	58.8	54.3	4.5	100.6	101.7	-1.1
Florida	46.7	49.2	-2.5	94.1	131.8	-37.7
EAST SOUTH CENTRAL:						
Kentucky	37.5	33.8	3.7	82.5	82.1	.4
Tennessee	38.6	39.9	-1.3	79.1	83.8	-4.7
Alabama	44.3	45.7	-1.4	81.9	94.6	-12.7
Mississippi	33.2	36.1	-2.9	86.8	111.7	-24.9
WEST SOUTH CENTRAL:						
Arkansas	31.2	36.3	-5.1	83.3	92.5	-9.2
Louisiana	31.4	35.2	-3.8	80.3	106.8	-26.5
Oklahoma	70.0	78.0	-8.0	175.9	174.5	1.4
Texas	51.5	56.5	-5.0	293.7	306.7	-13.0

Source: "Average Acreage per Farm of Negro and White operators, by Sections, Southern Divisions, and States: 1930 and 1920," *Negroes in the United States, 1920-1932*, 1935, p. 576. Primary source: U.S. Bureau of the Census. *Negroes in the United States, 1920-1932*. Washington, D.C.: U.S. Government Printing Office, 1935. *Note:* 1. Includes Mexicans and Hindus.

★ 101 ★

Farms and Farmers

Acreage/Square Miles: Distribution of Acreage on Southern Farms, 1910

SIZE OF FARM	Number			Distribution per 1,000		Colored farms per 1,000 all farms
	Total	Colored farms	White farms	Colored farms	White farms	
Total	3,097,547	890,141	2,207,406	1,000	1,000	287
Under 3 acres	2,928	402	2,526	[1]	1	137
3 to 9 acres	157,320	61,953	95,277	70	43	394
10 to 19 acres	340,456	151,894	188,562	171	85	446
20 to 49 acres	955,907	426,540	529,367	479	240	446
50 to 99 acres	694,737	152,244	542,493	171	246	219
100 to 174 acres	561,724	68,599	492,945	77	223	122
175 to 259 acres	187,549	17,394	170,155	20	77	93
260 to 499 acres	135,063	8,779	126,284	10	57	65
500 to 990 acres	41,183	1,881	30,302	2	18	46
1,000 acres or more	20,950	455	20,495	1	9	22

Source: "Farms in the South: 1910," *Negro Population, 1790-1915*, 1918, p. 567. Primary source: U.S. Bureau of the Census. *Negro Population, 1790-1915.* Washington, D.C.: Government Printing Office, 1918. *Note:* 1. Less than 1.

★ 102 ★

Farms and Farmers

Acreage/Square Miles: Distribution of Total Farm Acreage in the South, 1900 and 1910 - I

DIVISION AND SIZE OF FARM	FARMS Total number	
	1910	1900
THE SOUTH		
Total	3,097,547	2,620,391
Under 3 acres	2,928	12,972
3 to 9 acres	157,320	112,528
10 to 19 acres	340,456	259,922
20 to 49 acres	955,907	764,114
50 to 99 acres	694,737	583,047
100 to 174 acres	561,724	518,836
175 to 159 acres	187,549	176,087
260 to 499 acres	135,063	127,899
500 to 999 acres	41,183	42,015
1,000 acres and over	20,950	22,971

[Continued]

★ 102 ★

Acreage/Square Miles: Distribution of Total Farm Acreage in the South, 1900 and 1910 - I

[Continued]

DIVISION AND SIZE OF FARM	FARMS Total number	
	1910	1900
SOUTH ATLANTIC		
Total	1,111,881	962,225
EAST SOUTH CENTRAL		
Total	1,042,480	903,313
WEST SOUTH CENTRAL		
Total	913,186	754,853

Source: "Size of Farms—Farms Operated by Colored and by White Farmers, Classified by Size, for Southern States: 1910 and 1900," *Negro Population, 1790-1915*, 1918, p. 603. Primary source: U.S. Bureau of the Census. *Negroes in the United States, 1790-1915.* Washington, D.C.: U.S. Government Printing Office, 1918. *Notes:* 1. A minus sign (-) denotes decrease. 2. Less than 1.

★ 103 ★

Farms and Farmers

Acreage/Square Miles: Distribution of Total Farm Acreage in the South, 1900 and 1910 - II

DIVISION AND SIZE OF FARM	FARMS												
	Operated by colored farmers							Operated by white farmers					
	Number		Per 1,000 farms of specified size		Increase:[1] 1900 1910	Distribution per 1,000		Number		Increase:[1]	1900	1900-1910	Distribution per 1,000	
	1910	1900	1910	1900		1910	1900	Increase:[1] 1910	1900				1910	1900
THE SOUTH													
Total	800,141	740,670	287	283	149,471	1,000	1,000	2,207,406	1,879,721	327,685			1,000	1,000
Under 3 acres	402	4,300	137	331	-3,898	...	6	2,526	8,672	-6,146			1	5
3 to 9 acres	61,953	50,004	394	444	11,949	70	68	95,277	62,524	32,753			43	33
10 to 19 acres	151,891	118,876	446	457	33,018	171	160	188,562	141,046	47,516			85	75
20 to 49 acres	426,540	340,106	446	445	86,434	479	459	529,367	424,008	105,359			240	226
50 to 99 acres	152,241	132,350	219	227	19,894	171	179	542,493	450,697	91,796			246	240
100 to 174 acres	68,599	66,501	122	128	2,098	77	90	492,945	452,335	40,610			223	241
175 to 159 acres	17,391	16,545	93	91	849	20	22	170,155	159,542	10,613			77	85
260 to 499 acres	8,779	8,995	65	70	-216	10	12	126,284	118,904	7,380			57	63
500 to 999 acres	1,881	2,292	46	55	-411	2	3	39,302	39,723	-421			18	21
1,000 acres and over	455	701	22	31	-246	1	1	20,495	22,270	-1,775			9	12
SOUTH ATLANTIC													
Total	355,862	288,871	320	300	66,991	1,000	1,000	756,019	673,354	82,665			1,000	1,000
EAST SOUTH CENTRAL													
Total	325,218	267,895	312	297	57,323	1,000	1,000	717,262	635,418	81,844			1,000	1,000
WEST SOUTH CENTRAL													
Total	209,061	183,904	222	244	25,157	1,000	1,000	734,125	570,949	163,176			1,000	1,000

Source: "Size of Farms—Farms Operated by Colored and by White Farmers, Classified by Size, for Southern States: 1910 and 1900," *Negro Population, 1790-1915*, 1918, p. 603. Primary source: U.S. Bureau of the Census. *Negroes in the United States, 1790-1915.* Washington, D.C.: U.S. Government Printing Office, 1918. *Notes:* 1. A minus sign (-) denotes decrease. 2. Less than 1.

★ 104 ★

Farms and Farmers

Acreage/Square Miles: Farm Acreage of Farm Managers 1920 and 1930, and Change for 1920-1930 by Location of Farm

SECTION AND DIVISION	LAND IN FARMS (ACRES)					
	Negro managers			White managers[1]		
	1930	1920	Increase or decrease (-)	1930	1920	Increase or decrease (-)
United States	249,072	406,088	-157,016	61,549,583	53,653,478	7,896,105
The North	15,138	38,335	-13,197	9,056,203	11,803,417	-2,747,214
The South	229,938	355,749	-125,811	27,295,725	22,073,344	5,222,381
The West	3,996	12,004	-8,008	25,197,655	19,776,717	5,420,938
New England	1,075	3,910	-2,835	750,125	976,421	-226,296
Middle Atlantic	4,176	9,448	-5,272	1,272,151	1,913,201	-641,050
East North Central	3,640	8,427	-4,787	2,090,899	2,857,754	-766,855
West North Central	6,247	16,550	-10,303	4,943,028	6,056,041	-1,113,013
South Atlantic	109,107	145,948	-36,841	3,640,876	4,256,070	-615,184
East South Central	49,992	85,834	-35,842	1,236,683	1,442,654	-204,971
West South Central	70,839	123,967	-53,128	22,417,166	16,374,630	6,042,536
Mountain	1,550	10,230	-8,680	18,035,018	12,939,972	5,095,046
Pacific	2,446	1,774	672	7,162,637	6,836,745	325,892

Source: "Number of Negro and White Farm Operators with Acreage, by Tenure, by Sections, Divisions, and States: 1930 and 1920," *Negroes in the United States, 1920-1932*, 1935, pp. 593-595. Primary source: U.S. Bureau of the Census. *Negroes in the United States, 1920-1932*. Washington, D.C.: U.S. Government Printing Office, 1935. *Note:* 1. Includes Mexicans and Hindus.

★ 105 ★

Farms and Farmers

Acreage/Square Miles: Farm Acreage of Farm Owners 1920 and 1930, and Change for 1920-1930 by Location of Farm

SECTION AND DIVISION	LAND IN FARMS (ACRES)					
	Negro owners			White owners[1]		
	1930	1920	Increase or decrease (-)	1930	1920	Increase or decrease (-)
United States	11,198,893	13,948,512	-2,749,619	604,595,531	620,070,823	-15,475,292
The North	332,520	435,075	-102,555	272,174,162	287,317,789	-15,143,627
The South	10,785,312	13,434,106	-2,648,794	178,621,215	206,525,033	-27,903,818
The West	81,061	79,331	1,730	153,800,154	126,228,001	27,572,153
New England	7,297	10,121	-2,824	12,584,539	14,693,218	-2,108,679
Middle Atlantic	26,758	28,516	-1,758	27,720,458	28,969,267	-1,248,809
East North Central	114,748	138,109	-23,361	72,222,278	76,345,020	-4,122,742
West North Central	183,717	258,329	-74,612	159,646,887	167,310,284	-7,663,397
South Atlantic	4,214,663	5,483,254	-1,268,591	47,393,132	56,279,975	-8,886,843
East South Central	3,516,640	3,930,410	-413,770	41,765,792	50,088,549	-8,322,757

[Continued]

★ 105 ★

Acreage/Square Miles: Farm Acreage of Farm Owners 1920 and 1930, and Change for 1920-1930 by Location of Farm

[Continued]

SECTION AND DIVISION	LAND IN FARMS (ACRES)					
	Negro owners			White owners[1]		
	1930	1920	Increase or decrease (-)	1930	1920	Increase or decrease (-)
West South Central	3,054,009	4,020,442	-966,433	89,462,291	100,156,509	-10,694,218
Mountain	59,689	54,574	5,115	113,405,424	90,040,400	23,365,024
Pacific	21,372	24,757	-3,385	40,394,730	36,187,601	4,207,129

Source: "Number of Negro and White Farm Operators with Acreage, by Tenure, by Sections, Divisions, and States: 1930 and 1920," *Negroes in the United States, 1920-1932*, 1935, pp. 593-595. Primary source: U.S. Bureau of the Census. *Negroes in the United States, 1920-1932*. Washington, D.C.: U.S. Government Printing Office, 1935. *Note:* 1. Includes Mexicans and Hindus.

★ 106 ★

Farms and Farmers

Acreage/Square Miles: Farm Acreage of Farm Tenants by Location of Farm, 1920 and 1930, and Change for 1920-1930

SECTION, DIVISION, AND STATE	LAND IN FARMS (ACRES)					
	Negro tenants			White tenants[1]		
	1930	1920	Increase or decrease (-)	1930	1920	Increase or decrease (-)
United States	26,149,167	27,077,582	-928,415	279,537,920	237,214,893	42,323,027
The North	373,214	294,543	78,671	142,733,476	131,244,422	11,489,054
The South	25,743,324	26,754,386	-1,011,152	99,363,713	80,204,960	19,158,753
The West	32,719	28,653	4,066	37,440,731	25,765,511	11,675,220
New England	1,025	5,221	-4,196	938,127	1,300,337	-362,210
Middle Atlantic	24,874	34,933	-10,059	5,975,035	9,594,304	-3,619,269
East North Central	96,208	93,247	2,961	36,339,304	38,254,768	-1,915,464
West North Central	251,107	161,142	89,965	99,481,010	82,095,013	17,385,997
South Atlantic	10,226,681	12,521,869	-2,295,188	20,670,173	19,014,267	1,655,906
East South Central	8,351,425	8,088,733	262,692	17,882,827	15,252,588	2,630,239
West South Central	7,165,128	6,143,784	1,021,344	60,810,713	45,938,105	14,872,608
Mountain	15,989	12,445	3,544	25,005,449	13,359,385	11,646,064
Pacific	16,730	16,208	522	12,435,282	12,406,126	29,156

Source: "Number of Negro and White Farm Operators with Acreage, by Tenure, by Sections, Divisions, and States: 1930 and 1920," *Negroes in the United States, 1920-1932*, 1935, pp. 593-595. Primary source: U.S. Bureau of the Census. *Negroes in the United States, 1920-1932*. Washington, D.C.: U.S. Government Printing Office, 1935. *Note:* 1. Includes Mexicans and Hindus.

★ 107 ★

Farms and Farmers

Acreage/Square Miles: Improved and Unimproved Farm Acreage by Location of Farm, 1900 and 1910

DIVISION	ACRES IN FARMS							
	Improved land				Unimproved land			
	Farms operated by Negroes		Farms operated by whites		Farms operated by Negroes		Farms operated by whites	
	1910	1900	1910	1900	1910	1900	1910	1900
UNITED STATES	27,845,190	23,362,786	449,418,265	390,201,306	14,434,320	14,871,134	382,747,755	406,624,445
GEOGRAPHIC DIVISIONS:								
New England	5,669	5,708	7,248,822	8,128,180	9,090	7,330	12,449,801	12,406,049
Middle Atlantic	49,469	49,371	29,250,638	30,722,666	25,380	21,998	13,828,328	14,044,955
East North Central	222,774	221,550	88,702,567	86,429,877	64,739	63,056	28,887,330	29,557,497
West North Central	340,566	344,523	163,735,756	135,147,523	150,943	157,942	66,720,703	64,003,239
South Atlantic	10,956,415	8,874,506	37,489,664	37,204,364	6,649,073	6,699,055	48,617,209	51,455,877
East South Central	9,548,129	8,183,108	34,390,317	32,045,709	4,025,851	4,418,674	33,534,595	36,580,616
West South Central	6,665,869	5,663,170	51,075,128	33,643,413	3,439,134	3,447,924	106,736,830	132,494,326
Mountain	11,531	5,631	15,773,427	8,281,131	51,276	34,392	42,975,335	37,779,198
Pacific	44,768	15,219	21,751,946	18,598,443	18,834	20,763	28,997,624	28,302,688

Source: "Acreage Improved and Unimproved in Farms Operated by Negroes and by Whites, by Divisions and States: 1910 and 1900," *Negro Population, 1790-1915*, 1918, p. 590. Primary source: U.S. Bureau of the Census. *Negro Population, 1790-1915*. Washington, D.C.: Government Printing Office, 1918.

★ 108 ★

Farms and Farmers

Acreage/Square Miles: Increase in Improved and Unimproved Farm Acreage by Location of Farm, 1900-1910

DIVISION	INCREASE: 1900-1910[1]								
	Acres in farms			Acres improved			Acres unimproved		
	All farms	Negro farms	White farms	All farms	Negro farms	White farms	All farms	Negro farms	White farms
UNITED STATES	40,206,551	4,045,590	35,340,269	63,953,263	4,482,404	59,216,956	-23,746,712	-436,814	-23,876,700
GEOGRAPHIC DIVISIONS:									
New England	-834,068	1,721	-835,606	-879,499	-39	-879,358	45,431	1,760	43,752
Middle Atlantic	-1,669,034	3,480	-1,688,655	-1,465,317	98	-1,472,028	-203,717	3,382	-216,627
East North Central	1,588,387	2,907	1,602,523	2,276,957	1,224	2,272,690	-6,88,570	1,683	-670,167
West North Central	31,639,408	-10,956	31,305,697	28,641,034	-3,957	28,588,233	2,998,374	-6,999	2,717,464
South Atlantic	-515,251	2,031,927	-2,553,368	2,379,507	2,081,909	285,300	-2,984,758	-49,982	-2,838,668
East South Central	272,986	972,198	-701,413	3,709,509	1,365,021	2,344,608	-3,436,523	-392,823	-3,046,021
West South Central	-7,341,226	993,909	-8,325,781	18,493,743	1,002,699	17,431,715	-25,834,969	-8,790	-25,757,496
Mountain	13,136,136	22,784	12,688,433	7,512,426	5,900	7,492,296	5,623,710	16,884	5,196,137
Pacific	3,299,213	27,620	3,848,439	3,284,903	29,549	3,153,503	644,310	-1,929	694,936

Source: "Increase in Acreage—Total Improved and Unimproved—of Negro and White Farms, by Divisions and States: 1900-1910," *Negro Population, 1790-1915*, 1918, p. 591. Primary source: U.S. Bureau of the Census. *Negro Population, 1790-1915*. Washington, D.C.: Government Printing Office, 1918. *Note:* 1. A minus sign (-) denotes decrease.

★ 109 ★

Farms and Farmers

Acreage/Square Miles: Land (1930) and Crop Land Harvested (1929) on Owned Farms by Farm Location

[Colored farmers include Negroes, Indians, Chinese, Japanese, and all other nonwhite races. White includes Mexicans and Hindus]

| DIVISION AND STATE | ALL LAND IN FARMS, 1930 | | CROP LAND HARVESTED, 1929 | | | |
| | | | Number of acres | | Percent "All land in farms" Percent | |
	Colored	White	Colored	White	Colored	White
The South	11,478,898	178,621,215	4,122,806	45,085,636	35.9	25.2
SOUTH ATLANTIC	4,258,325	47,393,132	1,808,634	12,119,693	35.4	25.6
Delaware	13,781	466,704	6,039	207,770	43.8	44.5
Maryland	107,935	2,532,361	34,273	993,600	31.8	39.2
District of Columbia	28	697	11	416	39.3	59.7
Virginia	1,183,134	11,066,532	331,379	2,484,959	28.0	22.5
West Virginia	18,542	7,126,681	3,772	1,348,521	20.3	18.9
North Carolina	982,111	10,090,169	371,689	2,563,366	37.8	25.4
South Carolina	787,551	4,440,414	323,781	1,299,537	41.1	29.3
Georgia	883,324	8,971,316	323,737	2,447,112	36.6	27.3
Florida	281,919	2,698,258	113,953	774,412	40.4	28.7
EAST SOUTH CENTRAL	3,522,790	41,765,792	1,138,893	10,627,197	32.3	25.4
Kentucky	183,148	14,427,710	54,756	3,606,586	29.9	25.0
Tennessee	419,211	11,309,984	156,685	3,264,382	37.4	28.9
Alabama	1,189,873	8,214,031	420,125	2,218,415	35.3	27.0
Mississippi	1,730,558	7,814,067	507,327	1,537,814	29.3	19.7
WEST SOUTH CENTRAL	3,697,783	89,462,291	1,475,279	22,338,746	39.9	25.0
Arkansas	705,156	8,285,121	292,899	2,458,312	41.5	29.7
Louisiana	602,967	4,157,573	239,030	1,229,294	39.6	29.6
Oklahoma	914,689	15,556,837	325,508	6,764,319	35.6	43.5
Texas	1,474,971	61,462,760	617,842	11,886,821	41.9	19.3
SELECTED NORTHERN STATES[1]	275,792	104,858,240	115,117	48,495,136	41.7	46.2
New Jersey	7,682	1,227,874	3,251	546,553	42.3	44.5
Pennsylvania	10,256	11,945,213	4,018	4,953,985	39.2	41.5
Ohio	45,504	14,364,938	16,476	6,384,757	36.2	44.4
Indiana	14,607	12,271,620	6,245	6,015,323	42.8	49.0
Illinois	27,641	15,198,903	12,025	8,628,302	43.5	56.8
Missouri	76,296	22,141,050	29,205	8,217,867	38.3	37.1
Kansas	93,806	27,708,642	43,897	13,748,349	46.8	40.6

Source: "All Land, and Crop Land Harvested, in Farms of Colored and White Owners, by Southern Divisions, and States, and Selected Northern States: Census of 1930," *Negroes in the United States, 1920-1932,* 1935, p. 588. Primary source: U.S. Bureau of the Census. *Negroes in the United States, 1920-1932.* Washington, D.C.: U.S. Government Printing Office, 1935. *Notes:* 1. States having 200 or more Negro farmers who constitute 90 percent or more of the colored farmers in the State.

★ 110 ★

Farms and Farmers

Acreage/Square Miles: Percentage Distribution of Total, Improved, and Unimproved Land in Farms by Farm Location, 1910

SECTION AND DIVISION	All land in farms		Improved land in farms		Unimproved land in farms	
	Of Negroes	Of whites	Of Negroes	Of whites	Of Negroes	Of whites
United States	100.0	100.0	100.0	100.0	100.0	100.0
The South	97.6	37.5	97.6	27.4	97.8	49.4
South Atlantic	41.6	10.3	39.3	8.3	46.1	12.7
East South Central	32.1	8.2	34.3	7.7	27.9	8.8
West South Central	23.9	19.0	23.9	11.4	23.8	27.9
The North	2.1	49.4	2.2	64.3	1.7	31.8
The West	0.3	13.2	0.2	8.3	0.5	18.8

Source: [Untitled Table], *Negro Population, 1790-1915*, 1918, p. 556. Primary source: U.S. Bureau of the Census. *Negro Population, 1790-1915.* Washington, D.C.: U.S. Government Printing Office, 1918.

★ 111 ★

Farms and Farmers

Acreage/Square Miles: Square Miles on Farms by Location of Farm, 1920 and 1930

SECTION AND DIVISION	ALL LAND IN FARMS (SQUARE MILES)			SQUARE MILES OPERATED BY-					
	1930	1920	Increase or decrease (-)	Negroes		Whites[1]		Increase or decrease (-)	
				1930	1920	1930	1920	Negroes	Whites[1]
United States	1,541,830	1,493,568	48,262	58,745	64,737	1,477,630	1,423,343	-5,992	54,287
THE SOUTH	536,073	547,065	-10,992	57,435	63,350	477,001	482,505	-5,915	-5,504
South Atlantic	134,942	152,774	-17,832	22,735	28,361	112,038	124,297	-5,626	-12,259
East South Central	113,777	123,277	-9,500	18,622	18,914	95,135	104,350	-292	-9,215
West South Central	287,354	271,014	16,340	16,078	16,075	269,828	253,858	3	15,970
THE NORTH	665,171	675,425	-10,254	1,126	1,200	662,444	672,447	-74	-10,003
THE WEST	340,586	271,078	69,508	184	187	338,185	268,391	-3	69,794

Source: "All Farm Land in Square Miles Operated by Negro and White Farmers, by Sections, and Southern Divisions: 1930 and 1920," *Negroes in the United States, 1920-1932*, 1935, p. 578. Primary source: U.S. Bureau of the Census. *Negroes in the United States, 1920-1932.* Washington, D.C.: U.S. Government Printing Office, 1935. *Note:* 1. Includes Mexicans and Hindus.

★ 112 ★

Farms and Farmers

Acreage/Square Miles: Total Farm Acreage by Location of Farm, 1900 and 1910

DIVISION	ACRES IN FARMS						ACRES IN FARMS OPERATED BY NEGROES PER 1,000 ACRES IN ALL FARMS	
	All farms		Farms operated by Negroes		Farms operated by whites			
	1910	1900	1910	1900	1910	1900	1910	1900
UNITED STATES	878,798,325	838,591,774	42,279,510	38,233,920	832,166,020	796,835,751	48	46
GEOGRAPHIC DIVISIONS:								
New England	19,714,931	20,548,999	14,759	13,038	19,608,623	20,534,229	1	1
Middle Atlantic	43,191,056	44,860,090	74,849	71,369	43,078,966	44,767,621	2	2
East North Central	117,929,148	116,340,761	287,513	284,606	117,589,897	115,987,374	2	2
West North Central	232,648,121	201,008,713	491,509	502,465	230,456,459	199,150,762	2	2
South Atlantic	103,782,255	104,297,506	17,605,488	15,573,561	86,106,873	885,660,241	170	149
East South Central	81,520,629	81,247,643	13,573,980	12,601,782	67,924,912	68,626,325	167	155
West South Central	169,149,976	176,491,202	10,105,003	9,111,094	157,811,958	166,137,739	60	52
Mountain	59,533,420	46,397,284	62,807	40,023	58,748,762	46,060,329	1	1
Pacific	51,328,789	47,399,576	63,602	35,982	50,749,570	46,901,131	1	1

Source: "Acreage in Farms Operated by Negroes and by Whites, by Divisions and States: 1910 and 1900," *Negro Population, 1790-1915*, 1918, p. 589. Primary source: U.S. Bureau of the Census. *Negro Population, 1790-1915*. Washington, D.C.: Government Printing Office, 1918.

★ 113 ★

Farms and Farmers

Acreage/Square Miles: Trends in Average Farm Acreage in the South, 1900-1935

	Average Size of Farms in Acres									
	1935		1930		1920		1910		1900	
	White	Negro	White	Negro	White	Negro	White	Negro	White	Negro
The South	121.8	43.2	119.5	42.6	135.2	44.8	141.3	47.9	172.1	52.1
South Atlantic	90.3	52.2	90.5	48.8	102.6	47.5	113.9	49.7	131.7	54.1
E. South Central	80.1	36.3	80.7	37.0	89.7	39.4	94.7	41.8	108.0	47.1
W. South Central	190.2	41.3	179.8	42.3	212.6	47.4	215.0	54.2	291.0	56.3

Source: "Average Size of Farms in South of White and Negro Farmers by Geographic Division, 1935, 1930, 1920, 1910, 1900," *Negro Year Book: An Annual Encyclopedia of the Negro, 1937-1938*, 1937, p. 56. Primary source: U.S. Bureau of the Census. Published by permission.

★ 114 ★

Farms and Farmers

Acreage/Square Miles: Trends in Average Farm Acreage, 1910-1940

	Average Size of Farms Acres: All Land in Farms				Per cent 1910, 1930, and 1940 are of 1920			
	1940	1930	1920	1910	1940	1930	1920	1910
ALL FARMS IN U.S.A.	174.0	156.9	148.2	138.1	117.4	105.9	100	93.1
By Color of Operator:								
White Operator	188.8	176.0	165.6	152.9	113.5	106.3	100	92.3
Non-white operators	63.6	44.8	47.3	50.6	134.6	94.7	100	107.0

Source: "Trends in the Size of Farms (All land in Farms) in the United States by Color and Tenure of Operator, 1910-1940. (Decinnial Censuses)," *Negro Year Book: A Review of Events Affecting Negro Life, 1941-1946*, 1947, p. 166. Primary source: U.S. Bureau of the Census. Published by permission.

★ 115 ★

Farms and Farmers

Acreage: Improved and Unimproved Acreage on Black Farms by Location of Farm, 1910

SECTION AND DIVISION	Total	Improved	Unimproved		
			Total	Woodland	Other
United States	42,279,510	27,845,190	14,434,320	11,938,284	2,496,036
The South	41,284,471	27,170,413	14,114,058	11,797,439	2,316,619
South Atlantic	17,605,488	10,956,415	6,649,073	5,732,248	916,825
East South Central	13,573,980	9,548,129	4,025,851	3,196,381	829,470
West South Central	10,105,003	6,665,869	3,439,134	2,868,810	570,324
The North	868,630	618,478	250,152	129,660	120,492
The West	126,409	56,299	70,110	11,185	58,925

Source: "Acres in Farms Operated by Negroes: 1910," *Negro Population, 1790-1915*, 1918, p. 558. Primary source: U.S. Bureau of the Census. *Negro Population, 1790-1915*. Washington, D.C.: Government Printing Office, 1918.

★ 116 ★

Farms and Farmers

Conveniences: Modern Conveniences Available on Black Farms by Owner Status and Farm Location, 1930 - I

[Colored farmers include Negroes, Indians, Chinese, Japanese, and all other nonwhite races]

DIVISION AND STATE	FARMS REPORTING-											
	Telephones				Electric lights				Water piped into dwellings			
	Total	Owners	Tenants	Managers	Total	Owners	Tenants	Managers	Total	Owners	Tenants	Managers
The South	4,775	2,750	1,844	181	2,816	1,712	985	139	2,600	1,160	1,264	176
South Atlantic	1,015	515	406	94	1,359	846	439	74	902	379	429	94
East South Central	1,276	619	612	45	618	319	267	32	605	207	358	40
West South Central	2,484	1,616	826	42	839	547	259	33	1,093	574	477	42
Selected Northern States[1]	1,297	847	420	30	420	305	91	24	299	184	87	28

Source: "Farms of Colored Operators Reporting Telephones, Dwellings Lighted by Electricity, Water Piped into Dwellings and into Bathrooms, by Tenure of Operator, with Total Farm Motor Equipment, by Southern Divisions, and States, and Selected Northern States: 1930," *Negroes in the United States, 1920-1932,*1935, p. 591. Primary source: U.S. Bureau of the Census. *Negroes in the United States, 1920-1932.* Washington, D.C.: U.S. Government Printing Office, 1935. *Notes:* 1. States having 200 or more Negro farmers who constitute 90 percent or more of the colored farm operators in the State.

★ 117 ★

Farms and Farmers

Conveniences: Modern Conveniences Available on Black Farms by Owner Status and Farm Location, 1930 - II

[Colored farmers include Negroes, Indians, Chinese, Japanese, and all other nonwhite races]

DIVISION AND STATE	FARMS REPORTING Water piped into bathrooms				NUMBER OF-					
	Total	Owners	Tenants	Managers	Automobiles	Motor trucks	Tractors	Electric motors for farm work	Stationary gas engines	Farmers per automobile
The South	1,376	717	520	139	186,518	11,062	2,533	363	1,681	4.7
South Atlantic	482	201	207	74	78,764	5,101	1,221	137	1,008	3.8
East South Central	278	104	144	30	56,039	2,673	514	55	213	5.7
West South Central	616	412	169	35	51,715	3,288	798	171	460	5.1
Selected Northern States[1]	130	76	35	19	3,708	677	403	59	359	2.8

Source: "Farms of Colored Operators Reporting Telephones, Dwellings Lighted by Electricity, Water Piped into Dwellings and into Bathrooms, by Tenure of Operator, with Total Farm Motor Equipment, by Southern Divisions, and States, and Selected Northern States: 1930," *Negroes in the United States, 1920-1932,*1935, p. 591. Primary source: U.S. Bureau of the Census. *Negroes in the United States, 1920-1932.* Washington, D.C.: U.S. Government Printing Office, 1935. *Notes:* 1. States having 200 or more Negro farmers who constitute 90 percent or more of the colored farm operators in the State.

★ 118 ★

Farms and Farmers

Expenditures: Expenditures on All Black-Operated Farms by Location of Farm, 1930 - I

[Colored farmers include Negroes, Indians, Chinese, Japanese, and all other nonwhite races]

DIVISION AND STATE	All colored farm operators	Total selected expenditures	FEED		ELECTRIC CURRENT	
			Farm reporting	Amount expended	Farm reporting	Amount expended
ALL OPERATORS						
The South	881,687	$79,777,157	284,668	$18,063,402	1,535	$66,270
SOUTH ATLANTIC	298,379	42,935,633	92,062	4,856,476	841	27,816
Delaware	807	209,322	451	52,708	12	668
Maryland	5,267	1,006,941	2,917	233,182	73	2,870
District of Maryland	11	8,834	11	3,465	5	81
Virginia	39,673	4,337,510	14,724	664,305	171	6,965
West Virginia	491	48,551	262	19,439	27	1,879
North Carolina	76,873	14,364,765	28,723	1,722,734	271	7,154
South Carolina	77,425	10,530,517	19,549	841,864	125	2,548
Georgia	86,789	11,147,580	22,485	1,101,127	105	3,047
Florida	11,043	1,281,613	2,940	217,652	52	2,604
EAST SOUTH CENTRAL	320,959	20,705,322	95,458	6,268,837	354	12,305
Kentucky	9,104	435,146	2,879	161,515	43	1,658
Tennessee	35,138	1,339,838	10,515	506,848	85	3,214
Alabama	93,829	8,657,022	33,371	1,630,281	135	4,296
Mississippi	182,888	10,273,316	48,693	3,970,193	91	3,137
WEST SOUTH CENTRAL	262,349	16,136,202	97,148	6,938,089	340	26,149
Arkansas	79,579	5,034,344	32,220	2,828,447	56	6,422
Louisiana	73,770	4,388,016	25,760	1,656,867	41	1,557
Oklahoma	22,937	1,889,480	7,533	647,212	164	15,140
Texas	86,063	4,824,362	31,635	1,805,563	79	3,030
SELECTED NORTHERN STATES[1]	10,250	1,425,442	4,091	551,115	268	10,210
New Jersey	384	301,870	276	99,523	50	2,045
Pennsylvania	363	130,102	244	54,135	30	1,435
Ohio	1,237	189,387	630	61,458	56	2,002
Indiana	475	68,319	260	33,319	22	843
Illinois	894	107,229	474	45,974	21	679
Missouri	5,861	421,910	1,682	201,016	41	1,400
Kansas	1,036	206,625	525	55,690	48	1,806

Source: "Selected Farm Expenditures of Colored Farm Operators, with Farm Reporting, by Tenure, by Southern Divisions, and States, and Selected Northern States: 1930," *Negroes in the United States, 1920-1932*, 1935, pp. 608-610. Primary source: U.S. Bureau of the Census. *Negroes in the United States, 1920-1932*. Washington, D.C.: U.S. Government Printing Office, 1935. *Notes:* 1. States having 200 or more Negro farmers who constitute 90% or more of the colored farmers in the State.

★ 119 ★

Farms and Farmers

Expenditures: Expenditures on All Black-Operated Farms by Location of Farm, 1930 - II

[Colored farmers include Negroes, Indians, Chinese, Japanese, and all other nonwhite races]

DIVISION AND STATE	FARM LABOR		FARM IMPLEMENTS AND MACHINERY		FERTILIZER		
	Farms reporting	Amount expended	Farms reporting	Amount expended	Farms reporting	Quantity (tons)	Amount expended
ALL OPERATORS							
The South	160,460	$10,534,357	124,442	$6,464,666	447,424	1,354,339	$44,648,462
SOUTH ATLANTIC	68,531	4,981,573	58,473	2,283,872	244,620	969,099	30,785,896
Delaware	253	60,474	168	36,875	540	1,957	58,597
Maryland	1,781	325,281	893	143,113	3,721	9,803	302,495
District of Maryland	2	4,760	1	528	...	...	...
Virginia	7,796	855,729	5,683	511,528	25,646	73,361	2,298,983
West Virginia	114	16,366	43	5,510	218	250	5,357
North Carolina	18,770	1,127,379	12,384	527,274	68,000	344,842	10,980,224
South Carolina	16,199	938,726	14,497	413,428	66,690	269,033	8,333,951
Georgia	20,672	1,254,535	22,098	553,033	74,346	254,796	8,235,838
Florida	2,944	398,323	1,896	92,583	5,459	15,057	570,451
EAST SOUTH CENTRAL	43,780	2,144,224	36,612	1,975,165	143,525	289,574	10,304,791
Kentucky	1,943	168,995	535	60,742	2,061	1,587	42,236
Tennessee	5,357	250,542	3,191	258,312	7,830	9,580	320,922
Alabama	16,593	703,493	19,735	569,879	65,802	173,029	5,749,073
Mississippi	19,887	1,021,194	13,151	1,086,232	67,832	105,378	4,192,560
WEST SOUTH CENTRAL	48,149	3,408,560	29,357	2,205,629	59,279	95,666	3,557,775
Arkansas	14,461	810,878	8,186	572,507	13,263	21,179	816,090
Louisiana	10,761	749,677	8,577	470,863	24,865	40,470	1,509,052
Oklahoma	5,783	649,155	2,824	561,133	292	579	16,840
Texas	17,144	1,198,850	9,770	601,126	20,859	33,438	1,215,793
SELECTED NORTHERN STATES[1]	2,407	508,332	1,046	232,727	1,009	3,163	123,058
New Jersey	170	101,465	104	28,115	258	1,678	70,722
Pennsylvania	122	35,611	79	20,671	163	446	18,250
Ohio	309	67,916	157	37,602	395	680	20,409
Indiana	117	16,949	39	10,101	96	207	7,107
Illinois	242	43,485	95	13,899	27	50	3,192
Missouri	1,048	170,812	329	46,079	58	92	2,603
Kansas	399	72,094	243	76,260	12	10	775

Source: "Selected Farm Expenditures of Colored Farm Operators, with Farms Reporting, by Tenure, by Southern Divisions, and States, and Selected Northern States: 1930," *Negroes in the United States, 1920-1932*, 1935, pp. 608-610. Primary source: U.S. Bureau of the Census. *Negroes in the United States, 1920-1932*. Washington, D.C.: U.S. Government Printing Office, 1935. *Notes:* 1. States having 200 or more Negro farmers who constitute 90% or more of the colored farmers in the State.

★ 120 ★
Farms and Farmers

Expenditures: Expenditures on All Black-Owned Farms by Location of Farm, 1930 - I
[Colored farmers include Negroes, Indians, Chinese, Japanese, and all other nonwhite races]

DIVISION AND STATE	All colored farm operators	Total selected expenditures	FEED		ELECTRIC CURRENT	
			Farm reporting	Amount expended	Farm reporting	Amount expended
OWNERS (FULL AND PART)						
The South	182,019	$19,731,900	87,919	$5,086,770	993	$43,890
SOUTH ATLANTIC	80,503	10,003,811	35,137	1,766,071	546	17,670
Delaware	373	81,606	242	26,663	9	353
Maryland	2,941	449,690	1,908	142,896	51	1,533
District of Maryland	8	1,381	8	845	3	36
Virginia	24,448	2,091,051	10,814	464,740	140	5,607
West Virginia	373	23,424	206	12,691	19	1,163
North Carolina	19,711	3,262,539	9,652	509,146	173	4,617
South Carolina	15,992	1,986,527	5,555	232,780	62	1,394
Georgia	11,081	1,458,203	4,831	234,026	50	1,557
Florida	5,576	649,390	1,921	142,284	39	1,410
EAST SOUTH CENTRAL	50,588	4,630,441	24,662	1,366,045	202	7,263
Kentucky	4,175	234,229	2,028	100,859	37	1,473
Tennessee	7,832	475,899	4,326	206,284	53	1,637
Alabama	15,931	1,839,879	7,926	404,175	76	2,711
Mississippi	22,650	2,080,434	10,382	645,727	36	1,442
WEST SOUTH CENTRAL	50,928	5,097,648	28,120	1,954,654	245	18,957
Arkansas	11,455	1,247,018	7,617	615,098	27	1,620
Louisiana	10,503	1,000,119	5,527	318,649	27	1,033
Oklahoma	8,334	1,183,186	3,329	379,381	144	14,422
Texas	20,636	1,667,325	11,647	641,526	47	1,882
SELECTED NORTHERN STATES[1]	3,776	671,583	2,289	282,016	203	6,593
New Jersey	240	142,333	184	58,486	36	1,491
Pennsylvania	233	67,552	162	26,956	20	771
Ohio	783	107,903	455	43,807	43	1,440
Indiana	283	33,135	167	18,269	16	528
Illinois	460	56,651	278	24,151	17	413
Missouri	1,170	125,559	708	72,953	32	791
Kansas	607	138,450	335	37,394	39	1,159

Source: "Selected Farm Expenditures of Colored Farm Operators, with Farm Reporting, by Tenure, by Southern Divisions, and States, and Selected Northern States: 1930," *Negroes in the United States, 1920-1932*, 1935, pp. 608-610. Primary source: U.S. Bureau of the Census. *Negroes in the United States, 1920-1932.* Washington, D.C.: U.S. Government Printing Office, 1935. *Notes:* 1. States having 200 or more Negro farmers who constitute 90% or more of the colored farmers in the State.

★ 121 ★
Farms and Farmers

Expenditures: Expenditures on All Black-Owned Farms by Location of Farm, 1930 - II

[Colored farmers include Negroes, Indians, Chinese, Japanese, and all other nonwhite races]

DIVISION AND STATE	FARM LABOR		FARM IMPLEMENTS AND MACHINERY		FERTILIZER		
	Farms reporting	Amount expended	Farms reporting	Amount expended	Farms reporting	Quantity (tons)	Amount expended
OWNERS (FULL AND PART)							
The South	46,874	$3,348,313	34,198	$2,838,920	101,795	255,383	$8,414,007
SOUTH ATLANTIC	21,756	1,654,214	15,089	1,061,579	57,485	173,107	5,504,277
Delaware	108	15,173	83	21,509	253	555	17,908
Maryland	1,029	120,744	492	70,248	2,072	3,529	114,269
District of Maryland	1	500	...	...	...	...	...
Virginia	5,132	387,608	3,512	376,823	14,310	28,810	856,273
West Virginia	80	5,158	25	1,720	175	129	2,692
North Carolina	5,545	340,817	3,372	232,993	16,994	67,635	2,174,966
South Carolina	4,749	335,840	3,332	157,868	12,134	40,069	1,258,645
Georgia	3,594	257,847	3,247	138,779	8,798	25,685	825,994
Florida	1,518	190,527	1,026	61,639	2,749	6,695	253,530
EAST SOUTH CENTRAL	11,318	592,210	9,341	283,391	28,128	56,101	1,946,532
Kentucky	1,007	69,983	322	32,889	1,070	761	20,025
Tennessee	1,833	85,802	1,074	104,139	2,227	2,402	78,037
Alabama	4,376	237,208	4,316	200,544	12,334	29,661	995,241
Mississippi	4,102	199,217	3,629	380,819	12,497	23,277	853,229
WEST SOUTH CENTRAL	13,800	1,101,889	9,768	1,058,950	16,182	26,175	963,198
Arkansas	3,502	214,805	2,522	194,214	3,838	5,952	221,281
Louisiana	2,278	177,883	2,086	164,514	5,342	9,155	338,040
Oklahoma	2,598	362,243	1,379	416,467	170	363	10,673
Texas	5,422	346,958	3,781	283,755	6,832	10,705	393,204
SELECTED NORTHERN STATES[1]	1,060	197,347	566	135,297	628	1,301	50,330
New Jersey	89	40,219	64	15,466	154	590	26,671
Pennsylvania	74	18,028	48	14,762	110	209	7,035
Ohio	175	30,607	93	21,526	254	351	10,523
Indiana	69	7,468	20	4,571	53	76	2,299
Illinois	143	22,659	54	7,268	18	31	2,160
Missouri	252	31,008	134	19,860	29	34	947
Kansas	258	47,358	153	51,844	10	10	695

Source: "Selected Farm Expenditures of Colored Farm Operators, with Farms Reporting, by Tenure, by Southern Divisions, and States, and Selected Northern States: 1930," *Negroes in the United States, 1920-1932,* 1935, pp. 608-610. Primary source: U.S. Bureau of the Census. *Negroes in the United States, 1920-1932.* Washington, D.C.: U.S. Government Printing Office, 1935. *Notes:* 1. States having 200 or more Negro farmers who constitute 90% or more of the colored farmers in the State.

★ 122 ★
Farms and Farmers

Expenditures: Expenditures on Black Tenant Farms by Location of Farm, 1930 - I
[Colored farmers include Negroes, Indians, Chinese, Japanese, and all other nonwhite races]

DIVISION AND STATE	All colored farm operators	Total selected expenditures	FEED		ELECTRIC CURRENT	
			Farms reporting	Amount expended	Farms reporting	Amount expended
ALL TENANTS						
The South	698,839	$58,973,561	196,339	$12,778,593	472	$16,715
SOUTH ATLANTIC	217,397	32,287,473	56,702	3,011,845	247	5,927
Delaware	415	102,004	199	22,131	...	...
Maryland	2,206	417,658	949	77,318	12	784
District of Maryland	2	340	2	320	1	20
Virginia	15,148	2,126,252	3,874	189,020	24	608
West Virginia	111	14,886	51	5,147	4	82
North Carolina	57,139	11,072,506	19,059	1,206,266	92	2,184
South Carolina	61,362	8,479,256	13,971	602,230	60	1,009
Georgia	75,636	9,563,024	17,620	853,072	59	931
Florida	5,378	511,547	977	56,341	4	309
EAST SOUTH CENTRAL	270,230	15,846,638	70,716	4,842,112	138	4,046
Kentucky	4,914	195,019	846	49,806	5	175
Tennessee	27,272	823,115	6,167	289,843	23	936
Alabama	77,875	6,736,657	25,432	1,214,656	56	1,280
Mississippi	160,169	8,091,847	38,271	3,287,807	54	1,655
WEST SOUTH CENTRAL	211,212	10,839,450	68,921	4,924,636	87	6,742
Arkansas	68,101	3,761,974	24,590	2,207,504	27	4,687
Louisiana	63,213	3,329,919	20,207	1,322,426	13	454
Oklahoma	14,459	646,304	4,178	248,646	19	688
Texas	65,339	3,101,253	19,946	1,146,060	28	913
SELECTED NORTHERN STATES[1]	6,394	624,004	1,754	217,036	51	2,617
New Jersey	129	105,848	83	25,174	9	218
Pennsylvania	116	49,377	74	24,659	10	664
Ohio	442	68,285	166	15,826	11	367
Indiana	190	34,117	92	14,820	6	315
Illinois	428	42,488	194	17,573	4	266
Missouri	4,671	259,846	960	101,313	5	294
Kansas	418	64,043	185	17,671	6	493

Source: "Selected Farm Expenditures of Colored Farm Operators, with Farms Reporting, by Tenure, by Southern Divisions, and States, and Selected Northern States: 1930," *Negroes in the United States, 1920-1932*, 1935, pp. 608-610. Primary source: U.S. Bureau of the Census. *Negroes in the United States, 1920-1932*. Washington, D.C.: U.S. Government Printing Office, 1935. *Notes:* 1. States having 200 or more Negro farmers who constitute 90 percent or more of the colored farmers in the State.

★ 123 ★
Farms and Farmers

Expenditures: Expenditures on Black Tenant Farms by Location of Farm, 1930 - II

[Colored farmers include Negroes, Indians, Chinese, Japanese, and all other nonwhite races]

DIVISION AND STATE	FARM LABOR		FARM IMPLEMENTS AND MACHINERY		FERTILIZER		
	Farms reporting	Amount expended	Farms reporting	Amount expended	Farms reporting	Quantity (tons)	Amount expended
ALL TENANTS							
The South	113,067	$6,617,486	89,968	$3,511,479	345,147	1,093,285	$38,049,283
SOUTH ATLANTIC	46,446	2,980,123	43,224	1,165,230	186,759	791,109	25,124,348
Delaware	135	29,768	79	12,976	278	1,247	37,129
Maryland	663	117,096	366	63,460	1,554	5,193	159,000
District of Maryland	...	...	...	...	...	...	...
Virginia	2,610	397,134	2,145	120,151	11,280	43,875	1,419,339
West Virginia	28	4,963	16	2,941	36	93	1,753
North Carolina	13,209	774,673	9,003	298,132	50,983	276,884	8,796,251
South Carolina	11,407	572,530	11,138	250,692	54,500	228,217	7,052,795
Georgia	17,028	931,633	19,627	398,409	65,489	228,154	7,378,979
Florida	1,366	152,326	850	23,469	2,639	7,446	279,102
EAST SOUTH CENTRAL	32,379	1,438,165	27,215	1,226,399	115,332	232,844	8,335,916
Kentucky	931	96,117	209	26,853	986	820	22,068
Tennessee	3,506	142,045	2,105	148,444	5,591	7,148	241,847
Alabama	12,198	416,546	15,403	363,119	53,451	142,970	4,741,056
Mississippi	15,744	783,457	9,498	687,983	55,304	81,906	3,330,945
WEST SOUTH CENTRAL	34,242	2,199,198	19,529	1,119,850	43,056	69,332	2,589,024
Arkansas	10,949	583,623	5,654	372,788	9,418	15,183	563,372
Louisiana	8,453	538,735	6,473	299,299	19,506	31,260	1,169,005
Oklahoma	3,155	252,309	1,432	138,761	117	207	5,900
Texas	11,685	824,531	5,970	309,002	14,015	22,682	820,747
SELECTED NORTHERN STATES[1]	1,306	260,699	459	84,800	350	1,604	58,852
New Jersey	60	36,063	33	7,817	92	894	36,576
Pennsylvania	44	11,743	28	5,695	46	223	6,616
Ohio	125	31,229	60	12,126	133	300	8,737
Indiana	47	8,856	18	5,455	42	127	4,671
Illinois	98	16,986	41	6,631	9	19	1,032
Missouri	786	133,556	191	23,543	26	41	1,140
Kansas	137	22,266	88	23,533	2	1	80

Source: "Selected Farm Expenditures of Colored Farm Operators, with Farms Reporting, by Tenure, by Southern Divisions, and States, and Selected Northern States: 1930," *Negroes in the United States, 1920-1932*, 1935, pp. 608-610. Primary source: U.S. Bureau of the Census. *Negroes in the United States, 1920-1932.* Washington, D.C.: U.S. Government Printing Office, 1935. *Notes:* 1. States having 200 or more Negro farmers who constitute 90 percent or more of the colored farmers in the State.

★ 124 ★
Farms and Farmers

Expenditures: Expenditures on Farms with Black Managers by Location of Farm, 1930 - I

[Colored farmers include Negroes, Indians, Chinese, Japanese, and all other nonwhite races]

DIVISION AND STATE	All colored farm operators	Total selected expenditures	FEED		ELECTRIC CURRENT	
			Farms reporting	Amount expended	Farms reporting	Amount expended
		MANAGERS				
The South	829	$1,071,696	410	$198,039	70	$5,665
SOUTH ATLANTIC	479	644,349	223	78,560	48	4,219
Delaware	19	25,712	10	3,914	3	315
Maryland	120	139,593	60	12,968	10	553
District of Maryland	1	7,113	1	2,300	1	25
Virginia	77	120,207	36	10,545	7	750
West Virginia	7	10,241	5	1,601	4	634
North Carolina	23	29,720	12	7,322	6	353
South Carolina	71	64,734	23	6,854	3	145
Georgia	72	126,353	34	14,029	5	559
Florida	89	120,676	42	19,027	9	885
EAST SOUTH CENTRAL	141	228,243	80	60,680	14	996
Kentucky	15	5,898	5	1,850	1	10
Tennessee	34	40,824	22	10,721	9	641
Alabama	23	80,486	13	11,450	3	305
Mississippi	69	101,035	40	36,659	1	40
WEST SOUTH CENTRAL	209	199,104	107	58,799	8	450
Arkansas	23	25,352	13	5,845	2	115
Louisiana	54	57,978	26	15,792	1	70
Oklahoma	44	59,990	26	19,185	1	30
Texas	88	55,784	42	17,977	4	235
SELECTED NORTHERN STATES[1]	80	129,855	48	52,063	14	1,000
New Jersey	15	53,689	9	15,863	5	336
Pennsylvania	14	13,173	8	2,520	...	...
Ohio	12	13,199	9	1,825	2	195
Indiana	2	1,067	1	230	...	...
Illinois	6	8,090	2	4,250	...	...
Missouri	20	36,505	14	26,750	4	315
Kansas	11	4,132	5	625	3	154

Source: "Selected Farm Expenditures of Colored Farm Operators, with Farms Reporting, by Tenure, by Southern Divisions, and States, and Selected Northern States: 1930," *Negroes in the United States, 1920-1932*, 1935, pp. 608-610. Primary source: U.S. Bureau of the Census. *Negroes in the United States, 1920-1932*. Washington, D.C.: U.S. Government Printing Office, 1935. *Notes:* 1. States having 200 or more Negro farmers who constitute 90 percent or more of the colored farmers in the State. 2. Less than 1 ton per farm reported.

★ 125 ★
Farms and Farmers

Expenditures: Expenditures on Farms with Black Managers by Location of Farm, 1930 - II
[Colored farmers include Negroes, Indians, Chinese, Japanese, and all other nonwhite races]

DIVISION AND STATE	FARM LABOR		FARM IMPLEMENTS AND MACHINERY		FERTILIZER		
	Farms reporting	Amount expended	Farms reporting	Amount expended	Farms reporting	Quantity (tons)	Amount expended
MANAGERS							
The South	519	$568,558	276	$114,267	482	5,671	$185,167
SOUTH ATLANTIC	329	347,236	160	57,063	376	4,883	157,271
Delaware	10	15,533	6	2,300	9	155	3,560
Maryland	89	87,441	35	9,405	95	1,081	29,226
District of Maryland	1	4,260	1	528	...	...	...
Virginia	54	70,987	26	14,554	56	676	23,371
West Virginia	6	6,245	2	849	7	28	912
North Carolina	16	11,889	9	1,149	23	323	9,007
South Carolina	43	30,356	27	4,868	56	747	22,511
Georgia	50	65,055	34	15,845	59	957	30,865
Florida	60	55,470	20	7,475	71	916	37,819
EAST SOUTH CENTRAL	83	113,849	56	30,375	65	629	22,343
Kentucky	5	2,895	4	1,000	5	6	143
Tennessee	18	22,695	12	5,729	12	30	1,038
Alabama	19	49,739	16	6,216	17	398	12,776
Mississippi	41	38,520	24	17,430	31	195	8,386
WEST SOUTH CENTRAL	107	107,473	60	26,829	41	159	5,553
Arkansas	10	12,450	10	5,505	7	44	1,437
Louisiana	30	33,059	18	7,050	17	55	2,007
Oklahoma	30	34,603	13	5,905	5	9	267
Texas	37	27,361	19	8,369	12	51	1,842
SELECTED NORTHERN STATES[1]	41	50,286	21	12,630	31	258	13,876
New Jersey	12	25,183	7	4,832	12	194	7,475
Pennsylvania	4	5,840	3	214	7	14	4,599
Ohio	9	6,080	4	3,950	8	29	1,149
Indiana	1	625	1	75	1	4	137
Illinois	1	3,840	...	...	...	...	...
Missouri	10	6,248	4	2,676	3	17	516
Kansas	4	2,470	2	883	...	...	...

Source: "Selected Farm Expenditures of Colored Farm Operators, with Farm Reporting, by Tenure, by Southern Divisions, and States, and Selected Northern States: 1930," *Negroes in the United States, 1920-1932,* 1935, pp. 608-610. Primary source: U.S. Bureau of the Census. *Negroes in the United States, 1920-1932.* Washington, D.C.: U.S. Government Printing Office, 1935. *Notes:* 1. States having 200 or more Negro farmers who constitute 90 percent or more of the colored farmers in the State. 2. Less than 1 ton per farm reported.

★ 126 ★

Farms and Farmers

Farm Access: Type of Access Road Leading to Black Farms by Farm Location, 1930

[Colored farmers include Negroes, Indians, Chinese, Japanese, and all other nonwhite races]

DIVISION AND STATE	All farms	NUMBER OF FARMS LOCATED ON-								
		Concrete road	Brick road	Asphalt road	Macadam road	Gravel road	Sand-clay road	Improved dirt road	Unimproved dirt road	All other (including not reported)
The South	881,687	14,380	242	9,283	7,282	145,964	51,595	219,951	380,914	52,076
SOUTH ATLANTIC	298,379	7,297	145	4,106	3,459	15,464	38,638	78,748	131,937	18,585
Delaware	807	94	...	...	40	43	1	188	380	61
Maryland	5,267	368	1	2	404	693	49	791	2,666	293
District of Columbia	11	...	...	...	4	2	...	1	4	...
Virginia	39,673	662	6	518	1,548	3,977	4,136	7,871	18,977	1,978
West Virginia	491	13	...	12	49	21	20	74	265	37
North Carolina	76,873	3,029	97	1,657	883	5,299	10,922	19,705	28,889	6,392
South Carolina	77,425	1,998	13	824	239	2,829	12,718	18,670	36,741	3,393
Georgia	86,789	991	2	606	112	2,353	9,676	29,567	38,046	5,436
Florida	11,043	142	26	487	180	247	1,116	1,881	5,969	995
EAST SOUTH CENTRAL	320,959	3,746	91	1,090	2,676	86,199	9,132	75,156	126,444	16,425
Kentucky	9,104	34	...	119	1,524	2,024	13	1,028	3,385	977
Tennessee	35,138	909	1	537	1,051	7,806	174	7,001	15,293	2,366
Alabama	93,829	535	...	315	95	14,515	6,556	22,718	43,492	5,603
Mississippi	182,888	2,268	90	119	6	61,854	2,389	44,409	64,274	7,479
WEST SOUTH CENTRAL	262,349	3,337	6	4,087	1,147	44,301	3,825	66,047	122,533	17,066
Arkansas	79,579	1,238	1	2,071	183	11,886	771	15,666	41,651	6,112
Louisiana	73,770	848	...	270	390	23,092	250	15,499	29,970	3,451
Oklahoma	22,937	239	2	77	9	1,366	275	8,604	10,200	2,165
Texas	86,063	1,012	3	1,669	565	7,957	2,529	26,278	40,712	5,338
SELECTED NORTHERN STATES[1]	10,250	548	25	35	366	1,843	43	2,964	3,932	494
New Jersey	384	30	...	8	43	137	1	28	116	21
Pennsylvania	363	24	4	1	34	31	2	43	201	23
Ohio	1,237	21	16	3	206	460	...	65	400	66
Indiana	475	16	...	2	43	262	1	18	103	30
Illinois	894	47	1	1	6	222	...	134	429	54
Missouri	5,861	370	1	5	18	668	22	2,270	2,232	275
Kansas	1,036	40	3	15	16	63	17	406	451	25

Source: "Number of Farms of Colored operators Classified by Kind of Road on which Located, by Southern Divisions, and States, and Selected Northern States: 1930," *Negroes in the United States, 1920-1932*, 1935, p. 591. Primary source: U.S. Bureau of the Census. *Negroes in the United States, 1920-1932.* Washington, D.C.: U.S. Government Printing Office, 1935. *Notes:* 1. States having 200 or more Negro farmers who constitute 90 percent or more of the colored farmers in the State.

★ 127 ★

Farms and Farmers

Length of Occupancy: Percent Distribution of Length of Occupancy of Southern Black Croppers by Location of Farm 1930

Division and State	All Croppers	Total	Not reporting years on farm	Per Cent Distribution By Years on Farm								
				Less than 1 Years			One Year	Two to Four Years	10 Years and Over			
				Total	Three Mos. or Less	Four To Eleven Mos.			Five to Nine Years	Total	Ten to Fourteen	15 Years and Over
				NEGRO CROPPERS								
THE SOUTH	392,897	381,543	11,354	35.6	28.2	7.4	22.5	23.8	10.8	7.2	4.1	3.1
Geographic Divisions:												
South Atlantic	124,171	120,631	3,540	34.5	28.8	5.7	21.7	23.5	11.9	8.4	4.6	3.7
East South Central	150,239	145,873	4,366	33.9	26.3	7.6	23.0	25.3	10.8	7.0	4.1	2.9
W. South Central	118,487	115,039	3,448	39.0	30.1	8.9	22.8	22.3	9.6	6.3	3.6	2.7
South Atlantic:												
Delaware	60	59	1	22.0	10.2	11.9	22.0	28.8	20.3	6.8	6.8	0.0
Maryland	597	570	27	16.5	10.5	6.0	24.4	30.5	16.8	11.8	7.0	4.7
District of Columbia	0	0	0	0.0	0.0	0.0	0.0	0.0	0.0	0.0	0.0	0.0
Virginia	6,797	6,564	233	23.7	16.1	7.6	24.1	27.0	14.0	11.3	6.3	5.0
West Virginia	23	23	0	30.4	13.0	17.4	21.7	17.4	13.0	17.4	13.0	4.3
North Carolina	34,805	33,544	1,261	37.4	32.6	4.7	22.0	22.3	10.8	7.6	4.1	3.4
South Carolina	31,046	30,236	810	31.2	27.6	3.7	21.5	25.6	12.4	9.2	4.9	4.3
Georgia	49,450	48,298	1,152	36.3	29.1	7.2	21.2	22.6	12.1	7.9	4.4	3.4
Florida	1,393	1,337	56	30.6	20.9	9.6	25.8	22.3	10.6	10.7	5.8	4.9
East South Central												
Kentucky	3,116	3,011	105	32.5	29.1	3.4	25.6	22.9	9.9	9.0	4.3	4.7
Tennessee	16,559	15,868	691	35.5	30.3	5.2	23.9	24.7	9.8	6.2	3.5	2.7
Alabama	27,572	26,886	686	33.4	25.8	7.5	20.9	25.0	12.4	8.3	4.8	3.5
Mississippi	102,992	100,108	2,884	33.9	25.8	8.1	23.3	25.6	10.5	6.7	4.0	2.7
West South Central												
Arkansas	45,465	44,345	1,120	41.8	36.0	5.8	25.3	20.6	8.0	4.4	2.7	1.6
Louisiana	32,214	31,105	1,109	33.2	22.2	11.0	21.5	24.3	11.9	9.3	4.8	4.5
Oklahoma	4,560	4,409	151	54.1	45.5	8.6	21.1	16.6	5.6	2.7	1.6	1.1
Texas	36,248	35,180	1,068	38.7	27.7	11.0	21.2	23.4	10.2	6.6	3.8	2.7

Source: "Croppers in the South, Classified by Years on Farm and Color, with Per Cent Distribution, by Divisions and States: 1930," *Negro Year Book: An Annual Encyclopedia of the Negro, 1937-1938*, 1937, p. 54. Primary source: U.S. Bureau of the Census. Published by permission.

★ 128 ★

Farms and Farmers

Length of Occupancy: Percentage Distribution of Length of Occupancy of Southern Tenant Farmers, 1920 and 1930

	Less Than 1 Year		1 Year	1 Year	2 to 4 Years		5 to 9 Years		10 Years and over	
	1930	1920	1930	1920	1930	1920	1930	1920	1930	1920
All Tenants	35.6	20.6	20.3	27.1	22.3	30.4	12.1	12.5	9.7	9.4
Cash Tenants	26.7	13.5	18.0	21.0	24.3	31.9	15.6	16.9	15.5	16.6
Other Tenants	37.0	22.7	20.6	28.9	22.0	30.0	11.6	11.2	8.8	7.2
White Tenants	40.1	24.8	20.6	29.0	20.8	27.7	10.8	11.0	7.8	7.4
Cash Tenants	34.0	18.8	20.0	24.6	22.6	30.3	12.3	14.6	10.5	11.7

[Continued]

★ 128 ★

Length of Occupancy: Percentage Distribution of Length of Occupancy of Southern Tenant Farmers, 1920 and 1930
[Continued]

	Less Than 1 Year		1 Year	1 Year	2 to 4 Years		5 to 9 Years		10 Years and over	
	1930	1920	1930	1920	1930	1920	1930	1920	1930	1920
Other Tenants	41.0	26.3	20.6	30.1	20.5	27.1	10.5	10.2	7.4	6.4
Negro Tenants	28.6	15.4	19.8	24.7	24.8	33.8	14.2	14.2	12.7	11.8
Cash Tenants	16.2	8.8	15.1	17.7	26.6	33.4	19.7	19.1	22.5	21.0
Other Tenants	30.6	17.9	20.6	27.2	24.5	34.0	13.3	12.5	11.1	8.5

Source: "Percentage Distribution of White and Negro Tenants in the South by Number of Years on Farm: 1920-1930," *Negro Year Book: An Annual Encyclopedia of the Negro, 1937-1938,* 1937, p. 51. Primary source: Work, Monroe N. (Ed.), *Negro Year Book: An Annual Encyclopedia of the Negro, 1937-1938.* Tuskegee Institute, Ala.: The Negro Year Book Pub. Co., 1937. Published by permission.

★ 129 ★

Farms and Farmers

Length of Occupancy: Years on Farm of All Black Farmers by Farm Location, 1910 - I

CLASS OF FARM, SECTION, AND DIVISION	Number of farms	FARMS REPORTING OCCUPANCY: 1910						
		Total		Less than 1 year	1 year	2 to 4 years	5 to 9 years	10 years and over
		Number	Percent of all farms					
COLORED FARMS								
United States	929,883	837,227	90.9	191,808	105,781	242,724	131,354	165,560
The South	890,141	814,284	91.5	189,324	103,714	237,107	127,586	156,553
South Atlantic	355,862	326,932	91.9	67,259	41,506	95,713	52,222	70,232
East South Central	325,218	299,774	92.2	75,463	37,621	88,533	46,949	51,208
West South Central	209,061	187,578	89.7	46,602	24,587	52,861	28,415	35,113
The North	17,884	14,685	82.1	1,642	1,307	3,340	2,568	5,828
The West	12,858	8,258	64.2	842	760	2,277	1,200	3,179
WHITE FARMS								
United States	5,440,619	4,957,541	91.1	808,485	522,079	1,128,883	861,114	1,636,980
The South	2,207,406	1,997,830	90.5	434,268	229,434	474,524	312,140	547,464
South Atlantic	756,019	679,532	89.9	109,346	68,669	154,283	111,285	235,949
East South Central	717,262	651,455	90.8	137,353	71,627	152,703	102,357	187,415
West South Central	734,125	666,843	90.8	187,569	89,138	167,538	98,498	124,100
The North	2,872,734	2,630,982	91.6	324,662	252,097	558,228	486,122	1,009,873
The West	360,479	328,729	91.2	49,555	40,548	96,131	62,852	79,643

Source: "Colored and White Farms Classified by Terms of Occupancy, by Sections and Southern Divisions: 1910," *Negro Population, 1790-1915,* 1918, p. 568. Primary source: U.S. Bureau of the Census. *Negroes in the United States, 1790-1915.* Washington, D.C.: U.S. Government Printing Office, 1918.

★ 130 ★

Farms and Farmers

Length of Occupancy: Years on Farm of All Black Farmers by Farm Location, 1910 - II

CLASS OF FARM, SECTION, AND DIVISION	FARMS REPORTING OCCUPANCY: 1910 Distribution per cent by term of occupancy					
	Total	Less than 1 year	1 year	2 to 4 years	5 to 9 years	10 years and over
COLORED FARMS						
United States	100.0	22.9	12.6	29.0	15.7	19.8
The South	100.0	23.3	12.7	29.1	15.7	19.2
South Atlantic	100.0	20.6	12.7	29.3	16.0	21.5
East South Central	100.0	25.2	12.6	29.5	15.7	17.1
West South Central	100.0	24.9	13.1	28.2	15.2	18.7
The North	100.0	11.2	8.9	22.7	17.5	39.7
The West	100.0	10.2	9.2	27.6	14.5	38.5
WHITE FARMS						
United States	100.0	16.3	10.5	22.8	17.4	33.0
The South	100.0	21.7	11.5	23.8	15.6	27.4
South Atlantic	100.0	16.1	10.1	22.7	16.4	34.7
East South Central	100.0	21.1	11.0	23.4	15.7	28.8
West South Central	100.0	28.1	13.4	25.1	14.8	18.6
The North	100.0	12.3	9.6	21.2	18.5	38.4
The West	100.0	15.1	12.3	29.2	19.1	24.2

Source: "Colored and White Farms Classified by Terms of Occupancy, by Sections and Southern Divisions: 1910," *Negro Population, 1790-1915*, 1918, p. 568. Primary source: U.S. Bureau of the Census. *Negroes in the United States, 1790-1915.* Washington, D.C.: U.S. Government Printing Office, 1918.

★ 131 ★
Farms and Farmers

Length of Occupancy: Years on Farm of All Black Operators by Farm Location, 1930 - I
[Colored farmers include Negroes, Indians, Chinese, Japanese, and all other nonwhite races]

DIVISION AND STATE	All colored farm operators	NUMBER REPORTING YEARS ON FARM						
		Total Number	Percent of all farms	Less than 1 year	1 year	2 to 4 years	5 to 9 years	10 years and over
ALL OPERATORS								
The South	881,687	852,232	96.7	201,039	142,526	188,416	123,066	197,185
SOUTH ATLANTIC	298,379	288,210	96.6	62,243	43,823	58,757	42,902	80,485
Delaware	807	777	96.3	98	91	178	139	271
Maryland	5,267	5,026	95.4	492	530	940	865	2,199
District of Columbia	11	10	90.9	...	...	1	3	6
Virginia	39,673	38,132	96.1	3,224	3,645	6,100	5,897	19,266
West Virginia	491	476	96.9	34	36	60	91	255
North Carolina	76,873	73,723	95.9	17,947	12,045	14,688	10,531	18,512
South Carolina	77,425	75,260	97.2	15,382	11,458	16,815	11,876	19,729
Georgia	86,789	84,329	97.2	23,643	14,810	18,243	11,940	15,693
Florida	11,043	10,477	94.9	1,423	1,208	1,732	1,560	4,554
EAST SOUTH CENTRAL	320,959	310,752	96.8	71,152	54,091	74,619	46,586	64,304
Kentucky	9,104	8,734	95.9	1,588	1,345	1,601	1,136	3,064
Tennessee	35,138	33,485	95.3	8,116	6,052	7,628	4,358	7,331
Alabama	93,829	91,097	97.1	16,492	12,881	21,412	16,333	23,979
Mississippi	182,888	177,436	97.0	44,956	33,813	43,978	24,759	29,930
WEST SOUTH CENTRAL	262,349	253,270	96.5	67,644	44,612	55,040	33,578	52,396
Arkansas	79,579	77,355	97.2	24,312	16,172	16,277	8,691	11,903
Louisiana	73,770	70,938	96.2	15,960	11,891	16,767	10,818	15,502
Oklahoma	22,937	21,889	95.4	6,251	3,276	4,116	2,873	5,373
Texas	86,063	83,088	96.5	21,121	13,273	17,880	11,196	19,618
SELECTED NORTHERN STATES[1]	10,250	10,033	97.9	2,835	1,454	1,760	1,258	2,726
New Jersey	384	370	96.4	30	43	90	79	128
Pennsylvania	363	351	96.7	39	37	69	82	124
Ohio	1,237	1,200	97.0	173	118	207	176	526
Indiana	475	463	97.5	60	58	75	64	206
Illinois	894	856	95.7	101	129	144	132	350
Missouri	5,861	5,781	98.6	2,307	963	1,022	553	936
Kansas	1,036	1,012	97.7	125	106	153	172	456

Source: "Colored Farm Operators, by Years on Farm, and by Tenure, by Southern Divisions, and States, and Selected Northern States: 1930," *Negroes in the United States, 1920-1932,* 1935, pp. 607-608. Primary source: U.S. Bureau of the Census. *Negroes in the United States, 1920-1932.* Washington, D.C.: U.S. Government Printing Office, 1935.

★ 132 ★
Farms and Farmers

Length of Occupancy: Years on Farm of All Black Operators by Farm Location, 1930 - II

[Colored farmers include Negroes, Indians, Chinese, Japanese, and all other nonwhite races]

DIVISION AND STATE	PERCENT DISTRIBUTION BY YEARS ON FARM					
	Total	Less than 1 year	1 year	2 to 4 years	5 to 9 years	10 years and over
ALL OPERATORS						
The South	100.0	23.6	16.7	22.1	14.4	23.1
SOUTH ATLANTIC	100.0	21.6	15.2	20.4	14.9	27.9
Delaware	100.0	12.6	11.7	22.9	17.9	34.9
Maryland	100.0	9.8	10.5	18.7	17.2	43.8
District of Columbia	100.0	...	...	10.0	30.0	60.0
Virginia	100.0	8.5	9.6	16.0	15.5	50.5
West Virginia	100.0	7.1	7.6	12.6	19.1	53.6
North Carolina	100.0	24.3	16.3	19.9	14.3	25.1
South Carolina	100.0	20.4	15.2	22.3	15.8	26.2
Georgia	100.0	28.0	17.6	21.6	14.2	18.6
Florida	100.0	13.6	11.5	16.5	14.9	43.5
EAST SOUTH CENTRAL	100.0	22.9	17.4	24.0	15.0	20.7
Kentucky	100.0	18.2	15.4	18.3	13.0	35.1
Tennessee	100.0	24.2	18.1	22.8	13.0	21.9
Alabama	100.0	18.1	14.1	23.5	17.9	26.3
Mississippi	100.0	25.3	19.1	24.8	14.0	16.9
WEST SOUTH CENTRAL	100.0	26.7	17.6	21.7	13.3	20.7
Arkansas	100.0	31.4	20.9	21.0	11.2	15.4
Louisiana	100.0	22.5	16.8	23.6	15.2	21.9
Oklahoma	100.0	28.6	15.0	18.8	13.1	24.5
Texas	100.0	25.4	16.0	21.5	13.5	23.6
SELECTED NORTHERN STATES[1]	100.0	28.3	14.5	17.5	12.5	27.2
New Jersey	100.0	8.1	11.6	24.3	21.4	34.6
Pennsylvania	100.0	11.1	10.5	19.7	23.4	35.3
Ohio	100.0	14.4	9.8	17.3	14.7	43.8
Indiana	100.0	13.0	12.5	16.2	13.8	44.5
Illinois	100.0	11.8	15.1	16.8	15.4	40.9
Missouri	100.0	39.9	16.7	17.7	9.6	16.2
Kansas	100.0	12.4	10.5	15.1	17.0	45.1

Source: "Colored Farm Operators, by Years on Farm, and by Tenure, by Southern Divisions, and States, and Selected Northern States: 1930," *Negroes in the United States, 1920-1932,* 1935, pp. 607-608. Primary source: U.S. Bureau of the Census. *Negroes in the United States, 1920-1932.* Washington, D.C.: U.S. Government Printing Office, 1935.

★ 133 ★
Farms and Farmers

Length of Occupancy: Years on Farm of Black Farm Owners and Managers by Farm Location, 1930 - I

[Colored farmers include Negroes, Indians, Chinese, Japanese, and all other nonwhite races]

DIVISION AND STATE	All colored farm operators	NUMBER REPORTING YEARS ON FARM		Less than 1 year	1 year	2 to 4 years	5 to 9 years	10 years and over
		Total						
		Number	Percent of all farms					
OWNERS AND MANAGERS								
The South	182,848	174,626	95.5	7,418	8,273	20,665	27,019	111,251
SOUTH ATLANTIC	80,982	77,430	95.6	2,781	3,274	8,028	11,648	51,699
Delaware	392	375	95.7	13	19	56	69	218
Maryland	3,061	2,903	94.8	106	138	328	458	1,873
District of Columbia	9	8	88.9	...	...	...	2	6
Virginia	24,525	23,537	96.0	584	788	2,122	3,293	16,750
West Virginia	380	368	96.8	9	20	38	69	232
North Carolina	19,734	18,761	95.1	726	914		3,059	11,968
South Carolina	16,063	15,463	96.3	575	626	1,619	2,476	10,167
Georgia	11,153	10,681	95.8	557	498	1,207	1,442	6,977
Florida	5,665	5,334	94.2	211	271	564	780	3,508
EAST SOUTH CENTRAL	50,729	48,621	95.8	2,116	2,404	6,457	8,014	29,630
Kentucky	4,190	4,004	95.6	189	192	469	600	2,554
Tennessee	7,866	7,410	94.2	369	411	910	1,114	4,606
Alabama	15,954	15,305	95.9	668	639	1,929	2,513	9,556
Mississippi	22,719	21,902	96.4	880	1,162	3,149	3,787	12,914
WEST SOUTH CENTRAL	51,137	48,575	95.0	2,521	2,595	6,180	7,357	29,922
Arkansas	11,478	11,044	96.2	555	587	1,394	1,601	6,907
Louisiana	10,557	9,995	94.7	431	512	1,375	1,540	6,137
Oklahoma	8,378	7,789	93.0	596	495	1,088	1,348	4,262
Texas	20,724	19,747	95.3	939	1,001	2,323	2,868	12,616
SELECTED NORTHERN STATES	3,856	3,727	96.7	194	187	461	594	2,291
New Jersey	255	247	96.9	10	17	47	60	113
Pennsylvania	247	236	95.5	13	18	35	60	110
Ohio	795	774	97.4	55	34	93	128	464
Indiana	285	276	96.8	13	15	29	41	178
Illinois	466	446	95.7	20	20	52	61	293
Missouri	1,190	1,146	96.3	55	53	140	149	749
Kansas	618	602	97.4	28	30	65	95	384

Source: "Colored Farm operators, by Years on Farm, and by Tenure, by Southern Divisions, and States, and Selected Northern States: 1930," *Negroes in the United States, 1920-1932*, 1935, pp. 607-608. Primary source: U.S. Bureau of the Census. *Negroes in the United States, 1920-1932*. Washington, D.C.: U.S. Government Printing Office, 1935.

★ 134 ★
Farms and Farmers

Length of Occupancy: Years on Farm of Black Farm Owners and Managers by Farm Location, 1930 - II

[Colored farmers include Negroes, Indians, Chinese, Japanese, and all other nonwhite races]

DIVISION AND STATE	PERCENT DISTRIBUTION BY YEARS ON FARM					
	Total	Less than 1 year	1 year	2 to 4 years	5 to 9 years	10 years and over
			OWNERS AND MANAGERS			
The South	100.0	4.2	4.7	11.8	15.5	63.7
SOUTH ATLANTIC	100.0	3.6	4.2	10.4	15.0	66.8
Delaware	100.0	3.5	5.1	14.9	18.4	58.1
Maryland	100.0	3.7	4.8	11.3	15.8	64.5
District of Columbia	100.0	...	...	...	25.0	75.0
Virginia	100.0	2.5	3.3	9.0	14.0	71.2
West Virginia	100.0	2.4	5.4	10.3	18.8	63.0
North Carolina	100.0	3.9	4.9	11.2	16.3	63.8
South Carolina	100.0	3.7	4.0	10.5	16.0	65.8
Georgia	100.0	5.2	4.7	11.3	13.5	65.3
Florida	100.0	4.0	5.1	10.6	14.6	65.8
EAST SOUTH CENTRAL	100.0	4.4	4.9	13.3	16.5	60.9
Kentucky	100.0	4.7	4.8	11.7	15.0	63.8
Tennessee	100.0	5.0	5.5	12.3	15.0	62.2
Alabama	100.0	4.4	4.2	12.6	16.4	62.4
Mississippi	100.0	4.1	5.3	14.4	17.3	59.0
WEST SOUTH CENTRAL	100.0	5.2	5.3	12.7	15.1	61.6
Arkansas	100.0	5.0	5.3	12.6	14.5	62.5
Louisiana	100.0	4.3	5.1	13.8	15.4	61.4
Oklahoma	100.0	7.7	6.4	14.0	17.3	54.7
Texas	100.0	4.8	5.1	11.8	14.5	63.9
SELECTED NORTHERN STATES	100.0	5.2	5.0	12.4	15.9	61.5
New Jersey	100.0	4.0	6.9	19.0	24.3	45.7
Pennsylvania	100.0	5.5	7.6	14.8	25.4	46.6
Ohio	100.0	7.1	4.4	12.0	16.5	59.9
Indiana	100.0	4.7	5.4	10.5	14.9	64.5
Illinois	100.0	4.5	4.5	11.7	13.7	65.7
Missouri	100.0	4.8	4.6	12.2	13.0	65.4
Kansas	100.0	4.7	5.0	10.8	15.8	63.8

Source: "Colored Farm operators, by Years on Farm, and by Tenure, by Southern Divisions, and States, and Selected Northern States: 1930," *Negroes in the United States, 1920-1932*, 1935, pp. 607-608. Primary source: U.S. Bureau of the Census. *Negroes in the United States, 1920-1932.* Washington, D.C.: U.S. Government Printing Office, 1935.

★ 135 ★

Farms and Farmers

Length of Occupancy: Years on Farm of Black Tenant Farmers by Farm Location, 1930 - I

DIVISION AND STATE	All colored farm operators	NUMBER REPORTING YEARS ON FARM						
		Total		Less than 1 year	1 year	2 to 4 years	5 to 9 years	10 years and over
		Number	Percent of all farms					
ALL TENANTS								
The South	698,839	677,606	97.0	193,621	134,253	167,751	96,047	85,934
SOUTH ATLANTIC	217,397	210,780	97.0	59,462	40,549	50,729	31,254	28,786
Delaware	415	402	96.9	85	72	122	70	53
Maryland	2,206	2,123	96.2	386	392	612	407	326
District of Columbia	2	2	100.0	...	...	1	1	...
Virginia	15,148	14,595	96.3	2,640	2,857	3,978	2,604	2,516
West Virginia	111	108	97.3	25	16	22	22	23
North Carolina	57,139	54,962	96.2	17,221	11,131	12,594	7,472	6,544
South Carolina	61,362	59,797	97.4	14,807	10,832	15,196	9,400	9,562
Georgia	75,636	73,648	97.4	23,086	14,312	17,036	10,498	8,716
Florida	5,378	5,143	95.6	1,212	937	1,168	780	1,046
EAST SOUTH CENTRAL	270,230	262,131	97.0	69,036	51,687	68,162	38,572	34,674
Kentucky	4,914	4,730	96.3	1,399	1,153	1,132	536	510
Tennessee	27,272	26,075	95.6	7,747	5,641	6,718	3,244	2,725
Alabama	77,875	75,792	97.3	15,824	12,242	19,483	13,820	14,423
Mississippi	160,169	155,534	97.1	44,066	32,651	40,829	20,972	17,016
WEST SOUTH CENTRAL	211,212	204,695	96.9	65,123	42,017	48,860	26,221	22,474
Arkansas	68,101	66,311	97.4	23,757	15,585	14,883	7,090	4,996
Louisiana	63,213	60,943	96.4	15,529	11,379	15,392	9,278	9,365
Oklahoma	14,559	14,100	96.8	5,655	2,781	3,028	1,525	1,111
Texas	65,339	63,341	96.9	20,182	12,272	15,557	8,328	7,002
SELECTED NORTHERN STATES	6,394	6,304	98.6	2,641	1,267	1,299	664	435
New Jersey	129	123	95.3	20	26	43	19	15
Pennsylvania	116	115	99.1	26	19	34	22	14
Ohio	442	426	96.4	118	84	114	48	62
Indiana	190	187	98.4	47	43	46	23	28
Illinois	428	410	95.8	81	109	92	71	57
Missouri	4,671	4,635	99.2	2,252	910	882	404	187
Kansas	418	410	98.1	97	76	88	77	72

Source: "Colored Farm operators, by Years on Farm, and by Tenure, by Southern Divisions, and States, and Selected Northern States: 1930," *Negroes in the United States, 1920-1932*, 1935, pp. 607-608. Primary source: U.S. Bureau of the Census. *Negroes in the United States, 1920-1932*. Washington, D.C.: U.S. Government Printing Office, 1935. *Notes:* 1. States having 200 or more Negro farmers who constitute 90 percent or more of the colored farmers in the State.

★ 136 ★
Farms and Farmers

Length of Occupancy: Years on Farm of Black Tenant Farmers by Farm Location, 1930 - II

DIVISION AND STATE	PERCENT DISTRIBUTION BY YEARS ON FARM					
	Total	Less than 1 year	1 year	2 to 4 years	5 to 9 years	10 years and over
ALL TENANTS						
The South	100.0	28.6	19.8	24.8	14.2	12.7
SOUTH ATLANTIC	100.0	28.2	19.2	24.1	14.8	13.7
Delaware	100.0	21.1	17.9	30.3	17.4	13.2
Maryland	100.0	18.2	18.5	28.8	19.2	15.4
District of Columbia	100.0	...	...	50.0	50.0	...
Virginia	100.0	18.1	19.6	27.3	17.8	17.2
West Virginia	100.0	23.1	14.8	20.4	20.4	21.3
North Carolina	100.0	31.3	20.3	22.9	13.6	11.9
South Carolina	100.0	24.8	18.1	25.4	15.7	16.0
Georgia	100.0	31.3	19.4	23.1	14.3	11.8
Florida	100.0	23.6	18.2	22.7	15.2	20.3
EAST SOUTH CENTRAL	100.0	26.3	19.7	26.0	14.7	13.2
Kentucky	100.0	29.6	24.4	23.9	11.3	10.8
Tennessee	100.0	29.7	21.6	25.8	12.4	10.5
Alabama	100.0	20.9	16.2	25.7	18.2	19.0
Mississippi	100.0	28.3	21.0	26.3	13.5	10.9
WEST SOUTH CENTRAL	100.0	31.8	20.5	23.9	12.8	11.0
Arkansas	100.0	35.8	23.5	22.4	10.7	7.5
Louisiana	100.0	25.5	18.7	25.3	15.2	15.4
Oklahoma	100.0	40.1	19.7	21.5	10.8	7.9
Texas	100.0	31.9	19.4	24.6	13.1	11.1
SELECTED NORTHERN STATES	100.0	41.9	20.1	20.6	10.5	6.9
New Jersey	100.0	16.3	21.1	35.0	15.4	12.2
Pennsylvania	100.0	22.6	16.5	29.6	19.1	12.2
Ohio	100.0	27.7	19.7	26.8	11.3	14.6
Indiana	100.0	25.1	23.0	24.6	12.3	15.0
Illinois	100.0	19.8	26.6	22.4	17.3	13.9
Missouri	100.0	48.6	19.6	19.0	8.7	4.0
Kansas	100.0	23.7	18.5	21.5	18.8	17.6

Source: "Colored Farm operators, by Years on Farm, and by Tenure, by Southern Divisions, and States, and Selected Northern States: 1930," *Negroes in the United States, 1920-1932*, 1935, pp. 607-608. Primary source: U.S. Bureau of the Census. *Negroes in the United States, 1920-1932.* Washington, D.C.: U.S. Government Printing Office, 1935.

★ 137 ★

Farms and Farmers

Number/Percent: Black Farm Laborers by Regions and Southern States, 1940

	Total of all farm laborers[1]	NEGROES			Per cent Negroes are of total farm laborers	Per cent of Negro total	Per cent of Negro farm laborers that were female
		Total	Males	Females			
United States	3,411,306	827,564	617,353	210,211	24.2	100	25.4
Northeastern States	278,579	7,724	7,365	359	27.7	0.9	4.6
North Central States	903,196	11,096	10,507	589	1.2	1.3	5.3
West	397,178	3,861	3,719	142	9.7	0.5	3.7
South	1,832,353	804,790	595,670	209,120	43.9	97.2	26.0
Alabama	145,973	82,098	54,377	27,721	56.2	10.2[2]	33.7
Arkansas	114,451	42,047	33,206	8,841	36.7	5.2	21.0
Delaware	6,534	2,584	2,519	65	39.5	.3	2.5
Florida	75,178	45,974	34,099	11,875	61.1	5.7	25.8
Georgia	111,479	102,764	76,859	25,905	57.9	12.8	25.2
Kentucky	111,976	11,055	10,949	106	9.8	1.4	1.0
Louisiana	111,004	72,327	55,436	16,891	65.1	9.0	23.3
Maryland	37,724	14,878	14,195	683	39.4	1.8	4.6
Mississippi	146,554	109,499	65,172	44,327	74.7	13.6	40.5
North Carolina	162,337	78,768	62,459	16,309	48.5	9.8	20.7
Oklahoma	72,982	7,069	6,714	355	9.6	.9	5.0
South Carolina	139,076	102,538	64,842	37,696	73.7	12.7	36.8
Tennessee	111,520	27,154	22,620	4,534	19.5	3.4	16.7
Texas	289,189	64,834	54,635	10,199	22.4	8.0	15.7
Virginia	97,225	40,502	36,895	3,607	41.6	5.0	8.9
West Virginia	32,866	699	693	6	2.1	.1	0.9

Source: "Number of Negro Farm Laborers in the United States by Regions and for the Southern States—1940," *Negro Year Book: A Review of Events Affecting Negro Life, 1941-1946,* 1947, p. 161. Primary source: Sixteenth Census of the United States: 1940. Population, Volume 111, The Labor Force, Part I, tables 62 and 63, Parts 2-5, table 13. Published by permission. *Notes:* 1. Includes employed persons (except on public emergency work) and experienced workers seeking work. 2. The percentages for the States are based on the total number of Negro farm laborers in the South.

★ 138 ★

Farms and Farmers

Number/Percent: Black Farmers in the South by State, 1900 and 1910

State	Number of Negroes on farms		Increase	Per cent increase
	1910	1900		
Alabama	353,906	279,480	74,426	26.6
Arkansas	177,491	117,571	59,920	51.0
Delaware	5,345	4,024	1,321	32.8
District of Columbia	403	400	3	.8
Florida	70,697	43,245	27,452	63.5
Georgia	411,086	277,970	133,116	47.9
Kentucky	37,537	38,222	685[1]	1.8[1]
Louisiana	211,873	189,969	21,868	11.5
Maryland	33,551	27,193	6,358	23.4
Mississippi	472,594	337,940	134,654	39.8
North Carolina	226,525	160,194	66,331	41.4
Oklahoma	34,259	30,402	3,857	12.7
South Carolina	351,927	267,326	84,601	31.6
Tennessee	109,848	90,337	19,511	21.6
Texas	217,930	145,555	72,375	49.7
Virginia	127,730	103,521	24,209	23.4
West Virginia	2,450	2,116	334	15.8

Source: [Untitled Table], *Negro Education: A Study of the Private and Higher Schools for Colored People in the United States,* vol. I. Bulletin, 1916, No. 38, 1917, p. 98. Primary source: U.S. Office of Education. *Negro Education: A Study of the Private and Higher Schools for Colored People in the United States,* vol. I. Bulletin, 1916, No. 38. Washington, D.C.: Government Printing Office, 1917. *Note:* 1. Decrease.

★ 139 ★

Farms and Farmers

Number/Percent: Black and White Farm Operators by Region, in 1930 and 1940, and Change, 1930-1940

RACE	NUMBER OF OPERATORS		INCREASE 1930 to 1940	
	1940	1930	Number	Per Cent
United States				
All classes	6,096,799	6,288,648	-191,849	-3.1
Negro	681,790	882,850	-201,060	-22.8
White	5,377,728	5,372,578	5,150	0.1
The North				
All classes	2,579,959	2,561,785	18,174	0.7
Negro	8,898	11,104	-2,206	-19.9
White	2,567,257	2,545,829	21,428	0.8

[Continued]

★ 139 ★

Number/Percent: Black and White Farm Operators by Region, in 1930 and 1940, and Change, 1930-1940
[Continued]

RACE	NUMBER OF OPERATORS		INCREASE 1930 to 1940	
	1940	1930	Number	Per Cent
The South				
All classes	3,007,170	3,223,816	-216,646	-6.7
Negro	672,214	870,936	-198,722	-22.8
White	2,326,904	2,342,129	-15,225	-0.7
The West				
All classes	509,670	503,047	6,623	1.3
Negro	678	810	-132	-16.3
White	483,567	484,620	-1,053	-0.2

Source: "Farm Operators, by Race, for the United States, by Regions: 1940 and 1930," *Negro Year Book: A Review of Events Affecting Negro Life, 1941-1946,* 1947, p. 154. Primary source: United States Bureau of the Census. Published by Permission. *Note:* A minus sign (-) denotes decrease.

★ 140 ★

Farms and Farmers

Number/Percent: Change in Farmers and Population by Location of Farm 1920-1930

SECTION AND DIVISION	INCREASE OR DECREASE (-) 1920-30				FARM OPERATORS PER 1,000 POPULATION			
	Farm operators		Percent		Negro		White[1]	
	Negro	White[1]	Negro	White[1]	1930	1920	1930	1920
United States	-42,858	-125,876	-4.6	-2.3	74	88	49	58
THE SOUTH	-44,659	58,379	-4.9	2.6	93	103	85	95
South Atlantic	-86,344	-15,055	-22.6	-1.9	67	88	67	80
East South Central	13,594	-3,113	4.4	-.4	121	122	103	117
West South Central	28,091	76,547	12.4	10.0	111	110	92	94
THE NORTH	1,724	-204,374	18.4	-7.4	5	6	36	44
THE WEST	77	20,119	10.5	4.3	7	9	45	54

Source: "Increase in Number of Negro and White Farm Operators, 1920 to 1930, with Number of Operators per 1,000 Population, by Sections, and Southern Divisions: 1930 and 1920," *Negroes in the United States, 1920-1932,* 1935, p. 576. Primary source: U.S. Bureau of the Census. *Negroes in the United States, 1920-1932.* Washington, D.C.: U.S. Government Printing Office, 1935. *Note:* 1. Includes Mexican and Hindus.

★ 141 ★

Farms and Farmers

Number/Percent: Change in Farmers and Population, 1920-1930

| RACIAL CLASS | INCREASE OR DECREASE (-) | | | | FARM OPERATORS PER 1,000 POPULATION | |
| | Number | | Percent | | | |
	Population	Farm operators	Population	Farm operators	1930	1920
All classes	17,064,426	-159,695	16.1	-2.5	51	61
Negro	1,428,012	-42,858	13.6	-4.6	74	88
White[1]	15,466,448	-125,876	16.3	-2.3	49	58
Indian	87,960	10,137	36.0	60.8	81	68
Japanese	27,824	-1,052	25.1	-15.3	42	62
Chinese	13,315	-133	21.6	-21.8	6	10
All other nonwhite	40,867	87	585.4	...	2	...

Source: "Increase in Population and Number of Farm operators, by Racial Classes, with Number of per 1,000 Population of Each Class, for the United States: 1930 and 1920," *Negroes in the United States, 1920-1932*, 1935, p. 575. Primary source: U.S. Bureau of the Census. *Negroes in the United States, 1920-1932.* Washington, D.C.: U.S. Government Printing Office, 1935. *Note:* 1. Includes Mexicans and Hindus.

★ 142 ★

Farms and Farmers

Number/Percent: Counties Reporting Black Inhabitants and Black Farmers by State, 1930

| STATE | Total number of counties | COUNTIES REPORTING | |
		Negro inhabitants	Negro farmers
United States	3,100[1]	2,855	2,119
Alabama	67	67	66
Arizona	14	13	9
Arkansas	75	72	63
California	58	57	36
Colorado	63	54	20
Connecticut	8	8	8
Delaware	3	3	3
District of Columbia	1	1	1
Florida	67	67	65
Georgia	161	160	158
Idaho	44	30	9
Illinois	102	96	60
Indiana	92	86	60
Iowa	99	87	32
Kansas	105	99	78
Kentucky	120	120	114

[Continued]

★ 142 ★

Number/Percent: Counties Reporting Black Inhabitants and Black Farmers by State, 1930

[Continued]

STATE	Total number of counties	COUNTIES REPORTING	
		Negro inhabitants	Negro farmers
Louisiana	64	64	64
Maine	16	16	8
Maryland	24	24	22
Massachusetts	14	14	11
Michigan	83	76	56
Minnesota	87	71	18
Mississippi	82	82	82
Missouri	115	103	83
Montana	56	45	14
Nebraska	93	65	21
Nevada	17	15	3
New Hampshire	10	10	5
New Jersey	21	21	18
New Mexico	31	28	9
New York	62	62	44
North Carolina	100	100	99
North Dakota	53	33	10
Ohio	88	87	82
Oklahoma	77	73	71
Oregon	36	32	6
Pennsylvania	67	66	44
Rhode Island	5	5	4
South Carolina	46	46	46
South Dakota	69	45	23
Tennessee	95	95	92
Texas	254	243	189
Utah	29	13	2
Vermont	14	13	11
Virginia	124	124	106
Washington	39	33	20
West Virginia	55	54	39
Wisconsin	71	55	27
Wyoming	24	22	8

Source: "Number of Counties Reporting Negro Inhabitants and Negro Farmers, by States: 1930," Negroes in the United States, 1920-1932, 1935, p. 575. Primary source: U.S. Bureau of the Census. Negroes in the United States, 1920-1932. Washington, D.C.: U.S. Government Printing Office, 1935. Notes: 1. Includes Baltimore city, St. Louis city, 24 independent cities in Virginia, and that part of Yellowstone National Park located in Wyoming.

★ 143 ★

Farms and Farmers

Number/Percent: Employment in Agriculture in the U.S. and the South, 1940 and 1950

| Year | United States | | | | South | | | |
| | Total | | Nonwhite | | Total | | Nonwhite | |
	Number	Per Cent of all Employed	Number	Per Cent of all Employed	Number	Per Cent of all Employed	Number	Per Cent of all Employed
1940	8,372,222	18.7	1,541,807	33.1	4,342,096	31.8	1,449,023	40.4
1950	7,138,000	12.8	1,078,000	20.1	3,408,000	20.6	1,013,000	29.2

Source: "Agricultural Employment: 1940 and 1950," *1952 Negro Year Book: A Review of Events Affecting Negro Life,* 1952, p. 101. Primary source: U.S. Bureau of the Census, *Employment and Income in the United States, By Regions: 1950,* 1950 Census of Population, Preliminary Reports, Series PC-7, No. 2, Table 8. Published by permission.

★ 144 ★

Farms and Farmers

Number/Percent: Farmers and Population, 1900 and 1910

| RACIAL CLASS | POPULATION | | FARM OPERATORS | |
	1910	1900	1910	1900
	NUMBER			
All classes	91,972,266	75,994,575	6,361,502	5,737,372
Negro	9,827,763	8,833,934	893,370	746,715
White	81,731,957	66,809,196	5,440,619	4,969,608
Indian	265,683	237,196	24,251	19,910
Chinese	71,531	89,863	760	1,100
Japanese	72,157	24,326	2,502	39
Other	3,175	...	...	...
	PERCENTAGE DISTRIBUTION BY RACIAL CLASS			
All classes	100.0	100.0	100.0	100.0
Negro	10.7	11.6	14.0	13.0
White	88.9	87.6	85.5	86.6
Indian	0.3	0.3	0.4	0.3
Chinese	0.1	0.1	[1]	[1]
Japanese	0.1	[1]	[1]	[1]
Other	[1]	...	...	...

Source: [Untitled Table], *Negro Population, 1790-1915,* 1918, p. 553. Primary source: U.S. Bureau of the Census. *Negro Population, 1790-1915.* Washington, D.C.: Government Printing Office, 1918. *Note:* 1. Less than one-tenth of 1 per cent.

★ 145 ★

Farms and Farmers

Number/Percent: Farmers and Population, 1920 and 1930

RACIAL CLASS	POPULATION		FARM OPERATORS	
	1930	1920	1930	1920

NUMBER

All classes	122,770,046	105,710,620	6,288,648	6,448,343
Negro	11,891,143	10,463,131	882,850	925,708
White[1]	110,289,870	94,823,422	5,372,578	5,498,454
Indian	332,397	244,437	26,817	16,680
Japanese	138,834	111,010	5,840	6,892
Chinese	74,954	61,639	476	609
All other nonwhite	47,848	6,981	87	...

PERCENT DISTRIBUTION

All classes	100.0	100.0	100.0	100.0
Negro	9.7	9.9	14.0	14.4
White[1]	89.8	89.7	85.4	85.3
Indian	.3	.2	.4	.3
Japanese	.1	.1	.1	.1
Chinese	.1	.1	[2]	[2]
All other nonwhite	[2]	[2]	[2]	...

Source: "Population and Farm Operators, by Racial Classes, for the United States: 1930 and 1920," *Negroes in the United States, 1920-1932*, 1935, p. 575. Primary source: U.S. Bureau of the Census. *Negroes in the United States, 1920-1932*. Washington, D.C.: U.S. Government Printing Office, 1935. *Notes:* 1. Includes Mexicans and Hindus. 2. Less than 1/10 of 1 percent.

★ 146 ★

Farms and Farmers

Number/Percent: Farmers by Geographic Division, 1900 and 1910 - I

DIVISION AND STATE	FARM OPERATORS									
	1910					1900				
	Total	Colored			White	Total	Colored			White
		Total	Negro	Other			Total	Negro	Other	
UNITED STATES	6,361,502	920,883	893,370	27,513	5,440,619	5,737,372	767,764	746,715	21,049	4,969,608
GEOGRAPHIC DIVISIONS										
New England	188,802	342	310	32	188,460	191,888	294	264	30	191,594
Middle Atlantic	468,379	1,961	1,310	651	466,418	485,618	1,846	1,497	349	483,772
East North Central	1,123,489	5,717	4,843	874	1,117,772	1,135,823	6,013	5,179	834	1,129,810
West North Central	1,109,948	9,864	5,589	4,275	1,100,084	1,060,744	10,887	7,076	3,811	1,049,857
South Atlantic	1,111,881	355,862	354,530	1,332	756,019	962,225	288,871	287,933	938	673,354
East South Central	1,042,480	325,218	324,884	334	717,262	903,313	267,805	267,530	365	635,418

[Continued]

★ 146 ★

Number/Percent: Farmers by Geographic Division, 1900 and 1910 - I

[Continued]

DIVISION AND STATE	FARM OPERATORS									
	1910					1900				
	Total	Colored			White	Total	Colored			White
		Total	Negro	Other			Total	Negro	Other	
West South Central	943,186	209,061	201,422	7,639	734,125	754,853	183,904	176,899	7,005	570,949
Mountain	183,446	8,028	219	7,809	175,418	101,327	4,806	133	4,673	96,521
Pacific	189,891	4,830	263	4,567	185,061	141,581	3,248	204	3,044	138,333

Source: "Number of Colored, Negro, and White Farm Operators, by Divisions and States: 1910 and 1900," *Negro Population, 1790-1915,* 1918, p. 588. Primary source: U.S. Bureau of the Census. *Negro Population, 1790-1915.* Washington, D.C.: Government Printing Office, 1918.

★ 147 ★

Farms and Farmers

Number/Percent: Farmers by Geographic Division, 1900 and 1910 - II

DIVISION AND STATE	FARM OPERATORS Increase: 1900-1910[1]		NEGRO FARM OPERATORS		
			Per 1,000 Negro population		Per 1,000 colored operators: 1910
	Negro	White	1910	1900	
UNITED STATES	146,655	471,011	91	76	970
GEOGRAPHIC DIVISIONS					
New England	46	-3,134	5	4	906
Middle Atlantic	-187	-17,354	3	5	668
East North Central	-336	-12,038	16	20	847
West North Central	-1,487	50,227	23	30	567
South Atlantic	66,597	82,665	86	77	996
East South Central	57,354	81,844	122	107	999
West South Central	24,523	163,176	102	104	963
Mountain	86	78,897	10	9	27
Pacific	59	46,728	9	14	54

Source: "Number of Colored, Negro, and White Farm Operators, by Divisions and States: 1910 and 1900," *Negro Population, 1790-1915,* 1918, p. 588. Primary source: U.S. Bureau of the Census. *Negro Population, 1790-1915.* Washington, D.C.: Government Printing Office, 1918. *Note:* 1. A minus sign (-) denotes decrease.

★ 148 ★

Farms and Farmers

Number/Percent: Farmers by Location of Farm, 1900 and 1910

| SECTION AND DIVISION | FARM OPERATORS | | | |
| | Negro | | White | |
	1910	1900	1910	1900
NUMBER				
United States	893,370	746,715	5,440,619	4,969,608
The South	880,836	732,362	2,207,406	1,879,721
South Atlantic	354,530	287,933	756,019	673,354
East South Central	324,884	267,530	717,262	635,418
West South Central	201,422	176,899	734,125	570,949
The North	12,052	14,016	2,872,734	2,855,033
The West	482	337	360,479	234,854
PERCENTAGE DISTRIBUTION BY SECTIONS AND DIVISIONS				
United States	100.0	100.0	100.0	100.0
The South	98.6	98.1	40.6	37.8
South Atlantic	39.7	38.6	13.9	13.5
East South Central	36.4	35.8	13.2	12.8
West South Central	22.5	23.7	13.5	11.5
The North	1.3	1.9	52.8	57.4
The West	0.1	[1]	6.6	4.7

Source: "Farm Operators," *Negro Population, 1790-1915*, 1918, p. 554. Primary source: U.S. Bureau of the Census. *Negroes in the United States, 1790-1915*. Washington, D.C.: U.S. Government Printing Office, 1918. *Note:* 1. Less than 1/10 of 1 per cent.

★ 149 ★

Farms and Farmers

Number/Percent: Increase in Farmers and in Population, 1900-1910

| RACIAL CLASS | INCREASE: 1900-1910[1] | | | | FARM OPERATORS PER 1,000 POPULATION OF EACH CLASS | |
| | Number | | Per cent | | | |
	Population	Farm operators	Population	Farm operators	1910	1900
All classes	15,977,691	624,130	21.0	10.9	69	76
Negro	993,769	146,655	11.2	19.6	91	85
White	14,922,761	471,011	22.3	9.5	67	74
Indian	28,487	4,341	12.0	21.8	91	84
Chinese	-18,332	-340	-20.4	-30.9	11	12

[Continued]

★ 149 ★

Number/Percent: Increase in Farmers and in Population, 1900-1910

[Continued]

| RACIAL CLASS | INCREASE: 1900-1910[1] | | | | FARM OPERATORS PER 1,000 POPULATION OF EACH CLASS | |
| | Number | | Per cent | | | |
	Population	Farm operators	Population	Farm operators	1910	1900
Japanese	47,831	2,463	196.6	6,315.4	35	2
Other	3,175	...	...	...	...	...

Source: "Increase: 1900-1910," *Negro Population, 1790-1915*, 1918, p. 553. Primary source: U.S. Bureau of the Census. *Negro Population, 1790-1915.* Washington, D.C.: Government Printing Office, 1918. *Note:* 1. A minus sign (-) denotes decrease.

★ 150 ★

Farms and Farmers

Number/Percent: Minority Farm Operators by Location of Farm 1930

SECTION, DIVISION, AND STATE	Total	Negro	Indian	Japanese	Chinese	Other nonwhite[1]	Percent Negro of total colored
United States	916,070	882,850	26,817	5,840	476	87	96.37
The North	15,956	11,104	4,753	83	13	3	69.59
The South	881,687	870,936	10,637	87	26	1	98.78
The West	18,427	810	11,427	5,670	437	83	4.39
NEW ENGLAND	159	148	7	1	2	1	93.08
Maine	17	15	2	...	...	...	88.23
New Hampshire	8	6	1	...	1	...	75.00
Vermont	22	22	...	...	...	...	100.00
Massachusetts	64	63	...	...	...	1	98.43
Rhode Island	11	9	2	...	...	...	81.81
Connecticut	37	33	2	1	1	...	89.18
MIDDLE ATLANTIC	1,207	873	314	10	10	...	72.32
New York	460	148	303	6	3	...	32.17
New Jersey	384	372	2	4	6	...	96.87
Pennsylvania	363	353	9	...	1	...	97.24
EAST NORTH CENTRAL	3,488	3,065	406	10	1	1	87.99
Ohio	1,237	1,229	6	2	...	...	99.35
Indiana	475	461	10	4	...	...	97.05
Illinois	894	893	1	...	...	...	99.88
Michigan	561	427	131	1	1	1	76.11
Wisconsin	316	55	258	3	...	...	17.40
WEST NORTH CENTRAL	11,107	7,018	4,026	62	...	1	63.18
Minnesota	245	27	217	1	...	...	11.02
Iowa	154	118	35	1	...	...	76.62
Missouri	5,861	5,844	14	2	...	1	99.70

[Continued]

★ 150 ★

Number/Percent: Minority Farm Operators by Location of Farm 1930
[Continued]

SECTION, DIVISION, AND STATE	Total	Negro	Indian	Japanese	Chinese	Other nonwhite[1]	Percent Negro of total colored
North Dakota	801	10	791	...	...	...	1.24
South Dakota	2,740	40	2,698	2	...	...	1.45
Nebraska	270	38	176	56	...	...	14.07
Kansas	1,036	941	85	...	...	...	90.83

Source: "Number of Colored Farm Operators by Race, by Sections, Divisions, and States: 1930," *Negroes in the United States, 1920-1932*, 1935, p. 582. Primary source: U.S. Bureau of the Census. *Negroes in the United States, 1920-1932*. Washington, D.C.: U.S. Government Printing Office, 1935. *Note:* 1. Includes 56 Filipinos, 30 Koreans, and 1 Hawaiian.

★ 151 ★

Farms and Farmers

Number/Percent: Minority Farm Operators by Location of Farm in 1930 and 1940, and Change 1930-1940

DIVISION AND STATE	Number		Increase or decrease (-)	
	1940	1930	Number	Percent
United States	719,971	916,070	-196,999	-21.5
The North	12,702	15,956	-3,254	-20.4
The South	680,266	881,687	-201,421	-22.8
The West	26,103	18,427	7,676	41.7
New England	563	159	404	254.1
Maine	18	17	1	5.9
New Hamsphire	2	8	-6	-75.0
Vermont	12	22	-10	-45.4
Massachusetts	481	64	417	651.6
Rhode Island	5	11	-6	-54.5
Connecticut	45	37	8	21.6
Middle Atlantic	1,337	1,207	130	10.8
New York	567	460	107	23.3
New Jersey	448	384	64	16.7
Pennsylvania	322	363	-41	-11.3
East North Central	3,329	3,483	-154	-4.4
Ohio	1,099	1,237	-138	-11.2
Indiana	380	475	-95	-20.0
Illinois	785	894	-109	-12.2
Michigan	761	561	200	35.6
Wisconsin	304	316	-12	-3.8
West North Central	7,473	11,107	-3,634	-32.7
Minnesota	294	245	49	20.0
Iowa	127	154	-27	-17.5

[Continued]

★ 151 ★

Number/Percent: Minority Farm Operators by Location of Farm in 1930 and 1940, and Change 1930-1940
[Continued]

DIVISION AND STATE	Number		Increase or decrease (-)	
	1940	1930	Number	Percent
Missouri	3,690	5,861	-2,171	-37.0
North Dakota	593	801	-208	-26.0
South Dakota	1,741	2,740	-999	-36.5
Nebraska	283	270	13	4.8
Kansas	745	1,036	-291	-28.1
South Atlantic	230,906	298,379	-67,473	-22.6
Delaware	625	807	-182	-22.6
Maryland	4,051	5,267	-1,216	-23.1
District of Columbia	4	11	-7	-63.6
Virginia	35,090	39,673	-4,583	-11.6
West Virginia	671	491	180	36.7
North Carolina	60,268	76,873	-16,605	-21.6
South Carolina	61,307	77,425	-16,118	-20.8
Georgia	59,132	86,789	-27,657	-31.9
Florida	9,758	11,043	-1,285	-11.6
East South Central	266,426	320,959	-54,533	-17.0
Kentucky	5,547	9,104	-3,557	-39.1
Tennessee	27,975	35,138	-7,163	-20.4
Alabama	73,364	93,829	-20,465	-21.8
Mississippi	159,540	192,888	-23,348	-12.8
West South Central	182,934	262,349	-79,415	-30.3
Arkansas	57,025	79,579	-22,554	-28.3
Louisiana	59,584	73,770	-14,186	-19.2
Oklahoma	13,372	22,937	-9,365	-40.8
Texas	52,753	86,063	-33,310	-38.7
Mountain	17,243	10,923	6,320	57.9
Montana	1,076	1,184	-108	-9.1
Idaho	566	698	-132	-18.9
Wyoming	303	263	40	15.2
Colorado	402	601	-199	-33.1
New Mexico	5,564	3,345	2,219	66.3
Arizona	8,229	3,953	4,276	108.2
Utah	677	568	109	19.2
Nevada	426	311	115	37.0
Pacific	8,860	7,504	1,356	18.1
Washington	1,507	1,349	158	11.7
Oregon	623	683	-60	-8.8
California	6,730	5,472	1,258	23.0

Source: "Number of Non-white Farm Operators by Sections, Divisions, and States: 1940-1930," *The Negro Handbook*, 1942, p. 214. Primary source: U.S. Bureau of the Census. Published by permission.

★ 152 ★

Farms and Farmers

Number/Percent: Number of Blacks Farms, 1910 and 1930, and Change for 1910-1930 by Location of Farm

SECTION AND DIVISION	NUMBER OF NEGRO FARM OPERATORS			
	1930	1910	Increase or decrease (-) 1910-30	
			Number	Percent
United States	882,850	893,870	10,520	-1.2
The North	11,104	12,052	-948	-7.9
The South	870,936	880,836	-9,900	-1.1
The West	810	482	328	68.0
New England	148	310	-162	-52.3
Middle Atlantic	873	1,310	-437	-33.4
East North Central	3,065	4,843	-1,778	-36.7
West North Central	7,018	5,589	1,429	25.6
South Atlantic	295,934	354,530	-58,596	-16.5
East South Central	320,600	324,884	-4,284	-1.3
West South Central	254,402	201,422	52,980	26.3
Mountain	304	219	85	38.8
Pacific	506	263	243	92.4

Source: "Farm Operated by Negroes—Number, Farm Acreage, and Value of Land and Buildings, by Sections, Divisions, and States: 1930 and 1910," *Negroes in the United States, 1920-1932*, 1935, p. 601. Primary source: U.S. Bureau of the Census. *Negroes in the United States, 1920-1932*. Washington, D.C.: U.S. Government Printing Office, 1935.

★ 153 ★

Farms and Farmers

Number/Percent: Trends in Black Wage Farm Laborers in the U.S. and in the South, 1930-1945

	1930	1940	1945
United States			
Negroes	529,307	483,785	483,000[1]
Whites	2,008,038	1,410,175	1,150,000
Total	2,732,972	1,924,890	1,633,000
Per cent Negroes	19.7	25.1	29.6
South			
Negroes	...	468,126	459,000[1]
Whites	...	494,918	404,000

[Continued]

★ 153 ★

Number/Percent: Trends in Black Wage Farm Laborers in the U.S. and in the South, 1930-1945

[Continued]

	1930	1940	1945
Total	...	965,464	863,000
Per cent Negroes	...	48.5	53.2

Source: "Number of Negro Wage Farm Laborers in the United States, and in the South, 1930, 1940, and 1945," *Negro Year Book: A Review of Events Affecting Negro Life, 1941-1946*, 1947, p. 158. Primary source: The figures for 1930 were taken from the Fifteenth Census of the United States: 1930, Population, Volume 4; those for 1940, from the Sixteenth Census of the United States 1940, Population - Volume 111, Part 1, tables 62 and 63; Parts 2-5, table 13; those for 1945 from Survey of Negroes and Negro Wage Rates in Agriculture, Report number 4, Bureau of Agricultural Economics, U.S.D.A., October, 1945. *Notes:* 1. Includes all non-whites, but in the South almost all non-whites are Negroes.

★ 154 ★

Farms and Farmers

Number/Percent: Trends in Number of Black Farmers by State, 1900-1910 and 1910-1920

Divisions and States	1900	1910	1920	Increase 1900-1910	Increase 1900-1920
New England	264	310	242	46	-68
Maine	24	28	13	4	-15
New Hampshire	10	14	14	4	...
Vermont	8	20	28	12	8
Massachusetts	87	103	103	16	...
Rhode Island	28	40	19	12	-21
Connecticut	107	105	65	-2	-40
Middle Atlantic	1,497	1,310	1,227	-187	83
New York	443	295	245	-148	-50
New Jersey	469	472	531	3	59
Pennsylvania	585	543	451	-42	-92
East North Central	5,179	4,843	3,674	-336	-1,169
Ohio	1,966	1,948	1,616	-18	-332
Indiana	1,043	785	570	-258	-215
Illinois	1,486	1,422	892	-64	-530
Michigan	626	640	549	14	-91
Wisconsin	58	48	47	-10	-1
West North Central	7,076	5,589	4,237	-1,487	-1,352
Minnesota	31	29	33	-2	33
Iowa	200	187	109	-13	-78
Missouri	4,950	3,656	2,824	-1,294	-832
North Dakota	18	22	26	4	4
South Dakota	17	67	47	50	-20
Nebraska	78	96	63	18	-33

[Continued]

★ 154 ★

Number/Percent: Trends in Number of Black Farmers by State, 1900-1910 and 1910-1920

[Continued]

Divisions and States	1900	1910	1920	Increase 1900-1910	Increase 1900-1920
Kansas	1,782	1,532	1,135	-250	-397
South Atlantic	287,933	354,530	382,278	66,597	27,748
Delaware	817	922	872	105	-50
Maryland	5,842	6,370	6,208	528	-168
District of Columbia	17	12	20	-5	2
Virginia	44,795	48,039	47,690	3,244	-349
West Virginia	742	707	504	35	-203
North Carolina	53,996	64,456	74,849	10,460	10,393
South Carolina	85,381	96,772	109,005	11,391	12,233
Georgia	82,822	122,559	130,176	39,737	7,617
Florida	13,521	14,721	12,954	1,200	1,767
East South Central	267,530	324,884	307,006	57,354	17,878
Kentucky	11,227	11,709	12,624	482	915
Tennessee	33,883	38,300	38,181	4,417	-119
Alabama	94,069	110,387	95,200	16,318	-15,187
Mississippi	128,351	164,488	161,001	36,137	-3,487
West South Central	176,899	201,422	226,311	24,523	24,889
Arkansas	46,978	63,578	72,275	16,600	8,697
Louisiana	58,096	54,819	62,036	-3,277	7,217
Oklahoma	6,353	13,209	13,403	6,856	194
Texas	65,472	69,816	78,597	4,344	8,781
Mountain	133	219	349	86	130
Montana	21	29	31	8	2
Idaho	9	13	23	4	10
Wyoming	2	19	17	17	-2
Colorado	58	81	148	23	67
New Mexico	14	48	32	34	-16
Arizona	15	12	32	-3	20
Utah	11	11	61	...	50
Nevada	3	6	5	3	-1
Pacific	204	263	384	59	121
Washington	55	77	79	22	2
Oregon	14	27	15	13	-12
California	135	159	290	24	131

Source: "Total Negro Farmers by States, 1900, 1910, 1920, with Increase 1900- 1910 and 1910-1920," *Negro Year Book: An Annual Encyclopedia of the Negro, 1925-1926,* 1925, p. 374. Primary source: U.S. Bureau of the Census. Published by permission.

★ 155 ★

Farms and Farmers

Owner Status: Black Farmers in 1900 and 1910, by Owner Status and Farm Location - I

DIVISION	1910				1900			
	Total	Owners	Tenants	Managers	Total	Owners	Tenants	Managers
UNITED STATES	893,370	218,972	672,964	1,434	746,715	187,797	557,174	1,744
GEOGRAPHIC DIVISIONS:								
New England	310	240	51	19	264	197	54	13
Middle Atlantic	1,310	793	447	70	1,497	953	490	54
East North Central	4,843	3,095	1,677	71	5,179	3,064	2,070	45
West North Central	5,589	3,370	2,155	64	7,076	3,908	3,104	64
South Atlantic	354,530	101,135	252,676	719	287,933	84,389	202,578	966
East South Central	324,884	58,610	266,025	249	267,530	49,888	217,318	324
West South Central	201,422	51,342	149,858	222	176,899	45,141	131,487	271
Mountain	219	176	34	9	133	104	26	3
Pacific	263	211	41	11	204	153	47	4

Source: "Negro Farmers—Owners, Tenants, and Managers, by Divisions and States: 1910 and 1900," *Negro Population, 1790-1915*, 1918, p. 607. Primary source: U.S. Bureau of the Census. *Negro Population, 1790-1915*. Washington, D.C.: Government Printing Office, 1918.

★ 156 ★

Farms and Farmers

Owner Status: Black Farmers in 1900 and 1910, by Owner Status and Farm Location - II

[A minus sign (-) denotes decrease.]

DIVISION	INCREASE DURING DECADE							
	Total		Owners		Tenants		Managers	
	Number	Percent	Number	Percent	Number	Percent	Number	Percent
UNITED STATES	146,655	19.6	31,175	16.6	115,790	20.8	-310	-17.8
GEOGRAPHIC DIVISIONS:								
New England	46	17.4	43	21.8	-3	[1]	6	[1]
Middle Atlantic	-187	-12.5	-160	-16.8	-43	-8.8	16	[1]
East North Central	-336	-6.5	31	1.0	-393	-19.0	26	[1]
West North Central	-1,487	-21.0	-538	-13.8	-949	-30.6	-	-
South Atlantic	66,597	23.1	16,746	19.8	50,098	24.7	-247	-25.6
East South Central	57,354	21.4	8,722	17.5	48,707	22.4	-75	-23.1
West South Central	24,523	13.9	6,201	13.7	18,371	14.0	-49	-18.1
Mountain	86	64.7	72	69.2	8	[1]	6	[1]
Pacific	59	28.9	58	37.9	-6	[1]	7	[1]

Source: "Negro Farmers—Owners, Tenants, and Managers, by Divisions and States: 1910 and 1900," *Negro Population, 1790-1915*, 1918, p. 607. Primary source: U.S. Bureau of the Census. *Negro Population, 1790-1915*. Washington, D.C.: Government Printing Office, 1918. *Note:* 1. Per cent not shown where base is less than 100.

★ 157 ★

Farms and Farmers

Owner Status: Black Farms in 1900 and 1910, by Owner Status and Region

[A minus sign (-) denotes decrease.]

TENURE	1910	1900	Increase 1900-1910[1]	Percentage distribution by tenure	
				1910	1900
UNITED STATES					
Total	893,370	746,715	146,655	100.0	100.0
Owners	218,972	187,797	31,175	24.5	25.1
Tenants	672,964	557,174	115,790	75.3	74.6
Managers	1,434	1,744	-310	0.2	0.2
THE SOUTH					
Total	880,836	732,362	148,474	100.0	100.0
Owners	211,087	179,418	31,669	24.0	24.5
Tenants	668,559	551,383	117,176	75.9	75.3
Managers	1,190	1,561	-371	0.1	0.2
THE NORTH					
Total	12,052	14,016	-1,964	100.0	100.0
Owners	7,498	8,122	-624	62.2	57.9
Tenants	4,330	5,718	-1,388	35.9	40.8
Managers	224	176	48	1.9	1.3
THE WEST					
Total	482	337	145	100.0	100.0
Owners	387	257	130	80.3	76.3
Tenants	75	73	2	15.6	21.7
Managers	20	7	13	4.1	2.1

Source: "Negro Farm Operators," *Negro Population, 1790-1915,* 1918, p. 572. Primary source: U.S. Bureau of the Census. *Negro Population, 1790-1915.* Washington, D.C.: Government Printing Office, 1918.

★ 158 ★

Farms and Farmers

Owner Status: Black Farms, by Owner Status, Region, and Division, 1930 - I

SECTION, AND DIVISION	Total number	OWNERS		TENANTS			Managers
		Full	Part	Cash	Cropper	Other	
United States	882,850	139,114	41,902	98,246	394,928	207,737	923
The North	11,104	3,335	1,089	669	3,310	2,609	92
The South	870,936	135,394	40,736	97,495	391,547	204,959	805
The West	810	385	77	82	71	169	26
New England	148	119	9	9	2	3	6
Middle Atlantic	873	527	41	111	39	124	31
East North Central	3,065	1,453	439	259	192	698	24
West North Central	7,018	1,236	600	290	3,077	1,784	31
South Atlantic	295,934	60,017	19,666	29,277	123,478	63,019	477
East South Central	320,600	39,311	11,164	53,365	150,075	66,545	140
West South Central	254,402	36,066	9,906	14,853	117,994	75,395	188
Mountain	304	142	41	19	34	62	6
Pacific	506	243	36	63	37	107	20

Source: "Number of Farms Operated by Negroes, by Tenure, by Sections, Divisions, and States: 1930," *Negroes in the United States, 1920-1932*, 1935, p. 583. Primary source: U.S. Bureau of the Census. *Negroes in the United States, 1920-1932.* Washington, D.C.: U.S. Government Printing Office, 1935.

★ 159 ★

Farms and Farmers

Owner Status: Black Farms, by Owner Status, Region, and Division, 1930 - II

[Percent not shown when less than 1/10 of 1 percent]

SECTION, AND DIVISION	PERCENT DISTRIBUTION					
	Owners		Tenants			Managers
	Full	Part	Cash	Cropper	Other	
United States	15.8	4.7	11.1	44.7	23.5	0.1
The North	30.0	9.8	6.0	29.8	23.5	.8
The South	15.5	4.7	11.2	45.0	23.5	.1
The West	47.5	9.5	10.2	8.8	20.9	3.2
New England	80.4	6.1	6.1	1.4	2.0	4.1
Middle Atlantic	60.4	4.7	12.7	4.5	14.2	3.6
East North Central	47.4	14.3	8.5	6.3	22.8	.8
West North Central	17.6	8.5	4.1	43.8	25.4	.4
South Atlantic	20.3	6.6	9.9	41.7	21.3	.2
East South Central	12.3	3.5	16.6	46.8	20.8	-
West South Central	14.2	3.9	5.8	46.4	29.6	.1

[Continued]

★ 159 ★

Owner Status: Black Farms, by Owner Status, Region, and Division, 1930 - II
[Continued]

SECTION, AND DIVISION	PERCENT DISTRIBUTION					
	Owners		Tenants			Managers
	Full	Part	Cash	Cropper	Other	
Mountain	46.7	13.5	6.3	11.2	20.4	2.0
Pacific	48.0	7.1	12.5	7.3	21.1	4.0

Source: "Number of Farms Operated by Negroes, by Tenure, by Sections, Divisions, and States: 1930," *Negroes in the United States, 1920-1932*, 1935, p. 583. Primary source: U.S. Bureau of the Census. *Negroes in the United States, 1920-1932.* Washington, D.C.: U.S. Government Printing Office, 1935.

★ 160 ★

Farms and Farmers

Owner Status: Black-Operated Farms, by Owner Status, Region, and Division, 1920 and 1930

SECTION AND DIVISION	NUMBER OF NEGRO FARM OPERATORS							
	Total		Owner		Tenants		Managers	
	1930	1920	1930	1920	1930	1920	1930	1920
United States	882,850	926,708	181,016	218,612	700,911	705,070	923	2,026
The North	11,104	9,330	4,424	5,749	6,588	3,389	92	242
The South	870,936	915,595	176,130	212,365	694,001	701,471	805	1,759
The West	810	733	462	498	322	210	26	25
New England	148	242	128	192	14	33	6	17
Middle Atlantic	873	1,227	568	697	274	444	31	86
East North Central	3,065	3,674	1,892	2,335	1,149	1,273	24	66
West North Central	7,018	4,237	1,836	2,525	5,151	1,639	31	73
South Atlantic	295,934	382,278	79,683	102,056	215,774	279,266	477	956
East South Central	320,600	307,006	50,475	55,488	269,985	251,112	140	406
West South Central	254,402	226,311	45,972	54,821	208,242	171,093	188	397
Mountain	304	349	183	239	115	100	6	10
Pacific	506	384	279	259	207	110	20	15

Source: "Farms Operated by Negroes—Number, Farm Acreage, and Value of Land and Buildings, by Tenure, by Sections, Divisions, and States: 1930 and 1920," *Negroes in the United States, 1920-1932*, 1935, pp. 596-597. Primary source: U.S. Bureau of the Census. *Negroes in the United States, 1920-1932.* Washington, D.C.: U.S. Government Printing Office, 1935.

★ 161 ★

Farms and Farmers

Owner Status: Change in Black Farmers, by Owner Status and Region, 1900-1910 and 1910-1920

Class Farmers	NORTH						
	1900	1910	Increase 1900-1910		1920	Increase 1910-1920	
			Number	Per Ct		Number	Per Cent
Total	14,016	12,052	-1,914	-14.1	9,380	-2,572	-22.2
Owners	8,122	7,498	-624	-7.7	5,749	-1,649	-21.8
Managers	176	224	48	27.2	242	18	8.0
Tenants	5,718	4,330	-1,338	-24.3	3,389	-941	-21.7
	WEST						
Total	337	482	145	43.2	733	251	152.0
Owners	257	387	130	50.6	498	111	28.7
Managers	7	20	13	-	25	5	-
Tenants	73	75	2	-	210	135	-
	SOUTH						
Total	732,362	880,836	148,474	20.3	915,595	34,759	3.9
Owners	179,418	211,087	31,669	17.3	212,365	1,278	0.6
Managers	1,561	1,190	-371	-23.7	1,759	569	47.8
Tenants	551,383	668,559	117,176	21.2	701,471	32,912	4.9

Source: "Increase and Decrease by Sections of Country of Classes of Negro Farmers 1900-1910 and 1910-1920," *Negro Year Book: An Annual Encyclopedia of the Negro, 1925-1926,* 1925, p. 370. Primary source: Work, Monroe N. (Ed.), *Negro Year Book: An Annual Encyclopedia of the Negro, 1925-1926.* Tuskegee Institute, Ala.: The Negro Year Book Pub. Co., 1925.

★ 162 ★

Farms and Farmers

Owner Status: Change in Number Nonwhite Owners (Part and Full) and Tenants on Southern Farms from 1930 to 1940, by State

DIVISION AND STATE	Total 1940	Increase or decrease (-) percent	Full owners		Part owners		Tenants			
							Total 1940	Increase or decrease (-) percent	Croppers	
			1940	Increase or decrease (-) percent	1940	Increase or decrease (-) percent			1940	Increase or decrease (-) percent
Southern States	680,266	-22.8	141,902	1.0	31,361	-24.5	506,638	-27.5	299,118	-23.9
South Atlantic	230,906	-22.6	61,881	1.9	14,275	-27.9	154,544	-28.9	85,746	-30.9
Delaware	625	-22.6	301	-2.6	44	-31.2	272	-34.5	49	-18.3
Maryland	4,051	-23.1	2,059	-12.8	212	-63.4	1,758	-20.3	562	-5.9
District of Columbia	4	-63.6	1	-85.7	-	-100.0	2	-	-	-
Virginia	35,090	-11.6	18,930	-1.4	3,320	-36.7	12,804	-15.5	5,897	-13.2
West Virginia	671	36.7	396	20.7	31	-31.1	239	115.3	9	-60.9
North Carolina	60,268	-21.6	13,937	5.6	4,308	-33.8	41,994	-26.5	26,803	-23.0
South Carolina	61,307	-20.8	13,145	10.1	3,939	-2.9	44,194	-28.0	22,061	-28.9

[Continued]

★ 162 ★

Owner Status: Change in Number Nonwhite Owners (Part and Full) and Tenants on Southern Farms from 1930 to 1940, by State

[Continued]

DIVISION AND STATE	Total 1940	Increase or decrease (-) percent	Full owners		Part owners		Tenants				
			1940	Increase or decrease (-) percent	1940	Increase or decrease (-) percent	Total 1940	Increase or decrease (-) percent	Croppers	
									1940	Increase or decrease (-) percent
Georgia	59,132	-31.9	8,604	-4.5	1,414	-31.6	49,078	-35.1	29,303	-40.7
Florida	9,758	-11.6	4,508	3.4	1,007	-17.2	4,203	-21.8	1,062	-23.8
East So. Central	266,426	17.0	40,496	2.7	8,673	-22.3	217,176	-19.6	136,821	-8.9
Kentucky	5,547	-39.1	2,702	-11.6	462	-58.8	2,377	-51.6	1,507	-51.6
Tennessee	27,975	-20.4	5,393	-5.2	1,493	-30.4	21,079	-22.7	13,870	-16.2
Alabama	73,364	-21.8	11,776	3.1	3,916	-13.2	57,651	-26.0	19,334	-29.9
Mississippi	159,540	-12.8	20,625	7.1	2,802	-17.3	136,069	-15.0	102,110	-0.9
West So. Central	182,934	-30.3	39,525	-2.1	8,413	-20.4	134,918	-36.1	76,551	-35.4
Arkansas	57,025	-28.3	8,943	-3.1	1,610	-32.8	46,453	-31.8	33,122	-27.1
Louisiana	59,584	-19.2	9,526	8.4	1,661	-3.3	48,380	-23.5	27,549	-14.5
Oklahoma	13,572	-40.8	4,912	-25.0	1,171	-34.4	7,475	-48.7	1,008	-77.9
Texas	52,753	-38.7	16,144	1.1	3,971	-14.9	32,610	-50.1	14,872	-59.0

Source: "Number of Nonwhite Farm Operators, by Tenure, for the Southern States in 1940, Showing Increase or Decrease Since 1930," *The Negro Handbook*, 1942, p. 215. Primary source: U.S. Bureau of the Census.

★ 163 ★

Farms and Farmers

Owner Status: Change in Owner Status of Black Farmers, 1910-1920 and 1920-1930, by Location of Farm

TENURE	NUMBER OF FARM OPERATORS			INCREASE OR DECREASE (-)				PERCENT DISTRIBUTION		
				1920-30		1910-20				
	1930	1920	1910	Number	Percent	Number	Percent	1930	1920	1910
				United States						
Total	882,850	925,708	893,370	-42,858	-4.6	32,338	3.6	100.0	100.0	100.0
Owners	181,016	218,612	218,972	-37,596	-17.2	-360	-.2	20.5	23.6	24.5
Tenants	700,911	705,070	672,964	-4,159	-.6	32,106	4.8	79.4	76.2	75.3
Managers	923	2,026	1,434	-1,103	-54.5	592	41.3	.1	.2	.2
				THE SOUTH						
Total	870,936	915,595	880,836	-44,659	-4.9	34,759	3.9	100.0	100.0	100.0
Owners	176,130	212,365	211,087	-36,235	-17.1	1,278	.6	20.2	23.2	24.0
Tenants	694,001	701,471	668,559	-7,470	-1.1	32,912	4.9	79.7	76.6	75.9
Managers	805	1,759	1,190	-954	-54.2	569	47.8	9.1	.2	.1
				THE NORTH						
Total	11,104	9,380	12,052	1,724	18.4	-2,672	-22.2	100.0	100.0	100.0
Owners	4,424	5,749	7,498	-1,325	-23.0	-1,749	-23.3	39.8	61.3	62.2
Tenants	6,588	3,389	4,330	3,199	94.4	-941	-21.7	59.3	36.1	35.9
Managers	92	242	224	-150	-62.0	18	8.0	.8	2.6	1.9

[Continued]

★ 163 ★

Owner Status: Change in Owner Status of Black Farmers, 1910-1920 and 1920-1930, by Location of Farm

[Continued]

| TENURE | NUMBER OF FARM OPERATORS | | | INCREASE OR DECREASE (-) | | | | PERCENT DISTRIBUTION | | |
| | | | | 1920-30 | | 1910-20 | | | | |
	1930	1920	1910	Number	Percent	Number	Percent	1930	1920	1910
				THE WEST						
Total	810	733	482	77	10.5	251	52.1	100.0	100.0	100.0
Owners	462	498	387	-36	-7.2	111	180.0	57.0	67.9	80.3
Tenants	322	210	75	112	53.3	135	180.0	39.8	28.6	15.6
Managers	26	25	20	1	4.0	5	25.0	3.2	3.4	4.1

Source: "Number of Negro Operators by Tenure, by Sections: 1930, 1920, and 1910," *Negroes in the United States, 1920-1932*, 1935, p. 577. Primary source: U.S. Bureau of the Census. *Negroes in the United States, 1920-1932*. Washington, D.C.: U.S. Government Printing Office, 1935.

★ 164 ★

Farms and Farmers

Owner Status: Change in Owner Status of Farmers, 1900-1910 and 1910-1920

| Class Farmers | 1900 | 1910 | Increase 1900-1910 | | 1920 | Increase 1910-1920 | |
			Amount	Per Ct		Amount	Per Cent
			WHITE FARMERS				
Total	4,969,608	5,440,619	471,011	9.5	5,498,454	57,835	1.1
Owners	3,446,806	3,707,501	260,695	7.6	3,691,868	15,633	0.4
Managers	57,261	56,560	701	1.2	66,223	9,663	17.1
Tenants	1,465,541	1,676,558	211,017	14.4	1,740,363	63,805	3.8
			NEGRO FARMERS				
Total	746,717	893,370	146,655	19.6	925,708	32,388	3.7
Owners	187,797	218,972	31,175	16.6	218,612	-360	-0.2
Managers	1,744	1,434	-310	-17.7	2,026	592	41.3
Tenants	557,174	672,964	115,790	20.8	705,070	32,106	4.7

Source: "Increase and Decrease White and Negro Farmers. 1900-1910 and 1910-1920," *Negro Year Book: An Annual Encyclopedia of the Negro, 1925-1926*, 1925, p. 372. Primary source: Work, Monroe N. (Ed.), *Negro Year Book: An Annual Encyclopedia of the Negro, 1925-1926*. Tuskegee Institute, AL: The Negro Year Book Pub. Co., 1925.

★ 165 ★

Farms and Farmers

Owner Status: Farmers of Color (Black and Other), by Owner Status and Location of Farm, 1910

DIVISION	NUMBER OF FARMS: 1910											
	Total			Owners			Tenants			Managers		
	Colored	Negro	Other colored	Colored	Negro	Other colored	Colored	Negro	Other colored	Colored	Negro	Other colored
UNITED STATES	920,883	893,370	27,513	241,221	218,972	22,249	678,118	672,964	5,154	1,544	1,434	110
GEOGRAPHIC DIVISIONS:												
New England	342	310	32	271	240	31	52	51	1	19	18	-
Middle Atlantic	1,961	1,310	651	1,414	793	621	475	447	28	72	70	2
East North Central	5,717	4,843	874	3,908	3,095	813	1,735	1,677	58	74	71	3
West North Central	9,864	5,589	4,275	7,369	3,370	3,999	2,419	2,155	264	76	64	12
South Atlantic	355,862	354,530	1,332	101,961	101,135	826	253,181	252,676	505	720	719	1
East South Central	325,218	324,884	334	58,737	58,610	127	266,232	266,025	207	249	249	-
West South Central	209,061	201,422	7,639	57,769	51,342	6,427	151,061	149,858	1,203	231	222	9
Mountain	8,028	219	7,809	7,675	176	7,499	331	34	297	22	0	13
Pacific	4,830	263	4,567	2,117	211	1,906	2,632	41	2,591	81	11	70

Source: "Colored Farms of Owners, Tenants, and Managers Classified as Negro and Other Colored, by Divisions and States: 1910," *Negro Population, 1790-1915,* 1918, p. 608. Primary source: U.S. Bureau of the Census. *Negro Population, 1790-1915.* Washington, D.C.: Government Printing Office, 1918.

★ 166 ★

Farms and Farmers

Owner Status: Nonwhite Farmers, by Owner Status, 1900-1945

Tenure	1945	1940	1935	1930	1925	1920	1910	1900
All nonwhite Operators[2]	689,215	719,071	855,555	916,070	831,455	949,889	920,883	767,764
Owners	205,917	201,098	211,394	202,720	194,540	233,222	241,221	206,517
Managers	622	717	1,190	3,122	667	2,226	1,544	1,824
All Tenants	482,676	517,256	642,971	710,228	636,248	714,441	678,118	559,423
Croppers (So.)	270,296	299,118	368,408	392,897	344,322	333,713	373,551	284,760

Source: "Number of Nonwhite Farmers by Tenure for U.S.: 1900 to 1945," *1952 Negro Year Book: A Review of Events Affecting Negro Life,* 1952, p. 104. Primary source: U.S. Census of Agriculture, 1945. *Notes:* 1. Figures for 1925 are for South only. U.S. figures not available. 2. Nonwhite includes Negroes, Indians, Chinese, and Japanese. Negroes are about 95% of all nonwhite farmers in U.S. and 98% of those in the South.

★ 167 ★

Farms and Farmers

Owner Status: Nonwhite Owners (Part and Full) and Tenants on Southern Farms, by State, 1940

DIVISION AND STATE	Total 1940	Full Owners 1940	Part Owners 1940	Tenants	
				Total 1940	Croppers 1940
Southern States	680,266	141,902	31,361	506,638	299,118
South Atlantic	230,906	61,881	14,275	154,544	85,746
Delaware	625	301	44	272	49
Maryland	4,051	2,059	212	1,758	562
District of Columbia	4	1	-	2	-
Virginia	35,090	18,930	3,320	12,804	5,897
West Virginia	671	396	31	239	9
North Carolina	60,268	13,937	4,308	41,994	26,803
South Carolina	61,307	13,145	3,939	44,194	22,061
Georgia	59,132	8,604	1,414	49,078	29,303
Florida	9,758	4,508	1,007	4,203	1,062
East South Central	266,426	40,496	8,673	217,176	136,821
Kentucky	5,547	2,702	462	2,377	1,507
Tennessee	27,975	5,393	1,493	21,079	13,870
Alabama	73,364	11,776	3,916	57,651	19,334
Mississippi	159,540	20,625	2,802	136,069	102,110
West South Central	182,934	39,525	8,413	134,918	76,551
Arkansas	57,025	8,943	1,610	46,453	33,122
Louisiana	59,584	9,526	1,661	48,380	27,549
Oklahoma	13,572	4,912	1,171	7,475	1,008
Texas	52,753	16,144	3,971	32,610	14,872

Source: "Number of Nonwhite Farm Operators, by Tenure, for the Southern States: 1940," *The Negro Handbook,* 1942, p. 215. Primary source: U.S. Bureau of the Census.

Farms and Farmers

Owner Status: Number of Southern Farms, by Owner Status, 1910

DIVISION AND STATE	FARMS OPERATED BY COLORED FARMERS: 1910										
	Total	Owners and part owners				Tenants					Managers
		Total	Owners		Part owners	Total	Cash tenants	Share tenants	Share-cash tenants	Tenants not specified	
			Free	Mortgaged							
NUMBER OF FARMS											
THE SOUTH											
Total	890,141	218,467	128,557	46,733	43,177	670,474	260,966	370,306	14,218	24,984	1,200
South Atlantic	355,862	101,961	63,701	17,213	21,047	253,181	101,664	135,203	4,781	11,533	720
East South Central	325,218	58,737	28,906	17,414	12,417	266,232	126,968	126,229	4,990	8,045	249
West South Central	209,061	57,759	35,950	12,106	9,713	151,061	32,334	108,874	4,447	5,406	231
SOUTH ATLANTIC											
Delaware	922	406	198	149	59	500	55	421	4	20	16
Maryland	6,372	3,950	2,191	1,110	649	2,335	405	1,685	35	210	87
District of Columbia	12	8	3	3	2	3	3	-	-	-	1
Virginia	48,114	32,228	22,220	4,600	5,408	15,706	3,661	10,906	382	757	180
West Virginia	708	558	417	70	71	143	62	78	2	1	7
North Carolina	65,656	21,443	11,088	3,734	6,621	44,139	10,110	31,609	921	1,499	74
South Carolina	96,798	20,372	12,805	3,272	4,295	76,295	36,658	34,169	1,496	3,972	131
Georgia	122,559	15,698	9,649	3,210	2,839	106,738	46,451	54,464	1,795	4,028	123
Florida	14,721	7,298	5,130	1,065	1,103	7,322	4,259	1,871	146	1,046	101
EAST SOUTH CENTRAL											
Kentucky	11,730	5,929	3,488	978	1,463	5,761	473	5,013	146	129	40
Tennessee	38,308	10,700	5,826	1,914	2,960	27,557	11,038	15,257	499	763	51
Alabama	110,443	17,082	8,030	4,979	4,073	93,309	61,235	27,687	1,289	3,098	52
Mississippi	164,737	25,026	11,562	9,543	3,921	139,605	54,222	78,272	3,056	4,055	106
WEST SOUTH CENTRAL											
Arkansas	63,593	14,662	7,891	3,969	2,802	48,885	17,104	27,582	1,500	2,699	46
Louisiana	54,879	10,725	7,312	2,287	1,126	44,077	8,723	33,596	908	850	77
Oklahoma	20,671	11,150	7,713	2,206	1,231	9,494	1,398	7,249	248	599	27
Texas	69,918	21,232	13,034	3,644	4,554	48,605	5,109	40,447	1,791	1,258	81

Source: "Colored and White Farms Classified by Seven Tenures, with Percentage Distribution by Tenure, by Southern Divisions and States: 1910," *Negro Population, 1790-1915*, 1918, p. 610. Primary source: U.S. Bureau of the Census. *Negro Population, 1790-1915*. Washington, D.C.: Government Printing Office, 1918.

★ 169 ★
Farms and Farmers

Owner Status: Owner Status of Farms in 1910, by Region

TENURE	Total	Negro	Native white	Foreign-born white	Percentage distribution by tenure		
					Negro	Native white	Foreign born white

UNITED STATES

TENURE	Total	Negro	Native white	Foreign-born white	Negro	Native white	Foreign born white
Total	6,361,502	893,370	4,771,063	669,556	100.0	100.0	100.0
Owners	3,948,722	218,972	3,162,584	544,917	24.5	66.3	81.4
Tenants	2,354,676	672,964	1,558,392	118,166	75.3	32.7	17.6
Managers	58,104	1,434	50,087	6,473	0.2	1.0	1.0

THE SOUTH

TENURE	Total	Negro	Native white	Foreign-born white	Negro	Native white	Foreign born white
Total	3,097,547	880,836	2,153,945	53,461	100.0	100.0	100.0
Owners	1,544,511	211,087	1,290,070	35,974	24.0	59.9	67.3
Tenants	1,536,752	668,559	849,295	16,983	75.9	39.4	31.8
Managers	16,284	1,190	14,580	504	0.1	0.7	0.9

THE NORTH

TENURE	Total	Negro	Native white	Foreign-born white	Negro	Native white	Foreign born white
Total	2,890,618	12,052	2,340,612	532,122	100.0	100.0	100.0
Owners	2,091,434	7,498	1,640,930	437,542	62.2	70.1	82.2
Tenants	765,501	4,330	670,792	90,028	35.9	28.7	16.9
Managers	33,683	224	28,890	4,552	1.9	1.2	0.9

THE WEST

TENURE	Total	Negro	Native white	Foreign-born white	Negro	Native white	Foreign born white
Total	373,337	482	276,506	83,973	100.0	100.0	100.0
Owners	312,777	387	231,584	71,401	80.3	83.8	85.0
Tenants	52,423	75	38,305	11,155	15.6	13.8	13.3
Managers	8,137	20	6,617	1,417	4.1	2.4	1.7

Source: "Farm Operators: 1910," *Negro Population, 1790-1915*, 1918, p. 571. Primary source: U.S. Bureau of the Census. *Negro Population, 1790-1915*. Washington, D.C.: Government Printing Office, 1918.

★ 170 ★

Farms and Farmers

Owner Status: Owner Status of Southern Agricultural Workers, 1940

Tenure	Number		Per Cent	
	Negro	White	Negro	White
Total[1]	1,148,392	2,821,822	100	100
Owners and Managers	173,628	1,384,249	15.1	49.1
Cash tenants	64,684	189,667	5.6	6.7
Other tenants except croppers	142,836	510,815	12.5	18.1
Croppers	299,118	242,173	26.0	8.6
Wage Laborers	468,126	494,918	40.8	17.5

Source: "Negro and White Agricultural Workers in the South, by Tenure, 1940," *Negro Year Book: A Review of Events Affecting Negro Life, 1941-1946,* 1947, p. 158. Primary source: Data on owners, tenants, and croppers are from Sixteenth Census of the United States: 1940, Agriculture, Chapter 111, Volume 111, General Report on Agriculture, table 3. They include a small number of non-whites other than Negroes. The data on wage laborers in agriculture are from the Sixteenth Census of the United States: 1940, Population - Volume 111, Part 1, tables 62 and 63. *Note:* 1. Exclusive of unpaid family workers.

★ 171 ★

Farms and Farmers

Owner Status: Owner Status of Southern Farms, 1900 and 1910, and Change 1900-1910

OWNER STATUS	NUMBER OF FARMERS							
	Colored				White			
	1900	1910	Increase[1]		1910	1900	Increase[1]	
			Number	Percent			Number	Percent
THE SOUTH								
Total	890,141	740,670	149,471	20.2	2,207,406	1,879,721	327,685	17.4
Owners	175,290	158,479	16,811	10.6	1,154,100	1,078,635	75,465	7.0
Part owners	43,177	28,197	14,980	53.1	171,944	105,171	66,773	63.5
Share tenants[2]	384,524	280,699	103,825	37.0	636,817	491,655	145,162	29.5
Cash tenants[3]	285,950	271,702	14,248	5.2	229,461	187,088	42,373	22.6
Managers	1,200	1,593	-393	-24.7	15,084	17,172	-2,088	-12.2

Source: "Colored and White Farmers Classified by Tenure, 1910 and 1900,with Increase, 1900-1910, by Southern Divisions and States," *Negro Population, 1790-1915,* 1918, p. 609. Primary source: U.S. Bureau of the Census. *Negro Population, 1790-1915.* Washington, D.C.: Government Printing Office, 1918. *Notes:* "Colored" may include persons other than black. 1. A minus sign (-) denotes decrease. 2. Includes not specified tenure. 3. Includes share-cash tenants.

★ 172 ★

Farms and Farmers

Owner Status: Percentage Distribution of Black Farmers, by Owner Status and Region, 1900-1920

Tenure	Percentage Distribution		
	1900	1910	1920

UNITED STATES

Tenure	1900	1910	1920
Total	100.0	100.0	100.0
Owners	25.1	24.5	23.5
Managers	0.2	0.2	0.2
Tenants	74.6	75.3	76.3

THE SOUTH

Tenure	1900	1910	1920
Total	100.0	100.0	100.0
Owners	24.5	24.0	23.2
Managers	0.2	0.1	0.2
Tenants	75.3	75.9	76.6

THE NORTH

Tenure	1900	1910	1920
Total	100.0	100.0	100.0
Owners	57.9	62.2	61.3
Managers	1.3	1.9	2.5
Tenants	40.8	35.9	36.2

THE WEST

Tenure	1900	1910	1920
Total	100.0	100.0	100.0
Owners	76.3	80.3	67.9
Managers	2.1	4.1	3.4
Tenants	21.7	15.6	28.7

Source. "Percentage Distribution by Tenure Negro Farm Operators," Negro Year Book: An Annual Encyclopedia of the Negro, 1925 1926, 1925, p. 369. Primary source: U.S. Bureau of the Census.

★ 173 ★

Farms and Farmers

Owner Status: Percentage Distribution of Black Owner and Tenant Farms, by Region and State, 1910-1930

SECTION AND STATE	PERCENT OF FARMS OPERATED BY-					
	Owners			Tenants		
	1930	1920	1910	1930	1920	1910
United States	20.5	23.6	24.5	79.4	76.3	75.3
The North	39.8	61.3	62.2	59.3	36.1	35.9
The South	20.2	23.2	24.0	79.7	76.6	75.9
The West	57.0	67.9	80.3	39.8	28.6	15.6
NEW ENGLAND:						
Maine	93.3	100.0	85.7	6.7	-	10.7
New Hampshire	83.3	85.7	78.6	16.7	7.1	14.3
Vermont	77.3	75.0	85.0	18.2	14.3	10.0
Massachusetts	93.7	86.4	86.4	4.8	6.8	9.7
Rhode Island	88.9	68.4	70.0	-	26.3	30.0
Connecticut	75.8	67.7	67.6	15.2	24.6	21.0
MIDDLE ATLANTIC:						
New York	75.7	62.0	65.4	22.3	29.0	30.5
New Jersey	62.4	53.5	55.5	33.9	42.9	38.8
Pennsylvania	63.5	57.9	62.2	32.6	32.3	32.0
EAST NORTH CENTRAL:						
Ohio	63.5	65.2	67.3	35.6	32.6	31.3
Indiana	59.7	53.5	58.1	39.9	44.0	40.0
Illinois	51.4	59.8	55.3	47.9	39.2	43.4
Michigan	78.9	73.4	78.4	19.9	25.3	20.2
Wisconsin	74.5	87.2	81.3	25.5	12.8	16.7
WEST NORTH CENTRAL:						
Minnesota	70.4	72.7	55.2	29.6	27.3	41.4
Iowa	56.8	67.9	65.2	43.2	31.2	33.7
Missouri	19.9	58.2	57.5	79.8	40.1	41.3
North Dakota	50.0	42.3	81.8	50.0	50.0	18.2
South Dakota	65.0	70.2	85.1	32.5	27.7	14.9
Nebraska	42.1	49.2	78.1	57.9	44.4	21.9
Kansas	57.4	62.5	63.8	41.6	36.0	34.9
SOUTH ATLANTIC:						
Delaware	46.2	40.7	44.0	51.4	57.8	54.2
Maryland	55.8	57.2	62.0	41.9	40.4	36.6
District of Columbia	72.7	45.0	66.7	18.2	50.0	25.0
Virginia	61.6	64.8	67.0	38.2	34.8	32.7
West Virginia	75.9	80.0	78.8	22.7	18.5	20.2
North Carolina	25.4	29.0	32.1	74.5	70.9	67.8
South Carolina	20.7	20.9	21.0	79.3	79.0	78.8
Georgia	12.8	12.3	12.8	87.2	87.5	87.1
Florida	50.5	48.8	49.6	48.7	50.4	49.7

[Continued]

★ 173 ★

Owner Status: Percentage Distribution of Black Owner and Tenant Farms, by Region and State, 1910-1930

[Continued]

SECTION AND STATE	PERCENT OF FARMS OPERATED BY-					
	Owners			Tenants		
	1930	1920	1910	1930	1920	1910
EAST SOUTH CENTRAL:						
Kentucky	45.9	42.1	50.5	54.0	57.6	49.1
Tennessee	22.3	25.8	27.9	77.6	74.1	71.9
Alabama	17.0	18.1	15.4	83.0	81.8	84.5
Mississippi	12.4	14.4	15.2	87.6	85.5	84.8
WEST SOUTH CENTRAL:						
Arkansas	14.4	21.3	23.1	85.5	78.6	76.9
Louisiana	14.2	17.7	19.5	85.7	82.2	80.4
Oklahoma	22.8	37.0	36.5	77.1	62.4	63.4
Texas	23.9	29.9	30.3	76.0	69.9	69.5
MOUNTAIN:						
Montana	71.4	83.9	75.9	28.6	12.9	17.2
Idaho	43.8	69.6	100.0	43.8	30.4	-
Wyoming	66.7	100.0	89.5	33.3	-	3.5
Colorado	69.2	77.7	71.6	29.5	18.9	27.2
New Mexico	64.6	75.0	85.4	34.5	25.0	6.3
Arizona	46.0	59.4	83.3	50.6	31.3	16.7
Utah	80.1	31.1	100.0	20.0	67.2	-
Nevada	66.7	60.0	66.7	33.3	40.0	16.7
PACIFIC:						
Washington	83.6	82.3	83.1	13.7	17.7	14.3
Oregon	88.9	73.3	81.5	11.1	13.3	14.8
California	49.5	63.1	78.6	46.2	32.4	16.4

Source: "Percent Distribution of Owned and Tenant Farms Operated by Negroes, by Sections, and States: 1930, 1920, and 1910," *Negroes in the United States, 1920-1932*, 1935, p. 578. Primary source: U.S. Bureau of the Census. *Negroes in the United States, 1920-1932*. Washington, D.C.: U.S. Government Printing Office, 1935.

★ 174 ★
Farms and Farmers

Owner Status: Percentage Distribution of Southern Farms, by Owner Status, 1910

DIVISION AND STATE	Total	FARMS OPERATED BY COLORED FARMERS: 1910									Managers
		Owners and part owners				Tenants					
		Total	Owners		Part owners	Total	Cash tenants	Share tenants	Share-cash tenants	Tenants not specified	
			Free	Mortgaged							
			PERCENTAGE DISTRIBUTION OF FARMS BY TENURE								
THE SOUTH											
Total	100.0	24.5	14.4	5.3	4.9	75.3	29.3	41.6	1.6	2.8	0.1
South Atlantic	100.0	28.7	17.9	4.8	5.9	71.1	28.6	38.0	1.3	3.2	0.2
East South Central	100.0	18.1	8.9	5.4	3.8	81.9	39.0	38.8	1.5	2.5	0.1
West South Central	100.0	27.6	17.2	5.8	4.6	72.3	15.5	52.1	2.1	2.6	0.1
SOUTH ATLANTIC											
Delaware	100.0	44.0	21.5	16.2	6.4	54.2	6.0	45.7	0.4	2.2	1.7
Maryland	100.0	62.0	34.4	17.4	10.2	36.6	6.4	26.4	0.5	3.3	1.4
District of Columbia	100.0	66.7	25.0	25.0	16.7	25.0	25.0	-	-	-	8.3
Virginia	100.0	67.0	46.2	9.6	11.2	32.6	7.6	22.7	0.8	1.6	0.4
West Virginia	100.0	78.8	58.9	9.9	10.0	20.2	8.8	11.0	0.3	0.1	1.0
North Carolina	100.0	32.7	16.9	5.7	10.1	67.2	15.4	48.1	1.4	2.3	0.1
South Carolina	100.0	21.0	13.2	3.4	4.4	78.3	37.9	35.3	1.5	4.1	0.1
Georgia	100.0	12.8	7.9	2.6	2.3	87.1	37.9	44.4	1.5	3.3	0.1
Florida	100.0	49.6	34.8	7.2	7.5	49.7	28.9	12.7	1.0	7.1	0.7
EAST SOUTH CENTRAL											
Kentucky	100.0	50.5	29.7	8.3	12.5	49.1	4.0	42.7	1.2	1.1	0.3
Tennessee	100.0	27.9	15.2	5.0	7.7	71.9	28.8	39.8	1.3	2.0	1.0
Alabama	100.0	15.5	7.3	4.5	3.7	84.5	55.4	25.1	1.2	2.8	-
Mississippi	100.0	15.2	7.0	5.8	2.4	84.7	32.9	47.5	1.9	2.5	0.1
WEST SOUTH CENTRAL											
Arkansas	100.0	23.1	12.4	6.2	4.4	76.9	26.9	43.4	2.4	4.2	0.1
Louisiana	100.0	19.5	13.3	4.2	2.1	80.3	15.9	61.2	1.7	1.5	0.1
Oklahoma	100.0	53.9	37.3	10.7	6.0	45.9	6.8	35.1	1.2	2.9	0.1
Texas	100.0	30.4	18.6	5.2	6.5	69.5	7.3	57.8	2.6	1.8	0.1

Source: "Colored and White Farms Classified by Seven Tenures, with Percentage Distribution by Tenure, by Southern Divisions and States: 1910," *Negro Population, 1790-1915,* 1918, p. 610. Primary source: U.S. Bureau of the Census. *Negro Population, 1790-1915.* Washington, D.C.: Government Printing Office, 1918.

★ 175 ★

Farms and Farmers

Owner Status: Southern Farmers, by Owner Status, 1900-1935

	Number of Farmers									
	White					Negro				
	1935	1930	1920	1910	1900	1935	1930	1920	1910	1900
Total	2,606,176	2,342,129	2,288,750	2,207,406	1,879,721	815,747	881,687	922,914	890,141	740,670
Owners	1,388,601	1,233,656	1,379,636	1,326,044	1,183,806	186,065	182,019	217,589	218,467	186,676
Managers	15,401	16,529	16,548	15,084	17,172	381	829	1,770	1,200	1,593
Tenants	1,202,174	1,092,944	887,566	866,278	678,743	629,301	698,839	703,555	670,474	552,401

	Percentage Distribution									
Total	100.0	100.0	100.0	100.0	100.0	100.0	100.0	100.0	100.0	100.0
Owners	53.3	52.6	60.4	60.1	63.0	22.8	20.6	23.6	24.6	25.2
Managers	0.6	0.7	0.7	0.7	0.9	0.1	0.1	0.2	0.1	0.2
Tenants	46.1	46.7	38.9	39.2	36.1	77.1	79.3	76.2	75.3	74.6

Source: "Number of White and Negro Farmers in South, by Tenure: 1935, 1930, 1920, 1910, 1900," *Negro Year Book: An Annual Encyclopedia of the Negro, 1937-1938,* 1937, p. 48. Primary source: U.S. Bureau of the Census.

★ 176 ★

Farms and Farmers

Owner Status: Trends in Owner Status of Southern Nonwhite Farmers, 1930-1945

Tenure	Total	Nonwhite	
		Number	% of Total
1930			
All	3,223,816	881,687	27.3
All owners	1,415,675	182,019	12.8
Part owners	224,992	41,523	18.2
All tenants	1,790,783	698,839	39.0
Croppers	776,278	392,897	50.5
1935			
All	3,421,923	815,747	23.8
All owners	1,574,666	186,065	11.8
Part owners	234,720	35,952	15.3
All tenants	1,831,475	629,301	34.3
Croppers	716,256	368,408	51.4

[Continued]

★ 176 ★

Owner Status: Trends in Owner Status of Southern Nonwhite Farmers, 1930-1945
[Continued]

Tenure	Total	Nonwhite	
		Number	% of Total
1940			
All	3,007,170	680,266	22.6
All owners	1,544,297	173,263	11.2
Part owners	216,607	31,361	14.3
All tenants	1,449,293	506,630	35.0
Croppers	541,291	299,118	55.3
1945			
All	2,881,135	665,413	23.1
All owners	1,702,663	189,232	11.1
Part owners	193,607	28,252	14.4
All tenants	1,165,279	475,739	40.8
Croppers	446,556	270,296	60.5

Source: "Proportion of Nonwhite Farm Operators to All Operators According to Tenure in South, 1930 to 1945," *1952 Negro Year Book: A Review of Events Affecting Negro Life*, 1952, p. 102. Primary source: U.S. Census of Agriculture, 1945.

★ 177 ★

Farms and Farmers

Population: Black Rural Population, by Region, 1920 and 1930

SECTION	1930	1920	INCREASE OR DECREASE (-) 1920-30	
			Number	Percent
RURAL POPULATION				
United States	6,697,230	6,903,658	-206,428	-3.0
The South	6,395,252	6,661,262	-266,010	-4.0
The North	280,890	221,997	58,893	26.5
The West	21,088	20,399	689	3.4
RURAL FARM				
United States	4,680,523	5,099,963	-419,440	-8.2
The South	4,608,786	5,034,343	-425,557	-8.5
The North	65,601	61,865	3,736	6.0
The West	6,136	3,755	2,381	63.4

[Continued]

★ 177 ★

Population: Black Rural Population, by Region, 1920 and 1930

[Continued]

SECTION	1930	1920	INCREASE OR DECREASE (-) 1920-30	
			Number	Percent

RURAL NONFARM

United States	2,016,707	1,803,695	213,012	11.8
The South	1,786,466	1,626,919	159,547	9.8
The North	215,289	160,132	55,157	34.4
The West	14,952	16,644	-1,692	-10.2

Source: "Negro Rural Population, by Sections: 1930 and 1920," *Negroes in the United States, 1920-1932*, 1935, p. 575. Primary source: U.S. Bureau of the Census. *Negroes in the United States, 1920-1932*. Washington, D.C.: U.S. Government Printing Office, 1935.

★ 178 ★

Farms and Farmers

Population: Change in Southern Farm Population, 1920-1930 and 1930-1935, by Divisions and States

Divisions and States	Number Increase or Decrease in Farm Population 1920-1930, 1930-1935						Percentage Increase or Decrease in Farm Population 1920-1930, 1930-1935					
	Total		White		Negro		Total		White		Negro	
	1930 1935	1920 1930	1930 1935	1920 1930	1930 1935	1920 1930	1930 1935	1920 1930	1930 1935	1920 1930	1930 1935	1920 1930
The South	607,043	291,850	1,146,220	-456,682	-102,692	-488,200	3.7	1.8	10.1	-3.8	-2.2	-9.6
South Atlantic	305,416	-518,522	393,854	-161,320	-36,286	-409,354	3.2	-8.1	10.1	-3.9	-1.8	-17.4
Delaware	2,028	-4,682	3,168	-3,957	342	-2,207	4.4	-9.1	8.0	-9.4	5.1	-24.6
Maryland	4,140	-41,759	11,745	-70,491	-2,240	-18,713	1.7	-14.9	6.2	-27.2	-5.4	-29.7
District of Columbia	97	-459	466	0	0	0	22.2	-51.3	0.0	0.0	0.0	0.0
Virginia	102,712	-118,660	98,427	-69,137	10,042	-50,260	10.8	-10.7	14.3	-9.2	3.9	-16.3
West Virginia	112,805	-28,810	115,480	-31,688	440	-237	25.1	-6.0	26.1	6.7	11.5	-5.3
North Carolina	23,563	98,691	78,556	60,828	-36,510	19,380	1.5	6.6	7.2	5.9	-7.3	4.1
South Carolina	31,964	-158,222	23,324	-19,051	12,077	-142,608	3.5	-14.7	5.6	-4.4	2.4	-22.2
Georgia	-12,570	-266,699	23,352	-70,648	-30,433	-201,540	-0.8	-15.8	2.7	-7.6	-5.5	-26.6
Florida	40,677	-2,912	39,336	1,270	10,110	-12,951	14.6	-1.0	20.2	0.7	13.4	-14.6
East South Central	240,195	-87,841	318,767	-73,099	-58,692	-34,622	4.7	-1.7	8.9	-1.9	-3.9	-2.3
Kentucky	131,292	-128,338	139,612	-106,543	-4,536	-25,579	11.1	-9.8	12.4	-3.7	-9.5	-34.3
Tennessee	92,968	-56,256	101,255	-30,782	-4,598	-29,163	7.6	-4.4	9.8	-2.8	-2.6	-14.3
Alabama	45,797	4,892	58,078	17,268	-5,836	-19,321	3.4	0.3	6.9	2.1	-1.2	-3.7
Mississippi	-29,862	92,361	19,822	46,958	-43,722	39,441	-2.2	7.3	3.3	8.6	-5.7	5.4
West South Central	61,432	98,213	433,792	-222,209	-7,714	-44,224	1.2	1.8	11.5	-5.6	-0.7	-3.5
Arkansas	60,774	-27,585	70,018	-23,678	-3,544	-9,607	5.4	-2.4	8.8	-2.9	-1.1	-2.3
Louisiana	28,745	44,556	41,213	22,858	-1,356	10,586	3.4	5.7	9.2	5.4	-0.4	2.9
Oklahoma	-8,508	6,743	41,943	-25,994	19,122	-36,836	-0.8	0.7	4.8	-2.9	24.0	-31.6
Texas	-19,579	74,499	280,618	-195,395	-21,936	-8,367	-0.8	3.3	16.9	-10.5	-5.4	-2.0

Source: "Increase or Decrease by Number and Percent in Farm Population in South by Color for Divisions and States: 1920-1930, 1930-1935," *Negro Year Book: An Annual Encyclopedia of the Negro, 1937-1938*, p. 57. Primary source: Work, Monroe N. (Ed.), *Negro Year Book: An Annual Encyclopedia of the Negro, 1937-1938*. Tuskegee Institute, AL; The Negro Year Book Pub. Co., 1937. *Note:* A minus sign denotes decrease.

★ 179 ★

Farms and Farmers

Population: Southern Farm Population, by Divisions and States, 1920, 1930, and 1935

Divisions and States	Total Farm Population			White Farm Population			Negro Farm Population		
	1935	1930	1920	1935	1930	1920	1935	1930	1920
The South	16,926,727	16,319,684	16,027,834	12,420,633	11,274,220	11,730,848	4,506,094	4,608,786	5,096,986
South Atlantic	6,203,592	5,898,176	6,416,698	4,299,377	3,905,523	4,066,843	1,904,215	1,904,215	2,349,855
Delaware	48,558	46,530	51,212	41,461	38,293	42,250	7,097	6,755	8,962
Maryland	241,596	237,456	279,225	199,735	187,990	258,481	41,861	44,281	62,994
District of Columbia	532	435	894	466	0	676	66	0	218
Virginia	1,053,469	950,757	1,064,417	784,460	686,033	755,190	269,009	258,967	309,227
West Virginia	561,919	449,114	477,924	557,664	442,184	473,872	4,255	3,815	4,052
North Carolina	1,623,481	1,599,918	1,501,227	1,162,495	1,083,939	1,023,111	460,986	497,496	478,116
South Carolina	948,435	916,471	1,074,693	438,404	415,080	434,131	510,031	497,954	640,562
Georgia	1,405,944	1,418,514	1,685,213	880,613	857,261	927,909	525,331	555,764	757,304
Florida	319,658	278,981	281,893	234,079	194,743	193,473	85,579	75,469	88,420
East South Central	5,335,291	5,095,096	5,182,937	3,912,241	3,593,474	3,666,573	1,423,050	1,481,742	1,516,364
Kentucky	1,307,816	1,176,524	1,304,862	1,264,503	1,124,891	1,231,434	43,313	47,849	73,428
Tennessee	1,308,420	1,215,452	1,271,708	1,138,503	1,037,248	1,068,030	169,917	174,515	203,678
Alabama	1,386,074	1,340,277	1,335,885	895,368	837,290	820,022	490,706	496,542	515,863
Mississippi	1,332,981	1,362,843	1,270,482	613,867	594,045	547,087	719,114	762,836	723,395
West South Central	5,387,844	5,326,412	5,228,199	4,209,015	3,775,223	3,997,432	1,178,829	1,186,543	1,230,767
Arkansas	1,180,238	1,119,464	1,147,049	859,171	789,153	812,831	321,067	324,611	334,218
Louisiana	859,351	830,606	786,050	488,211	446,998	424,140	371,140	372,496	361,910
Oklahoma	1,015,562	1,024,070	1,027,327	916,926	874,983	900,977	98,636	79,514	116,350
Texas	2,332,693	2,352,272	2,227,773	1,944,707	1,664,089	1,859,484	387,986	409,922	418,289

Source: "Farm Population for the South by Color for Divisions and States: 1935, 1930, 1920," *Negro Year Book: An Annual Encyclopedia of the Negro, 1937- 1938*, p. 57. Primary source: Work, Monroe N. (Ed.), *Negro Year Book: An Annual Encyclopedia of the Negro, 1937-1938*. Tuskegee Institute, AL; The Negro Year Book Pub. Co., 1937.

★ 180 ★

Farms and Farmers

Purchases/Sales: Black Farm Managers' Production and Sales of Dairy Products, by Farm Location, 1929 - I

DIVISION AND STATE	COWS AND HEIFERS MILKED DAILY, APRIL 1, 1930		TOTAL MILK PRODUCED		TOTAL MILK SOLD	
	Farms reporting	Number	Farms reporting	Gallons	Farms reporting	Gallons
MANAGERS						
The South	421	1,979	481	1,114,656	120	684,975
South Atlantic	230	979	270	592,396	70	366,959
East South Central	85	509	91	272,239	28	184,724
West South Central	106	491	120	250,021	22	133,292
Selected Northern States[1]	50	291	57	223,012	25	178,981

[Continued]

★ 180 ★

Purchases/Sales: Black Farm Managers' Production and Sales of Dairy Products, by Farm Location, 1929 - I

[Continued]

DIVISION AND STATE	COWS AND HEIFERS MILKED DAILY, APRIL 1, 1930		TOTAL MILK PRODUCED		TOTAL MILK SOLD	
	Farms reporting	Number	Farms reporting	Gallons	Farms reporting	Gallons
New Jersey	6	73	7	64,241	5	58,866
Pennsylvania	11	67	12	42,961	6	37,710
Ohio	10	46	10	29,405	5	21,801
Indiana	2	8	2	3,900	1	3,300
Illinois	3	6	5	8,800	2	6,400
Missouri	12	62	14	50,846	4	33,052
Kansas	6	29	7	22,859	2	17,852

Source: "Specified Dairy Products Produced and Sold in 1929, with Number of Farms Reporting, by Tenure of Colored Operators, by Southern Divisions, and States, and Selected Northern States: 1929," *Negroes in the United States, 1920-1932*, 1935, pp. 624-625. Primary source: U.S. Bureau of the Census. *Negroes in the United States, 1920-1932*. Washington, D.C.: U.S. Government Printing Office, 1935. *Notes:* 1. States having 200 or more Negro farmers who constitute 90 percent or more of the colored farmers in the State.

★ 181 ★

Farms and Farmers

Purchases/Sales: Black Farm Managers' Production and Sales of Dairy Products, by Farm Location, 1929 - II

DIVISION AND STATE	CREAM SOLD AS BUTTERFAT		CREAM SOLD NOT AS BUTTERFAT		BUTTER CHURNED		BUTTER SOLD	
	Farms reporting	Number	Farms reporting	Gallons	Farms reporting	Gallons	Farms reporting	Pounds
MANAGERS								
The South	26	21,713	5	1,287	295	69,654	83	28,496
South Atlantic	10	9,037	2	620	149	34,930	47	15,561
East South Central	6	2,516	2	597	64	19,946	22	10,490
West South Central	10	10,160	1	70	82	14,778	14	2,445
Selected Northern States[1]	4	1,580	-	-	23	5,569	3	2,610
New Jersey	-	-	-	-	1	108	-	-
Pennsylvania	-	-	-	-	1	200	-	-
Ohio	2	1,030	-	-	4	505	-	-
Indiana	-	-	-	-	1	80	1	40
Illinois	-	-	-	-	2	195	-	-
Missouri	-	-	-	-	10	4,226	2	2,570
Kansas	2	550	-	-	4	255	-	-

Source: "Specified Dairy Products Produced and Sold in 1929, with Number of Farms Reporting, by Tenure of Colored Operators, by Southern Divisions, and States, and Selected Northern States: 1929," *Negroes in the United States, 1920-1932*, 1935, pp. 624-625. Primary source: U.S. Bureau of the Census. *Negroes in the United States, 1920-1932*. Washington, D.C.: U.S. Government Printing Office, 1935. *Notes:* 1. States having 200 or more Negro farmers who constitute 90 percent or more of the colored farmers in the State.

★ 182 ★
Farms and Farmers

Purchases/Sales: Black Farm Owners' Production and Sales of Dairy Products, by Farm Location, 1929 - I

DIVISION AND STATE	COWS AND HEIFERS MILKED DAILY, APRIL 1, 1930		TOTAL MILK PRODUCED		TOTAL MILK SOLD	
	Farms reporting	Number	Farms reporting	Gallons	Farms reporting	Gallons
ALL OWNERS						
The South	91,231	148,066	115,197	63,846,334	5,523	3,983,914
SOUTH ATLANTIC	34,547	46,368	43,992	20,410,060	1,630	893,944
Delaware	134	272	156	121,150	31	58,613
Maryland	793	1,301	1,108	674,802	172	232,862
District of Columbia	1	1	1	750	1	300
Virginia	11,992	15,053	15,257	7,511,082	353	225,660
West Virginia	196	310	264	188,902	39	20,570
North Carolina	7,048	8,410	9,001	4,186,404	315	86,161
South Carolina	6,736	8,343	8,599	3,358,333	319	123,601
Georgia	5,881	9,565	7,276	3,430,969	264	67,199
Florida	1,766	3,113	2,330	937,668	135	78,973
EAST SOUTH CENTRAL	29,761	52,660	37,075	22,406,976	2,514	2,033,829
Kentucky	2,071	3,511	2,689	2,035,854	209	144,032
Tennessee	4,370	6,978	5,591	3,604,021	348	252,161
Alabama	9,397	15,219	11,811	6,245,505	577	328,058
Mississippi	13,923	25,952	16,984	10,521,596	1,380	1,309,578
WEST SOUTH CENTRAL	26,923	49,058	34,130	21,029,298	1,378	1,056,141
Arkansas	6,089	9,798	7,963	4,359,075	310	116,067
Louisiana	5,290	9,201	6,760	3,464,682	197	242,228
Oklahoma	4,312	9,736	5,132	4,924,624	319	405,513
Texas	11,232	20,323	14,275	8,280,917	552	292,333
SELECTED NORTHERN STATES[1]	2,050	4,789	2,437	2,856,385	389	826,210
New Jersey	65	230	81	191,062	37	160,722
Pennsylvania	116	407	132	247,520	68	177,211
Ohio	462	1,067	553	646,850	97	190,040
Indiana	147	316	171	239,902	47	96,366
Illinois	237	458	282	257,178	42	47,187
Missouri	661	1,220	791	667,098	48	49,212
Kansas	362	1,091	427	606,775	50	105,472

Source: "Specified Dairy Products Produced and Sold in 1929, with Number of Farms Reporting, by Tenure of Colored operators, by Southern Divisions, and States, and Selected Northern States: 1929," *Negroes in the United States, 1920-1932,* 1935, pp. 624-625. Primary source: U.S. Bureau of the Census. *Negroes in the United States, 1920-1932.* Washington, D.C.: U.S. Government Printing Office, 1935. *Notes:* Colored farmers include Negroes, Indians, Chinese, Japanese, and all other nonwhite races. 1. States having 200 or more Negro farmers who constitute 90 percent or more of the colored farmers in the State.

★ 183 ★
Farms and Farmers

Purchases/Sales: Black Farm Owners' Production and Sales of Dairy Products, by Farm Location, 1929 - II

DIVISION AND STATE	CREAM SOLD AS BUTTERFAT		CREAM SOLD NOT AS BUTTERFAT		BUTTER CHURNED		BUTTER SOLD	
	Farms reporting	Pounds	Farms reporting	Gallons	Farms reporting	Pounds	Farms reporting	Pounds
ALL OWNERS								
The South	5,305	1,430,523	345	49,876	97,679	13,553,501	18,012	1,547,920
SOUTH ATLANTIC	751	192,328	89	21,091	36,392	4,718,244	10,133	813,226
Delaware	-	-	-	-	83	8,273	34	2,804
Maryland	4	1,161	1	250	770	69,835	230	21,790
District of Columbia	-	-	-	-	1	50	-	402,719
Virginia	328	107,820	35	17,299	14,453	1,926,248	5,265	-
West Virginia	12	5,035	-	-	250	38,422	98	11,105
North Carolina	58	8,312	13	650	7,955	1,115,024	1,880	152,202
South Carolina	33	10,015	20	1,022	5,404	617,248	1,054	79,824
Georgia	304	59,058	17	1,543	5,920	828,885	1,339	130,335
Florida	12	927	3	327	1,576	114,259	233	13,447
EAST SOUTH CENTRAL	2,770	669,410	143	14,998	32,486	4,641,098	4,203	392,683
Kentucky	874	208,296	31	2,075	2,268	264,611	387	50,906
Tennessee	662	155,026	45	5,238	5,019	760,689	1,010	104,866
Alabama	214	77,662	30	5,362	10,849	1,643,832	1,645	131,464
Mississippi	1,020	228,426	37	2,323	14,350	1,971,966	1,161	105,447
WEST SOUTH CENTRAL	1,784	568,785	113	13,787	28,801	4,193,159	3,676	342,018
Arkansas	204	37,524	18	3,044	7,426	1,226,494	1,037	89,134
Louisiana	81	22,141	4	513	4,550	549,849	377	28,508
Oklahoma	1,054	396,721	48	6,691	4,277	614,795	590	72,198
Texas	445	112,399	43	3,539	12,548	1,802,021	1,672	152,175
SELECTED NORTHERN STATES[1]	870	278,612	29	1,911	1,626	186,883	339	51,031
New Jersey	-	-	-	-	19	1,515	4	330
Pennsylvania	3	1,124	1	60	65	12,815	28	6,068
Ohio	242	74,058	4	392	287	39,215	64	13,211
Indiana	63	23,749	2	62	90	10,883	24	3,894
Illinois	89	24,924	3	240	193	23,621	70	9,813
Missouri	283	73,925	14	976	663	64,640	106	10,715
Kansas	190	80,832	5	181	309	34,194	43	7,000

Source: "Specified Dairy Products Produced and Sold in 1929, with Number of Farms Reporting, by Tenure of Colored operators, by Southern Divisions, and States, and Selected Northern States: 1929," *Negroes in the United States, 1920-1932*, 1935, pp. 624-625. Primary source: U.S. Bureau of the Census. *Negroes in the United States, 1920-1932*. Washington, D.C.: U.S. Government Printing Office, 1935. *Notes:* Colored farmers include Negroes, Indians, Chinese, Japanese, and all other nonwhite races. 1. States having 200 or more Negro farmers who constitute 90 percent or more of the colored farmers in the State.

★ 184 ★

Farms and Farmers

Purchases/Sales: Black Farmers' Purchases and Sales through Cooperatives, by Farm Location, 1929

[Colored farmers include Negroes, Indians, Chinese, Japanese, and all other nonwhite races]

DIVISION AND STATE	Total colored farm operators	Farms reporting cooperative sales	VALUE OF ALL PRODUCTS ON FARMS REPORTING COOPERATIVE SALES, 1929		VALUE OF PRODUCTS SOLD COOPERATIVELY			Farms reporting cooperative purchases	VALUE OF PRODUCTS PURCHASED COOPERATIVELY	
			Amount	Average per farm reporting	Amount	Percent of total product	Average per farm reporting		Amount	Average per farm reporting
The South	881,687	9,616	$10,941,241	$1,138	$6,479,795	59.2	$674	5,263	$880,048	$129
South Atlantic	298,379	3,436	4,891,412	1,424	2,781,747	56.9	810	958	175,261	183
East South Central	320,959	3,812	3,800,838	997	2,348,197	61.8	616	2,464	251,841	102
West South Central	262,349	2,368	2,248,991	950	1,349,851	60.0	570	1,841	252,946	137
Selected Northern States[1]	10,250	452	671,524	1,486	237,757	35.4	526	216	25,504	118

Source: "Sales and Purchases of Colored Farm Operators Through Farmers' Cooperative Organizations, and Value of All Products on Farms Reporting Cooperative Sales, by Southern Divisions, and States, and Selected Northern States: 1929," *Negroes in the United States, 1920-1932,* 1935, p. 589. Primary source: U.S. Bureau of the Census. *Negroes in the United States, 1920-1932.* Washington, D.C.: U.S. Government Printing Office, 1935.

★ 185 ★

Farms and Farmers

Purchases/Sales: Black Tenant Farmers' Production and Sales of Dairy Products, by Farm Location, 1929 - I

DIVISION AND STATE	COWS AND HEIFERS MILKED DAILY, APRIL 1, 1930		TOTAL MILK PRODUCED		TOTAL MILK SOLD	
	Farms reporting	Number	Farms reporting	Gallons	Farms reporting	Gallons
ALL TENANTS						
The South	195,982	264,827	253,358	111,024,905	6,442	4,284,921
SOUTH ATLANTIC	60,296	73,422	77,867	32,733,545	1,461	989,687
Delaware	153	464	182	227,445	61	161,358
Maryland	716	1,766	1,014	892,642	198	460,735
District of Columbia	-	-	-	-	-	-
Virginia	4,787	5,692	6,508	2,824,720	60	44,082
West Virginia	45	118	55	63,557	9	11,700
North Carolina	11,612	13,037	14,898	6,412,567	236	55,398
South Carolina	18,067	20,723	23,326	8,971,156	386	51,503
Georgia	23,624	29,534	30,214	12,735,762	478	172,530
Florida	1,292	2,088	1,670	605,296	33	32,381
EAST SOUTH CENTRAL	86,808	122,756	111,617	49,345,777	3,712	2,775,162
Kentucky	1,512	2,310	1,878	1,225,759	121	151,646
Tennessee	9,841	13,064	12,276	6,336,316	3054	217,367
Alabama	32,130	44,567	41,717	17,691,541	1,448	745,750
Mississippi	43,325	62,815	55,746	24,092,161	1,838	1,660,399

[Continued]

★ 185 ★

Purchases/Sales: Black Tenant Farmers' Production and Sales of Dairy Products, by Farm Location, 1929 - I

[Continued]

DIVISION AND STATE	COWS AND HEIFERS MILKED DAILY, APRIL 1, 1930		TOTAL MILK PRODUCED		TOTAL MILK SOLD	
	Farms reporting	Number	Farms reporting	Gallons	Farms reporting	Gallons
WEST SOUTH CENTRAL	48,878	68,649	63,874	28,945,983	1,269	520,072
Arkansas	12,940	16,519	17,568	7,450,533	479	81,158
Louisiana	14,477	19,919	18,477	6,968,131	201	76,367
Oklahoma	5,098	8,441	6,335	4,289,824	258	191,969
Texas	16,363	23,770	21,494	10,237,495	331	170,578
SELECTED NORTHERN STATES[1]	1,616	3,781	1,880	2,231,608	266	809,253
New Jersey	59	290	65	200,247	39	175,616
Pennsylvania	68	410	68	301,730	48	267,267
Ohio	268	767	283	411,496	76	166,489
Indiana	82	277	102	174,726	26	74,484
Illinois	150	305	167	184,581	26	60,814
Missouri	793	1,273	961	665,121	35	41,928
Kansas	196	459	234	293,697	16	22,655

Source: "Specified Dairy Products Produced and Sold in 1929, with Number of Farms Reporting, by Tenure of Colored operators, by Southern Divisions, and States, and Selected Northern States: 1929," *Negroes in the United States, 1920-1932*, 1935, pp. 624-625. Primary source: U.S. Bureau of the Census. *Negroes in the United States, 1920-1932*. Washington, D.C.: U.S. Government Printing Office, 1935. Notes: 1. States having 200 or more Negro farmers who constitute 90 percent or more of the colored farmers in the State.

★ 186 ★

Farms and Farmers

Purchases/Sales: Black Tenant Farmers' Production and Sales of Dairy Products, by Farm Location, 1929 - II

DIVISION AND STATE	CREAM SOLD AS BUTTERFAT		CREAM SOLD NOT AS BUTTERFAT		BUTTER CHURNED		BUTTER SOLD	
	Farms reporting	Pounds	Farms reporting	Gallons	Farms reporting	Pounds	Farms reporting	Pounds
ALL TENANTS								
The South	4,810	1,008,579	286	24,288	208,533	25,146,030	18,219	1,314,832
SOUTH ATLANTIC	834	161,456	66	4,092	65,245	8,208,872	8,696	603,929
Delaware	-	-	-	-	78	7,391	26	2,331
Maryland	11	3,623	-	-	667	55,734	103	10,175
District of Columbia	-	-	-	-	-	-	-	-
Virginia	46	18,648	6	1,476	6,091	798,829	1,107	75,217
West Virginia	12	6,405	-	-	45	8,666	17	2,701
North Carolina	48	5,075	9	323	12,754	1,672,726	1,675	111,932
South Carolina	54	7,038	22	422	18,639	2,145,358	2,147	127,692
Georgia	648	118,719	27	1,846	25,979	3,451,871	3,513	267,608
Florida	15	1,948	2	25	992	68,297	108	6,273

[Continued]

★ 186 ★

Purchases/Sales: Black Tenant Farmers' Production and Sales of Dairy Products, by Farm Location, 1929 - II
[Continued]

DIVISION AND STATE	CREAM SOLD AS BUTTERFAT		CREAM SOLD NOT AS BUTTERFAT		BUTTER CHURNED		BUTTER SOLD	
	Farms reporting	Pounds	Farms reporting	Gallons	Farms reporting	Pounds	Farms reporting	Pounds
EAST SOUTH CENTRAL	2,833	540,982	138	11,529	94,373	11,055,571	6,077	444,650
Kentucky	449	101,156	17	1,480	1,540	169,901	176	15,745
Tennessee	456	87,509	37	1,942	11,079	1,522,639	1,060	82,396
Alabama	647	116,443	36	4,006	37,645	4,618,998	3,117	226,880
Mississippi	1,281	235,874	48	4,101	44,109	4,744,033	1,724	119,629
WEST SOUTH CENTRAL	1,143	306,141	82	8,667	48,915	5,881,587	3,446	266,253
Arkansas	114	17,576	16	638	15,027	2,027,456	1,113	71,427
Louisiana	55	7,899	4	2,242	10,684	972,418	473	23,614
Oklahoma	665	204,864	38	3,216	5,175	688,480	539	54,144
Texas	309	75,802	24	2,571	18,029	2,193,233	1,321	117,068
SELECTED NORTHERN STATES[1]	419	163,408	12	1,870	1,161	137,408	167	19,965
New Jersey	-	-	-	-	11	764	1	10
Pennsylvania	2	2,700	-	-	13	3,167	7	2,046
Ohio	104	44,103	2	533	107	11,656	13	1,288
Indiana	37	10,725	1	20	48	7,311	9	2,952
Illinois	33	11,305	4	1,121	103	12,158	34	3,195
Missouri	144	37,904	4	96	740	90,066	95	9,709
Kansas	99	49,671	1	100	139	12,286	8	765

Source: "Specified Dairy Products Produced and Sold in 1929, with Number of Farms Reporting, by Tenure of Colored operators, by Southern Divisions, and States, and Selected Northern States: 1929," *Negroes in the United States, 1920-1932,* 1935, pp. 624-625. Primary source: U.S. Bureau of the Census. *Negroes in the United States, 1920-1932.* Washington, D.C.: U.S. Government Printing Office, 1935. *Notes:* 1. States having 200 or more Negro farmers who constitute 90 percent or more of colored farmers in the State.

★ 187 ★

Farms and Farmers

Relationships: Acreage and Average Acreage on Southern Farms, by Owner Status, 1910

TENURE	Colored	White	Percentage distribution by tenure		Average per farm	
			Colored	White	Colored	White
ALL LAND						
Total	42,609,117	311,843,743	100.0	100.0	47.9	141.3
Owners, free	8,835,857	134,584,147	20.7	43.2	68.7	148.2
Owners, mortgaged	4,011,491	46,759,094	9.4	15.0	85.8	190.2
Part owners	2,844,188	33,580,452	6.7	10.8	65.9	195.3
Cash tenants[1]	12,876,308	26,275,674	30.2	8.4	45.0	114.5
Share tenants[2]	13,691,494	46,328,127	32.1	14.9	35.6	72.4
Managers	349,779	24,316,249	0.8	7.8	291.5	1,612.1

[Continued]

★ 187 ★

Relationships: Acreage and Average Acreage on Southern Farms, by Owner Status, 1910
[Continued]

TENURE	Colored	White	Percentage distribution by tenure		Average per farm	
			Colored	White	Colored	White
IMPROVED LAND						
Total	27,735,743	122,955,109	100.0	100.0	131.2	55.7
Owners, free	4,005,552	50,780,626	14.5	41.3	31.2	55.9
Owners, mortgaged	1,893,013	16,588,921	6.8	13.5	40.5	67.5
Part owners	1,632,554	12,212,994	5.9	9.9	37.8	71.0
Cash tenants[1]	9,218,158	10,839,130	33.3	9.0	32.2	42.2
Share tenants[2]	10,878,217	29,407,345	39.3	23.9	28.3	16.2
Managers	108,249	3,126,093	0.4	2.5	90.2	207.2

Source: "Acres in Farms in the South: 1910," *Negro Population, 1790-1915*, 1918, p. 574. Primary source: U.S. Bureau of the Census. *Negro Population, 1790-1915*. Washington, D.C.: Government Printing Office, 1918. *Notes:* "Colored" may include persons other than black. 1. Includes not specified tenure. 2. Includes share-cash tenants.

★ 188 ★

Farms and Farmers

Relationships: Acreage on Black Farms, by Owner Status and Farm Location, 1920 and 1930

TENURE	ACRES IN FARMS		INCREASE OR DECREASE (-)		PERCENT DISTRIBUTION	
	1930	1920	Number	Percent	1930	1920
United States						
Total	37,597,132	41,432,182	-3,835,050	-9.3	100.0	100.0
Owners	11,198,893	13,948,512	-2,749,619	-19.7	29.8	33.7
Tenants	29,149,167	27,077,582	-928,415	-3.4	69.6	65.4
Managers	249,072	406,088	-157,016	-38.7	.7	1.0
THE SOUTH						
Total	36,758,484	40,544,241	-3,785,757	-9.3	100.0	100.0
Owners	10,785,312	13,434,106	-2,648,794	-19.7	29.3	33.1
Tenants	25,743,234	26,754,386	-1,011,152	-3.8	70.0	66.0
Managers	229,938	355,749	-125,811	-35.4	.6	.9
THE NORTH						
Total	720,872	767,953	-47,081	-6.1	100.0	100.0
Owners	332,520	435,075	-102,555	-23.6	46.1	56.7
Tenants	373,214	294,543	78,671	26.7	51.8	38.4
Managers	15,138	38,335	-23,197	-60.5	2.1	5.0

[Continued]

★ 188 ★

Relationships: Acreage on Black Farms, by Owner Status and Farm Location, 1920 and 1930
[Continued]

TENURE	ACRES IN FARMS		INCREASE OR DECREASE (-)		PERCENT DISTRIBUTION	
	1930	1920	Number	Percent	1930	1920
THE WEST						
Total	117,776	119,988	-2,212	-1.8	100.0	100.0
Owners	81,061	79,331	1,730	2.2	68.8	66.1
Tenants	32,719	28,653	4,066	14.2	27.8	23.9
Managers	3,996	12,004	-8,008	-66.7	3.4	10.0

Source: "Number of Acres in Farms Operated by Negro Farmers, by Tenure, by Sections: 1930 and 1920," *Negroes in the United States, 1920-1932*, 1935, p. 577. Primary source: U.S. Bureau of the Census. *Negroes in the United States, 1920-1932.* Washington, D.C.: U.S. Government Printing Office, 1935.

★ 189 ★

Farms and Farmers

Relationships: Acreage on Black Farms, by Owner Status, Region, and Division, 1920 and 1930

SECTION AND DIVISION	LAND IN FARMS (ACRES)				Tenants		Managers	
	Total		Owners					
	1930	1920	1930	1920	1930	1920	1930	1920
United States	37,597,132	41,432,182	11,198,893	13,948,512	26,149,167	27,077,582	249,072	406,088
The North	720,872	767,953	332,520	435,075	373,214	294,543	15,138	38,335
The South	36,758,484	40,544,241	10,785,312	13,434,106	25,743,234	26,754,386	229,938	355,749
The West	117,776	119,988	81,061	79,331	32,719	28,653	3,996	12,004
New England	9,397	19,252	7,297	10,121	1,025	5,221	1,075	3,910
Middle Atlantic	55,808	72,897	26,758	28,516	24,874	34,933	4,176	9,448
East North Central	214,596	239,783	114,748	138,109	96,208	93,247	3,640	8,427
West North Central	441,071	436,021	183,717	258,329	251,107	161,142	6,247	16,550
South Atlantic	14,550,451	18,151,071	4,214,663	5,483,254	10,226,681	12,521,869	109,107	145,948
East South Central	11,918,057	12,104,977	3,516,640	3,930,410	8,351,425	8,088,733	49,992	85,834
West South Central	10,289,976	10,288,193	3,054,009	4,020,442	7,165,128	6,143,784	70,839	123,967
Mountain	77,228	77,249	59,689	54,574	15,989	12,445	1,550	10,230
Pacific	40,548	42,739	21,372	24,757	16,730	16,208	2,446	1,774

Source: "Farms Operated by Negroes—Number, Farm Acreage, and Value of Land and Buildings, by Tenure, by Sections, Divisions, and States: 1930 and 1920," *Negroes in the United States, 1920-1932*, 1935, pp. 596-597. Primary source: U.S. Bureau of the Census. *Negroes in the United States, 1920-1932.* Washington, D.C.: U.S. Government Printing Office, 1935.

★ 190 ★

Farms and Farmers

Relationships: Acreage on Southern Farms, by Owner Status, 1900 and 1910

| | ACRES IN FARMS | | | | | | | | AVERAGE ACRES PER FARM | | | |
| DIVISION AND TENURE | Total | | Improved | | Increase 1900-1910[1] | | Percentage improved | | Total | | Improved | |
	1910	1900	1910	1900	1910	1900	1910	1900	1910	1900	1910	1900
THE SOUTH												
Colored operators												
Total	42,609,117	38,612,046	27,735,743	23,214,607	3,997,071	4,521,136	65.1	60.1	47.9	52.1	31.2	31.3
Owners	12,847,348	11,512,424	5,898,565	5,030,912	1,334,924	867,653	45.9	43.7	73.3	72.6	33.6	31.7
Part owners	2,844,188	1,846,260	1,632,554	995,893	997,928	636,661	57.4	53.9	65.9	65.5	37.8	35.3
Cash tenants	12,876,308	13,042,374	9,218,158	8,540,633	-166,066	677,525	71.6	65.5	45.0	48.0	32.2	31.4
Share tenants	13,691,494	11,782,470	10,878,217	8,519,427	1,909,024	2,358,790	79.5	72.3	35.6	40.0	28.3	30.4
Managers	349,779	428,518	108,249	127,742	-78,739	-19,493	30.9	29.8	201.5	269.0	90.2	80.2
White operators												
Total	311,843,743	323,424,305	122,955,109	102,893,486	-11,580,562	20,061,623	39.4	31.8	141.3	172.1	55.7	54.7
Owners	181,343,241	170,909,394	67,369,547	62,442,183	10,433,847	4,927,364	37.2	36.5	157.1	158.4	58.4	57.79
Part owners	33,580,452	38,847,090	12,212,994	7,497,960	-5,266,638	4,715,034	36.4	19.3	195.3	369.4	71.0	71.3
Cash tenants	26,275,674	26,245,180	10,839,130	8,827,588	30,494	2,011,542	41.3	33.6	114.5	140.3	42.2	47.2
Share tenants	46,328,127	36,545,215	29,407,345	21,074,171	9,782,912	8,333,174	63.5	57.7	72.4	74.3	46.2	41.9
Managers	24,316,249	50,877,426	3,126,093	3,051,584	-26,561,177	74,509	12.9	6.0	1,612.1	2,962.8	207.2	177.7

Source: "Colored and White Acreage, Total and Improved, by Tenure Classes with decennial Increase, and Average Acres Per Farm, by Southern Divisions: 1910 and 1900," *Negro Population, 1790-1915*, 1918, p. 577. Primary source: U.S. Bureau of the Census. *Negro Population, 1790-1915.* Washington, D.C.: Government Printing Office, 1918.

★ 191 ★

Farms and Farmers

Relationships: Age Group of Black Owners, by Farm Location, 1930 - I

[Colored farmers include Negroes, Indians, Chinese, Japanese, and all other nonwhite races]

| DIVISION AND STATE | AGE OF COLORED FARM OPERATORS | | | | | | |
	Total number reporting	Under 25 years	25 to 34 years	35 to 44 years	45 to 54 years	55 to 64 years	65 years and over
				OWNERS			
The South	177,604	3,393	14,915	33,111	52,540	43,036	30,609
SOUTH ATLANTIC	78,552	1,231	5,968	15,125	23,409	19,175	13,644
Delaware	367	3	19	67	101	97	80
Maryland	2,871	16	183	541	815	788	528
District of Columbia	8	-	-	-	4	3	1
Virginia	23,897	309	1,636	4,794	7,183	5,720	4,255
West Virginia	360	7	31	70	89	84	79
North Carolina	19,150	311	1,615	3,748	5,633	4,552	3,291
South Carolina	15,652	337	1,402	3,394	4,717	3,527	2,275
Georgia	10,862	169	692	1,578	3,310	2,959	2,154
Florida	5,385	79	390	933	1,557	1,445	981
EAST SOUTH CENTRAL	49,477	919	3,881	8,256	14,924	12,411	9,086
Kentucky	4,045	56	270	689	1,059	976	995
Tennessee	7,652	118	482	1,150	2,163	2,028	1,711

[Continued]

★ 191 ★

Relationships: Age Group of Black Owners, by Farm Location, 1930 - I
[Continued]

DIVISION AND STATE	AGE OF COLORED FARM OPERATORS						
	Total number reporting	Under 25 years	25 to 34 years	35 to 44 years	45 to 54 years	55 to 64 years	65 years and over
Alabama	15,628	270	1,086	2,328	5,425	3,853	2,666
Mississippi	22,152	475	2,043	4,089	6,277	5,554	3,714
WEST SOUTH CENTRAL	49,575	1,243	5,066	9,730	14,207	11,450	7,879
Arkansas	11,170	239	905	2,080	3,605	2,615	1,726
Louisiana	10,271	221	1,001	2,160	2,949	2,386	1,554
Oklahoma	8,056	293	1,346	1,716	2,069	1,625	1,007
Texas	20,078	490	1,814	3,774	5,584	4,824	3,592
SELECTED NORTHERN STATES[1]	3,684	19	191	587	938	997	952
New Jersey	236	1	19	43	68	64	41
Pennsylvania	230	3	12	41	75	58	41
Ohio	761	3	39	128	172	211	208
Indiana	272	-	8	37	65	75	87
Illinois	442	2	16	76	124	122	102
Missouri	1,144	6	57	155	276	315	335
Kansas	599	4	50	107	158	152	138

Source: "Colored Farm Owners and Tenants by Age, by Southern Divisions, and States, and Selected Northern States: 1930," Negroes in the United States, 1920-1932, 1935, p. 606. Primary source: U.S. Bureau of the Census. Negroes in the United States, 1920-1932. Washington, D.C.: U.S. Government Printing Office, 1935. Notes: 1. States having 200 or more Negro farmers who constitute 90 percent or more colored farmers in the State.

★ 192 ★

Farms and Farmers

Relationships: Age Group of Black Owners, by Farm Location, 1930 - II
[Colored farmers include Negroes, Indians, Chinese, Japanese, and all other nonwhite races]

DIVISION AND STATE	AGE OF COLORED FARM OPERATORS Percent distribution						
	Total	Under 25 years	25 to 34 years	35 to 44 years	45 to 54 years	55 to 64 years	65 years and over
				OWNERS			
The South	100.0	1.9	3.4	18.6	29.6	24.2	17.2
SOUTH ATLANTIC	100.0	1.6	7.6	19.3	29.8	24.4	17.4
Delaware	100.0	.8	5.2	18.3	27.5	26.4	21.8
Maryland	100.0	.6	6.4	18.8	28.4	27.4	18.4
District of Columbia	100.0	-	-	-	50.0	37.5	12.5
Virginia	100.0	1.3	6.8	20.1	30.1	23.9	17.8
West Virginia	100.0	1.9	8.6	19.4	24.7	23.3	21.9
North Carolina	100.0	1.6	8.4	19.6	29.4	23.8	17.2

[Continued]

★ 192 ★

Relationships: Age Group of Black Owners, by Farm Location, 1930 - II
[Continued]

DIVISION AND STATE	AGE OF COLORED FARM OPERATORS Percent distribution						
	Total	Under 25 years	25 to 34 years	35 to 44 years	45 to 54 years	55 to 64 years	65 years and over
South Carolina	100.0	2.2	9.0	21.7	30.1	22.5	14.5
Georgia	100.0	1.6	6.4	14.5	30.5	27.2	19.8
Florida	100.0	1.5	7.2	17.3	28.9	26.8	18.2
EAST SOUTH CENTRAL	100.0	1.9	7.8	16.7	30.2	25.1	18.4
Kentucky	100.0	1.4	6.7	17.0	26.2	24.1	24.6
Tennessee	100.0	1.5	6.3	15.0	28.3	26.5	22.4
Alabama	100.0	1.7	6.9	14.9	34.7	24.7	17.1
Mississippi	100.0	2.1	9.2	18.5	28.3	25.1	16.8
WEST SOUTH CENTRAL	100.0	2.5	10.2	19.6	28.7	23.1	15.9
Arkansas	100.0	2.1	8.1	18.6	32.3	23.4	15.5
Louisiana	100.0	2.2	9.7	21.0	28.7	23.2	15.1
Oklahoma	100.0	3.6	16.7	21.3	25.7	20.2	12.5
Texas	100.0	2.4	9.0	18.8	27.8	24.0	17.9
SELECTED NORTHERN STATES[1]	100.0	.5	5.2	15.9	25.5	27.1	25.8
New Jersey	100.0	.4	8.1	18.2	28.8	27.1	17.4
Pennsylvania	100.0	1.3	5.2	17.8	32.6	25.2	17.8
Ohio	100.0	.4	5.1	16.8	22.6	27.7	27.3
Indiana	100.0[1]	-	2.9	13.6	23.9	27.6	32.0
Illinois	100.0	.5	3.6	17.2	28.1	27.6	23.1
Missouri	100.0	.5	5.0	13.5	24.1	27.5	29.3
Kansas	100.0	.7	6.7	17.9	26.4	25.4	23.0

Source: "Colored Farm Owners and Tenants by Age, by Southern Divisions, and States, and Selected Northern States: 1930," *Negroes in the United States, 1920-1932*, 1935, p. 606. Primary source: U.S. Bureau of the Census. *Negroes in the United States, 1920-1932*. Washington, D.C.: U.S. Government Printing Office, 1935. *Notes:* 1. States having 200 or more Negro farmers who constitute 90 percent or more colored farmers in the State.

15,292

★ 193 ★
Farms and Farmers

Relationships: Age Group of Black Tenant Farmers, by Farm Location, 1930 - I

[Colored farmers include Negroes, Indians, Chinese, Japanese, and all other nonwhite races]

DIVISION AND STATE	AGE OF COLORED FARM OPERATORS						
	Total number reporting	Under 25 years	25 to 34 years	35 to 44 years	45 to 54 years	55 to 64 years	65 years and over
				TENANTS			
The South	675,104	95,352	153,331	152,101	151,208	84,971	38,141
SOUTH ATLANTIC	208,436	24,065	42,035	49,616	49,719	29,726	13,275
Delaware	400	13	55	105	125	64	38
Maryland	2,085	89	400	538	595	311	152
District of Columbia	2	-	-	-	1	1	-
Virginia	14,495	1,469	2,927	3,825	3,520	1,821	933
West Virginia	107	3	15	24	30	19	16
North Carolina	53,987	6,401	12,778	13,120	12,199	6,651	2,838
South Carolina	59,084	7,000	11,574	15,465	13,290	8,059	3,696
Georgia	73,132	8,763	13,399		18,529	11,978	5,171
Florida	5,144	327	887	1,247	1,430	822	431
EAST SOUTH CENTRAL	262,315	39,313	60,588	55,624	58,327	32,922	15,541
Kentucky	4,673	519	980	1,178	1,010	648	347
Tennessee	26,265	4,061	5,820	5,500	5,817	3,530	1,537
Alabama	76,119	8,551	15,048	14,268	21,721	10,851	5,680
Mississippi	155,258	26,191	38,740	34,678	29,779	17,893	7,977
WEST SOUTH CENTRAL	204,353	31,974	50,708	46,861	43,162	22,323	9,325
Arkansas	66,091	10,701	15,972	14,405	14,958	7,288	2,767
Louisiana	61,240	8,667	14,678	14,478	12,820	7,279	3,318
Oklahoma	14,126	1,671	3,393	3,305	3,260	1,812	685
Texas	62,896	10,935	16,665	14,673	12,124	5,944	2,555
SELECTED NORTHERN STATES[1]	6,281	614	1,190	1,587	1,531	940	419
New Jersey	121	2	24	42	32	18	3
Pennsylvania	110	4	13	27	32	27	7
Ohio	420	8	53	99	121	86	53
Indiana	187	7	215	48	49	37	21
Illinois	411	10	47	86	133	92	43
Missouri	4,619	553	959	1,163	1,066	616	262
Kansas	413	30	69	122	98	64	30

Source: "Colored Farm Owners and Tenants by Age, by Southern Divisions, and States, and Selected Northern States: 1930," *Negroes in the United States, 1920-1932*, 1935, p. 606. Primary source: U.S. Bureau of the Census. *Negroes in the United States, 1920-1932.* Washington, D.C.: U.S. Government Printing Office, 1935. *Notes:* 1. States having 200 or more Negro farmers who constitute 90 percent or more colored farmers in the State.

★ 194 ★

Farms and Farmers

Relationships: Age Group of Black Tenant Farmers, by Farm Location, 1930 - II

[Colored farmers include Negroes, Indians, Chinese, Japanese, and all other nonwhite races]

DIVISION AND STATE	AGE OF COLORED FARM OPERATORS Percent distribution						
	Total	Under 25 years	25 to 34 years	35 to 44 years	45 to 54 years	55 to 64 years	65 years and over
TENANTS							
The South	100.0	14.1	22.7	22.5	22.4	12.6	5.6
SOUTH ATLANTIC	100.0	11.5	20.2	23.8	23.9	14.3	6.4
Delaware	100.0	3.3	13.8	26.3	31.3	16.0	9.5
Maryland	100.0	4.3	19.2	25.8	28.5	14.9	7.3
District of Columbia	100.0	-	-	-	50.0	50.0	-
Virginia	100.0	10.1	20.2	26.4	24.3	12.6	6.4
West Virginia	100.0	2.8	14.0	22.4	28.0	17.8	15.0
North Carolina	100.0	11.9	23.7	24.3	22.6	12.3	5.3
South Carolina	100.0	11.8	19.6	26.2	22.5	13.6	6.3
Georgia	100.0	12.0	18.3	20.9	25.3	16.4	7.1
Florida	100.0	6.4	17.2	24.2	27.8	16.0	8.4
EAST SOUTH CENTRAL	100.0	15.0	23.1	21.2	22.2	12.6	5.9
Kentucky	100.0	10.9	21.0	25.2	21.6	13.9	7.4
Tennessee	100.0	15.5	22.2	20.9	22.1	13.4	5.9
Alabama	100.0	11.2	19.8	18.7	28.5	14.3	7.5
Mississippi	100.0	16.9	25.0	22.3	19.2	11.5	5.1
WEST SOUTH CENTRAL	100.0	15.6	24.8	22.9	21.1	10.9	4.6
Arkansas	100.0	16.2	24.2	21.8	22.6	11.0	4.2
Louisiana	100.0	14.2	24.0	23.6	20.9	11.9	5.4
Oklahoma	100.0	11.8	24.0	23.4	23.1	12.8	4.8
Texas	100.0	17.4	26.5	23.3	19.3	9.5	4.1
SELECTED NORTHERN STATES[1]	100.0	9.8	18.9	25.3	24.4	15.0	6.7
New Jersey	100.0	1.7	19.8	34.7	36.4	14.9	2.5
Pennsylvania	100.0	3.6	11.8	24.5	29.1	24.5	6.4
Ohio	100.0	1.9	12.6	23.6	28.8	20.5	12.6
Indiana	100.0	3.7	13.4	25.7	26.2	19.8	11.2
Illinois	100.0	2.4	11.4	20.9	32.4	22.4	10.5
Missouri	100.0	12.0	20.8	25.2	23.1	13.3	5.7
Kansas	100.0	7.3	16.7	29.5	23.7	15.5	7.3

Source: "Colored Farm Owners and Tenants by Age, by Southern Divisions, and States, and Selected Northern States: 1930," *Negroes in the United States, 1920-1932,* 1935, p. 606. Primary source: U.S. Bureau of the Census. *Negroes in the United States, 1920-1932.* Washington, D.C.: U.S. Government Printing Office, 1935. *Notes:* 1. States having 200 or more Negro farmers who constitute 90 percent or more colored farmers in the State.

★ 195 ★

Farms and Farmers

Relationships: Average Size and Value of Land, Buildings, and Equipment of Black Farms, by Owner Status and Location of Farm, 1930 - I

SECTION AND DIVISION	AVERAGE SIZE OF FARM (ACRES)		AVERAGE VALUE-							
			Land and Buildings				Land alone			
			Per farm		Per acre		Per farm		Per acre	
	Owners	Tenants	Owners	Tenants	Owners	Tenants	Owners	Tenants	Owners	Tenants
United States	61.9	37.3	$1,848	$1,503	$29.86	$40.29	$1,263	$1,174	$20.42	$31.47
The North	75.2	56.7	3,998	3,389	53.18	59.82	2,625	2,691	34.92	47.50
The South	61.2	37.1	1,783	1,482	29.12	39.95	1,220	1,156	19.93	31.18
The West	175.5	101.6	5,771	9,164	32.89	90.18	4,741	8,378	27.02	82.45
New England	57.0	73.2	5,088	4,791	89.26	65.43	2,364	2,266	41.46	30.95
Middle Atlantic	47.1	90.8	4,265	7,905	90.54	87.07	1,929	4,680	40.95	51.55
East North Central	60.6	83.7	3,592	5,303	59.23	63.33	2,255	4,006	37.18	47.84
West North Central	100.1	48.7	4,256	2,718	42.54	55.76	3,239	2,293	32.37	47.03
South Atlantic	52.9	47.4	1,703	1,585	32.20	33.43	1,070	1,169	20.22	24.67
East South Central	69.7	30.9	1,634	1,263	23.45	40.83	1,136	975	16.31	31.53
West South Central	66.4	34.4	2,087	1,659	31.41	48.22	1,573	1,378	23.68	40.05
Mountain	326.2	139.0	5,157	8,807	15.81	63.65	4,383	7,997	13.44	57.52
Pacific	76.6	80.8	6,173	9,362	80.59	115.83	4,977	8,589	64.97	106.27

Source: "Average Size of Farm, and Average Value of Specified Classes of Farm Property of Negro Farm operators, by Tenure, by Sections, Divisions, and States: 1930," *Negroes in the United States, 1920-1932*, 1935, p. 600. Primary source: U.S. Bureau of the Census. *Negroes in the United States, 1920-1932.* Washington, D.C.: U.S. Government Printing Office, 1935.

★ 196 ★

Farms and Farmers

Relationships: Average Size and Value of Land, Buildings, and Equipment of Black Farms, by Owner Status and Location of Farm, 1930 - II

SECTION AND DIVISION	AVERAGE VALUE-							
	Buildings				Implements and machinery			
	Per farm		Per acre		Per farm		Per acre	
	Owners	Tenants	Owners	Tenants	Owners	Tenants	Owners	Tenants
United States	$584	$329	$9.44	$8.82	$109	$57	$1.77	$1.53
The North	1,373	698	18.27	12.33	236	130	3.13	2.29
The South	563	325	9.20	8.77	106	56	1.72	1.51
The West	1,029	786	5.87	7.74	310	372	1.77	3.67
New England	2,725	2,525	47.79	34.48	345	330	6.04	4.51
Middle Atlantic	2,336	3,225	49.59	35.53	415	563	8.82	6.20
East North Central	1,338	1,297	22.05	15.49	184	184	3.03	2.20
West North Central	1,017	426	10.16	8.73	226	94	2.25	1.93
South Atlantic	634	415	11.98	8.76	93	54	1.75	1.14
East South Central	497	288	7.14	9.30	110	52	1.58	1.69
West South Central	513	281	7.73	8.17	123	63	1.85	1.84

[Continued]

★ 196 ★

Relationships: Average Size and Value of Land, Buildings, and Equipment of Black Farms, by Owner Status and Location of Farm, 1930 - II
[Continued]

SECTION AND DIVISION	AVERAGE VALUE-							
	Buildings				Implements and machinery			
	Per farm		Per acre		Per farm		Per acre	
	Owners	Tenants	Owners	Tenants	Owners	Tenants	Owners	Tenants
Mountain	774	810	2.37	5.83	347	367	1.06	2.64
Pacific	1,196	773	15.62	9.56	285	375	3.72	4.64

Source: "Average Size of Farm, and Average Value of Specified Classes of Farm Property of Negro Farm operators, by Tenure, by Sections, Divisions, and States: 1930," *Negroes in the United States, 1920-1932*, 1935, p. 600. Primary source: U.S. Bureau of the Census. *Negroes in the United States, 1920-1932*. Washington, D.C.: U.S. Government Printing Office, 1935.

★ 197 ★

Farms and Farmers

Relationships: Average Value of Southern Farms, by Owner Status, 1900 and 1910 - I

DIVISION AND TENURE	Per farm				Per acre			
	Colored operators		White operators		Colored operators		White operators	
	1910	1900	1910	1900	1910	1900	1910	1900
THE SOUTH								
Total	$1,254	$659	$3,559	$2,012	$26.21	$12.64	$25.19	$11.69
Owners	1,588	779	3,911	2,140	22.11	10.89	24.13	12.08
Tenants	1,130	607	2,582	1,363	28.52	13.50	30.81	14.73
Managers	10,050	4,640	28,629	18,861	34.48	17.25	17.76	6.37
South Atlantic	1,247	566	3,317	1,917	25.11	10.45	29.12	14.56
Owners	1,280	553	3,613	2,038	23.12	10.63	27.96	13.98
Tenants	1,212	558	2,330	1,439	25.83	10.27	30.89	15.34
Managers	8,847	3,397	17,562	8,363	43.82	16.39	41.34	20.89
East South Central	1,099	639	2,545	1,613	26.28	13.56	26.88	14.93
Owners	1,570	778	2,967	1,830	20.32	10.12	25.49	14.14
Tenants	983	601	1,646	1,083	29.15	14.99	31.30	17.41
Managers	13,146	4,628	17,421	7,404	42.87	24.83	34.69	20.71
West South Central	1,509	835	4,798	2,568	27.83	14.83	22.32	8.83
Owners	2,148	1,152	5,407	2,668	22.54	11.69	20.96	9.53
Tenants	1,251	693	3,478	1,546	33.13	17.95	30.60	13.01
Managers	10,460	8,687	55,045	47,988	18.87	15.55	12.56	4.85

Source: "Average Value of Farm Property," *Negro Population, 1790-1915*, 1918, p. 580. Primary source: U.S. Bureau of the Census. *Negro Population, 1790-1915*. Washington, D.C.: Government Printing Office, 1918. *Note:* "Colored" may include persons other than black.

★ 198 ★

Farms and Farmers

Relationships: Average Value of Southern Farms, by Owner Status, 1900 and 1910 - II

DIVISION AND TENURE	Per farm				Per acre			
	Colored operators		White operators		Colored operators		White operators	
	1910	1900	1910	1900	1910	1900	1910	1900
THE SOUTH								
Total	$1,254	$659	$3,559	$2,012	$26.21	$12.64	$25.19	$11.69
Owners	1,588	779	3,911	2,140	22.11	10.89	24.13	12.08
Tenants	1,130	607	2,582	1,363	28.52	13.50	30.81	14.73
Managers	10,050	4,640	28,629	18,861	34.48	17.25	17.76	6.37
South Atlantic	1,247	566	3,317	1,917	25.11	10.45	29.12	14.56
Owners	1,280	553	3,613	2,038	23.12	10.63	27.96	13.98
Tenants	1,212	558	2,330	1,439	25.83	10.27	30.89	15.34
Managers	8,847	3,397	17,562	8,363	43.82	16.39	41.34	20.89
East South Central	1,099	639	2,545	1,613	26.28	13.56	26.88	14.93
Owners	1,570	778	2,967	1,830	20.32	10.12	25.49	14.14
Tenants	983	601	1,646	1,083	29.15	14.99	31.30	17.41
Managers	13,146	4,628	17,421	7,404	42.87	24.83	34.69	20.71
West South Central	1,509	835	4,798	2,568	27.83	14.83	22.32	8.83
Owners	2,148	1,152	5,407	2,668	22.54	11.69	20.96	9.53
Tenants	1,251	693	3,478	1,546	33.13	17.95	30.60	13.01
Managers	10,460	8,687	55,045	47,988	18.87	15.55	12.56	4.85

Source: "Average Value of Farm Property," *Negro Population, 1790-1915,* 1918, p. 580. Primary source: U.S. Bureau of the Census. *Negro Population, 1790-1915.* Washington, D.C.: Government Printing Office, 1918. *Note:* "Colored" may include persons other than black.

★ 199 ★

Farms and Farmers

Relationships: Black Farm Acreage Per 1,000 Acres of Farm Land, for Total, Improved, and Unimproved Land in Farms, by Farm Location, 1900 and 1910

SECTION AND DIVISION	ACRES IN FARMS OPERATED BY NEGROES PER 1,000 ACRES IN ALL FARMS					
	All farm land		Improved farm land		Unimproved farm land	
	1910	1900	1910	1900	1910	1900
United States	48	46	58	56	36	35
The South	116	103	180	180	69	62
South Atlantic	170	149	226	193	120	115
East South Central	167	155	217	203	107	108
West South Central	60	52	114	142	31	25

[Continued]

★ 199 ★

Relationships: Black Farm Acreage Per 1,000 Acres of Farm Land, for Total, Improved, and Unimproved Land in Farms, by Farm Location, 1900 and 1910

[Continued]

SECTION AND DIVISION	ACRES IN FARMS OPERATED BY NEGROES PER 1,000 ACRES IN ALL FARMS					
	All farm land		Improved farm land		Unimproved farm land	
	1910	1900	1910	1900	1910	1900
The North	2	2	2	2	2	2
The West	1	1	1	1	1	1

Source: "Acres in Farms Operated by Negroes Per 1,000 Acres in All Farms," *Negro Population, 1790-1915,* 1918, p. 556. Primary source: U.S. Bureau of the Census. *Negro Population, 1790-1915.* Washington, D.C.: Government Printing Office, 1918.

★ 200 ★

Farms and Farmers

Relationships: Dwellings on Black Farms – Percentage Distribution by Owner Status, Dwelling Value, and Farm Location, 1930

SECTION AND DIVISION	Total number of farms	REPORTING VALUE OF DWELLINGS									Not reporting value
		Total	Under $500	$500 to $999	$1,000 to $1,999	$2,000 to $2,999	$3,000 to $4,999	$5,000 to $7,499	$7,500 to $9,999	$10,000 and over	
						TOTAL DWELLINGS					
United States	882,850	806,074	668,018	110,267	22,231	3,619	1,384	364	85	106	76,776
						PERCENT DISTRIBUTION					
United States	100.0	100.0	100.0	100.0	100.0	100.0	100.0	100.0	100.0	100.0	100.0
THE SOUTH	98.7	98.7	99.1	98.0	93.5	86.5	79.6	76.4	81.2	84.9	98.5
South Atlantic	33.5	34.1	31.3	45.0	57.8	56.7	52.7	48.1	48.2	55.7	27.4
East South Central	36.3	36.3	38.0	30.6	17.3	15.2	13.9	14.8	22.4	13.2	36.6
West South Central	28.8	28.3	29.7	22.4	18.4	14.6	13.1	13.5	10.6	16.0	34.4
THE NORTH	1.3	1.2	.9	1.8	6.0	12.5	19.0	22.8	17.6	13.2	1.5
THE WEST	.1	.1	.1	.1	.5	1.1	1.4	.8	1.2	1.9	.1
						DWELLINGS OF OWNERS[1]					
						PERCENT DISTRIBUTION					
United States	100.0	100.0	100.0	100.0	100.0	100.0	100.0	100.0	100.0	100.0	100.0
THE SOUTH	97.2	97.3	98.3	96.9	92.5	86.3	78.1	73.7	83.6	83.6	96.2
South Atlantic	44.1	44.2	41.2	49.1	54.6	54.5	50.1	44.9	49.1	55.7	40.8
East South Central	27.8	27.9	30.3	24.6	18.2	15.9	14.0	12.8	27.3	11.5	26.7
West South Central	25.4	25.3	26.8	23.1	19.7	15.9	14.1	16.0	7.3	16.4	28.7
THE NORTH	2.5	2.5	1.5	2.9	6.9	12.5	20.5	25.5	14.5	14.8	3.3
THE WEST	.3	.3	.2	.2	.6	1.2	1.4	.8	1.8	1.6	.5

[Continued]

★ 200 ★

Relationships: Dwellings on Black Farms – Percentage Distribution by Owner Status, Dwelling Value, and Farm Location, 1930

[Continued]

SECTION AND DIVISION	Total number of farms	REPORTING VALUE OF DWELLINGS									Not reporting value
		Total	Under $500	$500 to $999	$1,000 to $1,999	$2,000 to $2,999	$3,000 to $4,999	$5,000 to $7,499	$7,500 to $9,999	$10,000 and over	

DWELLINGS OF TENANTS

PERCENT DISTRIBUTION

United States	100.0	100.0	100.0	100.0	100.0	100.0	100.0	100.0	100.0	100.0	100.0
THE SOUTH	99.0	99.1	99.2	98.7	94.9	86.7	82.6	81.8	76.7	86.7	98.6
South Atlantic	30.8	31.3	29.2	42.8	62.2	60.5	57.9	54.5	46.7	55.6	26.2
East South Central	38.5	38.6	39.7	33.9	16.0	13.9	13.7	19.0	13.3	15.6	37.4
West South Central	29.7	29.1	30.3	22.1	16.7	12.3	11.1	8.3	16.7	15.6	34.9
THE NORTH	.9	.9	.7	1.2	4.7	12.5	16.1	17.4	23.3	11.1	1.3
THE WEST	2	2	2	.1	.4	.8	1.3	.8	-	2.2	.1

Source: "Number of Dwellings on Farms Operated by Negroes, by Value Groups, and by Tenure, by Sections, and Southern Divisions: 1930," *Negroes in the United States, 1920-1932,* 1935, p. 581. Primary source: U.S. Bureau of the Census. *Negroes in the United States, 1920-1932.* Washington, D.C.: U.S. Government Printing Office, 1935. *Notes:* 1. Includes 923 managers, 805 in the South, 92 in the North, and 26 in the West. 2. Less than 1/10 of 1 percent.

★ 201 ★

Farms and Farmers

Relationships: Farm Acreage on Southern Farms, by Owner Status, 1910 - I

DIVISION AND STATE	FARMS OPERATED BY COLORED FARMERS: 1910						
	Total	Owners and part owners			Tenants		Managers
		Owners		Part owners	Cash and not specified	Share and share cash	
		Free	Mortgaged				

NUMBER OF ACRES

THE SOUTH							
Total	42,609,117	8,835,857	4,011,491	2,844,188	12,876,308	13,691,494	349,779
South Atlantic	17,675,382	3,280,891	1,251,082	1,114,405	5,981,903	5,901,730	145,371
East South Central	13,595,717	2,149,433	1,556,778	833,741	5,348,300	3,631,105	76,360
West South Central	11,338,018	3,405,533	1,203,631	896,042	1,546,105	4,158,659	128,048
SOUTH ATLANTIC							
Delaware	56,973	6,439	4,999	2,177	4,112	36,851	2,395
Maryland	385,517	58,733	39,195	24,111	41,820	181,297	13,361
District of Columbia	95	15	3	40	33	-	4
Virginia	2,238,220	889,297	243,224	248,702	244,343	582,669	29,985
West Virginia	34,541	19,894	3,040	3,023	2,190	5,739	655

[Continued]

★ 201 ★

Relationships: Farm Acreage on Southern Farms, by Owner Status, 1910 - I

[Continued]

DIVISION AND STATE	FARMS OPERATED BY COLORED FARMERS: 1910						
	Total	Owners and part owners			Tenants		Managers
		Owners		Part owners	Cash and not specified	Share and share cash	
		Free	Mortgaged				
North Carolina	3,185,804	604,292	257,037	336,167	601,283	1,368,033	18,992
South Carolina	3,940,476	607,767	271,588	218,689	1,595,244	1,204,734	42,454
Georgia	7,092,051	785,895	346,221	217,387	3,272,972	2,442,025	27,551
Florida	768,705	308,559	85,775	64,109	219,906	80,382	9,974
EAST SOUTH CENTRAL							
Kentucky	440,777	143,507	51,080	60,776	25,139	155,957	4,318
Tennessee	1,606,078	307,399	125,686	157,591	525,125	472,595	17,682
Alabama	5,091,435	660,075	498,567	308,077	2,611,447	995,787	17,482
Mississippi	6,457,427	1,038,452	881,445	307,297	2,186,589	2,006,766	36,878
WEST SOUTH CENTRAL							
Arkansas	2,653,323	636,899	353,283	213,932	695,584	747,532	6,093
Louisiana	2,124,321	567,301	188,352	79,042	323,641	945,009	20,976
Oklahoma	2,276,711	1,100,167	289,952	209,536	203,293	467,468	6,295
Texas	4,283,663	1,101,166	372,044	393,532	323,587	1,998,650	94,684

Source: "Acres in Colored and White Farms, Classified by Tenure, by Southern Divisions, and States: 1910," *Negro Population, 1790-1915,* 1918, p. 612. Primary source: U.S. Bureau of the Census. *Negro Population, 1790-1915.* Washington, D.C.: Government Printing Office, 1918.

★ 202 ★

Farms and Farmers

Relationships: Farm Acreage on Southern Farms, by Owner Status, 1910 - II

DIVISION AND STATE	FARMS OPERATED BY WHITE FARMERS: 1910						
	Total	Owners and part owners			Tenants		Managers
		Owners		Part owners	Cash and not specified	Share and share cash	
		Free	Mortgaged				
	NUMBER OF ACRES						
THE SOUTH							
Total	311,843,743	134,584,147	46,759,094	33,580,452	26,275,674	46,328,127	24,316,249
South Atlantic	86,106,873	48,158,522	9,871,919	5,452,964	7,689,142	11,715,307	3,219,019
East South Central	67,924,912	38,000,187	8,929,447	5,662,386	5,245,221	8,560,564	1,527,107
West South Central	157,811,958	48,425,438	27,957,728	22,465,102	13,341,311	26,052,256	19,570,123

[Continued]

★ 202 ★

Relationships: Farm Acreage on Southern Farms, by Owner Status, 1910 - II
[Continued]

DIVISION AND STATE	FARMS OPERATED BY WHITE FARMERS: 1910						
	Total	Owners and part owners			Tenants		Managers
		Owners		Part owners	Cash and not specified	Share and share cash	
		Free	Mortgaged				
SOUTH ATLANTIC							
Delaware	981,893	286,098	161,003	16,111	67,545	432,367	18,769
Maryland	4,698,623	1,632,616	965,268	185,395	368,132	1,353,282	193,930
District of Columbia	5,968	1,866	336	169	2,069	76	1,452
Virginia	17,257,416	10,209,308	1,941,675	1,183,139	1,090,454	2,202,500	630,340
West Virginia	9,991,901	6,429,302	885,909	843,027	827,918	721,898	283,847
North Carolina	19,253,325	10,981,223	1,936,085	1,541,519	1,146,502	3,084,611	563,385
South Carolina	9,571,552	4,931,808	1,461,880	559,771	1,191,907	921,228	504,958
Georgia	19,861,362	10,614,095	2,050,484	837,210	2,761,942	2,846,060	751,571
Florida	4,484,833	3,072,206	469,279	286,623	232,673	153,285	270,767
EAST SOUTH CENTRAL							
Kentucky	21,748,350	12,708,031	2,744,751	1,754,610	1,180,895	3,049,121	310,942
Tennessee	18,435,579	10,347,702	1,785,151	1,949,108	1,204,724	2,831,647	317,247
Alabama	15,640,877	8,268,042	2,236,398	1,308,947	1,764,461	1,713,744	349,285
Mississippi	12,100,106	6,676,412	2,163,147	649,721	1,095,141	966,052	549,633
WEST SOUTH CENTRAL							
Arkansas	14,762,752	7,759,104	1,700,909	1,725,415	1,133,811	2,121,420	322,093
Louisiana	8,315,160	4,272,176	1,191,593	467,659	683,716	779,635	965,381
Oklahoma	26,582,642	4,974,762	4,037,695	5,384,683	4,288,425	7,474,693	422,384
Texas	108,151,404	31,419,396	21,027,531	14,887,345	7,280,359	15,676,508	17,860,265

Source: "Acres in Colored and White Farms, Classified by Tenure, by Southern Divisions, and States: 1910," *Negro Population, 1790-1915*, 1918, p. 612. Primary source: U.S. Bureau of the Census. *Negro Population, 1790-1915*. Washington, D.C.: Government Printing Office, 1918.

★ 203 ★

Farms and Farmers

Relationships: Improved Acreage on Southern Farms, by Owner Status, 1910 - I

DIVISION AND STATE	FARMS OPERATED BY COLORED FARMERS: 1910						
	Total	Owners and part owners			Tenants		Managers
		Owners		Part owners	Cash and not specified	Share and share cash	
		Free	Mortgaged				

NUMBER OF ACRES IMPROVED

THE SOUTH							
Total	27,735,743	4,005,552	1,893,013	1,632,554	9,218,158	10,878,217	108,249
South Atlantic	10,990,069	1,493,024	573,626	629,297	3,900,843	4,331,992	61,287
East South Central	9,556,529	988,088	735,893	489,664	4,170,455	3,146,192	26,237
West South Central	7,189,145	1,524,440	583,494	513,593	1,146,860	3,400,033	20,725
SOUTH ATLANTIC							
Delaware	37,076	4,070	3,458	1,746	2,647	23,121	2,034
Maryland	218,582	35,176	24,125	17,263	23,463	109,540	9,015
District of Columbia	95	15	3	40	33	-	4
Virginia	1,111,208	421,031	108,228	140,099	104,938	322,866	14,046
West Virginia	20,257	10,521	2,007	1,994	1,166	3,967	602
North Carolina	1,730,712	236,163	105,115	171,289	326,085	886,816	5,244
South Carolina	2,598,224	286,275	123,158	129,914	1,073,124	970,879	14,874
Georgia	4,791,562	352,940	163,893	127,563	2,189,038	1,946,912	11,216
Florida	482,353	146,833	43,639	39,389	180,349	67,891	4,252
EAST SOUTH CENTRAL							
Kentucky	343,694	98,385	36,681	50,723	18,795	135,533	3,577
Tennessee	1,162,276	168,597	74,137	106,958	397,328	408,478	6,778
Alabama	3,563,176	283,558	222,641	169,620	2,037,433	844,912	5,012
Mississippi	4,487,383	437,548	402,434	162,363	1,716,899	1,757,269	10,870
WEST SOUTH CENTRAL							
Arkansas	1,773,206	275,226	152,155	113,884	577,603	651,270	3,068
Louisiana	1,466,607	259,152	92,766	47,732	243,487	815,423	8,047
Oklahoma	1,172,819	459,420	156,867	118,307	102,533	334,208	1,484
Texas	2,776,513	530,642	181,706	233,670	223,237	1,599,132	8,126

Source: "Acres Improved in Colored and White Farms, Classified by Tenure, by Southern Divisions, and States: 1910," *Negro Population, 1790-1915,* 1918, p. 613.
Primary source: U.S. Bureau of the Census. *Negro Population, 1790-1915.* Washington, D.C.: Government Printing Office, 1918.

★ 204 ★

Farms and Farmers

Relationships: Improved Acreage on Southern Farms, by Owner Status, 1910 - II

DIVISION AND STATE	FARMS OPERATED BY WHITE FARMERS: 1910						
	Total	Owners and part owners			Tenants		Managers
		Owners		Part owners	Cash and not specified	Share and share cash	
		Free	Mortgaged				

NUMBER OF ACRES IMPROVED

DIVISION AND STATE	Total	Free	Mortgaged	Part owners	Cash and not specified	Share and share cash	Managers
THE SOUTH							
Total	122,955,109	50,780,626	16,588,921	12,212,994	10,839,130	29,407,345	3,126,093
South Atlantic	37,489,664	19,157,380	4,354,417	2,636,523	3,532,513	6,641,034	1,167,797
East South Central	34,390,317	17,563,414	4,466,366	3,140,497	2,815,572	5,851,914	552,554
West South Central	51,075,128	14,059,832	7,768,138	6,435,974	4,491,045	16,914,397	1,405,742
SOUTH ATLANTIC							
Delaware	676,462	186,182	114,928	11,693	44,802	303,304	15,553
Maryland	3,136,185	1,029,132	653,241	124,545	228,397	980,616	120,254
District of Columbia	5,038	1,640	262	167	1,645	65	1,259
Virginia	8,758,850	5,115,695	1,009,731	677,002	452,183	1,197,757	306,482
West Virginia	5,501,500	3,591,580	484,568	515,433	332,822	443,865	133,232
North Carolina	7,082,344	3,698,312	700,169	628,735	442,156	1,458,234	154,738
South Carolina	3,499,775	1,512,529	517,790	231,112	568,930	542,482	126,932
Georgia	7,506,455	3,197,819	725,350	363,730	1,343,048	1,639,374	237,134
Florida	1,323,055	824,491	148,378	84,106	118,530	75,337	72,213
EAST SOUTH CENTRAL							
Kentucky	14,010,777	7,776,139	1,874,722	1,250,094	669,792	2,245,899	171,131
Tennessee	9,728,208	5,032,536	962,808	1,116,463	664,998	1,842,263	109,140
Alabama	6,130,405	2,607,153	817,021	520,239	919,774	1,151,131	115,087
Mississippi	4,520,927	2,147,586	811,815	253,701	538,008	612,621	157,196
WEST SOUTH CENTRAL							
Arkansas	6,303,048	2,832,442	712,899	728,516	596,598	1,322,962	109,631
Louisiana	3,809,409	1,681,845	543,051	241,216	359,417	577,485	406,395
Oklahoma	16,378,518	2,807,653	2,528,269	3,251,649	2,295,853	5,319,651	175,443
Texas	24,584,153	6,737,892	3,983,919	2,214,593	1,239,177	9,694,299	714,273

Source: "Acres Improved in Colored and White Farms, Classified by Tenure, by Southern Divisions, and States: 1910," *Negro Population, 1790-1915,* 1918, p. 613. Primary source: U.S. Bureau of the Census. *Negro Population, 1790-1915.* Washington, D.C.: Government Printing Office, 1918.

★ 205 ★

Farms and Farmers

Relationships: Land and Building Value on Black Farms, by Owner Status and Location of Farm, 1930

SECTION AND DIVISION	VALUE OF LAND ALONE				VALUE OF ALL BUILDINGS			
	Total	Owners	Tenants	Managers	Total	Owners	Tenants	Managers
United States	$1,062,536,439	$228,709,700	$823,005,516	$10,821,223	$340,409,310	$105,741,696	$230,644,120	$4,023,544
THE SOUTH	1,026,877,643	214,907,952	802,581,553	9,388,138	328,304,024	99,192,480	225,789,875	3,321,669
South Atlantic	342,118,722	85,227,015	252,300,365	4,591,342	142,325,221	50,497,142	89,622,060	2,206,019
East South Central	323,130,648	57,360,605	263,328,563	2,441,480	103,398,196	25,092,461	77,634,070	671,665
West South Central	361,628,273	72,320,332	286,952,625	2,355,316	82,580,607	23,602,877	58,533,745	443,985
THE NORTH	30,366,748	11,611,190	17,726,373	1,029,185	11,301,474	6,073,789	4,601,110	626,575
New England	406,290	302,565	31,725	72,000	503,105	348,760	35,345	119,000
Middle Atlantic	2,687,260	1,095,865	1,282,195	309,200	2,452,995	1,326,810	883,685	242,505
East North Central	9,130,656	4,265,786	4,602,325	262,545	4,174,095	2,530,750	1,490,320	153,020
West North Central	18,142,542	5,946,974	11,810,128	385,440	4,171,279	1,867,469	2,191,760	112,050
THE WEST	5,292,048	2,190,558	2,697,590	403,900	803,862	475,427	253,135	75,300
Mountain	1,792,685	802,065	919,620	71,000	244,825	141,620	93,205	10,000
Pacific	3,499,363	1,388,493	1,777,970	332,900	559,037	333,807	159,930	65,300

PERCENT DISTRIBUTION

	Total	Owners	Tenants	Managers	Total	Owners	Tenants	Managers
United States	100.0	100.0	100.0	100.0	100.0	100.0	100.0	100.0
The South	96.6	94.0	97.5	86.8	96.4	93.8	97.9	82.6
The North	2.9	5.1	2.2	9.5	3.3	5.7	2.0	15.6
The West	.5	1.0	.3	3.7	.2	.5	.1	1.9

Source: "Value of Land in Farms and Value of All Buildings on Farms Operated by Negroes, by Tenure, by Sections, and Divisions: 1930," *Negroes in the United States, 1920-1932,* 1935, p. 580. Primary source: U.S. Bureau of the Census. *Negroes in the United States, 1920-1932.* Washington, D.C.: U.S. Government Printing Office, 1935.

★ 206 ★

Farms and Farmers

Relationships: Land and Building Value on Black-Owned Farms, by Mortgage Status and Farm Location, 1930

Figures relate only to farms wholly owned by their operators. Colored farmers include Negroes, Indians, Chinese, Japanese, and all other nonwhite races.

DIVISION AND STATE	Total	Reporting farms free mortgage	Reporting farms mortgaged	Unknown (no report)	PERCENT DISTRIBUTION BY MORTGAGE STATUS			PERCENT DISTRIBUTION OF TOTAL FOR SOUTH AND SELECTED NORTHERN STATES			
					Reporting farms free from mortgage	Reporting farms mortgaged	Unknown (no report)	Total	Reporting farms free from mortgage	Reporting farms mortgaged	Unknown (no report)
The South	$33,039,069	$143,615,598	$95,284,776	$24,138,695	54.6	36.3	9.2	100.0	100.0	100.0	100.0
South Atlantic	106,007,752	62,365,265	35,921,883	7,720,604	58.8	33.9	7.3	40.3	43.4	37.7	32.0
East South Central	65,075,305	30,315,560	29,257,867	5,501,878	46.6	45.0	8.5	24.7	21.1	30.7	22.8
West South Central	91,956,012	50,934,773	30,105,026	10,916,213	55.4	32.7	11.9	35.0	35.5	31.6	45.2
SELECTED NORTHERN STATES[1]	9,709,768	4,035,360	5,168,308	506,100	41.6	53.2	5.2	100.0	100.0	100.0	100.0
New Jersey	932,450	377,700	495,750	59,000	40.5	53.2	6.3	9.6	9.4	9.6	11.7
Pennsylvania	926,480	313,580	595,500	17,400	33.8	64.3	1.9	9.5	7.8	11.5	3.4
Ohio	2,076,060	857,845	1,080,575	137,640	41.3	52.0	6.6	21.4	21.3	20.9	27.2
Indiana	600,490	221,440	343,750	35,300	36.9	57.2	5.9	6.2	5.5	6.7	7.0
Illinois	874,714	399,895	413,569	61,250	45.7	47.3	7.0	9.0	9.9	8.0	12.1

[Continued]

★ 206 ★

Relationships: Land and Building Value on Black-Owned Farms, by Mortgage Status and Farm Location, 1930

[Continued]

DIVISION AND STATE	Total	Reporting farms free mortgage	Reporting farms mortgaged	Unknown (no report)	PERCENT DISTRIBUTION BY MORTGAGE STATUS			PERCENT DISTRIBUTION OF TOTAL FOR SOUTH AND SELECTED NORTHERN STATES			
					Reporting farms free from mortgage	Reporting farms mortgaged	Unknown (no report)	Total	Reporting farms free from mortgage	Reporting farms mortgaged	Unknown (no report)
Missouri	2,262,724	1,064,245	1,092,169	106,310	47.0	48.8	4.7	23.3	26.4	21.1	21.0
Kansas	2,036,850	800,655	1,146,995	89,200	39.3	56.3	4.4	21.0	19.8	22.2	17.6

Source: "Value of Farms (Land and Buildings) Operated by Colored Full Owners, by Mortgage Status, with Percent Distribution, by Southern Divisions, and States, and Selected Northern States: 1930," *Negroes in the United States, 1920-1932*, 1935, p. 584. Primary source: U.S. Bureau of the Census. *Negroes in the United States, 1920-1932.* Washington, D.C.: U.S. Government Printing Office, 1935. *Notes:* 1. States having 200 or more Negro farmers who constitute 90 percent or more of the colored farmers in the State.

★ 207 ★

Farms and Farmers

Relationships: Length of Occupancy on All Black Farms, by Owner Status and Division, 1910

DIVISION, STATE, AND TERM OF OCCUPANCY	COLORED FARMS: 1910						
	Total	Owners free	Owners mortgaged	Part owners	Cash tenants	Share tenants	Managers
UNITED STATES							
Total	920,883	145,924	49,885	45,412	289,944	388,174	1,544
Less than 1 year	191,808	3,198	2,097	3,677	51,385	131,155	296
1 year	105,781	3,904	2,503	3,353	35,669	60,176	176
2 to 4 years	242,724	18,613	9,499	10,229	94,331	109,633	419
5 to 9 years	131,354	24,558	10,202	9,402	49,056	37,861	275
10 years and over	165,560	65,605	17,724	15,561	41,616	24,808	246
Not reported	83,656	30,046	7,860	3,190	17,887	24,541	132

Source: "Colored Farms Classified by Tenure and Term of Occupancy, by Divisions and States: 1910," *Negro Population, 1790-1915*, 1918, pp. 638-641. Primary source: U.S. Bureau of the Census. *Negro Population, 1790-1915.* Washington, D.C.: Government Printing Office, 1918. *Note:* "Colored" may include persons other than black.

★ 208 ★
Farms and Farmers

Relationships: Length of Occupancy on Southern Black Farms (in percentages), by Owner Status, 1910 - I

DIVISION AND TERM OF OCCUPANCY	COLORED FARMERS: 1910 Percentage distribution by term of occupancy						
	Total	Owners free	Owners mortgaged	Part owners	Cash tenants	Share tenants	Managers
SOUTH ATLANTIC							
Total	100.0	100.0	100.0	100.0	100.0	100.0	100.0
Less than 1 year	18.9	1.8	4.0	7.0	16.8	32.0	14.6
1 year	11.6	2.4	5.1	6.9	12.8	16.4	9.6
2 to 4 years	26.9	13.3	19.2	22.2	33.1	29.7	30.4
5 to 9 years	14.7	17.3	19.2	20.1	17.3	10.0	21.2
10 years and over	19.7	47.8	36.8	36.8	14.9	6.2	15.7
Not reported	8.1	17.3	15.8	6.9	5.1	5.6	8.5
EAST SOUTH CENTRAL							
Total	100.0	100.0	100.0	100.0	100.0	100.0	100.0
Less than 1 year	23.2	2.1	4.0	8.8	17.9	37.2	18.1
1 year	11.6	2.9	4.6	7.2	11.6	14.8	11.2
2 to 4 years	27.2	13.8	19.4	24.1	32.4	26.2	28.1
5 to 9 years	14.4	18.5	21.4	21.6	17.2	9.1	12.1
10 years and over	15.8	47.0	35.7	32.0	14.6	5.8	20.1
Not reported	7.8	15.7	14.9	6.3	6.3	6.8	10.4
WEST SOUTH CENTRAL							
Total	100.0	100.0	100.0	100.0	100.0	100.0	100.0
Less than 1 year	22.3	2.9	4.5	9.8	19.7	32.3	24.7
1 year	11.8	2.9	5.4	8.6	12.8	15.2	11.3
2 to 4 years	25.3	12.1	18.4	21.9	30.9	28.6	19.5
5 to 9 years	13.6	17.8	21.6	21.5	15.2	10.2	18.6
10 years and over	16.8	43.1	31.9	30.0	12.5	7.1	15.6
Not reported	10.3	21.2	18.2	8.1	8.9	6.6	10.4

Source: "Percentage Distribution of Colored Farmers by Term of Occupancy and Tenure, by Southern Divisions: 1910," *Negro Population, 1790,1915,* 1918, p. 586. Primary source: U.S. Bureau of the Census. *Negro Population, 1790-1915.* Washington, D.C.: Government Printing Office, 1918. *Note:* "Colored" may include persons other than black.

★ 209 ★

Farms and Farmers

Relationships: Length of Occupancy on Southern Black Farms (in percentages), by Owner Status, 1910 - II

DIVISION AND TERM OF OCCUPANCY	COLORED FARMERS: 1910 Percentage distribution by tenure						
	Total	Owners free	Owners mortgaged	Part owners	Cash tenants	Share tenants	Managers
SOUTH ATLANTIC							
Total	100.0	17.9	4.8	5.9	31.8	39.3	0.2
Less than 1 year	100.0	1.7	1.0	2.2	28.2	66.7	0.2
1 year	100.0	3.8	2.1	3.5	35.0	55.4	0.2
2 to 4 years	100.0	8.9	3.4	4.9	39.1	43.5	0.2
5 to 9 years	100.0	21.1	6.3	8.1	37.6	26.7	0.3
10 years and over	100.0	43.4	9.0	11.0	24.0	12.4	0.2
Not reported	100.0	38.1	9.4	5.1	19.9	27.3	0.2
EAST SOUTH CENTRAL							
Total	100.0	8.9	5.3	3.8	41.5	40.3	0.1
Less than 1 year	100.0	0.8	0.9	1.4	32.0	64.7	0.1
1 year	100.0	2.2	2.1	2.4	41.7	51.6	0.1
2 to 4 years	100.0	4.5	3.9	3.4	49.3	38.9	0.1
5 to 9 years	100.0	11.4	7.9	5.7	49.5	25.5	0.1
10 years and over	100.0	26.5	12.1	7.8	38.5	14.9	0.1
Not reported	100.0	17.8	10.2	3.1	33.5	35.3	0.1
WEST SOUTH CENTRAL							
Total	100.0	17.2	5.8	4.6	18.0	54.2	0.1
Less than 1 year	100.0	2.2	1.2	2.0	16.0	78.5	0.1
1 year	100.0	4.2	2.6	3.4	19.7	70.0	0.1
2 to 4 years	100.0	8.2	4.2	4.0	22.0	61.4	0.1
5 to 9 years	100.0	22.6	9.2	7.4	20.1	40.6	0.1
10 years and over	100.0	44.1	11.0	8.3	13.5	23.0	0.1
Not reported	100.0	35.5	10.3	3.7	15.7	34.8	0.1

Source: "Percentage Distribution of Colored Farmers by Term of Occupancy and Tenure, by Southern Divisions: 1910," *Negro Population, 1790,1915,* 1918, p. 586. Primary source: U.S. Bureau of the Census. *Negro Population, 1790-1915.* Washington, D.C.: Government Printing Office, 1918. *Note:* "Colored" may include persons other than black.

★ 210 ★
Farms and Farmers

Relationships: Minority ("Colored") Farmers, by Owner Status and Farm Location, 1930

TENURE	NUMBER					PERCENT DISTRIBUTION			
	Total	Colored			White[2]	Colored			White[2]
		Negro	Indian	Other[1]		Negro	Indian	Other[1]	
UNITED STATES									
Total	6,288,648	882,850	26,817	6,403	5,372,578	100.0	100.0	100.0	100.0
Owners	3,568,394	181,016	20,658	1,046	3,365,674	20.5	77.0	16.3	62.6
Tenants	2,664,365	700,911	6,091	3,226	1,954,137	79.4	22.7	50.4	36.4
Managers	55,889	923	68	2,131	52,767	.1	.3	33.3	1.0
THE SOUTH									
Total	3,223,816	870,936	10,637	114	2,342,129	100.0	100.0	100.0	100.0
Owners	1,415,675	176,130	5,850	39	1,233,656	20.2	55.0	34.2	52.7
Tenants	1,790,783	694,001	4,766	72	1,091,944	79.7	44.8	63.2	46.6
Managers	17,358	805	21	3	16,529	.1	.2	2.6	.7
THE NORTH									
Total	2,561,785	11,104	4,753	99	2,545,829	100.0	100.0	100.0	100.0
Owners	1,768,206	4,424	3,929	35	1,759,818	39.8	82.7	35.4	69.1
Tenants	768,486	6,588	807	64	761,027	59.3	17.0	64.6	29.9
Managers	25,093	92	17	-	24,984	.8	.4	-	1.0
THE WEST									
Total	503,047	810	11,427	6,190	484,620	100.0	100.0	100.0	100.0
Owners	384,513	462	10,879	972	372,200	57.0	95.2	15.7	76.8
Tenants	105,096	322	518	3,090	101,166	39.8	4.5	49.9	20.9
Managers	13,438	26	30	2,128	11,254	3.2	.3	34.4	2.3

Source: "Number of Farms Operated by Color, and Tenure, by Sections: 1930," *Negroes in the United States, 1920-1932*, 1935, p. 577. Primary source: U.S. Bureau of the Census. *Negroes in the United States, 1920-1932*. Washington, D.C.: U.S. Government Printing Office, 1935. *Notes:* 1. Includes 5,840 Japanese, 476 Chinese, 56 Filipinos, 30 Koreans, and 1 Hawaiian. 2. Includes Mexicans and Hindus.

★ 211 ★
Farms and Farmers

Relationships: Mortgage Status of Black Farm Owners Under 25, by Age Group and Farm Location, 1920 and 1930 - I

| DIVISION AND STATE | ALL COLORED FULL OWNERS | | | | | UNDER 25 YEARS | | | | |
| | 1930 | | | 1920 | | 1930 | | | 1920 | |
	Reporting farms free from mortgage	Reporting farms mortgaged	Unknown (no report)	Reporting farms free from mortgage[1]	Reporting farms mortgaged	Reporting farms free from mortgage	Reporting farms mortgaged	Unknown (no report)	Reporting farms free from mortgage[1]	Reporting farms mortgaged
					PERCENT DISTRIBUTION					
The South	60.4	29.9	9.7	76.1	23.9	61.2	23.6	15.1	78.8	21.2
SOUTH ATLANTIC	65.7	26.1	8.2	79.4	20.6	70.5	17.6	11.9	84.0	16.0
Delaware	52.4	40.1	7.4	58.4	41.6	50.0	-	50.0	50.0	50.0
Maryland	61.3	34.5	4.2	70.2	29.8	60.0	40.0	-	75.0	25.0
District of Columbia	28.6	42.9	28.6	75.0	25.0	-	-	-	-	-
Virginia	73.3	21.8	4.9	82.3	17.7	73.7	19.7	6.6	80.7	19.3
West Virginia	78.7	14.6	6.7	86.3	13.7	100.0	-	-	75.0	25.0
North Carolina	58.1	32.3	9.6	77.1	22.9	63.3	20.2	16.5	82.3	17.7
South Carolina	64.9	27.3	7.8	81.1	18.9	72.5	14.9	12.6	88.0	12.0
Georgia	58.9	28.2	12.9	75.3	24.7	68.1	17.0	14.8	80.8	19.2
Florida	73.7	14.3	12.0	84.2	15.8	77.3	12.1	10.6	93.3	6.7
EAST SOUTH CENTRAL	52.4	38.3	9.3	72.9	27.1	49.7	34.8	15.5	71.8	28.2
Kentucky	62.1	22.3	15.5	74.8	25.2	30.2	18.6	51.2	66.7	33.3
Tennessee	60.8	28.8	10.4	78.5	21.5	51.9	28.4	19.8	73.9	26.1
Alabama	53.8	36.2	10.0	72.2	27.3	60.1	26.9	13.0	77.1	22.9
Mississippi	47.6	44.8	7.6	70.4	29.6	46.2	41.7	12.1	69.2	30.8
WEST SOUTH CENTRAL	60.2	27.3	12.5	73.6	26.4	60.5	21.6	17.9	76.5	23.5
Arkansas	49.9	38.6	11.5	62.5	37.5	45.7	37.5	16.8	65.8	34.2
Louisiana	57.8	30.3	11.9	79.5	20.5	56.2	25.9	17.8	78.2	21.8
Oklahoma	56.2	24.5	19.3	72.6	27.4	62.8	12.8	24.4	78.3	21.7
Texas	69.1	20.4	10.5	78.5	21.5	67.9	17.6	14.5	80.3	19.7
SELECTED NORTHERN STATES[1]	49.1	4.55	5.4	57.0	43.0	33.3	60.0	6.7	64.8	35.2
New Jersey	47.5	49.3	3.2	56.0	44.0	100.0	-	-	33.3	66.7
Pennsylvania	41.2	54.8	4.1	46.2	53.8	33.3	66.7	-	50.0	50.0
Ohio	50.6	41.4	8.0	69.4	30.6	33.3	33.3	33.3	80.0	20.0
Indiana	45.9	46.9	7.2	51.4	48.6	-	-	-	50.0	50.0
Illinois	48.5	45.3	6.1	56.0	44.0	-	100.0	-	83.3	16.7
Missouri	51.0	45.4	3.6	53.1	46.9	33.3	66.7	-	55.0	45.8
Kansas	49.9	44.6	5.5	54.0	46.0	25.0	75.0	-	75.0	25.0

Source: "Mortgage Status of Colored Full Owners and Percent Distribution, by Age, by Southern Divisions, and States, and Selected Northern States: 1930 and 1920," *Negroes in the United States, 1920-1932*, 1935, p. 586. Primary source: U.S. Bureau of the Census. *Negroes in the United States, 1920-1932*. Washington, D.C.: U.S. Government Printing Office, 1935. *Notes:* 1. Includes full owners whose mortgage status was not reported. 2. States having 200 or more Negro farmers who constitute 90 percent or more of the colored farmers in the State.

★ 212 ★

Farms and Farmers

Relationships: Mortgage Status of Black Farm Owners 25-44 Years Old, by Age Group and Farm Location, 1920 and 1930 - II

DIVISION AND STATE	25 TO 34 YEARS					35 TO 44 YEARS				
	1930			1920		1930			1920	
	Reporting farms free from mortgage	Reporting farms mortgaged	Unknown (no report)	Reporting farms free from mortgage[1]	Reporting farms mortgaged	Reporting farms free from mortgage	Reporting farms mortgaged	Unknown (no report)	Reporting farms free from mortgage[1]	Reporting farms mortgaged
PERCENT DISTRIBUTION										
The South	58.9	29.5	11.6	72.2	27.8	58.2	32.0	9.8	73.1	26.9
SOUTH ATLANTIC	66.6	23.5	9.9	76.8	23.2	65.2	26.9	7.9	77.3	22.7
Delaware	53.8	46.2	-	45.5	54.5	41.7	52.1	6.3	56.1	43.9
Maryland	53.3	40.7	6.0	63.9	36.1	56.4	40.3	3.4	62.9	37.1
District of Columbia	-	-	-	-	-	-	-	-	100.0	-
Virginia	73.7	20.8	5.5	76.8	23.1	70.7	24.6	4.7	80.8	19.5
West Virginia	85.2	14.8	-	71.0	29.0	78.6	16.1	5.4	88.0	12.0
North Carolina	56.9	30.9	12.2	73.6	26.4	56.3	34.2	9.4	72.2	27.8
South Carolina	70.2	20.5	9.3	81.4	18.6	67.0	24.4	8.6	80.1	19.9
Georgia	60.2	24.1	15.7	72.4	27.6	60.1	25.5	13.4	73.4	26.6
Florida	72.9	10.3	16.8	85.3	14.7	74.4	14.3	11.3	83.3	16.7
EAST SOUTH CENTRAL	48.1	40.5	11.4	66.8	33.2	47.5	43.3	9.2	68.1	31.9
Kentucky	52.8	20.1	27.1	61.8	38.2	55.4	26.1	18.5	66.3	33.7
Tennessee	58.0	30.5	11.5	68.1	31.9	57.4	33.9	8.7	72.6	27.4
Alabama	51.5	35.6	12.9	67.8	32.2	52.3	37.3	10.4	71.5	28.5
Mississippi	44.2	46.9	8.9	66.6	33.4	42.0	50.5	7.5	65.5	34.5
WEST SOUTH CENTRAL	58.4	27.8	13.7	69.6	30.4	56.9	30.1	13.0	70.0	30.0
Arkansas	53.3	37.2	9.5	59.3	40.7	47.8	40.7	11.5	57.4	42.6
Louisiana	57.1	28.3	14.6	76.7	23.3	55.7	31.9	12.4	77.8	22.2
Oklahoma	59.1	22.4	18.6	71.2	28.8	54.9	25.3	19.7	74.1	25.9
Texas	61.4	27.1	11.5	71.6	28.4	63.9	25.2	10.9	72.2	27.8
SELECTED NORTHERN STATES[1]	48.4	45.3	6.3	47.4	52.6	38.8	55.8	5.3	52.0	48.0
New Jersey	62.5	31.3	6.3	41.2	58.8	33.3	61.5	5.1	48.1	51.9
Pennsylvania	41.7	33.3	25.0	21.7	78.3	29.7	70.3	-	50.0	50.0
Ohio	41.9	51.6	6.5	56.1	43.9	37.9	54.4	7.8	68.9	31.1
Indiana	40.0	60.0	-	38.5	61.5	34.6	53.8	11.5	45.9	54.1
Illinois	57.1	42.9	-	64.3	35.7	41.3	52.2	6.5	49.3	50.7
Missouri	44.4	50.0	56.6	41.6	58.4	40.9	56.8	2.3	45.1	54.9
Kansas	57.1	42.9	-	52.8	47.2	47.3	47.3	5.5	44.0	56.0

Source: "Mortgage Status of Colored Full Owners and Percent Distribution, by Age, by Southern Divisions, and States, and Selected Northern States: 1930 and 1920," *Negroes in the United States, 1920-1932*, 1935, p. 586. Primary source: U.S. Bureau of the Census. *Negroes in the United States, 1920-1932*, Washington, D.C.: U.S. Government Printing Office, 1935. *Notes:* 1. Includes full owners whose mortgage status was not reported. 2. States having 200 or more Negro farmers who constitute 90 percent or more of the colored farmers in the State.

★ 213 ★

Farms and Farmers

Relationships: Mortgage Status of Black Farm Owners Up to 44 Years Old, by Age Group and Farm Location, 1920 and 1930 - I

[Colored farmers include Negroes, Indians, Chinese, Japanese, and all other nonwhite races]

DIVISION AND STATE	ALL COLORED FULL OWNERS					UNDER 25 YEARS				
	1930			1920		1930			1920	
	Reporting farms free from mortgage	Reporting farms mortgaged	Unknown (no report)	Reporting farms free from mortgage[1]	Reporting farms mortgaged	Reporting farms free from mortgage	Reporting farms mortgaged	Unknown (no report)	Reporting farms free from mortgage[1]	Reporting farms mortgaged
	NUMBER									
The South	84,861	41,964	13,671	135,944	42,614	1,643	636	406	3,447	928
South Atlantic	39,887	15,860	4,967	65,960	17,062	681	170	115	1,590	303
East South Central	20,659	15,087	3,674	33,375	12,427	355	249	111	642	252
West South Central	24,315	11,017	5,030	36,609	13,125	607	217	180	1,215	373
Selected Northern States[2]	1,369	1,270	151	2,199	1,658	5	9	1	35	19
New Jersey	103	107	7	145	114	1	-	-	1	2
Pennsylvania	91	121	9	110	128	1	2	-	2	2
Ohio	324	265	51	626	276	1	1	1	12	3
Indiana	95	97	15	109	103	-	-	-	1	1
Illinois	150	140	19	214	168	-	1	-	5	1
Missouri	416	370	29	693	612	1	2	-	11	9
Kansas	190	170	21	302	257	1	3	-	3	1

Source: "Mortgage Status of Colored Full Owners and Percent Distribution, by Age, by Southern Divisions, and States, and Selected Northern States: 1930 and 1920," *Negroes in the United States, 1920-1932*, 1935, p. 585. Primary source: U.S. Bureau of the Census. *Negroes in the United States, 1920-1932*. Washington, D.C.: U.S. Government Printing Office, 1935. *Notes:* 1. Includes full owners whose mortgage status was not reported. 2. States having 200 or more Negro farmers who constitute 90 percent or more of the colored farmers in the State.

★ 214 ★

Farms and Farmers

Relationships: Mortgage Status of Black Farm Owners Up to 44 Years Old, by Age Group and Farm Location, 1920 and 1930 - II

[Colored farmers include Negroes, Indians, Chinese, Japanese, and all other nonwhite races]

DIVISION AND STATE	25 to 34 YEARS					35 TO 44 YEARS				
	1930			1920		1930			1920	
	Reporting farms free from mortgage	Reporting farms mortgaged	Unknown (no report)	Reporting farms free from mortgage[1]	Reporting farms mortgaged	Reporting farms free from mortgage	Reporting farms mortgaged	Unknown (no report)	Reporting farms free from mortgage[1]	Reporting farms mortgaged
	NUMBER									
The South	6,572	3,298	1,297	13,440	5,166	13,900	7,648	2,333	26,529	9,757
South Atlantic	2,903	1,026	432	6,496	1,962	6,938	2,861	845	13,634	4,011
East South Central	1,433	1,207	340	2,828	1,406	2,887	2,632	558	5,698	2,664
West South Central	2,236	1,065	525	4,116	1,798	4,075	2,155	930	7,197	3,082
Selected Northern States[2]	62	58	8	137	152	153	220	21	332	307
New Jersey	10	5	1	7	10	13	24	2	26	28
Pennsylvania	5	4	3	5	18	11	26	-	15	15
Ohio	13	16	2	37	29	39	56	8	111	50
Indiana	2	3	-	5	8	9	14	3	17	20
Illinois	4	3	-	18	10	19	24	3	37	38

[Continued]

★ 214 ★

Relationships: Mortgage Status of Black Farm Owners Up to 44 Years Old, by Age Group and Farm Location, 1920 and 1930 - II

[Continued]

DIVISION AND STATE	25 to 34 YEARS					35 TO 44 YEARS				
	1930			1920		1930			1920	
	Reporting farms free from mortgage	Reporting farms mortgaged	Unknown (no report)	Reporting farms free from mortgage[1]	Reporting farms mortgaged	Reporting farms free from mortgage	Reporting farms mortgaged	Unknown (no report)	Reporting farms free from mortgage[1]	Reporting farms mortgaged
Missouri	16	18	2	37	52	36	50	2	82	100
Kansas	12	9	-	28	25	26	26	3	44	56

Source: "Mortgage Status of Colored Full Owners and Percent Distribution, by Age, by Southern Divisions, and States, and Selected Northern States: 1930 and 1920," *Negroes in the United States, 1920-1932,* 1935, p. 585. Primary source: U.S. Bureau of the Census. *Negroes in the United States, 1920-1932.* Washington, D.C.: U.S. Government Printing Office, 1935. *Notes:* 1. Includes full owners whose mortgage status was not reported. 2. States having 200 or more Negro farmers who constitute 90 percent or more of the colored farmers in the State.

★ 215 ★

Farms and Farmers

Relationships: Mortgage Status of Black-Owned Farms, by Farm Location, 1930

[Figures relate only to farms wholly owned by their operators. Colored farmers include Negroes, Chinese, Japanese, and all other nonwhite races]

DIVISION AND STATE	Total	Reported free from mortgage	Reported mortgaged	Unknown (no report)	PERCENT DISTRIBUTION		
					Reported free from mortgage	Reported mortgaged	Unknown (no report)
The South	140,496	84,861	41,964	13,671	60.4	29.9	9.7
SOUTH ATLANTIC	60,714	39,887	15,860	4,967	65.7	26.1	8.2
Delaware	309	162	124	23	52.4	40.1	7.4
Maryland	2,362	1,449	814	99	61.3	34.5	4.2
District of Columbia	7	2	3	2	28.6	42.9	28.6
Virginia	19,200	14,077	4,184	939	73.3	21.8	4.9
West Virginia	328	258	48	22	78.7	14.6	6.7
North Carolina	13,198	7,671	4,258	1,269	58.1	32.3	9.6
South Carolina	11,937	7,745	3,263	929	64.9	27.3	7.8
Georgia	9,014	5,311	2,541	1,162	58.9	28.2	12.9
Florida	4,359	3,212	625	522	73.7	14.3	12.0
EAST SOUTH CENTRAL	30,420	20,659	15,087	3,674	52.4	38.3	9.3
Kentucky	3,055	1,898	682	475	62.1	22.3	15.5
Tennessee	5,687	3,456	1,639	592	60.8	28.8	10.4
Alabama	11,417	6,140	4,135	1,142	53.8	36.2	10.0
Mississippi	19,261	9,165	8,631	1,465	47.6	44.8	7.6
WEST SOUTH CENTRAL	40,362	24,315	11,017	5,030	60.2	27.3	12.5
Arkansas	9,058	4,521	3,496	1,041	49.9	38.6	11.5
Louisiana	8,786	5,080	2,659	1,047	57.8	30.3	11.9
Oklahoma	6,550	3,682	1,604	1,264	56.2	24.5	19.3
Texas	15,968	11,032	3,258	1,678	69.1	20.4	10.5

[Continued]

★ 215 ★

Relationships: Mortgage Status of Black-Owned Farms, by Farm Location, 1930
[Continued]

DIVISION AND STATE	Total	Reported free from mortgage	Reported mortgaged	Unknown (no report)	PERCENT DISTRIBUTION		
					Reported free from mortgage	Reported mortgaged	Unknown (no report)
SELECTED NORTHERN STATES[1]	2,790	1,369	1,270	151	49.1	45.5	5.4
New Jersey	217	103	107	7	47.5	49.3	3.2
Pennsylvania	221	91	121	9	41.2	54.8	4.1
Ohio	640	324	265	51	50.6	41.4	8.0
Indiana	207	95	97	15	45.9	46.9	7.2
Illinois	309	150	140	19	48.5	45.3	6.1
Missouri	815	416	370	29	51.0	45.4	3.6
Kansas	381	190	170	21	49.9	44.6	5.5

Source: "Farms Operated by Colored Full Owners, Classified According to Mortgage Status, by Southern Divisions, and States, and Selected Northern States: 1930," *Negroes in the United States, 1920-1932*, 1935, p. 582. Primary source: U.S. Bureau of the Census. *Negroes in the United States, 1920-1932.* Washington, D.C.: U.S. Government Printing Office, 1935. *Notes:* 1. States having 200 or more Negro farmers who constitute 90 percent or more of the colored farm operators in the State.

★ 216 ★

Farms and Farmers

Relationships: Number and Owner Status of Farms, 1910-1940

	Number of Farms				Per cent 1910, 1930,and 1940 are of 1920			
	1940	1930	1920	1910	1940	1930	1920	1910
	(000)	(000)	(000)	(000)				
NO, FARMS (TOTAL)	6,097	6,289	6,448	6,362	94.5	97.5	100	98.6
By Color of Operators:								
White Operators	5,378	5,373	5,498	5,441	97.8	97.7	100	98.9
Non-white Operators	719	916	950	921	75.7	96.4	100	98.9
By Tenure of Operators:								
Full Owners	3,084	2,912	3,367	3,355	91.6	86.5	100	99.6
Part Owners	615	657	559	594	110.1	117.6	100	106.3
Managers	36	56	68	58	53.1	81.6	100	84.9
All Tenants	2,361	2,664	2,455	2,355	96.2	108.5	100	95.9
Proportion of Tenancy (%)	38.7	42.4	38.1	37.0	101.6	111.2	100	97.1
Croppers (Southern States)	541	776	561	[1]	96.5	138.2	100	-

Source: "Trends in the Number of Farms in the United States by Color and Tenure of Operators, 1910-1940. (Decennial Censuses)," *Negro Year Book: A Review of Events Affecting Negro Life, 1941-1946*, 1947, p. 163. Primary source: U.S. Bureau of the Census. *Note:* 1. Not available for 1910 census.

★ 217 ★

Farms and Farmers

Relationships: Occupational Status of Persons Employed in Agriculture for the U.S. and the South, 1940 and 1950

| Year and Class | United States | | | | South | | | |
| | Total | | Nonwhite | | Total | | Nonwhite | |
	Number	Per Cent	Number	Per Cent	Number	Per Cent	Number	Per Cent
1940								
All	8,372,000	100.0	1,541,000	100.0	4,342,000	100.0	1,449,000	100.0
Farmers and farm managers	5,143,614	61.4	700,602	45.5	2,583,937	59.5	666,929	46.0
Paid farm laborers	1,924,890	23.0	514,602	33.4	965,464	22.2	470,546	32.5
Unpaid family workers	1,165,120	13.9	308,722	20.0	746,440	17.2	298,312	20.6
Not reported	138,376	1.7	17,676	1.1	46,159	1.1	13,213	0.9
1950								
All	7,138,000	100.0	1,078,000	100.0	3,408,000	100.0	1,013,000	100.0
Farmers and farm managers	4,453,000	62.4	507,000	47.0	2,090,000	61.3	482,000	47.6
Paid farm laborers	1,562,000	21.9	345,000	32.0	709,000	20.8	312,000	30.8
Unpaid family workers	941,000	13.2	211,000	19.6	547,000	16.1	204,000	20.1
Not reported	182,000	2.5	15,000	1.4	62,000	1.8	15,000	1.5

Source: "Occupational Classification of Agriculturally Employed, 1940 and 1950," *1952 Negro Year Book: A Review of Events Affecting Negro Life*, 1952, p. 102. Primary source: U.S. Bureau of the Census, *Employment and Income in the United States, by Regions: 1950*, 1950 Census of Population, Preliminary Reports, Series PC-7, No. 2, Table 6.

★ 218 ★

Farms and Farmers

Relationships: Percent of Farmland Improved and Average Number of Acres Improved, by Location of Farm 1910

| DIVISION AND STATE | PERCENTAGE IMPROVED: 1910 | | AVERAGE NUMBER OF ACRES IMPROVED PER FARM: 1910 | |
	Of land in Negro farms	Of land in white farms	Negro farms	White farms
United States	65.9	54.0	31.2	82.6
The South	65.8	39.4	30.8	55.7
South Atlantic	62.2	43.5	30.9	49.6
East South Central	70.3	50.6	29.4	47.9
West South Central	66.0	32.4	33.1	69.6

[Continued]

★ 218 ★

Relationships: Percent of Farmland Improved and Average Number of Acres Improved, by Location of Farm 1910

[Continued]

DIVISION AND STATE	PERCENTAGE IMPROVED: 1910		AVERAGE NUMBER OF ACRES IMPROVED PER FARM: 1910	
	Of land in Negro farms	Of land in white farms	Negro farms	White farms
The North	71.2	70.3	72.1	100.6
The West	44.5	34.3	116.8	104.1
THE SOUTH				
South Atlantic:				
Delaware	65.0	68.9	40.2	68.2
Maryland	61.0	66.7	34.3	73.7
District of Columbia	100.0	84.4	7.9	24.6
Virginia	49.7	50.8	23.1	64.4
West Virginia	58.6	55.1	28.6	57.3
North Carolina	54.5	36.8	26.4	37.7
South Carolina	65.6	36.6	26.8	43.9
Georgia	67.6	37.8	39.1	44.6
Florida	62.8	29.5	32.8	37.5
East South Central:				
Kentucky	78.0	64.4	29.3	56.6
Tennessee	72.4	52.8	30.3	46.8
Alabama	70.1	39.2	32.3	40.2
Mississippi	79.5	37.4	27.2	41.2
West South Central:				
Arkansas	66.8	42.7	27.9	41.7
Louisiana	69.1	45.8	26.7	58.0
Oklahoma	62.3	61.6	50.3	96.6
Texas	64.8	22.7	39.6	70.7

Source: [Untitled Table]," *Negro Population, 1790-1915,* 1918, p. 558. Primary source: U.S. Bureau of the Census. *Negro Population, 1790-1915.* Washington, D.C.: Government Printing Office, 1918.

★ 219 ★
Farms and Farmers

Relationships: Percentage Distribution of Farm Acreage on Southern Farms, by Owner Status, 1910 - I

DIVISION AND STATE	Total	FARMS OPERATED BY COLORED FARMERS: 1910					
		Owners and part owners			Tenants		
		Owners		Part owners	Cash and not specified	Share and share cash	Managers
		Free	Mortgaged				

PERCENTAGE DISTRIBUTION OF ACREAGE, BY TENURE

DIVISION AND STATE	Total	Free	Mortgaged	Part owners	Cash and not specified	Share and share cash	Managers
THE SOUTH							
Total	100.0	20.7	9.4	6.7	30.2	32.1	0.8
South Atlantic	100.0	18.6	7.1	6.3	33.8	33.4	0.8
East South Central	100.0	15.8	11.4	6.1	39.3	26.7	0.6
West South Central	100.0	30.0	10.6	7.9	13.6	36.7	1.1
SOUTH ATLANTIC							
Delaware	100.0	11.3	8.8	3.8	7.2	64.7	4.2
Maryland	100.0	16.4	10.9	6.7	11.7	50.6	3.7
District of Columbia	100.0	15.8	3.2	42.1	34.7	-	4.2
Virginia	100.0	39.7	10.9	11.1	10.9	26.0	1.3
West Virginia	100.0	57.6	8.8	8.8	6.3	16.6	1.9
North Carolina	100.0	19.0	8.1	10.6	18.9	42.9	0.6
South Carolina	100.0	15.4	6.9	5.5	40.5	30.6	1.1
Georgia	100.0	11.1	4.9	3.1	46.1	34.4	0.4
Florida	100.0	40.1	11.2	8.3	28.6	10.5	1.3
EAST SOUTH CENTRAL							
Kentucky	100.0	32.6	11.6	13.8	5.7	35.4	1.0
Tennessee	100.0	19.1	7.8	9.8	32.7	29.4	1.1
Alabama	100.0	13.0	9.8	6.1	51.3	19.6	0.3
Mississippi	100.0	16.1	13.7	4.8	33.9	31.1	0.6
WEST SOUTH CENTRAL							
Arkansas	100.0	24.0	13.3	8.1	26.2	28.2	0.2
Louisiana	100.0	26.7	8.9	3.7	15.2	44.5	1.0
Oklahoma	100.0	48.3	12.7	9.2	8.9	20.5	0.3
Texas	100.0	25.7	8.7	9.2	7.6	46.6	2.2

Source: "Acres in Colored and White Farms, Classified by Tenure, by Southern Divisions, and States: 1910," *Negro Population, 1790-1915*, 1918, p. 612. Primary source: U.S. Bureau of the Census. *Negro Population, 1790-1915*. Washington, D.C.: Government Printing Office, 1918.

★ 220 ★
Farms and Farmers

Relationships: Percentage Distribution of Farm Acreage on Southern Farms, by Owner Status, 1910 - II

DIVISION AND STATE	Total	FARMS OPERATED BY WHITE FARMERS: 1910					
		Owners and part owners			Tenants		
		Owners		Part owners	Cash and not specified	Share and share cash	Managers
		Free	Mortgaged				
PERCENTAGE DISTRIBUTION OF ACREAGE, BY TENURE							
THE SOUTH							
Total	100.0	43.2	15.0	10.8	8.4	14.9	7.8
South Atlantic	100.0	55.9	11.5	6.3	8.9	13.6	3.7
East South Central	100.0	55.9	13.1	8.3	7.7	12.6	2.2
West South Central	100.0	30.7	17.7	14.2	8.5	16.5	12.4
SOUTH ATLANTIC							
Delaware	100.0	29.1	16.4	1.6	6.9	44.0	1.9
Maryland	100.0	34.7	20.5	3.9	7.8	28.8	4.1
District of Columbia	100.0	31.3	5.6	2.8	34.7	1.3	24.3
Virginia	100.0	59.2	11.3	6.9	6.3	12.8	3.7
West Virginia	100.0	64.3	8.9	8.4	8.3	7.2	2.8
North Carolina	100.0	57.0	10.1	8.0	6.0	16.0	2.9
South Carolina	100.0	51.5	15.3	5.8	12.5	9.6	5.3
Georgia	100.0	53.4	10.3	4.2	13.9	14.3	3.8
Florida	100.0	68.5	10.5	6.4	5.2	3.4	6.0
EAST SOUTH CENTRAL							
Kentucky	100.0	58.4	12.6	8.1	5.4	14.0	1.4
Tennessee	100.0	56.1	9.7	10.6	6.5	15.4	1.7
Alabama	100.0	52.9	14.3	8.4	11.3	11.0	2.2
Mississippi	100.0	55.2	17.9	5.4	9.1	8.0	4.5
WEST SOUTH CENTRAL							
Arkansas	100.0	52.6	11.5	11.7	7.7	14.4	2.2
Louisiana	100.0	51.4	14.3	5.6	7.7	9.4	11.6
Oklahoma	100.0	18.7	15.2	20.3	16.1	28.1	1.6
Texas	100.0	29.1	19.5	13.8	6.7	14.5	16.5

Source: "Acres in Colored and White Farms, Classified by Tenure, by Southern Divisions, and States: 1910," *Negro Population, 1790-1915*, 1918, p. 612. Primary source: U.S. Bureau of the Census. *Negro Population, 1790-1915.* Washington, D.C.: Government Printing Office, 1918.

★ 221 ★

Farms and Farmers

Relationships: Percentage Distribution of Improved Acreage on Southern Farms, by Owner Status, 1910 - I

DIVISION AND STATE	FARMS OPERATED BY COLORED FARMERS: 1910						
	Total	Owners and part owners			Tenants		Managers
		Owners		Part owners	Cash and not specified	Share and share cash	
		Free	Mortgaged				
	PERCENTAGE DISTRIBUTION OF IMPROVED ACREAGE, BY TENURE						
THE SOUTH							
Total	100.0	14.5	6.8	5.9	33.3	39.3	0.4
South Atlantic	100.0	13.7	5.2	5.8	35.7	39.6	0.6
East South Central	100.0	10.3	7.7	5.1	43.6	32.9	0.3
West South Central	100.0	21.2	8.1	7.1	15.9	47.3	0.3
SOUTH ATLANTIC							
Delaware	100.0	11.0	9.3	4.7	7.1	62.4	5.5
Maryland	100.0	16.1	11.0	7.9	10.7	50.1	4.1
District of Columbia	100.0	15.8	3.2	42.1	34.7	-	4.2
Virginia	100.0	40.1	10.3	13.3	10.0	30.7	1.3
West Virginia	100.0	51.9	9.9	9.8	5.8	19.6	3.0
North Carolina	100.0	13.6	6.1	9.9	18.8	51.2	0.3
South Carolina	100.0	11.0	4.7	5.0	41.2	37.4	0.6
Georgia	100.0	7.4	3.4	2.7	45.7	40.6	0.2
Florida	100.0	30.4	9.0	8.2	37.4	14.1	0.9
EAST SOUTH CENTRAL							
Kentucky	100.0	28.6	10.7	14.8	5.5	39.4	1.0
Tennessee	100.0	14.5	6.4	9.2	34.2	35.1	0.6
Alabama	100.0	8.0	6.2	4.8	57.2	23.7	0.1
Mississippi	100.0	9.8	9.0	3.6	38.3	39.2	0.2
WEST SOUTH CENTRAL							
Arkansas	100.0	15.5	8.6	6.4	32.6	36.7	0.2
Louisiana	100.0	17.7	6.3	3.3	16.6	55.6	0.5
Oklahoma	100.0	39.2	13.4	10.1	8.7	28.5	0.1
Texas	100.0	19.1	6.5	8.4	8.0	57.6	0.3

Source: "Acres Improved in Colored and White Farms, Classified by Tenure, by Southern Divisions, and States: 1910," *Negro Population, 1790-1915*, 1918, p. 613. Primary source: U.S. Bureau of the Census. *Negro Population, 1790-1915*. Washington, D.C.: Government Printing Office, 1918.

★ 222 ★
Farms and Farmers

Relationships: Percentage Distribution of Improved Acreage on Southern Farms, by Owner Status, 1910 - II

DIVISION AND STATE	Total	FARMS OPERATED BY WHITE FARMERS: 1910					Managers
		Owners and part owners			Tenants		
		Owners		Part owners	Cash and not specified	Share and share cash	
		Free	Mortgaged				

PERCENTAGE DISTRIBUTION OF IMPROVED ACREAGE, BY TENURE

DIVISION AND STATE	Total	Free	Mortgaged	Part owners	Cash and not specified	Share and share cash	Managers
THE SOUTH							
Total	100.0	41.3	13.5	9.9	9.0	23.9	2.5
South Atlantic	100.0	51.1	11.6	7.0	9.4	17.7	3.1
East South Central	100.0	51.1	13.0	9.1	8.2	17.0	1.6
West South Central	100.0	27.5	15.2	12.6	8.8	33.1	2.8
SOUTH ATLANTIC							
Delaware	100.0	27.5	17.0	1.7	6.6	44.8	2.3
Maryland	100.0	32.8	20.8	4.0	7.3	31.3	3.8
District of Columbia	100.0	32.6	5.2	3.3	32.7	1.3	25.0
Virginia	100.0	58.4	11.5	7.7	5.2	13.7	3.5
West Virginia	100.0	65.3	8.8	9.4	6.0	8.1	2.4
North Carolina	100.0	52.2	9.9	8.9	6.2	20.6	2.2
South Carolina	100.0	43.2	14.8	6.6	16.3	15.9	3.6
Georgia	100.0	42.6	9.7	4.8	17.9	21.8	3.2
Florida	100.0	62.3	11.2	6.4	9.0	5.7	5.5
EAST SOUTH CENTRAL							
Kentucky	100.0	55.5	13.4	8.9	4.9	16.0	1.2
Tennessee	100.0	51.7	9.9	11.5	6.8	18.9	1.1
Alabama	100.0	42.5	13.3	8.5	15.0	18.8	1.9
Mississippi	100.0	47.5	18.0	5.6	11.9	13.6	3.5
WEST SOUTH CENTRAL							
Arkansas	100.0	44.9	11.3	11.6	9.5	21.0	1.7
Louisiana	100.0	44.1	14.3	6.3	9.4	15.2	10.7
Oklahoma	100.0	17.1	15.4	19.9	14.0	32.5	1.1
Texas	100.0	27.4	16.2	9.0	5.0	39.4	2.9

Source: "Acres Improved in Colored and White Farms, Classified by Tenure, by Southern Divisions, and States: 1910," *Negro Population, 1790-1915*, 1918, p. 613. Primary source: U.S. Bureau of the Census. *Negro Population, 1790-1915*. Washington, D.C.: Government Printing Office, 1918.

★ 223 ★

Farms and Farmers

Relationships: Percentage Distribution of Mortgage Status of Black Farm Owners 45 Years Old and Over, by Age Group and Farm Location, 1920 and 1930 - I

[Colored farmers include Negroes, Indians, Chinese, Japanese, and all other nonwhite races]

| | 45 TO 54 YEARS | | | | | 55 TO 64 YEARS | | | | |
| | 1930 | | | 1920 | | 1930 | | | 1920 | |
DIVISION AND STATE	Reporting farms free from mortgage	Reporting farms mortgaged	Unknown (no report)	Reporting farms free from mortgage[1]	Reporting farms mortgaged	Reporting farms free from mortgage	Reporting farms mortgaged	Unknown (no report)	Reporting farms free from mortgage[1]	Reporting farms mortgaged
					NUMBER					
The South	22,353	12,753	3,480	38,106	13,786	20,640	10,493	2,980	28,693	7,992
South Atlantic	10,601	4,812	1,319	18,238	5,375	9,613	4,139	1,089	13,935	3,344
East South Central	5,497	4,641	918	9,525	4,080	5,228	3,785	848	7,456	2,440
West South Central	6,255	3,300	1,243	10,343	4,331	5,799	2,569	1,043	7,302	2,208
Selected Northern States[1]	297	342	34	476	446	367	325	38	588	410
New Jersey	24	35	1	32	41	34	26	+	46	26
Pennsylvania	27	42	2	28	39	19	32	3	29	27
Ohio	69	61	10	152	75	92	66	11	154	71
Indiana	21	28	3	22	23	26	25	3	23	27
Illinois	37	38	7	47	41	41	40	4	52	42
Missouri	80	90	8	129	165	119	92	6	214	156
Kansas	39	48	3	66	62	36	44	11	70	61

Source: "Mortgage Status of Colored Full Owners and Percent Distribution, by Age, by Southern Divisions, and States, and Selected Northern States: 1930 and 1920," *Negroes in the United States, 1920-1932*, 1935, p. 586. Primary source: U.S. Bureau of the Census. *Negroes in the United States, 1920-1932*. Washington, D.C.: U.S. Government Printing Office, 1935. *Notes:* 1. States having 200 or more Negro farmers who constitute 90 percent or more of the colored farmers in the State.

★ 224 ★

Farms and Farmers

Relationships: Percentage Distribution of Mortgage Status of Black Farm Owners 45 to 64 Years Old, by Age Group and Farm Location, 1920 and 1930 - I

| | 45 TO 54 YEARS | | | | | 55 TO 64 YEARS | | | | |
| | 1930 | | | 1920 | | 1930 | | | 1920 | |
DIVISION AND STATE	Reporting farms free from mortgage	Reporting farms mortgaged	Unknown (no report)	Reporting farms free from mortgage[1]	Reporting farms mortgaged	Reporting farms free from mortgage	Reporting farms mortgaged	Unknown (no report)	Reporting farms free from mortgage[1]	Reporting farms mortgaged
					PERCENT DISTRIBUTION					
The South	57.9	33.1	9.0	73.4	26.6	60.5	30.8	8.7	78.2	21.8
SOUTH ATLANTIC	63.4	28.8	7.9	77.2	22.8	64.8	27.9	7.3	80.6	19.4
Delaware	51.7	40.2	8.0	58.1	41.8	47.6	43.9	8.5	62.3	37.7
Maryland	56.7	40.0	3.3	67.4	32.6	63.7	32.2	4.1	74.3	25.7
District of Columbia	33.3	33.3	33.3	75.0	25.0	33.3	33.3	33.3	50.0	50.0
Virginia	71.8	23.6	4.6	80.8	19.2	73.3	22.7	4.1	84.1	15.9
West Virginia	78.2	12.8	9.0	83.9	16.1	72.0	16.0	12.0	85.7	14.3
North Carolina	54.7	36.0	9.3	74.2	25.8	58.0	33.8	8.2	79.4	20.6
South Carolina	63.1	30.0	6.9	78.4	21.6	61.2	31.7	7.1	81.4	18.6
Georgia	54.9	31.7	13.4	72.9	27.1	58.5	29.9	11.7	76.4	23.6
Florida	72.9	15.3	11.8	82.8	17.2	73.6	15.9	10.5	83.0	17.0
EAST SOUTH CENTRAL	49.7	42.0	8.3	70.0	30.0	53.0	38.4	8.6	75.3	24.7
Kentucky	60.8	26.8	12.4	72.8	27.2	64.8	23.4	11.8	78.3	21.7
Tennessee	57.9	32.3	9.7	75.9	24.1	60.1	29.2	10.7	80.5	19.5

[Continued]

★ 224 ★

Relationships: Percentage Distribution of Mortgage Status of Black Farm Owners 45 to 64 Years Old, by Age Group and Farm Location, 1920 and 1930 - I

[Continued]

| | 45 TO 54 YEARS | | | | | 55 TO 64 YEARS | | | | |
| | 1930 | | | 1920 | | 1930 | | | 1920 | |
DIVISION AND STATE	Reporting farms free from mortgage	Reporting farms mortgaged	Unknown (no report)	Reporting farms free from mortgage[1]	Reporting farms mortgaged	Reporting farms free from mortgage	Reporting farms mortgaged	Unknown (no report)	Reporting farms free from mortgage[1]	Reporting farms mortgaged
Alabama	51.6	39.6	8.8	68.9	31.1	52.5	37.4	10.2	73.7	26.3
Mississippi	44.5	48.5	7.0	68.2	31.9	49.4	44.1	6.6	73.4	26.6
WEST SOUTH CENTRAL	57.9	30.6	11.5	70.5	29.5	61.6	27.3	11.1	76.8	23.2
Arkansas	47.1	42.1	10.8	60.7	39.3	51.2	38.4	10.4	66.8	33.2
Louisiana	55.8	33.0	11.2	76.2	23.8	57.7	32.0	10.3	81.8	18.2
Oklahoma	55.4	25.7	18.9	69.6	30.4	54.3	27.7	18.0	68.8	31.2
Texas	67.4	22.3	9.3	75.6	24.4	71.9	18.4	9.6	83.2	16.8
SELECTED NORTHERN STATES[1]	44.1	50.8	5.1	51.6	48.4	50.3	44.5	5.2	58.9	41.1
New Jersey	40.0	58.3	1.7	43.8	56.2	56.7	43.3	-	63.9	36.1
Pennsylvania	38.0	59.2	2.8	41.8	58.2	35.2	59.3	5.6	51.8	48.2
Ohio	49.3	43.6	7.1	67.0	33.0	54.4	39.1	6.5	68.4	31.6
Indiana	40.4	53.8	5.8	48.9	51.1	48.1	46.3	5.6	46.0	54.0
Illinois	45.1	46.3	8.5	53.4	46.6	48.2	47.1	4.7	55.3	44.7
Missouri	44.9	50.6	4.5	43.9	56.1	54.8	42.4	2.8	57.8	42.2
Kansas	43.3	53.3	3.3	51.6	48.4	39.6	48.4	12.1	53.4	46.6

Source: "Mortgage Status of Colored Full Owners and Percent Distribution, by Age, by Southern Divisions, and States, and Selected Northern States: 1930 and 1920," *Negroes in the United States, 1920-1932*, 1935, p. 585. Primary source: U.S. Bureau of the Census. *Negroes in the United States, 1920-1932*. Washington, D.C.: U.S. Government Printing Office, 1935. *Notes:* 1. States having 200 or more Negro farmers who constitute 90 percent or more of the colored farmers in the State.

★ 225 ★

Farms and Farmers

Relationships: Percentage Distribution of Mortgage Status of Black Farm Owners 65 Years Old and Over, by Age Group and Farm Location, 1920 and 1930 - I

[Colored farmers include Negroes, Indians, Chinese, Japanese, and all other nonwhite races]

| | 65 YEARS AND OVER | | | | | AGE NOT REPORTED | | | | |
| | 1930 | | | 1920 | | 1930 | | | 1920 | |
DIVISION AND STATE	Reporting farms free from mortgage	Reporting farms mortgaged	Unknown (no report)	Reporting farms free from mortgage[1]	Reporting farms mortgaged	Reporting farms free from mortgage	Reporting farms mortgaged	Unknown (no report)	Reporting farms free from mortgage[1]	Reporting farms mortgaged
					NUMBER					
The South	17,779	6,230	2,665	24,226	4,530	1,974	906	510	1,503	455
South Atlantic	8,198	2,523	977	11,401	1,872	953	329	190	666	195
East South Central	4,844	2,269	765	6,785	1,461	415	304	134	441	124
West South Central	4,737	1,438	923	6,040	1,197	606	273	186	396	136
Selected Northern States[1]	456	281	43	578	306	29	35	6	53	18
New Jersey	18	16	3	31	7	3	1	-	2	-
Pennsylvania	28	12	1	29	27	-	3	-	2	-
Ohio	102	56	17	149	45	8	9	2	11	3
Indiana	34	25	2	38	23	3	2	4	3	1
Illinois	45	26	5	52	33	4	8	-	3	3
Missouri	155	110	11	196	119	9	8	-	24	11
Kansas	74	36	4	83	52	2	4	-	8	-

Source: "Mortgage Status of Colored Full Owners and Percent Distribution, by Age, by Southern Divisions, and States, and Selected Northern States: 1930 and 1920," *Negroes in the United States, 1920-1932*, 1935, p. 586. Primary source: U.S. Bureau of the Census. *Negroes in the United States, 1920-1932*. Washington, D.C.: U.S. Government Printing Office, 1935. *Notes:* 1. States having 200 or more Negro farmers who constitute 90 percent or more of the colored farmers in the State.

★ 226 ★

Farms and Farmers

Relationships: Percentage Distribution of Mortgage Status of Black Farm Owners 65 Years Old and Over, by Age Group and Farm Location, 1920 and 1930 - II

| DIVISION AND STATE | 65 YEARS AND OVER | | | | | AGE NOT REPORTED | | | | |
| | 1930 | | | 1920 | | 1930 | | | 1920 | |
	Reporting farms free from mortgage	Reporting farms mortgaged	Unknown (no report)	Reporting farms free from mortgage[1]	Reporting farms mortgaged	Reporting farms free from mortgage	Reporting farms mortgaged	Unknown (no report)	Reporting farms free from mortgage[1]	Reporting farms mortgaged
	PERCENT DISTRIBUTION									
The South	66.7	23.4	10.0	84.2	15.8	58.2	26.7	15.0	76.8	23.2
SOUTH ATLANTIC	70.1	21.6	8.4	85.9	14.1	64.7	22.4	12.9	77.4	22.6
Delaware	64.8	28.2	7.0	63.2	36.8	66.7	33.3	-	-	100.0
Maryland	72.6	22.8	4.6	80.1	19.9	51.7	35.0	13.3	72.4	27.6
District of Columbia	-	100.0	-	100.0	-	-	-	-	-	-
Virginia	77.9	16.3	5.8	88.4	11.6	73.9	17.9	8.2	78.0	22.0
West Virginia	81.1	14.9	4.1	94.4	5.6	81.8	18.2	-	100.0	-
North Carolina	64.1	26.0	9.9	85.1	14.9	58.7	28.7	12.6	83.1	16.9
South Carolina	66.0	26.3	7.6	86.2	13.8	70.1	20.5	9.4	73.8	26.2
Georgia	63.8	24.2	12.0	82.8	17.2	52.1	28.7	19.2	69.6	30.4
Florida	76.4	13.2	10.3	87.2	12.8	61.1	10.7	28.2	84.9	15.1
EAST SOUTH CENTRAL	61.5	28.8	9.7	82.3	17.7	48.7	35.6	15.7	78.1	21.9
Kentucky	68.8	16.9	14.4	85.7	14.3	58.5	17.0	24.5	80.5	19.5
Tennessee	68.1	21.6	10.3	88.2	11.8	50.7	31.9	17.4	76.1	23.9
Alabama	61.2	29.2	9.6	81.9	18.1	43.5	38.5	18.0	74.6	25.4
Mississippi	57.1	34.5	8.4	78.7	21.3	48.2	39.7	12.1	81.3	18.8
WEST SOUTH CENTRAL	66.7	20.3	13.0	83.5	16.5	56.9	25.6	17.5	74.4	25.6
Arkansas	53.3	32.4	14.3	71.1	28.9	55.0	32.1	12.8	55.7	44.3
Louisiana	64.2	23.0	12.8	86.7	13.3	59.7	29.6	10.8	85.5	14.5
Oklahoma	59.1	23.8	17.1	79.6	20.4	49.1	18.1	32.8	82.9	17.1
Texas	76.4	12.2	11.3	89.5	10.5	60.8	24.7	14.5	76.5	23.5
SELECTED NORTHERN STATES[1]	58.5	36.0	5.5	65.4	34.6	41.4	50.0	8.6	74.6	25.4
New Jersey	48.6	43.2	8.1	81.6	18.4	75.0	25.0	-	100.0	-
Pennsylvania	68.3	29.3	2.4	51.8	48.2	-	100.0	-	100.0	-
Ohio	58.3	32.0	9.7	76.8	23.2	42.1	47.4	10.5	78.6	21.4
Indiana	55.7	41.0	3.3	62.3	37.7	33.3	22.2	44.4	75.0	25.0
Illinois	59.2	34.2	6.6	61.2	38.8	33.3	66.7	-	50.0	50.0
Missouri	56.2	39.9	4.0	62.2	37.8	52.9	47.1	-	68.6	31.4
Kansas	64.9	31.6	3.5	61.5	38.5	33.3	66.7	-	100.0	-

Source: "Mortgage Status of Colored Full Owners and Percent Distribution, by Age, by Southern Divisions, and States, and Selected Northern States: 1930 and 1920," *Negroes in the United States, 1920-1932*, 1935, p. 585. Primary source: U.S. Bureau of the Census. *Negroes in the United States, 1920-1932.* Washington, D.C.: U.S. Government Printing Office, 1935. *Notes:* 1. States having 200 or more Negro farmers who constitute 90 percent or more of the colored farmers in the State.

★ 227 ★

Farms and Farmers

Relationships: Regional Change in Improved and Unimproved Farm Acreage, 1900-1910

SECTION AND DIVISIONS	INCREASE: 1900-1910[1]					
	Acres in farms		Improved acres in farms		Unimproved acres in farms	
	Of Negroes	Of whites	Of Negroes	Of whites	Of Negroes	Of whites
United States	4,045,590	35,340,269	4,482,404	59,216,959	-436,814	-23,876,690
The South	3,998,034	-11,580,562	4,449,629	20,061,623	-451,595	-31,642,185
The North	-2,848	30,383,959	-2,674	28,509,537	-174	1,874,422
The West	50,404	16,536,872	35,449	10,645,799	14,955	5,891,073

Source: [Untitled Table], *Negro Population, 1790-1915*, 1918, p. 555. Primary source: U.S. Bureau of the Census. *Negro Population, 1790-1915*. Washington, D.C.: Government Printing Office, 1918. *Note:* 1. A minus sign (-) denotes decrease.

★ 228 ★

Farms and Farmers

Relationships: Regional Change in Number of Farmers, 1900-1910, and Population in 1900 and 1910

SECTION AND DIVISION	INCREASE OF FARM OPERATORS: 1900-1910[1]				FARM OPERATORS PER 1,000 POPULATION OF EACH CLASS			
	Number		Per cent		Negro		White	
	Negro	White	Negro	White	1910	1900	1910	1900
United States	146,655	471,011	19.6	9.5	91	85	67	74
The South	148,474	327,685	20.3	17.4	101	92	107	114
South Atlantic	66,597	82,665	23.1	12.3	86	77	94	100
East South Central	57,354	81,844	21.4	12.9	122	107	125	126
West South Central	24,523	163,176	13.9	28.6	102	104	109	120
The North	-1,964	17,701	-14.0	0.6	12	16	53	62
The West	145	125,625	43.0	53.5	10	11	55	61

Source: [Untitled Table], *Negro Population, 1790-1915*, 1918, p. 555. Primary source: U.S. Bureau of the Census. *Negro Population, 1790-1915*. Washington, D.C.: Government Printing Office, 1918. *Note:* 1. A minus sign (-) denotes decrease.

★ 229 ★
Farms and Farmers

Relationships: Size Group (in Acreage) of Black Cash Tenant and Cropper Farms, by Farm Location, 1930 - I

| DIVISION AND STATE | All farms | UNDER 20 ACRES | | | | 20 to 49 acres | 50 to 99 acres | 100 to 174 acres |
		Total	Under 3 acres	3 to 9 acres	10 to 19 acres			
CASH TENANTS								
The South	97,920	25,805	96	9,689	16,020	49,881	14,471	5,384
South Atlantic	29,327	8,935	59	4,842	4,084	11,219	5,377	2,436
East South Central	53,371	12,654	9	3,815	8,830	30,398	7,305	2,178
West South Central	15,222	4,166	28	1,032	3,106	8,264	1,789	770
SELECTED NORTHERN STATES[1]	587	173	5	88	80	186	121	83
New Jersey	42	13	1	7	5	14	7	8
Pennsylvania	58	17	2	9	6	11	11	16
Ohio	122	27	-	10	17	36	25	26
Indiana	41	23	-	15	8	8	7	2
Illinois	65	21	1	7	13	24	15	3
Missouri	188	59	1	33	25	71	38	14
Kansas	71	13	-	7	6	22	18	14
CROPPERS								
The South	392,897	139,870	147	22,774	116,949	201,208	39,177	9,772
South Atlantic	124,171	26,800	108	6,047	20,645	66,459	22,532	6,388
East South Central	150,239	66,646	31	10,094	56,521	73,846	7,777	1,532
West South Central	118,487	46,424	8	6,633	39,783	60,903	8,868	1,852
SELECTED NORTHERN STATES[1]	3,300	1,478	1	262	1,215	1,483	227	72
New Jersey	16	1	-	-	1	3	4	7
Pennsylvania	21	-	-	-	-	-	6	10
Ohio	55	13	-	5	8	5	11	12
Indiana	31	16	1	8	7	5	5	4
Illinois	95	24	-	3	21	40	17	11
Missouri	3,017	1,423	-	245	1,178	1,399	162	25
Kansas	65	1	-	1	-	31	22	3

Source: "Number of Farms of Colored Operators, by Size, and Tenure, by Southern Divisions, and States, and Selected Northern States, *Negroes in the United States, 1920-1932*, 1935, pp. 602-605. Primary source: U.S. Bureau of the Census. *Negroes in the United States, 1920-1932*. Washington, D.C.: U.S. Government Printing Office, 1935. *Notes:* Colored farmers include Negroes, Indians, Chinese, Japanese, and all other nonwhite races. 1. States having 200 or more Negro farmers who constitute 90 percent or more colored farmers in the State.

★ 230 ★
Farms and Farmers

Relationships: Size Group (in Acreage) of Black Cash Tenant and Cropper Farms, by Farm Location, 1930 - II

DIVISION AND STATE	175 TO ACRES			500 to 999 acres	1,000 ACRES AND OVER			
	Total	175 to 259 acres	260 to 499 acres		Total	1,000 to 4,999 acres	5,000 to 9,999 acres	10,000 acres and over
CASH TENANTS								
The South	2,154	1,385	769	179	46	45	1	-
South Atlantic	1,171	752	419	117	22	22	-	-
East South Central	774	498	276	48	14	14	-	-
West South Central	209	135	74	14	10	9	1	-
SELECTED NORTHERN STATES[1]	24	18	6	-	-	-	-	-
New Jersey	-	-	-	-	-	-	-	-
Pennsylvania	3	2	1	-	-	-	-	-
Ohio	8	7	1	-	-	-	-	-
Indiana	1	1	-	-	-	-	-	-
Illinois	2	1	1	-	-	-	-	-
Missouri	6	5	1	-	-	-	-	-
Kansas	4	2	2	-	-	-	-	-
CROPPERS								
The South	2,697	1,875	822	147	26	26	-	-
South Atlantic	1,863	1,315	548	114	15	15	-	-
East South Central	418	277	141	16	4	4	-	-
West South Central	416	283	133	17	7	7	-	-
SELECTED NORTHERN STATES[1]	40	21	19	-	-	-	-	-
New Jersey	1	-	1	-	-	-	-	-
Pennsylvania	5	2	3	-	-	-	-	-
Ohio	14	9	5	-	-	-	-	-
Indiana	1	1	-	-	-	-	-	-
Illinois	3	1	2	-	-	-	-	-
Missouri	8	5	3	-	-	-	-	-
Kansas	8	3	5	-	-	-	-	-

Source: "Number of Farms of Colored Operators, by Size, and Tenure, by Southern Divisions, and States, and Selected Northern States, *Negroes in the United States, 1920-1932*, 1935, pp. 602-605. Primary source: U.S. Bureau of the Census. *Negroes in the United States, 1920-1932*. Washington, D.C.: U.S. Government Printing Office, 1935. *Notes:* Colored farmers include Negroes, Indians, Chinese, Japanese, and all other nonwhite races. 1. States having 200 or more Negro farmers who constitute 90 percent or more colored farmers in the State.

★ 231 ★

Farms and Farmers

Relationships: Size Group (in Acreage) of Black Full-Owner and Part-Owner Farms, by Owner Status and Farm Location, 1930 - I

[Colored farmers include Negroes, Indians, Chinese, Japanese, and all other nonwhite races]

DIVISION AND STATE	All farms	UNDER 20 ACRES				20 to 49 acres	50 to 99 acres	100 to 174 acres
		Total	Under 3 acres	3 to 9 acres	10 to 19 acres			
FULL OWNERS								
The South	140,496	27,750	272	10,962	16,516	47,128	38,305	20,123
South Atlantic	60,714	16,935	139	6,584	10,212	19,506	14,785	6,965
East South Central	39,420	5,692	61	2,466	3,165	12,951	11,481	6,705
West South Central	40,362	5,123	72	1,912	3,139	14,671	12,039	6,453
SELECTED NORTHERN STATES[1]	2,790	873	29	438	406	854	612	334
New Jersey	217	118	5	55	58	58	28	12
Pennsylvania	221	96	3	40	53	47	49	25
Ohio	640	177	5	94	78	187	180	75
Indiana	207	84	-	46	38	65	43	9
Illinois	309	80	1	38	41	128	55	40
Missouri	815	198	5	103	90	283	185	114
Kansas	381	120	10	62	48	86	72	59
PART OWNERS								
The South	41,523	8,948	7	2,244	6,697	16,194	10,515	4,137
South Atlantic	19,789	5,423	3	1,379	4,041	8,168	4,134	1,514
East South Central	11,168	2,342	2	598	1,742	4,275	2,945	1,129
West South Central	10,566	1,183	2	267	914	3,751	3,436	1,494
SELECTED NORTHERN STATES[1]	986	123	1	30	92	251	270	184
New Jersey	23	9	-	2	7	7	2	4
Pennsylvania	12	4	-	1	3	3	2	1
Ohio	143	23	-	5	18	35	44	34
Indiana	76	9	-	4	5	25	21	15
Illinois	151	17	-	1	16	49	52	20
Missouri	355	35	-	11	24	106	121	65
Kansas	226	26	1	6	19	26	28	45

Source: "Number of Farms of Colored Operators, by Size, and Tenure, by Southern Divisions, and States, and Selected Northern States, *Negroes in the United States, 1920-1932,* 1935, pp. 602-605. Primary source: U.S. Bureau of the Census. *Negroes in the United States, 1920-1932.* Washington, D.C.: U.S. Government Printing Office, 1935. *Notes:* 1. States having 200 or more Negro farmers who constitute 90% or more of the colored farmers in the State.

★ 232 ★
Farms and Farmers

Relationships: Size Group (in Acreage) of Black Full-Owner and Part-Owner Farms, by Owner Status and Farm Location, 1930 - II

[Colored farmers include Negroes, Indians, Chinese, Japanese, and all other nonwhite races]

DIVISION AND STATE	175 TO 499 ACRES			500 to 499 acres	1,000 ACRES AND OVER			
	Total	175 to 259 acres	260 to 499 acres		Total	1,000 to 4,999 acres	5,000 to 9,999 acres	10,000 acres and over
FULL OWNERS								
The South	6,783	4,742	2,041	346	61	57	4	-
South Atlantic	2,406	1,722	684	108	9	9	-	-
East South Central	2,450	1,692	758	124	17	16	1	-
West South Central	1,927	1,328	599	114	35	32	3	-
SELECTED NORTHERN STATES[1]	112	65	47	3	2	2	-	-
New Jersey	1	-	1	-	-	-	-	-
Pennsylvania	4	3	1	-	-	-	-	-
Ohio	21	15	6	-	-	-	-	-
Indiana	6	3	3	-	-	-	-	-
Illinois	5	4	1	-	1	1	-	-
Missouri	34	23	11	1	-	-	-	-
Kansas	41	17	24	2	1	1	-	-
PART OWNERS								
The South	1,599	1,072	527	94	36	28	4	4
South Atlantic	522	355	167	24	4	4	-	-
East South Central	446	307	139	27	4	4	-	-
West South Central	631	410	221	43	28	20	4	4
SELECTED NORTHERN STATES[1]	120	55	65	28	10	10	-	-
New Jersey	1	-	1	-	-	-	-	-
Pennsylvania	2	1	1	-	-	-	-	-
Ohio	7	5	2	-	-	-	-	-
Indiana	5	4	1	1	-	-	-	-
Illinois	13	4	9	-	-	-	-	-
Missouri	27	18	9	1	-	-	-	-
Kansas	65	23	42	26	10	10	-	-

Source: "Number of Farms of Colored Operators, by Size, and Tenure, by Southern Divisions, and States, and Selected Northern States, *Negroes in the United States, 1920-1932,* 1935, pp. 602-605. Primary source: U.S. Bureau of the Census. *Negroes in the United States, 1920-1932.* Washington, D.C.: U.S. Government Printing Office, 1935. *Notes:* 1. States having 200 or more Negro farmers who constitute 90% or more of colored farmers in the State.

★ 233 ★
Farms and Farmers

Relationships: Size Group (in Acreage) of Black Tenant (Unspecified) and Manager Farms, by Location, 1930 - I

| DIVISION AND STATE | All farms | UNDER 20 ACRES | | | | 20 to 49 acres | 50 to 99 acres | 100 to 174 acres |
		Total	Under 3 acres	3 to 9 acres	10 to 19 acres			
OTHER TENANTS								
The South	208,022	37,743	59	6,903	30,781	107,679	41,312	15,775
South Atlantic	63,899	9,828	34	2,793	7,001	28,396	15,686	6,993
East South Central	66,620	13,764	18	2,125	11,621	38,114	10,607	3,096
West South Central	77,503	14,151	7	1,985	12,159	41,169	15,019	5,686
SELECTED NORTHERN STATES[1]	2,507	258	-	73	185	902	632	448
New Jersey	71	8	-	4	4	8	24	24
Pennsylvania	37	4	-	1	3	6	12	13
Ohio	265	25	-	9	16	41	78	73
Indiana	118	9	-	4	5	24	40	32
Illinois	268	35	-	8	27	106	55	42
Missouri	1,466	156	-	41	115	682	356	179
Kansas	282	21	-	6	15	35	67	85
MANAGERS								
The South	829	63	3	20	40	130	130	172
South Atlantic	479	44	1	15	28	87	62	109
East South Central	141	7	-	1	6	15	28	23
West South Central	209	12	2	4	6	28	40	40
SELECTED NORTHERN STATES[1]	80	7	1	4	2	9	16	23
New Jersey	15	1	-	-	1	1	6	3
Pennsylvania	14	2	-	1	1	4	1	5
Ohio	12	-	-	-	-	1	2	3
Indiana	2	-	-	-	-	-	-	1
Illinois	6	-	-	-	-	1	2	2
Missouri	20	2	-	2	-	2	2	5
Kansas	11	2	1	1	-	-	3	4

Source: "Number of Farms of Colored Operators, by Size, and Tenure, by Southern Divisions, and States, and Selected Northern States, *Negroes in the United States, 1920-1932*, 1935, pp. 602-605. Primary source: U.S. Bureau of the Census. *Negroes in the United States, 1920-1932*. Washington, D.C.: U.S. Government Printing Office, 1935. *Notes:* Colored farmers include Negroes, Indians, Chinese, Japanese, and all other nonwhite races. 1. States having 200 or more Negro farmers who constitute 90 percent or more colored farmers in the State.

★ 234 ★

Farms and Farmers

Relationships: Size Group (in Acreage) of Black Tenant (Unspecified) and Manager Farms, by Location, 1930 - II

DIVISION AND STATE	175 TO 499 ACRES			500 to 999 acres	1,000 ACRES AND OVER			
	Total	175 to 259 acres	266 to 499 acres		Total	1,000 to 4,999 acres	5,000 to 9,999 acres	10,000 acres and over
OTHER TENANTS								
The South	5,115	3,451	1,664	344	54	54	-	-
South Atlantic	2,745	1,848	897	220	31	31	-	-
East South Central	977	638	339	55	7	7	-	-
West South Central	1,393	965	428	69	16	16	-	-
SELECTED NORTHERN STATES[1]	245	149	96	22	-	-	-	-
New Jersey	7	6	1	-	-	-	-	-
Pennsylvania	2	2	-	-	-	-	-	-
Ohio	44	27	17	4	-	-	-	-
Indiana	12	9	3	1	-	-	-	-
Illinois	29	18	11	1	-	-	-	-
Missouri	88	61	27	5	-	-	-	-
Kansas	63	26	37	11	-	-	-	-
MANAGERS								
The South	216	113	103	62	56	52	3	1
South Atlantic	132	73	59	29	16	16	-	-
East South Central	40	18	22	15	13	13	-	-
West South Central	44	22	22	18	27	23	3	1
SELECTED NORTHERN STATES[1]	21	14	7	3	1	1	-	-
New Jersey	4	2	2	-	-	-	-	-
Pennsylvania	1	1	-	1	-	-	-	-
Ohio	5	4	1	1	-	-	-	-
Indiana	1	1	-	-	-	-	-	-
Illinois	1	-	1	-	-	-	-	-
Missouri	8	5	3	1	-	-	-	-
Kansas	1	1	-	-	1	1	-	-

Source: "Number of Farms of Colored Operators, by Size, and Tenure, by Southern Divisions, and States, and Selected Northern States, *Negroes in the United States, 1920-1932*, 1935, pp. 602-605. Primary source: U.S. Bureau of the Census. *Negroes in the United States, 1920-1932*. Washington, D.C.: U.S. Government Printing Office, 1935. *Notes:* Colored farmers include Negroes, Indians, Chinese, Japanese, and all other nonwhite races. 1. States having 200 or more Negro farmers who constitute 90 percent or more colored farmers in the State.

Farms and Farmers

Relationships: Size Group (in Acreage) of Black Tenant Farms, by Farm Location, 1930 - I

DIVISION AND STATE	All farms	UNDER 20 ACRES				20 to 49 acres	50 to 99 acres	100 to 174 acres
		Total	Under 3 acres	3 to 9 acres	10 to 19 acres			
					ALL TENANTS			
The South	698,839	203,418	302	39,366	163,750	358,768	94,960	30,931
SOUTH ATLANTIC	217,397	45,613	201	13,682	13,730	106,074	43,595	15,817
Delaware	415	46	-	20	26	78	141	101
Maryland	2,206	470	2	176	292	406	409	570
District of Columbia	2	2	1	1	-	-	-	-
Virginia	15,148	4,212	16	1,209	2,987	5,493	3,043	1,613
West Virginia	111	34	-	20	14	31	16	15
North Carolina	57,139	15,251	25	3,668	11,558	26,546	10,770	3,549
South Carolina	61,362	17,341	6	6,130	11,205	30,682	9,498	2,753
Georgia	75,636	6,830	37	1,752	5,041	40,105	18,878	6,954
Florida	5,378	1,427	114	706	607	2,733	840	262
EAST SOUTH CENTRAL	270,230	93,064	58	16,034	76,972	142,358	25,689	6,806
Kentucky	4,014	2,617	31	1,075	1,511	1,542	410	230
Tennessee	27,272	7,850	6	1,409	6,435	14,722	3,467	976
Alabama	77,875	17,328	5	4,881	12,442	44,615	11,923	2,959
Mississippi	160,169	65,269	16	8,669	56,584	81,479	9,889	2,641
WEST SOUTH CENTRAL	211,212	64,741	43	9,650	55,048	110,336	25,676	8,308
Arkansas	68,101	28,160	9	3,535	24,616	35,057	3,844	812
Louisiana	63,213	24,947	25	4,388	20,534	33,226	3,858	889
Oklahoma	14,559	1,533	-	363	1,170	5,814	4,171	2,507
Texas	65,339	10,101	9	1,364	8,728	36,239	13,803	4,100
SELECTED NORTHERN STATES[1]	6,394	1,909	6	423	1,480	2,571	980	603
New Jersey	129	22	1	11	10	25	35	39
Pennsylvania	116	21	2	10	9	17	29	39
Ohio	442	65	-	24	41	82	114	111
Indiana	190	48	1	27	20	37	52	38
Illinois	428	80	1	18	61	170	87	56
Missouri	4,671	1,638	1	319	1,318	2,152	556	218
Kansas	418	35	-	14	21	88	107	102

Source: "Number of Farms of Colored Operators, by Size, and Tenure, by Southern Divisions, and States, and Selected Northern States, *Negroes in the United States, 1920-1932,* 1935, pp. 602-605. Primary source: U.S. Bureau of the Census. *Negroes in the United States, 1920-1932.* Washington, D.C.: U.S. Government Printing Office, 1935.

★ 236 ★

Farms and Farmers

Relationships: Size Group (in Acreage) of Black Tenant Farms, by Farm Location, 1930 - II

DIVISION AND STATE	175 TO 499 ACRES			500 to 499 acres	1,000 ACRES AND OVER			
	Total	175 to 259 acres	260 to 499 acres		Total	1,000 to 4,999 acres	5,000 to 9,999 acres	10,000 acres and over
ALL TENANTS								
The South	9,966	6,711	3,255	670	126	125	1	-
SOUTH ATLANTIC	5,779	3,915	1,864	451	68	68	-	-
Delaware	48	37	11	1	-	-	-	-
Maryland	333	211	122	15	3	3	-	-
District of Columbia	-	-	-	-	-	-	-	-
Virginia	710	461	249	69	8	8	-	-
West Virginia	14	8	6	1	-	-	-	-
North Carolina	971	683	288	46	6	6	-	-
South Carolina	981	636	345	91	16	16	-	-
Georgia	2,616	1,811	805	219	34	34	-	-
Florida	106	68	38	9	1	1	-	-
EAST SOUTH CENTRAL	2,169	1,413	756	119	25	25	-	-
Kentucky	110	77	33	4	1	1	-	-
Tennessee	248	178	70	4	5	5	-	-
Alabama	964	637	347	55	11	11	-	-
Mississippi	827	521	306	56	8	8	-	-
WEST SOUTH CENTRAL	2,018	1,383	635	100	33	32	1	-
Arkansas	215	131	84	8	5	5	-	-
Louisiana	270	175	95	19	4	4	-	-
Oklahoma	510	339	171	19	5	4	1	-
Texas	1,023	738	285	54	19	19	-	-
SELECTED NORTHERN STATES[1]	309	188	121	22	-	-	-	-
New Jersey	8	6	2	-	-	-	-	-
Pennsylvania	10	6	4	-	-	-	-	-
Ohio	66	43	23	4	-	-	-	-
Indiana	14	11	3	1	-	-	-	-
Illinois	34	20	14	1	-	-	-	-
Missouri	102	71	31	5	-	-	-	-
Kansas	75	31	44	11	-	-	-	-

Source: "Number of Farms of Colored Operators, by Size, and Tenure, by Southern Divisions, and States, and Selected Northern States, *Negroes in the United States, 1920-1932*, 1935, pp. 602-605. Primary source: U.S. Bureau of the Census. *Negroes in the United States, 1920-1932*. Washington, D.C.: U.S. Government Printing Office, 1935.

★ 237 ★
Farms and Farmers

Relationships: Size Group (in Acreage) of Black-Owned Farms, by Farm Location, 1930 - I

[Colored farmers include Negroes, Indians, Chinese, Japanese, and all other nonwhite races]

| DIVISION AND STATE | All farms | UNDER 20 ACRES | | | | 20 to 49 acres | 50 to 99 acres | 100 to 174 acres |
		Total	Under 3 acres	3 to 9 acres	10 to 19 acres			
				ALL OWNERS				
The South	182,019	36,698	279	13,206	23,213	63,322	48,820	24,260
SOUTH ATLANTIC	80,503	22,358	142	7,963	14,253	27,674	18,919	8,479
Delaware	373	154	-	66	88	124	71	20
Maryland	2,941	1,489	8	733	748	793	390	194
District of Columbia	8	8	5	2	1	-	-	-
Virginia	24,448	7,270	22	2,574	4,674	8,660	5,612	2,206
West Virginia	373	129	2	54	73	119	84	28
North Carolina	19,711	4,912	8	1,596	3,308	7,516	4,990	1,817
South Carolina	15,992	5,119	13	1,614	3,492	5,385	3,422	1,513
Georgia	11,081	1,714	39	669	1,006	2,830	3,284	2,204
Florida	5,576	1,563	45	655	863	2,247	1,066	497
EAST SOUTH CENTRAL	50,588	8,034	63	3,064	4,907	17,226	14,426	7,834
Kentucky	4,175	1,649	15	896	738	1,215	860	333
Tennessee	7,832	1,768	13	659	1,096	2,770	2,231	838
Alabama	15,931	2,238	11	757	1,470	5,540	4,379	2,583
Mississippi	22,650	2,379	24	752	1,603	7,701	6,956	4,080
WEST SOUTH CENTRAL	50,928	6,306	74	2,179	4,053	18,422	15,475	7,947
Arkansas	11,455	1,246	9	355	882	5,052	3,341	1,400
Louisiana	10,503	1,909	23	765	1,121	4,463	2,610	1,135
Oklahoma	8,334	651	21	223	407	2,311	2,463	1,985
Texas	20,636	2,500	21	836	1,643	6,596	7,061	3,427
SELECTED NORTHERN STATES[1]	3,776	996	30	468	498	1,105	882	518
New Jersey	240	127	5	57	65	65	30	16
Pennsylvania	233	100	3	41	56	50	51	26
Ohio	783	200	5	99	96	222	224	109
Indiana	283	93	-	50	43	90	64	24
Illinois	460	97	1	39	57	177	107	60
Missouri	1,107	233	5	114	114	389	306	179
Kansas	607	146	11	68	67	112	100	104

Source: "Number of Farms of Colored Operators, by Size, and Tenure, by Southern Divisions, and States, and Selected Northern States," *Negroes in the United States, 1920-1932*, 1935, pp. 602-605. Primary source: U.S. Bureau of the Census. *Negroes in the United States, 1920-1932.* Washington, D.C.: U.S. Government Printing Office, 1935. *Notes:* 1. States having 200 or more Negro farmers who constitute 90% or more of the colored farmers in the State.

★ 238 ★
Farms and Farmers

Relationships: Size Group (in Acreage) of Black-Owned Farms, by Farm Location, 1930 - II

DIVISION AND STATE	175 TO 499 ACRES			500 to 999 acres	1,000 ACRES AND A OVER		5,000 to 9,999 acres	10,000 acres and over
	Total	175 to 259 acres	260 to 499 acres		Total	1,000 to 4,999 acres		
ALL OWNERS								
The South	8,382	5,814	2,568	440	97	85	8	4
SOUTH ATLANTIC	2,928	2,077	851	132	13	13	-	-
Delaware	4	2	2	-	-	-	-	-
Maryland	74	57	17	1	-	-	-	-
District of Columbia	-	-	-	-	-	-	-	-
Virginia	667	495	172	29	4	4	-	-
West Virginia	11	7	4	2	-	-	-	-
North Carolina	459	333	126	15	2	2	-	-
South Carolina	524	376	148	26	3	3	-	-
Georgia	997	674	323	48	4	4	-	-
Florida	192	133	59	11	-	-	-	-
EAST SOUTH CENTRAL	2,896	1,999	897	151	21	20	1	-
Kentucky	114	84	30	4	-	-	-	-
Tennessee	219	177	42	6	-	-	-	-
Alabama	1,104	750	354	73	14	14	-	-
Mississippi	1,459	988	471	68	7	6	1	-
WEST SOUTH CENTRAL	2,558	1,738	820	157	63	52	7	4
Arkansas	407	292	115	8	1	1	-	-
Louisiana	361	247	114	20	5	5	-	-
Oklahoma	795	474	321	91	38	31	5	2
Texas	995	725	270	38	19	15	2	2
SELECTED NORTHERN STATES[1]	232	120	112	31	12	12	-	-
New Jersey	2	-	2	-	-	-	-	-
Pennsylvania	6	4	2	-	-	-	-	-
Ohio	28	20	8	-	-	-	-	-
Indiana	11	7	4	1	-	-	-	-
Illinois	18	8	10	-	1	1	-	-
Missouri	61	41	20	2	-	-	-	-
Kansas	106	40	66	28	11	11	-	-

Source: "Number of Farms of Colored Operators, by Size, and Tenure, by Southern Divisions, and States, and Selected Northern States," *Negroes in the United States, 1920-1932*, 1935, pp. 602-605. Primary source: U.S. Bureau of the Census. *Negroes in the United States, 1920-1932*. Washington, D.C.: U.S. Government Printing Office, 1935. *Notes:* 1. States having 200 or more Negro farmers who constitute 90% or more of the colored farmers in the State.

★ 239 ★

Farms and Farmers

Relationships: States with Decline in Farm Owners for 1900-1910 and 1910-1920 Decades

Geographical Division	Decrease 1900-1910		Decrease 1910-1920	
	White	Negro	White	Negro
New England	N.H. Mass. R.I.	Conn.	Me. N.H. Vt. Mass. Conn. R.I.	Me. R.I. Conn.
Middle Atlantic	N.Y.	N.Y. Pa. N.J.	N.Y. Pa. N.J.	N.Y. Pa.
East North Central	Ohio Ind. Ill.	Ind. Wis.	Ohio Ind. Ill. Mich.	Ohio Ind. Ill. Mich.
West North Central	Minn. Iowa Mo.	Minn. Mo. Kans.	Iowa Mo. N.D. S.D. Neb. Kans.	Iowa Mo. N.D. S.D. Neb. Kans.
South Atlantic			Del. Md. W. Va.	Del. Md. Va. W. Va. Fla.
East South Central				
West South Central				Ky. Tenn. Miss.
Mountain		Ariz.	N.M.	N.M. Nev.
Pacific				Oreg.

Source: "States Having Decrease of White and Negro Farm Owners, 1900-1910 and 1910-1920.," *Negro Year Book: An Annual Encyclopedia of the Negro, 1925-1926*, 1925, p. 372. Primary source: Work, Monroe N. (Ed.), *Negro Year Book: An Annual Encyclopedia of the Negro, 1925-1926.* Tuskegee Institute, AL: The Negro Year Book Pub. Co., 1925.

★ 240 ★
Farms and Farmers

Relationships: States with Decrease in Black Farm Managers and Black Tenant Farmers, 1900-1910 and 1910-1920

States Having Decrease of White and Negro Managers.

1900-1910 and 1910-1920

Geographical Division	Decrease 1900-1910		Decrease 1910-1920	
	White	Negro	White	Negro
New England	N.H.	R.I. N.H.	Me. Conn. Vt. Mass. R.I.	Me.
Middle Atlantic				N.J.
East North Central	Ohio Mich.			Ind. Ill. Mich. Wis.
West North Central	N.D. S.D. Neb. Kans.	Minn. Iowa Neb.		Minn. Iowa Kans.
South Atlantic	Del. Md. Va. W. Va. S.C. Ga.	Md. Va. W. Va. N.C. S.C. Ga.	N.C. S.C.	Del.
East South Central	Ky. Tenn. Ala. Miss.	Ky. Tenn. Ala. Miss.	Ky. Tenn.	Ky.
West South Central	Ark. La. Tex.	Ark. La. Tex. Okla.	Ark. La.	
Mountain	Colo. Wyo. Ariz. N. Mex. Utah	Ariz.	Nev.	Wyo. N. Mex. Mont.
Pacific				Wash.

[Continued]

★ 240 ★

Relationships: States with Decrease in Black Farm Managers and Black Tenant Farmers, 1900-1910 and 1910-1920
[Continued]

Geographical Division	Decrease 1900-1910		Decrease 1910-1920	
	White	Negro	White	Negro

STATES HAVING DECREASE OF WHITE AND NEGRO TENANTS

Geographical Division	White	Negro	White	Negro
New England	Me. N.H. Vt. Mass. R.I. Conn.	Mass. Conn.	Me. N.H. Vt. Mass. R.I. Conn.	Me. N.H. Mass. R.I. Conn.
Middle Atlantic	N.Y. Pa. N.J.	N.Y. Pa.	N.Y. Pa. N.J.	N.Y. Pa.
East North Central		Ohio Ind. Ill. Mich. Wis.	Ohio Ill.	Ohio Ind. Ill. Wis.
West North Central	Mo.	Iowa Mo. N.D. Neb. Kans.	Mo.	Minn. Iowa Mo. Kans.
South Atlantic	Del. Md. va. W. Va.	Md. Va. W. Va.	Del. Md. Va. W. Va.	W. Va. Fla.
East South Central		Ky.		Ala. Miss.
West South Central		La.	Okla.	Okla.
Mountain	Utah	Idaho N.M. Utah	Nev.	Mont. Wyo.
Pacific		Cal.		Oreg.

Source: "States Having Decrease of White and Negro Farm Managers, 1900-1910 and 1910-1920," and "States Having Decrease of White and Negro Tenants 1900- 1910 and 1910-1920," *Negro Year Book: An Annual Encyclopedia of the Negro, 1925-1926*, 1925, p. 373. Primary source: Work, Monroe N. (Ed.), *Negro Year Book: An Annual Encyclopedia of the Negro, 1925-1926*. Tuskegee Institute, AL: The Negro Year Book Pub. Co., 1925.

★ 241 ★

Farms and Farmers

Relationships: Value of Buildings on Southern Farms, by Owner Status, 1900 and 1910, and Change 1900-1910 - I

TENURE	VALUE OF FARM PROPERTY IN THE SOUTH					
	Colored farms		White farms		Increase: 1900-1910[1]	
	1910	1900	1910	1900	Colored farms	White farms

BUILDINGS

TENURE	1910	1900	1910	1900	Colored farms	White farms
Total	$162,500,212	$69,562,242	$1,264,655,914	$647,699,318	$92,937,970	$616,956,596
Owners	49,633,158	21,111,122	834,411,202	439,526,766	28,522,036	394,884,436
Free	35,775,640	[2]	643,867,091	[2]	[2]	[2]
Mortgaged	13,857,518	[2]	190,544,111	[2]	[2]	[2]
Part owners	11,083,509	3,511,370	98,811,108	39,472,610	7,572,139	69,338,498
Cash tenants	44,585,708	20,894,660	92,421,342	47,395,682	23,691,048	45,025,660
Share tenants	55,082,742	22,836,470	192,535,212	89,696,340	32,246,272	102,838,872
Managers	2,115,095	1,208,620	46,477,050	31,607,920	906,475	14,869,130

Source: "Value of Classes of Farm Property on Colored and White Farms, by Tenure of Classes, with Decennial Increase, Percentage Distribution by Tenure, and Average Per Farm: 1910," *Negro Population, 1790-1915*, 1918, p. 578. Primary source: U.S. Bureau of the Census. *Negro Population, 1790-1915*. Washington, D.C.: Government Printing Office, 1918. *Notes:* "Colored" may include persons other than black. 1. A minus sign (-) denotes decrease. 2. Data not available.

★ 242 ★

Farms and Farmers

Relationships: Value of Buildings on Southern Farms, by Owner Status, 1900 and 1910, and Change 1900-1910 - II

TENURE	VALUE OF FARM PROPERTY IN THE SOUTH							
	Percentage distribution				Average per farm			
	Colored farms		White farms		Colored farms		White farms	
	1910	1900	1910	1900	1910	1900	1910	1900

BUILDINGS

TENURE	1910	1900	1910	1900	1910	1900	1910	1900
Total	100.0	100.0	100.0	100.0	$183	$94	$573	$345
Owners	30.5	30.3	66.0	67.9	283	133	723	407
Free	22.0	[2]	50.9	[2]	278	[2]	709	[2]
Mortgaged	8.5	[2]	15.1	[2]	297	[2]	775	[2]
Part owners	6.8	5.0	7.8	6.1	257	125	575	375
Cash tenants	27.4	30.0	7.3	7.3	156	77	403	253

[Continued]

★ 242 ★

Relationships: Value of Buildings on Southern Farms, by Owner Status, 1900 and 1910, and Change 1900-1910 - II

[Continued]

TENURE	VALUE OF FARM PROPERTY IN THE SOUTH							
	Percentage distribution				Average per farm			
	Colored farms		White farms		Colored farms		White farms	
	1910	1900	1910	1900	1910	1900	1910	1900
Share tenants	33.9	32.8	15.2	13.8	143	81	302	182
Managers	1.3	1.7	3.8	4.9	1,763	759	3,081	1,841

Source: "Value of Classes of Farm Property on Colored and White Farms, by Tenure of Classes, with Decennial Increase, Percentage Distribution by Tenure, and Average Per Farm: 1910," *Negro Population, 1790-1915*, 1918, p. 578. Primary source: U.S. Bureau of the Census. *Negro Population, 1790-1915.* Washington, D.C.: Government Printing Office, 1918. *Notes:* "Colored" may include persons other than black. 1. A minus sign (-) denotes decrease. 2. Data not available.

★ 243 ★

Farms and Farmers

Relationships: Value of Implements and Machinery on Black Farms, by Owner Status, Region, and Division, 1930

SECTION AND DIVISION	Total	Owners	Tenants	Managers	Average value per owned farm
United States	$60,327,856	$19,784,411	$39,920,395	$623,050	$109
The North	1,971,346	1,042,391	855,340	73,615	236
The South	58,072,123	18,598,940	38,945,123	528,060	106
The West	284,387	143,080	119,932	21,375	310
New England	57,730	44,105	4,625	9,000	345
Middle Atlantic	414,576	235,976	154,140	24,460	415
East North Central	584,661	348,235	211,791	24,635	184
West North Central	914,379	414,075	484,784	15,520	226
South Atlantic	19,328,688	7,388,829	11,648,568	291,291	93
East South Central	19,776,031	5,560,624	14,087,943	127,464	110
West South Central	18,967,404	5,649,487	13,208,612	109,305	123
Mountain	112,654	63,502	42,252	6,900	347
Pacific	171,733	79,578	77,680	14,475	285

Source: "Value of Implements and Machinery on Farms Operated by Negroes, by Tenure, by Sections, Divisions, and States: 1930," *Negroes in the United States, 1920-1932*, 1935, p. 579. Primary source: U.S. Bureau of the Census. *Negroes in the United States, 1920-1932.* Washington, D.C.: U.S. Government Printing Office, 1935.

★ 244 ★

Farms and Farmers

Relationships: Value of Implements and Machinery on Southern Farms, by Owner Status, 1900 and 1910, and Change 1900-1910 - I

TENURE	VALUE OF FARM PROPERTY IN THE SOUTH					
	Colored farms		White farms		Increase: 1900-1910[1]	
	1910	1900	1910	1900	Colored farms	White farms

IMPLEMENTS AND MACHINERY

Total	$33,777,118	$18,586,225	$259,512,739	$161,424,950	$15,190,893	$98,087,789
Owners	10,798,831	5,795,970	158,755,449	98,161,120	5,002,861	60,594,329
Free	7,514,838	[2]	116,186,391	[2]	[2]	[2]
Mortgaged	3,283,993	[2]	42,569,058	[2]	[2]	[2]
Part owners	2,490,431	935,600	23,472,047	10,365,830	1,554,831	13,106,217
Cash tenants	11,337,009	6,405,775	20,110,267	11,303,060	4,931,234	8,807,207
Share tenants	8,841,943	5,247,960	43,911,243	22,957,740	3,593,983	20,953,503
Managers	308,904	200,920	13,263,733	18,637,200	107,984	-5,373,467

Source: "Value of Classes of Farm Property on Colored and White Farms, by Tenure of Classes, with Decennial Increase, Percentage Distribution by Tenure, and Average Per Farm: 1910," *Negro Population, 1790-1915,* 1918, p. 578. Primary source: U.S. Bureau of the Census. *Negro Population, 1790-1915.* Washington, D.C.: Government Printing Office, 1918. *Notes:* "Colored" may include persons other than black. 1. A minus sign (-) denotes decrease. 2. Data not available.

★ 245 ★

Farms and Farmers

Relationships: Value of Implements and Machinery on Southern Farms, by Owner Status, 1900 and 1910, and Change 1900-1910 - II

TENURE	VALUE OF FARM PROPERTY IN THE SOUTH							
	Percentage distribution				Average per farm			
	Colored farms		White farms		Colored farms		White farms	
	1910	1900	1910	1900	1910	1900	1910	1900

IMPLEMENTS

Total	100.0	100.0	100.0	100.0	$38	$25	$118	$86
Owners	32.0	3.2	61.2	60.8	62	37	138	91
Free	22.2	[2]	44.8	[2]	58	[2]	128	[2]
Mortgaged	9.7	[2]	16.4	[2]	70	[2]	173	[2]
Part owners	27.4	5.0	9.0	6.4	58	33	137	99
Cash tenants	33.6	34.5	7.7	7.0	40	24	88	60

[Continued]

★ 245 ★

Relationships: Value of Implements and Machinery on Southern Farms, by Owner Status, 1900 and 1910, and Change 1900-1910 - II

[Continued]

TENURE	VALUE OF FARM PROPERTY IN THE SOUTH							
	Percentage distribution				Average per farm			
	Colored farms		White farms		Colored farms		White farms	
	1910	1900	1910	1900	1910	1900	1910	1900
Share tenants	26.2	28.2	16.9	14.2	23	19	69	47
Managers	0.9	1.1	5.1	11.5	257	126	879	1,085

Source: "Value of Classes of Farm Property on Colored and White Farms, by Tenure of Classes, with Decennial Increase, Percentage Distribution by Tenure, and Average Per Farm: 1910," *Negro Population, 1790-1915*, 1918, p. 578. Primary source: U.S. Bureau of the Census. *Negro Population, 1790-1915*. Washington, D.C.: Government Printing Office, 1918. *Notes:* "Colored" may include persons other than black. 1. A minus sign (-) denotes decrease. 2. Data not available.

★ 246 ★

Farms and Farmers

Relationships: Value of Land and Buildings on Black Farms, by Owner Status and Region, 1920 and 1930

| TENURE | VALUE OF LAND AND BUILDINGS | | INCREASE OR DECREASE (-) | | PERCENT DISTRIBUTION | |
	1930	1920	Amount	Percent	1930	1920
	UNITED STATES					
Total	$1,402,945,799	$2,257,645,325	-$859,699,526	-37.9	100.0	100.0
Owners	334,451,396	554,158,003	-219,706,607	-39.6	23.8	24.5
Tenants	1,053,649,636	1,676,315,864	-622,666,228	-37.1	75.1	74.3
Managers	14,844,767	27,171,458	-12,326,691	-45.4	1.1	1.2
	THE SOUTH					
Total	$1,355,181,667	$2,191,005,642	-$835,823,975	-38.1	100.0	100.0
Owners	314,100,432	522,178,137	-208,077,705	-39.8	23.2	23.8
Tenants	1,028,371,428	1,647,447,607	-619,076,179	-37.6	75.9	75.2
Managers	12,709,807	21,379,898	-8,670,091	-40.6	.9	1.0
	THE NORTH					
Total	$41,668,222	$59,832,464	-$18,164,242	-30.4	100.0	100.0
Owners	17,684,979	28,481,761	-10,796,782	-37.9	42.4	47.6
Tenants	22,327,483	26,258,443	-3,930,960	-15.0	53.6	43.9
Managers	1,655,760	5,092,260	-3,436,500	-67.5	4.0	8.5
	THE WEST					
Total	$6,095,910	$6,807,219	-711,309	-10.4	100.0	100.0
Owners	2,665,985	3,498,105	-832,120	-23.8	43.7	51.4

[Continued]

★ 246 ★

Relationships: Value of Land and Buildings on Black Farms, by Owner Status and Region, 1920 and 1930

[Continued]

TENURE	VALUE OF LAND AND BUILDINGS		INCREASE OR DECREASE (-)		PERCENT DISTRIBUTION	
	1930	1920	Amount	Percent	1930	1920
Tenants	2,950,725	2,609,814	340,911	13.1	48.4	38.3
Managers	479,200	699,300	-220,100	-31.5	7.9	10.3

Source: "Value of Land and Buildings for Farms Operated by Negroes, by Tenure, by Sections: 1930 and 1920," *Negroes in the United States, 1920-1932*, 1935, p. 578. Primary source: U.S. Bureau of the Census. *Negroes in the United States, 1920-1932.* Washington, D.C.: U.S. Government Printing Office, 1935.

★ 247 ★

Farms and Farmers

Relationships: Value of Land and Buildings on Black Farms, by Owner Status, Region, and Division, 1920 and 1930

SECTION AND DIVISION	VALUE OF LAND AND BUILDINGS							
	Total		Owners		Tenants		Managers	
	1930	1920	1930	1920	1930	1920	1930	1920
United States	$1,402,945,799	$2,257,645,325	$334,451,396	$554,158,003	$1,053,649,636	$1,676,315,864	$14,844,767	$27,171,458
The North	41,688,222	59,832,464	17,684,979	28,481,761	22,327,483	26,258,443	1,655,760	5,092,260
The South	1,355,181,667	2,191,005,642	314,100,432	522,178,137	1,028,371,428	1,647,447,607	12,709,807	21,379,898
The West	6,095,910	6,807,219	2,665,985	3,498,105	2,950,725	2,609,814	479,200	699,300
New England	909,395	1,076,815	651,325	617,165	67,070	234,750	191,000	224,900
Middle Atlantic	5,140,255	6,937,600	2,422,675	2,294,225	2,165,880	2,854,710	551,700	1,788,665
East North Central	13,304,751	22,308,742	6,795,536	10,433,924	6,092,645	10,528,018	415,570	1,346,800
West North Central	22,313,821	29,509,307	7,814,443	15,136,447	14,001,888	12,640,965	497,490	1,731,895
South Atlantic	484,443,943	981,677,765	135,724,157	237,088,264	341,922,425	733,440,819	6,797,361	11,148,682
East South Central	426,528,844	645,828,371	82,453,066	127,401,052	340,962,633	513,777,358	3,113,145	4,649,961
West South Central	444,208,880	563,499,506	95,923,209	157,688,821	345,486,370	400,229,430	2,799,301	5,581,255
Mountain	2,037,510	2,523,814	943,685	1,273,200	1,012,825	916,214	81,000	334,400
Pacific	4,058,400	4,283,405	1,722,300	2,224,905	1,937,900	1,693,600	398,200	364,900

Source: "Farms Operated by Negroes—Number, Farm Acreage, and Value of Land and Buildings, by Tenure, by Sections, Divisions, and States: 1930 and 1920," *Negroes in the United States, 1920-1932*, 1935, pp. 596-597. Primary source: U.S. Bureau of the Census. *Negroes in the United States, 1920-1932.* Washington, D.C.: U.S. Government Printing Office, 1935.

★ 248 ★

Farms and Farmers

Relationships: Value of Land and Buildings on Black Farms, by Owner Status, Region, and Southern Division, 1920 and 1930

SECTION, DIVISION, AND TENURE	AVERAGE VALUE PER FARM				AVERAGE VALUE PER ACRE			
	1930	1920	Increase or decrease (-)		1930	1920	Increase or decrease (-)	
			Amount	Percent			Amount	Percent
United States	$1,589,	$2,439	-$850	-34.9	$37.32	$54.49	-$17.17	-31.5
Owners	1,848	2,535	-687	-27.1	29.86	39.73	-9.87	-24.8
Tenants	1,503	2,378	-875	-36.8	40.29	61.91	-21.62	-34.9
Managers	16,083	13,411	2,672	19.9	59.60	66.91	-7.31	-10.9
THE SOUTH	1,556	2,393	-837	-35.0	36.87	54.04	-17.17	-31.8
Owners	1,783	2,459	-676	-27.5	29.12	38.87	-9.75	-25.1
Tenants	1,482	2,349	-867	-36.9	39.95	61.58	-21.63	-35.1
Managers	15,789	12,155	3,634	29.9	55.27	60.10	-4.83	-8.0
SOUTH ATLANTIC	1,637	2,568	-931	-36.3	33.29	54.08	-20.79	-38.4
Owners	1,703	2,323	-620	-26.7	32.20	43.24	-11.04	-25.5
Tenants	1,585	2,626	-1,041	-39.6	33.43	58.57	-25.14	-42.9
Managers	14,250	11,662	2,588	22.2	62.30	76.39	-14.09	-18.4
EAST SOUTH CENTRAL	1,330	2,104	-774	-36.8	35.79	53.35	-17.56	-32.9
Owners	1,634	2,296	-662	-28.8	23.45	32.41	-8.96	-27.6
Tenants	1,263	2,046	-783	-38.3	40.83	63.52	-22.69	-35.0
Managers	22,237	11,453	10,784	94.2	62.27	54.17	8.10	15.0
WEST SOUTH CENTRAL	1,746	2,490	-744	29.9	43.17	54.77	-11.60	-21.2
Owners	2,087	2,876	-789	-27.4	31.41	39.22	-7.81	-19.9
Tenants	1,659	2,339	-680	-29.1	48.22	65.14	-16.92	-26.0
Managers	14,890	14,059	831	5.9	39.52	45.02	-5.50	-12.2
THE NORTH	3,753	6,379	-2,626	-41.2	57.80	77.91	-20.11	-25.8
Owners	3,998	4,954	-956	-19.3	53.18	65.46	-12.28	-18.8
Tenants	3,389	7,748	-4,359	-56.3	59.82	89.15	-29.33	-32.9
Managers	17,997	12,042	-3,045	-14.5	109.38	132.84	-23.46	-17.7
THE WEST	7,526	9,287	-1,761	-19.0	51.76	56.73	-4.97	-8.8
Owners	5,771	7,024	-1,253	-17.8	32.89	44.10	-11.21	-25.4
Tenants	9,164	12,428	-3,264	-26.3	90.18	91.08	-.90	-1.0
Managers	18,431	27,972	-9,541	-34.1	119.92	58.26	61.66	105.8

Source: "Average Value of Land and Buildings on Farms Operated by Negroes, by Tenure, by Sections, and Southern Divisions: 1930 and 1920," *Negroes in the United States, 1920-1932*, 1935, p. 579. Primary source: U.S. Bureau of the Census. *Negroes in the United States, 1920-1932*. Washington, D.C.: U.S. Government Printing Office, 1935.

★ 249 ★

Farms and Farmers

Relationships: Value of Land on Southern Farms, by Owner Status, 1900 and 1910, and Change 1900-1910 - I

TENURE	VALUE OF FARM PROPERTY IN THE SOUTH					
	Colored farms		White farms		Increase: 1900-1910[1]	
	1910	1900	1910	1900	Colored farms	White farms

LAND

TENURE						
Total	$737,632,122	$310,718,726	$5,188,642,947	$2,251,041,223	$426,913,396	$2,937,601,724
Owners	166,711,526	69,149,276	2,784,198,306	1,288,825,482	97,562,250	1,495,372,824
Free	114,480,372	[2]	2,018,861,909	[2]	[2]	[2]
Mortgaged	52,231,154	[2]	765,336,397	[2]	[2]	[2]
Part owners	45,564,045	12,847,560	506,514,471	179,997,100	32,716,485	326,517,371
Cash tenants	223,447,037	108,587,760	484,059,699	207,206,348	114,859,277	276,853,351
Share tenants	293,652,660	115,798,440	1,092,399,374	386,046,353	177,854,220	706,353,021
Managers	8,256,854	4,335,690	321,471,097	188,965,940	3,921,164	132,505,157

Source: "Value of Classes of Farm Property on Colored and White Farms, by Tenure of Classes, with Decennial Increase, Percentage Distribution by Tenure, and Average Per Farm: 1910," *Negro Population, 1790-1915*, 1918, p. 578. Primary source: U.S. Bureau of the Census, *Negro Population, 1790-1915*. Washington, D.C.: Government Printing Office, 1918. *Notes:* "Colored" may include persons other than black. 1. A minus sign (-) denotes decrease. 2. Data not available.

★ 250 ★

Farms and Farmers

Relationships: Value of Land on Southern Farms, by Owner Status, 1900 and 1910, and Change 1900-1910 - II

TENURE	VALUE OF FARM PROPERTY IN THE SOUTH							
	Percentage distribution				Average per farm			
	Colored farms		White farms		Colored farms		White farms	
	1910	1900	1910	1900	1910	1900	1910	1900

LAND

TENURE								
Total	100.0	100.0	100.0	100.0	$829	$420	$2,351	$1,198
Owners	22.6	22.3	53.7	57.3	951	436	2,412	1,195
Free	15.5	[2]	39.0	[2]	891	[2]	2,223	[2]
Mortgaged	7.1	[2]	14.8	[2]	1,118	[2]	3,113	[2]
Part owners	6.2	4.1	9.8	8.0	1,055	456	2,945	1,711
Cash tenants	30.3	34.9	9.3	9.2	781	400	2,110	1,108

[Continued]

★ 250 ★

Relationships: Value of Land on Southern Farms, by Owner Status, 1900 and 1910, and Change 1900-1910 - II
[Continued]

TENURE	VALUE OF FARM PROPERTY IN THE SOUTH							
	Percentage distribution				Average per farm			
	Colored farms		White farms		Colored farms		White farms	
	1910	1900	1910	1900	1910	1900	1910	1900
Share tenants	39.8	37.3	21.1	17.1	764	413	1,718	785
Managers	1.1	1.4	6.2	8.4	6,881	2,722	21,312	11,004

Source: "Value of Classes of Farm Property on Colored and White Farms, by Tenure of Classes, with Decennial Increase, Percentage Distribution by Tenure, and Average Per Farm: 1910," *Negro Population, 1790-1915,* 1918, p. 578. Primary source: U.S. Bureau of the Census, *Negro Population, 1790-1915.* Washington, D.C.: Government Printing Office, 1918. *Notes:* "Colored" may include persons other than black. 1. A minus sign (-) denotes decrease. 2. Data not available.

★ 251 ★

Farms and Farmers

Relationships: Value of Livestock on Southern Farms, by Owner Status, 1900 and 1910, and Change 1900-1910 - I

TENURE	VALUE OF FARM PROPERTY IN THE SOUTH					
	Colored farms		White farms		Increase: 1900-1910[1]	
	1910	1900	1910	1900	Colored farms	White farms
LIVE STOCK						
Total	$182,732,124	$89,182,043	$1,142,673,713	$721,639,992	$93,550,081	$421,033,721
Owners	48,179,712	27,698,028	659,607,543	396,168,555	20,481,684	263,438,988
Free	32,921,123[2]	[3]	474,921,450[2]	[3]	[3]	[3]
Mortgaged	13,641,333[2]	[3]	162,241,548[2]	[3]	[3]	[3]
Part owners	12,420,058	4,365,857	120,983,154	80,375,992	8,054,201	40,607,162
Cash tenants	63,018,214	30,887,862	104,629,233	64,683,765	32,130,352	39,990,468
Share tenants	57,735,590	24,583,913	206,830,206	95,792,850	33,151,677	111,037,356
Managers	1,378,550	1,646,383	50,623,577	84,603,830	-267,833	-34,040,253

Source: "Value of Classes of Farm Property on Colored and White Farms, by Tenure of Classes, with Decennial Increase, Percentage Distribution by Tenure, and Average Per Farm: 1910," *Negro Population, 1790-1915,* 1918, p. 578. Primary source: U.S. Bureau of the Census. *Negro Population, 1790-1915.* Washington, D.C.: Government Printing Office, 1918. *Notes:* "Colored" may include persons other than black. 1. A minus sign (-) denotes decrease. 2. Does not include value of poultry and bees included in total for owners. 3. Data not available.

★ 252 ★

Farms and Farmers

Relationships: Value of Livestock on Southern Farms, by Owner Status, 1900 and 1910, and Change 1900-1910 - II

TENURE	VALUE OF FARM PROPERTY IN THE SOUTH							
	Percentage distribution				Average per farm			
	Colored farms		White farms		Colored farms		White farms	
	1910	1900	1910	1900	1910	1900	1910	1900
LIVE STOCK								
Total	100.0	100.0	100.0	100.0	$205	$120	$518	$384
Owners	26.4	31.1	57.7	54.9	275	175	572	867
Free	18.6[2]	[3]	42.9[2]	[2]	256[2]	[2]	523[2]	[3]
Mortgaged	7.7[2]	[3]	14.7[2]	[3]	292[2]	[3]	660[2]	[2]
Part owners	6.8	4.9	10.6	11.1	288	155	704	764
Cash tenants	34.5	34.6	9.2	9.0	220	114	456	345
Share tenants	31.6	27.6	18.1	13.3	150	88	325	195
Managers	0.8	1.8	4.4	11.7	1,149	1,034	3,356	4,930

Source: "Value of Classes of Farm Property on Colored and White Farms, by Tenure of Classes, with Decennial Increase, Percentage Distribution by Tenure, and Average Per Farm: 1910," *Negro Population, 1790-1915*, 1918, p. 578. Primary source: U.S. Bureau of the Census. *Negro Population, 1790-1915*. Washington, D.C.: Government Printing Office, 1918. *Notes:* "Colored" may include persons other than black. 1. A minus sign (-) denotes decrease. 2. Does not include value of poultry and bees included in total for owners. 3. Data not available.

★ 253 ★

Farms and Farmers

Relationships: Value of Southern Farm Property, by Owner Status, 1900 and 1910, and Change 1900-1910 - I

TENURE	VALUE OF FARM PROPERTY IN THE SOUTH					
	Colored farms		White farms		Increase: 1900-1910[1]	
					Colored farms	White farms
	1910	1900	1910	1900		
ALL FARM PROPERTY						
Total	$1,116,641,576	$488,049,236	$7,855,485,313	$3,781,805,483	$628,592,340	$4,073,679,830
Owners	275,323,227	123,754,396	4,436,972,500	2,222,681,923	151,568,831	2,214,290,577
Free	190,691,973[2]	[3]	3,253,836,841[2]	[3]	[3]	[3]
Mortgaged	83,013,998[2]	[3]	1,160,691,114[2]	[3]	[3]	[3]
Part owners	71,558,043	21,660,387	749,780,780	310,211,532	49,897,656	439,569,248
Cash tenants	342,387,968	166,766,057	701,220,541	330,543,855	175,611,911	370,676,686

[Continued]

★ 253 ★

Relationships: Value of Southern Farm Property, by Owner Status, 1900 and 1910, and Change 1900-1910 - I

[Continued]

TENURE	VALUE OF FARM PROPERTY IN THE SOUTH					
	Colored farms		White farms		Increase: 1900-1910[1]	
					Colored farms	White farms
	1910	1900	1910	1900		
Share tenants	415,312,935	168,466,783	1,535,676,035	594,493,283	246,846,152	941,182,752
Managers	12,059,403	7,391,613	431,835,457	323,874,890	4,667,790	107,960,567

Source: "Value of Classes of Farm Property on Colored and White Farms, by Tenure of Classes, with Decennial Increase, Percentage Distribution by Tenure, and Average Per Farm: 1910," *Negro Population, 1790-1915*, 1918, p. 578. Primary source: U.S. Bureau of the Census, *Negro Population, 1790-1915*. Washington, D.C.: Government Printing Office, 1918. *Notes:* "Colored" may include persons other than black. 1. A minus sign (-) denotes decrease. 2. Does not include value of property and bees included in total for owners. 3. Data not available.

★ 254 ★

Farms and Farmers

Relationships: Value of Southern Farm Property, by Owner Status, 1900 and 1910, and Change 1900-1910 - II

TENURE	VALUE OF FARM PROPERTY IN THE SOUTH							
	Percentage distribution				Average per farm			
	Colored farms		White farms		Colored farms		White farms	
	1910	1900	1910	1900	1910	1900	1910	1900
	ALL FARM PROPERTY							
Total	100.0	100.0	100.0	100.0	$1,254	$659	$3,559	$2,012
Owners	24.7	25.4	56.5	58.8	1,571	781	3,845	2,061
Free	17.1	[3]	41.4	[3]	1,483	[3]	3,583	[3]
Mortgaged	7.4	[3]	14.8	[3]	1,776	[3]	4,720	[3]
Part owners	6.4	4.4	9.5	8.2	1,657	768	4,361	2,950
Cash tenants	30.7	34.2	8.9	8.7	1,197	614	3,056	1,767
Share tenants	37.2	34.5	19.5	15.7	1,080	600	2,411	1,209
Managers	1.1	1.5	5.5	8.6	10,050	4,640	28,629	18,861

Source: "Value of Classes of Farm Property on Colored and White Farms, by Tenure of Classes, with Decennial Increase, Percentage Distribution by Tenure, and Average Per Farm: 1910," *Negro Population, 1790-1915*, 1918, p. 578. Primary source: U.S. Bureau of the Census, *Negro Population, 1790-1915*. Washington, D.C.: Government Printing Office, 1918. *Notes:* "Colored" may include persons other than black. 1. A minus sign (-) denotes decrease. 2. Does not include value of property and bees included in total for owners. 3. Data not available.

★ 255 ★

Farms and Farmers

Summary Characteristics: 1920-1930 Change in Acreage on Black Farms, by Owner Status and Farm Location

SECTION AND DIVISION	LAND IN FARMS (ACRES)				Tenants		Managers	
	Total		Owners					
	Acres	Percent	Acres	Percent	Acres	Percent	Acres	Percent
United States	-3,835,050	-9.3	-2,749,619	-19.7	-928,415	-3.4	-157,016	-38.7
The North	-47,081	-6.1	-102,555	-23.6	78,671	26.7	-23,197	-60.5
The South	-3,785,757	-9.3	-2,648,794	-19.7	-1,011,152	-3.8	-125,811	-35.4
The West	-2,212	-1.8	1,730	2.2	4,066	14.2	-8,008	-66.7
New England	-9,855	-51.2	-2,824	-27.9	-4,196	-80.4	-2,835	-72.5
Middle Atlantic	-17,089	-23.4	-1,758	-6.2	-10,059	-28.8	-5,272	-55.8
East North Central	-25,187	-10.5	-23,361	-16.9	2,961	3.2	-4,787	-56.8
West North Central	5,050	1.2	-74,612	-28.9	89,965	55.8	-10,303	-62.3
South Atlantic	-3,600,620	-19.8	-1,268,591	-23.1	-2,295,188	-18.3	-36,841	-25.2
East South Central	-186,920	-1.5	-413,770	-10.5	262,692	3.2	-35,842	-41.8
West South Central	1,783	[1]	-966,433	-24.0	1,021,344	16.6	-53,128	-42.9
Mountain	-21	[1]	5,115	9.4	3,544	28.5	-8,680	-84.8
Pacific	-2,191	-5.1	-3,385	-12.7	522	3.2	672	37.9

Source: "Farms Operated by Negroes—Increase or Decrease (-) in Number, Farm Acreage, and Value of Land and Buildings, by Tenure, by Sections, Divisions, and States: 1920 to 1930," *Negroes in the United States, 1920- 1932*, 1935, pp. 598-599. Primary source: U.S. Bureau of the Census. *Negroes in the United States, 1920-1932*. Washington, D.C.: U.S. Government Printing Office, 1935.

★ 256 ★

Farms and Farmers

Summary Characteristics: 1920-1930 Change in Number on Black Farms, by Owner Status and Farm Location

SECTION AND DIVISION	NUMBER OF FARMS							
	Total		Owners		Tenants		Managers	
	Acres	Percent	Acres	Percent	Acres	Percent	Acres	Percent
United States	-42,858	-4.6	-37,596	-17.2	-4,159	-0.6	-1,103	-54.4
The North	1,724	18.4	-1,325	-23.0	3,199	94.4	-150	-62.0
The South	-44,659	-4.9	-36,235	-17.1	-7,470	-1.1	-954	-54.2
The West	77	10.5	-36	-7.2	112	53.3	1	4.0
New England	-94	-38.8	-64	-33.3	-19	-57.6	-11	-64.7
Middle Atlantic	-354	-28.9	-129	-18.5	-170	-38.3	-55	-64.0
East North Central	-609	-16.6	-443	-19.0	-124	-9.7	-42	-63.6
West North Central	2,781	65.6	-689	-27.3	3,512	214.3	-42	-57.5
South Atlantic	-86,344	-22.6	-22,373	-21.9	-63,492	-22.7	-479	-50.1
East South Central	13,594	4.4	-5,013	-9.0	18,873	7.5	-266	-65.5
West South Central	28,091	12.4	-8,849	-16.1	37,149	21.7	-209	-52.6

[Continued]

★ 256 ★

Summary Characteristics: 1920-1930 Change in Number on Black Farms, by Owner Status and Farm Location

[Continued]

SECTION AND DIVISION	NUMBER OF FARMS							
	Total		Owners		Tenants		Managers	
	Acres	Percent	Acres	Percent	Acres	Percent	Acres	Percent
Mountain	-45	-12.9	-56	-23.4	15	15.0	-4	-40.0
Pacific	122	31.8	20	7.7	97	88.2	5	33.3

Source: "Farms Operated by Negroes—Increase or Decrease (-) in Number, Farm Acreage, and Value of Land and Buildings, by Tenure, by Sections, Divisions, and States: 1920 to 1930," *Negroes in the United States, 1920- 1932,* 1935, pp. 598-599. Primary source: U.S. Bureau of the Census. *Negroes in the United States, 1920-1932.* Washington, D.C.: U.S. Government Printing Office, 1935.

★ 257 ★

Farms and Farmers

Summary Characteristics: 1920-1930 Change in Value of Land and Buildings on Black Farms, by Owner Status and Farm Location

SECTION AND DIVISION	VALUE OF LAND AND BUILDINGS							
	Total		Owners		Tenants		Managers	
	Value	Percent	Value	Percent	Value	Percent	Value	Percent
United States	-$854,699,526	-37.9	-$219,706,607	-39.6	-$622,668,228	-37.1	-$12,326,691	-45.4
The North	-18,164,242	-30.4	-10,796,782	-37.9	-3,930,960	-15.0	-3,436-500	-67.5
The South	-835,823,975	-38.1	-208,077,705	-39.8	-619,076,179	-37.6	-8,670,091	-40.6
The West	-711,309	-10.4	-832,120	-23.8	340,911	13.1	-220,100	-31.5
New England	-167,420	-15.5	34,160	5.5	-167,680	-71.4	-33,900	-15.1
Middle Atlantic	-1,797,345	-25.9	128,450	5.6	-688,830	-24.1	-1,236,965	-69.2
East North Central	-9,003,991	-40.4	-3,637,388	-34.9	-4,435,373	-42.1	-931,230	-69.1
West North Central	-7,195,486	-24.4	-7,322,004	-48.4	1,360,923	10.8	-1,234,405	-71.3
South Atlantic	-497,233-822	-50.7	-101,364,107	-42.8	-391,518,394	-53.4	-4,351,321	-39.0
East South Central	-219,299,527	-34.0	-44,947,986	-35.3	-172,814,725	-33.6	-1,536,816	-33.1
West South Central	-119,290,626	-21.2	-61,765,612	-39.2	-54,743,060	-13.7	-2,781,954	-49.8
Mountain	-486,304	-19.3	-329,515	-25.9	96,611	10.5	-253,400	-75.8
Pacific	-225,005	-5.3	-502,605	-22.6	244,300	14.4	33,300	9.1

Source: "Farms Operated by Negroes—Increase or Decrease (-) in Number, Farm Acreage, and Value of Land and Buildings, by Tenure, by Sections, Divisions, and States: 1920 to 1930," *Negroes in the United States, 1920- 1932,* 1935, pp. 598-599. Primary source: U.S. Bureau of the Census. *Negroes in the United States, 1920-1932.* Washington, D.C.: U.S. Government Printing Office, 1935.

★ 258 ★

Farms and Farmers

Summary Characteristics: Acreage and Value of Black-Owned Farms, by Division and State, 1920

Divisions and States	Number farms	Land in farms		Value of land and buildings
		Total	Improved	
United States	218,612	13,948,512	7,253,875	$554,158,000
New England	192	10,121	4,023	617,163
Maine	13	953	445	54,405
New Hampshire	12	1,121	410	18,200
Vermont	21	3,075	1,081	87,120
Massachusetts	89	3,003	1,305	243,355
Rhode Island	13	630	188	16,900
Connecticut	44	1,339	594	197,100
Middle Atlantic	697	28,516	18,927	2,294,220
New York	152	9,366	6,067	619,605
New Jersey	284	8,963	5,214	755,710
Pennsylvania	261	10,187	7,646	918,915
East North Central	2,335	138,109	102,021	10,433,920
Ohio	1,053		41,170	4,173,124
Indiana	305	17,284	14,324	1,831,914
Illinois	533	33,451	26,275	2,541,000
Michigan	403	28,372	18,649	1,643,890
Wisconsin	41	3,476	1,603	244,000
West North Central	2,525	258,329	162,323	15,136,440
Minnesota	24	1,657	581	75,327
Iowa	74	5,140	3,450	683,250
Missouri	1,643	111,946	77,896	8,449,930
North Dakota	11	4,711	2,056	85,147
South Dakota	33	14,205	4,849	357,310
Nebraska	31	13,556	2,528	445,545
Kansas	709	107,114	70,963	5,039,940
South Atlantic	102,0565	5,483,254	2,727,823	237,088,265
Delaware	355	12,512	8,424	681,304
Maryland	3,548	119,235	73,249	7,959,590
District of Columbia	9	25	24	40,307
Virginia	30,908	1,371,333	653,203	57,004,470
West Virginia	403	19,052	11,211	956,563
North Carolina	21,714	1,126,751	493,251	56,113,062
South Carolina	22,759	1,146,396	590,881	59,839,586
Georgia	16,040	1,331,278	693,500	45,465,433
Florida	6,320	356,682	204,080	9,027,950
East South Central	55,488	3,930,410	1,989,647	127,401,052
Kentucky	5,318	239,997	171,614	16,389,797
Tennessee	9,839	535,265	321,442	25,276,745
Alabama	17,2301	1,332,621	647,825	29,021,680
Mississippi	23,130	1,822,527	848,766	56,712,830
West South Central	54,821	4,020,442	2,226,275	157,688,821
Arkansas	15,369	1,042,047	540,366	45,536,138
Louisiana	10,975	746,701	382,852	25,438,223

[Continued]

★ 258 ★

Summary Characteristics: Acreage and Value of Black-Owned Farms, by Division and State, 1920

[Continued]

Divisions and States	Number farms	Land in farms		Value of land and buildings
		Total	Improved	
Oklahoma	4,958	438,567	272,490	19,227,142
Texas	23,519	1,793,127	1,030,567	67,487,318
Mountain	239	54,574	14,258	1,273,200
Montana	26	8,759	2,246	197,350
Idaho	16	1,523	662	83,200
Wyoming	17	6,702	1,098	131,410
Colorado	115	28,267	7,649	544,115
New Mexico	24	5,103	1,124	88,380
Arizona	19	2,178	785	117,500
Utah	19	1,804	618	94,240
Nevada	3	238	76	17,005
Pacific	259	24,757	8,578	2,224,905
Washington	65	5,803	1,713	378,960
Oregon	11	1,401	343	57,400
California	183	17,553	6,523	1,788,545

Source: "Farms Operated by Negro Owners, 1920," *Negro Year Book: An Annual Encyclopedia of the Negro, 1925-1926,* 1925, p. 378. Primary source: Work, Monroe N. (Ed.), *Negro Year Book: An Annual Encyclopedia of the Negro, 1925-1926.* Tuskegee Institute, Ala.: The Negro Year Book Pub. Co., 1925.

★ 259 ★

Farms and Farmers

Summary Characteristics: Acreage and Value of Farms, by Owner Status, 1940

	Size and Value of Farms					Croppers
	All operators	Owners	Part owners	Managers	All Tenants	
Size: Acres of land in farm						
White operators	145.8	122.3	342.1	2126.3	109.0	58.9
Non-white operators	45.4	58.7	68.3	479.3	40.0	30.2
Value: Land and buildings						
White operators	$3,818	$3,697	$7,016	$41,230	$2,819	$1,545
Non-white operators	1,222	1,403	1,657	20,562	1,132	1,049

Source: "Size and Value of Farms by Color of operator in Southern States in 1940," *Negro Year Book: A Review of Events Affecting Negro Life, 1941-1946,* 1947, p. 157. Primary source: U.S. Bureau of the Census.

★ 260 ★

Farms and Farmers

Summary Characteristics: Acreage and Value of Nonwhite Farms, by Division and State, 1940

Region, Division, and State	Farms of non-white operators (number)	Land in farms (acres)	Value of farms (land and buildings)
United States	719,071	45,739,931	$984,702,379
The North	12,702	1,447,452	32,292,818
The South	680,266	30,924,796	831,005,542
The West	26,103	13,376,683	121,404,019
New England	563	10,791	1,737,377
Maine	18	769	20,000
New Hampshire	2	220	8,300
Vermont	12	1,063	27,900
Massachusetts	481	6,347	1,394,020
Rhode Island	5	77	19,400
Connecticut	45	2,315	267,757
Middle Atlantic	1,337	72,045	4,497,350
New York	567	41,521	1,919,582
New Jersey	448	14,645	1,274,243
Pennsylvania	322	15,879	1,303,525
East North Central	3,329	183,923	8,775,067
Ohio	1,099	69,154	3,449,749
Indiana	380	17,285	1,162,214
Illinois	785	44,101	1,724,240
Michigan	761	40,191	1,863,495
Wisconsin	304	13,192	575,369
West North Central	7,473	1,180,693	17,283,024
Minnesota	294	22,269	599,286
Iowa	127	7,781	460,574
Missouri	3,690	174,668	6,880,637
North Dakota	593	123,936	1,178,185
South Dakota	1,741	712,051	4,059,376
Nebraska	283	30,130	1,338,054
Kansas	745	109,858	2,766,912
South Atlantic	230,906	12,605,318	338,881,618
Delaware	625	36,866	1,522,438
Maryland	4,051	236,197	10,575,990
District of Columbia	4	62	63,000
Virginia	35,090	1,782,602	50,083,201
West Virginia	671	23,741	906,110
North Carolina	60,268	2,858,389	113,121,849
South Carolina	61,307	2,781,837	77,059,331
Georgia	59,132	4,431,385	74,959,203

[Continued]

★ 260 ★

Summary Characteristics: Acreage and Value of Nonwhite Farms, by Division and State, 1940

[Continued]

Region, Division, and State	Farms of non-white operators (number)	Land in farms (acres)	Value of farms (land and buildings)
Florida	9,758	454,239	10,590,496
East South Central	266,426	10,258,747	264,026,221
Kentucky	5,547	240,804	9,826,638
Tennessee	27,975	1,070,191	36,535,445
Alabama	73,364	3,557,398	63,224,403
Mississippi	159,540	5,390,354	154,439,735
West South Central	182,934	8,060,731	228,097,703
Arkansas	57,025	1,870,918	64,034,632
Louisiana	59,584	1,928,441	66,888,058
Oklahoma	13,572	1,229,938	25,107,081
Texas	52,753	3,031,434	72,067,032
Mountain	17,243	12,820,979	34,360,167
Montana	1,076	436,260	3,687,770
Idaho	566	46,714	3,001,879
Wyoming	303	30,782	704,146
Colorado	402	50,042	3,027,911
New Mexico	5,564	3,516,482	7,642,529
Arizona	8,229	8,312,931	13,178,655
Utah	677	407,833	2,254,217
Nevada	426	19,935	863,060
Pacific	8,860	546,704	87,043,852
Washington	1,507	121,916	7,367,103
Oregon	623	69,018	3,872,715
California	6,730	355,770	75,904,034

Source: "Farms of Non-White Farm operators, by Acreage and Value, for the United States, by Divisions and States: 1940," *The Negro Handbook, 1942,* p. 216. Primary source: U.S. Bureau of the Census.

★ 261 ★

Farms and Farmers

Summary Characteristics: Acreage and Value of Southern Black Farms, by Owner Status, 1910 - I

DIVISION AND TENURE CLASS	FARMS OPERATED BY COLORED FARMERS					
	Acres in farms				Value of land and buildings	
	Total		Improved			
	1910	1900	1910	1900	1910	1900
THE SOUTH						
Total	42,609,117	38,612,046	27,735,743	23,214,607	$900,132,334	$380,280,968
Owners	15,691,536	13,358,684	7,531,119	6,026,805	272,992,238	106,619,328
Managers	349,779	428,518	108,249	127,742	10,371,949	5,544,310
Tenants	26,567,802	24,824,844	20,096,375	17,060,060	616,768,147	268,117,330
SOUTH ATLANTIC	17,675,382	15,637,265	10,990,069	8,895,862	367,707,068	133,387,758
Owners	5,646,378	4,427,439	2,695,947	2,099,232	105,586,619	36,982,908
Managers	145,371	201,074	61,287	66,764	5,727,681	2,937,580
Tenants	11,883,633	11,008,752	8,232,835	6,729,866	256,410,768	93,467,270
EAST SOUTH CENTRAL	13,595,717	12,621,318	9,556,529	8,191,628	279,667,758	131,453,610
Owners	4,539,952	3,837,853	2,213,645	1,714,020	70,937,214	28,539,910
Managers	76,360	60,388	26,237	25,866	2,572,270	1,282,910
Tenants	8,979,405	8,723,077	7,316,647	6,451,742	206,158,274	101,630,790
WEST SOUTH CENTRAL	11,338,018	10,353,463	7,189,145	6,127,117	252,757,508	115,439,600
Owners	5,505,206	5,093,392	2,621,527	2,213,553	96,486,405	41,096,510
Managers	128,048	167,056	20,725	35,112	2,071,998	1,323,820
Tenants	5,704,764	5,093,015	4,546,893	3,878,452	154,199,105	73,019,270

Source: "Colored Farm Acreage, Total and Improved, and Value of Land and Buildings, by Tenure of Farm, with Average Acreage per Farm, Percentage Improved of Farm Acreage, and Average Value of Land and Buildings per Farm and per Acre, by Southern Divisions and States: 1910," *Negro Population, 1790-1915*, 1918, pp. 625-626. Primary source: U.S. Bureau of the Census. *Negro Population, 1790-1915*. Washington, D.C.: Government Printing Office, 1918.

★ 262 ★

Farms and Farmers

Summary Characteristics: Acreage and Value of Southern Black Farms, by Owner Status, 1910 - II

DIVISION AND TENURE CLASS	FARMS OPERATED BY COLORED FARMERS									
	Average acres per farm				Percentage improved		Average value of land and buildings			
	Total		Improved		of farm acreage		Per farm		Per acre	
	1910	1900	1910	1900	1910	1900	1910	1900	1910	1900
THE SOUTH										
Total	47.9	52.1	31.2	31.3	65.1	60.1	$1,011	$513	$21.13	$9.85
Owners	71.8	71.6	34.5	32.3	48.0	45.1	125	571	17.40	7.98
Managers	291.5	269.0	90.2	80.2	30.9	29.8	8,643	3,480	29.65	12.94
Tenants	39.6	44.9	30.0	30.9	75.6	68.7	920	485	23.21	10.80
SOUTH ATLANTIC	49.7	54.1	30.9	30.8	62.2	56.9	1,033	462	20.80	8.53
Owners	55.4	52.0	26.4	24.7	47.7	47.4	1,035	435	18.70	8.35
Managers	201.9	207.3	85.1	68.8	42.2	33.2	7,955	3,028	39.40	14.61
Tenants	46.9	54.3	32.5	33.2	69.3	61.1	1,013	461	21.58	8.49
EAST SOUTH CENTRAL	41.8	47.1	29.4	30.6	70.3	64.9	860	491	20.57	10.42
Owners	77.3	76.9	37.7	34.3	48.8	44.7	1,208	572	15.63	7.44
Managers	306.7	186.4	105.4	79.8	34.4	42.8	10,330	3,960	33.69	21.24
Tenants	33.7	40.1	27.5	29.6	81.5	74.0	774	467	22.96	11.65
WEST SOUTH CENTRAL	54.2	56.3	34.4	33.3	63.4	59.2	1,209	628	22.29	11.15
Owners	95.3	98.6	45.4	42.9	47.6	43.5	1,670	796	17.53	8.07
Managers	554.3	558.7	89.7	117.4	16.2	21.0	8,970	4,427	16.18	7.92
Tenants	37.8	38.6	30.1	29.4	79.7	76.2	1,021	553	27.03	14.34

Source: "Colored Farm Acreage, Total and Improved, and Value of Land and Buildings, by Tenure of Farm, with Average Acreage per Farm, Percentage Improved of Farm Acreage, and Average Value of Land and Buildings per Farm and per Acre, by Southern Divisions and States: 1910," *Negro Population, 1790-1915*, 1918, pp. 625-626. Primary source: U.S. Bureau of the Census. *Negro Population, 1790-1915.* Washington, D.C.: Government Printing Office, 1918.

★ 263 ★

Farms and Farmers

Summary Characteristics: Average Acreage on Southern Black Farms, 1920-1930, and According to Land Use, 1924 and 1929, by Owner Status

[Colored farmers include Negroes, Indians, Chinese, Japanese, and all other nonwhite races]

REGION, USE OF LAND, AND YEAR	AVERAGE ACREAGE PER FARM						PERCENT DISTRIBUTION BY TENURE				
	All colored operators	Full owners	Part owners	Managers	Cash tenants	Other tenants	Full owners	Part owners	Managers	Cash tenants	Other tenants
THE SOUTH											
All land in farms 1930	42.9	64.1	59.5	321.8	41.8	36.6	23.8	6.5	0.7	10.8	58.1
1925	40.8	61.6	53.2	277.7	38.1	34.1	29.0	5.5	.5	8.9	56.1
1920	44.8	66.9	54.5	207.8	40.0	37.9	28.9	5.1	.9	9.7	55.3
Crop land harvested 1929	23.5	21.4	26.8	67.1	23.5	23.7	14.5	5.4	.3	11.1	68.7
1924	23.1	19.6	24.9	61.9	23.8	23.8	16.3	4.5	.2	9.8	69.2

[Continued]

★ 263 ★

Summary Characteristics: Average Acreage on Southern Black Farms, 1920-1930, and According to Land Use, 1924 and 1929, by Owner Status
[Continued]

REGION, USE OF LAND, AND YEAR	AVERAGE ACREAGE PER FARM						PERCENT DISTRIBUTION BY TENURE				
	All colored operators	Full owners	Part owners	Managers	Cash tenants	Other tenants	Full owners	Part owners	Managers	Cash tenants	Other tenants
Plowable pasture 1929	2.0	4.7	3.9	32.7	1.9	1.2	37.3	9.2	1.5	10.5	41.5
Other pasture 1929[1]	1.4	3.2	3.6	59.8	1.0	.9	35.5	11.9	3.9	7.6	41.1
SOUTH ATLANTIC											
All land in farms 1930	49.1	54.6	47.7	229.1	50.2	46.9	22.6	6.4	.7	10.0	60.2
1925	43.2	49.0	41,5	198.0	40.8	41.0	27.5	5.4	.6	7.5	59.1
1920	47.5	55.2	47.5	152.5	44.8	44.8	25.2	5.1	.8	6.6	62.3
Crop land harvested 1929	23.7	17.6	22.2	65.6	23.2	25.8	15.1	6.2	.4	9.6	68.6
1924	21.7	14.9	19.6	58.6	22.6	24.3	16.7	5.0	.3	8.2	69.7
Plowable pasture 1929	1.7	3.0	2.0	18.2	1.5	1.3	35.2	7.6	1.7	8.5	47.0
Other pasture 1929[1]	1.1	1.5	.9	6.1	.9	1.0	27.9	5.7	.9	8.6	56.9
EAST SOUTH CENTRAL											
All land in farms 1930	37.2	72.9	58.1	354.9	37.9	29.2	24.1	5.4	.4	17.0	53.1
1925	36.5	72.5	55.7	373.6	36.7	27.9	27.5	5.0	.5	15.8	51.2
1920	39.4	74.8	52.1	211.1	37.9	30.6	28.3	4.2	.7	17.7	49.1
Crop land harvested 1929	21.6	21.9	24.8	81.9	23.7	20.8	12.4	4.0	.2	18.2	65.2
1924	22.0	20.3	24.7	78.8	24.1	21.6	12.8	3.7	.2	17.7	65.7
Plowable pasture 1929	2.3	6.9	5.3	55.6	2.1	1.3	37.3	8.2	1.1	15.4	38.0
Other pasture 1929[1]	1.2	4.1	2.3	17.7	1.0	.7	40.8	6.5	.6	12.8	39.3
WEST SOUTH CENTRAL											
All land in farms 1930	42.8	69.9	82.9	511.9	39.3	34.8	25.2	7.8	1.0	5.3	60.7
1925	42.6	75.1	79.0	447.0	37.5	27.9	32.8	6.1	.6	3.4	57.1
1920	47.4	79.2	71.1	334.8	39.3	35.8	35.9	6.3	1.2	6.0	50.6
Crop land harvested 1929	25.6	26.8	37.3	60.7	23.2	24.9	16.1	5.9	.2	5.3	72.6
1924	26.5	28.0	38.3	56.3	23.2	25.8	19.6	4.7	.1	3.4	72.1
Plowable pasture 1929	2.0	5.2	6.0	50.5	2.0	1.1	39.4	12.0	2.0	5.7	41.0
Other pasture 1929[1]	2.1	4.9	10.0	211.5	1.2	.9	36.1	19.3	8.1	3.2	33.3

Source: "Average Acreage by Farm, and Percent Distribution of All Land in Farms 1930, 1925, and 1920; and of Specified Classes of Land According to Use in 1929 and 1924 (Based on All Farms), by Tenure of Colored Operators, by Southern Divisions, and States," *Negroes in the United States, 1920-1932*, 1935, pp. 612-613. Primary source: U.S. Bureau of the Census. *Negroes in the United States, 1920-1932*. Washington, D.C.: U.S. Government Printing Office, 1935. *Note:* 1. Other than plowable or woodland pasture.

★ 264 ★

Farms and Farmers

Summary Characteristics: Characteristics of Black-Owned Farms with Mortgages, by Location of Farm, 1930

[Colored farmers include Negroes, Indians, Chinese, Japanese, and all other nonwhite races]

DIVISION AND STATE	Number	Land in farms (acres)	Value of land and buildings	Amount of mortgage indebtedness	All charges 1929[1]	Ratio of charges per farm	Average charges per farm	AVERAGE VALUE, DEBT, AND EQUITY PER FARM		
								Value of land and buildings	Amount of mortgage debt	Owners' equity
The South	39,555	3,157,969	$90,681,315	$33,372,640	$2,436,459	7.30	$62	$2,293	$844	$1,449
SOUTH ATLANTIC	15,021	1,096,515	34,386,847	12,502,573	847,907	6.78	56	2,289	832	1,457
Delaware	119	5,710	302,550	130,671	7,867	6.02	66	2,542	1,098	1,444
Maryland	789	38,607	2,278,995	771,836	46,578	6.03	59	2,888	978	1,910
District of Columbia	3	6	20,000	4,550	298	6.55	99	6,667	1,517	5,150
Virginia	4,007	260,932	8,847,433	2,878,651	182,947	6.36	46	2,208	718	1,490
West Virginia	45	3,409	153,950	43,811	2,724	6.22	61	3,421	974	2,447
North Carolina	4,009	265,433	10,254,093	4,077,374	257,271	6.31	64	2,558	1,017	1,541
South Carolina	3,119	237,909	6,363,949	2,470,693	189,439	7.67	61	2,040	792	1,248
Georgia	2,361	240,359	4,798,877	1,805,196	134,074	7.43	57	2,033	765	1,268
Florida	569	44,150	1,367,000	319,791	26,709	8.35	47	2,402	562	1,840

[Continued]

★ 264 ★

Summary Characteristics: Characteristics of Black-Owned Farms with Mortgages, by Location of Farm, 1930

[Continued]

DIVISION AND STATE	Number	Land in farms (acres)	Value of land and buildings	Amount of mortgage indebtedness	All charges 1929[1]	Ratio of charges per farm	Average charges per farm	AVERAGE VALUE, DEBT, AND EQUITY PER FARM		
								Value of land and buildings	Amount of mortgage debt	Owners' equity
EAST SOUTH CENTRAL	14,159	1,219,653	27,579,239	10,636,390	783,696	7.37	55	1,948	751	1,197
Kentucky	638	40,350	1,539,473	588,701	35,654	6.06	56	2,413	923	1,490
Tennessee	1,544	105,603	3,424,674	1,378,001	98,850	7.17	64	2,218	892	1,326
Alabama	3,928	379,142	7,731,384	2,927,931	229,050	7.82	58	1,968	745	1,223
Mississippi	8,049	694,558	14,883,708	5,741,757	420,142	7.32	52	1,849	713	1,136
WEST SOUTH CENTRAL	10,375	841,801	28,715,229	10,233,677	804,856	7.86	78	2,768	986	1,782
Arkansas	3,305	225,160	7,182,025	2,681,799	228,659	8.53	69	2,173	811	1,362
Louisiana	2,485	168,734	5,590,514	1,910,978	146,939	7.69	59	2,250	769	1,481
Oklahoma	1,538	170,888	6,794,808	2,404,508	169,899	7.07	110	4,418	1,563	2,855
Texas	3,047	277,019	9,147,882	3,236,392	259,359	8.01	85	3,002	1,062	1,940
SELECTED NORTHERN STATES[2]	1,214	80,235	5,010,504	2,051,511	128,578	6.27	106	4,127	1,690	2,437
New Jersey	102	3,891	480,050	157,475	9,584	6.09	94	4,706	1,544	3,162
Pennsylvania	113	5,817	578,340	206,621	12,317	5.96	109	5,118	1,829	3,289
Ohio	253	13,935	1,043,175	431,358	26,100	6.05	103	4,123	1,705	2,418
Indiana	92	4,892	323,150	138,879	8,684	6.25	94	3,513	1,510	2,003
Illinois	135	8,406	403,369	178,070	11,904	6.69	88	2,988	1,319	1,669
Missouri	356	24,894	1,054,525	513,698	33,160	6.46	93	2,962	1,443	1,519
Kansas	163	18,400	1,127,895	425,410	26,829	6.31	165	6,920	2,610	4,310

Source: "Mortgaged Farms Operated by Colored Full Owners Reporting Both Amount of Debt and Charges—Number of Farms, Acreage, Value, Mortgage Indebtedness, and Charges, by Southern Divisions, and States, and Selected Northern States: 1930," *Negroes in the United States, 1920-1932*, 1935, p. 580. Primary source: U.S. Bureau of the Census. *Negroes in the United States, 1920-1932.* Washington, D.C.: U.S. Government Printing Office, 1935. *Notes:* 1. Interest, commissions, bonuses, and premiums charged. 2. States having 200 or more Negro farmers who constitute 90 percent or more of the colored farmers in the State.

★ 265 ★

Farms and Farmers

Summary Characteristics: Farms and Acreage on Farms, by Location, 1920 and 1930

SECTION AND DIVISION	NEGRO		WHITE[1]	
	1930	1920	1930	1920
NUMBER OF FARMS				
United States	882,850	925,708	5,372,578	5,498,454
THE SOUTH	870,936	915,595	2,342,129	2,283,750
South Atlantic	295,934	382,278	760,089	775,144
East South Central	320,600	307,006	741,255	744,368
West South Central	254,402	226,311	840,785	764,238
THE NORTH	11,104	9,380	2,545,829	2,750,203
THE WEST	810	733	484,620	464,501
PERCENT DISTRIBUTION				
United States	100.0	100.0	100.0	100.0
THE SOUTH	98.7	98.9	43.6	41.5
South Atlantic	33.5	41.3	14.1	14.1
East South Central	36.3	33.2	13.8	13.5

[Continued]

★ 265 ★

Summary Characteristics: Farms and Acreage on Farms, by Location, 1920 and 1930
[Continued]

SECTION AND DIVISION	NEGRO		WHITE[1]	
	1930	1920	1930	1920
West South Central	28.8	24.4	15.6	13.9
THE NORTH	1.3	1.0	47.4	50.0
THE WEST	.1	.1	9.0	8.4

LAND IN FARMS (acres)

United States	37,597,132	41,432,182	945,683,034	910,939,194
THE SOUTH	36,758,484	40,544,241	305,280,653	308,803,337
South Atlantic	14,550,451	18,151,071	71,704,181	79,550,302
East South Central	11,918,057	12,014,977	60,886,302	66,783,791
West South Central	10,289,976	10,288,193	172,690,170	162,469,244
THE NORTH	720,782	767,953	423,963,841	430,365,628
THE WEST	117,776	119,988	216,438,540	171,770,229

PERCENT DISTRIBUTION

United States	100.0	100.0	100.0	100.0
THE SOUTH	97.8	97.9	32.3	33.9
South Atlantic	38.7	43.8	7.6	8.7
East South Central	31.7	29.2	6.4	7.3
West South Central	27.4	24.8	18.3	17.8
THE NORTH	1.9	1.9	44.8	47.2
THE WEST	.3	.3	22.9	18.9

Source: "Number of Farms and Farm Acreage of Negro and White Operators, by Sections, and Southern Divisions: 1930 and 1920," *Negroes in the United States, 1920-1932,* 1935, p. 576. Primary source: U.S. Bureau of the Census. *Negroes in the United States, 1920-1932.* Washington, D.C.: U.S. Government Printing Office, 1935. *Note:* 1. Includes Mexicans and Hindus.

★ 266 ★
Farms and Farmers

Summary Characteristics: Farms, Farm Land, and Farm Value of Black Farms, by Owner Status, 1900-1940

Tenure	1940	1930	1920	1910	1900
			Number of farms		
Total	681,790	882,850	925,708	893,370	746,715
Owners	174,010	181,016	218,612	218,972	[1]
Managers	413	923	2,026	1,434	[1]
Tenants	507,367	700,911	705,070	672,964	[1]
			Land in farms (acres)		
Total	30,785,095	37,597,132	41,432,182	[1]	38,293,920
Owners	10,314,283	11,198,893	[1]	[1]	[1]
Managers	153,601	249,072	[1]	[1]	[1]
Tenants	20,317,211	26,149,167	[1]	[1]	[1]
			Value of land and buildings (dollars)		
Total	836,067,623	1,402,945,799	2,257,645,325	[1]	396,145,262
Owners	251,328,726	334,451,396	[1]	[1]	[1]
Managers	8,208,132	14,844,767	[1]	[1]	[1]
Tenants	576,530,765	1,053,649,636	[1]	[1]	[1]
			Value of buildings (dollars)		
Total	224,388,138	340,409,360	[1]	[1]	71,902,265
Owners	81,129,400	105,741,696	[1]	[1]	[1]
Managers	1,998,971	4,023,544	[1]	[1]	[1]
Tenants	141,259,767	230,644,120	[1]	[1]	[1]
			Value of implements and machinery (dollars)		
Total	40,193,537	60,327,856	[1]	[1]	18,859,757
Owners	15,671,208	19,784,411	[1]	[1]	[1]
Managers	539,663	623,050	[1]	[1]	[1]
Tenants	23,982,666	39,920,395	[1]	[1]	[1]

Source: "Farms of Negro Operators by Tenure—Number, Acreage, and Specified Values for the United States: 1900 to 1940," *Negro Year Book: A Review of Events Affecting Negro Life, 1941-1946.* 1947, p. 155. Primary source: Chapter III, Volume 3, General Report on Agriculture: 1940. *Notes:* (Data for 1940 and 1930 relate to April 1; for 1920 to January 1; for 1910 to April 15; and for earlier years of June 1). 1. Not available.

★ 267 ★

Farms and Farmers

Summary Characteristics: Mortgage Status of Owned Farms and Type of Tenancy on Tenant Farms in the South, 1910

TENURE	1910	1900	Increase: 1900-1910[1]	Percentage distribution by tenure	
				1910	1900
UNITED STATES					
Total	893,370	746,715	146,655	100.0	100.0
Owners	218,972	187,797	31,175	24.5	25.1
Tenants	672,964	557,174	115,790	75.3	74.6
Managers	1,434	1,744	-310	0.2	0.2
THE SOUTH					
Total	880,836	732,362	148,474	100.0	100.0
Owners	211,087	179,418	31,669	24.0	24.5
Tenants	668,559	551,383	117,176	75.9	75.3
Managers	1,190	1,561	-371	0.1	0.2
THE NORTH					
Total	12,052	14,016	-1,964	100.0	100.0
Owners	7,498	8,122	-624	62.2	57.9
Tenants	4,330	5,718	-1,388	35.9	40.8
Managers	224	176	48	1.9	1.3
THE WEST					
Total	482	337	145	100.0	100.0
Owners	387	257	130	80.3	76.3
Tenants	75	73	2	15.6	21.7
Managers	20	7	13	4.1	2.1

Source: "Farms in the South: 1910," *Negro Population, 1790-1915,* 1918, p. 572. Primary source: U.S. Bureau of the Census. *Negro Population, 1790-1915.* Washington, D.C.: Government Printing Office, 1918. *Note:* 1. A minus sign (-) denotes decrease.

★ 268 ★
Farms and Farmers

Summary Characteristics: Number, Acreage, and Value of Farms, by Owner Status and Farm Location: 1935 and 1945

	Number of Farms		Land in Farms, Acres		Average acres per farm 1945	Value of Land and Buildings	
	1945	1935	1945 (000)	1935 (000)		1945 (000)	1935 (000)
United States	5,859,169	6,812,350	1,141,615	1,054,515	194.8	$46,388,925	$32,858,844
Owners	3,961,863	3,899,091	783,609	657,609	197.8	31,135,665	20,339,784
Tenants[1]	1,858,421	2,865,155	251,634	336,802	135.4	12,898,697	10,952,747
Whites	5,169,954	5,956,795	1,100,858	1,015,710	212.9	45,112,676	31,930,394
Owners	3,755,946	3,687,697	767,477	664,209	204.3	30,680,053	20,075,488
Tenants	1,375,745	2,222,184	231,605	311,109	168.3	12,106,870	10,307,948
Nonwhites[2]	689,215	855,555	40,756	38,804	59.1	1,276,249	928,449
Owners	205,917	211,394	16,132	12,839	78.3	455,612	264,295
Tenants	482,676	642,971	20,028	25,692	41.5	791,826	644,798
North							
Whites	2,470,049	2,802,801	445,670	440,383	180.4	25,352,173	18,988,831
Owners	1,836,117	1,891,538	312,218	277,852	170.0	16,460,700	11,840,979
Tenants	616,706	890,566	123,972	153,406	201.1	8,171,446	6,602,542
Nonwhites	13,529	16,667	2,044	1,568	151.1	49,240	35,836
Owners	8,754	9,166	1,483	1,054	169.4	29,561	19,621
Tenants	4,704	7,433	458	488	97.4	17,376	15,200
West							
Whites	484,183	547,818	308,163	234,706	636.5	7,747,731	4,993,107
Owners	406,398	407,558	217,117	166,841	534.2	5,859,393	3,460,070
Tenants	69,499	129,444	27,563	41,639	396.6	1,064,672	1,034,686
Nonwhites	10,273	23,141	7,942	1,649	773.1	95,246	104,210
Owners	7,331	16,163	3,268	1,250	412.1	51,317	36,740
Tenants	2,233	6,237	423	331	189.8	29,635	55,497
South							
Whites	2,215,722	2,606,176	347,025	340,619	156.6	12,017,072	7,948,456
Owners	1,513,431	1,388,601	238,140	199,515	157.4	8,359,959	4,774,438
Tenants	689,540	1,202,174	80,069	116,063	116.1	2,870,751	2,670,719
Nonwhites	665,413	815,747	30,769	35,586	46.2	1,131,761	788,402
Owners	189,232	186,065	11,380	10,533	60.1	374,732	207,932
Tenants	475,739	629,301	19,146	24,872	40.2	744,814	574,100

Source: "Number of Farms, Land in Farms, Value of Land in Buildings, by Color and Tenure for U.S. and by Regions, 1935 and 1945," *1952 Negro Year Book: A Review of Events Affecting Negro Life*, 1952, p. 105. Primary source: U.S. Bureau of Agriculture, 1945. *Notes:* 1. Nonwhite includes Negroes, Indians, Chinese, and Japanese. Approximately 95% of all nonwhite farmers are Negroes; in the South, the percentage of Negroes increases to about 98. 2. Nonwhite includes Negroes, Indians, Chinese, and Japanese. Approximately 95% of all nonwhite owners are Negroes; in the South, the percentage of Negroes increases to about 98.

★ 269 ★

Farms and Farmers

Summary Characteristics: Southern Black Farms – Value and Acreage, by State, 1910

SECTION AND DIVISION	Farm acreage			Value of farm property		
	Total	Owned	Rented	Total	Owned	Rented
Total	42,259,247	15,691,478	26,567,769	$1,104,496,687	$346,829,358	$757,667,329
Alabama	5,073,953	1,466,719	3,607,234	96,856,685	22,506,427	74,350,258
Arkansas	2,647,230	1,204,114	1,443,116	86,871,173	27,139,889	59,731,284
Delaware	54,578	13,615	40,963	2,184,474	686,322	1,498,152
Florida	758,731	458,443	300,288	14,622,184	8,779,585	5,842,599
Georgia	7,064,500	1,349,503	5,714,997	156,988,269	25,679,922	131,308,347
Kentucky	436,459	255,363	181,096	17,519,312	8,908,927	8,610,385
Louisiana	2,103,345	834,695	1,268,650	55,834,314	16,494,075	39,340,239
Maryland	345,156	122,039	223,117	10,953,278	4,879,716	6,073,562
Mississippi	6,420,549	2,227,194	4,193,355	186,458,876	44,417,423	142,041,453
North Carolina	3,166,812	1,197,496	1,969,316	80,804,831	27,448,410	53,356,421
Oklahoma	2,270,416	1,599,655	670,761	58,674,493	40,590,030	18,084,463
South Carolina	3,898,022	1,098,044	2,799,978	117,281,487	27,340,950	89,940,537
Tennessee	1,588,396	590,676	977,720	53,181,362	16,411,350	36,770,012
Texas	4,188,979	1,866,742	2,322,237	111,736,262	39,873,225	71,863,037
Virginia	2,208,235	1,381,223	827,012	53,266,983	34,774,150	18,492,833
West Virginia	33,886	25,957	7,929	1,262,704	898,957	363,747

Source: "Acreage and Value of Farms operated by Colored Farmers: 1910," *Negro Education: A Study of the Private and Higher Schools for Colored People in the United States*, vol. I. Bulletin, 1916, No. 38, 1917, p. 103. Primary source: U.S. Office of Education. *Negro Education: A Study of the Private and Higher Schools for Colored People in the United States*, vol. I. Bulletin, 1916, No. 38. Washington, D.C.: Government Printing Office, 1917.

★ 270 ★

Farms and Farmers

Summary Characteristics: Southern Black-Owned Farms with Mortgages, 1910

| DIVISION AND STATE | FARMS OPERATED BY COLORED OWNERS: 1910 | | | | | | | | Mortgaged farms consisting of owned land only. | | | |
| | Number | | | | Percentage | | | | | Value of land buildings | Mortgage debt | |
	Total	Owners free	Owners mortgaged	No report	Total	Owners free	Owners mortgaged	No report	Number		Amount	Percent of value of land and buildings
THE SOUTH												
Total	218,467	152,426	59,662	6,379	100.0	69.8	27.3	2.9	41,432	$59,865,633	$16,953,463	28.3
South Atlantic	101,961	77,064	22,533	2,364	100.0	75.6	22.1	2.3	15,582	20,583,811	5,577,004	27.1
East South Central	58,737	35,023	21,942	1,772	100.0	59.6	37.4	2.0	15,268	19,804,163	6,391,842	32.3
West South Central	57,769	40,339	15,187	2,243	100.0	69.8	26.3	3.9	10,582	19,477,659	4,984,617	25.6
SOUTH ATLANTIC												
Delaware	406	231	171	4	100.0	56.9	42.1	1.0	137	197,500	62,794	31.8
Maryland	3,950	2,582	1,334	34	100.0	65.4	33.8	0.8	1,056	1,202,584	358,490	29.8
District of Columbia	8	4	3	1	100.0	50.0	37.5	12.5	3	12,000	4,600	38.3
Virginia	32,228	26,200	5,609	419	100.0	81.2	17.4	1.3	4,304	4,386,949	1,037,658	23.7
West Virginia	558	479	78	1	100.0	85.8	14.0	0.2	67	126,609	31,210	24.7
North Carolina	21,443	15,433	5,609	401	100.0	72.0	26.1	1.9	3,464	4,435,616	1,134,853	25.6

[Continued]

★ 270 ★

Summary Characteristics: Southern Black-Owned Farms with Mortgages, 1910
[Continued]

DIVISION AND STATE	FARMS OPERATED BY COLORED OWNERS: 1910											
	Number				Percentage				Mortgaged farms consisting of owned land only.			
									Number	Value of land buildings	Mortgage debt	
											Amount	Percent of value of land and buildings
	Total	Owners free	Owners mortgaged	No report	Total	Owners free	Owners mortgaged	No report				
South Carolina	20,372	15,268	4,386	718	100.0	75.0	21.5	3.5	2,842	4,870,642	1,333,696	27.4
Georgia	15,698	11,025	4,059	614	100.0	70.2	25.9	3.9	2,739	4,298,361	1,376,654	32.0
Florida	7,298	5,842	1,284	172	100.0	80.0	17.6	2.4	970	1,053,550	237,049	22.5
EAST SOUTH CENTRAL												
Kentucky	5,929	4,488	1,319	122	100.0	75.7	22.2	2.1	906	1,153,510	320,579	27.8
Tennessee	10,700	7,781	2,687	232	100.0	72.7	25.1	2.2	1,742	2,080,982	691,155	33.2
Alabama	17,082	9,951	6,551	580	100.0	58.3	38.3	3.4	4,293	4,778,354	1,612,895	33.8
Mississippi	25,026	12,803	11,385	838	100.0	51.2	45.5	3.3	8,327	11,791,317	3,767,213	31.9
WEST SOUTH CENTRAL												
Arkansas	14,662	9,111	4,913	638	100.0	62.1	33.5	4.4	3,521	5,308,624	1,408,613	26.5
Louisiana	10,725	7,736	2,637	352	100.0	72.1	24.6	3.3	1,971	2,631,991	784,216	29.8
Oklahoma	11,150	7,806	2,663	711	100.0	70.0	23.6	6.4	1,900	5,986,167	1,209,079	20.2
Texas	21,232	15,686	5,004	542	100.0	73.9	23.6	2.5	3,190	5,550,877	1,582,709	28.5

Source: "Mortgage Indebtedness of Colored Owners, by Southern States: 1910," *Negro Population, 1790-1915*, 1918, p. 587. Primary source: U.S. Bureau of the Census. *Negro Population, 1790-1915*. Washington, D.C.: Government Printing Office, 1918.

★ 271 ★

Farms and Farmers

Summary Characteristics: Total Acreage on Southern Black Farms, 1920-1930, and According to Land Use, 1924 and 1929, by Owner Status
[Colored farmers include Negroes, Indians, Chinese, Japanese, and all other nonwhite races]

REGION USE OF LAND, AND YEAR	Total	OWNERS		Managers	TENANTS	
		Full owners	Part owners		Cash	Other
THE SOUTH						
Number of farms 1930	881,687	140,496	41,523	829	97,920	600,919
1925	831,455	159,651	34,889	667	78,760	557,488
1920	922,914	178,558	39,031	1,770	100,275	603,280
All land in farms 1930	37,805,765	9,010,320	2,468,578	266,752	4,095,292	21,964,823
1925	33,894,038	9,828,895	1,855,972	185,195	3,003,423	19,020,553
1920	41,318,496	11,950,158	2,126,465	367,820	4,010,599	22,863,454
Crop land harvested 1929	20,726,437	3,011,824	1,110,982	55,636	2,299,938	14,248,057
1924	19,211,420	3,135,684	867,676	41,306	1,877,098	13,289,656
Plowable pasture 1929	1,770,492	660,890	162,416	27,087	185,150	734,949
Other pasture 1929[1]	1,265,072	449,438	150,243	49,598	95,913	519,880

Source: "Number of Farms, and Farm Acreage, 1930, 1925, and 1920; and Specified Classes of Land, According to Use in 1929 and 1924; by Tenure of Colored Operators, by Southern Divisions, and States," *Negroes in the United States, 1920-1932*, 1935, pp. 610-611. Primary source: U.S. Bureau of the Census. *Negroes in the United States, 1920-1932*. Washington, D.C.: U.S. Government Printing Office, 1935. *Note:* 1. Other than plowable or woodland pasture.

★ 272 ★

Farms and Farmers

Summary Characteristics: Total and Average Acreage on Mortgaged Black Farms, by Location of Farm, 1930 - I

[Figures relate only to farms wholly owned by their operators. Colored farmers include Negroes, Indians, Japanese, Chinese, and other nonwhite races.]

DIVISION AND STATE	ALL LAND IN FARMS (ACRES)				AVERAGE ACREAGE PER FARM			
	Total	Reporting farms free from mortgage	Reporting farms mortgaged	Unknown (no reporting)	Total	Reporting farms free from mortgage	Reporting farms mortgaged	Unknown (no report)
The South	9,010,320	4,911,661	3,325,882	772,777	64.4	57.9	79.3	56.5
SOUTH ATLANTIC	3,314,342	1,925,835	1,150,108	238,399	54.6	48.3	72.5	48.0
Delaware	11,050	4,209	5,836	1,005	35.8	26.0	47.1	43.7
Maryland	87,593	43,844	40,002	3,747	37.1	30.3	49.1	37.8
District of Columbia	13	3	6	4	1.9	1.5	2.0	2.0
Virginia	937,215	628,624	269,279	39,312	48.8	44.7	64.4	41.9
West Virginia	15,741	10,946	3,478	1,317	48.0	42.4	72.5	59.9
North Carolina	696,930	359,621	279,781	57,528	52.8	46.9	65.7	45.3
South Carolina	616,579	335,284	246,917	34,378	51.7	43.3	75.7	37.0
Georgia	726,112	387,879	258,326	79,907	80.6	73.0	101.7	68.8
Florida	223,109	155,425	46,483	21,201	51.2	48.4	74.4	40.6
EAST SOUTH CENTRAL	2,874,227	1,362,388	1,290,141	221,698	72.9	65.9	85.5	60.3
Kentucky	138,252	82,965	42,464	12,823	45.3	43.7	62.3	27.0
Tennessee	309,906	166,647	113,454	29,805	54.5	48.2	69.2	50.3
Alabama	916,880	438,853	397,886	80,141	80.3	71.5	96.2	70.2
Mississippi	1,509,189	673,923	736,337	98,929	78.4	73.5	85.3	67.5
WEST SOUTH CENTRAL	2,821,751	1,623,438	885,633	312,680	69.9	66.8	80.4	62.2
Arkansas	560,843	269,983	237,339	53,521	61.9	59.7	67.9	51.4
Louisiana	512,572	277,887	180,582	54,103	58.3	54.7	67.9	51.7
Oklahoma	623,258	342,557	175,631	105,070	95.2	93.0	109.5	83.1
Texas	1,126,078	733,011	292,081	99,986	70.5	66.4	89.7	59.6
SELECTED NORTHERN STATES[2]	156,104	66,673	82,413	7,018	56.0	48.7	64.9	46.5
New Jersey	6,415	2,289	3,993	133	29.6	22.2	37.8	19.0
Pennsylvania	9,600	3,388	5,999	213	43.4	37.2	49.6	23.7
Ohio	34,933	18,060	14,585	2,288	54.6	55.7	55.0	44.9
Indiana	8,495	2,945	5,035	495	41.0	31.2	51.9	33.0
Illinois	15,871	6,415	8,644	812	51.4	42.8	61.7	42.7
Missouri	47,940	21,182	25,469	1,289	58.8	50.9	68.8	44.4
Kansas	32,850	12,374	18,688	1,788	86.2	65.1	109.9	85.1

Source: "All Land in Farms Operated by Colored Full Owners, by Mortgage Status, with Average Acreage per Farm, and Percent Distribution, by Southern Divisions, and States, and Selected Northern States: 1930," *Negroes in the United States, 1920-1932*, 1935, p. 584. Primary source: U.S. Bureau of the Census. *Negroes in the United States, 1920-1932*. Washington, D.C.: U.S. Government Printing Office, 1935. *Notes:* 1. Less than 1/10 of 1 percent. 2. States having 200 or more Negro farmers who constitute 90 percent or more of the colored farm operators in each State.

★ 273 ★
Farms and Farmers

Summary Characteristics: Total and Average Acreage on Mortgaged Black Farms, by Location of Farm, 1930 - II

[Figures relate only to farms wholly owned by their operators. Colored farmers include Negroes, Indians, Japanese, Chinese, and other nonwhite races.]

| DIVISION AND STATE | PERCENT DISTRIBUTION OF LAND, BY MORTGAGE STATUS | | | PERCENT DISTRIBUTION OF LAND OPERATED BY FULL OWNERS | | | |
	Reporting farms free from mortgage	Reporting farms mortgaged	Unknown (no report)	Total	Reporting farms free from mortgage	Reporting farms mortgaged	Unknown (no report)
The South	54.5	36.9	8.6	100.0	100.0	100.0	100.0
SOUTH ATLANTIC	58.1	34.7	7.2	36.8	39.2	34.6	30.8
Delaware	38.1	52.8	9.1	.1	.1	.2	.1
Maryland	50.1	45.7	4.3	1.0	.9	1.2	.5
District of Columbia	23.1	46.2	30.8	1	1	1	1
Virginia	67.1	28.7	4.2	10.4	12.8	8.1	5.1
West Virginia	69.5	22.1	8.4	.2	.2	.1	.2
North Carolina	51.6	40.1	8.3	7.7	7.3	8.4	7.4
South Carolina	54.4	40.0	5.6	6.8	6.8	7.4	4.4
Georgia	53.4	35.6	11.0	8.1	7.9	7.8	10.3
Florida	69.7	20.8	9.5	2.5	3.2	1.4	2.7
EAST SOUTH CENTRAL	47.4	44.9	7.7	31.9	27.7	38.8	28.7
Kentucky	60.0	30.7	9.3	1.5	1.7	1.3	1.7
Tennessee	53.8	36.6	9.6	3.4	3.4	3.4	3.9
Alabama	47.9	43.4	8.7	10.2	8.9	12.0	10.4
Mississippi	44.7	48.8	6.6	16.7	13.7	22.1	12.8
WEST SOUTH CENTRAL	57.5	31.4	11.1	31.3	33.1	26.6	40.5
Arkansas	48.1	42.3	9.5	6.2	5.5	7.1	6.9
Louisiana	54.2	35.2	10.6	5.7	5.7	5.4	7.0
Oklahoma	55.0	28.2	16.9	6.9	7.0	5.3	13.6
Texas	65.2	26.0	8.9	12.5	14.9	8.8	12.9
SELECTED NORTHERN STATES[2]	42.7	52.8	4.5	100.0	100.0	100.0	100.0
New Jersey	35.7	62.2	2.1	4.1	3.4	4.8	1.9
Pennsylvania	35.3	62.5	2.2	6.1	5.1	7.3	3.0
Ohio	51.7	41.0	6.5	22.4	27.1	17.7	32.6
Indiana	34.9	59.3	5.8	5.4	4.4	6.1	7.1
Illinois	40.4	54.5	5.1	10.2	9.6	10.5	11.6
Missouri	44.2	53.1	2.7	30.7	31.8	30.9	18.4
Kansas	37.7	56.9	5.4	21.0	18.6	22.7	25.5

Source: "All Land in Farms Operated by Colored Full Owners, by Mortgage Status, with Average Acreage per Farm, and Percent Distribution, by Southern Divisions, and States, and Selected Northern States: 1930," *Negroes in the United States, 1920-1932,* 1935, p. 584. Primary source: U.S. Bureau of the Census. *Negroes in the United States, 1920-1932.* Washington, D.C.: U.S. Government Printing Office, 1935. *Notes:* 1. Less than 1/10 of 1 percent. 2. States having 200 or more Negro farmers who constitute 90 percent or more of the colored farm operators in each State.

★ 274 ★

Farms and Farmers

Support Programs: Black Borrowers through Farm Security Administration Program, 1941

Type of Program	Number
Rural Rehabilitation	53,322
Tenant Purchase Borrowers	3,061
Families on 22 Rental Cooperatives (Leasing Association)	967
Families on 35 Community Projects	1,889
Families on 6 Migratory Camps	1,199
Total	60,440

Source: "Negro Borrower Participation in Farm Security Administration Program, November 15, 1941—United States," *Negro Year Book: A Review of Events Affecting Negro Life, 1941-1946,* 1947, p. 177. Primary source: "Plain Facts About Negro Farming" by Constance E.H. Daniels - F.S.A. Publication 104. - Printed in "The Brown American," November, 1941.

★ 275 ★

Farms and Farmers

Support Programs: Family Status of Southern Black Families under Rural Rehabilitation Program, 1944

Item	Fourteen Southern States
Active Standard Negro Families...No.	37,763
No. of Families in Sample...No.	1,746
Size of Farm 1944...Acres	79
Land in Crops 1944...Acres	36
Total Owned...$	1,542
Total Owed....$	569
Net Worth...$	973
Working Capital End of '44...$	851
Total Amount Borrowers From FSA...$	1,254
Total RR Debt End of '44...$	488
Delinquency Status:	
Number Borrowers Delinquent...No.	19,714
Per cent of Borrowers Delinquent...%	52
Amount Delinquent for those Delinquent...$	243
Gross Family Income...$	1,221
Gross Farm Income...$	1,006
Total Non-Farm Income...$	215

[Continued]

★ 275 ★

Support Programs: Family Status of Southern Black Families under Rural Rehabilitation Program, 1944
[Continued]

Item	Fourteen Southern States
Farm Operating Expenses...$	316
Net Family Income...$	905
Net Farm Income...$	690
Value Home-Owned Food...$	337

Source: "Status of the Active Standard Rural Rehabilitation Negro Family at End of 1944 Crop Year in the Fourteen Southern States," *Negro Year Book: A Review of Events Affecting Negro Life, 1941-1946,* 1947, p. 178. Primary source: Data supplied by the Farm Security Administration, Washington, D.C.

★ 276 ★
Farms and Farmers

Type of Farm: Location of Black Farms, by Type and by Region and Geographic Division, 1930 - I

SECTION AND DIVISION	Total number of farms	Self-sufficing	Abnormal	Truck	Fruit	Cash grain
United States	882,850	42,987	64,250	7,041	2,904	3,256
The North	11,104	1,266	1,849	356	113	783
The South	870,936	41,683	62,169	6,661	2,739	2,448
The West	810	38	232	24	52	25
New England	148	21	46	7	23	-
Middle Atlantic	873	80	244	173	9	7
East North Central	3,065	516	691	135	69	230
West North Central	7,018	649	868	41	12	546
South Atlantic	295,934	24,044	29,822	3,847	1,189	860
East South Central	320,600	11,518	16,706	2,176	176	635
West South Central	254,402	6,121	15,461	638	1,374	953
Mountain	304	17	80	4	3	17
Pacific	506	21	152	20	49	8

Source: "Number of Farms Operated by Negroes, by Type of Farm, by Sections, Divisions, and States: 1930," *Negroes in the United States, 1920-1932,* 1935, p. 587. Primary source: U.S. Bureau of the Census. *Negroes in the United States, 1920-1932.* Washington, D.C.: U.S. Government Printing Office, 1935.

★ 277 ★

Farms and Farmers

Type of Farm: Location of Black Farms, by Type and by Region and Geographic Division, 1930 - II

SECTION AND DIVISION	Cotton	General	Crop-specialty	Dairy	Stock-ranch	Poultry	Animal specialty
United States	665,255	26,822	66,246	1,520	123	846	1,600
The North	3,593	1,585	256	438	6	253	606
The South	661,448	25,182	65,939	1,028	100	560	979
The West	214	55	51	54	17	33	15
New England	-	14	5	21	-	11	-
Middle Atlantic	-	136	32	135	-	51	6
East North Central	69	746	126	217	-	76	190
West North Central	3,524	689	93	65	6	115	410
South Atlantic	164,026	14,226	56,929	276	7	323	385
East South Central	274,092	6,738	7,490	612	15	83	359
West South Central	223,330	4,218	1,520	140	78	154	235
Mountain	99	31	22	12	10	6	3
Pacific	115	24	29	42	7	27	12

Source: "Number of Farms Operated by Negroes, by Type of Farm, by Sections, Divisions, and States: 1930," *Negroes in the United States, 1920-1932,* 1935, p. 587. Primary source: U.S. Bureau of the Census. *Negroes in the United States, 1920-1932.* Washington, D.C.: U.S. Government Printing Office, 1935.

★ 278 ★

Farms and Farmers

Type of Farm: Percentage Distribution of Location of Black Farms, by Type and by Region and Geographic Division, 1930

SECTION AND DIVISION	Total number of farms	PERCENT OF TOTAL REPORTED AS-					
		Cotton	Crop specialty	Abnormal	Self sufficing	General	All other
United States	882,850	75.4	7.5	7.3	4.9	3.0	2.0
THE SOUTH	870,936	75.9	7.6	7.1	4.8	2.9	1.7
South Atlantic	295,934	55.4	19.2	10.1	8.1	4.8	2.3
East South Central	320,600	85.5	2.3	5.2	3.6	2.1	1.3
West South Central	254,402	87.8	.6	6.1	2.4	1.7	1.4
THE NORTH	11,104	32.4	2.3	16.7	11.4	14.3	23.0
New England	148	-	3.4	31.1	14.2	9.5	41.9
Middle Atlantic	873	-	3.7	27.9	9.2	15.6	43.6
East North Central	3,065	2.3	4.1	22.5	16.8	24.3	29.9
West North Central	7,018	50.2	1.3	12.4	9.2	9.8	17.0
THE WEST	810	26.4	6.3	28.6	4.7	6.8	27.2

[Continued]

★ 278 ★

Type of Farm: Percentage Distribution of Location of Black Farms, by Type and by Region and Geographic Division, 1930

[Continued]

SECTION AND DIVISION	Total number of farms	PERCENT OF TOTAL REPORTED AS-					
		Cotton	Crop specialty	Abnormal	Self sufficing	General	All other
Mountain	304	32.6	7.2	26.3	5.6	10.2	18.1
Pacific	506	22.7	5.7	30.0	4.2	4.7	32.6

Source: "Percent Distribution by Type of Farm Operated by Negroes, by Sections, and Southern Divisions: 1930," *Negroes in the United States, 1920-1932,* 1935, p. 577. Primary source: U.S. Bureau of the Census. *Negroes in the United States, 1920-1932.* Washington, D.C.: U.S. Government Printing Office, 1935.

★ 279 ★

Farms and Farmers

Value: Aggregate and Increase in Total Value of Black Farms, by Region, 1900 and 1910

SECTION AND DIVISION	Aggregate			Average per farm		
	1910	1900	Increase: 1910-1900	1910	1900	Increase: 1910-1900
TOTAL						
United States	$1,141,792,526	$499,941,234	$641,851,292	$1,278	$669	$608
The South	1,083,658,351	469,506,555	614,151,796	1,230	641	589
South Atlantic	440,876,367	162,841,284	278,035,083	1,244	566	678
East South Central	356,089,149	170,985,641	186,003,508	1,099	639	460
West South Central	285,792,835	135,679,630	150,113,205	1,419	767	652
The North	53,473,329	29,384,290	24,089,039	4,437	2,096	2,341
New England	945,061	582,851	362,210	3,049	2,208	841
Middle Atlantic	6,123,854	4,193,394	1,930,460	4,675	2,801	1,874
East North Central	20,063,311	11,535,146	8,528,165	4,143	2,227	1,916
West North Central	26,341,103	13,072,899	13,268,204	4,713	1,847	2,866
The West	4,660,846	1,050,389	3,610,457	9,670	3,117	6,553
Mountain	1,610,050	382,943	1,227,107	7,352	2,879	4,473
Pacific	3,050,796	667,446	2,383,350	11,600	3,272	8,328

Source: "Value of Property on Farms Operated by Negroes," *Negroes Population, 1790-1915,* 1918, p. 560. Primary source: U.S. Bureau of the Census. *Negro Population, 1790-1915.* Washington, D.C.: Government Printing Office, 1918.

★ 280 ★

Farms and Farmers

Value: Average Value of Specific Items on Black Farms, 1900 and 1910, and Increase for 1900-1910 Decade

CLASS OF FARM PROPERTY	1910	1900	Increase: 1900-1910 Amount	Percent
Total	$1,278	$669	$609	91.0
Land	846	434	412	94.9
Buildings	187	96	91	94.8
Implements and machinery	38	25	13	52.0
Live stock	207	114	93	81.6

Source: "Average Value per Farm of Farm Property on Farms Operated by Negroes," *Negro Population, 1790-1915*, 1918, p. 559. Primary source: U.S. Bureau of the Census. *Negro Population, 1790-1915*. Washington, D.C.: Government Printing Office, 1918.

★ 281 ★

Farms and Farmers

Value: Land Value of Black Farms, by Region, 1900 and 1910

SECTION AND DIVISION	VALUE OF PROPERTY ON FARMS OPERATED BY NEGROES					
	Aggregate			Average per farm		
	1910	1900	Increase: 1910-1900	1910	1900	Increase: 1910-1900
	LAND					
United States	$756,158,264	$324,242,997	$431,915,267	$846	$434	$412
The South	714,988,872	302,933,342	412,055,530	812	414	398
South Atlantic	294,198,215	106,251,076	187,947,139	830	369	461
East South Central	227,012,113	108,254,534	118,757,579	699	405	294
West South Central	193,778,544	88,427,732	105,350,812	962	500	462
The North	37,584,524	20,590,880	16,993,644	3,119	1,469	1,650
New England	427,635	320,384	107,251	1,379	1,214	165
Middle Atlantic	3,432,477	2,344,334	1,088,143	2,620	1,566	1,054
East North Central	14,669,103	8,527,575	6,141,528	3,209	1,647	1,382
West North Central	19,055,309	9,308,587	9,658,722	3,409	1,328	2,081
The West	3,584,868	718,775	2,866,093	7,437	2,133	5,304
Mountain	1,033,530	241,285	792,245	4,719	1,814	2,905
Pacific	2,551,338	477,490	2,073,848	9,701	2,341	7,360

Source: "Value of Property on Farms Operated by Negroes," *Negroes Population, 1790-1915*, 1918, p. 561. Primary source: U.S. Bureau of the Census. *Negro Population, 1790-1915*. Washington, D.C.: Government Printing Office, 1918.

★ 282 ★

Farms and Farmers

Value: Percentage Distribution, by Region, of Value of Black Farms, 1900 and 1910

SECTION AND YEAR	Total	Land	Buildings	Implements and machinery	Live stock
United States:					
1910	100.0	100.0	100.0	100.0	100.0
1900	100.0	100.0	100.0	100.0	100.0
The South:					
1910	94.9	94.6	95.2	95.8	95.9
1900	93.9	93.4	93.7	94.9	95.7
The North:					
1910	4.7	5.0	4.6	3.9	3.7
1900	5.9	6.4	6.1	4.9	4.1
The West:					
1910	0.4	0.5	0.2	0.3	0.4
1900	0.2	0.2	0.2	0.2	0.2

Source: "Percentage Distribution, by Sections, of Value of Farm Property on Farms Operated by Negroes," *Negro Population, 1790-1915*, 1918, p. 560. Primary source: U.S. Bureau of the Census. *Negro Population, 1790-1915*. Washington, D.C.: Government Printing Office, 1918.

★ 283 ★

Farms and Farmers

Value: Percentage Distribution, by Region, of Value of Specific Items on Black Farms, 1900 and 1910

CLASS OF PROPERTY AND YEAR	United States	The South				The North	The West
		Total	South Atlantic division	East South Central division	West South Central division		
All farm property:							
1910	100.0	100.0	100.0	100.0	100.0	100.0	100.0
1900	100.0	100.0	100.0	100.0	100.0	100.0	100.0
Land:							
1910	66.2	66.0	66.7	63.6	67.8	70.3	76.9
1900	64.9	64.5	65.2	63.3	65.2	70.1	68.4
Buildings:							
1910	14.6	14.6	16.1	14.7	12.4	14.3	6.3
1900	14.4	14.4	16.4	13.5	13.0	15.0	10.6
Implements and machinery:							
1910	3.0	3.0	3.0	3.1	3.0	2.5	2.2
1900	3.8	3.8	3.6	4.0	3.8	3.2	3.4

[Continued]

★ 283 ★

Value: Percentage Distribution, by Region, of Value of Specific Items on Black Farms, 1900 and 1910

[Continued]

CLASS OF PROPERTY AND YEAR	United States	The South Total	South Atlantic division	East South Central division	West South Central division	The North	The West
Live stock:							
1910	16.2	16.4	14.2	18.6	16.9	12.9	14.6
1900	17.0	17.3	14.8	19.2	18.0	11.8	17.6

Source: "Percentage Distribution, by Class of Property, of Value of Farm Property on Farms Operated by Negroes," *Negro Population, 1790-1915,* 1918, p. 560. Primary source: U.S. Bureau of the Census. *Negro Population, 1790-1915.* Washington, D.C.: Government Printing Office, 1918.

★ 284 ★

Farms and Farmers

Value: Value of Buildings on Black Farms, by Region, 1900 and 1910

SECTION AND DIVISION	VALUE OF PROPERTY ON FARMS OPERATED BY NEGROES					
	Aggregate			Average per farm		
	1910	1900	Increase: 1910-1900	1910	1900	Increase: 1910-1900
BUILDINGS						
United States	$166,559,439	$71,902,265	$94,657,174	$187	$96	$91
The South	158,593,538	67,392,514	91,201,024	180	92	88
South Atlantic	70,870,030	26,658,379	44,211,651	200	93	107
East South Central	52,419,081	23,113,572	29,305,509	161	86	75
West South Central	35,304,427	17,620,563	17,683,864	175	100	75
The North	7,671,864	4,398,877	3,272,987	637	314	323
New England	374,725	195,330	179,395	1,209	740	469
Middle Atlantic	1,866,870	1,270,170	596,700	1,425	848	577
East North Central	2,808,546	1,468,470	1,340,076	580	284	296
West North Central	2,621,723	1,464,907	1,156,816	469	207	262
The West	294,037	110,874	183,163	610	329	281
Mountain	122,465	42,229	80,236	559	318	241
Pacific	171,572	68,645	102,927	652	336	316

Source: "Value of Property on Farms Operated by Negroes," *Negro Population, 1790-1915,* 1918, p. 561. Primary source: U.S. Bureau of the Census. *Negro Population, 1790-1915.* Washington, D.C.: Government Printing Office, 1918.

★ 285 ★

Farms and Farmers

Value: Value of Implements and Machinery on Black Farms, by Region, 1900 and 1910

| SECTION AND DIVISION | VALUE OF PROPERTY ON FARMS OPERATED BY NEGROES | | | | | |
| | Aggregate | | | Average per farm | | |
	1910	1900	Increase: 1910-1900	1910	1900	Increase: 1910-1900
	IMPLEMENTS AND MACHINERY					
United States	$34,178,052	$18,859,757	$15,318,295	$38	$25	$13
The South	32,755,291	17,893,841	14,861,450	37	24	13
South Atlantic	13,148,827	5,879,229	7,269,598	37	20	17
East South Central	11,163,547	6,847,843	4,315,704	34	26	8
West South Central	8,442,917	5,166,769	3,276,148	42	29	13
The North	1,322,473	929,902	392,571	110	66	44
New England	42,771	21,428	21,343	138	81	57
Middle Atlantic	250,259	185,349	64,910	191	124	67
East North Central	440,693	326,208	114,485	91	63	28
West North Central	588,750	396,917	191,833	105	56	49
The West	100,288	36,014	64,274	208	107	101
Mountain	47,564	14,698	32,866	217	111	106
Pacific	52,724	21,316	31,408	200	104	96

Source: "Value of Property on Farms Operated by Negroes," *Negro Population, 1790-1915,* 1918, p. 561. Primary source: U.S. Bureau of the Census. *Negro Population, 1790-1915.* Washington, D.C.: Government Printing Office, 1918.

★ 286 ★

Farms and Farmers

Value: Value of Land and Buildings on Black Farms, 1910 and 1930, and Change for 1910-1930 by Location of Farm

| SECTION AND DIVISION | VALUE OF LAND AND BUILDINGS | | | |
| | 1930 | 1910 | Increase or decrease (-) 1910-30 | |
			Amount	Percent
United States	$1,402,945,799	$922,717,703	$480,228,096	52.0
The North	41,668,222	45,256,388	-3,588,166	-7.9
The South	1,355,181,667	873,582,410	481,599,257	55.1
The West	6,095,910	3,878,905	2,217,005	57.2
New England	909,395	802,360	107,035	13.3
Middle Atlantic	5,140,255	5,299,347	-159,092	-3.0
East North Central	13,304,751	17,477,649	-4,172,898	-23.9
West North Central	22,313,821	21,677,032	636,789	2.9

[Continued]

★ 286 ★

Value: Value of Land and Buildings on Black Farms, 1910 and 1930, and Change for 1910-1930 by Location of Farm

[Continued]

SECTION AND DIVISION	VALUE OF LAND AND BUILDINGS			
	1930	1910	Increase or decrease (-) 1910-30	
			Amount	Percent
South Atlantic	484,443,943	365,068,245	119,375,698	32.7
East South Central	426,528,844	279,431,194	147,097,650	52.6
West South Central	444,208,880	229,082,971	215,125,909	93.9
Mountain	2,037,510	1,155,995	881,515	76.3
Pacific	4,058,400	2,722,910	1,335,490	49.0

Source: "Farms Operated by Negroes—Number, Farm Acreage, and Value of Land and Buildings, by Sections, Divisions, and States: 1930 and 1910," *Negroes in the United States, 1920-1932,* 1935, p. 601. Primary source: U.S. Bureau of the Census. *Negroes in the United States, 1920-1932.* Washington, D.C.: Government Printing Office, 1935.

★ 287 ★

Farms and Farmers

Value: Value of Specific Items on Black Farms, 1900 and 1910, and Increase for 1900-1910 Decade

CLASS OF FARM PROPERTY	Amount		Increase: 1900-1910		Percentage distribution	
	1910	1900	Amount	Percent	1910	1900
Total	$1,141,792,526	$499,941,234	$641,851,292	128.4	100.0	100.0
Land	756,158,264	324,242,997	431,915,267	133.2	66.2	64.9
Buildings	166,559,439	71,902,265	94,657,174	131.6	14.6	14.4
Implements and machinery	34,178,052	18,859,757	15,318,295	81.2	3.0	3.8
Live stock	184,896,771	84,936,215	99,960,556	117.7	16.2	17.0

Source: "Value of Farm Property on Farms Operated by Negroes," *Negro Population, 1790-1915,* 1918, p. 559. Primary source: U.S. Bureau of the Census. *Negro Population, 1790-1915.* Washington, D.C.: Government Printing Office, 1918.

★ 288 ★

Farms and Farmers

Value: Value per Farm and Per Acre of Black-Owned Farms, by Mortgage Status and Location of Farm, 1930

[Colored farmers include Negroes, Indians, Chinese, Japanese, and all other non-white races.]

DIVISION AND STATE	AVERAGE VALUE OF LAND AND BUILDINGS PER FARM				AVERAGE VALUE OF LAND AND BUILDINGS PER ACRE			
	Total	Reporting farms free from mortgage	Reporting farms mortgaged	Unknown (no report)	Total	Reporting farms free from mortgage	Reporting farms mortgaged	Unknown (no report)
The South	$1,872	$1,692	$2,271	$1,766	$29.19	$29.24	$28.65	$31.24
SOUTH ATLANTIC	1,746	1,564	2,265	1,554	31.98	32.38	31.23	32.39
Delaware	2,143	1,810	2,542	2,330	59.91	69.66	54.02	53.33
Maryland	2,286	1,919	2,863	2,913	61.63	63.40	58.25	76.97
District of Columbia	4,071	2,150	6,667	2,100	2,192.31	1,433.33	3,333,33	1,050.00
Virginia	1,739	1,613	2,188	1,612	35.62	36.13	33.99	38.51
West Virginia	2,260	2,054	3,318	2,359	47.08	48.42	45.79	39.41
North Carolina	2,044	1,810	2,533	1,816	38.70	38.60	38.54	40.07
South Carolina	1,464	1,252	2,025	1,261	28.34	28.92	26.77	34.09
Georgia	1,590	1,436	2,009	1,380	19.74	19.66	19.76	20.07
Florida	1,610	1,508	2,313	1,394	31.45	31.17	31.10	34.32
EAST SOUTH CENTRAL	1,651	1,467	1,939	1,498	22.64	22.25	22.68	24.82
Kentucky	1,744	1,621	2,366	1,345	38.55	37.08	38.00	49.84
Tennessee	1,802	1,594	2,241	1,806	33.07	33.05	32.37	35.87
Alabama	1,594	1,398	1,950	1,355	19.85	19.57	20.27	19.30
Mississippi	1,625	1,434	1,843	1,533	20.74	19.51	21.60	22.71
WEST SOUTH CENTRAL	2,278	2,095	2,733	2,170	32.59	31.37	33.99	34.91
Arkansas	1,915	1,762	2,165	1,740	30.93	29.50	31.89	33.84
Louisiana	1,863	1,716	2,218	1,678	31.94	31.37	32.66	32.47
Oklahoma	3,610	3,315	4,365	3,511	37.94	35.63	39.87	42.24
Texas	2,167	1,998	2,958	1,734	30.75	30.08	33.00	29.11
SELECTED NORTHERN STATES[1]	3,480	2,948	4,070	3,352	62.20	60.52	62.71	72.11
New Jersey	4,297	3,667	4,633	8,429	145.35	165.01	124.15	443.61
Pennsylvania	4,192	3,446	4,921	1,933	96.51	92.56	99.27	81.69
Ohio	3,244	2,648	4,078	2,699	59.43	47.50	74.09	60.16
Indiana	2,901	2,331	3,544	2,353	70.69	74.68	68.27	71.31
Illinois	2,831	2,666	2,954	3,224	55.11	62.34	47.84	75.43
Missouri	2,776	2,558	2,952	3,666	47.20	50.24	42.88	82.47
Kansas	5,346	4,214	6,747	4,248	62.00	64.70	61.38	49.89

Source: "Average Value of Land and Buildings per Farm and per Acre of Farms Operated by Colored Full Owners, by Mortgage Status, by Southern Divisions, and States, and Selected Northern States: 1930," *Negroes in the United States, 1920-1932*, 1935, p. 582. Primary source: U.S. Bureau of the Census. *Negroes in the United States, 1920-1932.* Washington, D.C.: Government Printing Office, 1935. *Notes:* 1. States having 200 or more Negro farmers who constitute 90 percent or more of the colored farmers in the State.

Chapter 2
BUSINESS AND ECONOMICS

Advertising Agencies

★ 289 ★

Black-Owned Advertising Agencies, 1973

NAME OF AGENCY	LOCATION	CHIEF EXECUTIVE OFFICER	YEAR STARTED	NUMBER OF EMPLOYEES	BILLINGS 1972
John F. Small, Inc.	New York, New York	John F. Small	1970	16	$7,000,000
Zebra Associates, Inc.	New York, New York	Joan Murray	1969	17	4,650,000
Junius Edwards, Inc.	New York, New York	Junius Edwards	1965	8	3,500,000
Uniworld Group, Inc.	New York, New York	Byron Lewis	1969	12	3,500,000
Vince Cullers Advertising, Inc.	Chicago, Illinois	Vine Cullers	1953	18	2,500,000
Burrell Mc Bain Inc.	Chicago, Illinois	Thomas J. Burrell	1971	8	2,000,000
Proctor & Gardner Advertising, Inc.	Chicago, Illinois	Barbara Gardner Proctor	1970	15	1,800,000
Phat Advertising Consultants, Inc.	New York, New York	Walter Long	1967	9	1,200,000
Howard Sanders Advertising, LTD.	New York, New York	Howard Sanders	1966	12	1,200,000
Eden Advertising & Communications, Inc.	New York, New York	Barbara-Simmons	1971	15	1,000,000
Vanguard Associates, Inc.	Minneapolis, Minnesota	Thomas Tipton	1969	7	1,000,000
Tom Cleveland and Associates	Detroit, Michigan	Tom Cleveland, Sr.	1954	7	850,000
Communicon, Inc.	Chicago, Illinois	Bill Fonville	1970	5	500,000
Wright Edelen Advertising Agency, Inc.	Los Angeles, California	Norman E. Edelen	1971	7	500,000
Few Hunter & Wilson	Atlanta, Georgia	Michael Wilson	1969	5	200,000
Provident Home Ind. Mutual Life Insurance Company	Pennsylvania	Edward W. Robinson, Jr.	1916	100	14,238,138
Golden Circle Life Insurance Company	Brownsville, Tennessee	C.A. Rawls	1958	82	14,787,959
Wright Mutual Insurance Company	Detroit, Michigan	Wardell C. Croft	1942	60	14,000,000
Winnfield Life Insurance Company	Natchitoches, Louisiana	Ben D. Johnson	1936	200	25,168,000
Gertrude Geddes Willis Life Insurance Company	New Orleans, Louisiana	Mrs. Maude V. Misshore	1945	61	16,597,924
Unity Burial & Life Insurance Company	Mobile, Alabama	Roger Allen	1928	100	15,527,099
Security Life Insurance Company	Jackson, Mississippi	W.H. Williams	1940	65	6,645,817
Christian Benevolent Burial Association	Mobile, Alabama	Mrs. Pearl J. Madison	1929	70	12,679,000
Southern Life Insurnace Company	Baltimore, Maryland	Owen Wilson	1906	35	3,146,741
National Service Industrial Life Insurance Company	New Orleans, Louisiana	Duplain Rhodes	1947	30	5,232,324
Keystone Life Insurance Company	New Orleans, Louisiana	George Liopis	1941	125	7,900,000
Bradford's Industrial Insurance Company	Birmingham, Alabama	Mrs. Marion K. Bradford	1932	28	5,331,587
Purple Shield Life Insurance Company	Baton Rouge, Louisiana	Homer J. Sheeler, Sr.	1949	100	20,000,000
Reliable Life Insurance Ccompany	Monroe, Louisiana	Joseph H. Miller, Jr.	1940	50	8,000,000
Benevolent Life Insurance Company	Shreveport, Louisiana	Granville L. Smith	1934	120	9,402,263
United Fidelity-Victory Life Insurance Company	New Orleans, Louisiana	Duplain Rhodes	1970	42	1,653,775
Majestic Life Insurance Company	New Orleans, Louisiana	James V. Haydel	1949	37	5,855,391
Lighthouse Life Insurance Company	Shreveport, Louisiana	Bunyan Jacobs, Sr.	1945	50	5,500,189
Lovett's Life & Burial Insurance Company	Mobile, Alabma	Mrs. L.M. Lovett	1950	40	4,780,000
Superior Life Insuarnce Company	Ruston, Louisiana	J.K. Haynes	1953	32	4,933,875

[Continued]

★ 289 ★

Black-Owned Advertising Agencies, 1973
[Continued]

NAME OF AGENCY	LOCATION	CHIEF EXECUTIVE OFFICER	YEAR STARTED	NUMBER OF EMPLOYEES	BILLINGS 1972
Progressive Industrial Life Insurance Company	New Orleans, Louisiana	C.L. Dennis	1948	23	1,199
People's Progressive Burial Insurance Company	Rayville, Louisiana	Mrs. Marion Gundy Hill	1929	45	3,828,966

Source: "Advertising Agencies," *Black Enterprise* 3 (June 1973), pp. 67-68. Published by permission.

Banks, Financial Institutions, Finances

★ 290 ★

Banking Institutions, Characteristics, 1939, 1940

	Deposits		Capital		Surplus and undivided profits	
	Dec 30, 1939	Dec. 31, 1940	Dec. 30, 1939	Dec.31, 1940	Dec.30, 1939	Dec.31, 1940
Citizens and Southern Bank and Trust Co., Philadelphia, Pa.	$585,000	$687,607	$125,000	$125,000	$5,000	$16,572[1]
Citizens Savings Bank and Trust Co., Nashville, Tenn.	207,000	237,655	60,000	60,000	6,000	5,831
Citizens Trust Company Atlanta, Ga.	558,000	631,180	72,500	72,250	12,500	14,820
Consolidated Bank and Trust Company Richmond, Va.	867,000	941,922	80,000	80,000	64,000	67,606
Crown Savings Bank Newport News, Va.	467,000	606,202	36,750	36,250	14,250	21,114[1]
Danville Savings Bank and Trust Company Danville, Va.	229,300	289,964	34,700	34,600	23,000	30,517
Farmers State Bank Boley, Okla.	40,000	91,384	15,000	15,000	5,000	4,825
Fraternal Bank and Trust Company Fort Worth, Texas	377,580	411,285	15,420	15,420	3,000	2,978[2]
Industrial Bank of Washington Washington, D.C.	817,000	1,104,296	50,000	50,000	42,000	54,091
Mechanics and Farmers Bank Durham, N.C.	1,016,000	1,063,257	214,000	210,000	36,000	41,664
Tuskegee Institute Savings Bank Tuskegee, Ala.	169,000	149,787	25,000	25,000	25,000[2]	14,047
Victory Savings Bank Columbia, S.C.	35,000	54,095	14,612	14,612	3,388	3,236

Source: "Banks." Murray, Florence, ed. *The Negro Handbook*. New York: Wendell Malliet, 1942, p. 13. *Notes:* 1. Reserve and Undivided Profits Together. 2. Surplus Only.

★ 291 ★

Banks, Financial Institutions, Finances

Banking Institutions, Characteristics, 1947

Bank and president	Total deposits	Capital	Total assets	Value of bank premises owned
Citizens Trust Co. Atlanta, Ga. Lorimer D. Milton	$3,793,718	$100,000	$4,009,666	$53,778
Citizens Savings Bank & Trust Co. Nashville, Tenn. Henry A. Boyd	1,436,314	80,000	1,554,815	8,420
Citizens & Southern Bank & Trust Co. Philadelphia, Pa. Emanuel C. Wright	2,812,136	125,000	2,978,502	39,500
Industrial; Bank of Washington Washington, D.C. Jesse H. Mitchell	5,365,110	100,000	5,670,385	50,000
Danville Savings Bank & Trust Co. Danville, Va. Irvin C. Taylor	1,096,389	50,000	1,294,453	50,000
Mechanics & Farmers Bank Durham, N.C. C.C. Spaulding	5,048,732	339,559	5,408,303	14,460
Farmers State Bank Boley, Okla. Forest Anderson	157,408	15,000	179,279	5,000
Consolidated Bank & Trust Co. Richmond, Va. Emmett C. Burke	3,478,404	80,000	3,706,562	50,000
Crown Savings Banks Newport News, Va. W.P. Dickerson	2,374,219	50,000	2,514,036	22,800
Fraternal Bank and Trust Co. Fort Worth, Texas W.C. McDonald	1,024,041	15,720	1,068,277	4,572
Victory Savings Bank Columbia, S.C. E.A. Adams	901,948	15,000	930,943	-
Tri-State Bank[1] Memphis, Tenn. Dr. J.E. Walker	1,083,419	200,000	1,322,217	-
Douglass State Bank[1] Kansas City, Kans. H.W. Ewing	302,545	125,000	458,561	58,831
Carver Savings Bank[1] Savannah, Ga. L.B. Toomer	119,775	100,000	239,594	2,000

Source: "Comparative Statements of Banking Institutions: As of December 31, 1947." Murray, Florence, ed. *The Negro Handbook, 1949.* New York: Macmillan, 1949, p. 200. Primary source: Bank statements, and U.S. Department of Commerce. *Note:* 1. Data supplied by Department of Commerce.

★ 292 ★

Banks, Financial Institutions, Finances

Banks Established by Region: 1900-1975

Area	Total number of banks in 1975	Period established			
		1900 to 1939	1940 to 1959	1960 to 1969	1970 to 1975
United States	45	8	2	11	24
South	19	8	1	2	8
North	21	-	1	6	14
Northeast	4	-	-	2	2
North Central	17	-	1	4	12
West	5	-	-	3	2

Source: "Black-Owned Banks by Period Established and Region: 1900-1939 to 1970- 1975," U.S. Department of Commerce, Bureau of the Census. *The Social and Economic Status of the Black Population in the United States: An Historical View, 1790-1978*, p. 79. Primary source: "Black Banks: An Overview," *Black Enterprise Magazine* (June 1977). Published by permission. *Notes:* - Represents zero. Figures exclude Black-owned banks which may have been established at an earlier time but were no longer in existence in 1975.

★ 293 ★

Banks, Financial Institutions, Finances

Banks in the United States, 1950

Fourteen banks owned and operated by blacks in 1950 had combined resources of approximately 35,000,000. At the end of the year they were serving approximately 110,000 depositors. At their 1950 meeting, the National Bankers Association stressed the problems of rising operating costs and gave special consideration to the limited sources available to blacks in business and the assistance which might be forthcoming from black banking institutions.

Source: Guzman, Jessie Parkhurst, ed., *Negro Year Book: A Review of Events Affecting Negro Life, 1941-1946*, p. 135.

★ 294 ★

Banks, Financial Institutions, Finances

Banks, Aggregate Totals of Investments, Resources, Liabilities, and Capital – 1939, 1940

	Dec. 31 1940	June, 29 1940	Dec. 30 1939
Resources			
Loans and discounts	$2,942,803	$2,761,524	$2,539,000
U.S. Government obligations	915,956	1,047,148	902,000
Obligations of state and city	120,630	188,833	202,000
Other bonds and notes	826,918	545,090	735,000
Total investments	1,863,504	1,781,071	1,839,000
Cash and exchange	2,002,685	2,140,396	1,683,000
Bank premises owned, etc.	422,552	155,763	83,000
Other real estate owned	140,228	113,765	154,000
Other resources	32,703	128,981	199,000
Total resources	7,404,475	7,081,500	6,497,000
Liabilities			
Demand deposits	815,033	678,559	2,402,580
Time deposits	690,565	1,037,744	2,948,300
Other deposits	4,753,296	4,242,264	17,000
Total deposits	6,258,894	5,958,567	5,367,880
Bills payable	17,283		
Other liabilities	35,888	39,226	67,000
Total liabilities	6,312,065	5,997,793	5,434,800
Capital accounts			
Capital	737,132	738,731	742,982
Surplus	209,352	200,432	191,138
Undivided profits	61,697	68,431	48,000
Reserves	84,229	76,113	80,000
Total capital accounts	1,092,410	1,083,707	1,062,120
Total liabilities and capital accounts	7,404,475	5,081,500	6,497,000

Source: "Aggregate Totals of All Negro Banks." Murray, Florence, ed. *The Negro Handbook.* New York: Wendell Malliet, 1942, p. 14.

★ 295 ★

Banks, Financial Institutions, Finances

Building and Loan Association, 1899

State	Number of institutions
Philadelphia, Pa.	3
Wilmington, N.C.	2
Anderson, S.C.	1
Augusta, Ga.	1
Hampton, Va.	1
Ocala, Fla.	1
Little Rock, Ark.	1
Portsmouth, Va.	1
Sacramento, Cal.	1
Washington, D.C.	1
Total	13

Source: W.E.B. DuBois, ed., *The Negro in Business*, p. 13. Primary source: Arranged by the Editors. *Notes:* In 1899 a number of brokers and money-lending institutions were established, especially in cities like Washington, D.C. where a large black salaried-class lived. This group included building and loan associations, of which thirteen were reported, as shown in the table below. Other institutions were unreported.

★ 296 ★

Banks, Financial Institutions, Finances

Building and Loan Associations, Black-Operated, 1947

Company	Total assets	Private repurchasable capital (deposits and investment certificates)
Atlanta Mutual Bldg., Loan & Savings Assn.,[1] Atlanta, Ga.	$662,987	$525,859
Berkley Citizens Mutual Bldg. & Loan Assn. Norfolk, Va.	293,345	155,373
The Berean Savings & Loan Assn.,[1] Philadelphia, Pa.	1,014,623	848,886
Broadway Savings & Loan Assn.[1] Los Angeles, Calif.	669,809	529,452
Cavalry Bldg. & Loan Assn. Philadelphia, Pa.	77,334	59,411
Columbia Savings & Loan Assn.[1] Milwaukee, Wis.	576,436	491,130
Community Bldg. & Loan Assn. Norfolk, Va.	20,920	9,574

[Continued]

★ 296 ★

Building and Loan Associations, Black-Operated, 1947

[Continued]

Company	Total assets	Private repurchasable capital (deposits and investment certificates)
East End Investment & Loan Assn. Cincinnati, Ohio	125,642	91,422
Eighth Ward Settlement Bldg. & Loan Assn. Philadelphia, Pa.	39,525	14,995
Home Federal Savings & Loan Assn.[1] Detroit, Mich.	159,500	158,837
Homeseekers Savings & Loan Assn. Kansas City, Mo.	22,859	-
Illinois Federal Savings & Loan Assn.[1] Chicago, Ill.	1,012,328	910,034
Imperial Bldg. & Loan Assn. Martinsville, Va.	29,975	26,110
Industrial Savings & Loan Assn. Cincinnati, Ohio	207,866	147,899
Liberty Building-Loan Assn.[1] Los Angeles, Calif.	1,539,806	1,234,136
Magic City Bldg. & Loan Assn. Roanoke, Va.	151,963	127,065
Morgan Park Savings & Loan Assn. Chicago, Ill.	44,931	34,314
Mutual Bldg. & Loan Assn.[1] Durham, N.C.	1,048,947	870,906
New Age Bldg. & Loan Assn.[1] St. Louis, Mo.	151,958	81,349
People's Bldg. & Loan Assn.[1] Hampton, Va.	649,037	422,355
Tuskegee Savings & Loan Assn.[1] Tuskegee, Ala.	229,242	148,725
Zoar Community Bldg. & Loan Assn. Philadelphia, Pa.	135,309	114,612
Total assets	8,864,342	

Source: "Black-Operated Building and Loan Associations As of December 31, 1947." Murray, Florence, ed. *The Negro Handbook, 1949.* New York: Macmillan, 1949, p. 204. Primary source: Unpublished data, Adviser on Negro Affairs, Department of Commerce. *Note:* 1. Members, Federal Home Loan Bank System.

★ 297 ★

Banks, Financial Institutions, Finances

Credit Unions, Assets of Black Associations Compared to Total, 1944

Item	Reporting Negro Associations	Reporting Federal Associations
Total number of associations	72	3,795
Actual membership as per cent		
Total membership	34	33
Average members per association	174	343
Total share capital	$642,711	$133,586,147
Average per association	$6,926	$35,200
Average per member	$51	$102
Total assets	$683,100	$144,266,156
Total loans outstanding	$230,756	$34,403,467
Per cent current	87	85
Per cent military loans	2	5
Per cent delinquent, 20 mos. or more	11	10
Reserves for bad loans as per cent of loans outstanding	9	13
Total loans since organization	$1,723,451	$657,786,637
Bad loans as per cent of total	0.09	0.13

Source: "Financial Strength of Sixty Member Companies, NNIA, 1950." Guzman, Jessie Parkhurst, ed. Guzman, Jessie Parkhurst, ed. *Negro Year Book: A Review of Events Affecting Negro Life, 1941-1946.* Tuskegee Institute, Ala.: Department of Records and Research, 1947, p. 187.

★ 298 ★

Banks, Financial Institutions, Finances

Directory of Black Banks, 1913

Location	Name of bank	Number
Alabama		
Anniston	Anniston Penny Savings Bank	
Birmingham	Alabama Penny Savings and Loan Company	
Birmingham	Peoples Investment and Savings	
Birmingham	Prudential Savings	
Mobile	Safety Banking and Realty Company	
Montgomery	Montgomery Penny Savings Bank	
Selma	Alabama Savings Bank	
Tuskegee	Tuskegee Institute Savings Department	
Total		8
District of Columbia		
Washington, D.C.	Industrial Savings Bank	
Total		1

[Continued]

★ 298 ★

Directory of Black Banks, 1913
[Continued]

Location	Name of bank	Number
Florida		
Jacksonville	Afro-American Insurance Company	
Jacksonville	Capitol Trust and Investment Company	
Jacksonville	National Mercantile Realty and Inprovement Company	
Key West	Progress Savings Bank	
Total		4
Georgia		
Atlanta	Atlanta Savings Bank	
Augusta	Penny Savings Loan & Investment Company	
Savannah	Mechanics' Investment Company	
Savannah	Wage Earners Loan and Investment Company	
Total		4
Illinois		
Chicago	American Bank	
Chicago	Jesse Binga Bank	
Springfield	Enterprise Savings Bank	
Total		3
Indiana		
Indianapolis	Pythian Bank and Loan Association	
Total		1
Maryland		
Baltimore	Baltimore Penny Savings Bank	
Salisbury	Houston Savings Bank	
Total		2
Massachusetts		
Boston	Eureka-Co-operative Bank	
Total		1
Mississippi		
Columbus	Penny Savings Bank	
Greenville	Delta Savings Bank	
Jackson	Southern Bank	
Indianola	Delta Penny Savings Bank	
Mound Bayou	Bank of Mound Bayou	
Natchez	Bluff City Savings Bank	
Total		6
North Carolina		
Durham	Mechanics and Farmers' Bank	
Kingston	Dime Bank	

[Continued]

★ 298 ★

Directory of Black Banks, 1913
[Continued]

Location	Name of bank	Number
Kinston	Holloway, Borden, Hicks & Company, Bankers	
Newbern	Isaac Smith Trust Company	
Newbern	Mutual Aid and Banking Company	
Winston-Salem	Forsyth Savings and Trust Company	
Total		6
Oklahoma		
Boley	Boley Bank and Trust Company	
Boley	Farmers' and Merchants' Bank	
Muskogee	Peoples' Bank and Trust Company	
Total		3
Pennsylvania		
Philadelphia	People's Savings Bank	
Total		1
Tennessee		
Memphis	Fraternal Savings Bank and Trust Company	
Memphis	Solvent Savings Bank and Trust Company	
Nashville	One Cent Savings Bank	
Nashville	Peoples' Savings Bank and Trust Company	
Total		4
Texas		
Fort Worth	Fraternal Bank and Trust Company	
Houston	Orgen Savings Bank	
Palestine	Farmers' and Citizen's Savings Bank	
Tyler	Farmers' and Merchants' Bank	
Waco	Farmers' Improvement Bank	
Total		5
Virginia		
Courtland	American Home & Missionary Banking Association	
Courtland	Sussex-Surrey Savings Bank	
Hare Valley (Exmore, R.D.)	Brickhouse Savings Bank	
Newport News	Crown Savings Bank	
Newport News	Sons and Daughters of Peace Penny, Nickel & Dime Savings Bank	
Norfolk	Brown Savings Bank	
Richmond	Mechanics Savings Bank	
Richmond	Nickel Savings Bank	
Richmond	St. Luke's Savings Bank	
Salem	Star of Zion Banking and Loan Assocation	
Stauton	People's Dime Savings Bank Trust	

[Continued]

★ 298 ★

Directory of Black Banks, 1913
[Continued]

Location	Name of bank	Number
Waynesboro Total	Southern One Cent Savings Bank	12
Grand Total		62

Source: "Directory of Negro Banks." Monroe N. Work, ed., *Negro Year Book and Annual Encyclopedia of the Negro, 1913*, pp. 231-234. Primary source: Rearranged by the Editors.

★ 299 ★

Banks, Financial Institutions, Finances

Federal Credit Unions, 1935-1940

Year	Number of active unions	Total Number of members in unions	Total loans made to members	Interest on loans	Returned in dividends	Loans to members out-standing	Savings (share balance)
1935	5	467	$4,360	$52	-	$2,460	$3,160
1936	18	1,251	16,552	427	38	7,541	10,134
1937	28	2,295	32,626	1,114	240	16,258	20,649
1938	44	3,680	63,320	2,463	622	30,239	37,810
1939	48	5,047	125,804	4,891	1,554	62,013	67,117
1940	51	6,462	202,529	8,855	3,028	102,403	108,796

Source: "Federal Credit Unions," *Negro Handbook*, 1944, p. 162.

★ 300 ★

Banks, Financial Institutions, Finances

Federal Credit Unions, 1942, 1950

	December 31, 1942				December 31, 1950			
	All fed C.U		Fed. C.U. Among Negroes		All Fed. C.U.		Fed. C.U. Among Negroes	
Fed. C.U. chartered	4,980	100%	84	100%	7,046	100%	153	100%
Fed. C.U. operating	4,145	83%	72	86%	4,984	71%	122	80%
Fed. C.U. canceled and inoperative	835	17%	12	14%	2,062	29%	31	20%
Fed. Cr. Un. reporting	4,070		70		4,984		122	
Membership								
Potential	3,780,251		36,048		5,411,152		96,912	
Actual	1,347,519		10,706		2,126,823		23,254	
Percentage actual to potention		35%		30%		39%		24%
Average no. members per FCU	331		153		427		191	
Total assets	$119,232,893		$301,863		$405,834,976		$2,270,434	

[Continued]

★ 300 ★

Federal Credit Unions, 1942, 1950

[Continued]

| | December 31, 1942 | | | | December 31, 1950 | | | |
	All fed C.U		Fed. C.U. Among Negroes		All Fed. C.U.		Fed. C.U. Among Negroes	
Loan statistics								
Total loans outstanding	$42,886,750	100%	$152,721	100%	$263,735,838	100%	$1,514,458	100%
Current loans	36,044,390	84%	122,639	80%	249,161,672	94%	1,308,195	86%
Delinquent 2 or more[1]	6,842,360	16%	30,082	20%	14,574,166	6%	206,263	14%
Legal reserve for bad loans	3,719,976		13,443		12,356,142		78,343	
Special reserve for delinquent loans	97,365		1,133		563,212		16,776	
Total amount loaned since organization	$502,187,358		$1,061,299		$2,124,264,706		$13,292,158	
Net amount charged off for bad loans	403,392		861		2,928,445		16,717	
Percentage of charge-off to amount loaned		0.08%		0.08%		.14%		.12%
Share statistics								
Total shareholdings	$109,498,801		$274,288		$361,924,778		$2,017,725	
Average holdings per FCU	26,903		3,918		72,617		16,539	
Average holdings per member	81		26		170		87	

Source: "Progress of Federal Credit Unions Among Negroes Compared to All Federal Credit Unions." Guzman, Jessie Parkhurst, ed. *Negro Year Book: A Review of Events Affecting Negro Life, 1941-1946.* New York: William H. Wise, 1952, p. 139. Primary source: Bureau of Federal Credit Unions Affairs, Department of Commerce. *Note:* 1. Includes military loans.

★ 301 ★

Banks, Financial Institutions, Finances

Leading Banks, 1973

Name of company	Location	Chief executive officer	Year started	Number of employees	Total deposits	Total assets 1972
Seaway National Bank of Chicago	Chicago, Illinois	Harold Algar	1965	108	$45,899,103	$48,797,915
Freedom National Bank	New York, New York	Robert Boyd	1964	106	43,378,534	47,111,915
Independence Bank of Chicago	Chicago, Illinois	Alvin J. Boutte	1964	88	44,000,000	47,000,000
Citizens Trust Bank	Atlanta, Georgia	Charles M. Reynolds	1921	110	33,072,000	40,744,588
Industrial Bank of Washington	Washington, D.C.	B. Doyle Mitchell	1934	74	37,000,000	40,000,000
Mechanics and Farmers Bank	Durham, North Carolina	John H. Wheeler	1907	51	34,166,230	37,697,158
First Independence National Bank	Detroit, Michigan	David B. Harper	1970	40	27,632,574	30,000,000
Bank of Finance	Los Angeles, California	Edward E. Tillmon	1964	75	27,500,000	29,000,000
National Industrial Bank of Miami	Miami, Florida	Garth C. Reeves	1964	27	25,855,403	26,865,545
United Community National Bank	Washington, D.C.	Samuel L. Foggie	1964	38	21,000,000	23,254,000
Douglass State Bank	Kansas City, Kansas	Sharnia Buford	1947	42	17,000,000	20,000,000
Consolidated Bank & Trust Co.	Richmond, Virginia	V. W. Henley	1903	40	18,000,000	19,617,243
Tri-State Bank of Memphis	Memphis, Tennessee	A. Maceo Walker	1946	35	17,800,000	19,600,000
Gateway National Bank	St. Louis, Missouri	I. Owen Funderburg	1965	39	14,000,000	16,700,000
North Milwaukee State Bank	Milwaukee, Wisconsin	Felmers O. Chaney	1971	27	13,879,478	14,568,453
Unity Bank and Trust Company	Roxbury, Massachusetts	Marvin Peck	1968	30	14,000,000	14,000,000
First Plymouth National Bank	Minneapolis, Minnesota	John Warder	1969	29	12,500,000	14,000,000
Swope Parkway National Bank	Kansas City, Missouri	Edward V. Kerrigan	1968	33	10,500,000	12,000,000
Vanguard National Bank	Hempstead, New York	John Bates	1972	17	9,000,000	12,000,000
Highland Community Bank	Chicago, Illinois	George Brokemond	1970	21	10,547,800	11,627,500

Source: "Banks," *Black Enterprise* 4 (June 1973), pp. 55, 57. Published by permission.

★ 302 ★
Banks, Financial Institutions, Finances

Leading Banks, 1974

Company	Location	Chief Executive	Year Started	Employees	Total Deposits (Dollars)[1]	Total Assets (Dollars)[1]
Independence Bank of Chicago	Chicago, Illinois	Alvin J. Boutte	1964	80	48,816,325	55,594,474
Seaway National Bank of Chicago	Chicago, Illinois	Richard Linyard	1965	105	41,122,712	45,299,983
Freedom National Bank	New York, New York	Daniel Limerick	1964	75	41,558,805	44,787,675
Industrial Bank of Washington	Washington, D.C.	B. Doyle Mitchell	1934	75	36,164,351	39,309,959
Mechanics & Farmers Bank	Durham, North Carolina	John H. Wheeler	1907	55	35,232,134	39,141,848
Citizens Trust Bank	Atlanta, Georgia	Charles M. Reynolds	1921	110	28,394,384	35,965,744
First Independence National Bank	Detroit, Michigan	David B. Harper	1970	40	31,851,892	34,064,730
Bank of Finance	Los Angeles, California	Edward Ballard	1964	64	27,885,828	29,782,688
Consolidated Bank & Trust Co.	Richmond, Virginia	V.W. Henley	1903	46	20,923,741	22,914,863
Tri-State Bank of Memphis	Memphis, Tennessee	A. Maceo Walker	1946	51	19,985,360	22,351,776
Gateway National Bank	St. Louis, Missouri	I. Owen Funderburg	1965	51	18,012,182	19,889,231
Douglass State Bank	Kansas City, Kansas	Sharina Buford	1947	39	17,339,994	19,519,586
United Community National Bank	Washington, D.C.	Samuel L. Foggie	1964	56	16,421,741	18,277,645
First Enterprise Bank	Oakland, California	William Pickens	1972	15	15,951,626	17,077,866
Gateway National Bank	Chicago, Illinois	Joseph Bertrand	1955	34	15,460,217	16,055,707
Vanguard National	Hempstead,					

[Continued]

★ 302 ★

Leading Banks, 1974
[Continued]

Company	Location	Chief Executive	Year Started	Employees	Total Deposits (Dollars)[1]	Total Assets (Dollars)[1]
Bank	New York	Richard F. Smith	1972	17	13,137,593	15,776,052
Highland Community Bank	Chicago, Illinois	George Brokemond	1970	35	13,144,483	14,321,127
Unity Bank & Trust Company	Roxbury, Massachusetts	Marvin Peck	1968	28	11,508,449	13,593,763
National Industries Bank of Miami	Miami, Florida	John W. Roberts	1964	35	12,007,572	13,025,475
First Plymouth National Bank	Minneapolis, Minnesota	John Warder	1969	30	11,675,424	13,099,188
Riverside National Bank	Houston, Texas	Dr. Carl Carroll	1963	27	9,308,983	10,627,202
Swope Parkway National Bank	Kansas City, Missouri	E.V. Kerrigan	1968	21	9,404,648	10,622,974
Midwest National Bank	Indianapolis, Indiana	James Sedwick	1972	41	8,066,338	10,358,227
Citizens Savings Bank & Trust Co.	Nashville, Tennessee	M.G. Ferguson	1904	15	8,091,181	8,737,398
Unity State Bank	Dayton, Ohio	Robert L. Davis	1970	24	7,302,817	8,415,687
Liberty Bank & Trust Company	New Orleans, Louisiana	Alden J. McDonald, Jr.	1972	16	5,831,675	8,302,704
North Milwaukee State Bank	Milwaukee, Wisconsin	Felmers O. Chaney	1971	25	7,031,273	8,251,181
First State Bank	Danville, Virginia	L. Wilson York	1919	13	6,997,818	7,919,824
Liberty Bank of Seattle	Seattle, Washington	James C. Purnell	1968	21	6,713,992	7,483,833
Carver State Bank	Savannah, Georgia	Robert E. James	1947	14	5,460,865	7,374,120
Atlantic National	Norfolk,					

[Continued]

★ 302 ★

Leading Banks, 1974
[Continued]

Company	Location	Chief Executive	Year Started	Employees	Total Deposits (Dollars)[1]	Total Assets (Dollars)[1]
Bank	Virginia	L. Willis	1971	17	6,063,302	6,927,631
Guaranty Bank & Trust Company	Chicago, Illinois	Oscar S. Williams	1972	25	6,129,000	6,785,000
Peoples National Bank of Springfield	Springfield, Illinois	Leon H. Stewart	1970	12	5,158,224	5,719,619
Freedom Bank of Finance	Portland, Oregon	V.F. Booker	1969	14	4,561,462	5,219,940
Victory Savings Bank	Columbia, South Carolina	Henry D. Monteith	1921	14	4,416,854	5,015,573
Greensboro National Bank	Greensboro, North Carolina	Henry Frye	1971	13	3,965,000	4,803,000
American State Bank	Tulsa, Oklahoma	Gerald B. Nelson	1970	17	3,337,662	3,966,788

Source: "Banks," *Black Enterprise* 4 (June 1974), pp. 47,49. Published by permission. *Note:* 1. As of December 31, 1973.

★ 303 ★

Banks, Financial Institutions, Finances

Leading Banks, 1975

Company	Location	Chief executive	Year started	Employees	Total assets (million$)[1]	Total deposits (million $)[1]
Independence Bank of Chicago	Chicago, Illinois	Alvin J. Boutte	1964	87	60.692	50.717
Seaway National Bank of Chicago	Chicago, Illinois	Richard Linyard	1965	87	48.114	44.721
Industrial Bank of Washington	Washington, D.C.	B. Doyle Mitchell	1934	75	41.208	37.940
Freedom National Bank	New York, New York	Hughlyn F. Fierce	1964	69	36.787	35.691
Mechanics & Farmers Bank	Durham, North Carolina	John Wheeler	1907	63	38.922	35.016
First Independence National Bank	Detroit, Michigan	David R. Harper	1970	65	31.749	29.648
Bank of Finance	Los Angeles, California	LaVannes Squires	1964	68	29.827	28.423
United National Bank of Washington	Washington, D.C.	Samuel Foggie	1964	60	26.097	26.745
Tri-State Bank of Memphis	Memphis, Tennessee	Jesse H. Turner, Sr.	1946	50	23.468	20.758
South Side Bank	Chicago, Illinois	T.P. Lewis	1973	40	19.566	18.467
First Enterprise Bank	Oakland, California	Lloyd A. Edwards	1972	44	19.180	18.127
The Douglass State Bank	Kansas City, Missouri	Sharina Buford	1947	36	19.743	17.976
Highland Community Bank	Chicago, Illinois	George R. Brokemond	1970	32	18.316	16.811
Gateway National Bank	St. Louis, Missouri	John H. Harris	1965	42	18.704	15.720
Gateway National Bank of Chicago	Chicago, Illinois	Joseph G. Bertrand	1972	35	16.985	15.524
Midwest National Bank	Indianapolis, Indiana	John P. Kelly	1972	42	15.450	13.266
First Plymouth National Bank	Minneapolis, Minnesota	John Warder	1969	23	15.309	11.814
Riverside National Bank	Houston, Texas	Dr. Carl M. Carroll, Jr.	1962	30	12.663	11.182
City National Bank of New Jersey	Newark, New Jersey	Charles L. Whigham	1973	21	11.747	10.450
Unity Bank & Trust Co.	Roxbury, Massachusetts	Marvin Peck	1968	26	12.220	10.390

[Continued]

★ 303 ★

Leading Banks, 1975
[Continued]

Company	Location	Chief executive	Year started	Employees	Total assets (million$)[1]	Total deposits (million $)[1]
Vanguard National Bank	Hempstead, New York	C.R. Merolla	1972	30	11.452	9.773
Liberty Bank & Trust Co.	New Orleans, Louisiana	Alden J. McDonald, Jr.	1972	30	12.543	9.392
Unity State Bank	Dayton, Ohio	Robert L. Davis	1970	32	10.537	9.250
Guaranty Bank & Trust Co.	Chicago, Illinois	Oscar S. Williams	1972	25	10.218	9.184
Liberty Bank of Seattle	Seattle, Washington	J.C. Purnell	1968	21	9.131	8.344
Citizens Savings Bank & Trust Co.	Nashville, Tennessee	M.G. Ferguson	1904	15	9.355	8.302
First State Bank	Danville, Virginia	Wilson York	1919	14	8.957	7.942
Carver State Bank	Savannah, Georgia	Robert Earl James	1927	21	10.279	7.691
North Milwaukee State Bank	Milwaukee, Wisconsin	Clifford M. Wilson, Jr.	1971	23	9.159	7.448
Atlantic National Bank	Norfolk, Virginia	Charles M. Reynolds, Jr.	1971	16	7.664	6.650
Peoples National Bank of Springfield	Springfield, Illinois	Richard H. Rush	1970	11	5.885	5.303
Victory Savings Bank	Columbia, South Carolina	Henry D. Monteith	1921	13	5.792	5.121
Greensboro National Bank	Greensboro, North Carolina	William Pickens	1971	14	5.358	4.364
Freedom Bank of Finance	Portland, Oregon	V.F. Booker	1969	12	4.771	4.139
American State Bank	Tulsa, Oklahoma	Leroy Thomas, Sr.	1970	16	4.858	4.008
Pacific Coast Bank	San Diego, California	Richard F. Smith, Jr.	1971	15	4.944	3.926
Medical Center State Bank	Oklahoma City, Oklahoma	Donald E. Jacobs	1973	16	4.000	3.521
Community Bank of Nebraska	Omaha, Nebraska	Glenn M. Manning	1973	9	3.294	2.680

Source: "Banks," *Black Enterprise* 4 (June 1975), pp. 46-47. Published by permission. *Notes:* 1. As of December 31, 1974. Note that, in a change from previous years, companies are ranked by deposits rather than assets.

★ 304 ★

Banks, Financial Institutions, Finances

Leading Savings and Loan Association, 1975

Company	Location	Managing Officer	Year Started	Employees	Total Assets (million$)[1]	Total Deposits (million$)[1]
Carver Federal Savings & Loan Assn.	New York, New York	Richard T. Greene	1949	60	61,653	52,877
Broadway Federal Savings & Loan Assn.	Los Angeles, California	Elbert T. Hudson	1946	43	53,413	39,770
Illinois Federa Savings & Loan Assn.	Chicago, Illinois	Louise Q. Lawson	1934	25	40,193	37,229
Family Savings & Loan Assn.	Los Angeles, California	Robert Bowdoin	1948	26	32,893	25,479
Citizens Federal Savings & Loan Assn.	Birmingham, Alabama	H.J. Willis	1957	15	18,125	16,723
Home Federal Savings & Loan Assn.	Detroit, Michigan	Wilburn R. Phillips	1947	18	18,200	16,413
Independent Federal Savings & Loan Assn.	Washington, D.C.	William B. Fitzgerald	1968	16	22,403	19,238

[Continued]

★ 304 ★

Leading Savings and Loan Association, 1975
[Continued]

Company	Location	Managing Officer	Year Started	Employees	Total Assets (million$)[1]	Total Deposits (million$)[1]
Mutual Federal Savings & Loan Assn.	Atlanta, Georgia	Fletcher Coombs	1925	15	14,469	13,069
Allied Federal Savings & Loan Assn.	Jamaica, New York	Frank L. Thompson	1958	15	14,256	12,185
Service Federal Savings & Loan Assn.	Chicago, Illinois	Harry M. Hardwick	1950	14	12,573	11,309
Advance Federal Savings & Loan Assn.	Baltimore, Maryland	W.O. Bryson, Jr.	1957	16	12,217	11,238
Mutual Savings & Loan Assn.	Durham, North Carolina	John S. Stewart	1921	8	14,559	10,558
United Federal Savings & Loan Assn.	New Orleans, Louisiana	Samuel O'Neal	1964	10	11,613	10,435
New Age Federal Savings & Loan Assn.	St. Louis, Missouri	Ernest Carter	1915	10	11,014	9,499
Quincy Savings & Loan Assn.	Cleveland, Ohio	Arthur B. Heard	1952	9	9,616	8,295
First Federal Savings & Loan Assn. of Scotlandville	Baton Rouge, Louisiana	L.L. Eames	1956	8	8,867	7,822
Enterprise Savings & Loan Assn.	Compton, California	Cornell R. Kirkland	1963	10	9,686	7,146
Peoples Building & Loan Assn.	Hampton, Virginia	Johnnie H. Sykes	1889	8	8,130	6,557
Connecticut Federal Savings & Loan Assn.	Hartford, Connecticut	Edward J. Barlow, Jr.	1968	5	7,775	6,529
American Federal Savings & Loan Assn.	Greensboro, North Carolina	Albert S. Webb	1959	6	8,278	6,313
Berean Savings & Loan Assn.	Philadelphia, Pennsylvania	I. Maximillian Martin	1888	8	8,371	6,271
Standard Savings Assn.	Houston, Texas	Shirley Bradford	1958	6	6,249	5,637

[Continued]

★ 304 ★

Leading Savings and Loan Association, 1975

[Continued]

Company	Location	Managing Officer	Year Started	Employees	Total Assets (million$)[1]	Total Deposits (million$)[1]
Tuskegee Federal Savings & Loan Assn.	Tuskegee, Alabama	Richad Harvey	1894	4	6,200	5,400
Berkley Citizens Mutual Savings & Loan Assn.	Norfolk, Virginia	Elbert Stewart	1913	6	5,970	5,077
Community Federal Savings & Loan Assn.	Nashville, Tennessee	Alfred C. Galloway	1961	4	5,059	4,596
Major Industrial Federal Savings & Loan Assn.	Cincinnati, Ohio	Pauline Strayhorne	1921	7	5,335	4,506
Columbia Savings & Loan Assn.	Milwaukee, Wisconsin	Thalia B. Winfield	1924	8	4,772	4,136
Dwelling House Savings & Loan Assn.	Pittsburgh, Pennsylvania	Robert R. Lavelle	1890	4	4,343	3,955
State Mutual Federal Savings & Loan Assn.	Jackson, Mississippi	Herman E. Pride	1955	6	4,500	3,700
Gulf Federal Savings & Loan Assn.	Mobile, Alabama	H. Leroy Davis	1964	5	3,790	3,586
Community Federal Savings & Loan Assn.	Tampa, Florida	James T. Hargett, Jr.	1967	5	3,397	3,172
Washington Shores Federal Savings & Loan Assn.	Orlando, Florida	Charles J. Hawkins	1963	6	3,798	3,077
Union Mutual Savings & Loan Assn.	Richmond, Virginia	G.F. Childs	1961	5	3,012	2,511
Security Federal Savings & Loan Assn.	Chattanooga, Tennessee	Edward C. Lott	1971	2	2,500	1885
Morgan Park Savings & Loan Assn.	Chicago, Illinois	Roy E. Conley	1921	5	1,810	1,658
Equity Savings & Loan Assn.	Denver, Colorado	Earl M. West	1959	6	1,650	1,500
Ideal Building & Loan Assn.	Baltimore, Maryland	E. Gaines Lansey	1920	2	1,530	1,267

[Continued]

★ 304 ★

Leading Savings and Loan Association, 1975
[Continued]

Company	Location	Managing Officer	Year Started	Employees	Total Assets (million$)[1]	Total Deposits (million$)[1]
Imperial Savings & Loan Assn.	Martinsville, Virginia	W.B. Muse, Jr.	1929	3	1,171	1,087
Community Savings & Loan Assn.	Newport News, Virginia	Samuel L. Urquhart	1957	2	0.707	0.612
Cosmopolitan Savings & Loan Assn.	Philadelphia, Pennsylvania	Robert G. Nelson	1906	3	0.550	0.450

Source: "Banks," *Black Enterprise* 5 (June 1975), pp. 53,55. Published by permission. *Notes:* 1. As of December 31, 1974. Note that, in a change from previous years, companies are ranked by deposits rather than assets.

★ 305 ★

Banks, Financial Institutions, Finances

Savings and Loan Companies, 1973

Name of company	Location	Chief executive officer	Year started	Number of employees	Total deposits	Total assets 1972
Broadway Federal Savings & Loan Assn.	Los Angles, California	Elbert Hudson	1947	45	$47,863,938	$60,451,990
Carver Federal Savings & Loan Assn.	New York, New York	Richard T. Greene	1948	60	50,000,000	60,000,000
Illinois Federal Savings & Loan Assn.	Chicago, Illinois	A. W. Williams	1934	27	31,463,000	34,500,000
Family Savings & Loan Assn.	Los Angeles, California	M. Earl Grant	1948	23	24,085,200	30,196,000
Hyde Park Federal Savings & Loan Assn.	Chicago, Illinois	Paul H. Berger	1961	15	22,029,189	26,641,104
Independence Federal Savings & Loan Assn.	Washington, D.C.	William B. Fitzgerald	1968	11	18,500,000	21,000,000
Home Federal Savings & Loan Assn. of Detroit	Detroit, Michigan	W.R. Philips	1947	16	14,653,700	15,966,000
Citizens Federal Savings & Loan Assn.	Birmingham, Alabama	A. G. Gaston	1957	15	13,000,000	15,000,000
Mutual Savings & Loan Assn.	Durham, North Carolina	John S. Stewart	1921	8	9,802,854	13,194,647
Mutual Federal Savings & Loan Assn.	Atlanta, Georgia	Fletcher Coombs	1925	16	11,500,000	12,500,000
Service Federal Savings & Loan Assn.	Chicago, Illinois	Harold Thatcher	1950	12	10,213,382	11,857,343
Allied Federal Savings & Loan Assn. of New York	New York, New York	Frank L. Thompson	1958	17	8,135,957	10,254,768
Advance Federal Savings & Loan Assn.	Baltimore, Maryland	W.O. Bryson, Jr.	1957	12	8,268,515	10,012,285
New Age Federal Savings & Loan Assn.	St. Louis, Missouri	Henry Harding	1915	11	9,139,498	10,000,567
United Federal Savings & Loan Assn.	New Orleans, Louisiana	Anthony J. Hackett	1964	9	7,984,875	9,601,189
Enterprise Savings & Loan Assn.	Compton, California	Cornell R. Kirkland	1963	12	7,100,000	9,600,000
Quincy Savings & Loan Company	Cleveland, Ohio	Charles V. Carr	1952	9	7,894,689	9,145,094
Connecticut Savings & Loan Assn.	Hartford, Connecticut	Edward J. Barlow	1968	8	6,700,000	7,500,000
Berean Savings Assn.	Philadelphia, Pennsylvania	Robert Horton	1888	8	6,000,000	7,500,000
Peoples Building & Loan Assn.	Hampton, Virginia	Lawrence Barbour	1889	8	5,822,405	7,320,827

Source: "Savings & Loan Associations," *Black Enterprise* 4 (June 1973), pp. 61, 63. Published by permission.

Business Owners and Operators

★ 306 ★

Black Proprietorship Sales of Each Group of Stores, 1929

25,701 stores with sales of $101,146,043.

Group of stores	Percent
Food	36.25
Restaurants and eating places	21.09
All other retail stores	20.87
Automotive	9.68
General stores	4.78
Apparel	2.99
Lumber and building	1.25
Furniture and household	1.15
Secondhand stores	0.97
General merchandise	0.97

Source: "Negro Proprietorship—Sales of Each Group of Stores." U.S. Bureau of the Census. *Negroes in the United States: 1920-32.* Washington, D.C.: Government Printing Office, 1935, p. 496.

★ 307 ★

Business Owners and Operators

Black-Owned Firms: Industry and Organization, 1969

Line number	1969										Percent changes 1969 to 1972	
	All firms		With paid employees					Without paid employees				
	Firms (number)	Gross receipts ($1,000)	Firms (number)	Employees (number)	Gross receipts ($1,000)	Average employees per firm (number)	Average receipts per firm ($1,000)	Firms (number)	Gross receipts ($1,000)	Average receipts per firm ($1,000)	All firms	Gross receipts for all firms
1	163,073	4,474,191	38,304	151,996	3,653,363	4	95	124,769	820,828	7	20	60
2	148,135	2,512,024	30,131	88,194	1,752,530	3	58	118,004	759,494	6	23	65
3	11,424	646,341	5,149	23,357	591,841	5	115	6,275	54,500	9	-26	25
4	3,514	1,315,826	3,024	40,445	1,308,992	13	433	490	6,834	14	15	68
5	16,235	464,343	3,886	17,900	375,239	5	97	12,349	89,104	7	24	77
6	14,907	246,576	2,977	10,317	164,326	3	55	11,930	82,250	7	24	104
7	936	79,227	562	3,248	73,344	6	131	374	5,883	16	25	38
8	392	138,540	347	4,335	137,569	12	396	45	971	22	40	49
9	2,981	302,648	1,566	12,306	292,448	8	187	1,415	10,200	7	38	77
10	2,136	49,404	893	3,338	40,889	4	46	1,243	8,515	7	48	108
11	367	38,186	236	1,698	37,056	7	157	131	1,130	9	-7	24
12	478	215,058	437	7,270	214,503	17	491	41	555	14	26	80
13	16,733	210,808	2,141	7,520	121,081	4	57	14,592	89,727	6	30	102
14	16,222	158,946	1,825	4,833	70,917	3	39	14,397	88,029	6	31	112
15	351	14,804	175	675	13,292	4	76	176	1,512	9	-8	113
16	160	37,058	141	2,012	36,872	14	262	19	186	10	22	54

[Continued]

★ 307 ★

Black-Owned Firms: Industry and Organization, 1969
[Continued]

Line number	All firms		With paid employees					Without paid employees			Percent changes 1969 to 1972	
	Firms (number)	Gross receipts ($1,000)	Firms (number)	Employees (number)	Gross receipts ($1,000)	Average employees per firm (number)	Average receipts per firm ($1,000)	Firms (number)	Gross receipts ($1,000)	Average receipts per firm ($1,000)	All firms	Gross receipts for all firms
17	1,660	385,039	742	5,601	368,711	8	497	918	16,328	18	26	98
18	1,068	65,206	297	1,121	52,503	4	177	771	12,703	16	35	132
19	258	58,296	152	996	56,258	7	370	106	2,038	19	-2	52
20	334	261,537	293	3,484	259,950	12	887	41	1,587	39	20	100
21	45,220	1,932,363	17,208	55,159	1,651,899	3	96	28,012	280,464	10	25	51
22	40,998	1,293,262	14,237	36,405	1,032,927	3	73	26,761	260,335	10	28	54
23	3,345	295,438	2,154	8,820	275,989	4	128	1,191	19,449	16	-7	22
24	877	343,663	817	9,934	342,983	12	420	60	680	11	20	65
25	7,612	287,471	1,390	8,952	260,261	6	187	6,222	27,210	4	5	59
26	4,683	46,607	674	1,898	26,920	3	40	4,009	19,687	5	52	188
27	2,466	41,389	394	1,125	34,823	3	88	2,072	6,566	3	-77	-
28	463	199,475	322	5,929	198,518	18	617	141	957	7	-29	41
29	56,077	663,236	8,728	38,182	424,139	4	49	47,349	239,097	5	22	59
30	52,950	477,226	7,110	25,622	252,864	4	36	45,840	224,362	5	23	59
31	2,478	79,501	1,060	5,561	66,450	5	63	1,418	13,051	9	-7	40
32	649	106,509	558	6,999	104,825	13	188	91	1,684	19	31	73
33	3,407	63,699	663	2,127	47,001	3	71	2,744	16,698	6	26	39
34	3,109	42,791	499	1,402	26,914	3	54	2,610	15,877	6	31	59
35	214	11,971	101	398	11,246	4	111	113	725	6	-18	20
36	84	8,937	63	327	8,841	5	140	21	96	5	-52	-28
37	13,148	164,584	1,980	4,249	112,584	2	57	11,168	52,000	5	-28	-41
38	12,062	132,006	1,619	3,258	84,270	2	52	10,443	47,736	5	-23	-30
39	1,009	27,529	315	836	23,383	3	74	694	4,146	6	-83	-83
40	77	5,049	46	155	4,931	3	107	31	118	4	-83	-81

Source: "Selected Statistics by Industry Division and Legal Form of Organization for Black-Owned Firms: 1972 and 1969," U.S. Bureau of the Census, 1972 Survey of Minority Business Enterprises, *Minority Owned Businesses—Black*, p. 161.

★ 308 ★
Business Owners and Operators

Black-Owned Firms: Receipts by Industry: 1969 and 1972

[Receipts in millions on dollars, 1972]

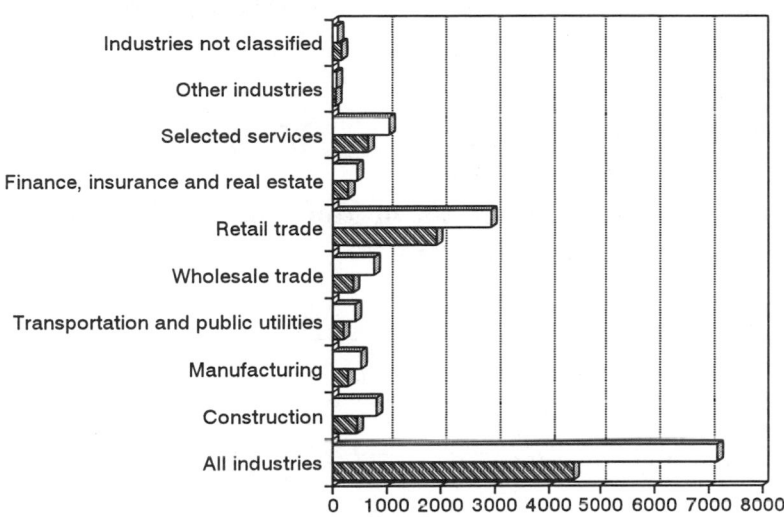

1969   1972

Receipts in millions of dollars.

	Percent change	1969	1972
All industries	60%	4,474	7,168
Construction	77%	464	820
Manufacturing	77%	303	537
Transportation and public utilities	102%	211	425
Wholesale trade	98%	385	764
Retail trade	51%	1932	2925
Finance, insurance and real estate	59%	287	457
Selected services	59%	663	1054
Other industries	39%	64	89
Industries not classified	-41%	165	97

Source: "Receipts of Black-Owned Firms by Industry: 1969 and 1972," U.S. Bureau of the Census, 1972 Survey of Minority Business Enterprises, *Minority Owned Businesses—Black*, p. 2.

★ 309 ★

Business Owners and Operators

Business Enterprises

There were approximately 43,000 black business enterprises in 1913. The annual volume of business was approximately $1 billion.

Source: Monroe N. Work, *The Negro Year Book and Annual Encyclopedia of the Negro, 1913*, p. 300.

★ 310 ★

Business Owners and Operators

Business Enterprises in Which 200 or More Blacks Were Engaged, 1913

Employment Office Keepers	213
Buyers and Shippers of Grain and Livestock etc.	214
Fruit Dealers	216
Saw and Planning Mill Proprietors	219
Jewelry	24
Ice Dealers	253
Furniture	256
Dry Goods, Fancy Goods and Notions	262
Stock Raising	296
Garage Keepers and Managers	309
Manufacturers and Proprietors of Clothing Factories	340
Fruit Growers	345
Dairying	526
Candy and Confectionery	573
Produce and Provisions	689
General Stores	884
Drug Stores	910
Proprietors of Transfer Companies	990
Hotel Keepers and Managers	1,020
Junk Dealers	1,132
Real Estate Dealers	1,369
Builders and Contractors	1,454
Undertakers	1,558
Billiard and Pool Room Keepers, etc.	1,582
Coal and Wood Dealers	1,754
Undesignated Retail Dealers	2,128
Butchers and Meat Dealers	3,009
Hucksters and Peddlers	3,194
Truck Gardners	6,242

[Continued]

★ 310 ★

Business Enterprises in Which 200 or More Blacks Were Engaged, 1913

[Continued]

Grocers	6,339
Restaurant Cafe and Lunch Room Keepers	7,511

Source: "Business Enterprises in Which 200 or More Negroes Are Engaged." Monroe N. Work, *The Negro Year Book and Annual Encyclopedia of the Negro, 1913*, pp. 390-391.

★ 311 ★

Business Owners and Operators

Business Establishments, 1863-1913

KINDS OF BUSINESS 1863	KINDS OF BUSINESS 1913
Bakery	Automobile Service and Garage
Barbering	Architecture
Blacksmithing	Bakery
Boot and Shoe Repairing	Banking
Cabinetmaking	Barbering
Catering	Blacksmithing and Wheelwrighting
Dressmaking	Bottling and Soda Water Making
Fish and Oyster Business	Broom making
Hairdressing	Cabinet making
Sailmaking	Carriage making
Shopkeeping	Catering
Vending	Confectionery
Total 12	Contracting and Building
	Cigarmaking
	Dairying
	Delicatessen Business
	Dressmaking
	Drug Store
	Drygoods Store
	Electrical Business
	Employment Bureau
	Fish and Oyster Business
	Floral Culture
	Fruit Raising
	Furmaking and Repairing
	Furniture Store
	General Store
	Grocery Store
	Haberdashery
	Hair goods manufacturing
	Hairdressing, Manicuring and Massaging
	Hack Business

[Continued]

★ 311 ★

Business Establishments, 1863-1913
[Continued]

Hospitals and Sanitarian Management
Hotelkeeping
Huckstering
Insurance
Jewelry
Loan and Investment Business
Laundrying-Steam and Hand
Livery Business
Lumber Business
Meat Market
Mine Operating
Millinery
Painting and House Decorating
Photography
Plumbing
Poultry Raising
Printing and Publishing
Produce and Provisions
Real Estate
Restaurant keeping
Regalia making
Sawmilling
Saloons
Shoemaking and Repairing
Shoe Store
Stationery
Stockraising
Tailoring
Theatre and Amusement Park
Truck gardening
Tea and Coffee Business
Tinsmithing Business
Undertaking
Upholstering
Vacuum House Cleaning
Wood and Coal
Wine and Liquor Business
Total 72

Source: "Fifty Year Business Progress-1683-1913," Monroe N. Work, *The Negro Year Book and Annual Encyclopedia of the Negro, 1913*, pp. 300-301.

★ 312 ★

Business Owners and Operators

Business Investment, 1899

A list of some of the larger investment is as follows:	
$10,000	2 real estate dealers, Houston, Texas,
	1 real estate dealer, New York City,
	1 builder and contractor, Brooklyn, N.Y.,
	1 builder and contractor, Carlisle, Penn.,
	1 builder and contractor, Raleigh, N.C.,
	1 builder and contractor, St. Louis, Mo.,
	1 publishing house, Nashville, Tenn.,
	1 publishing house, Jackson, Tenn.,
	1 undertaker, Washington, D.C.,
	1 merchant and planter, Dougherty county Ga.,
	1 banker and merchant, Kinston, N.C.
$12,000	1 building and loan assocation, Brooklyn, N.Y.
$15,000	1 proprietor of transfer wagons, Nashville, Tenn.
$20,000	1 brick contractor and druggist, Durham, N.C.,
	1 club house, New York city,
$25,000	1 real estate agent, New York city,
	1 hardware and crockery store, Mobile, Ala,
	1 undertaker, Chicago, Ill.,
	1 hotel, Chicago, Ill.,
	1 fish dealer and capitalist, Concord, N.C.,
	1 caterer, Chicago, Ill.,
	1 banking association, Jacksonville, Fla.,
$30,000	1 planter and contractor, Dougherty county, Ga.,
	1 merchant and planter, Dougherty county, Ga.,
	1 publishing house, Nashville, Tenn.,
	1 bank, Richmond, Va.,
$50,000	1 real estate dealer, Houston, Tex.,
	1 building and loan association, Washington, D.C.
$60,000	1 relief society, New York city.
$100,000	1 dealer in real estate, Cleveland, O.,
	1 bank, Richmond, Va.
$120,000	1 public hall association, New York city.
$150,000	2 real estate agents, New York city,

[Continued]

★ 313 ★

Business Owners and Operators

Business Men of Seattle, Washington, 1899

KINDS OF BUSINESS	YEARS IN BUSINESS	CAPITAL INVESTED
Real Estate	5 "	$10,000
Stock Broker	3 "	2,500
Hotel	2 "	1,500
Club House	2 "	700
Barber	6 "	3,000
Saloon	2 "	1,000
Barber	3 "	500
Restaurant	4 "	900
Restaurant	9 "	1,000
Newspaper	6 "	2,000

Source: "Negro Business Men of Seattle, Wash." W.E.B. DuBois, ed., *The Negro in Business*, p. 37.

★ 314 ★

Business Owners and Operators

Business Owners by State, 1899

State	Businesses	State	Businesses
Alabama	136	Maryland	49
Arkansas	94	Mississippi	78
California	43	Missouri	49
Colorado	8	New Jersey	36
Delaware	16	New York	80
District of Columbia	50	North Carolina	98
Florida	78	Ohio	14
Georgia	324	Oklahoma	7
Indiana	4	Pennsylvania	47
Indian Territory	7	South Carolina	123
Illinois	23	Tennessee	131
Kansas	30	Texas	159
Kentucky	72	Virginia	105
Louisiana	11	Washington	10
Massachusetts	14	West Virginia	9
Total			1,906
Condensing this table the following statistics are reported:			
The north, east of the Mississippi	218		
The south, east of the Mississippi	1,281		

[Continued]

★ 314 ★

Business Owners by State, 1899
[Continued]

State	Businesses	State	Businesses
West of the Mississippi	407		
Total	1,906		

Source: "Negro Business Men by States." W.E.B. DuBois, ed., *The Negro in Business*, p. 6.

★ 315 ★

Business Owners and Operators

Business Reporting Net Sales of $1,000,000 and Over with Black Proprietors, 1929

Kind of business	Number of stores	Proprietors and firm members (not on payroll)	Number of employees (full time)	Total payroll (including part time)	Stocks on hand end of year (at cost)	Net sales		
						Amount	Percent of total	Average per store
United States, total	25,701	28,243	12,561	$8,528,306	$10,657,000	$101,146,043	100.0	$3,935
Principal kinds of business, total	22,969	24,979	10,398	6,483,714	7,541,310	83,372,335	82.4	3,630
Grocery stores	8,450	9,118	1,475	857,251	2,857,690	28,369,178	28.0	3,357
Restaurants, cafeterias, and lunch rooms	5,729	6,209	4,742	2,358,331	431,950	17,284,126	17.1	3,017
Drug stores	712	852	955	790,465	1,566,750	7,253,921	7.2	10,188
General stores – groceries with dry goods, apparel, or general merchandise	761	892	229	151,947	1,161,880	4,828,700	4.8	6,345
Lunch counters, refreshment stands, etc.	2,189	2,321	683	369,552	140,100	4,049,072	4.0	1,850
Filling stations (automobile)	799	869	302	258,220	217,100	3,429,826	3.4	4,293
Motor-vehicle dealers (automobile – new and used)	39	46	166	245,535	331,750	3,149,837	3.1	80,765
All other food stores	631	707	182	171,379	107,290	2,880,145	2.8	4,564
Meat markets (including sea foods)	537	576	252	188,200	68,150	2,829,147	2.8	5,269
Candy and confectionery stores	1,137	1,193	230	124,841	207,480	2,584,053	2.6	2,273
Garages and repair shops	732	838	525	481,317	184,310	2,543,898	2.5	3,475
Coal and wood yards – ice dealers	549	594	337	250,079	125,900	2,117,474	2.1	3,857
Cigar stores and cigar stands	704	764	320	236,597	140,690	2,052,958	2.0	2,916

Source: "Kind of Retail Business Reporting Net sales of $1,000,000 and Over, Operated by Negro Proprietors in the United States: 1929." U.S. Bureau of the Census. *Negroes in the United States: 1920-32.* Washington, D.C.: Government Printing Office, 1935, p. 499.

★ 316 ★

Business Owners and Operators

Businesses in Selected Cities, 1939

CITY	KIND OF BUSINESS							
	Auto Repairs and Garages	Barber Shops	Beauty Parlors	Cleaning Pressing	Under-takers	Printing Shops	Shoe Repairs	Shoe Shine Parlors
Baltimore	54	179	217	87	26	5	49	119
Birmingham	9	41	19	22	10	4	27	28
Chicago	71	250	262	217	41	25	58	95
Cleveland	49	85	99	56	8	7	10	68
Detroit	30	105	145	105	24	13	31	37
Jacksonville	4	32	19	16	5	...	18	4
Houston	39	84	79	33	13	9	22	62
Los Angeles	27	66	118	55	3	7	17	460
Memphis	20	92	49	45	13	3	36	82
New Orleans	17	137	57	82	3	9	24	10
New York	104	266	567	298	63	54	63	205
Richmond	17	89	70	26	17	7	31	23
St. Louis	42	130	140	72	30	4	18	111
Washington	17	175	249	68	32	17	25	56

Source: "Negro Businesses in Selected Cities 1939." Jessie Parkhurst Guzman, ed., *Negro Year Book: A Review of Events Affecting Negro Life, 1941-1946*, p. 184. Primary source: Census of Business, Vol. 3, Series Establishments, 1939.

★ 317 ★

Business Owners and Operators

Businessmen by Occupations, 1899

Type of Business	Business men	Type of Business	Business men
Grocers	432	Caterers	24
General merchandise dealers	166	Plumbing, tinware, and	
Barbers with $500 or more		hardware shops	17
invested	162	Shoe dealers and repairers	17
Publishers and job printers	89	Fish dealers	15
Undertakers	80	Furniture dealers	13
Saloon-keepers	68	Building and loan association	13
Druggists	64	Jewelers	11
Restaurant-keepers	61	Market gardeners and planters	11
Hackmen and expressmen,		Clothing-dealers	10
owning outfits	53	Wall-paper and paint-shops	10
Builders and contractors	48	Bakers, with shops	10
Dealers in meat	47	Dry-goods dealers	9
Merchant tailors	40	Cotton gin proprietors	9
Dealers in fuel	27	Steam laundries	8
Dealers in real estate	36	Proprietors of machine shops	8

[Continued]

★ 317 ★

Businessmen by Occupations, 1899
[Continued]

Type of Business	Business men	Type of Business	Business men
Wagon-makers and blacksmiths	32	Cigar manufactures	8
Hotels	30	Photographers	8
Green grocers, dairymen, etc.	30	Brokers and money lenders	8
Livery-stable keepers	26	Dealers in feed	7
Confectioners	25	Dealers in fruit	6
Milliners	5		
Banks			
Second-hand stores	Businesses		
Harness-shops	With Four	Ice cream depots	
Employment agencies	Persons En-	Wire goods man'fr's	
Florists	gaged in each	Dressmaking shops	Two per-
Crokery-stores		Private cemeteries	sons in
Carpet-cleaning works		Bicycle-stores	Each
		M'ch'ncs' with shops	
Upholstering shops		Shirt factory	
Hair goods stores		Toilet supply shop	
Lumber mills	Three Persons	Broom manufactory	
Cl'n'ng & dyeing shops	In Each	Cotton mill	
Brick contractors		Assembly hall	One
Dealers in cotton		Naval store dealer	Person
		School of music	In Each
		Fan manufactory	
		Carpet manufactory	
		Handle factory	
		Rubber goods shop	
		Book-store	
Miscellaneous, undersignated		82	
Total		1,906	

Source: "Negro Business Men, According to Occupations." W.E.B. DuBois, ed., *The Negro in Business*, pp. 7-8.

★ 318 ★

Business Owners and Operators

Characteristics of Insurance Companies, 1913

Black insurance companies grew out of sick and death benefit societies established among free blacks during the days of slavery. The first Black insurance company organized in the United States was the American Insurance Company of Philadelphia, established in 1810. Its headquarters were at 159, later 525 Lombard Street, and it had a capital of $5,000.

[Continued]

★ 318 ★

Characteristics of Insurance Companies, 1913
[Continued]

Insurance was one of the most flourishing lines of business in which blacks were engaged in 1913 and at that time was the largest field of business from the standpoint of capital concentrated. Assets and other characteristics of insurance companies operated by blacks in 1913 were approximated as follows: assets, $7,500,000; income, $10,000,000; disbursements, $9,500,000; annual amount of insurance written, $100,000,000; and value of policies in force, $250,000,000.

Source: "Negro Insurance Companies." Monroe No. Work, *The Negro Year Book and Annual Encyclopedia of the Negro, 1913,* p. 391.

★ 319 ★

Business Owners and Operators

Construction Industry: 1972

Industry				With paid employees					Without paid employees		
	All firms		Gross receipts ($1,000)	Firms (number)	Employees (number)	Gross receipts ($1,000)	Average employees per firm (number)	Average receipts per firm ($1,000)	Firms (number)	Gross receipts ($1,000)	Average receipts per firm ($1,000)
	Code	Firms (number)									
ALL INDUSTRIES, TOTAL		194,986	7,168,491	31,893	196,596	5,101,280	6	160	163,093	2,067,211	13
CONSTRUCTION, TOTAL		20,151	819,661	4,437	29,741	579,614	7	131	15,714	240,047	15
General Building contractors	15	3,166	232,317	912	6,850	178,396	8	196	2,254	53,921	24
Residential building construction	152	672	69,324	518	2,811	64,846	5	125	154	4,478	29
Operative builders	153	72	7,013	32	287	6,266	9	196	40	747	19
Nonresidential building construction	154	40	27,198	35	890	27,097	25	774	5	101	20
General building contractors, n.s.k.	15-	2,382	128,782	327	2,862	80,187	9	245	2,055	48,595	24
Heavy construction contractors	16	561	45,028	197	1,360	35,678	7	181	364	9,350	26
Highway and street construction	161	215	22,901	94	(D)	(D)	(D)	(D)	121	(D)	(D)
Heavy construction, except highway	162	338	22,002	102	769	16,633	8	163	236	5,369	23
Heavy construction contractors, n.s.k.	16-	8	125	1	(D)	(D)	(D)	(D)	7	(D)	(D)
Special trade contractors	17	16,352	535,431	3,302	21,366	359,914	6	109	13,050	175,517	13
Plumbing, heating, and air conditioning	171	1,481	71,297	325	1,845	52,600	6	162	1,156	18,697	16
Painting, paperhanging, and decorating	172	3,121	44,934	288	1,333	21,002	5	73	2,833	23,932	8
Electrical work	173	989	61,710	280	1,880	47,359	7	169	709	14,351	20
Masonry, stonework, and plastering	174	3,184	131,243	1,084	7,996	94,582	7	87	2,100	36,661	17
Masonry and other stonework	1741	1,098	66,234	843	6,168	59,174	7	70	255	7,060	28
Plastering, drywall, and insulation	1742	216	24,984	168	1,474	23,681	9	141	48	1,303	27
Terazzo, tile, marble, and mosaic work	1743	71	6,139	53	215	5,753	4	109	18	386	21
Masonry	174-	1,799	33,886	20	139	5,974	7	299	1,779	27,912	16
Carpeting and flooring	175	3,069	54,584	299	1,542	29,143	5	97	2,770	25,441	9
Carpeting	1751	256	22,680	183	1,124	20,834	6	114	73	1,846	25
Floor laying and floorwork, n.e.c.	1752	128	7,716	104	394	7,244	4	70	24	472	20
Carpeting and flooring, n.s.k.	175-	2,685	24,188	12	24	1,065	2	89	2,673	23,123	9
Roofing and sheet metal work	176	425	25,661	122	974	19,880	8	163	303	4,781	16
Concrete work	177	1,574	63,696	531	3,304	43,504	6	82	1,043	20,192	19
Water well drilling	178	66	2,261	17	64	1,521	4	89	49	740	15
Miscellaneous special trade contractors	179	2,443	81,045	356	2,428	50,323	7	141	2,087	30,722	15
Structural steel erection	1791	12	2,333	8	(D)	(D)	(D)	(D)	4	(D)	(D)
Glass and glazing work	1793	21	3,243	19	(D)	(D)	(D)	(D)	2	(D)	(D)

[Continued]

★ 319 ★

Construction Industry: 1972
[Continued]

| Industry | | | | 1972 | | | | | | | |
| | All firms | | Gross receipts ($1,000) | With paid employees | | | | | Without paid employees | | |
	Code	Firms (number)		Firms (number)	Employees (number)	Gross receipts ($1,000)	Average employees per firm (number)	Average receipts per firm ($1,000)	Firms (number)	Gross receipts ($1,000)	Average receipts per firm ($1,000)
Excavating and foundation work	1794	89	8,982	64	350	8,299	5	130	25	683	27
Wrecking and demolition work	1795	31	3,499	24	153	3,292	6	137	7	207	30
Installing building equipment, n.e.c.	1796	3	1,188	3	61	1,188	20	396	-	-	-
Special trade contractors, n.e.c.	1799	2,287	61,800	238	1,662	32,033	7	135	2,049	29,767	15
Subdividers and developers, n.e.c.	6552	72	6,885	26	165	5,626	6	216	46	1,259	27

Source: "Selected Statistics for Industry for Black-Owned Firms: 1972 and 1969," U.S. Bureau of the Census, 1972 Survey of Minority Business Enterprises, *Minority Owned Businesses—Black*, p. 14. *Note:* - Represents zero.

★ 320 ★

Business Owners and Operators

Distribution of Businesses: Cities Having Twenty or More Black Merchants, 1899

Birmingham, Ala., 32	
Grocers	8
Barbers	6
Banks and Brokers	5
Druggists	4
Tailors	4
Miscellaneous	5
Mobile, Ala., 25	
Grocers	2
Fuel-dealers	2
Barbers	2
Saloon	1
Hardware-store	1
General Merchandise	1
Confectionery	1
Fish and Oysters	1
Undertakers	2
Publisher	1
Hotels	2
Shoe-store	1
Drug-store	1
Miscellaneous	7

[Continued]

★ 320 ★

Distribution of Businesses: Cities Having Twenty or More Black Merchants, 1899
[Continued]

Montgomery, Ala., 20	
Grocers	6
Undertakers	2
Drug-stores	2
Butcher	1
Dry-goods	1
Builder and Contractor	1
Miscellaneous	7
Little Rock, Ark., 42	
Grocers	14
Tailors	3
Confectioners	3
Publishers	3
Hotels	2
Jewelers	2
Druggists	2
Fuel-dealers	2
Undertakers	2
General Merchandise	2
Wholesale Grocer	1
Shirt Manufacturer	1
Miscellaneous	5
Washington, D.C., 49	
Grocers	9
Druggists	4
Restaurants	2
Undertakers	3
Caterers	2
Newspapers	2
Job Printers	2
Saloons	2
Coal-dealers	2
Green Grocers	2
Hardware	1
Fish-dealer	1
Photographer	1
Hotels	2
General Merchandise	1
Undertaker	1
Book-store	1
Grain and Feed	1

[Continued]

★ 320 ★

Distribution of Businesses: Cities Having Twenty or More Black Merchants, 1899

[Continued]

Miscellaneous	7
Atlanta, Ga., 50	
Grocers	19
Meat-markets	6
General Merchandise	5
Fuel-dealers	5
Undertakers	2
Real Estate	2
Tailor	1
Drug-store	1
Publisher	1
Wagon Builder	1
Miscellaneous	7
Savannah, Ga., 30	
Grocers	7
Saloons	5
Meat Markets	7
Plumber	1
General Merchandise	1
Printer	1
Cotton Merchants	2
Miscellaneous	6
Macon, Ga., 27	
Grocers	7
Broom Manufacturers	2
General Merchandise	3
Contractors and Builders	2
Real Estate	1
Tailor	1
Coal-dealer	1
Druggist	1
Saloon	1
Barbers	4
Miscellaneous	7
Louisville, Ky., 35	
Grocers	5
Expressmen	4
Saloons	3

[Continued]

★ 320 ★

Distribution of Businesses: Cities Having Twenty or More Black Merchants, 1899
[Continued]

Feed-stores	3
Publishers	2
Restaurants	2
Real Estate	2
Undertakers	2
Drug-stores	2
Milliner	1
Furniture	1
Fish-dealer	1
Photographer	1
Miscellaneous	6
Baltimore, Md., 31	
Undertakers	5
Caterers	5
Furniture	3
Butchers	2
Printers	2
Green Groceries	2
Coal and Wood	2
Pork Butcher	1
Tailor	1
China Store	1
Ice Cream Manufactory	1
Stationary	1
Cigar Manufacturer	1
Grocer	1
Miscellaneous	3
Vicksburg, Miss., 21	
Saloons	2
Jeweler	2
Clothiers and Tailors	2
Drug-stores	2
Newspapers	2
Dry-goods	2
Undertaker	1
Confectioners	2
Upholsterer	1
Butcher	1
Fish and Oysters	1
Miscellaneous	3

[Continued]

★ 320 ★

Distribution of Businesses: Cities Having Twenty or More Black Merchants, 1899

[Continued]

St. Louis, Mo., 12	
Grocers	3
Express	2
Coal-dealers	2
Stock-dealer	1
Painter and Paper-hanger	1
Paving Business	1
Wall Paper	1
Tailor	1
Contractor and Builder	1
Undertaker	1
Publisher	1
Miscellaneous	5
New York City, N.Y., 63	
Caterers	6
Express	5
Intelligence Offices	4
Real Estate	4
Undertakers	4
Newsdealers	3
Printers	3
Hotels	2
Restaurants	2
Machinists	2
Coal-dealer	1
Saloons	2
Grocer	1
Tailors	2
Fuel-dealer	1
Publisher	1
Manufacturer of Wire Goods	1
Bicycle Manufacturer	1
Druggist	1
Miscellaneous	18
Wilmington, N.C., 20	
Grocers	5
Undertakers	4
Druggists	2
Merchant Tailors	2
General Merchandise	1
Broker	1

[Continued]

★ 320 ★

Distribution of Businesses: Cities Having Twenty or More Black Merchants, 1899

[Continued]

Contractor and Miscellaneous	5
Philadelphia, Penn., 45	
Caterers	5
Undertakers	4
Grocers	4
Building and Loan Associations	3
Saloons	3
Bicycle Shops	2
Real Estate	2
Crockery-stores	2
Publishers	2
Printers	2
Cigar and Tobacco	2
Upholsterers	2
Expressmen	1
Steam Carpet Cleaning	1
Restaurants	2
Rubber Goods Dealer	1
China-store	1
Market	1
Dairy	1
Fancy Goods	1
Florist	1
Miscellaneous	2
Charleston, S.C., 58	
Undertakers	7
Barbers	6
Green Grocers	6
Tailors	5
Grocers	4
Contractors	4
Fruit and Vegetables	3
Printers	3
Livery Stables	3
Shoe-store	2
Wheelwrights	2
Photographer	1
Fan-maker	1
Drug-store	1
Steam Dye Works	1
Miscellaneous	9

[Continued]

★ 320 ★

Distribution of Businesses: Cities Having Twenty or More Black Merchants, 1899

[Continued]

Nashville, Tenn., 45	
Contractors	9
Grocers	6
Undertakers	2
Saloons	2
Drug-stores	2
Second-hand Stores	2
Livery-stables	2
Publishers	2
Tailors	2
Coal and Ice	1
Produce Merchant	1
Furniture	1
Transfer Wagons	1
Restaurant and Grocer	1
Grocer and Saloon	1
Second-hand Furniture	1
Miscellaneous	9
San Antonio, Tex., 24	
Saloons	8
Expressmen	3
Real Estate	1
Newspaper	1
Tailor	1
Contractor	1
Green Grocer	1
Miscellaneous	8
Houston, Tex., 37	
Grocers	10
Real Estate	6
Contractors	4
Saloons	3
Dairy	1
Coal and Wood-dealers	2
Pawn Broker	1
Caterer	1
Miscellaneous	9
Richmond, Va., 28	
Insurance Societies	5

[Continued]

★ 320 ★

Distribution of Businesses: Cities Having Twenty or More Black Merchants, 1899
[Continued]

Grocers	4
Undertakers	4
Fish-dealers	4
Banks	2
Druggist	1
Newspaper	1
Dry-goods	1
Miscellaneous	6

Source: " W.E.B. DuBois, ed., *The Negro in Business*, pp. 25-28.

★ 321 ★

Business Owners and Operators

Distribution of Firms by State: 1972

State	Number of firms
Alabama	2500-4999
Alaska	0-2499
Arizona	0-2499
Arkansas	0-2499
California	7500 or more
Colorado	0-2499
Connecticut	0-2499
Delaware	0-2499
District of Columbia	5000-7499
Florida	7500 and more
Georgia	7500 and more
Hawaii	0-2499
Idaho	0-2499
Illinois	7500 and more
Indiana	2500-4999
Iowa	0-2499
Kansas	0-2499
Kentucky	0-2499
Louisiana	7500 and more
Maine	0-2499
Maryland	5000-7499
Massachusetts	0-2499
Michigan	7500 and more
Minnesota	0-2499
Mississippi	2500-4999
Missouri	2500-4999
Montana	0-2499

[Continued]

★ 321 ★

Distribution of Firms by State: 1972
[Continued]

State	Number of firms
Nebraska	0-2499
Nevada	0-2499
New Hampshire	0-2499
New Jersey	5000-7499
New Mexico	0-2499
New York	7500 and more
North Carolina	7500 and more
North Dakota	0-2499
Ohio	7500 and more
Oklahoma	0-2499
Oregon	0-2499
Pennsylvania	7500 and more
Rhode Island	0-2499
South Carolina	5000-7499
South Dakota	0-2499
Tennessee	2500-4999
Texas	7500 and more
Utah	0-2499
Vermont	0-2499
Virginia	7500 and more
Washington	0-2499
West Virginia	0-2499
Wisconsin	0-2499
Wyoming	0-2499

Source: "Distribution of Black-Owned Firms by State: 1972," U.S. Bureau of the Census, 1972 Survey of Minority Business Enterprises, *Minority Owned Businesses—Black*, p. 3.

★ 322 ★

Business Owners and Operators

Fifty Years of Business Progress, 1865-1915

KINDS OF BUSINESS 1865	KINDS OF BUSINESS 1915
Bakery	Automobile service and garage
Barbering	Architecture
Blacksmithing	Bakery
Boot and shoe repair	Banking
Cabinetmaking	Barbering
Catering	Blacksmithing and wheelwrighting
Dressmaking	Bottling and soda water making
Fish and oyster business	Brick making
Hairdressing	Broom making
Sailmaking	Cabinet making

[Continued]

★ 322 ★

Fifty Years of Business Progress, 1865-1915
[Continued]

Shopkeeping	Carriage making
Vending	Catering
Total 12	Confectionery
	Contracting and building
	Cigar making
	Dairying
	Delicatessen business
	Dressmaking
	Drug store
	Drygoods store
	Electrical business
	Employment bureau
	Fish and oyster business
	Floral culture
	Fruit raising
	Furmaking and repairing
	Furniture store
	General store
	Grocery store
	Haberdashery
	Hair goods manufacturing
	Hairdressing, manicuring, and massaging
	Hack business
	Hospitals and sanitarium management
	Hotelkeeping
	Huckstering
	Insurance
	Jewelry
	Loan and investment business
	Laundrying--steam and hand
	Livery business
	Lumber business
	Meat market
	Mine operating
	Millinery
	Painting and house decorating
	Photography
	Plumbing
	Poultry raising
	Printing and publishing
	Produce and provisions
	Real estate
	Restaurant keeping
	Regalia making
	Sawmilling
	Saloons
	Shoemaking and repairing
	Shoe store
	Stationery

[Continued]

★ 322 ★

Fifty Years of Business Progress, 1865-1915
[Continued]

Stockraising
Tailoring
Theater and amusement park
Truck gardening
Tea and coffee business
Tinsmithing business
Undertaking
Upholstering
Vacuum house cleaning
Wholesale merchandising
Wood and coal
Wine and liquor business
Total 71

Source: "Fifty Years Business Progress 1865-1915," Monroe Work, ed., *Negro Year Book: An Annual Encyclopedia of the Negro, 1916-1917,* pp. 318-320.

★ 323 ★

Business Owners and Operators

Finance, Insurance, and Real Estate: 1972

Industry	Code	All firms		With paid employees					Without paid employees		
		Firms (number)	Gross receipts ($1,000)	Firms (number)	Employees (number)	Gross receipts ($1,000)	Average employees per firm (number)	Average receipts per firm ($1,000)	Firms (number)	Gross receipts ($1,000)	Average receipts per firm ($1,000)
FINANCE, INSURANCE, AND REAL ESTATE, TOTAL		8,001	456,781	1,130	17,771	392,686	16	348	6,871	64,095	9
Banking	60	100	40,476	43	1,601	39,494	37	918	57	982	17
Credit agencies other than banks	61	116	25,799	81	1,210	25,312	15	312	35	487	14
Savings and loan associations	612	50	16,931	50	660	16,931	13	339	-	-	-
Personal credit institutions	614	19	2,812	16	132	2,744	8	172	3	68	23
Credit agencies, n.e.c. and n.s.k.	61-	47	6,056	15	418	5,637	28	376	32	419	13
Security and commodity brokers and services	62	171	11,624	15	268	9,920	18	661	156	1,704	11
Security brokers and dealers	621	116	8,236	13	(D)	(D)	(D)	(D)	103	(D)	(D)
Security brokers and services, n.s.k.	621-	55	3,388	2	(D)	(D)	(D)	(D)	53	(D)	(D)
Insurance carriers	63	73	201,606	71	(D)	(D)	(D)	(D)	2	(D)	(D)
Insurance agents, brokers, and services	64	1,988	49,105	259	1,272	33,903	5	131	1,729	15,202	9
Real estate	65pt.	5,272	115,242	593	2,842	71,852	5	121	4,679	43,390	9
Real estate operators and lessors	651	1,889	44,490	278	1,245	30,178	4	109	1,611	14,312	9
Real estate agents and managers	653	3,295	62,611	289	1,356	35,774	5	124	3,006	26,837	9
Title abstract offices	654	17	1,225	7	39	966	6	138	10	259	26
Subdividers and developers, n.e.c.	655	42	4,163	10	135	2,947	14	295	32	1,216	38
Real estate, n.s.k.	65-	29	2,753	9	67	1,987	7	221	20	766	38
Combined real estate, insurance, etc.	66	232	6,996	58	230	5,238	4	90	174	1,758	10
Holding and other investment offices	67pt.	49	5,933	10	120	5,369	12	537	39	564	14

Source: "Selected Statistics for Industry for Black-Owned Firms: 1972 and 1969," U.S. Bureau of the Census, 1972 Survey of Minority Business Enterprises, *Minority Owned Businesses—Black,* p. 24. *Notes:* - Represents zero. D = Withheld to avoid disclosing figures for individual companies.

★ 324 ★

Business Owners and Operators

Firms in Cities, Compared with States: 1972

City	City		State		Percent city to state	
	Firms (number)	Receipts ($1,000)	Firms (number)	Receipts ($1,000)	Firms	Receipts
New York	9,996	322,015	14,377	466,363	70	69
Chicago, IL	8,308	437,757	11,458	609,423	73	72
Washington, DC	7,102	155,877	(X)	(X)	(X)	(X)
Los Angeles, CA	7,042	229,511	19,282	703,512	37	33
Detroit, MI	4,984	268,395	7,964	401,511	63	67
Houston, TX	4,673	132,038	15,001	483,920	31	27
Philadelphia, PA	4,482	185,899	7,579	344,606	59	54
Baltimore, MD[1]	3,043	107,122	7,019	244,843	43	44
Cleveland, OH	2,667	93,054	10,524	332,793	25	28
St. Louis, MO[1]	2,249	69,028	4,685	149,021	48	46

Source: "Largest Cities in Number of Black-Owned Firms and Comparison with States: 1972," U.S. Bureau of the Census, 1972 Survey of Minority Business Enterprises, *Minority Owned Businesses—Black*, p. 5. *Notes:* X Not applicable. 1. Independent city.

★ 325 ★

Business Owners and Operators

Firms in Counties, Compared with States: 1972

County	County		State		Percent county to state	
	Firms (number)	Receipts ($1,000)	Firms (number)	Receipts ($1,000)	Firms	Receipts
Los Angeles, CA	11,061	358,685	19,282	703,512	57	51
Cook, IL	9,284	514,058	11,458	609,423	81	84
District of Columbia	7,102	155,877	(X)	(X)	(X)	(X)
Wayne, MI	5,719	308,958	7,964	401,511	72	77
Harris, TX	5,011	142,556	15,001	483,920	33	29
Philadelphia, PA	4,482	185,899	7,579	344,606	59	54
Cuyahoga, OH	3,320	117,313	10,524	332,793	32	35
Kings, NY	3,299	85,298	14,377	466,363	23	18
Baltimore, MD[1]	3,043	107,122	7,019	244,843	43	44
New York, NY	2,538	148,339	14,377	466,363	18	32

Source: "Largest Counties in Number of Black-Owned Firms and Comparison with States: 1972," U.S. Bureau of the Census, 1972 Survey of Minority Business Enterprises, *Minority Owned Businesses—Black*, p. 5. *Notes:* X Not applicable. 1. Independent city.

★ 326 ★

Business Owners and Operators

Firms in SMSA's, Compared with States: 1972

Standard metropolitan statistical area	SMSA		State		Percent SMSA to state	
	Firms (number)	Receipts ($1,000)	Firms (number)	Receipts ($1,000)	Firms	Receipts
New York, NY-NJ	11,282	363,724	14,377[1]	466,363[1]	78	78
Los Angeles-Long Beach, CA	11,057	358,533	19,282	703,512	57	51
Washington, DC-MD-VA	9,726	251,074	(X)	(X)	(X)	(X)
Chicago, IL	9,718	533,643	11,458	609,423	85	88
Philadelphia, PA-NJ	6,278	273,515	7,579[2]	344,606[2]	83	79
Detroit, MI	6,146	335,855	7,964	401,511	77	84
Houston, TX	5,477	151,928	15,001	483,920	37	31
San Francisco-Oakland, CA	4,313	170,821	19,282	703,512	22	24
Baltimore, MD	3,994	139,379	7,019	244,843	57	57
St. Louis, MO-IL	3,619	129,616	4,685[3]	149,021[3]	77	87

Source: "Largest SMSA's in Number of Black-Owned Firms and Comparison with States: 1972," U.S. Bureau of the Census, 1972 Survey of Minority Business Enterprises, *Minority Owned Businesses—Black*, p. 4. *Notes:* X Not applicable. 1. NY data only. 2. PA data only. 3. MO data only.

★ 327 ★

Business Owners and Operators

Growth in Retail Proprietorships, 1929-1939

YEAR	Negro population	Stores	Sales
1939	12,808,073	29,827	$71,466,000
1935	...	22,756	47,968,000
1929	11,891,143	24,969	98,602,000

Source: Untitled Table. Florence Murray, ed., *The Negro Handbook*, 1942, p. 18. Primary source: Joseph R. Houchins, Chief, Negro Statistics, Bureau of the Census, Department of Commerce.

★ 328 ★

Business Owners and Operators

Growth of Businesses, 1863-1913

Numbers in thousands.

Year	Total Black businesses	Change over preceding date --	
		Number	Percent
1863	2	(X)	(X)
1873	4	2	100
1883	10	6	150
1893	17	7	70
1903	25	8	47
1913	40	15	60

Source: "Number of Black Businesses for Selected Years: 1863 to 1913," U.S. Department of Commerce, Bureau of the Census. *The Social and Economic Status of the Black Population in the United States: An Historical View, 1790-1978*, p. 78. Primary source: Monroe N. Work, ed. *Negro Yearbook, An Annual Encyclopedia of the Negro 1914-1915*. Tuskegee, Alabama: The Negro Yearbook Publishing Company Tuskegee Institute, 1914. Published by permission. *Note:* X Not applicable.

★ 329 ★

Business Owners and Operators

Increase in Business Enterprises, 1866-1926

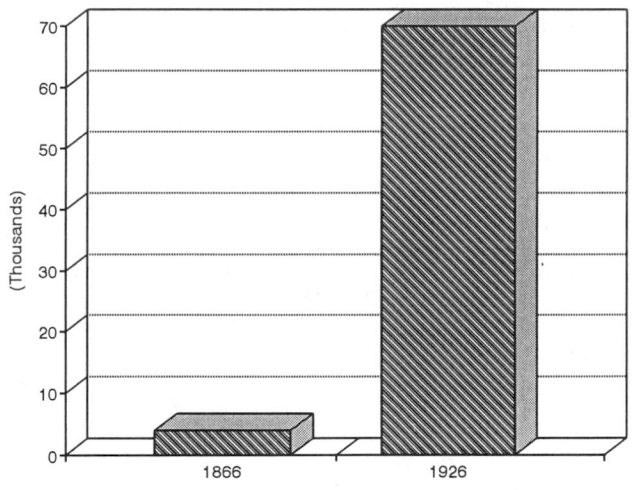

Number of Negroes Engaged in Business	
1866	4,000
1926	70,000

Source: "Increase in Kinds of Negro Businesses." Monroe N. Work, *The Negro Year Book and Annual Encyclopedia of the Negro, 1913*, p. 390.

★ 330 ★
Business Owners and Operators

Industry and Organization, 1972

Industry	All firms		With paid employees					Without paid employees		
	Firms (number)	Gross receipts ($1,000)	Firms (number)	Employees (number)	Gross receipts ($1,000)	Average employees per firm (number)	Average receipts per firm ($1,000)	Firms (number)	Gross receipts ($1,000)	Average receipts per firm ($1,000)
ALL INDUSTRIES, TOTAL	194,986	7,168,491	31,893	196,596	5,101,280	6	160	163,093	2,067,211	13
Sole proprietorships	182,530	4,143,692	23,754	98,791	2,206,451	4	93	158,776	1,937,241	12
Partnerships	8,422	809,136	4,312	25,181	684,975	6	159	4,110	124,161	30
Corporations	4,034	2,215,663	3,287	72,624	2,209,854	19	577	207	5,809	28
Construction, total	20,151	819,661	4,437	29,741	579,614	7	131	15,714	240,047	15
Sole proprietorships	18,432	503,393	3,251	16,779	281,841	5	87	15,181	221,552	15
Partnerships	1,169	109,482	660	4,486	91,696	7	139	509	17,786	35
Corporations	550	206,786	526	8,476	206,077	16	392	24	709	30
Manufacturing, total	4,116	536,619	1,706	20,390	502,385	12	294	2,410	34,234	14
Sole proprietorships	3,170	102,608	914	4,305	72,448	5	79	2,256	30,160	13
Partnerships	342	47,213	217	1,750	43,701	8	201	125	3,512	28
Corporations	604	386,798	575	14,335	386,236	25	672	29	562	19
Transportation and public utilities, total	21,738	425,467	1,680	10,714	209,736	6	125	20,058	215,731	11
Sole proprietorships	21,221	336,612	1,344	6,351	125,366	5	93	19,877	211,246	11
Partnerships	322	31,601	157	1,528	27,417	10	175	165	4,184	25
Corporations	195	57,254	179	2,835	56,953	16	318	16	301	19
Wholesale trade, total	2,091	764,178	926	7,691	734,087	8	793	1,165	30,091	26
Sole proprietorships	1,438	151,460	374	1,744	126,253	5	338	1,064	25,207	24
Partnerships	253	88,461	172	970	84,371	6	491	81	4,090	50
Corporations	400	524,257	380	4,977	523,463	13	1,378	20	794	40
Retail trade, total	56,617	2,925,459	12,215	58,326	1,976,237	5	162	44,402	949,222	21
Sole proprietorships	52,443	1,997,656	9,501	34,374	1,111,584	4	117	42,942	886,072	21
Partnerships	3,122	360,607	1,701	8,681	299,000	5	176	1,421	61,607	43
Corporations	1,052	567,196	1,013	15,271	565,653	15	558	39	1,543	40
Finance, insurance, and real estate, total	8,001	456,781	1,130	17,771	392,686	16	348	6,871	64,095	9
Sole proprietorships	7,117	134,323	564	3,283	76,271	6	135	6,553	58,052	9
Partnerships	557	41,254	261	1,230	35,594	5	136	296	5,660	19
Corporations	327	281,204	305	13,258	280,821	43	921	22	383	17
Selected services, total	68,469	1,054,057	9,192	49,102	645,353	5	70	59,277	408,704	7
Sole proprietorships	65,305	757,725	7,329	29,995	370,998	4	51	57,976	386,727	7
Partnerships	2,311	111,572	1,057	6,040	90,679	6	86	1,254	20,893	17
Corporations	853	184,760	806	13,067	183,676	16	228	47	1,084	23
Other industries, total	4,283	88,782	428	2,282	44,752	5	105	3,855	44,030	11
Sole proprietorships	4,067	68,021	328	1,544	27,675	5	84	3,739	40,346	11
Partnerships	176	14,329	65	408	11,036	6	170	111	3,293	30
Corporations	40	6,432	35	330	6,041	9	173	5	391	78
Industries not classified, total	9,520	97,487	179	579	16,430	3	92	9,341	81,057	9
Sole proprietorships	9,337	91,894	149	416	14,015	3	94	9,188	77,879	8
Partnerships	170	4,617	22	88	1,481	4	67	148	3,136	21
Corporations	13	976	8	75	934	9	117	5	42	8

Source: "Selected Statistics by Industry Division and Legal Form of Organization for Black-Owned Firms: 1972 and 1969," U.S. Bureau of the Census, 1972 Survey of Minority Business Enterprises, *Minority Owned Businesses—Black*, p. 160.

★ 331 ★

Business Owners and Operators

Landmarks in Business Enterprises

	Year
The Fourteenth Amendment to the Constitution adopted. Legalized right of Negroes, anywhere in the country, to engage in any occupation in which other persons are engaged.	1868
The Freedman's Savings Bank and Trust Company fails. The loss thereby of many millions of dollars greatly retards the development of Negro enterprises.	1873
About this time the operating of Negro beneficial societies develops into a regular business. The operating of industrial insurance companies by Negroes becomes a regular business.	1880-85
First Negro banks organized. 1888, the Capital Savings Bank of Washington begins business. 1889, the True Reformers Bank of Richmond and the Mutual Bank and Trust Company of Chattanooga begin business. 1890, the Penny Savings Bank of Birmingham begins business.	1888-90
The National Negro Business League organized.	1900
First reserve legal (old line) insurance company among Negroes, the Standard Life of Atlanta, Georgia, organized with a paid in capital of $100,000.	1912

Source: "Landmarks in Negro Business Enterprises." Monroe N. Work, *The Negro Year Book and Annual Encyclopedia of the Negro, 1913*, p. 391.

★ 332 ★

Business Owners and Operators

Loans to Minority-Operated Businesses, 1968-1970

For years ending June 30.

Year	Number of loans approved			Value of loans approved		
	Total loans	Minority		Total (mil. dol.)	Minority	
		Total	Percent of total		Total (mil. dol.)	Percent of total
1968	13,100	2,335	18	624.3	41.3	7
1969	14,523	4,654	32	699.3	104.6	15
1970	15,102	6,262	41	709.6	160.4	23

Source: "Loans to Minority-Operated Small Businesses: 1968 to 1970," *Statistical Abstract of the United States*, 1971, p. 442. Primary source: Small Business Administration, unpublished data.

★ 333 ★

Business Owners and Operators

Major Industry Groups in Receipts of Black-Owned Firms: 1972

Industry group	SIC code	Firms (number)	Receipts (million dollars)
Automotive dealers and service stations	55	7,287	951
Food stores	54	12,271	649
Eating and drinking places	58	15,154	537
Special trade contractors	17	16,352	535
Miscellaneous retail	59	16,441	487
Wholesale trade – durable goods	50	1,236	449
Personal services	72	35,473	355
Wholesale trade – nondurable goods	51	318	300
Trucking and warehousing	42	10,187	294
General building contractors	15	3,166	232

Source: "Largest Major Industry Groups in Receipts of Black-Owned Firms, 1972," U.S. Bureau of the Census, 1972 Survey of Minority Business Enterprises, *Minority Owned Businesses—Black*, p. 2.

★ 334 ★

Business Owners and Operators

Manufacturing Industry: 1972

Industry	Code	All firms — Firms (number)	All firms — Gross receipts ($1,000)	With paid employees — Firms (number)	With paid employees — Employees (number)	With paid employees — Gross receipts ($1,000)	With paid employees — Average employees per firm (number)	With paid employees — Average receipts per firm ($1,000)	Without paid employees — Firms (number)	Without paid employees — Gross receipts ($1,000)	Without paid employees — Average receipts per firm ($1,000)
MANUFACTURING, TOTAL		4,116	536,619	1,706	20,390	502,385	12	294	2,410	34,234	14
Food and kindred products	20	153	88,310	97	2,333	87,103	24	898	56	1,207	22
Meat products	201	31	42,006	26	901	41,888	35	1,611	5	118	24
Dairy products	202	8	12,486	6	(D)	(D)	(D)	(D)	2	(D)	(D)
Preserved fruits and vegetables	203	6	5,459	6	208	5,459	35	910	-	-	-
Grain mill products	204	10	(D)	7	52	1,861	7	266	3	(D)	(D)
Bakery products	205	20	5,733	16	208	5,712	13	357	4	21	5
Sugar and confectionery products	206	3	(D)	3	(D)	(D)	(D)	(D)	-	-	-
Beverages	208	16	11,049	12	(D)	(D)	(D)	(D)	4	(D)	(D)
Miscellaneous food and kindred products	209	59	8,658	21	314	7,758	15	369	38	900	24
Tobacco manufacturers	21	4	119	2	(D)	(D)	(D)	(D)	2	(D)	(D)
Textile mill products	22	54	8,791	16	331	8,428	21	527	38	363	10
Apparel and other textile products	23	247	30,601	109	2,092	28,619	19	263	138	1,982	14
Men's and boys' furnishings	232	9	4,803	6	(D)	(D)	(D)	(D))	3	(D)	(D)
Women's and misses' outerwear	233	31	9,615	31	761	9,615	25	310	-	-	-
Women's and misses' blouses and waists	2331	2	(D)	2	(D)	(D)	(D)	(D)	-	-	-
Women's and misses' dresses	2335	16	3,416	16	320	3,416	20	214	-	-	-
Women's and misses' suits and coats	2337	5	(D)	5	(D)	(D)	(D)	(D)	-	-	-
Women's and misses' outerwear, n.e.c.	2339	8	4,250	8	302	4,250	38	531	-	-	-

[Continued]

★ 334 ★

Manufacturing Industry: 1972

[Continued]

Industry	Code	All firms		With paid employees					Without paid employees		
		Firms (number)	Gross receipts ($1,000)	Firms (number)	Employees (number)	Gross receipts ($1,000)	Average employees per firm (number)	Average receipts per firm ($1,000)	Firms (number)	Gross receipts ($1,000)	Average receipts per firm ($1,000)
Women's and children's undergarments	234	11	60	-	-	-	-	-	11	60	5
Miscellaneous fabricated textile products	239	196	16,123	72	(D)	(D)	(D)	(D)	124	(D)	(D)
Lumber and wood products	24	1,649	73,969	695	3,645	59,507	5	86	954	14,462	15
Logging camps and logging contractors	241	717	26,182	577	2,008	23,880	3	41	140	2,302	16
Sawmills and planing mills	242	83	21,812	73	(D)	(D)	(D)	(D)	10	(D)	(D)
Sawmills and planing mills, general	2421	80	20,770	72	931	20,497	13	285	8	273	34
Sawmills and planing mills, n.e.c.	242-	3	1,042	1	(D)	(D)	(D)	(D)	2	(D)	(D)
Millwork, plywood, and structural members	243	15	6,424	13	(D)	(D)	(D)	(D)	2	(D)	(D)
Wood containers	244	3	1,656	3	85	1,656	28	552	-	-	-
Miscellaneous wood products	249	831	17,895	29	332	6,133	11	211	8052	11,762	15
Furniture and fixtures	25	149	18,187	52	484	16,891	16	325	97	1,296	13
Household furniture	251	38	13,663	30	692	13,388	23	446	8	275	34
Wood household furniture	2511	12	6,340	11	(D)	(D)	(D)	(D)	1	(D)	(D)
Upholstered household furniture	2512	6	3,790	6	205	3,790	34	632	-	-	-
Mattresses and bedsprings	2515	15	2,979	10	119	2,750	12	275	5	229	46
Household furniture, n.s.k.	251-	5	554	3	(D)	(D)	(D)	(D)	2	(D)	(D)
Office furniture	252	-	-	-	-	-	-	-	-	-	-
Public building and related furniture	253	5	49	-	-	-	-	-	5	49	10
Partitions and fixtures	254	15	2,050	11	84	2,024	8	184	4	26	7
Miscellaneous furniture and fixtures	259	91	2,425	11	72	1,479	6	134	80	946	12
Paper and allied products	26	16	4,732	15	(D)	(D)	(D)	(D)	1	(D)	(D)
Printing and publishing	27	744	76,767	224	2,255	69,978	10	312	520	6,789	13
Newspapers	271	63	11,510	48	530	11,254	11	234	15	256	17
Periodicals	272	15	(D)	11	(D)	(D)	(D)	(D)	5	68	17
Books	273	8	4,669	7	(D)	(D)	(D)	(D)	1	(D)	(D)
Miscellaneous publishing	274	11	2,469	8	(D)	(D)	(D)	(D)	3	(D)	(D)
Commercial printing	275	138	22,692	112	909	22,173	8	198	26	519	20
Commercial printing, letterpress	2751	75	7,522	65	404	7,376	6	113	10	146	15
Commercial printing, lithographic	2752	42	13,087	34	432	12,957	13	381	8	130	16
Commercial printing, n.s.k.	275-	21	2,083	13	73	1,840	6	142	8	243	30
Blankbooks and bookbinding	278	6	(D)	5	45	1,561	9	312	1	(D)	(D)
Printing trade services	279	17	2,718	9	97	2,582	11	287	8	136	17
Printing and publishing, n.s.k.	27-	486	8,368	24	115	2,617	5	109	462	5,751	12
Chemicals and allied products	28	79	41,246	54	957	40,986	18	759	25	260	10
Petroleum and coal products	29	13	938	6	55	867	9	145	7	71	10
Rubber and miscellaneous plastics products	30	30	6,004	17	286	5,711	17	336	13	293	23
Leather and leather products	31	28	1,210	'9	75	895	8	99	19	315	17
Stone, clay, and glass products	32	125	19,520	50	888	18,941	18	379	75	579	8
Concrete, gypsum, and plaster products	327	50	16,252	41	684	16,045	17	391	9	207	23
Stone, clay, and glass products, n.s.k.	32-	75	3,268	9	204	2,896	23	322	66	372	6
Primary metal industries	33	58	15,711	19	464	15,158	24	798	39	553	14
Fabricated metal products	34	162	45,093	99	1,887	43,977	19	444	63	1,116	18
Metal cans and shipping containers	341	14	245	-	-	-	-	-	14	245	18

[Continued]

★ 334 ★

Manufacturing Industry: 1972

[Continued]

Industry	Code	All firms		With paid employees					Without paid employees		
								1972			
		Firms (number)	Gross receipts ($1,000)	Firms (number)	Employees (number)	Gross receipts ($1,000)	Average employees per firm (number)	Average receipts per firm ($1,000)	Firms (number)	Gross receipts ($1,000)	Average receipts per firm ($1,000)
Fabricated structural metal products	344	34	12,478	30	479	12,407	16	414	4	71	18
Fabricated structural metal	3441	6	2,359	4	(D)	(D)	(D)	(D)	2	(D)	(D)
Metal doors, sash, and trim	3442	8	3,584	8	106	3,584	13	448	-	-	-
Sheet metal work	3444	10	2,011	9	(D)	(D)	(D)	(D)	1	(D)	(D)
Architectural metal work	3446	7	(D)	6	50	1,116	8	186	1	(D)	(D)
Fabricated structural metal products, n.e.c.	344-	3	(D)	3	(D)	(D)	(D)	(D)	-	-	-
Screw machine products, bolts, etc.	345	6	658	6	42	658	7	110	-	-	-
Metal forgings and stampings	346	11	11,389	10	(D)	(D)	(D)	(D)	1	(D)	(D)
Metal services, n.e.c.	347	36	6,568	33	342	6,482	10	196	3	86	29
Miscellaneous fabricated metal products	349	16	8,284	15	(D)	(D)	(D0	(D)	1	(D)	(D)
Fabricated metal products, n.s.k.	34-	45	5,471	5	(D)	(D)	(D)	(D)	40	(D)	(D)
Machinery, except electrical	35	132	33,972	92	1,274	33,353	14	363	40	619	15
Construction and related machinery	353	8	(D)	4	56	1,037	14	259	4	(D)	(D)
Metalworking machinery	354	23	3,122	18	150	2,992	8	166	5	130	26
Special industry machinery	355	4	(D)	3	(D)	(D)	(D)	(D)	1	(D)	(D)
General industrial machinery	356	6	4,746	5	(D)	(D)	(D)	(D)	1	(D)	(D)
Miscellaneous machinery, except electrical	359	91	23,799	62	932	23,338	15	376	29	461	16
Electrical and electronic equipment	36	90	40,744	66	1,625	40,141	25	608	24	603	25
Electric distributing equipment	361	5	2,107	5	136	2,107	27	421	-	-	-
Electrical industrial apparatus	362	5	2,975	5	153	2,975	321	595	-	-	-
Household appliances	363	1	(D)	1	(D)	(D)	(D)	(D)	-	-	-
Electric lighting and wiring equipment	364	9	4,460	9	173	4,460	19	496	-	-	-
Radio and television receiving equipment	365	7	(D)	4	(D)	(D)	(D)	(D)	3	71	24
Communication equipment	366	5	3,257	5	122	3,257	24	651	-	-	-
Electronic components and accessories	367	27	11,548	26	(D)	(D)	(D)	(D)	1	(D)	(D)
Miscellaneous electrical equipment and supplies	369	31	2,039	11	(D)	(D)	(D)	(D)	20	(D)	(D)
Transportation equipment	37	32	7,630	19	384	7,536	20	397	13	94	7
Instruments and related products	38	26	3,693	16	176	3,615	11	226	10	78	8
Miscellaneous manufacturing industries	39	325	19,382	49	612	15,889	12	324	276	3,493	13

Source: "Selected Statistics for Industry for Black-Owned Firms: 1972 and 1969," U.S. Bureau of the Census, 1972 Survey of Minority Business Enterprises, *Minority Owned Businesses—Black*, pp. 14, 16, 18. *Notes:* - Represents zero. D = Withheld to avoid disclosing figures for individual companies.

★ 335 ★

Business Owners and Operators

Merchants of Americus, Georgia, 1899

KINDS OF BUSINESS	YEARS IN BUSINESS	CAPITAL INVESTED
Grocery and Farming	14 years	$1,500
Grocery and Restaurant	10 "	1,200
Grocery	9 "	1,500
Druggist	5 "	1,000
Grocery	2 "	225
Grocery	6 "	300
Furniture	7 "	3,000

[Continued]

★ 335 ★

Merchants of Americus, Georgia, 1899
[Continued]

KINDS OF BUSINESS	YEARS IN BUSINESS	CAPITAL INVESTED
Grocery	4 "	300
Grocery	10 "	270
Grocery	8 "	300
Grocery	8 "	375
Grocery	5 "	300
Grocery	12 "	1,000
Restaurant and Barber-shop	9 "	500
Market	7 "	1,000
Wood Yard	22 "	1,000
Grocery	9 "	500
Cigars and Tobacco	4 "	500

Source: "Negro Merchants of Americus, Ga." W.E.B. DuBois, ed., *The Negro in Business,* p. 35.

★ 336 ★

Business Owners and Operators

Merchants of Athens, Georgia, 1899

BUSINESS	YEARS IN BUSINESS	CAPITAL	LARGEST DAILY INCOME	AVERAGE DAILY AM'NT
Grocery	2	$300	$70.50	$25
Grocery	4	650	350.00	35
Grocery	8	150	12.00	6
Barber	25	500	85.00	7
Livery-stable	3	360	15.00	6
Barber	4	350	63.35	10

Source: "Negro Merchants of Athens, Ga.," W.E.B. DuBois, ed., *The Negro in Business,* p. 39.

★ 337 ★

Business Owners and Operators

Merchants of Charleston, South Carolina, 1899

KINDS OF BUSINESS	YEARS IN BUSINESS	CAPITAL INVESTED
Steam Dye Works	7 years	$1,500
Undertakers	21 "	5,000
Undertakers	16 "	2,000
Undertakers	3 "	300

[Continued]

★ 337 ★

Merchants of Charleston, South Carolina, 1899
[Continued]

KINDS OF BUSINESS	YEARS IN BUSINESS	CAPITAL INVESTED
Undertakers	3 "	700
Undertakers	1 "	400
Undertakers	6 mos.	500
Groceries and Provisions	2 years	800
Groceries and Provisions	- "	400
Groceries and Provisions	1 "	1,000
Groceries and Provisions	- "	600
Groceries and Provisions	5 "	700
Fish, Oysters and Game	30 "	30,000
Livery Stables	- "	20,000
Livery Stables	- "	5,000
Livery Stables	- "	2,000
Wagon Maker and Wheelwright	15 "	5,000
Wagon Maker and Wheelwright	2 "	500
Printing Office	8 "	-
Printing Office	8 "	-
Job Office	- "	-
Drug-store	5 "	3,000
Shoe-store	1 "	1,000
Fan Maker	30 "	-
Tailor-shop	20 "	500
Upholsterer	- "	-
Barber	12 "	600
Barber	5 "	600
Contractors	- "	-
Stair Builder	30 "	-
Contractor	- "	-
Contractor	25 "	-
Green Grocer	10 "	2,500
Photographer	12 "	-
Green Grocers	30 "	2,000
Green Grocers	25 "	3,000
Green Grocers	25 "	1,500
Stone Cutter	15 "	1,000
Contractor	- "	-
Tailor	6 "	300
Truck-Farm	30 "	100,000
Tailor-shop	25 "	400
Barber	25 "	700
Green Grocer	4 "	500
Tailor	- "	-
Green Grocer	- "	500
Fruit and Vegetables	11"	2,000
Fruit and Vegetables	10 "	2,000
Fruit and Vegetables	-	500
Shoes	1 "	500

[Continued]

★ 337 ★

Merchants of Charleston, South Carolina, 1899
[Continued]

KINDS OF BUSINESS	YEARS IN BUSINESS	CAPITAL INVESTED
Undertaker	-	300
Tinner	-	-
Paint Store	10 "	1,000
Barber	-	1,000
Barber	-	500
Barber	-	700
Tailor-shop	8 "	500

Source: "Negro Merchants of Charleston, S.C." W.E.B. DuBois, ed., *The Negro in Business*, p. 34-35.
Notes: No other city has so many black businessmen as the metropolis of the state of South Carolina. This table is a partial list of the more successful ones.

★ 338 ★

Business Owners and Operators

Merchants of Cleveland, Ohio, 1899

KINDS OF BUSINESS	YEARS IN BUSINESS	CAPITAL INVESTED	MEN EMPLOYED
Barber Shop	11"	$10,000	18 men.
Barber Shop	20 "	5,000	20"
Barber Shop	10"	$6,000	12 men.
Hair Workers, Wigs, etc.	10 "	2,000	5"
Grocers	1 "	600	5"
Baker and Grocer	30 "	1,500	3"
Druggist	2 "	300	2"
Groceries	2 "	800	4"
Builder and Contractor	12 "	3,000	15"
Plasterer	7 "	500	4"
Merchant Tailor	45 "	3,000	5"
Blacksmith and Wagon Builder	10 "	1,5000	5"

Source: "Negro Merchants of Cleveland, Ohio." W.E.B. DuBois, ed., *The Negro in Business*, p. 37-38.

★ 339 ★

Business Owners and Operators

Merchants of Griffin, Georgia, 1899

KINDS OF BUSINESS	YEARS IN BUSINESS	CAPITAL INVESTED
Grocer	12 "	$500
Barber	18 "	600
Liveryman	20 "	7,000
Drayman	16 "	800
Grocer and Baker	10 "	600
Grocers and Undertakers	2 "	400

Source: "Negro Merchants of Griffin Ga." W.E.B. DuBois, ed., *The Negro in Business*, p. 31.

★ 340 ★

Business Owners and Operators

Merchants of Guthrie, Oklahoma, 1899

KINDS OF BUSINESS	YEARS IN BUSINESS	CAPITAL INVESTED
Grocery	8	$3,000
Grocery	7	1,000
Grocery	3	800
Grocery	5	700
Newspaper	6	500
Newspaper	8	800
Barber	4	500

Source: "Negro Merchants of Guthrie, Oklahoma." W.E.B. DuBois, ed., *The Negro in Business*, p. 32.

★ 341 ★

Business Owners and Operators

Merchants of Houston, Texas, 1899

KINDS OF BUSINESS	YEARS IN BUSINESS	CAPITAL INVESTED
Grocery	4	$1,500
Grocery	3	1,000
Grocery	5	2,000
Grocery		1,000
Real Estate Dealer	15	10,000

[Continued]

★ 341 ★

Merchants of Houston, Texas, 1899

[Continued]

KINDS OF BUSINESS	YEARS IN BUSINESS	CAPITAL INVESTED
Real Estate Dealer	18	50,000
Contractor	12	10,000
Contractor	12	8,000
Barber	20	1,000
Barber	18	1,200
Barber	16	1,000
Saloon	14	4,000
Hair Dressing	20	1,000
Real Estate Broker	3	6,000
Real Estate Broker	20	40,000
Real Estate Broker	30	75,000
Grocer	5	350
Grocer	15	1,200
Contractor, Builder	6	7,000
Grocer	3	200
Contractor, Builder	30	5,000
Grocer	10	3,000
Grocer and Real Estate Broker	10	15,000

Source: "Negro Merchants of Houston, Texas." W.E.B. DuBois, ed., *The Negro in Business*, p. 29.

★ 342 ★

Business Owners and Operators

Merchants of Jacksonville, Florida, 1899

KINDS OF BUSINESS	YEARS IN BUSINESS	CAPITAL INVESTED
Dry Goods and Millinery	7"	$5,000
Groceries	2 "	1,000
Millinery	3 "	700
Tinware	6 "	1,000
Cement-Work	5 "	-
Curios, Jewelry Store, etc.	2 "	3,000
Commission Merchants	9 "	3,000
Shoe Store	5 "	7,000
Lumber Mill	5 "	-
Newspaper and Jobbing	3 "	5,000
Drug Store	4 "	1,000
Contractor and Builder	15 "	6,000

Source: "Negro Merchants of Jacksonville, Fla.," W.E.B. DuBois, ed., *The Negro in Business*, p. 93.

★ 343 ★

Business Owners and Operators

Merchants of Kansas City, Kansas, 1899

KINDS OF BUSINESS	YEARS IN BUSINESS	CAPITAL INVESTED
Coal, Wood, Flour, Feed, etc.	9	$500
Drug Store	3	1,500
Grocery	2	300
Builders and Owners of a Hall	9	2,500
Bridge Contractor	10	1,000
Grocery	2	
Newspaper	10	500
New and Second-band Furniture and Stoves	3	1,200
Dry-goods and Groceries	10	1,500
Meat Market	2	250
Confectioner	1	100
Dairyman	3	1,000
Confectioner	9	500
Restaurant and Hotel	3	1,000
Restaurant and Hotel	1	1,000
Barber	8	500
Jeweler	10	2,000

Source: "Negro Merchants of Kansas City, Kan." W.E.B. DuBois, ed., *The Negro in Business*, p. 30-31.

★ 344 ★

Business Owners and Operators

Merchants of Lexington, Kentucky, 1899

KINDS OF BUSINESS	YEARS IN BUSINESS	CAPITAL INVESTED
Drug Store	5 "	$2,000
Barber	20 "	1,000
Tinner	16 "	2,000
Brick Contractor	20 "	10,000
New and Second-hand Furniture	16 "	1,500
Stock Company	27 "	5,000
Undertakers, Livery Stable	6 "	5,000
Undertakers	2 "	1,500
Barber	25 "	700
Dressmaker and Milliners	2 "	500
Barbers	18 "	500

Source: "Negro Merchants of Lexington, Ky." W.E.B. DuBois, ed, *The Negro in Business*, p. 31.

★ 345 ★

Business Owners and Operators

Merchants of Mobile, Alabama, 1899

KINDS OF BUSINESS	YEARS IN BUSINESS	CAPITAL INVESTED
Hardware, Crockery, Glassware, etc.	32 years	$25,000
Funeral Director and Livery Stable Keeper	5 "	3,000
Grocer	30 "	2,500
Wholesale and Retail Candy Manufacturer	9 "	2,200
Grocer	20 "	1,500
Undertaker	5 "	5,000
Printing Establishment	5 "	1,000
Coal and Wood	4 "	1,600
Wood and Coal	6 "	2,000
Restaurant	18 "	2,500
Restaurant	6 "	1,200
Barber	22 "	2,000

Source: "Negro Merchants of Mobile, Alabama," W.E.B. DuBois, ed., *The Negro in Business*, p. 33.

★ 346 ★

Business Owners and Operators

Merchants of Montgomery, Alabama, 1899

KINDS OF BUSINESS	YEARS IN BUSINESS	CAPITAL INVESTED
Hacks and Undertakers, Coal & Wood, etc.	-years	$-
Dry Goods	9 "	8,000
Groceries	12 "	4,000
Groceries	11 "	-
Groceries	5 "	3,000
Drug Store	10 "	5,000
Drug Store	4 "	3,000
Undertaker	-	2,000
Undertakers	-	-
Manufacturers of Boots and Shoes	18 "	500
Harness Maker	15 "	700

Source: "Negro Merchants of Montgomery, Ala." W.E.B. DuBois, ed., *The Negro in Business*, p. 35-36.

★ 347 ★

Business Owners and Operators

Merchants of Mound Bayou, Mississippi, 1899

KINDS OF BUSINESS	YEARS IN BUSINESS	CAPITAL INVESTED	ASSESSED REAL ESTATE
General Merchandise	10	$5,000	$3,000
Merchandise and Ginning	8	1,000	2,000
General Merchandise	2	300	500
General Merchandise	8	150	800
General Merchandise	3	750	...
Merchandise and Blacksmith	7	150	800
Merchandise and Saw Mill	10	1,000	10,000

Source: "Negro Merchants of Mound Bayou, Miss." W.E.B. DuBois, ed, *The Negro in Business*, p. 32. *Note:* The all-black town also has a black government.

★ 348 ★

Business Owners and Operators

Merchants of New Bedford, Massachusetts, 1899

KINDS OF BUSINESS	YEARS IN BUSINESS	CAPITAL INVESTED
Merchant Tailor	14	$1,000
Drugstore	17	4,000
Portrait Photographer	10	3,000
Expressman	-	-
Expressman	-	-
Baker, bread, pies, cake, etc.	4	1,000
Shoe dealer	2	1,500
Druggists	3	3,000
Hair store	35	
Hair store	20	-

Source: "Negro Merchants of New Bedford, Mass." W.E.B. DuBois, ed., *The Negro in Business*, p. 39.

★ 349 ★

Business Owners and Operators

Merchants of Norfolk, Virginia, 1899

KINDS OF BUSINESS	YEARS IN BUSINESS	CAPITAL INVESTED
Undertaker	18"	$5,000
Undertaker	9 "	2,500
Coal and Wood	5 "	3,000
Grocer	15 "	2,500
Groceries	1 "	1,000
Florist	6 "	1,500
Groceries	6 mos.	1,000
Publishers	6 years	2,000
Restaurant	28 "	3,000
Bakery	10 "	2,000
Undertaker	4 "	1,500
Undertaker	25 "	1,500

Source: "Negro Merchants of Norfolk, Va." W.E.B. DuBois, ed., *The Negro in Business*, p. 38.

★ 350 ★

Business Owners and Operators

Merchants of Petersburg, Virginia: 1899

KINDS OF BUSINESS	YEARS IN BUSINESS	CAPITAL INVESTED
Grocery	34 years	$300
Boots, Shoes and Books	6 mos.	1,250
Grocery	12 years	500
Grocery	13 "	500
Grocery	28 "	50
Grocery	7 "	200
Druggist	12 "	500
Confectioneries	10 "	200
Grocery	8 "	150
Grocery	20 "	250
Butcher	10 "	1,000
Butchers	10 "	750
Grocery	10 mos.	100
Grocery	6 years	75
Grocery	15 "	150
Grocery	4 "	200
Grocery	1 mo.	50
Grocery	30 years	100

Source: "Negro Merchants of Petersburg, Va." W.E.B. DuBois, ed., *The Negro in Business*, p. 32.
Notes: No account has been made for hucksters, fish-dealers, and other small tradespeople.

★ 351 ★

Business Owners and Operators

Merchants of Portsmouth, Virginia, 1899

KINDS OF BUSINESS	YEARS IN BUSINESS	CAPITAL INVESTED
Huckster	42"	$400
Barber	35 "	1,500
Grocer	20 "	2,300
Wood-dealers & Contractors for Sand & Shells	16 "	1,500
Loaning Money on Real Estate, etc.	16 "	11,000
Huckster	15 "	300
Undertaker and Embalmer	12 "	6,500
Grocer	8 "	1,000
Liquors and Tobacco	7 "	3,600
Grocer	5 "	2,400
Druggist	3 "	2,000
Oyster Planter	40 "	1,500

Source: "Negro Merchants of Portsmouth, Va." W.E.B. DuBois, ed., *The Negro in Business*, p. 38.

★ 352 ★

Business Owners and Operators

Merchants of San Francisco, California, 1899

KINDS OF BUSINESS	YEARS IN BUSINESS	CAPITAL INVESTED
Hairdressing, Toilet Articles, etc.	22"	$8,000
Expressing	3 "	2,000
Electrician	3 "	500
Weekly Newspaper	5"	3,000
Barber	2 "	500
Expressman	15 "	2,000
Expressmen	15 "	3,000
"Nabob" Restaurant	5 "	5,000
Stove Store	30 "	2,000
Barber Shop	17 "	3,000
Barber Shop	4 "	2,500
Restaurant	4 "	4,000
Groceries and Fruit	2 "	1,500
Cleaning Suits	3 "	500
Newspaper and Printing	5 "	1,000
Newspaper and Printing	13 "	800
Fancy Goods, Embroidery	1 "	500
Real Estate	25 "	100,000

Source: "Negro Merchants of San Francisco, Cal." W.E.B. DuBois, ed., *The Negro in Business*, pp. 83-84.

★ 353 ★

Business Owners and Operators

Merchants of Tallahassee, Florida, 1899

KINDS OF BUSINESS	YEARS IN BUSINESS	CAPITAL INVESTED	SALES PER YEAR
Groceries and Dry Goods	-years	$1,500	$6,000
Meat Market	-	1,000	4,680
Meat Market	-	250	832
Groceries	-	400	1,500
General Merchandise	-	150	
General Merchandise	-	150	

Source: "Negro Merchants of Tallahassee, Fla.," W.E.B. DuBois, ed., *The Negro in Business*, p. 33.

★ 354 ★

Business Owners and Operators

Merchants of Washington, D.C., 1899

KINDS OF BUSINESS	YEARS IN BUSINESS	CAPITAL INVESTED
Ice Cream Manufacturer and Restaurant	5"	$700
Undertaker	15 "	10,000
Groceries and Provisions	10 "	15,000
Jeweler and Watchmaker	9 "	800
Newspaper Publisher	18 "	700
Job Printer	6 "	500
Undertaker		
Druggist	8 "	1,000
Druggist	5 "	1,500
Restaurant	8 "	500
Grain and Feed	25 "	2,000
Pork Business	7 "	3,000
Vegetable Business	25 "	5,000
Grocer	4 "	1,000
Green-grocer	4 "	700
Fish-dealer		15,000
Grocery	12 "	5,000
Tinner and Hardware work	3 "	5,000
Coal	15 "	8,000
Caterer and Confectioner	22 "	5,000
Grocery	13 "	300
Grocery	5 "	500
Wood, Coal and Fertilizers	12 "	10,000
Undertaker	20 "	10,000
Undertaker	6 "	5,000
Restaurant	1 "	3,000

[Continued]

★ 354 ★

Merchants of Washington, D.C., 1899
[Continued]

KINDS OF BUSINESS	YEARS IN BUSINESS	CAPITAL INVESTED
Sign Writer	15 "	5,000
Barber	15 "	500
Barber	15 "	500
Grocery	6 "	800
Grocery	7 "	500
Confectioners, Caterers, Bakers, etc.	1 "	3,000
Old Books, Documents Magazines, etc.	7 "	1,000
Photographer and Artist	12 "	1,200
Bakery	6 "	800
Saloon and Restaurant	1/2 "	5,000
Saloon and Restaurant	4 "	5,000
Newspaper	6 "	3,500
Saloon, Cafe and Hotel.	1/2 "	6,000
Hotel	2 "	1,000
Book and Job Printer	13 "	1,200
Druggist	5 "	1,500
Dying and Cleaning	30 "	700

Source: "Negro Merchants of Washington, D.C." W.E.B. DuBois, ed., *The Negro in Business*, pp. 28-29.

★ 355 ★

Business Owners and Operators

Merchants of Williamsburg, Virginia, 1899

KINDS OF BUSINESS	YEARS IN BUSINESS	CAPITAL INVESTED
General Merchant	26	40,000
General Merchant	2	3,000
General Merchant	6	2,000
General Merchant	5	1,500
Restaurant	12	1,200
Barber	12	300

Source: "Negro Merchants of Williamsburg, Va.," W.E.B. DuBois, ed., *The Negro in Business*, p. 40.

★ 356 ★

Business Owners and Operators

Merchants of Wilmington, North Carolina, 1899

KINDS OF BUSINESS	YEARS IN BUSINESS	CAPITAL INVESTED
Grocer	15 years	$2,000
Grocer	- "	1,800
Grocer	- "	800
Grocer	- "	2,000
Grocer	- "	1,200
Druggist	- "	1,900
Druggist	15 "	1,000
Contractor and Pain-dealer	- "	2,500
Undertaker	- "	2,800
Undertaker	- "	2,000
Undertaker	- "	1,500
Broker	- "	3,000
Merchant Tailor	- "	1,200
Merchant Tailor	- "	1,500
Grocer	- "	1,600
Grocer	3 "	2,000
Building and Loan Association	8 "	20,000
Building and Loan Association	7 "	11,000
Wood Yard	- "	2,000
Wood Yard	- "	2,500

Source: "Negro Merchants of Wilmington, N.C." W.E.B. DuBois, ed., *The Negro in Business*, p. 33.
Notes: In addition, blacks held $500,000 in real and personal property, owned fifteen churches, five of which were worth $90,000; two public halls worth $20,000, and had four physicians and four lawyers.

★ 357 ★

Business Owners and Operators

Minority-Owned Business by Industry, 1972

Number and employment in thousands and receipts in billions of dollars, except as indicated. Based on a mail canvass, various published and unpublished source listings, and personal contacts with knowledgeable community and governmental representatives, and records of the Internal Revenue Service and the Social Security Administration. "Minority" identified to include the following groups: Black, Chinese, Japanese, Puerto Rican, Mexican or Latin American, American Indian, Filipino, Korean, Hawaiian, etc.

Industry	All U.S. firms[1]	Firms owned by--					Percent change from 1969			
		All minorities		Black	Spanish origin	Other	All minorities	Black	Spanish origin	Other
		Total	Percent of all firms							
Number of firms, total	8,730	382	4.4	195	120	67	19	20	20	14
With paid employees	(X)	76	(X)	32	29	15	-16	-17	-12	-22
With no paid employees	(X)	306	(X)	163	91	52	32	31	36	31
Construction	1,020	40	3.9	20	17	3	34	24	67	-11
Manufacturing	437	9	2.1	4	4	1	18	38	-	19

[Continued]

★ 357 ★

Minority-Owned Business by Industry, 1972
[Continued]

| Industry | All U.S. firms[1] | Firms owned by-- | | | | | Percent change from 1969 | | | |
| | | All minorities | | Black | Spanish origin | Other | All minorities | Black | Spanish origin | Other |
		Total	Percent of all firms							
Transport, and public util.[2]	432	30	6.9	22	6	2	28	30	29	3
Wholesale trade	560	7	1.3	2	3	2	31	26	41	20
Retail trade	2,381	121	5.1	57	42	22	25	25	26	22
Finance, ins., real estate	1,318	19	1.4	8	6	5	-15	5	-22	-31
Selected services	2,212	120	5.4	68	32	20	19	22	11	21
Other industries[3]	370	36	9.7	14	10	12	-	-28	6	24
Business receipts, total	2,381.2	16.6	0.7	7.2	5.3	4.1	56	60	58	46
Firms with –										
Paid employees	(X)	12.1	(X)	5.1	3.7	3.3	35	31	32	32
No paid employees	(X)	4.5	(X)	2.1	1.6	.8	163	152	193	143
Construction	146.2	1.7	1.2	.8	.6	.3	84	77	125	38
Manufacturing	875.3	1.3	0.1	.5	.5	.3	95	77	126	88
Transport, and public util.[2]	159.5	.7	0.4	.4	.2	.1	79	102	50	56
Wholesale trade	349.4	1.8	0.5	.8	.5	.5	91	98	91	82
Retail trade	474.9	7.5	1.6	2.9	2.5	2.1	44	51	43	37
Finance, ins., real estate	252.8	.9	0.4	.5	.2	.2	59	59	64	54
Selected services	95.5	2.1	2.2	1.1	.6	.4	47	59	30	49
Other industries[3]	27.6	.6	2.2	.2	.2	.2	5	-18	29	17
Employment, total	56,466	456	0.8	197	150	109	23	29	18	20
Construction	3,398	57	1.7	30	21	6	63	66	78	23
Manufacturing	18,696	54	0.3	20	21	13	73	66	80	76
Transport, and public util.[2]	3,895	19	0.5	11	5	3	40	42	42	28
Wholesale trade	4,075	19	0.5	8	6	5	44	37	39	63
Retail trade	11,648	173	1.5	58	59	56	3	6	-4	10
Finance, ins., real estate	3,901	28	0.7	18	4	6	91	99	74	85
Selected services	9,576	98	1.0	49	31	18	21	29	15	12
Other industries[3]	1,277	8	0.6	3	3	2	-40	-55	-31	-24

Source: "Minority-Owned Business Firms—Number and Receipts, by Industry: 1972," *Statistical Abstract of the United States,* 1975, p. 493. Primary source: U.S. Bureau of the Census, *Minority-Owned Businesses: 1972. Notes:* - Represents zero. X Not applicable. 1. Based on data from U.S. Internal Revenue Service, Preliminary Report, *Statistics of Income, Business Income Tax Returns, 1972,* for number of firms and receipts; and from Bureau of the Census, *County Business Patterns, 1972,* for employment. 2. Excludes railroads. 3. Includes firms not allocable to specific industries.

★ 358 ★

Business Owners and Operators

Minority-Owned Businesses: Characteristics, 1968

Based on interviews conducted during the summer of 1968 with a sample of businesses filing business tax returns with Internal Revenue Service in 1966. "Minority" identified to include the following groups: Negro, Chinese, Japanese, Puerto Rican, and Mexican or Latin American. "Share of business" refers to percent of all businesses operated by specified group.

| Characteristic | Percent share of business | | | | Percent distribution by characteristic | | | |
| | Minority groups | | | Nonminority | Minority groups | | | Nonminority |
	All	Negro	Other		All	Negro	Other	
All locations	3.8	2.3	1.5	96.2	100.0	100.0	100.0	100.0
Ghetto	27.9	18.3	9.6	72.1	31.2	33.3	27.7	3.2
Central city, nonghetto	4.7	2.7	2.0	95.3	37.6	35.1	41.7	30.4
Suburbs	1.1	0.7	0.4	98.9	3.2	3.5	2.8	11.9
Urban, 2,500-50,000 population	2.0	1.4	0.6	98.0	17.2	19.3	13.9	33.6
Under 2,500 population and rural	2.0	1.0	1.0	98.0	10.8	8.8	13.9	20.9
All industries	3.7	2.3	1.4	96.3	100.0	100.0	100.0	100.0
Personal services	12.3	8.4	3.9	87.7	26.8	29.9	22.2	7.3
Other services	2.8	1.4	1.4	97.4	15.1	12.3	19.4	20.3
Construction	4.3	2.6	1.7	95.7	10.8	10.4	11.1	9.0
Manufacturing	1.2	1.2	-	98.8	2.2	3.5	-	6.9
Retail trade	3.6	1.9	1.7	96.4	34.4	29.9	41.7	34.9
Other	1.8	1.5	0.4	98.2	10.8	14.0	5.6	21.6
Owned facility	3.4	2.2	1.3	96.6	50.0	52.0	47.0	54.0
Leased facility	4.0	2.3	1.6	96.0	50.0	48.0	53.0	46.0

Source: "Minority- and Nonminority-Operated Businesses—Specific Characteristics: 1968," *Statistical Abstract of the United States*, 1971, p. 462. Primary source: U.S. Senate, Select Committee on Small Business: *Review of Small Business Administration's Programs and Policies—1969*. (91st Congress, 1st Session). *Note:* - Represents zero.

★ 359 ★

Business Owners and Operators

Miscellaneous Industries: 1972

| Industry | SIC codes | 1972 | | | | | | | | | |
| | | All firms | | With paid employees | | | | | Without paid employees | | |
		Firms (number)	Gross receipts ($1,000)	Firms (number)	Employees (number)	Gross receipts ($1,000)	Average employees per firm (number)	Average receipts per firm ($1,000)	Firms (number)	Gross receipts ($1,000)	Average receipts per firm ($1,000)
OTHER INDUSTRIES, TOTAL		4,283	88,782	428	2,282	44,752	5	105	3,855	44,030	11
Agricultural services	07	2,688	50,241	318	1,618	24,976	5	79	2,370	25,265	11
Soil preparation services	071	77	8,176	18	(D)	(D)	(D)	(D)	59	(D)	(D)
Crop services	072	118	8,335	38	362	7,505	4	85	30	830	28
Animal services, except veterinary	075	184	1,264	2	(D)	(D)	(D)	(D)	182	(D)	(D)
Landscape and horticultural services	078	2,162	29,560	205	931	12,054	5	59	1,957	17,506	9
Agricultural services, n.s.k.	07-	147	2,906	5	70	534	14	107	142	2,372	17
Forestry	08	822	13,275	17	60	1,868	4	110	805	11,407	14
Fishing, hunting, and trapping	09	544	6,263	35	118	1,907	3	54	509	4,356	9

[Continued]

★ 359 ★

Miscellaneous Industries: 1972
[Continued]

Industry	SIC codes	All firms		With paid employees					Without paid employees		
		Firms (number)	Gross receipts ($1,000)	Firms (number)	Employees (number)	Gross receipts ($1,000)	Average employees per firm (number)	Average receipts per firm ($1,000)	Firms (number)	Gross receipts ($1,000)	Average receipts per firm ($1,000)
Other industries	-	229	19,003	58	486	16,001	8	276	171	3,002	18
Industries not classified		9,520	97,487	179	579	16,430	3	92	9,341	81,057	9

Source: "Selected Statistics for Industry for Black-Owned Firms: 1972 and 1969," U.S. Bureau of the Census, 1972 Survey of Minority Business Enterprises, *Minority Owned Businesses—Black*, p. 26. *Note:* D = Withheld to avoid disclosing figures for individual companies.

★ 360 ★

Business Owners and Operators

Moving Picture Theaters by State, 1943

State	Towns	Total theaters	Negro theaters
Alabama	179	229	18
Arizona	64	99	-
Arkansas	192	299	6
California	413	1,179	8
Colorado	134	254	-
Connecticut	89	213	-
Delaware	20	36	1
District of Columbia	1	65	13
Florida	142	335	40
Georgia	186	353	20
Idaho	138	200	-
Illinois	474	1,123	21
Indiana	235	537	6
Iowa	512	703	-
Kansas	309	461	4
Kentucky	204	348	4
Louisiana	181	383	22
Maine	133	206	-
Maryland	94	245	17
Massachusetts	185	454	-
Michigan	297	728	7
Minnesota	349	446	-
Mississippi	131	242	18
Missouri	387	701	14
Montana	141	198	-
Nebraska	267	384	1
Nevada	31	47	-
New Hampshire	70	111	-
New Jersey	194	542	9
New Mexico	65	113	-

[Continued]

★ 360 ★

Moving Picture Theaters by State, 1943
[Continued]

State	Towns	Total theaters	Negro theaters
New York	464	1,433	39
North Carolina	232	452	20
North Dakota	171	200	-
Ohio	360	1,015	17
Oklahoma	229	492	6
Oregon	138	253	-
Pennsylvania	561	1,313	19
Rhode Island	29	65	-
South Carolina	120	200	9
South Dakota	162	205	-
Tennessee	138	292	17
Texas	564	1,322	30
Utah	127	200	-
Vermont	45	68	-
Virginia	183	246	20
Washington	173	333	-
West Virginia	219	345	4
Wisconsin	259	474	-
Wyoming	49	65	-

Source: "Moving Picture Theaters in the United States, with Number of Negro Theaters, by States: 1943," *Negro Handbook*, 1944, p. 260. Primary source: Film Daily Year Book of Motion Pictures.

★ 361 ★

Business Owners and Operators

Net Sales of Selected Types of Businesses Compared, by Cities of 50,000 or More Black Inhabitants: 1929

CITY	Net sales in order of size	Percent of total	CITY	Net sales in order of size	Percent of total
RESTAURANTS AND EATING PLACES			DRUG STORES		
Total	$7,371,584	100.0	Total	$2,789,586	100.00
New York, N.Y.	1,003,713	13.62	Chicago, Ill.	632,063	22.66
Chicago, Ill.	989,569	13.42	Detroit, Mich.	392,044	14.05
Detroit, Mich.	813,454	11.03	St. Louis, Mo.	270,885	9.71
Philadelphia, Pa.	678,769	9.21	Washington, D.C.	238,281	8.54
New Orleans, La.	551,713	7.48	Philadelphia, Pa.	220,407	7.90
Memphis, Tenn.	495,847	6.73	New York, N.Y.	212,805	7.63
Washington, D.C.	481,812	6.54	Memphis, Tenn.	152,724	5.48
Atlanta, Ga.	467,974	6.35	New Orleans, La.	147,804	5.30
Houston, Tex.	466,624	6.33	Houston, Tex.	106,336	3.81
St. Louis, Mo.	432,391	5.86	Pittsburgh, Pa.	99,645	3.57
Cleveland, Ohio	343,383	4.66	Baltimore, Md.	87,537	3.14
Baltimore, Md.	216,387	2.94	Atlanta, Ga.	80,670	2.89
Pittsburgh, Pa.	191,843	2.60	Richmond, Va.	68,375	2.45
Birmingham, Ala.	172,563	2.34	Birmingham, Ala.	58,680	2.10
Richmond, Va.	65,542	.89	Cleveland, Ohio	21,430	.77

[Continued]

★ 361 ★

Net Sales of Selected Types of Businesses Compared, by Cities of 50,000 or More Black Inhabitants: 1929

[Continued]

CITY	Net sales in order of size	Percent of total	CITY	Net sales in order of size	Percent of total
COMBINATION STORES (GROCERIES AND MEATS)			GROCERY STORES (WITHOUT MEATS)		
Total	$2,929,856	100.0	Total	$2,682	100.0
Detroit, Mich.	626,242	21.37	New York, N.Y.	534,598	19.93
Chicago, Ill.	498,924	17.03	Chicago, Ill.	430,434	16.05
Memphis, Tenn.	419,481	14.32	New Orleans, La.	377,493	14.07
Atlanta, Ga.	266,064	9.08	Philadelphia, Pa.	279,520	10.42
St. Louis, Mo.	248,470	8.48	Detroit, Mich.	214,607	8.00
Houston, Tex.	147,961	5.05	Cleveland, Ohio	171,163	6.38
Richmond, Va.	142,431	4.86	Memphis, Tenn.	161,537	6.02
Cleveland, Ohio	138,286	4.72	Atlanta, Ga.	119,801	4.47
Washington, D.C.	84,035	2.87	Houston, Tex.	90,533	3.38
Philadelphia, Pa.	80,400	2.75	Birmingham, Ala.	60,009	2.24
Birmingham, Ala.	75,440	2.57	St. Louis, Mo.	54,140	2.02
Baltimore, Md.	74,900	2.56	Baltimore, Md.	53,410	1.99
New Orleans, La.	66,100	2.26	Pittsburgh, Pa.	48,400	1.80
New York, N.Y.	32,880	1.12	Washington, D.C.	46,511	1.73
Pittsburgh, Pa.	28,182	.96	Richmond, Va.	40,342	1.50

Source: "Net Sales of Selected Kind of Business Compared, by Cities of 50,000 or more Negro Inhabitants: 1929." U.S. Bureau of the Census. *Negroes in the United States: 1920-32.* Washington, D.C.: Government Printing Office, 1935, pp. 518.

★ 362 ★

Business Owners and Operators

Net Sales of Stores With Black Proprietors, Geographical Areas, 1929

Section and division	Number of stores	Net sales	
		Amount	Average per store
United States	25,701	$101,146,043	$3,935
The South	18,864	57,036,307	3,024
South Atlantic	9,622	27,347,636	2,842
East South Central	4,359	13,248,290	3,039
West South Central	4,883	16,440,381	3,367
The North	6,475	40,335,397	6,229
New England	232	1,929,224	8,316
Middle Atlantic	2,514	14,883,293	5,920
East North Central	2,728	17,191,719	6,302
West North Central	1,001	6,331,161	6,325
The West	362	3,774,339	10,426

[Continued]

★ 362 ★

Net Sales of Stores With Black Proprietors, Geographical Areas, 1929

[Continued]

Section and division	Number of stores	Net sales	
		Amount	Average per store
Mountain	68	557,044	8,192
Pacific	294	3,217,295	10,943

Source: "Net Sales of Stores Operated by Negro Proprietors, for the United States, by Sections, and Divisions: 1929." U.S. Bureau of the Census. *Negroes in the United States: 1920-32.* Washington, D.C.: Government Printing Office, 1935, p. 498.

★ 363 ★

Business Owners and Operators

Owners by Geographic Division, State, and Industry: 1972. Part I. New England

Industry	All firms		With paid employees					Without paid employees		
	Firms (number)	Gross receipts ($1,000)	Firms (number)	Employees (number)	Gross receipts ($1,000)	Average employees per firm (number)	Average receipts per firm ($1,000)	Firms (number)	Gross receipts ($1,000)	Average receipts per firm ($1,000)
United States	194,986	7,168,491	31,893	196,596	5,101,280	6	160	163,093	2,067,211	13
New England	3,512	125,630	622	3,890	87,600	6	141	2,890	38,030	13
Maine	58	2,466	11	89	1,988	8	181	46	478	10
Construction	10	754	4	(D)	(D)	(D)	(D)	6	(D)	(D)
Manufacturing	3	(D)	1	(D)	(D)	(D)	(D)	2	(D)	(D)
Transportation and public utilities	2	(D)	-	-	-	-	-	2	(D)	(D)
Wholesale trade	-	-	-	-	-	-	-	-	-	-
Retail trade	15	545	2	(D)	(D)	(D)	(D)	13	(D)	(D)
Finance, insurance, and real estate	2	(D)	-	-	-	-	-	2	(D)	(D)
Selected services	19	176	4	16	138	4	35	15	38	3
Other industries	3	20	-	-	-	-	-	3	20	7
Industries not classified	4	(D)	-	-	-	-	-	3	(D)	(D)
New Hampshire	49	2,356	8	34	1,704	4	213	41	652	16
Construction	4	44	1	(D)	(D)	(D)	(D)	3	(D)	(D)
Manufacturing	-	-	-	-	-	-	-	-	-	-
Transportation and public utilities	1	(D)	-	-	-	-	-	1	(D)	(D)
Wholesale trade	2	(D)	1	(D)	(D)	(D)	(D)	1	(D)	(D)
Retail trade	15	771	4	(D)	(D)	(D)	(D)	11	(D)	(D)
Finance, insurance, and real estate	-	-	-	-	-	-	-	-	-	-
Selected services	24	365	2	(D)	(D)	(D)	(D)	22	(D)	(D)
Other industries	-	-	-	-	-	-	-	-	-	-
Industries not classified	3	24	-	-	-	-	-	3	24	8
Vermont	31	722	7	46	529	7	76	24	193	8
Construction	4	22	1	(D)	(D)	(D)	(D)	3	(D)	(D)
Manufacturing	2	(D)	1	(D)	(D)	(D)	(D)	1	(D)	(D)
Transportation and public utilities	1	(D)	-	-	-	-	-	1	(D)	(D)
Wholesale trade	-	-	-	-	-	-	-	-	-	-
Retail trade	7	148	1	(D)	(D)	(D)	(D)	6	(D)	(D)
Finance, insurance, and real estate	-	-	-	-	-	-	-	-	-	-
Selected services	16	329	4	28	223	7	56	12	106	9

[Continued]

★ 363 ★

Owners by Geographic Division, State, and Industry: 1972. Part I. New England
[Continued]

Industry	1972									
	All firms		With paid employees					Without paid employees		
	Firms (number)	Gross receipts ($1,000)	Firms (number)	Employees (number)	Gross receipts ($1,000)	Average employees per firm (number)	Average receipts per firm ($1,000)	Firms (number)	Gross receipts ($1,000)	Average receipts per firm ($1,000)
Other industries	-	-	-	-	-	-	-	-	-	-
Industries not classified	1	(D)	-	-	-	-	-	1	(D)	(D)
Massachusetts	1,610	72,278	288	2,191	56,842	8	197	1,322	15,436	12
Construction	182	12,377	37	393	9,741	11	263	145	2,636	18
Manufacturing	46	6,036	21	373	5,755	18	274	25	281	11
Transportation and public utilities	92	2,774	12	77	1,537	6	128	80	1,237	15
Wholesale trade	15	7,046	6	64	6,890	11	1,148	9	156	17
Retail trade	370	25,937	96	571	20,234	6	211	274	5,703	21
Finance, insurance, and real estate	89	3,288	7	80	2,587	11	370	82	701	9
Selected services	711	13,050	105	590	8,979	6	86	606	4,071	7
Other industries	17	1,234	4	43	1,119	11	280	13	115	9
Industries not classified	87	536	-	-	-	-	-	87	536	6
Rhode Island	196	4,974	36	147	3,299	4	92	160	1,675	10
Construction	19	695	6	24	569	4	95	13	126	10
Manufacturing	5	272	4	(D)	(D)	(D)	(D)	1	(D)	(D)
Transportation and public utilities	30	1,056	2	(D)	(D)	(D)	(D)	28	(D)	(D)
Wholesale trade	-	-	-	-	-	-	-	-	-	-
Retail trade	56	2,072	15	37	1,321	2	88	41	751	18
Finance, insurance, and real estate	3	27	-	-	-	-	-	3	27	9
Selected services	76	752	8	27	260	3	33	68	492	7
Other industries	3	(D)	1	(D)	(D)	(D)	(D)	2	(D)	(D)
Industries not classified	4	(D)	-	-	-	-	-	4	(D)	(D)
Connecticut	1,568	42,834	272	1,383	23,238	5	85	1,296	19,596	15
Construction	171	4,306	25	95	2,298	4	92	146	2,008	14
Manufacturing	23	1,124	7	58	912	8	130	16	212	13
Transportation and public utilities	124	2,887	12	64	1,309	5	109	112	1,578	14
Wholesale trade	15	397	4	8	263	2	66	11	134	12
Retail trade	418	21,050	80	279	10,966	3	137	338	10,084	30
Finance, insurance, and real estate	83	1,179	6	21	560	4	93	77	619	8
Selected services	640	10,808	135	845	6,568	6	49	505	4,240	8
Other industries	36	628	2	(D)	(D)	(D)	(D)	34	(D)	(D)
Industries not classified	58	455	1	(D)	(D)	(D)	(D)	57	(D)	(D)

Source: "Selected Statistics by Geographic Division, State, and Industry Division, for Black-Owned Firms: 1972 and 1969," U.S. Bureau of the Census, 1972 Survey of Minority Business Enterprises, *Minority Owned Businesses—Black*, p. 30. *Notes:* - Represents zero. D = Withheld to avoid disclosing figures for individual companies.

★ 364 ★

Business Owners and Operators

Owners by Geographic Division, State, and Industry: 1972. Part II. Middle Atlantic

Industry	All firms		With paid employees					Without paid employees		
	Firms (number)	Gross receipts ($1,000)	Firms (number)	Employees (number)	Gross receipts ($1,000)	Average employees per firm (number)	Average receipts per firm ($1,000)	Firms (number)	Gross receipts ($1,000)	Average receipts per firm ($1,000)
Middle Atlantic	28,099	1,066,138	4,498	24,078	745,802	5	166	23,601	320,336	14
New York	14,377	466,363	2,103	11,015	326,958	5	155	12,274	139,405	11
Construction	1,060	41,894	171	1,378	30,881	8	181	889	11,013	12
Manufacturing	300	34,863	125	1,619	33,006	13	264	175	1,857	11
Transportation and public utilities	1,412	24,812	114	519	10,420	5	91	1,298	14,392	11
Wholesale trade	237	53,801	79	435	50,650	6	641	158	3,151	20
Retail trade	3,496	173,555	762	2,863	114,506	4	150	2,734	59,049	22
Finance, insurance, and real estate	806	25,087	107	827	19,826	8	185	699	5,261	8
Selected services	6,128	101,639	722	3,218	64,081	4	89	5,406	37,558	7
Other industries	134	2,312	11	111	845	10	77	123	1,467	12
Industries not classified	804	8,400	12	45	2,743	4	229	792	5,657	7
New Jersey	6,143	255,169	1,073	5,497	183,506	5	171	5,070	71,663	14
Construction	616	29,484	123	673	20,527	5	167	493	8,957	18
Manufacturing	88	17,007	50	616	16,357	12	327	38	650	17
Transportation and public utilities	1,033	31,321	113	539	17,409	5	154	920	13,912	15
Wholesale trade	85	33,295	35	254	32,112	7	917	50	1,183	24
Retail trade	1,392	91,349	344	1,536	65,872	4	191	1,048	25,477	24
Finance, insurance, and real estate	199	12,460	26	374	10,835	14	417	173	1,625	9
Selected services	2,243	35,101	371	1,475	19,806	4	53	1,872	15,295	8
Other industries	114	1,470	9	(D)	(D)	(D)	(D)	105	(D)	(D)
Industries not classified	373	3,682	2	(D)	(D)	(D)	(D)	371	(D)	(D)
Pennsylvania	7,579	344,606	1,322	7,566	235,338	6	178	6,257	109,268	17
Construction	677	32,508	127	681	18,172	5	143	550	14,336	26
Manufacturing	134	21,431	59	976	19,893	17	337	75	1,538	21
Transportation and public utilities	609	17,389	82	554	9,136	7	111	527	8,253	16
Wholesale trade	95	31,785	49	285	29,293	6	598	46	2,492	54
Retail trade	2,242	167,234	536	2,492	112,869	5	211	1,706	54,365	32
Finance, insurance, and real estate	248	20,105	63	470	18,073	7	287	185	2,032	11
Selected services	3,250	50,246	394	2,074	26,914	5	68	2,856	23,332	8
Other industries	64	1,196	6	19	469	3	78	58	727	13
Industries not classified	260	2,712	6	15	519	3	87	254	2,193	9

Source: "Selected Statistics by Geographic Division, State, and Industry Division, for Black-Owned Forms: 1972 and 1969," U.S. Bureau of the Census, 1972 Survey of Minority Business Enterprises, *Minority Owned Businesses—Black*, p. 32. *Notes:* - Represents zero. D = Withheld to avoid disclosing figures for individual companies.

★ 365 ★

Business Owners and Operators

Owners by Geographic Division, State, and Industry: 1972. Part III. East North Central

Industry	All firms		With paid employees					Without paid employees		
	Firms (number)	Gross receipts ($1,000)	Firms (number)	Employees (number)	Gross receipts ($1,000)	Average employees per firm (number)	Average receipts per firm ($1,000)	Firms (number)	Gross receipts ($1,000)	Average receipts per firm ($1,000)
East North Central	34,563	1,510,329	6,428	38,571	1,124,730	6	175	28,135	385,599	14
Ohio	10,524	332,793	1,721	8,918	230,411	5	134	8,803	102,382	12
Construction	1,069	44,419	197	1,285	32,130	7	163	872	12,289	14
Manufacturing	121	16,184	41	634	15,212	15	371	80	972	12
Transportation and public utilities	1,293	29,352	117	456	14,844	4	127	1,176	14,508	12
Wholesale trade	75	20,387	38	241	19,621	6	516	37	766	21
Retail trade	2,826	155,079	751	3,405	111,521	5	148	2,075	43,558	21
Finance, insurance, and real estate	651	13,706	59	292	9,087	5	154	592	4,619	8
Selected services	3,962	48,411	497	2,556	27,383	5	55	3,465	21,028	6
Other industries	111	1,462	7	17	353	2	50	104	1,109	11
Industries not classified	416	3,793	14	32	260	2	19	402	3,533	9
Indiana	3,281	120,978	618	3,771	87,884	6	142	2,663	33,094	12
Construction	337	13,232	74	541	9,612	7	130	263	3,620	14
Manufacturing	38	3,925	15	176	3,723	12	248	23	202	9
Transportation and public utilities	367	8,484	27	192	4,178	7	155	340	4,306	13
Wholesale trade	42	14,911	22	173	14,409	8	655	20	502	25
Retail trade	948	54,226	280	1,327	39,567	5	141	668	14,659	22
Finance, insurance, and real estate	132	2,282	18	71	1,204	4	67	114	1,078	9
Selected services	1,214	21,638	174	1,257	14,688	7	84	1,040	6,950	6
Other industries	33	1,028	5	(D)	(D)	(D)	(D)	28	(D)	(D)
Industries not classified	170	1,252	3	(D)	(D)	(D)	(D)	167	(D)	(D)
Illinois	11,458	609,423	2,217	14,860	470,980	7	212	9,241	138,443	15
Construction	672	41,794	142	1,171	33,007	8	232	530	8,787	17
Manufacturing	208	69,220	92	1,613	67,219	18	731	116	2,001	17
Transportation and public utilities	823	26,794	85	706	16,264	8	191	738	10,530	14
Wholesale trade	170	56,898	69	446	54,003	6	783	101	2,895	29
Retail trade	4,173	285,206	1,067	5,467	210,107	5	197	3,106	75,099	24
Finance, insurance, and real estate	588	40,455	112	1,640	35,659	15	318	476	4,796	10
Selected services	4,179	81,970	625	3,701	53,370	6	85	3,554	28,600	8
Other industries	77	1,987	7	64	733	9	105	70	1,254	18
Industries not classified	568	5,099	18	52	618	3	34	550	4,481	8
Michigan	7,964	401,511	1,650	9,945	306,607	6	186	6,314	94,904	15
Construction	589	30,955	113	815	22,658	7	201	476	8,297	17
Manufacturing	110	29,506	55	780	28,590	14	520	55	916	17
Transportation and public utilities	738	16,250	81	563	7,718	7	95	657	8,532	13
Wholesale trade	91	52,968	40	558	51,727	14	1,293	51	1,241	24
Retail trade	2,563	194,409	797	3,681	146,232	5	183	1,766	48,177	27
Finance, insurance, and real estate	489	17,064	67	581	12,627	9	188	422	4,437	11
Selected services	2,938	54,502	475	2,913	35,115	6	74	2,463	19,387	8
Other industries	129	2,507	12	28	1,350	2	113	117	1,157	10
Industries not classified	317	3,350	10	26	590	3	59	307	2,760	9
Wisconsin	1,336	45,624	222	1,077	28,848	5	130	1,114	16,776	15
Construction	50	1,285	11	43	853	4	78	39	432	11
Manufacturing	24	2,411	9	122	2,304	14	256	15	107	7
Transportation and public utilities	121	1,530	6	32	435	5	73	115	1,095	10
Wholesale trade	15	(D)	4	(D)	(D)	(D)	(D)	11	156	14
Retail trade	591	23,861	110	377	12,580	3	114	481	11,281	23
Finance, insurance, and real estate	50	1,315	8	52	902	7	113	42	413	10
Selected services	410	6,140	72	376	3,813	5	53	338	2,327	7

[Continued]

★ 365 ★

Owners by Geographic Division, State, and Industry: 1972. Part III. East North Central

[Continued]

Industry	1972								
	All firms		With paid employees					Without paid employees		
	Firms (number)	Gross receipts ($1,000)	Firms (number)	Employees (number)	Gross receipts ($1,000)	Average employees per firm (number)	Average receipts per firm ($1,000)	Firms (number)	Gross receipts ($1,000)	Average receipts per firm ($1,000)
Other industries	9	238	2	(D)	(D)	(D)	(D)	7	(D)	(D)
Industries not classified	66	(D)	-	-	-	-	-	66	(D)	(D)

Source: "Selected Statistics by Geographic Division, State, and Industry Division, for Black-Owned Forms: 1972 and 1969," U.S. Bureau of the Census, 1972 Survey of Minority Business Enterprises, *Minority Owned Businesses—Black*, pp. 32, 34. *Notes:* - Represents zero. D = Withheld to avoid disclosing figures for individual companies.

★ 366 ★

Business Owners and Operators

Owners by Geographic Division, State, and Industry: 1972. Part IV. West North Central

Industry	1972								
	All firms		With paid employees					Without paid employees		
	Firms (number)	Gross receipts ($1,000)	Firms (number)	Employees (number)	Gross receipts ($1,000)	Average employees per firm (number)	Average receipts per firm ($1,000)	Firms (number)	Gross receipts ($1,000)	Average receipts per firm ($1,000)
West North Central	6,837	277,073	1,225	8,784	211,990	7	173	5,612	65,083	12
Minnesota	541	38,590	131	1,418	32,937	11	251	410	5,653	14
Construction	52	3,385	15	105	2,162	7	144	37	1,223	33
Manufacturing	12	(D)	3	(D)	(D)	(D)	(D)	9	55	6
Transportation and public utilities	33	856	8	26	469	3	59	25	387	15
Wholesale trade	5	847	2	(D)	(D)	(D)	(D)	3	(D)	(D)
Retail trade	153	19,957	55	447	18,015	8	328	98	1,942	20
Finance, insurance, and real estate	27	(D)	4	(D)	(D)	(D)	(D)	23	170	7
Selected services	221	8,996	39	588	7,650	15	196	182	1,346	7
Other industries	7	410	4	(D)	(D)	(D)	(D)	3	(D)	(D)
Industries not classified	31	432	1	(D)	(D)	(D)	(D)	30	(D)	(D)
Iowa	419	34,798	96	924	31,791	10	331	323	3,007	9
Construction	30	8,086	9	66	7,776	7	864	21	310	15
Manufacturing	7	3,204	6	(D)	(D)	(D)	(D)	1	(D)	(D)
Transportation and public utilities	36	3,542	6	67	3,198	11	533	30	344	11
Wholesale trade	8	5,795	7	(D)	(D)	(D)	(D)	1	(D)	(D)
Retail trade	113	7,783	33	268	6,653	8	202	80	1,130	14
Finance, insurance, and real estate	21	3,274	7	87	3,156	12	451	14	118	8
Selected services	169	2,194	23	240	1,272	10	55	146	922	6
Other industries	10	369	4	15	305	4	76	6	64	11
Industries not classified	25	551	1	(D)	(D)	(D)	(D)	24	(D)	(D)
Missouri	4,685	149,021	726	4,608	103,273	6	142	3,959	45,748	12
Construction	349	15,156	68	517	11,549	8	170	281	3,607	13
Manufacturing	61	9,157	30	403	8,729	13	291	31	428	14
Transportation and public utilities	621	9,560	35	249	3,904	7	112	586	5,656	10
Wholesale trade	8	5,795	7	(D)	(D)	(D)	(D)	1	(D)	(D)
Retail trade	113	7,783	33	268	6,653	8	202	80	1,130	14
Finance, insurance, and real estate	21	3,274	7	87	3,156	12	451	14	118	8
Selected services	169	2,194	23	240	1,272	10	55	146	922	6
Other industries	10	369	4	15	305	4	76	6	64	11
Industries not classified	25	551	1	(D)	(D)	(D)	(D)	24	(D)	(D)

[Continued]

★ 366 ★

Owners by Geographic Division, State, and Industry: 1972. Part IV. West North Central

[Continued]

Industry	All firms		With paid employees					Without paid employees		
						1972				
	Firms (number)	Gross receipts ($1,000)	Firms (number)	Employees (number)	Gross receipts ($1,000)	Average employees per firm (number)	Average receipts per firm ($1,000)	Firms (number)	Gross receipts ($1,000)	Average receipts per firm ($1,000)
Missouri	4,685	149,021	726	4,608	103,273	6	142	3,959	45,748	12
Construction	349	15,156	68	517	11,549	8	170	281	3,607	13
Manufacturing	61	9,157	30	403	8,729	13	291	31	428	14
Transportation and public utilities	621	9,560	35	249	3,904	7	112	586	5,656	10
Wholesale trade	41	14,293	16	142	13,677	9	855	25	616	25
Retail trade	1,308	67,538	334	1,705	44,938	5	135	974	22,600	23
Finance, insurance, and real estate	238	6,049	19	205	4,193	11	221	219	1,856	8
Selected services	1,787	23,671	212	1,333	14,312	6	68	1,575	9,359	6
Other industries	46	2,175	9	40	1,924	4	214	37	251	7
Industries not classified	234	1,422	3	14	47	5	16	231	1,375	6
North Dakota	28	2,164	7	78	1,740	11	249	21	424	20
Construction	7	665	2	(D)	(D)	(D)	(D)	5	(D)	(D)
Manufacturing	1	(D)	1	(D)	(D)	(D)	(D)	-	-	-
Transportation and public utilities	1	(D)	-	-	-	-	-	1	(D)	(D)
Wholesale trade	1	(D)	1	(D)	(D)	(D)	(D)	-	-	-
Retail trade	7	372	2	(D)	(D)	(D)	(D)	5	(D)	(D)
Finance, insurance, and real estate	1	(D)	-	-	-	-	-	1	(D)	(D)
Selected services	8	31	-	-	-	-	-	8	31	4
Other industries	1	(D)	1	(D)	(D)	(D)	(D)	-	-	-
Industries not classified	1	(D)	-	-	-	-	-	1	(D)	(D)
South Dakota	22	525	6	23	351	4	59	16	174	11
Construction	1	(D)	1	(D)	(D)	(D)	(D)	-	-	-
Manufacturing	-	-	-	-	-	-	-	-	-	-
Transportation and public utilities	-	-	-	-	-	-	-	-	-	-
Wholesale trade	-	-	-	-	-	-	-	-	-	-
Retail trade	9	264	3	(D)	(D)	(D)	(D)	6	(D)	(D)
Finance, insurance, and real estate	2	(D)	-	-	-	-	-	2	(D)	(D)
Selected services	9	162	1	(D)	(D)	(D)	(D)	8	(D)	(D)
Other industries	1	(D)	1	(D)	(D)	(D)	(D)	-	-	-
Industries not classified	-	-	-	-	-	-	-	-	-	-
Nebraska	301	18,616	90	669	16,202	7	180	211	2,414	11
Construction	41	2,535	16	100	2,271	6	142	25	264	11
Manufacturing	5	(D)	3	(D)	(D)	(D)	(D)	2	(D)	(D)
Transportation and public utilities	21	1,104	5	50	902	10	180	16	202	13
Wholesale trade	4	(D)	4	(D)	(D)	(D)	(D)	-	-	-
Retail trade	87	7,815	32	193	6,591	6	206	55	1,224	22
Finance, insurance, and real estate	9	110	2	(D)	(D)	(D)	(D)	7	(D)	(D)
Selected services	117	1,917	24	136	1,342	6	56	93	575	6
Other industries	4	634	3	(D)	(D)	(D)	(D)	1	(D)	(D)
Industries not classified	13	87	1	(D)	(D)	(D)	(D)	12	(D)	(D)
Kansas	841	33,359	169	1,064	25,696	6	152	672	7,663	11
Construction	74	3,884	12	109	2,867	9	239	62	1,019	16
Manufacturing	16	3,254	13	119	3,251	9	250	3	3	1
Transportation and public utilities	107	3,332	17	77	2,253	5	133	90	1,079	12
Wholesale trade	10	2,881	5	(D)	(D)	(D)	(D)	5	(D)	(D)
Retail trade	244	12,062	64	329	8,964	5	140	180	3,098	17
Finance, insurance, and real estate	31	1,532	3	(D)	(D)	(D)	(D)	28	(D)	(D)
Selected services	294	5,229	48	326	3,734	7	78	246	1,495	6

[Continued]

★ 366 ★

Owners by Geographic Division, State, and Industry: 1972. Part IV. West North Central

[Continued]

Industry	1972									
	All firms		With paid employees					Without paid employees		
	Firms (number)	Gross receipts ($1,000)	Firms (number)	Employees (number)	Gross receipts ($1,000)	Average employees per firm (number)	Average receipts per firm ($1,000)	Firms (number)	Gross receipts ($1,000)	Average receipts per firm ($1,000)
Other industries	13	660	6	20	487	3	81	7	173	25
Industries not classified	52	525	1	(D)	(D)	(D)	(D)	51	(D)	(D)

Source: "Selected Statistics by Geographic Division, State, and Industry Division, for Black-Owned Forms: 1972 and 1969," U.S. Bureau of the Census, 1972 Survey of Minority Business Enterprises, *Minority Owned Businesses—Black*, pp. 34, 36. *Notes:* - Represents zero. D = Withheld to avoid disclosing figures for individual companies.

★ 367 ★

Business Owners and Operators

Owners by Geographic Division, State, and Industry: 1972. Part V. South Atlantic

Industry	1972									
	All firms		With paid employees					Without paid employees		
	Firms (number)	Gross receipts ($1,000)	Firms (number)	Employees (number)	Gross receipts ($1,000)	Average employees per firm (number)	Average receipts per firm ($1,000)	Firms (number)	Gross receipts ($1,000)	Average receipts per firm ($1,000)
South Atlantic	54,510	1,770,923	9,194	55,267	1,197,852	6	130	45,316	573,071	13
Delaware	683	23,906	106	589	15,574	6	147	577	8,332	14
Construction	77	3,054	21	112	1,997	5	95	56	1,057	19
Manufacturing	11	360	1	(D)	(D)	(D)	(D)	10	(D)	(D)
Transportation and public utilities	145	3,522	18	100	1,479	6	82	127	2,043	16
Wholesale trade	5	(D)	3	(D)	(D)	(D)	(D)	2	(D)	(D)
Retail trade	141	12,637	37	230	9,837	6	266	104	2,800	27
Finance, insurance, and real estate	11	(D)	1	(D)	(D)	(D)	(D)	10	93	9
Selected services	256	2,532	21	104	834	5	40	235	1,698	7
Other industries	9	328	4	27	299	7	75	5	29	6
Industries not classified	28	320	-	-	-	-	-	28	320	11
Maryland	7,019	244,843	914	5,269	152,578	6	167	6,105	92,265	15
Construction	585	23,051	114	637	13,025	6	114	471	10,026	21
Manufacturing	62	21,355	28	707	20,120	25	719	34	1,235	36
Transportation and public utilities	1,998	24,336	80	327	5,222	4	65	1,918	19,114	10
Wholesale trade	49	28,668	19	261	27,565	14	1,451	30	1,103	37
Retail trade	1,576	105,779	382	1,907	65,459	5	171	1,194	40,320	34
Finance, insurance, and real estate	239	6,722	33	232	4,563	7	138	206	2,159	10
Selected services	2,061	30,828	249	1,175	16,213	5	65	1,812	14,610	8
Other industries	209	2,135	6	13	275	2	46	203	1,860	9
Industries not classified	240	1,969	3	10	131	3	44	237	1,838	8
District of Columbia	7,102	155,877	773	4,682	98,392	6	127	6,329	57,485	9
Construction	297	8,844	39	218	3,182	6	82	258	5,662	22
Manufacturing	59	3,376	22	147	2,697	7	123	37	679	18
Transportation and public utilities	3,202	21,010	51	359	4,153	7	81	3,151	16,857	5
Wholesale trade	20	839	5	15	472	3	94	15	367	24
Retail trade	913	68,608	309	1,527	52,123	5	169	604	16,485	27
Finance, insurance, and real estate	270	7,648	26	509	5,958	20	229	244	1,690	7
Selected services	2,050	42,899	315	1,899	29,674	6	94	1,735	13,225	8
Other industries	31	561	1	(D)	(D)	(D)	(D)	30	(D)	(D)
Industries not classified	260	2,092	5	(D)	(D)	(D)	(D)	255	(D)	(D)

[Continued]

★ 367 ★

Owners by Geographic Division, State, and Industry: 1972. Part V. South Atlantic

[Continued]

Industry	All firms		With paid employees					Without paid employees		
	Firms (number)	Gross receipts ($1,000)	Firms (number)	Employees (number)	Gross receipts ($1,000)	Average employees per firm (number)	Average receipts per firm ($1,000)	Firms (number)	Gross receipts ($1,000)	Average receipts per firm ($1,000)
Virginia	8,173	234,538	1,568	8,368	160,733	5	103	6,605	73,805	11
Construction	1,298	44,928	348	2,060	32,279	6	93	950	12,649	13
Manufacturing	356	13,618	148	888	11,324	6	77	208	2,294	11
Transportation and public utilities	1,142	24,406	136	878	13,573	6	100	1,006	10,833	11
Wholesale trade	88	18,721	21	250	17,458	12	931	67	1,263	19
Retail trade	2,015	84,170	465	2,031	56,147	4	121	1,550	28,023	18
Finance, insurance, and real estate	169	9,903	40	472	8,713	12	218	129	1,190	9
Selected services	2,495	30,532	373	1,601	17,909	4	48	2,122	12,623	6
Other industries	248	4,944	28	167	3,157	6	113	220	1,787	8
Industries not classified	362	3,316	9	21	173	2	19	353	3,143	9
West Virginia	481	13,271	87	440	9,755	5	112	394	3,516	9
Construction	34	366	6	13	177	2	30	28	189	7
Manufacturing	5	387	3	(D)	(D)	(D)	(D)	2	(D)	(D)
Transportation and public utilities	31	639	8	55	336	7	42	23	303	13
Wholesale trade	6	1,748	5	(D)	(D)	(D)	(D)	1	(D)	(D)
Retail trade	143	5,848	30	132	4,234	4	141	113	1,614	14
Finance, insurance, and real estate	5	39	-	-	-	-	-	5	39	8
Selected services	218	3,681	30	163	2,532	5	84	188	1,149	6
Other industries	17	430	5	15	359	3	72	12	71	6
Industries not classified	22	133	-	-	-	-	-	22	133	6
North Carolina	8,082	288,783	1,432	9,873	206,637	7	144	6,650	82,146	12
Construction	1,216	39,257	380	2,419	26,285	6	69	836	12,972	16
Manufacturing	278	19,960	92	1,013	17,991	11	196	186	1,969	11
Transportation and public utilities	655	9,968	60	(D)	(D)	(D)	(D)	595	(D)	(D)
Wholesale trade	86	33,429	41	331	32,420	8	791	45	1,009	22
Retail trade	2,512	98,202	389	1,681	58,070	4	149	2,123	40,132	19
Finance, insurance, and real estate	146	46,086	29	(D)	(D)	(D)	(D)	117	(D)	(D)
Selected services	2,611	36,103	423	2,090	22,037	5	52	2,188	14,066	6
Other industries	179	2,391	13	144	580	11	45	166	1,811	11
Industries not classified	399	3,387	5	13	133	3	27	394	3,254	8
South Carolina	5,910	150,187	946	5,520	83,409	6	88	4,964	66,778	13
Construction	1,102	31,177	294	1,697	19,845	6	68	808	11,332	14
Manufacturing	249	10,818	113	641	8,653	6	77	136	2,165	16
Transportation and public utilities	350	5,393	30	111	2,366	4	79	320	3,027	9
Wholesale trade	34	7,614	16	108	7,171	7	448	18	443	25
Retail trade	2,179	67,808	252	1,974	32,360	8	128	1,927	35,448	18
Finance, insurance, and real estate	88	2,315	16	75	1,677	5	105	72	638	9
Selected services	1,559	18,468	208	780	8,643	4	42	1,351	9,825	7
Other industries	149	4,243	12	113	2,131	9	178	137	2,112	15
Industries not classified	200	2,351	5	21	563	4	113	195	1,788	9
Georgia	8,310	327,804	1,633	10,360	240,662	6	147	6,677	87,142	13
Construction	1,332	46,070	347	2,200	31,860	6	92	985	14,210	14
Manufacturing	289	16,260	134	750	14,045	6	105	155	2,215	14
Transportation and public utilities	722	9,633	55	302	4,058	5	74	667	5,575	8
Wholesale trade	89	29,976	42	304	29,090	7	693	47	886	19
Retail trade	2,616	118,458	574	2,351	76,722	4	134	2,042	41,736	20
Finance, insurance, and real estate	279	49,411	49	2,065	46,805	42	955	230	2,606	11
Selected services	2,481	49,037	398	2,275	34,155	6	86	2,083	14,882	7
Other industries	217	5,530	26	75	3,367	3	130	191	2,163	11
Industries not classified	285	3,429	8	38	560	5	70	277	2,869	10

[Continued]

★ 367 ★

Owners by Geographic Division, State, and Industry: 1972. Part V. South Atlantic
[Continued]

| Industry | 1972 | | | | | | | | | |
| | All firms | | With paid employees | | | | | Without paid employees | | |
	Firms (number)	Gross receipts ($1,000)	Firms (number)	Employees (number)	Gross receipts ($1,000)	Average employees per firm (number)	Average receipts per firm ($1,000)	Firms (number)	Gross receipts ($1,000)	Average receipts per firm ($1,000)
Florida	8,750	331,714	1,735	10,160	230,112	6	133	7,015	101,602	14
Construction	1,139	52,061	378	2,347	38,892	6	103	761	13,169	17
Manufacturing	164	19,191	84	903	17,804	11	212	80	1,387	17
Transportation and public utilities	734	21,253	71	584	11,759	8	166	663	9,494	14
Wholesale trade	89	32,606	48	288	31,668	6	660	41	938	23
Retail trade	2,754	133,551	603	2,892	86,147	5	143	2,151	47,404	22
Finance, insurance, and real estate	206	13,650	42	774	11,448	18	273	164	2,202	13
Selected services	2,725	41,470	415	1,973	25,810	5	62	2,310	15,660	7
Other industries	662	13,488	87	384	6,081	4	70	575	7,407	13
Industries not classified	277	4,444	7	15	503	2	72	270	3,941	15

Source: "Selected Statistics by Geographic Division, State, and Industry Division, for Black-Owned Forms: 1972 and 1969," U.S. Bureau of the Census, 1972 Survey of Minority Business Enterprises, *Minority Owned Businesses—Black*, pp. 36, 38. *Notes:* - Represents zero. D = Withheld to avoid disclosing figures for individual companies.

★ 368 ★

Business Owners and Operators

Owners by Geographic Division, State, and Industry: 1972. Part VI. East South Central

| Industry | 1972 | | | | | | | | | |
| | All firms | | With paid employees | | | | | Without paid employees | | |
	Firms (number)	Gross receipts ($1,000)	Firms (number)	Employees (number)	Gross receipts ($1,000)	Average employees per firm (number)	Average receipts per firm ($1,000)	Firms (number)	Gross receipts ($1,000)	Average receipts per firm ($1,000)
East South Central	15,162	582,123	2,575	16,753	416,670	7	162	12,587	165,453	13
Kentucky	2,085	69,722	335	2,350	51,149	9	153	1,750	18,573	11
Construction	264	6,631	55	272	4,248	5	77	209	2,383	11
Manufacturing	20	4,318	8	245	3,990	31	499	12	328	27
Transportation and public utilities	202	(D)	26	(D)	(D)	(D)	(D)	176	2,028	12
Wholesale trade	17	5,711	11	73	5,679	7	516	6	32	5
Retail trade	567	31,018	129	666	23,276	5	180	438	7,742	18
Finance, insurance, and real estate	46	(D)	7	(D)	(D)	(D)	(D)	39	561	14
Selected services	807	8,657	93	388	4,379	4	47	714	4,278	6
Other industries	26	985	6	32	634	5	106	20	351	18
Industries not classified	136	870	-	-	-	-	-	136	870	6
Tennessee	4,305	196,774	783	5,193	151,558	7	194	3,522	45,216	13
Construction	649	30,490	148	978	23,363	7	158	501	7,127	14
Manufacturing	64	20,794	20	449	19,993	22	1,000	44	801	18
Transportation and public utilities	328	5,655	32	211	3,047	7	95	296	2,608	9
Wholesale trade	43	27,375	23	267	26,982	12	1,173	20	393	20
Retail trade	1,397	64,899	317	1,214	41,611	4	131	1,080	23,288	22
Finance, insurance, and real estate	126	23,770	31	1,012	22,681	33	732	95	1,089	11
Selected services	1,410	18,870	200	1,008	11,739	5	59	1,210	7,131	6
Other industries	47	653	5	20	193	4	39	42	460	11
Industries not classified	241	4,268	7	34	1,949	5	278	234	2,319	10
Alabama	4,749	182,655	925	5,788	133,988	6	145	3,824	48,667	13
Construction	654	20,504	157	1,017	14,568	6	93	497	5,936	12
Manufacturing	240	21,278	108	814	19,509	8	181	132	1,769	13

[Continued]

★ 368 ★

Owners by Geographic Division, State, and Industry: 1972. Part VI. East South Central
[Continued]

Industry	1972									
	All firms		With paid employees					Without paid employees		
	Firms (number)	Gross receipts ($1,000)	Firms (number)	Employees (number)	Gross receipts ($1,000)	Average employees per firm (number)	Average receipts per firm ($1,000)	Firms (number)	Gross receipts ($1,000)	Average receipts per firm ($1,000)
Transportation and public utilities	278	12,043	39	492	9,103	13	233	239	2,940	12
Wholesale trade	50	25,677	31	245	25,299	8	816	19	378	20
Retail trade	1,682	64,836	316	1,342	38,426	4	122	1,368	26,410	19
Finance, insurance, and real estate	81	14,014	33	671	13,558	20	411	48	456	10
Selected services	1,453	19,346	216	1,112	11,998	5	56	1,237	7,348	6
Other industries	116	2,416	20	77	1,025	4	51	96	1,391	14
Industries not classified	195	2,541	5	18	502	4	100	190	2,039	11
Mississippi	4,023	132,972	532	3,422	79,975	6	150	3,491	52,997	15
Construction	592	17,083	103	631	10,572	6	103	489	6,511	13
Manufacturing	97	5,466	31	258	4,836	8	156	66	630	10
Transportation and public utilities	309	9,665	19	376	7,256	20	382	290	2,409	8
Wholesale trade	47	21,438	25	295	20,531	12	821	22	907	41
Retail trade	1,566	55,511	205	800	22,980	4	112	1,361	32,531	24
Finance, insurance, and real estate	104	7,294	12	487	6,654	41	555	92	640	7
Selected services	1,062	12,610	131	551	6,288	4	48	931	6,322	7
Other industries	87	1,234	5	(D)	(D)	(D)	(D)	82	(D)	(D)
Industries not classified	159	2,671	1	(D)	(D)	(D)	(D)	158	(D)	(D)

Source: "Selected Statistics by Geographic Division, State, and Industry Division, for Black-Owned Forms: 1972 and 1969," U.S. Bureau of the Census, 1972 Survey of Minority Business Enterprises, *Minority Owned Businesses—Black,* pp. 38, 40. *Notes:* - Represents zero. D = Withheld to avoid disclosing figures for individual companies.

★ 369 ★

Business Owners and Operators

Owners by Geographic Division, State, and Industry: 1972. Part VII. West South Central

Industry	1972									
	All firms		With paid employees					Without paid employees		
	Firms (number)	Gross receipts ($1,000)	Firms (number)	Employees (number)	Gross receipts ($1,000)	Average employees per firm (number)	Average receipts per firm ($1,000)	Firms (number)	Gross receipts ($1,000)	Average receipts per firm ($1,000)
West South Central	26,779	917,522	3,877	23,955	634,371	6	164	22,902	283,151	12
Arkansas	2,118	63,156	221	1,578	39,776	7	180	1,897	23,380	12
Construction	298	7,519	30	215	4,217	7	141	268	3,302	12
Manufacturing	66	4,960	18	266	3,975	15	221	48	985	21
Transportation and public utilities	176	1,997	6	17	127	3	21	170	1,870	11
Wholesale trade	18	9,461	10	106	9,413	11	941	8	48	6
Retail trade	700	28,410	90	511	16,512	6	183	610	11,898	20
Finance, insurance, and real estate	41	788	8	37	532	5	67	33	256	8
Selected services	602	7,086	54	385	4,329	7	80	548	2,757	5
Other industries	87	1,894	5	41	671	8	134	82	1,223	15
Industries not classified	130	1,041	-	-	-	-	-	130	1,041	8
Louisiana	7,958	323,257	1,131	8,053	225,202	7	199	6,827	98,055	14
Construction	1,095	40,040	173	1,331	27,560	8	159	922	12,480	14
Manufacturing	151	15,480	67	622	14,141	9	211	84	1,339	16
Transportation and public utilities	906	17,932	61	445	11,067	7	181	845	6,865	8
Wholesale trade	72	67,112	48	770	65,774	16	1,370	24	1,338	56
Retail trade	2,873	121,960	452	1,938	64,095	4	142	2,421	57,865	24

[Continued]

★ 369 ★

Owners by Geographic Division, State, and Industry: 1972. Part VII. West South Central
[Continued]

Industry	1972									
	All firms		With paid employees					Without paid employees		
	Firms (number)	Gross receipts ($1,000)	Firms (number)	Employees (number)	Gross receipts ($1,000)	Average employees per firm (number)	Average receipts per firm ($1,000)	Firms (number)	Gross receipts ($1,000)	Average receipts per firm ($1,000)
Finance, insurance, and real estate	196	26,272	54	1,667	25,207	31	467	142	1,065	7
Selected services	2,118	25,461	252	1,169	14,081	5	56	1,866	11,380	6
Other industries	219	5,685	22	(D)	(D)	(D)	(D)	197	(D)	(D)
Industries not classified	328	3,315	2	(D)	(D)	(D)	(D)	326	(D)	(D)
Oklahoma	1,702	47,189	243	1,557	30,862	6	127	1,459	16,327	11
Construction	190	5,773	34	201	3,864	6	114	156	1,909	12
Manufacturing	19	4,262	9	186	3,942	21	438	10	320	32
Transportation and public utilities	118	1,691	3	17	33	6	11	115	1,658	14
Wholesale trade	13	4,339	7	55	4,307	8	615	6	32	5
Retail trade	499	17,166	93	359	10,068	4	108	406	7,098	17
Finance, insurance, and real estate	94	2,523	15	87	1,835	6	122	79	688	9
Selected services	633	9,550	77	611	6,278	8	82	556	3,272	6
Other industries	32	1,073	5	41	535	8	107	27	538	20
Industries not classified	104	812	-	-	-	-	-	104	812	8
Texas	15,001	483,920	2,282	12,737	338,531	6	148	12,719	145,389	11
Construction	1,602	64,208	322	2,272	45,515	7	141	1,280	18,693	15
Manufacturing	252	39,297	94	1,002	36,737	11	391	158	2,560	16
Transportation and public utilities	1,586	32,714	130	842	15,704	6	121	1,456	17,010	12
Wholesale trade	138	56,007	70	609	53,680	9	767	68	2,327	34
Retail trade	4,783	202,343	993	4,471	136,106	5	137	3,790	66,237	17
Finance, insurance, and real estate	555	14,556	70	478	10,744	7	153	485	3,812	8
Selected services	4,974	60,031	552	2,884	35,648	5	65	4,422	24,383	6
Other industries	392	7,355	36	173	2,996	5	83	356	4,359	12
Industries not classified	719	7,409	15	36	1,401	2	93	704	6,008	9

Source: "Selected Statistics by Geographic Division, State, and Industry Division, for Black-Owned Forms: 1972 and 1969," U.S. Bureau of the Census, 1972 Survey of Minority Business Enterprises, *Minority Owned Businesses—Black*, p. 40. *Notes:* - Represents zero. D = Withheld to avoid disclosing figures for individual companies.

★ 370 ★

Business Owners and Operators

Owners by Geographic Division, State, and Industry: 1972. Part VIII. Mountain

Industry	1972									
	All firms		With paid employees					Without paid employees		
	Firms (number)	Gross receipts ($1,000)	Firms (number)	Employees (number)	Gross receipts ($1,000)	Average employees per firm (number)	Average receipts per firm ($1,000)	Firms (number)	Gross receipts ($1,000)	Average receipts per firm ($1,000)
Mountain	2,487	105,548	429	4,158	84,221	10	196	2,058	21,327	10
Montana	46	4,233	13	132	3,553	10	273	33	680	21
Construction	7	(D)	1	(D)	(D)	(D)	(D)	6	95	16
Manufacturing	-	-	-	-	-	-	-	-	-	-
Transportation and public utilities	2	(D)	2	(D)	(D)	(D)	(D)	-	-	-
Wholesale trade	1	(D)	1	(D)	(D)	(D)	(D)	-	-	-
Retail trade	13	2,354	5	(D)	(D)	(D)	(D)	8	(D)	(D)
Finance, insurance, and real estate	4	38	-	-	-	-	-	4	38	10
Selected services	17	207	4	9	144	2	36	13	63	5
Other industries	1	(D)	-	-	-	-	-	1	(D)	(D)

[Continued]

★ 370 ★

Owners by Geographic Division, State, and Industry: 1972. Part VIII. Mountain
[Continued]

Industry	All firms		With paid employees					Without paid employees		
	Firms (number)	Gross receipts ($1,000)	Firms (number)	Employees (number)	Gross receipts ($1,000)	Average employees per firm (number)	Average receipts per firm ($1,000)	Firms (number)	Gross receipts ($1,000)	Average receipts per firm ($1,000)
Industries not classified	1	(D)	-	-	-	-	-	1	(D)	(D)
Idaho	40	2,120	5	(D)	(D)	(D)	(D)	35	(D)	(D)
Construction	8	146	1	(D)	(D)	(D)	(D)	7	(D)	(D)
Manufacturing	-	-	-	-	-	-	-	-	-	-
Transportation and public utilities	2	(D)	1	(D)	(D)	(D)	(D)	1	(D)	(D)
Wholesale trade	1	(D)	-	-	-	-	-	1	(D)	(D)
Retail trade	10	(D)	1	(D)	(D)	(D)	(D)	9	104	12
Finance, insurance, and real estate	4	(D)	1	(D)	(D)	(D)	(D)	3	(D)	(D)
Selected services	13	83	1	(D)	(D)	(D)	(D)	12	(D)	(D)
Other industries	2	(D)	-	-	-	-	-	2	(D)	(D)
Industries not classified	-	-	-	-	-	-	-	-	-	-
Wyoming	51	1,276	12	(D)	(D)	(D)	(D)	39	(D)	(D)
Construction	10	539	2	(D)	(D)	(D)	(D)	8	(D)	(D)
Manufacturing	-	-	-	-	-	-	-	-	-	-
Transportation and public utilities	1	(D)	1	(D)	(D)	(D)	(D)	-	-	-
Wholesale trade	-	-	-	-	-	-	-	-	-	-
Retail trade	18	398	3	(D)	(D)	(D)	(D)	15	(D)	(D)
Finance, insurance, and real estate	2	(D)	-	-	-	-	-	2	(D)	(D)
Selected services	20	303	6	25	225	4	38	14	78	6
Other industries										
Industries not classified	-	-	-	-	-	-	-	-	-	-
Colorado	1,087	54,154	172	2,312	45,790	13	266	915	8,364	9
Construction	100	12,086	36	477	11,251	13	313	64	835	13
Manufacturing	19	6,973	11	361	6,942	33	631	8	31	4
Transportation and public utilities	86	1,629	5	36	677	7	135	83	952	11
Wholesale trade	16	1,851	5	(D)	(D)	(D)	(D)	11	(D)	(D)
Retail trade	289	13,413	62	520	10,571	8	171	227	2,842	13
Finance, insurance, and real estate	96	11,479	12	472	10,825	39	902	84	654	8
Selected services	394	6,106	39	392	3,941	10	101	355	2,165	6
Other industries	26	289	2	(D)	(D)	(D)	(D)	24	(D)	(D)
Industries not classified	59	328	-	-	-	-	-	59	328	6
New Mexico	270	10,835	62	499	8,557	8	138	208	2,278	11
Construction	30	2,299	13	108	2,040	8	157	17	259	15
Manufacturing	6	1,267	5	(D)	(D)	(D)	(D)	1	(D)	(D)
Transportation and public utilities	8	518	4	34	437	9	109	4	81	20
Wholesale trade	6	177	1	(D)	(D)	(D)	(D)	5	(D)	(D)
Retail trade	95	4,532	20	135	3,314	7	166	75	1,218	16
Finance, insurance, and real estate	10	155	2	(D)	(D)	(D)	(D)	8	(D)	(D)
Selected services	93	1,604	14	146	1,217	10	87	79	387	5
Other industries	7	199	3	14	192	5	64	4	7	2
Industries not classified	15	84	-	-	-	-	-	15	84	6
Arizona	637	22,492	106	807	16,525	8	156	531	5,967	11
Construction	55	5,997	19	275	5,153	14	271	36	844	23
Manufacturing	11	352	3	35	287	12	96	8	65	8
Transportation and public utilities	31	871	3	(D)	(D)	(D)	(D)	28	(D)	(D)
Wholesale trade	6	1,024	5	(D)	(D)	(D)	(D)	1	(D)	(D)
Retail trade	184	6,744	35	163	4,561	5	130	149	2,183	15
Finance, insurance, and real estate	41	510	5	12	152	2	30	36	358	10
Selected services	254	6,353	34	274	4,773	8	140	220	1,580	7
Other industries	23	417	2	(D)	(D)	(D)	(D)	21	(D)	(D)

[Continued]

★ 370 ★

Owners by Geographic Division, State, and Industry: 1972. Part VIII. Mountain

[Continued]

Industry	1972									
	All firms		With paid employees					Without paid employees		
	Firms (number)	Gross receipts ($1,000)	Firms (number)	Employees (number)	Gross receipts ($1,000)	Average employees per firm (number)	Average receipts per firm ($1,000)	Firms (number)	Gross receipts ($1,000)	Average receipts per firm ($1,000)
Industries not classified	32	224	-	-	-	-	-	32	224	7
Utah	77	2,166	13	88	1,260	7	97	64	906	14
Construction	5	524	1	(D)	(D)	(D)	(D)	4	(D)	(D)
Manufacturing	2	(D)	2	(D)	(D)	(D)	(D)	-	-	-
Transportation and public utilities	7	(D)	1	(D)	(D)	(D)	(D)	6	(D)	(D)
Wholesale trade	1	(D)	-	-	-	-	-	1	(D)	(D)
Retail trade	22	828	5	23	565	5	113	17	263	15
Finance, insurance, and real estate	2	(D)	-	-	-	-	-	2	(D)	(D)
Selected services	32	402	4	17	200	4	50	28	202	7
Other industries	-	-	-	-	-	-	-	-	-	-
Industries not classified	6	10	-	-	-	-	-	6	10	2
Nevada	279	8,272	46	226	5,869	5	128	233	2,403	10
Construction	14	549	5	36	486	7	97	9	63	7
Manufacturing	4	193	1	(D)	(D)	(D)	(D)	3	(D)	(D)
Transportation and public utilities	2	(D)	1	(D)	(D)	(D)	(D)	1	(D)	(D)
Wholesale trade	1	(D)	1	(D)	(D)	(D)	(D)	-	-	-
Retail trade	85	4,948	20	118	3,854	6	193	65	1,094	17
Finance, insurance, and real estate	8	247	1	(D)	(D)	(D)	(D)	7	(D)	(D)
Selected services	152	1,826	16	49	920	3	58	136	906	7
Other industries	6	35	-	-	-	-	-	6	35	6
Industries not classified	7	(D)	1	(D)	(D)	(D)	(D)	6	(D)	(D)

Source: "Selected Statistics by Geographic Division, State, and Industry Division, for Black-Owned Forms: 1972 and 1969," U.S. Bureau of the Census, 1972 Survey of Minority Business Enterprises, *Minority Owned Businesses—Black*, pp. 42, 44. Notes: - Represents zero. D = Withheld to avoid disclosing figures for individual companies.

★ 371 ★

Business Owners and Operators

Owners by Geographic Division, State, and Industry: 1972. Part IX. Pacific

Industry	1972									
	All firms		With paid employees					Without paid employees		
	Firms (number)	Gross receipts ($1,000)	Firms (number)	Employees (number)	Gross receipts ($1,000)	Average employees per firm (number)	Average receipts per firm ($1,000)	Firms (number)	Gross receipts ($1,000)	Average receipts per firm ($1,000)
Pacific	20,912	766,238	2,986	20,775	581,777	7	195	17,926	184,461	10
Washington	988	35,560	171	1,220	27,171	7	159	817	8,389	10
Construction	65	2,822	17	148	1,870	9	110	48	952	20
Manufacturing	23	2,836	8	72	2,766	9	346	15	70	5
Transportation and public utilities	44	778	2	(D)	(D)	(D)	(D)	42	(D)	(D)
Wholesale trade	15	904	2	(D)	(D)	(D)	(D)	13	(D)	(D)
Retail trade	250	16,463	67	469	13,936	7	204	183	2,824	15
Finance, insurance, and real estate	64	5,423	9	167	4,638	19	515	55	785	14
Selected services	464	5,897	61	340	3,674	6	60	403	2,223	6
Other industries	25	305	4	8	61	2	15	21	244	12
Industries not classified	38	132	1	(D)	(D)	(D)	(D)	37	(D)	(D)
Oregon	393	18,464	69	577	14,838	8	215	324	3,626	11

[Continued]

★ 371 ★

Owners by Geographic Division, State, and Industry: 1972. Part IX. Pacific

[Continued]

Industry	1972								
	All firms		With paid employees					Without paid employees		
	Firms (number)	Gross receipts ($1,000)	Firms (number)	Employees (number)	Gross receipts ($1,000)	Average employees per firm (number)	Average receipts per firm ($1,000)	Firms (number)	Gross receipts ($1,000)	Average receipts per firm ($1,000)
Construction	31	1,334	7	76	875	11	125	24	459	19
Manufacturing	8	1,365	3	52	1,185	17	395	5	180	36
Transportation and public utilities	18	1,045	2	(D)	(D)	(D)	(D)	16	(D)	(D)
Wholesale trade	5	(D)	2	(D)	(D)	(D)	(D)	3	(D)	(D)
Retail trade	92	4,255	27	102	2,988	4	111	65	1,267	19
Finance, insurance, and real estate	15	(D)	2	(D)	(D)	(D)	(D)	13	101	8
Selected services	197	2,315	25	133	1,193	5	48	172	1,122	7
Other industries	9	39	1	(D)	(D)	(D)	(D)	8	(D)	(D)
Industries not classified	18	120	-	-	-	-	-	18	120	7
California	19,282	703,512	2,709	18,710	533,272	7	197	16,573	170,240	10
Construction	1,093	57,743	223	1,875	45,426	8	204	870	12,317	14
Manufacturing	414	78,404	154	2,930	75,389	19	490	260	3,015	12
Transportation and public utilities	942	26,396	106	632	13,354	6	126	836	13,042	16
Wholesale trade	240	72,134	99	605	69,022	6	697	141	3,112	22
Retail trade	5,108	257,404	936	5,454	197,079	6	211	4,172	60,325	14
Finance, insurance, and real estate	1,295	50,665	122	1,235	39,196	10	321	1,173	11,469	10
Selected services	8,200	135,157	1,008	5,572	82,829	6	82	7,192	52,328	7
Other industries	558	12,084	32	284	8,052	9	252	526	4,032	8
Industries not classified	1,432	13,525	29	121	2,925	4	101	1,403	10,600	8
Alaska	152	4,673	24	134	2,931	6	122	128	1,742	14
Construction	17	(D)	2	(D)	(D)	(D)	(D)	15	(D)	(D)
Manufacturing	3	(D)	1	(D)	(D)	(D)	(D)	2	(D)	(D)
Transportation and public utilities	4	(D)	1	(D)	(D)	(D)	(D)	3	(D)	(D)
Wholesale trade	-	-	-	-	-	-	-	-	-	-
Retail trade	33	1,347	5	20	719	4	144	28	628	22
Finance, insurance, and real estate	6	(D)	1	(D)	(D)	(D)	(D)	5	(D)	(D)
Selected services	75	1,772	14	86	1,223	6	87	61	549	9
Other industries	8	21	-	-	-	-	-	8	21	3
Industries not classified	6	(D)	-	-	-	-	-	6	(D)	(D)
Hawaii	97	4,029	13	134	3,565	10	274	84	464	6
Construction	3	(D)	2	(D)	(D)	(D)	(D)	1	(D)	(D)
Manufacturing	1	(D)	-	-	-	-	-	1	(D)	(D)
Transportation and public utilities	3	(D)	1	(D)	(D)	(D)	(D)	2	(D)	(D)
Wholesale trade	3	(D)	1	(D)	(D)	(D)	(D)	2	(D)	(D)
Retail trade	29	97	1	(D)	(D)	(D)	(D)	28	(D)	(D)
Finance, insurance, and real estate	8	96	-	-	-	-	-	8	96	12
Selected services	43	1,800	8	108	1,562	14	195	35	238	7
Other industries	-	-	-	-	-	-	-	-	-	-
Industries not classified	7	(D)	-	-	-	-	-	7	(D)	(D)
Not specified by area	2,125	46,967	59	365	16,267	6	276	2,066	30,700	15
Construction	274	5,778	4	14	1,484	4	371	270	4,294	16
Manufacturing	38	481	2	(D)	(D)	(D)	(D)	36	(D)	(D)
Transportation and public utilities	239	4,686	3	49	1,213	16	404	236	3,473	15
Wholesale trade	22	3,013	2	(D)	(D)	(D)	(D)	20	(D)	(D)
Retail trade	440	18,918	24	157	8,777	7	366	416	10,141	24
Finance, insurance, and real estate	121	1,572	1	(D)	(D)	(D)	(D)	120	(D)	(D)
Selected services	585	5,744	16	73	1,095	5	68	569	4,649	8

[Continued]

★ 371 ★

Owners by Geographic Division, State, and Industry: 1972. Part IX. Pacific
[Continued]

Industry	All firms		With paid employees					Without paid employees		
	Firms (number)	Gross receipts ($1,000)	Firms (number)	Employees (number)	Gross receipts ($1,000)	Average employees per firm (number)	Average receipts per firm ($1,000)	Firms (number)	Gross receipts ($1,000)	Average receipts per firm ($1,000)
Other industries	79	1,519	4	9	112	2	28	75	4,060	19
Industries not classified	327	5,256	3	7	1,196	2	399	324	4,060	13

Source: "Selected Statistics by Geographic Division, State, and Industry Division, for Black-Owned Forms: 1972 and 1969," U.S. Bureau of the Census, 1972 Survey of Minority Business Enterprises, *Minority Owned Businesses—Black*, p. 44. *Notes:* - Represents zero. D = Withheld to avoid disclosing figures for individual companies.

★ 372 ★

Business Owners and Operators

Payroll and Wages in Retail Stores with Black Proprietors, Percent of Total Sales, 1929

Section and division	Total annual pay roll	Wage cost (percent of total sales)
United States	$8,528,306	8.43
The South	4,333,477	7.60
South Atlantic	2,097,912	7.67
East South Central	1,046,500	7.90
West South Central	1,189,065	7.23
The North	3,760,864	9.32
New England	173,286	8.98
Middle Atlantic	1,364,432	9.17
East North Central	1,640,070	9.54
West North Central	583,076	9.21
The West	433,965	11.50
Mountain	62,201	11.17
Pacific	371,764	11.56

Source: "Pay Roll and Wage Cost (Percent of Total Sales) in Retail Stores Operated by Negro Proprietors, for the United States, by Sections, and Divisions: 1929." U.S. Bureau of the Census. *Negroes in the United States: 1920-32*. Washington, D.C.: Government Printing Office, 1935, p. 498.

★ 373 ★

Business Owners and Operators

Payroll and Wages in Retail Stores with Black Proprietors, Type of Business, 1929

Kinds of Business	Total annual pay roll	Wage cost (percent of total sales)
Total	$8,528,306	8.43
Food group	1,341,671	3.66
Candy and confectionery stores	124,841	4.83
Grocery stores (without meats)	336,608	2.29
Combination stores (groceries and meats)	520,643	3.81
Meat markets (including sea foods)	188,200	6.65
Other food stores	171,379	5.95
General stores – groceries with dry goods, apparel or general merchandise	151,947	3.15
General merchandise group	67,496	6.89
Dry-goods stores	27,418	7.19
General-merchandise stores	31,048	6.81
Variety, 5-and-10, and to-a-dollar stores	9,030	6.34
Automotive group	1,058,269	10.81
Motor-vehicle dealers (new and used)	245,535	7.80
Filling stations	258,220	7.53
Garages and repair shops	481,317	18.92
Other automotive establishments	73,197	10.93
Apparel group	322,620	10.65
men's and boy's clothing and furnishings stores	59,816	6.53
Family clothing stores – men's, women's, and children's	29,295	6.86
Women's ready-to-wear specialty stores – apparel and accessories	28,237	8.94
Women's accessories stores	32,649	10.58
Other apparel stores	139,385	19.47
Shoe stores	33,238	9.62
Furniture and household group	133,500	11.51
Furniture stores	56,410	14.07
Floor coverings, drapery, curtain, and upholstery stores	3,588	18.45
Household appliances stores	500	6.41
Other home-furnishings and appliances stores	15,414	19.42
Radio and music stores	57,588	8.83
Restaurants and eating places	2,727,883	12.79
Restaurants, cafeterias, and lunch rooms	2,358,331	13.64
Lunch counters, refreshment stands, etc.	369,552	9.13

[Continued]

★ 373 ★

Payroll and Wages in Retail Stores with Black Proprietors, Type of Business, 1929
[Continued]

Kinds of Business	Total annual pay roll	Wage cost (percent of total sales)
Lumber and building group	202,778	15.99
Lumber and building-material dealers	73,175	12.42
Electrical shops (without radio)	36,565	22.87
Heating and plumbing shops	69,147	19.50
Paint and glass stores	23,891	14.53
Other retail stores	2,411,120	11.42
Hardware stores	34,606	7.27
Hardware and farm-implement stores	20,286	6.05
Farmers' supplies	45,880	4.94
Book stores	4,933	9.37
Cigar stores and cigar stands	236,597	11.52
Coal and wood yards – ice dealers	250,079	11.81
Drug stores	790,465	10.90
Jewelry stores	45,596	11.74
Miscellaneous classifications (combined)	982,678	13.09
Second-hand stores	111,022	11.29

Source: "Pay Roll and Wage Cost (Percent of Total Sales) in Retail Stores Operated by Negro Proprietors, by Kind of Business for the United States: 1929." U.S. Bureau of the Census. *Negroes in the United States: 1920-32.* Washington, D.C.: Government Printing Office, 1935, p. 498.

★ 374 ★

Business Owners and Operators

Proprietors of Businesses in Cities With 50,000 or More Blacks: St. Louis, Missouri, 1929

Kind of business	Number of stores	Proprietors and firm members (not on pay roll)	Number of employees		Total pay roll (including part time)	Stocks on hand, end of year (at cost)	Net sales	
			Full time	Part time			Amount	Percent of total
Total	310	328	213	45	$149,516	$116,670	$1,457,427	100.00
Food group	80	82	26	7	23,015	24,830	422,794	29.01
Candy and confectionery stores	50	52	12	2	6,054	4,300	120,184	8.25
Grocery stores (without meats)	14	14	2	1	1,400	3,480	54,140	3.71
Combination stores (groceries and meats)	16	16	12	4	15,561	17,050	248,470	17.05
General merchandise group	3							
Dry goods stores	2	3	-	-	-	3,400	10,918	.75
Variety, 5-and-10, and to-a-dollar stores	1							
Automotive group	17	22	16	-	14,652	2,140	80,765	5.54
Filling stations	4	4	4	-	3,780	1,680	36,425	2.50
Garage and repair shops	13	18	12	-	10,872	460	44,340	3.04
Apparel group	10	11	8	1	4,678	7,710	33,760	2.32
Family clothing – men's, women's, and children's	1							
Women's ready-to-wear specialty stores – apparel and accessories	2	4	3	-	2,028	7,010	21,010	1.44
Women's accessories stores	1							
All other apparel stores	6	7	5	1	2,650	700	12,750	.87

[Continued]

★ 374 ★

Proprietors of Businesses in Cities With 50,000 or More Blacks: St. Louis, Missouri, 1929
[Continued]

Kind of business	Number of stores	Proprietors and firm members (not on pay roll)	Number of employees		Total pay roll (including part time)	Stocks on hand, end of year (at cost)	Net sales	
			Full time	Part time			Amount	Percent of total
Restaurants and eating places	120	123	97	24	54,414	7,070	432,391	29.67
Restaurants, cafeterias, and lunch rooms								
Cafeterias	1	] 72	26	12	12,259	2,795	162,315	11.14
Lunch rooms	70							
Restaurants with table service	15	17	60	8	34,956	1,505	189,282	12.99
Lunch counters, refreshment stands, etc.								
Lunch counters	24	24	9	4	5,959	1,870	58,976	4.05
Refreshment stands	3	3	1	-	1,000	190	7,980	.35
Soft-drink stands	7	7	1	-	240	710	13,838	.95
Other retail stores	75	82	64	13	50,977	70,430	466,399	82.00
Hardware stores	2	] 4	2	1	1,580	5,950	14,149	.97
Jewelry stores	2							
Farmers' supplies stores	3	3	-	-	-	240	8,700	.60
Cigar stores and cigar stands	11	12	7	-	5,130	950	40,890	2.81
Coal and wood yards – ice dealers	22	21	7	3	3,943	1,200	40,124	2.75
Drug stores								
Drug stores without fountains	7	8	14		10,630	31,200	96,825	6.64
Drug stores with fountains	10	11	22	7	19,519	24,340	174,080	11.94
Miscellaneous classifications (combined)[1]	18	23	12	2	10,175	6,550	91,651	6.29
Second-hand stores	5	5	2	-	1,780	1,000	10,400	.71

Source: "Stores Operated by Negro Proprietors, by Kind of Business, for Cities Having 50,000 or More Negro Inhabitants: 1929," U.S. Bureau of the Census, *Negroes in the United States: 1920-32*, p. 528. *Notes:* 1. Includes 2 florists, 2 foods stores, 5 printers and lithographers, 2 radio and music stores, 1 sanitary supplies store, and 6 undertakers' and funeral supplies stores.

★ 375 ★

Business Owners and Operators

Proprietors of Businesses in Cities With 50,000 or More Blacks: Washington, D.C., 1929

Kind of business	Number of stores	Proprietors and firm members (not on pay roll)	Number of employees		Total pay roll (including part time)	Stocks on hand, end of year (at cost)	Net sales	
			Full time	Part time			Amount	Percent of total
Total	244	284	195	63	$162,063	$102,820	$1,495,854	100.00
Food group	71	80	15	5	10,509	12,590	289,590	19.36
Candy and confectionery stores	9	10	2	1	1,766	1,330	12,895	.86
Grocery stores (without meats)	17	18	-	-	-	3,640	46,511	3.11
Combination stores (groceries and meats)	16	17	1	1	770	4,530	84,035	5.62
Meat markets (including sea foods)	17	20	9	3	6,285	1,760	103,362	6.91
All other food stores	12	15	3	-	1,688	1,330	42,787	2.86
Automotive group	15	18	12	2	12,893	4,770	68,815	4.60
Filling stations	3	3	3	-	2,160	480	20,900	1.40
Garage and repair shops	8	10	6	2	7,453	960	25,575	1.71
All other automotive establishments	4	5	3	-	3,280	3,330	22,340	1.49
Apparel group	6	7	5	2	5,740	10,200	35,595	2.38
Men's and boys' clothing and furnishings stores	1	(x)	-	-	-	(x)	(x)	(x)
Women's ready-to-wear specialty stores – apparel and accessories	1	(x)	-	-	-	(x)	(x)	(x)
Women's accessories stores	1	(x)	-	-	-	(x)	(x)	(x)
All other apparel stores	3	3	5	2	5,740	4,100	16,920	1.13
Furniture and household group	5	7	-	-	-	1,180	10,620	.71
Floor coverings, drapery, and upholstery	1	(x)	-	-	-	(x)	(x)	(x)
All other home furnishings and appliances stores	2	(x)	-	-	-	(x)	(x)	(x)
Radio and music stores	2	(x)	-	-	-	(x)	(x)	(x)
Restaurants and eating places	68	83	108	6	64,703	6,260	481,812	32.21
Restaurants, cafeterias, and lunch rooms	62	77	106	6	63,507	5,950	475,152	31.76
Lunch counters, refreshment stands, etc.	6	6	2	-	1,196	310	6,660	.45
Other retail stores	72	82	52	48	65,563	66,360	597,452	39.94
Farmers' supplies stores	1	(x)	-	-	-	(x)	(x)	(x)

[Continued]

★ 375 ★

Proprietors of Businesses in Cities With 50,000 or More Blacks: Washington, D.C., 1929

[Continued]

Kind of business	Number of stores	Proprietors and firm members (not on pay roll)	Number of employees		Total pay roll (including part time)	Stocks on hand, end of year (at cost)	Net sales	
			Full time	Part time			Amount	Percent of total
Cigar stores and cigar stands	10	10	4	1	2,520	1,830	25,530	1.71
Coal and wood yards – ice dealers	16	18	11	2	8,836	3,880	106,316	7.11
Drug stores	23	24	16	25	18,654	45,160	238,281	15.93
Jewelry stores	1	(x)	-	-	-	(x)	(x)	(x)
Miscellaneous classifications (combined)[1]	21	26	21	20	35,553	15,150	217,365	14.53
Second-hand stores	7	7	3	-	2,655	1,460	11,970	.80

Source: "Stores Operated by Negro Proprietors, by Kind of Business, for Cities Having 50,000 or More Negro Inhabitants: 1929," U.S. Bureau of the Census, *Negroes in the United States: 1920-32*, p. 529. *Notes:* 1. Includes 1 beauty shop, 4 florists, 2 news dealers, 1 novelty shop, 1 optical shop, 1 patent medicine shop, 2 printers and lithographers, and 9 undertakers' and funeral supplies stores.

★ 376 ★

Business Owners and Operators

Proprietors, Stores by Sections and Divisions, 1929

Section and division	Negro population[1]	Number of stores	Proprietors and firm members (not on pay roll)	Number of employees (full time)	Total pay roll (including part time)	Stocks on hand, end of year (at cost)	Net sales
United States	11,891,143	25,701	28,243	12,561	$8,528,306	$10,657,000	$101,146,043
The South	9,361,577	18,864	20,753	7,762	4,333,477	6,335,200	57,036,307
South Atlantic	4,421,388	9,622	10,412	3,516	2,097,912	3,175,340	27,347,636
East South Central	2,658,238	4,359	4,839	2,050	1,046,500	1,351,960	13,248,290
West South Central	2,281,951	4,883	5,502	2,196	1,189,065	1,807,900	16,440,381
The North	2,409,219	6,475	7,081	4,371	3,760,864	4,025,100	40,335,397
New England	94,086	232	254	143	173,286	231,710	1,929,224
Middle Atlantic	1,052,899	2,514	2,709	1,464	1,364,432	1,609,400	14,883,293
East North Central	930,450	2,728	3,009	1,980	1,640,070	1,471,150	17,191,719
West North Central	331,784	1,001	1,109	784	583,076	712,840	6,331,161
The West	120,347	362	409	428	433,965	296,700	3,774,339
Mountain	30,225	68	79	71	62,201	47,870	557,044
Pacific	90,122	294	330	357	371,764	248,830	3,217,295
Percent distribution							
United States	100.0	100.0	100.0	100.0	100.0	100.0	100.0
The South	78.73	73.40	73.48	61.79	50.81	59.45	56.39
South Atlantic	37.18	37.44	36.87	27.99	24.60	29.80	27.04
East South Central	22.35	16.96	17.13	16.32	12.27	12.69	13.10
West South Central	19.19	19.00	19.48	17.48	13.94	16.96	16.25
The North	20.26	25.19	25.07	34.80	44.10	37.77	39.88
New England	.79	.90	.90	1.14	2.03	2.17	1.91

[Continued]

★ 376 ★

Proprietors, Stores by Sections and Divisions, 1929

[Continued]

Section and division	Negro population[1]	Number of stores	Proprietors and firm members (not on pay roll)	Number of employees (full time)	Total pay roll (including part time)	Stocks on hand, end of year (at cost)	Net sales
Middle Atlantic	8.85	9.78	9.59	11.66	16.00	15.10	14.17
East North Central	7.82	10.61	10.65	15.76	19.23	13.80	17.00
West North Central	2.79	3.89	3.93	6.24	6.84	6.69	6.26
The West	1.01	1.41	1.45	3.41	5.09	2.78	3.73
Mountain	.25	.26	.28	.57	.73	.45	.55
Pacific	.76	1.14	1.17	2.84	4.36	2.33	3.18

Source: "Retail Business, by Specified Racial Classes, for the United States: 1929." U.S. Bureau of the Census. *Negroes in the United States: 1920-32.* Washington, D.C.: Government Printing Office, 1935, p. 497. *Note:* 1. Enumerated Apr. 1, 1930.

★ 377 ★

Business Owners and Operators

Proprietors, Stores by Sections, Divisions, and States, Characteristics, 1929

Division or state	Negro population[1]	Number of stores	Proprietors and firm members (not on pay roll)	Number of employees (full time)	Total pay roll (including part time)	Stocks on hand, end of year (at cost)	Net sales			
							Amount	Percent distribution	Per capita of Negro population	Average per store
United States	11,891,143	25,701	28,243	12,561	$8,528,306	$10,657,000	$101,146,043	100.00	$8.51	$3,935
The North	2,409,219	6,475	7,081	4,371	3,760,864	4,025,100	40,335,397	39.88	16.74	6,229
The South	9,361,577	18,864	20,753	7,762	4,333,477	6,335,200	57,036,307	56.39	6.09	3,024
The West	120,347	362	409	428	433,965	296,700	3,774,339	3.73	31.36	10,426
Geographic divisions										
New England	94,086	232	254	143	173,286	231,710	1,929,224	1.91	20.50	8,316
Middle Atlantic	1,052,899	2,514	2,709	1,464	1,364,432	1,609,400	14,883,293	14.71	14.14	5,920
East North Central	930,450	2,728	3,009	1,980	1,640,070	1,471,150	17,191,719	17.00	18.48	6,302
West North Central	331,784	1,001	1,109	784	583,076	712,840	6,331,161	6.26	19.08	6,325
South Atlantic	4,421,388	9,622	10,412	3,516	2,097,912	3,175,340	27,347,636	27.04	6.19	2,842
East South Central	2,658,238	4,359	4,839	2,050	1,046,500	1,351,960	13,248,290	13.10	4.98	3,039
West South Central	2,281,951	4,883	5,502	2,196	1,189,065	1,807,900	16,440,381	16.25	7.20	3,367
Mountain	30,225	68	79	71	62,201	47,870	557,044	.55	18.43	8,192
Pacific	90,122	294	330	357	371,764	248,830	3,217,295	3.18	35.70	10,943
New England										
Maine	1,096	4	5	2	4,689	2,300	46,917	.05	42.81	11,729
New Hampshire	790	4	4	5	4,005	5,950	26,791	.03	33.91	6,698
Vermont	568	3	5	4	4,286	9,830	76,462	.08	134.62	25,487
Massachusetts	52,365	121	135	86	98,139	123,380	1,149,686	1.14	21.96	9,502
Rhode Island	9,913	41	43	16	22,485	39,310	194,469	.19	19.62	4,743
Connecticut	29,354	59	62	30	39,682	50,940	434,899	.43	14.82	7,371
Middle Atlantic										
New York	412,814	611	682	510	500,533	564,790	5,625,743	5.56	13.63	9,207
New Jersey	208,828	577	624	294	264,386	349,900	2,737,685	2.71	13.11	4,745
Pennsylvania	431,257	1,326	1,403	660	599,513	694,710	6,519,865	6.45	15.12	4,917
East North Central										
Ohio	309,304	790	870	498	415,958	433,170	4,411,775	4.36	14.26	5,585
Indiana	111,982	342	383	260	189,328	131,350	2,021,677	2.00	18.05	5,911
Illinois	328,972	1,058	1,136	696	602,798	622,740	6,466,323	6.39	19.66	6,112
Michigan	169,453	488	563	465	379,949	229,970	3,817,530	3.77	22.53	7,823
Wisconsin	10,739	50	57	61	52,037	53,920	474,414	.47	44.18	9,488
West North Central										
Minnesota	9,445	71	86	72	54,410	100,870	585,676	.58	62.01	8,249

[Continued]

★ 377 ★

Proprietors, Stores by Sections, Divisions, and States, Characteristics, 1929
[Continued]

Division or state	Negro population[1]	Number of stores	Proprietors and firm members (not on pay roll)	Number of employees (full time)	Total pay roll (including part time)	Stocks on hand, end of year (at cost)	Net sales			
							Amount	Percent distribution	Per capita of Negro population	Average per store
Iowa	17,380	57	64	54	44,543	48,630	573,577	.57	33.00	10,063
Missouri	223,840	575	628	453	315,947	290,470	3,200,109	3.16	14.30	5,565
North Dakota	377	15	16	11	9,735	17,920	198,584	.20	526.75	13,239
South Dakota	646	13	14	15	18,319	23,940	129,862	.13	201.02	9,989
Nebraska	13,752	52	60	55	34,782	86,160	435,433	.43	31.66	8,374
Kansas	66,344	218	241	124	105,340	144,850	1,207,920	1.19	18.21	5,541
South Atlantic										
Delaware	32,602	61	62	27	18,811[1]	27,780	260,766	.26	8.00	4,275
Maryland	276,379	515	525	198	164,492	125,700	1,690,747	1.67	6.12	3,283
District of Columbia	132,068	244	284	195	162,063	102,820	1,495,854	1.48	11.33	6,131
Virginia	650,165	1,878	2,043	645	378,446	885,720	4,986,347	4.93	7.67	2,655
West Virginia	114,893	310	344	177	117,419	160,070	1,169,006	1.16	10.17	3,771
North Carolina	918,647	1,907	2,077	577	369,369	707,720	5,770,830	5.71	6.28	3,026
South Carolina	793,681	1,230	1,320	350	180,739	201,010	2,298,672	2.27	2.90	1,869
Georgia	1,071,125	2,099	2,253	763	380,600	525,970	5,147,040	5.09	4.81	2,452
Florida	431,828	1,378	1,504	584	325,973	438,550	4,528,374	4.48	10.49	3,286
East South Central										
Kentucky	226,040	683	778	310	191,080	260,760	2,144,159	2.12	9.49	3,139
Tennessee	477,646	973	1,100	537	311,748	327,960	3,728,674	3.69	7.81	3,832
Alabama	944,834	1,297	1,406	643	264,895	393,280	3,566,565	3.53	3.77	2,750
Mississippi	1,009,718	1,406	1,555	560	278,777	369,960	3,808,892	3.77	3.77	2,709
West South Central										
Arkansas	478,463	933	1,029	300	144,416	343,450	2,468,727	2.44	5.16	2,646
Louisiana	776,326	1,668	1,884	577	262,787	369,770	4,504,809	4.45	5.80	2,701
Oklahoma	172,198	546	626	320	211,888	419,040	2,833,144	2.80	16.45	5,189
Texas	854,964	1,736	1,963	999	569,974	675,640	6,633,701	6.56	7.76	3,821
Mountain										
Montana	1,256	6	7	7	6,036	5,730	49,497	.05	39.41	8,250
Idaho	668	2	(X)	(X)	(X)	(X)	(X)	(X)	(X)	(X)
Wyoming	1,250	3	3	4	4,678	3,250	24,176	.02	19.34	8,059
Colorado	11,828	41	49	44	39,827	20,100	335,893	.33	28.40	8,193
New Mexico	2,850	1	(X)	(X)	(X)	(X)	(X)	(X)	(X)	(X)
Arizona	10,749	8	9	11	7,754	670	34,283	.03	3.19	4,285
Utah	1,108	5	6	5	2,951	14,500	83,945	.08	75.76	16,789
Nevada	516	2	(X)	(X)	(X)	(X)	(X)	(X)	(X)	(X)
Pacific										
Washington	6,840	18	21	18	17,899	10,440	175,521	0.17	25.66	9,751
Oregon	2,234	14	16	27	34,036	34,310	329,541	0.33	147.51	23,539
California	81,048	262	293	312	319,829	204,080	2,712,233	2.68	33.46	10,352

Source: "Stores Operated by Negro Proprietors, by Sections, Divisions, and States: 1929." U.S. Bureau of the Census. *Negroes in the United States: 1920-32.* Washington, D.C.: Government Printing Office, 1935, p. 500. *Notes:* An (X) indicates the amount must be withheld to avoid disclosure of individual operations, but it is included in the totals. 1. Enumerated Apr. 1, 1930.

★ 378 ★

Business Owners and Operators

Proprietors, Stores by State, 1929

State	Ranked by--				
	Population[1]	Number of stores	Stocks on hand, end of year (at cost)	Net sales	
				Per capita of Negro population	Average per store
Georgia	1	1	7	44	47
Mississippi	2	6	12	46	43
Alabama	3	9	11	45	42
North Carolina	4	2	2	40	41
Texas	5	4	4	38	36
South Carolina	6	10	21	48	49
Louisiana	7	5	13	42	44
Virginia	8	3	1	39	45
Arkansas	9	13	15	43	46
Tennessee	10	12	16	37	35
Florida	11	7	8	33	38
Pennsylvania	12	8	3	26	29
New York	13	16	6	30	13
Illinois	14	11	5	19	23
Ohio	15	14	9	29	25
Maryland	16	20	25	41	39
Kentucky	17	15	18	35	40
Missouri	18	18	17	28	26
New Jersey	19	17	14	31	30
Oklahoma	20	19	10	24	28
Michigan	21	21	19	17	19
District of Columbia	22	25	27	32	22
West Virginia	23	23	22	34	37
Indiana	24	22	24	23	24
California	25	24	20	11	6
Kansas	26	26	23	22	27
Massachusetts	27	27	26	18	10
Delaware	28	29	35	36	33
Connecticut	29	30	31	27	20
Iowa	30	31	32	12	7
Nebraska	31	32	29	13	14
Colorado	32	34	37	14	17
Arizona	33	40	48	47	32
Wisconsin	34	33	30	7	11
Rhode Island	35	35	33	20	31
Minnesota	36	28	28	6	16
Washington	37	36	40	16	9
New Mexico	38	49	49	49	48
Oregon	39	38	34	3	2
Montana	40	41	43	9	15
Wyoming	41	46	44	21	18
Utah	42	42	39	5	3
Maine	43	43	46	8	5
New Hampshire	44	44	42	10	21

[Continued]

★ 378 ★

Proprietors, Stores by State, 1929

[Continued]

| State | Ranked by-- | | | | |
| | Population[1] | Number of stores | Stocks on hand, end of year (at cost) | Net sales | |
				Per capita of Negro population	Average per store
Idaho	45	47	45	15	12
South Dakota	46	39	36	2	8
Vermont	47	45	41	4	1
Nevada	48	48	47	25	34
North Dakota	49	37	38	1	4

Source: "Stores Operated by Negro Proprietors by States: 1929." U.S. Bureau of the Census. *Negroes in the United States:1920-32.* Washington, D.C.: Government Printing Office, 1935, p. 498. *Note:* 1. Enumerated April 1, 1930.

★ 379 ★

Business Owners and Operators

Proprietors, Stores by Type of Business, Characteristics, 1929

| Kind of business | Number of stores | Proprietors and firm members (not on pay roll) | Number of employees (full time) | Total pay roll (including part time) | Stocks on hand end of year (at cost) | Net sales | |
						Amount	Percent of total
Total	25,701	28,243	12,561	$8,528,306	$10,657,000	$101,146,043	100.00
Food group	10,755	11,594	2,139	1,341,671	3,240,610	36,662,523	36.25
Candy and confectionery stores	1,137	1,193	230	124,841	207,480	2,584,053	2.55
Grocery stores (without meats)	6,248	6,690	707	336,608	1,709,750	14,714,500	14.55
Combination stores (groceries and meats)	2,202	2,428	768	520,643	1,147,940	13,654,678	13.50
Meat markets (including sea foods)	537	576	252	188,200	68,150	2,829,147	2.80
All other food stores	631	707	182	171,379	107,290	2,880,145	2.85
General stores – groceries with dry goods, apparel, or general merchandise	761	892	229	151,947	1,161,880	4,828,700	4.78
General merchandise group	128	153	81	67,496	323,790	979,799	.97
Dry goods stores	61	76	33	27,418	165,900	381,111	.38
General merchandise stores	37	47	37	31,048	139,270	456,156	.45
Variety, 5-and-10, and to-a-dollar stores	30	30	11	9,030	18,620	142,532	.14
Automotive group	1,679	1,873	1,059	1,058,269	819,040	9,793,196	9.68
Motor-vehicle dealers (new and used)	39	46	166	245,535	331,750	3,149,837	3.11
Filling stations	799	869	302	258,220	217,100	3,429,826	3.39
Garages and repair shops	732	838	525	481,317	184,310	2,543,898	2.52
Other automotive establishments	109	120	66	73,197	85,880	669,635	.66
Apparel group	477	519	355	322,620	698,830	3,027,917	2.99
Men's and boys' clothing and furnishings stores	66	71	59	59,816	266,660	915,500	.90
Family clothing stores – men's, women's, and children's	32	37	27	29,295	149,040	426,756	.42
Women's ready-to-wear specialty stores – apparel and accessories	57	62	33	28,237	72,290	315,762	.31
Women's accessories stores	54	57	28	32,649	56,080	308,710	.31

[Continued]

★ 379 ★

Proprietors, Stores by Type of Business, Characteristics, 1929
[Continued]

Kind of business	Number of stores	Proprietors and firm members (not on pay roll)	Number of employees (full time)	Total pay roll (including part time)	Stocks on hand end of year (at cost)	Net sales	
						Amount	Percent of total
Other apparel stores	220	240	176	139,385	62,960	715,764	.71
Shoe stores	48	52	32	33,238	91,800	345,425	.34
Furniture and household group	149	174	125	133,500	240,290	1,160,120	1.15
Furniture stores	54	62	53	56,410	104,250	401,056	.40
Floor coverings, drapery, curtain, and upholstery stores	7	7	6	3,588	2,220	19,450	.02
Household appliances stores	3	3	1	500	1,030	7,800	.01
Other home furnishings and appliances stores	30	33	19	15,414	25,770	79,364	.08
Radio and music stores	55	69	46	57,588	107,020	652,450	.64
Restaurants and eating places	7,918	8,530	5,425	2,727,883	572,050	21,333,198	21.09
Restaurants, cafeterias, and lunch rooms	5,729	6,209	4,742	2,358,331	431,950	17,284,126	17.09
Lunch counters, refreshment stands, etc.	2,189	2,321	683	369,552	140,100	4,049,072	4.00
Lumber and building group	96	112	170	202,778	180,380	1,268,024	1.25
Lumber and building material dealers	26	31	72	73,175	98,070	589,155	.58
Electrical shops (without radio)	23	29	30	36,565	18,010	159,862	.16
Heating and plumbing shops	26	30	45	69,147	29,020	354,537	.35
Paint and glass stores	21	22	23	23,891	35,280	164,470	.16
Other retail stores	3,365	3,994	2,858	2,411,120	3,231,540	21,109,630	20.87
Hardware stores	40	49	22	34,606	179,110	476,048	.47
Hardware and farm implement stores	11	16	22	20,286	92,160	335,348	.33
Farmers' supplies	107	123	50	45,880	97,850	927,859	.92
Book stores	8	9	9	4,933	22,120	52,661	.05
Cigar stores and cigar stands	704	764	320	236,597	140,960	2,052,958	2.03
Coal and wood yards – ice dealers	549	594	337	250,079	125,900	2,117,474	2.09
Drug stores	712	852	955	790,465	1,566,750	7,253,921	7.17
Jewelry stores	67	74	33	45,596	231,650	388,282	.39
Miscellaneous classifications (combined)	1,167	1,513	1,110	982,678	775,040	7,505,079	7.42
Second-hand stores	373	402	120	111,022	188,590	982,936	.97

Source: "Stores Operated by Negro Proprietors, by Kind of Business, for the United States: 1929." U.S. Bureau of the Census. *Negroes in the United States: 1920-32.* Washington, D.C.: Government Printing Office, 1935, p. 499.

★ 380 ★

Business Owners and Operators

Proprietors, Stores in Cities Having 50,000 or More Black Inhabitants, Number and Characteristics, 1929

Cities	Negro population[1]	Number of stores	Number of employees		Total pay roll (including part time)	Stocks on hand, end of year (at cost)	Net sales			
			Full time	Part time			Amount	Percent of total	Per capita of Negro population	Average per store
Total	1,927,569	5,741	5,979	3,576	770	$2,674,564	$2,151,758	$27,862,020	100.0	$14	$4,853
Atlanta, Ga.	90,075	391	424	192	70	95,636	56,710	1,151,850	4.1	13	2,946
Baltimore, Md.	142,106	282	283	132	76	123,198	48,135	1,062,946	3.8	7	3,769
Birmingham, Ala.	99,077	200	228	144	6	64,044	43,790	601,916	2.2	6	3,010
Chicago, Ill.	233,903	815	866	576	147	497,349	435,130	4,826,897	17.3	21	5,923

[Continued]

★ 380 ★

Proprietors, Stores in Cities Having 50,000 or More Black Inhabitants, Number and Characteristics, 1929

[Continued]

Cities	Negro population[1]	Number of stores	Number of employees		Total pay roll (including part time)	Stocks on hand, end of year (at cost)	Net sales				
			Full time	Part time			Amount	Percent of total	Per capita of Negro population	Average per store	
Cleveland, Ohio	71,899	215	240	161	34	108,666	108,810	1,156,859	4.1	16	5,381
Detroit, Mich.	120,066	358	413	369	38	304,713	154,963	2,951,471	10.6	25	8,244
Houston, Tex.	63,337	259	272	259	22	155,511	82,000	1,343,588	4.8	21	5,188
Memphis, Tenn.	96,550	379	304	217	32	132,858	97,300	1,552,583	5.6	16	4,097
New Orleans, La.	129,632	771	906	238	22	126,252	130,140	2,300,374	8.3	18	2,984
New York, N.Y.	327,706	391	245	313	63	293,482	346,240	3,322,274	11.9	10	8,497
Bronx Borough	12,930	19	19	15	2	14,750	50,110	316,112	1.1	24	16,637
Brooklyn Borough	68,921	94	62	48	2	43,043	52,090	543,047	2.0	8	5,777
Manhattan Borough	224,670	258	142	243	56	227,414	229,990	2,261,677	8.1	10	8,766
Queens Borough	18,609	17	19	7	2	8,125	13,400	190,838	.7	10	11,226
Richmond Borough	2,576	3	3	-	1	150	650	10,600	[2]	4	3,533
Philadelphia, Pa.	219,599	787	819	337	96	300,747	266,480	3,150,007	11.3	14	4,003
Pittsburgh, Pa.	54,983	150	168	128	20	99,327	94,810	830,013	3.0	15	5,533
Richmond, Va.	52,988	189	199	102	36	61,202	67,760	657,961	2.4	12	3,481
St. Louis, Mo.	93,580	310	328	213	45	149,516	116,670	1,457,427	5.2	16	4,701
Washington, D.C.	132,068	244	284	195	63	162,063	102,820	1,495,854	5.4	11	6,131

Source: "Stores Operated by Negro Proprietors for Cities Having 50,000 or More Negro Inhabitants: 1929." U.S. Bureau of the Census. *Negroes in the United States: 1920-32.* Washington, D.C.: Government Printing Office, 1935, pp. 518. *Notes:* 1. Enumerated Apr. 1, 1930. 2. Less than 1/10 of 1 percent.

★ 381 ★

Business Owners and Operators

Proprietors, Stores in Cities Having 50,000 or More Black Inhabitants, Ranked, 1929

Cities	Ranked by--				
	Population[1]	Number of stores	Stocks on hand, end of year (at cost)	Net sales	
				Per capita of Negro population	Average per store
New York, N.Y.	1	5	2	13	1
Chicago, Ill.	2	1	1	2	4
Philadelphia, Pa.	3	2	3	9	10
Baltimore, Md.	4	9	14	14	11
Washington, D.C.	5	11	8	12	3
New Orleans, La.	6	3	5	4	14
Detroit, Mich.	7	7	4	1	2
Birmingham, Ala.	8	13	15	15	13
Memphis, Tenn.	9	6	9	6	9
St. Louis, Mo.	10	8	6	7	8
Atlanta, Ga.	11	4	13	10	15
Cleveland, Ohio	12	12	7	5	6
Houston, Tex.	13	10	11	3	7

[Continued]

★ 381 ★

Proprietors, Stores in Cities Having 50,000 or More Black Inhabitants, Ranked, 1929

[Continued]

| Cities | Ranked by-- | | | | |
| | | | | Net sales | |
	Population[1]	Number of stores	Stocks on hand, end of year (at cost)	Per capita of Negro population	Average per store
Pittsburgh, Pa.	14	15	10	8	5
Richmond, Va.	15	14	12	11	12

Source: "Stores Operated by Negro Proprietors in Cities Having 50,000 or More Negro Inhabitants: 1929." U.S. Bureau of the Census. *Negroes in the United States: 1920-32.* Washington, D.C.: Government Printing Office, 1935, p. 519. *Note:* 1. Enumerated Apr. 1, 1930.

★ 382 ★

Business Owners and Operators

Proprietors, Stores in Alabama, 1929

| Kind of business | Number of stores | Proprietors and firm members (not on pay roll) | Number of employees (full time) | Total pay roll (including part time) | Stocks on hand, end of year (at cost) | Net sales | |
						Amount	Percent of total
Total	1,297	1,406	643	$264,895	$393,280	$3,566,565	100.0
Food group	616	667	154	60,137	180,760	1,598,656	44.83
Candy and confectionery stores	29	31	5	1,741	3,280	27,693	.78
Grocery stores (without meats)	405	435	69	26,004	105,580	847,286	23.76
Combination stores (groceries and meats)	136	155	55	24,123	65,760	602,750	16.90
Meat markets (including sea foods)	42	42	22	7,809	5,940	114,387	3.21
Other food stores	4	4	3	460	200	6,540	.18
General stores – groceries with dry goods or apparel	56	62	16	11,012	69,940	354,854	9.95
General merchandise group	6	8	5	3,366	21,140	28,939	.81
Dry goods stores – piece goods stores	3	5	2	1,766	14,580	17,104	.48
General merchandise stores	3	3	3	1,600	6,560	11,835	.33
Automotive group	50	57	23	15,028	5,200	126,146	3.54
Filling stations	21	22	5	2,186	2,940	33,999	.95
Garage and repair shops	23	28	15	11,426	1,330	69,057	1.94
Other automotive establishments	6	7	3	1,416	930	23,090	.65
Apparel group	16	17	15	10,253	11,250	65,375	1.83
Men's and boys' clothing and furnishings stores	2	(x)	(x)	(x)	(x)	(x)	(x)
Family clothing stores – men's, women's, and children's	1	(x)	(x)	(x)	(x)	(x)	(x)
Other apparel stores	9	10	9	5,126	2,020	29,275	.82
Shoe stores	4	4	2	2,220	1,280	12,400	.35
Restaurants, cafeterias, and eating places	452	482	297	83,989	21,720	762,644	21.38
Restaurants, cafeterias, and lunch rooms	294	318	248	68,607	14,240	579,859	16.26
Lunch counters, refreshment stands, etc.	158	164	49	15,382	7,480	182,785	5.12
Lumber and building group	4	6	10	9,836	4,750	53,417	1.50
Lumber and building material dealers	1	(x)	(x)	(x)	(x)	(x)	(x)
Electrical shops (without radio)	1	(x)	(x)	(x)	(x)	(x)	(x)
Heating and plumbing shops	2	(x)	(x)	(x)	(x)	(x)	(x)
Other retail stores[1]	91	101	120	69,537	77,780	566,484	15.88
Farmers' supplies	3	3	-	-	1,050	3,960	.11
Cigar stores and cigar stands	3	3	7	2,642	1,100	14,256	.40
Coal and wood yards – ice dealers	16	18	21	12,663	3,780	89,178	2.50

[Continued]

★ 382 ★

Proprietors, Stores in Alabama, 1929
[Continued]

Kind of business	Number of stores	Proprietors and firm members (not on pay roll)	Number of employees (full time)	Total pay roll (including part time)	Stocks on hand, end of year (at cost)	Net sales	
						Amount	Percent of total
Drug stores	25	28	47	25,282	46,150	256,510	7.19
Miscellaneous classifications (combined)	42	47	45	28,950	24,800	200,930	5.64
Second-hand stores	6	6	3	1,737	740	10,050	.28

Source: "Stores Operated by Black Proprietors, by States: 1929." U.S. Bureau of the Census. *Negroes in the United States: 1920-32.*Washington, D.C.: Government Printing Office, 1935, p. 502. Adapted by the Editors. *Notes:* X - amount must be withheld to avoid disclosure of individual operations, but it is included in totals. 1. Includes 4 custom tailors.

★ 383 ★

Business Owners and Operators

Proprietors, Stores in California, 1929

Kind of business	Number of stores	Proprietors and firm members (not on pay roll)	Number of employees (full time)	Total pay roll (including part time)	Stocks on hand, end of year (at cost)	Net sales	
						Amount	Percent of total
Total	262	293	312	$319,829	$204,080	$2,712,233	100.00
Food group	56	63	12	10,201	29,210	327,343	12.07
Candy and confectionery stores	6	6	4	2,704	910	18,071	.67
Grocery stores (without meats)	36	41	1	1,148	16,870	148,815	5.49
Combination stores (groceries and meats)	9	9	4	3,200	10,650	114,236	4.21
All other food stores	5	7	3	3,149	780	46,221	1.70
General merchandise group	3	4	4	3,399	15,710	24,075	.89
Dry goods stores – piece goods stores	3	4	4	3,399	15,710	24,075	.89
Automotive group	40	48	52	95,728	46,890	975,649	35.97
Motor-vehicle dealers (new and used)	4	6	25	58,699	37,450	707,771	26.10
Filling stations	11	10	15	20,510	4,810	165,297	6.09
Garages and repair shops	18	24	10	13,440	1,260	77,151	2.84
Other automotive establishments	7	8	2	3,079	3,370	25,430	.94
Apparel group	14	15	13	13,181	41,950	134,891	4.97
Men's and boys' clothing and furniture stores	6	6	9	9,543	34,110	74,901	2.76
Family clothing stores – men's, women's, and children's	3	3	1	1,058	2,700	20,224	.75
Women's ready-to-wear specialty stores – apparel and accessories	2	(x)	(x)	(x)	(x)	(x)	(x)
Other apparel stores	2	(x)	(x)	(x)	(x)	(x)	(x)
Shoe stores	1	(x)	(x)	(x)	(x)	(x)	(x)
Furniture and household group	3	4	1	1,690	6,320	33,392	1.23
Furniture stores	2	(x)	(x)	(x)	(x)	(x)	(x)
Radio and music stores	1	(x)	(x)	(x)	(x)	(x)	(x)
Restaurants, cafeterias, and eating places	55	58	164	130,811	9,510	714,156	26.33
Restaurants, cafeterias, and lunch rooms	47	48	154	125,801	9,130	671,892	24.77
Lunch counters, refreshment stands, etc.	8	10	10	5,010	380	42,264	1.56
Lumber and building group	4	7	17	14,054	1,850	85,313	3.15
Lumber and building material dealers	1	(x)	(x)	(x)	(x)	(x)	(x)
Electrical shops (without radio)	2	(x)	(x)	(x)	(x)	(x)	(x)
Heating and plumbing shops	1	(x)	(x)	(x)	(x)	(x)	(x)
Other retail stores	70	76	42	42,844	34,710	367,922	13.57
General stores	2	(x)	(x)	(x)	(x)	(x)	(x)
Farmers' supplies stores (including feeds and fertilizers)	1	(x)	(x)	(x)	(x)	(x)	(x)
Cigar stores and cigar stands	45	48	22	17,957	4,410	111,727	4.12

[Continued]

★ 383 ★

Proprietors, Stores in California, 1929

[Continued]

Kind of business	Number of stores	Proprietors and firm members (not on pay roll)	Number of employees (full time)	Total pay roll (including part time)	Stocks on hand, end of year (at cost)	Net sales	
						Amount	Percent of total
Drug stores	3	3	10	14,404	10,680	71,320	2.63
Jewelry store	1	(x)	(x)	(x)	(x)	(x)	(x)
Miscellaneous classifications (combined)	18	20	8	8,829	6,110	104,982	3.87
Second-hand stores	17	18	7	7,921	17,930	49,492	1.82

Source: "Stores Operated by Black Proprietors, by States: 1929." U.S. Bureau of the Census. *Negroes in the United States: 1920-32.* Washington, D.C.: Government Printing Office, 1935, pp. 502-503. Adapted by the Editors. *Notes:* X - amount must be withheld to avoid disclosure of individual operations, but it is included in totals.

★ 384 ★

Business Owners and Operators

Proprietors, Stores in Colorado, 1929

Kind of business	Number of stores	Proprietors and firm members (not on pay roll)	Number of employees (full time)	Total pay roll (including part time)	Stocks on hand, end of year (at cost)	Net sales	
						Amount	Percent of total
Total	41	49	44	$39,827	$20,100	$335,893	100.00
Food group	5	5	-	-	630	19,245	5.73
Candy and confectionery stores	2	(x)	(x)	(x)	(x)	(x)	(x)
Grocery stores (without meats)	1	(x)	(x)	(x)	(x)	(x)	(x)
Combination stores (groceries and meats)	1	(x)	(x)	(x)	(x)	(x)	(x)
Other food stores	1	(x)	(x)	(x)	(x)	(x)	(x)
Automotive group	10	14	12	12,735	9,560	150,779	44.89
Motor-vehicle dealers (new and used)	3	3	8	8,412	8,460	109,010	32.46
Garages and repair shops	5	8	3	3,348	350	27,757	8.26
All other automotive establishments	2	3	1	975	750	14,012	4.17
Restaurants, cafeterias, and eating places	11	13	20	12,085	270	65,241	19.42
Other retail stores	15	17	12	15,007	9,640	100,628	29.96
Hardware stores	1	(x)	(x)	(x)	(x)	(x)	(x)
Farmers' supplies stores, including feed and fertilizer	1	(x)	(x)	(x)	(x)	(x)	(x)
Cigar stores and cigar stands	1	(x)	(x)	(x)	(x)	(x)	(x)
Coal and wood yards – ice dealers	6	7	4	4,800	550	40,904	12.18
Drug stores	1	(x)	(x)	(x)	(x)	(x)	(x)
Miscellaneous classifications (combined)	3	4	-	-	850	2,910	.87
Second-hand stores	2	(x)	(x)	(x)	(x)	(x)	(x)

Source: "Stores Operated by Black Proprietors, by States: 1929." U.S. Bureau of the Census. *Negroes in the United States: 1920-32.* Washington, D.C.: Government Printing Office, 1935, p. 503. Adapted by the Editors. *Notes:* X - amount must be withheld to avoid disclosure of individual operations, but it is included in totals.

★ 385 ★

Business Owners and Operators

Proprietors, Stores in Connecticut, 1929

Kind of business	Number of stores	Proprietors and firm members (not on pay roll)	Number of employees (full time)	Total pay roll (including part time)	Stocks on hand, end of year (at cost)	Net sales	
						Amount	Percent of total
Total	59	62	30	$39,682	$50,940	$434,899	100.00
Food group	24	-	3	4,652	15,220	179,928	41.37
Candy and confectionery stores	2	-	-	-	180	2,785	.64
Grocery stores (without meats)	15	-	2	1,970	9,140	100,655	23.14
Combination stores (groceries and meats)	5	-	1	2,500	5,700	66,245	15.23
Meat markets (including sea foods)	2	-	-	182	200	10,243	2.36
Automotive group	9	-	8	9,215	3,760	40,475	9.31
Garages and repair shops	6	-	5	2,955	1,130	14,644	3.37
All other automotive establishments	3	-	3	6,260	2,630	25,831	5.94
Miscellaneous apparel, including shoes	2	-	3	6,000	1,950	52,500	12.07
Radios and home furnishings	2	-	3	3,330	6,770	18,759	4.31
Restaurants, cafeterias, and eating places	11	-	5	4,770	1,020	43,423	9.98
Restaurants, cafeterias, and lunch rooms	10	-	5	4,770	870	40,323	9.27
Lunch counters, refreshment stands, etc.	1	-	-	-	150	3,100	.71
Other retail stores	11	-	8	11,715	22,220	99,814	22.95
Drug stores	4	-	5	8,415	17,790	81,288	18.69
All other stores (including 2 cigar stands and 2 second-hand stores)	7	-	3	3,300	4,430	18,526	4.26

Source: "Stores Operated by Black Proprietors, by States: 1929." U.S. Bureau of the Census. *Negroes in the United States: 1920-32.* Washington, D.C.: Government Printing Office, 1935, p. 503. Adapted by the Editors.

★ 386 ★

Business Owners and Operators

Proprietors, Stores in Delaware, 1929

Kind of business	Number of stores	Proprietors and firm members (not on pay roll)	Number of employees (full time)	Total pay roll (including part time)	Stocks on hand, end of year (at cost)	Net sales	
						Amount	Percent of total
Total	61	62	27	$18,811	$27,780	$260,766	100.00
Food group							
Candy and confectionery stores	3	3	1	800	180	6,286	2.41
Grocery stores (without meats)	5	5	-	-	2,400	15,650	6.00
Combination stores (groceries and meats)	1	(x)	(x)	(x)	(x)	(x)	(x)
Meat markets (including sea foods)	2	(x)	(x)	(x)	(x)	(x)	(x)
Other food stores	2	(x)	(x)	(x)	(x)	(x)	(x)
Dry-goods stores – piece-goods stores	1	(x)	(x)	(x)	(x)	(x)	(x)

[Continued]

★ 386 ★

Proprietors, Stores in Delaware, 1929

[Continued]

Kind of business	Number of stores	Proprietors and firm members (not on pay roll)	Number of employees (full time)	Total pay roll (including part time)	Stocks on hand, end of year (at cost)	Net sales	
						Amount	Percent of total
Automotive group							
Motor-vehicle dealers (new and used)	1	(x)	(x)	(x)	(x)	(x)	(x)
Filling stations	7	7	-	-	1,310	12,650	4.85
Garages and repair shops	2	(x)	(x)	(x)	(x)	(x)	(x)
Restaurants, cafeterias, and eating places							
Restaurants, cafeterias, and lunch rooms	15	15	7	3,108	1,230	32,351	12.41
Lunch counters and refreshment stands	2	(x)	(x)	(x)	(x)	(x)	(x)
Other retail stores							
Cigar stores and cigar stands	11	11	4	1,806	840	24,471	9.38
Drug stores	4	5	5	5,263	7,610	39,350	15.09
Miscellaneous classifications	3	3	1	1,280	1,300	20,800	7.98
Second-hand stores	2	(x)	(x)	(x)	(x)	(x)	(x)

Source: "Stores Operated by Black Proprietors, by States: 1929." U.S. Bureau of the Census. *Negroes in the United States: 1920-32.* Washington, D.C.: Government Printing Office, 1935, p. 503. Adapted by the Editors. *Notes:* x - amount withheld to avoid disclosure of individual operations, but it is included in totals.

★ 387 ★

Business Owners and Operators

Proprietors, Stores in the District of Columbia, 1929

Kind of business	Number of stores	Proprietors and firm members (not on pay roll)	Number of employees (full time)	Total pay roll (including part time)	Stocks on hand, end of year (at cost)	Net sales	
						Amount	Percent of total
Total	244	284	195	$162,063	$102,820	$1,495,854	100.0
Food group	71	80	15	10,509	12,590	289,590	19.36
Candy and confectionery stores	9	10	2	1,766	1,330	12,895	.86
Grocery stores (without meats)	17	18	-	-	3,640	46,511	3.11
Combination stores (groceries and meats)	16	17	1	770	4,530	84,035	5.62
Meat markets (including sea foods)	17	20	9	6,285	1,760	103,362	6.91
Other food stores	12	15	3	1,688	1,330	42,787	2.86
Automotive group	15	18	12	12,893	4,770	68,815	4.60
Filling stations	3	3	3	2,160	480	20,900	1.40
Garage and repair shops	8	10	6	7,453	960	25,575	1.71
Other automotive establishments	4	5	3	3,280	3,330	22,340	1.49
Apparel group	6	7	5	5,740	10,200	35,595	2.38
Men's and boys' clothing and furnishings stores	1	(x)	-	-	(x)	(x)	(x)
Women's ready-to-wear specialty stores – apparel and accessories	1	(x)	-	-	(x)	(x)	(x)
Women's accessories stores	1	(x)	-	-	(x)	(x)	(x)
Other apparel stores	3	3	5	5,740	4,100	16,920	1.13
Furniture and household group	5	7	-	-	1,180	10,620	.71

[Continued]

335

★ 387 ★

Proprietors, Stores in the District of Columbia, 1929
[Continued]

Kind of business	Number of stores	Proprietors and firm members (not on pay roll)	Number of employees (full time)	Total pay roll (including part time)	Stocks on hand, end of year (at cost)	Net sales Amount	Percent of total
Floor coverings, draperies, curtains, and upholstery stores	1	(x)	-	-	(x)	(x)	(x)
Other home furnishings and appliances stores	2	(x)	-	-	(x)	(x)	(x)
Radio and music stores	2	(x)	-	-	(x)	(x)	(x)
Restaurants, cafeterias, and eating places	68	83	108	64,703	6,260	481,812	32.21
Restaurants, cafeterias	62	77	106	63,507	5,950	475,152	31.76
Lunch counters and refreshment stands	6	6	2	1,196	310	6,660	.45
Other retail stores	72	82	52	65,563	66,360	597,452	39.94
Farmers' supplies	1	(x)	-	-	(x)	(x)	(x)
Cigar stores and cigar stands	10	10	4	2,520	1,830	25,530	1.71
Coal and wood yards – ice dealers	16	18	11	8,836	3,880	106,316	7.11
Drug stores	23	24	16	18,654	45,160	238,281	15.93
Jewelry stores	1	(x)	-	-	(x)	(x)	(x)
Miscellaneous classifications (combined)	21	26	21	35,553	15,150	217,365	14.53
Second-hand stores	7	7	3	2,655	1,460	11,970	.80

Source: "Stores Operated by Black Proprietors, by States: 1929." U.S. Bureau of the Census. *Negroes in the United States: 1920-32.*Washington, D.C.: Government Printing Office, 1935, p. 502. Adapted by the Editors. *Notes:* X - the amount must be withheld to avoid disclosure of individual operations, but it is included in totals.

★ 388 ★

Business Owners and Operators

Proprietors, Stores in Georgia, 1929

Kind of business	Number of stores	Proprietors and firm members (not on pay roll)	Number of employees (full time)	Total pay roll (including part time)	Stocks on hand, end of year (at cost)	Net sales Amount	Percent of total
Total	2,099	2,253	763	$380,600	$525,970	$5,147,040	100.0
Food group	1,005	1,069	176	74,788	242,990	2,493,500	48.45
Candy and confectionery stores	65	65	9	2,361	7,870	112,483	2.19
Grocery stores (without meats)	713	759	84	29,740	158,120	1,342,548	26.08
Combination stores (groceries and meats)	154	165	55	25,976	70,460	778,039	15.12
Meat markets (including sea foods)	46	50	20	12,935	5,090	173,799	3.38
Other food stores	27	30	8	3,776	1,450	86,631	1.68
General stores – groceries with dry goods or apparel	31	38	7	3,165	25,030	109,738	2.13
General merchandise group	10	13	11	6,702	56,010	125,125	2.43
Dry goods stores	7	10	6	3,066	15,500	39,425	.77
General merchandise stores	2	(x)	(x)	(x)	(x)	(x)	(x)
Variety, 5-and-10, and to-a-dollar stores	1	(x)	(x)	(x)	(x)	(x)	(x)
Automotive group[1]	80	84	44	30,649	11,590	294,374	5.72
Filling stations	44	44	13	8,579	3,990	129,964	2.53
Garage and repair shops	28	31	17	11,607	1,600	47,908	.93
Other automotive establishments	6	5	6	4,233	1,350	32,448	.63
Apparel group[1]	10	10	19	14,250	5,050	51,629	1.00

[Continued]

★ 388 ★

Proprietors, Stores in Georgia, 1929
[Continued]

Kind of business	Number of stores	Proprietors and firm members (not on pay roll)	Number of employees (full time)	Total pay roll (including part time)	Stocks on hand, end of year (at cost)	Net sales Amount	Net sales Percent of total
Other apparel stores	9	9	17	13,386	4,450	45,451	.88
Furniture and household group[1]	5	5	2	1,664	3,700	8,780	.17
Other home furnishings and appliances stores	4	4	2	1,664	3,200	7,280	.14
Restaurants, cafeterias, and eating places	775	807	307	98,911	35,210	1,115,491	21.67
Restaurants, cafeterias, and lunch rooms	473	497	242	74,802	19,870	729,395	14.17
Lunch counters, refreshment stands, etc.	302	310	65	24,109	15,340	386,096	7.50
Other retail stores[1]	176	219	193	146,709	144,400	921,487	17.91
Farmers' supplies	4	6	6	4,958	4,950	63,000	1.22
Cigar stores and cigar stands	9	9	7	3,188	510	16,080	.31
Coal and wood yards – ice dealers	38	39	26	12,334	2,710	50,232	.98
Drug stores	30	33	59	40,090	66,550	321,494	6.25
Jewelry stores	9	10	4	1,685	2,150	19,220	.38
Miscellaneous classifications (combined)	84	120	86	82,654	63,680	435,961	8.47
Second hand stores	7	8	4	3,762	1,990	26,916	.52

Source: "Stores Operated by Black Proprietors, by States: 1929." U.S. Bureau of the Census. *Negroes in the United States: 1920-32.* Washington, D.C.: Government Printing Office, 1935, pp. 504-505. Adapted by the Editors. *Notes:* X - amount must be withheld to avoid disclosure of individual operations, but it is included in totals. 1. Includes 4 custom tailors.

★ 389 ★

Business Owners and Operators

Proprietors, Stores in Kentucky, 1929

Kind of business	Number of stores	Proprietors and firm members (not on pay roll)	Number of employees (full time)	Total pay roll (including part time)	Stocks on hand, end of year (at cost)	Net sales Amount	Net sales Percent of total
Total	683	778	310	$191,080	$260,760	$2,144,159	100.0
Food group	201	230	38	20,907	63,600	601,372	28.05
Candy and confectionery stores	19	21	5	2,726	2,400	36,568	1.70
Grocery stores (without meats)	114	132	13	4,970	38,520	277,749	12.96
Combination stores (groceries and meats)	57	65	15	9,625	21,320	230,145	10.73
Meat markets (including sea foods)	4	4	2	1,300	340	28,450	1.33
Other food stores	7	8	3	2,286	1,020	28,460	1.33
General stores	18	19	8	4,850	37,750	113,493	5.29
General merchandise group	4	5	–	–	8,010	9,725	.45
Dry goods stores	2	(x)	(x)	(x)	(x)	(x)	(x)
General merchandise stores	1	(x)	(x)	(x)	(x)	(x)	(x)
Variety, 5-and-10, and to-a-dollar stores	1	(x)	(x)	(x)	(x)	(x)	(x)
Automotive group	28	29	12	8,888	10,720	103,010	4.81
Filling stations	4	4	3	1,250	310	29,510	1.38
Garage and repair shops	21	22	5	2,838	1,020	19,800	.92
All other automotive establishments	3	3	4	4,800	9,390	53,700	2.51
Apparel group	11	11	6	2,898	20,440	62,269	2.90
Men's and boys' clothing and furnishings stores	1	(x)	(x)	(x)	(x)	(x)	(x)
Family clothing stores – men's, women's, and children's	1	(x)	(x)	(x)	(x)	(x)	(x)
Women's accessories stores	1	(x)	(x)	(x)	(x)	(x)	(x)

[Continued]

★ 389 ★

Proprietors, Stores in Kentucky, 1929

[Continued]

Kind of business	Number of stores	Proprietors and firm members (not on pay roll)	Number of employees (full time)	Total pay roll (including part time)	Stocks on hand, end of year (at cost)	Net sales	
						Amount	Percent of total
Other apparel stores	5	5	4	1,658	2,280	15,542	.72
Shoe stores	3	3	1	720	2,400	9,727	.45
Furniture and household group	3	3	1	500	1,850	8,391	.39
Furniture stores	2	(x)	(x)	(x)	(x)	(x)	(x)
Radio and music stores	1	(x)	(x)	(x)	(x)	(x)	(x)
Restaurants, cafeterias, and eating places	274	298	142	68,500	20,410	544,818	25.41
Restaurants, cafeterias	185	201	102	50,819	16,050	389,035	18.14
Lunch counters, refreshment stands, etc.	89	97	40	17,681	4,360	155,783	7.27
Lumber and building group	3	3	1	850	2,500	13,000	.61
Lumber and building material dealers	2	(x)	(x)	(x)	(x)	(x)	(x)
Heating and plumbing shops	1	(x)	(x)	(x)	(x)	(x)	(x)
Other retail stores	133	170	102	83,687	93,700	683,356	31.87
Farmers' supplies stores (including feed and fertilizers)	3	3	-	-	580	11,560	.54
Cigar stores and cigar stands	11	12	12	5,198	1,720	34,607	1.61
Coal and wood yards – ice dealers	48	51	8	4,344	1,320	35,181	1.64
Drug stores	16	21	35	23,971	47,360	198,812	9.27
Miscellaneous classifications (combined)	55	83	47	50,174	42,720	403,196	18.81
Second hand stores	8	10	-	-	1,780	4,725	.22

Source: "Stores Operated by Black Proprietors, by States: 1929." U.S. Bureau of the Census. *Negroes in the United States: 1920-32.*Washington, D.C.: Government Printing Office, 1935, p. 507. Adapted by the Editors. *Notes:* X - amount must be withheld to avoid disclosure of individual operations, but it is included in totals.

★ 390 ★

Business Owners and Operators

Proprietors, Stores in Louisiana, 1929

Kind of business	Number of stores	Proprietors and firm members (not on pay roll)	Number of employees (full time)	Total pay roll (including part time)	Stocks on hand, end of year (at cost)	Net sales	
						Amount	Percent of total
Total	1,668	1,884	577	$262,787	$369,770	$4,504,809	100.0
Food group	810	905	94	41,359	147,690	2,126,708	47.21
Candy and confectionery stores	38	45	3	1,080	3,160	47,651	1.06
Grocery stores (without meats)	423	458	41	19,361	110,370	992,471	22.03
Combination stores (groceries and meats)	61	68	12	5,070	24,350	261,064	5.80
Meat markets (including sea foods)	34	40	13	6,868	2,160	115,915	2.57
Other food stores	254	294	25	8,980	7,650	709,607	15.75
General stores (groceries with apparel or dry goods)	43	52	17	6,499	54,120	231,216	5.13
Automotive group	59	70	27	15,706	9,990	179,479	3.98
Filling stations	33	39	11	6,662	7,150	121,344	2.69
Garage and repair shops	24	29	16	9,044	2,140	53,040	1.18
Other automotive establishments	2	2	-	-	700	5,095	.11
Apparel group	18	20	9	7,522	10,660	51,421	1.14
Men's and boys' clothing and furnishings stores	1	(x)	(x)	(x)	(x)	(x)	(x)
Family clothing stores – men's, women's, and children's	2	(x)	(x)	(x)	(x)	(x)	(x)
Women's accessories stores	2	(x)	(x)	(x)	(x)	(x)	(x)
Other apparel stores	11	12	5	4,818	2,080	21,365	.47
Shoe stores	2	(x)	(x)	(x)	(x)	(x)	(x)
Furniture and household group	7	8	9	6,600	3,660	30,936	.69
Furniture stores	6	7	7	5,300	2,660	24,324	.54

[Continued]

★ 390 ★

Proprietors, Stores in Louisiana, 1929
[Continued]

Kind of business	Number of stores	Proprietors and firm members (not on pay roll)	Number of employees (full time)	Total pay roll (including part time)	Stocks on hand, end of year (at cost)	Net sales	
						Amount	Percent of total
Other home furnishings and appliances stores	1	1	2	1,300	1,000	6,612	.15
Restaurants, cafeterias, and eating places	567	622	293	103,260	28,490	1,134,580	25.19
Restaurants, cafeterias, and lunch rooms	329	353	254	84,717	18,790	791,180	17.56
Lunch counters, refreshment stands, etc.	238	269	39	18,543	9,700	343,400	7.63
Other retail stores	161	204	116	75,341	109,701	728,359	16.17
Paint and glass stores	1	(x)	(x)	(x)	(x)	(x)	(x)
Farmers' supplies stores (including feeds and fertilizers)	2	(x)	(x)	(x)	(x)	(x)	(x)
Cigar stores and cigar stands	18	19	9	5,964	950	25,201	.56
Coal and wood yards – ice dealers	74	93	14	4,823	7,260	172,038	3.82
Drug stores	41	54	48	27,957	74,750	316,579	7.03
Jewelry stores	4	5	-	-	780	7,715	.17
Miscellaneous classifications (combined)	21	30	43	34,917	23,470	188,585	4.19
Second hand stores	3	3	12	6,500	5,450	22,110	.49

Source: "Stores Operated by Black Proprietors, by States: 1929." U.S. Bureau of the Census. *Negroes in the United States: 1920-32.* Washington, D.C.: Government Printing Office, 1935, p. 507. Adapted by the Editors. *Notes:* X - amount must be withheld to avoid disclosure of individual operations, but it is included in totals.

★ 391 ★

Business Owners and Operators

Proprietors, Stores in Mississippi, 1929

Kind of business	Number of stores	Proprietors and firm members (not on pay roll)	Number of employees (full time)	Total pay roll (including part time)	Stocks on hand, end of year (at cost)	Net sales	
						Amount	Percent of total
Total	1,406	1,555	560	$278,777	$369,960	$3,808,892	100.00
Food group	697	753	148	78,264	165,070	1,850,049	48.57
Candy and confectionery stores	9	9	6	5,853	890	26,153	.69
Grocery stores (without meats)	554	592	81	38,675	115,120	1,194,041	31.35
Combination stores (groceries and meats)	93	111	46	27,172	45,030	535,710	14.06
Meat markets (including sea foods)	37	37	15	6,539	3,960	92,295	2.42
Other food stores	4	4	-	25	70	1,850	.05
General stores (groceries with dry goods or apparel)	74	97	22	13,490	68,560	338,228	8.88
General merchandise group[1]	6	7	2	1,109	1,890	42,350	1.11
General merchandise stores	5	6	2	1,109	1,860	42,300	1.11
Automotive group[1]	72	79	48	37,012	45,030	339,078	8.90
Filling stations	33	34	8	3,911	6,620	80,601	2.12
Garages and repair shops	38	44	28	14,923	4,100	73,603	1.93
Apparel group[1]	15	19	11	6,961	4,040	28,160	.74
Other apparel stores	9	13	5	2,630	2,700	10,310	.27
Shoe stores	4	4	4	3,023	980	16,100	.42
Restaurants, cafeterias, and eating places	472	503	225	70,983	23,840	699,342	18.36
Restaurants, cafeterias, and lunch rooms	343	364	204	65,461	17,860	575,040	15.10
Lunch counters, refreshment stands, etc.	129	139	21	5,522	5,980	124,302	3.26
Lumber and building group	4	4	1	600	930	4,070	.11
Lumber and building material dealers	2	(x)	(x)	(x)	(x)	(x)	(x)

[Continued]

★ 391 ★

Proprietors, Stores in Mississippi, 1929
[Continued]

Kind of business	Number of stores	Proprietors and firm members (not on pay roll)	Number of employees (full time)	Total pay roll (including part time)	Stocks on hand, end of year (at cost)	Net sales	
						Amount	Percent of total
Electrical shops (without radio)	1	(x)	(x)	(x)	(x)	(x)	(x)
Heating and plumbing shops	1	(x)	(x)	(x)	(x)	(x)	(x)
Other retail stores	63	89	99	69,160	59,690	499,665	13.12
Furniture stores	1	(x)	(x)	(x)	(x)	(x)	(x)
Farmers' supplies	5	5	7	3,894	4,780	71,082	1.87
Cigar stores and cigar stands	2	(x)	(x)	(x)	(x)	(x)	(x)
Coal and wood yards – ice dealers	2	(x)	(x)	(x)	(x)	(x)	(x)
Drug stores	19	24	22	13,738	23,090	136,062	3.57
Jewelry stores	2	(x)	(x)	(x)	(x)	(x)	(x)
Miscellaneous classifications (combined)	32	52	65	48,708	29,760	257,869	6.77
Second hand stores	3	4	4	1,198	910	7,950	.21

Source: "Stores Operated by Black Proprietors, by States: 1929." U.S. Bureau of the Census. *Negroes in the United States: 1920-32.* Washington, D.C.: Government Printing Office, 1935, p. 509. Adapted by the Editors. *Notes:* X - amount must be withheld to avoid disclosure of individual operations, but it is included in totals. 1. Indicates 4 custom tailors.

★ 392 ★

Business Owners and Operators

Proprietors, Stores in North Carolina, 1929

Kind of business	Number of stores	Proprietors and firm members (not on pay roll)	Number of employees (full time)	Total pay roll (including part time)	Stocks on hand, end of year (at cost)	Net sales	
						Amount	Percent of total
Total	1,907	2,077	577	$369,369	$707,720	$5,770,830	100.0
Food group	956	1,009	144	91,256	279,590	2,679,821	46.44
Candy and confectionery stores	48	49	1	913	3,630	55,187	.96
Grocery stores (without meats)	640	669	59	27,326	158,810	1,183,944	20.51
Combination stores (groceries and meats)	210	227	60	45,078	111,410	1,106,373	19.17
Meat markets (including sea foods)	54	60	22	17,239	5,260	324,787	5.63
Other food stores	4	4	2	700	480	9,530	.17
General stores	62	65	12	6,475	89,040	337,699	5.85
General merchandise group	8	17	6	7,842	22,130	98,226	1.70
Dry goods stores – piece goods stores	4	7	2	2,164	4,790	17,325	.30
General merchandise stores	2	(x)	(x)	(x)	(x)	(x)	(x)
Variety, 5-and-10, and to-a-dollar stores	2	(x)	(x)	(x)	(x)	(x)	(x)
Automotive group	192	204	46	33,639	27,220	495,799	8.60
Filling stations	143	154	25	20,824	22,450	414,770	7.19
Garages and repair shops	46	47	21	12,815	4,240	77,738	1.35
Other automotive establishments	3	3	-	-	530	3,291	.06
Apparel group	22	25	11	11,088	13,160	70,650	1.22
Men's and boys' clothing and furniture stores	1	(x)	(x)	(x)	(x)	(x)	(x)
Women's ready-to-wear specialty stores – apparel and accessories	1	(x)	(x)	(x)	(x)	(x)	(x)

[Continued]

★ 392 ★

Proprietors, Stores in North Carolina, 1929
[Continued]

Kind of business	Number of stores	Proprietors and firm members (not on pay roll)	Number of employees (full time)	Total pay roll (including part time)	Stocks on hand, end of year (at cost)	Net sales	
						Amount	Percent of total
Women's accessories stores	2	(x)	(x)	(x)	(x)	(x)	(x)
Other apparel stores	14	16	8	8,228	6,270	53,885	.93
Shoe stores	4	5	3	2,860	3,690	9,200	.16
Furniture and household group	3	4	9	12,910	23,900	95,200	1.65
Furniture stores	3	4	9	12,910	23,900	95,200	1.65
Restaurants, cafeterias, and eating places	487	521	206	89,781	37,120	911,935	15.80
Restaurants, cafeterias, and lunch rooms	336	362	182	73,520	25,480	680,223	11.79
Lunch counters, refreshment stands, etc.	151	159	24	16,261	11,640	231,712	4.01
Lumber and building group	3	4	4	4,268	3,900	24,150	.42
Lumber and building material dealers	1	(x)	(x)	(x)	(x)	(x)	(x)
Electrical shops (without radio)	1	(x)	(x)	(x)	(x)	(x)	(x)
Paint and glass stores	1	(x)	(x)	(x)	(x)	(x)	(x)
Other retail stores	161	213	136	109,939	204,900	1,034,140	17.92
Cigar stores and cigar stands	9	10	3	1,396	1,440	17,775	.31
Coal and wood yards – ice dealers	23	24	9	5,131	3,970	38,163	.66
Drug stores	48	57	61	42,137	88,420	404,776	7.01
Jewelry stores	3	3	-	-	3,300	4,390	.08
Miscellaneous classifications (combined)	78	119	63	61,275	107,770	569,036	9.86
Second hand stores	13	15	3	2,171	6,760	23,210	.40

Source: "Stores Operated by Black Proprietors, by States: 1929." U.S. Bureau of the Census. *Negroes in the United States: 1920-32.* Washington, D.C.: Government Printing Office, 1935, p. 511-512. Adapted by the Editors. *Notes:* X - amount must be withheld to avoid disclosure of individual operations, but it is included in totals.

★ 393 ★

Business Owners and Operators

Proprietors, Stores in Oklahoma, 1929

Kind of business	Number of stores	Proprietors and firm members (not on pay roll)	Number of employees (full time)	Total pay roll (including part time)	Stocks on hand, end of year (at cost)	Net sales	
						Amount	Percent of total
Total	546	626	320	$211,888	$419,040	$2,833,144	100.00
Food group	199	228	66	40,015	90,090	1,001,775	35.36
Candy and confectionery stores	14	18	6	2,508	2,710	36,985	1.31
Grocery stores (without meats)	92	105	8	4,123	26,660	254,338	8.98
Combination stores (groceries and meats)	93	105	52	33,384	60,720	710,452	25.07
General stores – Groceries with dry goods or apparel	43	45	14	10,774	90,100	306,951	10.84
Other food stores							
General merchandise group	9	10	5	4,120	29,590	71,128	2.51
Dry goods stores	6	7	2	1,740	25,790	40,462	1.43
General merchandise stores	3	3	3	2,380	3,800	30,666	1.08
Automotive group	50	56	21	20,053	19,690	197,551	6.97
Filling stations	33	35	11	13,073	6,140	141,652	5.00
Garages and repair shops	16	20	7	5,780	12,550	50,899	1.80
Other automotive establishments	1	1	3	1,200	1,000	5,000	.17
Apparel group	7	7	11	9,888	49,900	104,642	3.69

[Continued]

★ 393 ★

Proprietors, Stores in Oklahoma, 1929
[Continued]

Kind of business	Number of stores	Proprietors and firm members (not on pay roll)	Number of employees (full time)	Total pay roll (including part time)	Stocks on hand, end of year (at cost)	Net sales	
						Amount	Percent of total
Men's and boys' clothing and furniture stores	1	(x)	(x)	(x)	(x)	(x)	(x)
Family clothing stores – men's, women's, and children's	3	3	8	7,400	46,600	88,192	3.11
Women's accessories stores	2	(x)	(x)	(x)	(x)	(x)	(x)
Other apparel stores	1	(x)	(x)	(x)	(x)	(x)	(x)
Furniture and household group	5	6	3	1,375	3,050	9,260	.33
Radio and music stores	3	4	1	220	1,800	4,660	.17
Restaurants, cafeterias, and eating places	170	195	142	74,033	13,900	593,358	20.94
Restaurants, cafeterias, and lunch rooms	129	148	124	64,035	11,410	474,899	16.76
Lunch counters, refreshment stands, etc.	41	47	18	9,998	2,490	118,459	4.18
Other retail stores	63	79	58	51,630	122,720	548,479	19.36
Lumber and building material dealers	1	(x)	(x)	(x)	(x)	(x)	(x)
Electrical shops (without radio)	1	(x)	(x)	(x)	(x)	(x)	(x)
Hardware stores	3	4	1	1,860	9,620	16,989	.60
Hardware and farm implement stores	2	(x)	(x)	(x)	(x)	(x)	(x)
Farmers' supplies stores	7	7	5	5,168	9,150	65,132	2.30
Book stores	1	(x)	(x)	(x)	(x)	(x)	(x)
Cigar stores and cigar stands	9	12	12	7,783	1,890	38,866	1.37
Coal and wood yards – ice dealers	1	(x)	(x)	(x)	(x)	(x)	(x)
Drug stores	20	23	21	18,766	57,820	214,032	7.55
Jewelry stores	1	(x)	(x)	(x)	(x)	(x)	(x)
Miscellaneous classifications (including 2 second-hand stores)	17	22	13	11,438	9,340	79,470	2.81

Source: "Stores Operated by Black Proprietors, by States: 1929." U.S. Bureau of the Census. *Negroes in the United States: 1920-32*. Washington, D.C.: Government Printing Office, 1935, pp. 512-513. Adapted by the Editors. *Notes:* X - amount must be withheld to avoid disclosure of individual operations, but it is included in totals.

★ 394 ★

Business Owners and Operators

Proprietors, Stores in South Carolina, 1929

Kind of business	Number of stores	Proprietors and firm members (not on pay roll)	Number of employees (full time)	Total pay roll (including part time)	Stocks on hand, end of year (at cost)	Net sales	
						Amount	Percent of total
Total	1,230	1,320	350	$180,739	$201,010	$2,298,672	100.00
Food group	671	704	69	33,023	92,860	1,065,240	46.34
Candy and confectionery stores	16	17	4	2,625	1,200	18,207	.79
Grocery stores (without meats)	505	527	39	14,819	70,020	692,035	30.11
Combination stores (groceries and meats)	101	106	13	8,000	18,740	231,732	10.08
Meat markets (including sea foods)	41	45	11	7,219	2,630	114,042	4.96
Other food stores	8	9	2	360	270	9,224	.40
General stores	48	50	8	3,245	19,260	119,396	5.19
General merchandise group[1]	4	4	3	2,387	4,660	14,285	.62
Dry goods stores – piece goods stores	3	3	3	2,387	4,580	13,685	.59
Automotive group	93	104	31	19,781	12,450	168,828	7.35
Filling stations	56	62	13	7,554	10,010	108,912	4.74

[Continued]

★ 394 ★

Proprietors, Stores in South Carolina, 1929

[Continued]

Kind of business	Number of stores	Proprietors and firm members (not on pay roll)	Number of employees (full time)	Total pay roll (including part time)	Stocks on hand, end of year (at cost)	Net sales Amount	Net sales Percent of total
Garages and repair shops	37	42	18	12,227	2,440	59,916	2.61
Apparel group[1]	13	14	18	12,376	1,420	33,875	1.47
Apparel stores	12	12	16	11,960	1,070	32,425	1.41
Restaurants, cafeterias, and eating places	278	291	90	30,831	7,870	316,041	13.75
Restaurants, cafeterias, and lunch rooms	219	228	77	24,777	5,770	233,064	10.14
Lunch counters, refreshment stands, etc.	59	63	13	6,054	2,100	82,977	3.61
Other retail stores[1]	116	145	127	77,412	60,860	572,888	24.93
Farmers' supplies	3	4	2	1,742	3,550	38,480	1.67
Coal and wood yards – ice dealers	21	21	19	5,635	850	44,251	1.93
Drug stores	20	24	16	7,961	17,320	113,748	4.95
Miscellaneous classifications (combined)	70	94	84	55,643	33,220	325,440	14.16
Second-hand stores	7	8	4	1,684	1,630	8,119	.35

Source: "Stores Operated by Black Proprietors, by States: 1929." U.S. Bureau of the Census. *Negroes in the United States: 1920-32*. Washington, D.C.: Government Printing Office, 1935, pp. 514. Adapted by the Editors. *Notes:* X - amount must be withheld to avoid disclosure of individual operations, but it is included in totals.
1. Includes 4 custom tailors.

★ 395 ★

Business Owners and Operators

Proprietors, Stores in Tennessee, 1929

Kind of business	Number of stores	Proprietors and firm members (not on pay roll)	Number of employees (full time)	Total pay roll (including part time)	Stocks on hand, end of year (at cost)	Net sales Amount	Net sales Percent of total
Total	973	1,100	537	$311,748	$327,960	$3,728,674	100.00
Food group	360	394	89	48,164	138,790	1,489,115	39.94
Candy and confectionery stores	8	8	9	3,704	810	27,700	.75
Grocery stores (without meats)	196	216	25	11,896	66,070	592,021	15.88
Combination stores (groceries and meats)	136	145	40	21,490	69,450	776,370	20.82
Meat markets (including sea foods)	17	22	9	7,330	2,120	79,584	2.13
Other food stores	3	3	6	3,744	340	13,440	.36
General stores	18	26	4	2,126	17,600	84,800	2.27
General merchandise group	3	6	2	1,200	3,200	11,840	.32
Dry goods stores – piece goods stores	3	6	2	1,200	3,200	11,840	.32
Automotive group	55	66	47	43,757	9,560	217,890	5.84
Filling stations	15	18	15	12,931	5,950	89,973	2.41
Garages and repair shops	39	47	32	30,826	3.580	127,517	3.42
Apparel group	8	10	8	6,072	15,490	61,578	1.65
Men's and boys' clothing and furnishings store	1	(x)	(x)	(x)	(x)	(x)	(x)
Family clothing stores – men's, women's, and children's	1	(x)	(x)	(x)	(x)	(x)	(x)
Other apparel stores	4	4	4	2,452	2,800	22,418	.60
Shoe stores	2	(x)	(x)	(x)	(x)	(x)	(x)
Furniture and household group	4	4	4	2,462	1,020	14,340	.39
Furniture stores	2	(x)	(x)	(x)	(x)	(x)	(x)
Other home furnishings and appliances stores	2	(x)	(x)	(x)	(x)	(x)	(x)
Restaurants, cafeterias, and eating places	427	449	233	99,202	30,350	1,006,873	27.00

[Continued]

★ 395 ★

Proprietors, Stores in Tennessee, 1929

[Continued]

Kind of business	Number of stores	Proprietors and firm members (not on pay roll)	Number of employees (full time)	Total pay roll (including part time)	Stocks on hand, end of year (at cost)	Net sales Amount	Net sales Percent of total
Restaurants, cafeterias, and lunch rooms	291	310	206	89,364	23,040	787,890	21.13
Lunch counters, refreshment stands, etc.	136	139	27	9,838	7,310	218,983	5.87
Other retail stores	92	139	150	108,765	109,500	834,883	22.39
Hardware stores	1	(x)	(x)	(x)	(x)	(x)	(x)
Hardware and farm implement stores	2	(x)	(x)	(x)	(x)	(x)	(x)
Farmers' supplies (including feeds and fertilizers)	1	(x)	(x)	(x)	(x)	(x)	(x)
Coal and wood yards – ice dealers	1	(x)	(x)	(x)	(x)	(x)	(x)
Drug stores	35	47	60	40,806	53,610	345,201	9.26
Jewelry stores	1	(x)	(x)	(x)	(x)	(x)	(x)
Miscellaneous classifications (combined)	51	83	84	64,679	40,900	441,358	11.84
Second-hand stores	6	6	-	-	2,450	7,355	.20

Source: "Stores Operated by Black Proprietors, by States: 1929." U.S. Bureau of the Census. *Negroes in the United States: 1920-32.* Washington, D.C.: Government Printing Office, 1935, pp. 514. Adapted by the Editors. *Notes:* X - amount must be withheld to avoid disclosure of individual operations, but it is included in totals.

★ 396 ★

Business Owners and Operators

Proprietors, Stores in Texas, 1929

Kind of business	Number of stores	Proprietors and firm members (not on pay roll)	Number of employees (full time)	Total pay roll (including part time)	Stocks on hand, end of year (at cost)	Net sales Amount	Net sales Percent of total
Total	1,736	1,963	999	$569,974	$6,75,640	$6,633,701	100.00
Food group	610	674	137	70,662	178,420	2,060,579	31.06
Candy and confectionery stores	65	70	19	7,931	7,920	106,526	1.61
Grocery stores (without meats)	351	377	43	16,473	89,050	775,330	11.69
Combination stores (groceries and meats)	156	186	58	32,780	75,840	939,603	14.16
Meat markets	14	14	11	9,808	1,540	118,160	1.76
Other food stores	24	27	6	3,670	4,070	120,960	1.82
General stores – groceries with dry goods or apparel	28	31	8	8,092	107,980	459,192	6.92
Automotive group	149	165	85	63,453	57,670	728,937	10.99
Filling stations	84	89	34	22,398	11,770	326,737	4.93
Garages and repair shops	60	71	37	26,688	27,950	188,003	2.83
Other automotive establishments	4	4	3	2,823	2,180	19,660	.30
Apparel group	32	35	36	32,909	72,480	312,411	4.71
Men's and boys' clothing and furnishings stores	4	4	6	5,888	20,670	63,996	.96
Women's accessories stores	7	7	15	15,576	25,260	132,346	2.00
Other apparel stores	16	18	9	6,145	2,060	47,019	.71
Shoe stores	3	3	1	600	300	4,050	.06
Furniture and household group	4	4	3	4,111	3,180	44,104	.67
Furniture stores	3	3	3	4,111	2,680	41,554	.63
Restaurants, cafeterias, and eating places	707	785	488	238,496	39,610	1,736,710	26.18
Restaurants, cafeterias, and lunch rooms	520	586	410	191,932	28,020	1,300,351	19.60
Lunch counters, refreshment stands, etc.	187	199	78	46,564	11,590	436,359	6.58
Other retail stores	195	257	234	145,805	203,670	1,259,209	18.98

[Continued]

★ 396 ★

Proprietors, Stores in Texas, 1929

[Continued]

Kind of business	Number of stores	Proprietors and firm members (not on pay roll)	Number of employees (full time)	Total pay roll (including part time)	Stocks on hand, end of year (at cost)	Net sales	
						Amount	Percent of total
Dry goods stores	2	(x)	(x)	(x)	(x)	(x)	(x)
General merchandise stores	1	(x)	(x)	(x)	(x)	(x)	(x)
Electrical shops (without radio)	1	(x)	(x)	(x)	(x)	(x)	(x)
Heating and plumbing shops	2	(x)	(x)	(x)	(x)	(x)	(x)
Paint and glass stores	1	(x)	(x)	(x)	(x)	(x)	(x)
Hardware and farm implement stores	1	(x)	(x)	(x)	(x)	(x)	(x)
Farmers' supplies	7	9	2	964	3,880	27,091	.41
Cigar stores and cigar stands	12	13	17	8,882	1,290	63,148	.95
Coal and wood yards – ice dealers	25	28	21	10,044	3,890	75,424	1.14
Drug stores	77	99	114	61,786	106,610	544,098	8.20
Jewelry stores	3	3	1	1,980	7,320	13,350	.20
Miscellaneous classifications	63	93	63	48,036	43,110	385,933	5.82
Second-hand stores	11	12	8	6,446	12,630	32,559	.49

Source: "Stores Operated by Black Proprietors, by States: 1929." U.S. Bureau of the Census. *Negroes in the United States: 1920-32.* Washington, D.C.: Government Printing Office, 1935, pp. 515. Adapted by the Editors. *Notes:* X - amount must be withheld to avoid disclosure of individual operations, but it is included in totals.

★ 397 ★

Business Owners and Operators

Proprietors, Stores in Virginia, 1929

Kind of business	Number of stores	Proprietors and firm members (not on pay roll)	Number of employees (full time)	Total pay roll (including part time)	Stocks on hand, end of year (at cost)	Net sales	
						Amount	Percent of total
Total	1,878	2,043	645	$378,446	$885,720	$4,986,347	100.00
Food group	964	1,015	165	85,863	276,000	2,128,400	42.68
Candy and confectionery stores	103	109	21	7,548	19,120	180,688	3.62
Grocery stores (without meats)	562	595	49	21,814	161,960	926,487	18.58
Combination stores (groceries and meats)	197	205	47	29,309	88,480	734,223	14.72
Meat markets (including sea foods)	73	78	40	21,787	3,830	199,317	4.00
Other food stores	29	28	8	5,405	2,610	87,685	1.76
General stores	185	231	27	11,534	213,850	680,372	13.65
General merchandise group	11	12	11	5,107	11,270	24,149	.48
General merchandise stores	6	7	11	5,107	10,550	20,600	.41
Variety, 5-and-10, and to-a-dollar stores	3	3	-	-	270	2,549	.05
Automotive group	130	147	44	28,342	32,680	351,598	7.05
Filling stations	85	99	19	7,442	14,280	151,199	3.03
Garages and repair shops	43	45	18	12,757	5,030	72,790	1.46
Apparel group	16	16	21	14,046	7,810	54,686	1.10
Men's and boys' clothing and furnishings stores	2	(x)	(x)	(x)	(x)	(x)	(x)
Family clothing stores – men's, women's, and children's	1	(x)	(x)	(x)	(x)	(x)	(x)
Women's ready-to-wear specialty stores – apparel and accessories	1	(x)	(x)	(x)	(x)	(x)	(x)
Women's accessories stores	1	(x)	(x)	(x)	(x)	(x)	(x)
Other apparel stores	9	9	17	10,402	2,900	32,174	.64
Shoe stores	2	(x)	(x)	(x)	(x)	(x)	(x)

[Continued]

★ 397 ★

Proprietors, Stores in Virginia, 1929
[Continued]

Kind of business	Number of stores	Proprietors and firm members (not on pay roll)	Number of employees (full time)	Total pay roll (including part time)	Stocks on hand, end of year (at cost)	Net sales	
						Amount	Percent of total
Furniture and household group	6	7	10	11,868	5,070	35,862	.72
Furniture stores	3	4	3	4,652	3,370	19,662	.40
Other home furnishings and appliances stores	2	(x)	(x)	(x)	(x)	(x)	(x)
Radio and music stores	1	(x)	(x)	(x)	(x)	(x)	(x)
Restaurants, cafeterias, and eating places	355	365	172	61,134	28,890	529,306	10.62
Restaurants, cafeterias, and lunch rooms	296	305	166	58,920	24,970	483,407	9.70
Lunch counters, refreshment stands, etc.	59	60	6	2,214	3,920	45,899	.92
Lumber and building group	6	6	9	4,963	7,600	18,150	.36
Lumber and building material dealers	1	(x)	(x)	(x)	(x)	(x)	(x)
Electrical shops (without radio)	2	(x)	(x)	(x)	(x)	(x)	(x)
Paint and glass stores	3	3	6	3,178	1,900	8,050	.16
Other retail stores	197	236	184	154,645	297,680	1,148,568	23.03
Farmers' supplies	21	22	1	1,016	13,240	65,867	1.32
Cigar stores and cigar stands	16	16	12	6,868	1,440	32,096	.64
Coal and wood yard – ice dealers	37	38	23	11,919	4,640	92,304	1.85
Drug stores	21	23	26	17,989	60,120	215,376	4.32
Jewelry stores	4	4	13	26,070	152,920	140,718	2.82
Miscellaneous classifications (combined)	96	131	108	89,823	60,320	583,207	11.70
Second-hand stores	8	8	2	944	4,870	15,256	.31

Source: "Stores Operated by Black Proprietors, by States: 1929." U.S. Bureau of the Census. *Negroes in the United States: 1920-32*. Washington, D.C.: Government Printing Office, 1935, pp. 515. Adapted by the Editors. *Notes:* X - amount must be withheld to avoid disclosure of individual operations, but it is included in totals.

★ 398 ★

Business Owners and Operators

Proprietors, Stores, Sales, and Personnel by Kinds of Business, 1939

Kind of business	Number of stores	Sales (add 000)	Active proprietors of unincorporated business	Number of employees
United States total	29,827	$71,466	29,116	13,778
Food Group	11,038	24,037	10,586	2,164
Grocery stores (without fresh meats)	5,655	7,934	5,297	418
Combination stores (groceries – meats)	2,524	11,454	2,491	1,054
Dairy products stores, milk dealers	15	67	15	9
Meat markets, fish markets	493	935	486	144
Candy, nut, confectionery stores	1,713	2,084	1,671	201
Delicatessen stores	74	210	70	21
Fruit stores, vegetable markets	331	555	327	39
Bakeries, caterers	99	412	100	222
Egg and poultry dealers	109	331	107	50
Other food stores	25	55	22	6
General stores (with food)	149	404	144	22

[Continued]

★ 398 ★

Proprietors, Stores, Sales, and Personnel by Kinds of Business, 1939
[Continued]

Kind of business	Number of stores	Sales (add 000)	Active proprietors of unincorporated business	Number of employees
General merchandise group	83	256	86	37
Dry goods and general merchandise stores	43	161	44	25
Variety stores	40	95	42	12
Apparel group	333	779	344	137
Men's-boys' furnishings, hat stores	15	41	15	5
Men's-boys' clothing stores (and furnishings)	8	54	6	10
Family clothing stores	32	110	36	16
Women's ready-to-wear stores	65	156	70	16
Furriers, fur shops	2	12	4	1
Millinery stores	55	76	54	15
Women's accessories stores	46	90	46	11
Infants', other apparel stores	48	56	50	11
Custom tailors	46	129	48	41
Shoe/stores (all kinds)	16	55	15	11
Furniture – household--radio group	65	511	73	91
Furniture stores	19	95	21	14
Other home furnishings stores	17	18	17	8
Household appliance dealers	6	79	11	14
Radio – household appliance stores	12	298	13	51
Radio stores – other	11	21	11	4
Automotive group	46	638	52	64
Motor-vehicle dealers (new)	4	335	3	27
Used-car dealers	6	191	8	16
Accessory, tire, battery dealers	38	112	41	21
Filling stations	1,268	6,917	1,241	798
Lumber – building group	24	38	22	14
Lumber and building-materials dealers	15	26	13	11
Heating – plumbing equipment dealers	4	7	4	3
Paint, glass, wallpaper stores	5	5	5	-
Hardware group	17	58	17	5
Hardware stores	17	58	17	5
Eating places	9,750	15,136	9,556	5,417
Restaurants, cafeterias, lunch rooms	2,836	9,193	2,910	4,429
Lunch counters and stands	6,316	5,591	6,097	929
Soft drink, juice, ice cream stands	598	352	549	59
Drinking places	2,860	11,391	2,824	2,968

[Continued]

★ 398 ★

Proprietors, Stores, Sales, and Personnel by Kinds of Business, 1939

[Continued]

Kind of business	Number of stores	Sales (add 000)	Active proprietors of unincorporated business	Number of employees
Drug stores	548	4,470	550	846
Drug store with fountain	276	3,084	284	568
Drug stores – other	272	1,386	266	278
Liquor stores (packaged goods)	169	1,679	147	130
Other retail stores	3,040	4,685	3,044	985
Fuel, ice, fuel-oil dealers	2,240	2,959	2,229	754
Hay, grain and feed stores	7	104	6	7
Farm and garden supply stores	4	30	5	6
Jewelry stores	10	33	9	2
Book stores	15	35	11	9
Stationary stores	16	36	16	1
Cigar stores, cigar stands	348	695	360	76
Florists	128	210	133	26
Gift, novelty, souvenir shops	18	66	18	15
News dealers	99	287	104	52
Office, school supply and equipment dealers 1 store combined with "Other retail stores."				
Opticians	7	16	7	2
Photographic supply – camera stores 1 store combined with "Other retail stores."				
Other retail stores	148	214	146	35
Second hand stores	437	467	430	100

Source: "Proprietorships—Stores, Sales and Personnel, by Kinds of Business: 1939." Murray, Florence, ed. *The Negro Handbook*. New York: Wendell Malliet, 1942, p. 21.

★ 399 ★

Business Owners and Operators

Proprietors, Type of Business for Cities Having 50,000 or More Black Inhabitants, 1929

Kind of business	Number of stores	Proprietors and firm members (not on pay roll)	Number of employees		Total pay roll (including part time)	Stocks on hand, end of year (at cost)	Net sales	
			Full time	Part time			Amount	Percent of total
Total	5,741	5,979	3,576	770	$2,674,564	$2,151,758	$27,862,020	100.0
Food group	1,923	2,002	420	183	335,248	566,530	9,366,532	33.6
Candy and confectionery stores	378	367	79	16	46,464	76,340	1,073,339	3.9
Grocery stores (without meats)	650	650	88	31	61,872	230,420	2,682,498	9.6
Combination stores (groceries and meats)	363	388	108	47	87,959	178,630	2,929,856	10.5
Meat markets (including sea foods)	112	122	54	19	49,416	17,980	849,169	3.1
Bakeries – bakery goods stores (except manufacturing bakeries)	17	24	25	44	38,962	2,840	179,508	.6

[Continued]

★ 399 ★

Proprietors, Type of Business for Cities Having 50,000 or More Black Inhabitants, 1929
[Continued]

Kind of business	Number of stores	Proprietors and firm members (not on pay roll)	Number of employees		Total pay roll (including part time)	Stocks on hand, end of year (at cost)	Net sales	
			Full time	Part time			Amount	Percent of total
Coffee, tea, and spice dealers	3	4	4	-	2,312	1,350	30,520	.1
Dairy products stores (including ice cream)	29	41	15	2	6,112	5,750	132,329	.5
Delicatessen stores	88	90	10	5	9,077	38,660	447,084	1.6
Egg and poultry dealers	17	19	7	2	6,908	1,840	145,820	.5
Fruit stores and vegetable markets	266	297	30	17	26,166	12,720	896,409	3.2
General stores – groceries with dry goods, apparel, or general merchandise	5	5	-	-	-	2,370	16,098	.1
General merchandise group	33	38	8	-	8,611	63,990	154,389	.6
Dry goods stores	12	16	6	-	6,695	45,960	109,886	.4
General merchandise stores	7	8	1	-	1,500	11,900	20,435	.1
Variety, 5-and-10, and to-a-dollar stores	14	14	1	-	416	6,130	24,068	.1
Automotive group	262	301	246	44	250,178	114,320	1,679,327	6.0
Filling stations								
Filling stations – gasoline and oil	34	36	36	10	39,991	11,610	439,714	1.6
Filling stations with tires and accessories	26	28	34	4	34,285	49,010	354,947	1.3
Filling stations with other merchandise	10	12	10	3	6,869	1,820	39,055	.1
Garages and repair shops	142	166	137	23	141,114	20,520	613,240	2.2
Other automotive establishments	50	59	29	4	27,919	31,360	232,371	.8
Apparel group	191	202	119	31	108,594	179,640	951,592	3.4
Men's and boys' clothing and furnishings stores	15	16	10	3	9,145	43,270	156,484	.6
Family clothing stores – men's, women's, and children's	8	9	2	1	1,760	11,980	47,661	.2
Women's ready-to-wear specialty stores – apparel and accessories	34	37	20	2	15,988	29,500	137,184	.5
Women's accessories stores	26	27	18	10	20,490	36,820	186,489	.7
Other apparel stores	95	100	59	14	51,547	27,250	321,328	1.1
Shoe stores	13	13	10	1	9,664	30,820	102,446	.3
Furniture and household group	69	77	46	12	38,074	56,070	275,074	1.0
Furniture stores	15	16	11	-	7,230	6,770	37,583	.1
Floor coverings, drapery, curtain, and upholstery stores	2	⎰ 5	3	1	1,324	1,480	10,700	.1
Household appliance stores	3	⎱						
Other home furnishings and appliances stores	11	12	9	4	7,318	12,270	23,507	.1
Radio and music stores	38	44	23	7	22,202	35,550	203,284	.7
Restaurants and eating places	1,898	1,890	1,804	212	1,028,931	140,023	7,371,584	26.5
Restaurants, cafeterias, and lunch rooms								
Cafeterias	6	6	34	1	24,209	1,040	170,127	.6
Lunch rooms	1,058	999	817	104	441,955	69,533	3,728,269	13.4
Restaurants with table service	225	227	714	67	415,897	26,815	2,056,455	7.4
Lunch counters, refreshment stands, etc.								
Lunch counters	345	370	199	35	125,707	30,165	1,011,052	3.6
Refreshment stands	142	158	21	2	12,004	5,810	220,957	.8
Soft-drink stands	122	130	19	3	9,159	6,660	184,724	.7
Lumber and building group	28	33	45	2	59,651	26,940	329,156	1.2
Lumber and building material dealers	6	8	10	1	7,286	6,000	51,499	.2
Electrical shops (without radio)	7	9	8	-	6,773	2,640	40,930	.2
Heating and plumbing shops	8	8	21	-	34,826	4,980	150,976	.5
Paint and glass stores	7	8	6	1	10,766	13,320	85,751	.3
Other retail stores	1,132	1,216	834	271	800,156	925,055	7,230,335	26.0
Hardware store	10	12	3	-	2,300	19,640	52,348	.2
Farmers' supplies	15/							
Book stores	2/	20	8	3	6,424	5,480	101,627	.4
Cigar stores and cigar stands								
Cigar stores without fountains	163	154	34	12	31,568	47,940	529,985	1.9
Cigar stores with fountains	15	16	3	1	2,570	3,085	31,717	.1
Cigar stands (hotel lobbies, pool rooms, etc.)	94	99	66	8	46,382	13,960	284,999	1.0
Coal and wood yard – ice dealers	241	264	98	46	82,784	34,010	825,573	3.0

[Continued]

★ 399 ★

Proprietors, Type of Business for Cities Having 50,000 or More Black Inhabitants, 1929
[Continued]

Kind of business	Number of stores	Proprietors and firm members (not on pay roll)	Number of employees		Total pay roll (including part time)	Stocks on hand, end of year (at cost)	Net sales	
			Full time	Part time			Amount	Percent of total
Drug stores								
Drug stores without fountains	60	66	74	16	65,991	162,510	673,421	2.4
Drug stores with fountains	161	187	241	78	243,382	420,970	2,116,165	7.6
Jewelry stores	31	33	5	4	4,368	23,150	125,294	.5
Miscellaneous classifications (combined)	340	365	302	103	314,387	194,310	2,489,206	8.9
Second-hand stores	200	215	54	15	45,121	76,820	487,933	1.7

Source: "Stores Operated by Black Proprietors, by Kind of Business, for Cities Having 50,000 or More Negro Inhabitants: 1929." U.S. Bureau of the Census. *Negroes in the United States: 1920-32.* Washington, D.C.: Government Printing Office, 1935, pp. 517.

★ 400 ★

Business Owners and Operators

Proprietors: Businesses in Cities With 50,000 or More Blacks: Atlanta, Georgia, 1929

Kind of business	Number of stores	Proprietors and firm members (not on pay roll)	Number of employees		Total pay roll (including part time)	Stocks on hand, end of year (at cost)	Net sales	
			Full time	Part time			Amount	Percent of total
Total	391	424	192	70	$95,636	$56,710	$1,151,850	100.00
Food group	110	123	24	20	14,299	26,240	430,233	37.35
Grocery stores (without meat)	59	64	6	6	3,818	11,350	119,801	10.40
Combination stores (groceries and meats)	35	43	16	10	9,420	12,040	266,064	23.10
Candy and confectionery stores	14							
Delicatessen stores	1	16	2	4	1,061	2,850	44,368	3.85
Meat markets (including sea foods)	1							
Automotive group	13	16	19	2	12,559	1,850	87,629	7.61
Filling stations	4	5	4	1	2,575	280	38,220	3.32
Bicycle shops	3	2	5	1	3,692	1,100	24,500	2.13
Garages and repair shops	6	9	10	-	6,292	470	24,909	2.16
Apparel group	4	4	7	1	8,726	850	29,551	2.57
Restaurants and eating places	241	254	113	35	43,824	10,840	467,974	40.63
Restaurants, cafeterias, and lunch rooms								
Lunch rooms	130	136	59	15	21,093	4,510	220,035	19.10
Restaurants with table service	19	22	32	7	12,744	870	86,939	7.55
Lunch counters, refreshment stands, etc.								
Lunch counters	43	44	16	8	7,509	2,220	80,050	6.95
Refreshment stands	40	42	6	2	2,146	2,100	67,639	5.87
Soft-drink stands	9	10	-	3	332	1,140	13,311	1.16
Other retail stores	23	27	29	12	16,228	16,930	136,463	11.85
Cigar stores and cigar stands	4	4	5	2	2,392	310	7,740	.67
Coal and wood yards – ice dealers	4	3	3	3	3,510	180	8,220	.71
Drug stores	4	7	12	6	6,255	10,080	80,670	7.00
Jewelry stores	6	7	2	-	1,205	1,250	12,255	1.06
Miscellaneous classifications (combined)	5	6	7	1	2,866	5,110	27,578	2.39

Source: "Stores Operated by Negro Proprietors, by Kind of Business, for Cities Having 50,000 or More Negro Inhabitants: 1929," U.S. Bureau of the Census, *Negroes in the United States: 1920-32,* p. 520.

★ 401 ★

Business Owners and Operators

Proprietors: Businesses in Cities With 50,000 or More Blacks: Baltimore,Maryland, 1929

Kind of business	Number of stores	Proprietors and firm members (not on pay roll)	Number of employees		Total pay roll (including part time)	Stocks on hand, end of year (at cost)	Net sales	
			Full time	Part time			Amount	Percent of total
Total	282	283	132	76	$123,198	$48,135	$1,062,948	100.00
Food group	100	99	19	51	27,086	14,935	403,217	37.93
Candy and confectionery stores	43	43	4	1	2,111	3,820	94,348	8.88
Grocery stores (without meats)	23	23	1	3	683	2,825	53,410	5.02
Combination stores (groceries and meats)	10	10	-	1	60	2,980	74,900	7.05
Meat markets (including sea foods)	9	9	2	1	1,578	3,390	58,190	5.47
Fruit stores and vegetable markets	4	4	-	-	-	260	14,665	1.38
Bakeries – bakery goods stores (except manufacturing bakeries)	5	⎱ 5	8	44	19,254	810	81,883	7.70
Caterers	1							
All other food stores								
Coffee, tea, and spice dealers	1	⎱ 5	4	1	3,400	850	25,821	2.43
Dairy products stores (including ice cream)	1							
Delicatessen stores	1							
Egg and poultry dealers	2							
Automotive group	5	⎱ 6	2	1	550	620	12,323	1.16
Filling stations	1							
Garages and repair shops	4							
Apparel group	3	⎱ 3	2	-	624	1,320	5,250	.49
Men's and boys' clothing and furnishings stores	1							
Women's accessories stores	1							
Other apparel stores	1							
Furniture and household group	2	(x)	(x)	-	(x)	(x)	(x)	(x)
Restaurants and eating places	78	79	48	9	21,143	3,310	216,387	20.36
Restaurants, cafeterias, and lunch rooms								
Lunch rooms	60	61	34	4	13,711	2,290	170,168	16.01
Restaurants with table service	9	9	13	5	6,756	690	33,917	3.19
Lunch counters, refreshment stands, etc.								
Refreshment stands	2	⎱ 9	1	-	676	380	12,302	1.16
Soft-drink stands	7							
Lumber and building group	2	(x)	(x)	-	(x)	(x)	(x)	(x)
Other retail stores	78	79	47	15	45,819	23,500	279,925	26.33
Cigar stores and cigar stands	4	5	-	1	260	210	15,434	1.45
Coal and wood yards	37	37	5	5	3,424	1,350	67,270	6.33
Ice dealers	4	4	1	-	45	100	8,785	.83
Drug stores with fountains	12	12	20	7	17,731	13,320	87,537	8.24
Miscellaneous classifications (combined)	21	21	21	2	24,359	8,520	100,899	9.49
Second-hand stores	14	14	1	-	416	3,150	29,810	2.80

Source: "Stores Operated by Negro Proprietors, by Kind of Business, for Cities Having 50,000 or More Negro Inhabitants: 1929," U.S. Bureau of the Census, *Negroes in the United States: 1920-32*, p. 520.

★ 402 ★

Business Owners and Operators

Proprietors: Businesses in Cities With 50,000 or More Blacks: Birmingham, Alabama, 1929

Kind of business	Number of stores	Proprietors and firm members (not on pay roll)	Number of employees		Total pay roll (including part time)	Stocks on hand, end of year (at cost)	Net sales	
			Full time	Part time			Amount	Percent of total
Total	200	228	144	6	$64,644	$48,790	$661,918	100.00
Food group	64	75	13	2	5,086	12,000	150,434	24.99
Candy and confectionery stores	11	12	3	-	1,271	2,060	14,985	2.49

[Continued]

★ 402 ★

Proprietors: Businesses in Cities With 50,000 or More Blacks: Birmingham, Alabama, 1929
[Continued]

Kind of business	Number of stores	Proprietors and firm members (not on pay roll)	Number of employees		Total pay roll (including part time)	Stocks on hand, end of year (at cost)	Net sales	
			Full time	Part time			Amount	Percent of total
Grocery stores (without meats)	33	37	6	-	2,286	5,090	60,009	2.97
Combination stores (groceries and meats)	20	26	4	3	1,529	4,850	75,440	12.53
General stores – groceries with dry goods or apparel	1	(x)	(x)	(x)	(x)	(x)	(x)	(x)
General merchandise group	4	6	1	-	1,678	13,380	19,438	3.23
Dry goods stores	2	(x)	(x)	-	(x)	(x)	(x)	(x)
General merchandise stores	2	(x)	(x)	-	(x)	(x)	(x)	(x)
Automotive group	14	17	12	-	6,352	1,210	43,280	7.19
Garages and repair shops	8	10	8	-	4,456	320	18,940	5.15
All other automotive establishments	6	7	4	-	1,896	890	24,340	4.04
Apparel group	4							
Apparel stores	3	4	4	-	1,898	370	7,000	1.16
Shoe stores	1							
Restaurants and eating places	92	99	70	1	21,244	2,790	172,563	28.67
Restaurants, cafeterias, and lunch rooms								
Lunch rooms	43	48	32	-	8,326	1,310	73,775	12.26
Restaurants with table service	7	7	29	-	10,166	230	52,262	8.68
Lunch counters, refreshment stands, etc.								
Lunch counters	18	18	8	1	2,544	660	28,048	4.66
Refreshment stands	20	22	1	-	208	470	16,063	2.67
Soft-drink stands	4	4	-	-	-	120	2,415	.40
Lumber and building group	3	5	8	-	8,101	4,500	49,187	8.17
Lumber and building material dealers	1	(x)	(x)	-	(x)	(x)	(x)	(x)
Electrical shops (without radio)	1	(x)	(x)	-	(x)	(x)	(x)	(x)
Heating and plumbing shops	1	(x)	(x)	-	(x)	(x)	(x)	(x)
Other retail stores	15	18	34	3	18,645	8,050	149,895	24.90
Coal and wood yards – Ice dealers	4	5	10	2	7,375	1,700	56,800	9.44
Drug stores	4	4	6	1	2,768	1,550	58,680	9.75
Cigar stores and cigar stands	2	9	18	-	8,502	4,800	34,415	5.72
Miscellaneous classifications (combined)[1]	5							
Second-hand stores	3	(x)	(x)	(x)	(x)	(x)	(x)	(x)

Source: "Stores Operated by Negro Proprietors, by Kind of Business, for Cities Having 50,000 or More Negro Inhabitants: 1929," U.S. Bureau of the Census, *Negroes in the United States: 1920-32*, pp. 520-521. *Notes:* 1. Includes 1 photographer and illustrator, 4 undertakers' and funeral supplies stores.

★ 403 ★

Business Owners and Operators

Proprietors: Businesses in Cities With 50,000 or More Blacks: Chicago, Illinois, 1929

Kind of business	Number of stores	Proprietors and firm members (not on pay roll)	Number of employees		Total pay roll (including part time)	Stocks on hand, end of year (at cost)	Net sales	
			Full time	Part time			Amount	Percent of total
Total	815	866	576	147	$497,349	$435,130	$4,826,897	100.00
Food group	213	222	46	14	46,110	107,040	1,441,241	29.86
Candy and confectionery stores	16	16	3	-	1,548	5,660	48,451	1.00
Grocery stores (without meats)	76	81	11	3	10,048	37,680	430,434	8.92
Combination stores (groceries and meats)	44	44	19	8	19,056	31,760	498,924	10.34
Meat markets (including sea foods)	8	8	1	-	2,600	3,580	59,552	1.23
All other food stores	3	3	7	-	7,317	230	68,900	1.43
General merchandise group	9							
Dry goods stores	2	9	2	-	1,016	9,200	21,775	.45
Variety, 5-and-10, and to-a-dollar stores	7							
Automotive group	35	42	39	7	47,351	9,410	250,584	5.19

[Continued]

★ 403 ★

Proprietors: Businesses in Cities With 50,000 or More Blacks: Chicago, Illinois, 1929
[Continued]

Kind of business	Number of stores	Proprietors and firm members (not on pay roll)	Number of employees		Total pay roll (including part time)	Stocks on hand, end of year (at cost)	Net sales	
			Full time	Part time			Amount	Percent of total
Garages and repair shops	25	29	29	6	34,893	2,440	156,250	3.24
Filling stations	2	] 13	10	1	12,458	6,970	94,334	1.95
All other automotive establishments	8							
Apparel group	58	61	28	9	27,264	64,310	308,365	6.39
Men's and boys' clothing and furnishings stores	6							
Family clothing stores – men's, women's, and children's	1	] 8	6	2	7,159	38,180	122,137	2.53
Shoe stores	1							
Women's ready-to-wear specialty stores – apparel and accessories	14	17	9	1	7,620	14,800	63,048	1.31
Women's accessories stores	9	9	3	2	2,460	5,550	36,045	.75
Other apparel stores	27	27	10	4	10,025	5,780	87,135	1.81
Furniture and household group	13	15	12	2	13,089	11,230	87,635	1.82
Furniture stores	1							
Draperies, curtains, and upholstery stores	1	] 15	12	2	13,089	11,230	87,635	1.82
Radio and music stores	11							
Restaurants and eating places	207	218	247	39	153,736	20,070	989,569	20.50
Restaurants, cafeterias, and lunch rooms								
Lunch rooms	140	150	132	29	78,237	7,545	613,461	12.71
Restaurants with table services	14	14	74	1	40,666	1,870	188,718	3.91
Lunch counters, refreshment stands, etc.								
Lunch counters	45	47	40	9	34,353	10,105	175,100	3.63
Refreshment stands	2	] 7	1	-	480	550	12,290	.25
Soft-drink stands	5							
Lumber and building group	9	10	11	1	11,621	7,180	63,226	1.31
Electrical shops (without radio)	3	4	2	-	576	810	7,300	.15
Roofing (including tinner)	3	3	6	1	3,845	1,330	17,876	.37
Heating and plumbing shops	2	(x)	(x)	-	(x)	(x)	(x)	(x)
Paint and glass stores	1	(x)	(x)	-	(x)	(x)	(x)	(x)
Other retail stores	206	219	177	71	181,000	173,580	1,482,286	30.71
Hardware stores	2	(x)	-	(x)	(x)	(x)	(x)	(x)
Farmers' supplies stores	6	6	4	1	4,556	410	37,445	.78
Book stores	1	(x)	-	(x)	(x)	(x)	(x)	(x)
Cigar stores and cigar stands								
Cigar stores without fountains	9	] 10	4	1	3,770	1,560	22,680	.47
Cigar stores with fountains	1							
Cigar stands (hotel lobbies, pool rooms, etc.)	21	22	32	1	24,532	3,470	116,854	2.42
Coal and wood yards – Ice dealers	35	38	12	25	16,075	3,690	113,981	2.36
Drug stores								
Drug stores without fountains	13	15	18	6	17,835	35,590	162,395	3.36
Drug stores with fountains	30	30	53	11	59,032	90,390	469,668	9.73
Jewelry stores	2	(x)	-	(x)	(x)	(x)	(x)	(x)
Miscellaneous classifications (combined)[1]	86	93	54	25	55,056	34,640	546,793	11.33
Second-hand stores	65	70	14	4	16,162	33,110	182,216	3.78
Clothing and shoes	19	16	4	-	5,610	6,390	32,110	.67
Furniture stores	34	40	7	3	6,496	16,760	117,303	2.43
All other second-hand dealers	12	14	3	1	4,056	9,960	32,803	.68

Source: "Stores Operated by Negro Proprietors, by Kind of Business, for Cities Having 50,000 or More Negro Inhabitants: 1929," U.S. Bureau of the Census, *Negroes in the United States: 1920-32*, p. 521. *Note:* 1. Includes 4 custom tailors.

★ 404 ★

Business Owners and Operators

Proprietors: Businesses in Cities With 50,000 or More Blacks: Cleveland, Ohio, 1929

Kind of business	Number of stores	Proprietors and firm members (not on pay roll)	Number of employees		Total pay roll (including part time)	Stocks on hand, end of year (at cost)	Net sales	
			Full time	Part time			Amount	Percent of total
Total	215	240	161	34	$108,666	$108,810	$1,156,859	100.00
Food group	65	69	24	9	17,550	23,080	470,429	40.66
Candy and confectionery stores	9	10	7	-	2,668	3,040	53,414	4.02
Grocery stores (without meats)	28	29	5	2	4,125	9,680	171,163	14.80
Combination stores (groceries and meats)	15	16	7	1	5,968	7,280	138,286	11.95
Meat markets (including sea foods)	9	10	3	5	2,687	1,060	62,766	5.43
All other food stores	4	4	2	1	2,102	2,020	44,800	3.87
Automotive group	15	17	14	4	11,752	42,790	64,393	5.57
Filling stations	3	3	2	1	2,388	30,250	16,413	1.42
Garages and repair shops	7	8	11	3	7,774	7,360	27,930	2.41
All other automotive establishments	5	6	1	-	1,590	5,180	20,050	1.73
Apparel group	9	9	3	1	3,560	5,120	25,195	2.18
Women's ready-to-wear specialty stores – apparel and accessories	3	3	1	-	1,500	1,220	8,200	.71
Women's accessories stores	1	] 3	2	-	1,800	1,650	7,640	.66
Shoe stores	2							
All other apparel stores	3	3	-	1	260	2,250	9,355	.81
Furniture and household group	3							
Household appliance stores	1	] 3	1	1	250	2,300	16,500	1.43
Radio and music stores	2							
Restaurants and eating places	73	85	91	13	48,262	13,750	343,383	29.68
Restaurants, cafeterias, and lunch rooms								
Lunch rooms	35	41	20	7	12,261	7,570	98,468	8.51
Restaurants with table services	28	33	65	5	33,940	5,460	198,995	17.20
Lunch counters, refreshment stands, etc.								
Lunch counters	8	] 11	6	1	2,061	720	45,920	3.97
Soft-drink stands	2							
Other retail stores	35	40	21	3	21,536	18,600	201,417	17.41
Cigar stores and cigar stands								
Cigar stores without fountains	8	11	2	-	3,380	1,470	36,900	3.19
Cigar stands (hotel lobbies, pool rooms, etc.)	7	7	3	-	2,776	1,020	37,990	3.28
Coal and wood yards – Ice dealers	7	8	2	2	2,672	920	21,200	1.83
Drug stores	3	3	5	-	1,860	5,200	21,430	1.85
Jewelry stores	4	4	1	-	468	1,750	13,300	1.15
Miscellaneous classifications (combined)[1]	6	7	8	1	10,380	8,240	70,597	6.10
Second-hand stores	15	17	7	3	5,756	3,170	35,542	3.07
Automobile parts, tires, and batteries	6	7	5	1	4,394	1,090	15,452	1.34
Clothing and shoes	4	4	2	2	1,362	700	5,130	.44
Furniture	5	6	-	-	-	1,380	14,960	1.29

Source: "Stores Operated by Negro Proprietors, by Kind of Business, for Cities Having 50,000 or More Negro Inhabitants: 1929," U.S. Bureau of the Census, *Negroes in the United States: 1920-32*, p. 522. *Notes:* 1. Includes 1 glass and mirror store, 1 patent medicine store, 1 printer and lithographer, and 3 undertakers' and funeral supplies store.

★ 405 ★

Business Owners and Operators

Proprietors: Businesses in Cities With 50,000 or More Blacks: Detroit, Michigan, 1929

Kind of business	Number of stores	Proprietors and firm members (not on pay roll)	Number of employees		Total pay roll (including part time)	Stocks on hand, end of year (at cost)	Net sales	
			Full time	Part time			Amount	Percent of total
Total	358	413	369	38	$304,713	$154,963	$2,951,471	100.00
Food group	147	162	50	17	44,321	44,585	1,101,766	37.33
Candy and confectionery stores	52	55	12	1	6,320	9,540	162,551	5.51
Grocery stores (without meats)	39	44	9	2	7,072	9,695	214,607	7.27
Combination stores (groceries and meats)	48	54	18	8	17,531	23,870	626,242	21.22
Meat markets (including sea foods)	4	4	2	2	2,628	430	46,340	1.57
All other food stores	4	5	9	4	10,770	1,050	52,026	1.76
General merchandise group	3	4x)	-	-	-	8,370	22,360	.76
Dry goods stores	1	(x)	-	-	-	(x)	(x)	(x)
Variety, 5-and-10, and to-a-dollar stores	2	(x)	-	-	-	(x)	(x)	(x)
Automotive group	28	32	27	4	38,811	12,110	348,679	11.81
Filling stations								
Filling stations – gasoline and oil	5	6	7	1	10,315	2,750	132,475	4.49
Filling stations with tires and accessories	7	6	9	-	14,176	5,210	141,272	4.79
Garages and repair shops	7	9	5	1	7,390	320	31,662	1.07
All other automotive establishments	9	11	6	2	6,930	3,830	43,270	1.47
Apparel group	12	12	6	2	2,532	4,140	45,927	1.56
Men's and boys' clothing and furnishings stores	2	(x)	(x)	(x)	(x)	(x)	(x)	(x)
Women's ready-to-wear specialty stores – apparel and accessories	3	3	-	1	364	790	9,365	.32
Women's accessories stores	2	(x)	-	-	-	(x)	(x)	(x)
All other apparel stores	5	5	5	-	1,136	350	5,092	.17
Furniture and household group	4							
Furniture stores	1	4	2	-	1,291	1,050	24,700	.84
Radio and music stores	3							
Restaurants and eating places	97	116	233	8	161,426	7,893	813,454	27.56
Restaurants, cafeterias, and lunch rooms								
Lunch rooms	58	71	101	6	72,706	5,913	408,399	13.84
Restaurants with table services	14	16	82	-	56,792	990	230,288	7.80
Lunch counters, refreshment stands, etc.								
Lunch counters	21	25	48	2	29,708	760	164,232	5.56
Refreshments	2	(x)	(x)		(x)	(x)	(x)	(x)
Soft-drink stands	2	(x)	(x)	-	(x)	(x)	(x)	(x)
Other retail stores	54	68	46	6	51,237	73,005	531,938	18.02
Paint and glass stores	1	(x)	(x)		(x)	(x)	(x)	(x)
Hardware stores	1	(x)	-	-	-	(x)	(x)	(x)
Feed stores (flour, feed, grain, fertilizer)	2	(x)	(x)	-	(x)	(x)	(x)	(x)
Cigar stores and cigar stands								
Cigar stores without fountains	4	6	3	-	2,360	475	15,665	.53
Cigar stores with fountains	1							
Cigar stands (hotel lobbies, pool rooms, etc.)	15	18	8	3	5,508	3,490	41,529	1.41
Ice dealers	1	(x)	-	-	-	-	(x)	(x)
Drug stores								
Drug stores without fountains	7	8	7	1	8,536	15,830	115,314	3.91
Drug stores with fountains	15	19	23	2	30,153	44,680	276,730	9.38
Miscellaneous classifications (combined)[1]	5	8	3	-	3,640	3,490	37,870	1.28
Second-hand stores	13	15	5	1	5,095	3,810	62,647	2.12

Source: "Stores Operated by Negro Proprietors, by Kind of Business, for Cities Having 50,000 or More Negro Inhabitants: 1929," U.S. Bureau of the Census, *Negroes in the United States: 1920-32*, p. 522. *Notes:* 1. Includes 1 florist, 1 art and gift shop, 1 malt products supplies store, 1 printer and lithographer, and 1 janitors' supplies store.

★ 406 ★

Business Owners and Operators

Proprietors: Businesses in Cities With 50,000 or More Blacks: Houston, Texas, 1929

Kind of business	Number of stores	Proprietors and firm members (not on pay roll)	Number of employees		Total pay roll (including part time)	Stocks on hand, end of year (at cost)	Net sales	
			Full time	Part time			Amount	Percent of total
Total	259	272	259	22	$155,511	$82,000	$1,343,588	100.00
Food group	73	74	22	2	12,652	22,420	357,914	26.64
Candy and confectionery stores	8	8	4	1	3,284	1,430	24,120	1.80
Grocery stores (without meats)	21	21	6	-	2,400	4,480	90,533	6.74
Combination stores (groceries and meats)	28	28	8	1	4,544	14,430	147,961	11.01
Fruit stores and vegetable markets	11	11	-	-	-	1,570	50,900	3.79
Meat markets (including sea foods)	2	] 6	4	-	2,424	510	44,400	3.30
All other food stores	3							
Automotive group	22	25	21	3	12,602	3,490	143,833	10.71
Filling stations								
Filling stations – gasoline and oil	5	6	3	-	2,120	810	33,688	2.51
Filling stations with tires and accessories	6	6	8	2	5,580	1,200	70,750	5.27
Filling stations with other merchandise	3	4	5	1	3,128	210	10,750	.80
Garages and repair shops	7	] 9	5	-	1,774	1,270	28,645	2.13
All other automotive establishments	1							
Apparel group	12	1	18	9	17,945	24,600	156,348	11.64
Women's accessories stores	3	3	12	6	14,226	23,260	123,296	9.18
All other apparel stores	6	8	5	3	3,119	1,040	29,002	2.16
Shoe stores	3	3	1	-	600	300	4,050	.30
Furniture and household group	1	(x)	(x)	(x)	(x)	(x)	(x)	(x)
Restaurants and eating places	113	117	160	4	86,317	8,320	466,624	34.73
Restaurants, cafeterias, and lunch rooms								
Cafeterias	1	] 50	63	3	32,368	4,590	180,746	13.45
Lunch rooms	50							
Lunch counters, refreshment stands, etc.								
Lunch counters	22	25	30	1	21,344	1,540	124,545	9.27
Refreshment stands	16	16	5	-	2,036	610	29,318	2.18
Soft-drink stands	6	6	-	-	-	300	7,425	.55
Other retail stores	38	42	38	4	25,995	23,170	218,869	16.29
Cigar stores and cigar stands	1	(x)	(x)	(x)	(x)	(x)	(x)	(x)
Coal and wood yards	11	11	6	-	3,312	1,020	31,550	2.35
Ice dealers	3	3	-	-	-	150	4,324	.32
Drug stores								
Drug stores without fountains	3	3	3	-	2,000	1,950	16,780	1.25
Drug stores with fountains	12	13	16	1	10,586	8,770	89,556	6.67
Jewelry stores	1	(x)	(x)	(x)	(x)	(x)	(x)	(x)
Miscellaneous classifications (combined)[1]	7	9	10	1	7,517	7,260	65,177	4.85

Source: "Stores Operated by Negro Proprietors, by Kind of Business, for Cities Having 50,000 or More Negro Inhabitants: 1929," U.S. Bureau of the Census, *Negroes in the United States: 1920-32*, p. 523. *Notes:* 1. Includes 1 florist, 1 printer, 2 toilet articles shops, and 3 undertakers' and funeral supplies stores.

★ 407 ★

Business Owners and Operators

Proprietors: Businesses in Cities With 50,000 or More Blacks: Memphis, Tennessee, 1929

Kind of business	Number of stores	Proprietors and firm members (not on pay roll)	Number of employees		Total pay roll (including part time)	Stocks on hand, end of year (at cost)	Net sales	
			Full time	Part time			Amount	Percent of total
Total	379	304	217	32	$132,858	$97,300	$1,552,583	100.00
Food group	121	126	24	9	12,531	44,310	598,073	38.52
Candy and confectionery stores	1	(x)	(x)	-	(x)	(x)	(x)	(x)
Grocery stores (without meats)	50	51	6	1	3,321	12,860	161,537	10.40
Combination stores (groceries and meats)	62	65	15	8	7,826	30,850	419,481	27.02
Meat markets (including sea foods)	6	7	2	-	1,020	290	9,655	.62
All other food stores	2	(x)	(x)	-	(x)	(x)	(x)	(x)
General stores – groceries with dry goods	1	(x)	(x)	(x)	(x)	(x)	(x)	(x)
Automotive group	22	26	20	5	23,489	5,810	97,480	6.28
Filling stations								
Filling stations – gasoline and oil	5	4	6	3	5,841	3,800	45,770	2.95
Filling stations with tires and accessories	1	] 5	4	1	2,992	1,180	22,393	1.44
Filling stations with other merchandise	3							
Garages and repair shops	12	] 17	10	1	14,656	830	29,317	1.89
All other automotive establishments	1							
Apparel group	5	]						
Men's and boys' clothing and furnishings stores	1							
Family clothing stores – men's, women's, and children's	1	6	7	-	4,402	4,390	28,848	1.86
All other apparel stores	3	]						
Furniture and household group	1	(x)	(x)	(x)	(x)	(x)	(x)	(x)
Restaurants and eating places	200	103	106	10	45,985	9,660	495,847	31.94
Restaurants, cafeterias, and lunch rooms								
Lunch rooms	113	14	80	5	35,272	5,870	322,809	20.79
Restaurants with table service	3	3	11	-	5,472	490	31,025	2.00
Lunch counters, refreshment stands, etc.								
Lunch counters	69	70	12	5	3,945	2,780	118,835	7.65
Refreshment stands	5	6	-	-	-	210	8,816	.57
Soft-drink stands	10	10	3	-	1,296	310	14,362	.93
Other retail stores	29	43	60	8	46,451	33,130	332,335	21.41
Hardware stores	1	(x)	(x)	(x)	(x)	(x)	(x)	(x)
Farmers' supplies stores	1	(x)	(x)	(x)	(x)	(x)	(x)	(x)
Coal and wood yards – Ice dealers	1	(x)	(x)	(x)	(x)	(x)	(x)	(x)
Drug stores								
Drug stores without fountains	3	4	7	-	4,340	2,820	33,624	2.17
Drug stores with fountains	10	13	16	6	13,117	19,770	119,100	7.67
Miscellaneous classifications (combined)[1]	12	19	35	-	27,592	7,060	159,407	10.27
Second-hand stores	1	(x)	(x)	(x)	(x)	(x)	(x)	(x)

Source: "Stores Operated by Negro Proprietors, by Kind of Business, for Cities Having 50,000 or More Negro Inhabitants: 1929," U.S. Bureau of the Census, *Negroes in the United States: 1920-32,* p. 523. *Notes:* 1. Includes 1 novelty and souvenir shop, 3 patent medicine stores, and 8 undertakers' and funeral supplies stores.

★ 408 ★

Business Owners and Operators

Proprietors: Businesses in Cities With 50,000 or More Blacks: New Orleans, Louisiana, 1929

Kind of business	Number of stores	Proprietors and firm members (not on pay roll)	Number of employees		Total pay roll (including part time)	Stocks on hand, end of year (at cost)	Net sales	
			Full time	Part time			Amount	Percent of total
Total	771	906	238	22	$126,252	$130,140	$2,300,374	100.00
Food group	376	438	42	8	22,826	43,700	1,201,996	52.25
Candy and confectionery stores	10	14	1	-	600	890	18,095	.79

[Continued]

★ 408 ★

Proprietors: Businesses in Cities With 50,000 or More Blacks: New Orleans, Louisiana, 1929
[Continued]

Kind of business	Number of stores	Proprietors and firm members (not on pay roll)	Number of employees		Total pay roll (including part time)	Stocks on hand, end of year (at cost)	Net sales	
			Full time	Part time			Amount	Percent of total
Grocery stores (without meats)	99	116	13	-	10,476	31,640	377,493	16.41
Combination stores (groceries and meats)	13	13	-	-	-	3,800	66,100	2.87
Meat markets (including sea foods)	9	11	4	-	3,060	200	41,278	1.79
Fruit stores and vegetable markets	219	245	11	7	4,262	6,160	604,321	26.27
All other food stores								
Dairy products stores	24							
Bakeries – bakery goods stores (except manufacturing bakeries)	2	] 39	13	1	4,428	1,010	94,709	4.12
General stores – groceries with dry goods or apparel	1	(x)	-	-	-	(x)	(x)	(x)
General merchandise group	1	(x)	-	-	-	(x)	(x)	(x)
Automotive group	13	16	9	2	5,073	2,900	55,284	2.40
Filling stations	7	10	8	-	4,453	2,430	42,384	1.84
Garages and repair shops	5							
Bicycle shops	1	] 6	1	2	620	470	12,900	.56
Apparel group	10	11	9	-	7,354	10,270	39,995	1.74
Family clothing stores – men's, women's, and children's	1	(x)	(x)	-	(x)	(x)	(x)	(x)
Women's accessories stores	1	(x)	(x)	-	(x)	(x)	(x)	(x)
All other apparel stores	7	8	5	-	4,650	2,070	18,595	.81
Shoe stores	1	(x)	(x)	(x)	(x)	(x)	(x)	(x)
Furniture and household group	5							
Furniture stores	4	] 6	8	-	6,300	2,510	24,107	1.05
Other home furnishings and appliances stores	1							
Restaurants and eating places	260	302	114	5	45,423	12,400	551,713	23.98
Restaurants, cafeterias, and lunch rooms								
Lunch rooms	79	91	46	5	15,318	4,290	207,722	9.03
Restaurants with table service	9	10	42	-	18,010	670	92,703	4.03
Lunch counters, refreshment stands, etc.								
Lunch counters	56	67	7	-	1,566	2,960	82,436	3.58
Refreshment stands	51	62	6	-	4,738	1,870	76,719	3.34
Soft-drink stands	65	72	13	-	5,791	2,610	92,133	4.01
Lumber and building group[1]	1	(x)	-	-	-	(x)	(x)	(x)
Other retail stores	104	130	56	7	39,276	56,960	412,984	17.95
Cigar stores and cigar stands	4	5	3	-	1,480	100	3,666	.16
Coal and wood yards – ice dealers	71	90	13	-	4,567	7,090	165,338	7.19
Drug stores								
Drug stores without fountains	10	11	8	-	5,856	26,470	66,454	2.89
Drug stores with fountains	8	13	8	2	5,743	13,990	81,350	3.54
Jewelry stores	2							
Miscellaneous classifications (combined)[2]	9	] 11	24	5	21,630	9,310	96,176	4.18

Source: "Stores Operated by Negro Proprietors, by Kind of Business, for Cities Having 50,000 or More Negro Inhabitants: 1929," U.S. Bureau of the Census, *Negroes in the United States: 1920-32*, p. 524. *Notes:* 1. Includes 1 paint and glass store. 2. Includes 1 chemicals store, 1 florist, 1 photographer and illustrator, 2 printers and lithographers, 1 second-hand store, and 2 undertakers' and funeral supplies stores.

★ 409 ★

Business Owners and Operators

Proprietors: Businesses in Cities With 50,000 or More Blacks: New York City and Boroughs, 1929

Kind of business	Number of stores	Proprietors and firm members (not on pay roll)	Number of employees		Total pay roll (including part time)	Stocks on hand, end of year (at cost)	Net sales	
			Full time	Part time			Amount	Percent of total
New York, N.Y.								
Total	391	245	313	63	$293,482	$346,240	$3,322,274	100.00
Food group	127	58	40	10	44,458	90,540	1,186,432	35.71
Candy and confectionery stores	40	11	5	-	3,610	14,210	187,627	5.65

[Continued]

★ 409 ★

Proprietors: Businesses in Cities With 50,000 or More Blacks: New York City and Boroughs, 1929

[Continued]

Kind of business	Number of stores	Proprietors and firm members (not on pay roll)	Number of employees		Total pay roll (including part time)	Stocks on hand, end of year (at cost)	Net sales	
			Full time	Part time			Amount	Percent of total
Grocery stores (without meats)	51	6	12	8	11,281	57,320	534,598	16.09
Combination stores (groceries and meats)	3	4	-	-	-	2,700	32,880	.99
Meat markets (including sea foods)	12	13	7	-	10,676	2,210	193,538	5.83
Fruit stores and vegetable markets	7	9	1	1	522	980	37,015	1.11
All other food stores								
Bakeries – bakery goods stores (except manufacturing bakeries)	4	5	10	-	13,832	1,120	59,487	1.79
Dairy products stores	3	3	1	-	824	4,600	39,200	1.18
Coffee, tea, and spice dealers	1	(x)	(x)	-	(x)	(x)	(x)	(x)
Delicatessen stores	4	3	1	1	968	6,900	46,567	1.40
Egg and poultry dealers	2	(x)	(x)	-	(x)	(x)	(x)	(x)
General merchandise group	5	5	2	-	4,100	23,340	50,580	1.52
Dry goods stores	2	(x)	(x)	-	(x)	(x)	(x)	(x)
General merchandise stores	2	(x)	(x)	-	(x)	(x)	(x)	(x)
Variety 5-and-10, and to-a-dollar stores	1	(x)	(x)	-	(x)	(x)	(x)	(x)
Automotive group	22	18	16	3	20,219	16,340	187,889	5.66
Garages and repair shops	13	7	10	2	13,886	3,440	85,043	2.56
Filling stations	1	] 11	6	1	6,333	12,900	102,846	3.10
All other automotive establishments	8							
Apparel group	20	22	7	3	7,200	27,800	100,077	3.01
Men's and boys' clothing and furnishings stores	2	(x)	(x)	(x)	(x)	(x)	(x)	(x)
Family clothing stores – men's, women's, and children's	2	(x)	(x)	(x)	(x)	(x)	(x)	(x)
Women's ready-to-wear specialty stores – apparel and accessories	6	6	5	-	3,196	4,930	22,386	.67
Women's accessories stores	2	(x)	(x)	(x)	(x)	(x)	(x)	(x)
All other apparel stores	6	7	-	-	-	1,520	12,500	.38
Shoe stores	2	(x)	(x)	(x)	(x)	(x)	(x)	(x)
Furniture and household group	10							
All other home furnishings and appliances stores	1	] 11	6	3	5,028	8,600	26,398	.79
Radio and music stores	9							
Restaurants and eating places	81	32	193	26	151,486	15,780	1,003,713	30.21
Restaurants, cafeterias, and lunch rooms								
Cafeterias	2	(x)	(x)	-	(x)	(x)	(x)	(x)
Lunch rooms	46	12	89	5	62,392	6,190	482,836	14.53
Restaurants with table service	24	6	77	20	66,838	6,190	361,604	10.88
Lunch counters, refreshment stands, etc.								
Lunch counters	7	9	13	1	9,856	2,890	56,544	1.70
Soft-drink stands	2	(x)	-	-	-	(x)	(x)	(x)
Lumber and building group	5							
Lumber and building material dealers	1	] 7	7	-	7,147	5,330	58,430	1.76
Electrical shops (without radio)	3							
Paint and glass stores	1							
Other retail stores	106	76	40	17	53,004	152,200	682,610	20.55
Hardware stores	1	(x)	-	(x)	(x)	(x)	(x)	(x)
Cigar stores and cigar stands								
Cigar stores without fountains	20	3	8	3	9,268	15,120	105,915	3.19
Cigar stores with fountains	2	] 6	1	-	1,300	640	14,347	.43
Cigar stands (hotel lobbies, pool rooms, etc.)	5							
Coal and wood yards – ice dealers	2	(x)	-	(x)	(x)	(x)	(x)	(x)
Drug stores	9	10	18	2	26,928	83,840	212,705	6.40
Jewelry stores	5	5	-	-	-	9,800	56,450	1.70
Miscellaneous classifications (combined)[1]	62	48	13	11	15,008	38,520	277,763	8.36
Second-hand stores	15	16	2	1	840	6,310	26,145	.79
				Bronx Borough				
Total	19	19	15	2	$14,750	$50,110	$316,112	100.00
Food group	7	7	4	1	4,104	10,000	135,292	42.80
Candy and confectionery stores	2	(x)	(x)	(x)	(x)	(x)	(x)	(x)
Grocery stores (without meats)	2	(x)	(x)	(x)	(x)	(x)	(x)	(x)
All other food stores	3	3	2	-	1,604	4,300	56,400	17.84
Automotive group	1	(x)	(x)	-	(x)	(x)	(x)	(x)
Apparel group[2]	2	(x)	-	-	-	(x)	(x)	(x)

[Continued]

★ 409 ★

Proprietors: Businesses in Cities With 50,000 or More Blacks: New York City and Boroughs, 1929
[Continued]

Kind of business	Number of stores	Proprietors and firm members (not on pay roll)	Number of employees		Total pay roll (including part time)	Stocks on hand, end of year (at cost)	Net sales	
			Full time	Part time			Amount	Percent of total
Furniture and household group	1	(x)	-	-	-	(x)	(x)	(x)
Restaurants and eating places	2	(x)	(x)	-	(x)	(x)	(x)	(x)
Other retail stores	5							
Hardware stores	1	⎤						
Drug stores	3	⎥ 4	5	1	5,866	22,000	82,700	26.16
Miscellaneous classifications (combined)[3]	1	⎦						
Second-hand stores	1	(x)	-	-	-	(x)	(x)	(x)
				Brooklyn Borough				
Total	94	62	48	2	$43,043	$52,090	$543,047	100.00
Food group	31	11	8	1	5,616	18,930	240,752	44.33
Candy and confectionery stores	7	7	-	-	-	1,960	23,408	4.31
Grocery stores (without meats)	20	1	6	1	4,492	14,780	166,144	30.59
Meat markets (including sea foods)	2	(x)	(x)	-	(x)	(x)	(x)	(x)
All other food stores	2	(x)	(x)	-	(x)	(x)	(x)	(x)
General merchandise group[4]	2	(x)	(x)	-	(x)	(x)	(x)	(x)
Automotive group	13	8	10	-	12,369	4,000	83,739	15.42
Garages and repair shops	9	3	8	-	10,676	2,620	59,987	11.05
All other automotive establishments	4	5	2	-	1,693	1,380	23,752	4.37
Apparel group	4	4	-	-	-	970	4,600	.85
Men's and boys' clothing and furnishings stores	1	(x)	-	-	-	(x)	(x)	(x)
Women's ready-to-wear specialty stores – apparel and accessories	1	(x)	-	-	-	(x)	(x)	(x)
All other apparel stores	2	(x)	-	-	-	(x)	(x)	(x)
Furniture and household group[5]	1	(x)	-	-	-	(x)	(x)	(x)
Restaurants and eating places	16	8	22	-	16,283	1,960	109,823	20.22
Restaurants, cafeterias, and lunch rooms								
Cafeterias	1	(x)	(x)	-	(x)	(x)	(x)	(x)
Lunch rooms	9	-	8	-	6,642	670	45,994	8.47
Restaurants with table service	4	4	10	-	6,953	330	33,479	6.17
Lunch counters, refreshment stands, etc.								
Lunch counters	2	(x)	(x)	-	(x)	(x)	(x)	(x)
Lumber and building group[6]	2	(x)	(x)	-	(x)	(x)	(x)	(x)
Other retail stores	16	16	3	1	3,575	5,890	41,238	7.59
Cigar stores and cigar stands	2	(x)	(x)	-	(x)	(x)	(x)	(x)
Jewelry stores	2	(x)	(x)	-	(x)	(x)	(x)	(x)
Miscellaneous classifications (combined)[7]	12	12	2	1	2,275	2,230	30,368	5.59
Second-hand stores	9	10	2	-	800	4,200	17,440	3.21
				Manhattan Borough				
Total	258	142	243	56	$227,414	$229,990	$2,261,677	100.00
Food group	81	31	26	7	33,373	53,850	705,302	31.18
Candy and confectionery stores	29	-	2	-	1,270	10,470	124,467	5.50
Grocery stores (without meats)	28	2	5	5	5,264	36,590	289,445	12.80
Combination stores (groceries and meats)	2	⎤ 10	6	-	10,052	2,790	152,968	6.76
Meat markets (including sea foods)	7	⎦						
Fruit stores and vegetable markets	7	9	1	1	522	980	37,015	1.64
All other food stores								
Bakeries – bakery goods stores (except manufacturing bakeries)	4	5	10	-	13,832	1,120	59,487	2.63
Coffee, tea, spice dealers	1	⎤						
Delicatessen stores	2	⎥ 5	2	1	2,433	1,900	41,920	1.85
Egg and poultry dealers	1	⎦						
General merchandise group	3	3	1	-	1,500	10,000	14,500	.64
Dry goods stores	1	(x)	(x)	-	(x)	(x)	(x)	(x)
General merchandise stores	2	(x)	(x)	-	(x)	(x)	(x)	(x)
Automotive group	5							
Garages and repair shops	1	⎤ 6	2	2	2,290	4,620	24,854	1.10
All other automotive establishments	4	⎦						
Apparel group	14	15	7	3	7,200	16,430	68,917	3.05

[Continued]

★ 409 ★

Proprietors: Businesses in Cities With 50,000 or More Blacks: New York City and Boroughs, 1929
[Continued]

Kind of business	Number of stores	Proprietors and firm members (not on pay roll)	Number of employees		Total pay roll (including part time)	Stocks on hand, end of year (at cost)	Net sales	
			Full time	Part time			Amount	Percent of total
Family clothing stores – men's, women's, and children's	1	(x)	(x)	(x)	(x)	(x)	(x)	(x)
Women's ready-to-wear specialty stores – apparel and accessories	5	] 7	6	1	4,900	8,380	29,486	1.30
Women's accessories stores	2							
All other apparel stores	4	5	-	-	-	1,100	9,800	.43
Shoe stores	2	(x)	(x)	(x)	(x)	(x)	(x)	(x)
Furniture and household group	8	9	6	3	5,028	5,700	22,803	1.01
Radio and electrical shops	8	9	6	3	5,028	5,700	22,803	1.01
Restaurants and eating places	61	19	164	25	129,073	13,260	846,790	37.44
Restaurants, cafeterias, and lunch rooms								
Cafeterias	1	(x)	(x)	-	(x)	(x)	(x)	(x)
Lunch rooms	33	7	74	4	49,620	4,960	389,742	17.23
Restaurants with table service	20	2	67	20	59,885	5,860	328,125	14.51
Lunch counters, refreshment stands, etc.								
Lunch counters	5	6	11	1	8,568	1,990	41,944	1.85
Soft drink stands	2	(x)	(x)	-	(x)	(x)	(x)	(x)
Lumber and building group	3	5	5	-	5,347	5,030	49,830	2.20
Electrical shops (without radio)	2	(x)	(x)	-	(x)	(x)	(x)	(x)
Paint and glass stores	1	(x)	(x)	-	(x)	(x)	(x)	(x)
Other retail stores	79	50	32	15	43,563	119,640	524,776	23.20
Cigar stores and cigar stands								
Cigar stores without fountains	20	3	8	3	9,268	15,120	105,915	4.68
Cigar stores with fountains	1	] 3	-	-	-	280	5,337	.24
Cigar stands (hotel lobbies, pool rooms, etc.)	2							
Drug stores	6	7	14	1	22,752	69,840	153,505	6.79
Coal and wood yards – ice dealers	2	] 5	-	1	500	6,330	54,200	2.40
Jewelry stores	3							
Miscellaneous classifications (combined)[8]	45	32	10	10	11,043	28,070	205,819	9.10
Second-hand stores	4	4	-	1	40	1,460	3,905	.17

Queens Borough

Total	17	19	7	2	$8,125	$13,400	$190,838	100.00
Food group	7	8	2	1	1,365	7,460	102,486	53.70
Candy and confectionery stores	2	(x)	(x)	(x)	(x)	(x)	(x)	(x)
Grocery stores (without meats)	1	(x)	(x)	(x)	(x)	(x)	(x)	(x)
Combination stores (groceries and meats)	1	(x)	(x)	(x)	(x)	(x)	(x)	(x)
Meat markets (including sea foods)	2	(x)	(x)	(x)	(x)	(x)	(x)	(x)
All other food stores	1	(x)	(x)	(x)	(x)	(x)	(x)	(x)
Automotive group[9]	3	(x)	(x)	(x)	(x)	(x)	(x)	(x)
Restaurants and eating places	1	(x)	(x)	(x)	(x)	(x)	(x)	(x)
Other retail stores	5							
Cigar stores and cigar stands	1	] 5	-	-	-	4,370	27,396	14.36
Miscellaneous classifications (combined)[10]	4							
Second-hand stores	1	(x)	-	-	-	(x)	(x)	(x)

Richmond Borough

Total	3	3	-	1	$150	$650	$10,600	100.00
Meat markets (including sea foods)	1	(x)	-	(x)	(x)	(x)	(x)	(x)
Restaurants, cafeterias, and lunch rooms	1	(x)	-	(x)	(x)	(x)	(x)	(x)
Cigar stores and cigar stands	1	(x)	-	(x)	(x)	(x)	(x)	(x)

Source: "Stores Operated by Negro Proprietors, by Kind of Business, for Cities Having 50,000 or More Negro Inhabitants: 1929," U.S. Bureau of the Census, *Negroes in the United States: 1920-32*, pp. 524-526. *Notes:* 1. Includes 30 news dealers, 5 florists, 1 barbers' supplies store, 2 opticians, 3 malt products supplies stores, 5 patent medicine stores, 6 printers and lithographers, 2 regalia badges and emblems stores, 2 stationers and engravers, 1 typewriter shop, and 5 undertakers' and funeral supplies stores. 2. Includes 1 men's and boys' clothing and furnishings store and 1 family clothing store. 3. Includes 1 news dealer. 4. Includes 1 dry goods store and 1 variety, 5-and-10, and to-a-dollar store. 5. Includes 1 antique shop. 6. Includes 1 electrical shop (without radio), and 1 lumber and building material dealer. 7. Includes 2 florists, 1 news dealer, 1 optician, 3 patent medicine stores, 4 printers and lithographers, and 1 undertakers' and funeral supplies stores. 8. Includes 1 barbers' supplies store, 3 florists, 3 malt products supplies stores, 24 news dealers, 1 optician, 2 patent medicine stores, 2 printers and lithographers, 2 regalia badges and emblems stores, 2 stationers and engravers, 1 typewriter shop, and 4 undertakers' and funeral supplies stores. 9. Includes 3 garages and repair shops. 10. Includes 4 news dealers.

★ 410 ★

Business Owners and Operators

Proprietors: Businesses in Cities With 50,000 or More Blacks: Philadelphia, Pennsylvania, 1929

Kind of business	Number of stores	Proprietors and firm members (not on pay roll)	Number of employees		Total pay roll (including part time)	Stocks on hand, end of year (at cost)	Net sales	
			Full time	Part time			Amount	Percent of total
Total	787	819	337	96	$300,747	$266,480	$3,150,007	100.00
Food group	210	218	26	8	21,037	54,550	733,718	23.29
Candy and confectionery stores	64	64	6	1	2,501	12,450	121,385	3.85
Grocery stores (without meats)	97	102	3	1	1,958	30,330	279,520	8.87
Combination stores (groceries and meats)	14	12	3	-	2,040	5,060	80,460	2.55
Meat markets (including sea foods)	12	12	5	1	4,480	2,660	122,875	3.90
Fruit stores and vegetable markets	13	15	8	4	8,398	1,530	59,156	1.88
All other food stores								
Bakeries – bakery goods stores (except manufacturing bakeries)	2	⎤ 9	-	1	360	2,070	33,804	1.07
Delicatessen stores	4	⎦						
Egg and poultry dealers	4	4	1	-	1,300	450	36,518	1.16
General merchandise group	3	⎤						
Dry goods stores	1	⎟ 3	1	-	985	1,350	11,000	.35
General merchandise stores	1	⎟						
Variety 5-and-10, and to-a-dollar stores	1	⎦						
Automotive group	33	36	29	8	29,549	8,870	129,923	4.12
Filling stations	6	6	4	2	4,256	3,010	19,358	.61
Garage and repair shops	22	25	23	6	23,653	1,860	97,683	3.10
All other automotive establishments	5	5	2	-	1,640	4,000	12,882	.41
Apparel group	36	36	14	2	15,695	17,160	127,486	4.05
Men's and boys' clothing and furnishings stores	2	⎤						
Family clothing stores – men's, women's, and children's	2	⎟ 6	3	-	3,440	9,680	40,006	1.27
Shoe stores	2	⎦						
Women's ready-to-wear specialty stores – apparel and accessories	5	5	2	-	1,280	1,960	11,885	.38
Women's accessories stores	5	5	-	1	300	1,250	7,805	.25
Other apparel stores	20	20	9	1	10,675	4,270	67,790	2.15
Furniture and household group	17	18	10	2	6,696	15,600	45,455	1.44
Furniture stores	8	8	3	-	756	3,000	9,355	.30
All other home furnishings and appliances stores	5	6	3	1	2,500	7,800	6,100	.19
Radio and music stores	4	4	4	1	3,440	4,800	30,000	.95
Restaurants and eating places	183	188	141	26	94,952	16,060	678,769	21.55
Restaurants, cafeterias, and lunch rooms								
Lunch rooms	130	133	52	8	32,868	9,610	373,014	11.84
Restaurants with table service	31	33	85	16	57,384	3,240	254,878	8.09
Lunch counters, refreshment stands, etc.								
Lunch counters	20	⎤ 22	4	2	4,700	3,210	50,877	1.62
Soft-drink stands	2	⎦						
All other retail stores	250	261	112	45	128,268	136,690	1,336,785	42.44
Lumber and building material dealers	1	⎤						
Paint and glass stores	1	⎟ 4	-	-	-	700	8,960	.28
Hardware stores	1	⎟						
Farmers' supplies stores	1	⎦						
Cigar stores and cigar stands								
Cigar stores without fountains	102	105	7	8	7,092	27,220	279,305	8.87
Cigar stores with fountains	8	8	-	-	-	2,070	17,042	.54
Cigar stands (hotel lobbies, pool rooms, etc.)	25	25	3	1	2,570	2,520	29,510	.94
Coal and wood yards	5	4	19	-	25,063	11,180	171,675	5.45
Ice dealers	4	4	1	1	860	160	6,708	.21
Drug stores								
Drug stores without fountains	4	4	4	2	4,232	10,300	26,100	.83
Drug stores with fountains	20	24	24	9	29,569	44,310	194,307	6.17
Jewelry stores	4	4	-	1	155	1,450	14,885	.47
Miscellaneous classifications (combined)[1]	74	79	54	23	58,727	36,780	588,293	18.68
Second-hand stores	55	59	4	5	3,565	16,200	86,871	2.76
Automobile parts	1	⎤ 7	-	-	-	1,930	10,175	.32
Clothing and shoe stores	6	⎦						
Furniture stores	41	43	4	-	2,315	10,390	67,876	2.15
All other second-hand dealers	7	9	-	5	1,250	3,880	8,820	.28

Source: "Stores Operated by Negro Proprietors, by Kind of Business, for Cities Having 50,000 or More Negro Inhabitants: 1929," U.S. Bureau of the Census, *Negroes in the United States: 1920-32*, pp. 526-527. *Note:* 1. Includes 4 custom tailors.

★ 411 ★

Business Owners and Operators

Proprietors: Businesses in Cities With 50,000 or More Blacks: Pittsburgh, Pennsylvania, 1929

Kind of business	Number of stores	Proprietors and firm members (not on pay roll)	Number of employees		Total pay roll (including part time)	Stocks on hand, end of year (at cost)	Net sales	
			Full time	Part time			Amount	Percent of total
Total	150	168	128	20	$99,327	$94,810	$830,013	100.00
Food group	58	61	20	4	19,492	22,560	265,699	32.01
Candy and confectionery stores	33	36	13	3	11,318	11,160	115,445	13.91
Grocery stores (without meats)	15	15	2	1	1,514	7,030	48,400	5.83
Combination stores (groceries and meats)	4	4	1	-	520	3,090	28,182	3.40
Meat markets (including sea foods)	5	] 6	4	-	6,140	1,280	73,672	8.83
Fruit stores and vegetable markets	1							
Automotive group	5	] 7	8	3	12,970	1,880	98,619	11.88
Filling stations	1							
Garage and repair shops	4							
Apparel group	1	(x)	(x)	-	(x)	(x)	(x)	(x)
Furniture and household group[1]	3	4	2	-	1,248	9,580	20,959	2.53
Restaurants and eating places	50	55	60	1	27,622	4,170	191,843	23.11
Restaurants, cafeterias, and lunch rooms								
Lunch rooms	32	34	24	-	10,700	1,860	89,783	10.82
Restaurants with table service	13	15	32	1	16,106	1,850	83,396	10.05
Lunch counters, refreshment stands, etc.								
Lunch counters	5	6	4	-	816	460	18,664	2.25
Lumber and building group	4	] 5	4	1	3,506	3,860	22,838	2.75
Heating and plumbing shops	3							
Paint and glass stores	1							
Other retail stores	26	32	33	10	33,489	51,710	221,493	26.69
Farmers' supplies stores	1	(x)	(x)	-	(x)	(x)	(x)	(x)
Cigar stores and cigar stands	7	8	4	-	2,940	1,230	14,692	1.77
Drug stores	7	9	8	4	9,273	32,320	99,645	12.01
Jewelry stores	1	(x)	(x)	-	(x)	(x)	(x)	(x)
Miscellaneous classifications[2]	10	11	19	6	20,196	15,190	98,991	11.93
Second-hand stores	3	4	1	1	1,000	1,050	8,562	1.03

Source: "Stores Operated by Negro Proprietors, by Kind of Business, for Cities Having 50,000 or More Negro Inhabitants: 1929," U.S. Bureau of the Census, *Negroes in the United States: 1920-32*, p. 527. *Notes:* 1. Includes 3 radio and music stores. 2. Includes 1 beauty shop, 1 news dealer, 1 novelty and souvenir shop, and 7 undertakers' and funeral supplies stores.

★ 412 ★

Business Owners and Operators

Proprietors: Businesses in Cities With 50,000 or More Blacks: Richmond, Virginia, 1929

Kind of business	Number of stores	Proprietors and firm members (not on pay roll)	Number of employees		Total pay roll (including part time)	Stocks on hand, end of year (at cost)	Net sales	
			Full time	Part time			Amount	Percent of total
Total	189	199	102	36	$61,202	$67,760	$657,981	100.00
Food group	106	113	28	17	13,964	22,670	304,996	46.35
Candy and confectionery stores	18	21	5	2	2,508	3,890	54,396	8.27
Grocery stores (without meats)	28	29	6	3	1,490	3,320	40,342	6.13
Combination stores (groceries and meats)	35	36	4	3	3,134	14,340	142,431	21.65
Meat markets (including sea foods)	18	20	12	7	6,078	910	49,163	7.47
Fruit stores and vegetable markets	4	4	1	2	754	150	16,580	2.52

[Continued]

★ 412 ★

Proprietors: Businesses in Cities With 50,000 or More Blacks: Richmond, Virginia, 1929
[Continued]

Kind of business	Number of stores	Proprietors and firm members (not on pay roll)	Number of employees		Total pay roll (including part time)	Stocks on hand, end of year (at cost)	Net sales	
			Full time	Part time			Amount	Percent of total
Bakeries – bakery goods stores (except manufacturing bakeries)	3	3	-	-	-	60	2,084	.32
General stores – groceries with dry goods or apparel	2	(x)	-	-	-	(x)	(x)	(x)
General merchandise group	4	5	-	-	-	3,270	6,164	.94
Dry goods stores	1	(x)	-	-	-	(x)	(x)	(x)
General merchandise stores	2	(x)	-	-	-	(x)	(x)	(x)
Variety, 5-and-10, and to-a-dollar stores	1	(x)	-	-	-	(x)	(x)	(x)
Automotive group	3	3	2	-	1,356	130	9,831	1.49
Filling stations	2	(x)	(x)	-	(x)	(x)	(x)	(x)
Garage and repair shops	1	(x)	(x)	-	(x)	(x)	(x)	(x)
Apparel group[1]	1	(x)	(x)	(x)	(x)	(x)	(x)	(x)
Furniture and household group[2]	2	(x)	(x)	(x)	(x)	(x)	(x)	(x)
Restaurants and eating places	35	36	23	5	8,394	1,650	65,542	9.96
Restaurants, cafeterias, and lunch rooms								
Lunch rooms	25	26	11	1	3,942	950	36,689	5.58
Restaurants with table service	8	(x)	(x)	(x)	(x)	(x)	(x)	(x)
Lunch counters, refreshment stands, etc.	2	(x)	(x)	(x)	(x)	(x)	(x)	(x)
Other retail stores	33	34	46	10	34,404	35,340	254,308	38.65
Hardware stores	1	(x)	(x)	-	(x)	(x)	(x)	(x)
Cigar stores	1	(x)	(x)	-	(x)	(x)	(x)	(x)
Coal and wood yards – ice dealers	14	14	8	1	2,362	1,160	17,157	2.61
Drug stores								
Drug stores without fountains	1	} 8	7	2	4,756	21,600	68,375	10.39
Drug stores with fountains	6							
Jewelry stores	1	(x)	(x)	-	(x)	(x)	(x)	(x)
Miscellaneous classifications (combined)[3]	9	10	30	7	26,326	10,680	156,526	23.79
Second-hand stores	3	3	1	-	312	1,730	5,070	.77

Source: "Stores Operated by Negro Proprietors, by Kind of Business, for Cities Having 50,000 or More Negro Inhabitants: 1929," U.S. Bureau of the Census, *Negroes in the United States: 1920-32*, p. 528. *Notes:* 1. Includes 1 apparel store. 2. Includes 1 furniture store, 1 other household appliance store. 3. Includes 1 florist and 1 news dealer, 7 undertakers' and funeral supplies stores.

★ 413 ★
Business Owners and Operators

Proprietors: Service Establishments in the United States, 1935

Of the 22,172 service establishments operated by blacks, as reported in the 1935 U.S. business census, 8,710, or approximately 39.3 per cent, were in the North; 12,204, or 55 per cent, in the South; and 1,258, or about 5.7 per cent, in the West. The sectional distribution of the total receipts of $27,281,000 showed 46.2 per cent for the North; 49.1 per cent for the South; and 4.7 per cent for the West.

Kind of business	Number of establishments	Receipts (add 000)	Employees (full-time & part-time) average for year	Total; pay roll[1] (add 000)
Total for United States	22,172	$27,281	13,975	$5,710
Personal service				
Barber shops	6,821	7,355	5,586	2,270
Barber and beauty shops	60	130	131	59
Baths and masseurs' establishments (turkish, etc.)	27	41	27	11
Beauty parlors	2,940	2,952	1,698	655
Cleaning, dyeing, pressing, alteration, and repair shops	3,326	3,590	1,620	591

[Continued]

★ 413 ★

Proprietors: Service Establishments in the United States, 1935
[Continued]

Kind of business	Number of establishments	Receipts (add 000)	Employees (full-time & part-time) average for year	Total; pay roll[1] (add 000)
Funeral directors, embalmers, and crematories	1,458	6,949	2,385	1,223
Fur repair and storage shops	7	9	2	1
Laundries (not including power laundries)	315	332	148	47
Photographic studios	96	114	21	8
Rug cleaning and repairing shops	10	18	5	3
Shoe repair shops and shoe shine parlors (including hat cleaning)	3,633	2,650	964	299
Other personal services	24	14	1	[3]
Business services				
Adjustment and credit bureaus, and collection agencies	3	17	-	-
Billboard advertising service	3	2	2	[3]
Court reporting and public stenographic agencies	8	3	1	[3]
Dental laboratories	12	33	10	6
Disinfecting and exterminating service	3	3	1	1
Duplicating, addressing, mailing, and mailing list service	4	9	5	3
Employment agencies	73	98	41	19
Sign painting shops	84	68	9	3
Ticket agents and brokers, and travel bureaus	5	27	1	[3]
Window cleaning service	20	19	11	6
Other business services	33	48	15	6
Repair services and custom industries				
Automotive repairs and services (excluding general repair garages)				
Automobile laundries	187	231	152	66
Automobile paint shops	22	45	14	8
Automobile rental service	14	14	17	5
Automobile storage garages	162	358	166	92
Automobile top and body repair shops	25	29	9	4
Battery and ignition repair shops	28	33	9	3
Parking lots	57	65	17	8
Tire automotive repairs	5	9	4	1
Other repair services (except apparel and shoes)				
Bicycle repair shops	39	36	15	4
Blacksmith shops	750	373	129	35
Electrical appliance repair shops	10	10	2	1
Harness and leather goods repair shops	12	6	-	-
Locksmith and gunsmith shops	12	7	1	[3]
Piano and organ tuning and repair service	3	3	-	-

[Continued]

★ 413 ★

Proprietors: Service Establishments in the United States, 1935
[Continued]

Kind of business	Number of establishments	Receipts (add 000)	Employees (full-time & part-time) average for year	Total; pay roll[1] (add 000)
Radio repair shops	163	131	22	9
Saw and tool sharpening and repair shops	5	3	-	-
Upholstery and furniture repair shops	181	162	53	24
Watch, clock, and jewelry repair shops	118	110	10	7
Other repair services	222	151	45	17
Custom industries[2]				
Cabinetmaking shops (including woodworking)	28	18	2	1
Grist mills	87	22	15	2
Hemstitching, embroidering, and buttonholing shops	7	5	3	1
Machine shops	17	10	-	-
Mattress renovating and repair shops	18	20	8	3
Molasses, sorghum, and syrup mills	261	35	17	2
Printing and publishing shops	284	398	188	82
Saw mills and planing mills	62	53	93	18
Threshing, corn shelling, hay baling, and other agricultural services	138	52	61	9
Tinsmith shops	42	27	7	3
Welding shops	21	40	13	7
Other industries	50	69	83	17
Miscellaneous services				
Landscape gardening and tree surgery service	22	34	17	8
Other miscellaneous services	104	165	89	49

Source: "Service Establishments: 1935," Florence Murray, ed., *The Negro Handbook*, pp. 29-30. *Notes:* 1. Includes no compensation for proprietors and firm members of unincorporated business. 2. Includes custom industries, and small manufacturing plants not included in the Census of Manufacturers for the reason that the value of product of each establishment is less than the minimum necessary to be classed as a manufacturing plant. 3. Less than 500.

★ 414 ★

Business Owners and Operators

Proprietors: Stores and Sales by Geographic Divisions, 1935

Division and state	Number of stores			Sales (Add 000)		
	1939	1935	1929	1939	1935	1929
United States Total	29,827	22,756	24,969	$71,466	$47,968	$98,602
Geographic divisions						
New England	197	165	217	770	1,251	1,876
Middle Atlantic	3,182	2,681	2,427	12,010	8,256	14,315
East North Central	3,755	2,806	2,612	13,542	8,416	16,727

[Continued]

★ 414 ★

Proprietors: Stores and Sales by Geographic Divisions, 1935
[Continued]

Division and state	Number of stores			Sales (Add 000)		
	1939	1935	1929	1939	1935	1929
West North Central	1,138	994	962	2,706	2,430	6,072
South Atlantic	10,897	8,305	9,411	21,323	14,399	26,921
East South Central	4,219	3,449	4,238	7,414	5,025	12,959
West South Central	5,709	3,789	4,764	10,627	6,052	16,066
Mountain	174	104	62	530	330	526
Pacific	556	463	276	2,544	1,809	3,140
New England						
Maine	2	2	4	⎤		47
New Hampshire	-	2	4	45	15	27
Vermont	1	1	3	⎦		76
Massachusetts	114	101	116	401	1,062	1,131
Rhode Island	24	14	37	115	49	175
Connecticut	56	45	53	209	127	420
Middle Atlantic						
New York	1,450	1,085	586	6,265	4,370	5,377
New Jersey	628	580	557	2,085	1,670	2,591
Pennsylvania	1,104	1,016	1,284	3,660	2,216	6,347
East North Central						
Ohio	1,096	896	736	4,113	2,612	4,245
Indiana	370	297	327	1,408	769	1,987
Illinois	1,364	919	1,027	4,374	3,208	6,265
Michigan	856	635	474	3,272	1,548	3,762
Wisconsin	69	59	48	375	279	468
West North Central						
Minnesota	52	73	70	243	385	578
Iowa	56	60	55	149	153	542
Missouri	716	548	553	1,515	1,257	3,035
North Dakota	2	15	15	⎤ 21	12	199
South Dakota	3	1	11	⎦		116
Nebraska	58	61	52	256	189	435
Kansas	251	236	206	522	434	1,167
South Atlantic						
Delaware	119	90	59	292	110	259
Maryland	1,016	559	503	2,595	1,292	1,667
District of Columbia	300	271	236	2,327	1,572	1,470
Virginia	1,918	1,464	1,835	3,887	2,540	4,913
West Virginia	190	213	301	435	588	1,136
North Carolina	1,834	1,367	1,861	3,060	2,174	5,693
South Carolina	1,246	985	1,193	1,618	1,074	2,239
Georgia	2,268	2,001	2,071	3,414	2,530	5,099
Florida	2,006	1,355	1,352	3,695	2,519	4,445

[Continued]

★ 414 ★

Proprietors: Stores and Sales by Geographic Divisions, 1935
[Continued]

Division and state	Number of stores			Sales (Add 000)		
	1939	1935	1929	1939	1935	1929
East South Central						
Kentucky	554	561	662	965	851	2,124
Tennessee	1,044	1,099	934	2,448	2,094	3,602
Alabama	1,285	956	1,274	2,198	1,239	3,498
Mississippi	1,336	843	1,368	1,803	841	3,735
West South Central						
Arkansas	973	657	914	1,118	792	2,387
Louisiana	1,410	968	1,644	2,776	1,579	4,452
Oklahoma	647	485	530	1,381	969	2,782
Texas	2,679	1,679	1,676	5,352	2,712	6,445
Mountain						
Montana	5	5	6	26[1]	32	69[1]
Idaho	2	-	2	26[1]	-	69[1]
Wyoming	7	5	3	60	38	24
Colorado	61	44	36	247	170	309
New Mexico	27	11	1	41	11	2
Arizona	60	29	7	122	68	30
Utah	5	4	5	16	3	84
Nevada	7	6	2	18	8	8
Pacific						
Washington	32	44	18	141	274	175
Oregon	7	12	14	79	34	330
California	517	407	244	2,324	1,501	2,635

Source: "Summary—Comparison of Stores and Sales, by Geographic Divisions," Florence Murray, ed., *The Negro Handbook*, p. 20. *Note:* Data includes Montana and Idaho.

★ 415 ★

Business Owners and Operators

Proprietors: Stores in Atlanta, Georgia, 1935

Atlanta, eleventh city in size of Negro population (90,075 in 1930), ranked seventh in the number of retail stores operated by Negroes, and seventh in the amount of sales. A total of 297 stores in 1935 brought in $694,000 in sales. Both the number of stores and the amount of sales decreased between 1929 and 1935; the city reporting 391 stores in 1929 and $1,151,850 in sales. A total of 222 employees (excluding 286 proprietors and firm members) in 1935 received $69,938 in pay, 10.1 per cent of the total sales. Operating expenses for 1935 were $161,000, 23.2 per cent of total sales. Eating and drinking places accounted for 35.6 per cent of the total sales, and food stores, 28.7 per cent. Stores averaged $2,337 in sales.

Kind of business	No. of stores	Sales
Total	297	$694,000
Food stores, including bakeries and caterers	71	199,000
Automotive, including accessories, filling stations, and garages	16	38,000
Apparel	1	X
Furniture – household	1	X
Eating and drinking places	180	247,000
Drug stores	5	131,000
Other retail stores, including fuel and ice dealers (10), cigar stores (4)	21	55,000
Second-hand stores	2	X

Source: "Retail Stores in Fifteen Cities with Largest Negro Population: 1935," Florence Murray, ed., *The Negro Handbook*, pp. 25-26. *Notes:* X means that the amount is withheld to avoid disclosure of individual operator, but it is included in the total.

★ 416 ★

Business Owners and Operators

Proprietors: Stores in Baltimore, Maryland, 1935

Baltimore, fourth largest city in Negro population (142,106 in 1930), was fifth in the number of retail stores operated by Negroes, and sixth in the amount of sales in 1935. With 383 stores, a total of $893,000 was reported in sales. Although 101 more stores were reported in 1935 than in 1929, sales were $169,946 less than in 1929. With a total number of 257 employees (excluding 380 proprietors and firm members), the total pay roll for 1935 was $94,505 and the operating expenses were $246,000. Combined operating expenses totaled $246,000 or 27.5 per cent of the total sales.

Kind of business	No. of stores	Sales
Total	383	$89,000
Food stores, including bakeries and caterers	129	197,000
Automotive, including accessories, filling stations and garages	20	47,000
General merchandise	1	X
Apparel	10	23,000
Furniture – household	2	X
Lumber – building--hardware	1	X

[Continued]

★ 416 ★

Proprietors: Stores in Baltimore, Maryland, 1935
[Continued]

Kind of business	No. of stores	Sales
Eating and drinking places	128	487,000
Drug stores	2	X
Other retail stores, including fuel and ice dealers (69)	75	104,000
Second-hand stores	15	16,000

Source: "Retail Stores in Fifteen Cities with Largest Negro Population: 1935," Florence Murray, ed., *The Negro Handbook*, p. 25. *Notes:* X means that the amount is withheld to avoid disclosure of individual operator, but it is included in the total.

★ 417 ★

Business Owners and Operators

Proprietors: Stores in Birmingham, Alabama, 1935

Birmingham, eighth city in size of Negro population (99,077 in 1930), ranked fourteenth in the number of retail stores operated by Negroes in 1935, and fourteenth in the amount of sales. A total of 132 stores brought in $193,000. Both the number and the amount of sales decreased between 1929 and 1935, with the city having reported in 1929 200 stores and $601,916. A total of 89 employees (excluding 127 proprietors and firm members) were given pay amounting to $25,802 in 1935 and $75,000 was spent for operating expenses, which represented 38.9 per cent of total sales. Eating and drinking places constituted 31.1 per cent of total sales; and food stores, 27.5.

Kind of business	No. of stores	Sales
Total	132	$193,000
Food stores	30	53,000
Automotive, including filling stations, and garages, tires and batteries	9	11,000
General merchandise	1	X
Eating and drinking places, including drinking places only (1)	63	60,000
Drug stores	3	11,000
Other retail stores, including fuel and ice dealers (24)	26	56,000

Source: "Retail Stores in Fifteen Cities with Largest Negro Population: 1935," Florence Murray, ed., *The Negro Handbook*, p. 28. *Notes:* X means that the amount is withheld to avoid disclosure of individual operator, but it is included in the total.

★ 418 ★

Business Owners and Operators

Proprietors: Stores in Chicago, 1935

Chicago, second city in Negro population (233,903, in 1930) occupied third place, in 1935, in the number of retail stores operated by colored proprietors and second place in the value of sales. Both the number of stores and the value of sales showed a decrease from 1929, in which year 815 stores were reported, with a total of $4,826,897 in sales. In 1935 Chicago reported 724 stores, whose sales for the year totaled $2,735,000. These stores gave employment to 1,349 persons: 743 proprietors not on the pay roll, and 606 employees who received $361,061 in wages. Operating expenses amounted to $802,000. Fuel and ice dealers reported the largest total value of sales. The combined sales of food stores, and eating and drinking places amounted to $1,380,000 or slightly in excess of 50 per cent of the total sales. Average sales per store amounted to $3,778, as compared to the average of $2,085 for the entire country.

Kind of business	No. of stores	Sales
Total	724	$2,735,000
Food stores (includes bakeries and caterers)	259	555,000
Automotive group, including accessories, filling stations, and garages	33	95,000
General merchandise	5	6,000
Apparel group	35	65,000
Furniture – household, including radios	4	46,000
Lumber – building--hardware	5	8,000
Eating and drinking places	217	725,000
Drug stores	38	185,000
Other retail stores, including fuel and ice (47), beer and liquor (3)	87	1,014,000
Second-hand stores	41	36,000

Source: "Retail Stores in Fifteen Cities with Largest Negro Population: 1935," Florence Murray, ed., *The Negro Handbook*, p. 23.

★ 419 ★

Business Owners and Operators

Proprietors: Stores in Cleveland, Ohio, 1935

Cleveland, twelfth city in size of Negro population (71,899 in 1930), ranked twelfth in the number of retail stores operated by Negroes in 1935 and eleventh in the amount of sales. A total of 184 stores in 1935 brought in $550,000. Both the number of stores and the amount of sales showed a decrease from the 1929 figure, which gave 215 stores and $1,156,859. A total of 128 employees (excluding 193 proprietors and firm members) were paid $62,850 in 1935. Operating expenses were $118,000 and constituted 21.5 per cent of the sales. Food stores reported 44 per cent of the total and eating and drinking places, 21.5 per cent.

Kind of business	No. of stores	Sales
Total	184	$550,000
Food stores, including bakeries and caterers	49	242,000
Automotive, including used car dealers, filling stations and garages	29	138,000
General merchandise	1	X
Apparel	2	X
Lumber – building--hardware	4	6,000
Eating and drinking places, including drinking places only (9)	50	118,000
Drug stores	2	X
Other retail stores, including fuel and ice dealers (20)	30	26,000
Second-hand stores, including clothing, furniture, and auto accessories	17	6,000

Source: "Retail Stores in Fifteen Cities with Largest Negro Population: 1935," Florence Murray, ed., *The Negro Handbook*, p. 27. *Notes:* X means that the amount is withheld to avoid disclosure of individual operator, but it is included in the total.

★ 420 ★

Business Owners and Operators

Proprietors: Stores in Detroit, Michigan, 1935

Detroit, seventh city in Negro population (120,066 in 1930), ranked fourth in the number of retail stores, 504, and fifth in the amount of sales, $1,128,000 in 1935. The increase in the number of stores between 1929 and 1935 was 146, but total sales decreased, from $2,951,471 in 1929 to $1,128,000 in 1935. A total pay roll of $158,912 in 1935 went to 364 employees, excluding 502 proprietors and firm members, while total operating expenses were $308,000. Food stores in 1935 constituted 26.1 per cent of total sales; eating and drinking places, 25.1 per cent. The total pay roll amounted to 51.6 per cent of the operating expenses and 14.1 per cent of the total sales.

Kind of business	No. of stores	Sales
Total	504	$1,128,000
Food stores, including bakeries and caterers	169	294,000
Automotive, including accessories, filling stations and garages	44	210,000
General merchandise	1	X
Apparel	9	18,000

[Continued]

★ 420 ★

Proprietors: Stores in Detroit, Michigan, 1935
[Continued]

Kind of business	No. of stores	Sales
Furniture – household, including radios	4	7,000
Eating and drinking places	115	283,000
Drug stores	20	126,000
Other retail stores, including fuel and (86), cigar stands (13)	108	155,000
Second-hand stores	34	35,000

Source: "Retail Stores in Fifteen Cities with Largest Negro Population: 1935," Florence Murray, ed., *The Negro Handbook*, pp. 24-25. *Notes:* X means that the amount is withheld to avoid disclosure of individual operator, but it is included in the total.

★ 421 ★

Business Owners and Operators

Proprietors: Stores in Houston, Texas, 1935

Houston, thirteenth city in size of Negro population (63,337 in 1930), was tenth among the cities in number of retail stores operated by Negroes, and tenth in the amount of sales in 1935. A total of 252 stores in 1935 reported $565,000 in sales. Both the number of stores and the amount of sales decreased from 1929 to 1935, with seven more stores and sales of $1,343,588 in 1929.

Kind of business	No. of stores	Sales
Total	252	$565,000
Food stores, including bakeries and caterers	55	90,000
Automotive, including accessories, filling stations and garages	29	122,000
General merchandise	1	X
Apparel	2	X
Eating and drinking places, including drinking places only (7)	133	287,000
Drug stores	9	34,000
Other retail stores, including fuel and ice (12), beer and liquor (2)	19	21,000
Second-hand stores	4	2,000

Source: "Retail Stores in Fifteen Cities with Largest Negro Population: 1935," Florence Murray, ed., *The Negro Handbook*, pp. 26-27. *Notes:* X means that the amount is withheld to avoid disclosure of individual operator, but it is included in the total.

★ 422 ★

Proprietors: Stores in Indiana, 1929

Kind of business	Number of stores	Proprietors and firm members (not on pay roll)	Number of employees (full time)	Total pay roll (including part time)	Stocks on hand, end of year (at cost)	Net sales Amount	Net sales Percent of total
Total	342	383	260	$189,328	$131,350	$2,021,677	100.00
Food group	97	105	16	8,844	29,760	621,973	30.76
Candy and confectionery stores	9	10	3	1,974	1,380	29,880	1.48
Grocery stores (without meats)	28	29	-	-	6,320	88,794	4.39
Combination stores (groceries and meats)	50	55	9	5,491	19,930	473,793	23.43
Other food stores	10	11	4	1,379	2,130	29,506	1.46
Automotive group	22	24	16	14,529	3,580	91,767	4.54
Motor-vehicle dealers (new and used)	1	(x)	(x)	(x)	(x)	(x)	(x)
Filling stations	2	(x)	(x)	(x)	(x)	(x)	(x)
Garages and repair shops	15	17	11	10,141	1,740	35,356	1.75
Other automotive establishments	4	4	4	2,628	1,280	16,965	.84
Apparel group	10	12	4	2,106	3,380	31,897	1.58
Men's and boys' clothing and furnishings stores	1	(x)	(x)	(x)	(x)	(x)	(x)
Family clothing stores-men's, women's, and children's	1	(x)	(x)	(x)	(x)	(x)	(x)
Women's ready-to-wear specialty stores – apparel and accessories	1	(x)	(x)	(x)	(x)	(x)	(x)
Women's accessories stores	1	(x)	(x)	(x)	(x)	(x)	(x)
Other apparel stores	6	8	2	1,020	382	13,873	.69
Furniture and household group	3	3	2	2,236	1,250	11,400	.56
Furniture stores	1	(x)	(x)	(x)	(x)	(x)	(x)
Other home furnishings and appliances stores	2	(x)	(x)	(x)	(x)	(x)	(x)
Restaurants, cafeterias, and eating places	116	131	112	47,220	4,910	367,914	18.20
Restaurants, cafeterias, and lunch rooms	89	103	99	39,146	3,600	298,869	14.79
Lunch counters, refreshment stands, etc.	27	28	13	8,074	1,310	69,045	3.41
Lumber and building group	3	3	27	40,771	5,580	129,952	6.43
Lumber and building material dealers	1	(x)	(x)	(x)	(x)	(x)	(x)
Electrical shops (without radio)	1	(x)	(x)	(x)	(x)	(x)	(x)
Heating and plumbing shops	1	(x)	(x)	(x)	(x)	(x)	(x)
Other retail stores	77	91	78	68,110	74,490	692,852	34.27
Hardware stores	2	(x)	(x)	(x)	(x)	(x)	(x)
Hardware and farm implement stores	1	(x)	(x)	(x)	(x)	(x)	(x)
Farmers' supplies stores (including feeds and fertilizers)	3	4	3	3,594	7,180	121,550	6.01
Cigar stores and cigar stands	42	49	29	24,581	5,030	125,164	6.19
Coal and wood yards – ice dealers	6	7	22	14,603	11,380	259,409	12.83
Drug stores	9	10	9	11,116	23,600	80,130	3.97
Miscellaneous classifications (combined)	14	17	12	12,436	6,080	78,854	3.90
Second-hand stores	14	14	5	5,512	8,400	73,922	3.66

Source: "Stores Operated by Black Proprietors, by States 1929," U.S. Bureau of the Census. *Negroes in the United States: 1920-32*, pp. 505-506.

★ 423 ★

Business Owners and Operators

Proprietors: Stores in Iowa, 1929

Kind of business	Number of stores	Proprietors and firm members (not on pay roll)	Number of employees (full time)	Total pay roll (including part time)	Stocks on hand, end of year (at cost)	Net sales	
						Amount	Percent of total
Total	57	64	54	$44,543	$48,630	$573,577	100.00
Food group	9	13	6	4,379	14,450	210,694	36.73
Grocery stores (without meats)	4	5	5	3,935	12,190	134,105	23.38
Combination stores (groceries and meats)	4	7	1	314	1,530	26,589	4.63
Other food stores	1	1	-	130	730	50,000	8.72
General stores – groceries with dry goods or apparel	3	4	3	1,940	10,200	66,400	11.58
Automotive group	4	4	2	2,622	3,680	46,342	8.08
Apparel group	5	6	1	2,476	2,400	12,786	2.23
Restaurants, cafeterias, and eating places	23	24	32	15,004	1,430	97,926	17.07
Other retail stores	13	13	10	18,122	16,470	139,429	24.31
Radio and music stores	2	(x)	(x)	(x)	(x)	(x)	(x)
Heating and plumbing shops	2	(x)	(x)	(x)	(x)	(x)	(x)
Hardware and farm implement stores	1	(x)	(x)	(x)	(x)	(x)	(x)
Farmers' supplies	1	(x)	(x)	(x)	(x))	(x)	(x)
Cigar stores and cigar stands	4	5	-	-	370	8,300	1.45
Coal and wood yards – ice dealers	1	(x)	(x)	(x)	(x)	(x)	(x)
Drug stores	2	(x)	(x)	(x)	(x)	(x)	(x)

Source: "Stores Operated by Black Proprietors, by States 1929," U.S. Bureau of the Census. *Negroes in the United States: 1920-32*, p. 506.

★ 424 ★

Business Owners and Operators

Proprietors: Stores in Kansas, 1929

Kind of business	Number of stores	Proprietors and firm members (not on pay roll)	Number of employees (full time)	Total pay roll (including part time)	Stocks on hand, end of year (at cost)	Net sales	
						Amount	Percent of total
Total	218	241	124	$105,340	$144,850	$1,207,920	100.00
Food group	83	92	22	17,047	29,710	379,899	31.45
Candy and confectionery stores	11	11	4	1,239	1,920	19,590	1.62
Grocery stores (without meats)	30	32	3	1,864	5,990	84,738	7.01
Combination stores (groceries and meats)	41	48	14	13,224	21,650	272,971	22.60
All other food stores	1	1	1	720	150	2,600	.22
General stores	3	3	7	5,500	45,100	97,800	8.10
Automotive group	19	20	19	20,613	23,570	209,482	17.34
Motor-vehicle dealers (new and used)	1	(x)	(x)	(x)	(x)	(x)	(x)
Filling stations	4	4	3	3,447	1,690	51,100	4.23
Garage and repair shops	12	13	9	9,772	3,520	41,213	3.41
Other automotive establishments	2	(x)	(x)	(x)	(x)	(x)	(x)
Apparel group	5	6	2	2,570	10,350	24,652	2.04
Women's ready-to-wear specialty stores – apparel and accessories	2	(x)	(x)	(x)	(x)	(x)	(x)

[Continued]

★ 424 ★

Proprietors: Stores in Kansas, 1929
[Continued]

Kind of business	Number of stores	Proprietors and firm members (not on pay roll)	Number of employees (full time)	Total pay roll (including part time)	Stocks on hand, end of year (at cost)	Net sales	
						Amount	Percent of total
Women's accessories stores	1	(x)	(x)	(x)	(x)	(x)	(x)
Other apparel stores	1	(x)	(x)	(x)	(x)	(x)	(x)
Shoe stores	1	(x)	(x)	(x)	(x)	(x)	(x)
Furniture and household group	3	4	-	-	600	2,900	.24
Furniture stores	2	(x)	(x)	(x)	(x)	(x)	(x)
Other home furnishings and appliances stores	1	(x)	(x)	(x)	(x)	(x)	(x)
Restaurants, cafeterias, and eating places	65	72	32	19,909	4,890	203,533	16.85
Restaurants, cafeterias, and lunch rooms	50	56	29	17,849	3,860	150,372	12.45
Lunch counters, refreshment stands, etc.	15	16	3	2,060	1,030	53,161	4.40
Other retail stores	40	44	42	39,701	30,630	289,654	23.98
Electrical shops (without radio)	1	(x)	(x)	(x)	(x)	(x)	(x)
Hardware stores	1	(x)	(x)	(x)	(x)	(x)	(x)
Hardware and farm implement stores	1	(x)	(x)	(x)	(x)	(x)	(x)
Farmers' supplies stores (including feeds and fertilizers)	6	6	2	1,388	670	12,213	1.01
Cigar stores and cigar stands	6	6	1	1,791	1,430	22,950	1.90
Coal and wood yards – ice dealers	10	11	15	12,663	12,470	78,138	6.47
Drug stores	12	14	17	16,489	3,910	91,528	7.58
Miscellaneous classifications (combined)	3	3	1	1,900	2,150	8,600	.71

Source: "Stores Operated by Black Proprietors, by States 1929," U.S. Bureau of the Census. *Negroes in the United States: 1920-32*, p. 506.

★ 425 ★

Business Owners and Operators

Proprietors: Stores in Maryland, 1929

Kind of business	Number of stores	Proprietors and firm members (not on pay roll)	Number of employees (full time)	Total pay roll (including part time)	Stocks on hand, end of year (at cost)	Net sales	
						Amount	Percent of total
Total	515	525	198	$164,492	$125,700	$1,690,747	100.00
Food group	236	241	41	39,351	54,580	720,732	42.63
Candy and confectionery stores	66	67	8	4,450	7,380	130,902	7.74
Grocery stores (without meats)	96	96	11	6,241	29,450	213,942	12.66
Combination stores (groceries and meats)	44	47	7	3,240	12,100	166,215	9.83
Meat markets (including sea foods)	11	11	2	1,578	3,490	59,186	3.50
Other food stores	19	20	13	23,842	2,160	150,487	8.90
General stores (groceries with apparel or dry goods)	19	19	4	2,929	18,700	111,092	6.57
Automotive group	20	24	12	8,136	5,770	79,568	4.70
Motor-vehicle dealers (new and used)	1	(x)	(x)	(x)	(x)	(x)	(x)
Filling stations	6	(x)	(x)	(x)	(x)	(x)	(x)
Garages and repair shops	12	14	5	2,267	700	24,198	1.43
Other automotive establishments	1	(x)	(x)	(x)	(x)	(x)	(x)
Apparel group	4	4	2	624	1,470	7,075	.42
Men's and boys' clothing and furnishings stores	1	(x)	(x)	(x)	(x)	(x)	(x)
Women's accessories stores	1	(x)	(x)	(x)	(x)	(x)	(x)

[Continued]

★ 425 ★

Proprietors: Stores in Maryland, 1929
[Continued]

Kind of business	Number of stores	Proprietors and firm members (not on pay roll)	Number of employees (full time)	Total pay roll (including part time)	Stocks on hand, end of year (at cost)	Net sales Amount	Net sales Percent of total
Other apparel stores	2	(x)	(x)	(x)	(x)	(x)	(x)
Restaurants and eating places	120	121	64	31,211	8,480	280,287	16.58
Restaurants, cafeterias, and lunch rooms	99	100	60	29,745	7,070	260,551	15.41
Lunch counters, refreshment stands, etc.	21	21	4	1,466	1,410	19,736	1.17
Other retail stores	101	101	74	81,825	33,450	458,183	27.10
Household appliances stores	1	(x)	(x)	(x)	(x)	(x)	(x)
Radio and music stores	1	(x)	(x)	(x)	(x)	(x)	(x)
Heating and plumbing shops	2	(x)	(x)	(x)	(x)	(x)	(x)
Hardware stores	1	(x)	(x)	(x)	(x)	(x)	(x)
Farmers' supplies	1	(x)	(x)	(x)	(x)	(x)	(x)
Cigar stores and cigar stands	11	12	4	1,690	690	26,234	1.55
Coal and wood yards – ice dealers	44	44	6	3,825	2,130	84,783	5.02
Drug stores	15	15	26	21,643	16,560	104,697	6.19
Miscellaneous classifications (combined)	25	25	25	27,107	12,320	122,265	7.23
Second-hand stores	15	15	1	416	3,250	33,810	2.00

Source: "Stores Operated by Black Proprietors, by States 1929," U.S. Bureau of the Census. *Negroes in the United States: 1920-32*, pp. 507-508.

★ 426 ★

Business Owners and Operators

Proprietors: Stores in Massachusetts, 1929

Kind of business	Number of stores	Proprietors and firm members (not on pay roll)	Number of employees (full time)	Total pay roll (including part time)	Stocks on hand, end of year (at cost)	Net sales Amount	Net sales Percent of total
Total	121	135	86	$98,139	$123,380	$1,149,686	100.00
Food group	49	56	12	11,419	23,760	285,969	24.87
Candy and confectionery stores	6	7	1	680	680	14,660	1.28
Grocery stores (without meats)	32	38	3	2,578	14,060	114,839	9.99
Combination stores (groceries and meats)	8	8	7	6,853	8,630	137,095	11.92
Other food stores	3	3	1	1,308	390	19,375	1.69
Automotive group	21	21	15	22,700	8,720	231,094	20.10
Filling stations	12	12	5	3,350	1,370	65,444	5.69
Garages and repair shops	6	6	3	5,350	420	19,800	1.72
Other automotive establishments	3	3	7	14,000	6,930	145,850	12.69
Apparel group	9	9	10	13,858	59,720	244,179	21.24
Men's and boys' clothing and furnishings stores	5	3	7	11,058	56,570	214,064	18.62
Other apparel and furnishings stores	4	6	3	2,800	2,700	30,115	2.62
Furniture and household group	2	3	-	-	5,120	54,830	4.77
Home furnishings and appliances stores	2	3	-	-	5,120	54,830	4.77
Restaurants, cafeterias, and eating places	21	24	39	36,143	2,230	178,942	15.56
Restaurants, cafeterias, and lunch rooms	14	16	32	30,755	1,340	142,950	12.43
Lunch counters, refreshment stands, etc.	7	8	7	5,388	890	35,992	3.13
Other retail stores	15	17	8	12,644	23,150	146,572	12.75

[Continued]

★ 426 ★

Proprietors: Stores in Massachusetts, 1929

[Continued]

Kind of business	Number of stores	Proprietors and firm members (not on pay roll)	Number of employees (full time)	Total pay roll (including part time)	Stocks on hand, end of year (at cost)	Net sales	
						Amount	Percent of total
Cigar stores and cigar stands	3	3	-	312	900	8,880	.77
Drug stores	3	4	4	5,052	15,500	70,506	6.13
Miscellaneous classifications	9	10	4	7,280	6,750	67,186	5.84
Second-hand stores	4	5	2	1,375	1,130	8,100	.70

Source: "Stores Operated by Black Proprietors, by States 1929," U.S. Bureau of the Census. *Negroes in the United States: 1920-32*, p. 508.

★ 427 ★

Business Owners and Operators

Proprietors: Stores in Memphis, Tennessee, 1935

Memphis, ninth city in size of Negro population (96,550 in 1930) was, in 1935, sixth in the number of retail stores operated by Negro proprietors, and ninth in the amount of sales. With a total of 324 stores, $566,000 was reported in sales. A decrease of 55 stores was reported from 1929 to 1935, and a decrease in sales from $1,552,583 to the above figure. A total of 144 employees (excluding the 318 proprietors and firm members) were paid $44,519 in 1935, while the total operating expenses were $122,000. Food stores brought in 45.4 per cent of the total sales, while eating and drinking places accounted for 24.2 per cent.

Kind of business	No. of stores	Sales
Total	324	$566,000
Food stores, including bakeries and caterers	84	257,000
Automotive, including accessories, filling stations and garages	15	57,000
Furniture – household	1	X
Eating and drinking places, including drinking places only (7)	119	137,000
Drug stores	13	84,000
Other retail stores, including fuel and ice dealers (8)	89	27,000
Second-hand stores	3	X

Source: "Retail Stores in Fifteen Cities with Largest Negro Population: 1935," Florence Murray, ed., *The Negro Handbook*, p. 26. *Notes:* X means that the amount is withheld to avoid disclosure of individual operator, but it is included in the total.

★ 428 ★

Business Owners and Operators

Proprietors: Stores in Michigan, 1929

Kind of business	Number of stores	Proprietors and firm members (not on pay roll)	Number of employees (full time)	Total pay roll (including part time)	Stocks on hand, end of year (at cost)	Net sales Amount	Net sales Percent of total
Total	488	563	465	$379,949	$229,970	$3,817,530	100.00
Food group	182	200	59	51,898	58,220	1,296,837	33.97
Candy and confectionery stores	56	60	12	6,320	10,240	170,311	4.46
Grocery stores (without meats)	53	60	10	8,020	15,420	262,103	6.87
Combination stores (groceries and meats)	64	70	26	24,160	31,070	765,857	20.06
Meat markets (including sea foods)	4	4	2	2,628	430	46,340	1.21
Other food stores	5	6	9	10,770	1,060	52,226	1.37
General merchandise group	3	4	-	-	8,370	22,360	.59
Dry-goods stores – piece-goods stores	1	(x)	(x)	(x)	(x)	(x)	(x)
Variety, 5-and-10, to-a-dollar stores	2	(x)	(x)	(X)	(x)	(x)	(x)
Automotive group	53	65	39	53,842	23,140	543,319	14.23
Filling stations	27	33	25	33,851	12,630	407,432	10.67
Garages and repair shops	14	17	8	13,061	1,060	55,647	1.46
Other automotive establishments	12	15	6	6,930	9,450	80,240	2.10
Apparel group	15	16	14	9,737	9,220	72,988	1.91
Women's ready-to-wear specialty stores – apparel and accessories	3	3	-	364	790	9,365	.24
Women's accessories stores	3	3	-	-	660	3,770	.10
Other apparel stores	7	8	13	8,341	5,420	32,003	.84
Furniture and household group	4	4	2	1,291	1,160	18,640	.49
Furniture stores	1	(x)	(x)	(x)	(x)	(x)	(x)
Other home furnishings and appliances stores	1	(x)	(x)	(x)	(x)	(x)	(x)
Radio and music stores	2	(x)	(x)	(x)	(x)	(x)	(x)
Restaurants and eating places	136	161	279	183,398	10,340	993,888	26.04
Restaurants, cafeterias, and lunch rooms	104	125	225	148,594	9,110	804,697	21.08
Lunch counters, refreshment stands, etc.	32	36	54	34,804	1,230	189,191	4.96
Other retail stores	79	95	66	73,088	115,130	804,826	21.08
General stores	2	(x)	(x)	(x)	(x)	(x)	(x)
Hardware stores	2	(x)	(x)	(x)	(x)	(x)	(x)
Farmers' supplies	2	(x)	(x)	(x)	(x)	(x)	(x)
Cigar stores and cigar stands	29	35	14	8,928	5,270	81,647	2.14
Coal and wood yards – ice dealers	4	4	5	7,129	6,730	69,594	1.82
Drug stores	26	31	35	43,777	81,150	430,466	11.28
Jewelry stores	2	(x)	(x)	(x)	(x)	(x)	(x)
Miscellaneous classifications (combined)	12	16	6	5,826	6,540	72,770	1.90
Second-hand stores	16	18	6	6,695	4,390	64,672	1.69

Source: "Stores Operated by Black Proprietors, by States 1929," U.S. Bureau of the Census. *Negroes in the United States: 1920-32,* p. 508.

★ 429 ★

Proprietors: Stores in Missouri, 1929

Kind of business	Number of stores	Proprietors and firm members (not on pay roll)	Number of employees (full time)	Total pay roll (including part time)	Stocks on hand, end of year (at cost)	Net sales	
						Amount	Percent of total
Total	575	628	453	$315,947	$290,470	$3,200,109	100.00
Food group	165	182	69	61,222	72,170	1,072,134	33.50
Candy and confectionery stores	57	61	14	6,502	5,620	137,459	4.30
Grocery stores (without meats)	49	56	8	4,808	15,040	188,658	5.89
Combination stores (groceries and meats)	50	53	43	47,208	49,880	712,762	22.27
Other food stores	9	12	4	2,704	1,630	33,255	1.04
General stores	6	7	3	3,080	11,960	70,289	2.20
General merchandise group	5	4	-	-	6,400	29,071	.91
Dry-goods stores – piece-goods stores	3	3	-	-	4,850	11,037	.35
Automotive group	34	40	39	34,127	29,960	297,901	9.31
Motor-vehicle dealers (new and used)	2	(x)	(x)	(x)	(x)	(x)	(x)
Filling stations	9	9	8	7,252	4,040	64,154	2.00
Garages and repair shops	22	28	26	23,995	9,370	164,667	5.15
Other automotive establishments	1	(x)	(x)	(x)	(x)	(x)	(x)
Apparel group	14	16	10	6,283	11,710	74,060	2.31
Family clothing stores – men's, women's, and children's	1	(x)	(x)	(x)	(x)	(x)	(x)
Women's ready-to-wear specialty stores – apparel and accessories	5	6	4	3,113	7,000	53,400	1.67
Women's accessories stores	1	(x)	(x)	(x)	(x)	(x)	(x)
Other apparel stores	6	7	5	2,650	700	12,750	.40
Shoe stores	1	(x)	(x)	(x)	(x)	(x)	(x)
Furniture and household group[1]	6	8	5	4,528	13,150	39,750	1.24
Radio and music stores	5	7	2	1,818	2,670	15,250	.48
Restaurants, cafeterias, and eating places	229	245	219	111,853	16,630	876,534	27.39
Restaurants, cafeterias, and lunch rooms	166	179	186	93,735	12,440	667,610	20.86
Lunch counters, refreshment stands, etc.	63	66	33	18,118	4,190	208,924	6.53
Other retail stores	107	117	103	89,020	122,110	702,090	21.94
Hardware stores	3	3	2	1,340	5,300	13,339	.42
Hardware and farm implement stores	1	(x)	(x)	(x)	(x)	(x)	(x)
Farmers' supplies stores (including feeds and fertilizers)	5	5	2	2,000	3,200	30,700	.96
Book stores	1	(x)	(x)	(x)	(x)	(x)	(x)
Cigar stores and cigar stands	14	15	7	5,442	1,090	43,850	1.37
Coal and wood yards – ice dealers	30	31	19	20,552	9,150	114,404	3.57
Drug stores	22	25	41	33,571	65,320	311,623	9.74
Jewelry stores	2	(x)	(x)	(x)	(x)	(x)	(x)
Miscellaneous classifications (combined)	29	35	25	19,002	18,440	143,146	4.47
Second-hand stores	9	9	5	5,834	6,380	38,280	1.20

Source: "Stores Operated by Black Proprietors, by States 1929," U.S. Bureau of the Census. *Negroes in the United States: 1920-32,* pp. 509-510. *Notes:* 1. This includes 1 classification in which the number of stores is less than 3, and concerning which no information can be disclosed.

★ 430 ★

Business Owners and Operators

Proprietors: Stores in Montana, and Nevada, 1929

Kind of business	Number of stores	Proprietors and firm members (not on pay roll)	Number of employees (full time)	Total pay roll (including part time)	Stocks on hand, end of year (at cost)	Net sales	
						Amount	Percent of total
Montana							
Total	6	7	7	$6,036	$5,730	$49,497	100.00
Nevada							
Total	9	(x)	(x)	(x)	(x)	(x)	100.00

Source: "Stores Operated by Black Proprietors, by States 1929," U.S. Bureau of the Census. *Negroes in the United States: 1920-32*, p. 510.

★ 431 ★

Business Owners and Operators

Proprietors: Stores in Nebraska, 1929

Kind of business	Number of stores	Proprietors and firm members (not on pay roll)	Number of employees (full time)	Total pay roll (including part time)	Stocks on hand, end of year (at cost)	Net sales	
						Amount	Percent of total
Total	52	60	55	$34,782	$86,160	$435,433	100.00
Food group	11	13	7	3,444	7,380	87,136	20.01
Grocery stores (without meats)	4	5	1	420	600	5,002	1.15
Combination stores (groceries and meats)	5	6	5	2,520	6,700	76,500	17.57
All other food stores	2	2	1	504	80	5,634	1.29
Automotive group	4	4	5	2,070	6,500	25,634	5.89
Apparel group	4	6	1	520	1,760	6,000	1.38
Men's and boys' clothing and furnishings stores	1	(x)	(x)	(x)	(x)	(x)	(x)
Family clothing stores – men's, women's, and children's	2	(x)	(x)	(x)	(x)	(x)	(x)
Other apparel stores	1	(x)	(x)	(x)	(x)	(x)	(x)
Furniture and household group	3	3	-	-	1,000	3,650	.84
Restaurants, cafeterias, and eating places	18	21	31	17,263	1,970	114,593	26.31
Restaurants, cafeterias, and lunch rooms	15	18	30	16,315	1,450	104,488	23.98
Lunch counters, refreshment stands, etc.	3	3	1	948	520	10,155	2.33
Other retail stores	12	13	11	11,485	67,550	198,420	45.57
General stores	2	(x)	(x)	(x)	(x)	(x)	(x)
Lumber and building material dealers	1	(x)	(x)	(x)	(x)	(x)	(x)
Farmers' supplies (including feeds and fertilizers)	2	(x)	(x)	(x)	(x)	(x)	(x)
Cigar stores and cigar stands	3	3	3	1,948	650	10,640	2.44
Drug stores	3	5	3	3,841	20,570	68,964	15.84
Jewelry stores	1	(x)	(x)	(x)	(x)	(x)	(x)

Source: "Stores Operated by Black Proprietors, by States 1929," U.S. Bureau of the Census. *Negroes in the United States: 1920-32*, p. 510.

★ 432 ★

Proprietors: Stores in New Jersey, 1929

Kind of business	Number of stores	Proprietors and firm members (not on pay roll)	Number of employees (full time)	Total pay roll (including part time)	Stocks on hand, end of year (at cost)	Net sales	
						Amount	Percent of total
Total	577	624	294	$264,386	$349,900	$2,737,685	100.00
Food group	216	228	28	29,337	82,350	868,861	31.74
Candy and confectionery stores	56	58	11	9,149	18,270	178,163	6.51
Grocery stores (without meats)	108	114	6	5,972	46,380	371,661	13.58
Combination stores (groceries and meats)	19	22	2	2,832	9,930	125,360	4.58
Meat markets (including sea foods)	13	13	4	2,730	1,360	77,517	2.83
Other food stores	20	21	5	8,654	6,510	116,160	4.24
General merchandise group	5	5	-	-	7,850	13,420	.49
Dry goods stores – piece goods stores	5	5	-	-	7,850	13,420	.49
Automotive group	37	41	39	28,326	14,490	222,061	8.11
Filling stations	14	14	6	5,240	4,630	55,252	2.02
Garages and repair shops	20	24	29	28,110	3,360	146,309	5.34
Other automotive establishments	3	3	4	4,976	6,500	20,500	.75
Apparel group	20	23	6	8,635	43,790	110,282	4.03
Men's and boys' clothing and furnishings stores	7	8	3	3,267	30,600	67,498	2.47
Family clothing stores – men's, women's, and children's	1	(x)	(x)	(x)	(x)	(x)	(x)
Women's ready-to-wear specialty stores – apparel and accessories	2	(x)	(x)	(x)	(x)	(x)	(x)
Women's accessories stores	2	(x)	(x)	(x)	(x)	(x)	(x)
Other apparel stores	7	9	2	3,764	1,090	21,669	.70
Shoe stores	1	(x)	(x)	(x)	(x)	(x)	(x)
Furniture and household group	11	13	10	7,312	30,800	86,074	3.15
Floor coverings, draperies, curtains, and upholstery stores	3	3	2	1,100	650	5,250	.19
Other home furnishings and appliances stores	3	4	2	1,196	6,700	20,444	.75
Radio and music stores	5	6	6	5,016	23,450	60,380	2.21
Restaurants, cafeterias, and eating places	133	146	134	94,403	20,020	608,301	22.22
Restaurants, cafeterias, and lunch rooms	118	129	134	94,385	18,910	584,287	21.34
Lunch counters, refreshment stands, etc.	15	17	-	18	1,110	24,014	.88
Lumber and building group	7	7	9	18,977	22,350	123,840	4.52
Electrical shops (without radio)	3	2	3	3,975	6,310	37,247	1.36
Heating and plumbing shops	2	(x)	(x)	(x)	(x)	(x)	(x)
Painting and glass stores	2	(x)	(x)	(x)	(x)	(x)	(x)
Other retail stores	132	144	62	62,236	123,250	666,411	24.34
Hardware stores	4	4	-	-	12,000	23,800	.87
Farmers' supplies	3	5	-	-	1,500	6,700	.24
Cigar stores and cigar stands	61	65	25	19,356	13,340	178,701	6.53
Coal and wood yards – ice dealers	14	15	9	8,890	2,870	76,070	2.78
Drug stores	19	22	14	18,557	71,370	238,634	8.72
Miscellaneous classifications (combined)	29	31	14	15,433	20,970	138,306	5.05
Second-hand stores	16	17	6	5,160	5,000	38,435	1.40

Source: "Stores Operated by Black Proprietors, by States 1929," U.S. Bureau of the Census. *Negroes in the United States: 1920-32*, p. 510.

★ 433 ★

Business Owners and Operators

Proprietors: Stores in New Orleans, Louisiana, 1935

New Orleans, sixth city in size of Negro population (129,632 in 1930), ranked eighth in the number of retail stores operated by Negroes, and eighth in the amount of sales in 1935. A total of 289 stores reported sales amounting to $574,000. The city lost 482 stores between 1929 and 1935, and sales decreased from $2,300,374 to the above figure. A total of 151 employees (excluding 294 proprietors and firm members), received $49,005 in pay, and total operating expenses for the year 1935 were $147,000. The pay roll amounted to 33.3 per cent of the operating expenses and 8.5 per cent of the total sales. Eating and drinking places and food stores accounted for 65.9 per cent of the total sales, and drinking places alone, 21.8 per cent.

Kind of business	No. of stores	Sales
Total	289	$574,000
Food stores, including bakeries and caterers	88	124,000
Automotive, including accessories, filling stations and garages	16	19,000
Apparel	1	X
Furniture – household	2	X
Eating and drinking places, including drinking places only (38)	112	254,000
Drug stores	11	71,000
Other retail stores, including fuel and ice (49)	53	63,000
Second-hand stores	6	35,000

Source: "Retail Stores in Fifteen Cities with Largest Negro Population: 1935," Florence Murray, ed., *The Negro Handbook*, p. 26. *Notes:* X means that the amount is withheld to avoid disclosure of individual operator, but it is included in the total.

★ 434 ★

Business Owners and Operators

Proprietors: Stores in New York City, 1935

New York City, with the largest Negro population (327,706 in 1930) of any city in the United States, reported 960 retail stores operated by colored proprietors in 1935, leading all other cities, an increase of 569 over 1929. Total value of sales increased from $3,322,000 in 1929 to $3,805,000 in 1935; and the total pay roll, which does not include salary of proprietors, increased from $293,482 to $472,186. Food stores and eating, and drinking places amounted to approximately 80 per cent of the total sales in 1935. Total operating expenses were $1,171,000 or 30.8 per cent of the total sales, and the total pay roll represented 40 per cent of the operating expenses. The stores gave employment to 1,801 persons—793 employees, and 1,008 active proprietors and firm members not on the pay roll. Average sales per store amounted to $3,964 as compared with $2,085 for the country.

Kind of business	No. of stores	Sales
Total	960	$3,805,000
Food stores, all classes, including bakeries and caterers	449	1,699,000
Automotive, including accessories, filling stations, and garages	48	158,000

[Continued]

★ 434 ★

Proprietors: Stores in New York City, 1935
[Continued]

Kind of business	No. of stores	Sales
General merchandise	5	12,000
Apparel	46	118,000
Furniture – household, including radios	4	11,000
Lumber – building--hardware	2	X
Eating and drinking places	172	1,344,000
Drug stores	6	29,000
Other retail stores, including fuel and ice (92), news dealers (39), beer and liquor (1)	205	397,000
Second-hand stores	23	29,000

Source: "Retail Stores in Fifteen Cities with Largest Negro Population: 1935," Florence Murray, ed., *The Negro Handbook*, p. 23. *Notes:* X means that the amount is withheld to avoid disclosure of individual operator, but it is included in the total.

★ 435 ★

Business Owners and Operators

Proprietors: Stores in Philadelphia, 1935

Philadelphia, third largest city in Negro population, (219,599 in 1930) although ranking second in the number of stores operated by colored proprietors, was third in the amount of sales, with a total of 729 stores, reporting $1,630,000 in sales. The number of stores decreased by 58 between 1929 and 1935, and 1929 sales were $3,150,007. Total pay roll for 1935 was $189,211, paid to 426 employees, not including the 727 proprietors and firm members; and operating expenses were $493,000. Food stores, with $554,000 in sales accounted for 34 per cent of the total sales; while restaurants, cafeterias and lunch rooms accounted for $294,000 or 54.2 per cent of sales; and drinking places, with $211,000, or 39 per cent.

Kind of business	No. of stores	Sales
Total	729	$1,630,000
Food stores, including bakeries and caterers	258	554,000
Automotive, including accessories, filling stations and garages	36	73,000
General merchandise	3	3,000
Apparel	15	13,000
Furniture – household, including radios	3	1,000
Lumber – building--hardware	1	X
Eating and drinking places	161	542,000
Drug stores	27	136,000
Other retail store, including cigar stores and stands (68), fuel and ice (52), beer and liquor stores (2)	159	251,000
Second-hand stores	66	56,000

Source: "Retail Stores in Fifteen Cities with Largest Negro Population: 1935," Florence Murray, ed., *The Negro Handbook*, p. 24. *Notes:* X means that the amount is withheld to avoid disclosure of individual operator, but it is included in the total.

★ 436 ★

Business Owners and Operators

Proprietors: Stores in Pittsburgh, Pennsylvania, 1935

Pittsburgh, fourteenth city in size of Negro population (54,983 in 1930), was fifteenth in the number of retail stores operated by Negroes in 1935 and fifteenth in the amount of sales. A total of 81 stores brought in $147,000 in 1935, showing a loss of 69 stores and an 82.3 per cent decrease in sales which were $830,013 in 1929. A total of 44 employees (excluding 84 proprietors and firm members), were paid $17,173 during 1935; and operating expenses were $43,000, 29.3 per cent of total sales. Eating and drinking places accounted for 43.5 per cent of the total sales; and food stores, for 29.9 per cent.

Kind of business	No. of stores	Sales
Total	81	$147,000
Food stores, including bakeries and caterers	27	44,000
Automotive, including filling stations and garages	6	6,000
Apparel	1	X
Eating and drinking places, including drinking places only (3)	36	64,000
Drug stores	6	27,000
Other retail stores, includes 1 cigar, 1 news dealer, and 1 other	3	X
Second-hand stores	2	X,000

Source: "Retail Stores in Fifteen Cities with Largest Negro Population: 1935," Florence Murray, ed., *The Negro Handbook*, pp. 28-29. *Notes:* X means that the amount is withheld to avoid disclosure of individual operator, but it is included in the total.

★ 437 ★

Business Owners and Operators

Proprietors: Stores in Richmond, Virginia, 1935

Richmond, fifteenth city in size of Negro population (52,988 in 1930), was thirteenth in the number of stores operated by Negroes in 1935, and thirteenth in the amount of sales. A total of 170 stores brought in $314,000 in sales. In 1929 the city reported 189 stores and $657,961 in sales, both amounts higher than in 1935. A total of 84 employees in 1935 (excluding 166 proprietors and firm members), were paid $28,256 in 1935; and operating expenses were $62,000, or 19.7 per cent of total sales. Food stores accounted for 39.8 per cent of the total sales, and eating and drinking places, 21.7 per cent.

Kind of business	No. of stores	Sales
Total	170	$314,000
Food stores, including bakeries and caterers	73	125,000
Automotive, including filling stations and garages	11	13,000
General merchandise	1	X
Furniture – household	1	X
Eating and drinking places, including drinking places only (2)	46	68,000
Drug stores	3	5,000

[Continued]

★ 437 ★

Proprietors: Stores in Richmond, Virginia, 1935
[Continued]

Kind of business	No. of stores	Sales
Other retail stores, including fuel and ice dealers (28)	31	89,000
Second-hand stores	4	3,000

Source: "Retail Stores in Fifteen Cities with Largest Negro Population: 1935," Florence Murray, ed., *The Negro Handbook*, p. 28. *Notes:* X means that the amount is withheld to avoid disclosure of individual operator, but it is included in the total.

★ 438 ★

Business Owners and Operators

Proprietors: Stores in St. Louis, Missouri, 1935

St. Louis, tenth city in size of Negro population (93,580 in 1930), ranked eleventh in the number of retail stores operated by Negroes, and twelfth in the amount of sales in 1935. A total of 250 stores brought in $521,000. Both the number of stores and the amount of sales decreased from 1929 to 1935, the former reported as 310 and the amount of sales as $1,457,427 in 1929. A total of 212 employees (excluding 247 proprietors and firm members) were paid $80,024 in 1935, while operating expenses were $182,000. Eating and drinking places accounted for 42.6 per cent of the total sales.

Kind of business	No. of stores	Sales
Total	250	$521,000
Food stores	37	55,000
Automotive, including accessories, filling stations and garages	22	58,000
General merchandise	2	X
Apparel	1	X
Furniture – household, including radios	2	X
Hardware	1	X
Eating and drinking places, including drinking places only (15)	107	222,000
Drug stores	7	51,000
Other retail stores, including fuel and ice dealers (54)	61	70,000
Second-hand stores	10	8,000

Source: "Retail Stores in Fifteen Cities with Largest Negro Population: 1935," Florence Murray, ed., *The Negro Handbook*, pp. 27-28. *Notes:* X means that the amount is withheld to avoid disclosure of individual operator, but it is included in the total.

★ 439 ★

Business Owners and Operators

Proprietors: Stores in Washington, D.C., 1935

Washington, fifth largest city in Negro population (132,068 in 1930), although ranking ninth in the number of retail stores operated by Negroes in 1935, was fourth in the amount of sales. With only 279 stores, sales amounted to $1,593,000. The stores, operated by 287 proprietors and firm members, represented an increase of 35 enterprises between 1929 and 1935. Total sales showed an increase of $97,146. Washington's stores ranked first as to average sales, with an average of $5,674 per store (1935). The total pay roll of $228,905 in 1935 went to 14,983 employees, not including 287 proprietors and firm members. Operating expenses, $570,000, constituted 35.8 per cent of the total sales; and 62.6 per cent of all operating expenses was incurred by the 88 eating and drinking places.

Kind of business	No. of stores	Sales
Total	279	$1,593,000
Food stores, including bakeries and caterers	66	244,000
Automotive, including accessories, filling stations and garages	25	191,000
General merchandise	3	27,000
Apparel	2	X
Furniture – household, including radios	1	X
Eating and drinking places	88	667,000
Drug stores	21	168,000
Other retail stores, including fuel and ice dealers (37), news dealers (15), beer and liquor (2)	70	271,000
Second-hand stores	3	X

Source: "Retail Stores in Fifteen Cities with Largest Negro Population: 1935," Florence Murray, ed., *The Negro Handbook*, p. 24. *Notes:* X means that the amount is withheld to avoid disclosure of individual operator, but it is included in the total.

★ 440 ★

Business Owners and Operators

Proprietors: Summary of Stores and Sales by Groups and Business, 1929, 1935, 1939

Kind of business	Number of stores			Sales (add 000)		
	1939	1935	1929	1939	1935	1929
Major business groups						
Total, all stores[1]	29,827	22,756	24,969	$71,466	$47,968	$98,602
Food group	11,038	9,038	10,755	24,037	17,267	36,663
General stores (with food)	149	321	761	404	1,081	4,829
General merchandise group	83	68	128	256	316	980
Apparel group	333	232	477	779	502	3,028
Furniture – household--radio group	65	74	149	511	472	1,160
Automotive group[1]	46	45	148	638	309	3,820
Filling stations	1,268	783	799	6,917	2,946	3,429
Lumber – building--hardware group	41	44	147	96	234	2,079
Eating and drinking places	12,610	8,568	7,918	26,527	15,718	21,333

[Continued]

★ 440 ★

Proprietors: Summary of Stores and Sales by Groups and Business, 1929, 1935, 1939

[Continued]

Kind of business	Number of stores			Sales (add 000)		
	1939	1935	1929	1939	1935	1929
Drug stores	548	608	712	4,470	3,760	7,254
Other stores	3,646	3,005	2,975	6,831	5,363	14,027
Principal kinds of business						
Food group	11,038	9,008	10,755	24,037	17,267	36,663
Grocery stores (without fresh meats)	5,655	4,553	6,248	7,934	6,270	14,715
Combination stores (groceries-meats)	2,524	1,811	2,202	11,454	7,351	13,655
Meat markets, fish markets	493	474	537	935	851	2,829
Candy, nut, confectionery stores	1,713	1,338	1,137	1,462	2,084	2,584
Fruit stores, vegetable markets	331	451	[2]	555	506	[2]
Other food stores	322	381	631	1,075	827	2,880
General stores (with food)	149	321	761	404	1,081	4,829
General merchandise group	83	68	128	256	316	980
Dry goods and general merchandise stores	43	51	98	161	196	837
Variety stores	40	17	30	95	120	143
Apparel group	333	232	477	779	502	3,028
Men's – boys' clothing, furnishings, hat stores	23	25	66	95	84	916
Family clothing stores	32	21	32	110	87	427
Women's ready-to-wear stores	65	64	57	156	98	316
Accessories, other apparel stores	197	108	274	363	195	1,024
Shoe stores (all kinds)	16	14	48	55	38	345
Furniture – household--radio group	65	74	149	511	472	1,160
Furniture stores	19	36	54	95	263	401
Other home furnishings stores	17	14	37	18	34	98
Household appliances, radio dealers	29	24	58	398	175	661
Automotive group[1]	46	45	148	638	309	3,820
Motor-vehicle dealers (new and used)	10	10	39	526	162	3,150
Accessory, tire, battery dealers and other automotive dealers	36	35	109	112	147	670
Filling stations	1,268	783	799	6,917	2,946	3,429
Lumber-building group	24	19	96	38	120	1,268
Hardware group	17	25	51	58	114	811
Eating places	9,750	7,487	7,918	15,136	11,396	21,333
Drinking places	2,860	1,081	-	11,391	4,322	-

[Continued]

★ 440 ★

Proprietors: Summary of Stores and Sales by Groups and Business, 1929, 1935, 1939

[Continued]

Kind of business	Number of stores			Sales (add 000)		
	1939	1935	1929	1939	1935	1929
Drug stores	548	608	712	4,470	3,760	7,254
Liquor stores (packaged goods)	169	73	-	1,679	339	-
Other retail stores	3,040	2,473	2,602	4,685	4,575	13,044
Fuel, ice, fuel-oil dealers	2,240	1,801	549	2,959	3,188	2,117
Feed stores and garden supply stores	11	17	107	134	123	928
Jewelry stores	10	11	67	33	26	388
Cigar stores, cigar stands	348	306	704	695	483	2,053
Florists	128	96	[2]	210	154	[2]
News dealers	99	103	[2]	287	168	[2]
Other retail stores	204	139	1,175	367	433	7,558
Second-hand stores	437	459	373	467	449	983

Source: "Summary-Comparison of Number of Stores and Sales by Major Groups and Principal Kinds of Business: 1939, 1935 and 1929," Florence Murray, ed., *The Negro Handbook*, p. 19. *Notes:* 1. Previously published totals for the United States and for the automotive group, for 1935 and 1929, are revised to exclude their sales of merchandise. These are now included in the Census of Service Establishments. 2. Data not available.

★ 441 ★

Business Owners and Operators

Proprietorship: Stores, Sales, Personnel, Payroll and Stocks by Geographic Area, 1935

Kind of business	Number of stores	Sales (add 000)	Active proprietors of unin-corporated business	Number of employees
United States Total	29,827	$71,466	29,116	13,778
Geographic divisions				
New England	197	770	203	132
Middle Atlantic	3,182	12,010	3,308	1,892
East North Central	3,755	13,542	3,754	2,745
West North Central	1,138	2,706	1,148	656
South Atlantic	10,897	21,323	10,305	4,138
East South Central	4,219	7,414	4,070	1,533
West South Central	5,709	10,627	5,584	2,099
Mountain	174	530	168	114
Pacific	556	2,544	576	469

[Continued]

★ 441 ★

Proprietorship: Stores, Sales, Personnel, Payroll and Stocks by Geographic Area, 1935
[Continued]

Kind of business	Number of stores	Sales (add 000)	Active proprietors of unincorporated business	Number of employees
New England				
Maine	2			
New Hampshire	-	] 45	4	10
Vermont	1			
Massachusetts	114	401	117	72
Rhode Island	24	115	24	11
Connecticut	56	209	58	39
Middle Atlantic				
New York	1,450	6,265	1,537	804
New Jersey	628	2,085	648	363
Pennsylvania	1,104	3,660	1,123	725
East North Central				
Ohio	1,096	4,113	1,083	717
Indiana	370	1,408	375	295
Illinois	1,364	4,374	1,365	873
Michigan	856	3,272	860	787
Wisconsin	69	375	71	73
West North Central				
Minnesota	52	243	56	72
Iowa	56	149	58	34
Missouri	716	1,515	722	369
North Dakota	2	] 21	3	5
South Dakota	3			
Nebraska	58	256	58	68
Kansas	251	522	251	108
South Atlantic				
Delaware	119	292	110	62
Maryland	1,016	2,595	1,020	472
District of Columbia	300	2,327	313	421
Virginia	1,918	3,887	1,811	705
West Virginia	190	435	188	107
North Carolina	1,834	3,060	1,725	537
South Carolina	1,246	1,618	1,121	308
Georgia	2,268	3,414	2,092	805
Florida	2,006	3,695	1,925	721
East South Central				
Kentucky	554	965	560	183

[Continued]

★ 441 ★

Proprietorship: Stores, Sales, Personnel, Payroll and Stocks by Geographic Area, 1935
[Continued]

Kind of business	Number of stores	Sales (add 000)	Active proprietors of unincorporated business	Number of employees
Tennessee	1,044	2,448	1,028	554
Alabama	1,285	2,198	1,216	437
Mississippi	1,336	1,803	1,266	359
West South Central				
Arkansas	973	1,118	934	181
Louisiana	1,410	2,776	1,382	515
Oklahoma	647	1,381	657	253
Texas	2,679	5,352	2,611	1,150
Mountain				
Montana	5	] 26	6	6
Idaho	2			
Wyoming	7	60	6	7
Colorado	61	247	61	61
New Mexico	27	41	27	8
Arizona	60	122	56	25
Utah	5	16	5	6
Nevada	7	18	7	1
Pacific				
Washington	32	141	34	34
Oregon	7	79	7	2
California	517	2,324	535	433

Source: "Proprietorships—Stores, Sales, Personnel, Pay Roll and Stocks by Geographic Divisions and States," Florence Murray, ed., *The Negro Handbook,* p. 22.

★ 442 ★

Business Owners and Operators

Retail Businesses by Race, 1929

Class or race	Population[1]	Number of stores	Proprietors and firm members (not on pay roll)	Number of employees (full time)	Total pay roll (including part time)	Stocks on hand, end of year (at cost)	Net sales
United States	122,775,046	1,543,158	1,510,607	3,833,581	$5,189,669,960	$7,262,582,920	$49,114,653,269
Negro	11,891,143	25,701	28,243	12,561	8,528,306	10,657,000	101,146,043
Oriental mutuals[2]	213,788	3,865	6,432	8,926	9,022,555	10,165,470	88,578,405
White[3]	110,670,115	1,513,592	1,475,932	3,812,094	5,172,119,099	7,241,760,450	48,924,928,821
				Percent distribution			
United States	100.00	100.00	100.00	100.00	100.00	100.00	100.00
Negro	9.69	1.67	1.87	.33	.16	.15	.21
Oriental mutuals[2]	.17	.25	.43	.23	.17	.14	.18
White[3]	90.14	98.08	97.70	99.44	99.67	99.71	99.61

Source: "Retail Business, by Specified Racial Classes, for the United States: 1929." U.S. Bureau of the Census. *Negroes in the United States: 1920-32*. Washington, D.C.: Government Printing Office, 1935, p. 497. *Notes:* 1. Enumerated Apr. 1, 1930. 2. Chinese and Japanese proprietors only. 3. Includes all other races.

★ 443 ★

Business Owners and Operators

Retail Trade: 1972

Industry	Code	All firms		With paid employees					Without paid employees		
		Firms (number)	Gross receipts ($1,000)	Firms (number)	Employees (number)	Gross receipts ($1,000)	Average employees per firm (number)	Average receipts per firm ($1,000)	Firms (number)	Gross receipts ($1,000)	Average receipts per firm ($1,000)
RETAIL TRADE, TOTAL		56,617	2,925,459	12,215	58,326	1,976,237	5	162	44,402	949,222	21
Building materials and garden supplies	52	632	79,675	197	1,492	69,130	8	351	435	10,545	24
Lumber and other building materials	521	160	36,848	66	680	34,827	10	528	94	2,021	22
Paint, glass, and wallpaper stores	523	38	12,164	24	256	11,773	11	491	14	391	28
Hardware stores	525	238	19,715	82	395	15,217	5	186	156	4,498	29
Retail nurseries and garden stores	526	105	3,745	8	74	2,305	9	288	97	1,440	15
Mobile home dealers	527	22	4,712	11	72	4,403	7	400	11	309	28
Building materials, garden supplies, n.s.k.	52-	69	2,491	6	15	605	3	101	63	1,886	30
General merchandise stores	53	1,040	50,174	214	1,025	31,427	5	147	826	18,747	23
Department stores	531	4	(D)	3	(D)	(D)	(D)	(D)	1	(D)	(D)
Variety stores	533	480	23,220	85	398	12,620	5	148	395	10,600	27
Miscellaneous general merchandise stores	539	445	19,919	117	396	13,243	3	113	328	6,676	20
General merchandise stores, n.s.k.	53-	111	(D)	9	(D)	(D)	(D)	(D)	102	(D)	(D)
Food stores	54	12,271	649,025	1,957	8,614	333,228	4	170	10,314	315,797	31
Grocery stores	541	9,587	549,379	1,655	7,155	283,675	4	171	7,932	265,704	33

[Continued]

★ 443 ★

Retail Trade: 1972

[Continued]

Industry	Code	All firms		With paid employees					Without paid employees		
		Firms (number)	Gross receipts ($1,000)	Firms (number)	Employees (number)	Gross receipts ($1,000)	Average employees per firm (number)	Average receipts per firm ($1,000)	Firms (number)	Gross receipts ($1,000)	Average receipts per firm ($1,000)
Meat markets and freezer provisions	542	515	29,968	95	433	19,233	5	202	420	10,735	26
Fruit stores and vegetable markets	543	290	6,595	17	33	2,363	2	139	273	4,233	16
Candy, nut, and confectionery stores	544	1,136	24,707	60	167	6,430	3	107	1,076	18,277	17
Dairy products stores	545	25	1,707	17	96	1,381	6	81	8	326	41
Retail bakeries	546	223	17,356	89	562	14,526	6	163	134	2,830	21
Miscellaneous food stores	549	436	15,794	19	79	3,337	4	176	417	12,457	30
Food stores, n.s.k.	54-	59	3,519	5	89	2,284	18	457	54	1,235	23
Automotive dealers and service stations	55	7,287	951,427	3,252	15,594	758,168	5	233	4,035	193,259	48
New and used car dealers	551	571	291,182	197	3,493	276,718	18	1,405	374	14,464	39
Auto and home supply stores	553	398	291,182	112	405	16,369	4	146	286	6,506	23
Gasoline service stations	554	6,180	628,551	2,919	11,600	457,925	4	157	3,261	170,626	52
Boat dealers	555	7	1,951	7	35	1,951	5	279	-	-	-
Automotive dealers	559	104	6,202	15	(D)	(D)	(D)	(D)	89	(D)	(D)
Automotive dealers, service stations, n.s.k.	55-	27	666	2	(D)	(D)	(D)	(D)	25	(D)	(D)
Apparel and accessory stores	56	1,952	79,690	415	2,422	60,569	6	146	1,537	19,121	12
Men's and boys' clothing and furnishings	561	169	27,669	95	716	25,891	8	273	74	1,778	24
Women's ready-to-wear stores	562	439	16,360	122	557	12,2134	5	99	317	4,226	13
Women's accessory and specialty stores	563	278	4,008	19	59	1,539	3	81	259	2,469	10
Children's and infants' wear stores	564	12	1,498	10	(D)	(D)	(D)	(D)	2	(D)	(D)
Family clothing stores	565	412	11,761	49	532	6,967	11	142	363	4,794	13
Shoe stores	566	234	9,373	63	80	7,344	4	117	171	2,029	12
Furriers and fur shops	568	14	722	1	(D)	(D)	(D)	(D)	13	(D)	(D)
Miscellaneous apparel and accessories	569	332	6,383	39	129	3,344	3	86	293	3,039	10
Apparel and accessory stores, n.s.k.	56-	62	1,916	17	70	1,253	4	74	45	663	15
Furniture and home furnishings stores	57	1,840	91,505	372	1,529	64,272	4	173	1,468	27,233	19
Furniture and home furnishings stores	571	673	48,056	184	887	39,200	5	213	489	8,856	18
Furniture stores	5712	350	30,009	103	521	24,929	5	242	247	5,080	21
Floor covering stores	5713	49	10,603	43	198	10,411	5	242	6	192	32
Drapery and upholstery stores	5714	37	1,739	20	69	1,458	3	73	17	281	17
Miscellaneous home furnishings stores	5719	237	5,705	18	99	2,402	5	133	219	3,303	15
Household appliance stores	572	152	11,249	36	186	9,173	5	255	116	2,076	18
Radio, television, and music stores	573	974	31,272	148	434	15,547	3	105	826	15,725	19
Radio and television stores	5732	791	18,561	43	127	5,391	3	125	748	13,170	18
Music stores	5733	163	11,122	102	(D)	(D)	(D)	(D)	61	(D)	(D)
Radio, television, music stores, n.s.k.	573-	20	1,589	3	(D)	(D)	(D)	(D)	17	(D)	(D)
Furniture, home furnishings, n.s.k.	57-	41	928	4	22	352	6	88	37	576	16
Eating and drinking places	58	15,154	536,547	4,035	19,764	343,109	5	85	11,119	193,438	17
Eating places	5812	9,456	283,806	2,220	10,131	170,646	5	77	7,236	113,160	16
Drinking places	5813	4,592	140,478	1,142	3,554	70,931	3	62	3,450	69,547	20
Eating and drinking places, n.s.k.	581-	1,106	112,263	673	6,079	101,532	9	151	433	10,731	25
Miscellaneous retail	59	16,441	487,416	1,773	7,886	316,334	4	178	14,668	171,082	12
Drug stores and proprietary stores	591	725	99,052	450	2,748	88,008	6	196	275	11,044	40
Liquor stores	592	1,715	180,275	678	2,270	120,998	3	178	1,037	59,277	57
Used merchandise stores	593	742	11,196	61	173	5,596	3	92	681	5,600	8
Miscellaneous shopping goods stores	594	1,692	29,229	131	577	17,759	4	136	1,561	11,470	7
Sporting goods and bicycle shops	5941	113	6,309	21	123	4,862	6	232	92	1,447	16
Book stores	5942	148	2,215	15	88	1,184	6	79	133	1,031	8
Stationery stores	5943	66	2,517	13	52	1,657	4	127	53	860	16
Jewelry stores	5944	338	6,717	29	126	4,812	4	166	309	1,905	6

[Continued]

★ 443 ★

Retail Trade: 1972
[Continued]

Industry	Code	All firms		With paid employees					Without paid employees		
		Firms (number)	Gross receipts ($1,000)	Firms (number)	Employees (number)	Gross receipts ($1,000)	Average employees per firm (number)	Average receipts per firm ($1,000)	Firms (number)	Gross receipts ($1,000)	Average receipts per firm ($1,000)
Hobby, toy, and game shops	5945	101	801	3	(D)	(D)	(D)	(D)	98	(D)	(D)
Camera and photographic supply stores	5946	66	1,135	5	12	714	2	143	61	421	7
Gift, novelty, and souvenir shops	5947	368	6,635	41	158	3,958	4	97	327	2,677	8
Luggage and leather goods stores	5948	13	191	1	(D)	(D)	(D)	(D)	12	(D)	(D)
Sewing, needlework, and piece goods	5949	479	2,709	3	(D)	(D)	(D)	(D)	476	(D)	(D)
Nonstore retailers	596	7,704	60,490	84	491	26,877	6	320	7,620	33,613	4
Mail order houses	5961	171	1,549	6	43	1,073	7	179	165	476	3
Merchandise machine operators	5962	345	8,300	15	70	4,235	5	282	330	4,065	12
Direct selling organizations	5963	7,188	50,641	63	378	21,569	1	342	7,125	29,072	4
Fuel and ice dealers	598	381	33,313	114	613	27,334	5	240	267	5,979	22
Fuel and ice dealers, n.e.c.	5982	275	7,343	32	71	2,132	2	67	243	5,211	21
Fuel oil dealers	5983	80	22,368	68	390	21,775	6	320	12	593	49
Liquefied petroleum gas dealers	5984	15	3,430	14	(D)	(D)	(D)	(D)	1	(D)	(D)
Fuel and ice dealers, n.s.k.	598-	11	172	6	(D)	(D)	(D)	(D)	5	(D)	(D)
Retail stores, n.e.c.	599	3,320	69,830	245	965	28,098	4	115	3,075	41,732	14
Florists	5992	610	14,600	119	387	8,925	3	75	491	5,675	12
Cigar stores and stands	5993	86	1,663	8	21	181	3	23	78	1,482	19
News dealers and newsstands	5994	19	695	11	26	508	2	46	8	187	23
Miscellaneous retail stores, n.e.c.	5999	2,556	49,468	101	419	15,775	4	155	2,455	33,693	14
Retail stores, n.s.k.	599-	49	3,404	6	112	2,709	19	452	43	695	16
Miscellaneous retail stores, n.s.k.	59-	162	4,031	10	49	1,664	5	166	152	2,367	16

Source: "Selected Statistics for Industry for Black-Owned Firms: 1972 and 1969," U.S. Bureau of the Census, 1972 Survey of Minority Business Enterprises, *Minority Owned Businesses—Black*, pp. 22, 24. *Notes:* - Represents zero. D = Withheld to avoid disclosing figures for individual companies.

★ 444 ★

Business Owners and Operators

Selected Business Services: 1972

Industry	Code	All firms		With paid employees					Without paid employees		
		Firms (number)	Gross receipts ($1,000)	Firms (number)	Employees (number)	Gross receipts ($1,000)	employees per firm (number)	Average receipts per firm ($1,000)	Average Firms (number)	Gross receipts ($1,000)	receipts per firm ($1,000)
SELECTED SERVICES, TOTAL		68,469	1,054,057	9,192	49,102	645,353	5	70	59,277	408,704	7
Hotels and other lodging places	70	2,344	63,557	539	3,618	45,387	7	84	1,805	18,170	10
Hotels, motels, and tourist courts	701	960	42,229	343	2,652	33,227	8	97	617	9,002	15
Rooming and boarding houses	702	1,208	18,093	185	827	10,463	4	57	1,023	7,630	7
Camps and trailering parks	703	137	1,757	5	17	579	3	116	132	1,178	9
Sporting and recreational camps	7032	48	759	3	(D)	(D)	(D)	(D)	45	(D)	(D)
Trailering parks for transients	7033	78	884	1	(D)	(D)	(D)	(D)	77	(D)	(D)
Camps and trailering parks, n.s.k.	703	11	114	1	(D)	(D)	(D)	(D)	10	(D)	(D)
Hotels and other lodging places, n.s.k.	70	39	1,478	6	122	1,118	20	186	33	360	12
Personal services	72	35,473	355,130	3,854	13,465	171,252	3	44	31,619	183,878	6
Laundry, cleaning, and garment services	721	5,103	100,795	1,388	5,651	61,501	4	44	3,715	39,294	11
Power laundries, family and commercial	7211	2,270	27,340	30	392	4,365	13	146	2,240	22,975	10
Coin-operated laundries and cleaning	7215	1,383	19,816	194	556	7,163	3	37	1,189	12,653	11
Dry cleaning plants, except rug	7216	878	35,769	767	3,356	34,051	4	44	111	1,718	15
Laundry, cleaning, and garment services, n.s.k.	721-	572	17,870	397	1,347	15,922	3	40	175	1,948	11
Photographic studios, portrait	722	943	7,460	36	155	2,516	4	70	907	4,944	5

[Continued]

★ 444 ★

Selected Business Services: 1972
[Continued]

Industry	Code	All firms		With paid employees					Without paid employees		
		Firms (number)	Gross receipts ($1,000)	Firms (number)	Employees (number)	Gross receipts ($1,000)	employees per firm (number)	Average receipts per firm ($1,000)	Average Firms (number)	Gross receipts ($1,000)	receipts per firm ($1,000)
Beauty shops	723	13,423	65,398	698	1,989	18,064	3	26	12,725	47,334	4
Barber shops	724	9,059	47,850	706	1,566	11,663	2	17	8,353	36,187	4
Shoe repair and hat cleaning shops	725	1,241	11,659	138	276	3,851	2	28	1,103	7,808	7
Funeral service and crematories	726	1,880	90,448	655	2,854	61,014	4	93	1,225	29,434	24
Miscellaneous personal services	729	3,476	21,861	66	378	5,271	6	80	3,410	16,590	5
Personal services, n.s.k.	72-	348	9,659	167	596	7,372	4	44	181	2,287	13
Business services	73	10,846	215,130	1,677	14,564	151,986	9	91	9,169	63,144	7
Advertising	731	289	15,790	35	201	13,500	6	386	254	2,290	9
Credit reporting and collection	732	18	(D)	12	(D)	(D)	(D)	(D)	6	(D)	(D)
Mailing, reproduction, and stenographic	733	32	2,088	24	144	1,987	6	83	8	101	13
Services to buildings	734	5,820	99,553	1,192	9,607	69,043	8	58	4,628	30,510	7
Window cleaning	7341	4,234	28,930	58	228	3,521	4	61	4,176	25,409	6
Disinfecting and exterminating	7342	59	2,747	44	242	2,472	6	56	15	275	18
Building maintenance services, n.e.c.	7349	1,430	66,424	1,073	9,054	62,325	8	58	357	4,099	11
Services to buildings, n.s.k.	734-	97	1,452	17	83	725	5	43	80	727	9
News syndicates	735	4	(D)	2	(D)	(D)	(D)	(D)	2	(D)	(D)
Personnel supply services	736	52	4,191	39	250	3,963	6	102	13	228	18
Computer and data processing services	737	53	580	3	(D)	(D)	(D)	(D)	50	(D)	(D)
Miscellaneous business services	739	4,415	87,447	353	4,085	58,733	12	166	4,062	28,714	7
Research and development laboratories	7391	10	1,272	8	(D)	(D)	(D)	(D)	2	(D)	(D)
Management and public relations	7392	1,564	32,114	111	1,305	23,241	12	209	1,453	8,873	6
Detective and protective services	7393	91	14,598	79	1,570	14,303	20	181	12	295	25
Equipment rental and leasing	7394	329	6,023	23	138	2,896	6	126	306	3,127	10
Photo finishing laboratories	7395	11	1,126	9	(D)	(D)	(D)	(D)	2	(D)	(D)
Business services, n.e.c.	7399	2,393	31,204	116	900	14,990	8	129	2,277	16,214	7
Miscellaneous business services, n.s.k.	739-	17	1,110	7	69	985	10	141	10	125	13
Business services, n.s.k.	73-	163	3,963	17	121	2,970	7	175	146	993	7
Automotive repair	75	5,607	123,499	1,145	3,978	72,427	3	63	4,462	51,072	11
Automotive rentals, without driver	751	117	3,005	12	(D)	(D)	(D)	(D)	105	(D)	(D)
Automobile parking	752	129	2,717	42	465	2,018	4	48	87	699	8
Automotive repair shops	753	4,261	97,467	886	2,661	57,271	3	65	3,375	40,196	12
Top and body repair shops	7531	1,074	28,261	286	885	17,674	3	62	788	10,587	13
Tire retreading and repair shops	7534	64	5,432	52	210	4,916	4	95	12	516	43
Paint shops	7535	54	2,777	42	127	2,581	3	61	12	196	16
General automotive repair shops	7538	2,619	49,495	430	1,169	25,307	3	59	2,189	24,188	11
Automotive repair shops, n.e.c.	7539	434	11,124	73	251	6,603	3	90	361	4,521	13
Automotive repair shops, n.s.k.	753-	16	378	3	19	190	6	63	13	188	14
Automotive services, except repairs	754	1,033	19,564	202	1,080	11,021	5	55	831	8,543	10
Car washes	7542	932	15,433	135	857	7,264	6	54	797	8,189	10
Automotive services, n.e.c.	7549	60	2,314	50	176	2,214	4	44	10	100	10
Automotive services, except repairs, n.s.k.	754-	41	1,797	17	47	1,543	3	91	24	254	11
Auto repairs, services, and garages, n.s.k.	75-	67	746	3	(D)	(D)	(D)	(D)	64	(D)	(D)
Miscellaneous repair services	76	4,155	53,119	384	1,238	25,670	3	67	3,771	27,449	7
Electrical repair shops	762	1,913	21,561	155	396	9,554	3	62	1,758	12,007	7
Radio and television repair	7622	1,556	15,097	114	276	5,936	2	52	1,442	9,161	7
Refrigeration service and repair	7623	28	1,843	18	(D)	(D)	(D)	(D)	10	(D)	(D)
Electrical repair shops, n.e.c.	7629	316	4,129	21	55	1,713	3	82	295	2,416	8
Electrical repair shops, n.s.k.	762-	13	492	2	(D)	(D)	(D)	(D)	11	(D)	(D)
Watch, clock, and jewelry repair	763	12	787	6	(D)	(D)	(D)	(D)	6	(D)	(D)
Reupholstery and furniture repair	764	944	12,123	113	357	5,502	3	49	831	6,621	8
Miscellaneous repair shops	769	1,216	17,632	107	443	9,421	4	88	1,109	8,211	7
Welding repair	7692	28	1,664	17	(D)	(D)	(D)	(D)	11	(D)	(D)
Armature rewinding shops	7694	10	1,684	8	(D)	(D)	(D)	(D)	2	(D)	(D)
Repair services, n.e.c.	7699	1,178	14,284	82	280	6,347	3	77	1,096	7,937	7
Miscellaneous repair services, n.s.k.	76-	70	1,016	3	(D)	(D)	(D)	(D)	67	(D)	(D)
Motion pictures	78	161	4,337	32	331	3,459	10	108	129	878	7
Motion picture production and services	781	104	1,867	13	(D)	(D)	(D)	(D)	91	(D)	(D)
Motion picture distribution and services	782	1	(D)	1	(D)	(D)	(D)	(D)	-	-	-

[Continued]

★ 444 ★

Selected Business Services: 1972
[Continued]

Industry	Code	All firms		With paid employees					Without paid employees		
		Firms (number)	Gross receipts ($1,000)	Firms (number)	Employees (number)	Gross receipts ($1,000)	employees per firm (number)	Average receipts per firm ($1,000)	Average Firms (number)	Gross receipts ($1,000)	receipts per firm ($1,000)
Motion picture theaters	783	39	2,093	17	262	1,835	15	108	22	258	12
Motion pictures, n.s.k.	78-	17	(D)	1	(D)	(D)	(D)	(D)	16	(D)	(D)
Amusement and recreation services	79	4,560	70,991	393	1,948	40,029	5	102	4,167	30,962	7
Dance halls, studios, and schools	791	13	381	10	27	329	3	33	3	52	17
Producers, orchestras, and entertainers	792	2,364	41,331	148	696	24,120	5	163	2,216	17,211	8
Bowling and billiard establishments	793	814	11,435	142	594	6,813	4	48	672	4,622	7
Billiard and pool establishments	7932	730	7,646	101	257	3,322	3	33	629	4,324	7
Bowling alleys	7933	56	3,321	32	317	3,180	10	99	24	141	6
Bowling and billiard establishments, n.s.k.	793-	28	468	9	20	311	2	35	19	157	8
Miscellaneous amusement and recreation	799	1,152	15,130	85	559	7,807	7	92	1,067	7,323	7
Amusement and recreation services, n.s.k.	79-	217	2,714	8	72	960	9	120	209	1,754	8
Health services	80pt.	2,463	77,533	431	4,950	58,213	11	135	2,032	19,320	10
Nursing and personal care facilities	805	1,744	17,154	23	158	2,556	7	111	1,721	14,598	8
Medical and dental laboratories	807	284	7,243	80	285	4,488	4	56	204	2,755	14
Medical laboratories	8071	94	3,508	37	145	2,758	4	75	57	750	13
Dental laboratories	8072	185	3,705	43	140	1,730	3	40	142	1,975	14
Medical and dental laboratories, n.s.k.	807-	5	30	-	-	-	-	-	5	30	6
Health and allied services, n.e.c.	809	224	39,590	193	3,753	38,884	19	201	31	706	23
Health services, n.s.k.	80-	211	13,546	135	754	12,285	6	91	76	1,261	17
Education services	82	2,006	42,238	416	2,676	33,911	6	82	1,590	8,327	5
Museums and botanical and zoological gardens	84	3	10	-	-	-	-	-	3	10	3
Services, n.s.k.	-	851	48,513	321	2,334	43,019	7	134	530	5,494	10

Source: "Selected Statistics for Industry for Black-Owned Firms: 1972 and 1969," U.S. Bureau of the Census, 1972 Survey of Minority Business Enterprises, *Minority Owned Businesses—Black*, pp. 26, 28. *Notes:* - Represents zero. D = Withheld to avoid disclosing figures for individual companies.

★ 445 ★
Business Owners and Operators

Stores Operated by Black Proprietors by Kind of Business for the United States, 1920-1932

KIND OF BUSINESS	Number of Stores	Proprietors and firm members (not on payroll)	Number of employees (full-time)	Total payroll (including part-time)	Stocks on hand end of year (at cost)	NET SALES	
						Amount of total	Per Cent
Total	25,701	28,243	12,561	$8,528,306	$10,657,000	$101,146,043	100.0
Food Group	10,755	11,594	2,139	1,341,671	3,240,610	36,662,523	36.25
Candy and Confectionery Stores	1,137	1,193	230	124,841	207,480	2,584,053	2.55
Grocery Store (without meats)	6,248	6,690	707	336,608	1,709,750	14,714,500	14.55
Combination Stores (groceries and meats)	2,202	2,428	768	520,643	1,147,940	13,654,678	13.50
Meat Markets (including sea foods)	537	576	252	188,200	68,150	2,829,147	2.80
All Other Food Stores	631	707	182	171,379	107,290	2,880,145	2.85
General Stores - Groceries with Dry Goods, Apparel, or General Merchandise	761	892	229	151,947	1,161,880	4,828,700	4.78
General Merchandise Group	128	153	81	67,496	323,790	979,799	.97
Dry Goods Stores	61	76	33	27,418	165,900	381,111	.33
General Merchandise Stores	37	47	37	31,048	139,270	456,156	.45
Variety, 5-and-10, and To-a-dollar Stores	30	30	11	9,030	18,620	142,532	.14
Automotive Group	1,679	1,873	1,059	1,058,269	819,040	9,793,196	9.68
Motor-vehicle dealers (new and used)	39	46	166	245,535	331,750	3,149,837	3.11
Filling Stations	799	869	302	258,220	217,100	3,429,826	3.39
Garages and Repair Shops	732	838	525	481,317	184,310	2,543,898	2.52

[Continued]

★ 445 ★

Stores Operated by Black Proprietors by Kind of Business for the United States, 1920-1932

[Continued]

KIND OF BUSINESS	Number of Stores	Proprietors and firm members (not on payroll)	Number of employees (full-time)	Total payroll (including part-time)	Stocks on hand end of year (at cost)	NET SALES Amount of total	NET SALES Per Cent
Other Automotive Establishments	109	120	66	73,197	85,880	669,635	.66
Apparel Group	477	519	355	322,620	698,830	3,027,917	2.99
Men's and Boys' Clothing and Furnishings Stores	66	71	59	59,816	266,660	915,500	.90
Family Clothing Stores-Men's, Women's and Children's	32	37	27	29,295	149,040	426,756	.42
Women's Ready-to-wear Specialty Stores-Apparel and Accessories	57	62	33	28,237	72,290	315,762	.31
Women's Accessories Stores	54	57	28	32,649	56,080	308,710	.31
Other Apparel Stores	220	240	176	139,385	62,960	715,764	.71
Shoe Stores	48	52	32	33,238	91,800	345,425	.34
Furniture and Household Group	149	174	125	133,500	240,290	1,160,120	1.15
Furniture Stores	54	62	53	56,410	104,250	401,056	.40
Floor Coverings, Drapery, Curtain, and Upholstery Stores	7	7	6	3,588	2,220	19,450	.02
Household Appliances Stores	3	3	1	500	1,030	7,800	.01
Other Home Furnishings and Appliances Stores	30	33	19	15,414	25,770	79,634	.08
Radio and Music Stores	55	69	46	57,588	107,020	652,450	.64
Restaurants and Eating Places	7,918	8,530	5,425	2,727,050	572,050	21,333,198	21.09
Restaurants, Cafeterias, and Lunch Rooms	5,729	6,209	4,742	2,358,331	431,950	17,284,126	17.09
Lunch Counters, Refreshment Stands, etc.	2,189	2,321	683	369,552	140,100	4,049,072	4.00
Lumber and Building Group	96	112	170	202,778	180,380	1,268,024	1.25
Lumber and Building Material Dealers	26	31	72	73,175	98,070	589,155	.58
Electrical Shops (without radio)	23	29	30	36,565	18,010	159,362	.16
Heating and Plumbings Shops	26	30	45	69,147	29,020	354,537	.35
Paint and Glass Stores	21	22	23	28,891	35,280	164,470	.16
Other Retail Stores	3,365	3,994	2,858	2,411,120	3,231,540	21,109,630	20.87
Hardware Stores	40	49	22	34,606	179,110	476,048	.47
Hardware and Farm Implement Stores	11	16	22	20,286	92,160	335,348	.33
Farmers' Supplies	107	123	50	45,880	97,850	927,859	.92
Book Stores	8	9	9	4,933	22,120	52,661	.05
Cigar Stores and Cigar Stands	704	764	320	236,597	140,960	2,052,958	2.03
Coal and Wood Yards-Ice Dealers	549	594	337	250,079	125,900	2,117,474	2.09
Drug Stores	712	852	955	790,465	1,566,750	7,253,921	7.17
Jewelry Stores	67	74	33	45,596	231,650	388,282	.39
Miscellaneous Classifications (Combined)	1,167	1,513	1,110	982,678	775,040	7,505,079	7.42
Second-hand Stores	373	402	120	111,022	188,590	982,936	.97

Source: "Stores Operated by Negro Proprietors, by Kind of Business, for the United States—1920-30." Monroe N. Work, *The Negro Year Book and Annual Encyclopedia of the Negro, 1927-38*, pp.

★ 446 ★

Business Owners and Operators

Top 100 Black Businesses, 1975

Company	Location	Chief executive	Business	Year started	Employees	1974 sales[1]
Motown Industries	Los Angeles, California	Berry Gordy, Jr.	Entertainment	1959	375	45.00
Johnson Publishing Co., Inc.	Chicago, Illinois	John H. Johnson	Publishing	1942	300	34.00
Johnson Products Co., Inc.	Chicago, Illinois	George E. Johnson	Cosmetics manufacturing	1954	410	33.20
Fedco Foods Corp.	Bronx, New York	J. Bruce Llewllyn	Supermarkets	1969	450	30.00
Garland Foods, Inc.	Dallas, Texas	Mildren M. Montgomery	Meat processing	1969	180	17.20
The Great Philadelphia Trading Co., Ltd/Assorted Music, Inc.	Philadelphia, Pennsylvania	Kenny Gamble, Leon Huff, Thom Bell	Record production, music publishing	1967	35	17.00
H.G. Parks, Inc.	Baltimore, Maryland	Henry G. Parks, Jr.	Meat product manufacturing	1951	300	15.00
Wallace & Wallace Chemical & Oil Corp.	St. Albans, New York	Charles Wallace	Refinery & pipeline construction & operation	1972	23	14.00
Al Johnson Cadillac, Inc.	Chicago, Illinois	Al W. Johnson, Sr.	Automobile dealership	1967	92	13.65
F.W. Eversley & Co., Inc.	New York, New York	F.W. Eversley, Jr.	General contracting	1967	65	13.60
Dick Gidron Cadillac, Inc.	Bronx, New York	Richard D. Gidron	Automobile dealership	1972	63	11.68
Capitol City Liquor Co., Inc.	Washington, D.C.	Chester C. Carter	Liquor & wine distribution & import	1970	60	11.00
TAW International Leasing, Inc.	New York, New York	Thomas A. Wood	Equipment leasing	1968	5	11.00
Webb, Brooks & Brooker, Inc.	New York, New York	Eugene H. Webb	Real estate management	1969	158	10.10
Sivart Mortage Corp.	Chicago, Illinois	Dempsey J. Travis	Mortgage brokerage	1953	12	10.00
E.G. Bowman Co., Inc.	Brooklyn, New York	Ernesta G. Procope	Insurance brokerage	1953	20	9.80

[Continued]

★ 446 ★

Top 100 Black Businesses, 1975

[Continued]

Company	Location	Chief executive	Business	Year started	Employees	1974 sales[1]
Big V Supermarkets	Washington, D.C.	Harold Perry	Supermarkets	1971	85	9.00
H.J. Russell & Co.	Atlanta, Georgia	Herman J. Russell	Construction, property management	1959	250	8.50
Drummond Distributing Co., Inc.	Compton, California	Lancelot E. Drummond	Liquor distributorship	1969	43	8.00
Century Chevrolet, Inc.	Upper Darby, Pennsylvania	Robert L. Myers, Jr.	Automobile dealership	1971	54	7.75
The Kenwood Co., Inc.	New York, New York	Kenneth N. Sherwood	Supermarkets, office furnishings, real estate management	1965	65	7.70
Urban Mechanical Co., Inc.	Bronx, New York	Frederick Clarke	Plumbing & mechanical contracting	1969	153	7.54
All-Pro Enterprises, Inc.	Pittsburgh, Pennsylvania	Brady Keys, Jr.	Fast-food franchising	1968	785	7.52
J.H. Copeland & Sons Construction, Inc.	Miami, Florida	John H. Copeland	Construction	1970	50	7.26
Conyers Ford, Inc.	Detroit, Michigan	Nathan G. Conyers	Automobile & truck dealership	1970	70	7.20
Robert Martin Construction Co., Inc.	Chicago, Illinois	Robert Martin	Construction	1946	39	6.50
Super Pride/Hilton Court, Inc.	Baltimore, Maryland	Charles Burns	Supermarkets, pharmacies	1970	98	6.50
Watts Manufacturing Corp.	Lynwood, California	Mark E. Rivers, Jr.	Metal & fabric products manufacturing	1970	230	6.50
Mitchom General Contracting Co.	East St. Louis, Illinois	Robert L. Mitchom	General contracting, diversified services	1969	65	6.20
Universal Real Estate, Inc.	Miami, Florida	Sonny Wright	Real estate & property management	1962	25	6.01
Bayou Pontiac, Inc.	New Orleans, Louisiana	Robert Green, Jr.	Automobile dealership	1973	85	6.00
Nartrans Manufacturing Co.	Canoga Park, California	Norman H. Casson	Electronic manufacturing	1972	200	6.00
Sengstacke Enterprises, Inc.	Chicago, Illinois	John H. Sengstacke	Publishing	1936	190	6.00
Travis Realty Co.	Chicago, Illinois	Dempsey J. Travis	Property management	1949	10	6.00
Porterfield Wilson Pontiac, Inc.	Detroit, Michigan	Porterfield Wilson	Automobile dealership	1970	50	6.00
Wallace & Wallace Fuel Oil Co.	St. Albans, New York	Charles Wallace	Fuel oil distributorship	1968	35	6.00
Tuesday Publications, Inc.	Chicago, Illinois	W. Leonard Evans, Jr.	Publishing	1965	35	5.78
Trans-Bay Engineers & Builders Inc.	Oakland, California	Ray Dones	General contracting	1967	64	5.60
Bill Nelson Chevrolet, Inc.	Richmond, California	William W. Nelson	Automobile dealership	1969	55	5.50
David Getz Buick, Inc.	Philadelphia, Pennsylvania	Darrell R. Gordon	Automobile dealership	1966	30	5.10
Chioke International Corp.	Jamaica, New York	Christopher E. Chioke	Automotive parts wholesaling & export	1970	8	5.00
Cocoline Chocolate Co., Inc.	Brooklyn, New York	Thomas A. Bourelly	Chocolate products manufacturing	1973	100	5.00
Jenkins Electric Co., Inc.	Brooklyn, New York	William E. Jenkins	Electrical contracting	1946	200	5.00
KC Dodge, Inc.	San Francisco, California	Todd S. Cochran	Automobile & truck dealership	1968	35	5.00
Parker House Sausage Co.	Chicago, Illinois	Daryl F. Grisham	Sausage manufacturing	1921	115	5.00
Sussex Records, Inc.	Los Angeles, California	Clarence Avant	Record production, music publishing	1969	15	5.00
Syphax Enterprises	Arlington, Virginia	William T. Syphax	Construction, property management	1969	75	5.00
G.E. Wash Construction, Inc.	Detroit, Michigan	Glenn E. Wash	General contracting	1967	30	5.00
Art-Ley Ford, Inc.	Brooklyn, New York	Arthur L. Bailey	Automobile dealership	1972	50	4.75
Progress Aerospace Enterprises, Inc.	Philadelphia, Pennsylvania	Frederick E. Miller	Mechanical & electrical manufacturing	1968	130	4.54
Willie Davis Distributing Co.	Los Angeles, California	Willie Davis	Beer distributorship	1970	43	4.51
Vassall Motors, Inc.	Philadelphia, Pennsylvania	Ivan Vassall	Automobile dealership	1969	38	4.50
Bob Smith Chevrolet, Inc.	Louisville, Kentucky	Robert W. Smith	Automobile dealership	1972	56	4.49
T.W.O./Hillman's Inc.	Chicago, Illinois	Lawrence W. Carroll	Supermarkets	1970	55	4.30
Fiesta Lincoln-Mercury, Inc.	Queens Village, New York	William J. Phillips	Automobile dealership	1969	29	4.20
Green Gardens, Inc.	Jersey City, New Jersey	Rudolph V. Green	Supermarkets	1972	82	4.20
California Golden Oak Products, Inc.	Los Angeles, California	William M. Alexander	Furniture manufacturing	1968	117	4.10
Wilson-McIntosh Buick, Inc.	Washington, D.C.	Maurice W, McIntosh	Automobile dealership	1970	50	4.09
Micon Construction & Development Corp.	Lynbrook, New york	Robert Rowley	Construction	1972	3	4.03
Lawndale Packaging Corp.	Chicago, Illinois	Dennis Manthe	Container manufacturing	1970	65	4.00
Thacker Construction Co.	Edwardsville, Illinois	Floyd Thacker	Construction	1970	250	4.00
VIP Lincoln-Mercury, Inc.	New Rochelle, New York	Daniel E. Brown	Automobile dealership	1969	22	4.00
Electroque Associates, Inc.	Brooklyn, New York	David L. Blaine	Electrical contracting	1968	150	3.96
Friendly Chrysler-Plymouth, Inc.	Los Angeles, California	Herbert Stephenson	Automobile dealership	1970	41	3.95
Main Food Service of Buffalo, Inc.	Buffalo, New York	Carl A. Mackin	Supermarkets	1970	70	3.86
Lowery Distributing Co.	Chicago, Illinois	Mannie A. Lowery, Jr.	Beer distributorship	1969	18	3.80
R.L. Dukes Oldsmobile, Inc.	Chicago, Illinois	Rufus L. Dukes	Automobile dealership	1971	37	3.73
Blanchard Management Corp.	New York, New York	Blanchard W. Robinson	Food service management	1973	156	3.70
Unique Plastics, Inc.	Cincinnati, Ohio	Samuel A. Reece	Plastics manufacturing	1968	31	3.62
Essence Communications, Inc.	New York, New York	Edward Lewis	Publishing	1969	36	3.50
Metro Lincoln-Mercury, Inc.	East St. Louis, Illinois	Sam Johnson	Automobile dealership	1973	25	3.50
Moss Plumbing Co., Inc.	Miami, Florida	Moses Moss	Contracting	1958	50	3.50
Renmuth Inc.	Detroit, Michigan	Robert Renfroe	Metal products manufacturing	1969	109	3.50
James Produce Co.	Charleston, West Virginia	Charles H. James II	Food wholesaling	1883	28	3.34
Chuck White Buick, Inc.	Chicago, Illinois	Charles H. White	Automobile dealership	1971	30	3.32
The Afro-American Co.	Baltimore, Maryland	John H. Murphy III	Publishing	1907	200	3.30
AVI Manufacturing, Inc.	Gardena, California	E.E. Barrington	Subassembly manufacturing	1971	200	3.30
Magnificent Products, Inc.	Los Angeles, California	Wilbur Jackson	Cosmetics manufacturing	1965	37	3.20
Roberts Motels, Inc.	Chicago, Illinois	Herman Roberts	Motel chain	1961	230	3.18
James Pontiac, Inc.	Oakland, California	Claude I. James	Automobile dealership	1971	33	3.10
Ault, Inc.	Minneapolis, Minnesota	Luther T. Prince	Electronic manufacturing	1962	120	3.00
D&H Tire Co.	Kansas City, Kansas	Luther D. White	Tire retailing	1965	41	3.00
C.J. Mack Improvement Co.	Detroit, Michigan	C.J. Mack, Sr.	Construction	1956	110	3.00
Willows Convalescent Centers, Inc.	Minneapolis, Minnesota	Archie Givens, Jr.	Convalescent care	1969	390	2.97

[Continued]

★ 446 ★

Top 100 Black Businesses, 1975

[Continued]

Company	Location	Chief executive	Business	Year started	Employees	1974 sales[1]
Earl G. Graves Publishing Co., Inc.	New York, New York	Earl G. Graves	Publishing	1970	30	2.90
Ozanne Construction Co., Inc.	Cleveland, Ohio	Leroy Ozanne	Construction	1956	10	2.90
Mercer Cadillac, Inc.	Alton, Illinois	Clavin Mercer	Automobile dealership	1973	31	2.87
Jim Bradley Pontiac-GMC, Inc.	Ann Arbor, Michigan	James H. Bradley, Jr.	Automobile & truck dealership	1973	35	2.86
Richfield Packing Co., Inc.	Palmetto, Florida	James Woodson	Produce cultivation & distribution	1972	375	2.83
Horace Noble Lincoln/Mercury, Inc.	Chicago, Illinois	Horace Noble	Automobile dealership	1970	38	2.80
Fighton, Inc.	Rochester, New York	William M. McGhee, Jr.	Electrical & metal products manufacturing	1968	85	2.78
Ebony Oil Corp.	Jamaica, New York	Lawrence J. Cormier	Fuel oil distributorship	1954	25	2.75
Tombs & Sons, Inc.	Bonner Springs, Kansas	Leroy C. Tombs	Diversified services	1972	1,000	2.75
Delta Enterprises, Inc.	Greenville, Mississippi	Charles D. Bannerman	Diversified manufacturing	1969	200	2.70
All-Stainless, Inc.	Hingham, Massachusetts	Eugene V. Roundtree	Metal parts wholesaling	1952	32	2.68
JWM Corp.	Philadelphia, Pennsylvania	J.J. Williams, Jr.	Electronic manufacturing	1969	150	2.65
Oasis Ford, Inc.	Newhall, California	David J. Babb	Automobile dealership	1972	31	2.63
Amnews, Inc.	New York, New York	John L. Procope	Publishing	1909	125	2.60
Ewing Enterprises, Inc.	Indianapolis, Indiana	Robert L. Ewing	Supermarkets	1972	40	2.60
Yonkers Plate Glass, Inc.	Yonkers, New York	Delton Walker	Glass & metal products subcontracting	1960	45	2.50

Source: "Banks," *Black Enterprise* 4 (June 1975), pp. 37, 43-45. Published by permission. *Note:* 1. Million dollars.

★ 447 ★

Business Owners and Operators

Transportation and Public Utilities: 1972

Industry	Code	All firms		With paid employees					Without paid employees		
		Firms (number)	Gross receipts ($1,000)	Firms (number)	Employees (number)	Gross receipts ($1,000)	Average employees per firm (number)	Average receipts per firm ($1,000)	Firms (number)	Gross receipts ($1,000)	Average receipts per firm ($1,000)
TRANSPORTATION AND PUBLIC UTILITIES, TOTAL		21,738	425,467	1,680	10,714	209,736	6	125	20,058	215,731	11
Local and interurban passenger transit	41	8,936	68,052	316	2,004	20,388	6	65	8,620	47,664	6
Local and suburban transportation	411	23	1,457	17	150	1,370	9	81	6	87	15
Local and suburban transit	4111	3	(D)	1	(D)	(D)	(D)	(D)	2	(D)	(D)
Local passenger transportation, n.e.c.	4119	20	(D)	16	(D)	(D)	(D)	(D)	4	(D)	(D)
Taxicabs	412	7,685	53,781	222	1,305	13,373	6	60	7,463	40,408	5
Intercity highway transportation	413	3	(D)	3	(D)	(D)	(D)	(D)	-	-	-
Transportation charter service	414	3	(D)	2	(D)	(D)	(D)	(D)	1	(D)	(D)
School buses	415	68	3,406	58	(D)	(D)	(D)	(D)	10	(D)	(D)
Bus terminal and service facilities	417	-	-	-	-	-	-	-	-	-	-
Local and interurban passenger transit, n.s.k.	41-	1,154	9,078	14	170	1,989	12	142	1,140	7,089	6
Trucking and warehousing	42	10,187	294,464	1,177	7,182	151,346	6	129	9,010	143,118	16
Trucking, local and long distance	421	9,155	225,884	644	4,197	91,660	7	142	8,511	134,224	16
Public warehousing	422	18	(D)	16	304	8,986	19	562	2	(D)	(D)
Trucking terminal facilities	423	2	(D)	2	(D)	(D)	(D)	(D)	-	-	-
Trucking and warehousing, n.s.k.	42-	1,012	59,216	515	(D)	(D)	(D)	(D)	497	(D)	(D)
Water transportation	44	51	3,956	21	(D)	(D)	(D)	(D)	30	(D)	(D)
Transportation by air	45	42	1,499	3	(D)	(D)	(D)	(D)	39	(D)	(D)
Transportation services	47	1,064	31,413	74	543	20,564	7	278	990	10,849	11
Freight forwarding	471	3	(D)	3	(D)	(D)	(D)	(D)	-	-	-
Arrangement of transportation	472	209	11,680	27	130	9,699	5	359	182	1,981	11
Passenger transportation arrangement	4722	76	693	-	-	-	-	-	76	693	9
Freight transportation arrangement	4723	109	2,488	5	(D)	(D)	(D)	(D)	104	(D)	(D)
Arrangement of transportation, n.s.k.	472-	24	8,499	22	(D)	(D)	(D)	(D)	2	(D)	(D)
Miscellaneous transportation services	478	17	(D)	14	(D)	(D)	(D)	(D)	3	46	15
Transportation services, n.s.k.	47-	835	17,997	30	268	9,175	9	306	805	8,822	11
Communication	48	58	9,080	30	470	8,581	16	286	28	499	18

[Continued]

★ 447 ★

Transportation and Public Utilities: 1972

[Continued]

Industry	Code	All firms		With paid employees					Without paid employees		
		Firms (number)	Gross receipts ($1,000)	Firms (number)	Employees (number)	Gross receipts ($1,000)	Average employees per firm (number)	Average receipts per firm ($1,000)	Firms (number)	Gross receipts ($1,000)	Average receipts per firm ($1,000)
Radio and television broadcasting	483	22	7,957	21	(D)	(D)	(D)	(D)	1	(D)	(D)
Communication services, n.e.c.	489	8	685	7	(D)	(D)	(D)	(D)	1	(D)	(D)
Communication, n.s.k.	48-	28	438	2	(D)	(D)	(D)	(D)	26	(D)	(D)
Electric, gas, and sanitary services	49	1,394	16,889	59	305	4,139	5	70	1,335	12,750	10
Transportation and public utilities, n.s.k.	--	6	114	-	-	-	-	-	6	144	19

Source: "Selected Statistics for Industry for Black-Owned Firms: 1972 and 1969," U.S. Bureau of the Census, 1972 Survey of Minority Business Enterprises, *Minority Owned Businesses—Black*, p. 18. *Notes:* - Represents zero. D = Withheld to avoid disclosing figures for individual companies.

★ 448 ★

Business Owners and Operators

Types of Businesses according to Capital Invested, 1899

KINDS OF BUSINESS	UNDER $100	$100 to $500	$500 to 1000	$1,000 to 2,500	$2,500 to 5,000	$5,000 to 10,000	$10,000 to 50,000	$50,000 and Over	Capital Unknown	Actual Total
General M'd'se	...	29	39	57	18	4	2	...	17	$1,423,075
Real Estate	...	...	4	6	8	10	3	5	...	742,700
Groceries	8	137	125	114	5	5	4	...	34	405,038
Liquor Saloons	...	6	6	25	15	13	...	1	2	291,300
Banking and Insurance	...	...	...	1	2	4	...	3	1	270,900
Undertakers	...	9	4	21	11	19	4	...	12	229,450
Publishers and Printers	1	18	17	25	15	4	4	...	5	226,975
Market Gardeners, etc.	...	...	1	2	2	4	...	1	1	205,700
Barbers	...	...	60	63	12	3	...	...	24	197,325
Building & Loan Ass'ns	...	...	...	...	2	...	6	1	4	165,000
Builders and Contractors	...	...	10	14	4	8	5	...	7	140,200
Hall, for renting etc.,	...	...	...	...	...	...	...	1	...	120,000
Drugs and Medicines	..	5	9	35	9	2	1	...	3	119,150
Hotels	...	5	1	13	7	2	2	...	6	92,200
Fuel-dealers	1	4	8	10	5	3	2	...	4	81,500
Caterers	...	1	1	5	5	4	2	,,,	6	79,395
Expressmen and Hackmen	...	8	16	20	9	...	...	...	...	78,875
Fish-dealers	1	2	4	4	1	...	2	...	1	67,744
Livery-stables	...	3	2	14	2	3	1	...	1	62,860
Miscellaneous	...	8	18	25	2	...	...	...	3	59,355
Restaurants	...	4	14	19	12	5	...	...	7	51,925
Plumbing and Tin-shops and Hardware stores	...	3	4	5	1	1	2	...	1	45,250
Green Grocers, Dairymen, etc.	...	7	6	12	3	2	...	...	...	43,475
Tailor-shops	...	12	10	9	3	1	...	...	5	37,125
Furniture, New and 2nd Hand	...	2	1	6	2	1	1	...	...	32,800
Wagon-makers, Blacksmiths, and Wheelwrights	...	8	11	9	3	1	...	...	...	31,700
Meat-shops	3	13	9	13	2	...	...	...	7	31,055
Dry-goods	...	...	1	4	1	3	...	...	...	28,200
Brokers and Money-lenders	...	1	...	2	1	1	1	...	1	27,500
Cotton Factory	...	...	...	...	...	...	1	...	...	25,000
Shoe-dealers	1	1	4	9	1	1	...	...	...	23,210
Cotton Gin Proprietors	...	...	...	2	4	1	...	...	2	21,000
Confectioners	1	9	6	4	1	1	...	...	3	19,175
Jewelers	...	2	3	2	1	...	1	...	2	18,850
New and 2nd Hand Clothing	...	1	2	3	2	1	...	...	1	17,050
Bakers	...	3	3	3	1	...	...	...	...	13,250

[Continued]

★ 448 ★

Types of Businesses according to Capital Invested, 1899
[Continued]

KINDS OF BUSINESS	UNDER $100	$100 to $500	$500 to 1000	$1,000 to 2,500	$2,500 to 5,000	$5,000 to 10,000	$10,000 to 50,000	$50,000 and Over	Capital Unknown	Actual Total
Steam Laundries	...	1	2	1	3	...	...	...	1	15,300
Feed-stores	...	1	1	2	1	1	...	...	1	12,700
Fruit-stores	...	2	...	3	1	...	...	...	1	12,000
Machine-shops	...	...	4	3	1	...	...	...	...	11,000
Paper-hanger and Paint-shops	...	1	3	2	...	1	...	...	3	10,750
Brick Contractors	...	...	...	...	...	...	1	...	2	10,000
Second-hand Stores	...	...	...	1	1	1	...	...	...	10,000
Lumber Mills	...	...	...	1	1	1	...	...	...	10,000
Stationers and Newsdealers	...	1	4	2	1	...	...	...	1	8,950
Photographers	...	2	1	3	1	...	...	...	1	7,600
Cigar Man'fc'rs	...	2	...	5	...	...	...	...	1	7,450
Wire-goods Manufactory	...	...	...	1	...	1	...	...	...	7,000
Carpet Man'fct'ry	...	...	...	...	...	1	...	...	...	7,000
Florists	...	...	1	2	1	...	...	...	...	6,200
Hair-goods	...	1	...	3	...	...	...	...	1	5,350
Handle Factory	...	...	...	...	...	1	...	...	...	5,000

Source: "Kinds of Business According to Capital Invested." W.E.B. DuBois, ed., *The Negro in Business*, pp. 16-18.

★ 449 ★

Business Owners and Operators

Types of Businesses according to Number of Years Engaged, 1899

KINDS OF BUSINESS	UNDER 1 YR.	1-3 YR'S	3-5 YR'S	5-10 YR'S	10-20 YR'S	20-30 YR'S	30 and OVER	Actual Av'r'ge
General Merchandise	5	26	21	44	34	9	...	9
Real Estate	1	1	1	7	14	3	1	14
Groceries	26	80	67	110	78	20	2	12
Liquor Saloons	5	20	9	6	15	8	...	7
Banking and Insurance	...	...	...	6	...	...	...	7
Undertakers	2	11	8	11	15	8	1	10
Publishers and Printers	...	7	6	16	10	3	...	8
Market Gardeners, etc.	...	...	...	2	7	1	...	15
Barbers	...	7	8	27	53	46	13	16
Building & Loan Ass'ns	...	...	...	3	2	...	...	10
Builders and Contractors	...	1	13	6	20	8	5	17
Drugs and Medicines	...	12	14	14	5	2	4	8
Hotels	...	5	3	6	7	2	...	8
Fuel-dealers	1	2	4	10	8	8	...	10
Caterers	...	...	1	3	5	4	3	19
Expressmen and Hackmen	...	4	6	15	15	7	1	3
Fish-dealers	...	4	1	2	3	3	...	9
Livery-stables	...	...	6	6	6	3	...	9
Restaurants	2	8	7	19	8	2	1	7
Plumbing and Tin-shops and Hardware-stores	...	1	2	5	3	1	2	12
Green-grocers and Dairymen	...	...	5	8	14	5	2	13
Tailor-shops	1	8	3	10	5	5	1	8

[Continued]

★ 449 ★

Types of Businesses according to Number of Years Engaged, 1899
[Continued]

KINDS OF BUSINESS	UNDER 1 YR.	1-3 YR'S	3-5 YR'S	5-10 YR'S	10-20 YR'S	20-30 YR'S	30 and OVER	Actual Av'r'ge
Furniture, new and second-hand	...	2	1	6	2	...	...	8
Meat-shops	...	7	...	11	3	4	4	12
Dry-goods	...	2	1	3	2	...	...	7
Brokers, etc.,	...	1	...	2	1	...	...	8
Shoe-dealers	1	4	...	1	...	2	1	4
Cotton Gin Proprietors	1	1	1	4	1	...	...	6
Confectioners	1	6	7	7	1	1	...	5
Jewelers	...	3	...	1	5	...	1	11
Clothiers	...	...	1	1	4	...	...	10
Bakers	...	2	2	1	1	4	...	14
Stationers and Newsdealers	...	1	...	2	1	1	...	9
Photographers	...	...	...	3	2	...	...	9
Cigar Manufactures	1	...	...	...	2	...	...	8
All other manufacturers	1	...	...	...	...	1	3	...
Florists	...	...	...	...	1	2	1	17
Dealers in Hair-goods	...	1	...	1	1	1	1	12
All other businesses	...	11	16	28	29	11	5	...

Source: "Kinds of Business According to the Number of Years Engaged." W.E.B. DuBois, ed., *The Negro in Business*, pp. 21-23.

★ 450 ★

Business Owners and Operators

Wholesale Trade: 1972

Industry	Code	1972									
		All firms		With paid employees					Without paid employees		
		Firms (number)	Gross receipts ($1,000)	Firms (number)	Employees (number)	Gross receipts ($1,000)	Average employees per firm (number)	Average receipts per firm ($1,000)	Firms (number)	Gross receipts ($1,000)	Average receipts per firm ($1,000)
WHOLESALE TRADE, TOTAL		2,091	764,178	926	7,691	734,087	8	793	1,165	30,091	26
Wholesale trade – durable goods	50	1,236	449,263	638	4,979	431,210	8	675	598	18,053	30
Motor vehicles and automotive equipment	501	184	76,063	113	851	74,031	8	655	71	2,032	29
Automobiles and other motor vehicles	5012	13	10,512	11	(D)	(D)	(D)	(D)	2	(D)	(D)
Automotive parts and supplies	5013	88	57,371	83	(D)	(D)	(D)	(D)	5	(D)	(D)
Tires and tubes	5014	17	3,538	13	52	3,462	4	266	4	76	19
Motor vehicles and automotive, n.s.k.	501-	66	4,642	6	19	2,922	3	487	60	1,720	29
Furniture and home furnishings	502	96	22,700	26	207	22,011	8	847	70	689	10
Lumber and construction materials	503	92	24,347	31	221	23,511	7	758	61	836	14
Sporting goods, toys, and hobby goods	504	157	36,369	22	336	31,284	15	1,422	135	5,085	38
Metals and minerals, except petroleum	505	88	8,879	14	126	6,873	9	491	74	2,006	27
Electrical goods	506	55	24,201	38	220	23,557	6	620	17	644	38
Electrical apparatus and equipment	5063	28	20,196	24	176	19,973	7	832	4	223	56
Electrical appliances, TV, and radios	5064	3	661	3	7	661	2	220	-	-	-
Electronic parts and equipment	5065	12	2,784	10	(D)	(D)	(D)	(D)	2	(D)	(D)
Electrical goods, n.s.k.	506-	12	560	1	(D)	(D)	(D)	(D)	11	(D)	(D)
Hardware, plumbing and heating equipment	507	63	35,691	40	287	34,872	7	872	23	819	36
Hardware	5072	13	7,015	11	(D)	(D)	(D)	(D)	2	(D)	(D)

[Continued]

★ 450 ★

Wholesale Trade: 1972
[Continued]

Industry	Code	All firms		With paid employees					Without paid employees		
		Firms (number)	Gross receipts ($1,000)	Firms (number)	Employees (number)	Gross receipts ($1,000)	Average employees per firm (number)	Average receipts per firm ($1,000)	Firms (number)	Gross receipts ($1,000)	Average receipts per firm ($1,000)
Plumbing and hydronic heating supplies	5074	14	18,523	14	131	18,523	9	1,323	-	-	-
Warm air heating and air conditioning	5075	7	5,739	7	68	5,739	10	820	-	-	-
Hardware, and plumbing and heating equipment, n.s.k.	507-	29	4,414	8	(D)	(D)	(D)	(D)	21	(D)	(D)
Machinery, equipment, and supplies	508	228	95,721	176	1,172	93,696	7	532	52	2,025	39
Commercial machines and equipment	5081	32	9,090	27	123	8,996	5	333	5	94	19
Construction and mining machinery	5082	6	6,554	5	(D)	(D)	(D)	(D)	1	(D)	(D)
Farm machinery and equipment	5083	28	14,151	22	174	13,900	8	632	6	251	42
Industrial machinery and equipment	5084	19	19,447	18	(D)	(D)	(D)	(D)	1	(D)	(D)
Industrial supplies	5085	3	(D)	2	(D)	(D)	(D)	(D)	1	(D)	(D)
Professional equipment and supplies	5086	15	12,549	14	(D)	(D)	(D)	(D)	1	(D)	(D)
Service establishment equipment	5087	92	25,226	81	449	24,858	6	307	11	368	33
Transportation equipment and supplies	5088	4	(D)	4	(D)	(D)	(D)	(D)	-	-	-
Machinery, equipment, supplies, n.s.k.	508-	29	1,474	3	19	503	6	168	26	971	37
Miscellaneous durable goods	509	273	125,292	178	1,559	121,375	9	682	95	3,917	41
Scrap and waste materials	5093	85	26,577	64	393	25,825	6	404	21	752	36
Jewelry, watches, and precious stones	5094	2	(D)	2	(D)	(D)	(D)	(D)	-	-	-
Durable goods, n.e.c.	5099	186	(D)	112	(D)	(D)	(D)	(D)	74	3,165	43
Wholesale trade-nondurable goods	51	318	300,487	278	2,675	298,537	10	1,074	40	1,950	49
Paper and paper products	511	27	20,612	21	203	20,453	10	974	6	159	27
Drugs, proprietaries, and sundries	512	19	14,266	16	164	14,169	10	886	3	97	32
Apparel, piece goods, and notions	513	24	23,107	23	(D)	(D)	(D)	(D)	1	(D)	(D)
Piece goods	5133	8	9,307	8	60	9,307	8	1,163	-	-	-
Notions and other dry goods	5134	4	(D)	4	(D)	(D)	(D)	(D)	-	-	-
Men's clothing and furnishings	5136	3	(D)	3	(D)	(D)	(D)	(D)	-	-	-
Women's and children's clothing	5137	6	1,558	5	(D)	(D)	(D)	(D)	1	(D)	(D)
Footwear	5139	3	(D)	3	(D)	(D)	(D)	(D)	-	-	-
Groceries and related products	514	132	159,449	120	1,351	158,712	11	1,323	12	737	61
Groceries	5141	8	10,284	8	74	10,284	9	1,286	-	-	-
Frozen foods	5142	4	(D)	4	(D)	(D)	(D)	(D)	-	-	-
Dairy products	5143	7	16,813	7	245	16,813	35	2,402	-	-	-
Poultry and poultry products	5144	6	3,997	5	(D)	(D)	(D)	(D)	1	(D)	(D)
Confectionery	5145	9	2,514	8	(D)	(D)	(D)	(D)	1	(D)	(D)
Fish and seafoods	5146	8	5,327	8	96	5,327	12	666	-	-	-
Meats and meat products	5147	23	47,410	21	(D)	(D)	(D)	(D)	2	(D)	(D)
Fresh fruits and vegetables	5148	24	38,712	22	(D)	(D)	(D)	(D)	2	(D)	(D)
Groceries and related products, n.e.c.	5149	42	29,621	37	202	29,439	5	796	5	182	36
Groceries, n.s.k.	514-	1	(D)	-	-	-	-	-	1	(D)	(D)
Farm-product raw materials	515	16	19,639	12	162	19,303	14	1,609	4	336	84
Livestock	5154	8	13,196	7	(D)	(D)	(D)	(D)	1	(D)	(D)
Farm-product raw materials, n.s.k.	515-	8	6,443	5	(D)	(D)	(D)	(D)	3	(D)	(D)
Chemicals and allied products	516	8	3,827	6	(D)	(D)	(D)	(D)	2	(D)	(D)
Petroleum and petroleum products	517	39	15,511	33	180	15,118	5	458	6	393	66
Beer, wine, and distilled beverages	518	22	30,682	20	(D)	(D)	(D)	(D)	2	(D)	(D)
Miscellaneous nondurable goods	519	31	13,394	27	129	13,328	5	494	4	66	17
Farm supplies	5191	15	3,911	14	(D)	(D)	(D)	(D)	1	(D)	(D)
Tobacco and tobacco products	5194	5	6,432	5	39	6,432	8	1,286	-	-	-
Nondurable goods, n.s.k.	5199	11	3,051	8	(D)	(D)	(D)	(D)	3	(D)	(D)
Wholesale trade, n.s.k.	-	537	14,428	10	37	4,340	4	434	527	10,088	19

Source: "Selected Statistics for Industry for Black-Owned Firms: 1972 and 1969," U.S. Bureau of the Census, 1972 Survey of Minority Business Enterprises, *Minority Owned Businesses—Black*, pp. 20, 22. *Notes:* - Represents zero. D = Withheld to avoid disclosing figures for individual companies.

Insurance Companies

★ 451 ★

Black-Operated Insurance Companies, Part 1. Industrial Legal Reserve Companies, 1949

Name of company	Location	Premium income	Total income	Insurance in force	Increase in insurance in force	Admitted assets
Douglas Life Insurance Co.	New Orleans, La.	$126,001	$139,118	$1,876,113	$-188,054	$152,747
The Federal Life Insurance Co.	Washington, D.C.	165,072	183,259	3,662,691	679,954	344,123
Good Citizens' Life Insurance Co.	New Orleans, La.	769,212	814,071	7,022,111	1,017,803	380,322
Keystone Life Insurance Co.	New Orleans, La.	305,759	324,109	4,092,510	236,293	213,137
Lincoln Industrial Life Insurance Co.	Birmingham, Ala.	105,944	109,097	1,716,274	106,419	111,960
People's Industrial Life Insurance Co.	New Orleans, La.	794,150	863,605	11,252,508	1,684,628	1,135,156
People's Life Insurance Company Inc.	Mobile, Ala.	216,568	223,810	2,901,682	-350,119	205,955
Protective Industrial Insurance Co.	Birmingham, Ala.	286,787	298,548	2,489,901	-255,176	140,740
Protective Mutual Life Insurance Co.	Chicago, Ill.	48,478	53,309	1,503,948	39,310	76,808
Provident Home Industrial Mutual Life Insurance Co.	Philadelphia, Pa.	564,827	585,253	7,782,069	-426,233	541,407
Security Life Insurance Co.	Jackson, Miss.	141,011	143,207	2,040,035	67,049	70,034
Southern Life Insurance Co.	Baltimore, Md.	102,924	146,073	2,133,523	-10,112	377,446
Standard Industrial Life Insurance Co.	New Orleans, La.	426,391	468,621	6,910,684	188,976	743,716
St. John Berchman's Industrial Life Insurance Co.	New Orleans, La.	59,799	61,391	778,048	123,278	55,161
Supreme Industrial Life Insurance Co.	New Orleans, La.	164,944	175,520	2,786,758	000	153,305
Union Protective Assurance Co.	Memphis, Tenn.	476,541	493,992	8,300,020	1,642,740	622,181
Unity Mutual Life Insurance Co.	Chicago, Ill.	451,437	473,107	11,823,492	-487,278	442,273
Victory Industrial Life Insurance Co.	New Orleans, La.	102,774	103,513	1,377,642	134,676	83,824
Total for 18 Industrial Legal Reserve Companies		5,308,619	5,659,603	80,450,009	4,204,154	5,850,295

Source: "Negro Operated Insurance Companies, 1949." Guzman, Jessie Parkhurst, ed. *Negro Year Book: A Review of Events Affecting Negro Life 1952.* New York: William H. Wise, 1952, p. 132. Primary source: Research Department, North Carolina Mutual Life Insurance Company, 1950.

★ 452 ★

Insurance Companies

Black-Operated Insurance Companies, Part 2. Assessment and Mutual Aid Associations, 1949

Name of company	Location	Premium income	Total income	Insurance in force	Increase in insurance in force	Admitted assets
Carver Mutual Insurance Co.	Detroit, Mich.	$36,240[1]	$37,390[1]	$911,020[1]	$391,020[1]	$21,732[1]
Diamond Mutual Insurance Co.	Detroit, Mich.	36,729	38,452	778,676	6,911	39,751
Fireside Mutual Insurance Co.	Columbus, Ohio	152,557	162,043	818,250	17,100	79,844
Keystone Aid Society	Philadelphia, Pa.	19,927	20,039	227,028	-53,200	12,143
Pilot Mutual Insurance Co.	Cleveland, Ohio	45,130[2]	48,229[2]	595,400[2]	-103,930[2]	16,068[2]
Safety Industrial Life Insurance and Sick Benefit Association	New Orleans, La.	118,904	124,706	1,762,929	-21,720	240,772
Superior Life Insurance Society of Michigan	Detroit, Mich.	333,850	343,927	5,272,085	711,530	203,134
Union Mutual Association	Philadelphia, Pa.	73,897	77,347	919,940	92,969	39,690
Western Mutual Insurance Co.	Detroit, Mich.	52,765	56,826	1,506,976	-118,881	92,433

[Continued]

★ 452 ★

Black-Operated Insurance Companies, Part 2. Assessment and Mutual Aid Associations, 1949
[Continued]

Name of company	Location	Premium income	Total income	Insurance in force	Increase in insurance in force	Admitted assets
Wright Mutual Insurance Co.	Detroit, Mich.	194,642	200,176	4,602,415	-654,610	173,562
Totals for 10 Assessment and Mutual Aid Associations		1,064,641	1,109,135	17,394,998	267,189	919,129

Source: "Negro Operated Insurance Companies, 1949." Guzman, Jessie Parkhurst, ed. *Negro Year Book: A Review of Events Affecting Negro Life 1952.* New York: William H. Wise, 1952, p. 132. Primary source: Research Department, North Carolina Mutual Life Insurance Company, 1950. *Notes:* 1. 1948 report. 2. 1947 report.

★ 453 ★

Insurance Companies

Black-Operated Insurance Companies, Part 3. Old Line Legal Reserve Companies, 1949

Name of company	Location	Premium income	Total income	Insurance in force	Increase in insurance in force	Admitted assets
Afro-American Life Insurance Co.	Jacksonville, Fla.	$2,507,329	$2,715,849	$39,776,875	$-123,532	$5,099,919
Atlanta Life Insurance Co.	Atlanta, Ga.	7,323,283	7,892,382	136,315,242	3,131,908	21,490,194
Central Life Insurance	Tampa, Fla.	968,773	1,026,089	16,450,899	476,107	1,347,375
Domestic Life and Accident Insurance Co.	Louisville, Ky.	1,184,853	1,314,609	22,078,399	250,000	2,735,352
The Dunbar Life Insurance Co.	Cleveland, Ohio	375,699	447,058	6,978,345	511,154	637,148
Excelsior Life Insurance Co.	Dallas, Texas	578,956	613,483	9,917,162	387,514	1,493,312
Guaranty Life Insurance Co.	Savannah, Ga.	454,520	507,368	8,435,322	521,667	977,029
Golden State Mutual Life Insurance Co.	Los Angeles, Calif.	3,268,273	3,496,663	50,598,002	3,672,995	4,270,204
The Great Lakes Mutual Life Insurance Co.	Detroit, Mich.	1,049,387	1,123,624	32,147,670	1,175,093	1,996,530
Jackson Mutual Life Insurance Co.	Chicago, Ill.	492,363	564,563	10,122,534	196,774	802,333
Louisiana Life Insurance Co.	New Orleans, La.	827,468	875,978	14,478,246	1,481,065	1,570,022
Mammoth Life and Accident Insurance Co.	Louisville, Ky.	2,106,861	2,219,193	30,258,731	4,540,170	2,596,374
Metropolitan Mutual Assurance Co.	Chicago, Ill.	2,311,124	2,473,733	50,017,269	3,281,768	4,090,821
Mutual Benefit Society of Baltimore	Baltimore, Md.	638,305	713,112	12,713,626	-490,286	1,888,066
North Carolina Mutual Life Insurance Co.	Durham, N.C.	8,766,276	10,159,056	146,241,142	6,372,906	26,250,001
Pilgrim Health and Life Insurance Co.	Augusta, Ga.	2,310,694	2,503,806	46,434,446	1,306,024	5,281,229
Richmond Beneficial Life Insurance Co.	Richmond, Va.	712,707	764,401	11,021,653	184,680	1,474,814
Southern Aid Life Insurance Co. Inc.	Richmond, Va.	797,680	906,622	10,919,245	-15,452	2,547,228
Supreme Liberty Life Insurance Co.	Chicago, Ill.	3,214,522	3,708,743	114,374,189	1,294,481	9,442,051
United Mutual Life Insurance Co.	New York, N.Y.	678,000	784,422	18,215,810	1,515,810	1,768,050
Universal Life Insurance Co.	Memphis, Tenn.	3,251,558	3,540,013	62,781,820	3,999,647	7,304,398
Victory Mutual Life Insurance Co.	Chicago, Ill.	717,223	842,883	22,822,064	1,676,761	3,070,958
Virginia Mutual Benefit Life Insurance Co.	Richmond, Va.	573,188	617,092	9,210,504	-122,307	970,146
Watchtower Life Insurance Co.	Houston, Texas	202,425	228,318	3,947,068	-135,458	455,716
Winston Mutual Life Insurance Co.	Winston-Salem, N.C.	596,331	685,009	9,568,535	180,430	1,728,866
Total for 25 Old Line Legal Reserve Companies		45,907,798	50,724,069	895,824,798	35,269,919	111,288,136
Totals for 18 Industrial Legal Reserve Companies		5,308,619	5,659,603	80,450,009	4,204,154	5,850,295
Totals for 10 Assembly and Mutual Aid Associations		1,064,641	1,109,135	17,394,998	267,189	919,129
Grand totals for 53 companies		52,281,058	57,492,807	993,669,805	39,741,262	118,057,560

Source: "Negro Operated Insurance Companies, 1949." Guzman, Jessie Parkhurst, ed. *Negro Year Book: A Review of Events Affecting Negro Life 1952.* New York: William H. Wise, 1952, p. 132. Primary source: Research Department, North Carolina Mutual Life Insurance Company, 1950.

★ 454 ★

Insurance Companies

Financial Strength of Sixty National Negro Insurance Company Members, 1950

Capital and surplus funds	$30,193,158.56
Insurance in force	1,287,216,075.10
Assets	137,708,766.07
Premium income	54,409,366.62
Total income	60,684,609.45
Benefit payments to policyholders	13,742,016.88
Staff payroll	16,518,714.00
Medical examinations and inspection fees	275,000.00
Bonds	75,463,734.00
Mortgage loans	27,491,928.00

Source: "Financial Strength of Sixty Member Companies, NNIA, 1950." Guzman, Jessie Parkhurst, ed. *Negro Year Book: A Review of Events Affecting Negro Life, 1952.* New York: William H. Wise, 1952, p. 131. Primary source: Murray J. Marvin, Jr., Executive Director, National Negro Insurance Company.

★ 455 ★

Insurance Companies

Insurance Companies Established by Region: 1900-1975

Area	Total number of insurance companies in 1975	Period established				
		1890 to 1909	1910 to 1939	1940 to 1959	1960 to 1969	1970 to 1975
United States	41	8	17	13	2	1
South	34	8	13	12	-	1
North	4	-	3	1	-	-
Northeast	1	-	1	-	-	-
North Central	3	-	2	1	-	-
West	3	-	1	-	2	-

Source: "Black-Owned Life Insurance Companies by Period Established and Region: 1890-1909 to 1970-1975," U.S. Department of Commerce, Bureau of the Census. *The Social and Economic Status of the Black Population in the United States: An Historical View, 1790-1978,* p. 80. Primary source: "Insurance Companies: An Overview," *Black Enterprise Magazine* (June 1977). Published by permission. *Notes:* - Represents zero. Figures exclude Black-owned life insurance companies which may have been established at an earlier time but were no longer in existence in 1975.

★ 456 ★

Insurance Companies

Leading Life Insurance Companies, 1974

Company	Location	Chief Executive	Year Started	Employees	Insurance in Force (Dollars)[1]	Total Assets (Dollars)[1]
North Carolina Mutual Life Insurance Co.	Durham, North Carolina	William J. Kennedy III	1898	1,354	1,729,610,019	135,682,962
Atlanta Life Insurance Co.	Atlanta, Georgia	Jesse Hill, Jr.	1905	1,500	346,225,931	84,493,743
Golden State Mutual Life Insurance Co.	Los Angeles, California	Ivan J. Houston	1925	650	1,436,446,714	48,884,687
Supreme Life Insurance Co. of America	Chicago, Illinois	John H. Johnson	1919	500	1,087,541,959	42,622,723
Universal Life Insurance Co.	Memphis, Tennessee	A.M. Walker, Sr.	1923	820	275,297,915	42,580,791
Chicago Metropolitan Mutual Assurance Co.	Chicago, Illinois	Anderson M. Schweich	1927	460	394,565,888	29,762,154
Mammouth Life & Accident Insurance Co.	Louisville, Kentucky	Julius E. Price, Sr.	1915	219	131,462,730	21,723,092
Pilgrim Health & Life Insurance Co.	Augusta, Georgia	W.S. Hornsby, Jr.	1898	300	91,248,304	14,305,551
Booker T. Washington Insurance Co.	Birmingham, Alabama	Dr. A. G. Gaston	1923	500	112,121,911	11,948,748
Afro-American Life Insurance Co.	Jacksonville, Florida	I.H. Burney II	1901	350	250,612,167	11,199,243
American Woodmen's Life Insurance Co.	Denver, Colorado	James H. Browne	1901	40	27,813,124	9,933,270
United Mutual Life Insurance Co.	New York, New York	Nathaniel Gibbon, Jr.	1933	32	43,926,975	9,032,002
Central Life Insurance Co. of Florida	Tampa, Florida	Edward D. Davis	1922	172	33,197,480	6,751,768
Winston Mutual Life Insurance Co.	Winston-Salem, North Carolina	George E. Hill	1906	150	45,187,800	4,741,704
Peoples Life Insurance Co. of Louisiana	New Orleans, Louisiana	Benjamin J. Johnson	1922	2256	31,576,943	3,993,085
Virginia Mutual Benefit	Richmond,					

[Continued]

★ 456 ★

Leading Life Insurance Companies, 1974

[Continued]

Company	Location	Chief Executive	Year Started	Employees	Insurance in Force (Dollars)[1]	Total Assets (Dollars)[1]
Life Insurance Co.	Virginia	Booker T. Bradshaw	1933	160	19,290,856	3,971,837
Southern Aid Life Insurance Co.	Richmond, Virginia	E.S. Thomas III	1893	105	23,675,378	3,858,719
Protective Industrial Insurance Co. of Alabama	Birmingham, Alabama	Virgil L. Harris	1923	136	26,783,952	3,775,147
Union Protective Life Insurance Co.	Memphis, Tennessee	C.A. Rawls	1933	112	18,499,619	3,137,157
Provident Home Industrial Mutual Life Insurance Co.	Philadelphia, Pennsylvania	Edward W. Robinson, Jr.	1916	117	15,000,000	2,700,000
Golden Circle Life Insurance Co.	Brownsville, Tennessee	C.A. Rawls	1958	81	15,117,484	2,626,186
Wright Mutual Insurance Co.	Detroit, Michigan	Wardell C. Croft	1942	75	14,864,795	2,449,065
Winnfield Life Insurance Co.	Natchitoches, Louisiana	Ben D. Johnson	1936	150	31,360,847	2,306,096
Gertrude Geddes Willis Life Insurance Co.	New Orleans, Louisiana	Maude V. Misshore	1941	60	15,925,780	1,460,874
Unity Burial & Life Insurance Co.	Mobile, Alabama	Roger Allen	1928	100	17,106,216	1,455,565
Christian Benevolent Burial Association	Mobile, Alabama	Pearl J. Madison	1926	75	11,674,445	1,103,842
Southern Life Insurance Co.	Baltimore, Maryland	Owen Wilson	1906	32	4,000, 000	1,066,000
Keystone Life Insurance Co.	New Orleans, Louisiana	George Liopis	1941	70	8,217,896	1,015,341
Security Life Insurance Co. of the South	Jackson, Mississippi	Walter H. Williams, Sr.	1940	81	6,840,774	965,899
Bradford's Industrial Insurance Co.	Birmingham, Alabama	Daniel Kennon, Jr.	1932	25	5,870,507	934,907
National Service Industrial	New Orleans,					

[Continued]

★ 456 ★

Leading Life Insurance Companies, 1974
[Continued]

Company	Location	Chief Executive	Year Started	Employees	Insurance in Force (Dollars)[1]	Total Assets (Dollars)[1]
Life Insurance Co.	Louisiana	Duplain W. Rhodes, Jr.	1948	35	5,942,677	824,511
Purple Shield Life Insurance Co.	Baton Rouge, Louisiana	Homer J. Sheeler, Sr.	1949	100	21,758,114	787,055
Benevolent Life Insurance Co.	Shreveport, Louisiana	Granville L. Smith	1934	95	9,587,848	741,173
Reliable Life Insurance Co.	Monroe, Lousiana	Joseph H. Miller, Jr.	1940	65	10,316,794	649,260
United Fidelity-Victory Life Insurance Co.	New Orleans, Louisiana	Duplain W. Rhodes, Jr.	1971	40	5,900,898	571,606
Majestic Life Insurance Co.	New Orleans, Louisiana	Adam R. Haydel	1947	38	6,097,901	487,109
Lighthouse Life Insurance Co.	Shreveport, Louisiana	Bunyan Jacobs	1945	12	5,394,755	401,747
Lovett's Life & Burial Insurance Co.	Mobile, Alabama	L.M. Lovett	1950	30	4,873,000	384,082
Superior Life Insurance Co.	Ruston, Louisiana	J.K. Haynes	1954	32	6,022,034	248,171
People's Progressive Burial Insurance Co.	Rayville, Louisiana	Marion Gundy Hill	1929	48	4,020,473	197,176
Progressive Industrial Life Insurance Co.	New Orleans, Louisiana	C.L. Dennis	1948	20	1,176,276	186,818

Source: "Life Insurance Companies," *Black Enterprise* 4 (June 1974), pp. 55,57. *Note:* 1. As of December 31, 1973.

Leading Businesses

★ 457 ★

Revenue Profile of Leading Businesses, 1973

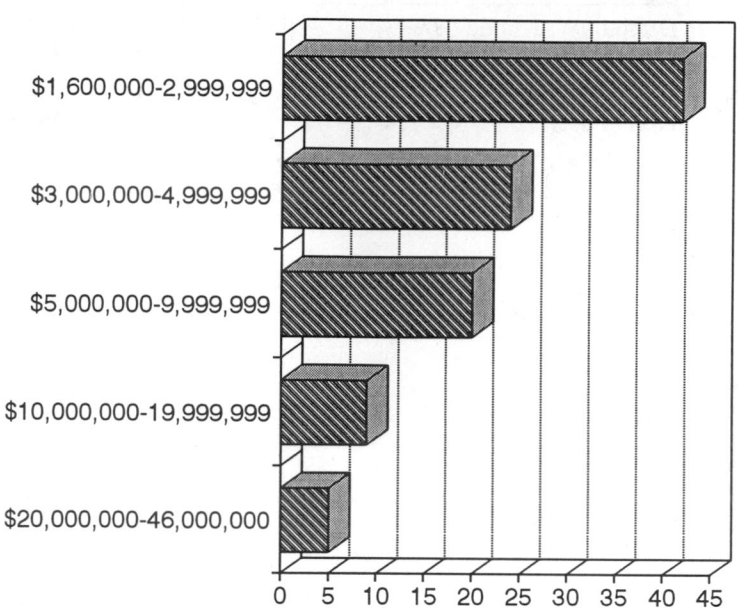

	Number of Companies
$20,000,000-46,000,000	5
$10,000,000-19,999,999	9
$5,000,000-9,999,999	20
$3,000,000-4,999,999	24
$1,600,000-2,999,999	42

Source: "Revenue Profile of the BE 100," *Black Enterprises* 4 (June 1974), p. 31. Published by permission. *Notes:* No surprises emerge when the BE 100 are grouped according to 1973 sales volume-as the volume decreases, the number of companies at that revenue level increases about as might be expected. The height of the bars indicates the median sales volume, while the width indicates the number of companies in each category. (The median sales volume of the five companies above $20 million, for example, is $26 million).

★ 458 ★
Leading Businesses

Top 100 Companies by Economic Sector, 1972-1973

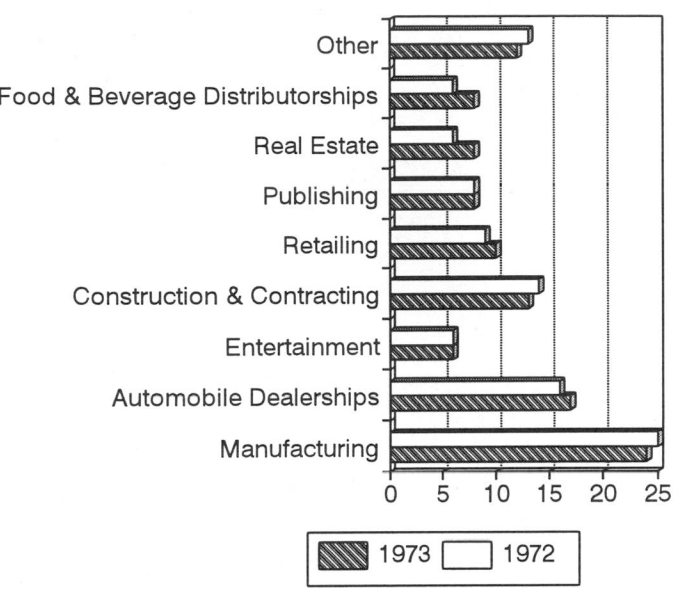

	Companies	
	1973	1972
Manufacturing	24	25
Automobile Dealerships	17	16
Entertainment	6	6
Construction & Contracting	13	14
Retailing	10	9
Publishing	8	8
Real Estate	8	6
Food & Beverage Distributorships	8	6
Other	12	13

Source: "The BE 100 by Economic Sector," *Black Enterprise* 4 (June 1974), p. 45. *Notes:* A 1972 vs 1973 comparison of the BE 100 on a functional basis provides evidence of considerable stability. In four categories of business, the number of BE 100 companies did not change at all, and in none of the others did it change by more than one. This breakdown also shows that the manufacturing, entertainment and real estate companies made the strongest contributions to the growth of the BE 100 in 1973. As might be expected, on the other hand, automobile dealers and construction firms showed less growth and in fact lagged behind the pace of inflation. (The total of companies on this graph slightly exceeds 100 for both 1972 and 1973, because several of the BE 100 are engaged in more than one of the categories of business shown here).

★ 459 ★

Leading Businesses

Top 100 Companies with Black Proprietors, 1973

Company	Location	Chief Executive(s)	Business	Year Started	Employees	1973 Sales[1]
Motown Industries	Los Angeles, California	Berry Gordy, Jr.	Entertainment	1959	375	46.0
Johnson Publishing Co., Inc.	Chicago, Illinois	John H. Johnson	Publishing	1942	245	27.8
Fedeo Food Corp.	New York, New York	J. Bruce Liewellyn	Supermarkets	1969	480	26.0
Johnson Products, Co., Inc.	Chicago, Illinois	George E. Johnson	Cosmetics manufacturing	1954	400	25.0
The Stax Organization	Memphis, Tennessee	Al Bell	Record production	1959	175	20.0
F.W. Eversley & Co., Inc.	New York, New York	F. W. Eversley, Jr.	Construction	1964	60	18.9
Jenkins Electric Co. Inc.	Brooklyn, New York	William E. Jenkins	Electrical contracting	1946	250	17.6
H.G. Parks, Inc.	Baltimore, Maryland	Henry G. Parks, Jr.	Sausage & pork products manufacturing	1951	296	15.0
Slvart Mortgage Corp.	Chicago, Illinois	Dempsey J. Travis	Mortgaging, banking	1960	16	15.0
Garland Foods, Inc.	Dallas, Texas	Mildren M. Montgomery	Meat processing	1970	155	14.2
Al Johnson Cadillac, Inc.	Chicago, Illinois	A. W. Johnson, Sr.	Automobile dealership	1971	97	13.8
TAW International Leasing, Inc.	New York, New York	Thomas A. Wood	Equipment leasing	1969	150	13.6
Capital City Liquor Co.	Washington, D.C.	Chester C. Carter	Wine & liquor distributorship	1970	55	11.5
Webb, Brooks & Brooker, Inc.	New York, New York	Eugene H. Webb	Real estate management	1969	20	10.0
Wright Ford Sales, Inc.	Marina del Rey, California	A. Gordon Wright	Automobile dealership	1968	76	9.7
Big V Supermarkets	Washington, D.C.	Joseph Yeats	Supermarkets	1971	100	8.5
E.G. Bowman Co., Inc.	Brooklyn, New York	Ernesta G. Procope	Insurance brokerage	1953	18	8.2
Myers Century Chevrolet, Inc.	Upper Darby, Pennsylvania	Robert L. Myers, Jr.	Automobile dealership	1971	60	8.2
H.J. Russell & Co.	Atlanta, Georgia	Herman J. Russell	General contracting	1959	300	8.15
Syphax Enterprise Inc.	Arlington,	William T. Syphax,	General contracting,			

[Continued]

★ 459 ★

Top 100 Companies with Black Proprietors, 1973
[Continued]

Company	Location	Chief Executive(s)	Business	Year Started	Employees	1973 Sales[1]
	Virginia	Margarita R. Syphax	real estate management	1953	53	8.1
G.E. Wash Constrction, Inc.	Detroit, Michigan	Glen Wash	General contracting	1967	24	8.0
The Great Philadelphia Trading Co., Ltd.	Philadelphia, Pennsylvania	Kenny Gamble	Record production, music publishing	1967	25	8.0
Conyers Ford, Inc.	Detroit, Michigan	Nathan G. Conyers	Automobile dealership	1970	75	7.7
Drummond Distributing, Inc.	Compton, California	Lance E. Drummond	Liquor distributorship	1969	34	7.5
Watis Manufacturing Corp.	Lynwood, California	Mark E. Rivers, Jr.	Metal products manufacturing	1966	347	7.5
All-Pro Enterprise, Inc.	Pittsburgh, Pennsylvania	Brady Keys, Jr.	Fast-food franchising	1967	685	7.3
The Kenwood Co., Inc.	New York, New York	Kenneth N. Sherwood	Furnishings & liquor retailing real estate management	1965	60	7.2
Porterfield Wilson Pontiac, Inc.	Detroit, Michigan	Proterfield Wilson	Automobile dealership	1972	56	6.6
Tuesday Publications, Inc.	Chicago Illinois	W. Leonard Evans, Jr.	Publising	1965	45	6.1
Wilson-McIntosh Buick-Opal, Inc.	Washigton, D.C.	Maurice McIntosh, Joseph I. Wilson	Automobile dealership	1970	65	6.0
VIP Lincoln Mercury, Inc.	New Rochelle, New York	Daniel E. Brown	Automobile dealership	1967	22	5.6
Bill Nelson Chevrolet, Inc.	Richmond, California	William W. Nelson	Automobile dealership	1969	58	5.2
K C Dodge, Inc.	San Francisco, California	Todd S. Cochran, Roy J. Knight	Automobile dealership	1968	37	5.1
Sengstacke Enterprise, Inc.	Chicago, Illinois	John H. Sengstacke	Publishing	1905	150	5.0
Parker House Sausage Co.	Chicago, Illinois	Daryl F. Grisham	Sausage manufacturing	1921	115	4.8
Super Pride/Hilton Court, Inc.	Balitmore, Maryland	Charles Burns	Supermarkets, pharmaries	1970	98	4.75
Chioke Internatinoal Corp. Inc.	New York, New York	Christopher Chioke	Automotive export	1970	30	4.5
Willie Davis Distributing Co.	Los Angeles, California	Willie D. Davis	Beer distributorship	1970	30	4.5
Sussex Records, Inc.	Los Angeles, California	Clarence Avant	Record production, music publishing	1969	20	4.4

[Continued]

413

★ 459 ★

Top 100 Companies with Black Proprietors, 1973
[Continued]

Company	Location	Chief Executive(s)	Business	Year Started	Employees	1973 Sales[1]
Barrett Group Corp.	Brooklyn, New York	Lieweilyn Barrett	Electronic manufacturing	1968	120	4.1
Joe Louis Milk, Co., Inc.	Chicago, Illinois	Helen Thornton Jones	Dairy product wholesaling	1935	20	4.1
Electorque Associates, Inc.	Brooklyn, New York	David L. Blaine	Electrical contracting	1968	108	4.0
Flesta Lincoln Mercury, Inc.	Queens Village, New York	William J. Phillips	Automobile dealership	1969	28	4.0
Robert Martin Constructino Co., Inc.	Chicago, Illinois	Robert Martin	Construction	1946	35	4.0
Travis Realty Co.	Chicago, Illinois	Dempsey J. Travis	Real estate management	1949	20	4.0
Vassail Motor, Inc.	Philadelphia, Pennsylvania	Ivan Vassail	Automobile dealership	1969	42	4.0
TWO/Hillman's, Inc.	Chicago, Illinois	Lawrence W. Carroll	Supermarkets	1970	55	3.8
Analytic Construction Co., Inc.	Utica, New York	Ronald O. Rohadfox	General contracting	1968	15	3.7
Progress Aerospace Enterprise, Inc.	Philadelphia, Pennsylvania	Frederick E. Miller	Sysbystem manufacturing	1968	212	3.65
Friendly Chrysler-Plymouth Inc.	Los Angeles, California	Herbert Stephenson	Automobile dealership	1970	45	3.6
Tinsley Buick-Opel, Inc.	Redwood City, California	Donald P. Tinsley	Automobile dealership	1971	35	3.5
Horce Noble Lincoln Mercury, Inc.	Chicago, Illinois	Horace Noble	Automobile dealership	1971	38	3.25
Magnificent Products, Inc.	Los Angeles, California	Wilbur Jackson	Cosmetics manufacturing	1965	37	3.2
California Golden Oak Products Inc.	Los Angeles, California	W.M. Alexander, Jr.	Furniture manufacturing	1968	130	3.1
Clipper International Corp.	Detroit, Michigan	Samuel Gorman	Component manufacturing	1962	80	3.1
Ault Inc.	Minneapolis, Minnesota	Luther T. Prince	System & component manufacturing	1961	170	3.0
R.A. Banks & Co.	Atlanta, Georgia	R.A. Banks	General contracting	1965	18	3.0
Renmuth, Inc.	Detroit, Michigan	Robert Renfroe	Metal fabrication	1970	120	3.0
Afro-American Co.	Baltimore, Maryland	John Murphy	Publishing	1892	205	2.9

[Continued]

★ 459 ★

Top 100 Companies with Black Proprietors, 1973
[Continued]

Company	Location	Chief Executive(s)	Business	Year Started	Employees	1973 Sales[1]
James Produce Co.	Dumbar, W. Virginia	C.H. James II	Food wholesaling	1883	22	2.85
Lawndale Packaging Corp.	Chicago, Illinois	William Franklin, Jr.	Container manufacturing	1970	65	2.85
AVI Manufacturing Inc.	Gardena, California	E.E. Barrington	Subassemly manufacturing	1971	175	2.8
Lowery Distributing Co., Inc.	Chicago, Illinois	Mannie A. Lowery, Jr.	Beer distributing	1969	19	2.8
Roberts Motels, Inc.	Chicago, Illinois	Herman Roberts	Motel chain	1961	200	2.8
National Black Network	New York, New York	Eugene D. Jackson	Network radio programming	1972	51	2.75
Alliance Food Corp.	Los Angeles, California	Robert E. Bell	Restaurants	1970	200	2.6
Amnews Inc.	New York, New York	Clarence B. Jones	Publishing	1908	130	2.6
Glopack Corp.	Passaic, New Jersey	Harold Martin	Container manufactuing	1966	50	2.6
Bowers Realty & Investment Co.	Detroit, Michigaan	France O. Bowers	Real estate	1968	30	2.5
Earl G. Graves Publishing Co., Inc.	New York, New York	Earl G. Graves	Publishing	1970	38	2.4
The Hollingsworth Group, Inc.	New York, New York	Edward Lewis	Publishing	1969	32	2.4
Ozanne Construction Co., Inc.	Cleveland, Ohio	Leroy Ozanne	General contracting	1956	12	2.4
Progress Laboratories, Inc.	Los Angeles, California	Clarence B. Lofton	Pharmaceutical manufacturing	1968	63	2.4
Trans-Bay Engineers & Builders, Inc.	Oakland, California	Ray Dones	General contracting	1967	36	2.4
Central News-Wave Publications, Inc.	Los Angeles, California	Chester L. Washington	Publishing	1971	80	2.35
Lance Investigation Service, Inc.	Bronx, New York	Ralph V. Johnson	Security services	1962	350	2.25
Ebony Oil Corp.	Jamaica, New York	Lawrence J. Cormier	Fuel&oil retailing	1954	47	2.2
Summit Laboratories, Inc.	Chicago, Illinois	H. Ray Welch, Jr.	Cosmetics manufacturing	1957	70	2.2
D&H Tire Service	Kansas City, Kansas	Luther D. White	Tire sales & service	1965	37	2.1

[Continued]

★ 459 ★

Top 100 Companies with Black Proprietors, 1973
[Continued]

Company	Location	Chief Executive(s)	Business	Year Started	Employees	1973 Sales[1]
Quinco Manufacturing Corp.	Calumet Park, Illinois	Monroe L. Hutt	Metal products manufacturing	1969	65	2.1
Southend Janitorial Supply Co., Inc.	Los Angeles, California	John A. Leday	Janitorial equipment manufacturing	1962	7	2.1
All-Stainless, Inc.	Boston, Massachusetts	Eugene V. Roundtree	Industrial steel distributorship	1952	30	2.0
Fighton, Inc.	Rochester, New York	William M. McGhee, Jr.	Electrical equipment & metal product manufacturing	1968	108	2.0
Hi-Pro Foods, Inc.	Los Angeles, California	R.E. Collins	Macaroni manufacturing	1967	25	2.0
Hubert Enterprises, Inc.	Newark, New Jersey	Frank Hubert	Manufacturing consulting, radio broadcasting, food brokerage	1969	61	2.0
A. McFaddin Pontiac Inc.	Los Angeles, California	William A. McDowell	Automobile dealership	1967	22	2.0
Northtown Big Star	Nashville, Tennessee	Flem B. Otey III	Supermarkets	1904	40	2.0
Vanguard Volkswagen	Pagedale, Missouri	James E. Hurt, Jr.	Automobile dealership	1970	22	2.0
The BLK Group, Inc.	Washington, D.C.	Kenneth R. Vallis	Management consulting	1969	25	1.9
IGT Travel, Inc.	Jamaica, New York	Earl Jackson	Travel agency	1967	7	1.9
Clean-Rite Maintenance Co., Inc.	Washington, D.C.	Nathaniel D. Williams	Janitorial & maintenance services	1969	167	1.85
Blatche's Food Inc.	Hartford, Connecticut	Emerson Blatche	Supermarket	1972	23	1.8
Menelek Construction Co., Inc.	Buffalo, New York	Emanuel I. Humes	General construction	1971	25	1.8
Optimum Computer Sytems, Inc.	New York, New York	Wilbert F. Boyce	Management consulting	1968	60	1.7
Competition Motors Ltd. Inc.	Chicago, Illinois	Robert P. Neal	Automobile dealership	1966	22	1.65
Henderson Travel Service	Atlanta, Georgia	Jacob R. Henderson	Travel agency	1954	15	1.65
Behrmann Iron Works, Inc.	Brooklyn, New York	Serge Behrmann	Steel fabrication & erection	1972	22	1.6
Builders Urban Development Co., Inc.	Tucson, Arizona	Nathaniel S. Russell	Constructing engineering & contracting	1969	5	1.6
George Christian Electric	Portland,					

[Continued]

★ 459 ★

Top 100 Companies with Black Proprietors, 1973
[Continued]

Company	Location	Chief Executive(s)	Business	Year Started	Employees	1973 Sales[1]
Co., Inc.	Oregon	George Christian	Electrial contracting	1972	20	1.6
JWM Corp.	Philadelphia, Pennsylvania	J.J. Williams	Electronic manufacturing	1969	150	1.6

Source: "The Top 100," *Black Enterprise* 4 (June 1974), pp. 35, 37, 39, 41. *Note:* 1. Million dollars.

Chapter 3
CRIME, LAW ENFORCEMENT, AND LEGAL JUSTICE

Crime

★ 460 ★

Black Crime Victims in Selected Cities, 1972 and 1973

(Rate per 1,000 population age 12 and over).

Year of survey	Selected Cities	All crimes against persons	Crimes of violence				Crimes of theft	
			Total	Rape	Robbery	Assault	Personal larceny with contact	Personal larceny without contact
a	Atlanta	115	38	2	15	21	13	64
a	Baltimore	120	58	2	30	26	15	47
b	Boston	171	70	2[1]	32	36	26	75
b	Buffalo	128	57	2	22	34	7	64
a	Chicago	163	72	4	39	29	18	72
b	Cincinnati	170	65	1	17	46	8	96
a	Cleveland	146	66	2	34	30	12	67
a	Dallas	96	34	3	11	20	4	58
a	Denver	182	65	2	14	49	8	110
a	Detroit	173	78	2	40	36	11	83
b	Houston	178	58	3	25	31	8	112
a	Los Angeles	166	79	5	29	45	6	81
b	Miami	88	39	2[1]	16	22	7	42
b	Milwaukee	203	74	3	25	46	11	118
b	Minneapolis	206	66	4[1]	19	44	7[1]	133
a	Newark	105	52	2	37	13	18	34
b	New Orleans	116	40	3	16	21	11	65
a	New York	81	42	1	30	11	11	27
b	Oakland	129	44	2	15	27	7	77
a	Philadelphia	179	88	2	44	42	18	73
b	Pittsburgh	139	61	3	20	39	11	67
a	Portland	219	67	2	16	49	8	143
b	San Diego	173	47	1[1]	10	36	2[1]	124
b	San Francisco	174	64	4[1]	23	36	16	94

[Continued]

★ 460 ★

Black Crime Victims in Selected Cities, 1972 and 1973
[Continued]

Year of survey	Selected Cities	All crimes against persons	Crimes of violence				Crimes of theft	
			Total	Rape	Robbery	Assault	Personal larceny with contact	Personal larceny without contact
a	St. Louis	87	36	2	18	16	8	44
b	Washington, D.C.	73	26	1	16	9	10	37

Source: "Personal Victimization Rates for Black Residents of Selected Cities, by Type of Crime: 1972 and 1973," *Current Population Reports,* Series P-23, No. 54. *The Social and Economic Status of the Black Population in the United States, 1974,* 1975, p. 169. Primary source: U.S. Department of Justice, Law Enforcement Assistance Administration. *Notes:* (A) Survey covers year 1972. (B) Survey covers year 1973. Statistics on criminal victimization for the 26 cities were gathered as part of the National Crime Panel by the Bureau of the Census for the Department of Justice, Law Enforcement Assistance Administration. The victimization rate for crimes against persons is a measure of occurrence among population groups at risk and is computed on the basis of the number of victimizations per 1,000 population, age 12 and over. 1. Estimate based on about 10 or fewer sample cases is statistically unreliable.

★ 461 ★
Crime

Family Income of Crime Victims by Type of Crime, 1973

(Rate per 1,000 population 12 years and over).

Family income, race of victim	All crimes against persons	Crimes of violence				Crimes of theft
		Total	Rape and attempted rape	Robbery and attempted robbery	Assault	
BLACK						
Under $3,000	133	63	3	16	44	70
$3,000 to $7,499	130	49	2^1	14	33	81
$7,500 to $9,999	115	29	1^1	11	17	86
$10,000 to $14,999	142	37	-	16	21	104
$15,000 and over	151	32	2^1	12	18	119
WHITE						
Under $3,000	127	46	2	10	34	80
$3,000 to $7,499	115	37	1	7	29	78
$7,500 to $9,999	124	33	1	6	26	91
$10,000 to $14,999	128	30	1	5	24	98
$15,000 and over	145	27	1	4	22	118

Source: "Victimization Rates for Crimes Against Persons, by Family Income of Victims by Type of Crime: 1973, *Current Population Reports,* Series P-23, No. 54. *The Social and Economic Status of the Black Population in the United States, 1974,* 1975, p. 166. Primary source: U.S. Department of Justice, Law Enforcement Assistance Administration. *Notes:* - Rounds to zero. Income refers to annual income at the time of the survey interview. 1. Estimate based on 10 or fewer sample cases is statistically unreliable.

★ 462 ★

Crime

Homicide: Homicide Victims in Atlanta, 1938-1945

Year	Negro Victims	White Victims	Coefficient of Frequency For Negroes
1938	94	13	14.5
1939	90	9	20.0
1940	100	10	20.0
1941	107	9	23.8
1942	76	8	19.0
1943	42	12	7.0
1944	50	20	5.0
1945	76	15	5.1
Totals	635	86	14.8

Source: "Racial Distribution of Homicides in Atlanta 1938-1945," *Negro Year Book: A Review of Events Affecting Negro Life, 1941-1946,* 1947, p. 314. Primary source: Crime Bureau of the Police Department, Atlanta, Georgia.

★ 463 ★

Crime

Male and Female Victims of "Serious" Crimes, 1965 to 1966

(Rates per 100,000 population).

Type of serious crime	Negro and other races		White	
	Male	Female	Male	Female
Crimes of violence (homicide, rape, robbery, and aggravated assault)	523	849	394	164
Burglary and larceny (over $50)	2,393	1,157	2,446	579
Vehicle theft	348	231	231	114

Source: "Victims of Serious Crimes, by Sex: 1965 to 1966," Current Population Reports, Special Studies, Series P-23, No. 38, *The Social and Economic Status of the Black Population in the United States, 1970,* 1970, p. 102. Primary source: President's Commission on Law Enforcement and Administration of Justice.

★ 464 ★

Crime

Number of Specific Male Felony Offenses, 1940

OFFENSE	Total	Native white	Foreign born white	Negro	Other races
Total	60,083	40,028	2,624	16,706	725
Murder	1,595	663	87	826	19
Manslaughter	1,327	600	56	650	21
Robbery	5,273	3,618	115	1,515	25
Aggravated assault	3,108	1,269	118	1,663	58
Burglary	12,137	7,917	232	3,992	96
Larceny, except auto theft	10,239	6,771	239	3,093	136
Auto theft	3,476	2,977	55	412	32
Embezzlement and fraud	1,954	1,720	100	129	5
Stolen property	513	331	25	155	2
Forgery	5,167	4,320	162	615	70
Rape	1,867	1,315	107	404	41
Commercialized vice	406	314	26	56	10
Other sex offenses	1,207	954	94	142	17
Violating drug laws	1,532	907	137	397	91
Carrying and possessing weapons	277	153	9	111	4
Nonsupport or neglect	495	424	25	45	1
Violating liquor laws	6,401	3,356	311	2,171	63
Violating traffic laws	296	220	10	65	1
All other offenses	2,813	1,699	716	365	33

Source: "Male Felony Prisoners Received from Court, by Race and Nativity, by Offense: 1940," *The Negro Handbook, 1944,* 1944, p. 164. Primary source: Bureau of the Census.

★ 465 ★

Crime

Offender/Victim Relationships by Type of Crime, 1973

Subject	All crimes against persons[1]	Crimes of violence				Personal larceny with contact
		Total	Rape	Robbery	Assault	
BLACK VICTIMS						
Perceived Race of Offender by Victim						
All offenders...thousands	519	468	26	83	359	51
Percent[2]	100	100	100	100	100	100
Black	87	88	89	93	87	71

[Continued]

★ 465 ★

Offender/Victim Relationships by Type of Crime, 1973
[Continued]

Subject	All crimes against persons[1]	Crimes of violence				Personal larceny with contact
		Total	Rape	Robbery	Assault	
White	8	8	11	-	10	13
Relation of Offender to Victim						
All offenders...thousands	519	468	26	83	359	51
Percent	100	100	100	100	100	100
Stranger	51	47	74	74	39	84
Not stranger	49	53	26	26	61	16
WHITE VICTIMS						
Perceived Race of Offender by Victim						
All offenders...thousands	3,060	2,916	96	358	2,463	144
Percent[2]	100	100	100	100	100	100
Black	21	20	31	41	16	43
White	74	75	62	52	79	41
Relation of Offender to Victim						
All offenders...thousands	3,060	2,916	96	358	2,463	144
Percent	100	100	100	100	100	100
Stranger	59	57	71	76	54	91
Not stranger	41	43	29	24	46	9

Source: "Perceived Race of Offender and the Relationship of Offender to Victim by Type of Crime: 1973," Current Population Reports, Special Studies, Series P-23, No. 54. *The Social and Economic Status of the Black Population in the United States, 1974*, 1975, p. 167. Primary source: U.S. Department of Justice, Law Enforcement Assistance Administration. *Notes:* - Represents zero. Includes only crimes committed by a single offender. 1. Excludes crimes of personal larceny without contact. 2. Includes other racial groups and "don't' know," not shown separately.

★ 466 ★
Crime

Offender/Victim Relationships in Selected Cities, 1967

Subject and race	Type of crime--				
	Homicide	Aggravated assault	Rape	Armed robbery	Unarmed robbery
Total crimes	3,274	75,198	7,908	54,942	51,255
Race of victims and assailants					
Percent total	100	100	100	100	100
Negro victims	70	68	60	40	38
With Negro assailants	66	66	60	38	37
With white assailants	4	2	-	2	1
White victims	31	32	41	60	62
With Negro assailants	7	8	11	47	44
With white assailants	24	24	30	13	18

Source: "Victims and Assailants by Type of Crime in 17 Cities: 1967," Current Population Reports, Special Studies, Series P-23, No. 38. *The Social and Economic Status of the Black Population in the United States, 1970*, 1970, p. 103. Primary source: National Commission of Causes and Prevention of Violence. *Notes:* - Represents zero. The 17 cities included are: Atlanta, Boston, Chicago, Cleveland, Dallas, Denver, Detroit, Los Angeles, Miami, Minneapolis, New Orleans, New York City, Philadelphia, St. Louis, San Francisco, Seattle, Washington, D.C.

★ 467 ★
Crime

Offender/Victim Relationships in Violent Crimes, 1973

Victim's relationship to offender	Race of victim	
	Black	White
Total, crimes of violence...thousands	468	2,916
Percent	100	100
Family members	11	8
Spouse or exspouse	6	5
Parent, own child, sibling	2	2
Other relative	4	2
Acquaintances	42	34
Close friend[1]	27	18
Casual acquaintance	15	17
Stranger	47	57

Source: "Crimes of Violence Against Persons by Relationship of Offender to Victim: 1973," Current Population Reports, Special Studies, Series P-23, No. 54. *The Social and Economic Status of the Black Population in the United States, 1974*, 1975, p. 168. Primary source: U.S. Department of Justice, Law Enforcement Assistance Administration. *Notes:* Includes only crimes of violence—rape, robbery, and assault—committed by a single offender. 1. Also includes non-family members (lodger) living in same household.

★ 468 ★

Crime

Offenses: Offenses of Male Prisoners, 1945

Type of Institution and Offense	Total	White	Negro
All institutions	40,852	27,911	12,428
Murder	1,281	529	737
Manslaughter	1,001	423	555
Robbery	3,479	2,045	1,420
Aggravated assault	2,403	1,099	1,265
Burglary	7,168	4,659	2,454
Larceny, except auto theft	7,009	4,735	2,210
Auto theft	3,114	2,608	466
Embezzlement and fraud	1,130	1,000	124
Stolen property	424	275	148
Forgery	2,373	1,969	374
Rape	1,868	1,235	603
Commercialized vice	242	183	57
Other sex offenses	1,060	908	138
Violating drug laws	990	664	238
Carrying and possessing weapons	190	97	91
Nonsupport or neglect	419	359	55
Violating liquor laws	2,062	1,316	735
Violating traffic laws	92	64	28
Violating National Defense laws	2,303	1,841	412
Other offenses	2,244	1,902	318
Federal institutions	11,399	8,387	2,761
Murder	130	45	79
Manslaughter	77	38	33
Robbery	133	101	30
Aggravated assault	263	112	134
Burglary	213	158	42
Larceny, except auto theft	1,333	890	427
Auto theft	1,266	1,114	142
Embezzlement and fraud	521	461	56
Stolen property	143	105	38
Forgery	560	368	186

Source: "Male Felony Prisoners Received from Court, by Type of Institutions, Offense, and Race, for the United States: 1945," *The Negro Handbook, 1949,* 1949, p. 87. Primary source: *U.S. Bureau of the Census. Notes:* Excludes statistics for Michigan, Georgia and Mississippi. Total includes "Other Races," for which figures are not shown in table.

★ 469 ★
Crime

Offenses: Prisoner and Juvenile Delinquent Offenses, by Region, 1910

OFFENSE	PRISONERS AND JUVENILE DELINQUENTS COMMITTED IN 1910											
	United States			The South			The North			The West		
	Total	Negro		Total	Negro		Total	Negro		Total	Negro	
		Number	Percent		Number	Percent		Number	Percent		Number	Percent
All offenses	493,934	108,268	21.9	130,684	77,022	58.9	305,008	29,145	9.6	57,255	1,858	3.2
Grave homicide	967	512	56.0	637	474	74.4	222	58	26.1	94	8	2
Lesser homicide	1,935	949	49.0	1,195	808	67.6	576	129	22.3	152	10	6.6
Assault	22,670	9,324	41.1	8,907	6,784	76.2	12,010	2,381	19.8	1,717	130	7.6
Robbery	1,728	575	33.3	443	318	71.8	1,008	225	22.3	241	16	6.6
Burglary	8,922	2,725	30.5	2,839	1,954	68.8	4,791	655	13.7	1,145	59	5.2
Larceny	42,716	13,591	31.8	13,615	9,865	72.5	24,302	3,527	14.5	4,704	169	3.6
Fraud	8,936	1,484	16.6	2,316	1,076	46.5	5,662	380	6.7	889	23	2.6
Forgery	2,156	315	14.6	639	244	38.2	1,028	53	5.2	447	7	1.6
Rape	1,480	380	25.7	372	247	66.4	955	122	12.8	144	6	4.2
Prostitution and fornication	6,450	2,166	33.6	1,539	982	63.8	4,620	1,132	24.5	291	52	17.9
Drunkenness and disorderly conduct	262,905	41,760	15.9	57,763	29,424	50.9	176,417	11,735	6.7	28,725	601	2.1
Vagrancy	50,302	8,256	16.4	8,399	4,794	57.1	30,429	2,970	9.8	11,474	492	4.3
Violating liquor laws	7,713	2,458	31.9	3,980	2,053	51.6	2,921	376	12.9	755	22	2.9
Malicious mischief and trespass	10,145	2,186	21.5	3,247	1,657	51.0	6,534	500	7.7	354	19	5.4
Offenses peculiar to children	7,803	839	10.8	1,105	230	20.8	6,084	574	9.4	614	35	5.7
Offense ill-defined or not reported	7,909	2,229	28.2	3,278	1,864	56.9	2,576	328	12.7	1,990	27	1.4
All others	49,197	18,489	37.6	20,410	14,248	69.8	24,873	4,000	16.1	3,510	182	5.2

Source: [Untitled Table], *Negro Population, 1790-1915*, 1918, p. 438. Primary source: U.S. Bureau of the Census. *Negro Population, 1790-1915.* Washington, D.C.: Government Printing Office, 1918. *Notes:* 1. Includes figures of the United States penitentiaries, which are not shown separately in this table. 2. Per cent not shown where base is less than 100.

★ 470 ★
Crime

Percentage Distribution of Male Felony Offenses in the South, 1940

OFFENSE	Native white	Negro
Total	100.0	10.0
Murder	3.2	6.8
Manslaughter	3.2	5.2
Robbery	8.2	6.4
Aggravated assault	5.7	13.4
Burglary	24.8	23.3
Larceny, except auto theft	22.9	22.6
Auto theft	3.1	1.6
Embezzlement and fraud	3.0	0.8
Stolen property	1.1	0.9
Forgery	10.6	2.6
Rape	2.6	2.3
Commercialized vice	0.3	0.1

[Continued]

★ 470 ★

Percentage Distribution of Male Felony Offenses in the South, 1940

[Continued]

OFFENSE	Native white	Negro
Other sex offenses	1.1	0.5
Violating drug laws	0.6	0.3
Carrying and possessing weapons	0.1	0.4
Nonsupport or neglect	1.2	0.4
Violating liquor laws	3.3	4.0
Violating traffic laws	0.9	0.5
All other offenses	4.3	2.5
Number of offenders	10,431	9,292

Source: "Percentage Distribution, by Offense, of Native White and Negro Male Felony Prisoners Received from Court, in 15 Southern States: 1940," *The Negro Handbook, 1944,* 1944, p. 164. Primary source: Bureau of the Census.

★ 471 ★

Crime

Race, Age, and Gender of Crime Victims, by Type of Crime, 1973

(Rate per 1,000 population 12 years and over).

Sex, age, and race of victim	All crimes against persons	Crimes of violence				Crimes of theft
		Total	Rape and attempted rape	Robbery and attempted robbery	Assault and attempted assault	
BLACK						
Total	132	47	2	14	31	85
Sex						
Male	161	59	-	23	36	102
Female	108	37	3	7	26	71
Age						
12 to 19 years	191	76	3	17	56	115
20 to 34 years	169	52	3	15	34	116
35 to 49 years	102	37	0	14	23	64
50 to 64 years	61	20	-	11	9	41
65 years and over	48	18	-	12	6	30
WHITE						
Total	127	32	1	6	26	95

[Continued]

★ 471 ★

Race, Age, and Gender of Crime Victims, by Type of Crime, 1973
[Continued]

Sex, age, and race of victim	All crimes against persons	Crimes of violence				Crimes of theft
		Total	Rape and attempted rape	Robbery and attempted robbery	Assault and attempted assault	
Sex						
Male	151	45	-	9	36	107
Female	105	21	2	3	16	84
Age						
12 to 19 years	245	62	2	10	51	182
20 to 34 years	162	47	2	7	38	115
35 to 49 years	95	20	-	4	16	75
50 to 64 years	61	12	-	4	8	49
65 years and over	30	8	-	4	3	22

Source: "Victimization Rates for Crimes Against Persons, by Sex and Age of Victims by Type of Crime: 1973," Current Population Reports, Special Studies, Series P-23, No. 54. The Social and Economic Status of the Black Population in the United States, 1974, 1975, p. 165. Primary source: U.S. Department of Justice, Law Enforcement Assistance Administration. Note: - Represents or rounds to zero.

★ 472 ★

Crime

Rates by Race: Racial "Criminality" in 1904

It is interesting to find that the Negro has a relatively lower percentage of crime that the emigrant races which are now coming to this country. The commitments to prison in 1904 per 1,000 of certain nationalities were: Mexicans, 4.7; Italians, 4.4; Austrians, 3.6; French, 3.4; Canadians, 3.0; Russians, 2.8; Polies, 2.7; Negroes, 2.7.

It is of still greater interest to compare the commitments for rape. In 1904 the commitments for this crime per 100,000 of the total population were: all whites, 0.6; colored, 1.8; Italians, 5.3; Mexicans, 4.8; Austrians, 3.2; Hungarians, 2.0; French, 1.9; Russians, 1.9; the per cent committed for rape was, for colored, 1.9; all whites, 2.3; foreign white, 2.6; Irish, 1.3; Germans, 1.8; Poles, 2.1; Mexicans, 2.7; Canadians, 3.0; Russians, 3.0; French, 3.1; Austrians, 4.2; Italians, 4.4; Hungarians, 4.7. The report, 1911, of the Immigration Commission, on "Immigration and Crime" gives the following concerning the per cent rape forms of all offenses by Negro and whites: of convictions, New York City Court of General Sessions, Negro, .5; foreign whites, 1.8; native white, .8; of Chicago police arrests, Negro, .34; of alien white prisoners, 1908, in the United States, 2.9.

Source: "Comparison of the Criminality of the Different Races," *Negro Year Book and Annual Encyclopedia of the Negro*, 1913, pp. 236-237. Primary source: Work, Monroe N. (Ed.), *Negro Year Book and Annual Encyclopedia of the Negro*. Tuskegee Institute, Ala.: Negro Year Book Co., 1913. *Notes:* 1. If to the colored all those who are lynched for rape were added, the change in the figures would be less than one-fourth of one percent.

★ 473 ★

Crime

Relationships: Offenses of 1910 Prisoners and Juvenile Delinquents as Related to Gender and Race

OFFENSE	RATIO OF COMMITMENT[1]					
	Male		Female		Coefficient of difference	
	Negro A	White B	Negro C	White D	Male A+B	Female C+D
All offenses	1,792.9	840.2	418.3	70.0	2.1	6.0
Grave homicide	10.8	1.0	0.3	[2]	11.3	18.3
Lesser homicide	17.8	2.2	1.6	0.1	8.1	21.3
Assault	166.7	30.5	23.9	0.7	5.5	32.9
Robbery	11.1	2.7	0.6	[2]	4.1	41.4
Burglary	54.7	14.6	1.4	0.1	3.7	18.1
Larceny	248.6	66.2	29.2	2.6	3.8	14.4
Fraud	29.9	17.5	0.5	0.1	4.7	3.3
Forgery	6.2	4.3	0.3	0.1	1.4	4.7
Rape	7.8	2.6	-	-	2.2	-
Prostitution and fornication	9.8	3.5	34.2	7.0	3.2	4.6

[Continued]

★ 473 ★

Relationships: Offenses of 1910 Prisoners and Juvenile Delinquents as Related to Gender and Race
[Continued]

OFFENSE	RATIO OF COMMITMENT[1]					
	Male		Female		Coefficient of difference	
	Negro A	White B	Negro C	White D	Male A+B	Female C+D
Drunkenness and disorderly conduct	628.6	477.7	223.5	44.0	1.3	5.4
Vagrancy	136.1	94.4	32.5	5.4	1.4	6.0
Violating liquor laws	45.9	11.4	5.3	0.6	3.9	9.2
Malicious mischief and trespass	42.7	18.7	2.1	0.2	2.3	10.3
Offenses peculiar to children	12.4	13.4	4.7	3.3	0.9	1.4
Offense ill-defined or not reported	38.9	12.8	6.7	0.5	3.0	12.4
All others	325.9	66.9	54.9	5.3	4.9	10.0

Source: [Untitled Table], *Negro Population, 1790-1915*, 1918, p. 446. Primary source: U.S. Bureau of the Census. *Negro Population, 1790-1915.* Washington, D.C.: Government Printing Office, 1918. *Notes:* 1. Number of prisoners and juvenile delinquents committed in 1910 per 100,000 population of the same race and sex. 2. Less than one-tenth of 1 per 100,000.

★ 474 ★
Crime

Relationships: Ratio of Black/White Commitments of Prisoners and Juvenile Delinquents in 1910

SEX	PRISONERS AND JUVENILE DELINQUENTS COMMITTED IN 1910				
	Number		Ratio of commitments[1]		
			Negro A	White B	Coefficient of difference A+B
	Negro	White			
Both sexes	108,268	382,052	1,101.7	467.4	2.4
Male	87,598	354,367	1,792.9	840.2	2.1
Female	20,670	27,685	418.3	70.0	6.0

Source: [Untitled Table], *Negro Population, 1790-1915*, 1918, p. 445. Primary source: U.S. Bureau of the Census. *Negro Population, 1790-1915.* Washington, D.C.: Government Printing Office, 1918.

★ 475 ★
Crime

Relationships: Total and Black Prisoner and Juvenile Delinquent Offenses in 1910, by Gender

OFFENSE	PRISONERS AND JUVENILE DELINQUENTS COMMITTED IN 1910					
	Total		Negro			
			Number		Percentage	
	Male	Female	Male	Female	Among males	Among females
All offenses	445,368	48,566	87,598	20,670	19.7	42.6
Grave homicide	944	23	526	16	55.7	[1]
Lesser homicide	1,825	110	869	80	47.6	72.7
Assault	21,201	1,469	8,145	1,179	38.4	80.3
Robbery	1,691	37	544	31	32.2	[1]
Burglary	8,847	75	2,673	52	30.2	[1]
Larceny	40,246	2,470	12,146	1,445	30.2	58.5
Fraud	8,858	78	1,461	23	16.5	[1]
Forgery	2,121	35	302	13	14.2	[1]
Rape	1,480	-	380	-	25.7	-
Prostitution and fornication	1,976	4,474	477	1,689	24.1	37.8
Drunkenness and disorderly conduct	234,343	28,562	30,713	11,047	13.1	38.7
Vagrancy	46,560	3,742	6,651	1,605	14.3	42.9
Violating liquor laws	7,219	494	2,197	261	30.4	52.8
Malicious mischief and trespass	9,962	183	2,084	102	20.9	55.7
Offenses peculiar to children	6,260	1,543	606	233	9.7	15.1
Offense ill-defined or not reported	7,363	546	1,899	330	25.8	60.4
All others	44,472	4,725	15,925	2,564	35.8	54.3

Source: [Untitled Table], *Negro Population, 1790-1915*, 1918, p. 446. Primary source: U.S. Bureau of the Census. *Negro Population, 1790-1915*. Washington, D.C.: Government Printing Office, 1918. *Note:* 1. Per cent not shown where base is less than 100.

★ 476 ★
Crime

Suicide: Death Rates from Suicide, by Race, Gender, and Age Group, 1960-1973 - I

AGE	MALE							
	White				Negro and other			
	1960	1970[1]	1972[1]	1973[1]	1960	1970[1]	1972[2]	1973[1]
Total	17.6	18.0	10.3	18.8	7.2	8.5	18.8	10.0
5-14 yr.	0.5	0.5	-	0.7	0.1	0.2	0.5	0.3
15-24 yr.	8.6	13.9	16.7	17.4	5.3	11.3	15.5	14.0
25-34 yr.	14.9	19.9	20.9	21.8	12.9	19.8	20.9	22.6
35-44 yr.	21.9	23.3	15.8	22.8	13.5	12.6	23.0	14.3
45-54 yr.	33.7	29.5	13.2	28.4	12.8	14.1	29.7	13.4
55-64 yr.	40.2	35.0	11.9	32.4	16.9	10.5	33.5	12.1
65 yr. and over	46.7	41.1	11.6	40.7	12.4	10.8	42.2	11.9

Source: "Suicide Mortality Rates, by Sex, Race, and Age Groups: 1960 to 1973," *Statistical Abstract of the United States, 1975*, p. 155. Primary source: U.S. National Center for Health Statistics, *Vital Statistics of the United States*, annual. *Notes:* - Represent zero. 1. Excludes nonresident aliens.

★ 477 ★

Crime

Suicide: Death Rates from Suicide, by Race, Gender, and Age Group, 1960-1973 - II

| AGE | FEMALE | | | | | | | |
| | White | | | | Negro and other | | | |
	1960	1970[1]	1972[1]	1973[1]	1960	1970[1]	1972[2]	1973[1]
Total	5.3	7.1	7.3	7.0	2.0	2.9	3.0	3.0
5-14 yr.	0.1	0.1	0.2	0.2	-	0.2	0.1	0.1
15-24 yr.	2.3	4.2	4.6	4.3	1.5	4.1	4.1	4.1
25-34 yr.	5.8	9.0	9.2	8.5	3.5	5.8	5.3	5.3
35-44 yr.	8.1	13.0	12.6	12.2	3.7	4.3	5.4	5.4
45-54 yr.	10.9	13.5	13.4	13.7	3.2	4.5	3.2	3.2
55-64 yr.	10.9	12.3	13.3	12.0	3.4	2.2	4.4	4.4
65 yr. and over	8.8	8.5	8.5	8.2	3.9	3.6	2.4	3.1

Source: "Suicide Mortality Rates, by Sex, Race, and Age Groups: 1960 to 1973," *Statistical Abstract of the United States, 1975*, p. 155. Primary source: U.S. National Center for Health Statistics, *Vital Statistics of the United States*, annual. *Notes:* - Represent zero. 1. Excludes nonresident aliens.

★ 478 ★

Crime

Victimizations Reported and Not Reported To Police by Victim, 1973

| Subject | Race of victim | |
	Black	White
Total victimizations...thousands[1]	921	5,024
Percent	100	100
Victimizations reported to police	44	44
Victimizations not reported to police	55	55
Unknown whether reported victimizations to police	2	1
Percent of victimizations reported to police by type of crime:		
Crimes of violence	47	45
Rape and attempted rape	52	41
Robbery and attempted robbery	50	52
Assault	45	43
Personal larceny with contact	29	34

Source: "Personal Victimizations, by Whether Reported to the Police by Victim: 1973," Current Population Reports, Special Studies, Series P-23, No. 54. *The Social and Economic Status of the Black Population in the United States, 1974*, 1975, p. 168. Primary source: U.S. Department of Justice, Law Enforcement Assistance Administration. *Note:* 1. Excludes crimes or personal larceny without contact.

★ 479 ★

Crime

Victimizations by Type, in 1973

Race of victim and type of crime	Victimizations		Victimization rate[1]
	Number (thousands)	Percent	
BLACK			
Total	2,255	100	132
Crimes of violence	801	36	47
Rape and attempted rape	29	1	2
Robbery and attempted robbery	245	11	14
Assault and attempted assault	527	23	31
Crimes of theft	1,454	64	85
Personal larceny with contact	118	5	7
Personal larceny without contact	1,336	59	78
WHITE			
Total	18,211	100	127
Crimes of violence	4,642	25	32
Rape and attempted rape	129	1	1
Robbery and attempted robbery	856	5	6
Assault and attempted assault	3,657	20	26
Crimes of theft	13,569	75	95
Personal larceny with contact	381	2	3
Personal larceny without contact	13,188	72	92

Source: "Number and Rate of Personal Victimizations, by Type of Crime: 1973," Current Population Reports, Special Studies, Series P-23, No. 54. *The Social and Economic Status of the Black Population in the United Sates, 1974,* 1975, p. 164. Primary source: U.S. Department of Justice, Law Enforcement Assistance Administration. *Notes:* Data on criminal victimization in 1973 were gathered from surveys of a National Crime Panel, conducted by the Bureau of the Census. The surveys were sponsored by the Department of Justice, Law Enforcement Assistance Administration. 1. The victimization rate, a measure of occurrence among population groups at risk, was computed on the basis of the number of victimizations per 1,000 population age 12 and over.

★ 480 ★
Crime

Victims: Crime Victims, by Type of Crime, 1965

[Number per 100,000 population.]

CHARACTERISTICS OF VICTIMS	Total	Forcible rape	Robbery	Aggravated assault	Burglary	Larceny-$50 and over	Motor vehicle theft
Total	2,117	43	94	218	949	607	206
White	1,860	22	58	186	822	608	164
Negro and other races	2,592	82	204	347	1,306	367	286

Source: "Victims of Crime: 1965," *Statistical Abstract of the United States, 1971*, p. 143. Primary source: Executive Office of the President, The President's Commission on Law Enforcement and Administration of Justice; *The Challenge of Crime in a Free Society*, 1967.

★ 481 ★
Crime

Victims: Homicide and Suicide Victims, by Race and Gender, 1930-1973

YEAR	HOMICIDE VICTIMS					SUICIDES				
	Total	White		Negro and other		Total	White		Negro and other	
		Male	Female	Male	Female		Male	Female	Male	Female
NUMBER										
1930	10,331[1]	4,605[1]	1,236[1]	3,628[1]	862[1]	18,323	13,877	3,863	442	141
1935	10,396[1]	4,200[1]	1,116[1]	4,167[1]	913[1]	18,214	13,465	4,094	477	178
1940	8,329	2,977	796	3,670	886	18,907	13,990	4,294	476	147
1945	7,547	2,759	791	3,210	787	14,782	10,374	3,920	380	108
1950	7,942	2,586	952	3,503	901	17,145	12,755	3,713	542	135
1955	7,418	2,439	922	3,191	866	16,760	12,430	3,662	531	137
1960	8,464	2,832	1,154	3,437	1,041	19,041	13,825	4,296	714	206
1965	10,712	3,660	1,379	4,488	1,185	21,507	14,624	5,718	866	299
1968	14,686	5,106	1,700	6,417	1,463	21,372	14,520	5,692	859	301
1969	15,477	5,215	1,801	6,951	1,510	22,364	14,886	6,152	971	355
1970[2]	16,848	5,865	1,938	7,413	1,632	23,480	15,591	6,468	1,038	383
1971[2]	18,787	6,455	2,106	8,357	1,869	24,092	15,802	6,775	1,058	457
1972[2]	19,638	6,820	2,156	8,822	1,840	25,004	16,476	6,788	1,292	448
1973[2]	20,465	7,411	2,575	8,429	2,050	25,118	16,823	6,589	1,285	421
RATE[3]										
1930	12.4[1]	12.1[1]	3.3[1]	92.6[1]	21.8[1]	22.1	36.4	10.4	11.3	3.6
1935	11.2[1]	9.9[1]	2.7[1]	94.4[1]	20.2[1]	19.6	31.8	9.8	10.8	3.9
1940	8.4	6.7	1.8	79.9	18.5	19.2	31.3	9.6	10.4	3.1
1945	7.7	6.8	1.7	71.4	15.2	15.1	25.6	8.2	8.5	2.1

[Continued]

★ 481 ★

Victims: Homicide and Suicide Victims, by Race and Gender, 1930-1973
[Continued]

YEAR	HOMICIDE VICTIMS					SUICIDES				
	Total	White		Negro and other		Total	White		Negro and other	
		Male	Female	Male	Female		Male	Female	Male	Female
1950	7.2	5.3	1.9	67.4	16.2	15.6	26.0	7.4	10.4	2.4
1955	6.4	4.8	1.7	57.8	14.4	14.5	24.5	6.9	9.6	2.3
1960	6.9	5.3	2.0	56.2	15.6	15.4	25.7	7.6	11.7	3.1
1965	8.0	6.3	2.2	66.6	15.9	16.1	25.3	9.2	12.9	4.0
1968	10.5	8.5	2.6	90.0	18.2	15.2	24.2	8.8	12.1	3.8
1969	10.9	8.6	2.7	95.1	18.3	15.7	24.4	9.3	13.3	4.3
1970[2]	11.6	9.5	2.9	95.9	18.5	16.2	25.3	9.6	13.4	4.3
1971[2]	12.6	10.2	3.1	105.9	20.7	16.2	25.0	9.9	13.4	4.8
1972[2]	13.0	10.6	3.1	108.3	19.7	16.5	25.6	9.7	15.9	4.8
1973[2]	13.3	11.3	3.6	100.7	21.4	16.3	25.7	9.3	15.4	4.4

Source: "Homicide Victims and Suicides, by Race and Sex: 1930 to 1973," *Statistical Abstract of the United States, 1975,* p. 154. Primary source: U.S. National Center for Health Statistics, *Vital Statistics of the United States,* annual. *Notes:* 1. Excludes legal executions. 2. Excludes nonresident deaths. 3. Per 100,000 resident population fifteen years old and over, enumerated as of April 1, 1930, 1940, 1950, 1960, and 1970; estimated as of July 1, for other years.

★ 482 ★

Crime

Victims: Victimization Rates, by Race, for Selected Crimes, 1971-1973

Rates per 100,000 persons, 12 years old and over. U.S. Data cover victimizations occurring during January-June 1973. Data are estimates subject to sampling error.

RACE, SEX, AND CITY	Total	Rape	ROBBERY[1]		ASSAULT[2]		Personal larceny
			With injury	Without injury	Aggravated	Simple	
Total[3]	64.0	0.5	1.2	2.3	5.1	8.1	46.7
White	63.5	0.4	1.0	2.0	4.7	8.1	47.2
Negro	70.1	1.2	2.2	5.2	9.0	7.9	44.6
Male[3]	75.2	[4]	1.6	3.6	7.7	10.3	52.1
White	74.3	[4]	1.4	3.0	7.2	10.5	52.2
Negro	85.0	[4]	2.8	8.5	12.4	8.2	53.0
Female[3]	53.9	1.0	0.8	1.2	2.8	6.1	42.0
White	53.5	0.8	0.7	1.1	2.4	5.9	42.6
Negro	57.6	2.0	1.7	2.5	6.1	7.6	37.7

Source: "Victimization Rates of Crimes Against Persons, by Race and Sex of Victim, and for Selected Cities: 1971-1973," *Statistical Abstract of the United States,* 1975, p. 153. Primary source: U.S. Law Enforcement Assistance Administration, *Crime in the Nation's Five Largest Cities,* Advance Report, April 1974; *Crime in Eight American Cities,* Advance Report, July 1974; and *Criminal Victimization in the United States, January-June 1973,* vol. 1, November 1974. *Notes:* 1. Includes attempted robbery. 2. Includes attempted assault. 3. Includes races not shown separately. 4. Rate not shown because estimated number of victimizations too small to be statistically reliable.

Juvenile Delinquents and Delinquency

★ 483 ★

Arrests: Racial Distribution of Arrests, 1932-1970

[In thousands].

Year	Persons arrested[1]	Race		
		White	Negro	Other
1970	6,257	4,373	1,688	196
1969	5,577	3,843	1,559	175
1968	5,349	3,700	1,472	178
1967	5,265	3,631	1,463	172
1966	4,798	3,329	1,316	152
1965	4,743	3,235	1,348	160
1964	4,381	3,054	1,194	133
1963	4,259	2,943	1,187	129
1962[1]	3,923	2,602	1,196	126
1961[1]	3,608	2,425	1,073	110
1960[2]	3,499	2,321	1,065	113
1959[2]	2,613	1,742	789	82
1958[2]	2,340	1,583	696	61
1957[2]	2,069	1,406	616	47
1956[2]	2,071	1,391	634	46
1955[2]	1,862	1,310	510	41
1954[2]	1,689	1,206	440	43
1953[2]	1,791	1,270	481	40
1952[2]	1,111	808	281	21
1951	831	599	219	14
1950	794	576	206	12
1949	792	582	199	11
1948	760	557	192	11
1947	734	537	188	10
1946	645	478	159	8
1945	544	390	146	8
1944	489	352	129	8
1943	491	358	125	7
1942	586	432	147	7
1941	631	475	148	7
1940	609	463	139	7
1939	577	445	126	6
1938	554	428	121	6
1937	520	400	114	6
1936	462	350	105	6
1935	392	296	91	5
1934	344	258	81	5

[Continued]

★ 483 ★

Arrests: Racial Distribution of Arrests, 1932-1970
[Continued]

Year	Persons arrested[1]	Race		
		White	Negro	Other
1933	320	236	76	8
1932[2]	-	-	-	-

Source: "Persons Arrested, by Race, Sex, and Age: 1932 to 1970," *Historical Statistics of the United States: Colonial Times to 1970, Part I,* 1975, p. 415. Primary source: U.S. Bureau of the Census. *Historical Statistics of the United States: Colonial Times to 1970, Part I.* Bicentennial Edition. Washington, D.C.: Government Printing Office, 1975. *Notes:* 1. Each person arrested is counted rather than the number of charges filed against one person. Includes persons for whom age was not known. Prior to 1952, arrest data determined by examination of fingerprint cards. 2. City arrest data. 3. February 1 through December 31.

★ 484 ★

Juvenile Delinquents and Delinquency

Correctional Facilities: Institutions in Southern States for Black Delinquents in the 1930s

State	No. Institutions	FOR:		Both or Not Specified
		Boys	Girls	
Alabama	2	1	1	--
Arkansas	1	1	--	--
Delaware	1	--	1	--
District of Columbia	3	1	1	1
Florida	2	1	1	--
Georgia	6	2	1	3
Kentucky	2	--	--	2
Maryland	3	1	2	--
Missouri	3	2	1	--
North Carolina	4	3	1	--
Oklahoma	2	2	--	--
South Carolina	2	1	1	--
Tennessee	5	--	1	4
Texas	3	1	1	1
Virginia	2	1	1	--
West Virginia	2	1	1	--
Total	43	18	14	11

Source: Adapted by the editors from "Institutions in the South for Negro Juvenile Delinquents or which Receive Them" *The Negro Yearbook: An Annual Encyclopedia of the Negro, 1937-1938,* 1937, p. 151. Primary source: U.S. Bureau of the Census.

★ 485 ★

Juvenile Delinquents and Delinquency

Correctional Facilities: Juvenile Delinquents in Public Facilities in 1933, by Geographic Division

Area	Present Jan. 1	Received from courts			
		Total	White	Negro	Other Races
United States	30,501	17,017	12,959	3,610	448
New England	2,326	279	1,193	45	1
Middle Atlantic	7,312	4,493	3,534	951	8
E. No. Central	3,225	1,494	1,223	253	18
W. No. Central	3,921	1,929	1,668	219	42
South Atlantic	6,009	3,320	1,907	1,412	1
E. So. Central	2,708	1,244	804	440	0
W. So. Central	2,184	1,394	1,085	206	103
Mountain	1,307	701	531	18	152
Pacific	1,509	1,203	1,014	66	123

Source: Adapted by the editors from "Juvenile Delinquents in Public Institutions for Juvenile Delinquents by States: 1933, *Negro Year Book: An Annual Encyclopedia of the Negro, 1937-1938,* 1937, p. 152. Primary source: U.S. Bureau of the Census.

★ 486 ★

Juvenile Delinquents and Delinquency

Court Cases of Juvenile Delinquency Settled in 1945 by Gender of Delinquent, 1945

State	#Areas/ Cities	All races	RANGE		AVERAGE Negro & other[1]	
			Boys	Girls	Boys	Girls
Total Cases		122,851	15,802	3,996	--	--
Areas with 100,000 or more population	--	108,469	15,058	3,823	--	--
Arkansas	1	1,437	408	141	408	141
California	3	9,095	63-305	25-78	150	44
Colorado	3	4,538	87-119	19-37	98	31
District of Columbia	1	3,202	1,601	270	1,601	270
Indiana	5	5,943	37-626	11-124	184	45
Iowa	1	839	23	6	23	6
Louisiana	1	671	111	49	111	49
Michigan	2	2,546	14-387	10-104	200	57
Minnesota	1	632	10	4	10	4
Missouri	3	4,253	45-356	21-224	223	106
New York	1	7,037	2,110	438	2,110	438

[Continued]

★ 486 ★

Court Cases of Juvenile Delinquency Settled in 1945 by Gender of Delinquent, 1945

[Continued]

State	#Areas/ Cities	All races	RANGE		AVERAGE Negro & other[1]	
			Boys	Girls	Boys	Girls
Ohio	10	13,081	21-713	1-221	209	59
Oklahoma	1	1,143	160	105	160	105
Pennsylvania	4	13,959	15-3,669	0-651	1,074	219
Rhode Island	1	1,960	120	20	120	20
South Carolina	1	340	103	40	103	40
Texas	2	5,195	173-463	65-173	318	119
Virginia	1	1,085	380	74	380	74
Wisconsin	1	6,583	274	96	274	96

Source: Compiled by the editors from "Juvenile Delinquency Cases: 1945; Boys' and Girls' Cases, by Race, Disposed of by 88 Courts Serving Areas with Populations of 100,000 or More and by 286 Courts Serving Areas with Populations Less than 100,000," *The Negro Handbook, 1949,* 1949, pp. 90-91. Primary source: Children's Bureau, U.S. Department of Labor. *Note:* 1. Includes other minority races.

★ 487 ★

Juvenile Delinquents and Delinquency

Number/Percent: Court Cases in Areas with Less than 100,000 Population, 1945

Areas with less than 100,000	All races Total	White		Negro and Other Nonwhite	
		Boys	Girls	Boys	Girls
Indiana: 34 courts	2,121	1,578	432	92	19
Louisiana: East Baton Rouge Parish	343	114	46	152	31
Missouri: 112 courts	1,990	1,531	313	66	15
Montana: Yellowstone County	400	324	65	7	4
Ohio: 38 courts	3,879	2,764	641	211	49
Virginia: Danville-city	573	257	45	216	55

Source: "Juvenile Delinquency Cases: 1945; Boys' and Girls' Cases, by Race, Disposed of by 88 Courts Serving Areas with Population of 100,000 or More and by 286 Courts Serving Areas with Population Less than 100,000," *The Negro Handbook, 1949,* 1949, p. 91. Primary source: Children's Bureau, U.S. Department of Labor.

★ 488 ★

Juvenile Delinquents and Delinquency

Number/Percent: Delinquents in Training Schools and Detention Homes, 1960 and 1970

[1960 based on 25-percent sample, 1970 on 20-percent sample. Comparability of figures is affected by differences in classification].

CHARACTERISTIC	1960				1970			
	Training schools for juvenile delinquents			Detention homes	Training schools for juvenile delinquents			Detention homes
	Total	Public	Private		Total	Public	Private	
Total	45,695	38,359	7,336	10,821	66,457	57,691	8,766	10,272
White	31,294	24,900	6,394	7,342	39,757	33,428	6,329	6,754
Negro and other	14,401	13,459	942	3,479	26,700	24,263	2,437	3,518

Source: "Persons in Custody in Training Schools for Juvenile Delinquents and in Detention Homes: 1960 and 1970," *Statistical Abstract of the United States, 1973*, p.162. Primary source: U.S. Bureau of the Census; *U.S. Census of Population: 1960, and 1970*, vol. II.

★ 489 ★

Juvenile Delinquents and Delinquency

Number/Percent: Race and Region of Delinquents in Relation to Population, 1890-1910

DIVISIONS	WHITE			NEGRO		
	1890	1904	1910	1890	1904	1910
United States	23.5	29.7	25.7	25.4	34.4	39.2
North Atlantic States	39.6	48.6	34.9	215.4	208.9	199.0
North Central States	21.8	26.9	27.6	147.9	200.7	226.0
South Atlantic States	13.9	20.9	19.2	15.7	23.9	25.1
South Central States	2.8	4.3	7.4	4.3	4.6	10.8
Western States	12.1	28.4	24.0	5.7	45.9	244.5

Source: "Juvenile Delinquents Per 100,000 of Population," *Negro Year Book: An Annual Encyclopedia of the Negro, 1918-1919*, 1919, p. 372. Primary source: Federal Census.

★ 490 ★

Juvenile Delinquents and Delinquency

Relationships: Racial and Gender Distribution of Delinquents in Relation to Population, 1933

Color or Race	Number			Ratio		
	Total	Male	Female	Total	Male	Female
Total	17,017	13,153	3,864	34.1	52.4	15.6
White	12,959	9,716	3,243	29.8	44.3	15.1
Negro	3,610	3,057	553	67.4	116.7	20.2
Mexican	336	312	24			
All other	112	68	44	44.4	74.2	13.7

Source: "Juvenile Delinquents Received from Courts by Color or Race or Sex: 1933," *The Negro Yearbook: An Annual Encyclopedia of the Negro, 1937-1938,* 1937, p. 151. Primary source: U.S. Bureau of the Census.

★ 491 ★

Juvenile Delinquents and Delinquency

Source of and Reason for Court Reference, Age of Delinquents, and Case Disposition for Boys, 1942

Reason for reference to court, disposition of case, age of child when referred, and source of reference	DELINQUENCY CASES					
	Total All Races	Per cent	White[1]		Negro and other Nonwhite	
			Number	Percent	Number	Per cent
BOYS' CASES						
Reason for reference to court	21,455	100	17,121	100	4,334	100
Stealing	9,215	43	6,690	39	2,525	58
Act of carelessness or mischief	4,143	19	3,244	19	899	21
Sex offense	439	2	365	2	74	2
Ungovernable behavior or running away	2,208	10	1,841	11	367	8
Other reasons	5,450	26	4,981	29	469	11
Disposition of case	21,455	100	17,121	100	4,334	100
Probation officer to supervise	4,326	20	3,418	20	908	21
Dismissed, adjusted, or held open without further action	12,647	59	10,402	61	2,245	52
Committed or referred to an institution	1,639	8	1,041	6	598	14
Other disposition	2,843	13	2,260	13	583	13
Age when referred to court	21,455	100	17,121	100	4,334	100
Under 10 years	1,074	5	819	5	255	6
10 years, under 12	1,973	9	1,381	8	592	14
12 years, under 14	3,769	18	2,748	16	1,021	23
14 years, under 16	7,017	33	5,542	32	1,475	34
16 years and over	7,603	35	6,617	39	986	23
Age not reported	19	[2]	14	[2]	5	[2]

[Continued]

★ 491 ★

Source of and Reason for Court Reference, Age of Delinquents, and Case Disposition for Boys, 1942
[Continued]

Reason for reference to court, disposition of case, age of child when referred, and source of reference	DELINQUENCY CASES					
	Total All Races	Per cent	White[1]		Negro and other Nonwhite	
			Number	Percent	Number	Per cent
Source of reference to court	21,455	100	17,121	100	4,334	100
Police	17,850	83	14,199	83	3,651	84
Parents or relatives	659	3	477	3	182	4
Other individuals	1,337	6	1,096	6	241	6
School Department	1,060	5	935	6	125	3
All other	549	3	414	2	135	3

Source: "Juvenile Delinquency Cases: 1942," *The Negro Handbook, 1944,* 1944, p. 173. Primary source: Bureau of the Census. *Notes:* 1. Includes all Mexicans. 2. Less than 1 per cent.

★ 492 ★

Juvenile Delinquents and Delinquency

Source of and Reason for Court Reference, Age of Delinquents, and Case Disposition for Girls, 1942

Reason for reference to court, disposition of case, age of child when referred, and source of reference	DELINQUENCY CASES					
	Total All Races	Per cent	White[1]		Negro and other Nonwhite	
			Number	Percent	Number	Per cent
GIRLS' CASES						
Reason for reference to court	4,338	100	3,342	100	996	100
Stealing	703	16	450	13	253	25
Act of carelessness or mischief	411	10	272	8	139	14
Sex offense	519	12	431	13	88	9
Ungovernable behavior or running away	1,928	44	1,559	47	369	37
Other reasons	777	18	630	19	147	15
Disposition of case	4,388	100	3,342	100	996	100
Probation officer to supervise	1,171	27	986	29	185	19
Dismissed, adjusted, or held open without further action	1,823	42	1,295	39	528	53
Committed or referred to an institution	591	14	440	13	151	15
Other disposition	753	17	621	19	132	13
Age when referred to court	4,338	100	3,342	100	996	100
Under 10 years	89	2	73	2	16	2
10 years, under 12	193	5	129	4	64	6
12 years, under 14	744	17	485	14	259	26
14 years, under 16	1,822	42	1,393	42	429	43
16 years and over	1,487	34	1,259	38	228	23
Age not reported	3	2	3	2	-	-

[Continued]

★ 492 ★

Source of and Reason for Court Reference, Age of Delinquents, and Case Disposition for Girls, 1942

[Continued]

Reason for reference to court, disposition of case, age of child when referred, and source of reference	DELINQUENCY CASES					
	Total All Races	Per cent	White[1]		Negro and other Nonwhite	
			Number	Percent	Number	Per cent
Source of reference to court	4,338	100	3,242	100	996	100
Police	2,460	57	1,856	55	604	60
Parents or relatives	705	16	516	15	189	19
Other individuals	289	7	221	7	68	7
School Department	485	11	427	13	58	6
All other	399	9	322	10	77	8

Source: "Juvenile Delinquency Cases: 1942," The Negro Handbook, 1944, 1944, p. 173. Primary source: Bureau of the Census. Notes: 1. Includes all Mexicans. 2. Less than 1 per cent.

Law Enforcement

★ 493 ★

Age, Education, and Marital Status of People in Jail, 1972

Subject	Black	White
AGE		
Total...thousands	59	80
Percent	100	100
Under 19 years	10	9
19 and 20 years	15	13
21 to 24 years	26	24
25 to 29 years	19	15
30 years and over	31	40
EDUCATIONAL ATTAINMENT		
Total...thousands	59	80
Percent	100	100
Not high school graduate	69	62
Elementary school only	19	25
High school, 1 to 3 years	51	37
High school graduate	31	38
Some college	7	13

[Continued]

★ 493 ★

Age, Education, and Marital Status of People in Jail, 1972

[Continued]

Subject	Black	White
MARITAL STATUS		
Total...thousands	59	80
Percent	100	100
Single	58	43
Married	23	25
Separated, divorced, or widowed	19	32

Source: "Selected Social and Economic Characteristics of Jail Inmates: 1972," Current Population Reports, Series P-23, No. 54. *The Social and Economic Status of the Black Population in the United States, 1974*, 1975, p. 172. Primary source: U.S. Department of Justice, Law Enforcement Assistance Administration.

★ 494 ★

Law Enforcement

Arrests: Arrests, by Offense, 1971

In thousands. Represents arrests reported by 5,610 agencies with a total 1971 population of 146,564,000 as estimated by FBI.

Offense charged	Total	White	Negro	Other
Total	6,626.1	4,623.9	1,791.5	210.7
Serious crimes	1,301.4	805.9	468.6	27.0
Murder and nonnegligent manslaughter	13.3	4.7	8.3	0.3
Manslaughter by negligence	2.7	2.0	0.6	0.1
Forcible rape	15.5	7.4	7.8	0.3
Robbery	83.9	26.5	55.7	1.7
Aggravated assault	126.7	64.5	59.4	2.7
Burglary	297.1	192.8	98.7	5.7
Larceny-theft	640.4	432.0	195.4	13.0
Auto theft	121.8	75.9	42.6	3.2
All other				
Other assaults	290.8	174.3	111.1	5.4
Forgery and counterfeiting	41.1	27.8	12.9	0.4
Embezzlement, fraud	99.7	73.9	25.0	0.8
Stolen property	61.4	38.6	22.0	0.9
Weapons (carrying, etc.)	105.8	49.7	54.1	2.1
Prostitution and commercialized vice	44.9	16.2	28.1	0.5
Sex offenses	48.2	36.6	10.5	1.1
Narcotic drug laws	354.8	273.7	76.7	4.4
Gambling	74.9	20.4	51.6	2.9

[Continued]

★ 494 ★

Arrests: Arrests, by Offense, 1971
[Continued]

Offense charged	Total	White	Negro	Other
Offenses against family and children	55.7	38.6	16.4	0.7
Driving intoxicated	480.8	383.1	81.4	16.3
Liquor laws	226.1	197.0	23.7	5.4
Drunkenness	1,472.9	1,085.2	291.3	96.4
Disorderly conduct	606.3	387.6	200.5	18.2
Vagrancy	60.1	43.2	15.3	1.6
Other, except traffic	1,301.1	972.1	302.4	26.6

Source: "Arrests—Number, by Race: 1971," *Statistical Abstract of the United States*, 1973, p. 154. Primary source: U.S. Federal Bureau of Investigation, *Uniform Crime Reports for the United States*, 1971.

★ 495 ★

Law Enforcement

Arrests: Offenses of Blacks Arrested in 1949 and 1950

Offense Charged	Total All Races		Negro		Per Cent Negro of Total in each offense	
	1949	1950	1949	1950	1949	1950
Criminal homicide	6,436	6,336	2,918	2,889	45.3	45.6
Robbery	21,623	19,779	7,745	7,060	35.8	35.9
Assault	58,870	59,496	26,769	27,619	45.5	46.4
Burglary	45,892	43,673	12,569	11,534	27.4	26.4
Larceny	67,647	66,031	20,788	20,672	30.7	31.3
Auto theft	19,119	18,398	3,437	3,500	18.0	19.0
Embezzlement	22,245	21,439	2,797	2,962	12.6	13.8
Stolen property	3,268	3,289	986	1,050	30.2	31.9
Arson	1,097	1,054	234	241	21.3	22.9
Forgery	11,231	11,743	1,567	1,689	13.9	14.4
Rape	9,449	9,323	2,911	2,717	30.8	29.1
Prostitution	9,208	8,579	3,315	3,260	36.0	38.0
Other sex offenses	18,448	19,725	2,836	3,473	15.4	17.6
Narcotic drug law	6,546	8,539	2,677	4,262	41.0	49.9
Weapons	11,358	10,376	5,478	5,198	48.2	50.1
Offenses against the family	15,342	15,238	2,903	3,415	18.9	22.4
Liquor laws	9,934	11,260	4,157	5,306	41.8	47.1
Driving while intoxicated	42,907	51,318	4,055	5,706	9.4	11.1
Road and driving laws	10,595	14,571	2,357	3,662	22.2	25.1
Parking violations	162	309	42	98	25.9	31.7
Other traffic	9,695	13,052	2,794	3,431	23.7	26.3
Disorderly conduct	49,085	45,438	14,293	13,610	29.1	29.9
Drunkenness	178,776	178,165	28,740	30,040	16.1	16.9
Vagrancy	54,511	48,604	12,191	10,657	22.4	21.9
Gambling	16,274	15,490	7,452	7,462	45.8	48.2
Suspicion	47,114	46,194	12,778	13,054	27.1	28.2

[Continued]

★ 495 ★

Arrests: Offenses of Blacks Arrested in 1949 and 1950

[Continued]

Offense Charged	Total All Races		Negro		Per Cent Negro of Total in each offense	
	1949	1950	1949	1950	1949	1950
Not stated	7,228	7,930	1,388	1,555	19.2	19.6
All other offenses	37,969	38,322	8,919	9,454	23.5	24.7

Source: "Distribution of Arrests According to Race and Type of Offense, 1949 and 1950," 1952 *Negro Year Book: A Review of Events Affecting Negro Life,* 1952, p. 269. Primary source: *Uniform Crime Reports for the United States and Its Possessions,* Vols. 20 and 21.

★ 496 ★

Law Enforcement

Arrests: Racial Distribution of Arrests, 1960-1973

Item	1960	1965	1967	1968	1969	1970	1971	1972	1973
RACE									
Agencies reporting	1	4,043	4,508	4,758	4,627	5,208	5,610	6,114	5,914
Population represented (mil.)	73	125	135	136	133	142	147	151	145
Persons arrested[2] (1,000)	3,499	4,743	5,265	5,349	5,577	6,257	6,626	6,707	6,248
White (1,000)	2,321	3,235	3,631	3,700	3,843	4,373	4,624	4,664	4,459
Percent of total	66.3	68.2	69.0	69.2	68.9	69.9	69.8	69.5	71.4
Negro (1,000)	1,065	1,348	1,463	1,472	1,559	1,688	1,791	1,848	1,636
Other (1,000)	113	160	172	178	175	196	211	195	153

Source: "Persons Arrested—Race, Sex, and Age: 1960 to 1973," *Statistical Abstract of the United States,* 1975, p. 157. Primary source: U.S. Federal Bureau of Investigation, *Uniform Crime Reports for the United States,* annual. Notes: 1. For 2,446 cities with population over 2,500. 2. Each person arrested is counted rather than the number of charges filed against one person.

★ 497 ★

Law Enforcement

Arrests: Racial Distribution of Arrests, by Offense, 1973

In thousands. Represents arrests reported by 5,914 agencies with a total 1973 population of 144,956,000 as estimated by FBI. Represents persons arrested, not charged.

Offense charged	Total	White	Negro	Other
Total	6,248	4,458.6	1,636.2	153.5
Serious crimes	1,284	819.8	444.9	19.5
Murder and nonnegligent manslaughter	13	5.2	7.5	.2

[Continued]

★ 497 ★

Arrests: Racial Distribution of Arrests, by Offense, 1973
[Continued]

Offense charged	Total	White	Negro	Other
Manslaughter by negligence	3	2.1	.7	.1
Forcible rape	17	8.8	8.0	.3
Robbery	84	29.7	53.2	1.1
Aggravated assault	137	74.8	60.3	2.3
Burglary	297	203.1	90.2	4.0
Larceny-theft	626	425.9	190.5	9.3
Auto theft	107	70.1	34.5	2.2
All other				
Other assaults	261	162.9	93.8	4.0
Forgery and counterfeiting	39	26.0	12.6	0.4
Embezzlement, fraud	88	63.2	23.7	.7
Stolen property	64	40.3	23.4	.7
Weapons (carrying, etc.)	106	52.9	51.9	1.4
Prostitution and commercialized vice	42	16.9	24.7	.4
Sex offenses	46	35.0	10.4	.6
Narcotic drug laws	463	373.9	85.8	3.8
Gambling	53	15.5	36.9	.5
Offenses against family and children	42	30.0	11.6	.5
Driving intoxicated	641	521.5	101.2	18.3
Liquor laws	181	156.2	20.0	5.2
Drunkenness	1,179	866.7	245.7	66.1
Disorderly conduct	432	299.4	124.7	8.3
Vagrancy	36	23.1	11.2	1.3
Other, except traffic	1,291	955.3	313.8	21.7

Source: "Arrests—Number, by Race: 1973," *Statistical Abstract of the United States,* 1975, p. 159. Primary source: U.S. Federal Bureau of Investigation, *Uniform Crime Reports for the United States,* 1973.

★ 498 ★

Law Enforcement

Felony and Misdemeanor Commitments of Prisoners, 1940

Race and Nativity	Received from Court			Commitments	
	Total	Male	Female	Felony	Misdemeanor
Total	73,456	69,743	3,713	62,692	10,764
White	51,631	49,394	2,237	44,258	7,373
Native	47,620	45,520	2,100	41,541	6,079
Foreign-born	4,011	3,874	137	2,717	1,294
Negro	20,954	19,519	1,435	17,677	3,277
Other races	871	830	41	757	114

[Continued]

★ 498 ★

Felony and Misdemeanor Commitments of Prisoners, 1940

[Continued]

Race and Nativity	Received from Court			Commitments	
	Total	Male	Female	Felony	Misdemeanor
Indian	661	621	40	562	99
Chinese	123	122	1	112	11
Filipino	58	58	...	56	2
All other	29	29	...	27	2

Source: "Prisoners Received from Court, by Type of Commitment and Sex, by Race and Nativity, by Offense: 1940," *The Negro Handbook, 1944,* 1944, p. 163. Primary source: Bureau of the Census.

★ 499 ★

Law Enforcement

Male Felony Prisoners by Geographic Division, 1940

Area	Total	Native white	Foreign born white	Negro
United States	60,083[1]	40,028	2,624	16,706
Federal institutions	12,621	8,204	1,236	2,878
New England	1,682	1,455	124	98
Middle Atlantic	6,749	4,528	390	1,814
East North Central	8,506	6,400	329	1,733
West North Central	4,884	4,104	108	572
South Atlantic	8,118	3,769	62	4,257
East South Central	5,666	2,994	4	2,668
West South Central	6,162	3,668	82	2,361
Mountain	2,359	2,098	85	112
Pacific	3,336	2,808	204	207

Source: Compiled by the editors from "Male Felony Prisoners Received from Court, by Race, by Geographic Areas, and by States: 1940," *The Negro Handbook, 1944,* p. 165. Primary source: Bureau of the Census. *Notes:* 1. This total includes 531 Indians, 111 Chinese. 56 Filipinos, and 27 persons of other races, not otherwise listed in this table.

★ 500 ★

Law Enforcement

Money Earned and Employment Status of Prisoners, Prior to Imprisonment, 1972

Subject	Black	White
PREARREST ANNUAL INCOME		
Total reporting...thousands	57	78
Percent	100	100
Less than $2,000	47	43
$2,000 to $2,999	12	11
$3,000 to $7,499	33	32
$7,500 or more	7	14
PREARREST EMPLOYMENT STATUS		
Total reporting...thousands	47	62
Percent	100	100
Employed	57	58
Full time	43	48
Part time	13	10
Unemployed	43	42

Source: "Selected Social and Economic Characteristics of Jail Inmates: 1972," Current Population Reports, Series P-23, No. 54. *The Social and Economic Status of the Black Population in the United States, 1974,* 1975, p. 172. Primary source: U.S. Department of Justice, Law Enforcement Assistance Administration.

★ 501 ★

Law Enforcement

Number and Confinement Status of Local Jail Inmates, 1972

Race	Total inmates	Confinement status		
		Serving sentence	Awaiting trial	Other[1]
Total...thousands[2]	142	60	51	31
Black...thousands	59	23	24	12
White...thousands	80	35	26	18
PERCENT DISTRIBUTION				
Total[2]	100	100	100	100
Black	42	38	47	39
White	56	58	51	58

[Continued]

★ 501 ★

Number and Confinement Status of Local Jail Inmates, 1972
[Continued]

Race	Total inmates	Confinement status		
		Serving sentence	Awaiting trial	Other[1]
PERCENT BY CONFINEMENT STATUS				
Total[2]	100	42	36	22
Black	100	39	41	20
White	100	44	33	23

Source: "Inmates of Local Jails, by Confinement Status: 1972," Current Population Reports, Special Studies, Series P-23 , No. 54. *The Social and Economic Status of the Black Population in the United States, 1974,* 1975, p. 171. Primary source: U.S. Department of Justice, Law Enforcement Assistance Administration. *Notes:* The jail or inmate population is the number of persons confined in a local jail, i.e., a locally administered institution that has the authority to retain adults for 48 hours or longer. Statistics on inmates of local jails are from a survey conducted in the summer of 1972 by the Bureau of the Census for the Department of Justice, Law Enforcement Assistance Administration. 1. The confinement status of these inmates is one of the following categories: (1) not yet arraigned before a judge; (2)being held for other authorities; (3) awaiting immediate transfer to another institution; (4) convicted but under appeal; or (5) convicted and awaiting sentence. 2. Includes inmates of "other" races not shown separately.

★ 502 ★

Law Enforcement

Offense, Age, and Level of Education of Prisoners Sentenced to Die, 1973

Subject	Total under death sentence[1]	Black	White
TYPE OF OFFENSE AND AREA			
United States			
Total, offenses[2]	162	81	79
Murder	146	71	73
Rape	13	9	4
South			
Total, offenses[2]	73	46	26
Murder	59	36	22
Rape	13	9	4
North and West			
Total, offenses[2]	89	35	53
Murder	87	35	51
Rape	-	-	-

[Continued]

★ 502 ★

Offense, Age, and Level of Education of Prisoners Sentenced to Die, 1973
[Continued]

Subject	Total under death sentence[1]	Black	White
AGE			
Total	162	81	79
Percent	100	100	100
Under 24 years	23	35	9
25 to 34 years	42	40	46
35 to 44 years	21	19	24
45 years and over	14	7	22
Median age	30.9	28.9	34.0
EDUCATIONAL ATTAINMENT			
Total, reporting	128	66	61
Percent	100	100	100
Elementary: 8 years or less	41	38	43
High school: 1 to 3 years	32	32	33
4 years or more	27	30	25

Source: "Selected Characteristics of Prisoners Under Death Sentence: December 31, 1973," Current Population Reports, Series P-23, No. 54. *The Social and Economic Status of the Black Population in the United States, 1974*, 1975, p. 176. Primary source: U.S. Department of Justice, Law Enforcement Assistance Administration. *Notes:* - Represents zero. Data on prisoners are from a survey conducted annually by the Bureau of the Census for the Department of Justice, Law Enforcement Assistance Administration, as part of the National Prisoner Statistics (NPS) program. 1. Includes prisoners of "other" races not shown separately. 2. Includes a small number of other offenses, not shown separately.

★ 503 ★

Law Enforcement

Police Officers: Southern Cities with Black Police Officers in 1946

State and City	Number of Negro Policemen	Number of Negro Policewomen
ARKANSAS		
Little Rock	8	
FLORIDA		
Dayton Beach	6	
Deland	1	
Fort Myers	2	
Miami	18	

[Continued]

★ 503 ★

Police Officers: Southern Cities with Black Police Officers in 1946
[Continued]

State and City	Number of Negro Policemen	Number of Negro Policewomen
Sanford	2	
Sarasota	1	
Tampa	4	
Ocala	1	
KENTUCKY		
Lexington	3	
Louisville	25	1
Owensboro	1	
MISSOURI		
Jefferson City	1	
Kansas City	1	
Sedalia	1	
St. Louis	1	
NORTH CAROLINA		
Ahoskie	1	
Asheville	2	
Charlotte	6	2
Durham	6	
Greensboro	4	
High Point	2	
Raliegh	2	2
Winston-Salem	3	
OKLAHOMA		
McAlester	1	
Muskoegee	2	
Oklahoma City	12	
Tulsa	14	
SOUTH CAROLINA		
Beaufort	1	
York	1	
Summerton	1	
TENNESSEE		
Chattanooga	2	
Knoxville	5	
TEXAS		
Austin	3	
Beaumont	2	
El Paso	4	
Galveston	14	
Houston	5	
Port Arthur	1	
San Antonio	9	
VIRGINIA		
Newport News	1	

[Continued]

★ 503 ★

Police Officers: Southern Cities with Black Police Officers in 1946
[Continued]

State and City	Number of Negro Policemen	Number of Negro Policewomen
Norfolk	6	
Richmond	4	
Roanoke	2	
WEST VIRGINA		
Charleston	1	
Wheeling	1	

Source: "A List of Southern Cities Using Negro Policemen, 1946," *Negro Year Book: A Review of Events Affecting Negro Life, 1941-1946*, 1947, p. 318. *Note:* 1. Exact number of policemen not known.

★ 504 ★

Law Enforcement

Police Officers: Southern Cities with Black Police Officers in 1948 and 1949

City	Uniformed	Plain-clothes	Police-women
Dothan, Ala.	1	-	-
Hot Springs, Ark.	2	-	-
Little Rock, Ark.	6	-	-
Clearwater, Fla.	-	2	-
Cocoa, Fla.	1	-	-
Dania, Fla.[1]	1	-	-
Daytona Beach, Fla.	5	-	-
Deland, Fla.	2	-	-
Ft. Myers, Fla.	2	-	-
Gainesville, Fla.	-	2	-
Key West, Fla.	2	-	-
Melbourne, Fla.	1	-	-
Miami, Fla.	30	-	-
Sanford, Fla.	1	-	-
St. Petersburg, Fla.	4	-	-
Tampa, Fla.	6	-	-
West Palm Beach, Fla.	4	-	-
Atlanta, Ga.	6	-	-
Macon, Ga.	2	-	-
Savannah, Ga.	10	2	-
Lexington, Ky.	2	-	1
Louisville, Ky.	26	6	2
Owensboro, Ky.	2	-	-
Gulfport, Miss.	2	-	-
Ahoskie, N.C.	1	-	-

[Continued]

★ 504 ★

Police Officers: Southern Cities with Black Police Officers in 1948 and 1949

[Continued]

City	Uniformed	Plain-clothes	Police-women
Asheville, N.C.[1]	2	-	-
Burlington, N.C.	2	-	-
Charlotte, N.C.	10	-	-
Durham, N.C.	8	-	-
Fayetteville, N.C.	2	-	-
Gastonia, N.C.	5	-	-
Goldsboro, N.C.	2	-	-
Greensboro, N.C.	5	-	-
High Point, N.C.	4	-	-
Raleigh, N.C.	2	-	2
Winston-Salem, N.C.	7	-	-
Muskogee, Okla.	2	-	-
Oklahoma City, Okla.	7	5	-
Tulsa, Okla.[1]	13	-	1
Clover, S.C.	1	-	-
Columbia, S.C.	2	-	-
Conway, S.C.	2	-	-
Rock Hill, S.C.	2	-	-
Chattanooga, Tenn.	7	-	-
Knoxville, Tenn.[1]	7	-	-
Nashville, Tenn.	6	-	-
Austin, Tex.	6	-	-
Beaumont, Tex.[1]	2	-	-
Corpus Christi, Tex.	2	-	-
Dallas, Tex.	4	-	-
El Paso, Tex.	4	-	-
Galveston, Tex.	9	6	-
Houston, Tex.[1]	16	1	
Port Arthur, Tex.	10	-	-
San Antonio, Tex.	7	4	-
Cape Charles, Va.	1	-	-
Newport News, Va.	5	-	-
Norfolk, Va.	4	5	-
Petersburg, Va.	-	-	1
Portsmouth, Va.	1	-	-
Richmond, Va.	7	-	-
Roanoke, Va.	6	-	-
Totals (12 states, 63 cities)	301	33	7

Source: "Negro Policemen in Southern Cities," *1952 Negro Year Book: A Review of Events Affecting Negro Life,* 1952, p. 274. Primary source: *New South,* September 1949, Vol. 4, No. 9. *Note:* 1. Most recent figures: September 1948.

★ 505 ★

Law Enforcement

Prisoners Serving Time and Prisoners Waiting to be Tried, 1972

Type of crime	Total inmates[1]		Confinement status			
			Serving sentences		Awaiting trial	
	Black	White	Black	White	Black	White
Total crimes...thousands	59	80	23	35	24	26
Percent	100	100	100	100	100	100
Crimes of violence	37	17	21	10	49	24
Murder or kidnaping	10	4	5	2	14	8
Rape	2	2	1	-	4	3
Robbery	19	6	10	2	24	8
Assault	6	5	6	6	7	5
Aggravated	3	2	2	2	5	3
Simple and unspecified	2	3	4	4	2	2
Crimes of theft	27	24	28	20	27	26
Larceny	11	7	15	9	8	6
Grand	4	3	5	2	4	4
Petty and unspecified	7	5	10	7	5	3
Burglary	13	13	11	10	16	17
Auto theft	3	3	3	2	3	3
Other serious crimes	25	36	32	32	19	39
Forgery or fraud	3	6	5	4	2	8
Drugs[2]	9	12	9	10	9	17
Sale	3	3	2	3	4	5
Possession or use	6	8	7	7	5	10
Other offenses	13	19	18	19	8	14
Minor crimes	10	23	19	38	5	11
Nonsupport	1	1	2	2	-	1
Drunkenness or vagrancy	6	13	10	21	2	6
Traffic offenses	4	9	7	14	2	5

Source: "Jail Inmates by Type of Crime and Confinement Status: 1972," Current Population Reports, Series P-23, No. 54. *The Social and Economic Status of the Black Population in the United States, 1974,* 1975, p. 173. Primary source: U.S. Department of Justice, Law Enforcement Assistance Administration. *Notes:* - Rounds to zero. 1. Includes inmates of "other" confinement status. 2. Includes unspecified drug charges, not shown separately.

★ 506 ★

Law Enforcement

Prisoners: Age Group of Prisoners, by type of Facility, 1950 and 1960

1950 excludes Alaska and Hawaii. 1960 based on 25-percent sample. Comparability of figures may be affected by minor differences in classification.

Characteristic	1950			1960		
	Total	Federal and State prisons and reformatories	Local jails and workhouses	Total	Federal and State prisons and reformatories	Local jails and workhouses
All races	264,557	178,065	86,492	349,298	229,306	119,992
Negro and other (exc. white)	91,960	62,941	29,019	133,249	87,401	45,848
Under 15 years	197	123	74	324	68	256
15-19 years	6,360	4,040	2,320	11,197	6,639	4,558
20-24 years	19,971	13,456	6,515	24,019	15,242	8,777
25-39 years	45,701	31,701	14,000	67,469	45,582	21,887
40-59 years	17,764	12,278	5,486	27,644	18,200	9,444
60 years and over	1,967	1,343	624	2,596	1,670	926

Source: "Persons in Correctional Institutions: 1950 and 1960," *Statistical Abstract of the United States*, 1970, p. 156. Primary source: Dept. of Commerce, Bureau of the Census; U.S. *Census of the Population: 1950*, Vol. IV, Part 2, Chapter C; and *1960*, Series PC(2)-8A.

★ 507 ★

Law Enforcement

Prisoners: Blacks Imprisoned in the South and North in Relation to Population, 1870-1904

Year	Northern States	Southern States
Negro Prisoners in:		
1870	2025	6031
1880	3774	12973
1890	5635	19244
1904	7527	18550
Prisoners per 100,000 of Negro Population:		
1870	372	136
1880	515	221
1890	773	284
1904	765	220

Source: [Untitled Table], *Negro Year Book and Annual Encyclopedia of the Negro*, 1913, p. 236. Primary source: Federal Census.

★ 508 ★
Law Enforcement

Prisoners: Characteristics of 1930, 1931, and 1932 Inmates of Federal and State Institutions - I

Ratios based upon estimated population of July 1 of each year.

RACE AND NATIVITY	1932			1931			1930		
	Total	Male	Female	Total	Male	Female	Total	Male	Female
Total	67,477	64,546	2,931	71,520	68,483	3,037	66,013	62,957	3,056
Negro	14,613	13,822	791	15,441	14,605	836	14,771	13,908	863
White	50,889	48,805	2,084	54,160	51,995	2,165	49,331	47,178	2,153
Native	47,488	45,574	1,914	50,265	48,265	2,000	45,495	43,510	1,985
Foreign born	3,401	3,231	170	3,895	3,730	165	3,836	3,668	168
Mexican	1,311	1,291	20	1,274	1,255	19	1,322	1,315	17
Indian	402	370	32	420	403	17	387	364	23
Chinese	152	150	2	126	126	-	103	103	-
Japanese	23	21	2	22	22	-	12	12	-
Other races	87	87	-	77	77	-	77	77	-

Source: "Persons in State and Federal prisons and Reformatories 1930, 1931, and 1932," *Negro Year Book: An Annual Encyclopedia of the Negro, 1937-1938,* 1937, p. 149. Primary source: U.S. Bureau of the Census. *Negroes in the United States, 1920-1932.* Washington, D.C.: U.S. Government Printing Office, 1935.

★ 509 ★
Law Enforcement

Prisoners: Characteristics of 1930, 1931, and 1932 Inmates of Federal and State Institutions - II

Ratios based upon estimated population of July 1 of each year.

RACE AND NATIVITY	Number Per 100,000 of Population 15 Years Old and Over					
	1932		1931		1930	
	Male	Female	Male	Female	Male	Female
Total	153.1	7.1	161.8	7.4	149.5	7.4
Negro	483.8	27.2	478.8	26.7	416.3	25.2
White	128.0	5.6	136.2	5.8	124.0	5.8
Native	146.2	6.1	154.7	6.4	140.0	6.4
Foreign born	46.3	2.8	53.4	2.7	52.6	2.8
Mexican						
Indian						
Chinese	253.2	10.4	252.6	6.8	256.1	7.7
Japanese						
Other races						

Source: "Persons in State and Federal prisons and Reformatories 1930, 1931, and 1932," *Negro Year Book: An Annual Encyclopedia of the Negro, 1937-1938,* 1937, p. 149. Primary source: U.S. Bureau of the Census. *Negroes in the United States, 1920-1932.* Washington, D.C.: U.S. Government Printing Office, 1935.

★ 510 ★

Law Enforcement

Prisoners: Characteristics of Federal Sentenced Prisoners in 1950

Offense	Total	White		Negro		Other	
		Number	Per Cent	Number	Per Cent	Number	Per Cent
Total	18,063	13,301	73.7	4,172	23.1[1]	590	3.2
Male	17,351	12,899	74.4	3,390	22.6	522	3.0
Female	712	402	56.4	242	34.0	68	9.6
Counterfeiting	260	175	67.3	84	32.3	1	.4
Embezzlement	230	189	82.2	41	17.8	-	-
Forgery	1,274	639	50.2	619	48.6	16	1.2
Fraud	379	199	52.6	176	46.4	4	1.0
Immigration	3,463	3,428	99.0	28	.8	7	.2
Juvenile Delinquency Act	658	555	84.3	83	12.6	20	3.1
Kidnaping	41	36	87.8	5	12.2	-	-
Larceny-Theft (Total)	3,914	3,018	77.1	856	21.9	40	1.0
Liquor laws	2,304	1,545	67.1	738	32.0	21	.9
Narcotic-Drug laws (Total)	2,029	1,055	52.0	916	45.2	58	2.8
National-Defense laws (Total)	266	215	80.8	39	14.6	12	4.6
Robbery	92	82	89.1	10	10.9	-	-
White Slave Traffic Act	185	165	89.2	18	9.7	2	1.1
Other and Unclassifiable	1,110	960	86.5	120	10.8	30	2.7
Military court-martial cases (Total)	713	593	83.2	115	16.1	5	.7
Government reservation, D.C., high seas and territorial cases	1,145	447	39.0	324	28.3	374	32.7

Source: "Federal Sentenced Prisoners Received from Courts, by Nativity, Race and Offense, Fiscal Year Ended June 30, 1950," *1952 Negro Year Book: A Review of Events Affecting Negro Life,* 1952, p 270 Primary source: U.S. Bureau of the Census. *Note:* 1. If immigration cases were excluded this percentage would be 28.4.

★ 511 ★

Law Enforcement

Prisoners: Characteristics of Prisoners in State Institutions, by Region, 1945

Race, Nativity, and Sex	Number					Percent Distribution				
	United States	The Northeastern States	The North Central States	The South	The West	United States	The Northeastern Central States	The North Central States	The South	The West
Total	31,450	6,321	7,984	12,141	5,004	100.0	100.0	100.0	100.0	100.0
White	20,840	4,425	6,104	6,163	4,148	66.3	70.0	76.5	50.8	82.9
Native	20,206	4,218	5,978	6,063	3,947	64.2	66.7	74.9	49.9	78.9
Foreign born	634	207	126	100	201	2.0	3.3	1.6	0.8	4.0
Negro	10,330	1,879	1,787	5,928	736	32.8	29.7	22.4	48.8	14.7
Other races	280	17	93	50	120	0.9	0.3	1.2	0.4	2.4
Male	29,453	5,680	7,483	11,473	4,817	100.0	100.0	100.0	100.0	100.0
White	19,524	3,947	5,702	5,875	4,000	66.3	69.5	76.2	51.2	83.0

[Continued]

★ 511 ★
Prisoners: Characteristics of Prisoners in State Institutions, by Region, 1945
[Continued]

Race, Nativity, and Sex	Number					Percent Distribution				
	United States	The Northeastern States	The North Central States	The South	The West	United States	The Northeastern Central States	The North Central States	The South	The West
Native	18,928	3,762	5,581	5,779	3,806	64.3	66.2	74.6	50.4	79.0
Foreign born	596	185	121	96	194	2.0	3.3	1.6	0.8	4.0
Negro	9,667	1,718	1,693	5,554	702	32.8	30.2	22.6	48.4	14.6
Other races	262	15	88	44	115	0.9	0.3	1.2	0.4	2.4
Female	1,997	641	501	668	187	100.0	100.0	100.0	100.0	100.0
White	1,316	478	402	288	148	65.9	74.6	80.2	43.1	79.1
Native	1,278	456	397	284	141	64.0	71.1	79.2	42.5	75.4
Foreign born	38	22	5	4	7	1.9	3.4	1.0	0.6	3.7
Negro	663	161	94	374	34	33.2	25.1	18.8	56.0	18.2
Other races	18	2	5	6	5	0.9	0.3	1.0	0.9	2.7

Source: "Felony Prisoners Received from Court in State Institutions, by Race, Nativity, and Sex, by Regions: 1945," *The Negro Handbook, 1949,* 1949, p. 86. Primary source: Murray, Florence (Ed.), *The Negro Handbook, 1949.* New York: The Macmillan Co., 1949.

★ 512 ★
Law Enforcement
Prisoners: Federal and State Prisoners, 1941-1945

Race and Nativity	Number					Percent Distribution				
	1945	1944	1943	1942	1941	1945	1944	1943	1942	1941
All classes	43,281	41,058	40,273	47,761	56,023	100.0	100.0	100.0	100.0	100.0
White	29,539	28,280	27,616	32,482	38,927	68.2	68.9	68.6	68.0	69.5
Native	27,825	26,584	25,888	30,179	36,423	64.3	64.7	64.3	63.2	65.0
Foreign born	1,714	1,696	1,728	2,303	2,504	4.0	4.1	4.3	4.8	4.5
Negro	13,207	12,165	12,131	14,660	16,355	30.5	29.6	30.1	30.7	29.2
Other races	535	613	526	619	714	1.2	1.5	1.3	1.3	1.3

Source: "Felony Prisoners Received from Court in Federal and State Institutions, by Race and Nativity, for the United States: 1941-1945," *The Negro Handbook, 1949,* 1949, p. 85. Primary source: *U.S. Bureau of the Census.*

★ 513 ★

Law Enforcement

Prisoners: Offenses of Prisoners in 1930 and 1931

Offense	1930 NEGRO			1930 WHITE			1931 NEGRO			1931 WHITE		
	Total	Male	Female	Total	Male	Female	Total	Male	Female	Total	Male	Female
All offenses	14,771	13,908	863	49,331	47,178	2,153	15,441	14,605	836	54,160	51,985	2,165
Homicide	1,647	1,466	181	1,768	1,705	63	1,650	1,462	188	2,010	1,925	85
Robbery	1,475	1,439	36	5,419	5,377	42	1,600	1,561	39	6,925	6,850	75
Aggravated Assault] Other Assault	1,395	1,299	96	1,378	1,343	35	1,578	1,473	105	1,474	1,451	23
Burglary	3,477	3,433	44	8,589	8,537	52	3,755	3,726	29	10,169	10,108	61
Larceny, except auto theft] Auto Theft	2,775	2,650	125	9,246	9,233	193	3,066	2,928	148	10,268	10,022	246
Embezzlement and Fraud	98	93	5	1,306	1,275	31	115	106	9	1,381	1,327	54
Stolen Property	307	286	21	1,788	1,752	36	344	329	15	1,887	1,846	41
Forgery	464	445	19	3,640	3,504	136	487	464	23	4,003	3,845	158
Rape	302	302	--	1,512	1,512	--	304	304	--	1,415	1,415	--
Other Sex Offense	216	129	87	1,446	925	521	160	98	62	1,610	1,078	532
Violating Drug Laws	395	345	50	1,106	974	132	261	225	36	1,307	1,164	143
Violating Liquor Laws	1,095	1,032	63	6,454	6,194	260	970	885	85	6,620	3,343	277
Other Offenses	1,125	989	136	5,499	4,847	652	1,151	1,049	102	5,091	4,621	470

Source: Adapted by the editors from "Prisoners Received from Courts, by Race, Sex, and Classification of Offense for the United States: 1932, 1931, and 1930," *The Negro Yearbook: An Annual Encyclopedia of the Negro, 1937-1938*, 1937, p. 150. Primary source: U.S. Bureau of the Census.

★ 514 ★

Law Enforcement

Prisoners: Race and Age of Male Felony Prisoners in 1937

AGE	TOTAL	NATIVE WHITE	FOREIGN-BORN WHITE	NEGRO	OTHER RACES
Total	56,754	38,855	2,666	14,507	726
Under 15 years	27	7	2	18	-
15 to 17 years	2,629	1,761	37	822	9
18 years	2,660	1,929	19	694	18
19 years	3,015	2,209	38	748	20
20 years	2,840	2,058	40	718	24
21 to 24 years	11,213	7,918	219	2,906	170
25 to 29 years	10,386	7,026	313	2,908	139
30 to 34 years	7,664	5,186	378	1,995	105
35 to 39 years	6,086	4,017	390	1,588	91
40 to 44 years	3,901	2,599	388	858	56
46 to 49 years	2,623	1,706	324	565	28
50 to 54 years	1,624	1,064	236	296	28
55 to 59 years	1,031	681	149	186	15
60 to 64 years	529	348	83	89	9

[Continued]

★ 514 ★

Prisoners: Race and Age of Male Felony Prisoners in 1937
[Continued]

AGE	TOTAL	NATIVE WHITE	FOREIGN-BORN WHITE	NEGRO	OTHER RACES
65 to 69 years	317	214	30	66	7
70 years and over	149	97	18	28	6
Not reported	60	35	2	22	1
Median age	27.9	27.5	38.7	27.3	29.4

Source: "Male 'Felony' Prisoners Received from Courts, by Race, Nativity, and Age: 1937," *The Negro Handbook, 1942*, p. 55. Primary source: U.S. Bureau of the Census.

★ 515 ★
Law Enforcement

Prisoners: Race and Gender of Felony Prisoners in 1939

RACE	TOTAL		MALE		FEMALE	
	Number	Percent	Number	Percent	Number	Percent
Total	62,000	100.0	59,432	100.0	2,568	100.0
White	44,990	72.6	43,417	73.1	1,573	61.3
Native	42,648	68.8	41,157	69.3	1,491	58.1
Foreign-born	2,342	3.8	2,260	3.8	82	3.2
Negro	16,309	26.3	15,340	25.8	969	37.7
Other races	701	1.1	675	1.1	26	1.0
Indian	521	0.8	498	0.8	23	0.9
Chinese	112	0.2	109	0.2	3	0.1
Filipino	44	0.1	44	0.1	-	-
Other races	24	1	24	1	-	-

Source: "Felony Prisoners Received from Courts, by Sex and Race: 1939," *The Negro Handbook*, 1942, p. 53. Primary source: U.S. Bureau of the Census. *Note:* 1. Less than one-tenth of 1 percent.

★ 516 ★
Law Enforcement

Prisoners: Race and Offense of Male Felony Prisoners in 1939

OFFENSE	TOTAL	NATIVE WHITE	FOREIGN-BORN WHITE	NEGRO	OTHER RACES
Total	59,432	41,157	2,260	15,340	675
Murder	1,713	684	83	907	39
Manslaughter	1,289	578	58	636	17

[Continued]

★ 516 ★

Prisoners: Race and Offense of Male Felony Prisoners in 1939

[Continued]

OFFENSE	TOTAL	NATIVE WHITE	FOREIGN-BORN WHITE	NEGRO	OTHER RACES
Robbery	5,562	3,982	168	1,466	36
Aggravated assault	3,012	1,307	138	1,526	41
Burglary	12,555	8,424	257	3,795	79
Larceny, except auto theft	10,543	7,342	238	2,860	103
Auto theft	3,127	2,674	40	358	55
Embezzlement and fraud	1,869	1,620	105	133	11
Stolen property	726	539	40	144	3
Forgery	4,969	4,178	172	558	61
Rape	2,030	1,530	109	363	28
Other sex offenses	1,733	1,381	145	179	28
Violating drug laws	1,992	1,208	164	530	90
Carrying, etc., weapons	294	155	18	118	3
Non-support or neglect	507	456	21	26	4
Violating liquor laws	5,016	3,344	224	1,408	40
Violating traffic laws	357	277	19	58	3
All other offenses	2,138	1,568	261	275	34

Source: "Male Felony Prisoners Received from Courts, by Race and by Offense: 1939," *The Negro Handbook, 1949,* 1949, p. 55. Primary source: U.S. Bureau of the Census.

★ 517 ★

Law Enforcement

Prisoners: Race and State Origins of Male Felony Prisoners in 1939

STATE	TOTAL	NATIVE WHITE	FOREIGN-BORN WHITE	NEGRO	OTHER RACES
United States	59,432	41,157	2,260	15,340	675
Federal institutions	11,108	7,739	693	2,390	286
State institutions	48,324	33,418	1,567	12,950	389
Maine	297	270	26	-	1
New Hampshire	94	87	7	-	-
Vermont	246	232	13	1	-
Massachusetts	681	588	61	30	2
Rhode Island	157	135	12	9	1
Connecticut	368	310	35	23	-
New York	2,860	1,894	299	657	10
New Jersey	1,369	914	91	364	-
Pennsylvania	2,244	1,586	69	587	2
Ohio	2,331	1,755	67	506	3
Indiana	1,332	1,080	18	233	1
Illinois	1,503	1,068	60	373	2

[Continued]

★ 517 ★

Prisoners: Race and State Origins of Male Felony Prisoners in 1939
[Continued]

STATE	TOTAL	NATIVE WHITE	FOREIGN-BORN WHITE	NEGRO	OTHER RACES
Michigan	2,422	1,775	145	477	25
Wisconsin	1,226	1,061	85	54	26
Minnesota	1,022	929	53	18	22
Iowa	713	666	8	37	2
Missouri	1,990	1,490	14	486	-
North Dakota	232	193	16	3	20
South Dakota	240	205	2	2	31
Nebraska	622	558	1	55	8
Kansas	831	721	6	98	6
Delaware	102	41	2	59	-
Maryland	1,738	677	19	1,041	1
District of Columbia	643	180	7	456	-
Virginia	1,793	792	2	999	-
West Virginia	1,126	897	4	225	-
North Carolina	1,229	609	2	602	16
South Carolina	651	357	2	292	-
Florida	1,306	628	13	665	-
Kentucky	1,723	1,277	1	444	1
Tennessee	1,390	822	-	568	-
Mississippi	819	224	2	592	1
Arkansas	858	420	1	435	2
Louisiana	953	330	4	619	-
Oklahoma	2,098	1,504	1	525	68
Texas	3,001	1,901	72	1,026	2
Montana	350	303	21	7	19
Idaho	242	225	9	5	3
Wyoming	225	209	9	5	2
Colorado	833	777	21	35	-
New Mexico	365	328	6	22	9
Arizona	374	312	14	43	5
Utah	173	159	8	5	1
Nevada	153	137	12	2	2
Washington	781	683	46	29	23
Oregon	522	487	21	4	10
California	2,096	1,622	180	232	62

Source: "Male Felony Prisoners Received from Courts, by Race and by State: 1939," *The Negro Handbook,* 1942, p. 54. Primary source: U.S. Bureau of the Census.

★ 518 ★

Law Enforcement

Prisoners: Retention Reason and Selected Characteristics of Prisoners, 1972

[As of summer. A jail was defined as a locally administrated institution that has the authority to retain adults for 48 hours or longer.]

CHARACTERISTIC	Total	White	Black	Other	Characteristic	Total	White	Black	Other
Total inmates[1]	141,600	79,900	58,900	2,800	Marital status:				
Serving sentence	60,200	35,400	23,200	1,600	Never married	70,500	34,400	34,400	1,700
Awaiting trail	50,800	26,300	23,800	700	Separated, divorced,				
Other State of adjudication	30,500	18,200	11,900	500	or widowed	37,100	25,200	11,400	600
					Married	33,900	20,300	13,100	400
Educational					Prearrest annual income:				
attainment:					Less than 2,000	61,800	33,500	26,800	1,600
0-8 years	32,200	20,300	11,000	900	$2,000-$2,999	16,100	8,600	7,000	400
9-12 years	94,500	49,200	43,600	1,700	$3,000-$7,499	44,400	24,800	19,000	600
Over 12 years	14,300	10,300	4,100	2	$7,500 and over	15,100	10,800	4,300	2
					Unknown	4,300	2,200	2,000	2

Source: "Reason for Retention and Selected Socioeconomic Characteristics of Jail Inmates, by Race: 1972," *Statistical Abstract of the United States,* 1975, p.167. Primary source: U.S. Law Enforcement Assistance Administration, *Survey of Inmates of Local Jails: Advance Report. Notes:* 1. Educational attainment excludes 600 inmates for whom data were not available. 2. Less than 300.

★ 519 ★

Law Enforcement

Prisoners: Trends in Admissions to State and Federal Prisons, 1926-1975 - I

By race, United States, selected years 1926-75.

Year	Number of admissions to State and Federal prisons	Percent of State and Federal prison admissions				Number of admissions to State prisons	Percent of State prison admissions			
		Total	White	Black	Other		Total	White	Black	Other
1926	43,328	100%	78%	21%	1%	38,318	100%	75%[1]	23%	2%[1]
1927	44,062	100	78	21	1	39,041	100	77	22	1
1928	48,212	100	78	21	1	42,642	100	NA	NA	NA
1929	58,906	100	78	21	1	49,172	100	76	23	1
1930	66,013	100	77	22	1	56,213	100	75	24	1
1931	71,520	100	77	22	1	60,905	100	76	23	1
1932	67,477	100	77	22	1	57,825	100	76	23	1
1933	62,801	100	76	23	1	54,468	100	74	25	1
1934	62,251	100	75	24	1	52,976	100	73	26	1
1935	65,723	100	74	25	1	53,886	100	72	27	1
1936	60,925	100	73	26	1	49,466	100	72	27	1
1937	59,073	100	73	26	1	46,412[2]	100	72	27	1
1938	64,265	100	73	26	1	50,169[2]	100	72	27	1
1939	62,000	100	73	26	1	48,324[2]	100	72	27	1
1940	62,692	100	71	28	1	47,462[2]	100	70	29	1
1941	56,023	100	70	29	1	41,202[2]	100	69	30	1
1942	47,761	100	68	31	1	35,649	100	65	34	1
1943	40,273	100	69	30	1	29,537	100	65	34	1
1944	41,058	100	69	30	1	28,641	100	66	33	1
1945	43,281	100	68	31	1	31,450	100	66	33	1

[Continued]

★ 519 ★

Prisoners: Trends in Admissions to State and Federal Prisons, 1926-1975 - I
[Continued]

Year	Number of admissions to State and Federal prisons	Percent of State and Federal prison admissions				Number of admissions to State prisons	Percent of State prison admissions			
		Total	White	Black	Other		Total	White	Black	Other
1946	56,432	100	66	33	1	43,679	100	64	35	1
1947	51,016[2]	100	69	30	1	40,601[2]	100	68	31	1
1948	49,834[2]	100	70	29	1	39,899[2]	100	68	31	1
1949	54,370[2]	100	70	29	1	43,941[2]	100	69	30	1
1950	57,988	100	69	30	1	46,496	100	69	30	1
1960	84,068	100	66	32	2	69,235	100	65	34	1
1964	81,099	100	65	33	2	67,879	100	63	35	2
1970	48,497	100	61	39[3]	X	37,437	100	57	43[3]	X
1974	52,245	100	59	38	3	37,064	100	54	41	5
1975	42,351	100	64	35	1	25,796	100	60	38	2

Source: "Admissions to State and Federal Prisons," *Sourcebook of Criminal Justice Statistics—1992*, 1992, p. 618. Primary source: U.S. Department of Justice, Bureau of Justice Statistics, *Race of Prisoners Admitted to State and Federal Institutions, 1926-86*, NCJ-125618 (Washington, DC: U.S. Department of Justice, 1991), p. 5. *Notes:* X = not available separately. These data were collected by the U.S. Department of Justice, Bureau of Justice Statistics through the National Prisoner Statistics (NPS) program. The NPS is now administered by the U.S. bureau of Justice Statistics and data are collected and processed by the U.S. Bureau of the Census. Where admission data are available on "sentenced felons admitted to prison as new court commitments," these data are used. Where there are no data on new court commitments, data on a more broadly defined category of admitted prisoners are the source of the numbers for race. the more broadly defined category of prisoners admitted applies to the years 1926-36. For 1926-36, the only available data are for new court commitments that include both sentenced felons and a small number of sentenced misdemeanants. For 1926-36, felons were defined as all admissions regardless of sentence length. From 1937-60, felons were defined as prisoners with maximum sentences of 6 months or longer. No data were available for 1961-63. From 1964-70, felons were defined as prisoners with maximum sentences of 1 year or longer. After 1970, felons were defined as prisoners with maximum sentences longer than 1 year. No statistics were available for 1951-59, 1961-63, 1965-69, and 1971-73. The Federal Government apparently did not operate the NPS admission series during these years. The number of admissions to State and Federal prisons includes prisoners whose race was unknown. Percentages are based on figures that exclude cases where race was unknown. The "other races" category consists of Asians, American Indians, Alaska Natives, and Pacific Islanders. 1. For 1926, the "white" total shown excludes Mexicans and the "other races" total shown includes Mexicans. 2. Males only. 3. Includes blacks plus "other" races.

★ 520 ★
Law Enforcement

Prisoners: Trends in Admissions to State and Federal Prisons, 1926-1975 - II

By race, United States, selected years 1926-75.

Year	Number of admissions to Federal prisons	Percent of Federal prison admissions			
		Total	White	Black	Other
1926	5,010	100%	81%[1]	13%	6%[1]
1927	5,021	100	84	14	2
1928	5,570	100	NA	NA	NA
1929	9,734	100	86	12	2
1930	9,800	100	86	12	1
1931	10,615	100	87	11	2
1932	9,652	100	88	10	2
1933	8,333	100	88	10	2
1934	9,275	100	87	11	2
1935	11,837	100	84	14	2
1936	11,459	100	80	18	2

[Continued]

★ 520 ★

Prisoners: Trends in Admissions to State and Federal Prisons, 1926-1975 - II
[Continued]

Year	Number of admissions to Federal prisons	Percent of Federal prison admissions			
		Total	White	Black	Other
1937	10,34[2]	100	80	18	2
1938	11,664[2]	100	78	20	2
1939	11,108[2]	100	76	21	3
1940	12,621[2]	100	75	23	2
1941	12,586[2]	100	74	24	2
1942	12,112	100	76	22	2
1943	10,736	100	78	20	2
1944	12,417	100	76	21	3
1945	11,831	100	74	24	2
1946	12,753	100	73	25	2
1947	10,415[2]	100	75	23	2
1948	9,935[2]	100	76	22	2
1949	10,429[2]	100	74	24	2
1950	11,492	100	70	28	2
1960	14,833	100	71	25	4
1964	13,220	100	73	25	2
1970	11,060	100	73	27[3]	X
1974	15,181	100	71	29[3]	X
1975	16,555	100	70	30[3]	X

Source: "Admissions to State and Federal Prisons," *Sourcebook of Criminal Justice Statistics—1992,* 1992, p. 618. Primary source: U.S. Department of Justice, Bureau of Justice Statistics, *Race of Prisoners Admitted to State and Federal Institutions, 1926-86,* NCJ-125618 (Washington, DC: U.S. Department of Justice, 1991), p. 5. *Notes:* X = not available separately. These data were collected by the U.S. Department of Justice, Bureau of Justice Statistics through the National Prisoner Statistics (NPS) program. The NPS is now administered by the U.S. bureau of Justice Statistics and data are collected and processed by the U.S. Bureau of the Census. Where admission data are available on "sentenced felons admitted to prison as new court commitments," these data are used. Where there are no data on new court commitments, data on a more broadly defined category of admitted prisoners are the source of the numbers for race. the more broadly defined category of prisoners admitted applies to the years 1926-36. For 1926-36, the only available data are for new court commitments that include both sentenced felons and a small number of sentenced misdemeanants. For 1926-36, felons were defined as all admissions regardless of sentence length. From 1937-60, felons were defined as prisoners with maximum sentences of 6 months or longer. No data were available for 1961-63. From 1964-70, felons were defined as prisoners with maximum sentences of 1 year or longer. After 1970, felons were defined as prisoners with maximum sentences longer than 1 year. No statistics were available for 1951-59, 1961-63, 1965-69, and 1971-73. The Federal Government apparently did not operate the NPS admission series during these years. The number of admissions to State and Federal prisons includes prisoners whose race was unknown. Percentages are based on figures that exclude cases where race was unknown. The "other races" category consists of Asians, American Indians, Alaska Natives, and Pacific Islanders. 1. For 1926, the "white" total shown excludes Mexicans and the "other races" total shown includes Mexicans. 2. Males only. 3. Includes blacks plus "other" races.

★ 521 ★

Law Enforcement

Relationships: Age Distribution of Prisoners and Juvenile Delinquents in 1910, in Relation to Population

| AGE | PRISONERS AND JUVENILE DELINQUENTS COMMITTED IN 1910 | | | | Percentage Negro in the population 1910 |
| | Number | | | Percentage Negro | |
	Total	Negro	White		
All ages	493,934	108,268	382,052	21.9	10.7
Under 10 years	568	112	456	19.7	12.3
10 to 14 years	9,061	1,992	7,059	22.0	12.7
15 to 17 years	15,793	5,289	10,457	33.5	11.8
18 to 20 years	35,697	12,375	23,080	34.7	11.5
21 to 24 years	64,221	20,834	42,885	32.4	11.3
25 to 34 years	129,974	31,380	97,424	24.1	10.2
35 to 44 years	99,023	13,685	84,630	13.8	9.3
45 to 54 years	56,230	4,411	51,457	7.8	8.5
55 to 64 years	22,408	1,310	20,949	5.8	7.8
65 years and over	7,718	506	7,152	6.8	7.4
Age not reported	53,241	16,374	36,503	30.8	18.4

Source: [Untitled Table], *Negro Population, 1790-1915*, 1918, p. 443. Primary source: U.S. Bureau of the Census. *Negro Population, 1790-1915*. Washington, D.C.: Government Printing Office, 1918.

★ 522 ★

Law Enforcement

Relationships: Differences in Black/White Prisoner and Juvenile Delinquent Commitments, by Age, in 1910

| AGE | PRISONERS AND JUVENILE DELINQUENTS COMMITTED IN 1910 | | | | |
| | Number | | Ratio of commitments[1] | | |
	Negro	White	Negro A	White B	Coefficient of difference A÷B
All ages	108,268	382,052	1,101.7	467.4	2.4
Under 10 years	112	456	4.5	2.6	1.7
10 years	114	596	47.0	36.8	1.3
11 years	176	838	90.2	55.7	1.6
12 years	364	1,400	139.3	85.2	1.6
13 years	513	1,887	231.2	122.1	1.9
14 years	825	2,338	351.7	145.5	2.4
15 years	1,128	2,642	543.5	175.3	3.1
16 years	1,813	3,088	807.9	189.1	4.3

[Continued]

★ 522 ★

Relationships: Differences in Black/White Prisoner and Juvenile Delinquent Commitments, by Age, in 1910

[Continued]

	PRISONERS AND JUVENILE DELINQUENTS COMMITTED IN 1910				
	Number		Ratio of commitments[1]		
AGE			Negro A	White B	Coefficient of difference A+B
	Negro	White			
17 years	2,348	4,727	1,151.8	299.9	3.8
18 years	3,831	7,148	1,656.2	423.2	3.9
19 years	4,098	8,175	2,120.0	523.3	4.1
20 years	4,446	7,757	2,061.9	47.5	4.3
21 to 24 years	20,834	42,885	2,555.8	674.7	3.8
25 to 34 years	31,380	97,424	2,025.4	720.4	2.8
35 to 44 years	13,685	84,630	1,256.8	805.1	1.6
45 to 54 years	4,411	51,457	619.5	675.6	0.9
55 to 64 years	1,310	20,949	330.7	452.1	0.7
65 years and over	506	7,152	172.0	196.5	0.9
Age not reported	16,374	36,503	...	...	...

Source: [Untitled Table], *Negro Population, 1790-1915*, 1918, p. 443. Primary source: U.S. Bureau of the Census. *Negro Population, 1790-1915.* Washington, D.C.: Government Printing Office, 1918. *Note:* 1. Number committed per 100,000 population of the same race and age.

★ 523 ★

Law Enforcement

Relationships: Gender and Race Differences in Prisoners and Juvenile Delinquents Committed, in Relation to Population, by Age, in 1910

	RATIO OF COMMITMENTS					
	Males		Females		Coefficient of difference	
AGE					Among males A/B	Among females C/D
	Negro A	White B	Negro C	White D		
All ages	1,792.9	840.2	418.3	70.0	2.1	6.0
Under 10 years	8.4	4.6	0.6	0.4	1.8	1.3
10 years	86.3	68.4	6.7	4.4	1.3	1.5
11 years	165.9	104.6	15.3	6.2	1.6	2.5
12 years	256.0	155.4	21.5	12.8	1.6	1.7
13 years	390.1	219.5	74.3	23.1	1.8	3.2
14 years	584.7	240.7	121.3	47.4	2.4	2.6
15 years	889.9	288.1	209.2	61.4	3.1	3.4
16 years	1,360.2	325.1	307.5	53.6	4.2	5.7
17 years	1,865.5	540.9	462.1	53.4	3.4	8.7
18 years	2,747.5	806.4	695.2	46.8	3.4	14.9
19 years	3,474.1	970.3	919.4	62.0	3.6	14.8
20 years	3,493.2	904.0	986.8	61.8	3.9	16.0

[Continued]

★ 523 ★

Relationships: Gender and Race Differences in Prisoners and Juvenile Delinquents Committed, in Relation to Population, by Age, in 1910
[Continued]

AGE	RATIO OF COMMITMENTS					
	Males		Females		Coefficient of difference	
					Among males	Among females
	Negro A	White B	Negro C	White D	A/B	C/D
21 to 24 years	4,121.8	1,218.9	1,121.7	98.2	3.4	11.4
25 to 34 years	3,369.4	1,268.7	751.4	116.3	2.7	6.5
35 to 44 years	2,139.9	1,392.0	355.1	145.8	1.5	2.4
45 to 54 years	1,040.0	1,179.3	140.1	95.2	0.9	1.5
55 to 64 years	555.9	815.0	60.0	48.2	0.7	1.2
65 years and over	310.2	365.7	23.3	26.3	0.8	0.9

Source: [Untitled Table], *Negro Population, 1790-1915*, 1918, p. 447. Primary source: U.S. Bureau of the Census. *Negro Population, 1790-1915*. Washington, D.C.: Government Printing Office, 1918.

★ 524 ★

Law Enforcement

Relationships: Prisoners and Juvenile Delinquents, in Relation to Population, 1910

| RACIAL CLASS | Population: 1910 | PRISONERS AND JUVENILE DELINQUENTS: 1910 | | | | | | Percentage distribution of population: 1910 |
| | | Number | | Ratio per 100,000 population | | Percentage distribution | | |
		Enumerated January 1.	Committed during year	Enumerated January 1.	Committed during year	Enumerated January 1.	Committed during year	
Total	91,972,266	136,472	493,934	118.4	537.0	100.0	100.0	100.0
Negro	9,827,763	41,729	108,268	424.6	1,101.7	30.6	21.9	10.7
White	81,731,957	93,841	382,052	114.8	467.8	68.8	77.3	88.9
Other colored	412,546	902	3,614	218.6	876.0	0.7	0.7	0.4
Indian	265,683	[1]	2,963	[1]	1,115.2	[1]	0.6	0.3
Chinese, Japanese, and other	146,863	[1]	651	[1]	443.3	[1]	0.1	0.2

Source: [Untitled Table], *Negro Population, 1790-1915*, 1918, p. 436. Primary source: U.S. Bureau of the Census. *Negro Population, 1790-1915*. Washington, D.C.: Government Printing Office, 1918. *Note:* 1. Separate figures not available.

★ 525 ★
Law Enforcement

Relationships: Ratio of Black/White Prisoner and Juvenile Delinquent Commitments, by Offense, c. 1910

OFFENSE	RATIO OF COMMITMENTS[1]					
	The South			The North		
	Negro A	White B	Coefficient of difference A/B	Negro A	White B	Coefficient of difference A/B
All offenses	880.3	258.1	3.4	2,836.0	503.2	5.6
Grave homicide	5.4	0.8	6.8	5.6	0.3	18.7
Lesser homicide	9.2	1.9	4.8	12.6	0.8	15.8
Assault	77.5	10.2	7.6	231.7	17.5	13.2
Robbery	3.6	0.6	6.0	21.9	1.4	15.6
Burglary	22.3	4.3	5.2	63.7	7.6	8.4
Larceny	112.8	18.1	6.2	343.2	37.9	9.1
Fraud	12.3	6.0	2.1	37.0	9.6	3.9
Forgery	2.8	1.9	1.5	5.2	1.8	2.9
Rape	2.8	0.6	4.7	11.9	1.5	7.9
Prostitution and fornication	11.2	2.7	4.1	110.2	6.4	17.2
Drunkenness and disorderly conduct	336.3	135.9	2.5	1,141.9	300.5	3.8
Vagrancy	54.8	17.5	3.1	289.0	50.2	5.8
Violating liquor laws	23.5	9.2	2.6	36.6	4.5	8.1
Malicious mischief and trespass	18.9	7.7	2.5	48.7	11.0	4.4
Offenses peculiar to children	2.6	4.3	0.6	55.9	10.1	5.5
Offense ill-defined or not reported	21.3	6.8	3.1	31.9	4.1	7.8
All others	162.8	29.7	5.5	389.2	37.9	10.3

Source: [Untitled Table], *Negro Population, 1790-1915*, 1918, p. 439. Primary source: U.S. Bureau of the Census. *Negro Population, 1790-1915*. Washington, D.C.: Government Printing Office, 1918. *Notes:* 1. Number of prisoners and juvenile delinquents in 1910 per 100,000 population of the same race.

★ 526 ★

Law Enforcement

Relationships: Ratio of Black/White Prisoner and Juvenile Delinquent Commitments, by Region, in 1910

SECTION AND DIVISION	PRISONERS AND JUVENILE DELINQUENTS COMMITTED IN 1910				
	Number		Ratio of commitments[1]		
			Negro A	White B	Coefficient of difference A÷B
	Negro	White			
United States	108,268	382,052	1,101.7	467.4	2.4
The South	77,022	53,023	880.3	258.1	3.4
South Atlantic	41,226	25,620	1,002.5	317.4	3.2
East South Central	23,347	13,357	880.2	232.1	3.8
West South Central	12,449	14,046	627.3	269.0	3.0
The North	29,145	274,941	2,836.0	503.2	5.6
The West	1,858	53,379	3,667.4	815.7	1.5
United States penitentiaries	243	709	...	...	...

Source: [Untitled Table], *Negro Population, 1790-1915*, 1918, p. 437. Primary source: U.S. Bureau of the Census. *Negro Population, 1790-1915.* Washington, D.C.: Government Printing Office, 1918. *Note:* 1. Number committed per 100,000 population of the same race.

★ 527 ★

Law Enforcement

Relationships: Regional Distribution of Prisoners and Juvenile Delinquents, in Relation to Population, 1910

SECTION AND DIVISION	PERCENTAGE NEGRO: 1910		
	In total population	Among prisoners and juvenile delinquents	
		Enumerated Jan. 1.	Committed during year
United States	10.7	30.6	21.9
The South	29.8	70.1	58.9
South Atlantic	33.7	72.0	61.6
East South Central	31.5	73.1	63.6
West South Central	22.6	62.4	46.0
The North	1.8	13.1	9.6
New England	1.0	4.6	2.6
Middle Atlantic	2.2	12.8	9.4
East North Central	1.6	14.7	11.0
West North Central	2.1	20.8	14.4

[Continued]

★ 527 ★

Relationships: Regional Distribution of Prisoners and Juvenile Delinquents, in Relation to Population, 1910
[Continued]

SECTION AND DIVISION	PERCENTAGE NEGRO: 1910		
	In total population	Among prisoners and juvenile delinquents	
		Enumerated Jan. 1.	Committed during year
The West	0.7	5.9	3.2
Mountain	0.8	7.8	4.4
Pacific	0.7	4.6	2.5
United States penitentiaries	...	31.3	24.6

Source: [Untitled Table], *Negro Population, 1790-1915*, 1918, p. 437. Primary source: U.S. Bureau of the Census. *Negro Population, 1790-1915.* Washington, D.C.: Government Printing Office, 1918.

★ 528 ★

Law Enforcement

Relationships: Southern and Northern Black/White Differences in Prisoner and Juvenile Delinquent Commitments, by Age Group, in 1910

AGE	RATIO OF COMMITMENTS[1]					
	Negro			White		
	In the South A	In the North B	Coefficient of difference B÷A	In the South A	In the North B	Coefficient of difference B÷A
All ages	880.3	2,836.0	3.2	258.1	503.2	1.9
Under 15 years	40.5	287.8	7.1	12.6	37.4	3.0
15 to 17 years	682.9	2,557.6	3.7	139.1	253.5	1.8
18 to 20 years	1,619.6	4,812.7	3.0	287.9	514.6	1.8
21 to 24 years	2,040.0	6,225.4	3.1	399.8	715.6	1.8
25 to 34 years	1,557.2	4,472.8	2.9	395.6	774.6	2.0
35 to 44 years	916.7	2,950.0	3.2	383.9	904.0	2.4
45 to 55 years	433.0	1,680.9	3.9	276.5	780.7	2.8
55 to 64 years	232.3	959.0	4.1	170.8	530.4	3.1
65 years and over	106.0	592.1	5.6	74.7	223.8	3.0

Source: [Untitled Table], *Negro Population, 1790-1915*, 1918, p. 445. Primary source: U.S. Bureau of the Census. *Negro Population, 1790-1915.* Washington, D.C.: Government Printing Office, 1918. *Notes:* 1. Number of prisoners and juvenile delinquents committed in 1910 per 100,000 population of the same race and age.

Legal Justice

★ 529 ★

Executions, 1940

Includes 38 executions in addition to those reported by State prisons and reformatories.

STATE	ALL OFFENSES		MURDER		RAPE	
	White	Negro	White	Negro	White	Negro
Total	49	75	44	61	2	13
Connecticut	2	-	2	-	-	-
New York	12	1	10	1	-	-
New Jersey	1	-	1	-	-	-
Pennsylvania	1	3	1	3	-	-
Ohio	-	2	-	2	-	-
Illinois	3	1	3	1	-	-
Iowa	1	-	1	-	-	-
Missouri	1	1	1	1	-	-
Maryland	2	4	-	3	2	1
Virginia	1	3	1	2	-	1
West Virginia	1	1	1	-	-	1
North Carolina	1	9	1	6	-	3
South Carolina	-	5	-	4	-	1
Georgia	-	14	-	10	-	3
Florida	1	2	1	2	-	-
Kentucky	-	2	-	2	-	-
Tennessee	2	2	2	1	-	1
Alabama	1	8	1	7	-	1
Mississippi	1	5	1	5	-	-
Arkansas	-	4	-	4	-	-
Louisiana	1	3	1	3	-	-
Oklahoma	2	-	2	-	-	-
Texas	4	4	4	3	-	1
Wyoming	1	-	1	-	-	-
Arizona	1	-	1	-	-	-
Nevada	-	1	-	1	-	-
Washington	2	-	1	-	-	-
Oregon	1	-	1	-	-	-
California	6	-	6	-	-	-

Source: "Prisoners Executed for Murder and Rape by Race, by States: 1940," *The Negro Handbook, 1944*, 1944, p. 166. Primary source: Bureau of the Census.

★ 530 ★

Legal Justice

Executions: Executions and Reasons for Executions, 1930-1969

TYPE OF OFFENSE AND RACE	All years	1930-1939	1940-1949	1950-1959	1960-1964	1965	1966	1967	1968	1969
Total	3,859	1,667	1,284	717	181	7	1	2	-	-
White	1,751	827	490	336	90	6	1	1	-	-
Negro	2,066	816	781	376	91	1	-	1	-	-
Other	42	24	13	5	-	-	-	-	-	-
Murder	3,334	1,514	1,064	601	145	7	1	2	-	-
White[1]	1,664	803	458	316	79	6	1	1	-	-
Negro1	1,630	687	595	280	66	1	-	1	-	-
Other	40	24	11	5	-	-	-	-	-	-
Rape	455	125	200	102	28	-	-	-	-	-
White	48	10	19	13	6	-	-	-	-	-
Negro	405	115	179	89	22	-	-	-	-	-
Other	2	-	2	-	-	-	-	-	-	-
Other offenses[2]	70	28	20	14	8	-	-	-	-	-
White[3]	39	14	13	7	5	-	-	-	-	-
Negro	31	14	7	7	3	-	-	-	-	-

Source: "Prisoners Executed Under Civil Authority: 1930 to 1969," *Statistical Abstract of the United States, 1970*, p. 161. Primary source: Dept. of Justice, Bureau of Prisons; *National Prisoner Statistics*, Bulletin No. 46. *Notes:* Represents zero. 1. White includes 18 females; Negro, 12 females. 2. 25 armed robbery, 20 kidnaping, 11 burglary, 8 espionage (6 in 1942 and 2 in 1953), and 6 aggravated assault. 3. Includes 2 females, both executed in 1953, 1 for kidnapping and 1 for espionage.

★ 531 ★

Legal Justice

Executions: Executions for Rape, Murder, and All Offenses, by State, 1946

Includes 60 executions in addition to those reported by state prisons and reformatories.

State	All Offenses		Murder		Rape	
	White	Negro	White	Negro	White	Negro
Total	46	84	45	61	-	21
Connecticut	3	-	3	-	-	-
Massachusetts	1	-	1	-	-	-
New York	3	1	3	1	-	-
Pennsylvania	3	2	3	2	-	-
Ohio	2	-	2	-	-	-
Indiana	-	1	-	1	-	-
Iowa	2	-	2	-	-	-

[Continued]

★ 531 ★

Executions: Executions for Rape, Murder, and All Offenses, by State, 1946

[Continued]

State	All Offenses		Murder		Rape	
	White	Negro	White	Negro	White	Negro
Missouri	-	2	-	2	-	-
Delaware	-	1	-	1	-	-
Maryland	-	5	-	1	-	4
District of Columbia	2	2	2	2	-	-
Virginia	1	8	1	7	-	1
West Virginia	1	-	1	-	-	-
North Carolina	3	10	3	6	-	4
South Carolina	-	5	-	4	-	1
Georgia	3	13	3	10	-	3
Florida	1	4	1	2	-	2
Kentucky	2	2	2	2	-	-
Tennessee	2	3	2	2	-	1
Alabama	3	6	3	5	-	1
Mississippi	-	9	-	6	-	1
Arkansas	2	2	2	2	-	-
Louisiana	-	2	-	1	-	1
Oklahoma	1	-	1	-	-	-
Texas	1	4	1	2	-	2
New Mexico	1	-	1	-	-	-
Nevada	1	-	1	-	-	-
Washington	2	-	2	-	-	-
Oregon	2	-	2	-	-	-
California	4	2	3	2	-	-

Source: "Prisoners Executed, by Offense and Race, by States: 1946," *The Negro Handbook, 1949,* 1949, p. 88. Primary source: *U.S. Bureau of the Census.*

★ 532 ★

Legal Justice

Executions: Race and Offense of Persons Executed, 1930-1970 - I

Year	All offenses				Murder[2]		
	Total	White	Negro	Other[1]	Total[3]	White	Negro
1970	-	-	-	-	-	-	-
1969	-	-	-	-	-	-	-
1968	-	-	-	-	-	-	-
1967	2	1	1	-	2	1	1
1966	1	1	-	-	1	1	-

[Continued]

★ 532 ★

Executions: Race and Offense of Persons Executed, 1930-1970 - I

[Continued]

Year	All offenses				Murder[2]		
	Total	White	Negro	Other[1]	Total[3]	White	Negro
1965	7	6	1	-	7	6	1
1964	15	8	7	-	9	5	4
1963	21	13	8	-	18	12	6
1962	47	28	19	-	41	26	15
1961	42	20	22	-	33	18	15
1960	56	21	35	-	44	18	26
1959	49	16	33	-	41	15	26
1958	49	20	28	1	41	20	20
1957	65	34	31	-	54	32	22
1956	65	21	43	1	52	20	31
1955	76	44	32	-	65	41	24
1954	81	38	42	1	71	37	33
1953	62	30	31	1	51	25	25
1952	83	36	47	-	71	35	36
1951	105	57	47	1	87	55	31
1950	82	40	42	-	68	36	32
1949	119	50	67	2	107	49	56
1948	119	35	82	2	95	32	61
1947	153	42	111		129	40	89
1946	131	46	84	1	107	45	61
1945	117	41	75	1	90	37	52
1944	120	47	70	3	96	45	48
1943	131	54	74	3	118	54	63
1942	147	67	80	-	115	57	58
1941	123	59	63	1	102	55	46
1940	124	49	75	-	105	44	61
1939	160	80	77	3	145	79	63
1938	190	96	92	2	154	89	63
1937	147	69	74	4	133	67	62
1936	195	92	101	2	181	86	93
1935	199	119	77	3	184	115	66
1934	168	65	102	1	154	64	89
1933	160	77	81	2	151	75	74
1932	140	62	75	3	128	62	63

[Continued]

★ 532 ★

Executions: Race and Offense of Persons Executed, 1930-1970 - I
[Continued]

Year	All offenses				Murder[2]		
	Total	White	Negro	Other[1]	Total[3]	White	Negro
1931	153	77	72	4	137	76	57
1930	155	90	65	-	147	90	57

Source: "Prisoners Executed Under Civil Authority, by Race and Offense: 1930 to 1970," *Historical Statistics of the United States: Colonial Times to 1970, Part I,* 1975, p. 422. Primary source: U.S. Bureau of the Census. *Historical Statistics of the United States: Colonial Times to 1970, Part I.* Bicentennial Edition. Washington, D.C.: Government Printing Office, 1975. *Notes:* - Represents zero. 1. All were for murder except 2 for rape in 1943. 2. Includes 32 females: 20 white, 12 Negro. 3. Total includes other races, not shown separately.

★ 533 ★

Legal Justice

Executions: Race and Offense of Persons Executed, 1930-1970 - II

Year	Rape			Other offenses		
	Total	White	Negro	Total[1]	White[2]	Negro
1970	-	-	-	-	-	-
1969	-	-	-	-	-	-
1968	-	-	-	-	-	-
1967	-	-	-	-	-	-
1966	-	-	-	-	-	-
1965	-	-	-	-	-	-
1964	6	3	3	-	-	-
1963	2	-	2	1	1	-
1962	4	2	2	2	-	2
1961	8	1	7	1	1	-
1960	8	-	8	4	3	1
1959	8	1	7	-	-	-
1958	7	-	7	1	-	1
1957	10	2	8	1	-	1
1956	12	-	12	1	1	-
1955	7	1	6	4	2	2
1954	9	1	8	1	-	1
1953	7	1	6	4	4	-
1952	12	1	11	-	-	-
1951	17	2	15	1	-	1
1950	13	4	9	1	-	1
1949	10	-	10	2	1	1
1948	22	1	21	2	2	-

[Continued]

★ 533 ★

Executions: Race and Offense of Persons Executed, 1930-1970 - II

[Continued]

Year	Rape			Other offenses		
	Total	White	Negro	Total[1]	White[2]	Negro
1947	23	2	21	1	-	1
1946	22	-	22	2	1	1
1945	26	4	22	1	-	1
1944	24	2	22	-	-	-
1943	13[3]	-	11	-	-	-
1942	25	4	21	7	6	1
1941	20	4	16	1	-	1
1940	15	2	13	4	3	1
1939	12	-	12	3	1	2
1938	25	1	24	11	6	5
1937	13	2	11	1	-	1
1936	10	2	8	4	4	-
1935	13	2	11	2	2	-
1934	14	1	13	-	-	-
1933	7	1	6	2	1	1
1932	10	-	10	2	-	2
1931	15	1	14	1	-	1
1930	6	-	6	2	-	2

Source. "Prisoners Executed Under Civil Authority, by Race and Offense: 1930 to 1970," Historical Statistics of the United States: Colonial Times to 1970, Part I, 1975, p. 422. Primary source: U.S. Bureau of the Census. Historical Statistics of the United States: Colonial Times to 1970, Part I. Bicentennial Edition. Washington, D.C.: Government Printing Office, 1975. Notes: - Represents zero. 1. Includes 25 armed robbery, 20 kidnaping, 11 burglary, 6 sabotage, 6 aggravated assault, and 2 espionage. 2. Includes 2 females.

★ 534 ★

Legal Justice

Executions: Racial Distribution and Offense of Executed Prisoners in 1937, by State

Includes 45 executions in addition to those reported by State prisons and reformatories.

State	All Offenses				Murder			Rape	
	Total	White	Negro	Other races[1]	White	Negro	Other races[1]	White	Negro
Total	147	69	74	4	67	62	4	2	11
Connecticut	1	1	-	-	1	-	-	-	-
New York	14	9	4	1	9	4	1	-	-
Pennsylvania	8	5	3	-	5	3	-	-	-
Ohio	1	1	-	-	1	-	-	-	-

[Continued]

★ 534 ★

Executions: Racial Distribution and Offense of Executed Prisoners in 1937, by State
[Continued]

State	All Offenses				Murder			Rape	
	Total	White	Negro	Other races[1]	White	Negro	Other races[1]	White	Negro
Indiana	5	5	-	-	5	-	-	-	-
Illinois	7	5	2	-	5	2	-	-	-
Missouri	4	3	1	-	3	1	-	-	-
Delaware	2	-	2	-	-	2	-	-	-
Maryland	1	-	1	-	-	1	-	-	-
District of Columbia	2	-	2	-	-	2	-	-	-
Virginia	3	-	3	-	-	3	-	-	-
West Virginia	4	3	1	-	3	1	-	-	-
North Carolina	12	1	11	-	1	9	-	-	2
South Carolina	2	1	1	-	1	1	-	-	-
Georgia	16	4	12	-	3	11	-	1	1
Florida	6	1	5	-	1	3	-	-	2
Kentucky	5[2]	3	2	-	3	-	-	-	1
Tennessee	10	5	5	-	4	3	-	1	2
Alabama	4	3	1	-	3	-	-	-	1
Mississippi	6	-	6	-	-	6	-	-	-
Arkansas	5	1	4	-	1	3	-	-	1
Louisiana	4	2	2	-	2	2	-	-	-
Oklahoma	2	1	-	1	1	-	1	-	-
Texas	8	4	4	-	4	3	-	-	1
Wyoming	1	1	-	-	1	-	-	-	-
Colorado	1	1	-	-	1	-	-	-	-
Arizona	4	3	1	-	3	1	-	-	-
Nevada	1	1	-	-	1	-	-	-	-
California	8	5	1	2	5	1	2	-	-

Source: "Prisoners Executed, by Offense and Race, by States: 1937," *The Negro Handbook,* 1942, p. 58. *Notes:* Executions occurred in every one of the 17 States (including Georgia, Alabama, and Mississippi) in the Southern area. Of the 92 prisoners executed in these States, 29 were white, 62 were Negro, and 1 was Indian. There were 55 prisoners executed in the other 12 States, outside the South of which 40 were white, 12 were Negro, 1 was Chinese, and 2 were Filipinos. There were only 5 of all of the white prisoners executed who were foreign born. 1. Other races include 1 Chinese (New York); 1 Indian (Oklahoma); and 2 Filipinos (California). 2. Includes 1 Negro executed for robbery.

★ 535 ★

Legal Justice

Length and Appeal Status of Sentences by Type of Crime, 1972

Appeal status and type of crime	Number sentenced		Median number of months sentenced	
	Black	White	Black	White
NOT ON APPEAL				
Murder or kidnapping	1,182	515	66.1	5.8
Rape	126	147	10.7	5.9
Robbery	2,315	834	52.9	11.5
Burglary	2,459	3,370	10.5	10.8
Assault: Aggravated	517	695	13.3	11.1
Simple	649	1,153	6.0	2.6
Larceny: Grand	1,113	755	10.0	10.2
Petty	1,492	1,636	2.9	2.8
Auto theft	625	625	5.6	4.7
Drugs: Sale	1,596	2,388	9.3	5.0
Possession or use	424	951	11.2	5.4
ON APPEAL				
Murder or kidnapping	319	360	598.9	439.7
Rape	123	124	498.9	598.9
Robbery	660	245	236.1	166.8
Burglary	207	510	37.4	86.8

Source: "Length of Sentence for Persons Sentenced, by Appeal Status, for Selected Types of Crimes: 1972," Current Population Reports, Series P-23, No. 54. *The Social and Economic Status of the Black Population in the United States, 1974,* 1975, p. 174. Primary source: U.S. Department of Justice, Law Enforcement Assistance Administration.

★ 536 ★

Legal Justice

Prisoners: Method of Release of Male Prisoners, by Type of Institution, 1945

Excludes statistics for State institutions in Michigan, Georgia, and Mississippi.

Type of Institution and Race	Number Unconditional Release				Percent of All Releases Unconditional Release			
	Total	Expiration of Sentence	Executive Clemency	Conditional Release	Total	Expiration of Sentence	Executive Clemency	Conditional Release
All institutions	13,698	13,173	525	29,718	31.6	30.3	1.2	68.4
White	8,734	8,351	383	21,765	28.6	27.4	1.3	71.4
Negro	4,776	4,639	137	7,601	38.6	37.5	1.1	61.4
Other races	188	183	5	352	34.8	33.9	0.9	65.2
Federal institutions	3,129	3,105	24	7,654	29.0	28.8	0.2	71.0
White	2,396	2,376	20	6,012	28.5	28.3	0.2	71.5

[Continued]

★ 536 ★

Prisoners: Method of Release of Male Prisoners, by Type of Institution, 1945

[Continued]

Type of Institution and Race	Number Unconditional Release				Percent of All Releases Unconditional Release			
	Total	Expiration of Sentence	Executive Clemency	Conditional Release	Total	Expiration of Sentence	Executive Clemency	Conditional Release
Negro	658	654	4	1,472	30.9	30.7	0.2	69.1
Other races	75	75	-	170	30.6	30.6	-	69.4
State institutions	10,569	10,068	501	22,064	32.4	30.9	1.5	67.6
White	6,338	5,975	363	15,753	28.7	27.0	1.6	71.3
Negro	4,118	3,985	133	6,129	40.2	38.9	1.3	59.8
Other races	113	108	5	182	38.3	36.6	1.7	61.7

Source: "Male Felony Prisoners Released, by Type of Institution, Method of Release, and Race, for the United States: 1945," *The Negro Handbook, 1949*, 1949, p. 88. Primary source: *U.S. Bureau of the Census.*

★ 537 ★

Legal Justice

Prisoners: Method of Release of Prisoners in 1937, by Region of Institution

Race	Total released	Unconditional Release		Conditional release	Percent released conditionally
		Sentence expired	Executive clemency		
Federal Institutions					
Total	11,011	1,484	17	9,510	86.4
White	9,012	1,200	13	7,799	86.5
Negro	1,770	257	2	1,511	85.4
Other races	229	27	2	200	87.3
14 Southern States					
Total	18,315	12,563	88	5,664	30.9
White	10,144	6,512	78	3,554	35.0
Negro	8,059	5,956	10	2,093	26.0
Other races	112	95	-	17	15.2
32 Northern and Western States					
Total	27,861	6,191	278	21,392	76.8
White	23,443	5,263	266	17,914	76.4
Negro	4,043	818	6	3,219	79.6
Other races	375	110	6	259	69.1

Source: "Felony' Prisoners Released, by Method of Release and Race, by State Groups: 1937," *The Negro Handbook*, 1942, p. 56. Primary source: U.S. Bureau of the Census.

★ 538 ★

Legal Justice

Relationships: Black/White Differences in Commitments Excluding Drunkenness and Disorderly Conduct, by Geographic Division, c. 1910

SECTION AND DIVISION	RATIO OF COMMITMENTS[1]					
	For all offenses except drunkenness and disorderly conduct			For drunkenness and disorderly conduct		
	Negro A	White B	Coefficient of differences A/B	Negro A	White B	Coefficient of differences A/B
United States	676.7	199.6	3.4	424.9	267.8	1.6
The South	544.0	122.2	4.5	336.3	135.9	2.5
South Atlantic	578.5	128.0	4.5	423.9	189.4	2.2
East South Central	523.6	110.7	4.7	356.6	121.4	2.9
West South Central	499.7	124.9	4.0	127.6	84.0	1.5
The North	1,694.1	202.7	8.4	1,141.9	300.5	3.8
New England	1,307.6	242.6	5.4	723.9	536.8	1.3
Middle Atlantic	1,241.5	229.2	5.4	1,344.7	322.2	4.2
East North Central	1,841.9	177.9	10.4	1,287.4	243.6	5.3
West North Central	2,395.9	175.0	13.7	726.5	219.4	3.3
The West	2,481.1	406.5	6.1	1,186.3	409.2	2.9
Mountain	3,498.4	429.7	8.1	1,197.2	388.4	3.1
Pacific	1,733.2	391.9	4.4	1,178.3	422.2	2.8

Source: [Untitled Table], *Negro Population, 1790-1915,* 1918, p. 439. Primary source: U.S. Bureau of the Census. *Negro Population, 1790-1915.* Washington, D.C.: Government Printing Office, 1918. *Notes:* 1. Number of prisoners and juvenile delinquents committed in 1910 per 100,000 population of the same race.

★ 539 ★

Legal Justice

Relationships: Regional Distribution of Prisoners and Juvenile Delinquents Committed but Not Fined, 1910

DIVISION	PRISONERS AND JUVENILE DELINQUENTS COMMITTED IN 1910 UNDER SENTENCE OF IMPRISONMENT ONLY					
	Total		Receiving indeterminate sentence			
			Number		Per cent	
	Negro	White	Negro	White	Negro	White
UNITED STATES[1]	28,093	142,411	1,663	15,975	5.9	11.2
THE SOUTH						
South Atlantic	10,638	6,418	126	268	1.2	4.2
East South Central	3,904	2,942	90	80	2.3	2.7

[Continued]

★ 539 ★

Relationships: Regional Distribution of Prisoners and Juvenile Delinquents Committed but Not Fined, 1910

[Continued]

DIVISION	PRISONERS AND JUVENILE DELINQUENTS COMMITTED IN 1910 UNDER SENTENCE OF IMPRISONMENT ONLY					
	Total		Receiving indeterminate sentence			
			Number		Per cent	
	Negro	White	Negro	White	Negro	White
West South Central	2,953	2,822	138	176	4.7	6.2
THE NORTH						
New England	620	25,370	120	5,956	19.4	22.5
Middle Atlantic	4,382	51,145	402	3,750	9.2	7.3
East North Central	1,637	17,622	509	3,313	31.1	18.8
West North Central	2,880	15,875	190	926	6.6	5.8
THE WEST						
Mountain	494	7,054	64	901	13.0	12.8
Pacific	395	12,802	24	605	6.1	4.7

Source: [Untitled Table], *Negro Population, 1790-1915*, 1918, p. 441. Primary source: U.S. Bureau of the Census. *Negro Population, 1790-1915.* Washington, D.C.: Government Printing Office, 1918. *Notes:* 1. Includes figures for the United States penitentiaries which are not shown separately in this table.

★ 540 ★

Legal Justice

Relationships: Total Prisoners and Juvenile Delinquents and Those Committed to Prison for Failure to Pay Fine, by Geographic Division, 1910

DIVISION	PRISONERS AND JUVENILE DELINQUENTS COMMITTED IN 1910					
	Total		Imprisoned for nonpayment of fine			
			Number		Per cent	
	Negro	White	Negro	White	Negro	White
UNITED STATES	108,268	382,052	67,860	208,737	62.7	54.6
THE SOUTH						
South Atlantic	41,226	25,620	27,949	17,466	67.8	68.2
East South Central	23,347	13,357	15,659	8,496	67.1	63.6
West South Central	12,449	14,046	7,841	9,524	63.0	67.8
THE NORTH						
New England	1,347	50,511	532	20,226	39.5	40.0
Middle Atlantic	10,807	104,105	5,257	47,433	48.6	45.6

[Continued]

★ 540 ★

Relationships: Total Prisoners and Juvenile Delinquents and Those Committed to Prison for Failure to Pay Fine, by Geographic Division, 1910

[Continued]

DIVISION	PRISONERS AND JUVENILE DELINQUENTS COMMITTED IN 1910					
	Total		Imprisoned for nonpayment of fine			
			Number		Per cent	
	Negro	White	Negro	White	Negro	White
East North Central	9,414	75,550	5,412	47,758	57.5	63.2
West North Central	7,577	44,775	4,359	27,125	57.5	60.6
THE WEST						
Mountain	1,008	20,621	472	12,562	46.8	60.9
Pacific	850	32,758	379	18,147	44.6	55.4
United States penitentiaries	243	709	...	...	...	...

Source: [Untitled Table], *Negro Population, 1790-1915*, 1918, p. 441. Primary source: U.S. Bureau of the Census. *Negro Population, 1790-1915*. Washington, D.C.: Government Printing Office, 1918.

★ 541 ★

Legal Justice

Sentences: Prisoner and Juvenile Delinquent Average Sentence Length in 1910

| DIVISION | AVERAGE LENGTH OF SENTENCE OF PRISONERS AND JUVENILE DELINQUENTS COMMITTED IN 1910 FOR A DEFINITE TERM OF IMPRISONMENT WITHOUT FINE (MONTHS) | |
	Negro	White
United States	17.4	5.2
The South:		
South Atlantic	15.4	9.6
East South Central	31.7	16.2
West South Central	29.7	25.3
The North:		
New England	4.7	3.5
Middle Atlantic	4.9	3.3
East North Central	17.7	4.8
West North Central	9.1	4.5

[Continued]

★ 541 ★

Sentences: Prisoner and Juvenile Delinquent Average Sentence Length in 1910
[Continued]

DIVISION	AVERAGE LENGTH OF SENTENCE OF PRISONERS AND JUVENILE DELINQUENTS COMMITTED IN 1910 FOR A DEFINITE TERM OF IMPRISONMENT WITHOUT FINE (MONTHS)	
	Negro	White
The West:		
Mountain	5.1	6.2
Pacific	11.8	6.5

Source: [Untitled Table], *Negro Population, 1790-1915*, 1918, p. 443. Primary source: U.S. Bureau of the Census. *Negro Population, 1790-1915.* Washington, D.C.: Government Printing Office, 1918.

★ 542 ★

Legal Justice

Sentences: Prisoner and Juvenile Delinquent Sentences of Persons Committed but Not Fined, 1910

LENGTH OF SENTENCE	PRISONERS AND JUVENILE DELINQUENTS COMMITTED IN 1910 UNDER SENTENCE OF IMPRISONMENT ONLY			
	Number		Percentage distribution	
	Negro	White	Negro	White
Total	28,093	142,411	100.0	100.0
Life	490	281	1.7	0.2
Definite term	24,458	117,570	87.1	82.6
1 year or over	7,950	11,719	28.3	8.2
Less than 1 year	16,508	105,851	58.8	74.3
Minority	1,272	7,946	4.5	5.6
Indeterminate	1,663	15,975	5.9	11.2
Not reported	210	639	0.7	0.4

Source: [Untitled Table], *Negro Population, 1790-1915*, 1918, p. 441. Primary source: U.S. Bureau of the Census. *Negro Population, 1790-1915.* Washington, D.C.: Government Printing Office, 1918.

★ 543 ★

Legal Justice

Sentences: Regional Distribution of Prisoner and Juvenile Delinquent Sentences Less Than or Over 1 Year, 1910

SECTION AND RACE	PRISONERS AND JUVENILE DELINQUENTS COMMITTED IN 1910 FOR LIFE OR FOR A DEFINITE TERM OF IMPRISONMENT WITHOUT FINE						
		Number sentenced for-			Per cent sentenced for-		
	Total	1 year or over	Less than 1 year		1 year or over[1]	Less than 1 year	
			1 month or over	Less than 1 month		1 month or over	Less than 1 month
United States:							
Negro	24,948	8,440	11,170	5,338	33.8	44.8	21.4
White	117,851	12,000	60,443	45,408	10.2	51.8	38.5
The South:							
Negro	16,460	6,955	6,645	2,860	42.3	40.4	17.4
White	10,397	3,517	3,928	2,952	33.8	37.8	28.4
The North:							
Negro	7,546	1,207	4,035	2,304	16.0	53.5	30.5
White	89,580	6,196	48,264	35,120	6.9	53.9	39.2
The West:							
Negro	752	88	490	174	11.7	65.2	23.1
White	17,513	1,927	8,250	7,336	11.0	47.1	41.9
United States penitentiaries:							
Negro	190	190	...	...	100.0	...	...
White	361	360	1	...	99.7	0.2	...

Source: [Untitled Table], *Negro Population, 1790-1915*, 1918, p. 442. Primary source: U.S. Bureau of the Census. *Negro Population, 1790-1915*. Washington, D.C.. Government Printing Office, 1918. *Note:* 1. Includes life sentence.

★ 544 ★

Legal Justice

Sentences: Sentences of Black and White Prisoners and Juvenile Delinquents, 1910

SENTENCE	PRISONERS AND JUVENILE DELINQUENTS COMMITTED IN 1910					
	All classes	Negro		White	Percentage distribution	
		Number	Percent of all classes		by sentence	
					Negro	White
Total	493,934	108,268	21.9	382,052	100.0	100.0
Death	130	49	37.7	80	[1]	[1]
Imprisonment only	171,383	28,093	16.4	142,411	25.9	37.3
One year or more[2]	20,616	8,440	40.9	12,000	7.8	3.1
Less than one year	123,004	16,508	13.4	105,851	15.2	27.7
During minority	9,229	1,272	13.8	7,946	1.2	2.1

[Continued]

★ 544 ★

Sentences: Sentences of Black and White Prisoners and Juvenile Delinquents, 1910
[Continued]

| SENTENCE | PRISONERS AND JUVENILE DELINQUENTS COMMITTED IN 1910 | | | | | |
| | All classes | Negro | | White | Percentage distribution by sentence | |
		Number	Percent of all classes		Negro	White
Indeterminate sentence	17,681	1,663	9.4	15,975	1.5	4.2
Length of sentence not reported	853	210	24.6	639	0.2	0.2
Imprisonment and fine	42,006	11,877	28.3	29,742	11.0	7.8
Imprisoned for nonpayment of fine	278,914	67,860	24.3	208,737	62.7	54.6
Nature of sentence not reported	1,501	389	25.9	1,082	0.4	0.3

Source: [Untitled Table], *Negro Population, 1790-1915*, 1918, p. 440. Primary source: U.S. Bureau of the Census. *Negro Population, 1790-1915*. Washington, D.C.: Government Printing Office, 1918. *Notes:* 1. Less than one-tenth of 1 per cent. 2. Includes life sentence.

★ 545 ★
Legal Justice

Sentences: Sentences of Unfined Prisoners and Juvenile Delinquents in 1910

| LENGTH OF SENTENCE | PRISONERS AND JUVENILE DELINQUENTS IN 1910 COMMITTED FOR LIFE OR FOR A DEFINITE TERM OF IMPRISONMENT WITHOUT FINE | | | | |
| | Negro | | White | Percentage distribution by length of sentence | |
	Number	Percent of total		Negro	White
Total	24,948	17.4	117,851	100.0	100.0
1 year or over	8,440	40.9	12,000	33.8	10.2
Life	490	62.6	281	2.0	0.2
10 years or over	913	54.8	734	3.7	0.6
5 to 9 years	1,260	46.0	1,465	5.1	1.2
2 to 4 years	3,001	40.4	4,377	12.0	3.7
1 year	2,776	34.7	5,143	11.1	4.4
Less than year	16,508	13.4	105,851	66.2	89.8
7 to 11 months	640	36.8	1,094	2.6	0.9
6 months	2,165	18.9	9,232	8.7	7.8
4 to 5 months	863	22.7	2,919	3.5	2.5
3 months	2,282	14.1	13,871	9.1	11.8
2 months	1,703	15.4	9,318	6.8	7.9
1 month	3,517	12.7	24,009	14.1	20.4
Less than 1 month	5,338	10.5	45,408	21.4	38.5

Source: [Untitled Table], *Negro Population, 1790-1915*, 1918, p. 442. Primary source: U.S. Bureau of the Census. *Negro Population, 1790-1915*. Washington, D.C.: Government Printing Office, 1918.

★ 546 ★

Legal Justice

Time Served: Male Prisoners' Median Time Served in Southern States in 1937, by Offense

Race and Offense	All Offenses		Expirations		Paroles, Pardons, Etc.	
	Total	Median (months)	Total	Median (months)	Total	Median (months)
White						
All offenses	9,923	16.4	6,373	16.9	3,550	15.1
Murder	334	58.0	109	58.2	225	57.9
Manslaughter	352	21.8	97	27.2	255	19.9
Robbery	903	37.3	449	40.0	454	33.5
Aggravated assault	483	14.5	304	13.9	179	15.3
Burglary	2,771	18.1	2,002	19.2	769	14.7
Larceny, fraud, and stolen property	2,938	12.0	1,937	12.3	1,001	11.6
Auto theft	326	24.0	256	28.2	70	15.6
Forgery	768	14.0	534	14.4	234	13.5
Rape	212	26.4	117	28.8	95	23.3
Other sex offenses	118	15.6	81	14.9	37	17.3
All other offenses	718	11.1	487	10.7	231	12.9
Negro						
All offenses	7,637	19.5	5,646	19.1	1,991	20.7
Murder	417	72.8	167	69.8	250	74.3
Manslaughter	399	34.5	230	35.1	169	33.3
Robbery	574	37.3	359	38.4	215	35.4
Aggravated assault	838	16.0	640	15.4	198	17.5
Burglary	2,508	20.8	2,003	20.9	505	20.1
Larceny, fraud, and stolen property	1,983	12.4	1,553	12.2	430	12.7
Auto theft	162	20.3	98	21.6	64	19.0
Forgery	177	17.6	138	18.3	39	15.8
Rape	159	33.4	119	32.7	40	36.0
Other sex offenses	52	18.0	42	22.5	10	...
All other offenses	368	10.6	297	10.1	71	18.3

Source: "Median Time Served by Male Prisoners, by Method of Release, Race, and Offense, in 14 Southern States: 1937," *The Negro Handbook*, 1942, p. 57. Primary source: U.S. Bureau of the Census. *Notes:* No computations of time served made where less than 25 cases. 1. Computations based on 25 to 50 cases, should be used with caution.

Lynching

★ 547 ★

Causes: Presumed Causes of Lynchings, 1882-1951

Causes	Number	Per Cent
Homicides	1,937	41.0
Felonious assault	204	4.3
Rape	910	19.2
Attempted rape	288	6.1
Robbery and theft	232	4.9
Insult to white person	84	1.8
All other causes	1,075	22.7
Totals	4,730	100.0

Source: "Causes of Lynchings Classified, 1882-1951," *1952 Negro Year Book: A Review of Events Affecting Negro Life,* 1952, p. 278. Primary source: Guzman, Jessie Parkhurst (Ed.), *1952 Negro Year Book: A Review of Events Affecting Negro Life.* New York: Wm. H. Wise & Co., Inc. 1952.

★ 548 ★

Lynching

Causes: Southern and Northern Newspapers' Judged Causes of and Remedies for a 1946 Lynching in Georgia

	Southern Papers	Northern Papers	Total
Causes			
Election of Talmadge, Activities of KKK	23	63	86
Race hatred	9	15	24
Southern living standards	2	5	7
Sadistic tendencies of lynch-minded persons	3	2	5
Postwar reaction	2	2	4
Outside agitators	3	1	4
Governor Arnall's liberalism	1	...	1
Results of capitalism	...	1	1
Total	43	89	132
Remedies			
Federal anti-lynch law	6	20	26
State anti-lynch law	2	4	6
Education, Religion	2	4	6
Harsh penalties for lynchers	2	...	2
Better local law enforcement officers	1	...	1
More all-Negro, all-white communities	1	...	1

[Continued]

★ 548 ★

Causes: Southern and Northern Newspapers' Judged Causes of and Remedies for a 1946 Lynching in Georgia
[Continued]

	Southern Papers	Northern Papers	Total
Unity of liberal forces	...	1	1
Total	14	29	43

Source: "Causes Attributed and Remedies Proposed by Editors of 217 Northern and Southern Newspapers in Discussing the Lynching of Four Negroes in Georgia, July 25, 1946," *Negro Year Book: A Review of Events Affecting Negro Life, 1941-1946*, 1947, p. 303. Primary source: Guzman, Jessie Parkhurst (Ed.), *Negro Year Book: A Review of Events Affecting Negro Life, 1941-1946*. Tuskegee Institute, Ala.: Department of Records and Research, 1947.

★ 549 ★

Lynching

Number/Percent: Lynchings from 1882-1951, by State

State	Whites	Negroes	Total
Alabama	48	299	347
Arizona	31	0	31
Arkansas	58	226	284
California	41	2	43
Colorado	66	2	68
Delaware	0	1	1
Florida	25	257	282
Georgia	39	491	530
Idaho	20	0	20
Illinois	15	19	34
Indiana	33	14	47
Iowa	17	2	19
Kansas	35	19	54
Kentucky	63	142	205
Louisiana	56	335	391
Maryland	2	27	29
Michigan	7	1	8
Minnesota	5	4	9
Mississippi	40	534	574
Missouri	53	69	122
Montana	82	2	84
Nebraska	52	5	57
Nevada	6	0	6
New Jersey	0	1	1
New Mexico	33	3	36
New York	1	1	2
N. Carolina	15	84	99
N. Dakota	13	3	16
Ohio	10	16	26
Oklahoma	82	40	122

[Continued]

★ 549 ★

Number/Percent: Lynchings from 1882-1951, by State
[Continued]

State	Whites	Negroes	Total
Oregon	20	1	21
Pennsylvania	2	6	8
S. Carolina	4	156	160
S. Dakota	27	0	27
Tennessee	47	204	251
Texas	141	352	493
Utah	6	2	8
Virginia	17	83	100
Washington	25	1	26
W. Virginia	20	28	48
Wisconsin	6	0	6
Wyoming	30	5	35
Total	1,293	3,437	4,730

Source: "Lynchings, by States and Race, 1882-1951," *1952 Negro Year Book: A Review of Events Affecting Negro Life*, 1952, p. 277. Primary source: U.S. Bureau of the Census.

★ 550 ★

Lynching

Number/Percent: Lynchings in a 5- and in 10-Year Periods, 1882-1946

Period	Whites	Negroes	Total
1937-1946	2	42	44
1927-1936	14	136	150
1917-1926	44	419	463
1907-1916	62	608	670
1897-1906	146	884	1,030
1887-1896	548	1,035	1,583
1882-1886[1]	475	301	776
Totals	1,291	3,425	4,716

Source: "Lynchings, Whites and Negroes, by Periods 1882-1946," *Negro Year Book: An Review of Events Affecting Negro Life, 1941-1946*, 1947, p. 308. Primary source: U.S. Bureau of the Census. *Notes:* 1. Indicates a five-year period. The other intervals are ten-year periods.

★ 551 ★
Lynching

Number/Percent: Number Lynching Victims and Number Prevented Lynchings, 1914-1936

Year	Number Persons Lynched	Number Persons Prevented Being Lynched	Ratio of Persons Lynched to Number Prevented being Lynched
1914	52	24	2.17
1915	67	25	2.68
1916	54	25	2.16
1917	38	23	1.65
1918	64	19	3.37
1919	83	43	1.93
1920	61	84	0.72
1921	64	108	0.59
1922	57	114	0.55
1923	35	56	0.59
1924	16	61	0.26
1925	17	53	0.32
1926	30	40	0.75
1927	16	68	0.24
1928	11	40	0.28
1929	10	34	0.29
1930	21	60	0.35
1931	13	91	0.14
1932	8	43	0.19
1933	28	48	0.58
1934	15	74	0.20
1935	20	84	0.24
1936	8	79	0.10

Source: "Number of Persons Lynched and Number Prevented Being Lynched, 1914- 1936," *The Negro Yearbook: A Annual Encyclopedia of the Negro, 1937-1938*, 1937, p. 157. Primary source: Work, Monroe N. (Ed.), *Negro Year Book: An Annual Encyclopedia of the Negro, 1937-1938*. Tuskegee Institute, AL: The Negro Year Book Pub. Co., 1937.

★ 552 ★
Lynching

Number/Percent: Number Lynching Victims and Number Prevented Lynchings, 1937-1946

Year	Number of Persons Lynched	Number of Persons Prevented From Being Lynched
1937	8	77
1938	6	53
1939	3	25
1940	5	28
1941	4	21
1942	5	17
1943	3	11
1944	2	8
1945	1	5
1946	6	28

Source: "Number of Persons Lynched and Number Prevented from Being Lynched, 1937-1946," *The Negro Yearbook: A Review of Events Affecting Negro Life, 1941-1946,* 1947, p. 309. Primary source: Guzman, Jessie Parkhurst (Ed.), *Negro Year Book: A Review of Events Affecting Negro Life, 1941-1946.* Tuskegee Institute, AL: Department of Records and Research, 1947.

★ 553 ★
Lynching

Number/Percent: Number Lynching Victims and Number Prevented Lynchings, 1947-1951

Year	Number Lynched	Prevented Lynchings
1947	1	31
1948	2	6
1949	3	14
1950	2	7
1951	1	3
Total	9	61

Source: "Number of Persons Lynched and Number Prevented Lynchings, 1947-1951," *The Negro Yearbook: A Review of Events Affecting Negro Life, 1952,* 1952, p. 278. Primary source: Guzman, Jessie Parkhurst (Ed.), *1952 Negro Year Book: A Review of Events Affecting Negro Life.* New York: Wm. H. Wise & Co., Inc., 1952.

★ 554 ★

Lynching

Number/Percent: Persons Lynched in Each Year, 1882-1970

[No lynchings occurred in 1952-1954, 1956, 1958, 1960, 1962, and 1965-1970].

Year	Total	White	Negro
1964[1]	3	2	1
1963	1	-	1
1961	1	-	1
1959	1	-	1
1957	1	1	-
1955	8	-	8
1951	1	-	1
1950	2	1	1
1949	3	-	3
1948	2	1	1
1947	1	-	1
1946	6	-	6
1945	1	-	1
1944	2	-	2
1943	3	-	3
1942	6	-	6
1941	4	-	4
1940	5	1	4
1939	3	1	2
1938	6	-	6
1937	8	-	8
1936	8	-	8
1935	20	2	18
1934	15	-	15
1933	28	4	24
1932	8	2	6
1931	13	1	12
1930	21	1	20
1929	10	3	7
1928	11	1	10
1927	16	-	16
1926	30	7	23
1925	17	-	17
1924	16	-	16
1923	33	4	29
1922	57	6	51
1921	64	5	59
1920	61	8	53
1919	83	7	76

[Continued]

★ 554 ★

Number/Percent: Persons Lynched in Each Year, 1882-1970

[Continued]

Year	Total	White	Negro
1918	64	4	60
1917	38	2	36
1916	54	4	50
1915	69	13	56
1914	55	4	51
1913	52	1	51
1912	63	2	61
1911	67	7	60
1910	76	9	67
1909	82	13	69
1908	97	8	89
1907	60	2	58
1906	65	3	62
1905	62	5	57
1904	83	7	76
1903	99	15	84
1902	92	7	85
1901	130	25	105
1900	115	9	106
1899	106	21	85
1898	120	19	101
1897	158	35	123
1896	123	45	78
1895	179	66	113
1894	192	58	134
1893	152	34	118
1892	230	69	161
1891	184	71	113
1890	96	11	85
1889	170	76	94
1888	137	68	69
1887	120	50	70
1886	138	64	74
1885	184	110	74
1884	211	160	51

[Continued]

★ 554 ★

Number/Percent: Persons Lynched in Each Year, 1882-1970

[Continued]

Year	Total	White	Negro
1883	130	77	53
1882	113	64	49

Source: "Persons Lynched, by Race: 1882 to 1970," *Historical Statistics of the United States: Colonial Times to 1970, Part I*, 1975, p. 422. Primary source: U.S. Bureau of the Census. *Historical Statistics of the United States: Colonial Times to 1970, Part I*. Bicentennial Edition. Washington, D.C.: Government Printing Office, 1975. *Notes:* - Represents zero. 1. No lynchings, 1965-1970.

★ 555 ★

Lynching

Number/Percent: Regional Incidence of Lynchings, 1882-1946

	Whites	Negroes	Total	Per Cent of U.S. Total
Northern Eastern States	3	8	11	0.2
North Central States	270	154	424	9.0
Southern States	660	3,245	3,905	82.8
Western States	358	18	376	8.0
Totals All Regions	1,291	3,425	4,716	100.0

Source: "Lynchings by Regions 1882-1946," *Negro Year Book: A Review of Events Affecting Negro Life, 1941-1946*, 1947, p. 309. Primary source: U.S. Bureau of the Census.

Chapter 4
EDUCATION

★ 556 ★

Academic Honors: Colleges and Universities with Black Inductees into Phi Beta Kappa, 1874-1916

Year	Institution(s)
1874	Yale
1878	Dartmouth
1891	Rutgers
1892	Western Reserve, Williams
1894	Harvard
1901	Oberlin
1902	Harvard
1903	Harvard
1904	Yale
1905	Amherst, Cornell
1906	Dartmouth
1907	Dartmouth, Harvard
1908	Oberlin
1910	Bowdoin, University of Michigan
1912	Bowdoin, Brown, Williams, University of Michigan
1915	Amherst, Yale
1916	Oberlin

Source: Adapted by the editors from "Negroes who Have Made Phi Beta Kappa," *Negro Year Book: An Annual Encyclopedia of the Negro, 1916-1917,* 1918, p. 245. Primary source: Work, Monroe N. (Ed.), *Negro Year Book: Annual Encyclopedia of the Negro, 1916-1917.* Tuskegee Institute, Ala: The Negro Year Book Pub., Co., 1918.

★ 557 ★

Achievements and Milestones

Academic Honors: National Interracial Honor Societies at Black Institutions, c. 1951

Honor Society	Academic Area	No. Institutions with Chapter
Alpha Kappa Delta	Sociology	2
Arnold Air Society	Aeronautics	4
Scabbard and Blade	Military	3
Delta Phi Alpha	German	1
Omicron Kappa Epsilon	Dental	1
Phi Kappa Lambda	Music	1
Phi Mu Epsilon	Mathematics	1
Psi Chi	Psychology	1
Sigma Pi Sigma	Physics	2
Sigma Xi	Science	1
Sigma Rho Sigma	Social Science	1
Gamma Theta Upsilon	Geography	1
Kappa Delta Pi	Education	1
Pi Omega Pi	Business	1
Simga Delta Pi	Spanish	1
Theta Alpha Pi	Drama	1
The American Veterinary Medical Association	Veterinary Medicine	1
Pershing Rifles	Military	1

Source: "Compiled by the editors from "Interracial Honor Societies," *1952 Negro Year Book: A Review of Events Affecting Negro Life*, 1952, p. 230. Primary source: Guzman, Jessie Parkhurst (Ed.), *1952 Negro Year Book: A Review of Events Affecting Negro Life*. New York: Wm. H. Wise & Co., Inc., 1952.

★ 558 ★

Achievements and Milestones

Early Schools: Schools Established During and Just After the Civil War

On September 17, 1861, the American Missionary Association established at Fortress Monroe, Virginia, the first day school among the Freedmen. This school laid the foundation of the Hampton Institute. In 1862, schools were established at Portsmouth, Norfolk and Newport News. Virginia; Newbern and Roanoke Island, North Carolina and Port Royal, South Carolina. On December 17, 1862, Col. John Eaton, under the orders of General Grant, assumed the general supervision of Freedmen in Arkansas. Schools were immediately established. After the Emancipation Proclamation of January 1, 1863, Negro schools multiplied in all parts of the South, occupied by the Federal armies. General Banks established the first public schools in Louisiana. Schools in Virginia, North Carolina, South Carolina, Tennessee and Arkansas multiplied. March 3, 1865, the Freedmen's Bureau was created, and the education of the Freedmen became one of its special objects, until 1870, when the Bureau was discontinued.

Source: "Education during the Civil War," *Negro Year Book and Annual Encyclopedia of The Negro,* 1912, p. 100. Primary source: Work, Monroe N. (Ed.), *Negro Year Book and Annual Encyclopedia of the Negro.* Tuskegee, AL: Tuskegee Normal and Industrial Institute, 1912.

★ 559 ★

Achievements and Milestones

Early Schools: Schools Established or Headed by Black Educators, 1798-1853

Year	Achievement/ Milestone
1798	First separate school for black children opened in a private home in Massachusetts.
1807	First schoolhouse in Washington, D.C. for black children erected by three black men.
1823	School for black children established in Washington, D.C. by 19-year-old black woman.
1830	School opened by black 15-year-old girl in Georgetown; she was named principal of the first Washington, D.C. seminary for black girls in 1827.

[Continued]

★ 559 ★

Early Schools: Schools Established or Headed by Black Educators, 1798-1853

[Continued]

Year	Achievement/ Milestone
1844	The "Cincinnati Colored High School" was founded by a black man.
1853	Black man named principal of the first Normal school for black teachers, established in New York City.

Source: Adapted by the editors from "Educators," *Negro Year Book and Annual Encyclopedia of the Negro*, 1913, p. 142. Primary source: Work, Monroe N. (Ed.), *Negro Year Book and Annual Encyclopedia of the Negro*. Tuskegee Institute, Ala.: Negro Year Book Co., 1913.

★ 560 ★

Achievements and Milestones

Test Results: Grade 1 and Grade 12 Median Test Scores on Selected Tests, 1965

[As of fall. Estimates based on survey of public elementary and secondary schools. Represents results of standard achievement tests of such skills as reading, writing, calculating, and problem solving. Scores on each test were standardized so that the average over the national sample equaled 50 and the standard deviation equaled 10].

GRADE AND TYPE OF TEST	White	Negro	Puerto Ricans	Indian Americans	Mexican Americans	Oriental Americans
GRADE 1						
Nonverbal	54.1	43.4	45.8	53.0	50.1	56.6
Verbal	53.2	45.4	44.9	47.8	46.5	51.6
GRADE 12						
Nonverbal	52.0	40.9	43.3	47.1	45.0	51.6
Verbal	52.1	40.9	43.1	43.7	43.8	49.6
Reading	51.9	42.2	42.6	44.3	44.2	48.8
Mathematics	51.8	41.8	43.7	45.9	45.5	51.3
General information	52.2	40.6	41.7	44.7	43.3	49.0
Five tests, average	52.0	41.1	43.1	45.1	44.4	50.1

Source: "Achievement Tests—Median Scores for Students in Grades 1 and 12, by Race or Ethnic Group: 1965," *Statistical Abstract of the United States, 1967*, p. 125. Primary source: Dept. of Health, Education, and Welfare, Office of Education: *Equality of Educational Opportunity*, 1966.

Adult Education

★ 561 ★

Number/Percent: Black Participation In and Cost of Adult Programs in Selected Cities, 1943-44

City	Total Population	Negro Population	Enrollment in Adult Programs	Approximate Annual Costs
Atlanta	302,288	104,533	1,900	$60,000
Baltimore	859,100	165,843	1,884	30,000
Birmingham	267,583	108,938	661	...
Chattanooga	128,163	36,404	...	1,083
Durham	60,185	23,347	...	4,000
Jacksonville	173,065	61,782	...	2,200
Knoxville	111,580	16,094	221	4,000
Louisville	319,077	47,158	400	15,000
Montgomery	78,720	34,535	75	1,000
Norfolk	144,332	45,893	618	...
Oklahoma City	204,424	19,344	400	1,875
Richmond	193,042	61,251	1,031	9,000
St. Louis	816,048	108,765	950	14,122
Washington, D.C.	663,091	187,226	2,032	...
Winston-Salem	79,815	36,018	150	2,500
Totals	4,400,523	1,057,131	10,322	$144,780

Source: "Negro Participation in Adult Education Programs in 15 Cities," *Negro Year Book: A Review of Events Affecting Negro Life 1941-1946*, 1947, p. 106. Primary source: Journal of Negro Education, Summer Number, 1945, p. 315.

★ 562 ★

Adult Education

Number/Percent: Source of Instruction of Adult Students (in percentages), 1972

SOURCE OF INSTRUCTION	RACE		
	White	Negro	Other
Total participants 1,000	14,518	1,011	205
Percent:[1]			
Public schools	13.6	17.4	23.4
Two-year colleges and tech. institutes	16.2	19.8	7.3
Four-year colleges and universities	21.7	16.9	21.0

[Continued]

★ 562 ★

Number/Percent: Source of Instruction of Adult Students
(in percentages), 1972
[Continued]

SOURCE OF INSTRUCTION	RACE		
	White	Negro	Other
Community organizations	12.7	12.9	10.2
Private trade, vocational, and business schools	8.6	12.9	6.8
Tutor or private instructor	6.3	0.9	6.3
Employer	16.8	14.4	16.6
Labor unions and professional assns.	5.6	3.4	8.3
Other	10.6	8.2	6.3

Source: "Adult Education—Percent Participation, by Sex, Race, Age, and Source of Instruction: 1972," *Statistical Abstract of the United States, 1973,* p. 143. Primary source: U.S. National Center for Education Statistics (see text, p. 107) *Participation in Adult Education, 1972. Notes:* 1. Percentages total more than 100, since some adults received instruction from more than one source.

★ 563 ★

Adult Education

Number/Percent: Type of Adult Education
Participation, 1969

SOURCE OF INSTRUCTION	RACE		
	White	Negro	Other
Total participants 1,000	12,036	981	133
Percent:[1]			
Public or private schools	27.1	33.8	36.8
College or university, part-time	25.5	21.9	21.8
Job training	27.4	28.7	21.8
Correspondence courses	8.3	4.6	4.5
Community organizations	13.6	11.4	15.8
Tutor or private instructor	5.9	3.3	10.5
Other	10.3	9.4	12.8

Source: "Adult Education—Participation, by Sex, Race, Age, and Source of Instruction: 1969," *Statistical Abstract of the United States, 1973,* p. 138. Primary source: U.S. Office of Education, *Participation in Adult Education, 1969: Initial Report.* Also in *Digest of Educational Statistics, 1970. Notes:* 1. Percentages total more than 100, since some adults received instruction from more than one source.

Characteristics

★ 564 ★

Black Enrollees, Illiterates, and Graduates in Cities with "Large" (100,000 or More) Black Populations, 1970

Selected cities	Number of Negro children enrolled in grades 1-12 (thousands)	Percent Negro of children in public elementary school	Negro population 25 years old and over		
			Percent functional illiterates[1]	Percent high school graduates	Percent college graduates
New York, N.Y.	414	37	7	41	4
Chicago, Ill.	316	56	8	39	4
Detroit, Mich.	174	64	8	37	4
Philadelphia, Pa.	173	61	9	32	3
Washington, D.C.	134	93	7	44	8
Los Angeles, Calif.	126	25	6	50	6
Baltimore, Md.	121	67	11	28	4
Houston, Texas	86	32	11	35	6
Cleveland, Ohio	81	57	8	35	3
New Orleans, La.	78	68	15	26	4
Atlanta, Ga.	66	65	15	34	7
St. Louis, Mo.	72	65	11	31	4
Memphis, Tenn.	73	51	16	24	4
Dallas, Tex.	58	34	10	37	5
Newark, N.J.	58	72	9	33	2
Indianapolis, Ind.	37	23	8	36	4
Birmingham, Ala.	35	53	18	29	4
Cincinnati, Ohio	34	46	12	29	3
Oakland, Calif.	36	57	8	43	4
Jacksonville, Fla.	34	28	17	29	5
Kansas City, Mo.	32	32	8	40	5
Milwaukee, Wis.	33	28	8	34	3
Pittsburgh, Pa.	28	42	9	35	3
Richmond, Va.	29	57	14	26	4
Boston, Mass.	27	32	5	45	4
Columbus, Ohio	28	26	7	41	5

Source: "Educational Characteristics of the Black Population for Cities with 100,000 or More Blacks: 1970," Current Population Reports, Special Studies, Series P-23, No. 42. *The Social and Economic Status of the Black Population in the United States, 1971,* 1972, p. 127. Primary source: U.S. Department of Commerce, Social and Economic Statistics Administration, Bureau of the Census. *Note:* 1. Less than 5 years of school completed.

★ 565 ★

Characteristics

Enrollees, Attendees, High School Graduates, and Pupil/Term Characteristics of Southern Black Public Schools by State, 1946

| State or District of Columbia | Enrollment | | | | Average Daily Attendance | Average Length of School Term | Average Number of Days Attended by Each Pupil Enrolled | Percent of Pupils Enrolled in High School | Total Number of High School Graduates |
| | Elementary | | Secondary | | | | | | |
	Boys	Girls	Boys	Girls					
Total	995,810	998,247	100,366	171,797	1,853,040	170.1	139.1	12.0	32,732
Alabama	99,894	100,823	8,248	16,639	187,297	167.2	138.7	11.0	2,803
Arkansas	43,761	43,809	3,035	5,095	76,926	151.3	121.7	8.5	977
Delaware	3,089	2,898	571	725	6,073	183.1	153.7	17.8	143
Florida	43,476	44,067	5,378	8,896	90,332	176.3	156.4	14.0	2,063
Georgia	115,745	116,345	9,225	17,796	196,989	179.0	136.1	10.4	3,068
Kentucky	15,296	14,833	2,419	3,657	29,793	173.1	142.4	16.8	941
Louisiana	76,247	77,227	4,012	8,220	139,032	160.0	134.4	7.4	2,391
Maryland	27,020	26,950	3,758	5,432	53,116	186.0	156.4	14.6	1,162
Mississippi	122,089	122,623	4,292	9,796	212,032	140.7	121.3	5.4	1,522
Missouri	21,014	20,919	3,966	4,988	40,315	192.3	152.3	17.6	1,403
North Carolina	109,484	111,866	10,536	19,421	211,565	179.9	151.5	11.9	1,925
Oklahoma	15,202	14,957	2,864	3,672	31,043	175.0	148.0	17.8	839
South Carolina	87,193	88,463	8,726	16,638	154,174	164.2	125.9	12.6	2,079
Tennessee	43,686	44,160	5,412	8,810	89,914	171.5	142.7	13.9	1,894
Texas	83,931	82,033	12,929	18,661	157,109	169.0	134.4	16.0	4,256
Virginia	62,136	60,660	9,490	15,413	124,715	180.0	152.0	16.9	3,222
West Virginia	9,809	9,427	2,389	3,232	22,875	175.7	161.6	22.6	1,098
District of Columbia	16,738	16,187	3,116	4,706	34,740	177.3	151.1	19.2	946

Source: "Enrollment, Attendance, and High School Graduates in Negro Public Schools in 17 States and the District of Columbia, 1946," *The Negro Handbook, 1949,* 1949, p. 113. Primary source: U.S. Office of Education.

★ 566 ★

Characteristics

Summary Characteristics: Free Black Persons Attending School and Free Black Persons Unable to Read, by State, 1850

| STATE | Population | ATTENDING SCHOOL | | | ADULTS UNABLE TO READ | | |
		Males	Females	Total	Male	Females	Total
Alabama	2,265	33	35	68	108	127	235
Arkansas	608	6	5	11	61	55	116
California	962	1	0	1	88	29	117
Connecticut	7,693	689	575	1,264	292	273	567

[Continued]

★ 566 ★

Summary Characteristics: Free Black Persons Attending School and Free Black Persons Unable to Read, by State, 1850
[Continued]

STATE	Population	ATTENDING SCHOOL			ADULTS UNABLE TO READ		
		Males	Females	Total	Male	Females	Total
Delaware	18,073	92	95	187	2,724	2,921	5,645
Florida	932	29	37	66	116	154	270
Georgia	2,931	1	0	1	208	259	467
Illinois	5,436	162	161	323	605	624	1,229
Indiana	11,262	484	443	927	1,024	1,146	2,170
Iowa	333	12	5	17	15	18	33
Kentucky	10,011	128	160	288	1,432	1,588	3,019
Louisiana	17,462	629	590	1,219	1,038	2,351	3,389
Maine	1,356	144	137	281	77	58	135
Maryland	74,723	886	730	1,616	9,422	11,640	21,062
Massachusetts	9,064	726	713	1,439	375	431	806
Michigan	2,583	106	101	207	201	168	369
Mississippi	930	0	0	0	75	48	123
Missouri	2,618	23	17	40	271	226	497
New Hampshire	520	41	32	73	26	26	52
New Jersey	23,810	1,243	1,083	2,326	2,167	2,250	4,417
New York	49,069	2,840	2,607	5,447	3,387	4,042	7,429
North Carolina	27,463	113	104	217	3,099	3,758	6,857
Ohio	25,279	1,321	1,210	2,531	2,366	2,624	4,990
Pennsylvania	53,626	3,385	3,114	6,499	4,115	5,229	6,344
Rhode Island	3,670	304	247	551	130	137	267
South Carolina	8,960	54	26	80	421	459	880
Tennessee	6,422	40	30	70	506	591	1,097
Texas	397	11	9	20	34	24	58
Vermont	718	58	32	90	32	19	51
Virginia	54,333	37	27	64	5,141	6,374	11,515
Wisconsin	635	32	35	67	55	37	92

Source: Woodson, *The Education of the Negro Prior to 1861,* "Statistics of the Free Colored Population of the United States in 1850," 1915, p. 237. Primary source: Woodson, C.G. *The Education of the Negro Prior to 1861: A History of the Colored People of the United States from the Beginning of Slavery to the Civil War.* New York and London: G.P. Putnam's Sons, 1915.

County Training Schools

★ 567 ★

Curriculum: Schools and Grades Teaching Specific Subjects in County Training Schools, c. 1920-21

Numbers of Schools	107	103	89	79	39	21	9
Grades	6	7	8	9	10	11	12
SUBJECTS:							
Reading	88	70	20	1	...	...	...
Spelling	104	93	57	26	7	...	...
English	62	57	52	44	14	...	3
Grammar	53	48	41	17	4	4	...
Rhetoric	...	...	21	33	21	5	1
Literature	...	...	14	18	22	22	7
U.S. History	75	95	59	31	14	...	...
State History	33	11	10	1	...	...	...
Civics	29	51	42	21	10	3	...
General History	...	...	17	33	13	11	1
Geography	101	94	45	13	...	...	...
Com. Phy. Geog.	...	...	...	...	...	...	4
General Science	...	...	39	43	13	7	4
Physiology	48	56	22	4	...	2	...
Hygiene	28	25	8	2	...	...	...
Sanitation	9	6	...	2	...	...	...
Nature Study	2	2	...	...	...	...	...
Physics	...	...	...	4	10	11	5
Chemistry	...	...	...	...	3	4	6
Arithmetic	107	103	80	47	10	...	...
Algebra	...	...	52	76	30	6	...
Geometry	...	...	...	10	18	21	6
Bookkeeping	...	...	...	3	1	2	1
Bible	1	2	...	...	...	...	...
Languages	...	...	13	25	17	12	2
Writing	60	51	31	...	...	...	...
Drawing	38	22	31	...	...	...	...
Music	11	8	10	5	2	...	1
Physical Training	5	7	4	2	...	...	...
Total Times Subjects Listed	854	801	637	461	217	103	41
Different Subjects	18	18	21	23	17	13	12

Source: Favrot, *A Study of County Training Schools for Negroes in the South*, "Showing Number of Schools and Grades in which Different Academic Subjects are Taught as Reported by 107 County Training Schools," 1923, p. 73. Primary source: Favrot, Leo Mortimer. *A Study of County Training Schools for Negroes in the South.* Charlottesville, Va.: 1923; bound in Slater Fund. *Occasional Papers.* Nos. 21-27.[Publication information not given.].

★ 568 ★

County Training Schools

Curriculum: Schools, Pupils, Teachers, and Funding of Vocational Programs in County Training Schools, 1920-21

States	V.A.	V.H.E.	V.A.	V.H.E.	V.A.	V.H.E.	V.A.	V.H.E.
Alabama	5	5	5	5	152	178	$2660	$499
Arkansas	6	1	6	1	199	20	2216	100
Georgia	7		8		295		2983	
Louisiana	9	15	11	5	270		5139	1040
Kentucky	1	1	1	1			900	125
Maryland	1		1		10		250	
Mississippi	4	4	8	4	56	92	873	105
N. Carolina	18	5	18	5	388	250	9370[1]	2120
S. Carolina	5	1	5	1	118	23	1645	420
Tennessee	7		7		504		4250	
Texas	6	2	6	2	116	72	3111	800
Virginia	4		4		78		4177	
Total	73	24	80	24	2186	685	$38574	$5209

Source: Favrot, *A Study of County Training Schools for Negroes in theSouth,* "Showing Some Important Facts Regarding the Teaching of Vocational Agriculture and Vocational Home Economics in County Training Schools in 1920-21," 1923, p. 75. Primary source: Favrot, Leo Mortimer. *A Study of Country Training Schools for the Negroes in the South.* Charlottesville, Va.: 1923; bound in Slater Fund. *Occasional Papers.* Nos. 21-27. [Publication information not given.] *Notes:* V.A. = Vocational Agriculture. V.H.E. = Vocational Home Economics. 1. Number of county training schools in which vocational agriculture was taught in 1920-21. 2. Number of teachers employed to teach vocational agriculture. 3. Number of pupils taking vocational agriculture. 4. Total Federal funds (Smith-Hughes) expended during 1920-21 on salaries or anything else in county training schools. The four facts above enumerated for vocational home economics also. 1. Estimated.

★ 569 ★

County Training Schools

Curriculum: Specific Vocational Courses for Boys' and Girls' Industries and in Teacher Training in County Training Schools, c. 1920-21

Boys' Industries		Girls' Industries		Teacher-Training	
SUBJECTS	TIMES LISTED	SUBJECTS	TIMES LISTED	SUBJECTS	TIMES LISTED
AGRICULTURE-	64	HOME ARTS-		PRINCIPLES	
Animal Husbandry	14	Sewing	62	OF TEACHING	20
Plant Husbandry	13	Domestic Art	12	Practice Teaching	20
Project Work	5	Needle Work	6	Methods	17
Gardening	4	Dressmaking	2	School Management	15
Farm Accounts	3	Nursing	2	Review State Examination	1
Horticulture	2	Laundering	1	Normal Course	1
Agronomy	2	Millinery	1		
Poultry	2	Designing	1		

[Continued]

★ 569 ★

Curriculum: Specific Vocational Courses for Boys' and Girls' Industries and in Teacher Training in County Training Schools, c. 1920-21

[Continued]

Boys' Industries		Girls' Industries		Teacher-Training	
Soils	1				
Farm Tools	1	HOME SCIENCE-			
		Domestic Science	12		
SHOP WORK-	29	Cooking	54		
Manual Training	16	Home Economics	15		
Wood Work	12	Housekeeping	7		
Carpentry	8	Canning	1		
Mechanics	6	Food & Health	1		
Painting	3				
Drawing	3	FARM-WIFERY-			
Brickmasonry	1	Agriculture	5		
		Gardening	4		
HANDICRAFT-	2	Poultry	2		
Basketry	7	Farm Accounts	1		
Chair Caning	5	Horticulture	1		
Broom-making	4	Plant Husbandry	1		
Shoe-making	2				
Cobbling	2	HANDICRAFT-	22		
Shuck-work	2	Basketry	3		
		Weaving	1		
		Chair-caning	1		
Total times Listed	213		230		74
Different Subjects	26		26		6

Source: Favrot, *A Study of County Training Schools for Negroes in the South*, "Showing Subjects Listed under Boys' Industries, and Teacher-Training, and Number of the Times Listed by Principals of 107 County Training Schools," 1923, p. 74. Primary source: Favrot, Leo Mortimer. *A Study of County Training Schools for Negroes in the South.* Charlottesville, Va.: 1923; bound in Slater Fund. *Occasional Papers.* Nos. 21-27.[Publication information not given.].

★ 570 ★

County Training Schools

Enrollment: Black Pupils Enrolling in County Training Schools from September (Opening Month) through January, 1920-21

	Sch.	Pup.
Sept.	56	10125
Oct.	44	5883
Nov.	6	1506
Jan.	2	736
Total	108	18250

[Continued]

★ 570 ★

Enrollment: Black Pupils Enrolling in County Training Schools from September (Opening Month) through January, 1920-21

[Continued]

	Sch.	Pup.
Total Entering Late	10325	
Percent Entering Late	36	

Source: Favrot, *A Study of County Training Schools for Negroes in the South,* "Showing Number of Pupils Enrolled at the Opening of School and Number Entering a Month or More Late," 1923, p. 78. Primary source: Favrot, Leo Mortimer. *A Study of County Training Schools for Negroes in the South.* Charlottesville, Va.: 1923; bound in Slater Fund. *Occasional Papers.* Nos. 21-27.[Publication information not given.] Published by permission.

★ 571 ★

County Training Schools

In/Out of School: Entrance and Dropout Patterns in County Training Schools for Black Pupils, by Month, 1920-21

Enrollment Status	Entering	Dropping out
Sept.	10125	71
Oct.	7364	234
Nov.	4232	384
Dec.	1812	374
Jan.	3444	378
Feb.	984	524
Mar.	344	789
Apr.	174	826
May	80	594
June	16	5
Total	28575	4179

Dropout percentages:
  Total   14.5%
  Sept.-Jan.   5.0%
  Feb.-June   9.5%

No. Schools = 108

Source: Adapted by the editors from Favrot, *A Study of County Training Schools for Negroes in the South,*" Showing the Number of Pupils Entering and Dropping Out of County Training Schools in the Different Months, Session 1920-21," 1923, p. 78. Primary source: Favrot, Leo Mortimer. *A Study of County Training Schools for Negroes in the South.* Charlottesville, Va.: 1923; bound in Slater Fund. *Occasional Papers.* Nos. 21-27.[Publication information not given.] Published by permission.

★ 572 ★

County Training Schools

Number/Percent: Growth of County Training Schools in Personnel, Pupils, and other Characteristics, 1911-12 through 1920-21

Session	No. of schools	No. of teachers	Pupils in High School Grades	For Salaries from Public Tax Funds	For Salaries through Slater Board	Average Amount for Salaries from Public Tax Funds	Appropriation of General Education Board for Building and Equipment
1911-12	4	20	77	$3,344	$2,000	$838	$
1912-13	4	23	74	4,612	2,000	1,153	
1913-14	8	41	184	10,696	4,000	1,337	
1914-15	17	85	267	17,986	8,500	1,058	
1915-16	27	135	404	37,395	13,500	1,385	6,392
1916-17	42	252	630	55,020	21,000	1,310	9,864
1917-18	52	308	948	78,533	27,552	1,510	12,374
1918-19	70	402	1,130	131,158	39,037	1,874	20,460
1919-20	107	624	1,649	239,252	52,894	2,236	61,290
1920-21	142	848	2,247	340,821[1]	62,400	2,422	75,271[2]

Source: Favrot, *A Study County of Training Schools for Negroes in the South,* "Showing Interesting Facts in the Growth of Country Training Schools," 1923, p. 65. Primary source: Favrot, Leo Mortimer. *A Study of County Training Schools for Negroes in the South.* Charlottesville, Va.: 1923; bound in Slater Fund. *Occasional Papers.* Nos. 21-27.[Publication information not given.] *Notes:* 1. Total amount, session 1920-21, for all purposes from Public Tax Funds, $648,415.00 2. The General Education Board is also contributing to salaries in diminishing amounts for a period of five years beginning with the session 1920-21, when the amount was $75,113.00.

★ 573 ★

County Training Schools

Progress Through School: County Training School Pupils At, Under, and Over Age, by Gender and Grade, c. 1921

Grades	Under-Age			At Age			Over-Age			% of %		Cumulative
	Boys	Girls	Both	Boys	Girls	Both	Boys	Girls	Both	Total	Total	
1st				1953	2258	4211	2802	2129	4931	9142	31.7	31.7
2nd	62	67	129	418	531	949	1627	1372	2999	4077	14.2	45.9
3rd	27	62	89	272	399	671	1434	1297	2731	3491	12.1	58.0
4th	33	72	105	255	360	615	1261	1344	2605	3325	11.6	69.6
5th	20	38	58	203	261	464	964	1147	2101	2623	9.1	78.7
6th	21	66	87	141	237	378	674	981	1655	2120	7.4	86.1
7th	12	34	46	145	217	362	523	808	1331	1739	6.0	92.1
8th	8	29	37	97	148	245	315	577	892	1174	4.07	96.17
9th	13	24	37	73	155	228	167	289	456	721	2.5	98.67
10th	3	5	8	39	72	111	85	96	181	300	1.0	99.67
11th	1	10	11	4	19	23	21	32	53	87	.3	99.97
12th				1	1	2	3	3	6	8	.03	100.00

[Continued]

★ 573 ★

Progress Through School: County Training School Pupils At, Under, and Over Age, by Gender and Grade, c. 1921

[Continued]

Grades	Under-Age			At Age			Over-Age			% of %		Cumulative
	Boys	Girls	Both	Boys	Girls	Both	Boys	Girls	Both	Total	Total	
Total	200	407	607	3601	4658	8259	9866	10075	19941	28807	100.0	
% Total	.7	1.4	2.1	12.3	16.3	28.6	34.4	34.9	69.3			
% of B. of Total	1.5			26.3			72.2					
% G. of Total		2.6			30.7			66.7				

Source: Favrot, *A Study County of Training Schools for Negroes in the South,* "Showing Number of Under-Age, At Age and Over-Age Pupils by Sexes and by Grades At 101 County Training Schools," 1923, p. 80. Primary source: Favrot, Leo Mortimer. *A Study of County Training Schools for Negroes in the South.* Charlottesville, Va.: 1923; bound in Slater Fund. *Occasional Papers.* Nos. 21-27.[Publication information not given.].

★ 574 ★

County Training Schools

Summary Characteristics: Attendance and Enrollment of Pupils, in County Training Schools, October 1920, January and April 1921

States	October			January			April		
	Enr.	Att.	%	Enr.	Att.	%	Enr.	Att.	%
Alabama	1141	791	69	2160	1603	74	1699	1164	68
Arkansas	1229	1018	82	1504	1262	82	1159	830	71
Georgia	939	736	78	1688	1345	79	1688	1133	78
Kentucky	602	500	83	663	503	76	644	490	76
Louisiana	1485	1234	83	2097	1638	78	1860	1336	72
Maryland	368	287	78	484	387	80	508	380	74
Mississippi	2607	2103	80	3202	2752	85	2973	2508	84
N. Carolina	2386	1645	69	2944	2200	74	2902	2101	72
Oklahoma	806	703	87	809	750	92	882	810	91
S. Carolina	2445	1964	80	3409	2516	74	3539	2385	67
Tennessee	1914	1312	69	2298	1523	67	2332	1469	65
Texas	783	594	76	1420	1177	83	1395	1007	72
Virginia	3231	2494	77	3747	2975	79	3162	2458	77
Total	19936	15390	77	26425	20631	78	24643	18271	74

Source: Favrot, *A Study County of Training Schools for Negroes in the South,* "Showing the Enrollment and Average Attendance in 100 County Training Schools for the Months of October, 1920, and January and April, 1921," 1923, p. 79. Primary source: Favrot, Leo Mortimer. *A Study of County Training Schools for Negroes in the South.* Charlottesville, Va.: 1923; bound in Slater Fund. *Occasional Papers.* Nos. 21-27.[Publication information not given.].

★ 575 ★

County Training Schools

Summary Characteristics: Schools, Teachers, Enrollment, and Property Value and Expenditure Characteristics of County Training Schools, by State, 1920-21

States	No. of Schools	No. of Teachers	Enrollment	No. above Grade 7	Property Value	Salary Expenditures	Total Expenditures (Including Building, Repairs, etc.)
Alabama	14	84	3,082	138	$187,465	$52,455	$78,398
Arkansas	7	55	2,677	163	76,868	37,722	47,192
Florida	1	7	150	13	8,708	4,550	7,225
Georgia	11	70	2,795	123	139,306	38,211	74,107
Kentucky	8	34	1,171	136	72,160	26,355	59,955
Louisiana	10	57	2,182	117	126,545	38,071	70,876
Maryland	2	12	491	39	25,950	6,675	16,900
Mississippi	11	54	2,674	275	181,338	33,909	178,782
N. Carolina	21	136	4,252	197	198,635	93,483	139,129
Oklahoma	1	4	188	58	12,900	2,966	14,445
S. Carolina	12	92	5,779	221	134,945	47,453	71,653
Tennessee	11	72	3,524	264	153,578	44,425	99,790
Texas	10	55	1,810	173	68,834	39,962	53,374
Virginia	23	116	4,542	330	203,030	63,620	95,795
Total	142	848	35,317	2,247	$1,590,262	$529,857	$1,007,732

Source: Favrot, *A Study County of Training Schools for Negroes in the South,* "Showing Status of County Training Schools by States for 1920-21 with Respect to Number of Schools and Teachers, Enrollment, Value of Property, and Total Expenditures," 1923, p. 66. Primary source: Favrot, Leo Mortimer. *A Study of County Training Schools for Negroes in the South.* Charlottesville, Va.: 1923; bound in Slater Fund. *Occasional Papers.* Nos. 21-27.[Publication information not given.].

★ 576 ★

County Training Schools

Teachers: Degree Status of Teachers in County Training Schools for Black Pupils, c. 1921

No. Sch.	131
No. Tchrs.	782
Number Holding	
Deg.	92
Dip.	544
Neither	146
Per Cent Holding	
Deg.	11.7
Dip.	69.6

[Continued]

★ 576 ★

Teachers: Degree Status of Teachers in County Training Schools for Black Pupils, c. 1921

[Continued]

Neither	18.7
Median Years Above Common School	
Deg.	8.3
Dip.	4.9
Neither	3.7

Source: Favrot, *A Study of County Training Schools for Negroes in the South,* "Showing Number of Teachers Holding Degrees, Diplomas, and No Diplomas and Median Number of Years of Schooling Above the Common School for Each Group," 1923, p. 70. Primary source: Favrot, Leo Mortimer. *A Study of County Training Schools for Negroes in the South.* Charlottesville, Va.: 1923; bound in Slater Fund. *Occasional Papers.* Nos. 21-27. [Publication information not given]. Published by permission.

★ 577 ★

County Training Schools

Teachers: Experience (in Years) of Teachers in County Training Schools, c. 1920-21

1 to 4.9 years	
1st	78 10.4%
2nd	58
3rd	61
4th	60
Total	267
5 to 9.9 years	170
10 to 14.9 years	103
15 to 19.9 years	91 64%
20 years and up	115 15%
Grand Total	746

Source: Favrot, *A Study of County Training Schools for Negroes in the South,* "Showing Experience and Tenure of Teachers in County Training Schools. Years' Experience as Teachers (746 Teachers)," 1923, p. 69. Primary source: Favrot, Leo Mortimer. *A Study of County Training Schools for Negroes in the South.* Charlottesville, Va.: 1923; bound in Slater Fund. *Occasional Papers.* Nos. 21-27. [Publication information not given]. Published by permission.

★ 578 ★

County Training Schools

Teachers: Number of Teachers in County Training Schools, by Level of Instruction, c 1920-21

	Schools	Teachers	Primary	Elementary	High School	Special
Alabama	9	59	20	14	14	11
Arkansas	6	36	12	9	8	7
Georgia	9	56	17	15	13	11
Kentucky	6	26	7	6	6	7
Louisiana	10	59	17	10	13	19
Maryland	2	11	4	2	3	2
Mississippi	9	56	17	12	17	10
N. Carolina	16	109	37	30	22	20
Oklahoma	3	24	6	5	10	3
S. Carolina	13	82	34	20	20	8
Tennessee	12	79	23	20	19	17
Texas	11	58	15	12	15	16
Virginia	21	110	39	35	27	9
Total	127	765	248	190	187	140
Per Cent. of Total			32.5	25	24.5	18

Source: Favrot, *A Study County of Training Schools for Negroes in the South*, "Showing Teachers in Training Schools Classified as Primary, Elementary, High School and Special," 1923, p. 71. Primary source: Favrot, Leo Mortimer. *A Study of County Training Schools for Negroes in the South*. Charlottesville, Va.: 1923; bound in Slater Fund. *Occasional Papers*. Nos. 21-27.[Publication information not given.] *Notes:* Primary = Grades 1 to 3; Elementary = Grades 4 to 6; H.S. = Grades 7 to 12.

★ 579 ★

County Training Schools

Teachers: Sources of Funding for Teacher Salaries in County Training Schools, by State, 1917-18 and 1920-21

States	Session 1917-18				Session 1920-21				Increase 48 Schools	
	A	B %	C %	D %	A	B %	C %	D %	A	E %
Alabama	7	63	31	6	14	51	34	15	7	93
Arkansas	5	83	15	2	7	71	14	15	3	90
Florida					1	61	19	20		
Georgia	4	57	27	16	11	53	34	13	4	82
Kentucky	3	76	20	4	8	69	24	7	1	83
Louisiana	3	69	25	6	10	67	19	14	1	53
Maryland					2	73	23	4		
Mississippi	3	61	32	7	11	69	20	11	3	168
N. Carolina	10	64	27	9	21	69	20	11	10	233
Oklahoma					1	83	17	0		
S. Carolina	4	75	18	7	12	64	31	5	4	97
Tennessee	5	85	15		11	63	26	11	5	23

[Continued]

★ 579 ★

Teachers: Sources of Funding for Teacher Salaries in County Training Schools, by State, 1917-18 and 1920-21
[Continued]

States	Session 1917-18				Session 1920-21				Increase 48 Schools	
	A	B %	C %	D %	A	B %	C %	D %	A	E %
Texas	4	61	18	21	10	69	19	12	4	127
Virginia	6	69	30	1	23	62	38	0	6	109
Totals	54	71	23	6	142	64	26	10	48	107

Source: Favrot, A Study County of Training Schools for Negroes in the South, "Showing A Comparison by States of the Per Cent. of Teachers' Salaries Derived from Various Sources for Sessions 1917-18 and 1920-21," 1923, p. 67. Primary source: Favrot, Leo Mortimer. A Study of County Training Schools for Negroes in the South. Charlottesville, Va.: 1923; bound in Slater Fund. Occasional Papers. Nos. 21-27.[Publication information not given.] Notes: A. Number of schools compared. B. Per cent. derived from public funds (all training schools). C. Per cent derived from philanthropic boards (Slater Fund and General Education Board). D. Per cent. derived from other sources. E. Per cent. of increase derived from public funds in 48 schools I.

★ 580 ★

County Training Schools

Teachers: Summer Training Experience of Teachers in County Training Schools, by State, 1919-1921

	Total	Teachers Attending Summer Schools			
		0 Years	1 Year	2 Years	3 Years
Alabama	67	16	27	13	11
Arkansas	36	5	8	7	16
Georgia	56	20	15	11	10
Kentucky	26	5	10	5	6
Louisiana	59	10	14	22	13
Maryland	11	5	5	1	
Mississippi	60	17	14	11	18
N. Carolina	109	19	27	39	24
Oklahoma	24	3	7	11	3
S. Carolina	82	15	29	21	17
Tennessee	81	15	17	26	23
Texas	58	22	21	9	6
Virginia	112	57	35	14	6
Total	781	209	229	190	153
Per cent	100%	26.7%	29.3%	24.3%	19.7%

Source: Favrot, A Study County of Training Schools for Negroes in the South, "Showing the Number of Training School Teachers Attending Summer Normals in the Years 1919, 1920, and 1921," 1923, p. 69. Primary source: Favrot, Leo Mortimer. A Study of County Training Schools for Negroes in the South. Charlottesville, Va.: 1923; bound in Slater Fund. Occasional Papers. Nos. 21-27.[Publication information not given.].

★ 581 ★

County Training Schools

Teachers: Weeks of Professional Training of Teachers in County Training Schools for Black Pupils, c. 1921

0 to 6	192
6.1 to 12	71
12.1 to 18	95
18.1 to 24	60
24.1 to 36	102
36.1 to 48	39
48.1 to 60	16
60.1 to 72	87
72.1 to 84	10
84.1 to 96	13
96.1 to 108	24
108 and up	72
Total	781

Source: Favrot, *A Study of County Training Schools for Negroes in the South,* "Showing Professional Training in Weeks Received by 781 Teachers in County Training Schools," 1923, p. 70. Primary source: Favrot, Leo Mortimer. *A Study of County Training Schools for Negroes in the South.* Charlottesville, Va.: 1923; bound in Slater Fund. *Occasional Papers.* Nos. 21-27. [Publication information not given]. Published by permission.

★ 582 ★

County Training Schools

Teachers: Years at Present School of Teachers in County Training Schools, c. 1920-21

2 to 4.9 years	
1st	311 42.5%
2nd	149
3rd	98
4th	46
Total	604
5 to 9.9 years	91
10 years and up	37
Grand Total	732

Source: Favrot, *A Study of County Training Schools for Negroes in the South,* "Showing Experience and Tenure of Teachers in County Training Schools. Years' Tenure in Present School (732 Teachers)," 1923, p. 69. Primary source: Favrot, Leo Mortimer. *A Study of County Training Schools for Negroes in the South.* Charlottesville, Va.: 1923; bound in Slater Fund. *Occasional Papers.* Nos. 21-27.[Publication information not given.] Published by permission.

★ 583 ★
County Training Schools

Teachers: Years of Advanced "Schooling" of Teachers in County Training Schools for Black Pupils, c. 1921

| | No. Tchrs. | YEARS | | | | | | | | | | Not given |
		1	2	3	4	5	6	7	8	9	10	
	782	6	36	74	243	115	121	52	63	10	9	52
Per Cent of Total		.8	4.6 14.6	9.2	31.1	14.7	15.5	6.7	8.1	1.3	1.2	6.8

Source: Favrot, *A Study of County Training Schools for Negroes in the South,* "Showing Number of Years of Schooling Above the Common School Reported by 782 County Training School Teachers,' 1923, p. 70. Primary source: Favrot, Leo Mortimer. *A Study of County Training Schools for Negroes in the South.* Charlottesville, Va.: 1923; bound in Slater Fund. *Occasional Papers.* Nos. 21-27. [Publication information not given]. Published by permission.

★ 584 ★
County Training Schools

Testing Results: Scores on Standardized Tests in County Training Schools for Black Pupils, c. 1921 - I

	Median Rate Scores			Median Comprehension Scores	
	No. of Pupils	Tr. Sch.	Standard	Tr. Sch.	Standard (Mid-year)
Test II.					
Sixth Grade	689	77.5	90.0	12.3	18.5
Seventh Grade	609	79.6	100.0	14.0	22.8
Eighth Grade	538	89.3	106.0	17.3	26.0
Test III.					
Ninth Grade	252	66.3	83.0	14.1	23.0
Tenth Grade	173	77.0	85.0	17.4	25.4
Eleventh Grade	55	59.2	90.0	19.4	27.2
Twelfth Grade	6	70.0	96.0	21.0	30.0

Source: Favrot, *A Study County of Training Schools for Negroes in the South,* "Showing Results of Standardized Tests in Training Schools," 1923, p. 82. Primary source: Favrot, Leo Mortimer. *A Study of County Training Schools for Negroes in the South.* Charlottesville, Va.: 1923; bound in Slater Fund. *Occasional Papers.* Nos. 21-27.[Publication information not given.].

★ 585 ★

County Training Schools

Testing Results: Scores on Standardized Tests in County Training Schools for Black Pupils, c. 1921 - II

	No. of Pupils	Tr. Sch.	Median Scores	
			Va. Tr. School	Standard (June)
Sixth Grade	671	17.7	19.2	28.5
Seventh Grade	586	20.1	22.0	31.0
Eighth Grade	557	21.7	25.5	33.0
Ninth Grade	193	23.9	26.7	-

Source: Favrot, *A Study County of Training Schools for Negroes in the South*, "Showing Results of Standardized Tests in Training Schools," 1923, p. 82. Primary source: Favrot, Leo Mortimer. *A Study of County Training Schools for Negroes in the South.* Charlottesville, Va.: 1923; bound in Slater Fund. *Occasional Papers.* Nos. 21-27.[Publication information not given.].

★ 586 ★

County Training Schools

Testing Results: Scores on Standardized Tests in County Training Schools for Black Pupils, c. 1921 - III

	No. of Pupils	Median Scores	
		Tr. School	Standard
Tenth Grade	140	5.35	6.5
Eleventh Grade	40	5.2	6.9

Source: Favrot, *A Study County of Training Schools for Negroes in the South*, "Showing Results of Standardized Tests in Training Schools," 1923, p. 82. Primary source: Favrot, Leo Mortimer. *A Study of County Training Schools for Negroes in the South.* Charlottesville, Va.: 1923; bound in Slater Fund. *Occasional Papers.* Nos. 21-27.[Publication information not given.].

Dropouts

★ 587 ★

Percent of 14 to 19-Year-Old Male and Female High School Dropouts, 1970 and 1971

Age	1970				1971			
	Black		White		Black		White	
	Male	Female	Male	Female	Male	Female	Male	Female
Total, 14 to 19 years	15.9	13.3	6.7	8.1	11.6	10.5	6.9	7.8
14 years old	0.9	2.9	1.4	1.1	0.9	0.4	1.0	1.1
15 years old	3.3	2.7	2.0	2.4	3.8	1.5	1.1	1.9
16 years old	10.9	11.1	5.0	6.7	7.2	4.2	5.3	6.2
17 years old	16.0	13.7	7.6	10.2	11.8	15.2	7.6	11.0
18 years old	29.8	27.8	13.6	14.1	22.7	20.8	12.8	13.6
19 years old	44.1	25.8	12.9	15.7	29.3	24.6	15.9	14.0

Source: "Percent High School Dropouts among Persons 14 to 19 Years Old, by Sex and Age: 1970 and 1971," Current Population Reports, Special Studies, Series P-23, No. 42. *The Social and Economic Status of the Black Population in the United States, 1971,* 1972, p. 81. Primary source: U.S. Department of Commerce, Social and Economic Statistics Administration, Bureau of the Census. *Notes:* Dropouts are persons who are not enrolled in school and who are not high school graduates.

★ 588 ★

Dropouts

Relationships: 16-21-Year-Old Dropouts and High School Graduates, Not in College, by Work Status, 1970-1974

[**In thousands, except percent**. Data for high school graduates relate to those not enrolled in college and include those who attended college prior to survey date; data for dropouts relate to persons not in regular school and not high school graduates. Based on samples and subject to sampling variability].

EMPLOYMENT STATUS, SEX, AND RACE	GRADUATES					DROPOUTS				
	1965	1970	1972[1]	1973[1]	1974[1]	1965	1970	1972[1]	1973[1]	1974[1]
Civilian population[2]	4,898	5,823	6,641	7,205	7,406	2,986	2,757	3,027	3,098	3,266
Percent of population	76.9	78.4	81.7	82.2	83.5	62.4	58.4	61.5	60.7	65.3
Employed	3,451	4,038	4,830	5,434	5,502	1,585	1,264	1,504	1,555	1,662
Percent of labor force	91.6	88.4	89.1	91.8	89.0	85.1	78.5	80.8	82.6	78.0
White	3,116	3,636	4,372	4,894	4,992	1,266	1,011	1,237	1,276	1,420
Negro and other	335	402	458	540	510	319	253	267	279	243
Unemployed	318	528	593	486	679	278	347	357	327	470

[Continued]

★ 588 ★

Relationships: 16-21-Year-Old Dropouts and High School Graduates, Not in College, by Work Status, 1970-1974
[Continued]

EMPLOYMENT STATUS, SEX, AND RACE	GRADUATES					DROPOUTS				
	1965	1970	1972[1]	1973[1]	1974[1]	1965	1970	1972[1]	1973[1]	1974[1]
Percent of labor force	8.4	11.6	10.9	8.2	11.0	14.9	21.5	19.2	17.4	22.0
White	259	429	430	366	532	203	232	263	221	338
Negro and other	59	99	163	120	145	75	115	94	106	130

Source: "High School Graduates Not Enrolled in College, and School Dropouts, 16 to 21 years, Old—Employment Status, by Sex and Race: 1965 to 1974," *Statistical Abstract of the United States, 1975,* p. 122. Primary source: U.S. Bureau of Labor Statistics, *Special Labor Force Report,* Nos. 66, 155, 168, and forthcoming report. *Notes:* 1. Based on population estimates consistent with 1970 census and not strictly comparable with earlier years, which are based on 1960 population. 2. Noninstitutional.

★ 589 ★

Dropouts

Relationships: 16-21-Year-Old Dropouts and High School Graduates, by Work Status, 1965-1969

[**In thousands, except as indicated**. As of October. Data for high school graduates relate to those not enrolled in college and include those who attended college prior to survey date; data for dropouts relate to persons not in regular school and not high school graduates. Based on samples and subject to sampling variability].

EMPLOYMENT STATUS, SEX AND RACE	GRADUATES				DROPOUTS			
	1965	1967	1968	1969	1965	1967	1968	1969
Civilian noninstitutional population	4,898	5,176	5,418	5,337	2,986	2,827	2,734	2,685
Percent of population	76.9	77.0	75.2	79.1	62.4	59.9	60.8	59.2
White	3,375	3,530	3,598	3,740	1,469	1,341	1,315	1,233
Negro and other	394	457	478	482	394	351	348	356
Employed	3,451	3,602	3,760	3,896	1,585	1,446	1,415	1,359
Percent of labor force	91.6	90.3	92.2	92.3	85.1	85.5	85.1	85.5
White	3,116	3,231	3,344	3,490	1,266	1,173	1,153	1,058
Negro and other	335	371	416	406	319	273	262	301
Unemployed	318	385	316	326	278	246	248	230
Percent of labor force	8.4	9.7	7.8	7.7	14.9	14.5	14.9	14.5
White	259	299	254	250	203	168	162	175
Negro and other	59	86	62	76	75	78	86	55

Source: "High School Graduates and School Dropouts, 16 to 21 Years Old—Employment Status by Sex and Race: 1965 to 1969," *Statistical Abstract of the United States, 1970,* p. 113. Primary source: Dept. of Labor, Bureau of Labor Statistics; *Special Labor Force Report,* Nos. 66, 100, 108, and forthcoming report.

Educational Attainment

★ 590 ★

Completion Levels: 25-34-Year Old High School and College "Completers," 1940, 1960, 1970, and 1975

[In percentages]

Year	Completed 4 years of high school or more		Completed 4 years of college or more	
	Black	White	Black	White
1940	11	39	2	7
1960	33	61	4	12
1970	52	74	6	17
1975	69	82	11	22

Source: "Selected Levels of Schooling Completed for Persons 25 to 34 Years Old: 1940, 1960, 1970, and 1975," *The Social and Economic Status of the Black Population in the United States: An Historical View, 1790-1978*, 1979, p. 85. Primary source: U.S. Department of Commerce. Bureau of the Census. *The Social and Economic Status of the Black Population in the United States: An Historical View, 1790-1978*. Current Population Reports. Special Studies, P-23, No. 80. Washington, D.C.: Government Printing Office, 1979. *Note:* The 1940 data for Black include persons of "other" races.

★ 591 ★

Educational Attainment

Completion Levels: Black-White Differences in Percent of High School Graduates, 1940-1975

Area, year, and race	Total (thousands)	Percent completed 4 years of high school or more		Median school years completed
		Total	4 years or more of college	
UNITED STATES				
1940				
Black[1]	2,228	11	2	6.9
White	19,111	39	7	10.4
Difference in level of schooling completed	(X)	28	5	3.5
1960				
Black	2,405	33	4	10.3

[Continued]

★ 591 ★

Completion Levels: Black-White Differences in Percent of High School Graduates, 1940-1975
[Continued]

Area, year, and race	Total (thousands)	Percent completed 4 years of high school or more		Median school years completed
		Total	4 years or more of college	
White	20,162	61	12	12.3
Difference in level of schooling completed	(X)	28	8	2.0
1970				
Black	2,664	52	6	12.0
White	21,800	74	17	12.6
Difference in level of schooling completed	(X)	22	11	0.6
1975				
Black	3,099	69	11	12.4
White	26,373	82	22	12.8
Difference in level of schooling completed	(X)	13	11	0.4

Source: "Selected Levels of Schooling Completed for Persons 25 to 34 Years old, by Region: 1940, 1960, 1970, and 1975," *The Social and Economic Status of the Black Population in the United States: An Historical View, 1790-1978*, 1979, pp. 94-95. Primary source: U.S. Department of Commerce, Bureau of the Census. *Notes:* X = Not applicable. 1. Includes persons of "other" races.

★ 592 ★

Educational Attainment

Completion Levels: Elementary, High School, and College Completers, 1947-1969
[Persons 25 years old and over as of March of year indicated, except as noted. Includes inmates of institutions and members of the Armed Forces living off post or with their families on post, but excludes all other members of the Armed Forces]

AGE AND YEAR	ALL RACES				NEGRO AND OTHER (except white)			
	Years completed (percent distribution)			Median school years completed[2]	Years completed (percent distribution)			Median school years completed[2]
	Elementary school, less than 5 years[1]	High school, 4 years or more	College 4 years or more		Elementary school, less than 5 years[1]	High school, 4 years or more	College, 4 years or more	
25 YEARS AND OVER								
1947[2]	10.6	33.1	5.4	9.0	32.2	13.6	2.5	6.9
1957	9.1	41.6	7.6	10.6	27.7	18.4	2.9	7.7
1960	8.3	41.1	7.7	10.5	23.5	21.7	3.5	8.2
1965	6.8	49.0	9.4	11.8	18.4	28.6	5.5	9.0
1968	5.9	52.6	10.5	12.1	17.3	32.5	5.5	9.5

[Continued]

★ 592 ★

Completion Levels: Elementary, High School, and College Completers, 1947-1969
[Continued]

AGE AND YEAR	ALL RACES				NEGRO AND OTHER (except white)			
	Years completed (percent distribution)			Median school years completed[2]	Years completed (percent distribution)			Median school years completed[2]
	Elementary school, less than 5 years[1]	High school, 4 years or more	College 4 years or more		Elementary school, less than 5 years[1]	High school, 4 years or more	College, 4 years or more	
1969	5.6	54.0	10.7	12.1	15.2	34.5	6.0	9.8
25-29 YEARS								
1947[3]	4.3	51.4	5.6	12.0	19.2	22.3	2.8	8.4
1957	2.7	60.2	10.4	12.3	8.7	31.6	4.1	9.9
1960	2.8	60.7	11.1	12.3	7.2	38.6	5.4	10.8
1965	2.0	70.3	12.4	12.4	4.8	52.2	8.3	12.1
1968	1.1	73.2	14.7	12.5	2.8	57.6	7.9	12.2
1969	1.3	74.7	16.0	12.6	2.5	57.5	9.1	12.2

Source: "Years of School Completed, by Race: 1947 to 1969" Statistical Abstract of the United States, 1970, p. 110. Primary source: Dept. of Commerce, Bureau of the Census, Current Population Reports, Series P-20, No. 194. Notes: 1. Includes persons reporting no school years completed. 2. As of April.

★ 593 ★

Educational Attainment

Completion Levels: Gender of 25-to 34-Year Old College "Completers," 1960, 1966, 1970, 1974

[In percentages]

Year	Black			White		
	Total	Male	Female	Total	Male	Female
1960	4.1	4.1	4.0	11.9	15.8	8.3
1966	5.7	5.2	6.1	14.6	18.9	10.4
1970	6.1	5.8	6.4	16.6	20.9	12.3
1974	8.1	8.8	7.6	21.0	24.9	17.2

Source: "Percent of Population 25 to 34 Years Old, Who Completed Four Years of College or More, by Sex: 1960, 1966, 1970, and 1974," Current Population Reports, Special Studies, Series P-23, No. 54. The Social and Economic Status of the Black Population in the United States, 1974, 1975, p. 97. Primary source: U.S. Department of Commerce, Social and Economic Statistics Administration, Bureau of the Census.

★ 594 ★

Educational Attainment

Completion Levels: Gender of Elementary, High School, and College Completers, 1960 and 1969

[**Persons 25 years old and over**. 1960 as of April 1, based on 25-percent sample; 1969 data as of March, based on Current Population Survey]

| YEAR, SEX, AND RACE | Persons 25 years old and over (1,000) | YEARS OF SCHOOL COMPLETED (percent distribution) | | | | | | | Median school years completed[1] |
| | | Elementary school | | | High school | | College | | |
		0-4 years	5-7 years	8 years	1-3 years	4 years	1-3 years	4 years or more	
1960, all races	99,438	8.3	13.8	17.5	19.2	24.6	8.8	7.7	10.6
Male	47,931	9.4	14.6	17.8	18.7	21.2	8.6	9.7	10.3
Female	51,508	7.4	13.1	17.3	19.7	27.8	9.0	5.8	10.9
White	89,581	6.7	12.8	18.1	19.3	25.8	9.3	8.1	10.9
Male	43,259	7.4	13.7	18.4	18.9	22.2	9.1	10.3	10.7
Female	46,322	6.0	11.9	17.8	19.6	29.2	9.5	6.0	11.2
Negro	9,054	23.8	24.2	12.9	19.0	12.9	4.1	3.1	8.2
Male	4,240	28.3	23.9	12.3	17.3	11.3	4.1	2.8	7.7
Female	4,814	19.8	24.5	13.4	20.5	14.3	4.1	3.3	8.6
1969, all races	107,750	5.6	9.4	13.7	17.2	33.5	9.8	10.7	12.1
Male	51,031	6.1	9.0	14.0	16.5	29.7	10.3	13.6	12.1
Female	56,719	5.1	9.0	13.5	17.9	36.9	9.3	8.1	12.1
White	96,822	4.5	8.5	14.0	16.7	34.8	10.3	11.2	12.2
Male	45,989	4.8	9.1	14.3	16.1	30.6	10.8	14.3	12.2
Female	50,833	4.2	8.1	13.7	17.3	38.5	9.8	8.5	12.2
Negro	9,918	15.5	18.3	11.5	22.4	22.3	5.4	4.6	9.6
Male	4,552	18.0	18.3	11.1	20.7	21.4	5.7	4.8	9.4
Female	5,366	13.4	18.3	11.9	23.9	23.0	5.1	4.5	9.8

Source: "Years of School Completed, by Sex and Race: 1960 and 1969," *Statistical Abstract of the United States, 1970*, p. 109. Primary source: Dept. of Commerce, Bureau of the Census, *U.S. Census of Population: 1960*, Vol. I and *Current Population Reports*, Series P-20, No. 194.

★ 595 ★
Educational Attainment

Completion Levels: Gender of High School "Completers," Aged 25 to 29 Years, 1960, 1966, 1970, 1971

[In percentages]

Year	Male		Female	
	Negro	White	Negro	White
1960	36[1]	63	41[1]	65
1966	49	73	47	74
1970	54	79	58	76
1971	54	81	61	78

Source: "Percent of Persons 25 to 29 Years Old Who Competed 4 Years of High School or More, by Sex: 1960, 1965, 1970, and 1971," Current Population Reports, Special Studies, Series P-23, No. 42. *The Social and Economic Status of the Black Population in the United States, 1971,* 1972, p. 83. Primary source: U.S. Department of Commerce, Social and Economic Statistics Administration, Bureau of the Census. *Note:* 1. Data for Negro and other races.

★ 596 ★
Educational Attainment

Completion Levels: Gender of "Completers" of High School and One or More Years of College, Aged 20 to 24 Years, 1960, 1965, 1970, 1974

[In percentages]

Level of schooling and year	Total		Male		Female	
	Black	White	Black	White	Black	White
Percent completed 4 years of high school or more:						
1960	42	66	39[1]	65	45[1]	68
1965	49	76	50	76	48	77
1970	65	83	62	83	67	83
1974	72	85	68	86	75	85
Percent completed 1 year of college or more:						
1960	12	25	12[1]	28	13[1]	22
1965	15	31	14	36	15	26
1970	23	39	23	44	23	35
1974	27	43	25	46	29	40

Source: "Level of Schooling Completed by Persons 20 to 24 Years Old, by Sex: 1960, 1965, 1970, and 1974," Current Population Reports, Special Studies, Series P-23, No. 54. *The Social and Economic Status of the Black Population in the United States, 1974,* 1975, p. 97. Primary source: U.S. Department of Commerce, Social and Economic Statistics Administration, Bureau of the Census. *Note:* 1. Includes persons of "other" races.

★ 597 ★

Educational Attainment

Completion Levels: Level of Education of Blacks in Low-Income Areas of Selected Cities, August 1970-March 1971

Subject	Total areas[1]	Low-income areas in--						
		New York	Chicago	Detroit	Philadelphia	Washington, D.C.	Los Angeles	Baltimore
EDUCATION								
Persons, 25 to 34 years old...thousands	841	158	77	44	49	52	39	38
Percent with less than 8 years of school	6	7	6	4	4	5	3	8
Percent with 4 years of high school or more	55	54	50	62	54	58	71	45
Median school years completed:								
Male	12.2	12.2	12.1	12.3	12.1	12.1	12.5	11.4
Female	12.1	12.0	11.7	12.2	12.1	12.2	12.4	11.8
Persons, 16 to 24 years old...thousands	1,004	145	85	59	62	51	41	57
Percent enrolled in school	45	44	47	38	40	47	53	43

Source: "Characteristics of the Black Population in Selected Low-Income, Areas," Current Population Reports, Special Studies, Series P-23, No. 42. *The Social and Economic Status of the Black Population in the United States, 1971,* 1972, p. 139. Primary source: U.S. Department of Commerce, Social and Economic Statistics Administration, Bureau of the Census. *Notes:* Statistics on low-income areas are based on information gathered in the Census Employment Survey (CES) conducted as part of overall program of the 1970 Census of Population and Housing. Interviewing for CES began August 1970 and was completed by March 1971. The period of interviewing in the selected low-income areas differed by city, and some cities were completed even before others began. The low-income areas were identified on the basis of several criteria-census tracts with a high proportion of families with "low income" in 1960, and other more recent socio-economic data, along with the views of local knowledgeable agencies. 1. Includes selected low-income areas in 44 other cities, not shown separately.

★ 598 ★

Educational Attainment

Completion Levels: Percent Distribution of Elementary, High School, and College Completers among Persons 25 and over, by Gender, 1970-1974

YEAR, RACE, AND SEX	Persons 25 years old and over (1,000)	PERCENT OF POPULATION COMPLETING-							Median school years completed
		Elementary school			High school		College		
		0-4 years	5-7 years	8 years	1-3 years	4 years	1-3 years	4 years or more	
1970, all races	109,310	5.3	9.1	13.4	17.1	34.0	10.2	11.0	12.2
White	98,112	4.2	8.3	13.6	16.5	35.2	10.7	11.6	12.2
Male	46,606	4.5	8.8	13.9	15.6	30.9	11.3	15.0	12.2
Female	51,506	3.9	7.8	13.4	17.3	39.0	10.1	8.6	12.2
Negro	10,089	15.1	16.7	11.2	23.3	23.4	5.9	4.5	9.9
Male	4,619	18.6	16.0	11.1	21.9	22.2	5.7	4.6	9.6
Female	5,470	12.1	17.3	11.3	24.5	24.4	6.0	4.4	10.2
1973, all races	112,866	4.5	8.0	11.4	16.3	35.8	11.4	12.6	12.3
White	100,818	3.6	7.2	11.6	15.7	37.0	11.8	13.1	12.3
Male	47,645	3.9	7.5	11.7	14.8	32.8	12.5	16.8	12.4
Female	53,173	3.4	6.9	11.5	16.5	40.7	11.1	9.9	12.3

[Continued]

★ 598 ★

Completion Levels: Percent Distribution of Elementary, High School, and College Completers among Persons 25 and over, by Gender, 1970-1974

[Continued]

| YEAR, RACE, AND SEX | Persons 25 years old and over (1,000) | PERCENT OF POPULATION COMPLETING- | | | | | | | Median school years completed |
| | | Elementary school | | | High school | | College | | |
		0-4 years	5-7 years	8 years	1-3 years	4 years	1-3 years	4 years or more	
Negro	10,585	12.6	14.8	10.1	23.2	25.8	7.5	6.0	10.6
Male	4,711	14.9	15.3	10.8	20.9	25.2	7.1	5.9	10.3
Female	5,874	10.7	14.5	9.6	25.1	26.3	7.8	6.0	10.8
1974, all races	115,005	4.4	7.6	10.8	15.9	36.1	11.9	13.3	12.3
White	102,524	3.5	6.8	11.1	15.2	37.1	12.2	14.0	12.4
Male	48,534	3.7	7.0	11.3	14.3	33.0	12.9	17.7	12.4
Female	53,990	3.3	6.6	11.0	16.1	40.8	11.7	10.6	12.3
Negro	10,899	12.9	14.7	9.0	22.7	27.0	8.3	5.5	10.7
Male	4,868	15.9	15.1	9.5	19.6	25.5	8.6	5.7	10.5
Female	6,030	10.4	14.3	8.5	25.2	28.2	8.0	5.3	10.9

Source: "Years of School Completed, by Race and Sex: 1960 to 1974,"*Statistical Abstract of the United States, 1975,* p. 118. Primary source: U.S. Bureau of the Census, *U.S. Census of Population: 1960,* vol. I, and *Current Population Reports,* series P-20, Nos. 207 and 274.

★ 599 ★

Educational Attainment

Completion Levels: Percent Distribution of Elementary, High School, and College Completion, by Age Group, 1974

[Persons 25 years old and over as of March 1974]

| RACE, SEX, AND AGE | Population (1,000) | PERCENT OF POPULATION COMPLETING- | | | | | | | Median school years completed |
| | | Elementary school | | | High school | | College | | |
		0-4 years	5-7 years	8 years	1-3 years	4 years	1-3 years	4 years or more	
All races	115,005	4.4	7.6	10.8	15.9	36.1	11.9	13.3	12.3
Negro	10,899	12.9	14.7	9.0	22.7	27.0	8.3	5.5	10.7
25-29 years	1,617	2.1	3.1	3.5	23.0	44.0	16.3	7.9	12.4
30-34 years	1,382	2.0	5.3	3.8	27.1	40.3	13.2	8.3	12.3
35-44 years	2,360	4.3	10.3	8.2	28.2	33.6	9.3	6.1	11.9
45-54 years	2,218	11.4	16.7	11.6	25.4	24.6	6.0	4.2	10.2
55 years and over	3,321	29.6	25.9	12.6	15.1	10.2	3.1	3.5	7.4

Source: "Years of School Completed, by Sex, Race, and Age: 1974," *Statistical Abstract of the United States, 1975,* p. 119. Primary source: U.S. Bureau of the Census, *Current Population Reports,* series P-20, No. 274.

★ 600 ★

Educational Attainment

Completion Levels: Percent Distribution of People at Educational Extremes – Less than 5 School Years and 4 High School Years or More, by Age, 1974 - I

[Persons 25 years old and over as of March 1974. All races include those not shown separately]

RACE	LESS THAN 5 YEARS OF SCHOOL						
	Total	25-29	30-34	35-44	45-55	55-64	65 and over
All races	4.4	1.2	1.3	2.2	3.4	5.3	11.9
White, total	3.5	1.1	1.2	1.9	2.5	3.6	9.4
Spanish origin[1]	19.4	9.1	9.6	16.3	23.1	29.8	47.4
Mexican	26.5	12.6	14.6	22.3	32.0	39.9	63.6
Puerto Rican	17.6	7.5	9.0	18.0	23.0	[2]	[2]
Negro	12.9	2.1	2.0	4.3	11.4	21.5	37.7

Source: "Percent of Population with Less than 5 Years of School and with 4 Years of High School or More, by Age and Race or Ethnic Origin: 1974," *Statistical Abstract of the United States, 1975*, p. 119. Primary source: U.S. Bureau of the Census, *Current Population Reports*, series P-20, No. 267. *Notes:* 1. Includes persons of Central or South American, Cuban, and other Spanish origin, not shown separately. 2. Not shown; base less than 75,000.

★ 601 ★

Educational Attainment

Completion Levels: Percent Distribution of People at Educational Extremes – Less than 5 School Years and 4 High School Years or More, by Age, 1974 - II

[Persons 25 years old and over as of March 1974. All races include those not shown separately]

RACE	4 YEARS OF HIGH SCHOOL OR MORE						
	Total	25-29	30-34	35-44	45-55	55-64	65 and over
All races	61.2	81.9	77.9	70.4	63.0	50.0	33.1
White, total	63.3	83.4	79.6	72.8	65.9	52.7	35.2
Spanish origin[1]	36.4	52.5	48.2	38.3	30.2	17.4	13.3
Mexican	29.1	46.7	41.9	31.0	20.6	9.6	5.2
Puerto Rican	29.6	39.6	40.3	29.5	18.8	[2]	[2]
Negro	40.8	68.2	61.8	48.9	34.9	22.1	11.5

Source: "Percent of Population with Less than 5 Years of School and with 4 Years of High School or More, by Age and Race or Ethnic Origin: 1974," *Statistical Abstract of the United States, 1975*, p. 119. Primary source: U.S. Bureau of the Census, *Current Population Reports*, series P-20, No. 267. *Notes:* 1. Includes persons of Central or South American, Cuban, and other Spanish origin, not shown separately. 2. Not shown; base less than 75,000.

★ 602 ★

Educational Attainment

Completion Levels: Percent Distribution of Selected Individual Years of School Completed, by Gender, 1966

[Persons 25 years old and over. As of March.]

RACE AND SEX	Persons 25 years old and over (1,000)	YEARS OF SCHOOL COMPLETED (percent distribution)							Median school years completed[2]
		Elementary school			High school		College		
		Less than 5 years[1]	5 to 7 years	8 years	1 to 3 years	4 years	1 to 3 years	4 years	
Total, all races	103,876	6.5	10.4	15.1	18.2	31.2	8.9	9.8	12.0
Male	49,410	7.3	10.7	15.6	17.4	27.7	8.8	12.5	11.8
Female	54,467	5.7	10.2	14.6	18.8	34.4	9.0	7.4	12.0
White	93,416	5.2	9.6	15.4	17.7	32.5	9.3	10.4	12.1
Male	44,537	5.7	10.1	15.8	17.1	28.8	9.2	13.3	12.0
Female	48,879	4.7	9.1	14.9	18.2	35.9	9.4	7.7	12.1
Negro	9,612	18.2	18.7	12.5	22.7	18.9	5.1	3.8	9.1
Male	4,444	23.2	17.2	13.4	20.4	17.2	4.7	3.9	8.7
Female	5,168	14.1	20.1	11.7	24.7	20.3	5.4	3.7	9.5

Source: "Years of School Completed, by Race and Sex: 1966" *Statistical Abstract of the United States, 1967,* p. 114. Primary source: Dept. of Commerce, Bureau of the Census, *Current Population Reports,* Series P-20, No. 158 and unpublished data. *Note:* 1. Includes persons reporting no school years completed.

★ 603 ★

Educational Attainment

Completion Levels: Percent of Minority College "Completers" in Relation to Male Population, 1960 and 1970 - I

	Raw Measure[1]			Social Indicator Values (Ratios of raw measures to the majority male population)		
	1960	1970	1976	1960	1970	1976
Males						
Amer. Ind./Alask. Nat.	03	08	08	.15	.36	.24[2]
Blacks	04	06	11	.20	.27	.32
Mexican Americans	04	05	11	.20	.23	.32
Japanese Americans	35	39	53	1.75	1.77	1.56
Chinese Americans	49	58	60	2.45	2.64	1.76
Pilipino Americans	19	28	34	.95	1.27	1.00
Puerto Ricans	04	04	06	.20	.18	.18
Majority	20	22	34	1.00	1.00	1.00
Females						
Amer. Ind./Alask. Nat.	02	05	04	.10	.23	.12
Blacks	06	08	11	.30	.36	.32
Mexicans Americans	02	03	05	.10	.14	.15

[Continued]

★ 603 ★

Completion Levels: Percent of Minority College "Completers" in Relation to Male Population, 1960 and 1970 - I

[Continued]

	Raw Measure[1]			Social Indicator Values (Ratios of raw measures to the majority male population)		
	1960	1970	1976	1960	1970	1976
Japanese Americans	13	31	35	.65	1.41	1.03
Chinese Americans	26	42	44	1.30	1.91	1.29
Pilipino Americans	16	50	51	.80	2.27	1.50
Puerto Ricans	01	03	04	.05	.14	.12
Majority	09	14	22	.45	.64	.65

Source: "High School Completion," *Social Indicators of Equality for Minorities and Women*, 1978, p. 14. Primary source: U.S. Commission on Civil Rights. *Social Indicators of Equality for Minorities and Women*. Washington, D.C.: 1978. *Notes:* 1. The percentage of persons from 25 to 29 years of age who have completed at least 4 years of college. 2. This can be interpreted as follows: "In 1976 the college completion rate for American Indian and Alaskan Natives male was 24 percent of (or 76 percent below) the rate for majority males."

★ 604 ★

Educational Attainment

Completion Levels: Percent of Minority College "Completers" in Relation to Male Population, 1960 and 1970 - II

	Raw Measure[1]			Social Indicator Values (Ratios of raw measures to the majority male population)		
	1960	1970	1976	1960	1970	1976
Males						
Amer. Ind./Alask. Nat.	33	58	70	.48	.70	
Blacks	41	59	74	.59	.71	
Mexican Americans	34	55	64	.49	.66	
Japanese Americans	89	94	98	1.29	1.13	2
Chinese Americans	84	90	88	1.22	1.08	
Pilipino Americans	81	77	81	1.17	.93	
Puerto Ricans	24	44	68	.35	.53	
Majority	69	83	87	1.00	1.00	
Females						
Amer. Ind./Alask. Nat.	29	56	58	.42	.67	.67
Blacks	42	62	74	.61	.75	.85
Mexicans Americans	35	51	58	.51	.61	.67
Japanese Americans	84	94	99	1.22	1.13	1.14
Chinese Americans	82	88	90	1.19	1.06	1.03
Pilipino Americans	76	84	78	1.10	1.01	.90

[Continued]

★ 604 ★

Completion Levels: Percent of Minority College "Completers" in Relation to Male Population, 1960 and 1970 - II
[Continued]

	Raw Measure[1]			Social Indicator Values (Ratios of raw measures to the majority male population)		
	1960	1970	1976	1960	1970	1976
Puerto Ricans	24	42	60	.351	.51	.69
Majority	70	82	86	1.01	.99	.99

Source: "High School Completion," *Social Indicators of Equality for Minorities and Women*, 1978, p. 12. Primary source: U.S. Commission on Civil Rights. *Social Indicators of Equality for Minorities and Women*. Washington, D.C.: 1978. *Notes:* 1. The percentage of persons from 20 to 24 years of age who have completed 12 or more years of school. 2. Figures missing from source table.

★ 605 ★

Educational Attainment

Completion Levels: Percentage of High School and College "Completers" (Aged 25 and Over) in Selected Cities, 1969

Standard metropolitan statistical area	4 years of high school or more	4 years of college or more	Standard metropolitan statistical area	4 years of high school or more	4 years of college or more
14 selected SMSA's:			New Orleans, La.:		
White	61	14	White	56	12
Negro and other races	43	7	Negro and other races	35	6
Atlanta, Ga.:			New York, N.Y.:		
White	64	17	White	58	14
Negro and other races	31	7	Negro and other races	45	6
Baltimore, Md.:			Newark, N.J.:		
White	51	10	White	57	12
Negro and other races	26	5	Negro and other races	46	4
Chicago, Ill.:			Philadelphia, Pa.-N.J.:		
White	61	13	White	57	13
Negro and other races	43	8	Negro and other races	37	5
Cleveland, Ohio:			St. Louis, Mo.-Ill.:		
White	62	14	White	51	11
Negro and other races	35	6	Negro and other races	32	2
Detroit, Mich.:			San Francisco-Oakland, Calif.:		
White	56	10	White	74	19
Negro and other races	40	5	Negro and other races	57	13
Houston, Tex.:			Washington, D.C.-Md.-Va.:		

[Continued]

★ 605 ★

Completion Levels: Percentage of High School and College "Completers" (Aged 25 and Over) in Selected Cities, 1969
[Continued]

Standard metropolitan statistical area	4 years of high school or more	4 years of college or more	Standard metropolitan statistical area	4 years of high school or more	4 years of college or more
White	59	13	White	81	30
Negro and other races	40	7	Negro and other races	47	11
Los Angeles-Long Beach, Calif.:					
White	69	15			
Negro and other races	58	11			

Source: "Percent of Persons 25 Years old and Over, Who Completed Four Years of High School or More and Four Years of College or More, for Selected Metropolitan Areas: 1969," Current Population Reports, Special Studies, Series P-23, No. 29. *The Social and Economic Status of the Black Population in United States, 1969,* 1969, p. 84. Primary source: U.S. Department of Commerce, Bureau of the Census.

★ 606 ★

Educational Attainment

Completion Levels: School Years Completed by Persons Aged 20 and Over, 1969 (in percentages)

	Less than 4 years high school	High school, 4 years	College, 1 years or more	Median years of school completed
NEGRO				
20 and 21 years old	42.1	36.6	21.2	12.2
22 to 24 years old	43.9	37.1	19.1	12.2
25 to 29 years old	44.3	40.1	15.7	12.1
30 to 34 years old	49.8	36.7	13.5	12.0
35 to 44 years old	62.8	26.8	10.5	10.6
45 to 54 years old	70.8	18.9	10.3	9.1
55 to 64 years old	85.2	8.7	6.2	7.6
65 to 74 years old	89.7	5.5	4.9	6.1
75 years old and over	92.4	4.1	3.5	5.2
WHITE				
20 and 21 years old	18.1	41.6	40.1	12.8
22 to 24 years old	19.6	44.7	35.7	12.7
25 to 29 years old	23.0	44.8	32.1	12.6
30 to 34 years old	27.3	44.9	27.6	12.5
35 to 44 years old	33.9	41.0	25.1	12.4
45 to 54 years old	40.7	39.3	20.0	12.2
55 to 64 years old	55.2	27.5	17.3	10.9

[Continued]

★ 606 ★

Completion Levels: School Years Completed by Persons Aged 20 and Over, 1969 (in percentages)
[Continued]

	Less than 4 years high school	High school, 4 years	College, 1 years or more	Median years of school completed
65 to 74 years old	67.6	18.9	13.4	8.9
75 years old and over	75.1	13.8	11.1	8.5

Source: "Percent Distribution by Years of School Completed for Persons 20 Years Old and Over, by Age, 1969," Current Population Reports, Special Studies, Series P-23, No. 29. *The Social and Economic Status of the Black Population in the United States, 1969,* 1969, p. 50. Primary source: U.S. Department of Commerce, Bureau of the Census.

★ 607 ★

Educational Attainment

Completion Levels: School Years Completed by Persons Aged 20 and Over, 1970

Age and race	Total (thousands)	Percent distribution by years of school completed				Median years of school completed
		Total	Less than 4 years high school	High school, 4 years	College, 1 years or more	
NEGRO						
20 and 21 years old	791	100	33	44	24	12.4
22 to 24 years old	1,035	100	37	42	21	12.3
25 to 29 years old	1,453	100	44	39	17	12.2
30 to 34 years old	1,198	100	50	38	12	12.0
35 to 44 years old	2,347	100	59	29	12	11.2
45 to 54 years old	2,128	100	71	20	9	9.3
55 to 64 years old	1,545	100	83	11	6	7.9
65 to 74 years old	840	100	90	5	5	6.1
75 years old and over	577	100	93	4	3	4.6
WHITE						
20 to 21 years old	5,403	100	18	40	43	12.8
22 to 24 years old	8,185	100	17	46	37	12.7
25 to 29 years old	11,893	100	22	45	33	12.6
30 to 34 years old	9,994	100	26	45	29	12.5
35 to 44 years old	20,392	100	33	42	25	12.4
45 to 54 years old	20,961	100	39	40	21	12.3
55 to 64 years old	16,731	100	54	28	18	11.2

[Continued]

★ 607 ★

Completion Levels: School Years Completed by Persons Aged 20 and Over, 1970

[Continued]

Age and race	Total (thousands)	Percent distribution by years of school completed				Median years of school completed
		Total	Less than 4 years high school	High school, 4 years	College, 1 years or more	
65 to 74 years old	11,131	100	67	18	15	8.9
75 years old and over	7,010	100	75	14	11	8.6

Source: "Highest Grade of School Completed by Persons 20 Years Old and Over, b y Age, 1970," Current Population Reports, Special Studies, Series P-23, No. 38. *The Social and Economic Status of the Black Population in the United States, 1970,* 1970, p. 79. Primary source: U.S. Department of Commerce, Bureau of the Census.

★ 608 ★

Educational Attainment

Level of Education: Race and Age Distribution of Schools Years Completed, 1947

Year, Age, Color and Sex, by Percent	Years of School Completed						
	Elementary School			High School		College	
	Less than 5 Years	5 and 6 Years	7 and 8 Years	1 to 3 Years	4 Years	1 to 3 Years	4 Years
(Totals in thousands)							
WHITE							
Total number 14 years and over	6,705	6,917	27,777	20,495	22,351	6,737	4,515
Percent							
14 years and over	6.9	7.2	28.7	21.2	23.1	7.0	4.7
14 to 17 years	2.6	7.1	34.2	53.5	2.2	0.2	-
18 to 19 years	1.7	3.3	13.6	35.9	37.8	7.4	-
20 to 24 years	2.0	3.2	13.0	24.6	43.5	10.5	2.6
25 years and over	8.3	7.9	31.1	16.7	21.7	7.1	5.7
25 to 29 years	2.5	3.3	16.2	22.9	38.8	9.8	5.9
30 to 34 years	2.9	4.3	21.7	22.1	33.1	8.3	7.0
35 to 44 years	4.5	5.7	30.5	19.4	22.9	8.6	7.6
45 to 54 years	8.8	9.4	37.0	16.1	15.5	6.6	5.0
55 to 64 years	14.4	11.5	38.7	10.9	12.9	5.2	3.9
65 years and over	18.8	13.7	3.8	7.9	10.3	3.7	3.5
(Totals in thousands)							
NONWHITE							
Total number 14 years and over	2,715	1,885	2,440	1,789	957	268	202
Percent							
14 years and over	25.9	18.0	23.3	17.1	9.1	2.6	1.9
14 to 17 years	11.6	21.9	32.9	30.9	2.2	0.1	-

[Continued]

★ 608 ★

Level of Education: Race and Age Distribution of Schools Years Completed, 1947
[Continued]

Year, Age, Color and Sex, by Percent	Years of School Completed						
	Elementary School			High School		College	
	Less than 5 Years	5 and 6 Years	7 and 8 Years	1 to 3 Years	4 Years	1 to 3 Years	4 Years
18 to 19 years	11.1	11.7	16.8	35.9	18.8	5.1	-
20 to 24 years	12.3	16.8	22.9	25.7	14.4	5.0	1.3
25 years and over	31.4	18.1	22.4	12.3	8.5	2.3	2.4
25 to 29 years	18.9	16.2	20.6	20.8	15.8	3.4	2.7
30 to 34 years	20.3	13.7	28.0	15.9	13.2	2.8	3.8
35 to 44 years	23.8	20.8	27.3	13.0	8.4	2.3	2.3
45 to 54 years	38.2	21.2	20.5	7.4	4.8	1.8	2.9
55 to 64 years	44.5	17.5	20.0	8.1	3.5	2.0	1.3
65 years and over	60.8	15.0	10.4	5.6	3.2	1.2	0.6

Source: "Years of School Completed by Persons 14 Years Old and Over, by Age, Color, by Percent, for the United States: Civilian Population, April 1947," *The Negro Handbook, 1949,* 1949, p. 118. Primary source: *U.S. Bureau of the Census. Notes:* Percent not shown where less than 0.1. 1. Includes persons reporting no school years completed.

★ 609 ★

Educational Attainment

Progress Through School: Normal and Slower-than-Normal School Progress at Ages 14-17, 1971
[In percentages]

Subject	Negro		White	
	Male	Female	Male	Female
IN MODAL GRADE[1]				
Total, 14 to 17 years old	44.3	52.1	65.5	72.1
14 years old	53.3	56.7	67.9	72.4
15 years old	43.9	54.9	63.3	70.7
16 years old	38.2	51.9	64.1	69.3
17 years old	39.7	41.7	66.8	76.5
TWO OR MORE YEARS BELOW MODE				
Total, 14 to 17 years old	14.3	9.7	5.4	3.1
14 years old	11.5	6.9	3.9	3.9
15 years old	11.8	7.8	4.6	3.4
16 years old	13.3	5.6	5.8	2.5
17 years old	22.0	22.5	7.0	2.4

Source: "Percent of Enrolled Persons 14 to 17 Years Old In Below Modal Grade, by Age: 1971," Current Population Reports, Special Studies, Series P-23, No. 42. *The Social and Economic Status of Black Population in the United States, 1971,* 1972, p. 80. Primary source: U.S. Department of Commerce, Social and Economic Statistics Administration, Bureau of the Census. *Notes:* 1. Modal grades are: 14 year olds, high school 1; 15 year olds, high school 2; 16 years old, high school 3; 17 year olds, high school 4.

★ 610 ★

Educational Attainment

Progress through School: 14-17-Year-Olds, Two or More Years Behind in School (in percentages), by Age, 1950, 1960, and 1970

Modal grade status, age, and race	1950[1]	1960[1]	1970
TWO OR MORE YEARS BELOW MODAL GRADE			
Black			
Total, 14 to 17 years	52.3	31.8	21.1
14 years	51.6	29.1	19.0
15 years	53.1	31.5	20.5
16 years	52.8	32.6	22.0
17 years	51.7	35.1	24.0
White			
Total, 14 to 17 years	21.1	12.6	9.0
14 years	21.3	11.8	8.8
15 years	22.8	13.1	9.1
16 years	21.1	13.0	9.1
17 years	18.6	12.5	9.1

Source: "Percent of Enrolled Persons 14 to 17 Years Old, Two or More Years Below Modal Grade, by Age: 1950, 1960, and 1970," *The Social and Economic Status by the Black Population in the United States: An Historical View, 1790- 1978,* 1979, p. 90. Primary source: U.S. Department of Commerce. Bureau of the Census. *Notes:* Model grades are: 14 years old, high school 1; 15 years old, high school 2; 16 years old, high school 3; and 17 years old, high school 4. Data in this table are for the population as of Spring of school year. 1. Data for Black include persons of "other" races.

★ 611 ★

Educational Attainment

Relationships: Percent Distribution of Selected Levels of Educational Attainment, for Persons 25 and over and 25-29 Years Old, 1940-1974

AGE AND YEAR	ALL PERSONS					NEGRO PERSONS				
	Percent-				Median	Percent-				Median
	Not high school graduates		With 4 years of high school or more		school	Not high school graduates		With 4 years of high school or more		school
	Total	With less than 5 years of school	Total	College, 4 years or more	years completed[1]	Total	With less than 5 years of school	Total	College, 4 years or more	years completed[1]
25 years and over:										
1940[1]	75.5	13.7	24.5	4.6	8.6	92.7	42.0	7.3	1.3	5.7
1950[1]	67.5	11.1	32.5	6.2	9.0	88.3	32.9	12.9	2.1	6.8
1960[1]	58.9	8.3	41.1	7.7	10.3	81.3	23.8	20.1	3.1	8.0
1970	44.8	5.3	55.2	11.0	12.2	66.3	15.1	33.7	4.5	9.9
1972	41.8	4.6	58.2	12.0	12.2	63.5	12.8	36.6	5.1	10.3

[Continued]

★ 611 ★

Relationships: Percent Distribution of Selected Levels of Educational Attainment, for Persons 25 and over and 25-29 Years Old, 1940-1974

[Continued]

	ALL PERSONS					NEGRO PERSONS				
	Percent-					Percent-				
	Not high school graduates		With 4 years of high school or more		Median school	Not high school graduates		With 4 years of high school or more		Median school
AGE AND YEAR	Total	With less than 5 years of school	Total	College, 4 years or more	years completed[1]	Total	With less than 5 years of school	Total	College, 4 years or more	years completed[1]
1973	40.2	4.5	59.8	12.6	12.3	60.8	12.6	39.2	6.0	10.6
1974	38.8	4.4	61.2	13.3	12.3	59.2	12.9	40.8	5.5	10.7
25-29 years:										
1940[1]	61.9	5.9	38.1	5.9	10.3	(NA)	27.7	11.6	1.6	7.0
1950[1]	49.5	4.7	52.8	7.7	12.0	80.4	16.8	22.2	2.7	8.6
1960[1]	39.3	2.8	60.7	11.1	12.3	62.3	7.0	37.7	4.8	9.9
1970	24.6	1.1	75.4	16.4	12.6	43.9	2.5	56.2	7.3	12.2
1972	20.2	0.8	79.8	19.0	12.7	36.0	1.3	64.1	8.3	12.3
1973	19.8	1.0	80.2	19.0	12.7	35.8	1.5	64.2	8.1	12.3
1974	18.1	1.2	81.9	20.7	12.8	31.7	2.1	68.2	7.9	12.4

Source: "Years of School Completed by Race: 1940 to 1974," *Statistical Abstract of the United States, 1975*, p. 118. Primary source: U.S. Bureau of the Census, *Census of Population: 1940, 1950, and 1960*, vol. I. and *Current Population Reports*, series P-20, Nos. 207, 229, 243, and 274. *Note:* 1. As of April.

★ 612 ★

Educational Attainment

Relationships: Percent of Minority College-Trained (1 Year or More)Persons in Jobs for which They were Overqualified, 1960 and 1970

	Raw Measure[1]			Social Indicator Values (Ratios of raw measures to the majority male population)		
	1960	1970	1976	1960	1970	1976
Males						
Amer. Ind./Alask. Nat.	51.6	49.2	51.9	1.21	1.18	1.16[2]
Blacks	58.8	52.6	55.0	1.38	1.26	1.23
Mexican Americans	46.9	47.3	46.5	1.10	1.13	1.04
Japanese Americans	52.4	44.3	49.4	1.23	1.06	1.10
Chinese Americans	48.2	38.3	51.3	1.13	.92	1.15
Pilipino Americans	48.1	45.1	56.2	1.13	1.08	1.26
Puerto Ricans	52.9	44.7	41.0	1.24	1.07	.92
Majority	42.7	41.7	44.7	1.00	1.00	1.00
Females						
Amer. Ind./Alask. Nat.	46.2	38.7	46.6	1.08	.93	1.04
Blacks	41.6	35.1	41.3	.97	.84	.92
Mexicans Americans	28.1	31.7	38.8	.66	.76	.87
Japanese Americans	32.3	35.0	41.1	.76	.84	.92
Chinese Americans	39.0	34.5	51.2	.91	.83	1.14

[Continued]

★ 612 ★

Relationships: Percent of Minority College-Trained (1 Year or More)Persons in Jobs for which They were Overqualified, 1960 and 1970

[Continued]

	Raw Measure[1]			Social Indicator Values (Ratios of raw measures to the majority male population)		
	1960	1970	1976	1960	1970	1976
Pilipino Americans	37.1	38.2	39.6	.87	.92	.89
Puerto Ricans	42.2	29.8	50.4	.99	.71	1.13
Majority	29.8	24.7	45.4	.70	.59	1.02

Source: "College Overqualification," *Social Indicators of Equality for Minorities and Women,* 1978, p. 20. Primary source: U.S. Commission on Civil Rights. *Social Indicators of Equality for Minorities and Women.* Washington, D.C.: 1978. *Notes:* 1. The percent of persons with at least 1 year of college who are employed in occupations which typically require less education than they have. 2. This can be interpreted as follows: "In 1976 the college overqualification rate for American Indian and Alaskan Native males was 16 percent higher than (or 1.16 times) the rate for majority males."

★ 613 ★

Educational Attainment

Relationships: Percent of Minority High School Graduates in Jobs for which They were Overqualified, 1960 and 1970

	Raw Measure[1]			Social Indicator Values (Ratios of raw measures to the majority male population)		
	1960	1970	1976	1960	1970	1976
Males						
Amer. Ind./Alask. Nat.	71.7[1]	59.5	60.5	1.78	1.58	1.37[2]
Blacks	70.2	66.1	67.2	1.75	1.76	1.52
Mexican Americans	55.6	56.8	59.6	1.38	1.51	1.35
Japanese Americans	51.8	43.4	48.4	1.29	1.15	1.10
Chinese Americans	34.6	33.8	43.3	.86	.90	.98
Pilipino Americans	62.6	49.3	49.5	1.56	1.31	1.12
Puerto Ricans	58.2	54.8	60.8	1.45	1.46	1.38
Majority	40.2	37.6	44.2	1.00	1.00	1.00
Females						
Amer. Ind./Alask. Nat.	56.5	48.0	53.0	1.40	1.28	1.20
Blacks	65.1	53.0	56.1	1.62	1.41	1.27
Mexicans Americans	42.8	42.0	52.5	1.06	1.12	1.19
Japanese Americans	44.5	35.4	50.8	1.11	.94	1.15
Chinese Americans	27.2	25.7	48.3	.68	.68	.79
Pilipino Americans	35.8	33.2	34.8	.89	.88	.79

[Continued]

★ 613 ★

Relationships: Percent of Minority High School Graduates in Jobs for which They were Overqualified, 1960 and 1970

[Continued]

	Raw Measure[1]			Social Indicator Values (Ratios of raw measures to the majority male population)		
	1960	1970	1976	1960	1970	1976
Puerto Ricans	54.0	38.5	59.0	1.34	1.02	1.33
Majority	33.4	29.9	49.0	.83	.80	1.11

Source: "College Overqualification," *Social Indicators of Equality for Minorities and Women*, 1978, p. 18. Primary source: U.S. Commission on Civil Rights. *Social Indicators of Equality for Minorities and Women*. Washington, D.C.: 1978. *Notes:* 1. The percent of high school graduates who are employed in occupations which require less than a high school degree. 2. This can be interpreted as follows: "In 1976 the high school overqualification rate for American Indian and Alaskan Native males was 37 percent higher than (or 1.37 times) the rate for majority males."

★ 614 ★

Educational Attainment

Relationships: School Years Completed, by Gender and Occupational Group, 1959-1974

[Relates to civilian noninstitutional population 18 years and over as of March of years indicated. Service includes private household workers.]

OCCUPATION GROUP	MALE				FEMALE			
	White		Negro		White		Negro	
	With less than 4 years of high school	With 4 or more years of high school	With less than 4 years of high school	With 4 or more years of high school	With less than 4 years of high school	With 4 or more years of high school	With less than 4 years of high school	With 4 or more years of high school
1959								
Total mil.	18.7	19.0	2.9	0.8	7.0	10.8	1.7	0.8
Percent:								
White collar	20.3	58.8	5.3	38.8	31.5	80.3	5.8	44.5
Blue collar	58.9	32.3	65.4	37.3	31.4	8.0	15.7	12.4
Service	7.2	4.0	12.6	20.2	31.6	10.0	73.8	42.6
Farm	13.7	4.9	16.7	3.7	5.5	1.6	4.7	6.5
1970								
Total mil.	14.7	27.7	2.6	2.0	6.9	18.1	2.6	2.0
Percent:								
White collar	18.5	58.0	8.8	42.1	30.3	77.9	8.8	42.1
Blue collar	64.8	34.6	71.6	47.3	35.6	9.0	71.6	47.3
Service	7.5	4.6	12.6	9.2	31.0	12.3	12.6	9.2
Farm	9.1	2.9	7.0	1.4	3.2	0.8	7.0	1.4

[Continued]

★ 614 ★

Relationships: School Years Completed, by Gender and Occupational Group, 1959-1974

[Continued]

| | MALE | | | | FEMALE | | | |
| | White | | Negro | | White | | Negro | |
OCCUPATION GROUP	With less than 4 years of high school	With 4 or more years of high school	With less than 4 years of high school	With 4 or more years of high school	With less than 4 years of high school	With 4 or more years of high school	With less than 4 years of high school	With 4 or more years of high school
1973								
Total mil.	13.1	31.4	2.4	2.5	6.4	20.5	1.5	2.4
Percent:								
White collar	16.0	54.0	7.2	39.7	29.5	75.5	12.8	60.7
Blue collar	66.8	37.1	68.7	46.4	35.9	9.9	24.1	13.8
Service	8.8	5.9	18.4	12.8	31.8	13.8	61.1	25.5
Farm	8.4	3.0	5.7	1.1	2.8	0.9	2.0	[1]
1974								
Total mil.	12.7	32.5	2.3	2.7	6.2	21.7	1.5	2.5
Percent:								
White collar	16.0	53.6	7.2	39.8	30.7	76.1	11.1	58.6
Blue collar	66.1	37.4	67.2	47.3	34.7	9.4	25.8	17.1
Service	9.0	5.9	18.8	12.1	31.9	13.6	61.5	24.3
Farm	8.9	3.1	6.8	0.8	2.7	1.0	1.6	[1]

Source: "Years of School Completed by Major Occupation Group of Employed Persons, by Sex and Race: 1959 to 1974," *Statistical Abstract of the United States, 1975,* p. 122. Primary source: U.S. Bureau of Labor Statistics, *Special Labor Force Report,* Nos. 1, 125, 161 and 170. *Note:* 1. Less than 0.05 percent.

Enrollment

★ 615 ★

Black Children In and Out of School, c. 1916

[In percentages]

State	Percent in school	Percent out of school
District of Columbia	88	12
Oklahoma	80	20
North Carolina	75	25
Kentucky	73.5	26.5
Tennessee	68.6	31.4
Mississippi	67.5	32.5
Georgia	65.4	34.6

[Continued]

★ 615 ★

Black Children In and Out of School, c. 1916
[Continued]

State	Percent in school	Percent out of school
West Virginia	60.4	39.6
Texas	58.8	41.2
South Carolina	58.4	41.6
Maryland	56.4	43.6
Virginia	56	44
Florida	54.8	45.2
Alabama	41.8	58.2
Louisiana	40.1	59.0

Source: "Per Cent Negro Children In School and Out," *Negro Year Book: An Annual Encyclopedia of the Negro, 1916-1917*, 1918, [no p. no.] Primary source: Not specifically identified.

★ 616 ★
Enrollment

Black Children In and Out of School, c. 1918
[In percentages]

State	Percent in school	Percent out of school
District of Columbia	88	12
Oklahoma	83	17
North Carolina	75.3	24.7
Georgia	70.8	29.2
Mississippi	70.4	29.6
West Virginia	70.0	30.0
Tennessee	67.9	32.1
Texas	67.4	32.6
Kentucky	63.0	37.0
Virginia	62.3	37.7
Arkansas	62.0	38.0
South Carolina	60.8	39.2
Maryland	60.6	39.4
Alabama	60.3	39.7
Florida	53.0	47.0
Louisiana	43.6	56.4

Source: "Percent Negro Children In School and Out," *Negro Yea Book: An Annual Encyclopedia of the Negro, 1918-1919*, 1919, p. 270. Primary source: Negro Education, Bulletin, 1916, No. 39, Vol. I. Bureau of Education.

★ 617 ★

Enrollment

Educational Level and Work Status of 16 to 21-Year-Old Males Not In School, 1970

Subject	Negro		White	
	Number (thousands)	Percent	Number (thousands)	Percent
Total	604	100	3,317	100
Not high school graduate	345	57	1,275	38
High school graduate	259	43	2,042	62
Not high school graduate	345	100	1,275	100
Employed or in Armed Forces	171	50	837	66
Unemployed or not in labor force	173	50	437	34
High school graduate	259	100	2,042	100
Employed or in Armed Forces	186	72	1,716	84
Unemployed or not in labor force	73	28	326	16

Source: "Men 16 to 21 Years Old Not Attending School, by Level of Education and Labor Force Status: 1970," Current Population Reports, Special Studies, Series P-23, No. 42. *The Social and Economic Status of the Black Population in the United States, 1971,* 1972, p. 82. Primary source: U.S. Department of Commerce, Social and Economic Statistics Administration, Bureau of the Census.

★ 618 ★

Enrollment

Elementary and Secondary: Black Elementary and Secondary Enrollment in Selected States, 1931-1932

State	Total estimated Population (thousands)	Population 5-17 years inclusive (estimated)	Enrollment in Kindergarten and Elementary Total	Enrollment in Secondary Total	Total Enrollment Total
Total, 18 States	9,644	2,903,700	2,217,339	135,981	2,353,320
Alabama	950	293,500	198,962	8,175	207,137
Arkansas	479	138,100	97,236	3,373	100,609
Delaware	33	8,100	6,223	684	6,907
District of Columbia	135	26,700	25,442	4,947	30,389
Florida	444	115,000	97,529	4,028	101,557
Georgia	1,055	338,100	254,309	8,792	263,101
Kentucky	225	54,100	43,307	4,677	47,984
Louisiana	785	227,000	153,285	7,244	160,529
Maryland	280	70,700	48,647	5,483	54,130
Mississippi	1,019	313,700	283,469	5,656	289,125

[Continued]

★ 618 ★

Elementary and Secondary: Black Elementary and Secondary Enrollment in Selected States, 1931-1932

[Continued]

State	Total estimated Population (thousands)	Population 5-17 years inclusive (estimated)	Enrollment in Kindergarten and Elementary Total	Enrollment in Secondary Total	Total Enrollment Total
Missouri	229	46,200	33,218	5,053	38,271
North Carolina	937	323,900	246,747	19,034	265,781
Oklahoma	175	49,400	45,515	4,783	50,298
South Carolina	785	289,700	214,299	9,411	223,710
Tennessee	481	128,300	105,357	8,240	113,597
Texas	869	242,700	191,790	22,606	214,396
Virginia	645	208,300	149,410	10,615	160,025
West Virginia	118	30,200	22,594	3,180	25,774

Source: "Distribution of Negro Population, Children of School Age, and School Enrollment in 16 Southern States: 1931-1932," *Negro Year Book: An Annual Encyclopedia of the Negro, 1937-1938,* 1937, p. 169. Primary source: U.S. Bureau of the Census. *Note:* 1. Estimate by the Bureau of the Census.

★ 619 ★

Enrollment

Elementary and Secondary: Black Enrollment in Public Elementary and Secondary Schools, by Geographic Area, 1970 and 1972

[As of fall. Excludes Hawaii. "Minority group" refers to Negroes, American Indians, Orientals, and Spanish-surnamed Americans]

ITEM	1970				1972			
	Total	32 Northern and Western States[1]	6 Border States and District of Columbia[2]	11 Southern States[3]	Total	32 Northern and Western States[1]	6 Border States and District of Columbia[2]	11 Southern States[3]
Total students 1,000	44,910	30,131	3,725	11,054	44,647	29,916	3,743	10,988
Negro 1,000	6,713	3,188	641	2,884	6,796	3,251	651	2,895
Percent Negro:								
Of total students	14.6	10.6	17.2	26.1	15.2	10.9	17.4	26.3
By minority group enrollment of schools:								
Under 50 percent	33.1	27.6	28.7	40.3	36.3	28.3	31.8	46.3
50-100 percent	66.9	72.4	71.3	59.7	63.7	71.7	69.2	53.7
95-100 percent	38.2	43.1	54.7	29.2	34.8	43.3	53.0	21.1
100 percent	14.0	11.7	24.1	14.4	11.2	10.9	23.6	8.7

Source: "Negro Group Enrollment in Public Elementary and Secondary Schools, by Specified Areas: 1970 and 1972," *Statistical Abstract of the United States, 1975,* p. 127. Primary source: U.S. Office for Civil Rights, *The Directory of Public Elementary and Secondary Schools in Selected Districts-Enrollment and Staff by Racial/Ethnic Group, Fall 1970,* and releases. *Notes:* 1. Alaska, Ariz., Calif., Colo., Conn., Idaho, Ill., Iowa, Kans., Maine, Mass., Mich., Minn., Mont., Nebr., Nev., N.H., N.J., N. Mex., N.Y., N. Dak., Ohio, Oreg., Pa., R.I., S. Dak., Utah, Vt., Wash., Wis., Wyo. 2. Del, Ky., Md., Mo., Okla., W. Va. 3. Ala., Ark., Fla., Ga., La., Miss., N.C., S.C., Tenn., Texas, Va.

★ 620 ★

Enrollment

Elementary and Secondary: Black Public School Enrollment by Degree of Segregation, by State, 1968

[Enrollment in thousands. As of fall. Excludes Hawaii.]

STATE	Total enrollment	NEGRO ENROLLMENT										
		Total	Percent of total enrollment	By minority group enrollment of schools								
				Under 50 percent		50-100 percent		95-100 percent		100 percent	
				Number	Percent	Number	Percent	Number	Percent	Number	Percent
Total	43,353.6	6,282.2	14.5	1,467.3	23.4	4,814.9	76.6	3,832.8	61.0	2,493.4	39.7
Ala.	770.5	269.2	34.9	22.3	8.3	246.9	91.7	244.7	90.9	230.4	85.6
Alaska	71.8	2.1	3.0	2.1	100.0	-	-	-	-	-	-
Ariz.	366.5	15.8	4.3	5.3	33.4	10.5	66.5	4.3	27.6	0.8	5.0
Ark.	415.6	106.5	25.6	24.1	22.6	82.4	77.4	78.9	74.1	75.8	71.1
Calif.	4,477.4	388.0	8.7	87.3	22.5	300.7	77.5	185.6	47.8	28.0	7.2
Colo.	519.1	17.8	3.4	5.4	30.5	12.4	69.5	8.0	45.0	-	-
Conn.	632.4	52.6	8.3	22.8	43.3	29.8	56.7	9.6	18.3	0.3	0.6
Del.	123.9	24.0	19.4	13.0	54.2	11.0	45.8	5.2	21.6	-	-
D.C.	148.7	139.0	93.5	1.3	0.9	137.8	99.1	123.9	89.2	38.7	27.8
Fla.	1,340.7	311.5	23.2	72.3	23.2	239.2	76.8	224.7	72.1	184.1	59.1
Ga.	1,001.2	314.9	31.5	44.2	14.0	270.7	86.0	262.7	83.4	240.5	76.4
Idaho	174.5	0.4	0.2	0.4	100.0	-	-	-	-	-	-
Ill.	2,252.3	406.4	18.0	55.4	13.6	351.0	86.4	294.1	72.4	156.9	38.6
Ind.	1,210.5	106.2	8.8	31.8	30.0	74.3	70.0	46.2	43.5	13.6	12.8
Iowa	651.7	9.6	1.5	7.0	73.1	2.6	26.9	0.3	3.6	-	-
Kans.	518.7	30.8	5.9	16.5	53.4	14.4	46.6	9.8	31.8	2.3	7.5
Ky.	695.6	64.0	9.2	34.4	53.7	29.6	46.3	17.0	26.6	3.3	5.2
La.	817.0	317.3	38.8	28.2	8.9	289.1	91.1	279.6	88.1	259.9	81.9
Maine	220.3	1.4	0.6	0.4	27.2	1.0	72.8	-	-	-	-
Md.	859.4	201.4	23.4	62.7	31.1	138.8	68.9	105.9	52.6	62.9	31.2
Mass.	1,097.2	46.7	4.3	23.9	51.2	22.8	48.8	8.6	18.3	0.1	0.2
Mich.	2,073.4	275.9	13.3	56.8	20.6	219.0	79.4	128.1	46.4	24.7	9.0
Minn.	856.6	9.0	1.1	7.1	79.0	1.9	21.0	0.4	4.0	-	-
Miss.	456.5	223.8	49.0	15.0	6.7	208.8	93.3	207.5	92.7	197.4	88.2
Mo.	954.6	138.4	14.5	34.0	24.6	104.4	75.4	91.4	66.0	46.3	33.4
Mont.	127.1	0.1	0.1	0.1	100.0	-	-	-	-	-	-
Nebr.	266.3	12.3	4.6	3.4	27.3	9.0	72.7	4.3	35.0	-	-
Nev.	119.2	9.2	7.7	4.9	53.1	4.3	46.9	3.6	39.5	-	-
N.H.	132.2	0.5	0.4	0.5	100.0	-	-	-	-	-	-
N.J.	1,401.9	208.5	14.9	70.6	33.9	137.9	66.1	68.4	32.8	15.2	7.3
N. Mex.	271.0	5.7	2.1	2.7	47.9	2.9	52.1	0.9	15.9	0.4	7.0
N.Y.	3,364.1	473.3	14.1	152.9	32.3	320.4	67.7	169.4	35.8	35.6	7.5
N.C.	1,199.5	352.2	29.4	99.7	28.3	252.5	71.7	229.4	65.1	207.7	59.0
N. Dak.	116.0	0.5	0.4	0.5	100.0	-	-	-	-	-	-
Ohio	2,400.3	287.4	12.0	79.8	27.7	207.7	72.3	123.1	42.8	37.9	13.2

[Continued]

★ 620 ★

Elementary and Secondary: Black Public School Enrollment by Degree of Segregation, by State, 1968
[Continued]

STATE	Total enrollment	NEGRO ENROLLMENT									
		Total	Percent of total enrollment	By minority group enrollment of schools							
				Under 50 percent		50-100 percent		95-100 percent		100 percent	
				Number	Percent	Number	Percent	Number	Percent	Number	Percent
Okla.	543.5	48.9	9.0	18.5	37.8	30.4	62.2	23.6	48.3	8.4	17.3
Oreg.	455.1	7.4	1.6	4.7	63.3	2.7	36.7	-	-	-	-
Pa.	2,296.0	268.5	11.7	73.9	27.5	194.6	72.5	118.4	44.1	11.8	4.4
R.I.	172.3	8.0	4.7	7.2	89.4	0.9	10.6	-	-	-	-
S.C.	603.5	238.0	39.4	33.8	14.2	204.2	85.8	200.2	84.1	188.7	79.3
S. Dak.	146.4	0.4	0.3	0.4	93.7	-	6.3	-	3.1	-	-
Tenn.	887.5	184.7	20.8	39.2	21.2	145.5	78.8	132.2	71.6	108.4	58.7
Texas	2,510.4	379.8	15.1	95.9	25.3	283.9	74.7	239.5	63.1	165.2	43.5
Utah	303.2	1.5	0.5	1.1	73.9	0.4	26.1	-	-	-	-
Vt.	73.6	0.1	0.1	0.1	100.0	-	-	-	-	-	-
Va.	1,041.1	245.0	23.5	65.9	26.9	179.1	73.1	167.2	68.2	142.2	58.0
Wash.	791.3	19.1	2.4	12.3	64.2	6.8	35.8	-	-	-	-
W. Va.	404.6	20.4	5.0	16.8	82.0	3.7	18.0	1.2	5.7	0.8	4.1
Wis.	942.4	37.3	4.0	8.4	22.5	28.9	77.5	14.8	39.6	4.8	12.9
Wyo.	79.1	0.7	0.8	0.5	72.5	0.2	27.5	-	-	-	-

Source: "Negro Enrollment in Public Elementary and Secondary Schools, by Extent of School Segregation—States: 1968," *Statistical Abstract of the United States, 1970,* p. 119. Primary source: Dept. of Health, Education, and Welfare, Office of the Secretary; news release, January 4, 1970. *Note:* - Represents zero.

★ 621 ★

Enrollment

In/Out of School: 1900-1910 Changes in School Participation, by Gender and Age Group - I

AGE AND CENSUS YEAR	POPULATION 5 TO 20 YEARS OF AGE Negro					
	In school			Not in school		
	Both sexes	Male	Female	Both sexes	Male	Female
5 to 20 years:						
1910	1,644,759	771,587	873,172	2,033,101	1,026,101	1,007,000
1900	1,083,516	503,099	580,417	2,415,671	1,218,659	1,197,012
Increase, 1900-1910	561,243	268,488	292,755	...	...	...
Decrease, 1900-1910	...	...	...	382,570	192,558	190,012
5 to 9 years:						
1910	514,014	248,936	265,078	732,539	370,239	362,300
1900	284,784	139,201	145,583	917,974	461,209	456,765
Increase, 1900-1910	229,230	109,735	119,495	...	...	...
Decrease, 1900-1910	...	...	...	185,435	90,970	94,465

[Continued]

★ 621 ★

In/Out of School: 1900-1910 Changes in School Participation, by Gender and Age Group - I
[Continued]

| AGE AND CENSUS YEAR | POPULATION 5 TO 20 YEARS OF AGE Negro | | | | | |
| | In school | | | Not in school | | |
	Both sexes	Male	Female	Both sexes	Male	Female
10 to 14 years:						
1910	791,995	379,486	412,509	363,271	198,588	164,683
1900	587,560	277,832	309,728	504,430	270,810	233,620
Increase, 1900-1910	204,435	101,654	102,781	...	...	...
Decrease, 1900-1910	...	...	...	141,159	72,222	68,937
15 to 20 years:						
1910	338,750	143,165	195,585	937,291	457,274	480,017
1900	211,172	86,066	125,106	993,267	486,640	506,627
Increase: 1900-1910	127,578	57,099	70,479	...	...	...
Decrease: 1900-1910	...	...	...	55,976	29,366	26,610

Source: "Negro and White Population 5 to 20 Years of Age In School and Not In School, by Sex and Age Periods: 1910 and 1900, *Negro Population, 1790-1915*, 1918, p. 377. Primary source: U.S. Bureau of the Census. *Negro Population, 1790-1915*. Washington, D.C.: Government Printing Office, 1918.

★ 622 ★

Enrollment

In/Out of School: 1900-1910 Changes in School Participation, by Gender and Age Group - II

| AGE AND CENSUS YEAR | POPULATION 5 TO 20 YEARS OF AGE Percentage in school | | | | | | Percentage not in school | | | | | |
| | Negro | | | White | | | Negro | | | White | | |
	Both sexes	Male	Female	Both sexes	Male	Female	Both sexes	Male	Female	Both sexes	Male	Female
5 to 20 years:												
1910	44.7	42.9	46.4	61.3	61.3	61.3	55.3	57.1	53.6	38.7	38.7	38.7
1900	31.0	29.2	32.7	53.6	53.4	53.9	69.0	70.8	67.3	46.4	46.4	46.1
Increase, 1900-1910	13.7	13.7	13.7	7.7	7.9	7.4	...	...	...	...	...	...
Decrease, 1900-1910	...	...	...	...	...	...	13.7	13.7	13.7	7.7	7.9	7.4
5 to 9 years:												
1910	41.2	40.2	42.3	64.8	64.7	65.0	58.8	59.8	57.7	35.2	35.3	35.0
1900	23.7	23.2	24.2	52.0	52.0	51.9	76.3	76.8	75.8	48.0	48.0	48.1
Increase, 1900-1910	17.5	17.0	18.1	12.8	12.7	13.1	...	...	...	...	...	...
Decrease, 1900-1910	...	...	...	...	...	...	17.5	17.0	18.1	12.8	12.7	13.1
10 to 14 years:												
1910	68.6	65.6	71.5	91.1	91.0	91.2	31.4	34.4	28.5	8.9	9.0	8.8
1900	53.8	50.6	57.0	84.0	83.2	84.8	46.2	49.4	43.0	16.0	16.8	15.2
Increase, 1900-1910	14.8	15.0	14.5	7.1	7.8	6.4	...	...	...	...	...	...
Decrease, 1900-1910	...	...	...	...	...	...	14.8	15.0	14.5	7.1	7.8	6.4

[Continued]

★ 622 ★

In/Out of School: 1900-1910 Changes in School Participation, by Gender and Age Group - II
[Continued]

AGE AND CENSUS YEAR	POPULATION 5 TO 20 YEARS OF AGE Percentage in school						Percentage not in school					
	Negro			White			Negro			White		
	Both sexes	Male	Female	Both sexes	Male	Female	Both sexes	Male	Female	Both sexes	Male	Female
15 to 20 years:												
1910	26.5	23.8	28.9	33.7	33.7	33.8	73.5	76.2	71.1	66.3	66.3	66.2
1900	17.5	15.0	19.8	28.3	27.8	28.8	82.5	85.0	80.2	71.7	72.2	71.2
Increase: 1900-1910	9.0	8.8	9.1	5.4	5.9	5.0	...	...	...	...	...	...
Decrease: 1900-1910	...	...	...	...	...	...	9.0	8.8	9.1	5.4	5.9	5.0

Source: "Negro and White Population 5 to 20 Years of Age In School and Not In School, by Sex and Age Periods: 1910 and 1900, *Negro Population, 1790-1915*, 1918, p. 377. Primary source: U.S. Bureau of the Census. *Negro Population, 1790-1915*. Washington, D.C.: Government Printing Office, 1918.

★ 623 ★

Enrollment

In/Out of School: Age Group and Regional Enrollment in 1900 and 1910

SECTION, DIVISION, AND AGE PERIOD	PERCENTAGE IN SCHOOL				INCREASE IN PERCENTAGE IN SCHOOL 1900-1910	
	1910		1900			
	Negro	White	Negro	White	Negro	White
UNITED STATES:						
5 to 20 years	44.7	61.3	31.0	53.6	13.7	7.7
5 to 9 years	41.2	64.8	23.7	52.0	17.5	12.8
10 to 14 years	68.6	91.1	53.8	84.0	14.8	7.1
15 to 20 years	26.5	33.7	17.5	28.3	9.0	5.4
THE SOUTH:						
5 to 20 years	43.7	58.3	29.6	45.9	14.1	12.4
5 to 9 years	39.5	53.1	21.7	34.6	17.8	18.5
10 to 14 years	67.0	85.1	51.6	74.0	15.4	11.1
15 to 20 years	26.6	39.5	17.3	31.4	9.3	8.1
THE NORTH:						
5 to 20 years	56.7	62.5	47.2	56.5	9.5	6.0
5 to 9 years	65.3	70.8	51.0	59.3	14.3	11.5
10 to 14 years	89.6	93.6	81.4	87.8	8.2	5.8
15 to 20 years	26.3	30.8	19.8	26.5	6.5	3.3
THE WEST:						
5 to 20 years	58.2	62.9	51.1	59.2	7.1	3.7
5 to 9 years	64.6	62.4	55.6	55.2	9.0	7.2
10 to 14 years	92.0	93.3	85.3	90.1	6.7	3.2
15 to 20 years	30.3	39.5	22.7	35.7	7.6	3.8

Source: "Percentage of Negroes and Whites In School, by Sections, Divisions, and Age Periods: 1910 and 1900, *Negro Population, 1790-1915*, 1918, p. 383. Primary source: U.S. Bureau of the Census. *Negro Population, 1790-1915*. Washington, D.C.: Government Printing Office, 1918.

★ 624 ★

Enrollment

In/Out of School: Black Children 10-14 In/Out of School, 1890-1910, by Geographic Division - I

[Parentage not shown where base is less than 100].

DIVISION AND STATE	NEGRO POPULATION 10 TO 14 YEARS OF AGE								
	1910	1900	1890	Number in school			Number not in school		
				1910	1900	1890	1910	1900	1890
UNITED STATES	1,155,266	1,091,990	1,033,701	791,995	587,560	534,864	363,271	504,430	498,837
GEOGRAPHIC DIVISIONS:									
New England	5,092	4,285	3,844	4,800	3,785	3,264	292	500	580
Middle Atlantic	29,648	23,932	19,943	26,760	19,224	15,000	2,888	4,708	4,943
East North Central	23,184	23,851	22,652	21,102	20,445	19,113	2,082	3,406	3,539
West North Central	20,281	25,529	27,063	17,397	19,699	20,099	2,884	5,830	6,964
South Atlantic	513,239	476,108	469,021	349,010	246,917	226,177	164,229	229,191	242,844
East South Central	320,476	316,984	299,473	215,349	162,205	155,861	105,127	154,779	143,612
West South Central	240,265	219,122	189,706	154,743	113,426	93,861	85,522	105,696	98,845
Mountain	1,286	984	768	1,166	832	546	120	152	222
Pacific	1,795	1,195	1,231	1,668	1,027	943	127	168	288

Source: "Negroes 10 to 14 Years of Age, In School and Not in School, by Divisions and States: 1910, 1900, and 1890," *Negro Population, 1790-1915*, 1918, p. 398. Primary source: U.S. Bureau of the Census. *Negro Population, 1790-1915*. Washington, D.C.: Government Printing Office, 1918.

★ 625 ★

Enrollment

In/Out of School: Black Children 10-14 In/Out of School, 1890-1910, by Geographic Division - II

[Parentage not shown where base is less than 100].

DIVISION AND STATE	PERCENTAGE IN SCHOOL OF CHILDREN 10 TO 14 YEARS OF AGE					
	Negro			Whites		
	1910	1900	1890	1910	1900	1890
UNITED STATES	68.6	53.8	51.7	91.1	84.0	84.6
GEOGRAPHIC DIVISIONS:						
New England	94.3	88.3	84.9	94.1	90.0	90.1
Middle Atlantic	90.3	80.3	75.2	92.9	85.8	85.3
East North Central	91.0	85.7	84.4	93.8	88.2	90.6
West North Central	85.8	77.2	74.3	93.8	88.6	90.6
South Atlantic	68.0	51.9	48.2	85.0	74.1	73.1
East South Central	67.2	51.2	52.0	84.8	73.4	74.8
West South Central	64.4	51.8	49.5	85.5	74.6	72.7
Mountain	90.7	84.6	71.1	91.9	87.1	81.9
Pacific	92.9	85.9	76.6	94.4	92.4	90.4

Source: "Negroes 10 to 14 Years of Age, In School and Not in School, by Divisions and States: 1910, 1900, and 1890," *Negro Population, 1790-1915*, 1918, p. 398. Primary source: U.S. Bureau of the Census. *Negro Population, 1790-1915*. Washington, D.C.: Government Printing Office, 1918.

★ 626 ★

Enrollment

In/Out of School: Black Male/Female Ratios In and Out of School, by Region and Age Group, 1910

SECTION, DIVISION, AND STATE	NEGRO POPULATION: 1910								
	Percentage in school						Males per 1,000 females in school		
	6 to 9 years of age		10 to 14 years of age		15 to 20 years of age		6 to 9 years of age	10 to 14 years of age	15 to 20 years of age
	Male	Female	Male	Female	Male	Female			
United States	48.2	50.5	65.6	71.5	23.8	28.9	942	920	732
The South	46.2	48.6	63.9	70.0	23.7	29.1	940	918	725
South Atlantic	47.8	50.2	64.6	71.4	22.4	28.8	939	909	691
East South Central	47.0	49.7	64.1	70.4	25.7	30.9	938	928	748
West South Central	41.7	43.8	62.2	66.6	23.5	27.5	946	927	764
The North	77.0	77.7	89.4	89.8	25.5	27.1	955	935	814
The West	77.1	77.3	91.7	92.3	27.5	32.9	961	933	764
THE SOUTH									
South Atlantic:									
Delaware	65.1	65.6	83.3	84.4	31.7	26.0	927	1,106	1,234
Maryland	60.0	61.9	77.5	80.1	22.9	23.2	934	944	886
District of Columbia	74.0	76.1	89.2	91.7	28.7	30.8	912	860	688
Virginia	43.1	45.9	68.3	73.2	23.4	30.5	922	941	707
West Virginia	68.7	69.5	80.8	84.6	18.3	29.7	915	975	802
North Carolina	53.2	54.9	70.3	75.4	33.4	39.7	954	931	765
South Carolina	43.0	45.4	63.2	69.3	24.0	30.5	943	915	695
Georgia	46.3	48.8	57.0	67.3	14.2	21.9	941	860	547
Florida	47.7	50.9	60.8	67.8	18.8	25.0	939	896	664
East South Central:									
Kentucky	58.3	59.9	77.3	80.7	26.3	34.2	961	964	729
Tennessee	47.3	50.3	66.9	72.3	24.5	31.1	938	937	742
Alabama	36.1	39.0	55.7	63.2	22.9	28.0	911	898	710
Mississippi	54.3	57.1	67.5	73.6	28.6	32.6	950	939	786
West South Central:									
Arkansas	48.6	49.7	63.6	68.9	31.0	34.1	959	906	816
Louisiana	28.2	30.6	42.3	46.8	11.7	15.7	923	903	642
Oklahoma	64.9	67.6	84.8	86.8	41.0	42.8	969	956	932
Texas	46.6	48.9	77.0	81.3	26.7	32.4	946	947	747

Source: "Urban and Rural Population—Negroes and Whites In School and Not In School, by Age Periods, by Sections, Divisions, and Southern States: 1910," *Negro Population, 1790-1915*, 1918, p. 387. Primary source: U.S. Bureau of the Census. *Negro Population, 1790-1915*. Washington, D.C.: Government Printing Office, 1918.

In/Out of School: Black School-Age Persons Not in School in 1910, by Age Group and Region - I

AGE	PERCENTAGE NOT IN SCHOOL: 1910										
	United States		The South								
			Negro	White	South Atlantic division		East South Central division		West South Central division		
	Negro	White			Negro	White	Negro	White	Negro	White	
6 to 20 years	52.7	35.5	53.6	37.9	53.0	37.8	52.7	36.9	56.3	38.8	
6 to 9 years	50.7	22.8	52.6	35.2	51.0	32.6	51.6	34.2	57.3	38.9	
10 to 14 years	31.4	8.9	33.0	14.9	32.0	15.0	32.8	15.2	35.6	14.5	
15 to 20 years	73.5	66.3	73.4	60.5	74.2	62.0	71.6	58.6	74.4	60.5	

Source: "Negro and White Percentage Not in School by Single Years of Age, by Sections and Southern Divisions: 1910," *Negro Population, 1790-1915*, 1918, p. 385. Primary source: U.S. Bureau of the Census. *Negro Population, 1790-1915*. Washington, D.C.: Government Printing Office, 1918.

In/Out of School: Black School-Age Persons Not in School in 1910, by Age Group and Region - II

AGE	PERCENTAGE NOT IN SCHOOL: 1910			
	The North		The West	
	Negro	White	Negro	White
6 to 20 years	40.8	34.7	39.2	33.5
6 to 9 years	22.7	16.7	22.8	24.2
10 to 14 years	10.4	6.4	8.0	6.7
15 to 20 years	73.7	69.2	69.7	60.5

Source: "Negro and White Percentage Not in School by Single Years of Age, by Sections and Southern Divisions: 1910," *Negro Population, 1790-1915*, 1918, p. 385. Primary source: U.S. Bureau of the Census. *Negro Population, 1790-1915*. Washington, D.C.: Government Printing Office, 1918.

★ 629 ★

Enrollment

In/Out of School: Black and Mulatto 6-20-Year-Olds In and Not In School, by Region and Age Group, 1910

| AGE | NEGRO POPULATION: 1910 | | | | | |
| --- | Black | | Mulatto | | Percentage in school | |
	In school	Not in school	In school	Not in school	Black	Mulatto
UNITED STATES						
6 to 20 years	1,230,843	1,465,328	388,856	337,130	45.7	53.6
6 to 9 years	369,352	411,993	119,602	89,903	47.3	57.1
10 to 14 years	607,401	305,247	184,594	58,024	66.6	76.1
15 to 20 years	254,090	748,088	84,660	189,203	25.4	30.9
THE SOUTH						
6 to 20 years	1,125,347	1,388,786	341,593	308,770	44.8	52.5
6 to 9 years	334,665	401,270	103,879	85,849	45.5	54.8
10 to 14 years	556,481	298,902	162,621	55,976	65.1	74.4
15 to 20 years	234,201	688,614	75,093	166,945	25.4	31.0
THE NORTH						
6 to 20 years	101,758	73,975	44,914	27,008	57.9	62.4
6 to 9 years	33,509	10,363	15,003	3,853	76.4	79.6
10 to 14 years	49,153	6,170	20,906	1,976	88.8	91.4
15 to 20 years	19,096	57,442	9,005	21,179	24.9	30.9
THE WEST						
6 to 20 years	3,738	2,567	2,349	1,352	59.3	63.5
6 to 9 years	1,178	360	720	201	76.6	78.2
10 to 14 years	1,767	175	1,067	72	91.0	93.7
15 to 20 years	793	2,032	562	1,079	28.1	34.2

Source: [Untitled Table], *Negro Population, 1790-1915,* 1918, p. 215. Primary source: U.S. Bureau of the Census. *Negro Population, 1790-1915.* Washington, D.C.: Government Printing Office, 1918.

★ 630 ★

Enrollment

In/Out of School: Cities with Largest Black Population and Children 6-14 In and Out of School, c. 1910

Order	CITY	Number in school	Order	CITY	Number not in school
1	Washington, D.C.	10,807	1	New Orleans, La.	4,544
2	New Orleans, La.	9,446	2	Baltimore, Md.	2,756
3	Baltimore, Md.	8,509	3	Richmond, Va.	2,413
4	Philadelphia, Pa.	8,051	4	Atlanta, Ga.	2,326
5	New York, N.Y.	7,783	5	Birmingham, Ala.	2,175
6	Birmingham, Ala.	5,807	6	Memphis, Tenn.	2,123
7	Atlanta, Ga.	5,685	7	Washington, D.C.	2,103
8	Richmond, Va.	4,514	8	Charleston, S.C.	1,859
9	Memphis, Tenn.	4,317	9	Savannah, Ga.	1,655
10	Nashville, Tenn.	4,098	10	Philadelphia, Pa.	1,553

Source: [Untitled Table], *Negro Population, 1790-1915,* 1918, p. 389. Primary source: U.S. Bureau of the Census. *Negro Population, 1790-1915.* Washington, D.C.: Government Printing Office, 1918.

★ 631 ★

Enrollment

In/Out of School: Enrollment in Relation to Population, 1910

SECTION AND DIVISION	POPULATION 6 TO 20 YEARS OF AGE: 1910						
	Negro			White, in school		Percentage distribution of population in school	
	Total	In school		Number	Percent	Negro	White
		Number	Percent				
United States	3,422,157	1,619,699	47.3	15,624,716	64.5	100.0	100.0
The South	3,164,496	1,466,940	46.4	4,279,812	62.1	90.6	27.4
South Atlantic	1,504,019	706,974	47.0	1,638,589	62.2	43.6	10.5
East South Central	944,880	447,230	47.3	1,225,752	63.1	27.6	7.8
West South Central	715,597	312,736	43.7	1,415,471	61.2	19.3	9.1
The North	247,655	146,672	59.2	10,208,409	65.3	9.1	65.3
New England	15,539	10,201	65.6	1,132,538	66.1	0.6	7.2
Middle Atlantic	95,194	54,780	57.5	3,313,591	63.0	3.4	21.2
East North Central	72,837	44,462	61.0	3,383,070	65.6	2.7	21.7
West North Central	64,085	37,229	58.1	2,379,210	68.1	2.3	15.2
The West	10,006	6,087	60.8	1,136,495	66.5	0.4	7.3

[Continued]

★ 631 ★

In/Out of School: Enrollment in Relation to Population, 1910
[Continued]

SECTION AND DIVISION	POPULATION 6 TO 20 YEARS OF AGE: 1910						
	Negro			White, in school		Percentage distribution of population in school	
	Total	In school		Number	Percent	Negro	White
		Number	Percent				
Mountain	4,170	2,531	60.7	476,502	67.1	0.2	3.0
Pacific	5,836	3,556	60.9	659,993	66.2	0.2	4.2

Source: "[Untitled Table], *Negro Population, 1790-1915*, 1918, p. 381. Primary source: U.S. Bureau of the Census. *Negro Population, 1790-1915*. Washington, D.C.: Government Printing Office, 1918.

★ 632 ★
Enrollment

In/Out of School: Gender, Age Group, and Geographic Division Distributions of Enrollment, Including those 6-9 and 10-14, 1910 - I

DIVISION AND STATE	NEGRO POPULATION: 1910							
	6 to 9 years of age				10 to 14 years of age			
	Number in school		Number not in school		Number in school		Number not in school	
	Male	Female	Male	Female	Male	Female	Male	Female
UNITED STATES	237,162	251,792	255,304	246,592	379,486	412,509	198,588	164,683
GEOGRAPHIC DIVISIONS:								
New England	1,736	1,828	276	274	2,288	2,512	146	146
Middle Atlantic	9,288	9,819	2,645	2,761	12,806	13,954	1,330	1,558
East North Central	7,065	7,399	1,860	1,836	10,344	10,758	1,033	1,019
West North Central	5,605	5,772	2,292	2,272	8,409	8,988	1,512	1,372
South Atlantic	104,856	111,609	114,736	110,821	166,162	182,848	91,056	73,164
East South Central	63,749	67,952	71,766	68,672	103,657	111,692	58,085	47,012
West South Central	43,933	46,445	61,452	59,672	74,452	80,291	45,293	40,229
Mountain	397	419	146	131	586	580	56	64
Pacific	533	549	131	153	782	886	68	59

Source: "Negro Males and Females In School and Not In School, by Age Periods, by Divisions and States: 1910, *Negro Population, 1790-1915*, 1918, p. 392. Primary source: U.S. Bureau of the Census. *Negro Population, 1790-1915*. Washington, D.C.: Government Printing Office, 1918.

★ 633 ★

Enrollment

In/Out of School: Gender, Age Group, and Geographic Division Distributions of Enrollment, Including those 15-20, Below 6 and Over 21, 1910 - II

DIVISION AND STATE	NEGRO POPULATION: 1910							
	15 to 20 years of age				Number under 6 years of age in school		Number 21 years of age and over in school	
	Number in school		Number not in school					
	Male	Female	Male	Female	Male	Female	Male	Female
UNITED STATES	143,165	195,585	457,274	480,017	13,452	15,108	10,604	11,787
GEOGRAPHIC DIVISIONS:								
New England	775	1,062	2,106	2,390	218	235	110	91
Middle Atlantic	4,054	4,859	14,068	18,052	856	939	566	473
East North Central	4,007	4,889	11,060	11,537	306	317	685	365
West North Central	3,773	4,682	9,654	9,754	303	345	402	314
South Atlantic	57,813	83,686	199,893	207,366	4,936	5,615	4,067	5,085
East South Central	42,880	57,300	123,839	128,246	4,690	5,203	2,619	3,046
West South Central	29,276	38,339	95,109	101,106	2,084	2,382	2,111	2,380
Mountain	243	306	584	658	20	31	23	14
Pacific	344	462	961	908	39	41	21	19

Source: "Negro Males and Females In School and Not In School, by Age Periods, by Divisions and States: 1910, *Negro Population, 1790-1915*, 1918, p. 392. Primary source: U.S. Bureau of the Census. *Negro Population, 1790-1915.* Washington, D.C.: Government Printing Office, 1918.

★ 634 ★

Enrollment

In/Out of School: Total Population Enrollment in 1910

RACIAL CLASS	POPULATION: 1910			PERCENTAGE DISTRIBUTION	
	Total	In school		Total population	Population in school
		Number	Percent		
All classes	91,972,266	18,009,891	19.6	100.0	100.0
Negro	9,827,763	1,670,650	17.0	10.7	9.3
White	81,731,957	16,279,292	19.9	88.9	90.4
Native white	68,386,412	15,627,786	22.9	74.4	86.8
Native parentage	49,488,575	11,110,583	22.5	53.8	61.7
Foreign or mixed parentage	18,897,837	4,517,203	23.9	20.5	25.1
Foreign born	13,345,545	651,506	4.9	14.5	3.6
Indian	265,688	53,458	20.1	0.3	0.3
Chinese	71,531	3,887	5.4	0.1	[1]
Japanese	72,157	2,512	3.5	0.1	[1]
All other	3,175	92	2.9	[1]	[1]

Source: [Untitled Table], *Negro Population, 1790-1915*, 1918, p. 375. Primary source: U.S. Bureau of the Census. *Negro Population, 1790-1915.* Washington, D.C.: Government Printing Office, 1918. *Note:* 1. Less than one-tenth of 1 per cent.

★ 635 ★
Enrollment

In/Out of School: Urban-Rural Residence and School Participation, by Region and Age Group, 1910 - I

[Percentage not shown where base is less than 100]

SECTION AND RACIAL CLASS	POPULATION 6 TO 9 YEARS OF AGE						POPULATION 10 TO 14 YEARS OF AGE					
	Urban		Rural		Percentage in school		Urban		Rural		Percentage in school	
	Number in school	Number not in school	Number in school	Number not in school	Urban	Rural	Number in school	Number not in school	Number in school	Number not in school	Urban	Rural
UNITED STATES:												
Negro	120,910	61,832	368,044	440,064	66.2	45.5	182,054	43,369	609,941	319,902	80.8	65.6
White	2,319,899	484,575	2,854,448	1,044,826	82.7	73.2	141,617	257,208	4,070,990	448,593	92.4	90.1
THE NORTH:												
Negro	35,227	8,543	13,285	5,673	80.5	70.1	49,661	4,896	20,398	3,250	91.0	86.3
White	1,913,499	338,465	1,596,097	365,766	85.0	81.4	2,541,733	190,981	2,207,656	136,187	93.0	94.2
THE SOUTH:												
Negro	84,175	52,900	354,369	434,219	61.4	44.9	130,186	38,315	588,916	316,563	77.3	65.0
White	253,172	106,992	1,059,482	605,953	70.3	63.6	377,954	51,884	1,576,457	290,376	87.9	84.4
THE WEST:												
Negro	1,598	389	390	172	79.5	69.4	2,207	158	627	89	93.3	87.6
White	153,228	39,118	198,869	73,107	79.7	73.1	221,930	14,343	286,877	22,030	93.9	92.9

Source: "Urban and Rural Population—Negroes and Whites In School and Not In School, by Age Periods, by Sections, Divisions, and Southern States: 1910," *Negro Population, 1790-1915,* 1918, p. 399. Primary source: U.S. Bureau of the Census. *Negro Population, 1790-1915.* Washington, D.C.: Government Printing Office, 1918.

★ 636 ★
Enrollment

In/Out of School: Urban-Rural Residence and School Participation, by Region and Age Group, 1910 - II

[Percentage not shown where base is less than 100]

SECTION AND RACIAL CLASS	POPULATION 15 TO 20 YEARS OF AGE					
	Urban		Rural		Percentage in school	
	Number in school	Number not in school	Number in school	Number not in school	Urban	Rural
UNITED STATES:						
Negro	70,927	243,572	267,823	693,719	22.6	27
White	1,256,338	3,324,440	1,981,424	3,036,510	27.4	39.9
THE NORTH:						
Negro	19,155	59,143	8,946	19,478	24.5	31.5
White	955,437	2,724,897	993,987	1,659,991	26.0	37.5
THE SOUTH:						
Negro	50,738	181,977	258,556	673,582	21.8	27.7
White	173,294	390,953	839,453	1,162,266	30.7	41.9

[Continued]

★ 636 ★

In/Out of School: Urban-Rural Residence and School Participation, by Region and Age Group, 1910 - II

[Continued]

SECTION AND RACIAL CLASS	POPULATION 15 TO 20 YEARS OF AGE					
	Urban		Rural		Percentage in school	
	Number in school	Number not in school	Number in school	Number not in school	Urban	Rural
THE WEST:						
Negro	1,634	2,452	321	659	29.7	32.8
White	127,607	208,590	147,984	214,253	38.0	40.9

Source: "Urban and Rural Population—Negroes and Whites In School and Not In School, by Age Periods, by Sections, Divisions, and Southern States: 1910," *Negro Population, 1790-1915*, 1918, p. 399. Primary source: U.S. Bureau of the Census. *Negro Population, 1790-1915*. Washington, D.C.: Government Printing Office, 1918.

★ 637 ★

Enrollment

Multi-Level Employment: Black Institutions and Students in Secondary and Higher Education, c. 1912

"There are more than 540 institutions devoted to the secondary and higher training of the Negro. The Statistics for 189 of these are: Teachers, 2,941; total students, 57,915; elementary students, 32,967; secondary students; 19,654; collegiate students, 3,214; professional students, 2,080; students being industrially trained, 29,954. Of the total number of students, 56.9 per cent are in elementary grades and 5.5 per cent are taking collegiate courses."

Source: "Secondary and Higher Education," *Negro Year Book and Annual Encyclopedia of the Negro*, 1912, p. 102. Primary source: Work, Monroe N. (Ed.), *Negro Year Book and Annual Encyclopedia of the Negro*. Tuskegee, Ala.: Tuskegee Normal and Industrial Institute, 1912.

★ 638 ★

Enrollment

Multi-Level Enrollment: 5-20-Year-Olds in School, by Gender and Age Group, 1890, 1910, and 1940

[In percentages]

Age and sex	Black			White		
	1890[1]	1910	1940	1890	1910	1940
MALE						
Total, 5 to 20 years	32	43	64	59	61	72
5 to 9 years	24	40	68	54	65	75
10 to 14 years	50	66	90	84	91	95

[Continued]

★ 638 ★

Multi-Level Enrollment: 5-20-Year-Olds in School, by Gender and Age Group, 1890, 1910, and 1940
[Continued]

Age and sex	Black			White		
	1890[1]	1910	1940	1890	1910	1940
15 to 20 years	20	24	37	36	34	52
FEMALE						
Total, 5 to 20 years	34	46	65	57	61	71
5 to 9 years	25	42	69	53	65	75
10 to 14 years	54	71	92	85	91	95
15 to 20 years	23	29	39	33	34	49

Source: "Percent of Persons 5 to 20 Years Old Enrolled in School, by Age and Sex: 1890, 1910, and 1940," *The Social and Economic Status of the Black Population in the United States: An Historical View, 1790-1978,* 1979, p. 89. Primary source: U.S. Department of Commerce, Bureau of the Census. *Note:* 1. Data include persons of "other" races.

★ 639 ★
Enrollment

Multi-Level Enrollment: 5-29-Year-Olds in School, by Gender and Age Group, 1950, 1960, 1970, and 1975
[In percentages]

Age and sex	Black[1]				White			
	1950	1960	1970	1975	1950	1960	1970	1975
MALE								
Total, 5 to 29 years	56	66	69	69	55	69	70	64
5 to 13 years	87	92	96	98	89	96	97	98
14 to 17 years	79	88	92	93	85	92	95	95
18 to 19 years	20	37	41	50	37	49	56	50
20 to 24 years	11	9	17	21	15	21	31	27
25 to 29 years	6	4	6	12	6	9	11	13
FEMALE								
Total, 5 to 29 years	47	62	64	63	49	61	62	59
5 to 13 years	87	93	96	98	89	95	98	99
14 to 17 years	72	85	92	91	84	90	94	93
18 to 19 years	26	32	39	45	24	30	42	44
20 to 24 years	3	6	12	19	5	8	15	19
25 to 29 years	1	2	4	8	-	2	4	7

Source: "Percent of Persons 5 to 29 Years Old Enrolled in School, by Age and Sex: 1950, 1960, 1970, and 1975," *The Social and Economic Status of the Black Population in the United States: An Historical View, 1790-1978,* 1979, p. 89. Primary source: U.S. Department of Commerce, Bureau of the Census. *Notes:* - Represents or rounds to zero. 1. Data for 1950 and 1960 includes persons of "other" races.

★ 640 ★

Enrollment

Multi-Level Enrollment: Black School Attendees 5 to 20 Years Old, 1900-1940

Year	Total Number	Number Attending school
1940	4,188,500	2,698,901
1930	4,128,998	2,477,311
1920	3,796,957	2,030,269
1910	3,677,860	1,644,759
1900	3,499,187	1,083,516

Source: "Negroes 5 to 20 Years of Age Attending School, for the United States: 1900 to 1940," *The Negro Handbook, 1944*, 1944, p. 276. Primary source: Murray, Florence (Ed.), *The Negro Handbook, 1944*. New York: Current Reference Publications, 1944.

★ 641 ★

Enrollment

Multi-Level Enrollment: Elementary and Secondary Day School Enrollment in Black Schools in Selected States, 1948-49

State	Total	Kindergarten and Elementary[1] Total	Secondary Pupils[2]			Per Cent Total Enrollment, Secondary Grades
			Total	Boys	Girls	
Alabama	233,699	202,347	31,352	12,606	18,746	13.4
Arkansas	110,992	100,004	10,988	4,751	6,237	9.9
Delaware	7,602	6,475	1,127	585	542	14.8
District of Columbia	44,456	36,252	8,204	3,408	4,796	18.5
Florida	111,781	94,031	17,750	7,965	9,785	15.9
Georgia	255,273	218,607	36,666	14,716	21,950	14.4
Kentucky	37,124	30,364	6,760	3,152	3,608	18.2
Louisiana	172,677	156,642	16,035	6,146	9,889	9.3
Maryland	69,522	51,713	17,809	7,731	10,078	25.6
Mississippi	261,805	243,353	18,452	7,382	11,070	7.0
Missouri	50,738	41,117	9,621	4,235	5,386	19.0
North Carolina	261,535	221,070	40,465	16,468	23,997	15.5
Oklahoma	36,214	28,729	7,485	3,551	3,934	20.7
South Carolina	215,559	192,971	22,588	8,695	13,893	10.5
Tennessee	104,704	87,975	16,729	7,318	9,411	16.0
Texas	201,281	167,605	33,676	14,913	18,763	16.7
Virginia	152,951	130,130	22,821	9,573	13,248	14.9

[Continued]

★ 641 ★

Multi-Level Enrollment: Elementary and Secondary Day School
Enrollment in Black Schools in Selected States, 1948-49
[Continued]

State	Total	Kindergarten and Elementary[1] Total	Secondary Pupils[2]			Per Cent Total Enrollment, Secondary Grades
			Total	Boys	Girls	
West Virginia	25,592	16,942	8,650	4,118	4,532	33.8
Total	2,353,505	2,026,327	327,178	137,313	189,865	13.9

Source: "Enrollment in Negro Elementary and Secondary Day Schools, 17 States and District of Columbia, 1948-19," *1952 Negro Year Book: A Review of Events Affecting Negro Life,* 1952, p. 202. Primary source: U.S. Office of Education, *Statistical Circular No. 286,* January 1951. *Notes:* 1. Elementary includes kindergarten through grade 8 (or grade 7 in 11- grade system. 2. Secondary includes 1st 4 years after elementary.

★ 642 ★

Enrollment

Multi-Level Enrollment: Elementary and Secondary Day School
Enrollment in Southern Black Public Schools, 1948-49

State	Total	Kindergarten and elementary[1] Total	Secondary Pupils[2]			Per Cent total Enrollment, Secondary Grades
			Total	Boys	Girls	
Alabama	233,699	202,347	31,352	12,606	18,746	13.4
Arkansas	110,992	100,004	10,988	4,751	6,237	9.9
Delaware	7,602	6,475	1,127	585	542	14.8
District of Columbia	44,456	36,252	8,204	3,408	4,796	18.5
Florida	111,781	94,031	17,750	7,965	9,785	15.9
Georgia	255,273	218,607	36,666	14,716	21,950	14.4
Kentucky	37,124	30,364	6,760	3,152	3,608	18.2
Louisiana	172,677	156,642	16,035	6,146	9,889	9.3
Maryland	69,522	51,713	17,809	7,731	10,078	25.6
Mississippi	261,805	243,353	18,452	7,382	11,070	7.0
Missouri	50,738	41,117	9,621	4,235	5,386	19.0
North Carolina	261,535	221,070	40,465	16,468	23,997	15.5
Oklahoma	36,214	28,729	7,485	3,551	3,934	20.7
South Carolina	215,559	192,971	22,588	8,695	13,893	10.5
Tennessee	104,704	87,975	16,729	7,318	9,411	16.0
Texas	201,281	167,605	33,676	14,913	18,763	16.7
Virginia	152,951	130,130	22,821	9,573	13,248	14.9

[Continued]

★ 642 ★

Multi-Level Enrollment: Elementary and Secondary Day School Enrollment in Southern Black Public Schools, 1948-49

[Continued]

State	Total	Kindergarten and elementary[1] Total	Secondary Pupils[2]			Per Cent total Enrollment, Secondary Grades
			Total	Boys	Girls	
West Virginia	25,592	16,942	8,650	4,118	4,532	33.8
Total	2,353,505	2,026,327	327,178	137,313	189,865	13.9

Source: "Enrollment in Negro Elementary and Secondary Day Schools, 17 States and District of Columbia, 1948-49," *1952 Negro Year Book: A Review of Events Affecting Negro Life*, 1952, p. 202. Primary source: U.S. Office of Education, *Statistical Circular No. 286*, January 1951. *Notes:* 1. Elementary includes kindergarten through grade 8 (or grade 7 in 11- grade system). 2. Secondary includes 1st 4 years after elementary.

★ 643 ★

Enrollment

Multi-Level Enrollment: Elementary and Secondary Enrollment in Southern Black Public Schools, 1933-34 through 1948-49

Periods	Elementary[1]	Secondary[1]	Total
1933-34	2,266,913	163,185	2,430,098
1935-36	2,250,045	188,936	2,438,981
1943-44	2,029,362	247,373	2,276,735
1945-46	1,994,057	272,163	2,266,220
1947-48	2,006,836	299,226	2,306,062
1948-49	2,026,327	327,178	2,353,505

Source: "Enrollment in Negro Public Schools in 17 States and the District of Columbia, by Periods," *1952 Negro Year Book: A Review of Events Affecting Negro Life*, 1952, p. 202. Primary source: U.S. Office of Education, *Statistical Circular, No. 286*, January 1951. *Notes:* 1. Elementary includes grades K to 8 (or K to 7). Secondary includes first 4 years after elementary.

★ 644 ★
Enrollment

Multi-Level Enrollment: Elementary, High School, and College Enrollment, by Age, 1960 and 1969

[In thousands, except percent. As of October.]

AGE	WHITE				NEGRO AND OTHER			
	Total enrolled	Elementary[1]	High school[1]	College[1]	Total enrolled	Elementary[1]	High school[1]	College[1]
1960								
Total, 5-34 years	40,348	27,884	9,122	3,342	5,910	4,556	1,127	227
5-13 years	27,723	27,149	574	-	4,336	4,285	51	-
14-17 years	9,028	731	8,084	214	1,213	268	937	8
18-24 years	2,854	4	431	2,420	312	2	132	178
25-34 years	743	1	33	709	49	1	7	41
1969								
Total, 5-34 years	50,531	31,117	12,588	6,827	8,187	5,614	1,966	607
5-13 years	30,627	30,237	394	-	5,372	5,318	56	-
14-17 years	12,489	860	11,407	222	1,962	294	1,648	20
18-24 years	6,006	5	654	5,347	724	1	230	493
25-34 years	1,408	17	131	1,259	128	4	30	95
Percent change, 1960-1969	25.2	11.6	38.0	104.3	38.5	23.2	74.2	167.4

Source: "School Enrollment, by Race, Level of School, and Age: 1960 and 1969," *Statistical Abstract of the United States, 1970*, p, 108. Primary source: Dept. of Commerce, Bureau of the Census; *Current Population Reports*, Series P-20, and unpublished data. *Notes:* - Represents zero. 1. Elementary includes kindergarten and nursery schools; high school, grades 9-12; college includes professional schools.

★ 645 ★
Enrollment

Multi-Level Enrollment: Elementary, High School, and College Enrollment, by Age, 1970-1974

[In thousands, except percent. As of October. Minus sign (-) denotes decrease]

YEAR AND AGE	WHITE				NEGRO AND OTHER			
	Total enrolled	Elementary[1]	High school[1]	College[1]	Total enrolled	Elementary[1]	High school[1]	College[1]
1970, total	51,719	32,237	12,723	6,759	8,639	5,993	1,992	654
3 and 4 years	1,181	1,181	-	-	281	281	-	-
5-13 years	30,460	30,133	327	-	5,482	5,415	67	-
14-17 years	12,769	898	11,639	230	2,027	295	1,703	30
18-24 years	5,979	14	661	5,304	701	5	196	499
25-34 years	1,326	5	95	1,224	150	-	24	125

[Continued]

★ 645 ★

Multi-Level Enrollment: Elementary, High School, and College Enrollment, by Age, 1970-1974
[Continued]

YEAR AND AGE	WHITE				NEGRO AND OTHER			
	Total enrolled	Elementary[1]	High school[1]	College[1]	Total enrolled	Elementary[1]	High school[1]	College[1]
1972, total	51,314	30,897	12,959	7,458	8,827	5,761	2,210	855
3 and 4 years	1,359	1,360	-	-	296	297	-	-
5-13 years	28,993	28,668	326	-	5,254	5,188	66	-
14-17 years	13,057	857	11,944	259	2,209	274	1,897	36
18-24 years	6,289	8	655	5,624	862	4	226	633
25-34 years	1,616	4	34	1,575	207	-	22	185
1973, total	50,617	30,202	13,091	7,324	8,776	5,665	2,256	855
3 and 4 years	1,364	1,363	-	-	328	327	-	-
5-13 years	28,373	28,028	341	-	5,144	5,077	68	-
14-17 years	13,109	792	12,063	253	2,246	254	1,949	42
18-24 years	6,095	9	651	5,440	846	2	225	616
25-34 years	1,676	7	37	1,631	212	2	13	196
1974, total	50,992	30,139	13,073	7,781	9,267	5,847	2,374	1,046
3 and 4 years	1,658	1,659	-	-	349	347	-	-
5-13 years	27,961	27,616	345	-	5,293	5,229	61	-
14-17 years	13,198	855	12,071	271	2,331	265	2,025	38
18-24 years	6,199	4	606	5,589	992	-	266	727
25-34 years	1,976	2	53	1,921	302	2	20	282
Percent change:								
1960-1970	28.1	15.6	39.5	102.2	46.2	31.5	76.8	188.1
1970-1974	-1.4	-6.5	2.8	15.1	7.3	-2.4	19.2	59.9

Source: "School Enrollment, by Race, Level, and Age: 1970 and 1974," *Statistical Abstract of the United States, 1970,* p, 116. Primary source: U.S. Bureau of the Census, *Current Population Reports,* series P-20, Nos. 110, 222, 260, 272, and unpublished data. *Notes:* - Represents zero. 1. Elementary includes kindergarten and, beginning 1970, nursery schools; high school, grades 9-12; college includes professional schools.

★ 646 ★

Enrollment

Multi-Level Enrollment: Enrollment and Population in Recent Slave States, by Race and State, 1876-77

States	White			Colored		
	School population	Enrollment	Percentage of the school population enrolled	School population	Enrollment	Percentage of the school population enrolled
Alabama	236,520[1]	86,485	37	168,706[1]	54,745	32
Arkansas	143,949	23,895[2]	17	43,518	7,255[2]	17
Delaware	31,849	22,398	70	3,800	1,663	44
Florida	40,606	14,948[2]	37	42,001	16,185[2]	39
Georgia	218,733	107,010	49	175,304	48,643	28
Kentucky	459,253[3]	228,000	50	53,126[3]	19,107	36
Louisiana	88,567	45,000[2]	51	108,548[4]	40,000[2]	37
Maryland	213,669[5]	125,737	59	63,591	24,539	39
Mississippi	150,504	84,374	56	174,485	76,154	44
Missouri	692,818	381,074	55	32,910	13,774	42
North Carolina	267,265	128,289	48	141,031	73,170	52
South Carolina	83,813	46,444	55	144,315	55,952	39
Tennessee	330,935	171,535	52	111,523	43,043	39
Texas	135,430[6]	85,620	63	30,587[6]	23,432	77
Virginia	280,149	140,363	50	202,640	65,043	32
West Virginia	178,780[1]	120,657[1]	67	5,980[1]	2,847[1]	48
District of Columbia	20,671	15,310	74	11,000	5,954	54
Total	3,573,511	1,827,139	-	1,513,065	571,506	-

Source: Robert, *Negro Civilization in the South*, "Table Showing the Comparative Population and Enrollment of the White and Colored Races in the Public Schools of the Recent Slave States for 1876-77," 1880, p. 131. Primary source: Robert, Charles Edwin. *Negro Civilization in the South; Educational, Social and Religious Advancement of the Colored People*. Nashville, Tenn.: Printed by Wheeler Bros, for the author, 1880. *Notes:* 1. For 1875-76. 2. Estimated by the Bureau. 3. For whites the school age is 6-20; for colored 6-16. 4. Exclusive of that of New Orleans. 5. Census of 1870. 6. The school age in Texas at our last report was 6-18; it has been made 8-14, considerably lessening the school population.

★ 647 ★
Enrollment

Multi-Level Enrollment: Enrollment from Elementary through College or Professional School, by Age Group, 1947

[Percent not shown where base is less than 100,000].

Age, Color, and Sex	Total Civilian Population	Total Enrolled	Enrolled in School By Type of School					
			Elementary School		High School		College or Professional School	
			Number Enrolled	Percent of Total Enrolled	Number Enrolled	Percent of Total Enrolled	Number Enrolled	Percent of Total Enrolled
Total Classes, Both Sexes, 5 to 29 Years	56,683	26,679	16,220	60.8	8,390	31.4	2,069	7.8
WHITE								
Male, 5 to 29 years	24,494	12,383	7,233	58.4	3,823	30.9	1,327	10.7
5 to 13 years	9,081	7,442	6,891	92.6	551	7.4	-	-
14 to 17 years	3,845	3,159	322	10.2	2,799	88.6	38	1.2
18 and 19 years	1,600	506	3	0.6	297	58.7	206	40.7
20 to 24 years	5,010	929	13	1.4	130	14.0	786	84.6
25 to 29 years	4,958	347	4	1.2	46	13.3	297	85.6
Female, 5 to 29 years	25,280	11,149	6,736	60.4	3,823	34.3	590	5.3
5 to 13 years	8,725	7,213	6,560	90.9	653	9.1	-	-
14 to 17 years	3,771	3,127	173	5.5	2,887	92.3	67	2.1
18 and 19 years	2,029	518	2	0.4	270	52.1	246	47.5
20 to 24 years	5,404	244	1	0.4	10	4.1	233	95.5
25 to 29 years	5,351	47	-	-	3	-	44	-
NONWHITE								
Male, 5 to 29 years	3,370	1,602	1,156	7.2	355	22.2	91	5.7
5 to 13 years	1,376	1,063	1,018	95.8	45	4.2	-	-
14 to 17 years	532	379	132	34.8	243	64.1	4	1.1
18 and 19 years	237	59	-	-	41	-	18	-
20 to 24 years	643	64	3	-	20	-	41	-
25 to 29 years	582	37	3	-	6	-	28	-
Female, 5 to 29 years	3,539	1,545	1,095	70.9	389	25.2	61	3.9
5 to 13 years	1,369	1,059	1,006	95.0	53	5.0	-	-
14 to 17 years	541	392	89	22.7	296	75.5	7	1.8
18 and 19 years	275	65	-	-	36	-	29	-
20 to 24 years	691	25	-	-	2	-	23	-
25 to 29 years	663	4	-	-	2	-	2	-

Source: "Type of School Attended by Civilian Population 5 to 29 Years Old, by Color, Age, and Sex for the United States, April 1947," *The Negro Handbook, 1949,* 1949, p. 120. Primary source: *U.S. Bureau of the Census.*

★ 648 ★

Enrollment

Multi-Level Enrollment: Enrollment from Nursery School Through College for 3- to 34-Year-Olds, 1970 and 1974

(Numbers in thousands. Minus sign (-) denotes decrease).

Level of school and race	1970	1974	Percent change, 1970 to 1974
BLACK			
Total enrolled	7,307	8,215	12.4
Nursery school	178	227	27.5
Kindergarten	426	463	8.7
Elementary school	4,868	4,585	-5.8
High school	1,834	2,125	15.9
College	522	814	55.9
WHITE			
Total enrolled	44,960	50,992	13.4
Nursery school	893	1,340	50.1
Kindergarten	2,706	2,745	1.4
Elementary school	28,638	26,051	-9.0
High school	12,723	13,073	2.8
College	6,759	7,781	15.1

Source: "School Enrollment of Persons 3 to 34 Years Old, by Level: 1970 and 1974," Current Population Reports, Special Studies, Series P-23, No. 54. *The Social and Economic Status of the Black Population in the United States, 1974,* 1975, p. 93. Primary source: U.S. Department of Commerce, Social and Economic Statistics Administration, Bureau of the Census.

★ 649 ★

Enrollment

Multi-Level Enrollment: Percent of 3- to 24-Year-Olds Enrolled in School by Age, 1960, 1965-1971, 1974

Race and Age	1960[1]	1965	1966	1967	1968	1969	1970	1971	1974
BLACK									
3 and 4 years	--	12[1]	14[1]	18	19	21	23	21	29
5 years	51	59	65	67	69	70	72	81	87
6 to 15 years	98	99	99	98	99	99	99	99	99
16 and 17 years	77	84	85	84	86	86	86	89	87
18 and 19 years	35	40	38	41	45	45	40	47	44
20 to 24 years	8	9	8	13	12	15	14	18	17

[Continued]

★ 649 ★

Multi-Level Enrollment: Percent of 3- to 24-Year-Olds
Enrolled in School by Age, 1960, 1965-1971, 1974
[Continued]

Race and Age	1960[1]	1965	1966	1967	1968	1969	1970	1971	1974
WHITE									
3 and 4 years	--	10	12	13	15	15	20	21	29
5 years	66	72	74	80	78	80	81	85	90
6 to 15 years	99	99	99	99	99	99	99	99	99
16 and 17 years	83	88	89	89	91	90	91	90	88
18 and 19 years	39	47	48	48	51	51	49	49	43
20 to 24 years	14	20	21	23	22	24	23	22	22

Source: Adapted by the editors from "Percent Enrolled in School, by Age, 1960, 1966, and 1968," Current Population Reports, Special Studies, Series P-23, No. 29. *The Social and Economic Status of the Black Population in the United States, 1969,* 9196, p. 48; "Percent Enrolled in School, by Age: 1965, 1967, 1969, and 1971," Current Population Reports, Special Studies, Series P-23, No. 42. *The Social and Economic Status of the Black Population in the United States, 1971,* 1971, p. 79; and "Percent Enrolled in School, by Age: 1965, 1970, and 1974," Current Population Reports, Special Studies, Series P-23, No. 54. *The Social and Economic Status of the Black Population in the United States, 1974,* 1975, p. 94.0 Primary source: U.S. Department of Commerce, Social and Economic Statistics Administration, Bureau of the Census. *Notes:*— Represents zero. 1. Negro and other races.

★ 650 ★
Enrollment

Multi-Level Enrollment: Percentage Distribution of Black Population Age 6-20 Enrolled in School, by Age Group, Region, and Division, 1910

SECTION AND DIVISION	PERCENTAGE IN SCHOOL OF NEGRO POPULATION 6 TO 20 YEARS OF AGE: 1910							
	Total		6 to 9 years of age		10 to 14 years of age		15 to 20 years of age	
	Black	Mulatto	Black	Mulatto	Black	Mulatto	Black	Mulatto
BOTH SEXES								
United States	45.6	53.6	47.3	57.1	66.6	76.1	25.4	30.9
The South	44.8	52.5	45.5	54.8	65.1	74.4	25.4	31.0
The North	57.9	62.4	76.4	79.6	88.8	91.4	24.9	29.8
The West	59.3	63.5	76.6	78.2	91.0	93.7	28.1	34.2
MALE								
United States	43.7	52.3	46.1	56.1	63.6	73.6	22.7	28.3
The South	42.7	51.1	44.3	53.6	62.0	71.7	22.6	28.3
South Atlantic	43.0	51.5	45.8	55.3	62.6	72.4	21.3	27.1
East South Central	43.6	52.9	45.0	55.7	62.1	72.9	24.5	31.1
West South Central	40.9	47.8	40.2	47.5	60.6	68.5	22.6	27.3
The North	57.9	63.0	75.8	79.8	88.6	91.3	24.3	28.6
New England	66.0	64.7	87.3	87.4	93.7	94.6	27.2	26.4
Middle Atlantic	58.2	62.8	77.3	79.6	90.0	92.7	21.5	25.7
East North Central	58.7	64.0	77.5	82.0	89.9	92.7	25.3	29.2
West North Central	55.1	61.2	68.9	75.5	83.8	86.9	26.8	31.3

[Continued]

★ 650 ★

Multi-Level Enrollment: Percentage Distribution of Black Population Age 6-20 Enrolled in School, by Age Group, Region, and Division, 1910
[Continued]

| SECTION AND DIVISION | PERCENTAGE IN SCHOOL OF NEGRO POPULATION 6 TO 20 YEARS OF AGE: 1910 | | | | | | | |
| | Total | | 6 to 9 years of age | | 10 to 14 years of age | | 15 to 20 years of age | |
	Black	Mulatto	Black	Mulatto	Black	Mulatto	Black	Mulatto
The West	57.7	63.2	76.5	78.0	90.8	99.3	24.7	32.8
Mountain	59.7	63.5	73.4	72.5	90.4	92.9	26.9	34.3
Pacific	56.2	63.1	79.5	81.3	91.0	93.5	23.2	31.9

Source: "Percentage in School of Negro Population 6 to 20 Years of Age: 1910," *Negro Population, 1790-1915*, 1918, p. 216. Primary source: U.S. Bureau of the Census. *Negro Population, 1790-1915*. Washington, D.C.: Government Printing Office, 1918.

★ 651 ★
Enrollment

Multi-Level Enrollment: Public School Enrollment in the South, 1876-1877

"The first report of enrollment in the public schools of the South was for the year 1876-1877, when 1,827,139, white children and 571,506 colored children were enrolled in the sixteen former slave States and the District of Columbia."

Source: [Untitled text], *Negro Year Book: An Annual Encyclopedia of the Negro, 1916-1917*, 1918, [no p. no]. Primary source: Work, Monroe N. (Ed.), *Negro Year Book and Annual Encyclopedia of the Negro 1916-1917*. Tuskegee Institute, Ala.: The Negro Year Book Pub. Co., 1918.

★ 652 ★
Enrollment

Preprimary: 3-5-Year Olds Enrolled in School, 1965-1974

[As of October. Civilian noninstitutional population. Includes public and nonpublic prekindergarten and kindergarten programs; excludes 5-year-olds enrolled in programs above kindergarten]

| YEAR | Population 3 to 5 years old (1,000) | ENROLLMENT, 3 TO 5 YEAR-OLDS | | | | | | | | | |
| | | Total | | White | | Negro and other | | Metropolitan areas[3] | | Nonmetropolitan areas[3] | |
		Number (1,000)	Percent of population[1]	Number (1,000)	Percent of population[1]	Number (1,000)	Percent of population[2]	Number (1,000)	Percent of population[4]	Number (1,000)	Percent of population[5]
1965	12,549	3,407	27.1	2,957	27.9	451	23.3	2,548	31.4	861	19.4
1967	12,242	3,868	31.6	3,267	31.8	601	30.7	2,769	36.0	1,098	24.1
1968	11,905	3,928	33.0	3,310	33.2	618	31.9	2,808	36.8	1,120	26.3
1969	11,424	3,949	34.6	3,312	34.8	637	33.5	2,810	38.4	1,139	27.7
1970	10,949	4,104	37.5	3,443	37.8	661	35.7	2,933	41.5	1,181	30.2
1971	10,610	4,148	39.1	3,469	39.4	679	37.5	2,947	44.0	1,201	30.7

[Continued]

★ 652 ★

Preprimary: 3-5-Year Olds Enrolled in School, 1965-1974
[Continued]

YEAR	Population 3 to 5 years old (1,000)	ENROLLMENT, 3 TO 5 YEAR-OLDS									
		Total		White		Negro and other		Metropolitan areas[3]		Nonmetropolitan areas[3]	
		Number (1,000)	Percent of population[1]	Number (1,000)	Percent of population[1]	Number (1,000)	Percent of population[2]	Number (1,000)	Percent of population[4]	Number (1,000)	Percent of population[5]
1972	10,166	4,231	41.6	3,542	41.4	689	42.9	3,108	45.3	1,123	34.0
1973	10,344	4,234	40.9	3,521	40.5	713	43.3	3,113	44.0	1,120	34.3
1974	10,393	4,699	45.2	3,941	45.5	759	44.0	3,424	48.8	1,276	37.8

Source: "Preprimary School Enrollment of Children 3 to 5 Years Old, by Race and Residence: 1965 to 1974," *Statistical Abstract of the United States, 1975,* p. 116. Primary source: Through 1972, U.S. National Center for Education Statistics *Preprimary Enrollment,* annual; beginning 1973, U.S. Bureau of the Census, *Current Population Reports,* series P-20, No. 278. *Notes:* 1. Base, 3 to 5 year-old white population. 2. Base, 3 to 5 year-old Negro and other population. 3. 1965-1970, refers to 212 SMSA's as defined in 1960 census reports; later data refer to 243 SMSA's as defined in 1970 census reports. 4. Base, 3 to 5 year-old metro area population. 5. Base, 3 to 5 years-old nonmetro area population.

★ 653 ★

Enrollment

Relationships: 1900-1910 Black and White Increases and Decreases in School Participation, by Age Group

AGE PERIOD AND SCHOOL ATTENDANCE CLASS	POPULATION 5 TO 20 YEARS OF AGE					
	Number		Increase: 1900-1910		Decrease: 1900-1910	
	1910	1900	Number	Percent	Number	Percent
NEGRO						
Total	3,677,860	3,499,187	178,673	5.1	...	...
In School	1,644,759	1,083,516	561,243	51.8	...	...
Not in School	2,033,101	2,415,671	...	...	382,570	15.8
5 to 9 years of age	1,246,553	1,202,758	43,795	3.6	...	...
In school	514,014	284,784	229,230	80.5	...	...
Not in school	732,539	917,974	...	...	185,435	20.2
10 to 14 years of age	1,155,266	1,091,990	63,276	5.8	...	...
In school	791,995	587,560	204,435	34.8	...	...
Not in school	363,271	504,430	...	...	141,159	28.0
15 to 20 years of age	1,276,041	1,204,439	71,602	5.9	...	...
In school	338,750	211,172	127,578	60.4	...	...
Not in school	937,291	993,267	...	...	55,976	5.6
WHITE						
Total	25,992,293	22,441,947	3,550,346	15.8	...	...
In School	15,945,412	12,039,594	3,905,818	32.4	...	...
Not in School	10,046,881	10,402,353	...	...	355,472	3.4

[Continued]

★ 653 ★

Relationships: 1900-1910 Black and White Increases and Decreases in School Participation, by Age Group

[Continued]

AGE PERIOD AND SCHOOL ATTENDANCE CLASS	POPULATION 5 TO 20 YEARS OF AGE					
	Number		Increase: 1900-1910		Decrease: 1900-1910	
	1910	1900	Number	Percent	Number	Percent
5 to 9 years of age	8,475,173	7,638,326	836,847	11.0	...	...
In school	5,495,043	3,971,175	1,523,858	38.4	...	...
Not in school	2,980,130	3,667,151	...	...	687,021	18.7
10 to 14 years of age	7,918,408	6,959,238	959,170	13.8	...	...
In school	7,212,607	5,846,411	1,366,196	23.4	...	...
Not in school	705,801	1,112,827	...	...	407,026	36.6
15 to 20 years of age	9,598,712	7,844,383	1,754,329	22.4	...	...
In school	3,237,762	2,222,008	1,015,754	45.7	...	...
Not in school	6,360,950	5,622,375	738,575	13.1	...	...

Source: "[Untitled Table], *Negro Population, 1790-1915*, 1918, p. 378. Primary source: U.S. Bureau of the Census. *Negro Population, 1790-1915*. Washington, D.C.: Government Printing Office, 1918.

★ 654 ★

Enrollment

Relationships: 1900-1910 School Participation Changes and Attribution of Cause of Change

ITEM	NEGRO POPULATION			
	5 to 20 years of age	5 to 9 years of age	10 to 14 years of age	15 to 20 years of age
Total, 1910	3,677,860	1,246,553	1,155,266	1,276,041
Percentage in school 1900	31.0	23.7	53.8	17.5
Corresponding proportion of 1910 population	1,140,273	295,433	621,533	223,307
Number in school:				
1910	1,644,759	514,014	791,995	338,759
1900	1,083,516	284,784	587,560	211,172
Increase of number in school, 1900-1910	561,243	229,230	204,435	127,578
Due to growth of population	56,757	10,649	33,973	12,135
Due to increased proportion in school	504,486	218,581	170,462	115,443

Source: "[Untitled Table], *Negro Population, 1790-1915*, 1918, p. 378. Primary source: U.S. Bureau of the Census. *Negro Population, 1790-1915*. Washington, D.C.: Government Printing Office, 1918.

★ 655 ★
Enrollment

Relationships: 5-17 Year Olds Enrolled in School, by Residence Area, 1970-1974

[**In millions**. As of October. Beginning 1970, includes nursery schools.]

RESIDENCE	WHITE					NEGRO AND OTHER				
	1960	1965	1970	1973[1]	1974[1]	1960	1965	1970	1973[1]	1974[1]
Total	36.8	40.9	43.2	41.5	41.2	5.5	6.6	7.5	7.4	7.6
Metropolitan	22.3	26.3	26.8	27.6	27.4	3.4	4.3	5.2	5.6	5.8
In central cities	9.6	9.8	9.2	9.8	9.5	2.6	3.4	3.9	4.4	4.3
Outside central cities	12.6	16.5	17.6	17.8	17.9	.8	.9	1.2	1.2	1.5
Nonmetrpolitan	14.5	14.6	16.4	13.9	13.8	2.2	2.2	2.3	1.8	1.9

Source: "School Enrollment of Persons 5 to 17 Years Old, by Race and Residence: 1960-1974," *Statistical Abstract of the United States, 1975,* p. 117. Primary source: U.S. Bureau of the Census, *Current Population Reports,* series P-20, and unpublished data. *Notes:* 1. Refers to metropolitan-nonmetropolitan residence as defined in 1970 census publications; earlier data based on 1960 census definitions.

★ 656 ★
Enrollment

Relationships: Black Public Elementary and Secondary Enrollment, by State and Percent of Minority Enrollment, 1970 and 1972 - I

[**Enrollment in thousands**. As of fall. Excludes Hawaii. "Minority group" refers to Negroes, American Indians, Orientals, and Spanish-surnamed Americans. Includes pre-kindergarten and kindergarten.]

STATE	NEGRO ENROLLMENT, 1970			Total enrollment, 1972 (1,000)
	Total (1,000)	Percent enrolled in schools with minority enrollment of-		
		Under 50 percent	100 percent	
Total	6,707.4	33.1	14.0	44,647
Ala.	270.0	36.5	20.0	762
Alaska	2.1	99.7	-	83
Ariz.	16.9	32.2	2.5	468
Ark.	106.1	43.0	8.6	417
Calif.	416.8	25.8	5.0	4,441
Colo.	19.0	50.1	-	557
Conn.	58.6	43.5	-	674
Del.	27.3	54.8	-	134
D.C.	137.5	1.2	33.5	140
Fla.	332.2	48.4	9.8	1,495

[Continued]

★ 656 ★

Relationships: Black Public Elementary and Secondary Enrollment, by State and Percent of Minority Enrollment, 1970 and 1972 - I
[Continued]

STATE	NEGRO ENROLLMENT, 1970			Total enrollment, 1972 (1,000)
	Total (1,000)	Percent enrolled in schools with minority enrollment of-		
		Under 50 percent	100 percent	
Ga.	365.2	35.9	16.8	1,085
Idaho	0.4	100.0	-	173
Ill.	421.4	14.3	36.2	2,263
Ind.	110.0	30.3	13.9	1,207
Iowa	10.3	70.4	-	633
Kans.	32.5	59.9	10.5	503
Ky.	66.2	55.0	3.3	722
La.	340.7	31.2	24.0	851
Maine	0.8	100.0	-	207
Md.	220.2	33.0	25.7	921
Mass.	52.4	48.0	6.1	1,178
Mich.	288.0	19.2	10.1	2,173
Minn.	10.1	64.1	-	926
Miss.	272.0	26.4	10.8	524
Mo.	144.6	20.1	30.2	1,005
Mont.	0.4	95.5	-	137
Nebr.	12.9	33.0	-	262
Nev.	10.5	65.7	4.9	131
N.H.	0.6	100.0	-	162
N.J.	225.2	32.0	6.6	1,469
N. Mex.	6.1	52.2	5.5	282
N.Y.	542.5	28.8	9.0	3,457
N.C.	351.7	54.1	6.8	1,180
N. Dak.	0.7	100.0	-	118
Ohio	295.5	27.2	14.0	2,405
Okla.	52.6	52.6	10.6	545
Oreg.	8.0	66.8	-	469
Pa.	275.5	26.3	4.7	2,306
R.I.	7.8	98.6	-	186
S.C.	260.9	44.8	7.0	630
S. Dak.	0.4	100.0	-	154
Tenn.	189.6	32.3	25.9	897
Texas	402.6	34.9	14.0	2,611
Utah	1.5	77.1	-	312

[Continued]

★ 656 ★

Relationships: Black Public Elementary and Secondary Enrollment, by State and Percent of Minority Enrollment, 1970 and 1972 - I

[Continued]

STATE	NEGRO ENROLLMENT, 1970			Total enrollment, 1972 (1,000)
	Total (1,000)	Percent enrolled in schools with minority enrollment of-		
		Under 50 percent	100 percent	
Vt.	0.1	100.0	-	72
Va.	259.2	41.4	10.3	1,060
Wash.	20.6	65.7	-	787
W. Va.	19.0	85.8	0.9	410
Wis.	41.2	22.8	-	984
Wyo.	0.8	80.1	-	80

Source: "Negro Enrollment in Public Elementary and Secondary Schools, by Increasing levels of Isolation-States: 1970 and 1972," *Statistical Abstract of the United States, 1975,* p. 128. Primary source: U.S. Office for Civil Rights, *The Directory of Public Elementary and Secondary Schools in Selected Districts-Enrollment and Staff by Racial/Ethnic Group, Fall 1970, and Fall 1972 Elementary and Secondary School Civil Rights Survey. Note:* - Represents zero.

★ 657 ★

Enrollment

Relationships: Black Public Elementary and Secondary Enrollment, by State and Percent of Minority Enrollment, 1970 and 1972 - II

[Enrollment in thousands. As of fall. Excludes Hawaii. "Minority group" refers to Negroes, American Indians, Orientals, and Spanish-surnamed Americans. Includes pre-kindergarten and kindergarten.]

STATE	Total, 1972 (1,000)	NEGRO ENROLLMENT, 1972							
		By minority group enrollment of schools							
		Under 50 percent		50-100 percent		95-100 percent		100 percent	
		Number (1,000)	Percent	Number (1,000)	Percent	Number (1,000)	Percent	Number (1,000)	Percent
Total	6,796.2	2,465.4	36.3	4,330.9	63.7	2,362.2	34.8	759.8	11.2
Ala.	251.6	103.5	41.1	148.1	58.9	84.4	33.5	41.3	16.4
Alaska	2.4	2.3	96.5	0.1	3.5	-	-	-	-
Ariz.	18.3	6.1	33.3	12.2	66.7	3.6	19.8	-	0.2
Ark.	100.3	50.6	50.5	49.6	49.5	2.3	2.3	1.9	1.9
Calif.	429.7	109.7	25.5	320.0	74.5	188.7	43.9	22.3	5.2
Colo.	22.2	12.4	55.7	9.8	44.3	5.6	25.1	-	-
Conn.	60.9	26.6	43.8	34.2	56.2	13.2	21.7	0.1	0.1
Del.	28.1	15.5	55.1	12.6	44.9	5.1	18.3	0.3	1.2
D.C.	133.6	0.5	0.4	133.2	99.6	125.0	93.5	47.7	35.7
Fla.	344.9	229.9	66.7	115.0	33.3	29.7	8.6	12.1	3.5

[Continued]

★ 657 ★

Relationships: Black Public Elementary and Secondary Enrollment, by State and Percent of Minority Enrollment, 1970 and 1972 - II
[Continued]

STATE	Total, 1972 (1,000)	NEGRO ENROLLMENT, 1972							
		By minority group enrollment of schools							
		Under 50 percent		50-100 percent		95-100 percent		100 percent	
		Number (1,000)	Percent	Number (1,000)	Percent	Number (1,000)	Percent	Number (1,000)	Percent
Ga.	371.0	150.4	40.5	220.7	59.5	83.3	22.5	48.9	13.2
Idaho	0.4	0.4	100.0	-	-	-	-	-	-
Ill.	423.7	62.3	14.7	361.4	85.3	300.8	71.0	156.0	37.0
Ind.	113.8	41.0	36.1	72.7	63.9	46.1	40.7	10.5	9.2
Iowa	10.7	7.6	70.6	3.2	29.4	-	-	-	-
Kans.	32.7	23.0	70.5	9.7	29.5	6.9	21.1	1.9	5.8
Ky.	62.6	38.6	61.7	24.0	38.3	16.6	26.5	4.6	7.4
La.	346.0	116.9	33.8	229.1	662.	119.5	34.5	58.9	17.0
Maine	0.4	0.4	100.0	-	-	-	-	-	-
Md.	232.0	79.0	34.1	153.0	65.9	106.3	45.8	55.7	24.0
Mass.	57.6	28.2	49.0	29.4	51.0	15.4	26.8	1.0	1.8
Mich.	304.9	66.0	21.7	238.8	78.3	152.1	49.9	22.6	7.4
Minn.	11.1	8.0	71.1	3.2	28.9	0.3	3.1	-	-
Miss.	265.0	68.8	26.0	196.1	74.0	69.8	26.4	22.4	8.5
Mo.	149.0	33.0	22.1	116.0	77.9	93.7	62.9	45.5	30.6
Mont.	0.3	0.3	94.7	-	5.3	-	-	-	-
Nebr.	13.5	6.1	45.1	7.4	54.9	3.3	24.1	-	-
Nev.	11.1	10.9	98.3	0.1	1.7	-	-	-	-
N.H.	0.6	0.6	100.0	-	-	-	-	-	-
N.J.	231.3	70.0	30.3	161.3	69.7	87.0	37.6	11.2	4.8
N. Mex.	6.2	3.2	51.2	3.0	48.8	0.6	9.1	0.1	1.5
N.Y.	556.2	154.5	27.8	401.7	72.2	223.1	40.1	30.6	5.5
N.C.	347.8	217.4	62.5	130.4	37.5	9.9	2.8	1.9	0.5
N. Dak.	0.5	0.5	100.0	-	-	-	-	-	-
Ohio	293.9	82.9	28.2	211.0	71.8	130.1	44.3	44.0	15.0
Okla.	55.3	39.3	71.0	16.0	29.0	3.2	5.8	-	-
Oreg.	8.5	6.1	72.1	2.4	7.9	0.4	4.3	-	-
Pa.	69	69.8	25.9	199.8	74.1	130.1	48.3	27.9	10.3
R.I.	7.8	7.5	96.9	0.2	3.1	-	-	-	-
S.C.	261.3	108.6	41.6	152.7	58.4	36.1	13.8	15.9	6.1
S. Dak.	0.4	0.4	99.1	-	0.9	-	-	-	-
Tenn.	192.5	79.2	41.1	113.3	58.9	74.8	38.9	38.5	20.0
Texas	418.3	158.3	37.8	260.0	62.2	162.4	38.8	29.9	71.
Utah	1.6	1.2	76.0	0.4	24.0	-	-	-	-
Vt.	0.1	0.1	100.0	-	-	-	-	-	-

[Continued]

★ 657 ★

Relationships: Black Public Elementary and Secondary Enrollment, by State and Percent of Minority Enrollment, 1970 and 1972 - II

[Continued]

STATE	Total, 1972 (1,000)	NEGRO ENROLLMENT, 1972							
		By minority group enrollment of schools							
		Under 50 percent		50-100 percent		95-100 percent		100 percent	
		Number (1,000)	Percent	Number (1,000)	Percent	Number (1,000)	Percent	Number (1,000)	Percent
Va.	261.0	124.5	47.7	136.5	52.3	7.6	2.9	1.7	0.6
Wash.	20.9	14.7	70.3	6.2	29.7	0.3	1.5	-	-
W. Va.	18.2	16.4	90.0	1.8	10.0	0.2	0.9	0.2	0.9
Wis.	45.4	11.2	24.7	34.2	75.3	24.6	54.2	3.3	7.3
Wyo.	0.8	0.6	82.5	0.1	17.5	-	-	-	-

Source: "Negro Enrollment in Public Elementary and Secondary Schools, by Increasing levels of Isolation-States: 1970 and 1972," *Statistical Abstract of the United States, 1975,* p. 128. Primary source: U.S. Office for Civil Rights, *The Directory of Public Elementary and Secondary Schools in Selected Districts-Enrollment and Staff by Racial/Ethnic Group, Fall 1970, and Fall 1972 Elementary and Secondary School Civil Rights Survey. Note:* - Represents zero.

★ 658 ★

Enrollment

Relationships: Black and Mulatto Population and Percent Black and Mulatto Enrollment of 6-20-Year-Olds, by Region, Division, and Southern State, 1910

SECTION, DIVISION, AND STATE	NEGRO POPULATION 6 TO 20 YEARS OF AGE				PERCENTAGE IN SCHOOL	
	Total	Black	Mulatto		Black	Mulatto
			Number	Percent		
United States	3,422,157	2,696,171	725,986	21.2	45.6	53.6
The South	3,164,496	2,514,133	650,363	20.6	44.8	52.5
The North	247,655	175,733	71,922	29.0	57.9	62.4
The West	10,006	6,305	3,701	37.0	59.3	63.5
The South:						
South Atlantic	1,504,019	1,186,665	317,354	21.1	45.3	53.2
East South Central	944,880	759,535	185,345	19.6	46.5	54.2
West South Central	715,597	567,933	147,664	20.6	42.4	48.9
The North:						
New England	15,539	9,860	5,679	36.5	65.4	66.1
Middle Atlantic	95,194	74,808	20,386	21.4	56.6	61.2
East North Central	72,837	46,717	26,120	35.9	59.7	63.5
West North Central	64,085	44,348	19,737	30.8	56.7	61.3
The West:						
Mountain	4,170	2,758	1,412	33.9	59.8	62.5
Pacific	5,836	3,547	2,289	39.2	58.9	64.0
THE SOUTH						
South Atlantic:						
Delaware	10,078	8,785	1,293	12.8	56.5	66.0
Maryland	73,230	59,194	14,036	19.2	51.5	56.6
District of Columbia	23,593	15,245	8,348	35.4	57.7	62.4

[Continued]

★ 658 ★

Relationships: Black and Mulatto Population and Percent Black and Mulatto Enrollment of 6-20-Year-Olds, by Region, Division, and Southern State, 1910
[Continued]

| SECTION, DIVISION, AND STATE | NEGRO POPULATION 6 TO 20 YEARS OF AGE | | | | PERCENTAGE IN SCHOOL | |
| | Total | Black | Mulatto | | Black | Mulatto |
			Number	Percent		
Virginia	242,413	160,037	82,376	34.0	44.9	51.5
West Virginia	18,481	11,818	6,663	36.1	51'.3	56.2
North Carolina	264,025	208,314	55,711	21.1	52.9	58.8
South Carolina	331,429	277,698	53,731	16.2	44.3	53.6
Georgia	439,485	361,255	78,230	17.8	40.5	49.5
Florida	101,285	84,319	16,966	16.8	43.0	49.5
East South Central:						
Kentucky	81,976	60,436	21,540	26.3	52.6	56.9
Tennessee	163,397	121,084	42,313	25.9	45.3	53.1
Alabama	327,176	270,891	56,285	17.2	39.9	48.7
Mississippi	372,331	307,124	65,207	17.5	50.3	58.8
West South Central:						
Arkansas	159,431	129,485	29,946	18.8	47.6	52.7
Louisiana	254,580	198,809	55,771	21.9	27.2	34.9
Oklahoma	48,718	34,004	14,714	30.2	62.0	67.9
Texas	252,868	205,635	47,233	18.7	50.5	57.0

Source: [Untitled Table], *Negro Population, 1790-1915*, 1918, p. 215. Primary source: U.S. Bureau of the Census. *Negro Population, 1790-1915*. Washington, D.C.: Government Printing Office, 1918.

★ 659 ★
Enrollment

Relationships: Mulatto Enrollment in Excess of Black Enrollment (in percentages), by Region and Age Group, 1910

| SECTION | EXCESS OF PERCENTAGE IN SCHOOL: MULATTOES OVER BLACKS | | | |
	Total 6 to 20 years of age	6 to 9 years of age	10 to 14 years of age	15 to 20 years of age
United States	8.0	9.8	9.5	5.5
The South	7.7	9.3	9.3	5.6
The North	4.5	3.2	2.6	4.9
The West	4.2	1.6	2.7	6.1

Source: "Excess of Percentage in School: Mulattoes Over Blacks," *Negro Population, 1790-1915*, 1918, p. 216. Primary source: U.S. Bureau of the Census. *Negro Population, 1790-1915*. Washington, D.C.: Government Printing Office, 1918.

★ 660 ★

Enrollment

Relationships: Percent Distribution of School Enrollment, by Age Group, 1960-1974

[As of October. Data based on sample and subject to sampling variability]

AGE (in years)	1960		1965		1970		1972		1973		1974	
	White	Negro and other	White	Negro and other	White	Negro and other	White	Negro and other	White	Negro and other	White	Negro and other
Total, 3-34	56.4[1]	55.9[1]	55.6	55.3	56.2	57.7	54.4	58.0	53.1	55.8	53.0	57.2
3 and 4	(NA)	(NA)	10.3	11.8	19.9	23.1	23.8	27.7	23.2	29.3	28.6	30.0
5 and 6	82.0	73.3	85.8	79.9	90.3	85.4	92.2	90.6	93.0	90.3	94.4	93.0
7-9	99.7	99.3	99.4	99.0	99.3	99.4	99.1	98.7	99.1	99.2	99.2	99.0
10-13	99.5	99.0	99.4	99.3	99.1	99.4	99.3	99.4	99.3	99.0	99.4	99.7
14 and 15	98.1	95.9	99.0	98.2	98.2	97.6	97.6	97.7	97.6	97.0	98.1	97.0
16 and 17	83.3	76.9	87.8	84.6	90.6	86.2	88.9	89.1	88.3	88.1	87.9	87.5
18 and 19	38.9	34.6	47.1	40.1	48.7	41.9	46.6	44.8	43.4	39.8	42.6	46.3
20-24	13.9	7.5	20.2	10.2	22.5	15.2	22.1	17.8	21.3	17.3	21.6	19.7
25-34	3.8	1.9	4.9	3.1	6.1	5.2	6.8	6.6	6.8	6.2	7.7	8.4

Source: "Percent Enrolled in School, by Age and Race: 1960 to 1974," *Statistical Abstract of the United States, 1975*, p. 115. Primary source: U.S. Bureau of the Census, *Current Population Reports*, series P-20, No. 278, and unpublished data. *Notes:* NA Not available. 1. Data are for persons 5 to 34 years of age.

★ 661 ★

Enrollment

Relationships: Percent Distribution of School Enrollment, by Age, 1955-1969

[As of October.]

AGE	1955		1960		1965		1969	
	White	Negro and other	White	Negro and other	White	Negro and other	White	Negro and other
Total 5-34	50.8	50.7	56.4	55.9	59.6	60.0	59.8	61.6
5 and 6 years	79.2	71.1	82.0	73.3	85.3	79.3	89.2	84.3
7-9 years	99.3[1]	98.2[1]	99.7	99.3	99.4	99.0	99.4	98.8
10-13 years	99.3[1]	98.2[1]	99.5	99.0	99.4	99.3	99.2	99.1
14 and 15 years	87.5[2]	82.8[2]	98.1	95.9	99.0	98.2	98.2	97.9
16 and 17 years	87.5[2]	82.8[2]	83.3	76.9	87.8	84.6	90.2	86.4
18 and 19 years	32.1	27.6	38.9	34.6	47.1	40.1	50.9	45.5
20-24 years	11.6	7.2	13.9	7.5	20.2	10.2	23.9	16.7
25-34 years	2.8	3.3	3.8	1.9	4.9	3.1	6.7	4.6

Source: "Percent Enrolled in School, by Age and Race: 1955 to 1969," *Statistical Abstract of the United States, 1975*, p. 109. Primary source: Dept. of Commerce, Bureau of the Census; *Current Population Reports*, Series P-20, and unpublished data. *Notes:* 1. Data includes ages 7 to 13 years. 2. Data includes ages 14 and 17 years.

★ 662 ★

Enrollment

Relationships: Percentage Distribution of Black and Mulatto Enrollment, by Gender and Age Group, 1910

AGE	PERCENTAGE IN SCHOOL: 1910			
	Male population		Female population	
	Black	Mulatto	Black	Mulatto
6 to 20 years	43.7	52.3	47.5	54.7
6 to 9 years	46.1	56.1	48.5	58.0
10 to 14 years	63.6	69.6	73.6	78.5
15 to 20 years	22.7	27.8	28.3	33.0

Source: [Untitled Table], *Negro Population, 1790-1915*, 1918, p. 215. Primary source: U.S. Bureau of the Census. *Negro Population, 1790-1915*. Washington, D.C.: Government Printing Office, 1918.

★ 663 ★

Enrollment

Relationships: School Enrollment of 5-17-Year Old, by Residence Area, 1960, 1965, and 1969

[Enrollment in thousands. As of October. Minus sign (-) denotes decrease.]

RESIDENCE	WHITE				NEGRO AND OTHER			
	1960	1965	1969	Percent change, 1960-69	1960	1965	1969	Percent change, 1960-69
Total	36,750	40,928	43,116	17.3	5,549	6,554	7,334	32.2
Metropolitan	22,279	26,300	26,915	20.8	3,378	4,344	5,106	51.2
In central cities	9,645	9,806	9,398	-2.6	2,615	3,433	3,898	49.1
Outside central cities	12,634	16,503	17,517	38.6	763	911	1,207	58.2
Nonmetropolitan	14,471	14,619	16,200	11.9	2,171	2,210	2,229	2.7

Source: "School Enrollment of Persons 5 to 17 Years Old, by Race and Residence: 1960, 1965, and 1969," *Statistical Abstract of the United States, 1970*, p. 109. Primary source: Dept. of Commerce, Bureau of the Census; *Current Population Reports*, Series P-20, and unpublished data.

Higher Education

★ 664 ★

Academic Environment: Number and Size of Classes in Selected Black Institutions, c. 1939 - I

[Total number of classes]

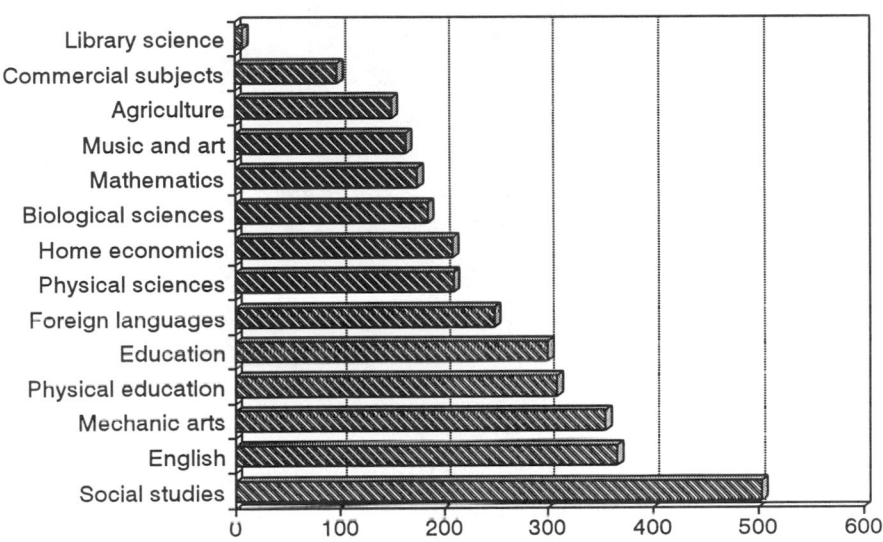

Field	Total number of classes	Number of classes, by class size				
		Below 10	10-19	20-29	30-39	40-49
Social studies	503	110	106	76	88	57
English	366	64	68	77	94	39
Mechanic arts	355	221	70	31	19	8
Physical education	309	77	71	60	42	27
Education	300	55	71	52	55	32
Foreign languages	248	76	41	55	49	20
Physical sciences	209	65	40	22	40	25
Home economics	208	61	74	39	18	5
Biological sciences	184	47	42	33	27	16
Mathematics	174	44	43	36	24	17
Music and art	163	19	57	22	33	14
Agriculture	150	39	39	36	16	3
Commercial subjects	97	30	43	15	5	2
Library science	7	6	1	...	...	...
Total, all subjects	3,273	914	766	554	510	265
Percent	...	27.9	23.4	16.9	15.6	8.1

Source: "Distribution of Size of Classes, according to Fields of Instruction, in 23 Colleges and Universities for Negroes," *National Survey of the Higher Education of Negroes.* Vol. 1, No. 6. *Socio-Economic Approach to Educational Problems,* 1942, p. 27. Primary source: U.S. Office of Education. *National Survey of the Higher Education of Negroes.* Vol. 1, No. 6. *Socio-Economic Approach to Educational Problems,* by Ida Corinne Brown. Washington, D.C.: U.S. Government Printing Office, 1942.

★ 665 ★

Higher Education

Academic Environment: Number and Size of Classes in Selected Black Institutions, c. 1939 - II

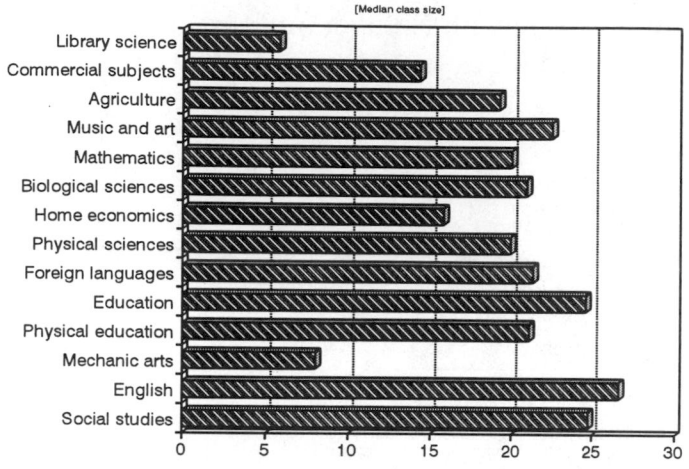

Field	Number of classes, by class size						Median class size
	50-59	60-69	70-79	80-89	90-100	Over 100	
Social studies	28	11	9	7	2	9	24.7
English	15	4	4	...	...	1	26.6
Mechanic arts	4	...	...	1	1	...	8.0
Physical education	14	7	3	2	1	5	21.1
Education	16	11	2	...	4	2	24.6
Foreign languages	2	3	1	1	...	...	21.3
Physical sciences	4	3	4	...	4	2	19.9
Home economics	6	3	2	...	...	...	15.8
Biological sciences	3	5	3	1	2	5	20.9
Mathematics	4	3	...	1	...	2	20.0
Music and art	3	3	6	1	1	4	22.5
Agriculture	6	6	3	2	...	...	19.2
Commercial subjects	2	...	...	...	...	...	14.3
Library science	...	...	...	...	...	...	5.8
Total, all subjects	107	59	37	16	15	30	19.4
Percent	3.3	1.8	1.1	.5	.4	.9	...

Source: "Distribution of Size of Classes, according to Fields of Instruction, in 23 Colleges and Universities for Negroes," *National Survey of the Higher Education of Negroes*. Vol. 1, No. 6. *Socio-Economic Approach to Educational Problems*, 1942, p. 27. Primary source: U.S. Office of Education. *National Survey of the Higher Education of Negroes*. Vol. 1, No. 6. *Socio-Economic Approach to Educational Problems*, by Ida Corinne Brown. Washington, D.C.: U.S. Government Printing Office, 1942.

★ 666 ★

Higher Education

Accreditation and Ratings: Accreditation Ratings of Selected Black Colleges, c. 1942

Highest accreditation of institution	Number of institutions	Weighted educational expenditure per student	
		Median	Range
Approved by the American Association of Universities	2	$530	$646-$415
Members of or rated "A" by their regional association	11	198	362-124
Rated "B" by their regional association	3	83	83-47
Not approved by a regional accrediting agency	9	83	184-20

Source: "[Untitled Table], *National Survey of Higher Education of Negroes.* Vol 1, No. 6. *Socio-Economic Approach to Educational Problems,* 1942, p. 107. Primary source: U.S. Office of Education. *National Survey of the Higher Education of Negroes.* Vol 1, No. 6. *Socio-Economic Approach to Educational Problems,* by Ida Corinne Brown. Washington, D.C.: U.S. Government Printing Office, 1942.

★ 667 ★

Higher Education

Accreditation and Ratings: Professional and Technical Education Ratings in Selected Black Colleges, c. 1939

Institution	Ratings on professional and technical edu		
	Offerings in professional and technical education	Competence to offer professional and technical education	Effectiveness of the plan
A	2	1	2
B	1	1	2
C	...	...	...
D	1	1	2
E	3	3	3
F	1	1	2
G	2	1	2
H	3	2	3
I	1	1	2
J	3	1	2
K	1	1	2
L	2	2	2
M	2	2	2
N	2	3	3
O	1	1	1
P	3	3	2
Q	1	1	1
R	2	2	2
S	2	2	2

[Continued]

★ 667 ★

Accreditation and Ratings: Professional and Technical Education Ratings in Selected Black Colleges, c. 1939
[Continued]

Institution	Ratings on professional and technical edu		
	Offerings in professional and technical education	Competence to offer professional and technical education	Effectiveness of the plan
T	3	1	3
U	4	2	2
V	3	2	3
W	3	3	3
X	1	1	1
Y	1	2	2

Source: "Ratings of Colleges and Universities for Negroes with Respect to Professional and Technical Education," *National Survey of the Higher Education of Negroes.* Vol. 1, No. 6. *Socio-Economic Approach to Educational Problems,* 1942, p. 51. Primary source: U.S. Office of Education, *National Survey of the Higher Education of Negroes.* Vol. 1, No. 6. *Socio-Economic Approach to Educational Problems,* by Ida Corinne Brown. Washington, D.C.: U.S. Government Printing Office, 1942. *Note:* 1. The highest rating obtainable is 5.

★ 668 ★

Higher Education

Accreditation and Ratings: Ratings of Selected Black Colleges on Several Criteria of Evaluation, c. 1939

Rating	Number of institutions				
	Range and thoroughness	Means of concern	Competence to offer advanced work	Effectiveness of the plan	Graduate work
5	0	0	1	0	0
4	1	4	1	2	0
3	6	13	3	6	2
2	7	4	6	10	0
1	9	2	11	4	3
0	0	0	1	1	0
X[1]	2	2	2	2	20

Source: "Distribution of 25 Colleges and Universities for Negroes with Respect to Their Ratings on Advanced Education," *National Survey of the Higher Education of Negroes.* Vol. 1, No. 6. *Socio-Economic Approach to Educational Problems,* 1942. p. 47. Primary source: U.S. Office of Education. *National Survey of the Higher Education of Negroes.* Vol. 1, No. 6. *Socio-Economic Approach to Educational Problems,* by Ida Corinne Brown. Washington, D.C.: U.S. Government Printing Office, 1942. *Notes:* 1. The letter "x" indicates that advanced education in academic subjects is not offered.

★ 669 ★

Higher Education

Accreditation and Ratings: Regional and National Accreditation of Black and White Institutions in the South, c. 1940 - I

	WHITE									
	Alabama	Arkansas	Delaware	District of Columbia	Florida	Georgia	Kentucky	Louisiana	Maryland	Mississippi
Association of American Universities:										
Public	2	1	1	...	2	1	2	1	1	1
All	4	2	1	3	2	4	4	2	3	3
Regional Accrediting Agency[1,2]										
Public	7	5	1	...	2	4	6	1	1	5
All	10	6	1	4	5	9	13	4	10	8
American Association of Teachers Colleges:										
Public	4	2	...	1	...	2	3	1	1	2
All	4	2	...	1	...	2	3	1	1	2
	NEGRO									
Association of American Universities:										
Public	...	...	...	...	...	...	...	...	...	...
All	...	...	...	1	...	...	...	...	...	...
Regional Accrediting Agency[1,2]										
Public	...	...	...	...	1	...	2	1	1	...
All	2	...	...	1	1	3	2	3	1	...
American Association of Teachers Colleges:										
Public	...	...	...	1	...	...	...	...	...	...
All	...	...	...	1	...	...	...	...	...	...

Source: "Number of Higher Institutions in 17 States and the District of Columbia which are Members of or are Approved by National and Regional Accrediting Agencies," *National Survey of the Higher Education of Negroes.* Vol. 1, No. 6. *Socio-Economic Approach to Educational Problems,* 1942, p. 16. Primary source: U.S. Office of Education, Educational Directory, 1941, Part III, Bulletin 1940, No. 1 (junior colleges are not included). *Notes:* Tabulation of the accreditation of professional schools is not included. 1. Southern Association of Colleges and Secondary Schools, North Central Association of Colleges and Secondary Schools or Middle States Association of Colleges and Secondary Schools. 2. Institutions rated class "B" by the Southern Association of Colleges and Secondary Schools are not included because they do not meet in full the standards of the association.

★ 670 ★

Higher Education

Accreditation and Ratings: Regional and National Accreditation of Black and White Institutions in the South, c. 1940 - II

	WHITE								
	Missouri	North Carolina	Oklahoma	South Carolina	Tennessee	Texas	Virginia	West Virginia	Total
Association of American Universities:									
Public	1	2	3	3	1	3	2	1	28
All	8	6	4	7	7	8	9	2	79
Regional Accrediting Agency[1,2]									
Public	7	4	3	4	5	11	6	3	75
All	20	14	5	13	14	18	16	4	174
American Association of Teachers Colleges:									
Public	7	3	6	...	3	7	4	6	52
All	7	4	6	...	3	7	4	6	53
	NEGRO								
Association of American Universities:									
Public	...	...	...	...	...	...	...	...	0
All	...	...	...	...	1	...	...	...	2

[Continued]

★ 670 ★

Accreditation and Ratings: Regional and National Accreditation of Black and White Institutions in the South, c. 1940 - II

[Continued]

	WHITE								
	Missouri	North Carolina	Oklahoma	South Carolina	Tennessee	Texas	Virginia	West Virginia	Total
Regional Accrediting Agency[1,2]									
Public	1	2	...	...	...	1	1	1	11
All	1	4	...	...	2	3	3	1	27
American Association of Teachers Colleges:									
Public	1	...	...	...	1	...	...	...	3
All	1	...	...	...	1	...	...	...	3

Source: "Number of Higher Institutions in 17 States and the District of Columbia which are Members of or are Approved by National and Regional Accrediting Agencies," *National Survey of the Higher Education of Negroes.* Vol. 1, No. 6. *Socio-Economic Approach to Educational Problems*, 1942, p. 16. Primary source: U.S. Office of Education, Educational Directory, 1941, Part III, Bulletin 1940, No. 1 (junior colleges are not included). *Notes:* Tabulation of the accreditation of professional schools is not included. 1. Southern Association of Colleges and Secondary Schools, North Central Association of Colleges and Secondary Schools or Middle States Association of Colleges and Secondary Schools. 2. Institutions rated class "B" by the Southern Association of Colleges and Secondary Schools are not included because they do not meet in full the standards of the association.

★ 671 ★

Higher Education

Black Enrollees (Partial List) and Degrees Awarded to Black Students by Predominately White Institutions, 1943

School	Number enrolled	A.B. or B.S.	School	Number enrolled	A.B or B.S.
Ohio State University	341	22	Smith College	4	-
Indiana University	196	6	Tufts College	4	2
University of Kansas	128	15			
Western Reserve University	108	7	Bradley Polytechnic Institute	2	-
University of Illinois	100	10	Briar Cliff College	2	-
Boston University	88	8	Clark University	2	2
College of City of New York	50	-	Harvard School of Divinity	2	2
Harvard Graduate School of Arts & Science	48	-	Syracuse University	2	-
Northwestern University	35	4	Butler University	-	1
University of Nebraska	27	2	Bates College	1	-
University of Arizona	21	4	Total	1303	101
Purdue University	20	1			
Pacific Union College	18	2	Master's degree		
Harvard College	14	4			
Drew University	12	-	Boston University		8
Union Theological Seminary	11	-	Ohio State University		9
Omaha University	11	1	Western Reserve		7
University of Denver	10	1	University of Kansas		4
Simmons College	10	2	Union Theological Seminary		3
Rutgers College	8	3	Indiana University		2
Bowdoin College	5	-	Northwestern University		2
University of Buffalo	5	-	University of Denver		1
Harvard Law School	5	-	University of New Mexico		1
Mass. Institute of Technology	5	-	Simmons College		1

[Continued]

★ 671 ★

Black Enrollees (Partial List) and Degrees Awarded to Black Students by Predominately White Institutions, 1943
[Continued]

School	Number enrolled	A.B. or B.S.	School	Number enrolled	A.B or B.S.
Harvard Graduate School of Education	4	-	Smith College		1
Mount Holyoke College	4	2	Total		39

Source: "Enrollment and Graduates," *The Negro Handbook, 1944*, 1944, p. 63. Primary source: Excerpts from a survey appearing in *The Crisis*, August, 1943. Published by permission.

★ 672 ★

Higher Education

Blacks in White Colleges: Black Faculty at Unsegregated, Predominantly White Schools, 1945-1948

"A total of 105 Negroes served on faculties of unsegreated, predominantly white colleges and universities between 1945 and the summer of 1948, according to a survey made by the *The Negro Handbook* in the summer of 1948... Sixty three of the total had regular full-time positions, two were library assistants with faculty rank, and one was a vocational guidance counselor, with faculty rank...The University of Illinois in Urbana had the largest number of Negroes on its faculty at the time the survey was taken—eleven. Other schools which had from four to ten Negroes on their faculties were the University of Chicago, Roosevelt College, College of the City of New York, Sampson College, and New York University."

Source: "Current Survey," *The Negro Handbook, 1949*, 1949, p. 138. Primary source: Murray, Florence (Ed.), *The Negro Handbook, 1949*. New York: The Macmillan Co., 1949.

★ 673 ★

Higher Education

Blacks in White Colleges: Date Opened and Fields Available to Black Students in Southern White Private Institutions, by State, 1951 - Part I

Institution	Date Opened to Negro Students	Date Students Accepted, Admitted or Enrolled	Fields of Study Opened
District of Columbia:			
American Univ., Washington	(No report)	(No report)	(No report)
The Catholic Univ. of American, Washington	1889	1889	No restrictions
Dunbarton College of Holy Cross (Women's), Washington	1835	1947	Liberal Arts: English

[Continued]

★ 673 ★

Blacks in White Colleges: Date Opened and Fields Available to Black Students in Southern White Private Institutions, by State, 1951 - Part I
[Continued]

Institution	Date Opened to Negro Students	Date Students Accepted, Admitted or Enrolled	Fields of Study Opened
Georgia:			
Columbia Theological Seminary (Presbyterian), Decatur	1948	Sept. 1948	Theology
Kentucky:			
Bellarmine College, Louisville	Oct. 1950	Oct. 1950	No restrictions: Business Administration Pre-Medical Lib. Arts
Berea College, Berea[1]	Sept. 1950	Sept. 1950	No restrictions
Louisville Presbyterian Theological Seminary, Louisville	May 1950	Sept. 1950	Theology
Nazareth Women's College, Louisville	June 1950	June 1950	No restrictions: Elementary Education Nursing Library Science
Southern Baptist Theological Seminary, Louisville	Sept. 10, 1951	Sept. 10, 1951	No restrictions
Ursuline College (Women's), Louisville	Sept. 1950	Fall 1950	Lib. Arts: Business (Special) Education (Special)
Louisiana:[2]			
New Orleans Baptist Theology Seminary, New Orleans	Sept. 4, 1951	(None to date)	Graduate

Source: "White Private Educational Institutions in the South Officially Admitting Negroes, 1951," *1952 Negro Year Book: A Review of Events Affecting Negro Life*, 1952, pp. 241-242. Primary source: *The New South*, Aug.- Sept. 1951, published by the Southern Regional Council, Atlanta, Ga.; press releases. *Notes:* 1. Berea College admitted Negroes 1866 to 1904, when it was prohibited by the Kentucky "Day Law." After law was amended in Spring 1950, Trustees voted to admit them again. 2. Another college in Louisiana admits a limited number of Negro students but does not wish publicity.

Blacks in White Colleges: Date Opened and Fields Available to Black Students in Southern White Private Institutions, by State, 1951 - Part II

Institution	Date Opened to Negro Students	Date Students Accepted, Admitted or Enrolled	Fields of Study Opened
Maryland: Johns Hopkins Univ., Baltimore	1946	(No report)	Undergraduate and graduate
Loyola College Eve. Sch. and Graduate Div., Baltimore	1943	1947	Lib. Arts and Graduate
Saint John's College, Annapolis	Sept. 1948	Sept. 24, 1948	Undergraduate
Missouri: Conservatory of Music, Kansas City	1945	Not given	No restrictions: Piano
Kansas City Art Inst. and Sch. of Design, Kansas City	1884	Not known	No restrictions
Park College, Parkville	June 5, 1950	Sept. 1950	College of Lib. Arts: English
Rockhurst College, Kansas City[1]	June 6, 1949	June 6, 1949	No restrictions: Liberal Arts
St. Louis Univ., St. Louis	(No report)	(No report)	
Washington Univ., St. Louis	June 1947	Medicine Graduate:	
		Spring 1948	Social Work
		Summer 1948	Arts and Sciences
		Fall 1949	Business and P.A.
		Fall 1949	Law
		Fall 1950	Engineering
Webster College (Women's), St. Louis	(No report)	(No report)	University College Evening Division
Texas: Amarillo College, Amarillo	Oct. 1, 1951	Oct. 3, 1951	Pre-Medical Pre-Nursing Home Economics
Austin Theological Seminary (Presbyterian), Austin	Sept. 1950	Sept. 1950	Theology
Southwestern Baptist Seminary, Fort Worth	May 25, 1951	May 25, 1951 Sept. 10, 1951	No restrictions
Southern Methodist Univ., Dallas	1950	(No report)	Graduate: Theology
Wayland College, Plainview	June 5, 1951	June 5, 1951	No restrictions:

[Continued]

585

★ 674 ★

Blacks in White Colleges: Date Opened and Fields Available to Black Students in Southern White Private Institutions, by State, 1951 - Part II

[Continued]

Institution	Date Opened to Negro Students	Date Students Accepted, Admitted or Enrolled	Fields of Study Opened
West Virginia: Wesleyan College, Buckinghannon	June 1, 1949	Sept. 1949	Education No restrictions: Education Pre-Engineering Pre-Medical Secretarial Studies

Source: "White Private Educational Institutions in the South Officially Admitting Negroes, 1951," *1952 Negro Year Book: A Review of Events Affecting Negro Life,* 1952, pp. 241-242. Primary source: *The New South,* Aug.- Sept. 1951, published by the Southern Regional Council, Atlanta, Ga.; press releases. *Notes:* 1. William Louis Blake, Liberty Mo., enrolled September 19, 1949, as transfer student: received B.S. degree, with education as major, Aug. 31, 1951.

★ 675 ★

Higher Education

Blacks in White Colleges: Southern States Admitting Black Students to White Public Colleges, 1951

State	No. institutions	Earliest date opened to Black students
Arkansas	1	January 30, 1948
Delaware	1	January 30,1948
Kentucky	2	March 30, 1949 September, 1950
Louisiana	1	1950
Maryland	2[1]	1935
Missouri	2	1948 1950
North Carolina	1	June 11, 1951
Oklahoma	2	October, 1948 Summer, 1949
Tennessee	1	January 10, 1952
Texas	2	1949 September, 1951

[Continued]

★ 675 ★

Blacks in White Colleges: Southern States Admitting Black Students to White Public Colleges, 1951

[Continued]

State	No. institutions	Earliest date opened to Black students
Virginia	5	1920 September 5, 1950 1951[2]
West Virginia	1	June 6, 1940

Source: Compiled by the editors from "White Public Colleges and Universities in South Officially Admitting Negroes, 1951," *1952 Negro Year Book: A Review of Events Affecting Negro Life*, 1952, p. 239. Primary source: Guzman, Jessie Parkhurst (Ed.), *1952 Negro Year Book: A Review of Events Affecting Negro Life*. New York: Wm. H. Wise & Co., Inc., 1952. *Notes:* 1. Two branches of the same institution. 2. Three different institutions.

★ 676 ★

Higher Education

College Faculty/Staff/Administration: Faculty 9-month and Total Salary Distributions at Selected Black Institutions, c, 1939

Salary interval	Teachers receiving salaries for-				Cumulative percent	
	Full-time 9 months' salary		Full-time total salary			
	Number	Percent	Number	Percent	9 months	12 months
$5,000 and over	1	.1	1	.1	100.0	100.0
$4,500-$4,999	...	...	...	...	...	...
$4,000-$4,499	18	2.2	18	2.2	99.9	99.9
$3,500-$3,999	...	...	10	1.2	...	97.7
$3,000-$3,499	24	3.0	20	2.5	97.7	96.5
$2,500-$2,999	29	3.6	59	7.3	94.7	94.0
$2,000-$2,499	104	12.9	141	17.5	91.1	86.7
$1,900-$1,999	16	2.0	16	3.2	78.2	69.2
$1,800-$1,899	83	10.3	91	11.3	76.2	66.0
$1,700-$1,799	20	2.5	21	2.6	65.9	54.7
$1,600-$1,699	29	3.6	62	8.0	63.4	52.1
$1,500-$1,599	56	7.0	69	8.6	59.8	44.1
$1,400-$1,499	34	4.2	22	2.7	52.8	35.5
$1,300-$1,399	80	10.0	56	7.0	48.6	32.8
$1,200-$1,299	90	11.2	49	6.1	38.6	25.8
$1,100-$1,199	93	11.6	56	7.0	27.4	19.7
$1,000-$1,099	30	3.7	29	3.6	15.8	12.7
$900-$999	52	6.5	42	5.2	12.1	9.1
$800-$899	12	1.5	7	.9	5.6	3.9
$700-$799	16	2.0	10	1.2	4.1	3.0
$600-$699	10	1.2	9	1.1	2.1	1.8
$500-$599	3	.4	2	.2	.9	.7
Under $500	4	.5	4	.5	.5	.5

[Continued]

★ 676 ★

College Faculty/Staff/Administration: Faculty 9-month and Total Salary Distributions at Selected Black Institutions, c, 1939
[Continued]

| Salary interval | Teachers receiving salaries for- | | | | Cumulative percent | |
| | Full-time 9 months' salary | | Full-time total salary | | | |
	Number	Percent	Number	Percent	9 months	12 months
Total	804	...	804	...	...	...
Median	$1,435	...	$1,676	...	...	...
Q3	1,889	...	2,170	...	...	...
Q1	1,180	...	1,284	...	...	...

Source: "Distribution of Teachers in 23 Colleges and Universities for Negroes, According to Annual Salaries," *National Survey of the Higher Education of Negroes.* Vol. 1, No. 6. *Socio-Economic Approach to Educational Problems,* 1942, p. 28. Primary source: U.S. Office of Education. *National Survey of the Higher Education of Negroes.* Vol. 1, No. 6. *Socio-Economic Approach to Educational Problems,* by Ida Corinne Brown. Washington, D.C.: U.S. Government Printing Office, 1942.

★ 677 ★

Higher Education

College Faculty/Staff/Administration: Faculty Development Activities at Selected Black Institutions, c. 1939

Aid to faculty growth	Number of institutions
Personal conferences with head of department or dean regarding problems	22
Traveling expenses in whole or in part for attendance at professional meetings	20
Library provision for books and periodicals relating to college education	20
Leave other than sabbatical	20
Observation of instruction by other faculty members, head of department, dean or president	19
Opportunity to visit classes and observe work of other instructors	18
Faculty groups organized for study of college and related educational problems	17
Special library facilities in teaching field	15
Counsel of specialists invited from outside the institution	15
Reduction of teaching load below normal for a semester or year without reduction of salary	11
Organized institutional effort to improve examination procedure by use of objective tests, comprehensive examinations, final course examinations, etc.	11
Special laboratory facilities in teaching field	10

[Continued]

★ 677 ★

College Faculty/Staff/Administration: Faculty Development Activities at Selected Black Institutions, c. 1939
[Continued]

Aid to faculty growth	Number of institutions
News letter on instructional problems from an administrative officer	10
Sabbatical leave with stipend	7
Systematic collection of alumni opinion regarding college improvement	5
Systematic courses in higher education offered by the institution	0

Source: "Aids to Faculty Growth Employed by 23 Colleges and Universities for Negroes," *National Survey of the Higher Education of Negroes*, Vol. 1, No. 6. *Socio-Economic Approach to Educational Problems*, 1942, p. 58. Primary source: U.S. Office Education. *National Survey of the Higher Education of Negroes*. Vol. 1, No. 6. *Socio-Economic Approach to Educational Problems*, by Ida Corinne Brown. Washington, D.C.: U.S. Government Printing Office, 1942.

★ 678 ★

Higher Education

College Faculty/Staff/Administration: Faculty Rank and Median Salary by Type of Institution, c. 1939

Type of institutions	Deans	Professors	Associate professors	Assistant professors	Instructors
52 white land-grant institutions	$5,050	$4,245	$3,272	$2,605	$1,937
17 white land-grant institutions in 17 Southern States	4,844	3,658	2,926	2,352	1,840
17 Negro land-grant institutions in 17 Southern States	2,625	1,821	1,701	1,560	1,293

Source: [Untitled Table], *National Survey of the Higher Education of Negroes*. Vol. 1, No. 6. *Socio-Economic Approach to Educational Problems*, 1942, p. 29. Primary source: U.S. Office of Education. *National Survey of the Higher Education of Negroes*. Vol. 1, No. 6. *Socio-Economic Approach to Educational Problems*, by Ida Corinne Brown. Washington, D.C.: U.S. government Printing Office, 1942.

★ 679 ★

Higher Education

College Faculty/Staff/Administration: Institutions from which Ten or More Black College Teachers Received First Degree, c. 1939

	Number of teachers
Institutions for Negroes	
Howard University	73 (20)
Hampton Institute	36
Fisk University	29
Tuskegee Institute	27 (23)
Lincoln University (Pa.)	25
Virginia Union University	24 (16)
Talladega College	20
Prairie View State College	15 (9)
Morehouse College	13
Wilberforce University	13
Alcorn A. and M. College	12 (9)
Johnson C. Smith University	11 (4)
West Virginia State College	11 (4)
Morris Brown College	10 (9)
Atlanta University	10
Shaw University	10
Morgan College	10 (10)
Non-segregated institutions	
University of Kansas	15
Iowa State College	14
Oberlin College	14
University of Pittsburgh	12
Columbia University	11
Ohio State University	11
Kansas State Agricultural College	10

Source: [Untitled Table], *National Survey of the Higher Education of Negroes*, Vol. 1, No. 6. *Socio-Economic Approach to Educational Problems*, 1942, p. 15. Primary source: U.S. Office Education. *National Survey of the Higher Education of Negroes*. Vol. 1, No. 6. *Socio-Economic Approach to Educational Problems*, by Ida Corinne Brown. Washington, D.C.: U.S. Government Printing Office, 1942. *Notes:* Figures in parentheses represent number of graduates of the institution included in the totals shown.

★ 680 ★

Higher Education

College Faculty/Staff/Administration: Length of Service of Administrators at Selected Black Institutions, c. 1939

Length of tenure in years	President	Dean	Registrar	Chief financial officer
10 or more	11	9	3	8
8-9	0	2	2	0
6-7	2	2	3	1
4-5	3	1	6	3
2-3	5	5	6	3
0-1	2	3	1	4
Approximate median	2	7	5	5

Source: [Untitled Table], *National Survey of the Higher Education of Negroes.* Vol. 1, No. 6. *Socio-Economic Approach to Educational Problems,* 1942, p. 31. Primary source: U.S. Office of Education. *National Survey of the Higher Education of Negroes.* Vol. 1, No. 6. *Socio-Economic Approach to Educational Problems,* by Ida Corinne Brown. Washington, D.C.: U.S. Government Printing Office, 1942.

★ 681 ★

Higher Education

College Faculty/Staff/Administration: Percent of Male and Female College Faculty Members, by Race, 1969

[**Percent distribution.** As of Spring. Covers all universities, 4-year colleges, and 2-year colleges, both publicly and privately controlled. Based on a sample survey]

CHARACTERISTIC	Total	Male	Female
Total	100.0	100.0	100.0
Race:			
White	96.3	96.6	94.7
Negro	2.2	1.8	3.9
Other	1.6	1.6	1.4

Source: "College Faculty Members—Characteristics, by Sex: 1969," *Statistical Abstract of the United States, 1973,* p. 134. Primary source: U.S. Office of Education, *Digest of Educational Statistics, 1971.*

★ 682 ★

Higher Education

College Faculty/Staff/Administration: Percentage Distribution of Annual Faculty Salaries in Selected Black Institutions, c. 1939

Salary	Percent
Under $500	0.5
$500-$999	11.6
$1,000-$1,499	40.7
$1,500-$$1,999	25.4
$2,000-$2,499	12.9
$2,500-$2,999	3.6
$3,000-$3,499	3.0
$3,500-$3,999	0.0
$4,000-$4,499	2.2
$4,000-$4,999	0.0
$5,000 & over	0.1

Source: [Untitled Figure], *National Survey of the Higher Education of Negroes.* Vol. 1, No. 6. *Socio-Economic Approach to Educational Problems,* 1942, p. 29. Primary source: U.S. Office of Education. *National Survey of the Higher Education of Negroes.* Vol. 1, No. 6. *Socio-Economic Approach to Educational Problems,* by Ida Corinne Brown. Washington, D.C.: U.S. government Printing Office, 1942.

★ 683 ★

Higher Education

College Faculty/Staff/Administration: Teachers and Administrators in Black Institutions, 1929-30, 1931-32, and 1939-40

Type of institution	Entire staff, excluding duplicates and staff for summer only		Administrators		Teachers			
					Preparatory		College and professional	
	Men	Women	Men	Women	Men	Women	Men	Women
Total								
1939-40	2,627	1,745	566	425	159	220	2,056	1,235
1929-30[1]	1,261	886	352[2]	305[2]	127	205	1,166	722
Four-year institutions								
Publicly controlled	798	461	142	107	38	33	594	341
Privately controlled	1,430	764	315	218	38	75	1,188	530
Teacher education institutions								
Publicly controlled	183	251	41	32	13	33	142	199
Privately controlled	41	50	17	13	18	16	17	24

[Continued]

★ 683 ★

College Faculty/Staff/Administration: Teachers and Administrators in Black Institutions, 1929-30, 1931-32, and 1939-40

[Continued]

| Type of institution | Entire staff, excluding duplicates and staff for summer only | | Administrators | | Teachers | | | |
| | | | | | Preparatory | | College and professional | |
	Men	Women	Men	Women	Men	Women	Men	Women
Junior colleges								
Publicly controlled	61	53	13	15	21	15	38	34
Privately controlled	114	166	38	40	31	48	77	107

Source: "Number of Teachers and Administrators in Institutions of Higher Education for Negroes, 1939-40, by Type of Instruction," *The Negro Handbook, 1944*, p. 57. Primary source: Murray, Florence (Ed.), *The Negro Handbook, 1944*. New York: Current Reference Publications, 1944. Published by permission. *Notes:* 1. Only 1929-30 data given for total group. 2. 1931-32.

★ 684 ★

Higher Education

College Faculty/Staff/Administration: Type of Institution Granting First Undergraduate and Graduate Degrees to Black Faculty, c. 1939

| Type of institution | Bachelor's, master's, and doctor's degrees received by instructors | | | | | |
| | Bachelor's | | Master's | | Doctor's | |
	Number	Percent of total	Number	Percent of total	Number	Percent of total
Institutions for Negroes	495	62.8	66	11.8	0	-
Public	119	15.1	4	.7	-	-
Private	376	47.7	62	11.1	-	-
Nonsegregated institutions	293	37.2	492	88.2	99	100.0
Public	185	23.5	250	44.8	42	42.4
Private	106	13.5	241	43.2	51	51.5
Foreign	2	.2	1	.2	6	6.1
Total	788	100.0	558	100.0	99	100.0

Source: "Institutions from which Teachers Received First Baccalaureate and Graduate Degrees, Classified According to Type," *National Survey of the Higher Education of Negroes*, Vol. 1, No. 6. *Socio-Economic Approach to Educational Problems*, 1942, p. 15. Primary source: U.S. Office Education. *National Survey of the Higher Education of Negroes*. Vol. 1, No. 6. *Socio-Economic Approach to Educational Problems*, by Ida Corinne Brown. Washington, D.C.: U.S. Government Printing Office, 1942.

★ 685 ★

Higher Education

College Faculty/Staff/Administration: Year of First Degree for Black Faculty in Selected Black Institutions, c. 1939

Year	Instructors	
	Number	Percent
1940	13	1.6
1925-1939	164	20.2
1930-1934	193	23.3
1925-1929	214	26.4
1920-1924	115	14.2
1915-1919	55	6.8
1910-1914	19	2.3
1905-1909	22	2.7
1900-1904	7	0.9
1895-1899	5	0.6
1890-1894	3	0.4
1885-1889	1	0.1
Total	811	100.0

Source: "Distribution of Teachers in 21 Colleges and Universities for Negroes, According to Year First Bachelor's Degree was Conferred," *National Survey of the Higher Education of Negroes.* Vol. 1, No. 6. *Socio-Economic Approach to Educational Problems*, 1942, p. 18. Primary source: U.S. Office of Education. *National Survey of the Higher Education of Negroes.* Vol. 1, No. 6. *Socio-Economic Approach to Educational Problems*, by Ida Corinne Brown. Washington, D.C.: U.S. Government Printing Office, 1942.

★ 686 ★

Higher Education

College Graduates: Black College Graduates, by Decade, 1820-1909

Decade	Number of Negro College Graduates
1820-1829	3
1830-1839	
1840-1849	7
1850-1859	12
1860-1869	44
1870-1879	313
1880-1889	738

[Continued]

★ 686 ★

College Graduates: Black College Graduates, by Decade, 1820-1909
[Continued]

Decade	Number of Negro College Graduates
1890-1899	1,126
1900-1909	1,613
Total	3,856

Source: [Untitled Table], *Negro Year Book and Annual Encyclopedia of the Negro*, 1913, p. 147. Primary source: Publication No. 15 of Atlanta University.

★ 687 ★

Higher Education

College Graduates: Black College Graduates, c. 1916-17

"In 1915...281 Negroes received the Bachelor's Degree in the arts and sciences. The total number of Negro college graduates is now about 5,350....About 700 Negroes have graduated from Northern colleges. Oberlin, which admitted Negroes for a number of years before the Civil War, has graduated a larger number of Negroes than any other Northern university or college. In Northern colleges and universities Negroes on a whole have made good records and have carried off many honors."

Source. "Negro College Graduates," *Negro Year Book: An Annual Encyclopedia of the Negro, 1916-1917*, 1918, p. 244. Primary source: Work, Monroe N. (Ed.), *Negro Year Book: An Annual Encyclopedia of the Negro, 1916-1917*. Tuskegee Institute, Ala.: The Negro Year Book Pub. Co., 1918. Published by permission.

★ 688 ★

Higher Education

College Graduates: Major of Black College Graduates, 1937-38 through 1939-40

Major subject	Number of students
History, social science, and psychology:	
History	531
Sociology	293
Social Science	251
Economics	64
Psychology	25

[Continued]

★ 688 ★

College Graduates: Major of Black College Graduates, 1937-38 through 1939-40
[Continued]

Major subject	Number of students
Political science	24
Total	1,188
Science and mathematics:	
Biology	287
Chemistry	186
Mathematics	179
General science	53
Zoology	49
Natural science	12
Botany	9
Physics	9
Total	784
English	409
Foreign language:	
French	107
Romance languages	21
Latin	20
Spanish	15
German	10
Modern foreign language	8
Languages	5
General language	2
Foreign language	1
Total	189
Philosophy and religion:	
Philosophy and religion	6
Philosophy	3
Religion	2
Total	11
Grand total	2,581

Source: "Major Subjects of 2,581 Students who Graduated in Arts and Science from 23 Colleges and Universities for Negroes in 1937-38, 1938-39, and 1939-40," U.S. Office of Education. *National Survey of the Higher Education of Negroes.* Vol. 1, No. 6. *Socio-Economic Approach to Educational Problems,* 1942, p. 49. Primary source: U.S. Office of Education. *National Survey of the Higher Education of Negroes.* Vol. 1, No. 6. *Socio-Economic Approach to Educational Problems,* by Ida Corinne Brown. Washington, D.C.: U.S. Government Printing Office, 1942.

★ 689 ★

Higher Education

College Students: Black Freshman and Senior Occupational Choices, c. 1937

Occupational choice	Freshmen		Seniors	
	Number	Percent	Number	Percent
Professions and semiprofessions	2,942	81.0	1,011	81.8
Business and commercial	276	7.6	142	11.5
Public service	27	.7	21	1.7
Trades and mechanic arts	333	9.6	34	2.6
Farming and allied occupations	50	1.8	29	2.3
Total	3,628	99.8	1,237[1]	99.9
Not given, undecided, etc.	116	-	309	-
Grand total	4,024	-	1,546	-

Source: "Distribution of Occupational Choices of Negro College Freshmen and Seniors," *National Survey of the Higher Education of Negroes.* Vol. 1, No. 6. *Socio-Economic Approach to Educational Problems,* 1942, pp. 56-57. Primary source: U.S. Office of Education, *National Survey of the Higher Education of Negroes.* Vol. 1, No. 6. *Socio-Economic Approach to Educational Problems,* by Ida Corinne Brown. Washington, D.C.: U.S. Government Printing Office, 1942. *Notes:* 1. Not included in this tabulation are the 64 women seniors who indicated "house wife" as the ultimate occupational choice.

★ 690 ★

Higher Education

College Students: Growth in Number Students at Black Institutions who were Receiving Actual College Instruction, 1913-c. 1922

"...there are [in 1922] two institutions that have only from 2% to 4% of their non-professional students enrolled in the college departments. These same two and six others were in this group in 1913. At that time [four institutions] had only from 5% to 9% of their non-professional students in the college departments. Two of these schools still fall in this group, but [one of them] now has 24% and [another of them] 34% of their enrollment in the college departments. Then there were only four out of twenty-two of the most advanced educational institutions for Negroes in America with more than 15% of their students in the college departments. Now there are twelve schools with from 20% to 100% of their non-professional students in their college departments."

Source: Williams, *Report on Negro Universities and Colleges,* [Untitled text], 1922, p. 9. Bound in Slater Fund. *Occasional Papers.* Nos. 21-27. Primary source: Williams, W.T.B. *Report on Negro Universities and Colleges,* [Publication information not given]: 1922. Bound in Slater Fund. *Occasional Papers.* Nos. 21-27. [Publication information not given.].

★ 691 ★

Higher Education

College Students: Major Field of Black Seniors, c. 1942

Major Field	Number	Percent
Art	5	0.3
Commerce and business	70	4.8
Mathematics	52	3.5
Philosophy	5	.3
Modern foreign lanaguage	42	2.8
Classical language	2	.1
English	169	11.5
Music	22	1.5
Biological science	134	9.1
General science	11	.8
Physical science (general)	1	.1
Chemistry	53	3.6
Physics	5	.3
Geography	1	.1
Social science	83	5.6
Economics	11	.8
History	108	7.3
Political science	7	.5
Psychology	4	.3
Sociology and Social work	73	5.0
Elementary education	283	19.3
Physical education	43	3.0
Religion and Religious education	2	.1
Home economics	148	10.0
Agriculture and agricultural education	79	5.4
Industrial Arts or education	27	2.0
Mechanic Arts	25	1.8
Pharmacy	1	.1
Total	1,466	100.0

Source: "Number and percent of Negro College Seniors According to Major Field," *National Survey of the Higher Education of Negroes*. Vol. 1, No. 6. *Socio- Economic Approach to Educational Problems*, 1942, p. 55. Primary source: U.S. Office of Education. *National Survey of the Higher Education of Negroes*. Vol. 1, No. 6. *Socio-Economic Approach to Educational Problems*, by Ida Corinne Brown. Washington, D.C.: U.S. Government Printing Office, 1942.

★ 692 ★

Higher Education

College Students: Number Students at Black Institutions who were Receiving Actual College Instruction and Instruction in Professions, by State, c. 1922

State	Number Schools	Total Enrollment[1]	Total College Enrollment	Total Professional Enrollment	Percent of Non-Professional Students Enrolled in College
Alabama	3	1,523	121	22	7.9
Florida	1	329	42	0	12.8
Georgia	4	2,439	326	62	13.4
Kansas	1	316	30	19	9.4
Kentucky	1	310	39	2	12.6
Louisiana	3	1,472	95	0	6.4
Mississippi	2	702	29	0	4.1
Missouri	1	500	68	0	13.6
North Carolina	3	924	241	65	26.1
Ohio	1	865	249	37	28.8
Pennsylvania	1	242	220	22	90.9
South Carolina	3	2,037	88	47	4.3
Tennessee	4	1,263	407	6	32.2
Texas	3	1,033	279	0	27.0
Virginia	1	356	135	31	37.9
District of Columbia	1	1,612	895	717	55.2
Total	33	15,923	3,264	1,020	20.5

Source: Williams, *Report on Negro Universities and Colleges,* [Untitled tables], 1922, p. 22-23. Bound in Slater Fund. *Occasional Papers.* Nos. 21-27. Primary source: Williams, W.T.B. *Report on Negro Universities and Colleges,* [Public information not given]: 1922. Bound in Slater Fund. *Occasional Papers.* Nos. 21-27. [Publication information not given.]
Notes: 1. Includes students receiving college and secondary instruction; excludes students receiving instruction in the professions of theology, law, and/or medicine.

★ 693 ★

Higher Education

College Students: Public and Private Northern Institutions Attended by Black Students, c. 1942 - I

	4 public institutions					
	University of Cincinnati	University of Illinois	University of Kansas	Ohio State University	Total reporting	Percent
Sex distribution:						
Male	24	48	27	82	181	53
Female	48	24	24	66	162	47
Total	...	...	...	...	343	...
Undergraduate students:						
Home address-						
In same State as college	56	55	30	101	242	90.6
In other Northern States	...	3	1	4	8	3.0
In Southern States	1	6	8	2	17	6.4
Total	57	64	39	107	267	...
Graduate and professional students:						
Home address-						
In same State as college	14	7	11	29	61	80.3
In other Northern States	...	...	1	2	3	3.9
In Southern States	1	1	...	10	12	15.8
Total	15	8	12	41	76	...
Total in same States as college	70	62	41	130	303	88.3
Percent	97.2	86.1	80.4	87.8	...	...
Total in other Northern States	...	3	2	6	11	3.2
Percent	...	4.2	3.9	4.1	...	...
Total in Southern States	2	7	8	12	29	8.5
Percent	2.8	9.7	15.7	8.1	...	...
Grand total	72	72	51	148	343	...

Source: "Negro students attending 8 northern institutions distributed according to sex and home address," *National Survey of the Higher Education of Negroes.* Vol. 1, No. 6. *Socio-Economic Approach to Educational Problems,* 1942, p. 79. Primary source: U.S. Office of Education. *National Survey of the Higher Education of Negroes.* Vol. 1, No. 6. *Socio-Economic Approach to Educational Problems,* by Ida Corinne Brown. Washington, D.C.: U.S. Government Printing Office, 1942.

★ 694 ★

Higher Education

College Students: Public and Private Northern Institutions Attended by Black Students, c. 1942 - II

	4 private institutions						Grand total reporting	Percent
	University of Chicago	Columbia (Teachers College)	New York University	Northwestern University	Total reporting	Percent		
Sex distribution:								
Male	18	23	50	14	105	37	286	46
Female	47	68	50	11	176	63	338	54
Total	...	...	...	...	281	...	624	...
Undergraduate students:								
Home address-								
In same State as college	13	8	52	10	83	75.4	325	86.2
In other Northern States	5	...	12	2	19	17.3	27	7.2
In Southern States	2	1	1	4	8	7.3	25	6.6
Total	20	9	65	16	110	...	377	...
Graduate and professional students:								
Home address-								
In same State as college	27	45	26	2	100	58.5	161	65.2
In other Northern States	4	12	3	1	20	11.7	23	9.3
In Southern States	14	25	6	6	51	29.8	63	25.5
Total	45	82	35	9	171	...	247	...
Total in same States as college	40	53	78	12	183	65.1	486	77.9
Percent	61.5	58.2	78.0	48.0	...	...	...	...
Total in other Northern States	9	12	15	3	39	13.9	50	8.0
Percent	13.9	13.2	15.0	12.0	...	...	...	...
Total in Southern States	16	26	7	10	59	21.0	88	14.1
Percent	24.6	28.6	7.0	40.0	...	...	...	...
Grand total	65	91	100	25	281	...	624	...

Source: "Negro students attending 8 northern institutions distributed according to sex and home address," *National Survey of the Higher Education of Negroes.* Vol. 1, No. 6. *Socio-Economic Approach to Educational Problems,* 1942, p. 79. Primary source: U.S. Office of Education. *National Survey of the Higher Education of Negroes.* Vol. 1, No. 6. *Socio-Economic Approach to Educational Problems,* by Ida Corinne Brown. Washington, D.C.: U.S. Government Printing Office, 1942.

★ 695 ★

Higher Education

Colleges and Universities: Campus and Non-Campus Acreage of Black Colleges by State, c. 1928

State	No. institutions	Range/No. of acres	Average[1]	Range of acreage		Average	
				Campus	Non-campus	Campus[1]	Non-campus
Alabama	4	30-1,850	678	7-110	24-1,740[3]	49	583[3]
Arkansas	3	4-20	83	4-40	182[3]	22	82[3]
Delaware	1	200	200	25	175	25	175
District of Columbia	1	25	25	25	-	25	-

[Continued]

★ 695 ★

Colleges and Universities: Campus and Non-Campus Acreage of Black Colleges by State, c. 1928
[Continued]

State	No. institutions	Range/No. of acres	Average[1]	Range of acreage		Average	
				Campus	Non-campus	Campus[1]	Non-campus
Florida	3	31-769	350	5-250	26-753[3]	90	390[3]
Georgia	9	6.5-164	74	6.5-60	44-150[3]	20	81[3]
Kentucky	2	5-444	224	5-50	394[3]	28	394[2]
Louisiana	5	2.31-500[2]	149[2]	2.31-35[2]	80-465[3]	13[2]	272[3]
Maryland	2	85-195	140	15-30	55-180	22	118
Mississippi	5	50-1,225	560	25-40	24-1,185	35	525
Missouri	1	98	98	30	68	30	68
North Carolina	12	20-1,129	195	20-60	6.5-1,079[3]	39	234[3]
Ohio	1	112	112	75	37	75	37
Oklahoma	1	320	40	280	320	40	280
Pennsylvania	2	137-145	141	7-25	120-130	16	125
South Carolina	5	20-141	56	5-50	20-91[3]	23	54[3]
Tennessee	8	1.5-375	96	1.5-75	70-300[3]	25	189[3]
Texas	8	15.5-1,435	317	13-300	0.5-1,360	62	255
Virginia	4	57-1,600	737	37-74	263-1,560[3]	52	913[3]
West Virginia	1	83	83	15	68	15	68
Total	78						

Source: Compiled by the editors from "Physical Plants of Negro Colleges," *Survey of Negro Colleges and Universities*. Bulletin, 1928, No. 7, 1929, pp. 952-954. Primary source: U.S. Bureau of Education. *Survey of Negro Colleges and Universities*. Bulletin, 1928, No. 7. Washington, D.C.: Government Printing Office, 1929. *Notes:* 1. Rounded to nearest whole number. 2. Excludes one institution with total and campus acreage reported as "1 block." 3. Information not furnished in source table for one or more institutions.

★ 696 ★

Higher Education

Colleges and Universities: Characteristics of Black Colleges and Universities, by State, 1877

States	Universities and colleges		
	Schools	Teachers	Pupils
Alabama	...	...	...
Georgia	1	5	33
Kentucky	1	13	129
Louisiana	3	23	337
Maryland	...	...	...
Mississippi	2	11	216
North Carolina	1	7	126
Ohio	1	16	145
Pennsylvania	1	9	134
South Carolina	...	...	...

[Continued]

★ 696 ★

Colleges and Universities: Characteristics of Black Colleges and Universities, by State, 1877

[Continued]

States	Universities and colleges		
	Schools	Teachers	Pupils
District of Columbia	1	7	57
Total	13	108	1270

Source: Robert, *Negro Civilization in the South,* "Summary of Statistics of Institutions for the Instruction of the Colored Race for 1877," 1880, p. 134. Primary source: Robert, Charles Edwin. *Negro Civilization in the South; Educational, Social, and Religious Advancement of the Colored People.* Nashville, Tenn.: Printed by Wheeler Bros, for the author, 1880.

★ 697 ★

Higher Education

Colleges and Universities: Characteristics of Higher Education Institutions with Predominantly Black Student Bodies, 1950, 1960, and 1964

ITEM	1950	1960	1964					
			Total	Universities, colleges, and professional schools		Teachers colleges[1]	Junior colleges[2]	
				Publicly controlled	Privately controlled		Publicly controlled	Privately controlled
Number of institutions	105	106	107	20	49	12	15	11
Faculty[3,4]	6,933	(NA)	9,968	3,858	4,316	1,109	414	211
Male	4,151	(NA)	6,209	2,394	2,791	622	284	118
Female	2,782	(NA)	3,759	1,464	1,525	487	190	93
RESIDENT DEGREE-CREDIT STUDENTS[4]								
Regular session:								
Total	76,561	88,859	105,495	45,838	38,558	14,902	4,273	1,924
Male	40,677	41,789	47,155	21,165	17,870	5,498	1,831	791
Female	35,884	47,070	58,340	24,673	20,688	9,404	2,442	1,133
Graduate	2,304	3,164	4,142	2,635	1,396	111	-	-
Male	1,161	1,440	1,771	958	777	36	-	-
Female	1,143	1,724	2,371	1,677	619	75	-	-
First time in any college	21,368	28,452	30,026	12,202	10,345	4,337	2,178	964
Male	10,613	13,234	13,297	5,812	4,459	1,659	951	416
Female	10,755	15,218	16,729	6,390	5,886	2,678	1,227	548
EARNED DEGREES CONFERRED								
Bachelor's and first professional	13,108	(NA)	14,058	5,611	5,908	2,539	(X)	(X)
Male	6,467	(NA)	5,667	2,414	2,439	814	(X)	(X)
Female	6,641	(NA)	8,391	3,197	3,469	1,725	(X)	(X)
Master's and second professional	768	(NA)	1,450	1,019	378	53	(X)	(X)
Male	335	(NA)	651	397	231	23	(X)	(X)
Female	433	(NA)	799	622	147	30	(X)	(X)
Doctor's	-	(NA)	7	1	6	(X)	(X)	(X)
Male	-	(NA)	5	1	4	(X)	(X)	(X)
Female	-	(NA)	2	-	2	(X)	(X)	(X)

[Continued]

★ 697 ★

Colleges and Universities: Characteristics of Higher Education Institutions with Predominantly Black Student Bodies, 1950, 1960, and 1964

[Continued]

ITEM	1950	1960	1964					
			Total	Universities, colleges, and professional schools		Teachers colleges[1]	Junior colleges[2]	
				Publicly controlled	Privately controlled		Publicly controlled	Privately controlled
OTHER TYPES OF STUDENTS[4]								
Extension degree-credit courses	(NA)	1,717	1,946	1,762	134	50	-	-
Terminal occupational education	(NA)	2,576	1,588	454	453	284	283	114

Source: "Institutions of Higher Education Attended Predominantly by Negroes—Summary: 1950, 1960, and 1964," *Statistical Abstract of the United States, 1966,* p. 137. Primary source: Dept. of Health, Education, and Welfare, Office of Education: *Biennial Survey of Education in the United States,* chapter on Statistics of Higher Education, and unpublished data. *Notes:* - Represents zero. NA Not available. X Not available. 1. All publicaly controlled. 2. Includes community colleges, technical institutes, normal schools, and other higher educational institutions restricted to less than 4 years of work on the undergraduate or terminal-occupational level. 3. Total number of different persons (not reduced to full-time basis). Includes administrative officers, extension service, correspondence courses, and organized research staff in addition to regular staff. 4. Data are for first term of academic year except 1964 data for "Resident degree-credit students" and "Other types of students" are for fall 1963.

★ 698 ★

Higher Education

Colleges and Universities: Historically Black Schools Founded 1830-1975, by Region

Period established	United States	South	North and West
Total, historically Black institutions institutions	107	100	7
1830-1849	1	-	1
1850-1859	3	1	2
1860-1869	21	20	1
1870-1879	22	22	-
1880-1889	19	18	1
1890-1899	15	14	1
1900-1909	10	10	-
1910-1919	2	2	-
1920-1929	2	2	-
1930-1939	2	1	1
1940-1949	3	3	-
1950-1959	3	3	-
1960-1969	4	4	-
1970-1975	-	-	-

Source: "Historically Black Colleges and Universities by Region and Period Founded: 1830-1849 to 1970-1975," *The Social and Economic Status of the Black Population in the United States: An Historical View, 1790-1978,* 1979, p. 96. Primary source: Institute for Services to Education, Inc., Division of Research and Evaluation. *Notes:* The definition of historically Black institutions used in this table includes those postsecondary institutions that were established *primarily* for Black Americans and which have continued to identify with Black- oriented issues. Excluded are some institutions which were established as historically Black institutions but which have under the desegregation mandate so altered the racial composition of their institution that they are no longer identified as functioning historically Black institutions. - Represents zero.

★ 699 ★

Higher Education

Colleges and Universities: Location, Denominational Affiliation, Instructors, and Students at Black Colleges and Universities, 1877

Name and class of institution	Location	Religious denomination	Instructors	Students
Atlanta University	Atlanta, Ga.	Cong	5	33
Berea College	Berea, Ky.	Cong	13[1]	129
Leland University	New Orleans, La.	Baptist	4	...
Straight University	New Orleans, La.	Cong	7	223
New Orleans University	New Orleans, La.	Meth	12[1]	110
Shaw University	Holly Springs, Miss.	Meth	6	130
Alcorn University	Rodney, Miss.	Non-sect	5	86
Biddle University	Charlotte, N.C.	Presb	7[1]	126
Wilberforce University	Xenia, Ohio	M.E.	16	145
Lincoln University	Oxford, Pa.	Presb	9	134
Central Tennessee College	Nashville, Tenn.	Cong	8	24
Fisk University	Nashville, Tenn.	Cong	9	69
Howard University	Washington, D.C.	Non-scct	7	57
Total			108	1270

Source: Robert, *Negro Civilization in the South*, "Universities and Colleges," 1880, pp. 132-133. Primary source: Robert, Charles Edwin. *Negro Civilization in the South; Educational, Social, and Religious Advancement of the Colored People.* Nashville, Tenn.: Printed by Wheeler Bros, for the author, 1880. *Note:* 1. For all departments.

★ 700 ★

Higher Education

Colleges and Universities: Location, Denominational Affiliation, Instructors, and Students at Black Normal Schools, 1877

Name and class of institution	Location	Religious denomination	Instructors	Students
NORMAL SCHOOLS				
Rust Normal Institute	Huntsville, Ala.	Meth	2	60
State Normal School for Colored Students	Huntsville, Ala.	...	...	81
Lincoln Normal University	Marion, Ala.	...	3	120
Emerson Institute	Mobile, Ala.	Cong	4	147
State Normal School for Colored Students	Pine Bluff, Ark.	...	2	83
Normal department of Atalanta University	Atlanta, Ga.	Presb	...	168
Lewis High School	Macon, Ga.	Cong	3	89
Haven Normal School	Waynesboro', Ga.	Meth	4	125
Peabody Normal School	New Orleans, La.	...	5	95
Baltimore Normal School for Colored Pupils	Baltimore, Md.	...	3	134
Centenary Biblical Instititute	Baltimore, Md.	Meth	4	77
Touglaoo University and Normal School	Tougaloo, Miss.	Cong	8	106
Lincoln Normal Institute	Jefferson, Mo.	...	6	122

[Continued]

★ 700 ★

Colleges and Universities: Location, Denominational Affiliation, Instructors, and Students at Black Normal Schools, 1877

[Continued]

Name and class of institution	Location	Religious denomination	Instructors	Students
State Normal School for Colored Students	Fayetteville, N.C.	...	3	71
Bennett Seminary	Greensboro', N.C.	Meth	2	75
St. Augustine's Normal School	Raleigh, N.C.	P.E.	4	127
Shaw University	Raleigh, N.C.	Baptist	5	240
Avery Normal Institute	Charleston, S.C.	Cong	9	315
Fairfield Normal Institute	Winnsboro', S.C.	Presb	...	340
Freedman's Normal Institute	Maryville, Tenn	Friends	13	204
LeMoyne Normal and Commercial School	Memphis, Tenn	Cong	9	295
Hampton Normal and Agricultural Institute	Hampton, Va	Cong[1]	14	274
Richmond Institute	Richmond, Va	Baptist	5	104
Richmond Normal School for Colored Pupils	Richmond, Va	...	6	232
Miner Normal School	Washington, D.C.	...	2	27
Normal department of Howard University	Washington, D.C.	Non-sect	3	74
Normal department of Wayland Seminary	Washington, D.C.	Baptist	[2]	[2]
Total			119	3785

Source: Robert, Negro Civilization in the South,1p7v0s0b5T "Statistics of Institutions for the Instruction of the Colored Race for 1877," 1880, pp. 131-132. Primary source: Robert, Charles Edwin, Negro Civilization in the South; Educational, Social and Religious Advancement of the Colored People. Nashville, Tenn.: Printed by Wheeler Bros, for the author, 1880. Notes: 1. In addition to the aid given by American Missionary Association, this institute has an appropriation from the state. 2. Reported under schools of theology.

★ 701 ★

Higher Education

Colleges and Universities: Property Holdings in Selected Black Institutions, 1910-1938

Type of institution by property holding	1910	1920	1930	1938
Buildings and grounds				
Public	$1,983,800	$4,423,574	$11,737,249	$16,481,722
Percent increase	-	+123	+165	+40
Private	$5,511,417	$9,506,805	$14,778,577	$20,839,737
Percent increase	-	+72	+55	+41
All	$7,495,217	$13,930,379	$26,515,826	$37,321,459
Percent increase	-	+86	+90	+41
Equipment				
Public	$468,710	$897,555	$2,357,761	$2,945,963
Percent increase	-	+91	+163	+25
Private	$750,687	$1,065,368	$2,043,500	$3,174,874
Percent increase	-	+42	+92	+55

[Continued]

★ 701 ★

Colleges and Universities: Property Holdings in Selected Black Institutions, 1910-1938
[Continued]

Type of institution by property holding	1910	1920	1930	1938
All	$1,219,397	$1,962,923	$4,401,261	$6,120,837
Percent increase	-	+61	+124	+39
Total				
Public	$2,452,510	$5,321,129	$14,095,010	$19,427,685
Percent increase	-	+177	+165	+38
Private	$6,262,104	$10,572,173	$16,822,077	$24,014,611
Percent increase	-	+69	+59	+43
All	$8,714,614	$15,893,302	$30,917,087	$43,442,296
Percent increase	-	+82	+95	+41

Source: "Distribution of Property Holdings in 20 Public and 16 Private Colleges, 1910-38," *National Survey of the Higher Education of Negroes.* Vol. 1, No. 6. *Socio-Economic Approach to Educational Problems,* 1942, p. 6. Primary source: U.S. Office of Education. *National Survey of the Higher Education of Negroes.* Vol. 1, No. 6. *Socio-Economic Approach to Educational Problems,* by Ida Corinne Brown. Washington, D.C.: U.S. Government Printing Office, 1942.

★ 702 ★

Higher Education

Colleges and Universities: Students, Teachers, Income, and Number of Denominational Affiliations in Black Institutions, 1912, 1913, 1916-17, 1918-19, and 1925-26

Year	Number of institutions	Number denominationally affiliated	Range of Students	Teachers	Income
1912	55	52	120-1577	7,104	$4,488-134,203
1913	55	52	54-1715	8-114	2,874-170,202
1916-17	61	58	3-567[1]	3-111	2,543-191,571
1918-19	62	59	6-482[1]	3-131	1,000-201,542
1925-26	68	64	3-1069[1]	2-174	5,000-443,144

Source: Compiled and adapted by the editors from "Educational Institutions: Universities and Colleges," *Negro Year Book and Annual Encyclopedia of the Negro,* 1912, [no p. no.]; 1913, p. 149; *Negro Year Book: An Annual Encyclopedia of the Negro, 1916-1917,* 1918, pp. 262-263; *Negro Year Book: An Annual Encyclopedia of the Negro, 1918-1919,* 1919, [no p. no.]; *Negro Year Book: An Annual Encyclopedia of the Negro, 1925-1926,* 1925, pp. 325-326. Primary source: Work, Monroe N. (Ed.), *Negro Year Book and Annual Encyclopedia of the Negro.* Tuskegee, Ala.: Tuskegee Normal and Industrial Institute, 1912; Work, Monroe N. (Ed.), *Negro Year Book and Annual Encyclopedia of the Negro.* Tuskegee Institute, Ala.: Negro Year Book Co., 1913; *Negro Year Book: An Annual Encyclopedia of the Negro, 1916-1917.* Tuskegee Institute, Ala.: The Negro Year Book Pub. Co., 1918, 1919, and 1925. Published by permission. *Note:* 1. Includes only those students taking college courses.

★ 703 ★
Higher Education

Colleges and Universities: Students, Teachers, and Income in Black Institutions by Type of Institution, c. 1937-38

Type of institution	Number of institutions	Range of students, teachers, income				
		College	High Sch.	Elem.	Teachers	Income
U.S. land-grant colleges for Negroes	16	43-1,253	29-296	45-578	9-99	$37,000-457,522
State and city normal schools and colleges	21	48-979	110-1,540	4-364	9-48	23,415-147,675
Private universities and colleges	101	4-1,727	6,464	15-695	6-300	1,088-941,020.09

Source: Complied and adapted by the editors from "United States Land-Grant Colleges for Negroes," "State and City Normal Schools and Colleges," and "Private Universities and Colleges," *Negro Year Book: An Annual Encyclopedia of the Negro, 1937-1938*, 1937, pp. 197-204. Primary source: Work, Monroe N. (Ed.), *Negro Year Book: An Annual Encyclopedia of the Negro, 1937-1938.* Tuskegee Institute, Ala.: The Negro Year Book Pub. Co., 1937. Published by permission.

★ 704 ★
Higher Education

Colleges and Universities: Summary Characteristics of Black Colleges and Universities, 1930-31

	Total number of teachers	Exclusively in college work	Total number of students	Students in four year coll. course	Total income for current purposes	Amount paid for teachers' salary	Amount received for permanent improvements	Debt on current expenses
Allen	25	13	417	160	$67,149	$20,111	$[1]	$4,683
Atlanta	26	24	38[1]	[1]	150,916	66,500	155,525	-
Benedict	27	10	399	236	70,563	20,301	[3]	
Bishop	22	22	324	276	91,528	38,941		18,049
Bennett	17	12	230	158	54,258	27,452	2,500	3,500
Clark	20	14	486	290	85,425	22,534	-	5,418
Claflin	32	10	408	115	89,236	26,186	-	-
Edward Waters	31	5	279	54	51,541	21,861	40,677	10,000
Jackson	15	5	251	74	25,097	11,231	-	-
Lane	19	9	586	321	30,068	20,050		21,100
Livingstone	28	13	261	240	63,162	26,866	-	-
Miles Memorial	19	4	228	69	23,814	14,956	-	42,611
Miss. Industrial	24	9	191	74	13,609	6,093	103	-
Morehouse	40	40	470	350	125,341	35,053	-	8,038
Morris Brown	22	12	443	217	69,301	17,018	9,000	3,373
New Orleans	31	15	696	485	62,598	30,411		900
Paine	22	12	216	85	50,455	23,382	24,467	-
Philander Smith	17	8	182	92	27,208	16,710	861	29,438
Rust	20	10	179	94	32,747	16,044	-	-
Samuel Huston	16	16	584	267	43,815	16,005	2,803	6,217
Shaw	20	20	301	286	71,420	28,872	400	-
Straight	32	11	340	134	85,857	31,343	-	-
St. Augustine	25	11	348	158	103,080	27,835	2,866	-
Talladega	46	21	520	288	173,885	61,600	-	18,625
Texas	18	7	284	156	21,372	13,314	-	-

[Continued]

★ 704 ★

Colleges and Universities: Summary Characteristics of Black Colleges and Universities, 1930-31
[Continued]

	Total number of teachers	Exclusively in college work	Total number of students	Students in four year coll. course	Total income for current purposes	Amount paid for teachers' salary	Amount received for permanent improvements	Debt on current expenses
Tougaloo	26	5	327	71	71,921	28,226	29,413	3,257
Virg. Theol. Sem. and Coll	16	9	170	102	51,036	9,745	-	-
Virginia Union	38	20	594	551	100,847	59,514	-	-
Wiley	31	22	424	380	71,487	37,241	-	8,202
Xavier	33	16	550	192	-	24,250	-	-

Source: The John F. Slater Fund, *Proceedings and Reports,* "A. Colleges and Universities," 1931, p. 13. Primary source: The John F. Slater Fund. *Proceedings and Reports.* For the Year Ending September 30th, 1931. *Notes:* 1. All graduate students. 2. Dotted line indicates failure to report. 3. Blank space indicates nothing to report.

★ 705 ★

Higher Education

Colleges and Universities: Summary Characteristics of Black Junior Colleges and Other Schools, 1930-31

	Total number of teachers	Exclusively in college work	Total number of students	Students in college and normal courses	Total income for current purposes	Amount paid for teachers' salary	Amount received for permanent improvements	Debt on current expenses
Bethune-Cookman	32	3	287	79	$75,215	$20,482	$8,294	$17,456
Bettis	18	1	668	25	15,301	6,291	[1]	-
Brick	16	1	175	53	47,213	16,662	8,915	475
Calhoun	17	0	291	0	93,084	24,771	-	5,810
Fort Valley	42	-	695	31	75,263	36,902	5,000	16,474
Kittrell	16	5	118	35	40,196	11,630	-	23,081
Le Moyne	27	10	465	191	38,040	21,000	30,000	[2]
National Training	9	1	68	6	30,513	6,331	8,435	-
Palmer Memorial	18	-	224	-	35,096	14,810	1,300	
Paul Quinn	7	2	91	79	20,576	7,881	-	19,897
Penn	30	-	283	6	52,240	20,929	15,120	5,799
Schofield	17	0	206	0	27,568	9,449	-	-
Selma Univ.	18	-	246	37	31,913	8,117	-	35,957
Snow Hill	13	0	211	4	20,928	11,922	33,100	1,762
Walker Memorial	14	-	225	-	12,468	6,640	3,600	10,125

Source: The John F. Slater Fund, *Proceedings and Reports,* "A. College and Universities," 1931, p. 14. Primary source: The John F. Slater Fund. *Proceedings and Reports.* For the Year Ending September 30th, 1931. *Notes:* 1. Dotted line indicates failure to report. 2. Blank space indicates nothing to report.

★ 706 ★

Higher Education

Colleges and Universities: Value of Black College Physical Plants by State, c. 1928

Amounts in thousands.

State	Number institutions	Range/amount of land value	Buildings (Average)	Equipment (Average)	Total value	Average
Alabama	4	33-234	132.6	811.7	178.2-2,201.5	1,039.0
Arkansas	3	20-104	61.3	109.2	165.8-195.5	182.4
Delaware	1	31	31.0	110.6	155.7	155.7
District of Columbia	1	744	744.0	1,031.1	2,254.7	2,254.7
Florida	3	42.1-246.4	121.2	229.4	358-500	421.4
Georgia	9	4-125	65.6	292.9	27.6-869.3	405.6
Kentucky	2	39.9-74.4	57.0	151.1	204.4-227.4	215.9
Louisiana	5	4.5-350	190.9	315.8[1]	4.5-708.4	460.9
Maryland	2	20-85	52.5	237.2	125.1-527.2	326.2
Mississippi	5	50-78	35.0	243.3	201.5-519.5	315.6
Missouri	1	80	80.0	313.0	447.8	447.8
North Carolina	12	11.1-300	129.3	322.8	231.7-986.3	508.0
Ohio	1	146.3	146.3	1,381.2	1,839.0	1,839.0
Oklahoma	1	16.6	16.6	225.7	259.0	259.0
Pennsylvania	2	28-30.8	29.4	322.0	318.5-478.6	398.6
South Carolina	5	15-165.3	82.5	286.6	246.0-747.3	436.7
Tennessee	8	12-88[1]	51.7[1]	298.0[1]	118.5-793.0[1]	386.0[1]
Texas	8	11.5-100	48.5	252.0	182.8-1,067.1	385.7
Virginia	4	75-250	230.0	619.5	495.2-1,125.0	789.8
West Virginia	1	83	83.0	781.8	1,025.8	1,025.8
Total	78	4.0-350.0	95.2	349.1	4.5-2,254.7	502.3

Source: Compiled by the editors from "Physical Plants of Negro Colleges," *Survey of Negro Colleges and Universities.* Bulletin, 1928, No. 7, 1929, pp. 952-954. Primary source: U.S. Bureau of Education. *Survey of Negro Colleges and Universities.* Bulletin, 1928, No. 7. Washington, D.C.: Government Printing Office, 1929. *Note:* 1. Information incomplete in source table for 1 or more institutions.

Higher Education

Curricula/Programs: Black "Colleges" and Level of Academic Work Offered, c. 1916

Characteristics	Number of schools	Students in college subjects	In professional subjects	All other students
College	3	722	972	717
Secondary and college	15	675	22	4,789
Schools offering college subjects[1]	15	246	0	4,583
Total	33	1,643	994	10,089

Source: [Untitled Table], *Negro Education: A Study of the Private and Higher Schools for Colored People in the United States*, vol. II Bulletin, 1916, No. 39, 1917, p. 16. Primary source: U.S. Office of Education. *Negro Education: A Study of the Private and Higher Schools for Colored People in the United States*, vol. II Bulletin, 1916, No. 39. Washington, D.C.: Government Printing Office, 1917. *Notes:* 1. Does not include Leland University, which had four colleges students at the time visit.

Higher Education

Curricula/Programs: Graduate Fields Available to Blacks and Whites in States with Segregation, 1939-40 - I

Type of institution by field	Alabama	Arkansas	Delaware	District of Columbia	Florida	Georgia	Kentucky	Louisiana	Maryland
				WHITE					
Arts and science:									
Public	18	19	11	...	24	17	24	28	17
All[2]	18	19	11	24	24	17	24	28	17
Education:									
Public	5	7	1	...	7	5	8	9	4
All	5	7	1	2	7	5	8	9	4
Agriculture:									
Public	10	7	2	...	13	10	11	13	14
All	10	7	2	...	13	10	11	13	14
Home economics:									
Public	6	2	...	...	5	5	3	1	2
All	6	2	...	...	5	5	3	1	2
Commerce:									
Public	5	7	...	...	1	2	2	5	5
All	5	7	...	2	1	2	2	5	5
Engineering and architecture:									
Public	15	4	4	...	6	10	7	7	4
All	15	4	4	...	6	10	7	7	7

[Continued]

★ 708 ★

Curricula/Programs: Graduate Fields Available to Blacks and Whites in States with Segregation, 1939-40 - I

[Continued]

Type of institution by field	Alabama	Arkansas	Delaware	District of Columbia	Florida	Georgia	Kentucky	Louisiana	Maryland
				NEGRO					
Arts and science:									
Public	...	...	...	...	...	...	...	...	...
All[2]	...	...	...	16	...	9	...	5	...
Education:									
Public	...	...	...	...	...	...	...	...	...
All	...	...	...	2	...	2	...	1	...
Agriculture:									
Public	...	...	...	...	...	...	...	...	...
All	...	...	...	...	...	...	...	...	...
Home economics:									
Public	...	...	...	...	...	...	...	...	...
All	...	...	...	...	...	...	...	...	...
Commerce:									
Public	...	...	...	...	...	1	...	...	...
All	...	...	...	...	...	...	...	...	...
Engineering and architecture:									
Public	...	...	...	...	...	...	...	...	...
All	...	...	...	...	...	...	...	...	...

Source: "Number of Graduate Fields of Specialization Available in Institutions of Higher Education in States Maintaining Separate Institutions, 1939-40," *National Survey of the Higher Education of Negroes*. Vol. 1, No. 6, *Socio- Economic Approach to Educational Problems*, 1942, p. 14. Primary source: U.S. Office of Education. *National Survey of the Higher Education of Negroes*. Vol. 1, No. 6. *Socio-Economic Approach to Educational Problems*, by Ida Corinne Brown. Washington, D.C.: U.S. Government Printing Office, 1942. Work. *Notes:* 1. This table is to be read as follows: Alabama - In institutions for the higher education white persons the following number of graduate fields are available: In arts and science, 18 fields in public institutions and 18 fields in both public institutions, etc. In institutions for the higher education of Negroes no graduate fields of specialization are available. 2. Includes both public and private institutions.

★ 709 ★

Higher Education

Curricula/Programs: Graduate Fields Available to Blacks and Whites in States with Segregation, 1939-40 - II

Type of institution by field	Mississippi	Missouri	North Carolina	Oklahoma	South Carolina	Tennessee	Texas	Virginia	West Virginia
				WHITE					
Arts and science:									
Public	23	24	28	27	18	21	27	23	17
All[2]	23	24	28	27	18	23	27	23	17
Education:									
Public	1	7	7	8	4	10	6	8	3
All	1	7	7	8	4	16	6	8	3
Agriculture:									
Public	11	13	12	12	...	10	14	10	7
All	11	13	12	12	...	10	14	10	7
Home economics:									
Public	...	2	1	12	...	5	6	6	...

[Continued]

★ 709 ★

Curricula/Programs: Graduate Fields Available to Blacks and Whites in States with Segregation, 1939-40 - II

[Continued]

Type of institution by field	Mississippi	Missouri	North Carolina	Oklahoma	South Carolina	Tennessee	Texas	Virginia	West Virginia
All	...	2	1	12	...	5	6	6	...
Commerce:									
Public	5	4	10	4	1	2	4	1	...
All	5	4	10	4	1	2	4	1	...
Engineering and architecture:									
Public	5	5	18	13	3	6	8	12	15
All	5	5	18	13	3	6	8	12	15
NEGRO									
Arts and science:									
Public	...	...	10	...	...	...	...	10	...
All[2]	...	...	10	...	...	6	...	10	...
Education:									
Public	...	...	1	...	...	...	2	6	...
All	...	...	1	...	...	1	2	6	...
Agriculture:									
Public	...	...	1	...	...	...	3	3	...
All	...	...	1	...	...	...	3	3	...
Home economics:									
Public	...	...	...	...	...	...	...	1	...
All	...	...	...	...	...	...	...	1	...
Commerce:									
Public	...	...	...	...	...	...	...	...	...
All	...	...	...	...	...	...	...	...	...
Engineering and architecture:									
Public	...	...	...	...	...	...	...	...	...
All	...	...	...	...	...	...	...	...	...

Source: "Number of Graduate Fields of Specialization Available in Institutions of Higher Education in States Maintaining Separate Institutions, 1939-40," *National Survey of the Higher Education of Negroes.* Vol. 1, No. 6, *Socio- Economic Approach to Educational Problems*, 1942, p. 14. Primary source: U.S. Office of Education. *National Survey of the Higher Education of Negroes.* Vol. 1, No. 6. *Socio-Economic Approach to Educational Problems*, by Ida Corinne Brown. Washington, D.C.: U.S. Government Printing Office, 1942. Work. *Notes:* 1. This table is to be read as follows: Alabama - In institutions for the higher education white persons the following number of graduate fields are available: In arts and science, 18 fields in public institutions and 18 fields in both public institutions, etc. In institutions for the higher education of Negroes no graduate fields of specialization are available. 2. Includes both public and private institutions.

★ 710 ★

Higher Education

Curricula/Programs: Majors Available in 25 Selected Black Institutions, c. 1939

Field	Number of institutions	Field	Number of institutions
English	23	Psychology	5
Chemistry	19	Foreign language	5
History	18	Latin	4
Biology, mathematics	17	German, political science,	

[Continued]

★ 710 ★

Curricula/Programs: Majors Available in 25 Selected Black Institutions, c. 1939
[Continued]

Field	Number of institutions	Field	Number of institutions
		Spanish	3
Sociology	13	Botany, general science,	
French	10	zoology	2
Economics, social science	9	Greek, natural science,	
Physics	6	philosophy, religion	1

Source: [Untitled Table], *National Survey of the Higher Education of Negroes.* Vol., 1, No. 6. *Socio-Economic Approach to Educational Problems*, 1942, p. 47. Primary source: U.S. Office of Education. *National Survey of the Higher Education of Negroes.* Vol. 1, No. 6. *Socio-Economic Approach to Educational Problems*, by Ida Corinne Brown. Washington, D.C.: U.S. Government Printing Office, 1942. Work.

★ 711 ★

Higher Education

Curricula/Programs: Professional, Technical, and Theology Program Areas at Black Institutions, c. 1939

Professional or technical field	Number of institutions offering-			
	A curriculum in the field	A major in the field	Some instruction, but less than a major	Total number offering instruction
Agriculture	9	...	...	9
Architecture	1	...	2	3
Fine arts	5	1	14	20
Commerce	6	3	3	12
Education	15	8	2	25
Engineering	2	...	...	2
Health and physical education	7	5	13	25
Home economics	15	3	2	20
Mechanic and industrial arts	9	...	1	10
Music	5	7	11	23
Nursing	4	...	...	4
Pharmacy	2	...	...	2
Theology	4	2	4	10

Source: "Number of Colleges and Universities for Negroes that Offer Instruction in Various Fields of Professional and Technical Education, not Including Instruction on the Graduate Level Except in Theology," U.S. Office of Education. *National Survey of the Higher Education of Negroes.* Vol. 1, No. 6. *Socio-Economic Approach to Educational Problems*, 1942, p. 51. Primary source: U.S. Office of Education. *National Survey of the Higher Education of Negroes.* Vol. 1, No. 6. *Socio-Economic Approach to Educational Problems*, by Ida Corinne Brown. Washington, D.C.: U.S. Government Printing Office, 1942.

★ 712 ★

Higher Education

Curricula/Programs: Undergraduate Fields Available to Blacks and Whites in States with Segregation, 1939-40 - I

Type of institution, by field of specialization[1]	Alabama		Arkansas		Delaware		District of Columbia	
	W[2]	N	W	N	W	N	W	N
Arts and science:								
Public	33	6	25	6	19	8	9	8
All[3]	33	16	27	15	19	8	28	25
Educational:								
Public	10	5	15	4	8	5	3	3
All	10	9	16	7	8	5	8	8
Commercial:								
Public	11	...	7	...	2	...	...	...
All	11	1	7	1	2	...	2	1
Agricultural:								
Public	14	2	8	2	5	3	...	...
All	14	9	8	2	5	3	...	...
Home economics:								
Public	9	2	4	2	4	5	...	...
All	9	4	4	2	4	5	1	2
Engineering and architectural:								
Public	21	...	4	...	4	...	...	...
All	21	2	6	...	4	...	3	3
Trades:								
Public	...	5	...	...	...	5	...	...
All	...	16	6	...	...	5	...	...

Source: "Number of Undergraduate Fields of Specialization Available in Institutions of Higher Education in States Maintaining Separate Institutions, 1939-40," *National Survey of the Higher Education of Negroes.* Vol. 1, No. 6, *Socio-Economic Approach to Educational Problems,* 1942, p. 10. Primary source: U.S. Office of Education. *National Survey of the Higher Education of Negroes.* Vol. 1, No. 6. *Socio-Economic Approach to Educational Problems,* by Ida Corinne Brown. Washington, D.C.: U.S. Government Printing Office, 1942. *Notes:* 1. This table to be read as follows: Alabama - In Arts and Science, 33 fields of specialization are available in public colleges and universities for white persons and 33 fields in both the public and private institutions; 6 fields of specialization are available in public higher institutions for Negroes and 16 fields in both the public and private institutions. 2. W for white; N for Negro 3. Includes both public and private institutions.

★ 713 ★

Higher Education

Curricula/Programs: Undergraduate Fields Available to Blacks and Whites in States with Segregation, 1939-40 - II

Type of institution, by field of specialization[1]	Florida		Georgia		Kentucky		Louisiana		Maryland	
	W	N	W	N	W	N	W	N	W	N
Arts and science:										
Public	29	12	26	7	31	14	30	9	22	16
All[3]	29	12	26	21	31	14	30	27	22	16
Educational:										
Public	14	8	9	4	11	6	13	11	8	10

[Continued]

★ 713 ★

Curricula/Programs: Undergraduate Fields Available to Blacks and Whites in States with Segregation, 1939-40 - II
[Continued]

Type of institution, by field of specialization[1]	Florida		Georgia		Kentucky		Louisiana		Maryland	
	W	N	W	N	W	N	W	N	W	N
All	14	8	9	7	11	6	13	11	8	10
Commercial:										
Public	3	...	7	2	5	...	9	2	4	1
All	3	...	7	2	5	...	9	2	4	1
Agricultural:										
Public	15	3	15	1	13	1	16	2	16	2
All	15	3	15	1	13	1	16	3	16	2
Home economics:										
Public	7	2	7	3	4	1	3	5	6	2
All	7	3	7	4	4	1	3	5	6	2
Engineering and architectural:										
Public	7	...	12	...	9	...	9	...	4	...
All	7	...	12	...	9	...	9	...	5	...
Trades:										
Public	...	13	...	8	...	...	...	4	...	...
All	...	13	...	8	...	...	...	4	...	...

Source: "Number of Undergraduate Fields of Specialization Available in Institutions of Higher Education in States Maintaining Separate Institutions, 1939-40," *National Survey of the Higher Education of Negroes.* Vol. 1, No. 6, *Socio-Economic Approach to Educational Problems,* 1942, p. 10. Primary source: U.S. Office of Education. *National Survey of the Higher Education of Negroes.* Vol. 1, No. 6. *Socio-Economic Approach to Educational Problems,* by Ida Corinne Brown. Washington, D.C.: U.S. Government Printing Office, 1942. *Notes:* 1. This table to be read as follows: Alabama - In Arts and Science, 33 fields of specialization are available in public colleges and universities for white persons and 33 fields in both the public and private institutions; 6 fields of specialization are available in public higher institutions for Negroes and 16 fields in both the public and private institutions. 2. W for white; N for Negro 3. Includes both public and private institutions.

★ 714 ★

Higher Education

Curricula/Programs: Undergraduate Fields Available to Blacks and Whites in States with Segregation, 1939-40 - III

Type of institution, by field of specialization	Mississippi		Missouri		North Carolina		Oklahoma		South Carolina	
	W	N	W	N	W	N	W	N	W	N
Arts and science:										
Public	28	9	31	18	30	16	31	11	24	6
All[3]	28	16	31	18	30	22	31	11	24	14
Educational:										
Public	9	7	15	6	13	11	10	9	12	7
All	9	7	15	6	13	11	10	9	12	7
Commercial:										
Public	7	2	6	2	9	2	7	1	5	1
All	7	2	6	2	9	2	7	1	5	1
Agricultural:										
Public	15	2	14	...	20	5	19	3	8	2
All	15	2	14	...	20	5	19	3	8	2

[Continued]

★ 714 ★

Curricula/Programs: Undergraduate Fields Available to Blacks and Whites in States with Segregation, 1939-40 - III

[Continued]

Type of institution, by field of specialization	Mississippi		Missouri		North Carolina		Oklahoma		South Carolina	
	W	N	W	N	W	N	W	N	W	N
Home economics:										
Public	4	2	5	2	8	2	12	1	2	1
All	4	3	5	2	8	3	12	1	2	2
Engineering and architectural:										
Public	7	...	9	...	20	3	18	1	11	...
All	7	...	9	...	20	3	18	1	11	...
Trades:										
Public	...	1	...	...	...	7	6	8	...	3
All	...	1	...	...	...	7	6	8	...	3

Source: "Number of Undergraduate Fields of Specialization Available in Institutions of Higher Education in States Maintaining Separate Institutions, 1939-40," *National Survey of the Higher Education of Negroes.* Vol. 1, No. 6, *Socio-Economic Approach to Educational Problems,* 1942, p. 10. Primary source: U.S. Office of Education. *National Survey of the Higher Education of Negroes.* Vol. 1, No. 6. *Socio-Economic Approach to Educational Problems,* by Ida Corinne Brown. Washington, D.C.: U.S. Government Printing Office, 1942. *Notes:* 1. This table to be read as follows: Alabama - In Arts and Science, 33 fields of specialization are available in public colleges and universities for white persons and 33 fields in both the public and private institutions; 6 fields of specialization are available in public higher institutions for Negroes and 16 fields in both the public and private institutions. 2. W for white; N for Negro 3. Includes both public and private institutions.

★ 715 ★

Higher Education

Curricula/Programs: Undergraduate Fields Available to Blacks and Whites in States with Segregation, 1939-40 - IV

Type of institution, by field of specialization	Tennessee		Texas		Virginia		West Virginia		Median	
	W	N	W	N	W	N	W	N	W	N
Arts and science:										
Public	26	8	34	16	30	14	29	18	29	10
All[3]	28	22	34	22	30	16	29	19	29	16
Educational:										
Public	12	7	14	8	13	11	12	10	12	7
All	19	9	14	9	13	11	12	10	12	8
Commercial:										
Public	8	1	18	2	3	2	2	2	6.5	1
All	8	1	18	2	3	2	2	2	6.5	1
Agricultural:										
Public	13	2	16	4	11	4	6	3	14	2
All	13	2	16	4	11	5	6	3	14	2.5
Home economics:										
Public	8	1	9	4	8	4	7	2	6.5	2
All	8	2	9	5	8	5	7	2	6.5	2.5
Engineering and architectural:										
Public	6	...	15	1	13	...	15	...	9	0
All	6	...	15	1	13	...	15	...	9	0

[Continued]

★ 715 ★

Curricula/Programs: Undergraduate Fields Available to Blacks and Whites in States with Segregation, 1939-40 - IV
[Continued]

Type of institution, by field of specialization	Tennessee		Texas		Virginia		West Virginia		Median	
	W	N	W	N	W	N	W	N	W	N
Trades:										
Public	...	...	...	14	...	6	...	4	0	4
All	...	...	...	14	...	15	...	4	0	4

Source: "Number of Undergraduate Fields of Specialization Available in Institutions of Higher Education in States Maintaining Separate Institutions, 1939-40," *National Survey of the Higher Education of Negroes.* Vol. 1, No. 6, *Socio-Economic Approach to Educational Problems*, 1942, p. 10. Primary source: U.S. Office of Education. *National Survey of the Higher Education of Negroes.* Vol. 1, No. 6. *Socio-Economic Approach to Educational Problems*, by Ida Corinne Brown. Washington, D.C.: U.S. Government Printing Office, 1942. *Notes:* 1. This table to be read as follows: Alabama - In Arts and Science, 33 fields of specialization are available in public colleges and universities for white persons and 33 fields in both the public and private institutions; 6 fields of specialization are available in public higher institutions for Negroes and 16 fields in both the public and private institutions. 2. W for white; N for Negro 3. Includes both public and private institutions.

★ 716 ★

Higher Education

Degrees Awarded to Black Students, 1929-30 and 1939-40

Number of degrees granted	1929-30	1939-40
Arts and sciences		
Men	665	1,733
Women	587	2,089
Professional		
Men	266	730
Women	171	1,155
Master's		
Men	11	94
Women	4	94
Honorary	21	45

Source: "College and University Statistics: 1929-30—1939-40," *The Negro Handbook, 1944*, 1944, p. 56. Primary source: Murray, Florence (Ed.), *The Negro Handbook, 1944*. New York: Current Reference Publications, 1944. Published by permission.

★ 717 ★

Higher Education

Degrees: Bachelor's and Master's Degrees Conferred by Black Institutions, 1900-1950

Year	Bachelor's Degree			Master's Degree		
	Men	Women	Total	Men	Women	Total
1900	134^2	22	156	1^1	1^1	1^1
1910	233^3	277^2	510^2	1^1	1^1	1^1
1920	818	191^3	$1,009^3$	4^3	1^3	5^3
1930	$1,200^3$	977^3	$2,177^3$	14^3	5^3	19^3
1940	2,463	3,244	5,707	58	94	152
1942	2,011	4,414	6,425	22	75	97
1944	840	4,036	4,876	46	86	132
1946	1,165	4,741	5,906	88	223	311
1948	3,062	5,442	8,504	184	249	433
1949	4,692	6,618	11,310	242	405	647
1950	6,467	6,641	13,108	335	433	768

Source: "Historical Summary of Earned Degrees Conferred, 1900 to 1950," *1952 Negro Year Book: A Review of Events Affecting Negro Life*, 1952, p. 218. Primary source: U.S. Office of Education, *Statistical Circular No. 293*, April 1951. *Notes:* 1. Data not available. 2. Includes 120 men and 28 women taking the bachelor's degree, and 113 men and 249 women taking normal school diplomas. 3. Estimated.

★ 718 ★

Higher Education

Degrees: Bachelor's, Master's, and Doctor of Philosophy Degrees Awarded Black Students in June 1941

Degree	BLACK SCHOOLS		WHITE SCHOOLS[1]	
	Number Enrolled	Number Graduates	Number Enrolled	Number Graduates
Bachelor's	37,203	4,181	2,790	273
Master's: Total Graduates, Black and and White Schools				310
Doctor of Philosophy	---	---	[2]	10

Source: Adapted by the editors from "College Enrollments and Graduates for June, 1941," *The Negro Handbook*, 1942, pp. 117-118. Primary source: The *Crisis* Magazine Poll, published in the August, 1941 issue. *Notes:* 1. Figures are not complete because some white schools that enroll black students do not keep records by race. 2. Information not given.

★ 719 ★

Higher Education

Degrees: Master's Degrees Conferred by Black Institutions, 1949-50

Institution	Master's Degrees Conferred 1949-50	
	Men	Women
A. & T. College of N. Carolina	3	8
Alabama State Teachers College	20	42
Atlanta University	72	108
Bishop College	-	-
Florida A. & M. College	2	2
FisK University	13	11
Hampton Institute	13	27
Howard University	52	58
Lincoln University (Mo.)	-	-
N. Carolina College at Durham	25	15
Prairie View A. & M. College	41	25
State A. & M. College of S. Carolina	6	5
Tennessee A. & I. State College (now Tennessee State University)	19	5
Texas State University for Negroes (now Texas Southern University)	38	86
Tuskegee Institute	18	13
Virginia State College	9	17
Xavier University	4	7

Source: "Negro Institutions Offering Graduate Work, Degrees Conferred 1949-50 and Enrolled 1950-51," *1952 Negro Year Book: A Review of Events Affecting Negro Life*, 1952, p. 219. Primary source: U.S. Office of Education, *Statistical Circular No. 293*, April 1951, and questionnaire.

★ 720 ★

Higher Education

Degrees: Range of Number of Degrees Offered by 25 Selected Black Institutions, c. 1939

Number of degrees offered	Number of institutions offering the degrees
1	2
2	8
3	6
4	2
7	3

[Continued]

★ 720 ★

Degrees: Range of Number of Degrees Offered by 25 Selected Black Institutions, c. 1939

[Continued]

Number of degrees offered	Number of institutions offering the degrees
9	3
19	1

Source: "Twenty-five Colleges and Universities for Negroes Distributed According to the Number of Different Degrees Offered," *National Survey of the Higher Education of Negroes.* Vol. 1, No. 6. *Socio-Economic Approach to Educational Problems,* 1942, p. 54. Primary source: U.S. Office of Education. *National Survey of the Higher Education of Negroes.* Vol. 1, No. 6. *Socio-Economic Approach to Educational Problems,* by Ida Corinne Brown. Washington, D.C.: U.S. Government Printing Office, 1942.

★ 721 ★

Higher Education

Degrees: Specific Degrees Offered by 25 Selected Black Institutions, c. 1939

Degree	Number of institutions conferring the degree
Arts and Sciences:	
Bachelor of Arts	22
Bachelor of Science	19
Bachelor of Philosophy	1
Technical and Professional Fields:	
Bachelor of Divinity	4
Bachelor of Music	3
Bachelor of Laws	2
Bachelor of Theology	2
Doctor of Medicine	1
Doctor of Dental Surgery	1
Bachelor of Public School Music	1
Bachelor of Arts in Education	2
Bachelor of Arts in Fine Arts	1
Bachelor of Science in Home Economics	9
Bachelor of Science in Education	6
Bachelor of Science in Agriculture	4
Bachelor of Science in Agricultural Education	2
Bachelor of Science in Art	2
Bachelor of Science in Commercial Education	2
Bachelor of Science in Elementary Education	2
Bachelor of Science in Industrial Arts	2

[Continued]

★ 721 ★

Degrees: Specific Degrees Offered by 25 Selected Black Institutions, c. 1939

[Continued]

Degree	Number of institutions conferring the degree
Bachelor of Science in Mechanic Arts	2
Bachelor of Science in Physical Education	2
Bachelor of Science in Animal Husbandry	1
Bachelor of Science in Architecture	1
Bachelor of Science in Business Administration	1
Bachelor of Science in Civil Engineering	1
Bachelor of Science in Commerce	1
Bachelor of Science in Commercial Dietetics	1
Bachelor of Science in Electrical Engineering	1
Bachelor of Science in Health and Physical Education	1
Bachelor of Science in Industrial Engineering	1
Bachelor of Science in Mechanical Engineering	1
Bachelor of Science in Nursing	1
Bachelor of Science in Pharmacy	1
Bachelor of Science in Public School Music	1
Bachelor of Science in Secondary Education	1
Bachelor of Science in Vocational Home Economics	1
Graduate Study:	
Master of Arts	3
Master of Science	2
Master of Arts in Education	1

Source: "Degrees Offered by 25 Colleges and Universities for Negroes and Number of Institutions Offering Each Degree," *National Survey of the Higher Education of Negroes.* Vol. 1, No. 6. *Socio-Economic Approach to Educational Problems,* 1942, p. 54. Primary source: U.S. Office of Education. *National Survey of the Higher Education of Negroes.* Vol. 1, No. 6. *Socio-Economic Approach to Educational Problems,* by Ida Corinne Brown. Washington, D.C.: U.S. Government Printing Office, 1942.

★ 722 ★

Higher Education

Enrollment: 14-34-Year-Olds Enrolled in College, by Gender, 1964-1974

[In thousands. As of October. Covers Civilian noninstitutional population]

SEX AND RACE	1964	1965	1966	1967	1968	1969	1970	1971	1972	1973	1974
Total, all races	4,643	5,675	6,085	6,401	6,801	7,435	7,413	8,087	8,313	8,179	8,827
Male	2,888	3,503	3,749	3,841	4,124	4,448	4,401	4,850	4,853	4,677	4,926
Female	1,755	2,172	2,337	2,560	2,677	2,987	3,013	3,236	3,460	3,502	3,901
White	4,337	5,317	5,708	5,905	6,255	6,827	6,759	7,273	7,458	7,324	7,781
Male	2,720	3,326	3,536	3,560	3,843	4,146	4,066	4,407	4,397	4,218	4,367
Female	1,617	1,991	2,172	2,345	2,412	2,681	2,693	2,867	3,061	3,105	3,413

[Continued]

★ 722 ★

Enrollment: 14-34-Year-Olds Enrolled in College, by Gender, 1964-1974

[Continued]

SEX AND RACE	1964	1965	1966	1967	1968	1969	1970	1971	1972	1973	1974
Negro	234	274	282	370	434	492	522	680	727	684	814
Male	120	126	154	199	221	236	253	363	384	358	422
Female	114	148	128	171	213	256	269	317	343	326	392

Source: "College Enrollment of the Population 14 to 34 Years Old, by Sex and Race: 1964 to 1974," *Statistical Abstract of the United States, 1975*, p. 137. Primary source: U.S. Bureau of the Census, *Current Population Reports*, series P-20, No. 278.

★ 723 ★

Higher Education

Enrollment: 16- to 34-Year-Olds Enrolled in Postsecondary School by Type of School, 1973

Numbers in thousands.

Subject	All races	Black	White
PERSONS 16 TO 34 YEARS OLD			
Total	61,546	7,152	53,464
Postsecondary students	8,524	678	7,659
Percent of total	14	9	14
Enrolled in college	7,354	549	6,639
University	4,032	252	3,698
4-year college	1,570	134	1,386
2-year college	1,752	163	1,555
Enrolled in vocational education school	1,170	128	1,020
Postsecondary Students			
Total	8,524	678	7,659
Percent	100	100	100
Enrolled in college	86	81	87
University	47	37	48
4-year college	18	20	18
2-year college	21	24	20
Enrolled in vocational education school	14	19	13
College students, excluding university			
Total	3,322	297	2,941
Percent	100	100	100
Enrolled in a 4-year college	47	45	47
Public	25	36	23
Private	21	8	23
Enrolled in 2-year college	53	55	53

[Continued]

★ 723 ★

Enrollment: 16- to 34-Year-Olds Enrolled in Postsecondary School by Type of School, 1973
[Continued]

Subject	All races	Black	White
Public	48	47	48
Private	3	5	3

Source: "Postsecondary Enrollment of Persons 16 to 34 Years Old, by type of School: 1973," Current Population Reports, Special Studies, Series P-23, No. 54, *The Social and Economic Status of the Black Population in the United States, 1974,* 1975, p. 99. Primary source: U.S. Department of Commerce, Social and Economic Statistics Administration, Bureau of the Census.

★ 724 ★

Higher Education

Enrollment: 18-24-Year-Olds In or Not in College, by Gender and Race, 1950-1975
[Numbers in thousands]

Enrollment status, sex, and race	1950[1]	1960[1]	1970	1975
BLACK				
Total men, 18 to 24 years	839	887	1,220	1,451
Number enrolled in college	41	63	192	294
Percent of total	5	7	16	20
Number enrolled below college level	95	131	116	148
Percent of total	11	15	10	10
Total women, 18 to 24 years	965	978	1,471	1,761
Number enrolled in college	42	66	225	372
Percent of total	4	7	15	21
Number enrolled below college level	74	111	77	106
Percent of total	8	11	5	6
WHITE				
Total men, 18 to 24 years	6,856	6,688	9,053	11,050
Number enrolled in college	1,025	1,267	3,096	3,326
Percent of total	15	19	34	30
Number enrolled below college level	622	664	429	420
Percent of total	9	10	5	4
Total women, 18 to 24 years	7,118	6,921	10,555	11,653
Number enrolled in college	558	811	2,209	2,790
Percent of total	8	12	21	24

[Continued]

★ 724 ★

Enrollment: 18-24-Year-Olds In or Not in College, by Gender and Race, 1950-1975
[Continued]

Enrollment status, sex, and race	1950[1]	1960[1]	1970	1975
Number enrolled below college level	425	474	246	250
Percent of total	6	7	2	2

Source: "Persons 18 to 24 Years Old Enrolled in College or Below College Level, by Sex: 1950, 1960, 1970, and 1975," *The Social and Economic Status of the Black Population in the United States: An Historical View, 1790-1978,* 1979, p. 90. Primary source: U.S. Department of Commerce, Bureau of the Census. *Note:* 1. Data for Black include persons of "other" races.

★ 725 ★

Higher Education

Enrollment: Average Enrollment in Black Institutions by State, 1922-23 through 1926-27

State	Number institutions	Average enrollment[1]					Average No.[2]	
							Women	Men
		1922	1923	1924	1925	1926	1926-27	1926-27
Alabama	4	64	57	68	91	105	50	53
Arkansas	3	35	38	35	37	34	13	7
Delaware	1	-	-	1	1	19	5	-
District of Columbia	1	1,761	1,667	1,813	2,063	2,268	798	1,470
Florida	3	52	60	22	41	54	28	26
Georgia	9	106	137	139	147	153	61	101
Kentucky	2	48	20	50	39	36	12	23
Louisiana	5	22	28	26	49	56	25	33
Maryland	2	131	190	203	196	194	119	150
Mississippi	5	22	28	26	49	56	25[2]	33[2]
Missouri	1	87	117	132	170	181	91	90
North Carolina	12	58	63	80	83	112	64	57
Ohio	1	497	559	557	586	549	239	310
Oklahoma	1	117	148	196	234	240	172	68
Pennsylvania	2	152	158	170	188	198	81	158
South Carolina	5	91	119	120	136	138	70	68
Tennessee	8	134	159	163	170	216	98	84
Texas	8	92	127	155	175	218	125	95
Virginia	4	145	179	185	250	325	151	162
West Virginia	1	140	199	233	312	370	209	173
Total	78	122	136	146	180	207	95	123

Source: Compiled and adapted by the editors from "Enrollment of Students in Negro Colleges, 1922-1927," *Survey of Negro Colleges and Universities.* Bulletin, 1928, No. 7, 1929, pp. 946-947. Primary source: U.S. Bureau of Education. *Survey of Negro Colleges and Universities.* Bulletin, 1928, No. 7, Washington, D.C.: Government Printing Office, 1929. *Notes:* 1. Average based on only those institutions that furnished data. 2. Averages based on coeducational schools and those that furnished enrollment data.

★ 726 ★

Higher Education

Enrollment: Black Freshmen and Seniors in 1936-37 by Age and Gender

Age in years	Number of seniors			Age in years	Number of freshmen		
	Total	Male	Female		Total	Male	Female
18	4	1	3	Under 15	2	-	2
19	66	16	50	15	20	8	12
20	194	41	153	16	161	48	113
21	325	101	224	17	605	175	430
22	310	140	170	18	1,174	414	760
23	225	121	104	19	927	401	526
24	126	85	41	20	582	332	250
25	82	58	24	21	269	184	85
26 or older	150	80	70	22 and over	284	176	108

Source: "Distribution of Negro College Freshmen and Seniors, according to Age and Sex," *National Survey of the Higher Education of Negroes.* Vol. 1, No. 6. *Socio-Economic Approach to Educational Problems,* 1942, p. 44. Primary source: U.S. Office of Education. *National Survey of the Higher Education of Negroes.* Vol. 1, No. 6. *Socio-Economic Approach to Educational Problems,* by Ida Corinne Brown. Washington, D.C.: U.S. Government Printing Office, 1942.

★ 727 ★

Higher Education

Enrollment: Black Students in Colleges and Universities by Type and Level of Study, 1929-30 and 1939-40

Number of students	1929-30	1939-40
Regular session		
Total, excluding duplicates		
Men	11,823	20,111
Women	14,487	28,503
Preparatory		
Boys	2,268	1,140
Girls	2,989	1,599
Collegiate		
Men	5,478	12,487
Women	4,825	16,665
Graduate		
Men	34	304
Women	22	367
Professional		
Men	4,069	6,216
Women	6,659	9,879
Summer schools		
Men	2,633	5,105

[Continued]

★ 727 ★

Enrollment: Black Students in Colleges and Universities by Type and Level of Study, 1929-30 and 1939-40
[Continued]

Number of students	1929-30	1939-40
Women	12,802	20,695
Extension and correspondence courses		
Men	1,110	2,094
Women	5,268	8,300
Laboratory schools		
Elementary		
Boys	1,236	1,190
Girls	1,386	1,497
Secondary		
Boys	744	233
Girls	789	340
Short courses		
Men	-	2,803
Women	-	1,760

Source: "College and University Statistics: 1929-30—1939-40," *The Negro Handbook, 1944,* 1944, p. 56. Primary source: Murray, Florence (Ed.), *The Negro Handbook, 1944.* New York: Current Reference Publications, 1944. Published by permission.

★ 728 ★

Higher Education

Enrollment: Blacks in Black Colleges, 1964 and 1968

Numbers in thousands.

	1964 (Fall)	1968 (Fall)	Change, 1964-68 Number	Change, 1964-68 Percent
Total enrollment	4,643	6,801	2,158	46
Total Negro enrollment	234	434	200	85
Percent of total enrollment	5	6	(X)	(X)
Enrollment in predominantly Negro colleges	120	156	36	30
Percent of all Negroes in college	51	36	(X)	(X)
Enrollment in other colleges	114	278	164	144
Percent of all Negroes in college	49	64	(X)	(X)

Source: "Negro College Students Enrolled in 1964 and 1968, by Type of Institution," Current Population Reports, Special Studies, Series P-23, No. 29. *The Social and Economic Status of the Black Population in the United States, 1969,* 1969, p. 53. Primary source: U.S. Department of labor, Bureau of Labor Statistics; U.S. Department of Commerce, Bureau of the Census; U.S. Department of Health, Education, and Welfare, Office of Education. *Note:* X Not applicable.

★ 729 ★
Higher Education

Enrollment: Blacks in Predominantly Minority and Predominantly Non-Minority Institutions by Region, 1970

Subject	Total	North and west	South[1]
Total, enrolled	356,836	161,580	195,256
Enrolled in predominantly minority institutions	158,500	31,181	127,319
Percent of total	44.4	19.3	65.2
Enrolled in other institutions (not predominantly minority)	198,336	130,399	67,937
Percent of total	55.6	80.7	34.8

Source: "Black Undergraduate Students Enrolled in College, by type and region of Institution: 1970," Current Population Reports, Special Studies, Series P- 23, No. 42. *The Social and Economic Status of the Black Population in the United States, 1971,* 1972, p. 88. Primary source: Department of Health, Education, and Welfare, Office for Civil Rights. *Notes:* 1. Includes the state of Missouri, not regularly included in census standard definition of the south.

★ 730 ★
Higher Education

Enrollment: Comparison of Freshman and Senior Enrollment for Two College Generations in the 1930s

Institution	Freshmen, 1930-31	Seniors, 1933-34	Percent seniors in 1930-31 were of freshmen in 1933-34	Freshmen, 1933-34	Seniors, 1936-37	Percent seniors in 1936-37 were of freshmen in 1933-34	Freshmen, 1936-37	Seniors, 1939-40	Percent seniors in 1939-40 were of freshmen in 1936-37
A	51	23	45	64	37	58	104	46	44
B	103	27	26	66	44	67	133	66	50
C	179	61	34	103	35	34	164	83	51
D	57	22	39	93	44	47	251	58	23
E	626	198	32	304	209	69	521	258	50
F	167	52	31	189	142	75	293	190	65
G	94	58	62	46	75	163	77	119	155
H	-	-	-	-	-	-	174	119	68
I	116	35	30	108	40	37	152	73	48
J	123	65	53	195	103	53	350	170	49
K	65	9	5	78	13	17	146	38	26
L	-	-	-	-	-	-	-	-	-
M	31	27	87	61	54	89	168	110	65
N	82	33	40	165	39	24	175	53	30
O	14	31	221	58	29	50	124	52	42
P	47	31	66	59	39	66	72	37	51
Q	39	22	56	65	51	78	123	70	57
R	106	83	78	131	70	53	147	133	90

[Continued]

★ 730 ★

Enrollment: Comparison of Freshman and Senior Enrollment for Two College Generations in the 1930s
[Continued]

Institution	Freshmen, 1930-31	Seniors, 1933-34	Percent seniors in 1930-31 were of freshmen in 1933-34	Freshmen, 1933-34	Seniors, 1936-37	Percent seniors in 1936-37 were of freshmen in 1933-34	Freshmen, 1936-37	Seniors, 1939-40	Percent seniors in 1939-40 were of freshmen in 1936-37
S	59	22	37	60	42	70	117	72	62
T	377	152	40	244	237	97	454	273	60
U	244	63	26	367	114	31	482	182	38
V	208	83	40	221	70	32	158	76	48
W	-	-	-	-	-	-	-	-	-
X	253	122	48	142	134	94	254	133	52
Y	149	55	37	137	60	44	297	106	36
Total	3,190	1,264	40	2,956	1,681	57	4,936	2,517	51

Source: "Freshmen and Seniors Enrolled in Stated Years in 23 Colleges and Universities for Negroes," *National Survey of the Higher Education of Negroes.* Vol. 1, No. 6. *Socio-Economic Approach to Educational Problems,* 1942, p. 49. Primary source: U.S. Office of Education. *National Survey of the Higher Education of Negroes.* Vol. 1, No. 6. *Socio-Economic Approach to Educational Problems,* by Ida Corinne Brown. Washington, D.C.: U.S. Government Printing Office, 1942.

★ 731 ★

Higher Education

Enrollment: Enrollment in Black Colleges in 1938-39, by Student State of Residence

State	Total enrollment in Negro colleges within the State 1938-39	Enrollment resident within the State		Enrollment resident in other Southern States		Enrollment resident outside of South[1]	
		Number	Percent	Number	Percent	Number	Percent
Alabama	3,238	1,930	59.6	977	30.1	319	9.8
Arkansas	959	786	82.0	121	12.6	51	5.3
Delaware	96	67	69.8	25	26.0	4	4.2
District of Columbia	2,141	1,428	66.7	290	13.5	388	18.1
Florida	1,636	1,514	92.5	79	4.8	43	2.6
Georgia[2]	3,121	2,290	73.4	533	17.1	229	7.3
Kentucky	869	788	90.7	23	2.6	58	6.7
Louisiana	2,361	2,053	87.0	230	9.7	70	3.0
Maryland	912	790	86.6	49	5.4	73	8.0
Mississippi[3]	950	744	78.3	52	5.5	16	1.7
Missouri[4]	866	718	81.0	41	4.6	119	13.4
North Carolina	4,724	3,760	79.6	642	13.6	319	6.7
Oklahoma[5]	1,474	1,174	70.6	35	2.4	15	1.0
South Carolina	2,253	2,131	94.6	84	3.7	38	1.7
Tennessee	2,654	1,767	66.6	537	20.2	343	12.9

[Continued]

★ 731 ★

Enrollment: Enrollment in Black Colleges in 1938-39, by Student State of Residence
[Continued]

State	Total enrollment in Negro colleges within the State 1938-39	Enrollment resident within the State		Enrollment resident in other Southern States		Enrollment resident outside of South[1]	
		Number	Percent	Number	Percent	Number	Percent
Texas[6]	4,218	3,479	82.5	271	6.4	91	2.1
Virginia[7]	2,936	1,664	56.7	602	20.5	555	18.9
West Virginia	1,275	913	71.6	196	15.4	166	13.0
Total	36,703	27,996	76.3	4,787	13.0	2,897	7.9

Source: "Enrollment in Negro Colleges and Place of Residence Distributed According to States, U.S. Office of Education. *National Survey of the Higher Education of Negroes.* Vol. 1, No. 6, *Socio-Economic Approach to Educational Problems,* 1942, p. 84. Primary source: U.S. Office of Education. *National Survey of the Higher Education for Negroes.* Vol. 1, No. 6. *Socio-Economic Approach to Educational Problems,* by Ida Corrine Brown. Washington, D.C.: U.S. Government Printing Office, 1942. *Notes:* 1. Does not include 105 students from outside the United States. This table is based on data supplied the U.S. Office of Education by the Negro College in each State. 2. Total includes 63 students whose residence was not given. 3. Total includes 136 students whose residence was not given. 4. Total includes 8 students whose residence was not given. 5. Total includes 200 students whose residence was not given. 6. Total includes 375 students whose residence was not given. 7. Total includes 103 students whose residence was not given.

★ 732 ★

Higher Education

Enrollment: Enrollment in Predominantly Black Institutions, by Type of Institution, 1964-1973

[In thousands.]

ENROLLMENT	1964[1]	1968	1969	1970	1971	1972	1973
Total	105.5	108.3	188.2	207.9	236.6	246.2	247.7
Public:							
2-year	4.3	23.1	24.3	33.0	49.8	53.7	53.2
4-year	60.7	99.6	106.9	115.8	124.6	130.3	132.7
Private:							
2-year	1.9	2.3	2.3	2.6	2.6	2.6	2.4
4-year	38.6	55.3	54.7	56.6	59.6	59.6	59.4

Source: "Institutions of Higher Education Attended Predominantly by Negroes—Enrollment, by Type: 1964 to 1973," *Statistical Abstract of the United States, 1975,* p. 139. Primary source: U.S. National Center for Education Statistics *Report on Higher Education, and Digest of Educational Statistics,* annual. *Notes:* 1. Enrollment figures represent resident degree-credit students, regular session, only.

★ 733 ★

Higher Education

Enrollment: Gender Distribution of Black Undergraduate Enrollment in Selected Public and Private Colleges, 1910-1940

Type of institution	1910			1920			1930			1940[1]		
	Total	Male	Female	Total	Male	Female	Total	Male	Female	Total	Male	Female
Public	960	506	454	677	310	367	5,763	2,233	3,530	13,147	5,963	7,184
Percent	...	53	47	...	46	54	...	39	61	...	45	55
Percent increase	...	...	...	-29[2]	...	...	+751	...	...	+128	...	...
Private	1,790	1,529	261	3,383	2,375	1,008	7,809	4,452	3,357	8,561	4,429	4,132
Percent	...	85	15	...	70	30	...	57	43	...	52	48
Percent increase	...	...	...	+89	...	...	+131	...	...	+10	...	...
Total	2,750[3]	2,035	715	4,060	2,685	1,375	13,572	6,685	6,887	21,708	10,392	11,316
Percent	...	74	26	...	66	34	...	49	51	...	48	52
Percent increase	...	...	...	+48	...	...	+234	...	...	+60	...	...

Source: "Undergraduate College Enrollment in 20 Public and 16 Private Colleges, 1910-40, Distributed According to Sex," U.S. Office of Education. *National Survey of the Higher Education of Negroes.* Vol. No. 6. *Socio-Economic Approach to Educational Problems,* 1942, p. 4. Primary source: U.S. Office of Education. *National Survey of the Higher Education for Negroes.* Vol. 1, No. 6. *Socio-Economic Approach to Educational Problems,* Washington, D.C.: U.S. Government Printing Office, 1942. *Notes:* 1. From Enrollment in Institutions of Higher Education of Negroes, 1940- 41, by Martin D. Jenkins. Journal of Negro Education, 10: 718, October 1941. 2. This abnormal decrease is attributable to a more accurate classification of students than in 1910 when undoubtedly the college enrollment lists contained many names of students below that level. 3. Totals in this column probably include some high-school and professional students.

★ 734 ★

Higher Education

Enrollment: Gender of 18 to 24-Year-Olds Enrolled in College, 1965, 1970, 1971, and 1974

Gender and college enrollment	Black				White			
	1965	1970	1971	1974	1965	1970	1971	1974
Both sexes								
Total persons, 18 to 24 years	2,041	2,692	2,866	3,105	16,505	19,608	20,533	22,141
Number enrolled in college	210	416	522	555	4,213	5,305	5,594	5,589
Percent of total	10	15	18	18	26	27	27	25
Male								
Total persons, 18 to 24 years	935	1,220	1,318	1,396	7,641	9,053	9,653	10,722
Number enrolled in college	99	192	262	280	2,593	3,096	3,284	3,035
Percent of total	11	16	20	20	34	34	34	28
Female								
Total persons, 18 to 24 years	1,106	1,471	1,547	1,709	8,864	10,555	10,880	11,419

[Continued]

★ 734 ★

Enrollment: Gender of 18 to 24-Year-Olds Enrolled in College, 1965, 1970, 1971, and 1974

[Continued]

Gender and college enrollment	Black				White			
	1965	1970	1971	1974	1965	1970	1971	1974
Number enrolled in college	111	225	259	277	1,620	2,209	2,310	2,555
Percent of total	10	15	17	16	18	21	21	22

Source: Adapted by the editors from "College Enrollment of Persons 18 to 24 Years Old, by Sex: 1965 and 1971," Current Population Reports, Special Studies, Series P-23, No. 42. *The Social and Economic Status of the Black Population in the United States, 1971,* 1972, p. 85; and "College Enrollment of Persons 18 to 24 Years Old by Sex: 1970 and 1974," Current Population Reports, Special Studies, Series P-23, No. 54. *The Social and Economic Status of the Black Population in the United States, 1974,* 1975, p. 94. Primary source: U.S. Department of Commerce, Social and Economic Statistics Administration, Bureau of the Census.

★ 735 ★

Higher Education

Enrollment: Minority College Enrollment, by Geographic Division, 1968

[**Enrollment in thousands.** As of fall. Excludes Alaska and Hawaii. Covers full-time undergraduate students taking credits equal to at least 75 percent of a normal load. Excludes federally controlled institutions.]

GEOGRAPHIC DIVISION	Number of institutions	Total enrollment	NEGRO ENROLLMENT		ENROLLMENT OF OTHER MINORITY GROUPS				
			Number	Percent	Total	Percent	American Indian	Oriental	Spanish surnamed
Total	2,054	4,820	287	6.0	169	3.5	29	48	91
New England	182	294	5	1.8	4	1.2	1	2	1
Middle Atlantic	309	685	23	3.3	14	2.0	2	5	7
East North Central	315	934	45	4.8	14	1.5	5	5	4
West North Central	256	477	12	2.4	8	1.6	3	3	2
South Atlantic	354	632	76	12.0	14	2.2	3	2	8
East South Central	153	290	41	14.0	3	0.9	1	1	1
West South Central	172	493	48	9.7	33	6.7	8	3	22
Mountain	86	263	3	1.2	18	6.8	3	3	12
Pacific	227	752	35	4.7	62	8.2	4	25	33

Source: "Enrollment in Institutions of Higher Education—Total and Specified Minority Groups, by Geographic Division: 1968," *Statistical Abstract of the United States, 1970,* p. 128. Primary source: Dept. of Health, Education, and Welfare, Office of Civil Rights; *Undergraduate Enrollment by Ethnic Group in Federally Funded Institutions of Higher Education,* Fall 1968.

★ 736 ★

Higher Education

Enrollment: Total and Veteran Enrollment in Black Colleges by Type and Control, 1947-48

College type	No. institutions	Total enrolled Fall, 1947-48	Vets, enrolled Fall, 1947-48	Percent veterans
Publicly controlled (with 4-yr. courses)	25	30,174	12,687	42.0
Privately controlled (with 4-yr. courses)	53	51,122	11,268	22.0
Teachers' colleges and normal schools (with 4-yr. courses)	13	7,155	1,659	23.2
Junior colleges and 2-yr. normal schools	17	2,757	793	28.8
Total	108	91,208	26,407	29.0

Source: Adapted and compiled by the editors from "Institutions of Higher Education for Negroes: 1947-48," *The Negro Handbook, 1949*, 1949, pp. 122-129. Primary source: United States Office of Education. Published by permission.

★ 737 ★

Higher Education

Entrance Criteria: Admissions Policies of Selected Black Colleges, c. 1942

Policy	Number of institutions	
	Public	Private
Selective admission which operates to exclude a large number of applicants	0	2
Selective admission which operates to exclude only a few applicants	1	1
None for selective admission, but occasionally excludes applicants whose high-school record is poor	0	3
Selective admission, but does not exclude applicants whose high-school record is poor	0	1
None for selective admission and does not exclude applicants whose high-school record is poor	11	6

Source: [Untitled Table], *National Survey of the Higher Education of Negroes*. Vol. 1, No. 6. *Socio-Economic Approach to Educational Problems*, 1942, p. 67. Primary source: U.S. Office of Education. *National Survey of the Higher Education of Negroes*. Vol. 1, No. 6. *Socio-Economic Approach to Educational Problems*, by Ida Corrine Brown. Washington, D.C.: U.S. Government Printing Office, 1942.

★ 738 ★

Higher Education

Entrance Criteria: Basis for Admission of Graduates from Unaccredited High Schools at Selected Black Institutions, c. 1942

	Number of institutions	
	Stated Policy	Actual Practice
Entrant must pass entrance examination	18	11
Entrant admitted on trial or placed on probation	4	3
Entrant admitted on same basic as graduates of accredited high school	2	10
Entrant required to take some additional high high-school subjects	4	1

Source: [Untitled Table], *National Survey of the Higher Education of Negroes.* Vol. 1, No. 6. *Socio-Economic Approach to Educational Problems,* 1942, p. 69. Primary source: U.S. Office of Education. *National Survey of the Higher Education of Negroes.* Vol. 1, No. 6. *Socio-Economic Approach to Educational Problems,* by Ida Corinne Brown. Washington, D.C.: U.S. Government Printing Office, 1942.

★ 739 ★

Higher Education

Entrance Criteria: Number of Tests Given on Entrance at Selected Black Colleges, c. 1942

Number of different tests administered	Number of institutions	Number of different tests administered	Number of institutions
6	1	3	3
5	2	2	11
4	5	1	1

Source: [Untitled Table], *National Survey of the Higher Education of Negroes.* Vol. 1, No. 6. *Socio-Economic Approach to Educational Problems,* 1942, p. 73. Primary source: U.S. Office of Education. *National Survey of the Higher Education of Negroes.* Vol. 1, No. 6. *Socio-Economic Approach to Educational Problems,* by Ida Corinne Brown. Washington, D.C.: U.S. Government Printing Office, 1942.

★ 740 ★

Higher Education

Entrance Criteria: Specific Tests Given on Entrance at Selected Black Colleges, c. 1942

Type of examination or test	Number
Psychological examinations:	
American Council on Education Psychological Examination	14
Otis Self-Administering Test of Mental Ability	3
Terman Group Test of Mental Ability	1
Detroit Advanced Intelligence Test	1
Achievement examinations-Standardized:	
Cooperative English Test	6
Barrett-Ryan English Test	5
Iowa Silent Reading Test	4
Iowa Placement Examination in English	2
Cross English Test	2
Shepherd English Test	1
Tressler English Minimum Essentials Test	1
Hudelson Typical Composition Ability Scale	1
Scores - Harry Achievement Tests	1
University System of Georgia Achievement Tests	1
Cooperative Mathematics Tests	1
Cooperative Algebra Test	1
Public School Achievement Test (Arithmetic)	1
Schorling-Clark-Potter Arithmetic Test	1
Cooperative French Test	1
Breslich French Test	1
Achievement examinations - Locally constructed:	
English	6
Mathematics	5
Music	2
Reading	1
Chemistry	1
Spelling	1
"Good Manners"	1

Source: "Types of Psychological and Achievement Tests Administered to Freshmen in 25 Colleges and Universities for Negroes," *National Survey of the Higher Education of Negroes.* Vol. 1., No. 6. *Socio-Economic Approach to Educational Problems*, 1942, p. 73. Primary source: U.S. Office of Education. *National Survey of the Higher Education of Negroes.* Vol. 1, No. 6. *Socio-Economic Approach to Educational Problems*, by Ida Corrine Brown. Washington, D.C.: U.S. Government Printing Office, 1942.

★ 741 ★

Higher Education

Entrance Criteria: Student Ability Level Preferred by Selected Black Colleges, c. 1942

The Institution prefers students who are of:	Number of institutions	
	Public	Private
High ability only	3	4
Average ability only	1	2
Low ability only	0	0
All levels of ability	8	7

Source: [Untitled Table], *National Survey of the Higher Education of Negroes.* Vol. 1, No. 6. *Socio-Economic Approach to Educational Problems,* 1942, p. 67. Primary source: U.S. Office of Education. *National Survey of the Higher Education of Negroes.* Vol. 1, No. 6. *Socio-Economic Approach to Educational Problems,* by Ida Corrine Brown. Washington, D.C.: U.S. Government Printing Office, 1942.

★ 742 ★

Higher Education

Financing College: Annual Fees (Excluding Board) at Selected Black Colleges, c. 1939

Total annual fees for nonboarding students	Number of institutions	
	Public	Private
$150-174	-	2
$125-$149	1	-
$100-$124	-	2
$75-$99	1	4
$50-$74	2	4
$25-$49	3	1
$0-$24	3	-
Median	$40	$78

Source: [Untitled Table], *National Survey of the Higher Education of Negroes,* Vol. 1, No. 6. *Socio-Economic Approach to Educational Problems,* 1942, p. 111. Primary source: U.S. Office of Education. *National Survey of the Higher Education of Negroes.* Vol. 1, No. 6. *Socio-Economic Approach to Educational Problems,* by Ida Corinne Brown. Washington, D.C.: Government Printing Office, 1942.

★ 743 ★

Higher Education

Financing College: Appropriations for and Students Assisted by Out-of-State Scholarships in Selected States, 1950-51

State	Date program began	Negro students aided through 1951	Amount appropriated 1950-51
Ala.	1945	413	$54,000
Ark.	1943	1,000	20,000
Del.[1]	-	-	-
Fla.	1945	895	10,000[2]
Ga.	1944	3,931	100,000
Ky.[3]	1936	1,200	10,000
La.	1946	1,135	75,000
Md.	1935	2,477	189,236[4]
Miss.	1948	482	24,000
N.C.	1939[5]	2,220[6]	69,337
Okla.	1935	1,495	30,000
S.C.	1946	60	25,000
Tenn.	1937	1,500	[7]
Texas	1939	3,000[8]	110,000
Va.	1936	4,163[9]	127,323.62
W. Va.	1927	67[10]	10,000

Source: "Out-of-State Scholarship Aid by States," *1952 Negro Year Book: A Review of Events Affecting negro Life*, 1952, p. 230. Primary source: Guzman, Jessie Parkhurst (Ed.), *1952 Negro Year Book: A Review of Events Affecting Negro Life.* New York: Wm, H. Wise & Co., Inc., 1952. Published by permission. *Notes:* 1. Out of state aid has not been provided for several years. 2. And additional funds as needed. 3. 1951-52 is last year of this program. 4. The amount actually used; $100,000 was appropriated. 5. Program administered by A.&T. College, Greensboro and N. Carolina College at Durham; the program at A.&T. College began 1943. 6. Students aided through A.&T. College not included. 7. Unlimited appropriation. 8. An approximation. 9. Number for 1940-51 only. 10. For 1940-51 only.

★ 744 ★

Higher Education

Financing College: Financial Independence of Postsecondary Students by Type of School, 1973

Subject	All schools	University	College 4-year	College 2-year	Vocational education school
All students					
Total (thousands)	9,667	4,375	1,715	2,075	1,502
Percent	100	100	100	100	100
Financially dependent	46	50	60	38	27
Financially independent	54	49	39	61	72

[Continued]

★ 744 ★

Financing College: Financial Independence of Postsecondary Students
by Type of School, 1973
[Continued]

Subject	All schools	University	College 4-year	College 2-year	Vocational education school
Percent by type of institution	100	45	18	21	16
Financially dependent	100	50	23	18	9
Financially independent	100	42	13	25	21
Median expected educational expenses					
Total	$784	$910	$1,318	$410	$533
Financially dependent	1,040	1,062	1,727	600	909
Financially independent	576	744	806	307	414
Black students					
Total (thousands)	789	279	150	202	158
Percent	100	100	100	100	100
Financially dependent	39	47	51	33	20
Financially independent	60	52	47	64	78
Percent by type of institution	100	35	19	26	20
Financially dependent	100	43	25	22	10
Financially independent	100	31	15	28	26
Median expected educational expenses					
Total	$745	$1,077	$1,278	$378	$538
Financially dependent	935	1,091	1,335	432	342
Financially independent	659	1,077	1,141	362	597

Source: "Postsecondary students 16 Years Old and Over, by Type of School and Financial Independence: 1973," Current Population Reports, Special Studies, Series P-23, No. 54. The Social and Economic Status of the Black Population in the United States, 1974, 1975, p. 100. Primary source: U.S. Department of Commerce, Social and Economic Statistics Administration, Bureau of the Census. Notes: In this table "financially dependent" or "independent" is a self- determined status, i.e., based on the response of students to a question which asked directly if they considered themselves to be financially independent of their parents. Expected educational expenses were for the period July 1973 to June 1974, and include tuition and fees, books and supplies, and transportation to and from class. Room and board are not included here as educational expenses.

★ 745 ★

Higher Education

Financing College: Income Source of Postsecondary Students 16 and Over, 1973

Source of income	All students Number (thousands)	All students Percent	Black students Number (thousands)	Black students Percent	Percent Black of all students
Total students	9,673	100	789	100	8
With income from specific source					
Personal savings	3,254	34	170	22	5
Earnings while taking courses	4,855	50	316	40	7

[Continued]

★ 745 ★

Financing College: Income Source of Postsecondary Students 16 and Over, 1973

[Continued]

Source of income	All students		Black students		Percent Black of all students
	Number (thousands)	Percent	Number (thousands)	Percent	
Spouses earnings or savings	1,809	19	125	16	7
Parents	3,924	41	211	27	5
College work-study program	441	5	93	12	21
National Defense student loan	524	5	81	10	15
Educational Opportunity grant	323	3	88	11	27
Federal guaranteed student loan program	513	5	52	7	10
Basic educational opportunity grant	105	1	19	2	18
Veterans Administration benefits	1,146	12	94	12	8
Personal loan	370	4	43	5	12
State scholarship or grant	775	8	74	9	10
Local scholarship or grant	699	7	62	8	9
Social Security benefits	395	4	59	7	15
Public assistance	104	1	25	3	24
Educational expenses from employer	488	5	24	3	5
Other sources	811	8	79	10	10
Not reported	246	3	32	4	13

Source: "Source of Income for Postsecondary Students 16 Years Old and Over: 1973," Current Population Reports, Special Studies, Series P-23, No. 54, *The Social and Economic Status of the Black Population in the United States, 1974*, 1975, p. 101. Primary source: U.S. Department of Commerce, Social and Economic Statistics Administration, Bureau of the Census. *Notes:* Detailed figures may not add to totals because some students received income from more than one source.

★ 746 ★

Higher Education

Financing college: Julius Rosenwald Funds Given for Black Fellowships, c. 1937

Fellowships classified as to subjects of study	Individuals	Amount
Agriculture	43	$48,226
The Arts (Painting, sculpture, dramatics)	6	12,060
Music	28	34,485
Literature	7	24,894
Accounting and Business Administration	14	6,384
Education	12	12,478
Home Economics	33	27,876
Library Administration	34	32,100
Physical Sciences (chemistry, physics, mathematics, engineering)	16	12,881
Biology and Medical Sciences	6	6,644
Social Sciences	27	31,360
Medicine and Surgery	45	68,946
Nursing	24	14,397
Hospital Administration and Health Service	13	8,023

[Continued]

★ 746 ★

Financing college: Julius Rosenwald Funds Given for Black Fellowships, c. 1937

[Continued]

Fellowships classified as to subjects of study	Individuals	Amount
Liberal Arts	18	11,069
Law	3	1,800
Social Work	40	29,189
Trades and Vocational Guidance	20	14,310
Total	389	$397,122
Grants-in-aid and special payments		40,493
		$437,615

Source: "Details of Appropriations for Negro Fellowships," *Negro Year Book: An Annual Encyclopedia of the Negro, 1937-1938,* 1937, p. 188. Primary source: Reports of the Julius Rosenwald Fund. Published by permission.

★ 747 ★

Higher Education

Institutional Expenditures: Categories of Expenditure in 103 Black Institutions, 1947-48

Item	Amount	Per cent of--Educational and general expenditures		Total current expenditures
		Except extension and research	All	
Educational and general expenditures				
Administration and general expense	$5,058,546	15.6	14.0	9.2
Resident instruction	18,233,634	56.2	50.3	33.2
Libraries	1,217,651	3.7	3.5	2.2
Plant operation and maintenance	6,717,785	20.7	18.5	12.3
Organized activities related to instruction	1,245,030	3.8	3.4	2.3
Subtotal	32,472,646	100.0	89.7	59.2
Organized research	1,520,915	-	4.2	2.8
Extension	2,222,358	-	6.1	4.0
Total education and general	36,215,919	-	100.0	66.0
Auxiliary enterprises and activities	17,248,601	-	-	31.4
Other noneducational expenditures	1,432,486	-	-	2.6
Total current expenditures	$54,897,006	-	-	100.0

Source: "Analysis of Current Expenditures of 103 Institutions, 1947-48," *1952 Negro Year Book: A Review of Events Affecting Negro Life,* 1952, p. 221. Primary source: U.S. Office of Education, *Statistical Circular No. 293,* April 1951. Published by permission.

★ 748 ★

Higher Education

Institutional Expenditures: Categories of Expenditure in Black Public and Private Institutions, c. 1939

	Percent
Administration and general	
Public	15.6
Private	24.8
All institutions	21.2
Instruction and departmental research	
Public	60.9
Private	55.6
All institutions	58.2
Library	
Public	3.2
Private	4.7
All institutions	4.6
Operation and maintenance	
Public	19.5
Private	15.0
All institutions	16.7

Source: [Untitled Figure], *National Survey of the Higher Education of Negroes.* Vol. 1, No. 6. *Socio-Economic Approach to Educational Problems,* 1942, p. 107. Primary source: U.S. Office of Education. *National Survey of the Higher Education of Negroes.* Vol. 1, No. 6. *Socio-Economic Approach to Educational Problems,* by Ida Corinne Brown. Washington, D.C.: U.S. Government Printing Office, 1942.

★ 749 ★

Higher Education

Institutional Expenditures: Expenditures in Public and Private Black Colleges, 1928-38

Type of institution by expenditure	1928	1930	1932	1934	1936	1938
Instruction						
Public	$1,138,183	$1,366,631	$1,207,302	$1,039,408	$1,316,798	$1,664,128
Percent increase	-	+20	-12	-16	+27	+26
Private	$1,317,597	$1,618,284	$1,979,085	$1,691,955	$1,686,027	$1,858,721
Percent increase	-	+23	+22	-15	-0.4	+10
All	$2,455,780	$2,984,915	$3,186,387	$2,731,363	$3,002,825	$3,522,849
Percent increase	-	+22	+7	-14	+10	+17
Total, education and general						
Public	$2,459,398	$2,740,085	$2,155,712	$1,898,108	$2,325,869	$2,896,129
Percent increase	-	+21	-21	-12	+23	+25

[Continued]

★ 749 ★

Institutional Expenditures: Expenditures in Public and Private Black Colleges, 1928-38
[Continued]

Type of institution by expenditure	1928	1930	1932	1934	1936	1938
Private	$2,678,951	$3,342,858	$3,642,408	$3,036,922	$3,012,264	$3,460,808
Percent increase	-	+25	+9	-17	-0.8	+15
All	$5,138,349	$6,082,943	$5,798,120	$4,935,030	$5,338,133	$6,356,937
Percent increase	-	+18	-5	-15	+8	+19
Capital outlay						
Public	$1,130,316	$911,055	$605,925	$312,976	$902,812	$1,000,073
Percent increase	-	-19	-35	-48	+188	+11
Private	$598,592	$1,725,144	$2,296,801	$1,140,367	$220,075	$1,124,096
Percent increase	-	+188	+33	-50	-81	+411[1]
All	$1,728,908	$2,636,199	$2,902,726	$1,453,343	$1,122,887	$2,124,169
Percent increase	-	+52	+10	-50	-23	+89

Source: "Distribution of Expenditures in 20 Public and 16 Private Colleges, 1928-38," *National Survey of the Higher Education of Negroes.* Vol. 1, No. 6. *Socio-Economic Approach to Educational Problems*, 1942, p. 6. Primary source: U.S. Office of Education. *National Survey of the Higher Education of Negroes.* Vol. 1, No. 6. *Socio-Economic Approach to Educational Problems*, by Ida Corinne Brown. Washington, D.C.: U.S. Government Printing Office, 1942. *Notes:* 1. This abnormal increase was due to the receipt by Howard University, a private institution receiving a major portion of its income from the Federal Government, of a large federal grant for a new building program. the otherwise actual increase would be comparable with that of the public colleges.

★ 750 ★

Higher Education

Ownership and Control: Property Value and Receipts of Public and Private Institutions, 1941

Type of institution	No. institutions	Value[1,2]	Receipts[1,2]
Publicly controlled 4-yr. schools			
Land-grant colleges	17	$57,877-1,687,610	$33,247-676,025
Non-land-grant colleges	15	237,767-875,209	27,546-295,115
Privately controlled 4-yr. schools	51	25,000-5,056,487	10,000-1,096,758
Publicly controlled junior colleges			
Land-grant colleges	1	656,000	67,952
Non-land-grant colleges	6	31,000-97,175[3]	4,800-58,947
Privately controlled junior colleges	23	18,500-579,500	9,645-262,296

Source: Compiled and adapted by the editors from "Institutions of Higher Education, 1941," *The Negro Handbook*, 1942, pp. 114-116. Primary source: Murray, Florence (Ed.), *The Negro Handbook.* New York: Wendell Malliet and Co., 1942. Published by permission. *Notes:* 1. As of 1936-37. 2. Information not provided for all institutions. 3. Value of leased institution not included.

★ 751 ★

Higher Education

Parents of College Students: Annual Income of Parents of Black Seniors, c. 1939

Annual income of parents	Number of seniors		
	All	Male	Female
$3,000 and over	55	23	32
$2,500-$2,999	37	15	22
$2,000-$2,499	99	41	58
$1,750-$1,999	42	16	26
$1,500-$1,749	94	44	50
$1,250-$1,499	54	18	36
$1,000-$1,249	269	124	145
$750-$999	217	107	110
$500-$749	181	91	90
Less than $500	147	63	84
Total	1,195	542	653
Median	$1,048	$1,022	$1,073
Q_3	1,575	1,520	1,623
Q_1	710	700	720

Source: "Distribution of Reported Annual Income of the Parents of Negro College Seniors, according to Sex," *National Survey of the Higher Education of Negroes.* Vol. 1, No. 6. *Socio-Economic Approach to Educational Problems,* 1942, p. 46. Primary source: U.S. Office of Education. *National Survey of the Higher Education of Negroes.* Vol. 1, No. 6. *Socio-Economic Approach to Educational Problems,* by Ida Corinne Brown. Washington, D.C.: U.S. Government Printing Office, 1942.

★ 752 ★

Higher Education

Parents of College Students: Father's Occupation and Test Scores of Black College Seniors, c. 1939

Score, by type of Test	Occupation of father							
	Professional	Clerical	Business	Skilled	Farming	Personal and Domestic	Unskilled	Semiskilled
General Culture Test:								
Number of cases	264	92	113	243	228	237	140	75
Median	109	113	100	91	61	89	76	88
Q3	149	160	148	130	98	131	123	136
Q1	73	73	76	62	39	54	50	50
Highest	Above 270	Above 270	Above 270	Above 270	240	Above 270	Above 270	240
Reading Test:								
Number of cases	266	90	112	245	229	237	143	77
Median	52.0	53.0	52.8	49.7	44.5	50.7	47.3	50.1
Q3	58.6	62.0	58.8	55.8	50.8	56.5	54.4	58.4

[Continued]

★ 752 ★

Parents of College Students: Father's Occupation and Test Scores of Black College Seniors, c. 1939

[Continued]

Score, by type of Test	Occupation of father							
	Professional	Clerical	Business	Skilled	Farming	Personal and Domestic	Unskilled	Semiskilled
Q1	45.7	46.9	48.3	44.6	40.0	44.7	42.3	44.4
Highest	Above 76	Above 76	Above 76	Above 76	69	Above 76	Above 76	73

Source: "Distribution of Scores Earned by Seniors on the General Culture and Reading Tests by Occupation of Father," *National Survey of the Higher Education of Negroes.* Vol. 1, No. 6, *Socio-Economic Approach to Educational Problems,* 1942, p. 62. Primary source: U.S. Office of Education. *National Survey of the Higher Education of Negroes.* Vol. 1, No. 6. *Socio-Economic Approach to Educational Problems,* by Ida Corrine Brown. Washington, D.C.: U.S. Government Printing Office, 1942.

★ 753 ★

Higher Education

Parents of College Students: Monthly Income of Parents of Black Freshmen, c. 1939

Monthly income of parents	Number of cases
More than $275	74
$250-$274	32
$225-$249	28
$200-$224	93
$175-$199	154
$150-$174	210
$125-$149	241
$100-$124	385
$75-$99	527
$50-$74	915
Less than $50	1,121
Total	3,770
Median	$71
Q_2	117
Q_1	42

Source: "Distribution of Reported Annual Income of the Parents of Negro College Freshmen," *National Survey of the Higher Education of Negroes.* Vol. 1, No. 6. *Socio-Economic Approach to Educational Problems,* 1942, p. 46. Primary source: U.S. Office of Education. *National Survey of the Higher Education of Negroes.* Vol. 1, No. 6. *Socio-Economic Approach to Educational Problems,* by Ida Corinne Brown. Washington, D.C.: U.S. Government Printing Office, 1942.

★ 754 ★

Higher Education

Parents of College Students: Occupation of Fathers of Black College Seniors in Relation to Black Male Population in 1930

Occupational group	Male Negro workers in United States (1930)[1]	Fathers of Negro college seniors	Excess or deficiency of groups in senior population in terms of statistical expectancy
	Percent of		
Professional	1.5	19.0	+1,266
Skilled labor	4.8	17.4	+362
Personal and domestic service	9.4	17.1	+181
Semi-skilled labor	9.0	5.4	-60
Farmers and farm laborers	40.9	16.6	-418
Unskilled labor	31.7	10.2	-322
Public service, business, and clerical	2.7	14.3	+529

Source: "A Comparison of the Social-Economic Grouping of Male Negro Workers in the United States (1930) and the Fathers of Negro College Seniors," *National Survey of the Higher Education of Negroes.* Vol. 1, No. 6. *Socio-Economic Approach to Educational Problems,* 1942, p. 45. Primary source: U.S. Office of Education. *National Survey of the Higher Education of Negroes.* Vol. 1, No. 6. *Socio-Economic Approach to Educational Problems,* by Ida Corinne Brown. Washington, D.C.: U.S. Government Printing Office, 1942. *Notes:* 1. Adapted from Alba Edwards, *A Social-Economic Grouping of the Gainful Workers of the United States (1930)* Washington, U.S. Government Printing Office, 1938. p. 13.

★ 755 ★

Higher Education

Parents of College Students: Occupational Group of Parents of Black College Freshmen and Seniors, c. 1939

Occupational group	Seniors				Freshmen			
	Fathers		Mothers		Fathers		Mothers	
	Number	Percent	Number	Percent	Number	Percent	Number	Percent
Professional	272	19.0	271	19.1	454	12.1	442	11.5
Business	114	7.9	14	1.0	184	4.9	51	1.3
Clerical and public service	92	6.4	15	1.0	190	5.0	48	1.3
Skilled labor	249	17.4	61	4.3	630	16.8	124	3.2
Personal and domestic service	245	17.1	218	15.4	758	20.2	1,079	28.1
Farming	238	16.6	55	3.9	763	20.3	263	6.9
Semi-skilled labor	78	5.4	3	.2	381	10.1	28	.7
Unskilled labor	147	10.2	15	1.0	398	10.6	49	1.3

[Continued]

★ 755 ★

Parents of College Students: Occupational Group of Parents of Black College Freshmen and Seniors, c. 1939
[Continued]

Occupational group	Seniors				Freshmen			
	Fathers		Mothers		Fathers		Mothers	
	Number	Percent	Number	Percent	Number	Percent	Number	Percent
Housewife	-	-	768	54.1	-	-	1,755	45.7
Total	1,435	100.0	1,420	100.0	3,758	100.0	3,839	100.0

Source: "The Occupations of Parents of Negro College Freshmen and Seniors Classified by Occupational Group," *National Survey of the Higher Education of Negroes.* Vol. 1, No. 6. *Socio-Economic Approach to Educational Problems,* 1942, p. 44. Primary source: U.S. Office of Education. *National Survey of the Higher Education of Negroes.* Vol. 1, No. 6. *Socio-Economic Approach to Educational Problems,* by Ida Corinne Brown. Washington, D.C.: U.S. Government Printing Office, 1942.

★ 756 ★

Higher Education

Relationships: 1930 Black Population and Black College-Age Population Attending Selected Black Colleges in 1938-39

State	Negro population resident in State in 1930	Negroes 15-19 resident in 1930	Negroes 20-24 resident in 1930	Number of Negroes from State attending Negro colleges in Ohio, Pennsylvania, and Kansas 1938-39	Number of Negroes from State attending Negro colleges in Southern States 1938-39	Total Negroes resident in State attending Negro colleges, 1938-39
Pennsylvania	431,257	33,213	31,895	347	494	841
New York	412,814	24,472	47,974	58	438	496
Illinois	328,972	23,363	33,264	30	392	422
Ohio	309,304	23,758	29,392	381	384	765
New Jersey	208,828	16,795	21,295	84	414	498
Michigan	169,453	10,888	17,731	15	112	127
Indiana	111,982	8,746	10,184	10	201	211
California	81,048	5,565	6,711	9	53	62
Kansas	66,344	5,434	5,486	38	78	116
Massachusetts	52,365	4,018	3,798	14	102	116
Connecticut	29,354	2,316	2,669	8	92	100
Iowa	17,380	1,414	1,363	1	25	26
Nebraska	13,752	962	1,122	0	11	11
Colorado	11,828	783	892	1	28	29
Arizona	10,749	788	1,128	0	10	10
Wisconsin	10,739	696	1,066	2	10	12
Total for 16 States	2,266,169	163,211	225,970	908	2,844	3,842

[Continued]

★ 756 ★

Relationships: 1930 Black Population and Black College-Age Population Attending Selected Black Colleges in 1938-39

[Continued]

State	Negro population resident in State in 1930	Negroes 15-19 resident in 1930	Negroes 20-24 resident in 1930	Number of Negroes from State attending Negro colleges in Ohio, Pennsylvania, and Kansas 1938-39	Number of Negroes from State attending Negro colleges in Southern States 1938-39	Total Negroes resident in State attending Negro colleges, 1938-39
15 other States outside South[1]	39,557	2,742	2,769	4	53	51
Grand Total	2,305,726	165,953	228,739	1,002	2,897	3,893

Source: "Distribution of Negro Population, According to Age and Attendance in Negro Colleges in a Selected Group of States," U.S. Office of Education. *National Survey of the Higher Education of Negroes.* Vol. 1, No. 6. *Socio- Economic Approach to Educational Problems,* 1942, p. 83. Primary source: U.S. Office of Education. *National Survey of the Higher Education of Negroes.* Vol. 1, No. 6. *Socio-Economic Approach to Educational Problems,* by Ida Corinne Brown. Washington, D.C.: U.S. Government Printing Office, 1942. *Notes:* 1. In the order of number of Negroes in the population these States are: Rhode Island, Minnesota, Washington, New Mexico, Oregon, Montana, Wyoming, Utah, Maine, New Hampshire, Idaho, South Dakota, Vermont, Nevada, and North Dakota; Rhode Island and Minnesota each have more than 9,000 Negroes. The 6 States last named have less than 1,000 each.

★ 757 ★

Higher Education

Relationships: Black Enrollment in Institutions in 3 Northern States, by Residence and Type of Institution, 1938-39

State	Residents of State attending Negro colleges	Residents of State attending Negro colleges within State	Residents of State attending other northern Negro colleges	Residents of State attending southern Negro colleges	Negroes from other Northern States enrolled in Negro colleges within State	Negroes from South enrolled in Negro colleges within State
Kansas	116	36	2	72	4	24
Ohio	765	376	5	380	132	110
Pennsylvania	841	306	41	494	148	84
Total	1,722	718	48	946	284	218

Source: [Untitled Table], U.S. Office of Education. *National Survey of the Higher Education of Negroes.* Vol. 1, No. 6. *Socio-Economic Approach to Educational Problems,* 1942. p. 83. Primary source: U.S. Office of Education. *National Survey of the Higher Education of Negroes.* Vol. 1, No. 6. *Socio-Economic Approach to Educational Problems,* by Ida Corinne Brown. Washington, D.C.: U.S. Government Printing Office, 1942.

★ 758 ★

Higher Education

Relationships: Black Students' Residence and Type of College Attended in 4 Selected States, 1939-40

| State | Negro population, 1930 | Percent of total | Negro students in 8 universities studied | | Negro residents of State attending Negro colleges, 1938-39 | |
			Total	Estimated number from South[1]	In North[2]	In South
New York	412,814	3.3	458	79	58	438
Illinois	328,972	4.3	269	55	30	392
Ohio	309,304	4.7	420	27	381	384
Kansas	66,814	3.5	106	17	38	78
Total	1,117,434	3.9	1,253	178	507	1,292

Source: "College Attendance and Percentage Distribution in the Population of Negro Residents in Four Selected States," U.S. Office of Education. *National Survey of the Higher Education of Negroes.* Vol. 1, No. 6. *Socio- Economic Approach to Educational Problems,* 1942, p. 80. Primary source: U.S. Office of Education. *National Survey of the Higher Education of Negroes.* Vol. 1, No. 6. *Socio-Economic Approach to Educational Problems,* by Ida Corinne Brown. Washington, D.C.: U.S. Government Printing Office, 1942. *Notes:* 1. Estimates based on the proportion of southern students in group replying to questionnaire from each institution. 2. Ohio, Pennsylvania, and Kansas.

★ 759 ★

Higher Education

Relationships: Institutional Expenditure per Student in Selected Black Institutions in Relation to Accreditation Rating, c. 1939

| Highest accreditation of institutions | Number of institutions | Weighted educational expenditure per student | |
		Median	Range
Approved by the American Association of Universities	2	$530	$646-$415
Members of or rated "A" by their regional association	11	198	362-124
Rated "B" by their regional association	3	83	83-47
Not approved by a regional accrediting agency	9	83	184-20

Source: [Untitled Table], *National Survey of the Higher Education of Negroes. Vol. 1, No. 6. Socio-Economic Approach to Educational Problems,* 1942, p. 107. Primary source: U.S. Office of Education. *National Survey of the Higher Education of Negroes. Vol. 1, No. 6. Socio-Economic Approach to Educational Problems,* by Ida Corinne Brown. Washington, D.C.: U.S. Government Printing Office, 1942.

★ 760 ★

Higher Education

Relationships: Type and Location of Elementary and Secondary Schools Attended by Black College Students, c. 1939

Kind of school	Elementary Number of seniors	Percent	Secondary Number of seniors	Percent	Elementary Number of freshmen	Percent	Secondary Number of freshmen	Percent
Southern urban								
Private	37	2.5	37	2.5	115	3.6	224	6.1
Public	784	53.0	845	57.5	1,397	44.0	1,837	49.9
Southern rural								
Private	29	2.0	56	3.8	25	.8	52	1.4
Public	204	13.8	103	7.0	503	16.0	311	8.4
Northern Private	3	.2	4	.3	13	.4	13	.4
Northern urban public	220	14.9	229	15.6	456	14.0	543	14.7
Northern rural public	21	1.4	19	1.3	51	2.0	34	.9
Border public	176	11.9	172	11.7	620	19.0	662	18.0
Foreign	5	.3	4	.3	7	.2	8	.2
Total								
Urban	1,220	82.5	1,287	87.6	2,601	81.6	3,279	89.0
Rural	254	17.2	178	12.1	579	18.2	397	10.8
Southern	1,054	71.3	1,041	70.9	2,040	64.0	2,424	65.8
Northern	244	16.5	252	17.1	520	16.3	590	16.0
Border	176	11.9	172	11.7	620	19.5	662	18.0
Public	1,405	95.0	1,368	93.1	3,027	95.0	3,387	91.9
Private	69	4.7	97	6.6	153	4.8	289	7.9
Number of students	1,479	100.0	1,469	100.0	3,187	100.0	3,684	100.0

Source: "Distribution of Place and Kinds of Elementary and Secondary Schools Attended by Negro College Seniors and Freshmen," *National Survey of the Higher Education of Negroes.* Vol. 1, No. 6. *Socio-Economic Approach to Educational Problems,* 1942, p. 47. Primary source: U.S. Office of Education. *National Survey of the Higher Education of Negroes.* Vol. 1, No. 6. *Socio-Economic Approach to Educational Problems,* by Ida Corinne Brown. Washington, D.C.: U.S. Government Printing Office, 1942.

★ 761 ★

Higher Education

Relationships: Type of Elementary and High School Attended by Black Students in Selected Northern Institutions, c. 1942 - I

Racial type of school attended	4 Public institutions University of Cincinnati	University of Illinois	University of Kansas	Ohio State University	Total reporting	Percent
Elementary:						
Negro	28	30	40	43	141	41.2
Mixed	39	38	9	100	186	54.4
Both	5	3	2	5	15	4.4

[Continued]

★ 761 ★

Relationships: Type of Elementary and High School Attended by Black Students in Selected Northern Institutions, c. 1942 - I

[Continued]

Racial type of school attended	4 Public institutions					
	University of Cincinnati	University of Illinois	University of Kansas	Ohio State University	Total reporting	Percent
Total	...	...	...	...	342	...
High school:						
Negro	6	17	31	22	76	22.2
Mixed	66	52	20	125	263	76.9
Both	...	2	...	1	3	.9
Total	...	...	...	...	342	...
College:[1]						
Negro	11	8	6	29	54	15.7
Mixed	61	64	45	119	289	84.3
Total	...	...	...	...	343	...

Source: "Negro Students Attending 8 Northern Institutions, Distributed According to Racial Type of Schools Attended," U.S. Office of Education. *National Survey of the Higher Education of Negroes.* Vol. 1, No. 6. *Socio-Economic Approach to Educational Problems,* 1942, p. 80. Primary source: U.S. Office of Education. *National Survey of the Higher Education of Negroes.* Vol. 1, No. 6. *Socio-Economic Approach to Educational Problems,* by Ida Corinne Brown. Washington, D.C.: U.S. Government Printing Office, 1942. *Notes:* 1. Some of the students reporting attendance at a Negro college had attended both Negro and mixed institutions. All students reporting were attending a mixed institution at the time the report was made.

★ 762 ★

Higher Education

Relationships: Type of Elementary and High School Attended by Black Students in Selected Northern Institutions, c. 1942 - II

Racial type of school attended	4 Private institutions						Grand total reporting	Percent
	University of Chicago	Columbia (Teachers College)	New York University	Northwestern University	Total reporting	Percent		
Elementary:								
Negro	34	56	35	13	138	49.1	279	44.8
Mixed	30	33	62	12	137	49.0	323	51.8
Both	1	2	3	...	6	.9	21	3.4
Total	...	...	...	...	281	...	623	...
High school:								
Negro	24	43	24	8	99	35.2	175	28.1
Mixed	40	46	74	17	177	63.0	440	70.6
Both	1	2	2	...	5	1.8	8	1.3
Total	...	...	...	...	281	...	623	...

[Continued]

★ 762 ★

Relationships: Type of Elementary and High School Attended by Black Students in Selected Northern Institutions, c. 1942 - II

[Continued]

Racial type of school attended	4 Private institutions						Grand total reporting	Percent
	University of Chicago	Columbia (Teachers College)	New York University	Northwestern University	Total reporting	Percent		
College:[1]								
Negro	24	44	17	9	94	33.5	148	23.7
Mixed	41	47	83	16	187	66.5	476	76.3
Total	...	...	...	...	281	...	624	...

Source: "Negro Students Attending 8 Northern Institutions, Distributed According to Racial Type of Schools Attended," U.S. Office of Education. *National Survey of the Higher Education of Negroes.* Vol. 1, No. 6. *Socio-Economic Approach to Educational Problems,* 1942, p. 80. Primary source: U.S. Office of Education. *National Survey of the Higher Education of Negroes.* Vol. 1, No. 6. *Socio-Economic Approach to Educational Problems,* by Ida Corinne Brown. Washington, D.C.: U.S. Government Printing Office, 1942. *Notes:* 1. Some of the students reporting attendance at a Negro college had attended both Negro and mixed institutions. All students reporting were attending a mixed institution at the time the report was made.

★ 763 ★

Higher Education

Special Curricula: Black Institutions Offering Courses in Civil Aviation in 1940 and 1941

Institution	No. Trainees
First Course (1940):	
Tuskegee Institute	19
Delaware State College	10
Howard University	9
Hampton Institute	19
West Virginia State College	14
Agricultural and Technical College (N.C.)	6
Second Course (1941):	
Tuskegee Institute	11
Agri. and Tech.	4
Hampton Institute	11
West Virginia State	10

Source: Adapted by the editors from Untitled figures, *The Negro Handbook,* 1942, p. 81. Primary source: Murray, Florence (Ed.), *The Negro Handbook.* New York: Wendell Malliet and Co., 1942.

★ 764 ★

Higher Education

Special Curricula: Characteristics of Black Institutions and Participants in Civilian Pilot Training and War Training Service Programs, 1943

Number of colleges participating, 9; number of non-college units participating, 3; number of schools in full time program (Army), 2.

Course	No. of trainees	No. completed	No. eliminated	Records incomplete
Elementary College	558	385	171	2
Elementary Non-College	51	36	15	-
Elementary Full Time (Army)	57	14	9	34
Secondary College	109	81	28	-
Secondary Full Time (Army)	20	8	1	11
Student Instructor	16	16	-	-
Advanced Instructor Refresher	1	1	-	-
Commercial Refresher	5	2	3	-
Type "B" Cross Country	18	16	2	-
Type "B" Instructor	16	15	-	1
Cross Country 43-C (Army)	6	-	-	6
Total	857	574	229	54

Source: "Negro Participation in the Civilian Pilot Training and War Training Service Programs (As of March 16, 1943)," *The Negro Handbook, 1944*, 1944, p. 120. Primary source: Murray, Florence (Ed.), *The Negro Handbook, 1944*. New York: Current Reference Publications, 1944. Published by permission.

★ 765 ★

Higher Education

Specialized Schools: Characteristics of "Aggie" Schools and Institutions for Women, 1912 and 1918-19

Type of institution	1912				1918-19			
	Number institutions	Average No.[1]			Number institutions	Average no.[1]		
		Students	Teachers	Income[3]		Students	Teachers	Income[3]
State Agricultural and Mechanical Colleges[2]	17	444.5	25.8	$51,202	17	627.9	35	$127,447
Institutions for Women[2]	13	232.2	17.6	$15,285	18	120.4	14.1	$11,001

Source: Compiled and adapted by the editors from "State Agricultural and Mechanical Colleges" and "Institutions for Women," *Negro Year Book and Annual Encyclopedia of the Negro*, [no p. no.], and *Negro Year Book: An Annual Encyclopedia of the Negro, 1918-19*, 1919, [no p. no.]. Published by permission. *Notes:* 1. Averages based on only those institutions that furnished data. 2. Some students below college level are included in student figures provided by both types of institutions. 3. Income includes both federal and state support.

★ 766 ★

Higher Education

Support for Colleges: Black Colleges' Sources of Income, 1926-27

Source	Amount	Percent of total
State appropriations	$2,207,221.82	25.9
Federal appropriations	485,520.29	5.7
Church appropriations	1,153,258.74	13.5
Interest on endowment fund	1,042,150.71	12.2
Gifts for current expenses	1,006,194.27	11.8
Student fees	1,677,453.66	19.7
Income for sales and services	448,365.30	5.3
Other sources	496,146.61	5.8
Total	$8,516,291.40	100.0

Source: "Different Sources of Income of Negro Colleges, with Percentage of Total Income from Each Source, 1926-27," *Survey of Negro Colleges and Universities*, Bulletin 1928, No. 7, 1929, pp. 954-956. Primary source: U.S. Bureau of Education. *Survey of Negro Colleges and Universities*. Bulletin, 1928, No. 7. Washington, D.C.: Government Printing Office, 1929.

★ 767 ★

Higher Education

Support for Colleges: Contributions of the United Negro College Fund, 1944-47

"The United Negro College Fund, a voluntary organization comprising 33 Negro private colleges, was founded in November, 1943, and incorporated on April 24, 1944, for the purpose of conducting annually a united appeal for funds with which to help meet the current operating expenses of the member institutions.... The first appeal was made in the spring of 1944 and resulted in the raising of $900,000. The second appeal, made in the spring of 1945, collected $1,069,000. During the 1946 and 1947 campaigns, $930,021 and $1,032,571, respectively, were collected. The 1948 goal was set at $1,400,000."

Source: "The United Negro College Fund," *The Negro Handbook, 1949*, 1949, p. 137. Primary source: Murray, Florence (Ed.), *The Negro Handbook, 1949*. New York: The Macmillan Co., 1949. Published by permission.

★ 768 ★

Higher Education

Support for Colleges: Endowment Growth in Black Institutions, 1922-23 to 1926-27

Name of institution	1922-23	1926-27	Increase
Alabama			
Talladega College	$246,000.00	$266,000.00	$20,000.00
Tuskegee Normal and Industrial Institute	[1]	6,177,005.71	None
District of Columbia			
Howard University[2]	231,327.21	592,532.90	361,205.69
Florida			
Bethune-Cookman College	50,000.00	50,000.00	None
Georgia			
Atlanta University	166,104.34	265,587.95	99,483.61
Clark University	56,000.00	195,000.00	139,000.00
Morehouse College	321,000.00	321,000.00	None
Paine College	30,000.00	30,000.00	None
Spelman College	48,848.76	53,813.48	4,964.72
Kentucky			
Lincoln Institute	267,770.31	278,791.63	11,021.32
Louisiana			
New Orleans University	100,000.00	105,000.00	5,000.00
Straight College	19,012.84	19,012.84	None
Maryland			
Morgan College	65,290.00	67,410.00	2,120.00
Mississippi			
Alcorn Agricultural and Mechanical College	96,236.20	96,236.20	None
Jackson College	-	1,000.00	1,000.00
Rust College	16,000.00	16,000.00	None
Tougaloo College	7,000.00	24,200.00	17,200.00
North Carolina			
Brick Junior College	222,000.00	222,000.00	None
Johnson C. Smith University	240,135.36	1,600,135.36	1,360,000.00
St. Augustine's School	94,136.19	141,726.63	47,590.44
Shaw University	54,700.00	355,000.00	300,300.00
Ohio			
Wilberforce University	14,373.91	14,373.91	None
Pennsylvania			
Lincoln University	691,102.82	696,880.19	5,777.37
South Carolina			
Benedict College	133,006.04	133,006.04	None
Claflin University	111,900.00	140,000.00	28,100.00
Tennessee			
Fisk University	262,277.03	293,543.44	31,266.41
Knoxville College	6,500.00	6,500.00	None
Lane College	31,000.00	31,150.00	150.00
Morristown Normal and Industrial University	-	35,000.00	35,000.00
Texas			
Bishop College	13,296.00	13,296.00	None
Jarvis Christian Institute	[1]	1,000.00	1,000.00
Wiley College	460.00	860.00	400.00

[Continued]

★ 768 ★

Support for Colleges: Endowment Growth in Black Institutions, 1922-23 to 1926-27

[Continued]

Name of institution	1922-23	1926-27	Increase
Virginia			
Hampton Normal and Agricultural Institute	4,837,583.44	7,958,763.73	3,121,180.29
St. Paul Normal and Industrial Institute	98,207.50	98,312.85	105.35
Virginia Union University	406,973.69	413,657.34	6,683.65
Total	8,938,241.64	9,176,573.19	5,598,548.85

Source: "Growth of Permanent Endowments, 1922-1927," *Survey of Negro Colleges and Universities*. Bulletin, 1928, No. 7, 1929, pp. 950-951. Primary source: U.S. Bureau of Education. *Survey of Negro colleges and Universities*. Bulletin, 1928, No. 7. Washington, D.C.: Government Printing Office, 1929. *Notes:* 1. Report not given for these years. 2. Represents endowments at beginning of year.

★ 769 ★

Higher Education

Support for Colleges: Endowments of Selected Black Institutions, 1951

Institution	Amount
Atlanta University, Atlanta, Ga.	$6,635,200.00
Barber-Scotia College, Concord, N.C.	850,000.00
Benedict College, Columbia, S.C.	353,906.79
Bennett College, Greensboro, N.C.	1,050,932.00
Bethune-Cookman College, Daytona Beach, Fla.	536,060.00
Bettis Academy and Junior College, Trenton, S.C.	35,075.28
Bishop College, Marshall, Texas	22,463.33
Claflin University, Orangeburg, S.C.	180,000.00
Clark College, Atlanta, Ga.	1,007,093.91
Dillard University, New Orleans, La.	3,300,000.00
Fisk University, Nashville, Tenn.	4,485,000.00
Fort Valley State College, Fort Valley, Ga.	63,824.86
Gammon Theological Seminary, Atlanta, Ga.	607,000.00
Hampton Institutute, Hampton, Va.	10,000,000.00
Howard University, Washington, D.C.	1,669,595.00
Jarvis Christian College, Hawkins, Texas	450,000.00
Johnson C. Smith University, Charlotte, N.C.	2,000,000.00
Knoxville College, Knoxville, Tenn.	536,800.00
Lane College, Jackson, Tenn.	36,667.21
Leland College, Baker, La.	109,000.00
LeMoyne College, Memphis, Tenn.	2,232.00
Lincoln University, Lincoln University, Pa.	1,012,416.00
Livingstone College, Salisbury, N.C.	75,000.00
Mississippi Vocational College, Itta Bena, Miss.	147,000.00
Morehouse College, Atlanta, Ga.	2,000,000.00
Morris Booker Memorial Baptist College, Dermott, Ark.	125,000.00
Morris Brown College, Atlanta, Ga.	18,000.00
Morristown N. and I. College, Morristown, Tenn.	82,928.12

[Continued]

★ 769 ★

Support for Colleges: Endowments of Selected Black Institutions, 1951
[Continued]

Institution	Amount
Paine College, Augusta, Ga.	795,360.75
Philander Smith College, Little Rock, Ark.	2,500,000.00
Rust College, Holly Springs, Miss.	29,099.82
Samuel Houston College, Austin, Texas	8,943.96
Shaw University, Raleigh, N.C.	500,000.00
Spelman College, Atlanta, Ga.	3,327,563.01
St. Augustine's College, Raleigh, N.C.	213,000.00
Stillman College, Tuscaloosa, Ala.	128,935.67
Talladega College, Talladega, Ala.	3,730,000.00
Tillotson College, Austin, Texas	1,500,000.000
Tougaloo College, Tougaloo, Miss.	48,521.08
Tuskegee Institute, Tuskegee Institute, Ala.	6,913,911.15
Virginia State College, Petersburg, Va.	173,000.00
Virginia Union University, Richmond, Va.	1,000,000.00
Voorhees School and Junior College, Denmark, S.C.	55,000.000
Wilberforce University, Wilberforce, Ohio	76,865.20
Wiley College, Marshall, Texas	600,000.00
Winston-Salem Teachers College, Winston-Salem, N.C.	100,000.00
Total	$59,091,395.14

Source: "Endowment of 46 Negro Colleges and Universities, 1951," *1952 Negro Year Book: A Review of Events Affecting Negro Life,* 1952, p. 222. Primary source: Reports of the institutions.

★ 770 ★
Higher Education

Support for Colleges: Funds Spent by Julius Rosenwald Fund for Black Private Colleges, c. 1937

Bennett College for Women	
Greensboro, North Carolina	$15,000
Bethune-Cookman College,	
Daytona Beach, Florida	9,000
Cardinal Gibbons Institute	
Institute, Maryland	6,000
Fort Valley Normal and Industrial School	
Fort Valley, Georgia	6,000
Lincoln Institute	
Shelby County, Kentucky	4,000
Lincoln University	
Chester County, Pennsylvania	91,342
Livingstone College	
Salisbury, North Carolina	2,500

[Continued]

★ 770 ★

Support for Colleges: Funds Spent by Julius Rosenwald
Fund for Black Private Colleges, c. 1937
[Continued]

Morgan College	
Baltimore, Maryland	10,000
Penn Normal, Industrial and Agricultural School	
St. Helena's Island, South Carolina	6,000
Philander Smith College	
Little Rock, Arkansas	4,000
St. Augustine's College	
Raleigh, North Carolina	17,500
Talladega College	
Talladega, Alabama	35,000
Tougaloo College	
Tougaloo, Mississippi	8,000
Wiley College	
Marshall, Texas	22,500
Methodist Episcopal Church,	
Joint Educational Survey	4,916
Southern Association of Colleges and Secondary Schools,	
surveys and meetings	4,084
	$245,842

Source: "Details of Expenditures, Negro Private Colleges," *Negro Year Book: An Annual Encyclopedia of the Negro, 1937-1938*, 1937, p. 186. Primary source: Reports of the Julius Rosenwald Fund. Published by Permission.

★ 771 ★

Higher Education

Support for Colleges: Funds Spent by Julius Rosenwald
Fund for Black State Colleges, c. 1937

State colleges	
Alabama Agricultural and Mechanical College, Huntsville	$38,358
Alabama Teachers College, Montgomery	21,642
Arkansas State College, Pine Bluff	33,000
Florida Agricultural and Mechanical College, Tallahassee	13,755
North Carolina Colored Normal School, Fayetteville	29,472
Tennessee Agricultural and Industrial Teachers College, Nashville	73,530
Virginia Normal and Industrial Institute, Petersburg	81,000

Source: "Details of Expenditures for Negro State Colleges, Summer Institutes, and High Schools," *Negro Year Book: An Annual Encyclopedia of the Negro, 1937-1938*, 1937, p. 187. Primary source: Reports of the Julius Rosenwald Fund. Published by permission.

★ 772 ★

Higher Education

Support for Colleges: Funds Spent by Julius Rosenwald Fund for Black University Centers, c. 1937

Washington	
Howard University	$286,479
Association for the Study of Negro Life and History	2,500
Atlanta	
Atlanta University	62,569
Spelman College	106,944
Morehouse College	118,744
Atlanta School for Social Work	25,500
Morris Brown University	5,000
Nashville	
Fisk University	213,970
Meharry Medical College	252,000
New Orleans	
Dillard University	202,802
	$1,276,508

Source: "Details of Expenditures, Negro University Centers," *Negro Year Book: An Annual Encyclopedia of the Negro, 1937-1938*, 1937, p. 185. Primary source: Reports of the Julius Rosenwald Fund. Published by permission.

★ 773 ★

Higher Education

Support for Colleges: Income Sources of Black Colleges as a Percent of Current Education-and-General Income, 1947-48

Item	Amount	Per cent of	
		Educational and general income	Total current income
Educational and general			
Students fees	$7,312,075	19.1	13.1
Federal government			
Veteran's education	6,581,892	17.2	11.8
Other purposes	4,273,509	11.2	7.6
State governments	10,881,932	28.4	19.4
Local governments	1,052,656	2.7	1.9
Endowment earnings	2,159,536	5.6	3.9
Private benefactions	3,715,734	9.7	6.6
Sales and services	1,348,906	3.5	2.4
Miscellaneous sources	992,014	2.6	1.8

[Continued]

★ 773 ★

Support for Colleges: Income Sources of Black Colleges as a Percent of Current Education-and-General Income, 1947-48
[Continued]

Item	Amount	Per cent of	
		Educational and general income	Total current income
Total educational and general	38,318,254	100.0	68.3
Auxiliary enterprises and activities	17,060,107	-	30.5
Other noneducational income	545,881	-	1.0
Total current income	$55,924,242	-	100.0

Source: "Analysis of Current Income of 103 Institutions, 1947-48," *1952 Negro Year Book: A Review of Events Affecting Negro Life,* 1952, p. 220. Primary source: U.S. Office of Education, Statistical Circular No. 293, April 1951. Published by permission.

★ 774 ★

Higher Education

Support for Colleges: State Appropriations for Black Senior Colleges, c. 1937

	1940-1941	1938-1939
Ark., A. & M.	$87,142.50	$46,230.00
Fla., A. & M.	277,442.00	277,450.00
Ga., Indus. Col.	35,000.00	30,000.00
Ky., Indus. Col.	110,000.00	160,000.00
La., Sou. Univ.	355,000.00	305,000.00
Md., St. T'ch. Col.	66,025.00	59,025.00
Miss., Alcorn A. & M.	46,419.00	46,419.00
Mo., Lincoln Univ.	805,000.00	806,000.00
N.C., A. & T.	615,000.00	550,000.00
Okla., Langston U.	186,749.00	199,673.00
S.C., A. & M.	90,000.00	89,997.00
Tenn., A. & I.	110,000.00	100,000.00
Tex., Prairie View	349,500.00	352,500.00
Va., St. College	121,041.00	121,041.00
W. Va., Te'ch. Col.	180,000.00	150,000.00
	$3,434,318.50	$3,293,335.00

Source: "Appropriations for Negro Senior Colleges, c. 1937-38," *Negro Year Book: An Annual Encyclopedia of the Negro, 1937-1938,* 1937, p. 43. Primary source: Work, Monroe N. (Ed.), *Negro Year Book: An Annual Encyclopedia of the Negro, 1937-1938.* Tuskegee Institute, Ala.: The Negro Year Book Pub. Co., 1937. Published by permission.

★ 775 ★

Higher Education

Support for Colleges: State and Federal Funds
Provided for Construction in Black and White Colleges,
c. 1937-38

	White est. cost	Negro est. cost
Alabama	$4,999,412	$89,091
Arkansas	5,625,654	285,631
Florida	2,335,012	367,282
Georgia	4,570,614	62,389
Kentucky	4,443,796	425,043
Louisiana	9,094,564	1,035,999
Maryland	3,222,751	521,245
Mississippi	1,946,161	63,636
Missouri	3,950,745	181,818
North Carolina	7,234,097	2,051,507
Oklahoma	6,557,956	215,236
South Carolina	5,324,327	61,100
Tennessee	1,369,068	-
Texas	10,317,349	100,000
Virginia	11,068,859	1,013,845
West Virginia	1,824,322	585,671
	$83,884,687	$7,059,493

Source: "Costs, State and Federal Funds for Construction," *Negro Year Book: An Annual Encyclopedia of the Negro, 1937-1938,* 1937, p. 43. Primary source: Work, Monroe N. (Ed.), *Negro Year Book: An Annual Encyclopedia of the Negro, 1937-1938.* Tuskegee Institute, Ala.: The Negro Year Book Pub. Co., 1937. Published by permission.

★ 776 ★

Higher Education

Support for Colleges: Summary Financial Characteristics
of Black Institutions, 1899-1948

Year	Education and General Income	Educational and General Expenditures	Physical Property	Endowment and other Nonexpendable Funds[1]
1899-1900	$1,111,783	[2]	$7,930,949	[2]
1909-1910	3,037,118	[2]	13,143,181	$2,155,014
1919-1920	4,193,333[3]	$3,729,960[3]	21,151,425[3]	12,915,015[3]
1929-1930	11,880,641[3]	8,158,313[3]	57,327,354[3]	36,604,552[3]
1939-1940	11,889,977	11,007,479	76,343,816	39,607,319
1941-1942	13,141,771	12,190,257	79,398,552	39,018,303
1943-1944	15,427,072	10,676,784	82,976,515	45,676,900

[Continued]

★ 776 ★

Support for Colleges: Summary Financial Characteristics
of Black Institutions, 1899-1948
[Continued]

Year	Education and General Income	Educational and General Expenditures	Physical Property	Endowment and other Nonexpendable Funds[1]
1945-1946	25,538,631	22,968,642	99,726,563[3]	49,308,992[3]
1947-1948	38,318,254	36,215,919	119,857,859	53,229,897

Source: "Historical Summary of Selected Financial Data, 1899-1900 to 1947-48 in Negro Institutions of Higher Education," *1952 Negro Year Book: A Review of Events Affecting Negro Life*, 1952, p. 219. Primary source: U.S. Office of Education, *Statistical Circular No. 293*, April 1951. *Notes:* 1. Value at end of fiscal year. 2. Data not available. 3. Estimated.

★ 777 ★

Higher Education

Test Scores: ACE Psychological Examination Scores for Black Students, by Major, c. 1942

Major field	Number	Score on A.C.E. Psychological Examination			
		Medians	Q1	Q3	Highest
Art	16	70	57	90	135
Commerce and business	154	54	39	76	155
Mathematics	121	63	49	84	145
Modern foreign language	24	65	47	85	145
Classical languages	3	103	...	...	105
English	394	50	36	68	155
Music	96	55	37	76	115
Biological science	249	74	49	96	165
General science	37	54	39	69	115
Physical science	15	65	55	93	135
Chemistry	108	70	50	88	155
Social sciences (general)	90	70	41	90	165
Economics	11	78	48	97	155
History	141	60	39	79	145
Political science (Government)	17	78	52	97	145
Psychology	3	45	...	...	95
Sociology and social work	120	70	54	94	135
Education	293	46	35	66	135
Physical education	111	67	50	86	145
Industrial arts education	26	65	51	82	125
Home economics	547	51	38	67	135
Agricultural education	221	49	36	68	115
Medicine	2	75	...	...	95
Dentistry	1	135	...	...	135
Law	5	93	62	99	105
Library science	8	80	50	90	105
Nursing	32	47	33	62	105

[Continued]

★ 777 ★

Test Scores: ACE Psychological Examination Scores for Black Students, by Major, c. 1942
[Continued]

Major field	Number	Score on A.C.E. Psychological Examination			
		Medians	Q1	Q3	Highest
Religion and religious education	3	45	...	...	95
Mechanic arts	309	61	45	78	155
Total	3,157	...	...	...	...

Source: "Distribution of scores earned by freshmen on American Council on Education Psychological Examination, by indicated major field," *National Survey of the Higher Education of Negroes*. Vol. 1, No. 6. *Socio-Economic Approach to Educational Problems*, 1942, p. 62. Primary source: U.S. Office of Education. *National Survey of the Higher Education of Negroes*. Vol. 1, No. 6. *Socio-Economic Approach to Educational Problems*, by Ida Corinne Brown. Washington, D.C.: U.S. Government Printing Office, 1942.

★ 778 ★

Higher Education

Test Scores: Freshman and Senior Scores on Test (of General Knowledge of the Negro) used by Black Colleges, c. 1942

Score	Seniors		Freshmen	
	Number	Cumulative Percent	Number	Cumulative Percent
90 and above	1	...	1	...
86-89	...	...	...	...
82-85	7	99	...	...
78-81	21	98	...	...
74-77	34	96	2	99
70-73	45	93	7	99
68-69	37	90	4	99
66-67	58	86	4	99
64-65	55	79	13	99
62-63	55	79	13	99
60-61	90	73	31	98
58-59	89	67	35	98
56-57	77	62	30	96
54-55	86	56	68	95
52-53	107	49	81	93
50-51	98	42	111	91
48-49	80	37	125	87
46-47	75	32	136	83
44-45	70	27	167	78
42-43	81	21	220	73
40-41	58	17	194	66
38-39	61	13	207	59
36-37	48	10	244	53
32-35	81	4	462	45

[Continued]

★ 778 ★

Test Scores: Freshman and Senior Scores on Test (of General Knowledge of the Negro) used by Black Colleges, c. 1942

[Continued]

Score	Seniors		Freshmen	
	Number	Cumulative Percent	Number	Cumulative Percent
28-31	40	2	410	29
24-27	19	1	289	16
20-23	5	...	197	7
Total	1,469	...	3,050	...
Median	52	...	37	...
Q^3	61	...	45	...
Q^1	43	...	31	...

Source: "Distribution of scores earned by 1,469 seniors and 3,050 freshmen on the Test of General Knowledge of the Negro, with cumulative percentages, *National Survey of the Higher Education of Negroes*. Vol. 1, No. 6. *Socio- Economic Approach to Educational Problems*, 1942, p. 53. Primary source: U.S. Office of Education. *National Survey of the Higher Education of Negroes*. Vol. 1, No. 6. *Socio-Economic Approach to Educational Problems*, by Ida Corinne Brown. Washington, D.C.: U.S. Government Printing Office, 1942.

★ 779 ★

Higher Education

Test Scores: Male/Female Differences in Scores on Selected Entrance Tests, c. 1942

Score, by type of test	Male	Female	D/PEd
A.C.E. Psychological Examination:			
Number of cases	1,611	2,073	...
Median	63	51	15.8
Q_3	84	69.8	...
Q_1	45	37	...
Highest	(160-169)	(150-159)	...
Reading Comprehension Test:			
Number of cases	1,287	1,900	...
Median	43.0	42.2	3.3
Q_3	49.3	47.2	...
Q_1	37.9	37.7	...
Highest	...	...	...
Test of General Knowledge of the Negro:			
Number of cases	1,242	1,808	...
Median	40	36	12.4
Q_3	47	43	...

[Continued]

★ 779 ★

Test Scores: Male/Female Differences in Scores on Selected Entrance Tests, c. 1942
[Continued]

Score, by type of test	Male	Female	D/PEd
Q$_1$	33	29	...
Highest	(74-77)	(Above 90)	...

Source: "Distribution of scores earned by freshmen on American Council on Education Psychological Examination, the Reading Comprehension Test, and the Test of General Knowledge of the Negro, by sex," *National Survey of the Highest Education of Negroes.* Vol. 1, No. 6. *Socio-Economic Approach to Educational Problems,* 1942, p. 59. Primary source: U.S. Office of Education. *National Survey of the Higher Education of Negroes.* Vol. 1, No. 6. *Socio-Economic Approach to Educational Problems,* by Ida Corinne Brown. Washington, D.C.: U.S. Government Printing Office, 1942. *Notes:* The last column of the table gives the result of a statistical test of significance.

★ 780 ★

Higher Education

Test Scores: Score Differences on Selected Entrance Tests, by Type of High School/Elementary School Attended, c. 1942

Score, by type of test	Southern urban public school	Southern rural public school	Southern private school	Northern private school	Border State public school
American Council Psychological Examination:					
Number of cases	1,837	311	276	577	662
Median	49.8	43	52.0	82.5	64
Q$_3$	66.0	57	68.3	100.6	85
Q$_1$	36.0	32	39.4	65.4	46
Highest	155	135	125	165	155
Reading Comprehension Test:					
Number of cases	1,397	503	140	507	620
Median	41.1	39.1	41.6	49.7	44.1
Q$_3$	45.5	43.4	45.5	55.2	49.7
Q$_1$	37.1	36.1	37.6	44.2	38.8
Highest	Above 76	Above 76	66	Above 76	Above 76
Test of General Knowledge of the Negro:					
Number of cases	1,448	220	200	510	657
Median	36.3	32.5	37.9	39.9	38.8
Q$_3$	43.6	39.4	46.7	47.8	45.9
Q$_1$	30.1	26.1	31.0	33.5	31.9
Highest	Above 90	65	76	72	76

Source: "Distribution of scores earned by freshmen on American Council on Education Psychological Examination and the Test of General Knowledge of the Negro, by place of secondary schooling, and on the Reading Comprehension Test, by place of elementary schooling," *National Survey of the Higher Education of Negroes.* Vol. 1, No. 6. *Socio-Economic Approach to Educational Problems,* 1942, p. 59. Primary source: U.S. Office of Education. *National Survey of the Higher Education of Negroes.* Vol. 1, No. 6. *Socio-Economic Approach to Educational Problems,* by Ida Corinne Brown. Washington, D.C.: U.S. Government Printing Office, 1942.

★ 781 ★

Higher Education

Test Scores: Scores of Black Seniors on General Culture Test, by Gender, c. 1942

Score, by type of test	Male	Female	D/PEd
Social studies			
Median	31	27	4.2
Q3	48	41	...
Q1	17	14	...
Highest score	105	95	...
Literature			
Median	14	17	5.0
Q3	25	28	...
Q1	7	9	...
Highest score	85	105	...
Fine arts			
Median	11	13	3.7
Q3	20	24	...
Q1	5	6	...
Highest score	85	85	...
Science			
Median	27	23	5.8
Q3	39	33	...
Q1	17	13	...
Highest score	75	65	...
Mathematics			
Median	10	8	4.8
Q3	19	15	...
Q1	5	4	...
Highest score	55	55	...

Source: "Distribution of scores earned by seniors on the sub-tests of the General Culture test, by sex," *National Survey of the Higher Education of Negroes.* Vol. 1, No. 6. *Socio-Economic Approach to Educational Problems*, 1942, p. 59. Primary source: U.S. Office of Education. *National Survey of the Higher Education of Negroes.* Vol. 1, No. 6. *Socio-Economic Approach to Educational Problems,* by Ida Corinne Brown. Washington, D.C.; U.S. Government Printing Office, 1942. *Notes:* The last column in the Table gives the results of a statistical test of significance.

★ 782 ★

Higher Education

Test Scores: Senior Scores on Selected Standardized Tests, c. 1942

General culture score	Median reading comprehension score	Median knowledge of Negro score
270 and above	70	71
250-269	70	63
230-249	68	64
210-229	66	66
190-209	63	61
170-189	60	60
150-169	56	60
140-149	57	57
130-139	55	57
120-129	54	57
110-119	50	53
100-109	49	55
90-99	50	53
80-89	49	49
70-79	48	49
60-69	45	46
50-59	45	45
40-49	42	45
30-39	41	41
20-29	41	41
10-19	42	47
0-9	43	44

Source: "Comparative scores earned by seniors on the General Culture, Reading Comprehension, and General Knowledge of the Negro tests," *National Survey of the Higher Education of Negroes.* Vol. 1, No. 6. *Socio-Economic Approach to Educational Problems,* 1942, p. 53. Primary source: U.S. Office of Education. *National Survey of the Higher Education of Negroes.* Vol. 1, No. 6. *Socio-Economic Approach to Educational Problems,* by Ida Corinne Brown. Washington, D.C.: U.S. Government Printing Office, 1942.

Illiteracy

★ 783 ★

Number/Percent of Illiterates at Age 21 and Over by Region, 1930

Section and division	Negro			White		
	Total number	Illiterate		Total number	Illiterate	
		Number	Percent		Number	Percent
United States	6,531,939	1,306,650	20.0	65,400,034	2,251,470	3.4
The South	4,848,072	1,212,258	25.0	15,016,965	711,862	4.7
South Atlantic	2,210,041	552,521	25.0	6,194,770	303,343	4.9
East South Central	1,402,055	392,519	28.0	3,816,222	235,387	6.2
West South Central	1,235,976	267,218	21.6	5,005,973	173,132	3.5
The North	1,598,098	91,052	5.7	43,363,284	1,429,140	3.3
The West	85,769	3,340	3.9	7,019,785	110,468	1.6

Source: "Illiteracy in the Negro and White Population 21 Years Old and Over, by Sections, and Southern Divisions: 1930," *Negroes in the United States, 1920-1932*, 1935, p. 233. Primary source: U.S. Bureau of the Census. *Negroes in the United States, 1920-1932*. Washington, D.C.: U.S. Government Printing Office, 1935.

★ 784 ★

Illiteracy

Number/Percent: Age and Gender Distribution of Black Illiterates, 1910

AGE PERIOD AND CENSUS YEAR	NEGRO ILLITERATES					
	Number			Per cent		
	Both sexes	Male	Female	Both sexes	Male	Female
10 years and over:						
1910	2,227,731	1,096,000	1,131,731	30.4	30.1	30.7
1900	2,853,194	1,371,432	1,481,762	44.5	43.1	45.8
1890[1]	3,042,668	1,438,923	1,603,745	57.1	54.5	59.8
10 to 14 years:						
1910	218,555	125,616	92,939	18.9	21.7	16.1
1900	328,992	183,540	145,452	30.1	33.5	26.8
1890[1]	411,726	220,414	191,312	39.8	41.9	37.7
15 to 19 years:						
1910	214,860	126,459	88,401	20.3	24.9	16.0
1900	312,094	173,891	138,203	31.8	36.7	27.2
1890[1]	371,076	192,853	178,223	42.6	45.7	39.7
20 to 24 years:						
1910	245,860	126,970	118,890	23.9	26.3	21.7

[Continued]

★ 784 ★

Number/Percent: Age and Gender Distribution of Black Illiterates, 1910
[Continued]

AGE PERIOD AND CENSUS YEAR	NEGRO ILLITERATES					
	Number			Per cent		
	Both sexes	Male	Female	Both sexes	Male	Female
1900	340,516	165,085	175,431	35.1	36.0	34.4
1890[1]	360,887	163,107	197,780	49.3	46.5	51.9
25 to 34 years:						
1910	380,742	183,993	196,749	24.6	24.4	24.7
1900	496,180	222,516	273,664	39.3	35.7	42.8
1890[1]	550,551	235,420	315,131	56.8	49.5	63.8
35 to 44 years:						
1910	351,858	152,132	199,726	32.3	27.7	37.1
1900	437,503	177,199	260,304	52.0	43.0	60.6
1890[1]	498,667	208,451	290,216	76.5	60.6	79.8
45 to 54 years:						
1910	334,930	147,542	187,388	47.0	38.9	56.3
1900	420,438	191,883	228,555	68.1	59.3	77.8
1890[1]	403,634	192,520	211,114	80.8	74.8	87.1
55 to 64 years:						
1910	249,584	120,046	129,538	63.0	55.5	72.0
1900	267,212	134,535	132,777	78.4	72.4	84.3
1890[1]	231,490	120,399	111,091	86.3	83.2	89.9
65 years and over:						
1910	219,255	107,877	111,378	74.5	70.7	78.6
1900	223,124	111,158	111,966	85.4	83.6	87.2
1890[1]	190,899	94,806	96,093	90.2	88.3	92.1
Age unknown:						
1910	12,087	5,365	6,722	38.9	31.4	48.1
1900	27,035	11,625	15,410	55.4	46.2	65.1
1890[1]	23,738	10,953	12,785	66.3	59.4	73.6

Source: [Untitled Table], *Negro Population, 1790-1915,* 1918, p. 406. Primary source: U.S. Bureau of the Census. *Negro Population, 1790-1915.* Washington, D.C.: Government Printing Office, 1918. *Notes:* 1. Figures for 1890 are exclusive of illiterate persons in Indian Territory and on Indian reservations specially enumerated but for which illiteracy statistics are not available.

★ 785 ★

Illiteracy

Number/Percent: Black Illiteracy by Geographic Division, 1890-1910 - I

[Per cent not shown where base is less than 100].

DIVISION AND STATE	NUMBER OF NEGRO ILLITERATES								
	Both sexes			Male			Female		
	1910	1900	1890[1]	1910	1900	1890[1]	1910	1900	1890[1]
UNITED STATES	2,227,731	2,853,194	3,042,668	1,096,000	1,371,432	1,438,923	1,131,731	1,481,762	1,603,745
GEOGRAPHIC DIVISIONS:									
New England	4,341	5,681	5,664	2,107	2,469	2,497	2,234	3,212	3,167
Middle Atlantic	27,811	38,594	41,092	12,573	18,141	19,182	15,238	20,453	21,910

[Continued]

★ 785 ★

Number/Percent: Black Illiteracy by Geographic Division, 1890-1910 - I
[Continued]

DIVISION AND STATE	NUMBER OF NEGRO ILLITERATES								
	Both sexes			Male			Female		
	1910	1900	1890[1]	1910	1900	1890[1]	1910	1900	1890[1]
East North Central	28,071	39,280	43,699	13,897	19,498	21,579	14,174	19,782	22,120
West North Central	30,436	48,634	63,696	14,678	23,271	30,355	15,758	25,363	33,341
South Atlantic	969,432	1,250,279	1,384,632	477,107	599,160	651,436	492,325	651,119	733,196
East South Central	681,507	887,838	922,664	337,893	429,984	438,397	343,614	457,854	484,267
West South Central	483,022	579,489	575,920	236,239	277,165	272,386	246,783	302,324	303,534
Mountain	1,497	1,840	2,467	754	967	1,444	743	873	1,023
Pacific	1,614	1,559	2,834	752	777	1,647	862	782	1,187

Source: [Untitled Table], *Negro Population, 1790-1915*, 1918, p. 419. Primary source: U.S. Bureau of the Census. *Negro Population, 1790-1915.* Washington, D.C.: Government Printing Office, 1918. *Notes:* 1. Figures for 1890 are exclusive of illiterate persons in Indian Territory and on Indian reservations, areas specially enumerated, but for which illiteracy statistics are not available.

★ 786 ★

Illiteracy

Number/Percent: Black Illiteracy by Geographic Division, 1890-1910 - II

DIVISION AND STATE	NUMBER OF NEGRO ILLITERATES								
	Both sexes			Male			Female		
	1910	1900	1890[1]	1910	1900	1890[1]	1910	1900	1890[1]
UNITED STATES	2,227,731	2,853,194	3,042,668	1,096,000	1,371,432	1,438,923	1,131,731	1,481,762	1,603,745
GEOGRAPHIC DIVISIONS:									
New England	4,341	5,681	5,664	2,107	2,469	2,497	2,234	3,212	3,167
Middle Atlantic	27,811	38,594	41,092	12,573	18,141	19,182	15,238	20,453	21,910
East North Central	28,071	39,280	43,699	13,897	19,498	21,579	14,174	19,782	22,120
West North Central	30,436	48,634	63,696	14,678	23,271	30,355	15,758	25,363	33,341
South Atlantic	969,432	1,250,279	1,384,632	477,107	599,160	651,436	492,325	651,119	733,196
East South Central	681,507	887,838	922,664	337,893	429,984	438,397	343,614	457,854	484,267
West South Central	483,022	579,489	575,920	236,239	277,165	272,386	246,783	302,324	303,534
Mountain	1,497	1,840	2,467	754	967	1,444	743	873	1,023
Pacific	1,614	1,559	2,834	752	777	1,647	862	782	1,187

Source: [Untitled Table], *Negro Population, 1790-1915*, 1918, p. 419. Primary source: U.S. Bureau of the Census. *Negro Population, 1790-1915.* Washington, D.C.: Government Printing Office, 1918. *Notes:* 1. Figures for 1890 are exclusive of illiterate persons in Indian Territory and on Indian reservations, areas specially enumerated, but for which illiteracy statistics are not available.

★ 787 ★

Illiteracy

Number/Percent: Black Illiteracy by Geographic Division, 1890-1910 - III

DIVISION AND STATE	PERCENTAGE ILLITERATE IN NEGRO POPULATION								
	Both sexes			Male			Female		
	1910	1900	1890[1]	1910	1900	1890[1]	1910	1900	1890[1]
UNITED STATES	30.4	44.5	57.1	30.1	43.1	54.4	30.7	45.8	59.8
GEOGRAPHIC DIVISIONS:									
New England	7.8	11.6	15.5	7.7	10.4	14.1	8.0	12.7	16.8
Middle Atlantic	7.9	14.2	22.3	7.4	13.6	21.0	8.4	14.8	23.6
East North Central	11.0	18.5	26.7	10.4	17.4	25.1	11.7	19.7	28.6
West North Central	14.9	25.4	37.4	13.8	23.6	34.7	16.2	27.1	40.2
South Atlantic	32.5	47.1	60.2	32.4	46.0	57.6	32.5	48.1	62.5
East South Central	34.8	49.2	61.5	34.8	48.1	58.9	34.7	50.4	63.9
West South Central	33.1	48.0	60.9	32.2	46.0	57.4	33.9	50.1	64.3
Mountain	8.0	13.5	21.8	7.2	11.9	19.2	9.0	15.9	27.1
Pacific	6.3	12.7	24.6	5.3	11.4	24.0	7.6	14.4	25.5

Source: [Untitled Table], *Negro Population, 1790-1915*, 1918, p. 419. Primary source: U.S. Bureau of the Census. *Negro Population, 1790-1915*. Washington, D.C.: Government Printing Office, 1918. *Notes:* 1. Figures for 1890 are exclusive of illiterate persons in Indian Territory and on Indian reservations, areas specially enumerated, but for which illiteracy statistics are not available.

★ 788 ★

Illiteracy

Number/Percent: Black Illiteracy, 1870-1930

Year	Illiterates Number	Percent
1930	1,513,892	16.3
1920	1,842,161	22.9
1910	2,227,731	30.4
1900	2,853,194	44.5
1890	3,042,668	57.1
1880	3,220,878	70.9
1870	2,789,689	81.4

Source: "Percentage of Negro Illiterates," *Negro Year Book: An Annual Encyclopedia of the Negro, 1937-1938*, 1937, p. 162. Primary source: U.S. Bureau of the Census.

★ 789 ★

Illiteracy

Number/Percent: Black Illiteracy, by State, 1910-1930

DIVISION AND STATE	NEGROES 10 YEARS OF AGE AND OVER											
	Urban: 1910			Rural: 1910			Cities of 25,000 or more population					
							1910			1900		
	Total	Illiterate		Total	Illiterate		Total	Illiterate		Total	Illiterate	
		Number	Percent		Number	Percent		Number	Percent		Number	Percent
UNITED STATES	2,231,353	393,273	17.6	5,086,569	1,834,458	36.1	1,378,149	201,010	14.6	945,909	230,711	24.6
GEOGRAPHIC DIVISIONS:												
New England	51,025	3,614	7.1	4,296	727	16.9	38,728	2,548	6.6	29,860	3,122	10.5
Middle Atlantic	288,414	20,089	7.0	63,132	7,722	12.2	237,292	15,268	6.4	165,358	18,795	11.4
East North Central	198,669	19,229	9.7	55,876	8,842	15.8	141,688	12,204	8.6	95,281	13,882	14.6
West North Central	141,823	17,454	12.3	61,818	12,982	21.0	94,439	9,790	10.4	71,376	13,460	18.9
South Atlantic	741,429	158,906	21.4	2,245,507	810,526	36.1	433,027	81,507	18.8	294,569	86,070	29.2
East South Central	421,529	100,257	23.8	1,539,369	581,250	37.8	223,866	47,261	21.1	167,741	59,149	35.3
West South Central	353,611	71,652	20.3	1,107,094	411,370	37.2	183,896	31,099	16.9	110,614	35,138	31.8
Mountain	13,505	939	7.0	5,250	558	10.6	8,131	539	6.6	4,858	571	11.8
Pacific	21,348	1,133	5.3	4,277	481	11.4	17,082	794	4.6	6,072	524	8.6

Source: "Percent Illiterate in Negro Population 10 Years Old and Over, 1910, 1920, and 1930 (Ranked as to percent illiterate in the Negro population, 1930),"
Negro Year Book: An Annual Encyclopedia of the Negro, 1937-1938, 1937, p. 163. Primary source: U.S. Bureau of the Census.

★ 790 ★

Illiteracy

Number/Percent: Black Illiterates in 1910, by Age Group and Region

SECTION AND DIVISION	PERCENTAGE ILLITERATE IN THE NEGRO POPULATION OF AGE SPECIFIED: 1910							
	10 years of age and over	10-14 years of age	15-24 years of age	25-34 years of age	35-44 years of age	45-54 years of age	55-64 years of age	65 years and over
United States	30.4	18.9	22.0	24.6	32.3	47.0	63.0	74.5
The South	33.3	20.2	24.1	28.1	36.8	51.9	67.6	78.5
South Atlantic	32.5	18.9	23.4	27.9	36.3	51.0	66.4	77.1
East South Central	34.8	20.7	24.9	29.1	38.1	54.1	70.0	80.8
West South Central	33.1	22.4	24.4	27.4	36.1	50.6	66.8	78.1
The North	10.5	1.7	3.7	5.4	9.6	19.2	32.9	47.9
New England	7.8	0.4	1.6	7.1	7.5	10.6	16.5	25.0
Middle Atlantic	7.9	1.0	3.2	4.6	8.1	15.5	25.1	36.4
East North Central	11.0	1.2	3.1	5.1	9.7	19.4	34.0	50.2
West North Central	14.9	3.6	4.7	6.9	12.8	27.3	46.3	63.6
The West	7.0	1.0	3.1	3.7	5.8	11.0	22.6	38.5
Mountain	8.0	1.6	3.9	4.3	7.2	12.4	25.8	41.4
Pacific	6.3	0.6	2.5	3.2	4.7	10.1	20.4	36.7

Source: [Untitled Table], *Negro Population, 1790-1915,* 1918, p. 412. Primary source: U.S. Bureau of the Census. *Negro Population, 1790-1915.* Washington, D.C.:
Government Printing Office, 1918.

★ 791 ★

Illiteracy

Number/Percent: Distribution of Illiteracy According to Gender by Region, 1930

Age 10 years and over	Negro population									Percent white population illiterate		
	Total			Male			Female					
	Total number	Illiterate		Total number	Illiterate		Total number	Illiterate		Total	Male	Female
		Number	Percent		Number	Percent		Number	Percent			
United States	9,292,556	1,513,892	16.3	4,564,690	801,949	17.6	4,727,866	711,943	15.1	2.7	2.7	2.7
The South	7,194,750	1,416,417	19.7	3,506,598	750,595	21.4	3,688,152	665,822	18.1	3.8	4.4	3.3
The North	1,994,085	94,034	4.7	1,005,003	49,720	4.9	989,082	44,314	4.5	2.6	2.4	2.8
The West	103,721	3,441	3.3	53,089	1,634	3.1	50,632	1,807	3.6	1.3	1.2	1.4

Source: "Illiteracy in Negro Population and Percent Illiteracy in Negro and White Population, by Sex, and Age Groups, by Sections: 1930," *Negroes in the United States, 1920-1932*, 1935, p. 235. Primary source: U.S. Bureau of the Census. *Negroes in the United States, 1920-1932*. Washington, D.C.: U.S. Government Printing Office, 1935.

★ 792 ★

Illiteracy

Number/Percent: Distribution of Illiteracy According to Race and Nativity at Age 10 and Over by Region, 1910-1930

Census year, color, and nativity	United States	The South				The North	The West
		Total	South Atlantic division	East South Central division	West South Central division		
				Number illiterate			
1930							
Negro	1,513,892	1,416,417	662,055	452,082	302,280	94,034	3,441
White							
Native	1,103,134	767,180	314,583	270,130	182,467	291,994	43,960
Foreign born	1,304,084	51,524	31,328	4,238	15,958	1,180,152	72,408
1920							
Negro	1,842,161	1,751,658	812,842	536,583	402,233	87,133	3,370
White							
Native	1,242,572	892,865	356,785	301,651	234,429	295,731	53,976
Foreign born	1,763,740	174,939	39,757	6,457	128,725	1,446,809	141,992
1910							
Negro	2,227,731	2,133,961	969,432	681,507	483,022	90,659	3,111
White							
Native	1,534,272	1,079,583	433,809	381,230	264,544	398,496	56,193
Foreign born	1,650,361	130,823	37,934	8,215	84,674	1,398,943	120,595
				Percent illiterate			
Negro							
1930	16.3	19.7	19.7	22.0	17.0	4.7	3.3
1920	22.9	26.0	25.2	27.9	25.3	7.0	4.9
1910	30.4	33.3	32.5	34.8	33.1	10.5	7.0

[Continued]

★ 792 ★

Number/Percent: Distribution of Illiteracy According to Race and Nativity at Age 10 and Over by Region, 1910-1930

[Continued]

| Census year, color, and nativity | United States | The South | | | | The North | The West |
		Total	South Atlantic division	East South Central division	West South Central division		
White							
Native							
1930	1.5	3.7	3.7	5.0	2.6	.6	.6
1920	2.0	5.2	5.1	6.4	4.1	.8	1.0
1910	3.0	7.5	7.6	9.2	5.8	1.2	1.4
Foreign born							
1930	9.9	9.8	10.4	7.4	9.4	10.5	5.1
1920	13.1	21.5	12.8	9.1	29.9	12.9	9.8
1910	12.7	18.8	13.5	9.7	·25.6	12.7	9.5

Source: "Illiteracy in the Population 10 Years Old and Over, by Color and Nativity, by Sections, and Southern Divisions: 1930, 1920, and 1910," *Negroes in the United States, 1920-1932*, 1935, p. 233. Primary source: U.S. Bureau of the Census. *Negroes in the United States, 1920-1932.* Washington, D.C.: U.S. Government Printing Office, 1935.

★ 793 ★

Illiteracy

Number/Percent: Gender Distribution of Black Illiterates, 1890-1910

| YEAR OF ENUMERATION | Age in years | NEGRO ILLITERATES | | | | | |
| | | Both sexes | | Male | | Female | |
		Number	Percent	Number	Percent	Number	Percent
1890	15-24	731,963	45.7	355,960	46.1	376,003	45.3
1900	25-34	496,180	39.3	222,516	35.7	273,664	42.8
1910	35-44	351,858	32.3	152,132	27.7	199,726	37.1
1890	25-34	550,551	56.8	235,420	49.5	315,131	63.8
1900	35-44	437,503	52.0	177,199	43.0	260,304	60.6
1910	45-54	334,930	47.0	147,542	38.9	187,388	56.3
1890	35-44	498,667	70.5	208,451	60.6	290,216	79.8
1900	45-54	429,438	68.1	191,883	59.3	228,555	77.8
1910	55-64	249,584	63.0	120,046	55.5	129,538	72.0
1900	15-24	626,610	33.4	383,976	36.3	313,634	30.8
1910	25-34	380,742	24.6	183,993	24.4	196,749	24.7
1910	15-24	460,720	22.0	253,429	25.6	207,291	18.8

Source: [Untitled Table], *Negro Population, 1790-1915*, 1918, p. 408. Primary source: U.S. Bureau of the Census. *Negro Population, 1790-1915.* Washington, D.C.: Government Printing Office, 1918.

★ 794 ★

Illiteracy

Number/Percent: Illiteracy among Blacks Aged 10 and Over by Region and Gender, 1910-1930

	Census year					
	Number illiterate			Decrease in number illiterate		
	1930	1920	1910	1930	1920	1910
The South						
Total	1,416,417	1,751,658	2,133,961	335,241	382,303	583,645
Male	750,595	895,490	1,051,239	144,895	155,749	255,070
Female	665,822	856,168	1,082,722	190,346	226,554	328,575
South Atlantic division						
Total	662,055	812,842	969,432	150,787	156,590	280,847
Male	353,459	417,569	477,107	64,110	59,538	122,053
Female	308,596	395,273	492,325	86,677	97,052	158,794
East South Central division						
Total	452,082	536,583	681,507	84,591	144,924	206,331
Male	240,348	274,925	387,893	34,577	62,968	92,091
Female	211,734	261,658	343,614	49,924	81,956	114,240
West South Central division						
Total	392,280	402,233	343,614	99,953	80,789	96,467
Male	156,788	202,996	286,239	46,208	33,243	40,926
Female	145,492	199,237	245,783	53,745	47,546	55,541
The North						
Total	94,034	87,133	90,659	+6,991	3,526	41,530
Male	49,720	45,136	43,255	+4,584	+1,881	20,124
Female	44,314	41,997	47,404	+2,317	5,407	21,406
The West						
Total	3,441	3,370	3,111	+71	+259	288
Male	1,634	1,742	1,506	108	+236	238
Female	1,807	1,628	1,605	+179	+23	50

Source: "Illiteracy in the Negro Population 10 Years Old and Over, by Sex, by Sections, and Southern Divisions: 1930, 1920, and 1910," *Negroes in the United States, 1920-1932,* 1935, p. 235. Primary source: U.S. Bureau of the Census. *Negroes in the United States, 1920-1932.* Washington, D.C.: U.S. Government Printing Office, 1935. *Note:* A plus sign (+) denotes increase.

★ 795 ★

Illiteracy

Number/Percent: Illiteracy among Southern Blacks
Over Age 20, 1860

State	Free Colored Population Over 20 Years	Illiterates Over 20 Years	Per Cent Illiterate	Per Cent Literate
Alabama	1,258	455	36.2	63.8
Arkansas	72	23	32.0	68.0
Delaware	9,030	6,508	72.1	27.9
District of Columbia	5,489	3,375	57.7	42.3
Florida	426	120	28.2	71.8
Georgia	1,677	573	34.2	65.8
Kentucky	5,619	2,463	43.8	56.2
Louisiana	9,855	1,202	12.2	87.8
Maryland	42,402	21,699	51.2	48.8
Mississippi	392	110	28.1	71.9
Missouri	2,161	885	41.0	59.0
North Carolina	13,343	6,849	51.3	48.7
South Carolina	4,505	1,416	31.4	68.6
Tennessee	3,308	1,695	51.2	48.8
Texas	163	62	38.0	62.0
Virginia	27,103	12,397	45.7	54.3
Totals	127,163	59,832	47.1	52.9

Source: [Untitled Table], *Negro Year Book: An Annual Encyclopedia of the Negro, 1937-1938,* 1937, p. 161. Primary source: United States Census for 1860.

★ 796 ★

Illiteracy

Number/Percent: Males 21 and Over who were Illiterate in 1910

SECTION AND DIVISION	MALE POPULATION 21 YEARS OF AGE AND OVER						
	Negro		Percentage illiterate				
			Negro population		White population, 1910		
	Total	Illiterate	1910	1900	Total	Native	Foreign born
United States	2,458,873	819,135	33.3	47.4	5.8	3.5	11.9
The South	2,086,639	777,181	37.2	51.9	8.9	8.4	16.1
South Atlantic	955,364	351,220	36.8	51.1	8.9	8.6	13.0
East South Central	642,460	252,677	39.2	53.6	10.6	10.7	7.8
West South Central	488,815	173,284	35.4	51.0	7.5	6.0	21.1

[Continued]

★ 796 ★

Number/Percent: Males 21 and Over who were Illiterate in 1910
[Continued]

SECTION AND DIVISION	MALE POPULATION 21 YEARS OF AGE AND OVER						
	Negro		Percentage illiterate				
			Negro population		White population, 1910		
	Total	Illiterate	1910	1900	Total	Native	Foreign born
The North	351,213	40,546	11.5	20.6	5.1	1.7	11.9
The West	21,021	1,408	6.7	13.4	3.8	1.2	9.3

Source: [Untitled Table], *Negro Population, 1790-1915*, 1918, p. 418. Primary source: U.S. Bureau of the Census. *Negro Population, 1790-1915.* Washington, D.C.: Government Printing Office, 1918.

★ 797 ★

Illiteracy

Number/Percent: Racial Distribution of Illiteracy by Region, 1890-1910

RACIAL CLASS AND YEAR	POPULATION 10 YEARS OF AGE AND OVER						
	United States	The South				The North	The West
		Total	South Atlantic division	East South Central division	West South Central division		
NUMBER ILLITERATE							
1910							
Negro	2,227,731	2,133,961	969,432	681,507	438,022	90,659	3,111
White:							
Native	1,534,272	1,079,583	433,809	381,230	264,544	398,496	56,193
Foreign born	1,650,361	130,823	37,934	8,215	84,674	1,398,943	120,595
1900							
Negro	2,853,194	2,717,606	1,250,279	887,838	579,489	132,189	3,399
White:							
Native	1,913,611	1,296,497	541,530	466,328	288,639	555,724	61,390
Foreign born	1,287,135	104,776	26,437	9,253	69,086	1,118,400	63,959
1890							
Negro	3,042,668	2,883,216	1,384,632	922,664	575,920	154,151	5,301
White:							
Native	2,065,003	1,326,834	571,899	499,699	255,236	666,225	71,944
Foreign born	1,147,571	86,149	24,053	9,411	52,685	993,709	67,713

Source: [Untitled Table], *Negro Population, 1790-1915*, 1918, p. 413. Primary source: U.S. Bureau of the Census. *Negro Population, 1790-1915.* Washington, D.C.: Government Printing Office, 1918.

★ 798 ★

Illiteracy

Number/Percent: Total Illiteracy and Age Distribution of Blacks, 1920

"In 1920 there were 4,931,905 persons 10 years of age and over in the United States who were illiterate. Of this number, 3,089,744 or 62.6 per cent were white and 1,842,161 or 37.3 per cent were Negroes. By age periods there were of the Negro illiterates, 166,416 or 9.1 per cent, 10 to 15 years of age; 162,758 or 8.8 per cent 16 to 20 years of age and 1,512,987 or 82.1 per cent 21 years of age and over."

Source: "Illiteracy," *Negro Year Book: An Annual Encyclopedia of the Negro, 1925-1926*, 1925, p. 295. Primary source: U.S. Bureau of the Census. Published by permission.

★ 799 ★

Illiteracy

Number/Percent: Urban-Rural Residence and Black Illiteracy in 1900 and 1910 - I

DIVISION AND STATE	NEGROES 10 YEARS OF AGE AND OVER Smaller cities and country districts					
	1910			1900		
	Total	Illiterate		Total	Illiterate	
		Number	Percent		Number	Percent
UNITED STATES	5,939,773	2,026,721	34.1	5,469,672	2,622,483	47.9
GEOGRAPHIC DIVISIONS:						
New England	16,593	1,793	10.8	19,159	2,559	13.4
Middle Atlantic	114,254	12,543	11.0	105,619	19,799	18.7
East North Central	112,857	15,867	14.1	117,440	25,398	21.6
West North Central	109,202	20,646	18.9	120,471	35,174	29.2
South Atlantic	2,533,909	887,925	34.8	2,361,264	1,164,209	49.3
East South Central	1,737,032	634,246	36.5	1,635,087	828,689	50.7
West South Central	1,276,809	451,923	35.4	1,095,700	544,351	49.7
Mountain	10,624	958	9.0	8,725	1,269	14.5
Pacific	8,493	820	9.7	6,207	1,035	16.7

Source: "Percent Illiterate in Negro Population 10 Years Old and Over, 1910, 1920, and 1930 (Ranked as to percent illiterate in the Negro population, 1930)," *Negro Year Book: An Annual Encyclopedia of the Negro, 1937-1938*, 1937, p. 163. Primary source: U.S. Bureau of the Census.

★ 800 ★

Illiteracy

Number/Percent: Urban-Rural Residence and Black Illiteracy in 1900 and 1910 - II

State	Per Cent Illiterate		
	1930	1920	1910
United States	16.3	22.9	30.4
South Carolina	26.9	29.3	38.7
Alabama	26.2	31.3	40.1
Louisiana	23.3	38.5	48.4
Mississippi	23.2	29.3	35.6
North Carolina	20.6	24.5	31.9
Georgia	19.9	29.1	36.5
Virginia	19.2	23.5	30.0
Florida	18.8	21.5	25.5
Arkansas	16.1	21.8	26.4
Kentucky	15.4	21.0	27.6
Tennessee	14.9	22.4	27.3
Texas	13.4	17.8	24.6
Delaware	13.2	19.1	25.6
Maryland	11.4	18.2	23.4
West Virginia	11.3	15.3	20.3
Oklahoma	9.3	12.4	17.7
Missouri	8.8	12.1	17.4
Rhode Island	8.1	10.2	9.5
Ohio	6.4	8.1	11.1
Indiana	6.0	9.5	13.7
New Mexico	6.0	4.3	14.2
Kansas	5.9	8.8	12.0
Iowa	5.4	8.1	10.3
Massachusetts	5.4	6.8	8.1
New Jersey	5.1	6.1	9.9
Connecticut	4.9	6.2	6.3
Vermont	4.9	6.2	4.8
Maine	4.8	5.9	8.0
Montana	4.6	6.0	7.0
Wisconsin	4.4	4.1	4.5
Idaho	4.2	5.4	6.4
Pennsylvania	4.2	6.1	9.1
Wyoming	4.2	5.3	5.0
District of Columbia	4.1	8.6	13.5
Arizona	4.0	4.6	7.2
Colorado	3.9	6.2	8.6
Nebraska	3.9	4.8	7.2
New Hampshire	3.9	6.7	10.6
Illinois	3.6	6.7	10.5
North Dakota	3.4	4.0	4.8
Utah	3.2	4.6	4.8
California	3.1	4.7	7.1
Michigan	3.0	4.2	5.7
Washington	2.9	4.0	4.3

[Continued]

★ 800 ★

Number/Percent: Urban-Rural Residence and Black Illiteracy in 1900 and 1910 - II
[Continued]

State	Per Cent Illiterate		
	1930	1920	1910
New York	2.5	2.9	5.0
Oregon	2.5	4.7	3.4
South Dakota	2.2	5.2	5.5
Minnesota	2.0	3.1	3.4
Nevada	1.5	5.1	5.5

Source: [Untitled Table], *Negro Population, 1790-1915*, 1918, p. 429. Primary source: U.S. Bureau of the Census. *Negro Population, 1790-1915*. Washington, D.C.: Government Printing Office, 1918.

★ 801 ★

Illiteracy

Relationships: Black Population and Illiterates, by Age Group, 1890-1910

CENSUS YEAR	NEGRO POPULATION								
	10 years of age and over	10 to 14 years	15 to 19 years	20 to 24 years	25 to 34 years	35 to 44 years	45 to 54 years	55 to 64 years	65 years and over
NUMBER OF ILLITERATES PER 1,000 POPULATION OF AGE SPECIFIED									
1910	304	189	203	239	246	323	470	630	745
1900	445	301	218	351	393	520	681	784	854
1890	571	398	426	493	568	705	808	863	902
DECREASE IN NUMBER OF ILLITERATES PER 1,000 POPULATION									
1890-1910	267	209	223	254	322	382	338	233	157
1900-1910	141	112	115	112	147	197	211	154	109
1890-1900	126	97	108	142	175	185	127	79	48

Source: [Untitled Table], *Negro Population, 1790-1915*, 1918, p. 407. Primary source: U.S. Bureau of the Census. *Negro Population, 1790-1915*. Washington, D.C.: Government Printing Office, 1918.

★ 802 ★

Illiteracy

Relationships: Black Illiterates per 1,000 Black Population, 1890-1910

| YEAR AND PERIOD | ILLITERATES PER 1,000 NEGRO POPULATION 10 YEARS OF AGE AND OVER | | | | | | |
| | United States | The South | | | | The North | The West |
		Total	South Atlantic division	East South Central division	West South Central division		
1910	304	333	325	348	331	105	70
1900	445	480	471	492	480	182	131
1890	571	607	601	615	609	278	232
Decrease: 1890-1910	267	274	276	267	278	173	162

Source: [Untitled Table], *Negro Population, 1790-1915*, 1918, p. 410. Primary source: U.S. Bureau of the Census. *Negro Population, 1790-1915*. Washington, D.C.: Government Printing Office, 1918.

★ 803 ★

Illiteracy

Relationships: Black Population and Illiterates, 1900-1910, by region

| SECTION AND DIVISION | INCREASE IN NEGRO POPULATION 10 YEARS OF AGE AND OVER, 1900-1910 | | DECREASE IN NUMBER OF NEGRO ILLITERATES, 1900-1910 | |
	Male	Female	Male	Female
United States	455,736	446,605	275,432	350,031
The South	374,729	368,835	255,070	328,575
South Atlantic	167,568	163,535	122,053	158,794
East South Central	77,369	80,701	92,091	114,240
West South Central	129,792	124,599	40,926	55,541
The North	71,289	69,020	20,124	21,406
The West	9,718	8,750	238	50

Source: [Untitled Table], *Negro Population, 1790-1915*, 1918, p. 411. Primary source: U.S. Bureau of the Census. *Negro Population, 1790-1915*. Washington, D.C.: Government Printing Office, 1918.

★ 804 ★

Illiteracy

Relationships: Changes in Black Illiteracy and Population by Gender and Region, 1920-1930

A plus sign (+) denotes increase.

Section and division	Increase in population 10 years old and over 1920-1930		Decrease in illiterate 1920-1930	
	Male	Female	Male	Female
United States	555,228	684,163	140,419	187,850
The South	186,254	275,068	144,895	190,346
South Atlantic	47,391	94,779	64,110	86,677
East South Central	55,502	72,735	34,577	49,924
West South Central	83,361	107,554	46,208	53,745
The North	355,849	387,528	+4,584	+2,317
The West	13,125	21,507	108	+179

Source: "Increase in Negro Population and Decrease in Number by Sections, and Southern Divisions: 1930," *Negroes in the United States, 1920-1932,* 1935, p. 233. Primary source: U.S. Bureau of the Census. *Negroes in the United States, 1920-1932.* Washington, D.C.: U.S. Government Printing Office, 1935.

★ 805 ★

Illiteracy

Relationships: Changes in Black Population and in Illiteracy of Blacks, 1890-1920

SECTION, DIVISION, AND YEAR	NEGRO POPULATION 10 YEARS OF AGE AND OVER			Decennial increase in population	Decennial decrease in number illiterate[1]
	Total	Illiterate			
		Number	Percent		
United States:					
1910	7,317,922	2,227,731	30.4	902,341	625,463
1900	6,415,581	2,853,194	44.5	1,086,609	189,474
1890	5,328,972	3,042,668	57.1	...	...
The South:					
1910	6,408,539	2,133,961	33.3	743,564	583,645
1900	5,664,975	2,717,606	48.0	913,212	165,610
1890	4,751,763	2,883,216	60.7	...	...
South Atlantic division:					
1910	2,986,936	969,432	32.5	331,103	280,847
1900	2,655,833	1,250,279	47.1	351,658	134,353
1890	2,304,175	1,384,632	60.1	...	...
East South Central division:					
1910	1,960,898	681,507	34.8	158,070	206,331
1900	1,802,828	887,838	49.2	301,398	34,826
1890	1,501,430	922,664	61.5	...	...

[Continued]

★ 805 ★

Relationships: Changes in Black Population and in Illiteracy of Blacks, 1890-1920
[Continued]

| SECTION, DIVISION, AND YEAR | NEGRO POPULATION 10 YEARS OF AGE AND OVER | | | Decennial increase in population | Decennial decrease in number illiterate[1] |
| | Total | Illiterate | | | |
		Number	Percent		
West South Central division:					
1910	1,460,705	483,022	33.1	254,391	96,467
1900	1,206,314	579,489	48.0	260,156	+3,569
1890	946,158	575,920	60.9	...	...
The North:					
1910	865,053	90,659	10.5	140,309	41,530
1900	724,744	132,189	18.2	170,357	21,962
1890	554,387	154,151	27.8	...	...
The West:					
1910	44,330	3,111	7.0	18,468	288
1900	25,862	3,399	13.1	3,040	1,902
1890	22,822	5,301	23.2	...	...

Source: [Untitled Table], *Negro Population, 1790-1915*, 1918, p. 409. Primary source: U.S. Bureau of the Census. *Negro Population, 1790-1915.* Washington, D.C.: Government Printing Office, 1918. *Note:* 1. A plus sign (+) denotes increase.

★ 806 ★

Illiteracy

Relationships: Changes in Black Population and in Illiteracy, 1890-1900 and 1900-1910

| AGE PERIOD | NEGRO POPULATION | | | |
| | 1900-1910 | | 1890-1900 | |
	Increase of population	Decrease in number of illiterates	Increase of population	Decrease in number of illiterates
10 years and over	902,341	625,463	1,086,609	189,474
10 to 14 years	63,276	110,437	58,289	82,734
15 to 19 years	78,394	97,234	110,904	58,982
20 to 24 years	61,623	94,656	237,624	20,371
25 to 34 years	287,230	115,438	292,558	54,371
35 to 44 years	246,959	85,645	134,322	61,164
45 to 54 years	94,608	85,508	117,692	16,804[2]
55 to 64 years	55,261	17,728	72,543	35,822[2]
65 years and over	32,761	3,869	49,679	32,225[2]
Age unknown	17,771[1]	14,948	12,998	3,297[2]

Source: [Untitled Table], *Negro Population, 1790-1915*, 1918, p. 406. Primary source: U.S. Bureau of the Census. *Negro Population, 1790-1915.* Washington, D.C.: Government Printing Office, 1918. *Notes:* 1. Decrease. 2. Increase.

★ 807 ★

Illiteracy

Relationships: Gender Distribution of Black Illiteracy in 1910, in Relation to Population

Ages by Years	Per Cent Negroes Illiterate		
	Of Total Pop.	Of Male Pop.	Of Female Pop.
Ten Years and Over	30.4	30.1	30.7
10 to 14 years	18.9	21.7	16.1
15 to 19 years	20.3	24.9	16.0
20 to 24 years	23.9	26.3	21.7
25 to 34 years	24.6	24.4	24.7
35 to 44 years	32.3	27.7	37.1
45 to 64 years	52.7	44.9	61.8
65 and over	74.5	70.7	78.6

Source: [Untitled Table], *Negro Year Book and Annual Encyclopedia of the Negro, 1913, p. 146.* Primary source: U.S. Bureau of the Census.

★ 808 ★

Illiteracy

Relationships: Illiteracy Among Persons 14 Years Old and Over by Age Group, 1959

Numbers in thousands.

Age and race	1959[1]			1969		
	Total persons 14 years and over	Illiterate		Total persons	Illiterate	
		Number	Percent of total		Number	Percent of total
Negro						
Total 14 years and over	12,210	910	7.5	14,280	509	3.6
14 to 24 years	3,121	38	1.2	4,528	21	0.5
25 to 44 years	4,851	247	5.1	4,784	61	1.3
45 to 64 years	3,207	362	11.3	3,586	197	5.5
65 years and over	1,031	263	25.5	1,381	230	16.7
White						
Total 14 years and over	109,163	1,709	1.6	127,449	891	0.7
14 to 24 years	21,997	106	0.5	31,949	76	0.2
25 to 44 years	41,292	328	0.8	41,151	170	0.4
45 to 64 years	31,998	567	1.8	37,068	248	0.7
65 years and over	13,876	708	5.1	17,280	397	2.3

Source: "Illiteracy of Persons 14 Years Old and Over, by Age: 1959 and 1969," Current Population Reports, Special Studies, Series P-23, No. 38. *The Social and Economic Status of the Black Population in the United States, 1970,* 1970, p. 78. Primary source: U.S. Department of Commerce, Bureau of the Census. *Note:* 1. Data are for Negro and other races.

★ 809 ★

Illiteracy

Relationships: Illiteracy in 1947 in Relation to School Years Completed, by Race and Gender

Age, Color, and Sex	Total Population	None	Years of School Completed			
			1 Year	2 Years	3 Years	4 Years
WHITE						
Total, 14 years and over	1.8	76.0	56.8	39.5	19.0	4.4
14 to 24 years	0.6	100.0[1]	85.7[1]	80.0[1]	32.6[1]	8.7
25 to 34 years	0.8	94.3[1]	73.9[1]	61.5[1]	19.0[1]	8.2
35 to 44 years	1.3	82.4	60.7[1]	47.8[1]	30.4	4.4
45 to 54 years	2.0	73.4	57.1[1]	26.3	16.3	4.2
55 to 64 years	4.2	74.5	56.5[1]	35.3	17.1	4.1
65 years and over	4.9	72.0	41.3[1]	34.1	14.1	2.6
Male, 14 years and over	1.9	72.0	62.9	39.8	22.4	5.7
Female, 14 years and over	1.7	79.5	49.3	39.0	15.1	2.9
NONWHITE						
Total, 14 years and over	11.0	89.9	80.2	55.6	19.4	5.5
14 to 24 years	4.4	82.4[1]	90.0[1]	60.5[1]	20.7[1]	9.7
25 to 34 years	7.2	93.9[1]	88.9[1]	68.4[1]	24.2	2.6
35 to 44 years	9.7	89.6[1]	83.3[1]	64.3[1]	20.7	6.2
45 to 54 years	13.8	91.9	80.6[1]	41.7[1]	10.3	4.8
55 to 64 years	19.1	85.9	75.0[1]	55.6[1]	19.0[1]	1.6
65 years and over	32.4	91.3	66.7[1]	46.3[1]	23.5[1]	8.5[1]
Male, 14 years and over	14.2	93.8	81.8	57.6	20.2	6.6
Female, 14 years and over	82.	84.9	76.9[1]	52.5	18.4	4.6

Source: "Percent Illiterate in the Civilian Noninstitutional Population 14 Years Old and Over, by Years of School Completed, Age, Color, and Sex, for the United States: October, 1947, *The Negro Handbook, 1949*, p. 116. Primary source: U.S. Bureau of the Census. *Notes:* 1. Percents computed where base is less than 100,000. These percents are presented in order to make available data which show a pattern of relationship of years of school completed and illiteracy, which is of much interest. Small differences between all percentages, especially those denoted by a (1), should be used with particular care.

★ 810 ★

Illiteracy

Relationships: Illiterate Blacks and Mulattoes in Relation to Population by Gender and Region, 1910

Section and southern division	Negro population 10 years of age and over:1910											
	Male		Female		Illiterate							
					Number				Per cent			
					Male		Female		Male		Female	
	Black	Mulatto	Black	Mulatto	Black	Mulatto	Black	Mulatto	Black	Mulatto	Black	Mulatto
United States	2,941,656	695,730	2,870,657	809,879	951,074	144,926	959,746	171,985	32.3	20.8	33.4	21.2
The South	2,593,275	580,888	2,547,131	687,245	914,427	136,812	920,811	161,911	35.3	23.6	36.2	23.6
South Atlantic	1,189,572	280,725	1,184,051	332,588	412,962	64,145	416,925	75,400	34.7	22.8	35.2	22.7
East South Central	803,975	166,946	788,310	201,667	297,375	40,518	295,172	48,442	37.0	24.3	37.4	24.0
West South Central	599,728	133,217	574,770	152,990	204,090	32,149	208,714	38,069	34.0	24.1	36.3	24.9
The North	330,833	107,745	310,547	115,928	35,500	7,755	37,722	9,682	10.7	7.2	12.1	8.4
The West	17,548	7,097	12,979	6,706	1,147	359	1,213	392	6.5	5.1	9.3	5.8

Source: "Illiteracy in the Black and Mulatto Population 10 Years of Age and Over, Classified by Sex, by Sections and Southern Divisions: 1910," *Negro Population, 1790-1915,* 1918, p. 217. Primary source: U.S. Bureau of the Census. *Negro Population, 1790-1915.* Washington, D.C.: Government Printing Office, 1918.

★ 811 ★

Illiteracy

Relationships: Population Increases and Illiteracy Decreases among Black Persons Aged 10 and Over by Region, 1910-1930

A minus (-) sign denotes decrease; a plus sign (+) denotes increase.

Census year, section, and division	Total number	Illiterate		Decennial increase in population	Decennial decrease in number illiterate
		Number	Percent		
United States					
1930	9,292,556	1,513,892	16.3	1,239,331	328,269
1920	8,053,225	1,842,161	22.9	735,303	385,570
1910	7,317,922	2,227,731	30.4	902,341	625,463
The South					
1930	7,194,750	1,416,417	19.7	461,322	335,241
1920	6,733,428	1,751,658	26.0	324,889	382,303
1910	6,408,539	2,133,961	33.3	743,564	583,645
South Atlantic division					
1930	3,363,864	662,055	19.7	142,170	150,787
1920	3,221,694	812,842	25.2	234,758	156,590
1910	2,986,936	969,432	32.5	331,103	280,847
East South Central division					
1930	2,052,951	452,082	2.0	128,237	84,501
1920	1,924,714	536,583	27.9	-36,184	114,924
1910	1,960,898	681,507	34.8	158,076	206,331
West South Central division					
1930	1,777,935	302,280	17.0	190,915	99,953

[Continued]

★ 811 ★

Relationships: Population Increases and Illiteracy Decreases among Black Persons Aged 10 and Over by Region, 1910-1930
[Continued]

Census year, section, and division	Total number	Illiterate		Decennial increase in population	Decennial decrease in number illiterate
		Number	Percent		
1920	1,587,020	402,233	25.3	126,315	80,789
1910	1,460,705	483,022	33.1	254,391	96,467
The North					
1930	1,994,085	94,034	4.7	743,377	+6,901
1920	1,250,708	87,133	7.0	385,655	3,526
1910	865,053	90,659	10.5	140,309	41,530
The West					
1930	103,721	3,441	3.3	34,632	+71
1920	69,089	3,370	4.9	24,759	+259
1910	44,330	3,111	7.0	18,468	288

Source: "Illiteracy in the Negro Population 10 Years Old and Over, by Sections, and Southern Divisions: 1930, 1920, and 1910," *Negroes in the United States, 1920-1932*, 1935, p. 233. Primary source: U.S. Bureau of the Census. *Negroes in the United States, 1920-1932*. Washington, D.C.: U.S. Government Printing Office, 1935.

★ 812 ★

Illiteracy

Relationships: Population Increases and Illiteracy Decreases among Black Persons by Age Group, 1920-1930 and 1910-1920

Age period	1920-1930		1910-1920	
	Increase[1] in population	Decrease in number illiterate	Increase[1] in population	Decrease[2] in number illiterate
10 years and over	1,239,331	328,269	735,303	385,570
10 to 14 years	14,628	74,654	81,648	77,663
15 to 19 years	167,313	41,887	22,799	61,862
20 to 24 years	148,344	32,774	24,052	66,736
25 to 34 years	328,697	36,037	58,288	93,679
35 to 44 years	244,691	45,997	244,770	41,320
45 to 54 years	183,956	49,282	238,720	11,006
55 to 64 years	121,468	22,753	33,974	36,902
65 years and over	40,006	19,804	38,589	+8,055
Unknown	-9,772	5,081	-7,537	4,457

Source: "Increase in Negro Population, and Decrease in Negro Illiterates for the United States in Each Age Group: 1910 to 1930," *Negroes in the United States, 1920-1932*, 1935, p. 233. Primary source: U.S. Bureau of the Census. *Negroes in the United States, 1920-1932*. Washington, D.C.: U.S. Government Printing Office, 1935. *Notes*: 1. A minus (-) sign denotes a decrease. 2. A plus (+) sign denotes an increase.

Libraries and Librarians

★ 813 ★

Employment of Librarians: Employment of Black First-Year Curriculum Completers Trained Outside the South, by Type of Library, in Selected States, 1939

| State | Types of libraries with graduates employed in each type[1] | | | |
	College or university	Public	School	Total graduates
Alabama	3	0	0	3
Florida	2	0	0	2
Georgia	1	0	0	1
Kentucky	1	1	0	2
Louisiana	1	0	0	1
Maryland	1	0	0	1
Mississippi	1	0	0	1
North Carolina	0	1	0	1
Tennessee	2	1	1	4
Texas	1	0	0	1
Virginia	2	0	0	2
West Virginia	1	0	0	1
Total graduates	16	3	1	20

Source: "Employment in States of Survey of Graduates who have Completed Only the First Year Curriculum in Schools Outside the South," *The Negro Handbook,* 1942, p. 130. *Notes:* 1. Information for all graduates of Hampton Institute Library School as of 1939.

★ 814 ★

Libraries and Librarians

Employment of Librarians: Employment of Black Librarians with 1 or More Years of Training, by Type of Library, in Selected States, 1939

| State | Types of libraries with graduates employed in each type[1] | | | |
	College or university	Public	School	Total librarians
Alabama	12	0	0	12
Arkansas	2	0	1	3
Florida	9	0	0	9
Georgia	12	1	3	16

[Continued]

★ 814 ★

Employment of Librarians: Employment of Black Librarians with 1 or More Years of Training, by Type of Library, in Selected States, 1939

[Continued]

| State | Types of libraries with graduates employed in each type[1] | | | |
	College or university	Public	School	Total librarians
Kentucky	4	1	2	7
Louisiana	4	0	1	5
Maryland	2	0	0	2
Mississippi	2	0	0	2
Missouri	1	1	3	5
North Carolina	12	3	8	23
Oklahoma	1	2	2	5
South Carolina	5	1	1	7
Tennessee	7	1	3	11
Texas	10	0	1	11
Virginia	7	1	3	11
West Virginia	2	0	0	2
Total librarians	92	11	28	131

Source: "Employment in States of Survey of Negro Librarians with One Year or More of Professional Training, 1929," *The Negro Handbook,* 1942, p. 130. Primary source: Murray, Florence (Ed.), *The Negro Handbook.* New York: Wendell Malliet and Co., 1942. *Notes:* 1. Data with information for all graduates of Hampton Institute Library School as of 1939.

★ 815 ★

Libraries and Librarians

Employment of Librarians: Employment of Graduates of Black Library Schools in Southern States, 1939

| State | Types of libraries with graduates employed in each type | | | |
	College or university	Public	School	Total graduates
Alabama	9	0	0	9
Arkansas	2	0	1	3
Florida	7	0	0	7
Georgia	10	1	3	14
Kentucky	3	0	2	5
Louisiana	3	0	1	4
Maryland	1	0	0	1
Mississippi	1	0	0	1
Missouri	1	1	2	5
North Carolina	12	2	8	22
Oklahoma	1	2	2	5

[Continued]

★ 815 ★

Employment of Librarians: Employment of Graduates of Black Library Schools in Southern States, 1939

[Continued]

| State | Types of libraries with graduates employed in each type | | | |
	College or university	Public	School	Total graduates
South Carolina	5	1	1	7
Tennessee	4	0	2	6
Texas	9	0	1	10
Virginia	5	1	3	9
West Virginia	1	0	0	1
Total graduates	74	8	27	109

Source: "Employment in 16 Southern States of Graduates of Hampton Institute Library School, 1939," *The Negro Handbook*, 1942, p. 129. Primary source: Murray, Florence (Ed.), *The Negro Handbook*. New York: Wendell Malliet and Co., 1942.

★ 816 ★

Libraries and Librarians

Employment of Librarians: Schools Attended and Employment of First Year Library Science Curriculum Completers, 1939

Library School	Liberians	Librarians employed
New York State College for Teachers, Albany	1	1
University of California	2	2
Columbia University	28	20[1]
Kansas State Teachers College of Emporia	1	[2]
University of Illinois	16	10[3]
McGill University	1	...
University of Michigan	2	1[4]
University of Minnesota	1	1
Carnegie Institute of Technology, Pittsburgh	1	...
Simmons College	5	3
University of Southern California	1	...
Syracuse University	1	...
Western Reserve University	5	2
University of Wisconsin	1	1
Total librarians	66	41

Source: "Negro Librarians who have Completed the First Year Curriculum in Library schools Outside the South and Number Employed, 1939," *The Negro Handbook*, 1942, p. 129. Primary source: Murray, Florence (Ed.), *The Negro Handbook*. New York: Wendell Malliet and Co., 1942. *Notes:* 1. Omits 2 who hold M.S. degree. 2. Subsequently completed work for M.A. in L.S. 3. Omits 1 M.S. 4. Omits 1 M.A. in L.S.

★ 817 ★

Libraries and Librarians

Expenditures: Cost of Library Operations in Selected States, Part I

Name of institution	Volumes in 1926-27	Average annual expenditures on libraries, 1922-27					Percentage of increase in expenditures since 1922-23
		Books	Magazines	Supplies and binding	Salaries	Total average	
Alabama							
Miles Memorial College	500[1]	-	-	-	-	-	-
Selma University	1,000	-	-	-	-	-	-
Talladega College	25,000	$634.00	$180.00	$526.00	$970.00	$2,310.00	77.7
Tuskegee Normal and Industrial Institute	21,167	500.00	-	-	-	500.00[2]	-
Arkansas							
Philander Smith College	2,800	600.00		-	-	600.00	100.0
Shorter College	-	330.00	18.00	-	-	348.00	90.6[3]
Agricultural, Mechanical, and Normal School	1,600	310.00	100.00	3.00	-	413.00	57.5
Delaware							
State College for Colored Students	3,364	385.00	16.00	5.46	90.00	496.46	100.0
District of Columbia							
Howard University[1]	43,500	1,083.10	331.95	4,241.86	5,943.20	11,600.11	23.3
Florida							
Bethune-Cookman College	3,000	33.00	13.25	16.00	774.00	836.25	72.2
Edward Waters College	850	90.00	15.00	61.00	352.00	518.00	730.0
Florida Agricultural and Mechanical College[1]	4,000	323.22	132.30	67.34	918.40	1,441.26	76.5
Georgia							
Agricultural and Mechanical School for Negroes	3,100	77.20	10.0	-	-	87.20	228.5
Atlanta University	16,243	335.40	113.60	149.00	1,232.60	1,830.60	38.3
Clark University	6,300	380.00	36.00	70.00	629.00	1,115.00	16.2
Georgia Normal and Agricultural College	1,500	300.00	-	-	-	300.00	-
Georgia State Industrial School	-	-	300.00	100.00	-	400.00	-
Morehouse College	8,400	920.00	110.00	50.00	1,000.00	2,080.00	927
Morris Brown University	-	200.00	11.80	381.78	310.14	903.72	3.0[3]
Paine College	5,244	309.00	58.79	-	-	367.79	31.4
Spelman College	9,192	974.06	100.28	347.27	648.71	2,070.32	532.6
Kentucky							
Lincoln Institute	10,000	2.40	-	-	100.00	102.40	12.0
Simmons University	3,035	14.00	8.00	40.00	72.00	134.00	-
Louisiana							
Coleman College	-	-	-	-	-	-	-
New Orleans University	5,040	-	-	180.00	241.00	421.00	246.1
Southern University and Agricultural and Mechanical College	11,000	300.00	50.00	100.00	900.00	1,350.00	38.0[3]
Straight College	7,100	257.87	76.14	37.70	754.65	1,126.36	109.3
Xavier College	3,931	519.00	50.00	46.20	-	615.20	180.9

Source: "Status of Libraries in Negro Colleges, 1922-1927," *Survey of Negro Colleges and Universities*, Bulletin, 1928, No. 7, 1929, pp. 948-950. Primary source: U.S. Bureau of Education, *Survey of Negro Colleges and Universities*. Bulletin, 1928, No. 7. Washington, D.C.: Government Printing Office, 1929. *Notes:* 1. Library occupies separate building. 2. No report of expenditures given. 3. Expenditures not itemized.

★ 818 ★

Libraries and Librarians

Expenditures: Cost of Library Operations in Selected States, Part II

Name of institution	Volumes in 1926-27	Average annual expenditures on libraries, 1922-27					Percentage of increase in expenditures since 1922-23
		Books	Magazines	Supplies and binding	Salaries	Total average	
Maryland							
Morgan College	6,500	$404.89	$72.24	$265.42	$911.00	$1,653.55	255.1
Princess Anne Academy	-	-	-	-	-	-	-
Mississippi							
Alcorn Agricultural and Mechanical College	2,334	175.49	103.53	54.18	66.00	399.20	27.4[1]

[Continued]

★ 818 ★

Expenditures: Cost of Library Operations in Selected States, Part II

[Continued]

Name of institution	Volumes in 1926-27	Average annual expenditures on libraries, 1922-27					Percentage of increase in expenditures since 1922-23
		Books	Magazines	Supplies and binding	Salaries	Total average	
Jackson College	2,326	175.00	47.00	-	-	222.00	100.0[1]
Rust College	6,825	-	37.82	15.64	603.10	656.56	-
Southern Christian Institute	2,725	-	26.58	.50	450.00	477.08	15.5
Tougaloo College	4,938	40.25	126.87	-	120.00	287.12	-
Missouri							
Lincoln University	10,236	1,260.00	95.40	71.60	1,102.00	2,529.00	100.0
North Carolina							
Agricultural and Technical College	5,063	868.52	21.05	155.60	886.00	1,931.17	490.3
Bennett College for Women	3,000	1,100.00	100.00	300.00	100.00	1,600.00	-
Brick Junior College	3,321	389.25	89.00	52.60	540.00	1,070.85	697.6
North Carolina College for Negroes	1,900	125.00	25.00	-	600.00	750.00	-
Johnson C. Smith University	13,500	355.94	44.20	53.64	1,694.50	2,148.28	34.3
Kittrell College	1,000	220.30	39.25	-	-	259.55	100.0
Livingstone College	9,714	1,902.00	161.00	518.00	1,600.00	4,181.00	-
St. Augustine's School	7,775	253.80	50.23	72.55	538.33	914.91	23.4
Shaw University	10,388	571.90	91.32	28.00	1,140.0	1,831.22	83.7
Winston-Salem Teachers College	2,150	604.43	97.20	91.70	600.00	1,393.33	51.6
State Normal School for Negroes	3,838	399.83	81.20	56.45	1,000.00	1,537.48	51.0[1]
North Carolina State Colored Normal School	1,878	122.50	228.95	15.87	666.00	1,033.32	40.0[1]
Ohio							
Wilberforce University	12,912	563.08	205.94	506.90	2,275.00	3,550.92	10.8
Oklahoma							
Colored Agricultural and Normal University	2,798	617.65	10.88	182.52	1,000.00	1,811.05	32.2
Pennsylvania							
Lincoln University[2]	40,000	1,287.85	55.36	-	687.31	2,030.52	320.0
Cheyney Training School for Teachers	7,609	1,369.41	153.87	106.25	2,544.55	38.0	

Source: "Status of Libraries in Negro Colleges, 1922-1927," Survey of Negro Colleges and Universities, Bulletin, 1928, No. 7, 1929, pp. 948-950. Primary source: U.S. Bureau of Education, Survey of Negro Colleges and Universities. Bulletin, 1928, No. 7. Washington, D.C.: Government Printing Office, 1929. Notes: 1. Decrease. 2. Library occupies separate building.

★ 819 ★

Libraries and Librarians

Expenditures: Cost of Library Operations in Selected States, Part III

Name of institution	Volumes in 1926-27	Average annual expenditures on libraries, 1922-27					Percentage of increase in expenditures since 1922-23
		Books	Magazines	Supplies and binding	Salaries	Total average	
South Carolina							
Allen University	-	$67.00	$28.40	-	$17.60	$113.00	-
Benedict College	$8,458	280.00	28.00	$17.50	1,000.00	1,325.50	-
Claflin University	5,300	184.00	50.80	4.00	873.00	1,111.80	65.1
Morris College	-	357.00	-	-	-	357.00	100.0
State Agricultural and Mechanical College	1,800	449.45	43.44	34.58	503.20	1,030.67	57.7
Tennessee							
Agricultural and Industrial State Normal School[2,4]	3,000	-	-	-	-	-	-
Fisk University[3]	12,400	1,507.83[1]	-	112.87	3,169.04	4,789.74	81.7
Knoxville College[3]	8,143	278.41	112.48	55.45	929.00	1,375.34	34.7
Lane College[4]	3,138	145.07	70.52	24.73	486.00	726.32	9.5
Le Moyne Junior College[3]	-	-	-	-	-	-	-
Morristown Normal and Industrial University	4,000	300.00	-	-	700.00	1,000.00	-
Roger Williams University	-	-	-	-	-	-	-

[Continued]

★ 819 ★

Expenditures: Cost of Library Operations in Selected States, Part III
[Continued]

Name of institution	Volumes in 1926-27	Average annual expenditures on libraries, 1922-27					Percentage of increase in expenditures since 1922-23
		Books	Magazines	Supplies and binding	Salaries	Total average	
Walden College	1,500	25.00	23.00	30.00	387.50	465.50	27.2
Texas							
Bishop College[4]	5,050	215.20	128.98	36.49	1,045.82	1,426.49	49.6
Samuel Houston College	6,290	720.00	43.00	550.00	843.00	2,156.00	221.0
Jarvis Christian Institute	2,450	173.14	10.80	-	-	183.94	8.1
Paul Quinn College	2,600	750.00	40.00	12.50	506.25	1,308.75	-
Prairie View State Normal and Industrial College	8,587	3,227.98[4]	-	-	-	3,227.98	135.2
Texas College	8,551	295.60	39.83	115.00	90.00	540.43	241.6
Tillotson College	3,000	-	-	-	-	-	-
Wiley College[3]	7,850	730.00	116.00	64.00	876.00	1,786.00	4.1
Virginia							
Virginia Union University	15,000	293.80	87.80	44.00	558.00	983.60	67.3
Virginia Normal and Industrial Institute	8,278	1,600.00	318.00	48.00	1,495.66	3,461.66	-
St. Paul Normal and Industrial School	-	235.00	30.00	315.00	740.00	1,320.00	77.2
Hampton Normal and Agricultural Institute[3]	57,750	579.92	1,008.95	358.11	6,087.72	8,034.70	57.8
West Virginia							
West Virginia Collegiate Institute	13,078	3,258.32	168.53	-	480.00	3,906.85	58.7
Total	418,695	37,357.06	6,043.53	10,792.26	53,217.75	107,410.60	-

Source: "Status of Libraries in Negro Colleges, 1922-1927," *Survey of Negro Colleges and Universities*, Bulletin, 1928, No. 7, 1929, pp. 948-950. Primary source: U.S. Bureau of Education, *Survey of Negro Colleges and Universities*. Bulletin, 1928, No. 7. Washington, D.C.: Government Printing Office, 1929. *Notes:* 1. Books and magazines. 2. Decrease 3. Library occupies separate building. 4. Expenditures not itemized.

★ 820 ★

Libraries and Librarians

Public and School Libraries: Number of Public Library Services Open to Blacks in the South by State, c. 1944

State	No. libraries
Alabama	3
Arkansas	2
Florida	6
Georgia	12
Kentucky	12
Louisiana	3
Mississippi	5
North Carolina	17
Oklahoma	8
South Carolina	6
Tennessee	4
Texas	17
Virginia	17
West Virginia	1

Source: Compiled by the editors from "Public Library Service to Negroes in 14 Southern States," *The Negro Handbook, 1944*, 1944, pp. 246-247. Primary source: American Library Association. Published by permission.

★ 821 ★

Libraries and Librarians

Public and School Libraries: Support for Library Buildings from the Carnegie Corporation, c. 1916

Agricultural and Mechanical College	Normal Ala.	$16,540
Atlanta University	Atlanta, Ga.	25,000
Benedict College	Columbia, S.C.	6,000
Biddle University	Charlotte, N.C.	12,500
Cheyney Institute for Colored Youth	Cheyney, Pa.	10,000
Fessenden Academy	Martin, Fla.	6,500
Fisk University	Nashville, Tenn.	20,000
Florida State Normal and Industrial College	Tallahassee, Fla.	10,000
Howard University	Washington, D.C.	50,000
Knoxville College	Knoxville, Tenn.	10,000
Livingstone Colllege	Salisbury, N.C.	12,500
Manassas Industrial Institute	Manassas, Va.	15,000
Talladega College	Talladega, Ala.	15,000
Tuskegee Institute	Tuskegee, Ala.	20,000
Wilberforce University	Wilberforce, Ohio	17,950
Wiley University	Marshall, Tex.	15,000

Source: [Untitled Table], U.S. Office of Education. *Negro Education: A Study of the Private and Higher Schools for Colored People in the United States*, vol. I Bulletin, 1916, No. 38, 1917, p. 173. Primary source: U.S. Office of Education. *Negro Education: A Study of the Private and Higher Schools for Colored People in the United States*, vol. I. Bulletin, 1916, No. 38. Washington, D.C.: Government Printing Office, 1917.

★ 822 ★

Libraries and Librarians

Public and School Libraries: for Black People, c. 1925-26

Location	Cost of Building
Public	
Atlanta, Georgia (Carnegie)	$25,000
Birmingham, Alabama	
Charlotte, N.C.	
Evansville, Indiana	
Galveston, Texas	
Guthrie, Oklahoma	
Houston, Texas (Carnegie)	15,000
Jacksonville, Florida	
Kansas City, Missouri	
Knoxville, Tennessee (Carnegie)	10,000
Louisville, Kentucky (Carnegie) - Eastern Branch	19,000

[Continued]

★ 822 ★

Public and School Libraries: for Black People, c. 1925-26
[Continued]

Location	Cost of Building
Western Branch	31,000
Lynchburg, Virginia	
Meridian, Mississippi (Carnegie)	8,000
Mound Bayou, Mississippi (Carnegie)	4,000
Nashville, Tennessee (Carnegie)	25,000
New Orleans, Louisiana (Carnegie)	25,000
Norfolk, Virginia	
Roanoke, Virginia	
Savannah, Georgia (Carnegie)	12,000
Tulsa, Oklahoma	

School

Location	
Alabama A. and M. College (Carnegie)	$16,540
Atlanta University (Carnegie)	25,000
Fisk University (Carnegie)	20,000
Florida A. and M. College (Carnegie)	16,540
Fort Valley (Georgia) High and Industrial School (Carnegie)	
Hampton Institute (Collis P. Huntington Memorial Library)	100,000
Howard University (Carnegie)	50,000
Talladega College (Carnegie)	15,000
Tuskegee Institute (Carnegie)	20,000
Wilberforce University (Carnegie)	18,000
Wiley University (Carnegie)	15,000

Source: "Libraries for Negroes," *Negro Year Book: An Annual Encyclopedia of the Negro, 1925-1926,* 1925, p. 323. Primary source: Work, Monroe N. (Ed.), *Negro Year Book: An Annual Encyclopedia of the Negro, 1925-1926.* Tuskegee Institute, Ala.: The Negro Year Book Pub. Co., 1925. *Note:* Funds furnished by The Carnegie Corporation where indicated.

★ 823 ★

Libraries and Librarians

Training of Librarians: Library Science Master's Recipients who Trained Outside the South- Employment, 1939

Library school	Graduates holding master's degrees	Graduates employed
University of California	2	1[1]
Columbia University	4	4
University of Illinois	1	1
University of Michigan	4	4
Total	11	10

Source: "Negro Graduates of Library Schools Outside the South who Hold Master's Degrees in Library Science and Number Employed, 1929," *The Negro Handbook,* 1942, p. 130. Primary source: Murray, Florence (Ed.), *The Negro Handbook.* New York: Wendell Malliet and Co., 1942. *Note:* 1. Student engaged in advanced study not counted.

★ 824 ★

Libraries and Librarians

Training of Librarians: Library Science Master's Recipients, by First and Second-Year School Attended, 1939

Negro librarians holding master's degrees in library science	Library school attended in first year of professional study	Library school from which master's degree was received
2	Columbia University	1 Columbia Univ. 1 Univ. of Mich.
1	Kansas State Teachers Col. of Emporia	1 Univ. of Mich.
5	Hampton Inst.	3 Colum. Univ. 1 Univ. of Mich. 1 Univ. of Calif.
2	Univ. of Ill.	1 Univ. of Ill. 1 Univ. of Calif.

[Continued]

★ 824 ★

Training of Librarians: Library Science Master's Recipients, by First and Second-Year School Attended, 1939
[Continued]

Negro librarians holding master's degrees in library science	Library school attended in first year of professional study	Library school from which master's degree was received
1	Univ. of Mich.	1 Univ. of Mich.
11	Total	11

Source: "Negro Librarians Holding Master's Degrees in Library Science with Library Schools in which First and Second Year Curricula Respectively were Completed, 1939," *The Negro Handbook*, 1942, p. 130. Primary source: Murray, Florence (Ed.), *The Negro Handbook*. New York: Wendell Malliet and Co., 1942.

★ 825 ★
Libraries and Librarians

Training of Librarians: Number of Library Schools Open to Blacks, 1943

"According to an inquiry conducted in the summer of 1943 by the American Library Association, one-half of the 34 accredited library schools admit Negro students who meet their admission requirements....The total of 17 accredited library schools includes the Schools of Library Service, Atlanta University (colored) and 16 library schools outside the Southern States."

Source: "Library Schools Admitting Negro Students," *The Negro Handbook, 1944*, 1944, p. 247. Primary source: American Library Association. Published by permission.

Professional Education

★ 826 ★

Degrees: Degrees in the Professions Awarded by Two Black Schools in June, 1941

Profession	Degrees Awarded	School(s) Awarding
Dentistry	27	Howard University and Meharry Medical College
Law	14	Howard University
Medicine	69	Howard University and Meharry Medical College
Nursing	10	Meharry Medical College
Pharmacy	8	Meharry Medical College
Religion	10	Howard University
Social Work	5	Howard University
Total	143	

Source: Adapted by the editors from "Howard University Professional Schools" and "Meharry Medical School," *The Negro Handbook,* 1942, p. 118. Primary source: Reports of the institutions.

★ 827 ★

Professional Education

Medicine: Black Medical Students in Black Institutions and in Northern Colleges, c. 1916

	Total	Medical	Dental	Pharmaceutical
All schools	878	431	287	160
Howard University	288	100	116	72
Meharry Medical College	482	291	137	54
Shaw University	22	9	...	13
Northern colleges	86	31	34	21

Source: [Untitled Table], *Negro Education: A Study of the Private and Higher Schools for Colored People in the United States,* vol. I. Bulletin, 1916, No. 38, 1917, p. 68. Primary source: U.S. Office of Education. *Negro Education: A Study of the Private and Higher Schools for Colored People in the United States,* vol. I. Bulletin, 1916, No. 38. Washington, D.C.: Government Printing Office, 1917.

★ 828 ★

Professional Education

Mixed Professions: Black Students at Black Institutions in Training for Professions, 1951

Professions and Institutions	Students Fall 1950-51
Anesthesia:	
Meharry Medical College (1876)	2
Chemical Laboratory Technology:	
Meharry Medical College	8
Dental Hygiene:	
Meharry Medical College	7
Dental Technology:	
Meharry Medical College	15
Dentistry:	
Howard University	203
Meharry Medical College	130
Engineering:	
A. & T. College of N. Carolina	97
Hampton Institute	33
Howard University	326
Lincoln University (Mo.)	8
Prairie View A. & M. College	213
State A. & M. College of S. Carolina	38
Tuskegee Institute·	11
Journalism:	
Lincoln University (Mo.)	31
Texas Southern University	30
Law:	
Florida A. & M. College	-
Howard University	120
North Carolina at Durham	26
Lincoln University (Mo.)	30
Southern University and A. & M. Col.	14
State A. & M. College of S. Carolina	19
Texas Southern University	29
Library Science:	
Atlanta University	37
N. Carolina College at Durham	12
State A.&M. College of S. Carolina	34
Texas Southern University	10
Medicine:	
Howard University	290
Meharry Medical College	251
Nurse Training:	
Florida A. & M. College	94
Hampton Institute	49
Howard University	36
Meharry Medical College	49
Prairie View A. & M. College	74
Tuskegee Institute	132

[Continued]

★ 828 ★

Mixed Professions: Black Students at Black Institutions
in Training for Professions, 1951
[Continued]

Professions and Institutions	Students Fall 1950-51
Pharmacy:	
Howard University	214
Xavier University	185
Texas Southern University	60
Social Work:	
Atlanta University	117
Howard University	117
Theology:	
(see Table 10)	700
Veterinary Medicine:	
Tuskegee Institute	35
Total	3,886

Source: "Professions Offered by Negro Colleges and Universities, 1951," *1952 Negro Year Book: A Review of Events Affecting Negro Life*, 1952, p. 228. Primary source: Guzman, Jessie Parkhurst (Ed.), *1952 Negro Year Book: A Review of Events Affecting Negro Life*. New York: Wm. H. Wise & Co., Inc., 1952.

★ 829 ★

Professional Education

Mixed Professions: Location, Denominational Affiliation, Instructors, and Students at
Black Schools Offering Medicine and Law, 1877

Name and class of institution	Location	Religious denomination	Instructors
SCHOOLS OF LAW			
Law department of Straight University	New Orleans, La.	4	8
Law department of Howard University	Washington, D.C.	2	6
Total		6	14
SCHOOLS OF MEDICINE			
Medical department of New Orleans University	New Orleans, La.	5	8
Meharry Medical department of Central Tennessee College	Nashville, Tenn.	...	18
Medical department of Howard University	Washington, D.C.	7	48
Total		12	74

Source: Robert, *Negro Civilization in the South*, "Statistics of Institutions for the Institutions for the Instruction of the Colored Race for 1877 - Universities and Colleges," 1880, p. 133. Primary source: Robert, Charles Edwin. *Negro Civilization in the South; Educational, Social, and Religious Advancement of the Colored People*. Nashville, Tenn.: Printed by Wheeler Bros. for the author, 1880.

★ 830 ★

Professional Education

Mixed Professions: Number of Schools Providing Professional Training for Black Students, 1912 to 1937-38

Profession	1912	1913	1916-17	1918-19	1937-38
Dentistry	2	3	[1]	3	2
Law	3	3	[1]	2	1
Medicine	5	6	[1]	3	2
Nursing	--	--	--	--	1
Pharmacy	4	4	5	3	2
Theology	23	29	20	35	4

Source: "Compiled and adapted by the editors from "Schools of Law," "Schools of Medicine," "Schools of Dentistry," "Schools of Pharmacy," "Schools of Theology," and "School of Nurse Training," *Negro Year Book and Annual Encyclopedia of the Negro,* 1912, [no page no.]. 1913, pp. 152 and 154; *Negro Year Book: An Annual Encyclopedia of the Negro, 1916-1917,* 1918, [no page no.]; *Negro Year Book; An Annual Encyclopedia of the Negro, 1918-1919,* 1919, [no page no.]; *Negro Year Book: An Annual Encyclopedia of the Negro, 1937-1938,* p. 205. Primary source: Reports of the institutions. *Note:* 1. Information not provided.

★ 831 ★

Professional Education

Mixed Professions: Professional Training Available for Blacks and Whites in States with Segregation, 1939-40 - I

Type of institutions, by curriculum	Alabama	Arkansas	Delaware	District of Columbia	Florida	Georgia	Kentucky	Louisiana	Maryland
				WHITE					
Dentistry:									
Public	...	...	...	...	...	...	X	...	X
All[2]	...	...	...	X	...	X	X	...	X
Law:									
Public	X	X	...	...	X	X	X	X	X
All	X	X	...	X	X	X	X	X	X
Medicine:									
Public	[3]	X	...	...	...	X	X	X	X
All	[3]	X	...	X	...	X	X	X	X
Pharmacy:									
Public	X	X	...	...	X	X	X	...	X
All	X	...	...	X	X	X	X	...	X
Social service:									
Public	x	...	...	...	x	...	X	X	X
All	X	...	...	...	X	...	X	X	X
Library science:									
Public	X	...	...	...	X	X	X	X	X
All	X	...	...	X	...	X	X	X	...
Graduate work leading to Ph.D.:									
Public	...	...	...	...	X	X	X	X	X
All	...	...	...	X	X	X	X	X	X
Theology[4]	...	...	...	...	...	...	...	...	...

[Continued]

★ 831 ★

Mixed Professions: Professional Training Available for Blacks and Whites in States with Segregation, 1939-40 - I
[Continued]

Type of institutions, by curriculum	Alabama	Arkansas	Delaware	District of Columbia	Florida	Georgia	Kentucky	Louisiana	Maryland
				NEGRO					
Dentistry:									
Public	...	...	...	...	...	...	...	...	...
All	...	...	...	X	...	...	...	...	...
Law:									
Public	...	...	...	...	...	...	...	...	...
All	...	...	...	X	...	...	...	...	...
Medicine:									
Public	...	...	...	...	...	...	...	...	...
All	...	...	...	X	...	...	...	...	...
Pharmacy:									
Public	...	...	...	...	...	...	...	...	...
All	...	...	...	X	...	...	...	X	...
Social service:									
Public	...	...	...	...	...	...	...	...	...
All	...	...	...	X	...	X	...	X	...
Library science:									
Public	...	...	...	...	...	...	...	...	...
All	...	...	...	...	...	...	...	...	...
Graduate work leading to Ph.D.:									
Public	...	...	...	...	...	...	...	...	...
All	...	...	...	...	...	...	...	...	...
Theology[4]	...	...	...	...	...	...	...	...	...

Source: "Professional Curricula Available In Institutions of Higher Education in States Maintaining Separate Institutions, 1939-40," *National Survey of the Higher Education of Negroes.* Vol. I., No. 6. *Socio-Economic Approach to Educational Problems,* 1942, p. 15. Primary source: U.S. Office of Education. *National Survey of the Higher Education of Negroes.* Vol. 1, No. 6. *Socio Economic Approach to Educational Problems,* by Ida Corrine Brown. Washington, D.C.: U.S. Government Printing Office, 1942. *Notes:* 1. This table is to be read as follows: Alabama - In institutions for the higher education of white persons the following professional curricula are available in public institutions: Law, medicine (2-year course only), pharmacy, social service, and library science; no additional curricula are available in both public and private institutions. The following curricula are to available in the State: Dentistry, medicine (last 2 years), graduate work leading to the Ph.D. degrees. 2. Includes both public and private institutions 3. 2-year medical course only. 4. Not checked due to nonavailability of catalog of small theological institutions.

★ 832 ★

Professional Education

Mixed Professions: Professional Training Available for Blacks and Whites in States with Segregation, 1939-40 - II

Type of institutions, by curriculum	Mississippi	Missouri	North Carolina	Oklahoma	South Carolina	Tennessee	Texas	Virginia	West Virginia
				WHITE					
Dentistry:									
Public	...	...	...	...	...	X	...	X	...
All[2]	...	X	...	...	...	X	X	X	...
Law:									
Public	X	X	X	X	X	X	X	X	X
All	X	X	X	X	X	X	X	X	X
Medicine:									
Public	[3]	[3]	[3]	X	X	X	X	X	[3]
All	[3]	X	X	X	X	X	X	X	[3]

[Continued]

★ 832 ★

Mixed Professions: Professional Training Available for Blacks and Whites in States with Segregation, 1939-40 - II

[Continued]

Type of institutions, by curriculum	Mississippi	Missouri	North Carolina	Oklahoma	South Carolina	Tennessee	Texas	Virginia	West Virginia
Pharmacy:									
Public	X	...	X	X	X	X	X	X	X
All	X	...	X	X	X	X	X	X	X
Social service:									
Public	...	X	X	X	X	...	...	...	...
All	...	X	X	X	X	...	...	...	...
Library science:									
Public	...	...	X	X	...	X	X	X	X
All	X	...	X	X	X	X	X	X	X
Graduate work leading to Ph.D.:									
Public	...	X	X	X	...	X	X	X	X
All	...	X	X	X	...	X	X	X	X
Theology[4]	...	...	...	...	...	...	...	...	...

NEGRO

Type of institutions, by curriculum	Mississippi	Missouri	North Carolina	Oklahoma	South Carolina	Tennessee	Texas	Virginia	West Virginia
Dentistry:									
Public	...	...	...	...	...	...	...	...	...
All	...	...	...	...	...	X	...	...	...
Law:									
Public	...	X	...	...	...	...	...	...	...
All	...	X	...	...	...	...	...	...	...
Medicine:									
Public	...	...	...	...	...	x	...	...	...
All	...	...	...	...	...	...	...	...	...
Pharmacy:									
Public	...	...	...	...	...	X	...	...	...
All	...	...	...	...	...	...	...	...	...
Social service:									
Public	...	...	...	...	...	...	...	...	...
All	...	...	...	...	...	...	...	...	...
Library science:									
Public	...	...	X	...	...	...	...	...	...
All	...	...	X	...	...	...	...	...	...
Graduate work leading to Ph.D.:									
Public	...	...	...	...	...	...	...	...	...
All	...	...	...	...	...	...	...	...	...
Theology[4]	...	...	...	...	...	...	...	...	...

Source: "Professional Curricula Available In Institutions of Higher Education in States Maintaining Separate Institutions, 1939-40," *National Survey of the Higher Education of Negroes.* Vol. I., No. 6. *Socio-Economic Approach to Educational Problems,* 1942, p. 15. Primary source: U.S. Office of Education. *National Survey of the Higher Education of Negroes.* Vol. 1, No. 6. *Socio-Economic Approach to Educational Problems,* by Ida Corrine Brown. Washington, D.C.: U.S. Government Printing Office, 1942. *Notes:* 1. This table is to be read as follows: Alabama - In institutions for the higher education of white persons the following professional curricula are available in public institutions: Law, medicine (2-year course only), pharmacy, social service, and library science; no additional curricula are available in both public and private institutions. The following curricula are to available in the State: Dentistry, medicine (last 2 years), graduate work leading to the Ph.D. degrees. 2. Includes both public and private institutions 3. 2-year medical course only. 4. Not checked due to nonavailability of catalog of small theological institutions.

★ 833 ★

Professional Education

Mixed Professions: Summary Characteristics of Black Schools of Theology, Law, and Medicine, 1877

State	THEOLOGY			LAW			MEDICINE		
	Schools	Teachers	Pupils	Schools	Teachers	Pupils	Schools	Teachers	Pupils
Alabama	3	2	18						
Georgia	1	2	85						
Louisiana	3	2	60	1	4	8	1	5	8
Maryland	1	5	24						
North Carolina	2	5	59						
Ohio	1	6	8						
Pennsylvania	1	5	20						
South Carolina	1	1	1						
Tennessee	2	7	68				1	1	18
District of Columbia	2	10	120	1	2	6	1	7	48
Total	17	44	462	2	6	14	3	12	74

Source: Adapted by the editors from Robert, *Negro Civilization in the South*, "Summary of Statistics of Institutions for the Instruction of the Colored Race for 1877," 1880, pp. 135. Primary source: Robert, Charles Edwin. *Negro Civilization in the South; Educational, Social, and Religious Advancement of the Colored People*. Nashville, Tenn.: Printed by Wheeler Bros. for the author, 1880. *Note:* 1. Information not provided in original source.

★ 834 ★

Professional Education

Nursing: Black Students Being Trained to be Nurses, 1941-1943

Year	Schools reporting	Number of students	Percent of increase
1941	32	1,405	
1942	32	1,580	12
1943	32	1,918	21

Source: "Negro Nurses in Training as of May, 1943," *The Negro Handbook, 1944*, 1944, p. 194. Primary source: National League of Nursing Education. Published by permission. *Notes:* There were 39 schools admitting Negro nurses at the end of June, 1943. One school in existence in 1941 and 1942 is now closed. Two schools did not report the number of students enrolled in 1941 and 1942, but in 1943 reported 8 and 30 respectively.

★ 835 ★

Professional Education

Nursing: Number of Black Nursing Schools by State, c. 1944

State/area	Number schools
Alabama	1
District of Columbia	1
Florida	2
Georgia	3
Illinois	1
Louisiana	1
Maryland	1
Missouri	3
New York	2
North Carolina	5
Pennsylvania	1
Tennessee	1
Texas	1
Virginia	2

Source: Compiled by the editors from "Negro Schools of Nursing," *The Negro Handbook, 1944,* 1944, p. 195. Primary source: National Association of Colored Graduate Nurses. Published by permission.

★ 836 ★

Professional Education

Theology: Black Institutions with Theology Curriculum, and Student Enrollment, 1950-51

Institutions	Denomination	Students Enrolled Fall 1950-51
American Baptist Theological Seminary, Nashville, Tenn.	Nat. Baptist	57
Benedict College, Columbia, S.C.	Baptist	72
Bishop College, Marshall Texas	Nat. Baptist	25
Butler College, Tyler, Texas	Baptist	18
Campbell College, Jackson, Miss.	A.M.E.	50
Conroe N. and I. College, Conroe, Texas	Baptist	10
Daniel Payne College, Birmingham, Ala.	A.M.E.	40
Edward Waters College, Jacksonville, Fla.	A.M.E.	9
Gammon Theological Seminary, Atlanta, Ga.	Methodist	59
Howard University, Washington, D.C.	Non-Sectarian	40
Immanuel Lutheran College, Greensboro, N.C.	Lutheran	9
Johnson C. Smith, College, Charlotte, N.C.	Presbyterian	29
Lincoln University, Lincoln University, Pa.	Non-Denom.	13
Livingstone College, Salisbury, N.C.	A.M.E.Z.	23

[Continued]

★ 836 ★

Theology: Black Institutions with Theology Curriculum, and Student Enrollment, 1950-51
[Continued]

Institutions	Denomination	Students Enrolled Fall 1950-51
Lomax-Hannon College, Greenville, Ala.	A.M.E.Z.	5
Morris Booker Memorial College, Dermott, Ark.	Baptist	24
Natchez College, Natchez, Miss.	Baptist	-
Paul Quinn College, Waco, Texas	A.M.E.	25
Selma University, Salem, Ala.	Baptist	47
Shaw University, Raleigh, N.C.	Nat. Baptist	22
Shorter College, North Little Rock, Ark.	A.M.E.	(N)
Simmons University, Louisville, Ky.	Miss. Baptist	(N)
St. Augustine's Seminary, Bay St. Louis, Miss.	R.C.	(N)
Virginia Theological Seminary, Lynchburg, Va.	Nat. Baptist	(N)
Virginia Union University, Richmond, Va.	Nat. Baptist	30
Wilberforce University, Wilberforce, Ohio	A.M.E.	87
Total		700

Source: "Theological Schools and Departments, 1951," *1952 Negro Year Book: A Review of Events Affecting Negro Life*, 1952, p. 229. Primary source: Guzman, Jessie Parkhurst (Ed.), *1952 Negro Year Book: A Review of Events Affecting Negro Life.* New York: Wm. H. Wise & Co., Inc., 1952. *Note:* (N) = No report received.

★ 837 ★

Professional Education

Theology: Black Students (and Their Teachers) in Theology Schools, c. 1916

Theological schools	Teachers	Students
Gammon Theological Seminary	6	78
Tuskegee Institute	3	77
Howard University	4	73
Lincoln University	6	54
Wilberforce University	4	30
Virginia Union University	6	24
Stillman Institute	2	21
Morehouse College	2	18
Bishop Payne Divinity School	4	15
Livingstone College	3	14
Talladega College	2	10
Shaw University	2	10
Paine College	2	9

[Continued]

★ 837 ★

Theology: Black Students (and Their Teachers) in Theology Schools, c. 1916

[Continued]

Theological schools	Teachers	Students
Biddle University	2	8
Total	48	441

Source: [Untitled Table], *Negro Education: A Study of the Private and Higher Schools for Colored People in the United States,* vol. I. Bulletin, 1916, No. 38, 1917. Primary source: U.S. Office of Education. *Negro Education: A Study of the Private and Higher Schools for Colored People in the United States,* vol. I. Bulletin, 1916, No. 38. Washington, D.C.: Government Printing Office, 1917.

★ 838 ★

Professional Education

Theology: Location, Denominational Affiliation, Instructors, and Students at Black Schools Offering Theology, 1877

Name and class of institution	Location	Religious denomination	Instructors	Students
		SCHOOLS OF THEOLOGY		
Rust Biblical and Normal Institute	Hunstville, Ala.	Meth	...	...
Theological department of Talladega College	Talladega, Ala.	Cong	2	18
Institute for the Education of Col'd Ministers	Tuscaloosa, Ala.	Presb	...	...
Augusta Institute	August, Ga.	Baptist	2	85
Theological department of Leland University	New Orleans, La.	Baptist	2	28
Thompson Biblical Institute (New Orleans University)	New Orleans, La.	M.E.	...	18
Theological department of Straight University	New Orleans,La.	Cong	...	14
Centenary Biblical Institute	Baltimore, Md.	M.E.	5	24
Theological department of Biddle University	Charlotte, N.C.	Presb	3	9
Theological department of Shaw University	Raleigh, N.C.	Baptist	2	50
Theological Seminary of Wilberforce Univer'y	Xenia, Ohio	M.E.	6	8
Theological department of Lincoln Univer'y	Oxford, Pa.	Presb	5	20
Baker Theological Seminary (Claflin Univer'y)	Orangeburg, S.C.	Meth	...	...
Theological course in Fisk University	Nashville, Tenn.	Cong	2	33
Theological department of Central Tennessee College	Nashville, Tenn.	M.E.	5	35
Theological department of Howard Univer'y	Washington, D.C.	Non-sect	4	32
Wayland Seminary	Washington, D.C.	Baptist	6	88
Total			44	462

Source: Robert, *Negro Civilization in the South,* "Statistics of Institutions for the Institutions for the Instruction of the Colored Race for 1877 - Universities and Colleges,", 1880, p. 133. Primary source: Robert, Charles Edwin. *Negro Civilization in the South; Educational, Social, and Religious Advancement of the Colored People.* Nashville, Tenn.: Printed by Wheeler Bros. for the author, 1880.

School Characteristics

★ 839 ★

Attendance, Teachers, Income, and Property Value at Black Schools with State Funding by State, c. 1916

State	Location of schools	Counted attendance				Teachers[1]	Income			Value of property
		Total	Elementary	Secondary	College		Total	State appropriations	Other sources	
Total	-	2,638	1,466	1,132	40	188	$246,834	$218,917	$27,917	$1,394,547
Alabama	Montgomery	714	575	139	-	31	21,500	16,000	5,500	70,000
Kansas	Topeka	82	45	37	-	14	15,830	12,000	3,830	131,305
Do.	Quindaro	106	27	79	-	26	38,148	28,766	9,382	195,300
Maryland	Bowie	50	12	38	-	8	8,053	7,167	886	33,500
New Jersey	Bordentown	93	72	21	-	18	27,755	27,755	-	99,159
North Carolina	Elizabeth City	249	181	68	-	8	6,074	5,360	714	45,000
Do.	Fayetteville	227	174	53	-	7	5,544	4,969	575	38,700
Do.	Winston-Salem	165	78	87	-	10	5,258	4,900	358	51,700
Ohio	Wilberforce	231	-	191	40	29	77,000	77,000	-	436,893
Virginia	Petersburg	573	282	291	-	25	27,898	22,000	5,898	233,900
West Virginia	Bluefield	148	20	128	-	12	13,774	13,000	774	59,000

Source: "Schools Maintained by State Funds," *Negro Education: A Study of the Private and Higher Schools for Colored People in the United States,* vol. I. Bulletin, 1916, No. 38, p. 117. Primary source: U.S. Office of Education. *Negro Education: A Study of the Private and Higher Schools for Colored People in the United States,* vol. I. Bulletin, 1916, No. 38. Washington, D.C.: Government Printing Office, 1917. *Note:* 1. All colored except two at Montgomery State Normal School.

★ 840 ★

School Characteristics

Attendance: Characteristics of Attendance in Selected States with Segregated Schools, 1948-49

State	Attendance			
	Average Daily Attendance	Average Number Days Schools were in Session	Average Number Days Attended per Pupil Enrolled	Per Cent Attendance is of Enrollment
Alabama	195,697	176.5	147.8	83.7
Arkansas	80,417	171.3	124.1	72.5
Delaware	6,793	182.4	163.0	89.4
District of Columbia	38,463	177.5	153.6	86.5
Florida	100,185	180.5	161.8	89.6
Georgia	200,075	178.0	139.5	78.4
Kentucky	31,415	176.8	149.6	84.6
Louisiana	148,039	180.0	154.3	85.7
Maryland	61,140	185.5	163.2	85.7

[Continued]

★ 840 ★

Attendance: Characteristics of Attendance in Selected States with Segregated Schools, 1948-49

[Continued]

State	Average Daily Attendance	Attendance		
		Average Number Days Schools were in Session	Average Number Days Attended per Pupil Enrolled	Per Cent Attendance is of Enrollment
Mississippi	220,142	148.0	124.4	84.1
Missouri	44,075	194.7	169.1	86.9
North Carolina	225,082	179.9	154.1	85.7
Oklahoma	31,993	180.0	159.0	88.4
South Carolina	171,191	170.3	135.2	79.4
Tennessee	91,609	180.0	157.4	87.5
Texas	169,525	172.4	145.2	84.2
Virginia	132,935	180.0	156.4	86.9
West Virginia	23,711	173.6	160.9	92.7
Total	1,971,487	174.4	146.1	83.8

Source: "Attendance in Negro Full-Time Schools in 17 States and District of Columbia which have Segregated Schools, 1948-49, *1952 Negro Year Book: A Review of Events Affecting Negro Life*, 1952, p. 204. Primary source: U.S. Office of Education, *Statistical Circular No. 286*, January 1951.

★ 841 ★

School Characteristics

Attendance: Elementary and Secondary School Attendance at Black Public Schools, 1918-19

State	Number institutions	Range of attendance		
		Total	Secondary	Elementary
Alabama	4	232-702	32-387	200-495
Arkansas	5	60-815	25-100	384-786
Delaware	1	485	60	425
District of Columbia	2	529-731	529-731	-
Florida	2	493-975	34-44	459-931
Georgia	1	321	40	281
Kansas	1	253	253	-
Kentucky	9	24-1,093	24-402	260-1,000
Maryland	1	669	669	-
Mississippi	1	699	49	650
Missouri	2	315-595	315-595	-
Oklahoma	5	85-799	40-138	67-719
South Carolina	1	1,465	138	1,327
Tennessee	5	166-857	26-232	140-777
Texas	13	151-986	28-243	82-743

[Continued]

★ 841 ★

Attendance: Elementary and Secondary School Attendance at Black Public Schools, 1918-19

[Continued]

State	Number institutions	Range of attendance		
		Total	Secondary	Elementary
Virginia	6	60-1,220	60-439	681-963
West Virginia	5	46-426	21-46	137-391

Source: Compiled and adapted by the editors from "Partial List Public High Schools for Negroes," *Negro Year Book: An Annual Encyclopedia of the Negro, 1918-1919,* 1919, [no p. no.]. Primary source: Work, Monroe N. (Ed.), *Negro Year Book: An Annual Encyclopedia of the Negro, 1918-1919.* Tuskegee Institute, Ala.: The Negro Year Book Pub. Co., 1919. Published by permission.

★ 842 ★

School Characteristics

Attendance: Number of Blacks and Mulattoes In and Out of School by Region and Age Group, 1910

Negro population 6 to 20 years of age: 1910	Section and division Both sexes			
	United States	The North	The South	The West
Total				
Black				
Number in school	1,230,843	1001,758	1,125,347	3,738
Number not in school	1,465,328	73,975	1,388,786	2,349
Mulatto				
Number in school	388,856	44,914	341,593	2,567
Number not in school	337,130	27,008	308,770	1,352
6 to 9 years of age				
Black				
Number in school	369,352	33,509	334,665	1,178
Number not in school	411,993	10,363	401,270	1,178
Mulatto				
Number in school	119,602	15,003	103,879	720
Number not in school	89,903	3,853	85,849	201
10 to 14 years of age				
Black				
Number in school	607,401	49,153	556,481	1,767
Number not in school	305,247	6,170	298,902	175
Mulatto				
Number in school	184,594	20,906	162,621	1,067
Number not in school	58,024	1,976	55,976	72

[Continued]

★ 842 ★

Attendance: Number of Blacks and Mulattoes In and Out of School by Region and Age Group, 1910
[Continued]

| Negro population 6 to 20 years of age: 1910 | Section and division Both sexes | | | |
	United States	The North	The South	The West
15 to 20 years of age				
Black				
Number in school	254,090	19,096	234,201	793
Number not in school	748,088	57,442	688,614	2,032
Mulatto				
Number in school	84,660	9,005	75,093	562
Number not in school	189,203	21,179	166,945	1,079

Source: "School Attendance of the Black and Mulatto Population—Number In School and Not In School, by Age Periods, by Sections, Southern Divisions, and States: 1910," *Negro Population, 1790-1915,* 1918, p. 230. Primary source: U.S. Bureau of the Census. *Negro Population, 1790-1915.* Washington, D.C.: Government Printing Office, 1918.

★ 843 ★
School Characteristics

Attendance: Percent Changes in Black Population and School Attendance by Age Group, 1910-1920 and 1920-1930

A minus sign (-) denotes decrease.

| Age period | 1920 to 1930 | | 1910 to 1920 | |
	Total	Attending school	Total	Attending school
5 to 20 years	8.7	22.0	3.2	23.4
5 and 6 years	7.5	23.4	-.4	38.6
7 to 13 years	4.2	18.8	5.5	26.0
14 and 15 years	7.0	21.5	4.5	23.1
16 and 17 years	16.7	37.9	.6	10.9
18 to 20 years	18.0	45.5	1.4	-6.2

Source: "Percent of Increase in Negro Population 5 to 20 Years and in Negroes Attending School, by Age Periods, for the United States: 1910 to 1930," *Negroes in the United States, 1920-1932,* 1935, p. 210. Primary source: U.S. Bureau of the Census. *Negroes in the United States, 1920-1932.* Washington, D.C.: U.S. Government Printing Office, 1935.

★ 844 ★

School Characteristics

Attendance: Percent of Minority 15-17-Year-Olds Not Attending School, in Relation to Male Population, 1960 and 1970

	Raw Measure[1]			Social Indicator Values (Ratios of raw measures to the majority male population)		
	1960	1970	1976	1960	1970	1976
Males						
Amer. Ind./Alask. Nat.	29	15	14	1.61	1.67	2.80
Blacks	21	16	07	1.17	1.78	1.40
Mexican Americans	26	13	11	1.44	1.44	2.20
Japanese Americans	02	06	02	.11	.67	.40
Chinese Americans	09	06	NA	.50	.67	NA
Pilipino Americans	12	08	06	.67	.89	1.20
Puerto Ricans	25	26	05	1.39	2.89	1.00
Majority	18	09	05	1.00	1.00	1.00
Females						
Amer. Ind./Alask. Nat.	24	16	15	1.33	1.78	3.00
Blacks	23	15	06	1.28	1.67	1.20
Mexicans Americans	31	17	14	1.72	1.89	2.80
Japanese Americans	03	06	01	.17	.67	.20
Chinese Americans	14	09	NA	.78	1.00	NA
Pilipino Americans	07	09	10	.39	1.00	2.00
Puerto Ricans	30	26	16	1.67	2.89	3.20
Majority	12	08	06	.67	.89	1.20

Source: "High School Completion," *Social Indicators of Equality for Minorities and Women*, 1978, p. 10. Primary source: U.S. Commission on Civil Rights. *Social Indicators of Equality for Minorities and Women.* Washington, D.C.: 1978. *Notes:* 1. The percent of 15-, 16-, and 17-year olds who were not enrolled in school on April 1. 2. NA indicates that a value was not reported due to an insufficient sample size. 3. This can be interpreted as follows: "In 1976 the high school nonattendance rate for American Indian and Alaskan Native males was 2.80 times greater than the rate for majority males."

★ 845 ★

School Characteristics

Attendance: School Attendance in U.S. Regions by Age Group, 1930 - I

Division or state and racial class	Total number of persons attending school	Persons 7 to 13 years old			Persons 14 and 15 years old			Persons 16 and 17 years old		
		Total number	Attending school		Total number	Attending school		Total number	Attending school	
			Number	Percent		Number	Percent		Number	Percent
United States										
Negro	2,553,151	1,811,015	1,580,624	87.3	493,897	385,502	78.1	502,710	232,648	46.3
White	24,973,932	15,065,790	14,457,737	96.6	4,110,385	3,716,963	90.4	4,086,139	2,405,061	58.9
The North										
Negro	430,796	264,683	255,177	96.4	65,844	60,132	91.3	68,300	36,479	53.4
White	15,888,164	9,400,734	9,199,458	97.9	2,594,446	2,388,626	92.1	2,555,473	1,475,716	57.7

[Continued]

★ 845 ★

Attendance: School Attendance in U.S. Regions by Age Group, 1930 - I
[Continued]

Division or state and racial class	Total number of persons attending school	Persons 7 to 13 years old			Persons 14 and 15 years old			Persons 16 and 17 years old		
		Total number	Attending school		Total number	Attending school		Total number	Attending school	
			Number	Percent		Number	Percent		Number	Percent
The South										
Negro	2,100,626	1,534,723	1,314,235	85.6	424,944	322,421	75.9	431,207	193,778	44.9
White	6,648,937	4,348,450	4,062,204	93.4	1,152,214	981,142	85.2	1,168,544	650,847	55.7
The West										
Negro	21,729	11,609	11,212	96.6	3,109	2,949	94.9	3,203	2,391	74.6
White	2,436,831	1,316,606	1,286,075	97.7	363,725	347,195	95.5	362,122	278,498	76.9

Source: "School Attendance of Negro and White Population by Age Periods, by Sections, Divisions, and States: 1930," *Negroes in the United States, 1920- 1932*, 1935, pp. 219-220. Primary source: U.S. Bureau of the Census. *Negroes in the United States 1920-1932*. Washington, D.C.: Government Printing Office, 1935.

★ 846 ★
School Characteristics

Attendance: School Attendance in U.S. Regions by Age Group, 1930 - II

Division or state and racial class	Persons 18 to 20 years old			Others attending school			
	Total number	Attending school		Under 5 years old	5 years old	6 years old	21 years and over
		Number	Percent				
United States							
Negro	765,928	102,038	13.3	4,813	34,748	141,751	71,027
White	5,929,322	1,338,189	22.6	56,374	458,629	1,502,550	948,429
The North							
Negro	121,226	16,464	13.6	1,588	12,795	31,991	16,212
White	3,726,755	790,086	21.2	42,806	365,553	1,031,674	594,202
The South							
Negro	639,388	94,218	13.2	3,090	21,229	108,378	53,277
White	1,657,578	369,668	22.3	7,606	49,183	331,933	196,354
The West							
Negro	5,314	1,356	25.5	135	766	1,382	1,538
White	544,989	178,435	32.7	5,962	43,850	138,943	157,873

Source: "School Attendance of Negro and White Population by Age Periods, by Sections, Divisions, and States: 1930," *Negroes in the United States, 1920- 1932*, 1935, pp. 219-220. Primary source: U.S. Bureau of the Census. *Negroes in the United States 1920-1932*. Washington, D.C.: Government Printing Office, 1935.

★ 847 ★

School Characteristics

Attendance: School Attendance of 5 to 20 Year-Olds by Region and Division, 1930

Region	Negro			White, attending school		Percent distribution attending school	
	Total	Number	Percent	Number	Percent	Negro	White
United States	4,128,998	2,477,311	60.0	23,969,129	71.5	100.0	100.0
The South	3,496,926	2,044,259	58.5	6,444,977	66.9	82.5	26.9
South Atlantic	1,721,330	983,407	57.1	2,611,374	66.4	39.7	10.9
East South Central	968,021	575,630	59.5	1,714,073	66.6	23.2	7.2
West South Central	807,575	485,222	60.1	2,119,530	67.7	19.6	8.8
The North	605,368	412,996	68.2	15,251,156	72.8	16.7	63.6
New England	26,401	19,262	73.0	1,733,928	73.7	.8	7.2
Middle Atlantic	263,331	174,159	66.1	5,339,867	71.5	7.0	22.3
East North Central	230,768	161,661	70.1	5,250,511	73.4	6.5	21.9
West North Central	84,868	57,914	68.2	2,926,850	73.7	2.3	12.2
The West	26,704	20,056	75.1	2,272,996	76.9	.8	9.5
Mountain	6,710	4,650	69.3	796,412	74.7	.2	3.3
Pacific	19,994	15,406	77.1	1,476,584	78.1	.6	6.2

Source: "The Number and Percent Attending School for Negroes and Whites from 5 to 20 Years, by Geographic Divisions, and Sections: 1930," *Negroes in the United States, 1920-1932,* 1935, p. 210. Primary source: U.S. Bureau of the Census. *Negroes in the United States, 1920-1932.* Washington, D.C.: U.S. Government Printing Office, 1935.

★ 848 ★

School Characteristics

Attendance: School Attendance of 7 to 15 Year-Olds in Cities with 50,000 or More Black Persons, 1930

City	Ranked by number attending school	Number attending school	City	Ranked by percent attending school	Percent attending school		
					Negro	White	Excess of white over Negro
New York, N.Y.	1	34,527	Cleveland, Ohio	1	97.0	98.3	1.3
Philadelphia, Pa.	2	28,424	Chicago, Ill.	2	96.1	96.9	.8
Chicago, Ill.	3	25,694	New York, N.Y.	3	95.9	96.9	1.0
Baltimore, Md.	4	18,598	Washington, D.C.	4	95.9	97.7	1.8
New Orleans, La.	5	17,955	Philadelphia, Pa.	5	95.3	96.6	1.3
Washington, D.C.	6	17,047	Pittsburgh, Pa.	6	94.3	96.9	2.6
Detroit, Mich.	7	14,468	St. Louis, Mo.	7	94.2	94.9	.7
Birmingham, Ala.	8	14,368	Houston, Tex.	8	93.2	95.1	1.9
Atlanta, Ga.	9	13,308	Baltimore, Md.	9	92.6	94.1	1.5
Memphis, Tenn.	10	11,378	Memphis, Tenn.	10	92.3	97.1	4.8
St. Louis, Mo.	11	10,692	Birmingham, Ala.	11	92.0	97.1	5.1
Cleveland, Ohio	12	9,286	Richmond, Va.	12	91.3	97.1	5.8
Richmond, Va.	13	8,149	Detroit, Mich.	13	90.9	97.8	6.9

[Continued]

★ 848 ★

Attendance: School Attendance of 7 to 15 Year-Olds in Cities with 50,000 or More Black Persons, 1930

[Continued]

City	Ranked by number attending school	Number attending school	City	Ranked by percent attending school	Percent attending school		
					Negro	White	Excess of white over Negro
Houston, Tex.	14	7,706	New Orleans, La.	14	90.9	94.3	3.4
Pittsburgh, Pa.	15	7,339	Atlanta, Ga.	15	86.6	95.2	8.6

Source: "Negro Children 7 to 15 Years of Age Attending School Ranked by Number and Percent, with the Percentage of White children Attending School, in Cities Having 50,000 or More Negro Inhabitants: 1930," *Negroes in the United States, 1920-1932*, 1935, p. 210. Primary source: U.S. Bureau of the Census. *Negroes in the United States, 1920-1932*. Washington, D.C.: U.S. Government Printing Office, 1935.

★ 849 ★

School Characteristics

Attendance: School Attendance of Black 7 to 15-Year Olds in Cities with 25,000 or More Black Persons, 1930

City	Total	Attending school		Number not attending school
		Number	Percent	
New York, N.Y.	35,999	34,527	95.9	1,472
Philadelphia, Pa.	29,832	28,424	95.3	1,408
Chicago, Ill.	26,732	25,694	96.1	1,038
Baltimore, Md.	20,089	18,598	92.6	1,491
New Orleans, La.	19,761	17,955	90.9	1,806
Washington, D.C.	17,783	17,047	95.9	736
Detroit, Mich.	15,925	14,468	90.9	1,457
Birmingham, Ala.	15,615	14,368	92.0	1,247
Atlanta, Ga.	15,368	13,308	86.6	2,060
Memphis, Tenn.	12,327	11,378	92.3	949
St. Louis, Mo.	11,356	10,692	94.2	664
Cleveland, Ohio	9,578	9,286	97.0	292
Richmond, Va.	8,925	8,149	91.3	776
Houston, Tex.	8,269	7,706	93.2	563
Pittsburgh, Pa.	7,779	7,339	94.3	440
Jacksonville, Fla.	7,320	6,646	90.8	674
Norfolk, Va.	6,869	6,242	90.9	627
Cincinnati, Ohio	6,495	6,239	96.1	256
Nashville, Tenn.	6,380	5,728	89.8	652
Indianapolis, Ind.	6,339	6,110	96.4	229
Louisville, Ky.	5,974	5,655	94.7	319
Newark, N.J.	5,550	5,278	95.1	272
Savannah, Ga.	5,458	4,560	83.5	898
Winston-Salem, N.C.	5,322	4,817	90.5	505
Chattanooga, Tenn.	5,219	4,815	92.3	404
Dallas, Tex.	5,110	4,615	90.3	495

[Continued]

★ 849 ★

Attendance: School Attendance of Black 7 to 15-Year Olds in Cities with 25,000 or More Black Persons, 1930
[Continued]

City	Total	Attending school		Number not attending school
		Number	Percent	
Charleston, S.C.	4,977	4,315	86.7	662
Montgomery, Ala.	4,897	4,348	88.8	549
Los Angeles, Calif.	4,647	4,516	97.2	131
Columbus, Ohio	4,609	4,425	96.0	184
Charlotte, N.C.	4,195	3,685	87.8	510
Kansas City, Mo.	4,089	3,822	93.5	267
Shreveport, La.	3,977	3,729	93.8	248
Miami, Fla.	3,931	3,689	93.8	242

Source: "School Attendance of Negro Children 7 to 15 Years of Age in Cities Having 25,000 or More Negro Inhabitants: 1930," *Negroes in the United States, 1920-1932*, 1935, p. 212. Primary source: U.S. Bureau of the Census. *Negroes in the United states, 1920-1932.* Washington, D.C.: U.S. Government Printing Office, 1935.

★ 850 ★
School Characteristics

Attendance: School Attendance of Black Persons in Urban, Rural-Farm, and Rural-Nonfarm Areas by Age Group, 1930 - I

Area and sex	Total number attending school	Persons 7 to 13 years			Persons 14 and 15 years			Persons 16 and 17 years		
		Total number	Attending school		Total number	Attending school		Total number	Attending school	
			Number	Percent		Number	Percent		Number	Percent
United States	2,553,151	1,811,015	1,580,624	87.3	493,897	385,502	78.1	502,710	232,648	46.3
Urban										
Total	954,641	607,212	571,918	94.2	159,822	133,839	83.7	172,312	84,703	49.2
Male	450,830	294,463	276,174	93.8	73,877	61,390	83.1	77,307	37,040	47.9
Female	503,811	312,749	295,744	94.6	85,945	72,449	84.3	95,005	47,663	50.2
Rural										
Total	1,598,510	1,203,803	1,008,706	83.8	334,075	251,663	75.3	330,398	147,945	44.8
Male	779,788	607,506	502,725	82.8	168,480	121,169	71.9	167,577	67,520	40.3
Female	818,722	596,297	505,981	84.9	165,595	130,494	78.8	162,821	80,425	49.4
Rural-farm										
Total	1,199,774	909,108	753,583	82.9	256,769	194,447	75.7	249,678	115,884	46.4
Male	587,716	461,294	377,614	81.9	130,554	93,945	72.0	128,766	53,437	41.5
Female	612,058	447,814	375,969	84.0	126,215	100,502	79.6	120,912	62,447	51.6
Rural-nonfarm										
Total	398,736	294,695	255,123	86.6	77,306	57,216	74.0	80,720	32,061	39.7

[Continued]

★ 850 ★

Attendance: School Attendance of Black Persons in Urban, Rural-Farm, and Rural-Nonfarm Areas by Age Group, 1930 - I
[Continued]

Area and sex	Total number attending school	Persons 7 to 13 years			Persons 14 and 15 years			Persons 16 and 17 years		
		Total number	Attending school		Total number	Attending school		Total number	Attending school	
			Number	Percent		Number	Percent		Number	Percent
Male	192,072	146,212	125,111	85.6	37,926	27,224	71.8	38,811	14,083	36.3
Female	206,664	148,483	130,012	87.6	39,380	29,992	76.2	41,909	17,978	42.9

Source: "School Attendance of the Negro Population by Age Periods and Sex, for the Urban, Rural-Farm, and Rural-Nonfarm Areas of the United States: 1930," *Negroes in the United States, 1920-1932*, 1935, p. 212. Primary source: U.S. Bureau of the Census. *Negroes in the United States, 1920-1932*. Washington, D.C.: U.S. Government Printing Office, 1935.

★ 851 ★

School Characteristics

Attendance: School Attendance of Black Persons in Urban, Rural-Farm, and Rural-Nonfarm Areas by Age Group, 1930 - II

Area and sex	Persons 18 to 20 years			Others attending school			
	Total number	Attending school		Under 5 years	5 years	6 years	21 years and over
		Number	Percent				
United States	765,928	102,038	13.3	4,813	34,748	141,751	71,027
Urban							
Total	304,094	42,396	13.9	3,005	20,384	63,487	34,909
Male	125,161	18,462	14.8	1,432	9,558	30,302	16,472
Female	178,933	23,934	13.4	1,573	10,826	33,185	18,437
Rural							
Total	461,834	59,642	12.9	1,808	14,364	78,264	36,118
Male	218,914	25,286	11.6	880	6,716	37,433	18,059
Female	242,920	34,356	14.1	928	7,648	40,831	18,059
Rural-farm							
Total	328,751	45,051	13.7	1,271	10,243	55,618	23,677
Male	157,245	18,954	12.1	617	4,857	26,745	11,547
Female	171,506	26,097	15.2	654	5,386	28,873	12,130
Rural-nonfarm							
Total	133,083	14,591	11.0	537	4,121	22,646	12,441
Male	61,669	6,332	10.3	263	1,859	10,688	6,512
Female	71,414	8,259	11.6	274	2,262	11,958	5,929

Source: "School Attendance of the Negro Population by Age Periods and Sex, for the Urban, Rural-Farm, and Rural-Nonfarm Areas of the United States: 1930," *Negroes in the United States, 1920-1932*, 1935, p. 212. Primary source: U.S. Bureau of the Census. *Negroes in the United States, 1920-1932*. Washington, D.C.: U.S. Government Printing Office, 1935.

★ 852 ★

School Characteristics

Attendance: School Attendance of Black and White 5 to 20-Year Olds by Age Group, 1920 and 1930

Age and census year	Percent attending school					
	Negro			White		
	Total	Male	Female	Total	Male	Female
5 to 20 years						
1930	60.0	59.4	60.5	71.5	71.7	71.2
1920	53.5	52.4	54.5	65.7	65.6	65.9
Increase, 1920-30	6.5	7.0	6.0	5.8	6.1	5.3
5 and 6 years						
1930	31.8	30.5	33.1	45.1	44.4	45.9
1920	27.7	26.7	28.7	42.7	42.2	43.3
Increase, 1920-30	4.1	3.8	4.4	2.4	2.2	2.6
7 to 13 years						
1930	87.3	86.4	88.2	96.6	96.5	96.7
1920	76.5	75.5	77.6	92.5	92.4	92.6
Increase, 1920-30	10.8	10.9	10.6	4.1	4.1	4.1
14 and 15 years						
1930	78.1	75.3	80.7	90.4	90.8	90.1
1920	68.7	65.0	72.3	81.5	81.4	81.6
Increase, 1920-30	9.4	10.3	8.4	8.9	9.4	8.5
16 and 17 years						
1930	46.3	42.7	49.7	58.9	58.4	59.3
1920	39.2	34.1	43.8	43.4	41.0	45.7
Increase, 1920-30	7.1	8.6	5.9	15.5	17.4	13.6
18 to 20 years						
1930	13.3	1.7	13.8	22.6	23.7	21.5
1920	10.8	9.7	11.7	15.2	15.4	15.1
Increase, 1920-30	2.5	3.0	2.1	7.4	8.3	6.4

Source: "Negro Population from 5 to 20 Years of Age, Attending and Not Attending School and Percentages for Negroes and Whites, by Sex and Age Periods: 1930 and 1920," *Negroes in the United States, 1920-1932*, 1935, p. 210. Primary source: U.S. Bureau of the Census. *Negroes in the United States, 1920-1932*. Washington, D.C.: U.S. Government Printing Office, 1935.

★ 853 ★

School Characteristics

Average White and Black Teacher Salaries in Elementary and Secondary Schools in Selected States, 1948-49 and 1949-50

State[1]	1949-50		1948-49	
	White	Negro	White	Negro
Alabama	$2,157	$1,870	$2,163	$1,778
Arkansas	-	-	1,718	1,262
District of Columbia	4,003	3,853	3,840	3,619
Florida	3,030	2,616	2,935	2,535
Georgia	2,148	1,655	-	-
Louisiana	2,957	2,329	2,938	2,388
Maryland	3,574	3,549	-	-
Mississippi	1,946	764	1,841	682
Missouri	2,325	2,788	2,265	2,793
North Carolina	2,600	2,650[2]	2,429	2,464
Oklahoma	2,769	2,707	2,299	2,174
South Carolina	-	-	2,019	1,403
Tennessee	-	-	1,845	1,843
Texas	3,051	2,976	2,579	2,175
Virginia	-	-	2,439[3]	2,364[3]

Source: "Average Salary per Member of Instructional Staff, 1948-49 and 1949-50," *1952 Negro Year Book: A Review of Events Affecting Negro Life*, 1952, p. 205. Primary source: State Dept. of Education; U.S. Office of Education, *Statistical Circular No. 286*, January 1951. Published by permission. *Notes:* 1. Figures only for those states that furnished basic data. 2. Estimate. 3. Corrected salaries for 1948-49.

★ 854 ★

School Characteristics

Characteristics of Enrollment and Staffing of School Population in Selected States, 1935-36

State	Population 5-17 years of age, inclusive		Percentage distribution of school population, by race		Percentage of school population enrolled in public schools		Number of teaching positions, supervisors, and principals	
	White	Negro	White	Negro	White	Negro	White	Negro
Total, 18 states	9,239,000	2,946,200	75.8	24.2	84.2	82.8	248,479	58,858
Alabama	542,000	293,000	64.9	35.1	82.3	78.9	13,667	5,043
Arkansas	410,000	150,000	73.2	26.8	85.1	74.7	10,131	2,451
Delaware	48,800	8,500	85.2	14.8	79.7	84.9	1,451	232
District of Columbia	68,000	28,000	68.7	31.3	95.1	125.5	2,036	1,020
Florida	271,000	122,500	68.9	31.1	105.0	82.7	9,513	2,896
Georgia	540,000	335,000	61.7	38.3	89.8	78.6	15,055	5,985
Kentucky	709,100	55,000	92.8	7.2	81.9	86.0	17,227	1,387
Louisiana	390,000	235,000	62.4	37.6	75.5	72.9	9,989	3,528
Maryland	342,300	69,700	83.1	16.9	70.0	83.8	7,169	1,631

[Continued]

★ 854 ★

Characteristics of Enrollment and Staffing of School Population in Selected States, 1935-36
[Continued]

State	Population 5-17 years of age, inclusive		Percentage distribution of school population, by race		Percentage of school population enrolled in public schools		Number of teaching positions, supervisors, and principals	
	White	Negro	White	Negro	White	Negro	White	Negro
Mississippi[1]	315,000	313,000	50.2	49.8	98.0	95.6	8,930	5,982
Missouri	810,300	50,000	94.2	5.8	82.0	93.5	24,190	1,408
North Carolina	739,000	330,000	69.1	30.9	83.7	81.9	17,402	6,833
Oklahoma	655,000	55,000	92.3	7.7	92.9	90.0	18,264	1,599
South Carolina	306,000	288,000	51.5	48.5	84.5	76.1	8,816	4,952
Tennessee	639,000	125,000	83.6	16.4	84.5	90.7	16,473	2,875
Texas	1,422,000	250,000	85.0	15.0	80.2	89.8	40,293	5,967
Virginia	518,000	206,000	71.5	28.5	83.4	77.8	13,064	4,101
West Virginia	513,500	32,500	94.0	6.0	82.0	88.2	14,809	968

Source: "Distribution of School Population—Enrollment in 17 States and the District of Columbia, 1935-36," *Negro Year Book: An Annual Encyclopedia of the Negro, 1937-1938*, 1937, p. 111. Primary source: U.S. Bureau of the Census. Published by permission. *Note:* 1. Enrollment and teacher statistics for 1934.

★ 855 ★
School Characteristics

Characteristics of Schools with Religious Boards of Control, c. 1918-19

Board	Number of schools				Total no. teachers	Number of students				
	Higher	Secondary	Elementary	Total		Collegiate	Professional	Secondary	Elementary	Total
American Baptist Home Mission Board	13	7	-	20	326	370	384	3,186	2,292	6,232
American Missionary Association	6	21	4	34	433	311	204	3,345	4,097	8,947
American Church Institute for Negroe's (Episcopal)	-	8	2	10	135	-	15	268	1,622	1,905
Board of Missions for Freedmen of the Presbyterian Ch. in the U.S.A.	2	25	113	140	434	152	30	1,610	16,316	18,108
Board of Missions for Freedmen of the United Presbyterian Church	1	5	9	15	151	30	8	650	2,570	3,258
Christian Woman's Board of Missions (Disciples)	-	2	4	6	67	-	-	84	491	575
Freedmen's Aid Society of the Methodist Episcopal Church	13	9	-	22	351	291	680	1,920	3,010	5,901
Woman's Home M. Society of the M.E. Church	-	-	18	18	-	-	-	-	-	-
Board of Colored Missions of the Evangelical Lutheran Synodical Conf. of North America	2[1]	-	8	10	26	-	4	78	2,262	2,344

Source: "Number of Schools for Negroes, Teachers and Students In, of Certain Religious Boards," *Negro Year Book: An Annual Encyclopedia of the Negro, 1918-1919*, 1919, p. 269. Primary source: Work, Monroe N. (Ed.), *Negro Year Book: An Annual Encyclopedia of the Negro, 1918-1919*. Tuskegee Institute, Ala.: The Negro Year Book Pub. Co., 1919. Published by permission. *Note:* 1. Both higher and secondary.

★ 856 ★

School Characteristics

Characteristics of Schools with Religious Boards of Control, c. 1937

Board	Number of schools				Total no. teachers	Number of students				
	Higher	Secondary	Elementary	Total		Collegiate	Professional	Secondary	Elementary	Total
American Baptist Home Mission Board	6	0	0	6	187	2,176	155	1,682	250	4,263
American Church Institute for Negroes (Episcopal)	6	3	0	9	190	670	12	1,779	1,628	4,089
American Missionary Association	5	10	1	16	260	1,358	0	1,511	1,023	3,892
Church of Christ (Disciples) United Christian Missionary Society	2	0	0	2	45	84	63	117	151	415
Lutheran Evangelical Synodical Conference of North America, Board Colored Missions	2	0	48	50	40	41	12	272	3,371	3,696
Methodist Episcopal Church, Board of Education, Institutions for Negroes	11	3	0	14	341	2,905	359	1,183	933	5,380
Methodist Episcopal Church Woman's Home Missionary Society	1	3	1	5	91	149	0	396	604	1,149
Presbyterian Church in the U.S.A., Division of Missions for Colored People	5	11	7	23	251	972	0	2,344	4,455	7,771
United Presbyterian Church Board of Missions for Freedmen	1	4	3	8	90	235	0	817	1,376	2,428

Source: "Schools for Negroes Under Certain Religious Boards," *Negro Year Book: An Annual Encyclopedia of the Negro, 1937-1938*, 1937, p. 174. Primary source: Work, Monroe N. (Ed.), *Negro Year Book: An Annual Encyclopedia of the Negro, 1937-1938*. Tuskegee Institute, Ala.: The Negro Year Book Pub. Co., 1937. Published by permission.

★ 857 ★

School Characteristics

Course Length, Attendance, High School Teachers, and Property Value in Black Public High Schools and Normal High Schools in Selected States, c. 1916

States	Number of schools			Attendance			High-school teachers			Value of property
	Total	Having four-year course	Less than four years	Total	Secondary	Elementary	Total	Male	Female	
Total	67[1]	45	19	29,630	8,707	20,923	484	243	220	$3,172,250
Alabama	4	2	2	1,852	541	1,311	19	6	13	21,500
Arkansas	5	3	2	1,828	253	1,575	22	11	11	105,000
Delaware	1	1	-	485	60	425	11	3	8	33,800
District of Columbia	3	2	-	1,375	1,375	-	96	48	48	985,000
Florida	2	1	1	1,468	78	1,390	6	3	3	190,000
Georgia	1	-	1	321	40	281	5	2	3	15,000
Kentucky	10	8	1	3,469	779	2,690	44	23	21	209,000
Maryland	2	1	-	781	781	-	42	17	25	80,000
Mississippi	1	-	1	699	49	650	3	2	1	14,000
Missouri	2	2	-	910	910	-	49	32	17	430,500
Oklahoma	5	5	-	1,796	368	1,428	27	17	10	166,750
South Carolina	1	-	1	1,465	138	1,327	6	2	4	15,300
Texas	13	10	3	6,300	1,212	5,088	63	33	30	370,300
Tennessee	5	1	4	1,947	650	1,297	25	15	10	117,000
Virginia	6	3	3	3,615	1,070	2,545	38	11	27	163,500
West Virginia	5	5	-	1,066	150	916	16	10	6	265,600
Kansas	1	1	-	253	253	-	12	8	4	70,000

Source: "Public High Schools and Normal Schools for Colored Pupils," *Negro Education: A Study of the Private and Higher Schools for Colored People in the United States*, vol. I. Bulletin, 1916, No. 38, 1917, p. 41. Primary source: U.S. Office of Education. *Negro Education: A Study of the Private and Higher Schools for Colored People in the United States*, vol. I. Bulletin, 1916, No. 38. Washington, D.C.: Government Printing Office, 1917. *Notes:* 1. Includes three normal schools which offer two-year courses above high-school grade, at Baltimore, Md., Louisville, Ky., and Washington, D.C.

★ 858 ★

School Characteristics

Enrollment, Attendance, and Related Characteristics in Black Public Elementary and Secondary Schools in the South, 1943-44 and 1945-46

Item	1943-44	1945-46
Enrollment of pupils		
Elementary		
Total	2,029,368	1,994,057
Boys	1,004,789	995,810
Girls	1,024,579	998,247
High school grades		
Total	247,374	272,163
Boys	84,886	100,366
Girls	162,488	171,797
Elementary and high school grades		
Total	2,276,742	2,266,220
Boys	1,089,675	1,096,176
Girls	1,187,067	1,170,044
Average daily attendance		
Total number of days attended by all pupils enrolled	303,802,159	315,256,045
Average number of days attended by each pupil enrolled	133	139
Average length of school term in days	164	170
Percent enrolled pupils in daily attendance	81.4	81.8
Percent of pupils in high school grades	10.9	12.0

Source. "Statistical Summary of Negro Public Elementary and Secondary Schools in 17 Southern States and the District of Columbia, 1945-46," *The Negro Handbook, 1949*, 1949, p. 112. Primary source: U.S. Office of Education. Published by permission.

★ 859 ★
School Characteristics

Expenditures: Per Capita Expenditures for Black and White Schools by Percentage of Black Population in Counties of 15 Southern States, c. 1916

County groups, percentage of Negroes in the population	White school population	Negro school population	Per capita for white	Per capita for Negro
Counties under 10 per cent	974,289	45,039	$7.96	$7.23
Counties 10 to 25 per cent	1,008,372	215,744	9.55	5.55
Counties 25 to 50 per cent	1,132,999	709,259	11.11	3.19
Counties 50 to 75 per cent	364,990	661,329	12.53	1.77
Counties 75 percent and over	40,003	207,900	22.22	1.78

Source: [Untitled figures], *Negro Education: A Study of the Private and Higher Schools for Colored People in the United States*, vol. II. Bulletin, 1916, No. 39, 1917, p. 11. Primary source: U.S. Office of Education. *Negro Education: A Study of the Private and Higher Schools for Colored People in the United States*, vol. II. Bulletin, 1916, No. 39. Washington, D.C.: Government Printing Office, 1917.

★ 860 ★
School Characteristics

Expenditures: Total and Per Child Expenditures of Public Schools in Selected States, c. 1925-26

States	Total expenditures		Average expenditures per child of school age		Per cent expenditures		Per cent each race of total population	
	For whites	For Negroes	For whites	For Negroes	For whites	For Negroes	For whites	For Negroes
Alabama	$12,900,274	$1,184,367	$26.57	$3.81	91	9	61.6	38.4
Arkansas	6,386,233	1,216,401	13.36	6.48	83	17	73.0	27.0
Delaware	3,125,872	500,000	60.00	52.90	86	14	86.6	13.4
D. Columbia	5,611,012	1,853,678	76.00	64.40	74	26	74.7	25.2
Florida	8,989,825	773,074	42.01	7.33	92	8	65.9	34.0
Georgia	13,547,310	2,175,338	25.84	5.78	86	14	58.3	41.7
Kentucky	12,521,958	1,093,175	16.61	15.40	92	8	90.2	9.2
Louisiana	11,329,241	1,256,869	33.73	5.48	90	10	61.0	38.9
Maryland	12,500,002	1,345,770	34.70	17.17	90	10	83.1	16.9
Mississippi	8,411,484	2,102,871	25.95	5.62	80	20	47.7	52.2
Missouri	39,220,839	1,279,100	45.32	29.59	97	3	94.7	5.2
N. Carolina	15,362,387	2,125,376	25.31	7.52	88	12	69.7	29.8
Oklahoma	21,406,075	1,064,205	33.08	21.04	95	5	89.8	7.4
S. Carolina	8,502,401	1,015,567	27.88	2.74	89	11	48.6	51.4
Tennessee	13,825,142	1,874,396	21.02	11.88	88	12	80.7	19.3
Texas	33,933,647	4,627,321	31.77	20.24	88	12	84.0	15.9
Virginia	18,534,620	2,312,365	40.27	10.47	89	11	70.1	29.9
W. Virginia	15,935,890	777,171	36.36	32.15	95	5	94.1	5.9
Total	$262,104,212	$28,577,044						

Source: "Annual Expenditures for Public Schools by States," *Negro Year Book: An Annual Encyclopedia of the Negro, 1925-1926*, 1925, p. 295. Primary source: U.S. Bureau of the Census. Published by permission.

★ 861 ★

School Characteristics

Expenditures: White and Black Per Pupil Expenditures in Selected States, 1948-48 and 1949-50

State	1949-50		1948-49	
	White	Negro	White	Negro
Alabama	$144.38	$80.76	$114.21	$77.75[1]
Arkansas	-	-	111.15	62.22
District of Columbia	270.71	209.45	281.41	210.42
Florida	185.89	131.32	188.35	131.67
Georgia	131.67	70.99	-	-
Maryland	187.82	172.11	-	-
Mississippi[2]	119.09	27.45	122.74	26.81
North Carolina	153.00	113.00	131.85	115.02
Oklahoma	-	-	166.31	175.32
South Carolina	-	-	148.48	69.65

Source: "Current Expenditures per Pupil in Average Daily Attendance," *1952 Negro Year Book: A Review of Events Affecting Negro Life,* 1952, p. 204. Primary source: State Depts. of Education and U.S. Office of Education, *Statistical Circular No. 286,* January 1951. Published by permission. *Notes:* Figures not available for either year for Del., Ky., La., Mo., Tenn., Texas., Va., W. Va. 1. Corrected figures for 1948-49. 2. In 1950-51, the figures are white $122.49; Negro $38.25.

★ 862 ★

School Characteristics

Facilities: Plant Value at Black Public Schools, 1918-19

State	Number institutions	Range of value (dollars)
Alabama	4	2,000-10,000
Arkansas	5	7,000-40,000
Delaware	1	33,800
District of Columbia	2	240,000-500,000
Florida	2	15,000-175,000
Georgia	1	15,000
Kansas	1	70,000
Kentucky	9	15,000-41,000
Maryland	1	65,000
Mississippi	1	14,000
Missouri	2	100,000-330,500
Oklahoma	5	6,000-70,000
South Carolina	1	15,300
Tennessee	5	12,000-35,000
Texas	13	4,000-68,000

[Continued]

★ 862 ★

Facilities: Plant Value at Black Public Schools, 1918-19
[Continued]

State	Number institutions	Range of value (dollars)
Virginia	6	14,000-41,500
West Virginia	5	26,750-88,000

Source: Compiled and adapted by the editors from "Partial List Public High Schools for Negroes," Negro Year Book: An Annual Encyclopedia of the Negro, 1918-1919, 1919, [no p. no.] Primary source: Work, Monroe N. (ed.), Negro Year Book: An Annual Encyclopedia of the Negro, 1918-1919. Tuskegee Institute, Ala.: The Negro Year Book Pub. Co., 1919. Published by permission.

★ 863 ★

School Characteristics

Income, Teachers, and Students in Black Private Schools, c. 1937-38

State	Number institutions	Range of students & teachers and income			
		High school	Elementary	Teachers	Income
Alabama	21	31-208	26-225	4-25	$1,000-31,000
Arkansas	2	5-273	120-127	5-13	[1]
Florida	3	57-100	55	8-13	6,342-20,000
Georgia	8	50-380	72-324	6-16	750-12,175
Kentucky	1	200	-	14	20,000
Louisiana	1	117	-	13	4,024.08
Maryland	1	14	18	9	[1]
Mississippi	5	24-90	32-317	8-10	300-3,478.50
Missouri	1	110	20	8	13,000
North Carolina	8	100-382	38-537	4-31	312-26,174.62
Ohio	1	200	-	10	30,000
Oklahoma	1	40	75	8	5,000
South Carolina	7	25-234	74-267	4-17	300-17,248.09
Tennessee	3	55-10	115-266	7-9	400-8,500
Texas	2	43-200	270	5-12	856[2]
Virginia	11	62-200	6-287	3-26	1,495.44-12,000
Total	76	9,060	8,295	775	$406,070.85

Source: Compiled by the editors from "Private High Schools and Academies," Negro Year Book: An Annual Encyclopedia of the Negro, 1937-1938, 1937, pp. 206-209. Primary source: Work, Monroe N. (Ed.), Negro Year Book: An Annual Encyclopedia of the Negro, 1937-1938. Tuskegee Institute, Ala.: The Negro Year Book Pub. Co., 1937. Published by permission. Notes: 1. No income information provided. 2. Information provided for only one school.

★ 864 ★

School Characteristics

Male and Female Teachers at Black Public Schools, 1918-19

State	Number institutions	Range		
		Total	Male	Female
Alabama	4	2-9	1-3	1-6
Arkansas	5	3-8	1-3	1-5
Delaware	1	11	3	8
District of Columbia	2	33-48	19-25	14-23
Florida	2	3	1-2	1-2
Georgia	1	5	2	3
Kansas	1	12	8	4
Kentucky	9	1-16	1-8	1-8
Maryland	1	34	15	19
Mississippi	1	3	2	1
Missouri	2	15-34	9-23	6-11
Oklahoma	5	2-8	1-5	1-4
South Carolina	1	6	2	4
Tennessee	5	2-7	2-5	2-3
Texas	13	2-12	1-6	1-6
Virginia	6	2-17	1-6	1-11
West Virginia	5	2-4	1-3	1-2

Source: Compiled and adapted by the editors from "Partial List Public High Schools for Negroes," *Negro Year Book: An Annual Encyclopedia of the Negro, 1918-1919*, 1919, [no p. no.]. Primary source: Work, Monroe N. (Ed.), *Negro Year Book: An Annual Encyclopedia of the Negro, 1918-1919*. Tuskegee Institute, Ala.: The Negro Year Book Pub. Co., 1919. Published by permission.

★ 865 ★

School Characteristics

Ownership and Control: Attendance, Teachers, Income, and Property Value of Land-Grant Schools by State, c. 1916

State	Location of schools	Counted attendance			Teachers[1]	Income			Value of property
		Total	Elementary	Secondary		Total	Land-grant funds	Other sources	
Total	-	4,875	2,595	2,268	400	$544,520	$259,851	$284,669	$2,576,142
Alabama	Normal	264	179	85	27	29,209	22,695	6,514	182,500
Arkansas	Pine Bluff	170	130	40	12	24,003	13,636	10,367	141,456
Delaware	Dover	71	-	71	8	13,159	10,000	3,159	42,150
Florida	Tallahassee	345[2]	185	148	34	34,168	25,193	8,975	131,421
Georgia	Savannah	390	280	110	21	25,369	16,667	8,702	68,449
Kentucky	Frankfort	234	108	126	19	22,327	8,505	13,822	156,700
Louisiana	Baton Rouge	160	102	58	23	31,384	21,102	10,282	95,250
Maryland	Princess Anne	123	38	85	12	15,528	10,000	5,528	44,950

[Continued]

★ 865 ★

Ownership and Control: Attendance, Teachers, Income, and Property Value of Land-Grant Schools by State, c. 1916
[Continued]

State	Location of schools	Counted attendance			Teachers[1]	Income			Value of property
		Total	Elementary	Secondary		Total	Land-grant funds	Other sources	
Mississippi	Alcorn	484	337	147	24	47,774	36,774	11,000	258,500
Missouri	Jefferson City	264	122	142	33	42,162	3,125	39,937	226,375
North Carolina	Greenboro	150	60	90	26	32,518	16,500	16,018	129,700
Oklahoma	Langston	408	219	189	28	46,400	10,400	36,000	153,827
South Carolina	Orangeburg	726	529	197	33	44,216	30,754	13,462	297,300
Tennessee	Nashville	300	119	181	25	39,819	12,000	27,819	193,915
Texas	Prairie View	552	115	437	46	49,985	12,500	37,485	237,200
West Virginia	Institute	234	72	162	29	46,499	10,000	36,499	216,449

Source: "Schools Maintained by Land-Grant Funds," *Negro Education: A Study of the Private and Higher Schools for Colored People in the United States*, vol. I. Bulletin, 1916, No. 38, 1917, p. 121. Primary source: U.S. Office of Education. *Negro Education: A Study of the Private and Higher Schools for Colored People in the United States*, vol. I. Bulletin, 1916, No. 38. Washington, D.C.: Government Printing Office. *Notes:* 1. All colored. 2. Includes 12 pupils of college grade at Florida Agricultural and Mechanical College.

★ 866 ★
School Characteristics

Ownership and Control: Characteristics of Schools with Religious Boards of Control, c. 1914-15

Board	Number of schools				Total No. Tchrs.	Number of students				
	Higher	Secondary	Elementary	Total		Collegiate	Profes'nal	Secondary	Elementary	Total
American Baptist Home Mission Board	13	11	-	24	408	342	327	3,302	3,380	7,351
American Missionary Association	7	27	31	65	587	353	161	2,246	9,337	12,097
American Church Institute for Negr's (Episcpl)	-	8	-	8	131	-	44	251	1,663	1,958
Board of Missions for Freedmen of the Presbyterian Church in the U.S.A.	2	22	112	136	444	112	55	3,233	13,027	16,427
Board of Freedmen's Missions of the United Presbyterian Church	1	5	11	17	139	25	3	769	3,464	4,261
Christian Women's Bo'd of Mis'ns (Disciples)	-	1	5	6	33	-	-	75	432	507
Freedmen's Aid Society of the Methodist Episcopal Church	13	9	-	22	479	266	632	1,933	3,757	6,588
Woman's Home Mis'ary Society of the Methodist Episcopal Church	-	-	18	18	-	-	-	-	-	-

Source: "Number of Schools for Negroes, Teachers and Students In, of Certain Religious Boards," *Negro Year Book: An Annual Encyclopedia of the Negro, 1914-15*, 1914, p. 215. Primary source: Work, Monroe N. (ed.), *Negro Year Book: An Annual Encyclopedia of the Negro, 1914-15*. Tuskegee Institute, Ala.: The Negro Year Book Pub. Co., 1914. Published by permission.

★ 867 ★

School Characteristics

Ownership and Control: Number of Schools and Multi-Level Attendance at Black Public and Private Schools, c. 1916

Ownership and control	Number of schools			Counted attendance			
	Total	Larger or important	Smaller or less important	Total	Elementary	Secondary	College and professional
All private and higher schools	747	388	359	107,206	80,376	24,189	2,641
Schools under public control	122	122	-	23,527	9,812	12,662	1,053
Federal schools	1	1	-	1,401	-	400	1,001
Land-grant schools	16	16	-	4,875	2,595	2,268	12
State schools	11	11	-	2,638	1,466	1,132	40
City high schools	67	67	-	8,707	-	8,707	-
County training schools	27	27	-	5,906	5,751	155	-
Schools under private control	625	266	359	83,679	70,564	11,527	1,588
Independent schools	118	46	72	14,851	12,273	1,841	737
Denominational schools	507	220	287	68,828	58,291	9,686	851
Under white boards	354	160	194	51,529	43,605	7,188	736
Under Negro boards	153	60	93	17,299	14,686	2,498	115

Source: "Colored Schools, Classified on the Basis of Ownership and Control," *Negro Education: A Study of the Private and Higher Schools for Colored People in the United States*, vol. I. Bulletin, 1916, No. 38, 1917, p. 115. Primary source: U.S. Office of Education. *Negro Education: A Study of the Private and Higher Schools for Colored People in the United States*, vol. I. Bulletin, 1916, No. 38. Washington, D.C.: Government Printing Office.

★ 868 ★

School Characteristics

Ownership and Control: Schools, Attendance, Teachers, Income, and Property Value at Black Schools with Black Baptist and Methodist Boards of Control, c. 1916

Name	Number of schools			Counted attendance				Teachers			Income for current expenses	Value of property
	Total	Large or important	Small or less important	Total	Elementary	Secondary	College	Total	White	Negro		
Total	153	60	93	17,299	14,686	2,498	115	828	2	826	$380,933	$2,305,054
Baptist local conventions	110	31	79	11,250	10,324	926	-	474	2	472	181,914	821,295
African Methodist Episcopal	17	13	4	3,212	2,096	1,028	88	187	-	187	129,778	800,609
African Methodist Episcopal Zion	11	9	2	1,207	923	267	17	77	-	77	37,600	316,950
Colored Methodist Episcopal	9	6	3	1,313	1,036	267	10	72	-	72	25,991	328,200
Five small church boards	6	1	5	317	307	10	-	18	-	18	5,650	38,000

Source: "Negro Church Boards Maintaining Schools," *Negro Education: A Study of the Private and Higher Schools for Colored People in the United States*, vol. I. Bulletin, 1916, No. 38, 1917, p. 151. Primary source: U.S. Office of Education. *Negro Education: A Study of the Private and Higher Schools for Colored People in the United States*, vol. I. Bulletin, 1916, No. 38. Washington, D.C.: Government Printing Office, 1917.

★ 869 ★

School Characteristics

Ownership and Control: Schools, Attendance, Teachers, Income, and Property Value at Black Schools with Independent Boards of Control, c. 1916

States	Number of schools			Counted attendance				Teachers			Income for current expenses	Value of property
	Total	Large or important	Small, less important	Total	Elementary	Secondary	College	Total	White	Negro		
Total	118	46	72	14,851	12,273	1,841	737	1,144	249	895	$1,099,224	$12,369,441
Alabama	23	11	12	4,887	4,415	472	-	331	23	308	369,544	4,279,566
Arkansas	2	-	2	70	70	-	-	2	-	2	1,100	3,700
Delaware	2	-	2	22	22	-	-	4	-	4	5,250	18,600
Florida	3	2	1	234	234	-	-	24	-	24	19,158	85,875
Georgia	21	6	15	2,654	2,227	383	44	97	29	68	72,888	493,673
Kentucky	3	1	2	177	122	55	-	19	8	11	20,351	529,698
Louisiana	7	2	5	702	671	31	-	34	-	34	10,831	118,037
Maryland	3	-	3	38	38	-	-	3	-	3	1,385	2,750
Mississippi	4	4	-	858	823	35	-	58	-	58	33,618	314,220
Missouri	1	1	-	19	19	-	-	6	-	6	2,837	38,500
North Carolina	9	3	6	597	537	60	-	55	-	55	18,389	120,000
South Carolina	11	4	7	1,012	954	58	-	84	3	81	51,235	416,205
Tennessee	3	2	1	1,061	112	256	693	78	33	45	103,305	733,058
Texas	4	2	2	363	317	46	-	23	-	23	10,364	42,000
Virginia	11	4	7	1,685	1,257	428	-	256	147	109	321,660	4,414,459
Northern States	11	4	7	472	455	17	-	70	6	64	57,309	759,100

Source: "White Church Boards Maintaining Schools for Colored People," *Negro Education: A Study of the Private and Higher Schools for Colored People in the United States,* vol. I. Bulletin, 1916, No. 38, 1917, p. 124. Primary source: U.S. Office of Education. *Negro Education:A Study of the Private and Higher Schools for Colored People in the United States,* vol. I. Bulletin, 1916, No. 38. Washington, D.C.: Government Printing Office, 1917.

★ 870 ★

School Characteristics

Ownership and Control: Teachers, Income, and Property Value at Black Public and Private Schools, c. 1916

Ownership and control	Teachers and workers			Income for current expenses	Value of property
	Total	White	Negro		
All private and higher schools	5,851	1,358	4,493	$4,241,572	$35,870,125
Schools under public control	1,317	38	1,279	1,215,112	7,373,179
Federal schools	106	33	73	172,257	1,756,920
Land-grant schools	400	-	400	544,520	2,576,142
State schools	188	2	186	246,834	1,394,547
City high schools	484	3	481	200,000[1]	1,500,000[1]
County training schools	139	-	139	51,501	145,570
Schools under private control	4,534	1,320	3,214	3,026,460	28,496,946
Independent schools	1,144	249	895	1,099,224	12,369,441
Denominational schools	3,390	1,071	2,319	1,927,236	16,127,505

[Continued]

★ 870 ★

Ownership and Control: Teachers, Income, and Property Value at Black Public and Private Schools, c. 1916

[Continued]

Ownership and control	Teachers and workers			Income for current expenses	Value of property
	Total	White	Negro		
Under white boards	2,562	1,069	1,493	1,546,303	13,822,451
Under Negro boards	828	2	826	380,933	2,305,054

Source: "Colored Schools, Classified on the Basis of Ownership and Control," *Negro Education: A Study of the Private and Higher Schools for Colored People in the United States*, vol. I. Bulletin, 1916, No. 38, 1917, p. 115. Primary source: U.S. Office of Education. *Negro Education: A Study of the Private and Higher Schools for Colored People in the United States*, vol. I. Bulletin, 1916, No. 38. Washington, D.C.: Government Printing Office. *Note:* 1. Estimated.

★ 871 ★

School Characteristics

Ownership and Control: Teachers, Income, and Property Value at Black Schools with White Boards of Major Religious Denominations, c. 1916

Denominational boards	Teachers			Income for current expenses	Value of property
	Total	White	Negro		
Total	2,562	1,069	1,493	$1,546,303	$13,822,451
Baptist					
American Home Mission Society	419	139	280	304,861	3,870,744
Woman's American Baptist Home Mission Society	14	11	3	7,746	16,500
Catholic Board of Missions	404	384	20	146,821	491,000
Christian Woman's Board of Missions	37	15	22	29,910	184,602
Congregational American Missionary Association	383	212	171	235,764	1,733,589
Friends Society and other Friends Agencies	96	12	84	63,868	915,900
Lutheran Board for Colored Missions	26	13	13	18,319	72,000
Methodist					
Freedman's Aid Society	266	65	201	230,160	2,605,687
Woman's Home Missionary Society	71	41	30	42,975	309,500
Presbyterian Board of Missions for Freedmen	423	84	339	200,124	2,151,321
Protestant Episcopal Boards, American Church Institute, and the Domestic and Foreign Missionary Society	176	12	164	118,526	628,743
United Presbyterian Church Boards of Freedman's Missions	166	44	122	88,512	455,600
Nine small church boards	81	37	44	58,717	387,265

Source: "White Church Boards Maintaining Schools for Colored People," *Negro Education: A Study of the Private and Higher Schools for Colored People in the United States*, vol. I. Bulletin, 1916, No. 38, 1917, p. 128. Primary source: U.S. Office of Education *Negro Education: A Study of the Private and Higher Schools for Colored People in the United States*, vol. I. Bulletin, 1916, No. 38. Washington, D.C.: Government Printing Office, 1917.

★ 872 ★

School Characteristics

Property Value Per Student and Expense Factors of Schools in Selected States by Race, 1946

State or District of Columbia	Value of school property per pupil enrolled		Current expense per pupil in average daily attendance		Percent increase of current expense since 1943-44	
	Negro	White	White	Negro	White	Negro
Total	$48	$250	$104.66	$57.57	22	35
Alabama	30	145	85.46	37.59	22	47
Arkansas	47	161	74.11	34.93	21	35
Delaware	-	-	158.04	125.12[1]	18	7
Florida	61	313	134.76	61.75	40	30
Georgia	41	200	82.57	31.14	12	32
Kentucky	-	-	90.05	98.35[1]	-	-
Louisiana	63	346	136.12	43.81[1]	12	9
Maryland	158	377	130.40	110.66[1]	13	22
Mississippi	-	-	75.19	14.74	5	23
Missouri	-	-	137.68	133.35[1]	37	27
North Carolina	70	217	86.05	70.36	20	41
Oklahoma	-	-	111.30	118.32	26	24
South Carolina	43	209	100.38	39.64	12	47
Tennessee	-	-	80.30	55.44[1]	24	10
Texas	95	298	123.14	91.22[1]	33	45
Virginia	100	239	104.29	53.15[1]	18	30
West Virginia	-	-	100.63	111.47[1]	-	-
District of Columbia	-	-	190.36	149.42	9	10

Source: "Value of School Property and Current Expense Per Pupil in Average Daily Attendance in 17 States and the District of Columbia, 1946," *The Negro Handbook, 1949,* 1949, pp. 114-115. Published by permission. Primary source: U.S. Office of Education. *Notes:* 1. Estimated proportion of state expense based on teachers' salaries, the only item available.

★ 873 ★

School Characteristics

Public School Salaries in Relation to Selected School Population Characteristics, c. 1916

	White	Colored
Total population	23,682,352	8,906,879
Population 6 to 14 years of age	4,889,762	2,023,108
Population 6 to 14[1]	3,552,431	1,852,181
Teachers' salaries in public schools[1]	$36,649,827	$5,860,876
Teachers' salaries per child 6 to 14[1]	$10.32	$2.89

[Continued]

★ 873 ★

Public School Salaries in Relation to Selected School
Population Characteristics, c. 1916
[Continued]

	White	Colored
Per cent of illiteracy	7.7	33.3
Per cent rural	76.9	78.8

Source: [Untitled figures], *Negro Education: A Study of the Private and Higher Schools for Colored People in the United States*, vol. II. Bulletin, 1916, No. 39, 1917, p. 9. Primary source: U.S. Office of Education. *Negro Education: A Study of the Private and Higher Schools for Colored People in the United States*, vol. II. Bulletin, 1916, No. 39. Washington, D.C.: Government Printing Office, 1917. *Note:* 1. In 1,055 counties.

★ 874 ★

School Characteristics

Public/Private: Attendance by Level in Public and Private Schools,
1916

Ownership of schools	Number of schools	Total attendance	Elementary	Secondary	College
Total private schools	625	83,679	70,564	11,527	1,588
Denominational	507	68,828	58,291	9,686	851
Independent	118	14,851	12,273	1,841	737
State and Federal	28	8,914	4,061	3,800	1,053

Source: [Untitled Table], *Negro Education: A Study of the Private and Higher Schools for Colored People in the United States*, vol. II. Bulletin, 1916, No. 39, 1917, p. 13. Primary source: U.S. Office of Education. *Negro Education: A Study of the Private and Higher Schools for Colored People in the United States*, vol. II. Bulletin, 1916, No. 39. Washington, D.C.: Government Printing Office, 1917.

★ 875 ★

School Characteristics

Public/Private: Black Private and Public Secondary School Enrollees in the South, c. 1916

Of the 24,189 colored secondary pupils in the Southern States, 11,527 are in private schools, 8,707 are in public schools and 3,800 are in State and Federal schools, While scarcely a fourth of the secondary pupils of the border States are in private schools, almost two-thirds of the pupils of the other Southern States are in private institutions. The courses of study of most of the schools follow closely the college preparatory or classical type.

Source: [Untitled text], *Negro Education: A Study of the Private and Higher Schools for Colored People in the United States*, vol. II. Bulletin, 1916, No. 39, 1917, p. 16. Primary source: U.S. Office of Education. *Negro Education: A Study of the Private and Higher Schools for Colored People in the United States*, vol. II. Bulletin, 1916, No. 39. Washington, D.C.: Government Printing Office, 1917.

★ 876 ★

School Characteristics

Relationships: Black Children's Projected School Term as Related to School Funding in 1918-19

Maryland	57
N. Carolina	55
Georgia	52
Virginia	52
Texas	47
Florida	39
Alabama	33
Louisiana	29
S. Carolina	25

Source: "Days of Schooling per Year if Each Negro Child of School Age Got His Share," *Negro Year Book: An Annual Encyclopedia of the Negro, 1918-1919*, 1919, p. 271. Primary source: Work, Monroe N. (Ed.), *Negro Year Book: An Annual Encyclopedia of the Negro, 1918-1919*. Tuskegee Institute, Ala.: The Negro Year Book Pub. Co., 1919.

★ 877 ★

School Characteristics

Relationships: Length of Term and Attendance Days for Selected States, 1935-36

State	Length of school term (days) in school for-		Average number of days attended by each pupil enrolled in schools for-	
	Whites	Negroes	Whites	Negroes
Total, 18 States	167	146	136	113
Alabama	144	127	115	102
Arkansas	156	132	123	102
Delaware	181	181	158	146
District of Columbia	176	176	145	142
Florida	174	168	139	132
Georgia	168	143	132	108
Kentucky	158	146	123	114
Louisiana	175	128	145	104
Maryland	188	179	162	144
Mississippi	145	119	111	86
Missouri	177	187	147	152
North Carolina	161	161	140	132
Oklahoma	174	172	132	125
South Carolina	173	127	141	91
Tennessee	167	158	131	125
Texas	171	157	137	115
Virginia	170	165	143	130
West Virginia	173	173	151	155

Source: "Average Length of School Term, and School Attendance by Race, in 17 States and the District of Columbia, 1935-36," *Negro Year Book: An Annual Encyclopedia of the Negro, 1936-1938*, 1937, p. 111. Primary source: Work, Monroe N. (Ed.), *Negro Year Book: An Annual Encyclopedia of the Negro, 1937-1938*. Tuskegee Institute, Ala.: The Negro Year Book Pub. Co., 1937.

★ 878 ★

School Characteristics

Relationships: Projected Days of Schooling in Selected States, 1914-15

State	Children of School Age	Attendance Total in Days	Average per Child
Texas	252,868	11,784,340	46
Florida	95,805	3,987,864	42
Maryland[1]	52,515	2,185,782	41
Virginia	217,760	8,865,374	41
North Carolina	247,318	8,777,354	36

[Continued]

★ 878 ★

Relationships: Projected Days of Schooling in Selected States, 1914-15
[Continued]

State	Children of School Age	Attendance Total in Days	Average per Child
Georgia	439,485	14,205,861	32
South Carolina	331,429	8,577,340	26
Alabama	328,024	8,038,487	24
Louisiana	222,111	4,878,901	22

Source: "Days of Schooling per Year if Each Negro Child of School Age Got His Share," *Negro Year Book: An Annual Encyclopedia of the Negro, 1914-15,* 1914, p. 219. Primary source: Work, Monroe N. (Ed.), *Negro Year Book: An Annual Encyclopedia of the Negro, 1914-15.* Tuskegee Institute, Ala.: The Negro Year Book Pub. Co., 1914. *Note:* 1. Exclusive of Baltimore City.

★ 879 ★

School Characteristics

Relationships: Projected Days of Schooling in Selected States, 1916-17

STATE	Children of School Age	Attendance Total in Days	Average per Child
Maryland	74,447	4,239,102	57
North Carolina	253,276	13,733,524	50
Georgia	366,473	17,761,077	48
Virginia	217,760	9,226,107	47
Texas	275,346	12,844,930	47
Florida	109,030	4,320,053	43
Alabama	342,425	9,515,480	27
South Carolina	348,000	9,061,348	26
Louisiana	227,557	5,332,643	23

Source: "Days of Schooling per Year if Each Negro Child of School Age Got His Share," *Negro Year Book: An Annual Encyclopedia of the Negro, 1918-1919,* 1919, p. 233. Primary source: Work, Monroe N. (Ed.), *Negro Year Book: An Annual Encyclopedia of the Negro, 1914-15.* Tuskegee Institute, Ala.: The Negro Year Book Pub. Co., 1918.

★ 880 ★

School Characteristics

Relationships: Projected Time Needed to Complete Elementary School, based on Average Days of Attendance in Selected States, 1914-15

State	Days Schools Are Open	Average Days a Child Attends	Years it Would Take to Complete Elementary Course
Maryland	138	73	19.7
Virginia	120	73	19.7
Texas	124	72	20
Florida	97	70	20
Alabama	97	60	24
Georgia	107	59	24.4
North Carolina	97.8	57	25
Louisiana	90.6	55	26
South Carolina	67	46	31

Source: "How Long it Would Take a Negro Child to Complete an Elementary Course on Basis of a Nine Months School Year," *Negro Year Book: An Annual Encyclopedia of the Negro, 1914-15,* 1914, p. 219. Primary source: Work, Monroe N. (Ed.), *Negro Year Book: An Annual Encyclopedia of the Negro, 1914-15.* Tuskegee Institute, Ala.: The Negro Year Book Pub. Co., 1914.

★ 881 ★

School Characteristics

Relationships: Projected Time Needed to Complete Elementary School, based on Average Days of Attendance in Selected States, 1916-17

STATE	Days Schools Are Open	Average Days a Child Attends	Years It Would Take to Complete Elementary Course
Maryland	163	91	16
Texas	124	80	18
Virginia	121.2	76	18.9
Georgia	123	74	19
Florida	98	72	20
North Carolina	114.8	72	20
Alabama	104	66	22

[Continued]

★ 881 ★

Relationships: Projected Time Needed to Complete Elementary School, based on Average Days of Attendance in Selected States, 1916-17

[Continued]

STATE	Days Schools Are Open	Average Days a Child Attends	Years It Would Take to Complete Elementary Course
Louisiana	86	58	25
South Carolina	67	44	33

Source: "How Long it Would Take a Negro Child to Complete an Elementary Course on Basis of a Nine Months School Year," *Negro Year Book: An Annual Encyclopedia of the Negro, 1916-1917,* 1918, p. 233. Primary source: Work, Monroe N. (Ed.), *Negro Year Book: An Annual Encyclopedia of the Negro, 1916-1917.* Tuskegee Institute, Ala.: The Negro Year Book Pub. Co., 1918.

★ 882 ★

School Characteristics

Salaries (by Gender) and Qualifying Certificates of Black Public School Teachers by State, c. 1916-17

State	Salaries		Total teachers	Grade certificates				
	Male	Female		Life	First grade	Second grade	Third grade	Temporary, etc.
Alabama	$169[1]	$153[1]	2,550	109	23	565	1,841	-
Arkansas	-	-	1,948	-	-	-	-	-
District of Columbia	-	-	567	-	-	-	-	-
Delaware	-	-	85	-	-	-	-	-
Florida	38.91[2]	30.47[2]	1,059	15	82	446	476	40
Georgia								
Counties	28.60	23.00	4,266	-	53	2,582	1,345	-
Special systems	57.00	30.00						
Kentucky	-	-	1,366	-	-	-	-	-
Louisiana	36.17	30.26	1,291	-	421	228	642	-
Maryland	-	-	940	-	-	-	-	-
Mississippi								
Exclusive of separate district	20.52							
Separate districts	30.00		4,160	-	864	1,012	1,767	-
Missouri	-		792	-	-	-	-	-
North Carolina	26.75		3,173	-	888	1,706	56	-
Oklahoma	-	-	912	-	-	-	-	-
South Carolina	133	107	2,884	-	-	-	-	-
Tennessee	-	-	2,104	-	-	-	-	-
Texas	-	-	3,195	-	-	-	-	-
Virginia	36.77	30.21	2,448	469	774	498	194	492

[Continued]

★ 882 ★

Salaries (by Gender) and Qualifying Certificates of Black Public School Teachers by State, c. 1916-17

[Continued]

State	Salaries		Total teachers	Grade certificates				
	Male	Female		Life	First grade	Second grade	Third grade	Temporary, etc.
West Virginia	-	-	428	-	-	-	-	
Total			34,128					

Source: "Number Negro Public School Teachers," *Negro Year Book: An Annual Encyclopedia of the Negro, 1916-1917*, 1918, p. 237. Primary source: Not specifically identified. Published by permission. *Notes:* 1. Annual. 2. Monthly.

★ 883 ★

School Characteristics

Salaries and Expenditures in Public and Private Schools, c. 1916

	Teachers' salaries in public schools	Annual expenditures in private schools	Total of teachers' salaries and private expenditures
White	$36,649,827	$6,000,000[1]	$42,649,827
Negro	5,860,876	3,026,460	8,887,336

Source: [Untitled figures], *Negro Education: A Study of the Private and Higher Schools for Colored People in the United States*, vol. II. Bulletin, 1916, No. 39, p. 12. Primary source: U.S. Office of Education. *Negro Education: A Study of the Private and Higher Schools for Colored People in the United States*, vol. II. Bulletin, 1916, No. 39. Washington, D.C.: Government Printing Office, 1917. *Notes:* 1. Includes 146 schools in southern states reporting income to the Bureau of Education.

★ 884 ★

School Characteristics

Salaries of Black and White School Personnel in Public Schools of Various Levels in Selected States, 1935-36

State	Supervisors	Principals	Elementary teachers	Junior high school teachers	Junior-senior high schools teachers	Senior high school teachers	Regular and vocational high school teachers	Total for all Negro schools	Total for all white schools	Excess of salaries of white personnel over those of Negro personnel, in %
Continental United States	1,204	1,248	439	1,206	526	784	814	510	833	63
Alabama	1,252	1,249	301	-	390	-	-	328	709	116
Arkansas	-	990	285	445	435	877	846	316	550	74
Delaware	-	-	1,701	-	1,543	-	-	1,664	1,538	8[1]
District of Columbia	-	-	-	-	-	-	-	2,376	2,376	0

[Continued]

★ 884 ★

Salaries of Black and White School Personnel in Public Schools of Various Levels in Selected States, 1935-36
[Continued]

State	Supervisors	Principals	Elementary teachers	Junior high school teachers	Junior-senior high schools teachers	Senior high school teachers	Regular and vocational high school teachers	Total for all Negro schools	Total for all white schools	Excess of salaries of white personnel over those of Negro personnel, in %
Florida	1,451	1,100	463	-	554	-	-	493	1,030	109
Georgia	-	-	247	-	611	-	-	282	709	151
Kentucky	-	-	597	-	-	647	-	607	802	32
Louisiana	-	-	377	-	-	654	-	403	931	131
Maryland	2,525	-	1,076	1,876	-	2,032	981	1,187	1,515	28
Mississippi	-	-	-	-	-	-	-	247	783	217
Missouri	-	1,929	1,023	-	1,020	-	2,339	1,332	1,031	23[1]
North Carolina	-	1,087	511	-	-	-	654	543	811	49
Oklahoma	-	-	-	-	-	-	-	821	926	13
South Carolina	-	1,311	280	-	-	-	509	302	825	173
Tennessee	-	-	-	-	-	-	-	520	752	45
Texas	-	1,155	532	1,027	-	-	773	604	91	64
Virginia	727	1,727	479	-	-	-	418	520	901	73

Source: "Average Annual Salaries of Negro Instructional Personnel Compared with Salaries of White Instructional Personnel in the Public Schools of 17 States, 1935-36," Negro Year Book: An Annual Encyclopedia of the Negro, 1937-1938, 1937, p..112. Primary source: Work, Monroe N. (Ed.), Negro Year Book: An Annual Encyclopedia of the Negro, 1937-1938. Tuskegee Institute, Ala.: The Negro Year Book Pub. Co., 1937. Published by permission. Notes: 1. Minus. (This lower percentage is due to the fact that most of the colored teachers in the state were in urban schools, while a much greater number of whites than colored were in rural schools which pay lower salaries.).

★ 885 ★
School Characteristics

Salaries of Public School Teachers in Selected Southern States, c. 1916

	White teachers	Negro teachers	Annual salaries, white	Annual salaries, Negro	Average annual salary white	Average annual salary Negro
Alabama	7,098	2,344	$2,523,550	$372,177	$355.53	$158.78
Florida	3,353	992	1,022,745	167,381	305.02	168.70
Georgia	9,053	4,052	2,884,580	483,622	318.63	119.35
Kentucky	10,503	1,294	3,389,354	401,208	322.70	310.05
Louisiana	5,306	1,322	2,807,103	211,376	529.04	159.89
North Carolina	8,716	2,875	1,715,994	340,856	196.83	118.59
South Carolina	4,363	2,760	1,454,098	305,084	333.28	110.54
Virginia	8,576	2,441	2,767,365	421,381	322.69	172.63

Source: [Untitled Table], Negro Education: A Study of the Private and Higher Schools for Colored People in the United States, vol. I. Bulletin, 1916, No. 38, 1917, p. 34. Primary source: U.S. Office of Education. Negro Education: A Study of the Private and Higher Schools for Colored People in the United States, vol. I. Bulletin, 1916, No. 38. Washington, D.C.: Government Printing Office, 1917.

★ 886 ★

School Characteristics

Salary and Qualifying Certificate of Public School Teachers in Selected States, c. 1925-26

State	Salaries		Total teachers	Grade certificate			
	Male	Female		First grade, Life, etc.	Second grade	Third grade	Temporary etc.
Alabama	$248.00	$299.00	3,066	238	772	2,051	-
Arkansas	61.00	52.00	2,095	984	957	353	-
Delaware	-	-	125	-	-	-	-
District of Columbia	[2]	-	575	-	-	-	-
Florida	65.73	50.18	1,253	140	456	512	68
Georgia	49.34		5,155	257	3,039	1,720	-
Kentucky	[1]	-	1,375	-	-	-	-
Louisiana	512.00	422.00	2,260	871	571	713	105
Maryland	465.00		1,143	-	-	-	-
Mississippi	30.58		3,716	1,554	1,165	997	-
Missouri	-	-	939	-	-	-	-
North Carolina	412.78		4,595	443	1,546	1,699	907
Oklahoma	716.71		1,170	630	322	218	-
South Carolina	245.00	224.00	3,575	-	-	-	-
Tennessee	68.44	52.49	2,305	1,327	859	129	-
Texas	420.00	360.00	4,286	2,605	1,681	-	-
Virginia	288.36		3,584	1,176	1,511	778	119
West Virginia	-	-	801	678	61	11	51
Total			42,018				

Source: "Number Negro Public School Teachers," *Negro Year Book: An Annual Encyclopedia of the Negro, 1925-1926*, 1925, p. 295. Primary source: Not specifically identified. Published by permission. *Notes:* 1. Annual. 2. Monthly.

★ 887 ★

School Characteristics

Schools and Attendance at Black Schools with White Boards of Miscellaneous Religious Denominations, c. 1916

Name	Number of schools			Counted attendance			
	Total	Large or important	Small or less important	Total	Elementary	Secondary	College
Total	12	6	6	1,570	1,362	194	81
Christian Advent Church	1	-	1	60	60	-	-
Christian Alliance	1	1	-	71	62	9	-
Christian Conventions (miscellaneous)	3	1	2	194	194	-	-
Methodist Episcopal Church South	1	1	-	202	82	106	14
Presbyterian Church South	1	1	-	51	30	21	-
Reformed Episcopal Church	1	-	1	95	95	-	-

[Continued]

★ 887 ★

Schools and Attendance at Black Schools with White Boards of Miscellaneous Religious Denominations, c. 1916

[Continued]

Name	Number of schools			Counted attendance			
	Total	Large or important	Small or less important	Total	Elementary	Secondary	College
Reformed Presbyterian Church	1	1	-	705	677	28	-
Seventh Day Adventist Church	2	1	1	136	106	30	-
Universalist Church	1	-	1	56	56	-	-

Source: "Miscellaneous Denominational Schools—White Boards," *Negro Education: A Study of the Private and Higher Schools for Colored People in the United States,* vol. I. Bulletin, 1916, No. 38, p. 150. Primary source: U.S. Office of Education. *Negro Education: A Study of the Private and Higher Schools for Colored People in the United States,* vol. I. Bulletin, 1916, No. 38. Washington, D.C.: Government Printing Office, 1917.

★ 888 ★

School Characteristics

Schools, Attendance, Teachers, Income, and Property Value at Black Schools with Black Boards of Miscellaneous Religious denominations, c. 1916

Denominational boards	Number of schools			Counted attendance				Teachers			Income for current expenses	Value of property
	Total	Large or important	Small, less important	Total	Elementary	Secondary	College	Total	White	Negro		
Total	6	1	5	317	307	10	-	18	-	18	$5,650	$38,000
Free Will Baptist Church	1	1	-	60	58	2	-	4	-	4	1,700	15,000
Methodist Episcopal local conventions	2	-	2	22	22	-	-	4	-	4	450	6,000
Afro-American Presbyterian Church	1	-	1	25	25	-	-	2	-	2	1,500	7,000
Church of Christ Sanctified	1	-	1	130	122	8	-	6	-	6	1,500	10,000
Colored Local Seventh Day Adventist Church	1	-	1	80	80	-	-	2	-	2	500	-

Source: "Miscellaneous Denominational Schools—Negro Boards," *Negro Education: A Study of the Private and Higher Schools for Colored People in the United States,* vol. I. Bulletin, 1916, No. 38, 1917, p. 159. Primary source: U.S. Office of Education. *Negro Education: A Study of the Private and Higher Schools for Colored People in the United States,* vol. I. Bulletin, 1916, No. 38. Washington, D.C.: Government Printing Office, 1917.

★ 889 ★

School Characteristics

Segregation/Desegregation: Enrollment and Segregation/Desegregation Status of Southern Public Elementary and Secondary Schools, 1955-1970

[As of May, except as indicated. Covers Ala., Ark., Del., D.C., Fla., Ga., Ky., La., Md., Miss., Mo., N.C., Okla., S.C., Tenn., Tex., Va., and W. Va. Desegregation refers to change in schools from segregated white and Negro status to biracial or multiracial status, either in practive or principle].

ITEM	1955	1960	1965	1966	1968, fall[1]	1970, fall[1]
School districts, total	10,569	7,016	5,457	5,372	3,015[2]	3,255[2]
With both white and Negro students	4,244	2,851	3,031	2,999	2,726	(NA)
Desegregated	159	755	1,476	4,804	(NA)	(NA)
Enrollment:						
White 1,000	8,544	10,004	11,179	11,573	10,559	10,880
In desegregated districts 1,000	(NA)	2,538[4]	6,704[4]	(NA)	(NA)	(NA)
Negro 1,000	2,639	3,057	3,481	3,573	3,579	3,818
In desegregated districts 1,000	(NA)	520	1,939	(NA)	(NA)	(NA)
Negro students in schools with white students, total	(NA)	195	380	569	1,418	3,220
Percent of Negro enrollment	(NA)	6.4	10.9	15.9	39.6	84.3

Source: "Public Elementary and Secondary Schools—Segregation-Desegregation Status, 17 Southern States: 1955 to 1970," *Statistical Abstract of the United States, 1975*, p. 127. Primary source: Except as noted, Race Relations Information Center (formerly Southern Education Reporting Service), Nashville, Tennessee, *Statistical Summary.*. February 1967. (Copyright). *Notes:* NA Not available. 1. Source: U.S. Office for Civil Rights, press release of June 18, 1971, and *Directory of Public Elementary Schools in Selected Districts-Enrollment and Staff by Racial/Ethnic Group, Fall 1968 and Fall 1970.* Based on universe of school districts with total enrollment of 300 and larger. 2. Estimated. 3. Districts ruled "In compliance" with Federal regulations of U.S. Office of Education. 4. Excludes Missouri.

★ 890 ★

School Characteristics

Segregation/Desegregation: Grade 1 and Grade 12 Public School Enrollments, by School Racial Composition, Region, and Area Type, 1965

[As of fall. Estimates based on survey of public elementary and secondary schools]

GRADE, AREA, AND REGION	RACIAL COMPOSITION OF SCHOOLS							
	0 to 10 percent Negro		10 to 20 percent Negro		20 to 80 percent Negro		80 to 100 percent Negro	
	Negro	White	Negro	White	Negro	White	Negro	White
All regions, grade 1	3.8	79.9	2.4	9.6	21.8	9.8	72.0	0.7
Metropolitan:								
North and West	3.8	79.7	4.5	9.1	47.2	9.9	44.5	1.3
South and Southwest	2.2	89.7	0.5	0.9	2.0	9.2	95.3	0.2
Nonmetropolitan:								
North and West	19.6	80.1	7.0	11.3	45.0	8.5	28.4	0.1
South and Southwest	4.2	70.9	2.1	16.6	15.9	12.1	77.8	0.4
All regions, grade 12	10.0	79.9	5.1	9.6	23.2	10.3	61.7	0.2
Metropolitan:								
North and West	13.0	74.2	8.3	8.2	54.8	17.4	23.9	0.2
South and Southwest	2.9	92.3	1.2	5.9	1.2	1.6	94.7	0.2

[Continued]

★ 890 ★

Segregation/Desegregation: Grade 1 and Grade 12 Public School Enrollments, by School Racial Composition, Region, and Area Type, 1965
[Continued]

GRADE, AREA, AND REGION	RACIAL COMPOSITION OF SCHOOLS							
	0 to 10 percent Negro		10 to 20 percent Negro		20 to 80 percent Negro		80 to 100 percent Negro	
	Negro	White	Negro	White	Negro	White	Negro	White
Nonmetropolitan:								
North and West	51.7	88.6	16.8	7.3	23.7	4.1	7.8	[1]
South and Southwest	7.7	71.5	3.6	20.2	5.5	8.2	83.2	0.1

Source: "Percent of Negro and White Students Enrolled in Grades 1 and 12, by Area and by Racial Composition of Schools: 1965," *Statistical Abstract of the United States, 1967*, p. 125. Primary source: Dept. of Health, Education, and Welfare, Office of Education: *Equality of Educational Opportunity*, 1966. *Note:* 1. Less than 0.05 percent.

★ 891 ★

School Characteristics

Segregation/Desegregation: Southern Public Elementary and Secondary Enrollment in All Districts and in Desegregated Districts, 1957-1965
[As of May, except as indicated.]

DATE	SCHOOL DISTRICTS			ENROLLMENT (1,000)				NEGRO STUDENTS IN SCHOOLS WITH WHITE STUDENTS	
	Total	With both white and Negro students	Desegregated	Total		In desegregated districts		Number (1,000)	Percent of Negro enrollment
				White	Negro	White	Negro		
1957	9,697	3,695	683	9,124	2,798	1,848[1]	325	110[2]	(NA)
1958	8,514	2,903	758	9,428	2,924	1,953[1]	377	132[1]	(NA)
1959	7,874	2,875	740	9,651	3,008	2,262[1]	447	146[1]	(NA)
1960	7,106	2,851	755	10,004	3,057	2,538[1]	520	195	6.4
1961	6,663	2,839	783	10,184	3,097	3,064[1]	706	217	7.0
1962	6,370	3,047	913	10,406	3,250	3,584[1]	918	247	7.6
1963	6,198	3,054	980	10,656	3,328	4,717	1,097	265	8.0
1964	6,120	3,027	1,161	10,941	3,421	5,356[1]	1,484	316	9.2
1965	5,457	3,031	1,476	11,179	3,481	6,704[1]	1,939	380	10.9
1965, December	5,372	2,999	4,804[3]	11,573	3,573	(NA)	(NA)	568	15.9

Source: "Public Elementary and Secondary Schools—Segregation-Desegregation Status, 17 Southern States: 1965," *Statistical Abstract of the United States, 1975*, p. 123. Primary source: Southern Education Reporting Service, Nashville, Tennessee; *Statistical Summary*... December 1965. (Copyright). *Notes:* NA Not available. 1. Excludes Missouri. 2. Excludes Missouri and West Virginia. 3. Number of school districts ruled "In compliance" with Federal regulations of U.S. Office of Education. Not all desegregated districts for 1965-66 school year were "In compliance."

★ 892 ★

School Characteristics

Segregation/Desegregation: Southern Public Elementary and Secondary Enrollment in Desegregated Districts, by State, 1965

[As of December.]

STATE	SCHOOL DISTRICTS			ENROLLMENT			NEGRO STUDENTS IN SCHOOLS	
				Total (1,000)		Covered by compliance acceptances, white and Negro (1,000)[2]	WITH WHITE STUDENTS	
	Total	With both white and Negro students	In compliance[1]	White	Negro		Number (1,00)	Percent of Negro enrollment
Total	5,372	2,999	4,804	11,573	3,573	13,468	568	15.9
Alabama	118	118	105	559[3]	296[2]	656	1[4]	0.4
Arkansas	410	217	400	338[3]	112[3]	472	5[4]	4.4
Delaware	58	47	59[5]	86	20	103	17	83.3
District of Columbia	1	1	1	15	129	-	109	84.8
Florida	67	67	67	1,057[4]	256[4]	1,210	25[4]	9.8
Georgia	196	180	192	785[4]	356[4]	919	9[4]	2.7
Kentucky	200	167	204[5]	713[3]	60	684	47	78.4
Louisiana	67	67	33	484	319	552	2	0.7
Maryland	24	23	24	584	179	729	99	55.6
Mississippi	149	149	118	309	297	398	2	0.6
Missouri	1,096	212	675	843	105	890	79[4]	75.1
North Carolina	170	170	165	829	349[3]	1,102	18[4]	5.2
Oklahoma	1,046	323	1,044	564[4]	46[4]	688	18[4]	38.3
South Carolina	108	108	86	374	264	555	4	1.5
Tennessee	152	129	149	714[4]	177	781	29	16.3
Texas	1,325	850	1,303	2,136[4]	349[4]	2,469	60	17.2
Virginia	130	127	124	757[3]	240[3]	827	28	11.5
West Virginia	55	44	55	425[4]	20[4]	433	16[4]	79.9

Source: "Public Elementary and Secondary Schools—Segregation-Desegregation Status, 17 Southern States: 1965," *Statistical Abstract of the United States, 1975,* p. 123. Primary source: Southern Education Reporting Service, Nashville, Tennessee; *Statistical Summary...* December 1965. (Copyright). *Notes:* - Represents zero. 1. U.S. Office of Education approval of the desegregation proposal offered by a school districts. Some school district have desegregated but are not officially "In compliance." 2. U.S. Office of Education data. 3. 1964-65 data. 4. Estimated. 5. U.S. Office of Education reports more districts "In compliance" than the total districts listed by the State Department of Education.

★ 893 ★

School Characteristics

Staff Categories, Average Salary, and Number of High School Graduates in Black Public Elementary and Secondary Schools in the South, 1943-44 and 1945-46

Item	1943-44	1945-46
Instructional staff		
Total	66,553	67,436
Elementary schools		
Supervisors	264	285
Principals	516	1,099
Men teachers	4,489	3,547
Women teachers	49,954	48,150
High schools		
Supervisors	34	77
Principals	789	959
Men teachers	3,658	4,582
Women teachers	6,849	8,737
Average salary, per member of		
instructional staff (those reporting)	$895	$1,139
High school graduates		
Total	31,180	32,732
Boys	8,338	10,275
Girls	22,842	22,457

Source: "Statistical Summary of Negro Public Elementary and Secondary Schools in 17 Southern States and the District of Columbia, 1945-46," *The Negro Handbook, 1949*, 1949, p. 112. Primary source: U.S. Office of Education. Published by permission.

★ 894 ★

School Characteristics

Summary Characteristics: Attendance, Enrollment, Teachers, and Other Characteristics of Black Public Schools in Selected States, 1933-36

ITEM	1933-34	1935-36
Negro children 5-17 years of age, inclusive	2,904,100	2,946,200
Pupils enrolled in elementary grades	2,266,913	2,250,045
Pupils enrolled in high schools (4-year)	163,185	188,936
Total enrolled in elementary and high school	2,430,098	2,438,981
Average daily attendance	1,893,995	1,885,690
Aggregate days attended	269,792,587	274,630,591
Average number of days attended by each pupil during the year	111	113
Average length of school term in days	142	146
Percent of school population enrolled	83.7	82.8

[Continued]

★ 894 ★

Summary Characteristics: Attendance, Enrollment, Teachers, and Other Characteristics of Black Public Schools in Selected States, 1933-36

[Continued]

ITEM	1933-34	1935-36
Percent of enrolled pupils in daily attendance	77.9	77.3
Percent of pupils in high school	6.72	7.75
Teachers in elementary schools:		
Men	7,361	7,756
Women	42,633	44,070
Teachers in high schools:		
Men	3,169	3,692
Women	3,149	3,439

Source: "Summary of Public School Statistics on Negroes in 17 States and the District of Columbia: 1935-36," *Negro Year Book: An Annual Encyclopedia of the Negro, 1937-1938*, 1937, p. 111. Primary source: Work, Monroe N. (Ed.), *Negro Year Book: An Annual Encyclopedia of the Negro, 1937-1938*. Tuskegee Institute, Ala.: The Negro Year Book Pub. Co., 1937.

★ 895 ★

School Characteristics

Summary Characteristics: Characteristics of Black Schools for Special Students, by State, 1877

States	Schools for the deaf and dumb and the blind		
	Schools	Teachers	Pupils
Maryland	1	11	31
North Carolina	1	14	68
Total	2	25	99

Source: Robert, *Negro Civilization in the South*, "Summary of Statistics of Institutions for the Instruction of the Colored Race for 1877," 1880, p. 135. Primary source: Robert, Charles Edwin. *Negro Civilization in the South; Educational, Social, and Religious Advancement of the Colored People*. Nashville, Tenn.: Printed by Wheeler Bros. for the author, 1880.

★ 896 ★

School Characteristics

Summary Characteristics: Enrollment and Teachers at Black Schools, by Type of School and State, 1877

States	Public schools		Normal schools			Institution for secondary instruction		
	School population	Enrollment	Schools	Teachers	Pupils	Schools	Teachers	Pupils
Alabama	168,706	54,745	4	9	408	2	10	375
Arkansas	43,518	7,255	1	2	83	...	...	...
Delaware	3,800	1,663	...	...	...	...	...	...
Florida	42,001	16,185	...	...	...	1	3	62
Georgia	175,304	48,643	3	7	382	2	7	185
Kentucky	53,126	19,107	...	...	...	...	...	...
Louisiana	108,548	40,000	1	5	95	1	...	...
Maryland	63,591	24,539	2	7	211	1	...	95
Mississippi	174,485	76,154	1	8	106	...	...	...
Missouri	32,910	13,774	1	6	122	...	...	...
North Carolina	141,031	73,170	4	14	513	3	15	436
Ohio	...	...	...	...	...	1	...	23
South Carolina	144,315	55,952	2	9	655	6	15	1007
Tennessee	111,523	43,043	2	22	499	2	7	295
Texas	30,587	23,432	...	...	...	1	2	53
Virginia	202,640	65,043	3	25	610	2	7	236
West Virginia	5,970	2,827	...	...	...	...	...	...
District of Columbia	11,000	5,954	3	5	101	1	...	40
Total	1,513,065	571,506	27	119	3785	23	66	2807

Source: Robert, *Negro Civilization in the South,* "Summary of Statistics of Institutions for the Instruction of the Colored Race for 1877," 1880, p. 134. Primary source: Robert, Charles Edwin. *Negro Civilization in the South; Educational, Social, and Religious Advancement of the Colored People.* Nashville, Tenn.: Printed by Wheeler Bros. for the author, 1880.

★ 897 ★

School Characteristics

Summary Characteristics: Location, Denominational Affiliation, Instructors, and Students at Black Schools for Students with Handicaps, 1877

Name and class of institution	Location	Religious denomination	Instructors	Students
SCHOOLS FOR THE DEAF AND DUMB AND THE BLIND				
Institution for the Colored Blind and Deaf Mutes	Baltimore, Md.	...	11	31
North Carolina Institution for the Deaf and Dumb and Blind (colored department)	Raleigh, N.C.	...	14[1]	68
Total			25	99

Source: Robert, *Negro Civilization in the South,* "Schools for the Deaf and Dumb and the Blind," 1880, p. 133. Primary source: Robert, Charles Edwin. *Negro Civilization in the South; Educational, Social, and Religious Advancement of the Colored People.* Nashville, Tenn.: Printed by Wheeler Bros. for the author, 1880. *Note:* 1. For all departments.

★ 898 ★

School Characteristics

Summary Characteristics: Location, Denominational Affiliation, Instructors, and Students at Institutions Providing Secondary Instruction for Black Students, 1877

Name and class of institution	Location	Religious denomination	Instructors	Students
Trinity School	Athens, Ala.	Cong	...	139
Talladega College	Talladega, Ala.	Cong	10	236
Cookman Institute	Jacksonville, Fla.	Meth	3	62
Clark University	Atlanta, Ga.	M.E.	4	110
St. Augustine's School	Savannah, Ga.	P.E.	3	75
La Teche Seminary	Baldwin, La.	Meth	...	...
St. Francis Academy for Colored Girls	Baltimore, Md.	R.C.	...	95
Scotia Seminary	Concord, N.C.	Presb	8	128
St. Augustine's School	Newbern, N.C.	P.E.	2	224
Williston Academy and Normal School	Wilmington, N.C.	Cong	5	84
Albany Enterprise Academy	Albany, Ohio	Non-sect	...	23
High School for Colored Pupils	Charleston, S.C.	P.E.	4	224
Wallingford Academy	Charleston, S.C.	Presb	...	220
Brainerd Institute	Chester, S.C.	Presb	3	277
Benedict Institute	Columbia, S.C.	Baptist	4	117
Brewer Normal School	Greenwood, S.C.	Cong	...	49
Claflin University	Orangeburg, S.C.	M.E.	4	120
Canfield School	Memphis, Tenn.	P.E.	1	100
Nashville Institute	Nashville, Tenn.	Baptist	6	195
Wiley University	Marshall, Tex.	M.E.	2	53
St. Stephen's School	Petersburg, Va.	P.E.	5	150
St. Philip's School	Richmond, Va.	P.E.	2	86

[Continued]

★ 898 ★

Summary Characteristics: Location, Denominational Affiliation, Instructors, and Students at Institutions Providing Secondary Instruction for Black Students, 1877

[Continued]

Name and class of institution	Location	Religious denomination	Instructors	Students
St. Mary's School	Washington, D.C.	P.E.	...	40
Total			66	2807

Source: Robert, *Negro Civilization in the South*, "Institutions for Secondary Instruction," 1880, p. 132. Primary source: Robert, Charles Edwin. *Negro Civilization in the South; Educational, Social, and Religious Advancement of the Colored People*. Nashville, Tenn.: Printed by Wheeler Bros. for the author, 1880.

★ 899 ★

School Characteristics

Summary Characteristics: Schools and School Enrollment in Black Schools, by Type and Level, 1877

Class of institution	Schools	Enrollm'nt
Public schools	10,792[1]	571,506
Normal schools	27	3,785
Institutions for secondary instruction	23	2,807
Universities and colleges	13	1,270
Schools of theology	17	462
Schools of law	2	14
Schools of medicine	3	74
Schools for the deaf and dumb and the blind	2	99
Total	10,879	580,017

Source: Robert, *Negro Civilization in the South*, "Summary of Statistics of Institutions for the Instruction of the Colored Race for 1877," 1880, p. 135. Primary source: Robert, Charles Edwin. *Negro Civilization in the South; Educational, Social, and Religious Advancement of the Colored People*. Nashville, Tenn.: Printed by Wheeler Bros. for the author, 1880. *Notes:* 1. To these may be added 315 schools, having an enrollment of 16,548 in reporting free States, making total number of colored public schools 11,107 and total enrollment in them 588,054; it will be observed that this augments the total number of schools above given by 315, and the enrollment by 16,548, making the total number of schools, as far as reported to use, 11,194, and total number of the colored race under instruction in them, 596,565; this, however, does not include the colored public schools of those States in which no separate reports are made.

★ 900 ★

School Characteristics

Teacher Salaries, Pupils Aged 6 to 14, and Per Capita Pupil Expenditure in Black Private Northern and Southern Schools, c. 1916

State	Number of schools	Attendance	Teachers	Income	Value of property
United States	625	83,679	4,534	$3,026,460	$28,496,946
Alabama	72	12,819	694	554,556	5,457,375
Arkansas	26	3,103	141	62,337	376,222
Delaware	3	102	22	28,250	93,600
District of Columbia	3	581	22	11,813	42,500
Florida	26	3,345	148	77,001	478,411
Georgia	78	11,580	549	339,736	2,647,541
Kentucky	17	1,176	74	48,549	667,548
Louisiana	64	9,210	302	122,031	1,116,987
Maryland	10	1,033	39	23,454	99,624
Mississippi	46	7,044	321	177,425	1,282,902
Missouri	3	158	29	15,843	117,500
North Carolina	72	7,828	453	262,032	2,282,486
Oklahoma	4	289	14	4,026	9,300
South Carolina	60	8,616	413	214,379	2,126,434
Tennessee	31	4,043	311	220,034	1,630,308
Texas	29	3,757	237	131,508	1,194,160
Virginia	55	6,368	579	536,187	6,234,321
West Virginia	1	110	23	17,581	222,178
Northern states	25	2,517	163	178,818	2,417,549

Source: [Untitled Table], *Negro Education: A Study of the Private and Higher Schools for Colored People in the United States,* vol. I. Bulletin, 1916, No. 38, 1917, p. 14. Primary source: U.S. Office of Education. *Negro Education: A Study of the Private and Higher Schools for Colored People in the United States,* vol. I. Bulletin, 1916, No. 38. Washington, D.C.: Government Printing Office, 1917.

★ 901 ★

School Characteristics

Teacher Salaries, Pupils Aged 6 to 14, and Per Capita Pupil Expenditure in Black Public Northern and Southern Schools, c. 1910-1912

	Amount of teachers' salaries[1]	Number of children 6 to 14	Per capita for each child
Northern states			
All children			
California	$11,381,662	313,584	$36.30
New York	36,169,811	1,423,729	25.40

[Continued]

★ 901 ★

Teacher Salaries, Pupils Aged 6 to 14, and Per Capita Pupil Expenditure in Black Public Northern and Southern Schools, c. 1910-1912

[Continued]

	Amount of teachers' salaries[1]	Number of children 6 to 14	Per capita for each child
Massachusetts	12,991,737	519,454	25.01
New Jersey	9,266,170	420,635	22.03
Ohio	15,243,563	773,270	19.71
Wisconsin	7,001,946	443,787	15.78
Southern states			
All children			
Maryland	2,849,540	230,462	12.36
Kentucky	3,799,572	464,128	8.17
Virginia	3,188,746	440,804	7.23
Alabama	2,895,727	476,731	6.07
South Carolina	1,759,182	357,509	4.92
North Carolina	2,056,850	494,589	4.16
Southern states			
White children			
Maryland	2,567,021	188,147	13.79
Kentucky	3,389,354	417,081	8.13
Virginia	2,767,365	286,973	9.64
Alabama	2,523,550	268,283	9.41
South Carolina	1,454,098	145,384	10.00
North Carolina	1,715,994	325,555	5.27
Southern states			
Negro children			
Maryland	282,519	44,315	6.38
Kentucky	401,208	47,047	8.53
Virginia	421,381	153,827	2.74
Alabama	372,177	208,548	1.78
South Carolina	305,084	212,125	1.44
North Carolina	340,856	169,034	2.02

Source: [Untitled Table], *Negro Education: A Study of the Private and Higher Schools for Colored People in the United States*, vol. I. Bulletin, 1916, No. 38, 1917, p. 23. Primary source: U.S. Office of Education. *Negro Education: A study of the Private and Higher Schools for Colored People in the United States*, vol. I. Bulletin, 1916, No. 38. Washington, D.C.: Government Printing Office, 1917. *Notes:* 1. Figures for Northern States are for the year 1910-11; those for Southern States for 1911-12. Later figures are available for only certain states. For purposes of comparison it was desirable to have figures as close as possible to the census year.

★ 902 ★

School Characteristics

Teachers, Income, and Property Value at Black Schools with White Boards of Miscellaneous Denominations, c. 1916

Name	Teachers			Income for current expenses	Value of property
	Total	White	Negro		
Total	81	37	44	$58,717	$387,265
Christian Advent Church	3	-	3	1,500	2,500
Christian Alliance	9	9	-	1,476	33,000
Christian Conventions (miscellaneous)	12	-	12	4,187	75,000
Methodist Episcopal Church South	19	6	13	23,050	125,000
Presbyterian Church South	5	5	-	7,300	51,000
Reformed Episcopal Church	2	-	2	300	2,000
Reformed Presbyterian Church	17	7	10	7,300	52,500
Seventh Day Adventist Church	11	10	1	12,404	42,765
Universalist Church	3	-	3	1,200	3,500

Source: "Miscellaneous Denominational Schools—White Boards," *Negro Education: A Study of the Private and Higher Schools for Colored People in the United States*, vol. I. Bulletin, 1916, No. 38, 1917, p. 150. Primary source: U.S. Office of Education. *Negro Education: A Study of the Private and Higher Schools for Colored People in the United States*, vol. I. Bulletin, 1916, No. 38. Washington, D.C.: Government Printing Office, 1917.

★ 903 ★

School Characteristics

Teaching Personnel in Black Segregated Day Schools by State, 1948-49

State	Instructional staff						
	Total	Supervisors	Principals	Teachers			
				Total	Men	Women	Per cent men teachers
Alabama	7,175	44	95	7,036	873	6,163	12.4
Arkansas	2,663	1	89	2,573	399	2,174	15.5
Delaware	302	6	18	278	64	214	23.0
District of Columbia	1,531	21	62	1,448	300	1,148	20.7
Florida	4,095	21	128	3,946	501	3,445	12.7
Georgia	7,336	91	73	7,172	810	6,362	11.3
Kentucky	1,397	5	56	1,336	245	1,091	18.3
Louisiana	5,050	32	133	4,885	661	4,224	13.5
Maryland	2,293	-	87	2,206	404	1,802	18.3
Mississippi	6,496	23	69	6,404	841	5,563	13.1
Missouri	1,741	-	116	1,625	303	1,322	18.6
North Carolina	7,590	10	306	7,274	1,136	6,138	15.6
Oklahoma	1,635	9	219	1,407	255	1,152	18.1
South Carolina	6,738	34	60	6,644	924	5,720	13.9
Tennessee	33,311	-	-	3,311	614	2,697	18.5

[Continued]

★ 903 ★

Teaching Personnel in Black Segregated Day Schools by State, 1948-49
[Continued]

State	Instructional staff						
	Total	Supervisors	Principals	Teachers			
				Total	Men	Women	Per cent men teachers
Texas	7,616	27	189	7,400	1,339	6,061	18.1
Virginia	4,866	83	618	4,165	490	3,675	11.8
West Virginia	968	2	162	804	180[1]	624[1]	22.4

Source: "Instructional Staff and Percentage of Men Teachers in Negro Full-Time Day Schools in 17 States and District of Columbia which have Segregated Schools, 1948-49," *1952 Negro Year Book: A Review of Events Affecting Negro Life*, 1952, p. 205. Primary source: U.S. Office of Education, *Statistical Circular No. 286*, January 1951. Published by permission. *Note:* 1. Estimated.

★ 904 ★
School Characteristics

Teaching Staff, Average Salary, and Pupil-Teacher Ratio in Black Public Elementary and Secondary Schools in the South, 1946

State or District of Columbia	Number of Negro instructional staff		Average salary per member of instructional staff		Pupil-teacher ratio in elementary and secondary schools	
	Elementary	Secondary	White	Negro	White	Negro
Total	53,000	14,436	$1,640	$1,139	28	35
Alabama	4,616	1,605	1,163	711	31	37
Arkansas	2,106	549	1,862	1,278	31	30
Delaware	175	84	2,244	1,976	25	29
Florida	2,450	1,069	1,862	1,278	26	30
Georgia	6,009	1,341	1,279	651	28	36
Kentucky	926	432	1,289	1,367	31	28
Louisiana	3,811	678	1,797	948	29	38
Maryland	1,313	575	2,297	2,127	32	35
Mississippi	5,513	732	1,165	427	30	42
Missouri	1,199	438	2,703	1,853	27	31
North Carolina	6,195	1,241	1,608	1,587	32	35
Oklahoma	1,099	429	1,807	1,688	30	27
South Carolina	5,288	932	1,365	864	27	33
Tennessee	2,487	652	1,330	1,044	30	33
Texas	5,004	1,701	1,695	1,315	28	31
Virginia	3,458	1,037	1,605	1,475	31	39
West Virginia	608	371	1,571	1,789	27	25
District of Columbia	743	570	2,637	2,637	27	33

Source: "Number of Instructional Staff, Salaries, and Pupil-Teacher Ratio in 17 States and the District of Columbia, 1946," *The Negro Handbook, 1949*, 1949, p. 114. Primary source: U.S. Office of Education. Published by permission.

★ 905 ★

School Characteristics

Total and Per Pupil Expenditures in Public Schools by Race and State in Relation to Population, c. 1916-17

States	Total expenditures		Average expenditure per child of school age		Per cent expenditures		Per cent each race of total population	
	For Whites	For Negroes	For Whites	For Negroes	For Whites	For Negroes	For Whites	For Negroes
Alabama	$3,898,129	$507,725	$9.0	$1.47	88	12	57.5	42.5
Arkansas	3,770,936	700,000	8.15	3.74	84	16	71.8	28.1
District of Columbia	1,660,347	645,792	33.00	32.00	73	27	71.3	28.5
Delaware	552,027	52,763	11.53	5.23	91	9	84.6	15.4
Florida	2,511,242	258,093	15.10	2.37	90.7	9.3	58.9	41.0
Georgia	4,332,717	768,173	10.09	2.08	85	15	54.9	45.1
Kentucky	6,160,454	609,000	10.30	8.91	91	9	88.6	11.4
Louisiana	5,103,998	413,514	16.44	1.81	92.6	7.4	56.8	43.1
Maryland	4,997,941	524,667	14.63	7.04	90.5	9.5	82.0	17.9
Mississippi	2,236,571	569,990	8.20	1.53	80	20	43.7	56.2
Missouri	13,121,031	450,000	14.80	12.13	96.7	3.3	95.2	4.8
North Carolina	3,875,312	674,842	7.38	2.66	85	15	68.0	31.6
Oklahoma	7,328,313	551,593	14.33	11.16	93	7	87.2	8.3
South Carolina	2,619,138	378,670	10.70	1.09	87	13	44.8	55.2
Tennessee	5,294,653	770,000	8.70	4.58	88	12	78.3	21.7
Texas	11,656,305	1,897,537	10.89	7.50	86	14	82.2	17.7
Virginia	4,471,555	698,000	11.47	3.20	87	13	67.4	32.6
West Virginia	4,169,522	200,000	10.94	10.38	95	5	94.7	5.3
Total	$87,760,491	$10,665,359						

Source: "Annual Expenditures for Public Schools by States," *Negro Year Book: An Annual Encyclopedia of the Negro, 1916-1917*, 1918, p. 236. Primary source: U.S. Bureau of the Census. Published by permission.

★ 906 ★

School Characteristics

Type of School and Family Income Group of Grade 1-8 Pupils (in percentages), 1968 and 1970

	1968				1970			
	Negro		White		Negro		White	
	Public	Parochial and other private	Public	Parochial and other private	Public	Parochial and other private	Public	Parochial and other private
Total (thousands)	4,569	147	24,628	4,053	4,670	195	24,950	3,728
Percent								
Total	97	3	86	14	96	4	87	13
Under $3,000	100	-	92	8	98	2	95	5
$3,000 to $4,999	98	2	92	8	99	1	94	6
$5,000 to $7,499	96	4	88	12	94	6	90	10
$7,500 to $9,999	95	5	85	15	94	6	87	13

[Continued]

★ 906 ★

Type of School and Family Income Group of Grade 1-8 Pupils (in percentages), 1968 and 1970

[Continued]

	1968				1970			
	Negro		White		Negro		White	
	Public	Parochial and other private	Public	Parochial and other private	Public	Parochial and other private	Public	Parochial and other private
$10,000 to $14,999	88	12	83	17	93	7	85	15
15,000 and over	86	14	79	21	84	16	80	20

Source: Adapted by the editors from "Percent of Pupils Enrolled in Grades 1 to 8, in Public, Parochial and Other Private Schools, by Family Income, 1968," Current Population Reports, Special Studies, Series P-23, No. 29. *The Social and Economic Status of the Black Population in the United States, 1969*, 1969, p. 49; and "Pupils 3 to 17 Years Old Enrolled in Grades 1 to 8, in Public, Parochial, and Other Private Schools, by Family Income: 1970," Current Population Reports, Special Studies, Series P-23, No. 38. *The Social and Economic Status of the Black Population in the United States, 1970*, 1970, p. 75. Primary source: U.S. Department of Commerce, Bureau of the Census. *Note:* - Represents or rounds to zero.

Support for Schools

★ 907 ★

Contributions of Black Individuals and Groups to Freedmen's Aid, 1862-1870

Channel	Year	Amount
African Methodist Episcopal Church Society	1862-1868	$166,660
Presbyterian Church	1865-66	3,174
	1866-1870	20,848
Baltimore Association, etc.	1865-66	6,000
	1866-67	23,371
Louisville Negroes	1865	4,000
South Carolina Negroes	1866-67	17,000
Eastern Sanitary Commission Negroes	1866	3,200
African Civilization Society	1868	53,737
New England Society	1868-1872	798
Miscellaneous	1866-1868	180,207
Total	-	$478,995

Source: "Negro Contributions to Freedmen's Aid, 1862-1870," *Negro Education: A Study of the Private and Higher Schools for Colored People in the United States*, vol. I. Bulletin, 1916, No. 38, 1917, p. 297. Primary source: U.S. Office of Education. *Negro Education: A Study of the Private and Higher Schools for Colored People in the United States*, vol. I, Bulletin, 1916, No. 38. Washington, D.C.: Government Printing Office, 1917.

★ 908 ★

Support for Schools

Contributions of the John F. Slater Fund to Black Schools, 1882-83 through 1914-15

Time	Number of schools	Amount
1882-83	12	$16,250
1883-84	18	17,106
1884-85	29	36,764
1889-90	37	42,910
1894-95	16	42,400
1900-1901	11	43,330
1904-5	27	53,550
1909-10	40	69,750
1914-15	68	69,250

Source: [Untitled Table], *Negro Education: A Study of the Private and Higher Schools for Colored People in the United States,* vol. I. Bulletin, 1916, No. 38, 1917, p. 164. Primary source: U.S. Office of Education. *Negro Education: A Study of the Private and Higher Schools for Colored People in the United States,* vol. I. Bulletin, 1916, No. 38. Washington, D.C.: Government Printing Office, 1917.

★ 909 ★

Support for Schools

Expenditures and Other Characteristics of Support for Black Schools with Religious Boards of Control, c. 1937

	Annual expenditures	Permanent funds for Negro education	Value of school plants, etc.
American Baptist Home Mission Board	$110,225.65	$1,632,394.32	$1,872,000.00
American Church Institute for Negroes (Episcopal)	251,000.00	429,000.00	2,224,000.00
American Missionary Association	475,000.00	9,850,000.00[1]	3,000,000.00
Church of Christ (Disciples) United Christian Missionary Society	52,357.65	10,000.00	480,000.00
Lutheran Evangelical Synodical Conference of North America, Board of Colored Missions	30,590.16	0	152,713.39
Methodist Episcopal Church, Board of Education, Institutions for Negroes	754,458.58	2,191,961.00	4,090,670.24
Methodist Episcopal Church, Woman's Home Missionary Society of	142,952.39	225,416.79	1,731,100.00
Presbyterian Church in the U.S.A., Division of Missions for Colored People	191,028.78	1,367,381.02	2,959,234.80

[Continued]

★ 909 ★

Expenditures and Other Characteristics of Support for Black Schools with Religious Boards of Control, c. 1937

[Continued]

	Annual expenditures	Permanent funds for Negro education	Value of school plants, etc.
United Presbyterian Church, Board of Missions for Freedmen	30,485.07	645,000.00	1,000,000.00

Source: "Annual Expenditures, etc., for Negro Education by Certain Religious Boards," *Negro Year Book: An Annual Encyclopedia of the Negro, 1937-1938,* 1937, p. 175. Primary source: Work, Monroe N. (Ed.), *Negro Year Book: An Annual Encyclopedia of the Negro, 1937-1938.* Tuskegee Institute, Ala.: The Negro Year Book Pub. Co., 1937. Published by permission. *Notes:* 1. $1,500,000 of this amount is the Daniel Hand Fund, which the American Missionary Association administers.

★ 910 ★

Support for Schools

Federal/State Programs: Expenditures for Public Schools in Selected States, c. 1925-26

State	Total expenditures		Average expenditure per child of school age		Per cent expenditures		Per cent each race of total population	
	For Whites	For Negroes	For Whites	For Negroes	For Whites	For Negroes	For Whites	For Negroes
Alabama	$12,900,274	$1,184,367	$26.57	$3.81	91	9	61.6	38.4
Arkansas	6,386,233	1,216,401	13.36	6.48	83	17	73.0	27.0
Delaware	3,125,872	500,000	60.00	52.90	86	14	86.6	13.4
District of Columbia	5,611,012	1,853,678	76.00	64.40	74	26	74.7	25.2
Florida	8,989,825	773,074	42.01	7.33	92	8	65.9	34.0
Georgia	13,547,310	2,175,338	25.84	5.78	86	14	58.3	41.7
Kentucky	12,521,958	1,093,175	16.60	15.40	92	8	90.2	9.2
Louisiana	11,329,241	1,256,869	33.73	5.48	90	10	61.0	38.9
Maryland	12,560,002	1,345,770	34.70	17.17	90	10	83.1	16.9
Mississippi	8,411,484	2,102,871	25.95	5.62	80	20	47.7	52.2
Missouri	39,220,839	1,279,100	45.32	29.59	97	3	94.7	5.2
North Carolina	15,362,387	2,125,376	25.31	7.52	88	12	69.7	29.8
Oklahoma	21,406,075	1,064,205	33.08	21.04	95	55	89.8	7.4
South Carolina	8,502,401	1,015,567	27.88	2.74	89	11	48.6	51.4
Tennessee	13,825,142	1,874,396	21.02	11.88	88	12	80.7	19.3
Texas	33,933,647	4,627,321	31.77	20.24	88	12	84.0	15.9
Virginia	18,534,620	2,312,365	40.27	10.47	89	11	70.1	29.9
West Virginia	15,935,890	777,171	36.36	32.15	95	5	94.1	5.9
Total	$262,104,212	$28,577,044						

Source: "Annual Expenditures for Public Schools by State," *Negro Year Book: An Annual Encyclopedia of the Negro, 1925-1926,* 1925, p. 295. Primary source: Work, Monroe N. (Ed.), *Negro Year Book: An Annual Encyclopedia of the Negro, 1925-1926.* Tuskegee Institute, Ala.: The Negro Year Book Pub. Co., 1925. Published by permission.

★ 911 ★

Support for Schools

Federal/State Programs: Funds for and Estimated Black Participation in School Lunch Program in Selected States, 1951-52

State	Apportionment	Estimated Negro participation
Alabama	$2,476,367	26,700
Arkansas	1,535,127	12,500
Florida	1,197,452	14,000
Georgia	2,297,469	20,600
Kentucky	2,083,856	5,300
Louisiana	1,619,286	100,000
Mississippi	2,185,658	35,000
Missouri	1,402,200	21,000
North Carolina	2,883,099	24,000
Oklahoma	1,260,228	8,000
South Carolina	1,826,302	32,000
Tennessee	2,223,479	35,000
Texas	3,397,057	29,000
Virginia	1,714,715	29,000
Total	$28,102,295[1]	392,100[2]

Source: "Apportionment of Funds in South for National School Lunch Program by States and Estimated Participation of Negro Children, 1951-52," *Negro Year Book: A Review of Events Affecting Negro Life,* 1952, p. 208. Primary source: U.S. Department of Agriculture, Release No. 2376-51, p. 1, June 1951. Published by permission. *Notes:* 1. For all school children in the states listed. 2. School year, 1949-50.

★ 912 ★

Support for Schools

Federal/State Programs: Special State Aid to State Normal and Other Schools, c. 1918-19

Name of institution	Location	No. of instructors	No. of students	Income From state	Other sources	Total
Montgomery State Normal School	Montgomery, Ala.	26	650	$16,000	-	$19,000
Myrtilla Miner Normal School	Washington, D.C.	16	278	-	-	-
Georgia Normal and Agricultural College	Albany, Ga.	12	276	-	-	2,642
Western University	Kansas City, Kans	23	298	28,766	-	32,750
Topeka Indus. & Educational Institute	Topeka, Kansas	13	135	12,000	-	15,830
Louisville Colored Normal School	Louisville, Ky.	18	32	-	-	2,100
Baltimore Colored Normal School	Baltimore, Md.	8	112	-	-	-
Maryland Nor. & Industrial Institute	Bowic, Md.	8	50	7,167	-	8,053
New Jersey Manual Training School for Colored Youth	Bordentown, N.J.	14	200	27,755	-	37,538
Elizabeth City State Normal School	Elizabeth City, N.C.	11	464	5,360	-	6,866
Fayetteville State Normal School	Fayetteville, N.C.	11	368	4,969	-	5,280
Slater Normal School	Winston-Salem, N.C.	20	502	4,900	-	5,864

[Continued]

★ 912 ★

Federal/State Programs: Special State Aid to State Normal and Other Schools, c. 1918-19
[Continued]

Name of institution	Location	No. of instructors	No. of students	Income		
				From state	Other sources	Total
Combined Normal and Industrial Department of Wilberforce Univ	Wilberforce, Ohio	-	-	77,000	-	77,000
Virginia Normal and Industrial Inst	Petersburgh, Va.	36	91	25,000	-	32,176
Bluefield Colored Institute	Bluefield, W. Va.	10	250	13,000	-	17,000

Source: "State Normal Schools and Schools Receiving Special State Aid," *Negro Year Book: An Annual Encyclopedia of the Negro, 1918-1919*, 1919, [no p. no.]. Primary source: Work, Monroe N. (Ed.), *Negro Year Book: An Annual Encyclopedia of the Negro, 1918-1919*. Tuskegee Institute, Ala.: The Negro Year Book Pub. Co., 1919. Published by permission.

★ 913 ★
Support for Schools

Freedmen's Aid Society: Educational Activities of Freedmen and the Freedmen's Bureau, 1866-1870

"In five years the [Freedmen's] bureau established 4,239 schools; employed 9,307 teachers, and instructed 247,333 pupils and expended for education $3,521,936; the benevolent associations cooperating with the bureau expended $1,572,287. In addition, the freedmen during the five years of the bureau's life, raised and expended for their education $785,700. Higher education for the Negro was begun under the auspices of the bureau."

Source: Text from "Education During the Civil War and Reconstruction Period," *Negro Year Book: An Annual Encyclopedia of the Negro, 1937-1938*, 1937, p. 161. Primary source: Work, Monroe N. (Ed.), *Negro Year Book: An Annual Encyclopedia of the Negro, 1937-1938*. Tuskegee Institute, AL: The Negro Year Book Pub. Co., 1937. Published by permission.

★ 914 ★
Support for Schools

Funds Appropriated by the General Education Board for Black Colleges and Schools, c. 1937

	Amount appropriated	Total
Colleges and schools		
Teachers' salary endowment and grants	$3,415,301.38	
General endowment, buildings and other purposes	23,005,753.52	
		$26,421,054.90
Natural sciences	49,650.00	
Social sciences	45,000.00	

[Continued]

★ 914 ★

Funds Appropriated by the General Education Board for Black Colleges and Schools, c. 1937

[Continued]

	Amount appropriated	Total
Medical sciences		
		$94,650.00
Schools of medicine	4,883,202.89	
Special projects	20,520.87	
Public education		
Summer schools	447,446.34	
Anna T. Jeanes Foundation	1,247,610.00	
County training schools	832,588.76	
John F. Slater Fund	692,224.89	
Rural school agents	2,003,302.44	
Fellowships	707,266.66	
Special divisions in State Departments of Education	12,750.00	
Teacher training	186,093.40	
Other purposes	103,084.68	
		$6,232,367.17
Miscellaneous	51,789.22	
Total for Negroes	$37,703,585.05	

Source: "Total Amounts Distributed by and through the John F. Slater Fund, 1882- 1935," *Negro Year Book: An Annual Encyclopedia of the Negro, 1937-1938,* 1937, p. 179. Primary source: Reports of the General Education Board. Published by permission.

★ 915 ★

Support for Schools

Funds Disbursed for Black Public and Private Schools, by State, 1882-1935

	Religious and private institutions	Public schools[1]	Totals
Alabama	$555,270	$220,961	$776,231
Arkansas	26,059	105,872	131,931
Florida	34,865	53,041	87,906
Georgia	363,124	158,921	522,045
Kentucky	6,350	79,354	85,704
Louisiana	110,740	108,436	219,176
Maryland	1,251	3,900	5,151
Mississippi	179,773	156,887	336,660
Missouri	-	3,600	3,600
North Carolina	212,419	199,060	411,479
Oklahoma	-	25,325	25,325
South Carolina	232,395	176,811	409,206
Tennessee	204,755	108,128	312,883

[Continued]

★ 915 ★

Funds Disbursed for Black Public and Private Schools, by State, 1882-1935
[Continued]

	Religious and private institutions	Public schools[1]	Totals
Texas	130,973	94,430	225,403
Virginia	423,157	211,627	634,784
West Virginia	-	500	500
Pennsylvania	500	1,080	1,580
Washington, D.C.	10,260	-	10,260
	$2,491,891	$1,707,933	$4,199,824

Source: "Total Amounts Distributed by and through the John F. Slater Fund, 1882- 1935," *Negro Year Book: An Annual Encyclopedia of the Negro, 1937-1938*, 1937, p. 179. Primary source: Work, Monroe N. (Ed.), *Negro Year Book: An Annual Encyclopedia of the Negro, 1937-1938*. Tuskegee Institute, Ala.: The Negro Year Book Pub. Co., 1937. Published by permission. *Note:* 1. Mainly to County Training Schools, first established in 1911-12.

★ 916 ★

Support for Schools

Funds Spent by the Julius Rosenwald Fund for Black Industrial High Schools, c. 1937

Industrial high schools	
Columbus, Georgia	$21,266
Greenville, South Carolina	9,936
Little Rock, Arkansas	65,000
Maysville, Kentucky	25,000
Winston-Salem, North Carolina	50,000
Architectural and other consultant fees	31,506

Source: "Details of Expenditures for Negro State Colleges, Summer Institutes, and High Schools," *Negro Year Book: An Annual Encyclopedia of the Negro, 1937-1938*, 1937, p. 187. Primary source: Reports of the Julius Rosenwald Fund. Published by permission.

★917★

Support for Schools

Funds Spent by the Julius Rosenwald Fund for Black Public School Buildings, c. 1937

State	No. of bldg.	Pupil capacity	Total cost
Alabama	407	40,410	$1,285,060
Arkansas	389	46,980	1,952,441
Florida	125	22,545	1,432,706
Georgia	261	37,305	1,878,859
Kentucky	158	18,090	1,081,710
Louisiana	435	51,255	1,721,506
Maryland	153	15,435	899,658
Mississippi	633	77,850	2,851,421
Missouri	4	1,260	257,959
North Carolina	813	114,210	5,167,042
Oklahoma	198	19,575	1,127,449
South Carolina	500	74,070	2,892,360
Tennessee	373	44,460	1,969,822
Texas	527	57,330	2,496,521
Virginia	381	42,840	1,894,006
Totals	5,357	663,615	$28,408,520

Source: "Negro Public School Buildings Aided by the Fund," *Negro Year Book: An Annual Encyclopedia of the Negro, 1937-1938*, 1937, p. 185. Primary source: Reports of the Julius Rosenwald Fund. Published by permission.

★918★

Support for Schools

Funds Spent by the Julius Rosenwald Fund for Black School Building Program, c. 1937

Construction: Schoolhouses, teachers' homes, and shops	$4,174,120
Special school projects	24,170
Building plans and specifications	9,722
Interstate service for schoolhouse planning	14,750
State building agents	42,100
Shop equipment and supervisors of shop work	43,997
Initiating bus transportation to consolidated schools	142,141
Extension of school terms	88,671
Rosenwald day programs	11,130
Studies of schools and new developments	50,707
Fellowships for southern school officials	16,009
Development of curriculum materials on the Negro	5,000
Libraries for elementary and high schools	94,621
Rehabilitation of rural schools	6,919

[Continued]

★ 918 ★

Funds Spent by the Julius Rosenwald Fund for Black School Building Program, c. 1937
[Continued]

Administration of the school program: (salaries of S.L. Smith and staff, and maintenance of Nashville office, 1920-1936)	441,224

Source: "Details of Expenditures, Negro School Building Program," *Negro Year Book: An Annual Encyclopedia of the Negro, 1937-1938,* 1937, p. 185. Primary source: Reports of the Julius Rosenwald Fund. Published by permission.

★ 919 ★
Support for Schools

Property Investments in Public Schools in Selected States, c. 1914

State	For Whites	For Negroes	Average value per child of school age	
			Whites	Negroes
District of Columbia	6,310,389	2,103,463	113.39	90.00
Missouri	41,611,128	1,500,000	45.16	39.17
Maryland	11,020,620	1,080,000	34.96	14.74
Louisiana	9,261,023	437,020	30.44	1.97
Delaware	1,449,905	126,000	30.29	12.50
Oklahoma	14,809,912	1,026,357	29.64	21.70
Florida	3,512,145	448,224	25.53	4.67
W. Virginia	9,020,504	365,000	23.84	19.76
Georgia	11,254,604	1,089,990	23.13	2.50
Texas	25,192,466	1,700,000	22.68	6.72
South Carolina	5,222,083	716,570	22.42	2.16
Arkansas	9,031,828	1,100,000	21.11	6.02
Virginia	8,081,975	1,200,000	20.30	5.51
Tennessee	10,992,663	1,200,000	18.72	7.06
Alabama	6,584,452	608,334	16.50	1.85
Kentucky	10,279,046	1,016,608	15.86	11.85
North Carolina	6,530,592	850,024	12.67	3.43
Mississippi	2,160,000	350,000	7.92	.93
Total	192,325,335	16,917,590		

Source: "Investment in Public School Property for Whites and Negroes," *Negro Year Book: An Annual Encyclopedia of the Negro, 1914-1915,* 1914, p. 221. Primary source: Work, Monroe N. (Ed.), *Negro Year Book: An Annual Encyclopedia of the Negro, 1914-1915.* Tuskegee Institute, Ala.: The Negro Year Book Pub. Co., 1914. Published by permission.

★ 920 ★

Support for Schools

Property Investments in Public Schools in Selected States, c. 1916-17

State	For Whites	For Negroes	Average value per child of school age	
			Whites	Negroes
District of Columbia	$9,067,137	$2,706,036	$181.32	$135.30
Florida	4,438,093	370,299	91.70	8.30
Missouri	40,664,776	1,900,000	52.63	50.00
Louisiana	12,718,766	579,414	49.54	2.54
Oklahoma	19,827,182	1,200,000	38.80	26.21
West Virginia	12,162,442	506,000	31.95	26.27
Maryland	9,935,862	972,000	29.09	13.05
Georgia	11,667,470	1,869,077	27.19	3.73
Virginia	10,722,376	1,745,503	26.90	8.00
South Carolina	5,692,753	833,153	23.30	2.39
Texas	25,192,466	1,700,000	22.68	6.72
Arkansas	10,350,315	1,600,000	22.37	8.55
Kentucky	13,631,495	913,397	22.19	13.36
Alabama	8,650,527	813,772	20.00	2.36
Tennessee	12,092,210	1,350,000	19.85	8.63
North Carolina	8,056,966	1,021,736	15.34	4.03
Mississippi	2,560,000	500,000	8.00	1.20
Total	$218,880,741	$20,206,387		

Source: "Investment in Public School Property for Whites and Negroes," *Negro Year Book: An Annual Encyclopedia of the Negro, 1916-1917*, 1918, [no p. no.]. Primary source: Work, Monroe N. (Ed.), *Negro Year Book: An Annual Encyclopedia of the Negro, 1916-1917*. Tuskegee Institute, Ala.: The Negro Year Book Pub. Co., 1918. Published by permission.

★ 921 ★

Support for Schools

Slater Fund: Awards for Blacks for Fellowships and Professorships in Theology, 1930-31

Award	Number	Total Amount	Average Amount
Fellowships	9	$11,500	$1,278
Professorships	2	5,000	2,500
Total	11	$16,500	$1,500

Source: Compiled and adapted by the editors from The John F. Slater Fund, *Proceedings and Reports*, "Special Fund for Theology Fellowships and Professorships," 1931, p. 16. Primary source: The John F. Slater Fund. *Proceedings and Reports*. For the Year Ending September 30th, 1931.

★ 922 ★

Support for Schools

Slater Fund: Contributions to Black Institutions from Emergency Fund, 1930-31

State	No. Institutions	Total Amount	Average Amount
Alabama	2	$3,875	$1,938
Arkansas	2	2,234	1,117
Florida	2	2,500	1,250
Georgia	1	1,000	1,000
Mississippi	1	984	984
North Carolina	2	3,237	1,618
Tennessee	2	3,000	1,500
Texas	2	2,500	1,250
Virginia	1	670	670
Total	15	$20,000	$1,333

Source: Compiled by the editors from the John F. Slater Fund, *Proceedings and Reports*, "Distribution of Emergency Fund," 1931, p. 15. Primary source: The John F. Slater Fund. *Proceedings and Reports.* For the Year Ending September 30th, 1931.

★ 923 ★

Support for Schools

Slater Fund: Contributions to Faculty Salaries in Black Schools, by State and Level of Institution, 1930-31

State	No. Institutions	Total Amount	Average Amount
Colleges			
Alabama	3	$6,950	$2,317
Arkansas	1	1,575	1,575
Florida	1	1,350	1,350
Georgia	5	8,325	1,865
Louisiana	3	3,825	1,275
Mississippi	4	6,652	1,663
North Carolina	5	8,415	1,683
South Carolina	3	5,400	1,800
Tennessee	1	1,350	1,350
Texas	4	6,525	1,631
Virginia	2	2,475	1,238
Total	32	$52,842	$1,651
Junior Colleges & Secondary Schools			
Alabama	2	$965	$482
District of Columbia	1	540	540

[Continued]

★ 923 ★

Slater Fund: Contributions to Faculty Salaries in Black Schools, by State and Level of Institution, 1930-31

[Continued]

State	No. Institutions	Total Amount	Average Amount
Florida	1	540	540
Georgia	2	1,080	540
North Carolina	2	1,080	540
South Carolina	3	1,620	540
Tennessee	1	540	540
Texas	1	900	900
Total	13	$7,265	$559
Grand Total	45	$60,107	$1,336

Source: Compiled by the editors from the John F. Slater Fund, *Proceedings and Reports*, "Contributions to Salaries in Colleges," 1931, pp. 10-12. Primary source: The John F. Slater Fund. *Proceedings and Reports.* For the Year Ending September 30th, 1931.

★ 924 ★

Support for Schools

Slater Fund: Contributions to Schools, by Control of Institution and State, 1882-1931

State	Religious and Private Institutions	Public Schools[1]	Totals
Alabama	$534,655[2]	$193,463	$728,118
Arkansas	21,334	83,429	104,763
Florida	19,225	42,020	61,245
Georgia	327,254	125,141	452,395
Kentucky	6,350	69,769	76,119
Louisiana	102,640	90,470	193,110
Maryland	576	3,400	3,976
Missouri	-	500	500
Mississippi	159,418	126,777	286,195
North Carolina	179,617	175,655	355,272
Oklahoma	-	20,925	20,925
South Carolina	204,175	142,981	347,156
Tennessee	193,110	90,945	284,055
Texas	94,980	79,370	174,350
Virginia	416,533[2]	175,782	592,315
W. Virginia	-	500	500

[Continued]

★ 924 ★

Slater Fund: Contributions to Schools, by Control of Institution and State, 1882-1931
[Continued]

State	Religious and Private Institutions	Public Schools[1]	Totals
Pennsylvania	-	1,080[3]	1,080
Washington, D.C.	8,640	-	8,640
	$2,268,507	$1,422,207	$3,690,714

Source: The John F. Slater Fund, *Proceedings and Reports*, "Total Amounts Distributed by and Through the John F. Slater Fund. 1882-1931," 1931, p. 9. Primary source: The John F. Slater Fund. *Proceedings and Reports*. For the Year Ending September 30th, 1931. *Notes:* 1. Mainly to County Training Schools, first established in 1911-12. 2. Enchanced by early donations to Hampton and Tuskegee. 3. Part of Blanchard donation for city school-and-home visitors.

★ 925 ★

Support for Schools

Slater Fund: Regular and Special Appropriations to Black Schools and Programs, 1901-02 through 1911-12

Year	REGULAR AWARDS		SPECIAL AWARDS		TOTAL AWARDS	
	No. Schools	Amount	No. Schools	Amount	No. Schools	Amount
1901-02	12	$52,800	5	$600	17	$53,400
1902-03	12	53,800	-	-	12	53,800
1903-04	12	54,800[1]	-	-	12	54,800
1904-05	13	49,500[2]	14	4,550	27	54,050
1905-06	[3]	[3]	[3]	[3]	[3]	[3]
1906-07	18	58,100	4	1,140	22	59,240
1907-08	18	57,000	21	7,590	39	64,590
1908-09	22	61,500	16	5,190	38	66,690
1909-10	34	66,950	6	2,800	40	69,750
1910-11	45	68,400	1	300	46	68,700
1911-12	51	69,750	-	-	51	69,750

Source: Compiled and adapted by the editors from The John F. Slater Fund. *Proceedings of the Trustees of the John F. Slater Fund for the Education of Freedmen,* "Appropriations, 1901-02," p. 44; "Appropriations, 1902-03," p. 14; "Appropriations, 1903-4," p. 9; "Appropriations, 1904-5," pp. 8- 9; "Appropriations, 1906-07," p. 5; "Appropriations, 1907-08," p. 9; "Appropriations, 1908-09," pp. 4-5; "Appropriations, 1909-10," pp. 4-5; "Appropriations, 1910-11," pp. 9-10; and "Appropriations, 1911-12," pp. 6-7; 1902-1911. Primary source: The John F. Slater Fund. *Proceedings of the Trustees of the John F. Slater Fund for the Education of Freedman. November 6, 1901; April 16, 1902; October 23, 1902.* Baltimore: 1902; New York: 1903, 1904, 1905, 1906, 1907, 1908, 1909; [City not designated in source]: 1909-1910, 1910-1911. *Notes:* 1. Includes $1,000 in funds to be matched by schools. 2. Includes $500 in funds to be matched by a school. 3. Information for this year not included in source.

★ 926 ★

Support for Schools

Southern Education Foundation – Jeanes Teachers Needed in Southern States, 1940-41

"[In 1940-41, the Southern Education Fund existed] mainly to support the Jeanes Teachers—teachers in rural areas whose salaries are supplied in whole or in part by the foundation. For that purpose a total of $57,000 was expended by the foundation during the school year 1940-41.

There are 1,415 counties in the Southern States. Of this number 611 had each fewer than ten Negro teachers and a considerable number had no Negro teachers at all. South Carolina was the only Southern State having no county without any Negro teachers at all. There were, therefore, 804 counties that because of the size of their Negro educational problem needed the services of a Jeanes teacher."

Source: "Southern Education Foundation," *Negro Year Book: A Review of Events Affecting Negro Life, 1941-1946,* 1947, p. 125. Primary source: Guzman, Jessie Parkhurst (Ed.), *Negro Year Book: A Review of Events Affecting Negro Life, 1941-1946.* Tuskegee Institute, AL: Department of Records and Research, 1947. Published by permission.

★ 927 ★

Support for Schools

Southern Education Foundation: Jeanes Teachers – Supplied and Unmet Needs by State, 1940-41

	Counties with Jeanes Teachers 1936-1937	Counties needing Jeanes Teachers 1936-1937
Alabama	37	22
Arkansas	19	25
Florida	26	26
Georgia	37	97
Kentucky	10	16
Louisiana	27	32
Mississippi	50	29
Missouri	4	3
North Carolina	57	25
Oklahoma	16	14
South Carolina	37	9
Tennessee	34	6
Texas	30	36
Virginia	68	12
	452	352

Source: [Untitled Table], *Negro Year Book: A Review of Events Affecting Negro Life, 1941-1946,* 1947, p. 125. Primary source: Guzman, Jessie Parkhurst (Ed.), *Negro Year Book: A Review of Events Affecting Negro Life, 1941-1946.* Tuskegee Institute, AL: Department of Records and Research, 1947. Published by permission.

★ 928 ★
Support for Schools

Teachers, Schools, and Scholars Supported by the New England Freedmen's Aid Society, 1865-1874

Date	South Carolina	North Carolina	District of Columbia	Virginia	Maryland	Georgia	Florida	Men	Women	Total teachers	Total schools	Total scholars
July, 1865	44	13	7	22	2	1	-	18	71	89	-	-
April, 1866	56	26	10	36	29	-	-	-	-	182	79	9,649
April, 1867	44	9	5	26	28	6	-	-	-	118	73	8,647
April, 1868	34	13	-	24	19	8	1	-	-	99	-	5,144
April, 1870	38	11	-	40	18	4	1	-	-	112	70	5,017
April, 1871	25	3	-	22	16	5	-	-	-	71	43	3,221
April, 1872	21	2	-	5	2	4	-	-	-	34	11	1,280
April, 1873	17	-	-	4	-	4	-	-	-	25	7	949
April, 1874	-	-	-	-	-	-	-	-	-	10	6	1,000

Source: "Distribution of Teachers of the New England Freedmen's Aid Society," *Negro Education: A Study of the Private and Higher Schools for Colored People in the United States*, vol. I. Bulletin, 1916, No. 38, 1917, p. 298. Primary source: Taken from the "Freedmen's Record," 1865-1874.

Vocational Education

★ 929 ★

Characteristics of Students, Teachers, and Costs in Federally-Aided Vocational Programs, 1950-1968

In thousands, except as indicated. For years ending June 30. Includes Puerto Rico for all years; Virgin Islands, beginning 1955; and Guam, beginning 1960.

Item	1950	1955	1960	1965	1966	1967	1968
Students, total	3,365	3,314	3,768	5,431	6,070	7,048	7,534
Adult	(NA)	(NA)	(NA)	2,379	2,531	2,941	2,987
Secondary	(NA)	(NA)	(NA)	2,819	3,048	3,533	3,843
Other	(NA)	(NA)	(NA)	233	491	574	704
Type of program							
Home economics	1,430	1,432	1,588	2,099	1,897	2,187	2,283
Office occupations	-	-	-	731	1,238	1,572	1,736
Trades and industry	805	871	938	1,088	1,269	1,491	1,629
Agriculture	765	776	796	888	907	935	851
other	365	235	445	626	758	862	1,035
Teachers	(NA)	(NA)	(NA)	123	145	154	160
Full-time	(NA)	(NA)	(NA)	54	64	72	80
Part-time	(NA)	(NA)	(NA)	70	81	81	90
Expenditures, total...mil. dol	129	165	239	605	800	1,004	1,192

[Continued]

★ 929 ★

Characteristics of Students, Teachers, and Costs in Federally-Aided Vocational Programs, 1950-1968
[Continued]

Item	1950	1955	1960	1965	1966	1967	1968
Federal.....mil. dol	27	30	45	157	234	260	263
Percent of total	20.7	18.4	19.0	26.0	29.2	25.9	22.0
Type of program							
Home economics....mil. dol	37	49	69	98	113	125	161
Office occupations....mil. dol	-	-	-	54	92	133	176
Trades and industry....mil. dol	48	56	73	145	186	236	268
Agriculture....mil. dol	39	54	67	87	89	103	110
Other....mil. dol	5	6	30	221	320	407	478

Source: "Vocational Programs, Federally Aided—Students Enrolled, Teachers, and Expenditures: 1950 to 1968," *Statistical Abstract of the United States,* 1970, p. 134. Primary source: Dept. of Health, Education, and Welfare, Office of Education; annual report, *Vocational and Technical Education. Note:* - Represents zero. NA Not available.

★ 930 ★

Vocational Education

Educational Programs Aimed toward the Labor Force, 1968 and 1969

For years ending June 30. Covers work and training programs administered by the U.S. Department of Labor.

Year and program	Total enrollees (1,000)	Male	Negro and other races[1]	Age in years			Education, by grade		
				Under 22	22-44	45 and over	Less than 9th	9th-11th	12th and over
1968									
Manpower Development and Training Program									
Institutional	140	55	49	39	50	11	19	40	41
On-the-job	101	68	36	36	53	11	16	34	50
Neighborhood Youth Corps									
In school[2]	118	52	43	100	-	-	15	84	7
Out of school[3]	94	49	50	99	1	-	28	65	1
Summer[4]	255	55	55	100	-	-	15	84	7
Operation Mainstream	13	84	40	4	52	44	57	26	11
New Careers	4	37	75	1	85	14	15	47	38
Concentrated Employment Program	53	48	85	36	55	9	23	55	22
1969									
Manpower Development and Training Program									
Institutional	135	56	44	38	52	10	19	39	42
On-the-job	85	65	39	36	54	10	17	35	48
Neighborhood Youth Corps									
In school[2]	84	52	46	100	-	-	18	81	1
Out of school[3]	75	46	52	97	3	-	27	69	4
Summer[4]	345	54	56	100	-	-	20	79	1
Operation Mainstream	11	82	32	2	40	58	60	24	16
New Careers	4	30	67	8	79	13	10	40	50
Concentrated Employment Program	127	58	72	37	52	11	26	44	30
JOBS Program[5]	51	71	87	48	48	4	14	53	32
Work Incentive Program	81	40	44	16	74	10	31	41	28

Source: "Work and Training Programs—Selected Characteristics of Enrollees: 1968 and 1969," *Statistical Abstract of the United States,* 1970, p. 134. Primary source: Dept. of Labor, Manpower Administration: *Manpower Report of the President and a Report on Manpower Requirements, Resources, Utilization, and Training,* 1970. *Notes:* - Represents zero. 1. Excludes whites. 2. Individuals enrolled September-May. 3. Individuals enrolled September-August. 4. Individuals enrolled June-August. 5. Job opportunities in the business sector.

★ 931 ★

Vocational Education

Federal and State Funds for Teachers and Administrators in Agricultural Educational Programs, c. 1937-38

	Total for all purposes	Agriculture: for salaries of teachers, supervisors and directors		
		Total amount	Federal funds	State funds
Alabama	$320,000	$210,000	$105,000	$105,000
Arkansas	228,000	162,000	81,000	81,000
Florida	168,000	78,000	39,000	39,000
Georgia	346,000	222,000	111,000	111,000
Kentucky	318,000	204,000	102,000	102,000
Louisiana	250,000	144,000	72,000	72,000
Maryland	182,000	72,000	36,000	36,000
Mississippi	248,000	186,000	93,000	93,000
Missouri	418,000	198,000	99,000	99,000
North Carolina	386,000	264,000	132,000	132,000
Oklahoma	284,000	174,000	87,000	87,000
South Carolina	208,000	150,000	75,000	75,000
Tennessee	312,000	192,000	96,000	96,000
Texas	688,000	384,000	192,000	192,000
Virginia	284,000	180,000	90,000	90,000
West Virginia	208,000	138,000	69,000	69,000
Grand total	4,848,000	2,958,000		

Source: "Allotment of Federal and State Vocational Educational Funds Each Year to Southern States," *Negro Year Book: An Annual Encyclopedia of the Negro, 1937-1938,* 1937, p. 46. Primary source: Not specifically identified. Published by permission.

★ 932 ★

Vocational Education

Federal and State Funds for Teachers and Maintenance of Teacher Training Programs, c. 1937-38

	Total for all purposes	Teacher-Tr.: Salaries of teachers maintenance of teacher training		
		Total amount	Federal funds	State funds
Alabama	$32,000	$44,000	$22,000	$22,000
Arkansas	228,000	30,000	15,000	15,000
Florida	168,000	24,000	12,000	12,000
Georgia	346,000	46,000	23,000	23,000
Kentucky	318,000	42,000	21,000	21,000
Louisiana	250,000	34,000	17,000	17,000

[Continued]

★ 932 ★

Federal and State Funds for Teachers and Maintenance of Teacher Training Programs, c. 1937-38
[Continued]

	Total for all purposes	Teacher-Tr.: Salaries of teachers maintenance of teacher training		
		Total amount	Federal funds	State funds
Maryland	182,000	26,000	13,000	13,000
Mississippi	248,000	32,000	16,000	16,000
Missouri	418,000	58,000	29,000	29,000
North Carolina	386,000	50,000	25,000	25,000
Oklahoma	284,000	38,000	19,000	19,000
South Carolina	208,000	28,000	14,000	14,000
Tennessee	312,000	42,000	21,000	21,000
Texas	688,000	94,000	47,000	47,000
Virginia	284,000	38,000	19,000	19,000
West Virginia	208,000	28,000	14,000	14,000
Grand total	4,848,000	654,000		

Source: "Allotment of Federal and State Vocational Educational Funds Each Year to Southern States," *Negro Year Book: An Annual Encyclopedia of the Negro, 1937-1938,* 1937, p. 46. Primary source: Not specifically identified. Published by permission.

★ 933 ★

Vocational Education

Federal and State Funds for Trade, Industrial, and Home Economics Teachers, c. 1937-38

	Total for all purposes	Trade, industry and home econ. salaries and teachers		
		Total amount	Federal funds	State funds
Alabama	$320,000	$66,000	$33,000	$33,000
Arkansas	228,000	36,000	18,000	18,000
Florida	168,000	66,000	33,000	33,000
Georgia	346,000	78,000	39,000	39,000
Kentucky	318,000	72,000	36,000	36,000
Louisiana	250,000	72,000	36,000	36,000
Maryland	182,000	84,000	42,000	42,000
Mississippi	248,000	30,000	15,000	15,000
Missouri	418,000	162,000	81,000	81,000
North Carolina	386,000	72,000	36,000	36,000
Oklahoma	284,000	72,000	36,000	36,000
South Carolina	208,000	30,000	15,000	15,000
Tennessee	312,000	78,000	39,000	39,000
Texas	688,000	210,000	105,000	105,000
Virginia	284,000	66,000	33,000	33,000

[Continued]

★ 933 ★

Federal and State Funds for Trade, Industrial, and Home Economics Teachers, c. 1937-38
[Continued]

	Total for all purposes	Trade, industry and home econ. salaries and teachers		
		Total amount	Federal funds	State funds
West Virginia	208,000	42,000	21,000	21,000
Grand total	4,848,000	1,236,000		

Source: "Allotment of Federal and State Vocational Educational Funds Each Year to Southern States," *Negro Year Book: An Annual Encyclopedia of the Negro, 1937-1938,* 1937, p. 46. Primary source: Not specifically identified. Published by permission.

★ 934 ★

Vocational Education

Industrial Education: Enrollment in Schools for Black Students that have Industrial Facilities, 1916

Industrial school groups	Number of schools	Pupils					
		Total	Above elementary grade	Industrial pupils			
				Total	Boys' industries	Girls' industries	Not classified
Total	61	17,146	5,524	6,295	2,326	3,776	193
State and Federal schools with industrial facilities	29	7,988	3,614	3,508	1,208	2,300	...
Land-grant schools	16	5,175	2,298	2,394	935	1,459	...
State schools	13	2,813	1,316	1,114	273	841	...
Private schools with industrial facilities	32	9,158	2,110	2,787	1,118	1,476	193
Large institutions-Hampton and Tuskegee Institutes	2	2,100	716	1,336	613	723	...
Smaller industrial schools offering industrial course for boys and girls	30	7,058	1,394	1,451	505	753	193

Source: "Schools with Industrial Facilities," *Negro Education: A Study of the Private and Higher Schools for Colored People in the United States,* vol. I. Bulletin, 1916, No. 38, 1917, p. 85. Primary source: U.S. Office of Education. *Negro Education: A Study of the Private and Higher Schools for Colored People in the United States,* vol. I Bulletin, 1916, No. 38. Washington, D.C.: Government Printing Office, 1917.

★ 935 ★

Vocational Education

Industrial Education: Resources in Schools for Blacks that had Industrial Facilities, 1916

Industrial school groups	Total annual income	Financial		
		Value of industrial plant		
		Total	Buildings	Equipment
Total	$1,914,587	$1,311,406	$881,390	$429,916
State and Federal schools with industrial facilities	828,073	658,963	494,450	164,513
Land-grant schools	543,623	360,494	238,500	121,994
State schools	284,450	298,469	255,950	42,519
Private schools with industrial facilities	1,086,514	652,443	386,940	265,403
Large institutions-Hampton and Tuskegee Institutes	557,444	384,553	234,140	150,413
Smaller industrial schools offering industrial course for boys and girls	529,070	267,890	152,800	114,990

Source: "Schools with Industrial Facilities," *Negro Education: A Study of the Private and Higher Schools for Colored People in the United States*, vol. I. Bulletin, 1916, No. 38, 1917, p. 86. Primary source: U.S. Office of Education. *Negro Education: A Study of the Private and Higher Schools for Colored People in the United States*, vol. I Bulletin, 1916, No. 38. Washington, D.C.: Government Printing Office, 1917.

★ 936 ★

Vocational Education

Industrial Education: Teachers in Schools for Blacks with Industrial Facilities, 1916

Industrial school groups	Teachers				
	Total	Industrial teachers			
		Total	Boys' industries	Girls' industries	Not classified
Total	1,588	424	261	154	9
State and Federal schools with industrial facilities	619	179	112	66	1
Land-grant schools	400	126	87	38	1
State schools	219	53	25	28	...
Private schools with industrial facilities	969	245	149	88	8
Large institutions-Hampton and Tuskegee Institutes	394	90	65	25	...
Smaller industrial schools offering industrial course for boys and girls	575	155	84	63	8

Source: "Schools with Industrial Facilities," *Negro Education: A Study of the Private and Higher Schools for Colored People in the United States*, vol. I. Bulletin, 1916, No. 38, 1917, p. 86. Primary source: U.S. Office of Education. *Negro Education: A Study of the Private and Higher Schools for Colored People in the United States*, vol. I Bulletin, 1916, No. 38. Washington, D.C.: Government Printing Office, 1917.

Manual Training/Household Arts: Schools for Blacks that Offered Manual Training and Household Arts Courses, 1916

School group and kind of work	Number of schools	Pupils		Teachers	
		Total	Above Elementary grade	Total	Industrial teachers
Total	174	34,143	8,548	1,960	311
Literary institutions offering manual training					
for boys and girls	73	18,155	5,678	1,075	173
Work fairly well done	39	11,978	4,443	728	118
Work poorly done	34	6,177	1,235	347	55
Literary institutions offering households					
arts courses only	101	15,988	2,870	885	138
Work fairly well done	45	9,254	1,836	507	90
Work poorly done	56	6,734	1,034	378	48

Source: "Schools with Manual Training and Household Arts Courses," *Negro Education: A Study of the Private and Higher Schools for Colored People in the United States,* vol. I. Bulletin, 1916, No. 38, 1917, p. 87. Primary source: U.S. Office of Education. *Negro Education: A Study of the Private and Higher Schools for Colored People in the United States,* vol. I Bulletin, 1916, No. 38. Washington, D.C.: Government Printing Office, 1917.

Chapter 5
THE FAMILY

Characteristics

★ 938 ★

Age and Number of Own Children of Families with Female Heads, 1970 and 1974

Selected characteristics	Black 1970	Black 1974	White 1970	White 1974
AGE OF FEMALE HEAD				
Total female heads (thousands)	1,349	1,849	4,185	4,853
Percent	100	100	100	100
Under 35 years	35	40	21	27
35 to 64 years	53	48	56	54
65 years and over	11	12	23	19
PRESENCE OF OWN CHILDREN UNDER 18 YEARS				
Total female heads (thousands)	1,349	1,849	4,185	4,853
Percent	100	100	100	100
With own children	67	70	48	56
With no own children	34	30	52	44
With own children (thousands)	898	1,289	2,007	2,732
Percent with 2 or more children	71	69	61	56
NUMBER OF OWN CHILDREN UNDER 18 YEARS				
Total children under 18 years in				
families headed by women	2,645	3,168	4,184	5,343
Percent of all children in families	29	39	7	10

Source: "Selected Characteristics of Families Headed by Women: 1970 and 1974," Current Population Reports, Special Studies, Series P-23, No. 54. *The Social and Economic Status of the Black Population in the United States, 1974*, 1975, p. 109. Primary source: U.S. Department of Commerce, Social and Economic Statistics Administration, Bureau of the Census.

★ 939 ★

Characteristics

Employment: Families with Homemakers, Employed and Unemployed, 1930

Employment status of homemaker	Negro		Native white		Foreign-born white	
	Number	Percent distribution	Number	Percent distribution	Number	Percent distribution
Families having homemaker	2,601,254	100.0	20,052,369	100.0	5,404,476	100.0
Not gainfully employed	1,624,814	62.5	17,698,711	88.3	4,852,931	89.8
Gainfully employed	976,440	37.5	2,354,158	11.7	551,545	10.2
Gainfully employed homemakers	976,440	100.0	2,354,158	100.0	551,545	100.0
Employed at home	331,225	33.9	357,413	15.2	59,289	10.7
Agricultural occupations	190,268	19.5	180,285	7.7	21,643	3.9
Other occupations at home	140,957	14.4	177,128	7.5	37,646	6.8
Employed away from home	642,369	65.8	1,992,100	84.6	491,501	89.1
Professional workers	23,117	2.4	328,346	13.9	35,189	6.4
Office workers	4,157	.4	443,088	18.8	53,053	9.6
Industrial workers	72,538	7.4	470,287	20.2	187,022	33.9
Servants, waitresses, etc.	464,608	47.6	352,449	15.0	130,318	23.6
Saleswomen	3,531	.4	224,326	9.5	42,387	7.7
Other occupations away from home	74,418	7.6	173,604	7.4	43,532	7.9
Employed, place not specified	2,846	.3	4,645	.2	755	.1

Source: "Families with Homemakers, by Color, and Nativity of Head, and Employment Status of Homemaker, for the United States: 1930," *Negroes in the United States, 1920-1932*, 1935, p. 255. Primary source: U.S. Bureau of the Census. *Negroes in the United States, 1920-1932.* Washington, D.C.: U.S. Government Printing Office, 1935.

★ 940 ★

Characteristics

Employment: Working Members in Black Farm and Nonfarm Families by Region, 1930

	United States	The North	The South	The West
All families having specified number of gainful workers				
Total	2,803,756	576,328	2,193,357	34,071
None	86,227	23,128	60,961	2,138
1	1,532,551	329,916	1,181,401	21,234
2	758,898	159,061	591,573	8,264
3	250,634	43,826	205,018	1,790
4 or more	175,446	20,397	154,404	645
Farm families having specified number of gainful workers				
Total	978,653	14,744	962,401	1,508
None	8,454	261	8,159	34

[Continued]

★ 940 ★

Employment: Working Members in Black Farm and Nonfarm Families by Region, 1930

[Continued]

	United States	The North	The South	The West
1	529,888	10,205	518,535	1,148
2	235,833	2,902	232,699	232
3	102,619	935	101,616	68
4 or more	101,859	441	101,392	26
Nonfarm families having specified number of gainful workers				
Total	1,825,103	561,584	1,230,956	32,563
None	77,773	22,867	52,802	2,104
1	1,002,663	319,711	662,866	20,086
2	523,065	156,159	358,874	8,032
3	148,015	42,891	103,402	1,722
4 or more	73,587	19,956	53,012	619

Source: "Negro Families Classified According to the Number of Gainful Workers, by Sections, Divisions, and States: 1930," *Negroes in the United States, 1920-1932,* 1935, p. 272. Primary source: U.S. Bureau of the Census. *Negroes in the United States, 1920-1932.* Washington, D.C.: U.S. Government Printing Office, 1935.

★ 941 ★

Characteristics

Family Earners, 1967 and 1970 to 1974

Families as of the following year.

Number of earners and race of head	1967	1970	1971	1972	1973	1974
BLACK						
Number of families (thousands)	4,589	4,928	5,157	5,265	5,440	5,498
Percent	100	100	100	100	100	100
No earners	10	12	14	15	15	17
1 earner	32	34	34	35	35	35
2 earners or more	58	55	51	50	50	48
2 earners	42	40	37	38	36	36
3 earners	11	9	10	8	9	8
4 earners or more	5	5	4	4	4	4
Average number of earners per family	1.76	1.67	1.58	1.53	1.55	1.52
WHITE						
Number of families (thousands)	44,814	46,535	47,641	48,477	48,919	49,451
Percent	100	100	100	100	100	100
No earners	8	9	9	9	10	11
1 earner	40	37	38	38	36	35

[Continued]

★ 941 ★

Family Earners, 1967 and 1970 to 1974
[Continued]

Number of earners and race of head	1967	1970	1971	1972	1973	1974
2 earners or more	52	54	53	53	54	54
2 earners	38	39	39	39	40	40
3 earners	10	10	10	10	10	10
4 earners or more	4	4	4	4	5	5
Average number of earners per family	1.67	1.68	1.67	1.67	1.68	1.68

Source: "Distribution of Families by Number of Earners: 1967 and 1970 to 1974," Current Population Reports, Special Studies, Series P-23, No. 54. *The Social and Economic Status of the Black Population in the United States, 1974,* 1975, p. 34. Primary source: U.S. Department of Commerce, Social and Economic Statistics Administration, Bureau of the Census.

★ 942 ★

Characteristics

Family Type: Age Group of Head in Families Headed by Males, 1930

Age of man head	Negro families		Native-white families		Foreign-born white families	
	Number	Percent distribution	Number	Percent distribution	Number	Percent distribution
All families having man head	2,262,443	100.0	18,474,735	100.0	5,019,418	100.0
Under 25 years	201,896	8.9	986,844	5.3	49,178	1.0
25 to 34 years	563,314	24.9	4,535,328	24.5	678,714	13.5
35 to 44 years	584,294	25.8	4,927,974	26.7	1,470,252	29.3
45 to 54 years	501,944	22.2	3,829,210	20.7	1,340,291	26.7
55 to 64 years	262,624	11.6	2,518,550	13.6	865,038	17.2
65 to 74 years	107,925	4.8	1,283,987	6.9	475,291	9.5
75 years and over	36,996	1.6	380,490	2.1	138,607	2.8
Unknown	3,450	.2	12,352	.1	2,047	[1]

Source: "Families Having Man Head, Classified by Age, Color, and Nativity of Head, for the United States: 1930," *Negroes in the United States, 1920-1932,* 1935, p. 254. Primary source: U.S. Bureau of the Census. *Negroes in the United States, 1920-1932.* Washington, D.C.: U.S. Government Printing Office, 1935. *Note:* 1. Less than 1/10 of 1 percent.

★ 943 ★

Characteristics

Family Type: Change in Family Heads, 1960 to 1970

Numbers in thousands.

Type of family	1960	1970	Change, 1960 to 1970	
			Number	Percent
Total families	3,863	4,774	911	23.6
Husband-wife	2,885	3,249	364	12.6
Other male head	135	176	41	30.4
Female head	843	1,349	506	60.0

Source: "Number of Negro Families, by Type and Change: 1960 to 1970," Current Population Reports, Special Studies, Series P-23, No. 38. *The Social and Economic Status of the Black Population in the United States, 1970,* 1970, p. 108. Primary source: U.S. Department of Commerce, Bureau of the Census.

★ 944 ★

Characteristics

Family Type: Characteristics of Female-Headed Families, 1950-1975

Selected characteristic	Black				White			
	1950[1]	1960	1970	1975	1950	1960	1970	1975
AGE								
Total, female head, no husband present (thousands)	605	843	1,349	1,940	2,966	3,297	4,185	5,212
Percent	100	100	100	100	100	100	100	100
14 to 34 years	26	29	35	42	12	15	21	29
35 to 64 years	59	58	53	48	61	59	56	54
65 years and over	15	13	11	10	27	26	23	17
PRESENCE OF OWN CHILDREN UNDER 18 YEARS								
Total, female head, no husband present (thousands)	605	890	1,349	1,940	2,966	3,306	4,185	5,212
Percent	100	100	100	100	100	100	100	100
With own children	47	56	67	71	33	42	48	57
With 2 or more own children	59	70	71	67	50	54	61	55
WIth no own children	53	44	34	29	67	58	52	43
MARITAL STATUS								
Total, female head, no husband present (thousands)	612	843	1,349	1,940	2,960	3,297	4,185	5,212
Percent	100	100	100	100	100	100	100	100
With disrupted marriage	35	40	48	50	21	28	37	48
Separated	27	29	34	31	8	10	11	15
Divorced	8	11	14	19	13	18	25	33
Other	65	60	52	50	79	72	63	52
Single (never married)	9	12	16	22	12	11	9	9

[Continued]

★ 944 ★

Family Type: Characteristics of Female-Headed Families, 1950-1975
[Continued]

Selected characteristic	Black				White			
	1950[1]	1960	1970	1975	1950	1960	1970	1975
Widowed	51	42	30	25	61	53	47	39
Husband temporarily absent	5	6	6	3	5	8	7	4

Source: "Selected Characteristics of Families Maintained by Women: 1950, 1960, 1970, and 1975," *The Social and Economic Status of the Black Population in the United States: An Historical View, 1790-1978,* 1979, p. 106. Primary source: U.S. Department of Commerce. Bureau of the Census. *Notes:* Totals for female family heads do not agree in some cases because data are from different tabulations. 1. Data include families of "other" races.

★ 945 ★

Characteristics

Family Type: Distribution of Families, by Type, 1940-1975

Year and race	All families (thousands)	Percent of all families			
		Total	Husband-wife	Male head, no, wife present	Female head, no, husband present[1]
BLACK					
1940[2]	2,699	100.0	77.1	5.0	17.9
1950[3]	3,432	100.0	77.7	4.7	17.6
1960	3,950	100.0	74.1	4.1	21.7
1970	4,774	100.0	68.1	3.7	28.3
1971	4,928	100.0	65.6	3.8	30.6
1972	5,157	100.0	63.8	4.4	31.8
1973	5,265	100.0	61.4	4.0	34.6
1974	5,440	100.0	61.8	4.2	34.0
1975	5,498	100.0	60.9	3.9	35.3
WHITE					
1940[2]	28,740	100.0	85.5	4.4	10.1
1950	35,021	100.0	88.0	3.5	8.5
1960	40,873	100.0	89.2	2.7	8.1
1970	46,022	100.0	88.7	2.3	9.1
1971	46,535	100.0	88.3	2.3	9.4
1972	47,641	100.0	88.2	2.3	9.4
1973	48,477	100.0	87.8	2.5	9.6
1974	48,919	100.0	87.7	2.4	9.9
1975	49,451	100.0	86.9	2.6	10.5

Source: "Percent Distribution of Families by Type: 1940 to 1970 and 1971 to 1975," *The Social and Economic Status of the Black Population in the United States: An Historical View, 1790-1978,* 1979, p. 103. Primary source: U.S. Department of Commerce, Bureau of the Census. *Notes:* 1. Includes widowed, divorced, and single women, women whose husbands are in the Armed Forces or otherwise away from home involuntarily, as well as those separated from their husbands through marital discord. 2. Data revised to exclude one-person families. 3. Data include families of "other" races.

★ 946 ★
Characteristics

Family Type: Distribution of Family Type (in percentages), 1940, 1960, and 1975 - I

[Percent]

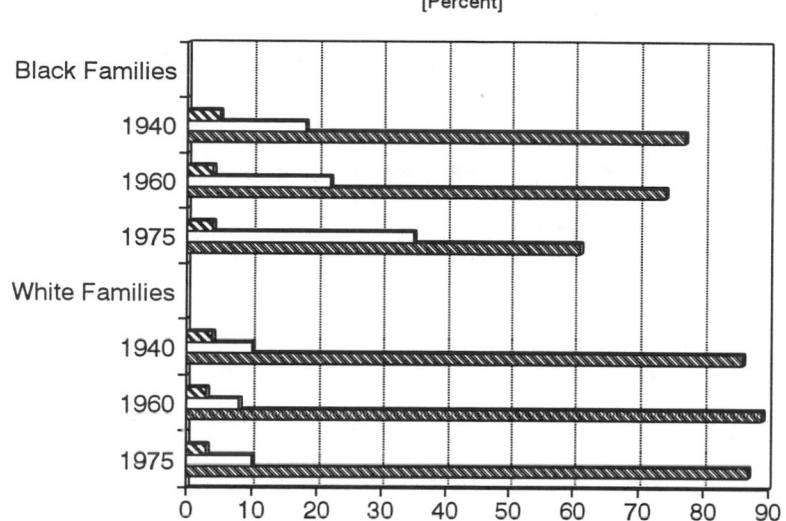

Husband/Wife Fams ▢ Single Mother Fams ▨ Single Father Fams

Year	Husband-wife families	Families maintained by a woman, no husband present	Families maintained by a man, no wife present
Black Families			
1940	77	18	5
1960	74	22	4
1975	61	35	4
White Families			
1940	86	10	4
1960	89	8	3
1975	87	10	3

Source: "Percent Distribution of Families by Type and Region: 1940, 1960, and 1975," *The Social and Economic Status of the Black Population in the United States: An Historical View, 1790-1978*, 1979, p. 99. Primary source: U.S. Department of Commerce. Bureau of the Census. *The Social and Economic Status of the Black Population in the United States: An Historical View, 1790-1978.* Current Population Reports. Special Studies, Series P- 23, No. 80. Washington, D.C.: Government Printing Office, 1979.

★ 947 ★

Characteristics

Family Type: Distribution of Family Type (in percentages), by Region: 1940, and 1975 - II

[Percent]

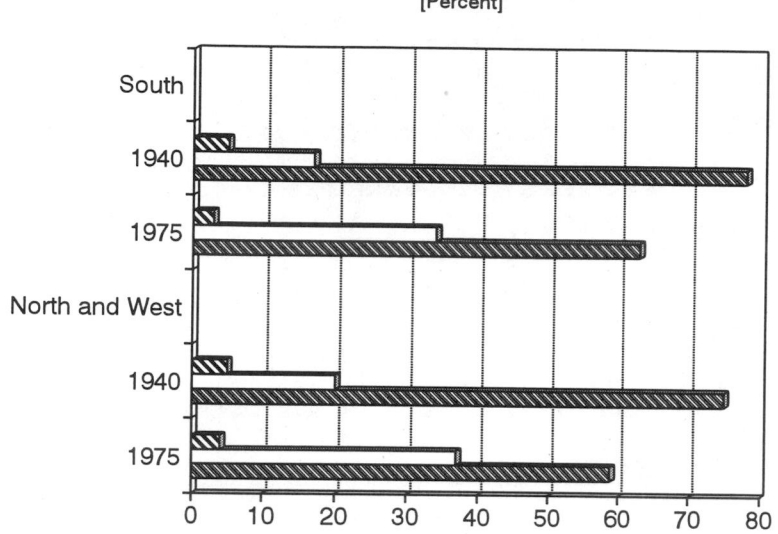

| Husband/Wife Fam | Single Mother Fam | Single Father Fam |

Year	Black Families, by Region		
	Husband-wife families	Families maintained by a woman, no husband present	Families maintained by a man, no wife present
South			
1940	78	17	5
1975	63	34	3
North and West			
1940	75	20	5
1975	59	37	4

Source: "Percent Distribution of Families by Type and Region: 1940, 1960, and 1975," *The Social and Economic Status of the Black Population in the United States: An Historical View, 1790-1978*, 1979, p. 99. Primary source: U.S. Department of Commerce. Bureau of the Census. *The Social and Economic Status of the Black Population in the United States: An Historical View, 1790-1978*. Current Population Reports. Special Studies, Series P- 23, No. 80. Washington, D.C.: Government Printing Office, 1979.

★ 948 ★

Characteristics

Family Type: Family Heads by Gender and Wife's Work Status, 1967 and 1970-1974

Families as of the following year.

Type of family and race of head	1967	1970	1971	1972	1973	1974
ALL FAMILIES						
Black						
Total (thousands)	4,589	4,928	5,157	5,265	5,440	5,498
Percent	100	100	100	100	100	100
Male head[1]	72	69	68	65	66	65
Married, wife present	68	66	64	61	62	61
Wife in paid labor force	34	36	34	33	32	33
Wife not in paid labor force	34	30	30	28	30	28
Female head	28	31	32	35	34	35
White						
Total (thousands)	44,814	46,535	47,641	48,477	48,919	49,451
Percent	100	100	100	100	100	100
Male head[1]	91	91	91	90	90	89
Married, wife present	89	88	88	88	88	87
Wife in paid labor force	32	34	34	35	36	37
Wife not in paid labor force	57	55	54	53	52	50
Female head	9	9	9	10	10	11
HUSBAND-WIFE FAMILIES						
Black						
Total (thousands)	3,118	3,235	3,289	3,233	3,360	3,346
Percent	100	100	100	100	100	100
Wife in paid labor force	50	54	52	54	51	54
Wife not in paid labor force	50	46	48	46	49	46
White						
Total (thousands)	39,821	41,092	42,039	42,585	42,894	42,969
Percent	100	100	100	100	100	100
Wife in paid labor force	35	38	39	40	41	42
Wife not in paid labor force	65	62	61	60	59	58

Source: "Distribution of Families, by Type of Family and Labor Force Status of Wife: 1967 and 1970 to 1974," Current Population Reports, Special Studies, Series P-23, No. 54. *The Social and Economic Status of the Black Population in the United States, 1974,* 1975, p. 32. Primary source: U.S. Department of Commerce, Social and Economic Statistics Administration, Bureau of the Census. *Note:* 1. Includes other male heads, not shown separately.

★ 949 ★

Characteristics

Family Type: Husbands and Wives and Other Family Heads (in percentages), 1950, 1955, 1960, and 1966-1972

Year	Husband-wife		Other male head		Female head[1]	
	Negro and other races	White	Negro and other races	White	Negro and other races	White
1950	77.7	88.0	4.7	3.5	17.6	8.5
1955	75.3	87.9	4.0	3.0	20.7	9.0
1960	73.6	88.7	4.0	2.6	22.4	8.7
1966	72.7	88.8	3.7	2.3	23.7	8.9
1967	72.6	88.7	3.9	2.1	23.6	9.1
1968	69.1	88.9	4.5	2.2	26.4	8.9
1969	68.7	88.8	3.9	2.3	27.3	8.9
1970	69.7	88.7	3.5	2.3	26.8	9.1
1971	67.4	88.3	3.7	2.3	28.9	9.4
1972[2]	65.7	88.2	4.2	2.3	30.1	9.4

Source: "Percent Distribution of Families by Type: 1950, 1955, 1960, and 1966 to 1972," Current Population Reports, Special Studies, Series P-23, No. 42. *The Social and Economic Status of the Black Population in the United States, 1971,* 1972, p. 100. Primary source: U.S. Department of Commerce, Social and Economic Statistics Administration, Bureau of the Census. *Notes:* A family consists of two or more persons living together and related by blood, marriage or adoption. 1. Female heads of families include widowed and single women, women whose husbands are in the armed services or otherwise away from home involuntarily, as well as those separated from their husbands through divorce or marital discord. 2. Data from the March 1972 Current Population Survey are tied in with figures using 1970 census-based population controls.

★ 950 ★

Characteristics

Family Type: Husbands and Wives and Other Family Heads (in percentages), 1965 and 1970-1975

Year and race	All families (thousands)	Percent of all families			
		Total	Husband-wife	Other male head	Female[1] head
Black					
1965[2]	4,752	100.0	73.1	3.2	23.7
1970	4,774	100.0	68.1	3.7	28.3
1971	4,928	100.0	65.6	3.8	30.6
1972[3]	5,157	100.0	63.8	4.4	31.8
1973[3]	5,265	100.0	61.4	4.0	34.6
1974[3]	5,440	100.0	61.8	4.2	34.0
1975[3]	5,498	100.0	60.9	3.9	35.3

[Continued]

★ 950 ★

Family Type: Husbands and Wives and Other Family Heads (in percentages), 1965 and 1970-1975

[Continued]

Year and race	All families (thousands)	Percent of all families			
		Total	Husband-wife	Other male head	Female[1] head
White					
1965	43,081	100.0	88.6	2.4	9.0
1970	46,022	100.0	88.7	2.3	9.1
1971	46,535	100.0	88.3	2.3	9.4
1972[3]	47,641	100.0	88.2	2.3	9.4
1973[3]	48,477	100.0	87.8	2.5	9.6
1974[3]	48,919	100.0	87.7	2.4	9.9
1975[3]	49,451	100.0	86.9	2.6	10.5

Source: "Percent Distribution of Families by Type: 1965 and 1970 to 1975," Current Population Reports, Special Studies, Series P-23, No. 54. *The Social and Economic Status of the Black Population in the United States, 1974*, 1975, p. 107. Primary source: U.S. Department of Commerce, Social and Economic Statistics Administration, Bureau of the Census. *Notes:* A family consists of two or more persons living together and related by blood, marriage, or adoption. 1. Female heads of families include widowed, divorced, and single women, women whose husbands are in the Armed Forces or otherwise away from home involuntarily, as well as those separated from their husbands through marital discord. 2. Includes persons of "other" races. 3. Based on 1970 census population controls.

★ 951 ★

Characteristics

Family Type: Intact Families, by Husband's Age, 1940-1975

Age of husband and race	1940[1]	1950[2]	1960	1970	1975
BLACK					
Husband-wife families...thousands	2,080	2,665	2,929	3,294	3,346
Percent	100	100	100	100	100
14 to 34 years	32	31	28	30	32
35 to 44 years	27	27	25	23	21
45 to 64 years	] 41	33	36	35	34
65 years and over		9	11	12	13
WHITE					
Husband-wife families...thousands	24,580	30,821	36,455	40,272	42,969
Percent	100	100	100	100	100
14 to 34 years	27	29	27	28	30
35 to 44 years	26	25	25	21	19

[Continued]

★ 951 ★

Family Type: Intact Families, by Husband's Age, 1940-1975
[Continued]

Age of husband and race	1940[1]	1950[2]	1960	1970	1975
45 to 64 years	] 47	35	37	38	36
65 years and over		10	12	13	14

Source: "Husband-Wife Families by Age of Husband: 1940 to 1975," *The Social and Economic Status of the Black Population in the United States: An Historical View, 1790-1978*, 1979, p. 105. Primary source: U.S. Department of Commerce, Bureau of the Census. *Notes:* 1. Data revised to exclude one-person families. 2. Data for Black include families of "other" races. 3. Data includes 45 years and over.

★ 952 ★

Characteristics

Family Type: Male and Female Family Heads in Cities with Largest Black Populations, 1970

Thirty cities with the largest Negro population in 1970.

Area	Total number of families	Percent of all families		
		Total	Male head	Female head
United States	4,815,197	100.0	72.1	27.9
Selected cities				
New York City, N.Y.	386,759	100.0	67.1	32.9
Chicago, Ill.	241,779	100.0	70.3	29.7
Detroit, Mich.	149,561	100.0	74.0	26.0
Philadelphia, Pa.	145,861	100.0	67.4	32.6
Washington, D.C.	119,678	100.0	71.3	28.7
Los Angeles, Calif.	116,414	100.0	67.8	32.2
Baltimore, Md.	89,327	100.0	67.8	32.2
Houston, Tex.	71,325	100.0	76.9	23.1
Cleveland, Ohio	66,359	100.0	70.2	29.8
New Orleans, La.	58,701	100.0	67.9	32.1
Atlanta, Ga.	57,009	100.0	69.5	30.5
St. Louis, Mo.	54,678	100.0	67.7	32.3
Memphis, Tenn.	50,809	100.0	71.0	29.0
Dallas, Tex.	46,682	100.0	73.7	26.3
Newark, N.J.	46,384	100.0	63.3	36.7
Indianapolis, Ind.	29,771	100.0	74.1	25.9
Birmingham, Ala.	28,176	100.0	72.3	27.7
Cincinnati, Ohio	28,046	100.0	68.8	31.2
Oakland, Calif.	28,773	100.0	71.5	28.5
Jacksonville, Fla.	25,605	100.0	68.7	31.3
Kansas City, Mo.	24,427	100.0	73.5	26.5
Milwaukee, Wis.	22,209	100.0	68.1	31.9
Pittsburgh, Pa.	23,953	100.0	66.3	33.7
Richmond, Va.	23,628	100.0	68.5	31.5
Boston, Mass.	23,197	100.0	60.0	40.0

[Continued]

★ 952 ★

Family Type: Male and Female Family Heads in Cities with Largest Black Populations, 1970
[Continued]

Area	Total number of families	Percent of all families		
		Total	Male head	Female head
Columbus, Ohio	22,248	100.0	71.1	28.9
San Francisco, Calif.	21,826	100.0	69.0	31.0
Buffalo, N.Y.	20,739	100.0	66.1	33.9
Gary, Ind.	20,394	100.0	77.0	23.0
Nashville-Davidson, Tenn.	18,569	100.0	72.3	27.7

Source: "Number of Negro Families, by Sex of Head, in 30 Selected Cities: 1970," Current Population Reports, Special Studies, Series P-23, No. 38. *The Social and Economic Status of the Black Population in the United States, 1970,* 1970, p. 112. Primary source: U.S. Department of Commerce, Bureau of the Census.

★ 953 ★
Characteristics

Family Type: Marital Status of Black Female Family Heads, 1960-1974

Marital status	1960	1967	1970	1974	Percent change, 1970-1974
Total female heads (thousands)	843	1,138	1,349	1,849	37
Percent	100	100	100	100	-
Single, never married	12	12	16	21	78
Separated or divorced	40	47	48	47	33
Separated	29	33	34	30	23
Divorced	11	13	14	16	56
Married, husband temporarily absent	6	7	6	3	-19
In Armed Forces	-	2	2	1	-68
Other reasons	6	5	4	3	13
Widowed	42	35	30	29	33

Source: Adapted by the editors from "Marital Status of Negro Female Heads of Families: 1960, 1967, and 1970," Current Population Reports, Special Studies, Series P-23, No. 38. *The Social and Economic Status of the Black Population in the United States, 1970,* 1970, p. 131; and "Marital Status of Female Family Heads: 1970 and 1974," Current Population Reports, Special Studies, Series P-23, No. 54. *The Social and Economic Status of the Black Population in the United States, 1974,* 1975, p. 108. Primary source: U.S. Department of Commerce, Social and Economic Statistics Administration, Bureau of the Census. *Notes:* Categories refer to marital status at time of enumeration. - Represents zero.

★ 954 ★

Characteristics

Housing: Change in Number/Percent of Black Families Owning and Renting by Region and Decade, 1900-1930

Figures for 1930 and 1900 represent private-family homes alone; those for 1920 and 1910 include the premises occupied by the small number of institutions and other quasifamily groups which were counted as families in the respective census.

Area and tenure	1900 to 1930		1920 to 1930		1910 to 1920		1900 to 1910	
	Number	Percent distribution	Number	Percent distribution	Number	Percent distribution	Number	Percent distribution
United States								
All homes	969,997	52.9	372,928	15.3	257,810	11.9	339,259	18.5
Owned	296,195	79.3	126,991	23.4	53,955	11.0	115,249	30.9
Rented	714,941	53.5	250,523	13.9	195,975	12.2	268,443	20.1
Tenure unknown	-41,139	-32.9	-4,586	-5.2	7,880	9.8	-44,433	-35.5
The North								
All homes	386,558	203.7	213,634	58.9	119,774	49.3	53,150	28.0
Owned	77,554	176.1	48,963	67.4	18,523	34.2	10,068	22.0
Rented	303,788	223.1	159,710	57.0	100,312	55.7	43,766	32.1
Tenure unknown	5,216	54.6	4,961	50.6	939	10.6	-684	-72
The South								
All homes	556,333	34.0	145,548	7.1	130,418	6.8	280,367	17.1
Owned	207,896	63.5	72,075	15.6	32,909	7.6	102,912	31.4
Rented	395,381	33.1	83,437	5.5	90,842	6.4	221,102	17.5
Tenure unknown	-46,944	-40.8	-9,964	-12.8	6,667	9.4	-543,647	-38.0
The West								
All homes	27,106	389.2	13,746	67.6	7,618	60.0	5,742	82.4
Owned	10,745	574.0	5,953	89.3	2,523	60.9	2,269	121.2
Rented	15,772	347.1	7,376	57.0	4,821	59.4	3,575	78.7
Tenure unknown	589	107.3	417	57.8	274	61.3	-102	-18.6

Source: "Homes of Negro Families by Tenure, by Sections, Divisions, and States: 1930, 1920, 1910, and 1900," *Negroes in the United States, 1920-1932*, 1935, p. 264. Primary source: U.S. Bureau of the Census. *Negroes in the United States, 1920-1932*. Washington, D.C.: U.S. Government Printing Office, 1935.

Housing: Number/Percent of Black Families Owning and Renting by Region and Decade, 1900-1930

Figures for 1930 and 1900 represent private-family homes alone; those for 1920 and 1910 include the premises occupied by the small number of institutions and other quasifamily groups which were counted as families in the respective census.

Area and tenure	1930		1920		1910		1900	
	Number	Percent distribution	Number	Percent distribution	Number	Percent distribution	Number	Percent distribution
United States								
All homes	2,803,756	100.0	2,430,828	100.0	2,173,018	100.0	1,833,759	100.0
Owned	669,645	23.9	542,654	22.3	488,699	22.5	373,450	20.4
Rented	2,050,217	73.1	1,799,694	74.0	1,603,719	73.8	1,335,276	72.8
Tenure unknown	83,894	3.0	88,480	3.6	80,600	3.7	125,033	6.8
The North								
All homes	576,328	100.0	362,694	100.0	242,920	100.0	189,770	100.0
Owned	121,595	21.1	72,632	20.0	54,109	222.3	44,041	23.2
Rented	439,971	76.3	280,261	77.3	179,949	74.1	136,183	71.8
Tenure unknown	14,762	2.6	9,801	2.7	8,862	3.6	9,546	5.0
The South								
All homes	2,193,357	100.0	2,047,809	100.0	1,917,391	100.0	1,637,024	100.0
Owned	535,433	24.4	463,358	22.6	430,449	22.4	327,537	20.0
Rented	1,589,930	72.5	1,506,493	73.6	1,415,651	73.8	1,194,549	73.0
Tenure unknown	67,994	3.1	77,958	3.8	71,291	3.7	114,938	7.0
The West								
All homes	34,071	100.0	20,325	100.0	12,707	100.0	6,965	100.0
Owned	12,617	37.0	6,664	32.8	4,141	32.6	1,872	26.9
Rented	20,316	59.6	12,940	63.7	8,119	63.9	4,544	65.2
Tenure unknown	1,138	3.3	721	3.5	447	3.5	549	7.9

Source: "Homes of Negro Families by Tenure, by Sections, Divisions, and States: 1930, 1920, 1910, and 1900," *Negroes in the United States, 1920-1932*, 1935, p. 264. Primary source: U.S. Bureau of the Census. *Negroes in the United States, 1920-1932.* Washington, D.C.: U.S. Government Printing Office, 1935.

★ 956 ★

Characteristics

Housing: Trends in Home Ownership, 1900-1930

Figures for 1930 and 1900 represent private-family homes alone; those for 1920 include the premises occupied by the small number of institutions and other quasi-family groups which were counted as families in that year.

Color and census year	All homes	Owned		Rented		Tenure unknown	
		Number	Percent	Number	Percent	Number	Percent
ALL FAMILIES							
1930	29,904,663	14,002,074	46.8	15,319,817	51.2	582,772	1.9
1920	24,351,676	10,866,960	44.6	12,943,598	53.2	541,118	2.2
1900	15,963,965	7,205,212	45.1	8,223,775	51.5	534,978	3.4
NEGRO FAMILIES							
1930	2,803,756	669,645	23.9	2,050,217	73.1	83,894	3.0
1920	2,430,828	542,654	22.3	1,799,694	74.0	88,480	3.6
1900	1,833,759	373,350	20.4	1,335,276	72.8	125,003	6.8
WHITE FAMILIES							
1930	26,705,294	13,224,389	49.5	13,004,800	48.7	476,105	1.8
1920	21,825,654	10,286,267	47.1	11,092,896	50.8	446,491	2.0
1900	14,063,791	6,788,069	48.3	6,871,037	48.9	404,685	2.9
OTHER FAMILIES							
1930	395,613	108,040	27.3	264,800	66.9	22,773	5.8
1920	95,194	38,039	40.0	51,008	53.6	6,147	6.5
1900	66,415	43,693	65.8	17,462	26.3	5,260	7.9

Increase or decrease (-)

Color and census year	All homes	Owned		Rented		Tenure unknown	
ALL FAMILIES							
1900-1930	13,940,698	6,796,862	94.3	7,096,042	86.3	47,794	8.9
1920-30	5,552,987	3,135,114	28.8	2,376,219	18.4	41,654	7.7
1900-1920	8,387,711	3,661,748	50.8	4,719,823	57.4	6,140	1.1
NEGRO FAMILIES							
1900-1930	969,997	296,195	79.3	714,941	53.5	-41.139	-32.9
1920-30	372,938	126,991	23.4	250,523	13.9	-4,586	-5.2
1900-1920	597,069	169,204	45.3	464,418	34.8	-36,553	-29.2
WHITE FAMILIES							
1900-1930	12,614,503	6,436,320	94.8	6,133,763	89.3	71,420	17.6
1920-30	4,879,640	2,938,122	28.6	1,911,904	17.2	29,614	6.6
1900-1920	7,761,863	3,498,198	51.5	4,221,859	61.4	41,806	10.3

[Continued]

★ 956 ★

Housing: Trends in Home Ownership, 1900-1930
[Continued]

Color and census year	All homes	Owned		Rented		Tenure unknown	
		Number	Percent	Number	Percent	Number	Percent
OTHER FAMILIES							
1900-1920	329,198	64,347	147.3	247,338	1,416.4	17,513	332.9
1920-30	300,419	70,001	184.0	213,792	419.1	16,626	270.5
1900-1920	28,779	-5,654	-12.9	33,546	192.1	887	16.9

Source: "Tenure of Homes, by Color of Head of Family, for the United States: 1930," *Negroes in the United States, 1920-1932,* 1935, p. 254. Primary source: U.S. Bureau of the Census. *Negroes in the United States, 1920-1932.* Washington, D.C.: U.S. Government Printing Office, 1935.

★ 957 ★

Characteristics

Housing: Trends in Percent of Black Farm and Nonfarm Homeowner Families by Region, 1910-1930

Section	All homes			Farm homes			Nonfarm homes		
	1930	1920	1910	1930	1920	1910	1930	1920	1910
United States	23.9	22.3	22.5	19.3	[1]	25.1	26.4	[1]	20.7
The South	24.4	22.6	22.4	19.1	[1]	24.6	28.6	[1]	20.7
The North	21.1	20.0	22.3	33.2	[1]	62.6	20.8	[1]	20.1
The West	37.0	32.8	32.6	30.9	[1]	77.4	37.3	[1]	30.7

Source: "Percent of Homes owned by Negro Families, by Sections: 1930, 1920, and 1910," *Negroes in the United States, 1920-1932,* 1935, p. 255. Primary source: U.S. Bureau of the Census. *Negroes in the United States, 1920-1932.* Washington, D.C.: U.S. Government Printing Office, 1935. *Note:* 1. Data not available.

★ 958 ★

Characteristics

Median Size of Black Families by Geographic Division and Urban-Rural Residence, 1930

Division	Total	Urban	Rural-farm	Rural-nonfarm
United States	3.15	2.70	4.05	2.96
New England	2.77	2.73	3.02	3.08
Middle Atlantic	2.79	2.76	3.49	3.01
East North Central	2.75	2.74	3.30	2.76
West North Central	2.50	2.45	3.20	2.57
South Atlantic	3.48	2.83	4.69	3.18
East South Central	3.16	2.58	3.74	2.79
West South Central	3.11	2.65	3.67	2.72

[Continued]

★958★

Median Size of Black Families by Geographic Division and Urban-Rural Residence, 1930
[Continued]

Division	Total	Urban	Rural-farm	Rural-nonfarm
Mountain	2.18	2.18	2.66	2.07
Pacific	2.32	2.32	2.74	2.19

Source: "Median Size of Urban, Rural-Farm and Rural-Nonfarm Negro Families, by Divisions, and States: 1930," *Negroes in the United States, 1920-1932,* 1935, pp. 255-256. Primary source: U.S. Bureau of the Census, *Negroes in the United States, 1920-1932.* Washington, D.C.: U.S. Government Printing Office, 1935.

★959★

Characteristics

Number/Percent: Change in Number of Families, by Region, 1940-1975

Area and year	All families (thousands)	Black families[1]			White families		
		Total (thousands)	Percent change over preceding date	Percent of all families	Total (thousands)	Percent change over preceding date	Percent of all families
UNITED STATES							
1940[2]	31,542	2,699	(X)	9	28,740	(X)	91
1950	38,454	3,432	27	9	35,021	22	91
1960	45,128	3,950	15	9	40,873	17	91
1970	51,237	4,774	21	9	46,022	13	90
1975	55,712	5,498	15	10	49,451	7	89
SOUTH							
1940[2]	9,492	2,094	(X)	22	7,380	(X)	78
1950	11,553	2,205	5	19	9,348	27	81
1960	13,512	2,290	4	17	11,189	20	83
1970	15,772	2,477	8	16	13,247	18	84
1975	18,101	2,823	14	16	15,154	14	84
NORTH AND WEST							
1940[2]	22,050	605	(X)	3	21,360	(X)	97
1950	26,901	1,227	103	5	25,674	20	95
1960	31,616	1,660	35	5	29,684	16	94
1970	35,467	2,297	38	6	32,777	10	92
1975	37,597	2,668	16	7	34,286	5	91

Source: "Number of Families by Region: 1940 to 1975," *The Social and Economic Status of the Black Population in the United States: An Historical View, 1790-1978,* 1979, p. 104. Primary source: U.S. Department of Commerce. Bureau of the Census. *Notes:* X Not applicable. A family consists of two or more persons living together and related by blood, marriage, or adoption. Comparable data for families are not available prior to 1940. Detailed figures may not add to total because of different tabulations. 1. Data for 1950 include families of "other" races. 2. Data revised to exclude one-person families.

★ 960 ★

Characteristics

Relationships: Family Size and Income in Families Above and Below Low-Income Level by City Residence Area, 1970

Type of residence	Negro		White		Ratio of Negro to white income per family member
	Average size of family	Income per family member	Average size of family	Income per family member	
BELOW LOW-INCOME LEVEL					
United States	4.7	$537	3.6	$577	93
Metropolitan areas	4.3	588	3.6	598	98
Central cities	4.2	597	3.7	623	96
Outside central cities	4.9	557	3.5	571	98
Outside metropolitan areas	5.2	476	3.6	558	85
ABOVE LOW-INCOME LEVEL					
United States	4.1	$2,328	3.5	$3,499	67
Metropolitan areas	4.0	2,488	3.5	3,765	66
Central cities	3.9	2,496	3.3	3,790	66
Outside central cities	4.2	2,460	3.6	3,751	66
Outside metropolitan areas	4.4	1,777	3.5	3,014	59

Source: "Average Size of Family and Income per Family Member, for Families Below and Above the Low-Income Level in 1970," Current Population Reports, Special Studies, Series P-23, No. 42. *The Social and Economic Status of the Black Population in the United States, 1971,* 1972, p. 44. Primary source: U.S. Department of Commerce, Social and Economic Statistics Administration, Bureau of the Census.

★ 961 ★

Characteristics

Relationships: Family Status of People at (100%) or Just Above (125%) Low-Income Level, 1959, 1966, and 1971

Family status and year	All races	Negro and other races	White	Negro and other races as a percent of all races
1959				
Total (millions)	15.5	2.1	13.4	14
Percent	100	100	100	(X)
In families	95	95	95	13
Head	22	21	23	13
65 years and over	4	2	5	8
Children under 18 years	46	47	45	14
Other family members	27	26	27	13

[Continued]

★ 961 ★

Relationships: Family Status of People at (100%) or Just Above (125%) Low-Income Level, 1959, 1966, and 1971

[Continued]

Family status and year	All races	Negro and other races	White	Negro and other races as a percent of all races
Unrelated individuals	5	5	5	14
65 years and over	2	1	2	4
1966				
Total (millions)	12.8	2.6	10.2	20
Percent	100	100	100	(X)
In families	92	96	91	21
Head	22	20	23	18
65 years and over	6	3	7	9
Children under 18 years	43	49	42	23
Other family members	27	27	27	20
Unrelated individuals	8	4	9	11
65 years and over	4	1	5	6
1971				
Total (millions)	10.9	2.5	8.4	23
Percent	100	100	100	(X)
In families	87	93	86	24
Head	22	21	23	21
65 years and over	6	4	7	16
Children under 18 years	40	47	38	27
Other family members	25	25	25	24
Unrelated individuals	13	7	14	13
65 years and over	8	3	9	9

Source: "Distribution of Persons Between 100 and 125 Percent of the Low-Income Level, by Family Status: 1959, 1966, and 1971," Current Population Reports, Special Studies, Series P-23, No. 42. *The Social and Economic Status of the Black Population in the United States, 1971,* 1972, p. 41. Primary source: U.S. Department of Commerce, Social and Economic Statistics Administration, Bureau of the Census. *Notes:* The average threshold for a nonfarm family of four below 125 percent of the low-income level was $5,171 in 1971, $4,146 in 1966, and $3,716 in 1959. (X) Not applicable.

★ 962 ★

Characteristics

Relationships: Wage/Salary Earners in Families Above and Below Low-Income Level, 1973

Families as the following year.

Subject	Black			White		
	Total	Above low-income level	Below low-income level	Total	Above low-income level	Below low-income level
Total, families (thousands)	5,440	3,913	1,527	48,919	45,700	3,219
Percent	100	100	100	100	100	100
No earners	15	6	38	10	8	38
One earner	35	33	42	36	35	42
Two or more earners	49	61	20	54	57	20
Total, one earner families (thousands)	1,918	1,282	636	17,436	16,081	1,355
Percent	100	100	100	100	100	100
Head an earner	80	82	76	88	89	84
Male	47	55	31	79	81	56
Female	33	27	44	9	7	28
Wife an earner	8	7	8	5	6	4
Other relative an earner	13	11	17	6	6	12
Total two or more earners (thousands)	2,692	2,385	307	26,597	25,960	637
Percent	100	100	100	100	100	100
Head and another family member(s)						
earners	95	96	81	98	98	91
Wife an earner	68	72	37	75	75	56
Other relatives(s) only other earner(s)	26	24	45	23	23	36
Head not an earner	5	4	19	2	2	9

Source: "Number of Earners by Relationship to Head and Low-Income Status of Families in 1973," Current Population Reports, Special Studies, Series P-23, No. 54. *The Social and Economic Status of the Black Population in the United States, 1974,* 1975, p. 47. Primary source: U.S. Department of Commerce, Social and Economic Statistics Administration, Bureau of the Census.

★ 963 ★

Characteristics

Size and Number of Black Families by Region, 1890-1910

Section and census year	Families			Persons to a family	
	Total number	Negro		Total population	Negro population
		Number	Percent		
United States					
1910	20,255,555	2,173,018	10.7	4.5	4.5
1900	16,187,715	1,833,759	11.3	4.7	4.8
1890	12,690,152	1,410,769	11.1	4.9	5.3
The South					
1910	6,163,207	1,917,391	31.1	4.7	4.6
1900	4,938,073	1,637,024	33.2	5.0	4.8
1890	3,758,887	1,262,707	33.6	5.3	5.4
The North					
1910	12,507,506	242,920	1.9	4.5	4.2
1900	10,318,990	189,770	1.8	4.6	4.6
1890	8,310,847	142,937	1.7	4.8	4.9
The West					
1910	1,584,842	12,707	0.8	4.3	4.0
1900	930,652	6,965	0.7	4.4	4.4
1890	620,418	5,125	0.8	4.9	5.3

Source: [Untitled Table], *Negro Population, 1790-1915*, 1918, p. 464. Primary source: U.S. Bureau of the Census. *Negro Population, 1790-1915*. Washington, D.C.: Government Printing Office, 1918.

★ 964 ★

Characteristics

Size of Black Families by Region, 1930

	United States	The North	The South	The West
All families	2,803,756	576,328	2,193,357	34,071
FAMILIES COMPRISING				
1 person	338,114	80,084	250,264	7,766
2 persons	739,812	183,678	544,285	11,849
3 persons	500,990	106,563	388,738	5,689
4 persons	361,880	72,550	285,962	3,368
5 persons	265,136	48,937	214,024	2,175
6 persons	193,720	32,724	159,692	1,304
7 persons	141,149	21,127	119,257	765
8 persons	99,800	13,119	86,176	505
9 persons	67,607	7,958	59,351	298

[Continued]

★ 964 ★

Size of Black Families by Region, 1930

[Continued]

	United States	The North	The South	The West
10 persons	43,573	4,574	38,841	158
11 persons	25,411	2,406	22,905	100
12 or more persons	26,564	2,608	23,862	94
PERCENT OF ALL FAMILIES				
1 person	12.1	13.9	11.4	22.8
2 persons	26.4	31.9	24.8	34.8
3 persons	17.9	18.5	17.7	16.7
4 persons	12.9	12.6	13.0	9.9
5 persons	9.5	8.5	9.8	6.4
6 or more persons	21.3	14.7	23.3	9.5

Source: "Negro Families by Size, by Sections, Divisions, and States: 1930," *Negroes in the United States, 1920-1932*, 1935, p. 273. Primary source: U.S. Bureau of the Census. *Negroes in the United States, 1920-1932*. Washington, D.C.: U.S. government Printing Office, 1935.

★ 965 ★

Characteristics

Summary Characteristics: Number, Size, Income, and Other Family Characteristics, 1960-61

[Annual averages based on national sample surveys and subject to sampling variability. Covers persons living alone as well as families of 2 or more persons].

CHARACTERISTIC	All families	RACE		
		White	Negro	Other
Number of families, 1,000[1]	55,307	49,392	5,321	593
Percent	100.0	89.3	9.6	1.1
Average:				
Family size, number	3.2	3.2	3.4	3.8
Money income before taxes	$6,246	$6,508	$3,838	$5,996
Age of head, years	48	48	47	44
Educational of head, years	10	10	8	8
Percent:				
Homeowners, all year	57	60	33	36
Auto owners, end of year	76	79	45	63
Nonwhite	11	(X)	100	100
Reporting savings increase	52	53	42	57
Reporting savings decrease	42	42	43	34
Average per family:[2]				
Receipts	$7,397	$7,746	$4,222	$6,807
Money income after taxes	5,557	5,772	3,584	5,388
Other money receipts	81	86	29	144
Decrease in assets	947	1,037	139	669
Increase in liabilities	812	851	470	606

[Continued]

★ 965 ★

Summary Characteristics: Number, Size, Income, and Other Family Characteristics, 1960-61

[Continued]

CHARACTERISTIC	All families	RACE		
		White	Negro	Other
Disbursements	7,583	7,934	4,399	6,906
Increase in assets	1,470	1,598	325	1,088
Decrease in liabilities	487	510	285	395
Personal insurance	299	311	187	306
Gifts and contributions	280	296	137	217
Expenditures for current consumption	5,047	5,219	3,465	4,900
Value of items received without expense	195	201	140	229

Source: "Financial and other Characteristics of Families, by Race, and by Education of Head: 1960-61," Statistical Abstract of the United States, 1966, p. 339. Primary source: Dept of Labor, Bureau of the Labor Statistics; Consumer Expenditures and Income, Total United States, Urban and Rural, 1960-61, Report No. 237- 93. Notes: X Not applicable. 1. Estimated. 2. Families interviewed were rarely able to give an exact account of their financial transactions over the 12-month period covered by the survey, therefore, receipts do not equal disbursements.

★ 966 ★

Characteristics

Trends in Number of Families, 1890-1930

The family figures for 1930 and 1900 represent private families only; those for 1920 and 1890 include the small number of institutions and other quasi-family groups which were counted as families in those years.

Color and nativity	1930		1920		1900		1890	
	Number	Percent	Number	Percent	Number	Percent	Number	Percent
All classes	26,904,663	100.0	24,351,676	100.0	15,963,965	100.0	12,690,152	100.0
Negro	2,803,756	9.4	2,430,828	10.0	1,833,759	11.5	1,410,769	11.1
White	26,705,294	89.3	21,825,654	89.6	14,063,791	88.1	11,255,169	88.7
Native	20,968,803	70.1	16,407,983	67.4	10,206,500	63.9	8,021,434	63.2
Foreign born	5,736,491	19.2	5,417,679	22.2	3,857,291	24.2	3,233,735	25.5
Other races[2]	395,613	1.3	95,194	.4	66,415	.4	24,214	.2

Source: "Families by Color, and Nativity of Head, with Total Population by Color, and Nativity, for the United States: 1890-1930," Negroes in the United States, 1920-1932, 1935, p. 258. Primary source: U.S. Bureau of the Census. Negroes in the United States, 1920-1932. Washington, D.C.: U.S. Government Printing Office, 1935. Notes: 1. Exclusive of 325,464 persons specially enumerated in Indian Territory and on Indian reservations, for whom family data are not available. 2. Figures for 1930 include Mexicans, who were for the most part classified as white at earlier census.

★ 967 ★

Characteristics

Trends in Urban-Rural Residence of Black Families by Region, 1910-1930

Section and census year	Number			Percent distribution		
	All homes	Farm homes	Nonfarm homes	All homes	Farm homes	Nonfarm homes
United States						
1930	2,803,756	981,038	1,822,718	100.0	100.0	100.0
1920	2,430,828	[1]	[1]	100.0	[1]	[1]
1910	2,173,018	877,648	1,295,370	100.0	100.0	100.0
The South						
1930	2,193,357	964,494	1,228,863	78.2	98.3	67.4
1920	2,047,809	[1]	[1]	84.2	[1]	[1]
1910	1,917,391	864,688	1,052,703	88.2	98.5	81.3
The North						
1930	576,328	15,000	561,328	20.6	1.5	30.8
1920	362,964	[1]	[1]	14.9	[1]	[1]
1910	242,920	12,437	230,483	11.2	1.4	17.8
The West						
1930	34,071	1,544	32,527	1.2	.2	1.8
1920	20,325	[1]	[1]	.8	[1]	[1]
1910	12,707	523	12,184	.6	.1	.9

Source: "Farm and Nonfarm Homes of Negro Families, by Sections: 1930," *Negroes in the United States, 1920-1932*, 1935, p. 256. Primary source: U.S. Bureau of the Census, *Negroes in the United States, 1920-1932*. Washington, D.C.: U.S. Government Printing Office, 1935. *Note:* 1. Data not available.

★ 968 ★

Characteristics

Work Status of Husband and Wife by Region and Age of Head, 1970 and 1973

Families as of the following year.

Race and earning status of husband and wife and work experience of wife	Total			Head under 35 years old		
	United States	North and West	South	United States	North and West	South
1970						
Earning status of husband and wife						
Black husband-wife families[1] (thousands)	3,235	1,545	1,690	965	515	450
Percent	100	100	100	100	100	100
Husband only earner	24	28	20	31	35	25
Husband and wife both earners	58	56	60	68	63	73

[Continued]

★ 968 ★

Work Status of Husband and Wife by Region and Age of Head, 1970 and 1973
[Continued]

Race and earning status of husband and wife and work experience of wife	Total			Head under 35 years old		
	United States	North and West	South	United States	North and West	South
White husband-wife families[1] (thousands)	41,092	29,175	11,918	11,516	8,054	3,463
Percent	100	100	100	100	100	100
Husband only earner	34	34	34	43	44	40
Husband and wife both earners	45	45	46	56	54	59
Work Experience of Wife						
Black wives with earnings (thousands)	1,880	864	1,016	651	323	327
Percent worked 50 to 52 weeks	55	57	54	47	52	41
White wives with earnings (thousands)	18,401	12,969	5,432	6,387	4,359	2,028
Percent worked 50 to 52 weeks	50	49	52	36	36	38
1973						
Earning Status of Husband and Wife						
Black husband-wife families[1] (thousands)	3,360	1,534	1,827	1,100	511	589
Percent	100	100	100	100	100	100
Husband only earner	25	28	22	28	34	22
Husband and wife both earners	55	52	57	68	61	75
White husband-wife families[1] (thousands)	42,894	29,899	12,995	12,857	8,665	4,192
Percent	100	100	100	100	100	100
Husband only earner	31	32	31	38	39	36
Husband and wife both earners	46	46	47	60	59	62
Work Experience of Wife						
Black wives with earnings (thousands)	1,836	797	1,039	750	308	441
Percent worked 50 to 52 weeks	57	61	54	47	52	44
White wives with earnings (thousands)	19,856	13,697	6,159	7,721	5,114	2,607
Percent worked 50 to 52 weeks	52	51	54	41	41	43

Source: "Distribution of Husband-Wife Families, by Earning Status of Husband and Wife in 1970 and 1973, Age of Head and Region," Current Population Reports, Special Studies, Series P-23, No. 54. *The Social and Economic Status of the Black Population in the United States, 1974,* 1975, p. 39. Primary source: U.S. Department of Commerce, Social and Economic Statistics Administration, Bureau of the Census. *Note:* 1. Includes other combinations, not shown separately.

★ 969 ★

Characteristics

Working Members of Husband-Wife Families with Young (Under 35) Heads, 1959 and 1970

Numbers in thousands.

Work experience of husband and wife	1959			1970		
	United States	North and West	South	United States	North and West	South
Negro, total	779	348	431	965	515	450
Only husband worked	334	157	177	296	182	114
Husband and wife worked	392	166	226	651	323	327
Percent of wives working year round	27	26	28	47	52	41
Other combinations	53	25	28	18	10	9
White, total	9,576	6,749	2,827	11,516	8,054	3,463
Only husband worked	5,392	3,825	1,567	4,905	3,528	1,377
Husband and wife worked	3,849	2,699	1,150	6,387	4,359	2,028
Percent of wives working year round	29	29	31	36	36	38
Other combinations	335	225	110	224	167	58
PERCENT DISTRIBUTION						
Negro, total	100	100	100	100	100	100
Only husband worked	43	45	41	31	35	25
Husband and wife worked	50	48	52	68	63	73
Other combinations	7	7	7	2	2	2
White, total	100	100	100	100	100	100
Only husband worked	56	57	55	43	44	40
Husband and wife worked	40	40	41	56	54	59
Other combinations	4	3	4	2	2	2

Source: "Distribution of Husband-Wife Families with Head Under 35 Years, by Work Experience of Husband and Wife: 1959 and 1970," Current Population Reports, Special Studies, Series P-23, No. 42. *The Social and Economic Status of the Black Population in the United States, 1971,* 1972, p. 35. Primary source: U.S. Department of Commerce, Social and Economic Statistics Administration, Bureau of the Census.

Children

★ 970 ★

Age Levels: Children Under 10 in Black Families by Region, 1930

	United States	The North	The South	The West
All families	2,803,756	576,328	2,193,357	34,071
FAMILIES HAVING SPECIFIED NUMBER OF CHILDREN UNDER 10 YEARS OLD				
None	1,655,217	389,364	1,239,876	25,977
1	467,575	82,797	380,878	3,900
2	288,572	48,509	237,951	2,112
3	190,380	29,236	159,991	1,153
4	121,107	16,338	104,179	590
5	58,180	7,367	50,577	236
6 or more	22,725	2,717	19,905	103
PERCENT OF ALL FAMILIES				
None	59.0	67.6	56.5	76.2
1	16.7	14.4	17.4	11.4
2	10.3	8.4	10.8	6.2
3	6.8	5.1	7.3	3.4
4	4.3	2.8	4.7	1.7
5	2.1	1.3	2.3	.7
6 or more	0.8	.5	.9	.3

Source: "Negro Families Classified by Number of Children Under 10 Years Old, by Sections, Divisions, and States: 1930," *Negroes in the United States, 1920-1932,* 1935, p. 271. Primary source: U.S. Bureau of the Census. *Negroes in the United States, 1920-1932.* Washington, D.C.: U.S. government Printing Office, 1935.

★ 971 ★

Children

Age Levels: Families with Some Young (Under 10) and Some Older (Under 21) Children, 1930

Number of children	Negro		Native White		Foreign-born White	
	Number	Percent distribution	Number	Percent distribution	Number	Percent distribution
All families	2,803,756	100.0	20,968,803	100.0	5,736,491	100.0
Families having						
No children under 10	1,655,217	59.0	12,216,802	58.3	3,544,030	61.8
1 child under 10	467,575	16.7	4,164,091	19.9	1,045,547	18.2
2 children under 10	288,572	10.3	2,542,041	12.1	636,073	11.1

[Continued]

★ 971 ★

Age Levels: Families with Some Young (Under 10) and Some Older (Under 21) Children, 1930

[Continued]

Number of children	Negro		Native White		Foreign-born White	
	Number	Percent distribution	Number	Percent distribution	Number	Percent distribution
3 children under 10	190,380	6.8	1,243,766	5.9	305,503	5.3
4 children under 10	121,107	4.3	560,506	2.7	138,653	2.4
5 children under 10	58,180	2.1	188,425	.9	50,993	.9
6 or more	22,725	.8	53,172	.3	15,692	.3
Families having						
No children under 21	1,151,361	41.1	8,197,010	39.1	2,132,426	37.2
1 child under 21	530,461	18.9	4,558,971	21.7	1,072,289	18.7
2 children under 21	356,826	12.7	3,485,729	16.6	944,760	16.5
3 children under 21	249,984	8.9	2,067,053	9.9	641,636	11.2
4 children under 21	177,914	6.3	1,198,678	5.7	401,049	7.0
5 children under 21	125,794	4.5	868,256	3.3	240,403	4.2
6 or more	211,416	7.5	775,106	3.7	303,928	5.3

Source: "Families Classified by Number of Children Under 10 and Under 21 Years Old, by Color, and Nativity of Head, for the United States: 1930," *Negroes in the United States, 1920-1932,* 1935, p. 255. Primary source: U.S. Bureau of the Census. *Negroes in the United States, 1920-1932.* Washington, D.C.: U.S. Government Printing Office, 1935.

★ 972 ★

Children

Relationships: Black Children Living with 1, 2, or No Parents and Parents' Marital Status by Child's Age Group, 1974

Subject	Total under 18 years	Age of child		
		Under 3 years	3 to 5 years	6 to 17 years
BLACK				
All children in families (thousands)	9,378	1,384	1,492	6,504
Percent	100	100	100	100
Living with two parents	52	49	51	52
Living with one parent	40	37	41	41
Mother only	38	36	40	39
Father only	2	1	1	2
Living with neither parent	8	15	8	7
Children living with one parent (thousands)	3,774	505	616	2,652
Marital status of parent				
Percent	100	100	100	100
Never married	20	43	31	13
Married	48	42	49	50
Separated	42	33	43	44

[Continued]

★ 972 ★

Relationships: Black Children Living with 1, 2, or No Parents and Parents' Marital Status by Child's Age Group, 1974
[Continued]

Subject	Total under 18 years	Age of child		
		Under 3 years	3 to 5 years	6 to 17 years
Divorced	18	11	12	20
Widowed	14	4	8	17

Source: "Living Arrangements of Children in Families and Marital Status of Parent by Age of Child: 1974," Current Population Reports, Special Studies, Series P-23, No. 54. *The Social and Economic Status of the Black Population in the United States, 1974,* 1975, p. 112. Primary source: U.S. Department of Commerce, Social and Economic Statistics Administration, Bureau of the Census. *Notes:* Universe is all children under 18 years old (regardless of marital status) living in families, but excluding heads and wives of heads of subfamilies.

★ 973 ★
Children

Relationships: Children Living with Both Parents, by Family Income (in percentages), 1960-1975
[Income in current dollars and refers to income received during 1959, 1969, and 1974]

Year and family income	Own Black children			Own White children		
	Total (thousands)	Percent living with--		Total (thousands)	Percent living with--	
		Both parents	One parent		Both parents	One parent
1960						
Total, own children	6,915	75	25	54,446	93	7
Under $4,000	3,842	64	36	8,674	77	23
$4,000 to $5,999	1,351	87	13	8,565	92	8
$6,000 to $7,999	945	92	8	12,633	96	4
$8,000 to $9,999	422	89	11	9,156	97	3
$10,000 and over	355	86	14	15,418	97	3
$10,000 to $14,999	307	87	13	10,485	97	3
$15,000 and over	48	81	19	4,933	97	3
1970						
Total, own children	8,944	65	35	58,244	91	9
Under $4,000	2,602	30	70	4,567	53	47
$4,000 to $5,999	1,860	63	37	5,166	79	21
$6,000 to $7,999	1,592	78	22	7,973	91	9
$8,000 to $9,999	1,088	90	10	9,399	95	5
$10,000 and over	1,804	91	9	31,138	97	3
$10,000 to $14,999	1,291	91	9	18,598	97	3
$15,000 and over	513	89	11	12,540	97	3

[Continued]

★ 973 ★

Relationships: Children Living with Both Parents, by Family Income (in percentages), 1960-1975
[Continued]

Year and family income	Own Black children			Own White children		
	Total (thousands)	Percent living with--		Total (thousands)	Percent living with--	
		Both parents	One parent		Both parents	One parent
1975						
Total, own children	8,721	54	46	54,266	87	13
Under $4,000	1,896	17	83	3,169	37	63
$4,000 to $5,999	1,348	29	71	3,069	61	39
$6,000 to $7,999	1,265	51	49	3,793	73	27
$8,000 to $9,999	926	66	34	4,677	83	17
$10,000 and over	3,284	82	18	39,557	95	5
$10,000 to $14,999	1,681	79	21	14,392	92	8
$15,000 and over	1,603	86	14	25,165	96	4

Source: "Total own Children and Percent of Own Children Living with Both Parents, by Family Income: 1960, 1970, and 1975," *The Social and Economic Status of the Black Population in the United States: An Historical View, 1790-1978*, 1979, p. 108. Primary source: U.S. Department of Commerce. Bureau of the Census. *Notes:* Universe is own unmarried children under 18 years old living in families where at least one parent is present.

★ 974 ★

Children

Relationships: Income Distribution in Families with Minor Children Living with One or Both Parents, 1971 and 1974

Income in current dollars and refers to income received during 1970 and 1973.

Year and family income	Own black children			Own white children		
	Total (thousands)	Percent living with--		Total (thousands)	Percent living with--	
		Both parents	One parent		Both parents	One parent
1971						
Under $4,000	2,542	27	73	4,637	52	48
$4,000 to $5,999	1,697	57	43	4,808	74	26
$6,000 to $7,999	1,344	76	24	7,013	87	13
$8,000 to $9,999	1,092	78	22	8,881	94	6
$10,000 and over	2,202	87	13	32,878	97	3
$10,000 to $14,999	1,515	88	12	18,533	97	3
$15,000 and over	687	85	15	14,345	97	3
1974						
Under $4,000	2,031	18	82	3,382	39	61
$4,000 to $5,999	1,472	35	65	3,413	66	34
$6,000 to $7,999	1,273	53	47	4,260	77	23
$8,000 to $9,999	914	78	22	5,321	88	12
$10,000 and over	2,910	88	12	38,949	96	4

[Continued]

★ 974 ★

Relationships: Income Distribution in Families with Minor Children Living with One or Both Parents, 1971 and 1974
[Continued]

Year and family income	Own black children			Own white children		
	Total	Percent living with--		Total	Percent living with--	
	(thousands)	Both parents	One parent	(thousands)	Both parents	One parent
$10,000 to $14,999	1,600	86	14	16,179	94	6
$15,000 and over	1,310	90	10	22,770	97	3

Source: "Own Children Under 18 Years by Presence of Parents and Family Income: 1971 and 1974," Current Population Reports, Special Studies,Series P-23, No. 54. *The Social and Economic Status of the Black Population in the United States, 1974,* 1975, p. 113. Primary source: U.S. Department of Commerce, Social and Economic Statistics Administration, Bureau of the Census. *Notes:* Universe is own unmarried children under 18 years old living in families where at least one parent is present.

★ 975 ★
Children

Relationships: Percent Distribution of Black Children Under 10 by Family Home Ownership Status and Urban-Rural Residence, 1930 - I

Number of children under 10 years old	All families				Urban families		
	Total	Owners	Tenants	Tenure unknown	Total	Owners	Tenants
	Percent distribution						
All families	100.0	100.0	100.0	100.0	100.0	100.0	100.0
Families having							
No children under 10	59.0	63.9	57.2	65.1	67.7	70.4	66.7
1 child under 10	16.7	15.3	17.1	16.2	15.1	14.1	15.5
2 children under 10	10.3	8.8	10.8	8.8	8.4	7.4	8.7
3 children under 10	6.8	5.8	7.2	5.2	4.8	4.3	5.0
4 children under 10	4.3	3.7	4.6	2.9	2.5	2.4	2.6
5 children under 10	2.1	1.8	2.2	1.3	1.0	1.0	1.1
6 or more	.8	.7	.9	.5	.4	.4	.4

Source: "Negro Families Classified by Number of Children Under 10 Years Old, by Tenure, Urban, Rural-Farm, and Rural Nonfarm Families, for the United States: 1930," *Negroes in the United States, 1920-1932,* 1935, p. 258. Primary source: U.S. Bureau of the Census. *Negroes in the United States, 1920-1932.* Washington, D.C.: U.S. Government Printing Office, 1935.

★ 976 ★

Children

Relationships: Percent Distribution of Black Children Under 10 by Family Home Ownership Status and Urban-Rural Residence, 1930 - II

Number of children under 10 years old	Rural-farm families			Rural-nonfarm families		
	Total	Owners	Tenants	Total	Owners	Tenants
Percent distribution						
All families	100.0	100.0	100.0	100.0	100.0	100.0
Families having						
No children under 10	47.0	53.6	45.0	59.6	63.3	57.2
1 child under 10	18.7	17.2	19.1	16.8	15.4	17.6
2 children under 10	12.9	10.9	13.5	10.3	9.0	11.1
3 children under 10	9.6	8.0	10.0	6.7	6.0	7.1
4 children under 10	6.8	5.9	7.1	4.1	3.8	4.4
5 children under 10	3.6	3.2	3.8	1.8	1.7	1.9
6 or more	1.5	1.3	1.5	.7	.7	.7

Source: "Negro Families Classified by Number of Children Under 10 Years Old, by Tenure, Urban, Rural-Farm, and Rural Nonfarm Families, for the United States: 1930," *Negroes in the United States, 1920-1932,* 1935, p. 258. Primary source: U.S. Bureau of the Census. *Negroes in the United States, 1920-1932.* Washington, D.C.: U.S. Government Printing Office, 1935.

★ 977 ★

Children

Relationships: Trends in Number of Children and Percent Living with Both Parents, 1965-1974

Number in thousands.

Year	Total own children (thousands)		Percent living with both parents	
	Black	White	Black	White
1965	8,922[1]	58,825	71[1]	91
1970	8,944	58,244	64	91
1971	8,876	58,217	61	90
1972	8,584	57,252	61	89
1973	8,676	56,138	56	89
1974	8,600	55,329	56	88

Source: "Total Own Children and Percent Children Living with Both Parents: 1965 and 1970 to 1974," Current Population Reports, Special Studies, Series P- 23, No. 54. *The Social and Economic Status of the Black Population in the United States, 1974,* 1975, p. 111. Primary source: U.S. Department of Commerce, Social and Economic Statistics Administration, Bureau of the Census. *Notes:* Universe is own unmarried children under 18 years old living in families with at least one parent present. "Own" child is a single (never married) son, daughter, stepchild, or adopted child of a married couple or of a family head or subfamily head. 1. Includes persons of "other" races.

Cost of Living

★ 978 ★

Expenditures: Average Annual Amount Families Spent on Food, Clothing, Shelter, and Other Items, 1960-61

EXPENDITURE	All families	White	Negro	Other
Number of families, 1,000[1]	55,307	49,392	5,321	593
Percent	100.0	89.3	9.6	1.1
Total expenditures	$5,047	$5,219	$3,465	$4,900
Food	1,235	1,269	886	1,454
Prepared at home	989	1,015	728	1,121
Other	246	254	158	333
Tobacco	91	93	75	67
Alcoholic beverages	78	79	65	76
Housing	1,461	1,507	1,061	1,233
Shelter	658	677	488	572
Owned dwelling	354	379	145	187
Rented dwelling (includes other shelter)	304	298	343	385
Other expenses[3]	803	830	573	661
Clothing and personal[4]	1,003	1,034	736	883
Recreation and education[5]	298	312	169	312
Transportation	770	808	419	756
Other	111	117	54	119
Percent of total	100.0	100.0	100.0	100.0
Food	24.5	24.3	25.6	29.7
Prepared at home	19.6	19.4	21.0	22.9
Other	4.9	4.9	4.6	6.8
Tobacco	1.8	1.8	2.2	1.4
Alcoholic beverages	1.5	1.5	1.9	1.6
Housing	28.9	28.9	30.6	25.2
Shelter	13.0	13.0	14.1	11.7
Owned dwelling	7.0	7.3	4.2	3.8
Rented dwelling (includes other shelter)	6.0	5.7	9.9	7.9
Other expenses[3]	15.9	15.9	16.5	13.5
Clothing and personal[4]	19.9	19.8	21.3	18.1
Recreation and education[5]	5.9	6.0	4.9	6.4
Transportation	15.3	15.5	12.1	15.4
Other	2.2	2.2	1.6	2.4

Source: "Average Annual Expenditures for Current Consumption by Families, by Residence and Race: 1960-61," *Statistical Abstract of the United States, 1966,* p. 340. Primary source: Dept of Labor, Bureau of the Labor Statistics; *Consumer Expenditures and Income, Total United States, Urban and Rural, 1960-61,* Report No. 237-93, and *Monthly Labor Review,* October 1965. *Notes:* 1. Estimated. 2. Comprises fuel, light, refrigeration, water, housefurnishings and equipment, and household operations. 3. Includes clothing materials and services, personal care, and medical care. 4. Includes reading matter.

★ 979 ★

Cost of Living

Housing: Monthly Rents of Black Nonfarm Families by Region, 1930

Median not shown where number of families reporting rental is less than 100.

	Section, division, and state			
	United States	The North	The South	The West
All rented nonfarm homes	1,290,697	430,466	840,908	19,323
Number of homes with monthly rental				
Under $10	479,539	27,708	450,070	1,761
$10 to $14	247,898	45,374	193,779	2,745
$15 to $19	133,854	56,358	74,712	2,784
$20 to $29	188,079	118,214	63,204	6,661
$30 to $49	149,096	118,362	26,578	4,156
$50 to $74	49,353	44,105	5,034	214
$75 to $99	8,838	8,299	504	35
$100 to $149	1,949	1,805	124	20
$150 to $199	452	416	31	5
$200 and over	147	121	26	-
Not reported	37,492	9,704	26,846	942
Median rental	$13.04	26.85	[1]	22.85

Source: "Rented Nonfarm Homes of Negro Families by Monthly Rental, with Median Rentals, by Sections, Divisions, and States: 1930," *Negroes in the United States, 1920-1932,* 1935, p. 270. Primary source: U.S. Bureau of the Census. *Negroes in the United States, 1920-1932.* Washington, D.C.: U.S. Government Printing Office, 1935. *Note:* 1. Less than $10.

★ 980 ★

Cost of Living

Housing: Percent Distribution of Value of Homes Owned by Black Nonfarm Families by Region, 1930

Percent not shown where less than 1/10 of 1 percent.

Value of monthly rentals	United States	The North	The South	The West
Owned nonfarm homes	100.0	100.0	100.0	100.0
Value under $1,000	39.3	14.8	48.5	9.3
$1,000 to $1,499	13.8	9.63	15.6	7.2
$15,000 to $1,999	8.8	8.2	9.1	6.7
$2,000 to $2,999	12.4	14.9	11.4	16.1
$3,000 to $4,999	12.4	23.1	8.2	31.3
$5,000 to $7,499	6.6	16.2	3.0	19.3
$7,500 to $9,999	2.1	5.6	.9	3.7

[Continued]

★ 980 ★

Housing: Percent Distribution of Value of Homes Owned by Black Nonfarm Families by Region, 1930

[Continued]

Value of monthly rentals	United States	The North	The South	The West
$10,000 to $14,999	1.4	3.9	.5	2.5
$15,000 to $19,999	.4	1.2	.1	.8
$20,000 and over	.3	.8	.1	.5
Not reported	2.5	2.1	2.7	2.7
Rented nonfarm homes	100.0	100.0	100.0	100.0
Rental under $10	37.2	6.4	53.5	9.1
$10 to $14	18.7	10.5	23.0	14.2
$15 to $19	10.4	13.1	8.9	14.4
$20 to $29	14.6	27.5	7.5	34.5
$30 to $49	11.6	27.5	3.2	21.5
$50 to $74	3.8	10.2	.6	1.1
$75 to $99	.7	1.9	.1	.2
$100 to $149	.2	.4	-	.1
$159 to $199	-	.1	-	-
$200 and over	-	-	-	-
Not reported	2.9	2.3	3.2	4.9

Source: "Percent Distribution of Nonfarm Homes of Negro Families, by Value or Monthly Rental, by Sections, and States: 1930," *Negroes in the United States, 1920-1932*, 1935, p. 269. Primary source: U.S. Bureau of the Census. *Negroes in the United States, 1920-1932*. Washington, D.C.: U.S. Government Printing Office, 1935.

★ 981 ★

Cost of Living

Relationships: Family Size and Housing Cost or Home Value among Nonfarm Families, 1930

Color and nativity of head	Median size of family	Median value of owned non-farm homes	Median monthly rental of rented non-farm homes
All classes	3.40	$4,778	$27.15
Negro	3.15	1,341	13.04
Native white	3.34	4,766	27.92
Foreign-born white	3.74	5,576	33.00
Other races	4.13	[1]	12.28

Source: "Median Size of Family, and Median Value or Rental of Nonfarm Homes, by Color and Nativity of Head, for the United States: 1930," *Negroes in the United States, 1920-1932*, 1935, p. 259. Primary source: U.S. Bureau of the Census. *Negroes in the United States, 1920-1932*. Washington, D.C.: U.S. Government Printing Office, 1935. *Note:* 1. Less than $1,000.

Income/Earnings

★ 982 ★

Black Family Median Income as Percent of White in Relation to Age of Head and Family Type, 1968

	All families	Husband-wife families
All ages	60	72
14 to 24 years	70	88
25 to 34 years	62	78
35 to 44 years	59	72
45 to 54 years	62	70
55 to 64 years	57	59
65 years and over	65	63

Source: "Median Income of Negro Families as a Percent of White, by Type of Family and Age of Family Head," Current Population Reports, Special Studies, Series P-23, No. 29. *The Social and Economic Status of the Black Population in the United States, 1969,* 1969, p. 18. Primary source: U.S. Department of Commerce, Bureau of the Census.

★ 983 ★

Income/Earnings

Family Income at or above $8,000 (in percentages), 1947-1963

Adjusted for price changes, in 1968 dollars. An $8,000 income in 1968 was equivalent in purchasing power to about $5,100 in 1947.

Area and year	Negro and other races	White	Area and year	Negro and other races	White
UNITED STATES			UNITED STATES		
1947	6	20	1964	20	47
1948	4	18	1965	21	50
1949	4	18	1966	25	53
1950	4	20	1967	29	55
1951	4	21	1968	32	58
1952	5	23			
1953	8	26	SOUTH		
1954	7	26	1966	14	44
1955	8	30	1967	17	48
1956	9	34	1968	19	50
1957	10	32			
1958	10	33	NORTH AND		
1959	12	37	WEST		
1960	15	39	1966	36	56
1961	15	41	1967	40	58

[Continued]

★ 983 ★

Family Income at or above $8,000 (in percentages), 1947-1963
[Continued]

Area and year	Negro and other races	White	Area and year	Negro and other races	White
1962	14	42	1968	43	61
1963	17	45			

Source: "Percent of Families with Income of $8,000 or More, 1947 to 1968" Current Population Reports, Special Studies, Series P-23, No. 29. *The Social and Economic Status of the Black Population in the United States, 1969,* 1969, p. 17. Primary source: U.S. Department of Commerce, Bureau of the Census.

★ 984 ★
Income/Earnings

Income Distribution of Male and Female Family Heads, 1965, 1970, and 1974

Adjusted for price change in 1974 dollars. Families as of the following year. Minus sign (-) denotes decrease.

Income	Black			White		
	1965	1970	1974	1965	1970	1974
Number of families (thousands)	4,424	4,928	5,498	43,500	46,533	49,451
Percent	100	100	100	100	100	100
Under $3,000	20	15	14	7	5	4
$3,000 to $3,999	10	8	9	4	3	3
$4,000 to $4,999	10	7	8	4	4	4
$5,000 to $6,999	17	13	14	9	8	8
$7,000 to $9,999	18	18	17	17	14	14
$10,000 to $11,999	8	9	8	13	11	11
$12,000 to $14,999	8	11	11	16	16	15
$15,000 and over	9	18	19	30	39	42
Median income	$6,072	$7,978	$7,808	$11,333	$13,000	$13,356
Net change over preceding date						
Amount	(X)	$1,906	$-170	(X)	$1,667	$356
Percent	(X)	31.4	-2.1	(X)	14.7	2.7

Source: "Distribution of Families by Income in 1965, 1970, and 1974," Current Population Reports, Special Studies, Series P-23, No. 29. *The Social and Economic Status of the Black Population in the United States, 1974,* 1975, p. 27. Primary source: U.S. Department of Commerce, Social and Economic Statistics Administration, Bureau of the Census. *Note:* X Not applicable.

★ 985 ★

Income/Earnings

Income Distribution of Male and Female Family Heads, 1968

Percent.

	Negro			White		
	Total	Female	Male	Total	Female	Male
All families	100	29	72	100	9	91
Under $3,000	100	56	44	100	27	73
$3,000 to $4,999	100	36	64	100	17	83
$5,000 to $6,999	100	22	78	100	12	88
$7,000 to $9,999	100	11	89	100	6	94
$10,000 to $14,999	100	9	91	100	4	96
$15,000 and over	100	7	93	100	3	98

Source: "Families by Sex of Head, by Income Group, 1968," Current Population Reports, Special Studies, Series P-23, No. 29. *The Social and Economic Status of the Black Population in the United States, 1969,* 1969, p. 73. Primary source: U.S. Department of Commerce, Bureau of the Census.

★ 986 ★

Income/Earnings

Income Distribution of Male and Female Family Heads, 1971

Family income in 1970	Negro			White		
	All families (thousands)	Percent of all families		All families (thousands)	Percent of all families	
		Male head	Female head		Male head	Female head
Total	4,928	69	31	46,540	91	9
Under $3,000	1,046	40	60	3,507	72	28
$3,000 to $4,999	857	54	46	4,424	80	20
$5,000 to $6,999	833	72	28	5,259	85	15
$7,000 to $9,999	890	84	16	9,361	91	9
$10,000 to $14,999	834	89	11	12,993	95	5
$15,000 and over	468	94	6	10,998	97	3

Source: "Families by Sex of Head and by Income: 1971," Current Population Reports, Special Studies, Series P-23, No. 42, *The Social and Economic Status of the Black Population in the United States, 1971,* 1972, p. 103. Primary source: U.S. Department of Commerce, Social and Economic Statistics Administration, Bureau of the Census.

★ 987 ★

Income/Earnings

Median Family Income 1950-1973

In current dollars.

Year	Race of head			Ratio: Black and other races to white	Ratio: Black to white
	Black and other races	Black	White		
1950	$1,869	(NA)	$3,445	0.54	(NA)
1951	2,032	(NA)	3,859	0.53	(NA)
1952	2,338	(NA)	4,114	0.57	(NA)
1953	2,461	(NA)	4,392	0.56	(NA)
1954	2,410	(NA)	4,339	0.56	(NA)
1955	2,549	(NA)	4,605	0.55	(NA)
1956	2,628	(NA)	4,993	0.53	(NA)
1957	2,764	(NA)	5,166	0.54	(NA)
1958	2,711	(NA)	5,300	0.51	(NA)
1959	3,161	$3,047	5,893	0.54	0.52
1960	3,233	(NA)	5,835	0.55	(NA)
1961	3,191	(NA)	5,981	0.53	(NA)
1962	3,330	(NA)	6,237	0.53	(NA)
1963	3,465	(NA)	6,548	0.53	(NA)
1964	3,839	3,724	6,858	0.56	0.54
1965	3,994	3,886	7,251	0.55	0.54
1966	4,674	4,507	7,792	0.60	0.58
1967[1]	5,094	4,875	8,234	0.62	0.59
1968	5,590	5,360	8,937	0.63	0.60
1969	6,191	5,999	9,794	0.63	0.61
1970	6,516	6,279	10,236	0.64	0.61
1971	6,714	6,440	10,672	0.63	0.60
1972	7,106	6,864	11,549	0.62	0.59
1973	7,596	7,269	12,595	0.60	0.58

Source: "Median Income of Families: 1950 to 1974," Current Population Reports, Special Studies, Series P-23, No. 54. *The Social and Economic Status of the Black Population in the United States, 1974,* 1975, p. 25. Primary source: U.S. Department of Commerce, Social and Economic Statistics Administration Bureau of the Census. *Notes:* Data for 1959 are from the 1960 census; figures for the remaining years are from Current Population Surveys. NA Not available. The ratio of black to white median family income first became available from this survey in 1964. 1. Revised, based on processing correction.

★ 988 ★

Income/Earnings

Median Family Income by Number Earners, 1967 and 1970-1974

In current dollars.

Number of earners and race of head	1967	1970	1971	1972	1973	1974
BLACK						
All families	$4,875	$6,279	$6,440	$6,864	$7,269	$7,808
No earners	1,991	2,235	2,607	2,696	3,006	3,324
1 earner	3,693	4,844	5,330	5,488	5,726	6,360
2 earners or more	6,482	8,885	9,439	10,639	11,224	12,281
WHITE						
All families	$8,234	$10,236	$10,672	$11,549	$12,595	$13,356
No earners	2,534	3,489	3,809	4,160	4,571	5,197
1 earner	7,247	8,713	9,173	9,969	10,813	11,482
2 earners or more	9,913	12,385	12,998	14,076	15,333	16,838
RATIO: BLACK TO WHITE						
All families	0.59	0.61	0.60	0.59	0.58	0.58
No earners	0.79	0.64	0.68	0.65	0.66	0.64
1 earner	0.51	0.56	0.58	0.55	0.53	0.55
2 earners or more	0.65	0.72	0.73	0.76	0.73	0.73

Source: "Median Income of Families, by Number of Earners: 1967 and 1970 to 1974," Current Population Reports, Special Studies, Series P-23, No. 54. *The Social and Economic Status of the Black Population in the United States, 1974,* 1975, p. 35. Primary source: U.S. Department of Commerce, Social and Economic Statistics Administration, Bureau of the Census.

★ 989 ★

Income/Earnings

Median Family Income by Number Earners, 1968

	All families	No earners	One earner	Two earners	Three earners	Four earners or more
Negro						
Percent	100	10	33	41	10	6
Median income	$5,359	$2,288	$4,151	$7,181	$7,891	$9,360
White						
Percent	100	8	39	39	10	4

[Continued]

★ 989 ★

Median Family Income by Number Earners, 1968

[Continued]

	All families	No earners	One earner	Two earners	Three earners	Four earners or more
Median income	$8,936	$2,940	$7,724	$10,000	$12,658	$14,566
Negro median income as a percent of white	60	78	54	72	62	64

Source: "Influence of Number of Earners on Family Income, 1968," Current Population Reports, Special Studies, Series P-23, No. 29. *The Social and Economic Status of the Black Population in the United States, 1969*, 1969, p. 19. Primary source: U.S. Department of Commerce, Bureau of the Census.

★ 990 ★

Income/Earnings

Median Family Income by Region, 1968 and 1971

Area	Median family income, 1968		Number of families 1972 (millions)		Median family income, 1971	
	Negro	White	Negro	White	Negro	White
United States	$5,359	$8,936	5,157	47,641	$6,440	$10,672
North and West	[1]	[1]	2,581	33,544	7,596	11,057
Northeast	6,460	9,318	1,068	11,447	7,601	11,291
North Central	6,910	9,259	1,057	13,582	7,603	11,019
West	7,506	9,462	456	8,515	7,623	10,803
South	4,278	7,963	2,576	14,097	5,414	9,706

Source: Adapted by the editors from "Median Family Income in 1968, and Negro Family Income, 1965-1968, as a Percent of White, by Region," Current Population Reports, Special Studies, Series P-23, No. 29. *The Social and Economic Status of the Black Population in the United States, 1969*, 1969, p. 15; and "Families by Median Income in 1971, and Negro Family Income as a Percent of White, by Region: 1959, 1966, and 1971," Current Population Reports, Special Studies, Series P-23, No. 42. *The Social and Economic Status of the Black Population in the United States, 1971*, 1972, p. 32. Primary source: U.S. Department of Commerce, Social and Economic Statistics Administration, Bureau of the Census. *Notes:* Number families not reported in 1969 source table. 1. North and West not combined in 1969 source table.

★ 991 ★

Income/Earnings

Median Family Income in Relation to Family Type and Wife's Work Status, 1967 and 1970-1974

[In current dollars]

Type of family and race and head	1967	1970	1971	1972	1973	1974
BLACK						
All families	$4,875	$6,279	$6,440	$6,864	$7,269	$7,808
Male head[1]	5,737	7,766	8,067	9,037	9,549	10,365
Married, wife present	5,808	7,816	8,178	9,166	9,729	10,530
Wife in paid labor force	7,272	9,721	10,274	11,336	12,266	12,982
Wife not in paid labor force	4,662	5,961	6,503	6,900	7,148	7,773
Female head	3,004	3,576	3,645	3,840	4,226	4,465
WHITE						
All families	$8,234	$10,236	$10,672	$11,549	$12,595	$13,356
Male head[1]	8,557	10,697	11,143	12,102	13,253	14,055
Married, wife present	8,588	10,723	11,191	12,137	13,297	14,099
Wife in paid labor force	10,196	12,543	13,098	14,148	15,654	16,825
Wife not in paid labor force	7,743	9,531	9,976	10,806	11,716	12,381
Female head	4,855	5,754	5,842	6,213	6,560	7,363
RATIO: BLACK TO WHITE						
All families	0.59	0.61	0.60	0.59	0.58	0.58
Male head[1]	0.67	0.73	0.72	0.75	0.72	0.74
Married, wife present	0.68	0.73	0.73	0.76	0.73	0.75
Wife in paid labor force	0.71	0.78	0.78	0.80	0.78	0.77
Wife not in paid labor force	0.60	0.63	0.65	0.64	0.61	0.63
Female head	0.62	0.62	0.62	0.62	0.64	0.61

Source: "Median Income of Families, by Type of Family and Labor Force Status of Wife: 1967 and 1970 to 1974," Current Population Reports, Special Studies, Series P-23, No. 54. *The Social and Economic Status of the Black Population in the United States, 1974,* 1974, p. 33. Primary source: U.S. Department of Commerce, Social and Economic Statistics Administration, Bureau of the Census. *Note:* 1. Includes other male heads, not shown separately.

★ 992 ★

Income/Earnings

Money Earned: Family Income in Selected Cities in the Mid 1940s

City or Area	$5,000 and over	$3,000 to $3,999	$2,000 to $2,999	$1,000 to $1,999	Under $1,000	Not Represented
New York	4.7	15.8	35.7	32.8	10.0	1.0
Newark, Northern New Jersey	5.7	22.1	45.0	23.6	-	3.6
SOUTH ATLANTIC - Durham, Winston-Salem, Columbia, Atlanta, Jacksonville, Miami, Tampa	4.8	13.5	26.7	40.9	10.4	3.7
EAST SOUTH CENTRAL- Greenville, Birmingham, Memphis, Meridian, Nashville	4.8	10.1	31.2	43.8	7.7	2.4
WEST SOUTH CENTRAL- New Orleans, Little Rock, San Antonio, Oklahoma City	4.4	9.6	30.0	47.5	8.5	-
EAST NORTH CENTRAL- Detroit, Cleveland, Chicago, Cincinnati	7.2	26.7	44.9	16.2	1.7	3.3
Los Angeles	5.6	23.1	33.1	25.0	6.9	6.3
WEST NORTH CENTRAL- Omaha, Kansas City, St. Louis	6.3	14.8	37.2	38.1	3.8	-
Pittsburgh[1]	1.1	2.6	21.7	59.3	15.3	-
Washington	6.0	27.0	33.8	27.9	5.3	-
Philadelphia	4.0	17.2	32.2	35.0	11.6	-
Baltimore	4.2	20.8	34.5	31.3	9.2	-
Boston	2.0	11.1	37.4	42.4	3.0	4.1

Source: "Income of Negro Families in Some Specific Areas, by Percent" *The Negro Handbook, 1949,* 1949, p. 16. Primary source: Research Company of America, 341 Madison Avenue, New York. Prepared for Interstate United Newspapers, Inc., during 1946, and in similar survey for the Afro-American Newspapers during 1945. Published in *Modern Industry,* issue in March 19, 1948. *Notes:* 1. The Pittsburgh figures were not taken from the survey made by the Research Company of America.

★ 993 ★

Income/Earnings

Money Earned: Income of Urban and Rural Families, by Region, 1946

Total Money Income Level	United States		The Northeastern States		The North Central States		The South		The West	
	White	Nonwhite	White	Nonwhite	White	Nonwhite	White	Nonwhite	White	Nonwhite
Urban and Rural non-farm Number of families and individuals (thousands)	33,368	3,697	11,021	808	10,475	674	7,070	1,994	4,802	221
Percent	100.0	100.0	100.0	100.0	100.0	100.0	100.0	100.0	100.0	100.0

[Continued]

★ 993 ★

Money Earned: Income of Urban and Rural Families, by Region, 1946

[Continued]

Total Money Income Level	United States		The Northeastern States		The North Central States		The South		The West	
	White	Nonwhite	White	Nonwhite	White	Nonwhite	White	Nonwhite	White	Nonwhite
Under $500	6.9	15.5	5.7	9.4	8.5	10.5	7.2	20.1	5.9	10.9
$500 to $999	7.5	15.9	6.0	15.7	7.9	10.8	8.1	18.1	8.7	11.8
$1,000 to $1,499	8.3	16.7	7.1	15.3	8.4	13.1	10.6	18.5	7.7	16.7
$1,500 to $1,999	9.5	15.7	8.8	17.5	8.9	13.1	11.8	16.3	8.7	11.3
$2,000 to $2,499	12.5	12.3	11.6	11.4	12.8	21.4	13.9	9.3	11.8	14.5
$2,500 to $2,999	11.1	8.3	11.5	10.4	11.0	11.9	10.6	6.6	11.0	5.4
$3,000 to $3,499	10.8	5.8	11.2	5.2	10.7	6.1	9.5	4.8	11.9	15.4
$3,500 to $3,999	7.6	3.0	8.3	3.1	7.3	3.7	6.6	2.6	7.5	4.5
$4,000 to $4,499	5.8	2.0	6.7	2.8	5.6	2.4	4.6	1.6	6.3	1.4
$4,500 to $4,999	4.5	1.5	4.7	2.5	4.7	1.9	3.7	0.9	4.8	3.2
$5,000 to $5,999	6.1	1.6	7.1	3.1	5.8	3.3	5.2	0.4	6.0	1.8
$6,000 to $9,999	7.3	1.7	8.7	3.6	6.9	1.9	5.9	0.9	6.8	1.8
$10,000 and over	2.2	0.1	2.5	-	1.5	-	2.2	-	2.7	1.4
Median income (dollars)	2,741	1,562	2,970	1,773	2,657	2,059	2,441	1,318	2,824	1,970

Source: "Percent Distribution of Urban and Rural - nonfarm Families and Individuals, by Total Money Income Level, by Color of Head, for the United States, by Regions: 1946," *The Negro Handbook, 1949,* 1949, p. 15. Primary source: U.S. Bureau of the Census.

★ 994 ★

Income/Earnings

Money Earned: Median Family Income in 1974 Dollars, 1947-1974

[Prior to 1960, excludes Alaska and Hawaii.]

YEAR	ALL RACES Families	WHITE Families	NEGRO AND OTHER RACES Families	NEGRO AND OTHER RACES COMPARED WITH WHITE	
				Ratio[1] Families	Absolute difference in median families
1947	$6,691	$6,970	$3,563	0.51	-$3,407
1950	6,800	7,057	3,828	0.54	-3,229
1955	8,137	8,495	4,685	0.55	-3,810
1960	9,358	9,716	5,379	0.55	-4,337
1965	10,874	11,333	6,242	0.55	-5,091
1970	12,531	13,000	8,275	0.64	-4,725
1972	13,103	13,614	8,376	0.62	-5,238
1973	13,373	13,977	8,429	0.60	-5,548
1974	12,836	13,356	8,265	0.62	-5,091

Source: "Money Income in Constant (1974) Dollars of Families and Individuals, by Race: 1947 to 1974," *Statistical Abstract of the United States, 1975,* p. 391. Primary source: U.S. Bureau of the Census, *Current Population Reports,* series P-60, No. 101, and earlier issues. *Notes:* 1. Ratios may differ from those calculated from current dollar distributors because of interpolation differences introduced in the derivation of constant dollar distributions.

★ 995 ★

Income/Earnings

Money Earned: Median Family Income, by Characteristics of Earners, 1959, 1970, and 1974

[Families and earners as of April 1960, March 1971, and March 1975.]

RACE AND AGE OF HEAD	1959			1970			1974		
	All families	Husband only earner	Husband and wife both earners	All families	Husband only earner	Husband and wife both earners	All families	Husband only earner	Husband and wife both earners
Total white	$5,928	$5,450	$6,984	$10,216	$9,357	$12,348	$13,271	$12,541	$16,553
Under 35 years	5,535	5,233	6,013	9,402	9,065	10,396	12,152	12,031	13,639
14-24 years	4,270	3,715	4,854	7,294	6,395	8,472	9,151	7,759	10,626
25-34 years	5,855	5,516	6,490	10,167	9,695	11,409	13,294	12,789	15,228
35-44 years	6,742	6,193	7,489	11,769	10,797	13,207	15,850	14,463	18,192
45-54 years	6,811	5,653	7,889	12,576	10,010	14,718	17,059	13,556	19,771
55-64 years	5,976	5,076	7,178	10,678	9,152	13,401	14,137	12,694	18,157
65 years and over	3,377	2,764	5,229	5,263	5,740	9,726	7,518	8,350	12,763
Total Negro	$3,010	$3,017	$4,174	$6,278	$6,024	$9,727	$7,807	$8,555	$13,316
Under 35 years	2,972	3,025	3,845	6,103	5,965	9,267	7,151	8,096	12,783
14-24 years	2,291	2,250	(B)	5,012	(B)	7,774	4,790	6,121	8,989
25-34 years	3,234	3,339	4,100	6,604	6,313	9,686	8,621	9,093	14,193
35-44 years	3,639	3,177	4,983	7,568	6,892	10,612	9,045	9,777	13,891
45-54 years	3,323	3,146	4,260	7,357	6,533	10,596	10,068	10,280	15,411
55-64 years	2,900	2,833	3,193	6,437	6,305	8,889	8,218	7,697	11,939
65 years and over	1,755	1,643	(B)	3,281	3,378	(B)	4,874	(B)	(B)
Negro as percent of white	50.8	55.4	59.8	61.5	64.4	78.8	58.8	68.2	80.4
Under 35 years	53.7	57.8	63.9	64.9	65.8	89.1	58.8	67.3	93.7
14-24 years	53.7	60.6	(X)	68.7	(X)	91.8	52.3	78.9	84.9
25-34 years	55.2	60.5	63.2	65.0	65.1	84.9	64.8	71.1	93.2
35-44 years	54.0	51.3	66.5	64.3	63.8	80.4	57.1	67.6	76.4
45-54 years	48.8	55.7	54.0	58.5	65.3	72.0	59.0	75.8	77.9
55-64 years	48.5	55.8	44.5	60.3	68.9	66.3	58.1	60.6	65.8
65 years and over	52.0	59.4	(X)	62.3	58.9	(X)	64.8	(X)	(X)

Source: "Median Money Income of Families—Earnings Status of Husband and Wife, by Race and Age of Head: 1959, 1970, and 1974," *Statistical Abstract of the United States, 1975*, p. 397. *Note:* B Base too small for reliability. X Not applicable.

★ 996 ★

Income/Earnings

Money Earned: Median Income of Husband-Wife and Other Families, in Selected Cities, 1935-36

City and type of family	Black	Native White	Ratio: Black to Native White
HUSBAND-WIFE FAMILIES			
New York, N.Y.	$980	$1,930	0.51
Chicago, Ill.	726	1,687	0.43
Columbus, Ohio	831	1,622	0.51
Atlanta, Ga.	632	1,876	0.34
Columbia, S.C.	576	1,876	0.31
Mobile, Ala.	481	1,419	0.34
OTHER FAMILIES			
Atlanta, Ga.	$332	$940	0.35
Columbia, S.C.	254	1,403	0.18
Mobile, Ala.	301	784	0.38

Source: "Median Income of Black and Native White Families in Selected Cities: 1935-36," *The Social and Economic Status of the Black Population in the United States: An Historical View, 1790-1978*, 1979, p. 30. Primary source: Gunnar Myrdal, et al. *An American Dilemma*. New York: Harper and Brothers, 1944. *Notes:* NA Not available. The 1935-1936 income data from the Department of Labor's Study of Consumer Purchases, presented in *An American Dilemma*, are the earliest data tabulated on Black families. Husband-wife families were designated as "Normal families" in *An American Dilemma*. A "Normal family" was defined as consisting of at least a husband and wife, living together, with or without children.

★ 997 ★

Income/Earnings

Money Earned: Median Income, Median Income Ratio, and Income Overlap of Blacks and Whites, 1947-1974

[Adjusted for price changes in 1974 dollars]

Year	Median Income			Median income ratio		Index of income overlap	
	Black and other races		White	Black and other races to White	Black to White	Black and other races to White	Black to White
	Total	Black					
1947	$3,563	(NA)	$6,970	0.51	(NA)	0.62	(NA)
1948	3,622	(NA)	6,781	0.53	(NA)	0.63	(NA)
1949	3,413	(NA)	6,686	0.51	(NA)	0.62	(NA)
1950	3,828	(NA)	7,057	0.54	(NA)	0.65	(NA)
1951	3,858	(NA)	7,326	0.53	(NA)	0.63	(NA)
1952	4,344	(NA)	7,643	0.57	(NA)	0.62	(NA)
1953	4,547	(NA)	8,110	0.56	(NA)	0.66	(NA)
1954	4,422	(NA)	7,061	0.56	(NA)	0.66	(NA)

[Continued]

★ 997 ★

Money Earned: Median Income, Median Income Ratio, and Income Overlap of Blacks and Whites, 1947-1974

[Continued]

Year	Median Income		White	Median income ratio		Index of income overlap	
	Black and other races			Black and other races to White	Black to White	Black and other races to White	Black to White
	Total	Black					
1955	4,685	(NA)	8,495	0.55	(NA)	0.65	(NA)
1956	4,768	(NA)	9,060	0.53	(NA)	0.64	(NA)
1957	4,843	(NA)	9,051	0.54	(NA)	0.65	(NA)
1958	4,624	(NA)	9,039	0.51	(NA)	0.64	(NA)
1959	5,348	$5,156	9,970	0.54	0.52	0.64	(NA)
1960	5,379	(NA)	9,716	0.55	(NA)	0.68	(NA)
1961	5,260	(NA)	9,859	0.53	(NA)	0.66	(NA)
1962	5,429	(NA)	10,168	0.53	(NA)	0.64	(NA)
1963	5,581	(NA)	10,547	0.53	(NA)	0.65	(NA)
1964	6,102	5,921	10,903	0.56	0.54	0.68	0.68
1965	6,242	6,072	11,333	0.55	0.54	0.67	0.66
1966	7,128	6,850	11,890	0.60	0.58	0.71	0.71
1967	7,524	7,201	12,162	0.62	0.59	0.72	0.69
1968	7,924	7,603	12,668	0.63	0.60	0.73	0.71
1969	8,328	8,074	13,175	0.63	0.61	0.73	0.71
1970	8,275	7,978	13,000	0.64	0.61	0.74	0.72
1971	8,175	7,844	12,995	0.63	0.60	0.74	0.72
1972	8,376	8,094	13,614	0.62	0.59	0.74	0.72
1973	8,429	8,068	13,977	0.60	0.58	0.73	0.71
1974	8,265	7,808	13,356	0.62	0.58	0.74	0.72

Source: "Selected Measures of Family Income: 1947 to 1974," *The Social and Economic Status of the Black Population in the United States: An Historical View, 1790-1978,* 1979, p. 31. Primary source: U.S. Department of Commerce, Bureau of the Census. *Notes:* NA Not available. All income data are from Current Population Survey with the exception of selected 1959 data. The 1959 income data are from the 1960 census. The Index of Income Overlap of White and Black is a statistical measure which summarizes the degree of overlap between the two distributions and is equal to 1.00 when the two distributions are identical.

★ 998 ★

Income/Earnings

Money Earned: Median Income, by Number of Earners, 1967 and 1974

NUMBER OF EARNERS	ALL FAMILIES, MEDIAN FAMILY INCOME (dollars)			FAMILIES WITH HEAD FULL-TIME WORKER[1]						RATIO OF NEGRO TO WHITE	
				Percent of all families			Median family income (dollars)			All families	Families with head full-time worker[1]
	All races	White	Negro	All races	White	Negro	All races	White	Negro		
All families, 1967	7,933	8,234	4,875	67.6	68.8	55.2	9,263	9,495	6,331	0.59	0.67
No earners	2,447	2,534	1,991	0.3	0.3	0.3	(B)	(B)	(B)	0.79	(X)
1 earner	6,980	7,247	3,693	70.3	71.6	53.4	7,854	8,031	4,598	0.51	0.57
2 earners	8,931	9,214	6,275	75.2	76.1	67.3	9,693	9,931	7,043	0.68	0.71
3 earners	11,221	11,590	6,957	79.7	81.5	64.5	11,741	11,987	8,036	0.60	0.67
4 earners or more	13,170	13,673	7,680	79.6	82.6	59.2	13,790	14,106	9,418	0.56	0.67
All families, 1974	12,836	13,356	7,808	62.4	64.1	47.3	16,072	16,467	12,137	0.58	0.74
No earners	4,835	5,197	3,324	0.1	0.1	-	(B)	(B)	(B)	0.64	(X)
1 earner	10,955	11,482	6,360	62.3	64.2	45.3	12,935	13,270	8,708	0.55	0.66
2 earners	14,746	15,055	11,820	73.9	74.9	64.6	16,722	16,986	13,777	0.79	0.81

[Continued]

★ 998 ★

Money Earned: Median Income, by Number of Earners, 1967 and 1974

[Continued]

NUMBER OF EARNERS	ALL FAMILIES, MEDIAN FAMILY INCOME (dollars)			FAMILIES WITH HEAD FULL-TIME WORKER[1]						RATIO OF NEGRO TO WHITE	
				Percent of all families			Median family income (dollars)			All families	Families with head full-time worker[1]
	All races	White	Negro	All races	White	Negro	All races	White	Negro		
3 earners	19,348	19,912	12,862	79.0	80.1	66.1	20,328	20,740	14,503	0.65	0.70
4 earners or more	22,784	23,401	16,648	82.4	84.4	69.5	23,829	24,234	18,838	0.71	0.78

Source: "Median Family Income, by Earners and Race: 1967 and 1974," *Statistical Abstract of the United States, 1975,* p. 396. *Notes:* - Represents zero. B Base less than 75,000. X Not applicable. 1. Employed year-round.

★ 999 ★

Income/Earnings

Money Earned: Percent Distribution of Family Income in 1950-1974 - I

Families as of March of following year. Prior to 1960, excludes Alaska and Hawaii. Based on sample. Includes members of the Armed Forces living off post or with their families on post (in March 1975, about 1,064,000) but excludes all other Armed Forces. Includes small number of families with no money income. Excludes inmates of institutions.

RACE OF HEAD AND YEAR	PERCENT DISTRIBUTION BY INCOME LEVEL						
	Under $1,000	$1,000-$1,999	$2,000-$2,999	$3,000-$3,999	$4,000-$4,999	$5,000-$5,999	$6,000-$6,999
ALL FAMILIES							
1950	11.5	13.2	17.8	20.7	13.6	9.0	5.2
1955	7.7	9.9	11.0	14.6	15.4	12.7	9.5
1960	5.0	8.0	8.7	9.8	10.5	12.9	10.8
1965	2.9	6.0	7.2	7.7	7.9	9.3	9.5
1970	1.6	3.0	4.3	5.1	5.3	5.8	6.0
1971	1.5	2.6	4.2	4.8	5.4	5.7	5.5
1972	1.3	2.2	3.7	4.5	4.9	5.0	5.2
1973	1.1	1.8	3.1	4.1	4.5	4.6	4.8
1974	1.3	1.3	2.7	3.6	4.1	4.4	4.4
WHITE							
1950	10.0	12.2	17.3	21.3	14.4	9.6	5.5
1955	6.6	8.7	10.4	14.3	16.0	13.4	9.9
1960	4.1	6.9	8.1	9.4	10.5	13.3	11.2
1965	2.5	5.2	6.3	6.9	7.6	9.3	9.8
1970	1.4	2.4	3.7	4.6	4.9	5.5	5.8
1971	1.3	2.1	3.5	4.3	5.0	5.4	5.4
1972	1.1	1.7	3.1	4.1	4.5	4.7	5.0
1973	1.0	1.3	2.6	3.5	4.1	4.3	4.5
1974	1.1	1.0	2.2	3.1	3.7	4.2	4.2
NEGRO AND OTHER							
1950	28.1	25.3	23.5	13.5	4.3	1.9	1.5
1955	19.0	20.7	17.6	17.2	11.1	5.8	4.8
1960	13.4	18.3	14.8	14.0	10.4	8.7	6.7

[Continued]

★ 999 ★

Money Earned: Percent Distribution of Family Income in 1950-1974 - I
[Continued]

RACE OF HEAD AND YEAR	PERCENT DISTRIBUTION BY INCOME LEVEL						
	Under $1,000	$1,000-$1,999	$2,000-$2,999	$3,000-$3,999	$4,000-$4,999	$5,000-$5,999	$6,000-$6,999
1965	7.1	13.6	14.6	14.8	10.8	9.5	6.8
1970	3.4	7.7	9.0	8.8	8.2	9.0	7.4
1971	2.9	6.6	9.9	8.7	8.9	8.1	7.1
1972	2.7	6.3	8.7	9.0	8.5	7.5	6.5
1973	2.5	5.3	7.6	8.4	8.3	7.2	6.8
1974	2.2	4.4	7.0	8.2	7.8	6.3	6.7

Source: "Money Income—Percent Distribution of Families, by Income Level, by Race of Head: 1950 to 1974," *Statistical Abstract of the United States, 1975*, p. 390.

★ 1000 ★

Income/Earnings

Money Earned: Percent Distribution of Family Income in 1950-1974 - II

Families as of March of following year. Prior to 1960, excludes Alaska and Hawaii. Based on sample. Includes members of the Armed Forces living off post or with their families with no money income. Excludes inmates of institutions.

RACE OF HEAD AND YEAR	PERCENT DISTRIBUTION BY INCOME LEVEL				MEDIAN	
	$7,000-$9,999	$10,000-$14,999	$15,000-$24,999	$25,000 and over	Income	Index (1950=100)
ALL FAMILIES						
1950	5.8	3.3[2]	3.3[2]	3.3[2]	3,319	100
1955	12.9	4.8	1.4[1]	1.4[1]	4,421	133
1960	20.0	10.6	3.7[1]	3.7[1]	5,620	169
1965	24.2	17.7	7.6[1]	7.6[1]	6,957	210
1970	19.9	26.8	22.3[1]	22.3[1]	9,867	297
1971	18.5	26.9	19.5	5.3	10,285	310
1972	16.8	26.1	23.0	7.3	11,116	335
1973	14.9	25.5	26.2	9.3	12,051	363
1974	13.8	24.3	28.3	11.5	12,836	387
WHITE						
1950	6.1	3.5[2]	3.5[2]	3.5[2]	3,445	100
1955	13.9	5.3	1.5[1]	1.5[1]	4,605	134
1960	21.3	11.2	4.1[1]	4.1[1]	5,835	169
1965	25.5	18.8	8.3[1]	8.3[1]	7,251	210
1970	20.1	27.9	23.7[1]	23.7[1]	10,236	297
1971	18.6	28.0	20.6	5.8	10,672	310
1972	16.7	27.0	24.2	8.0	11,549	335
1973	14.6	26.3	27.6	10.0	12,595	366
1974	13.5	25.1	29.7	12.4	13,356	388

[Continued]

★ 1000 ★

Money Earned: Percent Distribution of Family Income in 1950-1974 - II
[Continued]

| RACE OF HEAD AND YEAR | PERCENT DISTRIBUTION BY INCOME LEVEL | | | | MEDIAN | |
	$7,000-$9,999	$10,000-$14,999	$15,000-$24,999	$25,000 and over	Income	Index (1950=100)
NEGRO AND OTHER						
1950	1.7	0.3[3]	0.3[2]	0.3[2]	1,869	100
1955	3.1	0.6	(Z)[1]	(Z)[1]	2,549	136
1960	8.7	4.3	0.6[1]	0.6[1]	3,233	173
1965	13.7	7.6	1.4[1]	1.4[1]	3,994	214
1970	18.2	17.3	10.9[1]	10.9[1]	6,516	349
1971	17.8	17.9	10.5	1.7	6,714	359
1972	17.1	18.1	13.2	2.4	7,106	380
1973	16.9	19.1	14.4	3.5	7,596	406
1974	16.2	19.0	17.9	4.5	8,265	442

Source: "Money Income—Percent Distribution of Families, by Income Level, by Race of Head: 1950 to 1974," Statistical Abstract of the United States, 1975, p. 390. Notes: Z Less than 0.05 percent. 1. Data includes income level $10,000 and over. 2. Data includes income level $15,000 and over.

★ 1001 ★

Income/Earnings

Money Earned: Percent Distribution of Family Income in 1974 Dollars, 1970-1974

[Prior to 1960, excludes Alaska and Hawaii.]

| ITEM AND INCOME LEVEL | WHITE | | | NEGRO AND OTHER RACES | | |
	1970	1973	1974	1970	1973	1974
FAMILIES						
Under $3,000	5.1	4.1	4.3	14.5	13.3	13.5
$3,000-$4,999	6.7	6.6	6.8	14.0	15.1	16.0
$5,000-$6,999	8.1	7.7	8.4	13.6	13.2	13.1
$7,000-$9,999	13.9	12.9	13.5	17.6	16.5	16.1
$10,000-$11,999	11.0	9.8	10.5	9.3	9.2	8.3
$12,000-$14,999	15.7	14.8	14.6	11.0	10.8	10.7
$15,000-$24,999	29.1	31.1	29.7	16.2	17.1	17.9
$25,000 and over	10.3	13.1	12.4	3.7	4.8	4.4

Source: "Money Income—Percent Distribution of Families and Individuals, by Income Level and Race, in Constant (1974) Dollars: 1950 to 1974," Statistical Abstract of the United States, 1975, p. 390. Primary source: Bureau of the Census; Current Population Reports, Series P-60, No. 101.

★ 1002 ★

Income/Earnings

Money Earned: Percent Distribution of Family Income in Constant 1968 Dollars, 1950-1968

[Prior to 1960, excludes Alaska and Hawaii.]

ITEM AND INCOME LEVEL	WHITE					NEGRO AND OTHER RACES				
	1950	1955	1960	1965	1968[1]	1950	1955	1960	1965	1968[1]
Families	100.0	100.0	100.0	100.0	100.0	100.0	100.0	100.0	100.0	100.0
Under $3,000	23.4	18.4	15.5	12.1	8.9	55.4	45.7	40.5	31.4	22.8
$3,000-$4,000	26.8	19.4	15.5	12.9	11.0	29.7	26.9	22.7	24.7	21.9
$5,000-$6,999	22.9	23.3	20.6	16.1	14.3	9.2	15.4	16.1	16.7	16.5
$7,000-$9,999	16.6	23.1	24.5	25.6	24.0	3.7	9.4	12.9	15.3	17.7
$10,000-$14,999	10.2[1]	11.8	16.8	21.9	26.1	2.1[1]	2.3	6.3	9.4	14.7
$15,000 and over	10.2[1]	4.1	7.2	11.4	15.7	2.1[1]	0.3	1.6	2.6	6.3
Median income	$4,985	$5,991	$6,857	$7,995	$8,936	$2,704	$3,320	$3,794	$4,419	$5,590
Ratio, Negro and other to white	(X)	(X)	(X)	(X)	(X)	0.54	0.55	0.55	0.55	0.63

Source: "Money Income—Percent Distribution of Families and Unrelated Individuals, by Income Level and Race, in Constant (1968) Dollars: 1950 to 1968," *Statistical Abstract of the United States, 1970*, p. 322. Primary source: Dept. of Commerce, Bureau of the Census; *Current Population Reports*, Series P-60, and unpublished data. *Notes:* - Represents zero. X Not applicable. 1. Data includes income level $10,000 and over.

★ 1003 ★

Income/Earnings

Money Earned: Percent Distribution of Family Income, by Region, 1966

INCOME LEVEL	FAMILIES							UNRELATED INDIVIDUALS		
	All races	United States		North and West		South		All races	White	Negro
		White	Negro	White	Negro	White	Negro			
Under $1,000	3.0	2.6	7.6	1.9	3.2	4.1	11.3	23.6	22.4	31.3
$1,000 to $1,999	6.1	5.2	14.5	4.1	7.4	8.1	20.6	24.7	24.5	27.4
$2,000 to $2,999	7.4	6.6	15.2	5.9	11.6	8.3	18.3	12.6	12.4	12.2
$3,000 to $3,999	7.8	7.2	14.5	6.6	13.3	8.6	15.6	9.2	9.3	8.4
$4,000 to $4,999	8.0	7.8	10.7	7.1	11.4	9.4	10.2	8.0	8.0	7.2
$5,000 to $5,999	9.3	9.4	9.2	9.1	11.1	10.1	7.5	7.0	7.1	5.9
$6,000 to $6,999	9.3	9.5	6.9	9.5	8.6	9.6	5.4	4.9	5.1	3.5
$7,000 to $9,999	24.1	25.3	13.1	26.2	20.0	22.6	7.2	6.9	7.4	3.1
$10,000 and over	24.9	26.6	8.3	29.3	13.3	19.1	4.0	3.3	3.7	0.9
Median income[1]	$6,882	$7,170	$3,874	$7,546	$5,278	$6,141	$2,988	$2,110	$2,199	$1,555
Percent with income less than $3,000	16.5	14.4	37.3	11.9	22.2	20.5	50.2	60.9	59.3	71.0

Source: "Money Income—Percent Distribution of Families and Unrelated Individuals, by 1965 Income Levels, by Race and Region: 1966," *Statistical Abstract of the United States, 1967*, p. 335. Primary source: Dept. of Commerce, Bureau of the Census, *Current Population Reports*, Series P-20, forthcoming issue and Series P-60, No. 51.

★ 1004 ★

Income/Earnings

Money Earned: Share of Income, in Percentages, of Top 5% and in Each Fifth of Black and White Families, 1947-1974

Year and race of head	Number of families (thousands)	Lowest fifth	Second fifth	Middle fifth	Fourth fifth	Highest fifth	Top 5 percent	Mean income
BLACK AND OTHER RACES								
1947	3,117	4.3	10.4	16.1	23.8	45.3	16.4	$1,986
1953	(NA)	3.9	10.7	17.3	25.0	43.1	15.1	2,872
1959	4,239	4.0	9.7	16.6	25.3	44.4	15.6	3,463
1964	4,754	4.4	10.5	16.2	24.2	44.7	16.9	4,726
1969	5,215	4.8	10.9	16.9	24.7	42.7	15.2	7,255
1974	6,262	4.6	10.0	16.2	25.0	44.2	15.9	10,192
WHITE								
1947	34,120	5.5	12.2	17.0	22.9	42.5	17.4	$3,697
1953	(NA)	5.0	12.9	18.0	23.6	40.4	15.6	4,883
1959	40,872	5.4	12.7	17.8	23.6	40.5	15.7	6,235
1964	43,081	5.5	12.4	17.8	23.8	40.5	15.7	7,625
1969	46,022	5.9	12.7	17.8	23.5	40.1	15.4	10,953
1974	49,451	5.8	12.3	17.6	23.8	40.5	15.1	15,047

Source: "Percentage Share of Aggregate Income Received by Each Fifth and Top 5 Percent of Black and Other Races and White Families, for Selected Years: 1947 to 1974," *The Social and Economic Status of the Black Population in the United States: An Historical View, 1790-1978,* 1979, p. 34. Primary source: U.S. Department of Commerce. Bureau of the Census. *Note:* NA Not available.

★ 1005 ★

Income/Earnings

Money Earned: Upper Limit of Income in Each Fifth and Mean Income of Top 5% of Black and White Families, 1947-1974

[In current dollars. Families as of the following year]

Year and race of head	Number of families (thousands)	Income at selected positions					Mean income
		Upper limit of each fifth				Top 5 percent	
		Lowest	Second	Middle	Fourth		
BLACK AND OTHER RACES							
1947	3,117	$760	$1,319	$1,905	$2,921	$5,301	$1,986
1953	(NA)	1,038	2,033	2,991	4,359	7,066	2,872
1959	4,239	1,207	2,180	3,567	5,300	8,722	3,463
1964	4,754	1,857	3,100	4,630	7,000	11,400	4,726
1969	5,215	2,959	5,000	7,356	10,920	17,238	7,255
1974	6,262	3,798	6,548	10,200	15,868	24,267	10,192

[Continued]

★ 1005 ★

Money Earned: Upper Limit of Income in Each Fifth and Mean Income of Top 5% of Black and White Families, 1947-1974

[Continued]

Year and race of head	Number of families (thousands)	Income at selected positions					Mean income
		Upper limit of each fifth				Top 5 percent	
		Lowest	Second	Middle	Fourth		
WHITE							
1947	34,120	$1,756	$2,692	$3,589	$5,052	$8,304	$3,697
1953	(NA)	2,354	3,808	5,036	6,727	10,437	4,883
1959	40,872	3,000	4,872	6,300	8,600	13,050	6,235
1964	43,081	3,586	5,800	7,800	10,500	16,056	7,625
1969	46,022	5,360	8,375	11,090	15,021	23,298	10,953
1974	49,451	7,100	11,266	15,307	21,000	32,586	15,047
BLACK AND OTHER RACES TO WHITE							
1947	0.09	0.43	0.49	0.53	0.58	0.64	0.54
1953	(NA)	0.44	0.53	0.59	0.65	0.68	0.59
1959	0.10	0.40	0.45	0.57	0.62	0.67	0.56
1964	0.11	0.52	0.53	0.59	0.67	0.71	0.62
1969	0.11	0.55	0.60	0.66	0.73	0.74	0.66
1974	0.13	0.53	0.58	0.67	0.76	0.74	0.68

Source: "Income at Selected Positions Received by Each Fifth and Top 5 Percent of Black and Other Races and White Families, for Selected Years: 1947 to 1974," *The Social and Economic Status of the Black Population in the United States: An Historical View, 1790-1978*, p. 1979, p. 35. Primary source: U.S. Department of Commerce. Bureau of the Census. *Note:* NA Not available.

★ 1006 ★

Income/Earnings

Percentage Distribution of Family Income, 1947, 1960, and 1968

In 1968 dollars.

	Negro and other races			White		
	1947	1960	1968	1947	1960	1968
Number of families (in millions)	3,717	4,333	5,075	34,120	41,123	45,440
Percent	100	100	100	100	100	100
Under $3,000	60	41	23	23	16	9
$3,000 to $4,999	23	23	22	28	16	11
$5,000 to $6,999	9	16	17	23	21	14
$7,000 to $9,999	5	13	18	15	26	24
$10,000 to $14,999	3[1]	6	15	11[1]	17	26
$15,000 and over	3[1]	2	6	11[1]	7	16
Median income	$2,514	$3,794	$5,590	$4,916	$6,857	$8,937

[Continued]

★ 1006 ★

Percentage Distribution of Family Income, 1947, 1960, and 1968
[Continued]

	Negro and other races			White		
	1947	1960	1968	1947	1960	1968
Net change, 1947-1968						
Number	(X)	(X)	$3,076	(X)	(X)	$4,020
Percent	(X)	(X)	122.4	(X)	(X)	81.8

Source: "Distribution of Families by Income in 1947, 1960, and 1968," Current Population Reports, Special Studies, Series P-23, No. 29, *The Social and Economic Status of the Black Population in the United States, 1969*, 1969, p. 16. Primary source: U.S. Department of Commerce, Bureau of the Census. *Notes:* X Not applicable. Number includes $10,000 and over.

★ 1007 ★

Income/Earnings

Percentage of High-Range ($10,000 or more and $15,000 or more) Income Families by Region, 1965, 1970, and 1974

Adjusted for price change in 1974 dollars. Incomes of $10,000 and $15,000 in 1974 were equivalent in purchasing power to about $6,400 and $9,600, respectively, in 1965.

Year and area	Black		White	
	Income of $10,000 or more	Income of $15,000 or more	Income of $10,000 or more	Income of $15,000 or more
UNITED STATES				
1965	25	9	58	30
1970	38	18	66	39
1974	38	19	67	42
SOUTH				
1965	14	4	48	22
1970	28	13	60	34
1974	31	13	62	36
NORTH AND WEST				
1965	38	14	62	33
1970	49	24	69	42
1974	47	26	70	45

Source: "Percent of Families with Incomes of $10,000 or More and $15,000 or More, by Region: 1965, 1970, and 1974," Current Population Reports, Special Studies, Series P-23, No. 54. *The Social and Economic Status of the Black Population in the United States, 1974*, 1975, p. 27. Primary source: U.S. Department of Commerce, Social and Economic Statistics Administration, Bureau of the Census.

★ 1008 ★

Income/Earnings

Regional (1966-1970) and National (1947-1970) Percent of Families with Income of $10,000 or More

Adjusted for price changes, in 1970 dollars. A $10,000 income in 1970 was equivalent in purchasing power to about $5,800 in 1947.

Area and year	Negro and other races	White	Area and year	Negro and other races	White
UNITED STATES			UNITED STATES		
1947	4	15	1966	20	45
1948	2	13	1967	23	47
1949	2	13	1968	26	50
1950	3	14	1969	27	53
1951	2	14	1970	28	52
1952	3	16			
1953	6	19	SOUTH		
1954	4	19	1966	10	36
1955	4	22	1967	12	40
1956	6	25	1968	15	42
			1969	17	45
1957	7	24	1970	18	45
1958	7	25			
1959	9	29	NORTH AND		
1960	11	31	WEST		
1961	12	32	1966	26	48
1962	11	34	1967	33	50
1963	12	37	1968	36	53
1964	15	39	1969	37	56
1965	16	41	1970	38	54

Source: "Percent of Families with Income of $10,000 or More, 1947 to 1970, and by Regions: 1966 to 1970," Current Population Reports, Special Studies, Series P-23, No. 42. *The Social and Economic Status of the Black Population in the United States, 1971*, 1972, p. 31. Primary source: U.S. Department of Commerce, Social and Economic Statistics Administration, Bureau of the Census.

★ 1009 ★

Income/Earnings

Relationships: Black Median Family Income as Percent of White Median Family Income by Region and Age of Family Head, 1959, 1969, 1970, and 1973

Area and year	All families		Husband-wife families	
	Total	Head under 35 years	Total	Head under 35 years
UNITED STATES				
1959	51	54	57	62
1969	61	66	72	80
1970	61	65	73	82
1973	58	62	74	88
NORTH AND WEST				
1959	71	68	76	78
1969	73	74	86	91
1970	74	70	88	96
1973	65	61	86	93
SOUTH				
1959	46	50	50	55
1969	57	62	65	73
1970	57	62	66	74
1973	56	66	67	87

Source: "Median Family Income in 1959, 1969, 1970, and 1973 for All Black Families and Black Husband-Wife Families as a Percent of Corresponding White Families by Age of Head and Region," Current Population Reports, Special Studies, Series P-23, No. 54. *The Social and Economic Status of the Black Population in the United States, 1974,* 1975, p. 37. Primary source: U.S. Department of Commerce, Social and Economic Statistics Administration, Bureau of the Census.

★ 1010 ★

Income/Earnings

Relationships: Black Median Family Income as Percent of White Median Family Income by Region, 1959 and 1965-1971

Area	Negro income as a percent of white						
	1959	1965	1966	1967	1968	1970	1971
United States	51	54	58	59	60	61	60
North and West	71	[1]	71	[1]	[1]	74	69
Northeast	69	64	67	66	71	70	67
North Central	74	74	74	78	75	73	69

[Continued]

★ 1010 ★

Relationships: Black Median Family Income as Percent of White Median Family Income by Region, 1959 and 1965-1971
[Continued]

Area	Negro income as a percent of white						
	1959	1965	1966	1967	1968	1970	1971
West	72	69	72	74	80	77	71
South	51	49	51	54	54	57	56

Source: Adapted by the editors from "Median Family Income in 1968, and Negro Family Income, 1965-1968, as a Percent of White, by Region," Current Population Reports, Special Studies, Series P-23, No. 29, *The Social and Economic Status of the Black Population in the United States, 1969*, 1969, p. 15; and "Families by Median Income in 1971, and Negro Family Income as a Percent of White, by region: 1959, 1966, 1970, and 1971," Current Population Reports, Special Studies, Series P-23, No. 42. *The. Social and Economic Status of the Black Population in the United States, 1971*, 1972, p. 32. Primary source: U.S. Department of Commerce, Social and Economic Statistics Administration, Bureau of the Census. *Note:* 1. North and West not combined in 1969 source table.

★ 1011 ★

Income/Earnings

Relationships: Income and College Enrollment in Families with College-Age (18-24) Members, 1971

Enrollment status and race[1]	Total[2] (thousands)	Percent of total				
		Under $3,000	$3,000 to $9,999	$10,000 and over		
				Total	$10,000 to $14,999	$15,000
NEGRO						
Enrolled in college	408	12	60	27	16	11
Not enrolled in college	1,102	25	59	16	11	6
High school graduate	635	21	60	19	12	7
Not high school graduate	467	31	57	12	8	4
WHITE						
Enrolled in college	3,899	2	27	71	31	41
Not enrolled in college	5,053	7	43	49	29	20
High school graduate	3,970	5	39	56	32	24
Not high school graduate	1,082	18	58	24	17	7

Source: "Family Members 18 to 24 Years Old, by College Enrollment Status and Family Income: 1971," Current Population Reports, Special Studies, Series P-23, No. 42. *The Social and Economic Status of the Black Population in the United States, 1971*, 1972, p. 87. Primary source: U.S. Department of Commerce, Social and Economic Statistics Administration, Bureau of the Census. *Notes:* 1. Excludes family heads and wives and other family members who are married, spouse present. 2. Based on persons reporting on family income.

★ 1012 ★

Income/Earnings

Relationships: Income and College Enrollment in Families with College-Age (18-24) Members, 1974

Enrollment status and race	Total reporting on family income	Family income in 1973				
		Under $5,000	$5,000 to $9,999	$10,000 and over		
				Total	$10,000 to $14,999	$15,000 and over
BLACK						
Total, 18 to 24 years (thousands)	1,653	668	525	463	270	193
Percent	100	100	100	100	100	100
Enrolled in college	25	17	30	33	26	42
Not enrolled in college	75	83	70	67	74	58
High school graduate	46	37	49	54	56	50
Not high school graduate	29	46	21	14	18	8
WHITE						
Total, 18 to 24 years (thousands)	9,320	855	1,702	6,760	2,422	4,338
Percent	100	100	100	100	100	100
Enrolled in college	39	17	27	45	37	50
Not enrolled in college	61	83	73	55	63	50
High school graduate	48	44	53	47	52	45
Not high school graduate	13	39	21	7	11	5

Source: "Family Members 18 to 24 Years Old, by College Enrollment Status and Family Income: 1974," Current Population Reports, Special Studies, Series P-23, No. 54. *The Social and Economic Status of the Black Population in the United States, 1974,* 1975, p. 95. Primary source: U.S. Department of Commerce, Social and Economic Statistics Administration, Bureau of the Census. *Notes:* Universe includes only persons reporting on family income, and excludes family heads, wives, and other family members who are married, spouse present.

★ 1013 ★

Income/Earnings

Relationships: Mean Family Income of Families Above and Below Poverty Level, by Sex of Head, 1973

[Families as of March 1974.]

TYPE OF INCOME	ALL FAMILIES			FAMILIES, MALE HEAD			FAMILIES, FEMALE HEAD		
	Total	Below low income level	Above low income level	Total	Below low income level	Above low income level	Total	Below low income level	Above low income level
Mean income, dollars	13,622	2,616	14,680	14,524	2,672	15,209	7,228	2,549	9,453
White, dollars	14,163	2,445	14,988	14,841	2,524	15,436	8,003	2,311	9,582
Negro, dollars	8,807	2,975	11,083	10,646	3,200	12,001	5,236	2,847	7,895
Total families, 1,000	55,053	4,828	50,225	48,249	2,635	45,614	6,804	2,193	4,611

Source: "Families, by Low Income Status, and Type of Income: 1973," *Statistical Abstract of the United States, 1975*, p. 403. Primary source: U.S. Bureau of the Census, *Current Population Reports*, series P-60, Nos. 95 and 98. *Notes:* - Represents zero. 1. Some families receive more than one type of income. 2. Unemployment and workmen's compensation, government employees pensions, and veteran's payments. 3. Includes annuities.

★ 1014 ★
Income/Earnings

Relationships: Median Black Family Income, by Family Type and Wife's Earning Status, 1964, 1969, and 1974

[Median Income]

Income (Adjusted in 1974 dollars).

Year	Median income
All families	
1964	$5,921
1969	$8,074
1974	$7,808
Husband-wife families, wife in paid labor force	
1964	$8,631
1969	$12,287
1974	$12,982
Husband-wife families, wife not in paid labor force	
1964	$5,803
1969	$7,549
1974	$7,773
Families maintained by a woman, no husband present	
1964	$3,634

[Continued]

★ 1014 ★

Relationships: Median Black Family Income, by Family Type and Wife's Earning Status, 1964, 1969, and 1974

[Continued]

Year	Median income
1969	$4,494
1974	$4,465

Source: "Median Income of Black Families, by Type of Family and Labor Force Status of Wife: 1964, 1969, and 1974," *The Social and Economic Status of the Black Population in the United States: An Historical View, 1790-1978*, 1979, p. 23. Primary source: U.S. Department of Commerce, Bureau of the Census. *The Social and Economic Status of the Black Population in the United States: An Historical View, 1790-1978*. Current Population Reports. Special Studies, Series P-23, No. 80. Washington, D.C.: Government Printing Office, 1979.

★ 1015 ★

Income/Earnings

Relationships: Median Family Income in One- and Two-Earner Families by Region, 1970 and 1973

Race and earnings status of husband and wife	Total			Head under 35 years old		
	United States	North and West	South	United States	North and West	South
1970						
Black, total[1]	$7,816	$9,749	$6,427	$8,032	$9,560	$6,788
Husband only earner	6,024	7,329	4,370	5,965	7,104	5,196
Husband and wife both earners	9,727	11,725	7,773	9,267	11,045	7,464
White, total[1]	10,662	11,043	9,700	9,796	10,002	9,229
Husband only earner	9,357	9,680	8,520	9,065	9,373	8,210
Husband and wife both earners	12,348	12,798	11,276	10,396	10,578	9,948
Black as a percent of white						
Total[1]	73	88	66	82	96	74
Husband only earner	64	76	51	66	76	63
Husband and wife both earners	79	92	69	89	104	75
1973						
Black, total[1]	$9,729	$11,699	$8,063	$10,642	$11,653	$9,731
Husband only earner	7,345	8,402	5,960	7,942	8,556	6,412
Husband and wife both earners	12,281	15,238	10,216	11,873	13,235	10,628
White, total[1]	13,176	13,679	12,124	12,166	12,541	11,190
Husband only earner	11,764	12,211	10,603	11,014	11,629	9,845
Husband and wife both earners	15,352	15,894	14,192	12,962	13,332	12,180

[Continued]

★ 1015 ★

Relationships: Median Family Income in One- and Two-Earner Families by Region, 1970 and 1973

[Continued]

Race and earnings status of husband and wife	Total			Head under 35 years old		
	United States	North and West	South	United States	North and West	South
Black as a percent of white						
Total[1]	74	86	67	88	93	87
Husband only earner	62	69	56	72	74	65
Husband and wife both earners	80	92	72	92	99	87

Source: "Median Income in 1970 and 1973 of Husband-Wife Families, by Age of Head, Earnings Status of Husband and Wife, and Region," Current Population Reports, Special Studies, Series P-23, No. 54. *The Social and Economic Status of the Black Population in the United States, 1974*, 1975, p. 38. Primary source: U.S. Department of Commerce, Social and Economic Statistics Administration, Bureau of the Census. *Note:* 1. Includes other combinations not shown separately.

★ 1016 ★

Income/Earnings

Relationships: Percent Distribution of Family Income, 1947-1968 - I

[Families as of March of following year. Prior to 1960, excludes Alaska and Hawaii. Includes members of the Armed Forces living off post or with their families on post but excludes all other Armed Forces. Includes small number of families with no money income].

RACE OF HEAD AND YEAR	Total	INCOME LEVEL (percent distribution)					
		Under $1,000	$1,000-$1,999	$2,000-$2,999	$3,000-$3,999	$4,000-$4,999	$5,000-$5,999
ALL FAMILIES[1]							
1947	100.0	10.8	16.6	22.0	19.7	11.6	7.7
1950	100.0	11.5	13.2	17.8	20.7	13.6	9.0
1955	100.0	7.7	9.9	11.0	14.6	15.4	12.7
1960	100.0	5.0	8.0	8.7	9.8	10.5	12.9
1965	100.0	2.9	6.0	7.2	7.7	7.9	9.3
1967	100.0	2.1	4.4	6.0	6.3	6.5	7.8
1968	100.0	1.8	3.4	5.1	6.1	6.0	6.9
WHITE FAMILIES[1]							
1947	100.0	9.0	14.9	22.3	20.8	12.4	8.1
1950	100.0	10.0	12.2	17.3	21.3	14.4	9.6
1955	100.0	6.6	8.7	10.4	14.3	16.0	13.4
1960	100.0	4.1	6.9	8.1	9.4	10.5	13.3
1965	100.0	2.5	5.2	6.3	6.9	7.6	9.3
1967	100.0	1.8	3.8	5.2	5.8	6.1	7.6
1968	100.0	1.5	2.9	4.5	5.4	5.6	6.7

[Continued]

★ 1016 ★

Relationships: Percent Distribution of Family Income, 1947-1968 - I
[Continued]

RACE OF HEAD AND YEAR	INCOME LEVEL (percent distribution)						
	Total	Under $1,000	$1,000-$1,999	$2,000-$2,999	$3,000-$3,999	$4,000-$4,999	$5,000-$5,999
NEGRO AND OTHER FAMILIES							
1947	100.0	28.8	33.5	18.8	8.4	4.4	3.1
1950	100.0	28.1	25.3	23.5	13.5	4.3	1.9
1955	100.0	19.0	20.7	17.6	17.2	11.1	5.8
1960	100.0	13.4	18.3	14.8	14.0	10.4	8.7
1965	100.0	7.1	13.6	14.6	14.8	10.8	9.5
1967	100.0	4.9	9.4	12.8	11.5	10.0	9.7
1968	100.0	4.1	8.5	10.2	12.0	10.0	8.8

Source: "Money Income—Percent Distribution of Families, by Income Level, by Race of Head: 1947 to 1968," *Statistical Abstract of the United States, 1970*, p. 322. *Note:* 1. Beginning 1967, data based on revised methodology.

★ 1017 ★

Income/Earnings

Relationships: Percent Distribution of Family Income, 1947-1968 - II

[Families as of March of following year. Prior to 1960, excludes Alaska and Hawaii. Includes members of the Armed Forces living off post or with their families on post but excludes all other Armed Forces. Includes small number of families with no money income].

RACE OF HEAD AND YEAR	INCOME LEVEL (percent distribution)				MEDIAN	
	$6,000-$6,999	$7,000-$9,999	$10,000-$14,999	$15,000 and over	Income	Index (1947=100)
ALL FAMILIES[1]						
1947	8.9[3]	8.9[3]	2.7[2]	2.7[2]	$3,031	100
1950	5.2	5.8	3.3[3]	3.3[2]	3,319	110
1955	9.5	12.9	4.8	1.4	4,421	146
1960	10.8	20.0	10.6	3.7	5,620	185
1965	9.5	24.2	17.7	7.6	6,957	230
1967	8.3	24.3	22.4	12.0	7,974	263
1968	7.6	23.4	25.0	14.7	8,632	285
WHITE FAMILIES[1]						
1947	9.5[3]	9.5[3]	3.0[2]	3.0[2]	3,157	100
1950	5.5	6.1	3.5[2]	3.5[2]	3,445	109
1955	9.9	13.9	5.3	1.5	4,605	146
1960	11.2	21.3	11.2	4.1	5,835	185
1965	9.8	25.5	18.8	8.3	7,251	230
1967	8.4	25.1	23.6	12.9	8,274	262

[Continued]

★ 1017 ★

Relationships: Percent Distribution of Family Income, 1947-1968 - II

[Continued]

RACE OF HEAD AND YEAR	INCOME LEVEL (percent distribution)				MEDIAN	
	$6,000-$6,999	$7,000-$9,999	$10,000-$14,999	$15,000 and over	Income	Index (1947=100)
1968	7.6	24.0	26.2	15.7	8,937	283
NEGRO AND OTHER FAMILIES						
1947	3.0[3]	3.0[3]	0.1[2]	0.1[2]	1,614	100
1950	1.5	1.7	0.3[2]	0.3[2]	1,869	116
1955	4.8	3.1	0.6	(Z)	2,549	158
1960	6.7	8.7	4.3	0.6	3,233	200
1965	6.8	13.7	7.6	1.4	3,994	247
1967	8.0	16.9	11.7	5.0	5,141	319
1968	7.7	17.6	14.7	6.3	5,590	346

Source: "Money Income—Percent Distribution of Families, by Income Level, by Race of Head: 1947 to 1968," *Statistical Abstract of the United States, 1970,* p. 322. *Notes:* Z Less than 0.05 percent. 1. Beginning 1967, data based on revised methodology. 2. Data includes income level $10,000 and over. 3. Data includes income level from $6,000 to $7,000.

★ 1018 ★

Income/Earnings

Relationships: Percentage Distribution of Family Income, By Region, 1974

[As of March 1975]

RACE AND REGION	Number of families (1,000)	PERCENT DISTRIBUTUION, BY INCOME LEVEL										Median income
		Under $1,000	$1,000-$1,999	$2,000-$2,999	$3,000-$3,999	$4,000-$4,999	$5,000-$6,999	$7,000-$9,999	$10,000-$14,999	$15,000-$24,999	$25,000 and over	
All families[1]	55,712	1.3	1.3	2.7	3.6	4.1	8.8	13.8	24.3	28.3	11.5	$12,836
White	49,451	1.1	1.0	2.2	3.1	3.7	8.4	13.5	25.1	29.7	12.4	13,356
Northeast	11,447	0.8	0.6	1.5	3.0	3.2	7.0	13.0	25.0	31.7	14.2	14,164
North Central	13,827	0.9	0.7	1.7	2.4	3.1	7.8	12.4	26.0	32.1	12.8	14,017
South	15,147	1.5	1.5	3.0	3.7	4.5	9.4	14.7	25.4	25.7	10.4	12,050
West	9,029	1.3	1.0	2.2	3.0	3.7	9.0	13.9	23.0	30.0	12.7	13,339
Negro	5,498	2.3	4.7	7.4	8.9	8.2	13.5	16.5	19.1	16.2	3.2	7,808
Northeast	1,021	1.4	1.0	4.2	9.6	9.7	14.7	14.5	20.2	19.6	5.2	8,788
North Central	1,135	2.3	3.7	5.8	7.7	6.2	8.9	16.2	22.3	21.7	5.1	9,846
South	2,829	3.0	6.7	10.0	9.6	8.4	14.5	17.0	17.7	11.5	1.7	6,730
West	513	0.6	4.0	3.4	6.4	8.5	15.7	17.7	17.5	23.0	3.2	8,585

Source: "Money Income of Families—Race and Region by Income Level: 1974," *Statistical Abstract of the United States, 1975,* p. 393. Primary source: U.S. Bureau of the Census, *Current Population Reports,* series P-60, No. 101, and earlier issues. *Note:* 1. Includes races not shown separately.

Relationships: Percentage Distribution of Family Income, By Residence Area, 1974

[As of March 1975.]

RACE AND RESIDENCE	Number of families (1,000)	Under $2,000	$2,000-$2,999	$3,000-$3,999	$4,000-$4,999	$5,000-$6,999	$7,000-$8,999	$9,000-$11,999	$12,000-$14,999	$15,000-$24,999	$25,000 and over
White	49,451	2.1	2.2	3.1	3.7	8.4	8.8	15.2	14.6	29.7	12.4
In metropolitan areas	32,850	1.7	1.7	2.5	3.1	7.4	7.8	14.2	14.7	32.2	14.8
In central cities	12,388	2.0	2.1	3.3	3.9	9.1	9.4	15.3	14.0	28.9	11.8
Outside central areas	20,462	1.7	1.4	2.0	2.6	6.4	6.8	13.5	15.1	34.2	16.5
Outside metro areas	16,601	2.8	3.1	4.3	4.9	10.3	10.9	17.2	14.4	24.6	7.6
Nonfarm	14,768	2.4	3.0	4.2	4.9	10.1	10.9	17.4	14.9	24.9	7.4
Farm	1,833	6.7	4.2	4.5	4.7	11.5	11.3	15.4	10.4	22.0	9.2
Negro	5,499	7.0	7.4	8.9	8.2	13.5	11.5	13.4	10.7	16.2	3.2
In metropolitan areas	4,240	6.2	6.1	8.6	7.6	12.8	11.3	13.9	11.4	18.3	3.9
In central cities	3,271	6.6	6.5	9.0	8.1	12.8	11.7	13.5	12.1	16.5	3.2
Outside central cities	970	5.1	4.8	7.1	6.1	12.9	10.4	14.8	9.1	24.0	5.9
Outside metro areas	1,258	10.2	11.9	9.8	9.9	15.8	11.8	11.8	8.4	9.3	1.0
Nonfarm	1,159	9.9	11.8	9.7	10.2	15.8	11.8	11.8	8.7	9.7	0.8
Farm	99	14.4	14.5	12.0	7.4	15.7	12.2	10.5	5.1	4.6	3.5

Source: "Money Income of Families—Race and Residence, by Income Level: 1974," *Statistical Abstract of the United States, 1975*, p. 393. Primary source: U.S. Bureau of the Census, *Current Population Reports*, series P-60, No. 101, and earlier issues.

Relationships: Percentage Distribution of Family Income, by Educational Attainment, 1961 and 1968

RACE OF HEAD AND YEARS OF SCHOOL COMPLETED	Number of families (1,000)	Under $3,000	$3,000-$4,999	$5,000-$6,999	$7,000-$9,999	$10,000-$14,999	$15,000 and over	Median income[1]
1961								
White families	39,630	18.3	18.8	22.7	22.4	12.6	5.4	$6,100
Elementary school	13,525	32.9	24.2	19.3	15.0	6.7	1.9	4,419
High school	17,645	12.3	19.2	27.3	25.6	12.1	3.4	6,344
1-3 years	7,103	15.2	20.1	27.4	24.2	10.5	2.6	6,036
4 years	10,542	10.4	18.5	27.2	26.6	13.2	3.9	6,548
College	8,460	6.9	9.3	18.4	27.3	22.8	15.3	8,560
1-3 years	3,773	9.9	11.9	21.4	28.4	17.8	10.5	7,586
4 years or more	4,687	4.3	7.2	16.2	26.4	26.9	19.0	9,503
Negro and other families	4,190	45.7	24.7	14.4	9.3	4.8	1.3	3,340
Elementary school	2,416	57.4	24.2	10.7	5.1	2.0	0.7	2,593
High school	1,414	33.7	27.8	18.3	11.8	6.3	2.0	4,115
1-3 years	804	39.6	28.9	17.7	6.8	4.9	2.1	3,711
4 years	610	26.0	26.5	19.3	18.2	8.1	1.9	4,773
College	360	16.7	14.3	23.1	26.5	17.0	2.3	6,593
1-3 years	201	23.6	16.8	24.1	22.8	11.4	1.3	(B)
4 years	159	7.8	11.3	21.8	31.3	24.3	3.4	(B)

[Continued]

★ 1020 ★

Relationships: Percentage Distribution of Family Income, by Educational Attainment, 1961 and 1968

[Continued]

RACE OF HEAD AND YEARS OF SCHOOL COMPLETED	Number of families (1,000)	PERCENT DISTRIBUTION BY INCOME LEVEL						Median income[1]
		Under $3,000	$3,000-$4,999	$5,000-$6,999	$7,000-$9,999	$10,000-$14,999	$15,000 and over	
1968								
White families	42,506	8.6	10.3	13.5	23.8	27.0	16.7	9,179
Elementary school	11,268	19.1	18.9	17.4	21.9	16.2	6.3	6,328
Less than 8 years	5,460	24.0	20.8	17.4	19.8	13.5	4.7	5,589
8 years	5,808	14.8	17.3	17.4	23.8	18.7	7.7	7,041
High school	20,674	5.7	8.5	14.5	27.4	30.0	13.8	9,309
1-3 years	7,051	7.8	11.1	16.8	26.7	25.9	11.5	8,525
4 years	13,622	4.7	7.1	13.3	27.8	32.1	14.9	9,680
College	10,564	3.1	4.5	7.5	18.8	32.6	33.5	12,356
1-3 years	4,666	3.8	6.3	9.5	23.5	32.5	24.4	10,935
4 years or more	5,898	2.5	3.2	5.8	15.0	32.7	40.7	13,589
Negro and other families	4,692	22.4	21.8	16.4	17.3	15.5	6.7	5,684
Elementary school	2,076	31.7	26.9	16.7	13.6	8.9	2.2	4,297
Less than 8 years	1,558	33.7	28.0	16.3	11.8	8.4	1.8	4,088
8 years	519	25.4	23.4	18.0	18.8	10.6	3.9	5,116
High school	2,096	17.2	20.1	17.7	20.7	17.8	6.3	6,432
1-3 years	1,037	21.3	22.4	16.9	18.9	15.3	5.0	5,766
4 years	1,059	13.2	18.0	18.5	22.5	20.3	7.8	7,057
College	520	6.2	8.1	9.4	18.2	31.9	26.1	10,954
1-3 years	252	7.6	10.4	11.7	22.0	33.8	14.5	9,850
4 years or more	267	4.8	5.9	7.2	14.7	30.3	37.1	12,472

Source: "Money Income—Percent Distribution of Families, by Income level, by Years of School Completed and Race of Head: 1961 and 1968," *Statistical Abstract of the United States, 1970*, p. 325. Primary source: Dept. of Commerce, Bureau of the Census; *Current Population Reports*, Series P-60, No. 66, and unpublished data. *Note:* B Base less than 200,000.

★ 1021 ★

Income/Earnings

Relationships: Percentage Distribution of Income in Families Headed by persons 25 and Over, by Educational Attainment, 1974

RACE AND YEARS OF SCHOOL COMPLETED OF HEAD	Number of families (1,000)	PERCENT DISTRIBUTION BY INCOME LEVEL						Median income
		Under $3,000	$3,000-$4,999	$5,000-$6,999	$7,000-$9,999	$10,000-$14,999	$15,000 and over	
White families	45,877	3.8	6.5	8.0	12.7	24.7	44.3	$13,816
Elementary school: Less than 8 years	4,633	11.0	18.6	17.2	18.3	18.6	16.2	7,501
8 years	4,787	6.4	11.8	14.0	17.7	25.4	24.6	10,011
High school: 1-3 years	6,698	4.3	8.9	9.5	15.2	27.3	34.8	12,080
4 years	15,678	2.8	4.1	6.2	12.9	28.5	45.5	14,226
College: 1-3 years	6,157	2.1	2.9	5.2	10.0	25.5	54.3	16,139
4 years or more	7,924	1.4	1.8	3.2	5.9	17.7	70.1	20,267
Negro families	4,889	12.7	16.4	13.5	16.2	20.1	21.1	8,255
Elementary school: Less than 8 years	1,271	20.9	23.2	15.9	15.6	15.4	8.9	5,736
8 years	414	12.1	21.7	14.7	18.5	16.6	16.3	7,184

[Continued]

★ 1021 ★

Relationships: Percentage Distribution of Income in Families Headed by persons 25 and Over, by Educational Attainment, 1974

[Continued]

RACE AND YEARS OF SCHOOL COMPLETED OF HEAD	Number of families (1,000)	PERCENT DISTRIBUTION BY INCOME LEVEL						Median income
		Under $3,000	$3,000-$4,999	$5,000-$6,999	$7,000-$9,999	$10,000-$14,999	$15,000 and over	
High school: 1-3 years	1,163	14.9	18.5	15.2	18.1	18.3	15.1	7,238
4 years	1,336	7.8	12.2	12.0	16.6	25.5	25.8	10,283
College: 1-3 years	446	5.2	6.0	11.1	13.1	22.1	42.3	13,220
4 years or more	258	1.6	3.3	3.8	11.5	25.5	54.4	16,434

Source: "Money Income—Families with Heads 25 Years Old and Over, by Income level, by Race of Head and Years of School Completed: 1974," *Statistical Abstract of the United States, 1975,* p. 396. Primary source: U.S. Bureau of the Census, *Current Population Reports,* series P-60, No. 101, and earlier issues.

★ 1022 ★

Income/Earnings

Summary Characteristics: Median Income by Region, Family Type, and Husband's Work Experience, 1970 and 1974

Subject	Median income			Index of income overlap
	Black	White	Ratio: Black to White	
1970				
All families	$6,279	$10,236	0.61	72
Region:				
South	5,226	9,240	0.57	68
North and West	7,793	10,630	0.73	81
Northeast	7,774	10,939	0.71	78
North Central	7,718	10,508	0.73	81
West	8,001	10,382	0.77	84
Type of family:				
Male head[1]	7,766	10,697	0.73	79
Married, wife present	7,816	10,723	0.73	79
Wife in paid labor force	9,721	12,543	0.78	80
Wife not in paid labor force	5,961	9,531	0.63	70
Female head	3,576	5,754	0.62	76
Work experience of head:				
Worked	7,348	11,108	0.66	72
Worked at full-time jobs	8,000	11,405	0.70	75
50 to 52 weeks	8,880	12,016	0.74	76
Worked at part-time jobs	2,954	5,711	0.53	65

[Continued]

★ 1022 ★

Summary Characteristics: Median Income by Region, Family Type, and Husband's Work Experience, 1970 and 1974
[Continued]

Subject	Median income			Index of income overlap
	Black	White	Ratio: Black to White	
Did not work	2,811	4,466	0.63	72
1974				
All families	$7,808	$13,356	0.58	72
Region:				
South	6,730	12,050	0.56	69
North and West	9,271	13,906	0.67	77
Northeast	8,788	14,164	0.62	74
North Central	9,846	14,017	0.70	78
West	8,585	13,339	0.64	77
Type of family:				
Male head[1]	10,365	14,055	0.74	81
Married, wife present	10,530	14,099	0.75	82
Wife in paid labor force	12,982	16,825	0.77	82
Wife not in paid labor force	7,773	12,381	0.63	73
Female head	4,465	7,363	0.61	74
Work experience of head:				
Worked	9,813	14,717	0.67	74
Worked at full-time jobs	10,723	15,200	0.71	76
50 to 52 weeks	12,136	16,467	0.74	78
Worked at part-time jobs	4,655	8,117	0.57	70
Did not work	3,911	6,403	0.61	69

Source: "Measures of Income in 1970 and 1974, by Region, Type of Family, and Work Experience of Head," Current Population Reports, Special Studies, Series P-23, No. 54. *The Social and Economic Status of the Black Population in the United States, 1974,* 1975, p. 26. Primary source: U.S. Department of Commerce, Social and Economic Statistics Administration, Bureau of the Census. *Notes:* The Index of Income Overlap of White and Black is a statistical measure which summarizes the degree of overlap between the two distributions and is equal to 1.00 when the two distributions are identical. 1. Includes other male heads, not shown separately.

★ 1023 ★

Income/Earnings

Two-Income Families: Contributions of Working Wives in Nonfarm Families to Family Income (in percentages), 1968

	All income groups		Under $3,000 income	
	Negro and other races	White	Negro and other races	White
All earnings group	100	100	100	100
Less than 20 percent	37	34	46	44
20 to 30 percent	19	18	14	13
30 to 40 percent	19	19	13	11
40 to 50 percent	13	17	11	7
50 percent and over	11	12	16	25

Source: "Distribution of Nonfarm Husband-Wife Families by Percent of Total Family Income Contributed by Working Wife, 1968," Current Population, Special Studies, Series P-23, No. 29. *The Social and Economic Status of the Black Population in the United States, 1969,* 1969, p. 45. Primary source: U.S. Department of Labor, Bureau of Labor Statistics.

★ 1024 ★

Income/Earnings

Two-Income Families: Contributions of Working Wives in Nonfarm Families to Family Income (in percentages), May 1970

[Families where wife has had paid work experience during the year]

Income group	Husband-wife families with earnings (thousands)	Portion of family income contributed by wife					
		Total	For every dollar of income				
			Less than 20 cents	20 to 30 cents	30 to 40 cents	40 to 50 cents	50 cents and over
All income groups:							
Negro and other races	2,167	100	33	20	18	16	13
White	17,607	100	38	19	19	12	11
With incomes under $3,000:							
Negro and other races	116	100	47	19	8	11	15
White	391	100	46	13	13	4	25

Source: "Distribution of Nonfarm Husband-Wife Families by Portion of Total Family Income Contributed by Working Wife: May 1970," Current Population, Special Studies, Series P-23, No. 38. *The Social and Economic Status of the Black Population in the United States, 1970,* 1970, p. 129. Primary source: U.S. Department of Labor, Bureau of Labor Statistics.

★ 1025 ★

Income/Earnings

Two-Income Families: Mean Family Income When Both Husband and Wife Work by Region and Age of Head, 1973

Race and earnings of husband and wife and work experience of wife	Total			Husband under 35 years old		
	United States	North and West	South	United States	North and West	South
BLACK						
Mean family income	$13,319	$16,372	$10,978	$12,326	$14,290	$10,954
Mean earnings of husband	7,969	9,909	6,481	7,799	8,848	7,067
Mean earnings of wife	4,129	5,038	3,432	4,061	4,803	3,543
Earnings as a percent of family income	31	31	31	33	34	32
Wife worked 50 to 52 weeks	$5,550	$6,541	$4,699	$5,756	$6,678	$4,989
Earnings as a percent of family income	42	40	43	47	47	46
WHITE						
Mean family income	$16,749	$17,250	$15,635	$13,576	$13,984	$12,776
Mean earnings of husband	11,043	11,384	10,287	9,439	9,742	8,843
Mean earnings of wife	4,125	4,182	3,999	3,667	3,735	3,533
Earnings as a percent of family income	25	24	26	27	27	28
Wife worked 50 to 52 weeks	$5,928	$6,075	$5,623	$5,814	$6,024	$5,428
Earnings as a percent of family income	35	35	36	43	43	42
RATIO: BLACK TO WHITE						
Mean family income	0.80	0.95	0.70	0.91	1.02	0.86
Mean earnings of husband	0.72	0.87	0.63	0.83	0.91	0.80
Mean earnings of wife	1.00	1.20	0.86	1.11	1.29	1.00
Wife worked 50 to 52 weeks	0.94	1.08	0.84	0.99	1.11	0.92

Source: "Earnings of 1973 of Husband and Wife for Families in which Both Husband and Wife had Earnings, by Age of Head and Region," Current Population Reports, Special Studies, Series P-23, No. 54. *The Social and Economic Status of the Black Population in the United States, 1974,* 1975, p. 40. Primary source: U.S. Department of Commerce, Social and Economic Statistics Administration, Bureau of the Census.

★ 1026 ★
Income/Earnings

Two-Income Families: Mean Income of Husbands and Wives by Region, 1959 and 1970

[In current dollars]

Earnings of husband and wife	Total			Husband under 35 years		
	United States	North and West	South	United States	North and West	South
1970						
Negro						
Mean family income	$10,581	$12,430	$9,032	$9,905	$11,309	$8,516
Mean earnings of husband	6,209	7,247	5,326	6,225	6,978	5,481
Mean earnings of wife	3,327	4,015	2,742	3,307	3,903	2,719
Earnings as a percent of family income	31	32	30	33	35	32
White						
Mean family income	$13,563	$14,022	$12,467	$10,969	$11,215	$10,439
Mean earnings of husband	8,786	9,100	8,037	7,607	7,777	7,243
Mean earnings of wife	3,490	3,537	3,376	2,973	3,008	2,898
Earnings as a percent of family income	26	25	27	27	27	28
Negro as a Percent of White						
Mean family income	78	88	72	90	101	82
Mean earnings of husband	71	80	66	82	90	76
Mean earnings of wife	95	114	81	11	130	94
1959						
Negro						
Mean family income	$4,769	$6,237	$3,776	$4,560	$5,863	$3,603
Mean earnings of husband	2,887	3,764	2,293	2,883	3,510	2,422
Mean earnings of wife	1,323	1,804	998	1,340	1,881	942
Earnings as a percent of family income	28	29	26	29	32	26
White						
Mean family income	$7,814	$8,112	$6,986	$6,407	$6,662	$5,809
Mean earnings of husband	5,006	5,212	4,432	4,370	4,589	3,855
Mean earnings of wife	2,097	2,144	1,967	1,749	1,777	1,683
Earnings as a percent of family income	27	26	28	27	27	29
Negro as a Percent of White						
Mean family income	61	77	54	71	88	62

[Continued]

★ 1026 ★

Two-Income Families: Mean Income of Husbands and Wives by Region, 1959 and 1970

[Continued]

Earnings of husband and wife	Total			Husband under 35 years		
	United States	North and West	South	United States	North and West	South
Mean earnings of husband	58	72	52	66	76	63
Mean earnings of wife	63	84	51	77	106	56

Source: "Earnings of Husband and of Wife for Families in which Both the Husband and Wife Worked, by Region: 1959 and 1970," Current Population Reports, Special Studies, Series P-23, No. 42. *The Social and Economic Status of the Black Population in the United States, 1971,* 1972, p. 36. Primary source: U.S. Department of Commerce, Social and Economic Statistics Administration, Bureau of the Census.

★ 1027 ★

Income/Earnings

Two-Income Families: Working Wives' Contribution to Family Income, by Region and Husband's Race, 1970 and 1974

[Families as of March 1971 and March 1975]

RACE, REGION, AND CURRENT OCCUPATION GROUP OF WIFE	1970				1974			
	Husband wife, families both working (1,000)	Average (mean) family income	Earnings of wife		Husband wife families, both working (1,000)	Average (mean) family income	Earnings of wife	
			Average (mean)	Percent of family income			Average (mean)	Percent of family income
All white workers	18,401	$13,563	$3,490	25.7	20,101	$17,983	$4,483	24.9
North and West	12,969	14,022	3,537	25.2	13,733	18,599	4,575	24.6
South	5,432	12,467	3,376	27.1	6,367	16,654	4,286	25.7
White collar workers[1]	9,175	15,428	4,638	30.1	10,813	20,207	5,735	28.4
North and West	6,433	15,859	4,682	29.5	7,369	20,738	5,805	28.0
South	2,741	14,417	4,532	31.4	3,444	19,073	5,585	29.3
All Negro workers	1,880	10,581	3,327	31.4	1,821	14,317	4,645	32.4
North and West	864	12,403	4,015	32.4	815	16,801	5,525	32.9
South	1,016	9,032	2,742	30.4	1,006	12,305	3,932	32.0
White collar workers[1]	568	13,935	5,394	39.0	658	18,246	6,876	37.7
North and West	325	14,667	5,602	38.2	366	19,114	7,261	38.0
South	243	12,722	5,115	40.2	292	17,162	6,394	37.3

Source: "Wife's Contribution to Family Income—Families with Husband and Wife and Working, by Race of Husband: 1970 and 1974" *Statistical Abstract of the United States, 1975,* p. 397. Primary source: U.S. Bureau of the Census, *Current Population Reports,* series P-23, No. 39, and unpublished data. *Note:* 1. Includes professional, managerial, clerical, and sales workers.

Lifestyles and Conveniences

★ 1028 ★

Black Families with Radios by Region and Division, 1930

Section, division, and state	Negro families			Percent of all families having radio set
	Total number	Having radio set		
		Number	Percent	
United States	2,803,756	209,779	7.5	40.3
The North	576,328	151,633	26.3	51.1
The South	2,193,357	47,443	2.2	16.4
The West	34,071	10,703	31.4	44.0
New England	22,864	7,639	33.4	53.8
Middle Atlantis	243,371	72,427	29.8	55.3
East North Central	222,240	58,116	26.2	50.2
West North Central	87,853	13,451	15.3	43.1
South Atlantic	974,592	28,320	2.9	19.0
East South Central	653,847	9,222	1.4	12.3
West South Central	564,918	9,901	1.8	16.5
Mountain	8,743	1,337	15.3	30.9
Pacific	25,328	9,366	37.0	49.2

Source: "Negro Families Having Radio Set, by Sections, Divisions, and States: 1930," *Negroes in the United States, 1920-1932*, 1935, p. 259. Primary source: U.S. Bureau of the Census. *Negroes in the United States, 1920-1932*. Washington, D.C.: U.S. Government Printing Office, 1935.

★ 1029 ★

Lifestyles and Conveniences

Families With and Without Lodgers by Home Ownership Status, 1930

Number of lodgers and tenure	Negro families		Native-white families		Foreign-born white families	
	Number	Percent distribution	Number	Percent distribution	Number	Percent distribution
All families	2,803,756	100.0	20,968,803	100.0	5,736,491	100.0
Owner families	669,645	100.0	10,255,682	100.0	2,968,707	100.0
Families having						
No lodgers	584,856	87.3	9,366,136	91.3	2,690,961	90.6
1 lodger	49,952	7.5	621,394	6.1	181,997	6.1
2 lodgers	18,894	2.8	159,636	1.6	53,911	1.8
3 lodgers	7,558	1.1	55,264	.5	20,266	.7
4 lodgers	3,830	.6	24,814	.2	9,424	.3

[Continued]

★ 1029 ★

Families With and Without Lodgers by Home Ownership Status, 1930
[Continued]

Number of lodgers and tenure	Negro families		Native-white families		Foreign-born white families	
	Number	Percent distribution	Number	Percent distribution	Number	Percent distribution
5 lodgers	1,883	.3	12,214	.1	4,760	.2
6 or more lodgers	2,672	.4	16,224	.2	7,388	.2
Tenant families	2,050,217	100.0	10,314,500	100.0	2,690,300	100.0
Families having						
No lodgers	1,720,835	83.9	9,361,841	90.8	2,391,054	88.9
1 lodger	188,576	9.2	636,554	6.2	188,736	7.0
2 lodgers	76,590	3.7	172,838	1.7	59,855	2.2
3 lodgers	31,245	1.5	65,204	.6	23,408	.9
4 lodgers	15,376	.7	31,399	.3	11,060	.4
5 lodgers	7,842	.4	17,216	.2	5,703	.2
6 or more lodgers	9,753	.5	29,448	.3	10,485	.4
Tenure unknown	83,894	100.0	398,621	100.0	77,484	100.0
Families having						
No lodgers	72,838	86.8	355,495	89.2	67,250	86.8
1 lodger	6,635	7.9	26,849	6.7	5,880	7.6
2 lodgers	2,369	2.8	7,604	1.9	1,925	2.5
3 lodgers	987	1.2	3,344	.8	889	1.1
4 lodgers	483	.6	1,895	.5	460	.6
5 lodgers	225	.3	1,117	.3	313	.4
6 or more lodges	357	.4	2,317	.6	767	1.0

Source: "Families Classified According to Number of Lodgers, by Color, and Nativity of Head, and by Tenure, for the United States: 1930," *Negroes in the United States, 1920-1932*, 1935, p. 255. Primary source: U.S. Bureau of the Census. *Negroes in the United States, 1920-1932.* Washington, D.C.: U.S. Government Printing Office, 1935.

★ 1030 ★

Lifestyles and Conveniences

Families with Servants but Without Lodgers by Urban-Rural Residence and Home Ownership Status, 1930

Families designated as "having servants" include only those reporting servants living in the home and no lodgers. This combination was obtained as a byproduct of the tabulation by number of lodgers, but the mechanical restrictions were such that it was not possible to obtain data for families having both servants and lodgers.

Color and nativity and tenure	Total families			Urban families			Rural-farm families			Rural-nonfarm families		
	Total number	Having servants living in home		Total number	Having servants living in home		Total number	Having servants living in home		Total number	Having servants living in home	
		Number	Percent		Number	Percent		Number	Percent		Number	Percent
All families	29,904,663	523,922	1.8	17,372,524	376,104	2.2	6,604,637	57,919	0.9	5,927,502	89,899	1.5
Owner families	14,002,074	354,136	2.5	7,432,554	250,388	3.4	3,452,102	41,239	1.2	3,117,418	62,509	2.0
Negro	669,645	2,236	.3	315,584	1,022	.3	188,574	645	.3	165,487	569	.3
White	13,224,389	351,200	2.7	7,074,031	248,978	3.5	3,231,951	40,445	1.3	2,918,407	61,777	2.1
Native	10,255,682	304,452	3.0	4,941,762	211,482	4.3	2,840,831	36,825	1.3	2,473,089	56,145	2.3
Foreign-born	2,968,707	46,748	1.6	2,132,269	37,496	1.8	391,120	3,620	.9	445,318	5,632	1.3
Other races	108,040	700	.6	42,939	388	.9	31,577	149	.5	33,524	163	.5

[Continued]

★ 1030 ★

Families with Servants but Without Lodgers by Urban-Rural Residence and Home Ownership Status, 1930
[Continued]

Color and nativity and tenure	Total families			Urban families			Rural-farm families			Rural-nonfarm families		
	Total number	Having servants living in home		Total number	Having servants living in home		Total number	Having servants living in home		Total number	Having servants living in home	
		Number	Percent		Number	Percent		Number	Percent		Number	Percent
Tenant families	15,319,817	162,393	1.1	9,681,359	121,523	1.3	2,952,717	15,055	.5	2,685,741	25,815	1.0
Negro	2,050,217	6,049	.3	978,799	2,140	.2	758,014	2,215	.3	313,404	1,694	.5
White	13,004,800	155,575	1.2	8,565,849	118,907	1.4	2,125,854	12,710	.6	2,313,097	23,958	1.0
Native	10,314,500	127,958	1.2	6,213,093	94,872	1.5	2,022,067	11,726	.6	2,079,340	21,360	1.0
Foreign-born	2,690,300	27,617	1.0	2,352,756	24,035	1.0	103,787	984	.9	233,757	2,598	1.1
Other races	264,800	769	.3	136,711	476	.3	68,849	130	.2	59,240	163	.3

Source: "Families Having Servants Living in the Home, but No Lodgers, by Color, and Nativity of Head, for the United States: 1930," *Negroes in the United States, 1920-1932,* 1935, p. 259. Primary source: U.S. Bureau of the Census. *Negroes in the United States, 1920-1932.* Washington, D.C.: U.S. Government Printing Office, 1935.

★ 1031 ★

Lifestyles and Conveniences

"City" and "Country" Black Families with Radios, 1930

Area	Total number of families	Families having radio set	
		Number	Percent
All families	2,803,756	209,779	7.5
Urban families	1,328,170	191,790	14.4
Urban farm families	2,385	80	3.4
Rural-farm families	978,653	3,327	.3
Rural-nonfarm families	496,933	14,662	3.0
All farm families	981,638	3,407	.3

Source: "Negro Families Having Radio Set, in Urban, Rural-Farm, and Rural- Nonfarm Areas: 1930," *Negroes in the United States, 1920-1932,* 1935, p. 256. Primary source: U.S. Bureau of the Census. *Negroes in the United States, 1920-1932.* Washington, D.C.: U.S. Government Printing Office, 1935.

Poverty

★ 1032 ★

Black and White Families Below Poverty Level, 1959-1968

[Numbers in millions]

				Percent		
	Negro and other races	Negro	White	Negro and other races	Negro	White
1959	2.1	1.9	6.2	50	48	15
1960	2.1	(NA)	6.1	49	(NA)	15
1961	2.2	(NA)	6.2	49	(NA)	15
1962	2.2	(NA)	5.9	48	(NA)	14
1963	2.1	(NA)	5.5	44	(NA)	13
1964	1.9	(NA)	5.3	40	(NA)	12
1965	1.9	(NA)	4.8	40	(NA)	11
1966	1.7	(NA)	4.5	35	(NA)	10
Based on revised methodology[1]						
1966	1.7	1.6	4.1	34	36	9
1967[2]	1.6	1.6	4.1	32	34	9
1968	1.4	1.4	3.6	28	29	8

Source: "Families Below the Poverty Level, 1959-1968," Current Population Reports, Special Studies, Series P-23, No. 29. *The Social and Economic Status of the Black Population in the United States, 1969,* 1969, p. 22. Primary source: U.S. Department of Commerce, Bureau of the Census. *Notes:* NA Not available. The poverty concept used throughout this report is based on a revised definition adopted in 1969. The poverty threshold for a nonfarm family of four was $3,553 in 1968 and $2,973 in 1959. 1. Reflects improvements in statistical procedures used in processing the income data. 2. Due to a processing difference, data for 1967 are not strictly comparable with those shown for 1966 and 1968.

★ 1033 ★

Poverty

Families on Relief: Black and White Families on Relief in 1933 in States with "Large" Black Populations

CITY	NEGROES			WHITES		
	All persons, 1930	Relief persons, 1933	Ratio of Relief persons to all persons	All persons, 1930	Relief persons, 1933	Ratio of Relief persons to all persons
United States Total	11,891,143	2,117,644	17.8	108,864,207	10,309,844	9.5
Georgia	1,071,125	117,281	10.9	1,836,974	159,686	8.7
Mississippi	1,009,718	91,375	9.0	996,856	136,339	13.7
Alabama	944,834	179,727	19.0	1,700,775	275,049	16.2
North Carolina	918,647	104,124	11.3	2,234,948	147,435	6.6
Texas	854,964	75,535	8.8	4,283,491	232,954	5.4
South Carolina	793,681	218,806	27.6	944,040	184,421	19.5
Louisiana	776,326	134,849	17.4	1,318,160	190,140	14.4
Virginia	650,165	27,765	4.3	1,770,405	38,127	2.2
Arkansas	478,463	42,378	8.9	1,374,906	137,053	10.0
Tennessee	477,646	34,694	7.3	2,138,619	155,181	7.3
Florida	431,828	157,890	36.6	1,035,205	212,401	20.5
Pennsylvania	431,257	151,726	35.2	9,192,602	1,221,792	13.3
New York	412,814	104,396	25.3	12,150,293	1,128,079	9.3
Illinois	328,972	115,803	35.2	7,266,361	696,728	9.6
Ohio	309,304	117,498	38.0	6,331,136	640,695	10.1
Maryland	276,379	45,805	16.6	1,354,170	88,829	6.6
Kentucky	226,040	32,170	14.2	2,388,364	440,017	18.4
Missouri	223,840	45,427	20.3	3,398,887	157,195	4.6
New Jersey	208,828	58,571	28.0	3,829,209	286,334	7.5
Oklahoma	172,198	46,784	27.2	2,123,424	371,540	17.5
Michigan	169,453	48,547	28.6	4,650,171	555,754	12.0
District of Columbia	132,068	28,850	21.8	353,914	8,591	2.4
West Virginia	114,893	20,620	17.9	1,613,934	365,503	22.6
Indiana	111,982	33,018	29.5	3,116,136	263,084	8.4

Source: "Comparison of Persons in Negro Relief Families with Persons in White Relief Families, October, 1933, as Shown by Percentages of Total Negro Population and Total White Population, Respectively, for States Having More than 100,000 Negroes in 1930," *Negro Year Book: An Annual Encyclopedia of the Negro, 1937-1938*, 1937, p. 20. Primary source: Unemployment Relief Census. October, 1933.

★ 1034 ★

Poverty

Families on Relief: Black and White "Big City" Families on Relief in 1933

CITY	NEGROES			WHITES		
	All persons, 1930	Relief persons, 1933	Ratio of Relief persons to all persons	All persons, 1930	Relief persons, 1933	Ratio of Relief persons to all persons
New York City, N.Y.	327,706	78,262	23.9	6,587,225	607,762	9.2
Chicago, Illinois	233,903	80,542	34.4	3,117,731	316,014	10.1
Philadelphia, Pennsylvania	219,599	75,458	34.4	1,728,457	141,512	8.2
Baltimore, Maryland	142,106	40,923	28.8	662,124	61,872	9.3
Washington, D.C.	132,068	28,850	21.8	353,914	8,591	2.4
New Orleans, Louisiana	129,632	49,103	37.9	327,729	31,452	9.6
Detroit, Michigan	120,066	33,140	27.6	1,440,141	146,063	10.1
Birmingham, Alabama	99,077	26,220	26.5	160,551	17,567	10.9
Memphis, Tennessee	96,550	10,672	11.1	156,528	7,511	4.8
St. Louis, Missouri	93,580	32,110	34.3	726,879	52,132	7.2
Atlanta, Georgia	90,075	20,454	22.7	180,247	16,343	9.1
Cleveland, Ohio	71,899	30,939	43.0	827,090	102,950	12.4
Houston, Texas	63,337	13,122	20.7	214,687	19,186	8.9
Pittsburgh, Pennsylvania	54,983	23,871	43.4	614,317	96,345	15.7
Richmond, Virginia	52,988	5,660	10.7	129,871	4,751	3.7

Source: "Comparison of Persons in Negro Relief Families with Persons in White Relief Families, October, 1933, as Shown by Percentages of Total Negro Population and Total White Population, Respectively, for Cities Having More than 50,000 Negroes in 1930," *Negro Year Book: An Annual Encyclopedia of the Negro, 1937-1938,* 1937, p. 21. Primary source: 1930 Federal Census. *Note:* 1. Unemployment Relief Census, October, 1933.

★ 1035 ★

Poverty

Families on Relief: Public Assistance and Social Security Income for Families and Individuals Below Low-Income Level, 1970

[Numbers in thousands]

Subject	All families		Male head[1]		Female head[1]	
	Negro	White	Negro	White	Negro	White
FAMILIES						
Total	1,445	3,701	625	2,604	820	1,097
Receiving public assistance income	690	839	177	370	513	469
Percent	48	23	28	14	63	43
Receiving Social Security income	341	1,192	188	928	153	264
Percent	24	32	30	36	19	24

[Continued]

★ 1035 ★

Families on Relief: Public Assistance and Social Security Income for Families and Individuals Below Low-Income Level, 1970
[Continued]

Subject	All families		Male head[1]		Female head[1]	
	Negro	White	Negro	White	Negro	White
UNRELATED INDIVIDUALS						
Total	840	4,121	301	1,088	539	3,033
Receiving public assistance income	295	633	73	185	222	448
Percent	35	15	24	17	41	15
Receiving Social Security income	297	2,284	85	434	212	1,850
Percent	35	55	28	40	39	61

Source: "Families and Unrelated Individuals Below the Low-Income Level in 1970 Receiving Public Assistance and Social Security Income, by Sex of Head," Current Population Reports, Special Studies, Series P-23, No. 42. *The Social and Economic Status of the Black Population in the United States, 1971,* 1972, p. 47. Primary source: U.S. Department of Commerce, Social and Economic Statistics Administration, Bureau of the Census. *Note:* 1. For unrelated individuals, sex of individual.

★ 1036 ★

Poverty

Families on Relief: "Public Assistance" Recipients among Families and Individuals Below Low-Income Level, 1969
[Numbers in thousands]

Subject	All races	Negro	White
Low income families	4,946	1,326	3,555
Receiving public assistance	1,356	594	744
Percent	27	45	21
Low income unrelated individuals	4,851	806	3,962
Receiving public assistance	867	280	561
Percent	18	35	14

Source: "Families and Unrelated Individuals Below the Low-Income Level in 1969 Receiving Public Assistance," Current Population Reports, Special Studies, Series P-23, No. 38. *The Social and Economic Status of the Black Population in the United States, 1970,* 1970, p. 43. Primary source: U.S. Department of Commerce, Bureau of the Census.

★ 1037 ★
Poverty

Family Median Income in Six "Big City" Poverty Areas, July 1968-June 1969

	Atlanta	Chicago	Detroit	Houston	Los Angeles	New York City
Negro and other races	$4,700	$7,000	$6,200	$4,700	$5,800	$5,700
White	$6,200	(B)	$6,300	$6,000	$6,600	$5,300
Negro and other races as a percent of white	76	(NA)	98	78	88	108

Source: "Median Family Income in Poverty Areas of Six Large Cities, July 1968- June 1969," Current Population Reports, Special Studies, Series P-23, No. 29. *The Social Economic Status of the Black Population in the United States, 1969,* 1969, p. 96. Primary source: U.S. Department of Labor, Bureau of Labor Statistics. *Note:* NA Not available. B Base 2,000 or less.

★ 1038 ★
Poverty

Number Percent: Family Status of People Below Low-Income Level, 1959, 1966, and 1971

Family status and year	All races	Negro	White	Negro as a percent of all races
1959				
Total (millions)	38.8	9.9	28.3	26
Percent	100	100	100	(X)
In families	85	92	82	28
Head	21	19	21	23
65 years and over	5	3	5	16
Children under 18 years	41	51	37	32
Other family members	23	22	24	25
Unrelated individuals	15	8	18	14
65 years and over	6	2	7	10
1966				
Total (millions)	28.5	8.9	19.3	31
Percent	100	100	100	(X)
In families	84	91	80	34
Head	20	18	21	28
65 years and over	5	3	7	18
Children under 18 years	43	54	37	39
Other family members	21	19	21	29
Unrelated individuals	16	9	20	17
65 years and over	9	3	12	11

[Continued]

★ 1038 ★

Number Percent: Family Status of People Below Low-Income Level, 1959, 1966, and 1971

[Continued]

Family status and year	All races	Negro	White	Negro as a percent of all races
1971				
Total (millions)	25.6	7.4	17.8	29
Percent	100	100	100	(X)
In families	80	88	76	32
Head	21	20	21	28
65 years and over	4	3	5	20
Children under 18 years	40	52	36	37
Other family members	19	16	20	25
Unrelated individuals	20	12	24	17
65 years and over	10	4	12	12

Source: "Distribution of Persons Below the Low-Income Level, by Family Status: 1959, 1966, and 1971," Current Population Reports, Special Studies, Series P-23, No. 42. *The Social and Economic Status of the Black Population in the United States, 1971,* 1972, p. 40. Primary source: U.S. Department of Commerce, Social and Economic Statistics Administration, Bureau of the Census. *Note:* (X) Not applicable.

★ 1039 ★

Poverty

Number/Percent: Families and Non-Families Below Low-Income Level in Cities with Black Population of 100,000 or More, 1969

[Numbers in thousands]

Selected cities	Persons		Families			Unrelated individuals	
	Number	Percent of all black persons	Number	Percent of all black families	Percent of families with female head	Number	Percent of all black unrelated individuals
New York, N.Y.	399	24	81	21	63	58	31
Chicago, Ill.	274	25	51	21	66	38	37
Detroit, Mich.	143	22	28	19	63	24	39
Philadelphia, Pa.	165	26	32	21	66	28	40
Washington, D.C.	103	19	19	16	60	20	30
Los Angeles, Calif.	127	26	25	21	65	20	30
Baltimore, Md.	112	27	21	23	65	17	43
Houston, Tex.	93	30	18	25	49	12	46
Cleveland, Ohio	77	27	16	23	66	12	42
New Orleans, La.	116	44	23	39	54	11	57
Atlanta, Ga.	72	29	14	25	55	11	48

[Continued]

★ 1039 ★

Number/Percent: Families and Non-Families Below Low-Income Level in Cities with Black Population of 100,000 or More, 1969

[Continued]

Selected cities	Persons		Families			Unrelated individuals	
	Number	Percent of all black persons	Number	Percent of all black families	Percent of families with female head	Number	Percent of all black unrelated individuals
St. Louis, Mo.	79	31	14	26	60	11	46
Memphis, Tenn.	99	41	18	36	49	10	59
Dallas, Tex.	62	30	12	25	53	7	43
Newark, N.J.	56	27	11	24	68	6	34
Indianapolis, Ind.	29	22	5	18	57	4	39
Birmingham, Ala.	50	40	10	34	48	7	61
Cincinnati, Ohio	39	32	7	27	60	7	50
Oakland, Calif.	31	25	6	22	66	5	35
Jacksonville, Fla.	47	40	9	35	53	6	58
Kansas City, Mo.	28	25	5	20	55	5	42
Milwaukee, Wis.	28	27	6	25	64	3	38
Pittsburgh, Pa.	33	32	7	27	65	6	48
Richmond, Va.	30	30	6	25	63	5	47
Boston, Mass.	29	28	6	25	73	4	30
Columbus, Ohio	25	26	5	21	62	5	44

Source: "Black Persons, Families, and Unrelated Individuals Below the Low-Income Level in 1969 for Cities with 100,000 or More Blacks," Current Population Reports, Special Studies, Series P-23, No. 29. *The Social and Economic Status of the Black Population in the United States, 1969*, 1969, p. 132. Primary source: U.S. Department of Commerce, Social and Economic Statistics Administration, Bureau of the Census.

★ 1040 ★

Poverty

Number/Percent: Family Below Poverty Level and Income Deficit in 1975 Dollars, by Sex of Head, 1970-1973

[**Number in thousands; deficit in millions of 1973 dollars, except percent.** Families as of March of following year. Income deficit defined as the difference between the total income of families and unrelated individuals below low income level and their respective low income thresholds. In computing the income deficit families reporting a net loss are assigned zero dollars; for such cases, the deficit is equal to the low income level].

FAMILY STATUS AND RACE	NUMBER BELOW LOW INCOME LEVEL			AGGREGATE INCOME DEFICIT (1973 dollars)		
	1970	1972	1973	1970	1972	1973
All persons	25,420	24,460	22,973	13,241	12,781	11,975
Percent	100.0	100.0	100.0	100.0	100.0	100.0
In families	80.0	80.0	79.7	64.6	63.3	63.6
With male head	50.5	46.9	44.1	37.5	34.3	32.7
With female head	29.5	33.2	35.6	27.1	29.0	30.9
White, total	17,484	16,203	15,142	9,416	8,934	8,224
Percent	100.0	100.0	100.0	100.0	100.0	100.0
In families	76.2	75.7	75.4	60.3	58.6	59.1

[Continued]

★ 1040 ★

Number/Percent: Family Below Poverty Level and Income Deficit in 1975 Dollars, by Sex of Head, 1970-1973
[Continued]

FAMILY STATUS AND RACE	NUMBER BELOW LOW INCOME LEVEL			AGGREGATE INCOME DEFICIT (1973 dollars)		
	1970	1972	1973	1970	1972	1973
With male head	54.7	52.5	48.9	40.6	38.4	35.8
With female head	21.5	23.3	26.4	19.7	20.3	23.4
Negro and other	7,936	8,257	7,831	3,825	3,851	3,754
Percent	100.0	100.0	100.0	100.0	100.0	100.0
In families	88.3	88.5	87.9	75.1	74.1	73.3
With male head	41.2	35.9	34.6	30.0	24.9	26.1
With female head	47.1	52.6	53.3	45.1	49.2	47.2

Source: "Persons Below Low Income Level and Aggregate Income Deficit, by Race of Head and Family Status: 1959 to 1973," *Statistical Abstract of the United States, 1975*, p. 402. Primary source: U.S. Bureau of the Census, *Current Population Reports*, series P-60, No. 98 and earlier issues, and unpublished data.

★ 1041 ★

Poverty

Number/Percent: Family Status of People Below Poverty Level, 1959-1968

[**Persons in millions**. As of March of year following year shown. Covers persons with income below poverty level; Excludes inmates of institutions and Armed Forces living in barracks. The revised 1966 series and the 1968 data are based on a more refined method of imputing missing income data than used previously].

FAMILY STATUS AND RACE	NUMBER BELOW POVERTY LEVEL					PERCENT BELOW POVERTY LEVEL				
	1959	1963	1966	1966[1]	1968	1959	1963	1966	1966[1]	1968
All persons	39.5	36.4	30.4	28.5	25.4	22.4	19.5	15.7	14.7	12.8
In families	34.6	31.5	25.6	23.8	20.7	20.8	17.9	14.2	13.1	11.3
Head	8.3	7.6	6.2	5.8	5.0	18.5	15.9	12.7	11.8	10.0
Family members under 18 years[2]	17.2	15.7	12.9	12.1	10.7	26.9	22.8	18.4	17.4	15.3
Other family members	9.0	8.3	6.5	5.9	4.9	15.9	13.8	10.5	9.5	7.8
White	28.5	25.2	20.8	19.3	17.4	18.1	15.3	12.2	11.3	10.0
In families	24.4	21.1	16.7	15.4	13.5	16.5	13.6	10.5	9.7	8.4
Head	6.2	5.5	4.5	4.1	3.6	15.2	12.8	10.2	9.3	8.0
Family members under 18 years[2]	11.4	9.7	7.6	7.2	6.4	20.6	16.5	12.8	12.1	10.7
Other family members	6.9	5.9	4.6	4.1	3.6	13.3	11.0	8.2	7.4	6.3
Negro and other races	11.0	11.2	9.7	9.2	8.0	56.2	51.0	41.7	39.8	33.5
In families	10.1	10.3	8.9	8.4	7.1	56.0	50.5	41.1	38.9	32.4
Head	2.1	2.1	1.7	1.7	1.4	50.4	43.7	35.0	33.9	28.2
Family members under 18 years[2]	5.8	5.9	5.2	4.9	4.4	66.7	60.9	50.7	48.2	41.6
Other family members	2.2	2.3	1.9	1.8	1.4	42.5	38.9	30.2	27.7	20.9
Families with male head[3]	29.1	25.3	19.6	18.3	15.0	18.7	15.4	11.6	10.8	8.8
In families	27.5	23.9	18.3	16.9	13.7	18.2	14.9	11.2	10.3	8.3
Head	6.4	5.6	4.4	4.1	3.3	15.8	13.1	10.0	9.3	7.3
Family members under 18 years[2]	13.1	11.1	8.4	7.9	6.3	22.4	18.0	13.4	12.6	10.2
Other family members	8.1	7.1	5.6	5.0	4.1	15.3	12.9	9.6	8.7	7.0
Unrelated individuals 14 years and over	1.6	1.5	1.3	1.3	1.3	36.8	34.8	27.7	29.3	25.4
Families with female heard[3]	10.4	11.1	10.8	10.3	10.4	50.2	48.4	43.8	41.0	38.9
In families	7.0	7.6	7.3	6.9	7.0	49.4	47.7	43.1	39.8	38.7
Head	1.9	2.0	1.8	1.7	1.8	42.6	40.4	35.1	33.1	32.3
Family members under 18 years[2]	4.1	4.6	4.5	4.3	4.4	72.2	66.6	61.3	58.2	55.2

[Continued]

★ 1041 ★

Number/Percent: Family Status of People Below Poverty Level, 1959-1968
[Continued]

FAMILY STATUS AND RACE	NUMBER BELOW POVERTY LEVEL					PERCENT BELOW POVERTY LEVEL				
	1959	1963	1966	1966[1]	1968	1959	1963	1966	1966[1]	1968
Other family members	1.0	1.1	1.0	0.9	0.8	24.0	26.0	22.2	18.6	17.6
Unrelated individuals 14 years and over	3.4	3.5	3.5	3.4	3.4	52.1	50.0	45.4	43.5	39.2

Source: "Poor Persons—Number and Percent Below Poverty Level, by Family Status and Race: 1959 to 1968," *Statistical Abstract of the United States, 1970,* p. 328. Primary source: Dept. of Commerce, Bureau of the Census; *Current Population Reports,* Series P-60, No. 68, and unpublished data. *Notes:* 1. Revised series. 2. Other than head and wife.

★ 1042 ★

Poverty

Number/Percent: Heads of Families Below Low-Income Level, 1959 and 1967-1974

[Numbers in thousands]

Year	All families		Families with male head		Families with female head	
	Black	White	Black	White	Black	White
Number (thousands)						
1959	1,860	6,027	1,309	5,037	551	990
1967	1,555	4,056	839	3,019	716	1,037
1968	1,366	3,616	660	2,595	706	1,021
1969[1]	1,366	3,575	629	2,506	737	1,069
1970[1]	1,481	3,708	648	2,606	834	1,102
1971[1]	1,484	3,751	605	2,560	879	1,191
1972[1]	1,529	3,441	558	2,306	972	1,135
1973[1]	1,527	3,219	553	2,029	974	1,190
1974[1]	1,530	3,482	506	2,185	1,024	1,297
Percent below the low-income level						
1959	48.1	14.8	43.3	13.4	65.4	30.0
1967	33.9	9.0	25.3	7.4	56.3	25.9
1968	29.4	8.0	19.9	6.3	53.2	25.2
1969[1]	27.9	7.7	17.9	6.0	53.3	25.7
1970[1]	29.5	8.0	18.6	6.2	54.3	25.0
1971[1]	28.8	7.9	17.2	5.9	53.5	26.5
1972[1]	29.0	7.1	16.2	5.3	53.3	24.3
1973[1]	28.1	6.6	15.4	4.6	52.7	24.5
1974[1]	27.8	7.0	14.2	4.9	52.8	24.9

Source: "Families Below the Low-Income Level, by Sex of Head: 1959 and 1967 to 1974," Current Population Reports, Special Studies, Series P-23, No. 54. *The Social and Economic Status of the Black Population in the United States, 1974,* 1975, p. 43. Primary source: U.S. Department of Commerce, Social and Economic Statistics Administration, Bureau of the Census. *Notes:* 1. Based on 1970 census population controls; therefore, not strictly comparable to data for earlier years.

★ 1043 ★

Poverty

Number/Percent: Income Type and Sex of Head of Families Below Poverty Level, 1969, 1972, and 1974

[Families as of the following year]

Type of income and type of family	Black			White		
	1969	1972	1974	1969	1972	1974
ALL FAMILIES						
Total (thousands)	1,326	1,529	1,530	3,551	3,441	3,482
Percent[1]	100	100	100	100	100	100
With earnings	68	59	57	50	53	52
With income other than earnings:						
Public assistance income	45	55	60	21	28	32
Social Security income	24	21	22	35	27	25
Other transfer income[2]	8	6	7	9	10	11
Dividends, interest, and rent	3	3	3	20	17	18
Private pensions, alimony, etc.	9	7	8	11	9	12
FAMILIES WITH FEMALE HEAD, NO HUSBAND PRESENT						
Total (thousands)	737	972	1,024	1,069	1,135	1,297
Percent[1]	100	100	100	100	100	100
With earnings	59	51	51	48	49	46
With income other than earnings:						
Public assistance income	60	71	73	35	50	55
Social Security income	19	17	16	28	19	17
Other transfer income[2]	5	3	4	8	6	6
Dividends, interest, and rent	2	1	1	14	12	10
Private pensions, alimony, etc.	12	9	9	22	19	22

Source: "Families Below the Poverty Level by Type of Income and Sex of Head: 1969, 1972, and 1974," *The Social and Economic Status of the Black Population in the United States: An Historical View, 1790-1978,* 1979, p. 54. Primary source: U.S. Department of Commerce, Bureau of the Census. *Notes:* Data on families below the poverty level by type of income and race first became available from the Current Population Survey for 1969. 1. Detail does not add to total because some families have more than one of the type of income specified. 2. Includes unemployment and workmen's compensation, government employee pensions, and veterans' payments.

★ 1044 ★

Poverty

Relationships: Age Distribution of Black Women Receiving OEO Family Planning Services, 1971

Age	Number	Percent
All ages	83,681	100.0
Under 15 years old	808	1.0
15-19	19,483	23.3
20-24	29,666	35.5
25-29	15,902	19.0
30-34	9,171	11.0
35-39	5,113	6.1
40-44	2,485	3.0
45 years old and over	1,053	1.3

Source: Austin, "Black Women in OEO Funded Family Planning Services, by Age and Percent from 1/01/71 to 12/31/71," *The Black Woman: Myths and Realities*, 1975, p. 70. Primary source: Prepared by the National Urban League Research Department from data in U.S. Department of Health, Education, and Welfare, Family Planning Reporting Services, Reporting Period 01/01/71 to 12/31/71. *Note:* OEO = Office of Economic Opportunity.

★ 1045 ★

Poverty

Relationships: Black Family Characteristics in Low-Income Areas of Selected Cities, August 1970-March 1971

Subject	Low-income areas in--							
	Total urban areas[1]	New York	Chicago	Detroit	Philadelphia	Washington, D.C.	Los Angeles	Baltimore
Total, families (thousands)	1,612	270	144	93	106	83	69	79
Sex of head:								
Percent	100	100	100	100	100	100	100	100
Male	63	59	58	68	60	68	62	63
Female	37	41	42	32	40	32	38	37
Presence of children:								
Percent	100	100	100	100	100	100	100	100
No children under 18 years	33	31	31	39	34	35	31	32
Children 6 to 17 years only	30	33	30	26	31	29	30	34
Children under 6 years	37	36	40	35	35	36	40	35
Median income of families by sex of head:								
Male	$7,778	$7,809	$8,740	$8,866	$8,482	$7,575	$7,644	$8,505
Female	3,924	4,399	3,792	3,689	4,623	4,700	4,424	4,102
Work experience of head:								
Total, 16 to 64 years old (thousands)	1,403	242	126	70	90	73	60	70

[Continued]

★ 1045 ★

Relationships: Black Family Characteristics in Low-Income Areas of Selected Cities, August 1970-March 1971
[Continued]

Subject	Total urban areas[1]	Low-income areas in--						
		New York	Chicago	Detroit	Philadelphia	Washington, D.C.	Los Angeles	Baltimore
Percent	100	100	100	100	100	100	100	100
Worked	79	70	72	78	74	84	80	79
50 to 52 weeks	56	57	53	51	52	70	52	59
Full time	55	55	52	51	51	67	50	56
27 to 49 weeks	15	9	12	19	14	10	17	16
1 to 26 weeks	8	5	8	8	8	5	12	6
Did not work	21	29	28	22	26	16	20	21

Source: "Characteristics of Black Families in Selected Low-Income Areas," Current Population Reports, Special Studies, Series P-23, No. 42. *The Social and Economic Status of the Black Population in the United States, 1971*, 1972, p. 140. Primary source: U.S. Department of Commerce, Social and Economic Statistics Administration, Bureau of the Census. *Notes:* Statistics on low-income areas based on information gathered in the Census Employment Survey (CES), conducted during the period August 1970 to March 1971. 1. Includes selected low-income areas in 44 other cities, not shown separately.

★ 1046 ★
Poverty

Relationships: Characteristics of People Below Low-Income Level, 1959 and 1968

	Total	Negro	White	Negro as a percent of total
1959				
All persons (millions)	38.8	9.9	28.3	26
Percent	100	100	100	(X)
Family members	85	92	82	28
Heads	21	19	21	23
Children under 18 years	41	51	37	32
Other family members	23	22	24	25
Unrelated individuals	15	8	18	14
Male	6	3	7	14
Female	9	5	11	14
Persons 65 years and over	14	7	17	13
Persons under 65 years	86	93	83	28
1968				
All persons (millions)	25.4	7.6	17.4	30
Percent	100	100	100	(X)
Family members	82	90	78	33
Heads	20	18	21	27

[Continued]

★ 1046 ★

Relationships: Characteristics of People Below Low-Income Level, 1959 and 1968

[Continued]

	Total	Negro	White	Negro as a percent of total
Children under 18 years	42	55	37	39
Other family members	19	17	20	26
Unrelated individuals	18	10	22	17
Male	5	4	6	21
Female	13	6	16	15
Persons 65 years and over	18	9	23	14
Persons under 65 years	82	81	77	34

Source: "Distribution of Persons Below the Poverty Level, by Family Status and Age, in 1959 and 1968," Current Population Reports, Special Studies, Series P-23, No. 29. *The Social and Economic Status of the Black Population in the United States, 1969,* 1969, p. 25. Primary source: U.S. Department of Commerce, Bureau of the Census. *Note:* X Not applicable.

★ 1047 ★

Poverty

Relationships: Characteristics of People Below Low-Income Level, 1970 and 1974

[Persons as of the following year]

Family status and year	All races	Black	White	Black as a percent of all races
1970				
Total (thousands)	25,420	7,548	17,484	30
Percent	100	100	100	(X)
In families	80	89	76	33
Head	21	20	21	28
65 years and over	5	3	5	21
Related children under 18 years	40	52	35	38
Other family members	19	17	20	26
Unrelated individuals	20	11	24	17
65 years and over	11	5	14	12
1974				
Total (thousands)	24,260	7,467	16,290	31
Percent	100	100	100	(X)
In families	80	87	77	33
Head	21	20	21	30
65 years and over	3	2	3	23

[Continued]

★ 1047 ★

Relationships: Characteristics of People Below Low-Income Level, 1970 and 1974

[Continued]

Family status and year	All races	Black	White	Black as a percent of all races
Related children under 18 years	42	51	38	37
Other family members	17	15	18	28
Unrelated individuals	20	13	23	20
65 years and over	8	5	10	17

Source: "Distribution of Persons Below the Low-Income Level in 1970 and 1974, by Family Status," Current Population Reports, Special Studies, Series P-23, No. 54. *The Social and Economic Status of the Black Population in the United States, 1974*, 1975, p. 44. Primary source: U.S. Department of Commerce, Social and Economic Statistics Administration, Bureau of the Census. *Note:* X Not applicable.

★ 1048 ★

Poverty

Relationships: City Residence Area of Black Families Below Low-Income Level by Region, 1970

Area and type of residence	Total Negro families (thousands)	Below the low-income level		Percent distribution	
		Number (thousands)	Percent of total	Total	Below the low-income level
United States	4,928	1,445	29	100	100
Metropolitan areas[1]	3,583	828	23	73	57
Central cities	2,807	662	24	57	46
Outside central cities	776	166	21	16	11
Nonmetropolitan areas	1,345	617	46	27	43
North and West	2,390	492	21	100	100
Metropolitan areas[1]	2,219	461	21	93	94
Central cities	1,800	399	22	75	81
Outside central cities	419	62	15	18	13
Nonmetropolitan areas	170	29	17	7	6
South	2,538	953	38	100	100
Metropolitan areas[1]	1,363	365	27	54	38
Central cities	1,007	261	26	40	27
Outside central cities	356	104	29	14	11
Nonmetropolitan areas	1,175	589	50	46	62

Source: "Negro Families Below the Low-Income Level in 1970, by Region and Type of Residence," Current Population Reports, Special Studies, Series P-23, No. 42. *The Social and Economic Status of the Black Population in the United States, 1971*, 1972, p. 42. Primary source: U.S. Department of Commerce, Social and Economic Statistics Administration, Bureau of the Census. *Note:* 1. Metropolitan areas as defined in 1960.

★ 1049 ★
Poverty

Relationships: Education of Adult (Aged 25 and Over) Male and Female Family Heads Below Low-Income Level, 1969

Years of school completed	Male head		Female head	
	White	Negro	White	Negro
Total (thousands)	2,271	564	907	611
Percent	100	100	100	100
Elementary:				
Less than 8 years	38	60	25	37
8 years	20	8	13	11
High school:				
1 to 3 years	14	17	25	34
4 years	17	12	27	16
College:				
1 year or more	10	3	10	1

Source: "Years of School Completed by Family Heads 25 Years old and Over Below the Low-Income Level in 1969, by Sex of Head," Current Population Reports, Special Studies, Series P-23, No. 38. *The Social and Economic Status of the Black Population in the United States, 1970*, 1970, p. 39. Primary source: U.S. Department of Commerce, Bureau of the Census.

★ 1050 ★
Poverty

Relationships: Education of Adult (Aged 25 and Over) Male and Female Family Heads Below Low-Income Level, 1970

Years of school completed	Male head		Female head	
	Negro	White	Negro	White
Total (thousands)	591	2,340	708	926
Percent	100	100	100	100
Elementary:				
Less than 8 years[1]	59	35	32	23
8 years	10	20	14	16
High school:				
1 to 3 years	16	16	35	22
4 years	11	18	17	29
College:				
1 to 3 years	3	6	2	8
4 years or more	1	4	-	2

[Continued]

★ 1050 ★

Relationships: Education of Adult (Aged 25 and Over) Male and Female Family Heads Below Low-Income Level, 1970
[Continued]

Years of school completed	Male head		Female head	
	Negro	White	Negro	White
PERCENT BELOW THE LOW-INCOME LEVEL				
Total	19	6	53	23
Elementary:				
Less than 8 years[1]	33	19	61	32
8 years	20	9	61	26
High school:				
1 to 3 years	13	6	63	27
4 years	9	3	36	19
College:				
1 to 3 years	9	3	(B)	19
4 years or more	2	2	(B)	6

Source: "Years of school Completed by Family Heads 25 Years Old and over Below the Low-Income Level in 1970, by Sex of Head," Current Population Reports, Special Studies, Series P-23, No. 42. *The Social and Economic Status of the Black Population in the United States, 1971,* 1972, p. 43. Primary source: U.S. Department of Commerce, Social and Economic Statistics Administration, Bureau of the Census. *Notes:* - Represents zero. B Base less than 75,000. 1. Includes heads with no years of school completed.

★ 1051 ★
Poverty

Relationships: Employment and Work Experience of Male and Female Family Heads Below Low-Income Level, 1970
[Family heads as of March 1971]

Employment status and work experience of head	Male head		Female head	
	Negro	White	Negro	White
All family heads (thousands)	625	2,604	820	1,097
EMPLOYMENT STATUS OF HEAD IN MARCH 1971				
Percent	100	100	100	100
Employed	55	51	30	28
Unemployed	5	5	6	5
Not in civilian labor force	39	42	63	67
In Armed Forces	1	2	(X)	(X)
WORK EXPERIENCE OF HEAD IN 1970				
Percent	100	100	100	100
Worked	67	61	47	40
50 to 52 weeks	32	33	14	10

[Continued]

★ 1051 ★

Relationships: Employment and Work Experience of Male and Female Family Heads Below Low-Income Level, 1970
[Continued]

Employment status and work experience of head	Male head		Female head	
	Negro	White	Negro	White
Full time	27	28	9	7
1 to 49 weeks	35	28	33	30
Main reason for working part-year:				
Unemployed	15	12	5	6
Other	20	16	27	24
Did not work	32	38	53	60
In Armed Forces	1	2	(X)	(X)

Source: "Distribution of Family Heads Below the Low-Income Level in 1970 by Employment Status, Work Experience, and Sex of Head," Current Population Reports, Special Studies, Series P-23, No. 42. *The Social and Economic Status of the Black Population in the United States, 1971,* 1972, p. 45. Primary source: U.S. Department of Commerce, Social and Economic Statistics Administration, Bureau of the Census. *Note:* X Not applicable.

★ 1052 ★

Poverty

Relationships: Families Below Poverty Level, by Work Experience of Head, 1968
[**Number in thousands**. Families as of March 1969.]

CHARACTERISTIC	NUMBER OF POOR HOUSEHOLDS				INCIDENCE OF POVERTY[1]			
	Total	White	Negro and other races		Total	White	Negro and other races	
			Total	Negro			Total	Negro
FAMILIES								
Total[2]	5,047	3,616	1,431	1,366	10.0	8.0	28.2	29.4
Head worked in 1968, total	2,876	1,982	894	866	6.7	5.1	21.8	23.1
At full-time jobs	2,255	1,597	658	632	5.6	4.4	17.9	18.9
50-52 weeks	1,353	979	375	356	4.0	3.2	13.5	14.2
At part-time jobs	621	385	236	234	23.8	17.6	55.5	57.5
Head did not work in 1968	2,106	1,581	524	487	30.9	26.8	57.2	57.6

Source: "Families and Unrelated Individuals with Income Below Poverty Level, by Race and Work Experience of Head: 1968," *Statistical Abstract of the United States, 1970,* p. 330. Primary source: Dept. of Commerce, Bureau of the Census, *Current Population Reports,* series P-60, No. 68, and unpublished data. *Notes:* 1. Poor households as percent of total households in specified group. 2. Includes members of the Armed Forces, not shown separately by work experience.

★ 1053 ★

Poverty

Relationships: Family Size and Income in Families Below Low-Income Level, 1969

Area	All races		Negro		White	
	Persons per family	Income per family member	Persons per family	Income per family member	Persons per family	Income per family member
United States	3.9	$548	4.8	$505	3.6	$568
Metropolitan areas[1]	3.9	573	4.6	548	3.6	588
Central cities	4.0	584	4.5	552	3.6	613
Outside central cities	3.8	555	5.1	533	3.5	560
Outside metropolitan areas	4.0	523	5.0	458	3.6	551

Source: "Families Below the Low-Income Level in 1969, by Average Size of Family and Income per Family Member," Current Population Reports, Special Studies, Series P-23, No. 38. *Social and Economic Status of the Black Population in the United States, 1970,* 1970, p. 40. Primary source: U.S. Department of Commerce, Bureau of the Census. *Note:* 1. Metropolitan areas as defined in 1960 census.

★ 1054 ★

Poverty

Relationships: Family Status and Residence of People Below Poverty Level, 1959 and 1968

[**Numbers in thousands**. Persons as of April 1960 and March 1969.]

FAMILY STATUS AND RACE	NUMBER BELOW POVERTY LEVEL				PERCENT BELOW POVERTY LEVEL			
	Metropolitan areas		Outside metropolitan areas		Metropolitan areas		Outside metropolitan areas	
	1959[1]	1968	1959[1]	1968	1959[1]	1968	1959[1]	1968
All races	17,019	12,871	21,747	12,508	15.3	10.0	33.2	18.0
65 years and over	2,452	2,353	3,029	2,279	26.9	20.5	47.0	32.3
In families	13,546	9,958	19,326	10,727	13.2	8.4	31.5	16.4
Head	3,342	2,477	4,632	2,570	11.7	7.6	28.2	14.3
Family members under 18 years[2]	6,755	5,433	9,123	5,296	17.3	12.2	37.0	20.9
Other family members	3,449	2,047	5,571	2,860	9.8	5.0	27.3	12.9
White	11,825	8,474	16,511	8,887	12.0	7.6	28.2	14.2
65 years and over	2,151	2,037	2,593	1,902	25.5	19.3	43.9	29.3
In families	8,901	6,091	14,422	7,421	9.8	5.9	26.2	12.6
Head	2,369	1,657	3,658	1,957	9.2	5.7	24.3	11.8
Family members under 18 years[2]	4,128	2,957	6,496	3,379	12.2	7.9	30.3	15.3
Other family members	2,404	1,477	4,268	2,085	7.6	4.1	23.1	10.2
Negro	5,002	4,144	4,925	3,477	42.8	26.6	77.7	54.6
65 years and over	289	295	422	360	46.5	36.2	81.6	64.3
In families	4,487	3,660	4,625	3,185	42.2	25.6	77.7	53.6
Head	940	779	920	589	36.1	22.9	73.2	47.4

[Continued]

★ 1054 ★

Relationships: Family Status and Residence of People Below Poverty Level, 1959 and 1968

[Continued]

FAMILY STATUS AND RACE	NUMBER BELOW POVERTY LEVEL				PERCENT BELOW POVERTY LEVEL			
	Metropolitan areas		Outside metropolitan areas		Metropolitan areas		Outside metropolitan areas	
	1959[1]	1968	1959[1]	1968	1959[1]	1968	1959[1]	1968
Family members under 18 years[2]	2,541	2,358	2,481	1,844	53.9	34.9	84.2	61.9
Other family members	1,006	524	1,224	751	30.4	12.6	70.1	43.6

Source: "Persons Below Poverty Level, by Residence, Family Status, and Race: 1959 and 1968," *Statistical Abstract of the United States, 1970*, p. 330. Primary source: Dept. of Commerce, Bureau of the Census; unpublished data. *Notes:* 1. Data based on 1960 1-in-a-thousand sample. 2. Other than head or wife.

★ 1055 ★

Poverty

Relationships: Family Type of Low-Income Families, 1967 and 1970-1974

[Families as of the following year]

Type of family and race of head	1967	1970	1971	1972	1973	1974
BLACK						
Total (thousands)	1,555	1,481	1,484	1,529	1,527	1,530
Male head	839	648	605	558	553	506
Married wife present	(NA)	576	561	514	503	466
Female head	716	834	879	972	974	1,024
Percent	100	100	100	100	100	100
Male head	54	44	41	36	36	33
Married wife present	(NA)	39	38	34	33	30
Female head	46	56	59	64	64	67
WHITE						
Total (thousands)	4,056	3,708	3,751	3,441	3,219	3,482
Male head	3,019	2,606	2,560	2,306	2,029	2,185
Married wife present	(NA)	2,505	2,438	2,206	1,929	2,091
Female head	1,037	1,102	1,191	1,135	1,190	1,297
Percent	100	100	100	100	100	100
Male head	74	70	68	67	63	63
Married wife present	(NA)	68	65	64	60	60
Female head	26	30	32	33	37	37

Source: "Distribution of Low-Income Families, by Type of Family: 1967 and 1970 to 1974," Current Population Reports, Special Series P-23, No. 54. *The Social and Economic Status of the Black Population in the United States, 1974*, 1975, p. 45. Primary source: U.S. Department of Commerce, Social and Economic Statistics Administration, Bureau of the Census. *Note:* NA Not available.

★ 1056 ★

Poverty

Relationships: Income Source of Families Below Low-Income Level, 1973

[Families as of the following year]

Type of income	Total		Male head		Female head	
	Black	White	Black	White	Black	White
Total (thousands)	1,527	3,219	553	2,029	974	1,190
Percent	100	100	100	100	100	100
With income from earnings:						
Wage or salary income	59	52	77	53	49	50
Nonfarm self-employment income	3	12	6	17	1	3
Farm self-employment income	2	6	6	10	-	1
With income other than earnings:						
Social Security income	22	27	30	32	18	19
Public assistance income	57	30	25	18	75	52
Other transfer income[1]	6	10	13	12	3	7
Dividends, interest, and rent	2	16	5	19	1	11
Private pensions, alimony, etc.	8	10	3	5	10	19

Source: "Source of Income for Families Below the Low-Income level in 1973," Current Population Reports, Special Studies, Series P-23, No. 54. *The Social and Economic Status of the Black Population in the United States, 1974,* 1975, p. 48. Primary source: U.S. Department of Commerce, Social and Economic Statistics Administration, Bureau of the Census. *Notes:* - Rounds to zero. Detailed figures may not add to total because some families have more than one of the types of income specified. 1. Includes unemployment and workmen's compensation, government employee pensions, and veterans' payments.

★ 1057 ★

Poverty

Relationships: Number/Percent of Black and White Women in Poverty Receiving Family Planning Services, by Age, 1971

Age	All Groups	Black		White	
		Number	Percent	Number	Percent
All ages	249,003	83,681	33.6	108,108	43.4
Under 15 years old	1,208	808	66.9	301	24.9
15-19	55,826	19,483	34.9	29,788	53.4
20-24	88,099	29,666	33.7	41,565	47.2
25-29	48,345	15,902	32.9	18,056	37.3
30-34	27,406	9,171	33.5	9,198	33.6
35-39	15,804	5,113	32.4	4,845	30.7

[Continued]

★ 1057 ★

Relationships: Number/Percent of Black and White Women in Poverty Receiving Family Planning Services, by Age, 1971

[Continued]

Age	All Groups	Black		White	
		Number	Percent	Number	Percent
40-44	8,233	2,485	30.2	2,667	32.4
45 years old and over	4,082	1,053	25.8	1,688	41.4

Source: Austin, "Number and Percent of Patients in Poverty Status Receiving Family Planning Services, by Selected Ethnic Designation and Age," *The Black Woman: Myths and Realities*, 1975, p. 69. Primary source: Prepared by the National Urban League Research Department from data in U.S. Department of Health, Education, and Welfare, Family Planning Reporting Services, Reporting Period 01/01/71 to 12/31/71.

★ 1058 ★

Poverty

Relationships: Number/Percent of Black and White Women in Poverty Receiving OEO Funded Family Planning Services, by Age, 1971

Age	All Groups	Black		White	
		Number	Percent	Number	Percent
All ages	145,579	84,117	57.8	39,019	26.8
Under 15 years old	1,225	1,047	85.5	126	10.3
15-19	30,580	21,344	69.8	6,658	21.8
20-24	49,839	29,456	59.1	14,426	28.9
25-29	29,963	15,751	52.6	8,942	29.8
30-34	17,423	8,959	51.4	4,719	27.1
35-39	9,873	4,726	47.9	2,418	24.5
40-44	4,809	2,109	43.9	1,174	24.4
45 years old and over	1,867	725	38.8	556	29.8

Source: Austin, "Number and Percent of Patients in Poverty Status Receiving Family Planning Services, by Selected Ethnic Designation and Age," *The Black Woman: Myths and Realities*, 1975, p. 69. Primary source: Prepared by the National Urban League Research Department from data in U.S. Department of Health, Education, and Welfare, Family Planning Reporting Services, Reporting Period 01/01/71 to 12/31/71. *Note:* OEO = Office of Economic Opportunity.

★ 1059 ★
Poverty

Relationships: Selected Characteristics of Black Families Below Low-Income Level in Selected City Low-Income Areas, August 1970-March 1971

Subject	Total urban areas[1]	New York	Chicago	Detroit	Philadelphia	Washington, D.C.	Los Angeles	Baltimore
				Low-income areas in--				
Total, families (thousands)	438	60	50	23	25	18	17	20
Sex of head:								
Percent	100	100	100	100	100	100	100	100
Male	35	32	34	34	33	38	37	32
Female	65	68	66	66	67	62	63	68
Presence of children:								
Percent	100	100	100	100	100	100	100	100
No children under 18 years	17	15	16	26	19	20	16	15
With children 6 to 17 years only	31	37	28	24	29	26	33	33
With children under 6 years	52	48	56	50	52	54	51	51
Work experience of head:								
Percent, 16 to 64 years old	100	100	100	100	100	100	100	100
Worked	47	29	39	35	35	45	43	40
50 to 52 weeks	21	18	19	13	14	25	13	16
27 to 49 weeks	11	5	8	9	10	7	12	11
1 to 26 weeks	14	6	12	13	11	13	18	13
Did not work	53	71	61	65	65	55	57	60
PERCENT BELOW LOW-INCOME LEVEL								
Total	27	22	35	25	24	22	25	26
Male head	15	12	21	13	13	12	15	13
Female head	48	37	55	52	39	42	41	47

Source: "Characteristics of Black Families Below the Low-Income Level in Selected Low-Income Areas," Current Population Reports, Special Studies, Series P-23, No. 42. *The Social and Economic Status of the Black Population in the United States, 1971,* 1972, p. 143. Primary source: U.S. Department of Commerce, Social and Economic Statistics Administration, Bureau of the Census. *Notes:* Statistics on low-income areas based on information gathered in the Census Employment Survey (CES), conducted during the period August 1970 to March 1971. For the period covered by the CES, the low-income threshold was about $3,880 for a nonfarm family of four, headed by a male with a wife and two children under 18, and $6,904 for a nonfarm family with a male head and with 7 or more persons (none under 18 years old). 1. Includes selected low-income areas in 44 other cities, not shown separately.

★ 1060 ★

Poverty

Relationships: The Dollar Gap for Poor Households, 1959, 1963, and 1968

[Families, and presence of children as of March of year following year shown. Poverty gap defined as the difference between the total income of families and unrelated individuals below the poverty level and their respective poverty levels. In computing the income deficit, families reporting a net income loss are assigned zero dollars; for such cases the poverty gap is equal to the poverty level].

TYPE OF HOUSEHOLD	1959			1963			1968		
	Poor households (mil.)	Median income deficit (dol.)	Total deficit (bil. dol.)	Poor households (mil.)	Median income deficit (dol.)	Total deficit (bil. dol.)	Poor households (mil.)	Median income deficit (dol.)	Total deficit (bil. dol.)
Total households[1]	13.2	856	13.7	12.5	816	12.9	9.7	769	9.8
Families	8.3	956	9.8	7.6	998	9.4	5.0	993	6.5
Male head	6.4	895	7.2	5.6	889	6.3	3.3	875	3.8
Female head	1.9	1,165	2.7	2.0	1,386	3.1	1.8	1,290	2.7
White families	6.2	868	6.7	5.5	907	6.2	3.6	907	4.3
Male head	5.0	815	5.0	4.3	830	4.5	2.6	818	2.8
With children under age 18	2.9	971	3.5	2.4	1,057	3.1	1.4	1,022	1.9
Without children under age 18	2.1	636	1.6	1.8	653	1.4	1.2	660	1.0
Female head	1.2	1,085	1.6	1.2	1,277	1.7	1.0	1,176	1.5
With children under age 18	0.9	1,256	1.4	0.9	1,569	1.5	0.8	1,449	1.3
Without children under age 18	0.3	735	.2	0.3	723	.2	0.2	687	.2
Families of Negro and other races	2.1	1,280	3.1	2.1	1,335	3.2	1.4	1,260	2.1
Male head	1.5	1,259	2.1	1.3	1,154	1.8	0.7	1,112	1.0
With children under age 18	1.1	1,602	1.8	1.0	1,482	1.5	0.5	1,342	1.1
Without children under age 18	0.4	729	.3	0.3	663	.3	0.2	739	.2
Female head	0.7	1,330	1.0	0.8	1,538	1.4	0.7	1,445	1.2
With children under age 18	0.6	1,506	.9	0.7	1,724	1.3	0.7	1,552	1.1
Without children under age 18	0.1	(B)	(B)	0.1	(B)	(B)	0.1	(B)	(B)

Source: "Poor Households—Poverty Gap: 1959, 1963, and 1968," *Statistical Abstract of the United States, 1970,* p. 329. Primary source: Department of Commerce, Bureau of the Census; *Current Population Reports,* Series P-60, No. 68, and unpublished data. *Notes:* B: 1959 and 1963 base less than 200,00; 1968 base less than 75,000. 1. Families and unrelated individuals combined.

★ 1061 ★

Poverty

Relationships: Work Characteristics of Male and Female Family Heads Below Low-Income Level, 1973

[Families as of the following year]

Work experience	Male head		Female head	
	Black	White	Black	White
Total family (thousands)	553	2,029	974	1,190
Percent	100	100	100	100
Worked	65	61	38	40
50 to 52 weeks	32	30	13	8

[Continued]

★ 1061 ★

Relationships: Work Characteristics of Male and Female Family Heads Below Low-Income Level, 1973
[Continued]

Work experience	Male head		Female head	
	Black	White	Black	White
Full time	27	27	10	5
1 to 49 weeks	33	30	25	32
Did not work	35	38	62	60
Head in Armed Forces	1	1	(X)	(X)
Total, worked part year (thousands)	181	618	240	378
Main reason for working part year:				
Percent	100	100	100	100
Unemployed	43	42	23	21
Other	58	58	77	79
Total, did not work (thousands)	191	781	602	714
Main reason for not working:				
Percent	100	100	100	100
Ill or disabled	63	50	21	14
Keeping house	(X)	(X)	70	79
Going to school	5	4	3	3
Unable to find work	7	3	4	2
Retired	23	40	1	-
Other	3	2	-	-

Source: "Work Experience of Family Heads Below the Low-Income Level in 1973, by Sex of Head," Current Population Reports, Special Studies, Series P-23, No. 54. *The Social and Economic Status of the Black Population in the United States, 1974,* 1975, p. 45. Primary source: U.S. Department of Commerce, Social and Economic Statistics Administration, Bureau of the Census. *Note:* - Represents or rounds to zero. X Not applicable.

★ 1062 ★

Poverty

Relationships: Work Experience of Heads of Families in Poverty, 1973
[In thousands, except percent. Families as of March 1974.]

WORK EXPERIENCE	ALL RACES		WHITE		NEGRO	
	Male	Female	Male	Female	Male	Female
Total	2,635	2,193	2,029	1,190	553	974
Worked in 1973	1,630	852	1,236	476	358	372
Percent worked year-round full time	50.4	25.1	50.2	26.3	49.7	24.0
Did not work in 1973	990	1,340	781	714	191	602
Percent main reason for not working	100.0	100.0	100.0	100.0	100.0	100.0
Ill or disabled	52.6	17.1	50.3	13.9	62.8	21.1
Keeping house	-	74.7	-	78.6	-	69.6

[Continued]

★ 1062 ★

Relationships: Work Experience of Heads of Families in Poverty, 1973
[Continued]

WORK EXPERIENCE	ALL RACES		WHITE		NEGRO	
	Male	Female	Male	Female	Male	Female
In school	4.2	2.8	4.0	3.1	4.7	2.7
Unable to find work	4.1	3.3	3.5	2.4	7.3	4.5
Other 16	39.0	2.2	42.1	2.2	25.1	2.2
In Armed Forces in 1973	16	-	12	-	4	-

Source: "Work Experience of Family Heads Below the Low Income Level, by Sex and Race: 1973," *Statistical Abstract of the United States, 1975*, p. 404. Primary source: U.S. Bureau of the Census, *Current Population Reports*, Series P-60, No. 98. *Note:* - Represents zero.

★ 1063 ★

Poverty

Relationships: Working Mothers in Poverty and with Minor Children, by Work Experience, 1973
[As of March 1974.]

WORK EXPERIENCE	ALL RACES			WHITE			NEGRO		
	Total (1,000)	Below low income level		Total (1,00)	Below low income level		Total (1,000)	Below low income level	
		Number (1,000)	Percent		Number (1,000)	Percent		Number (1,000)	Percent
All women with own children	30,202	3,355	11.1	26,158	2,131	8.1	3,540	1,161	32.8
Worked in 1973	16,596	1,334	8.0	14,106	819	5.8	2,209	493	22.3
50-52 weeks	7,886	351	4.5	6,619	187	2.8	1,144	159	13.9
27-49 weeks	6,035	559	9.3	5,136	343	6.7	775	204	26.3
1-26 weeks	2,674	424	15.9	2,351	289	12.3	290	130	44.8
Did not work in 1973	13,606	2,020	14.8	12,052	1,311	10.9	1,332	668	50.2
Main reason: Keeping house	12,765	1,723	13.5	11,471	1,157	10.1	1,079	528	48.9
Families and subfamilies headed by women with own children	4,684	1,953	41.7	3,081	1,056	34.3	1,536	870	56.6
Worked in 1973	3,044	852	28.0	2,101	470	22.4	905	378	41.8
50-52 weeks	1,632	220	13.5	1,177	93	7.9	445	127	28.5
27-49 weeks	1,014	371	36.6	666	207	31.1	330	161	48.8
1-26 weeks	398	261	65.6	259	170	65.6	131	90	68.7
Did not work in 1973	1,640	1,101	67.1	979	586	59.9	631	492	78.0
Main reason: Keeping house	1,304	870	66.7	814	477	58.6	464	373	80.4

Source: "Working Mothers with Children Under 18, by Low Income Status, Work Experience, and Race; 1973," *Statistical Abstract of the United States, 1975*, p. 404. Primary source: U.S. Bureau of the Census, *Current Population Reports*, series P-60, No. 98.

★ 1064 ★

Poverty

Total Black Families and Black Families Below Poverty Level by City Area and Farm or Nonfarm Location, 1968

	Percent distribution of Negro families		Negro families below the poverty level in each location	
	Total	Below the poverty level	Number (thousands)	Percent
United States	100	100	1,366	29
Inside metropolitan areas	73	57	779	23
Central cities	59	45	620	23
Suburbs	14	12	159	24
Outside metropolitan areas	27	43	589	47
Farm	3	7	94	61
Nonfarm	23	36	496	46

Source: "Location of All Negro Families and of Negro Families Below the Poverty level, 1968," Current Population Reports, Special Studies, Series P-23, No. 29. *The Social and Economic Status of the Black Population in the United States, 1969,* 1969, p. 23. Primary source: U.S. Department of Commerce, Bureau of the Census.

Support Services

★ 1065 ★

Help for Children: Characteristics of Families Receiving Aid for Dependent Children, 1969

[Preliminary. Refers to federally aided State programs providing aid to needy children deprived of parental care or support. Based on a sample and subject to sampling variability.]

CHARACTERISTIC	Percent
Number of families 1,000	1,630.4
Percent distribution	100.0
Race:	
White	48.0

[Continued]

★ 1065 ★

Help for Children: Characteristics of Families Receiving Aid for Dependent Children, 1969

[Continued]

CHARACTERISTIC	Percent
Negro	45.1
Other[1]	6.9

Source: "Aid to Families with Dependent Children (AFDC)—Characteristics of Recipient Families: 1969," *Statistical Abstract of the United States, 1970,* p. 298. Primary source: Dept. of Health, Education, and Welfare, Social and Rehabilitation Service; *Characteristics of AFDC Families, 1969. Note:* 1. Includes unknown or not reported.

★ 1066 ★

Support Services

Help for Children: Percentage Distribution of Families with Dependent Children Receiving Help through Aid to Families With Dependent Children (AFDC), 1971 and 1973

CHARACTERISTIC	1971	1973
Number of families (1,000)	2,524	2,990
White	48.3	46.9
Negro	43.3	45.8
Other[1]	8.4	7.3

Source: "Aid to Families with Dependent Children (AFDC) Percent Distribution of Characteristics of Recipient Families: 1971 and 1973," *Statistical Abstract of the United States,* 1975, p. 389. Primary source: U.S. Social and Rehabilitation Service, *Findings of the 1971 AFDC Study,* December 1971 (Part I), and *Findings of the 1973 AFDC Study,* June 1974 (Part I). *Note:* 1. Includes unknown or not reported.

★ 1067 ★

Support Services

Planning Services: Age Distribution of Black Women Receiving Federally-Funded Family Planning Services, 1971

Age	Number	Percent
All ages	282,052	100.0%
Under 15 years old	2,476	.9%
15-19	68,588	24.3
20-24	104,589	37.1
25-29	53,050	18.8

[Continued]

★ 1067 ★

Planning Services: Age Distribution of Black Women Receiving Federally-Funded Family Planning Services, 1971

[Continued]

Age	Number	Percent
30-34	28,740	10.2
35-39	15,049	5.3
40-44	6,905	2.4
45 years old and over	2,655	.9

Source: Austin, "Black Women in Federally-Funded Family Planning, by Age and Percent," *The Black Woman: Myths and Realities*, 1975, p. 68. Primary source: Prepared by the National Urban League Research Department from data in U.S. Department of Health, Education, and Welfare Family Planning Reporting Service, Reporting Period 01/01/71 to 12/31/71.

★ 1068 ★

Support Services

Planning Services: Number/Percent of Black and White Women Receiving Federally-Funded Family Planning Services, by Age, 1971

Age	All Groups	Black Number	Black Percent	White Number	White Percent
All ages	798,129	282,052	35.3	352,125	44.1
Under 15 years old	3,712	2,476	66.7	903	24.3
15-19	190,690	68,588	36.0	99,724	52.3
20-24	299,355	104,589	34.9	142,409	47.6
25-29	152,438	53,050	34.8	58,404	38.3
30-34	79,566	28,740	36.1	26,938	33.9
35-39	42,523	15,049	35.4	13,157	30.9
40-44	20,686	6,905	33.4	6,771	32.7
45 years old and over	9,159	2655	29.0	3,819	41.7

Source: Austin, "Number and Percent of Patients Receiving Family Planning Services, by Selected Ethnic Designation and Age," *The Black Woman: Myths and Realities*, 1975, p. 68. Primary source: Prepared by the National Urban League Research Department from data in U.S. Department of Health, Education, and Welfare Family Planning Reporting Service, Reporting Period 01/01/71 to 12/31/71.

Chapter 6
HEALTH, DISABILITIES, AND HEALTH CARE

Disabilities

★ 1069 ★

Average Disability Days from July 1965 through June 1967, and in 1969

Type of Disability	JULY 1965--JUNE 1967		1969	
	Negro and other races	White	Negro and other races	White
Restricted-activity days	16.5[1]	15.4[1]	15.7	14.6
Bed-disability days	7.1	5.8	7.2	5.9
Work-loss days[2]	6.8	5.4	7.1	4.9
School-loss days[3]	4.2	5.3	4.7	5.5
Percent of persons with chronic conditions and activity limitations	11.2	11.5	[4]	[4]

Source: Adapted by the editors from "Days of Disability Per Person Per Year, July 1965-June 1967, and Percent of Population with Activity Limitations Resulting from Chronic Illnesses," Current Population Reports, Special Studies, Series P-23, No. 29. *The Social and Economic Status of the Black Population in the United States, 1969*, 1969, p. 67; and "Days of Disability Per Person Per Year, by Type of Disability: 1969," Current Population Reports, Special Studies, Series P-23, No. 38. *The Social and Economic Status of the Black Population in the United States, 1970*, 1970, p. 100. Primary source: U.S. Department of Health, Education, and Welfare. *Notes:* 1. For all types of illnesses, including chronic conditions, adjusted for age differences in the white population and that of Negro and other races. 2. Includes persons 17 years of age and over currently employed. 3. Includes children 6-16 years of age (data not age-adjusted). 4. Not reported in source document.

★ 1070 ★

Disabilities

Blindness: Gender of Blind Persons in 1910

RACIAL CLASS	BLIND POPULATION: 1910					
	Number				Per 100,000	
	Both sexes	Male	Female	Males to 1,000 females	Male	Female
All classes	57,272	32,443	24,829	1,307	68.5	55.6
Negro	8,819	4,971	3,878	1,282	101.7	78.5
White	47,585	26,994	20,591	1,311	64.0	52.1
Indian	804	451	353	1,278	333.7	270.4
Chinese, Japanese, and other	34	27	7	[1]	20.3	50.6

Source: [Untitled Table], *Negro Population, 1790-1915*, 1918, p. 451. Primary source: U.S. Bureau of the Census. *Negro Population, 1790-1915.* Washington, D.C.: Government Printing Office, 1918. *Note:* 1. Ratio not shown where number of females is less than 100.

★ 1071 ★

Disabilities

Blindness: Racial Distribution of Blind Persons in 1910

RACIAL CLASS	POPULATION: 1910				Blind per 100,000 of class specified
	Number		Distribution per cent		
	Total	Blind	Total	Blind	
All classes	91,972,266	57,272	100.0	100.0	62.3
Negro	9,827,763	8,849	10.7	15.5	90.0
White	81,731,957	47,585	88.9	83.1	58.2
Indian	265,683	804	0.3	1.4	302.6
Chinese, Japanese, and other	146,863	34	0.2	0.1	23.2

Source: [Untitled Table], *Negro Population, 1790-1915*, 1918, p. 451. Primary source: U.S. Bureau of the Census. *Negro Population, 1790-1915.* Washington, D.C.: Government Printing Office, 1918.

★ 1072 ★

Disabilities

Deafness: Communication Abilities of Deaf Persons in 1910

| MEANS OF COMMUNICATION | DEAF-MUTES 10 YEARS OF AGE AND OVER: 1910 | | | |
| | Number | | Percentage distribution | |
	Negro	White	Negro	White
Total	983	15,957	100.0	100.0
Able to use speech	119	4,056	12.1	25.4
Other means also	93	3,706	9.5	23.8
No other means	16	147	1.6	0.9
No report as to other means	10	113	1.0	0.7
Unable to use speech	850	11,850	86.5	74.3
Report other means	783	11,381	79.7	71.3
Report no means	11	87	1.1	0.5
No report as to other means	56	382	5.7	2.4
No report as to means	14	51	1.4	0.3
Number reporting:				
Speech	109	3,943	11.1	24.7
Writing	400	12,489	40.7	78.3
Finger spelling	415	12,284	42.2	77.0
Sign language	388	12,281	39.5	77.0
Miscellaneous methods	387	1,470	39.4	9.2

Source: "Means of Communication," *Negro Population, 1790-1915*, 1918, p. 454. Primary source. U.S. Bureau of the Census. *Negro Population, 1790-1915.* Washington, D.C.: Government Printing Office, 1918.

★ 1073 ★

Disabilities

Deafness: Instruction and School Abilities of Deaf Persons in 1910

| EDUCATION | DEAF-MUTES 5 YEARS OF AGE AND OVER: 1910 | | | |
| | Number | | Percentage distribution | |
	Negro	Native White	Negro	Native White
Total	1,061	15,889	...	...
No report as to education	16	186	...	...
Number reporting	1,045	15,703	100.0	100.0
Had attended school	548	13,743	52.4	87.5
Special school for the deaf	528	13,459	50.5	85.7
Other school only	20	284	1.9	1.8
Had not attended school	497	1,960	47.6	12.5

[Continued]

★ 1073 ★

Deafness: Instruction and School Abilities of Deaf Persons in 1910

[Continued]

| EDUCATION | DEAF-MUTES 5 YEARS OF AGE AND OVER: 1910 | | | |
| | Number | | Percentage distribution | |
	Negro	Native White	Negro	Native White
Private instruction at home	9	86	0.9	0.5
No instruction	488	1,874	46.7	11.9

Source: [Untitled Table], *Negro Population, 1790-1915*, 1918, p. 454. Primary source: U.S. Bureau of the Census. *Negro Population, 1790-1915.* Washington, D.C.: Government Printing Office, 1918.

★ 1074 ★

Disabilities

Deafness: Racial Distribution of Deaf Persons in 1910

| RACIAL CLASS | DEAF-MUTES: 1910 | | Percentage distribution of total population: 1910 |
	Number	Percentage distribution	
All classes	19,153	100.0	100.0
Negro	1,069	5.6	10.7
White	18,016	94.1	88.9
Indian	66	0.3	0.3
Chinese, Japanese, and other	2	1	0.2

Source: [Untitled Table], *Negro Population, 1790-1915*, 1918, p. 453. Primary source: U.S. Bureau of the Census. *Negro Population, 1790-1915.* Washington, D.C.: Government Printing Office, 1918.
Note: 1. Less than one-tenth of 1 per cent.

★ 1075 ★

Disabilities

Mental Conditions: Age Distribution of Northerners and Southerners Admitted to Hospitals for the Insane in 1910

| AGE | INSANE ADMITTED TO HOSPITALS: 1910 | | | | | |
| | United States | | The South | | The North | |
	Negro	White	Negro	White	Negro	White
	NUMBER					
All ages	4,384	56,182	3,193	10,161	1,105	41,118
Under 15 years	54	272	41	114	12	140
15 to 19 years	320	2,215	263	507	56	1,552

[Continued]

★ 1075 ★

Mental Conditions: Age Distribution of Northerners and Southerners Admitted to Hospitals for the Insane in 1910

[Continued]

AGE	INSANE ADMITTED TO HOSPITALS: 1910					
	United States		The South		The North	
	Negro	White	Negro	White	Negro	White
20 to 24 years	579	5,101	439	1,079	130	3,619
25 to 29 years	601	6,394	422	1,246	167	4,561
30 to 34 years	568	6,606	425	1,275	133	4,776
35 to 39 years	529	6,945	376	1,258	143	5,059
40 to 44 years	388	6,046	271	962	105	4,504
45 to 49 years	316	5,349	221	837	87	4,050
50 to 54 years	253	4,609	180	769	67	3,449
55 to 59 years	150	3,208	108	528	39	2,450
60 to 64 years	163	2,706	111	473	49	1,983
65 years and over	248	5,807	252	932	90	4,423
Age unknown	115	834	84	181	27	552

PER 100,000 POPULATION OF SPECIFIED AGE AND RACIAL CLASS

	Negro	White	Negro	White	Negro	White
All ages	44.6	68.7	36.5	49.5	107.5	75.3
Under 15 years	1.5	1.1	1.2	1.5	5.0	0.9
15 to 19 years	30.2	27.8	27.1	23.5	65.0	20.6
20 to 24 years	56.2	63.9	48.2	55.2	114.1	67.5
25 to 29 years	68.2	88.1	56.3	74.6	133.8	92.9
30 to 34 years	85.0	106.8	76.2	90.3	127.2	111.9
35 to 39 years	79.7	121.2	71.0	99.2	145.7	128.2
40 to 44 years	85.2	126.5	71.3	99.0	148.1	133.6
45 to 49 years	81.9	131.7	67.5	102.6	158.2	140.6
50 to 54 years	77.6	129.6	64.2	98.7	154.6	139.3
55 to 59 years	71.6	125.1	60.0	92.3	137.8	136.7
60 to 64 years	87.4	130.8	67.7	102.2	228.6	137.2
65 years and over	118.3	159.5	98.2	128.6	250.2	166.4

Source: [Untitled Table], *Negro Population, 1790-1915*, 1918, p. 449. Primary source: U.S. Bureau of the Census. *Negro Population, 1790-1915*. Washington, D.C.: Government Printing Office, 1918.

★ 1076 ★

Disabilities

Mental Conditions: Gender of the Hospitalized Insane in 1910, by Region

| DIVISION AND SEX | INSANE IN HOSPITALS PER 100,000 POPULATION OF SPECIFIED RACIAL CLASS AND SEX: 1910 | | | | | |
| | Enumerated on January 1 | | | Admitted during the year | | |
	Negro	Native white	Foreign born white	Negro	Native white	Foreign born white
UNITED STATES						
Male	133.8	175.0	377.7	47.2	64.0	117.5
Female	120.0	162.3	444.1	42.1	51.7	114.8
THE SOUTH						
South Atlantic:						
Male	128.9	166.4	579.0	49.0	63.1	131.3
Female	129.2	162.7	402.8	43.5	50.3	106.2
East South Central:						
Male	93.4	122.5	333.4	35.6	53.3	108.8
Female	97.9	120.8	311.2	36.1	39.5	82.6
West South Central:						
Male	74.6	90.6	216.5	18.0	38.1	69.1
Female	79.7	92.4	192.4	16.6	34.6	61.6
THE NORTH						
New England:						
Male	185.0	280.3	313.6	161.7	160.7	132.0
Female	862.4	251.0	420.7	146.2	86.8	136.9
Middle Atlantic:						
Male	384.3	222.7	343.2	111.6	68.4	106.3
Female	314.2	207.1	494.7	98.9	55.3	120.1
East North Central:						
Male	364.4	183.4	387.7	118.9	68.3	116.9
Female	277.0	166.3	407.3	81.7	55.4	100.3
West North Central:						
Male	274.9	155.7	436.6	112.8	56.6	108.6
Female	199.5	137.6	450.0	101.0	47.3	114.3
THE WEST						
Mountain:						
Male	272.0	102.9	347.2	136.0	60.9	135.7
Female	257.7	77.9	284.3	134.0	33.4	84.2
Pacific:						
Male	370.0	178.0	532.8	238.3	72.4	167.8
Female	264.2	142.0	471.3	143.4	47.1	125.0

Source: [Untitled Table], *Negro Population, 1790-1915*, 1918, p. 449. Primary source: U.S. Bureau of the Census. *Negro Population, 1790-1915*. Washington, D.C.: Government Printing Office, 1918.

★ 1077 ★

Disabilities

Mental Conditions: Hospitalized Insane Per 100,000 Population in 1910

DIVISION AND STATE	INSANE IN HOSPITALS PER 100,000 POPULATION OF SPECIFIED RACIAL CLASS: 1910			
	Enumerated on January 1		Admitted during the year	
	Negro	White	Negro	White
UNITED STATES	131.4	213.2	44.6	68.7
THE SOUTH				
South Atlantic	129.1	181.3	46.2	59.7
Delaware	282.2	206.3	73.8	60.8
Maryland	177.8	264.2	55.5	107.6
District of Columbia	686.1	946.5	158.8	188.0
Virginia	199.7	165.1	67.5	56.2
West Virginia	169.9	139.3	49.9	40.0
North Carolina	99.4	121.8	33.8	45.3
South Carolina	77.6	131.3	39.5	46.5
Georgia	83.2	150.4	33.5	50.1
Florida	125.7	103.7	49.6	38.8
East South Central	95.6	125.5	35.8	47.5
Kentucky	217.8	146.4	66.1	52.0
Tennessee	99.8	101.1	54.1	39.5
Alabama	74.1	111.2	27.2	47.5
Mississippi	81.4	146.9	27.1	33.2
West South Central	77.2	101.4	17.3	38.8
Arkansas	34.1	83.2	7.5	19.6
Louisiana	98.8	154.3	17.5	38.9
Oklahoma	93.0	65.6	34.9	47.2
Texas	79.3	108.4	19.9	41.8
THE NORTH				
New England	473.6	296.9	153.8	105.9
Middle Atlantic	363.7	269.1	105.1	75.3
East North Central	322.4	224.5	101.1	71.8
West North Central	238.6	194.1	107.1	63.3
THE WEST				
Mountain	265.5	137.6	135.1	62.6
Pacific	322.0	242.4	195.2	82.7

Source: [Untitled Table], *Negro Population, 1790-1915*, 1918, p. 448. Primary source: U.S. Bureau of the Census. *Negro Population, 1790-1915*. Washington, D.C.: Government Printing Office, 1918.

★ 1078 ★

Disabilities

Mental Conditions: Hospitalized Insane in 1910, by Urban-Rural Residence and Region

DIVISION AND RACIAL CLASS	INSANE ADMITTED TO HOSPITALS: 1910				
	Number			Per 100,000 population of specified racial class	
	From urban communities	From rural communities	Prior residence unknown	From urban communities	From rural communities
UNITED STATES	36,654	20,442	3,673	86.0	41.1
Negro	2,098	1,923	363	78.0	26.9
White	34,450	18,454	3,278	86.5	44.0
THE SOUTH					
South Atlantic	2,968	3,040	717	96.0	33.4
Negro	784	1,017	99	86.2	31.8
White	2,183	2,023	614	100.1	34.3
East South Central	1,058	2,264	363	67.2	33.1
Negro	242	537	171	47.5	25.1
White	816	1,725	191	76.6	36.8
West South Central	1,096	1,758	114	56.0	25.8
Negro	117	197	29	26.8	12.7
White	975	1,549	85	64.3	29.8
THE NORTH					
New England	5,804	1,009	173	106.4	91.9
Negro	90	10	2	147.8	184.2
White	5,692	999	171	105.6	91.6
Middle Atlantic	11,857	2,548	264	86.4	45.6
Negro	392	36	11	115.6	45.8
White	11,418	2,508	253	85.6	45.5
East North Central	8,132	4,698	451	84.6	53.4
Negro	216	49	9	106.7	69.7
White	7,874	4,553	440	83.9	53.3
West North Central	2,898	3,856	705	74.8	19.7
Negro	165	68	27	100.4	86.8
White	2,724	3,779	677	73.5	49.4
THE WEST					
Mountain	924	549	150	97.5	32.6
Negro	25	3	1	161.9	49.8
White	807	531	149	97.0	33.3

[Continued]

★ 1078 ★

Mental Conditions: Hospitalized Insane in 1910, by Urban-Rural Residence and Region
[Continued]

| DIVISION AND RACIAL CLASS | INSANE ADMITTED TO HOSPITALS: 1910 | | | | |
| | Number | | | Per 100,000 population of specified racial class | |
	From urban communities	From rural communities	Prior residence unknown	From urban communities	From rural communities
Pacific	1,917	810	736	80.5	44.8
Negro	37	6	14	151.9	124.1
White	1,841	787	698	80.2	45.5

Source: [Untitled Table], *Negro Population, 1790-1915*, 1918, p. 450. Primary source: U.S. Bureau of the Census. *Negro Population, 1790-1915.* Washington, D.C.: Government Printing Office, 1918.

★ 1079 ★
Disabilities

Mental Conditions: Institutionalized "Feeble-minded" Persons in Relation to Population in 1910

| RACIAL CLASS | FEEBLE-MINDED INSTITUTIONS: 1910 | | | | PERCENTAGE DISTRIBUTION: 1910 | | |
| | Number | | Per 100,000 of | | Feebleminded | | Total population |
	Enumerated on January 1	Admitted during the year	Enumerated on January 1	Admitted during the year	Enumerated on January 1	Admitted during the year	
All classes	20,731	3,825	22.5	4.2	100.0	100.0	100.0
Negro	280	85	2.8	0.9	1.4	2.2	10.7
White	20,441	3,737	25.0	4.6	98.6	97.7	88.9
Other	10	3	2.4	0.7	1	0.1	0.4

Source: [Untitled Table], *Negro Population, 1790-1915*, 1918, p. 450. Primary source: U.S. Bureau of the Census. *Negro Population, 1790-1915.* Washington, D.C.: Government Printing Office, 1918. *Note:* 1. Less than one-tenth of 1 per cent.

★ 1080 ★

Disabilities

Mental Conditions: Sex Ratios Among the Insane in 1910

RACIAL CLASS	INSANE IN HOSPITALS:1910				MALES TO 1,000 FEMALES: 1910		
	Enumerated on January 1		Admitted during the year		Insane in hospitals		Total population
					Enumerated on January 1	Admitted during the year	
	Male	Female	Male	Female			
All classes	98,695	89,096	34,116	26,653	1,108	1,280	1,060
Negro	6,536	6,374	2,304	2,080	1,025	1,108	989
White	91,617	82,607	31,646	24,536	1,109	1,290	1,066
Indian	90	76	32	19	[1]	[1]	1,035
Other	452	39	134	18	[1]	[1]	9,608

Source: [Untitled Table], *Negro Population, 1790-1915*, 1918, p. 448. Primary source: U.S. Bureau of the Census. *Negro Population, 1790-1915*. Washington, D.C.: Government Printing Office, 1918. *Note:* 1. Ratio not shown, the number of females being less than 100.

★ 1081 ★

Disabilities

Number/Percent: Characteristics of the Disabled, by Race, 1966

CHARACTERISTIC	BENEFICIARIES						SEVERELY DISABLED NONBENEFICIARIES[3]		
	Childhood disability[1]			Disabled worker[2]					
	Total	Men	Women	Total	Men	Women	Total	Men	Women
Number...1,000	136	67	69	842	624	217	4,475	1,509	2,966
White	89	88	89	86	86	85	78	80	77
Negro and other	11	12	11	14	14	15	22	20	23

Source: "Characteristics of Disabled Population: Spring 1966," *Statistical Abstract of the United States*, 1975, p. 280. Primary source: Dept. of Health, Education, and Welfare, Social Security Administration; *1966 Social Security Survey of Disabled Adults*. *Notes:* 1. Children aged 18 and over of retired, deceased, or disabled insured workers who are in receipt of disability benefits under the old-age, survivors, disability, and health insurance program as the result of disabilities that began before age 18. 2. Persons under age 65 who are in receipt of disability benefits under the OASDHI program because of their inability generally to engage in any substantial gainful activity. 3. Severely disabled persons who are not in receipt of any type of monthly cash benefit under OASDHI. "Severely disabled" is defined as unable to work altogether or unable to work regularly because of a chronic health condition or impairment lasting 7 or more months.

★ 1082 ★

Disabilities

Support Services: Percent of Black and White Disabled Persons Receiving Aid, 1962

[Refers to federally aided State programs providing public assistance to persons 18 years old and over who are permanently and totally disabled. Includes Puerto Rico and Virgin Islands. Based on sample and subject to sampling variability].

CHARACTERISTIC	Percent
Total	100.0
Race:	
White	63.4
Negro	30.0
Other[1]	6.4

Source: "Aid to the Disabled—Characteristics of Recipients: 1962," *Statistical Abstract of the United States, 1970*, p. 298. Primary source: Dept. of Health, Education, and Welfare, Social and Rehabilitation Service, *Characteristics of Recipients of Aid to the Permanently and Totally Disabled, Findings of the 1962 Survey: State Tables,* June 1964. *Note:* 1. Includes unknown or not reported.

Drug Abuse

★ 1083 ★

Addicts and Abusers: Average Number (1953-1973) and New Addicts/Abusers Reported in Individual Years (1965-1973)

["Addict/abuser" is defined as a person reported voluntarily by law enforcement agencies to the Drug Enforcement Administration as illegally using narcotic drugs. Average age of active addict/abusers as of Dec. 31, 1973, was 28.2 years.]

ITEM	NEW ADDICT/ABUSERS REPORTED									Active addict/ abusers Dec. 31, 1973
	Annual average 1953-1973	1965	1967	1968	1969	1970	1971	1972	1973	
Addict/abusers, total	10,507	6,012	6,417	7,219	14,606	12,201	23,881	24,692	16,446	98,988
White	4,877	3,562	3,585	3,785	7,553	6,813	10,485	9,849	6,843	44,738
Negro	5,543	2,419	2,817	3,425	7,008	5,345	13,363	14,775	9,562	53,993
Other	87	31	15	9	45	43	33	68	41	257

Source: "Reported Narcotic Addict/Abusers—Summary: 1953 to 1973," *Statistical Abstract of the United States, 1975*, p. 89. Primary source: U.S. Drug Enforcement Administration, 1965-1969, *Drug Abuse, and Law Enforcement Statistics;* thereafter, unpublished data.

Facilities

★ 1084 ★

Hospitals: Growth in Number of Hospital Serving Black Persons, c. 1920-1940

Twenty years ago the semblance of adequate hospitalization for Negroes was still in the conversational stage. The National Hospital Association, organized in St. Louis in 1923, assumed the responsibility to encourage better facilities for the training of Negroes in medicine and health.

Today there are 110 Negro hospitals scattered throughout the United States, with more than 10,000 beds specifically set aside to help care for Negroes. More than 70 per cent of these hospitals are privately owned, existing upon the incomes of a few patients who can pay their way, and the limited resources of their owners and organizers.

The last report of the American College of Surgeons, October, 1940, shows there were 22 fully approved and five provisionally approved Negro hospitals; 13 of which were approved for the training of interns by the Council on Medical Education and Hospitals of the American Medical Association. There are more than 20 schools connected with the hospitals for the training of nurses. Today, there are two Class-A medical schools for Negro Students- Meharry Medical College at Nashville, Tenn., and Howard University School of Medicine at Washington, which graduate about 85 per cent of all Negro graduates in medicine.

In some geographic areas where the population is predominantly Negro, there are as few as 75 beds set aside for over one million Negroes. A recent study made by Dr. T.R. Ponton, editor of *Hospital Management*, shows that Chicago hospitals, except Cook County Hospital which is devoted almost exclusively to the treatment of colored patients, either do not admit Negroes, or set them apart from other patients. The ratio of beds available is only 1.6 per thousand.

Source: "Some Facts and Figures on Hospitals," *The Negro Handbook*, 1942, p. 153. Primary source: Excerpts from a radio address given August 17, 1941, by E. R. Carney, president, National Hospital Association [colored].

★ 1085 ★

Facilities

Hospitals: Hospitals for Black Persons in 1944

Alabama	9	Mississippi	4
Arkansas	5	Missouri	7
Washington, D.C.	3	New Jersey	1
Florida	11	North Carolina	13
Georgia	8	New York	1
Illinois	2	Oklahoma	4
Indiana	2	Pennsylvania	3
Kansas	3	South Carolina	7
Louisiana	1	Tennessee	4
Michigan	10	Texas	7
Maryland	4	Virginia	10
Delaware	1	West Virginia	4

Source: "Negro Hospitals," *Negro Year Book: A Review of Events Affecting Negro Life, 1941-1946,* 1947, p. 336. Primary source: Eugene H. Bradley, "Health, Hospitals, and the Negro," *Modern Hospital,* August, 1946. Abstracted in National Negro Health News, (U.S. Public Health Service), Vol. 14, No. 2, April, June, 1946, pp. 14-15.

★ 1086 ★

Facilities

Hospitals: Hospitals for Black Persons in Southern and Border States in 1940

At least 5,838 new beds have been made available for colored patients in hospitals throughout the South during the past few years through the aid of grants and loans by the Public Works Administration, according to a report made by W.J. Trent, Jr., adviser on Negro affairs, at the end of the year 1940.

A total of 3,486 beds, or 59.7 per cent were provided for the insane; 1,469, or 25.2 per cent provided in general hospitals; and 883, or 15.1 per cent in tuberculosis sanitaria and other specialized hospitals.

The facilities ranged from seven-ward buildings accommodating 1,170 patients at the North Carolina State Hospital for the Insane at Goldsboro, N.C., to a five-bed ward at the Municipal General Hospital at Quitman, Ga.

Source: "Increase in Hospitalization,: *The Negro Handbook,* 1942, p. 152. Primary source: U.S. Bureau of the Census.

★ 1087 ★

Facilities

Hospitals: Hospitals for Negroes, with Professional Registration Credentials, 1948

State	No. hospitals	Range or No. Beds	Range or No. Bassinets
Alabama	8	12-2,203	1-24
Arkansas	3	21-196	0-6
Delaware	1	68	0
District of Columbia	2	23-498	8-54
Florida	7	30-105	0-25
Georgia	8	20-610	0-20
Illinois	2	28-180	7-28
Indiana	2	10-40	2-6
Kansas	1	50	14
Kentucky	1	57	10
Louisiana	1	97	20
Maryland	3	418-1,690	0-20
Michigan	9	29-125	0-34
Mississippi	4	20-65	1-2
Missouri	6	48-694	5-73
New Jersey	1	24	6
North Carolina	13	10-2,600	0-23
Oklahoma	2	44-800	0-10
Pennsylvania	2	84-104	16-24
South Carolina	5	15-32[1]	3-14[1]
Tennessee	3	26-160	2-21
Texas	9	18-150[1]	0-20[1]
Virginia	8	13-3,374	0-38
West Virginia	4	25-410	0-4

Source: Compiled by the editors from "Hospitals for Negroes, Registered by the American Medical Association and the American College of Surgeons: April 1, 1948," *The Negro Handbook, 1949,* 1949, pp. 36-44. Primary source: American Medical Association and American College of Surgeons. *Note:* 1. Information not provided for one of the hospitals in the State.

★ 1088 ★

Facilities

Hospitals: Negro Hospitals Not Registered by AMA in 1948

State	No. hospitals	Range or No. Beds	Range or No. Bassinets
Alabama	4	50-68[1]	6[1]
Florida	4	95-304[1]	25-32[1]
Georgia	3	40[1]	10[1]
Michigan	1	[2]	[2]
Mississippi	1	[2]	[2]
North Carolina	1	[2]	[2]
South Carolina	1	[2]	[2]
Tennessee	1	[2]	[2]

Source: Compiled by the editors from "[Hospitals for Negroes] Not Registered by the American Medical Association," *The Negro Handbook, 1949*, pp. 44-46. Primary source: National Conference of Hospital Administrators. *Notes:* 1. Incomplete information. 2. No information provided.

★ 1089 ★

Facilities

Hospitals: Negro Hospitals with 50 or More Beds (Partial List), c. 1951

State	No. hospitals
Alabama	1
District of Columbia	1
Florida	2
Georgia	2
Kansas	1
Louisiana	1
Michigan	2
Mississippi	1
North Carolina	3
South Carolina	1
Tennessee	2
Virginia	1
Total	18

Source: Compiled by the editors from "Partial List of Negro Hospitals with 50 Beds or More," *1952 Negro Year Book: A Review of Events Affecting Negro Life*, 1952, p. 167. Primary source: Taken from a list of 132 hospitals of record.

★ 1090 ★

Facilities

Nursing Homes: Nursing Home Residents, 1964, 1969, and 1973-74

ITEM	1964	1969	1973-1974
RESIDENTS IN NURSING AND PERSONAL CARE HOMES			
Total 1,000	554	815	1,075
White 1,000	(NA)	779	1,009
Negro and other 1,000	(NA)	37	65

Source: "Nursing Homes: Selected Characteristics, Resident Charges, and Primary Sources of Payment: 1964, 1969, and 1973-74," *Statistical Abstract of the United States, 1975*, p. 82. Primary source: U.S. National Center for Health Statistics, *Vital and Health Statistics*, series 12, Nos. 5,9,21, and 23. *Notes:* NA Not available. 1. Excludes those providing personal care, domiciliary care, or room and board only (an additional 5,600 homes in 1973-74.).

★ 1091 ★

Facilities

State Hospital Facilities for Black Tuberculosis Patients, 1942

State	Total institutions		Institutions exclusively for Negroes		Other institutions making specific provisions for Negroes	
	Number of institutions	Number of beds	Number of institutions	Number of beds	Number of institutions	Number of beds
United States	134	7,066	24	2,002	110	5,064
Alabama	6	187			6	187
Arizona	1	8			1	8
Arkansas	2	208	1	196	1	12
California	4	41	1	32	3	9
Colorado	1	4			1	4
Connecticut						
Delaware	1	68	1	68		
District of Columbia	3	717	1	150	2	567
Florida	11	295	2	60	9	235
Georgia	5	280			5	280
Idaho						
Illinois	5	126			5	126
Indiana	5	112			5	112
Iowa						
Kansas	2	21			2	21
Kentucky	2	141			2	141
Louisiana	5	347			5	347
Maine						
Maryland	3	636	1	485	2	151

[Continued]

★ 1091 ★

State Hospital Facilities for Black Tuberculosis Patients, 1942
[Continued]

State	Total institutions		Institutions exclusively for Negroes		Other institutions making specific provisions for Negroes	
	Number of institutions	Number of beds	Number of institutions	Number of beds	Number of institutions	Number of beds
Massachusetts						
Michigan	9	533	3	178	6	355
Minnesota						
Mississippi	3	74			3	74
Missouri	5	477	2	91	3	386
Montana						
Nebraska	1	16			1	16
Nevada						
New Hampshire						
New Jersey	1	20			1	20
New Mexico						
New York						
North Carolina	16	699	1	10	15	689
North Dakota						
Ohio	10	332			10	332
Oklahoma	2	62	1	10	1	52
Oregon						
Pennsylvania	2	81	1	21	1	60
Rhode Island						
South Carolina	6	340	1	12	5	328
South Dakota						
Tennessee	5	290	1	8	4	282
Texas	10	328	4	254	6	74
Utah						
Vermont						
Virginia	7	479	2	283	5	196
Washington						
West Virginia	1	144	1	144		
Wisconsin						
Wyoming						

Source: "Number of Tuberculosis Institutions and Beds with Exclusive or Special Provision for Negroes, Classified by State: United States, 1942," *The Negro Handbook, 1944,* 1944, p. 185. Primary source: National Tuberculosis Association.

★ 1092 ★

Facilities

State Hospital Facilities that Accepted Black Persons with Tuberculosis, 1947

State	Total institutions		Institutions Exclusively for Negroes		Other Institutions Making Specific Provisions for Negroes	
	Number	Beds	Number	Beds	Number	Beds
United States	100	7,350	16	1,825	84	5,525
Alabama	6	224	-	-	6	224
Arizona	1	8	-	-	1	8
Arkansas	1	195	1	195	-	-
California	1	4	-	-	1	4
Delaware	1	68	1	68	-	-
District of Columbia	3	521	1	150	2	371
Florida	5	383	1	48	4	335
Georgia	4	832	-	-	4	832
Illinois	5	99	-	-	5	99
Indiana	4	131	-	-	4	131
Iowa	1	15	-	-	1	15
Kentucky	2	215	-	-	2	215
Louisiana	5	341	-	-	5	341
Maryland	2	615	1	475	1	140
Michigan	6	374	2	150	4	224
Mississippi	3	74	-	-	3	74
Missouri	5	517	2	84	3	433
New Jersey	1	15	-	-	1	15
North Carolina	18	758	1	10	17	748
Ohio	3	324	-	-	3	324
Oklahoma	1	57	-	-	1	57
South Carolina	6	358	-	-	6	358
Tennessee	5	315	1	8	4	307
Texas	4	277	2	213	2	64
Virginia	6	505	2	299	4	206
West Virginia	1	125	1	125	-	-

Source: "Number of Tuberculosis Institutions and Beds with Exclusive or Special Provision for Negroes, Classified by State: United States, 1947," *The Negro Handbook, 1949,* 1949, p. 27. Primary source: National Tuberculosis Association. *Note:* States with no beds for exclusive use of Negroes are not listed.

Health Care

★ 1093 ★

Health Insurance Coverage for Those Under 65 by Age and Family Income, 1972

| Subject | Black and other races | | | | White | | | |
| | Total | Family income | | | Total | Family income | | |
		Under $5,000	$5,000 to $9,999	$10,000 and over		Under $5,000	$5,000 to $9,999	$10,000 and over
Persons under 65 years (thousands)	21,989	8,941	7,578	5,470	151,647	21,125	46,976	83,546
HOSPITAL INSURANCE COVERAGE								
Total (thousands)	12,489	2,813	5,026	4,650	121,411	9,464	36,038	75,909
Percent of persons under 65	57	31	66	85	80	45	77	91
Percent in each age group with hospital insurance coverage:								
Under 17 years	50	26	60	84	78	32	73	90
17 to 24 years	54	36	62	76	73	52	72	84
25 to 44 years	66	36	73	88	84	40	79	92
45 to 64 years	63	38	75	89	84	54	83	93
SURGICAL INSURANCE COVERAGE								
Total (thousands)	12,210	2,634	4,929	4,647	119,203	9,136	35,301	74,766
Percent of persons under 65	56	29	65	85	79	43	75	89
Percent in each age group with surgical insurance coverage:								
Under 17 years	49	24	59	84	77	32	72	89
17 to 24 years	53	34	61	75	72	50	70	83
25 to 44 years	65	33	71	89	82	39	78	91
45 to 64 years	61	35	73	88	82	52	81	92

Source: "Persons Under 65 Years of Age by Hospital and Surgical Insurance Coverage, by Age and Family Income: 1972," Current Population Reports, Special Studies, Series P-23, No. 54. *The Social and Economic Status of the Black Population in the United States, 1974*, 1975, p. 129. Primary source: U.S. Department of Health, Education, and Welfare, National Center for Health Statistics. *Notes:* The data presented in this table are from the Health Interview Survey conducted during 1972. The family income refers to the total of all income received by members of the family in the 12-month period ending with the week of interview.

★ 1094 ★

Health Care

Visits to Physicians and Dentists by Family Income, 1969

Subject	Family income			
	$3,000 to $4,999		$7,000 to $9,999	
	Negro and other races	White	Negro and other races	White
Total persons in families	4,878	17,361	3,570	37,651
Percent with one or more visits to–				
Physician	59.5	68.8	66.6	69.8
Dentist	24.4	34.0	31.4	46.5
Total physician's visits	15,871	84,454	13,125	155,733
Percent of all visits to physicians made in–				
Physician's office	61.2	70.1	63.6	71.9
Hospital clinic	21.5	12.0	15.2	8.1
Other (mainly by telephone)	17.3	17.9	21.2	20.0

Source: "Percent of Population with One or More Physician or Dental Visits for Selected Family Income Groups: 1969," Current Population Reports, Special Studies, Series P-23, No. 38. *The Social and Economic Status of the Black Population in the United States, 1970*, 1970, p. 99. Primary source: U.S. Department of Health, Education, and Welfare. *Notes:* Physician's office visit includes prepaid insurance group; hospital clinic includes hospital emergency room; other includes home, company, health department, and unknown visits.

★ 1095 ★

Health Care

Visits to Physicians and Dentists by Family Income, 1973

Subject	Total	Family income		
		Under $5,000	$5,000 to $9,999	$10,000 and over
BLACK AND OTHER RACES				
Total persons (thousands)	25,991[1]	8,788	7,481	7,202
Percent with one or more visits to:				
Physician	71	70	69	75
Dentist	34	29	34	42
Total physician visits (thousands)	116,802	44,946	30,564	33,086
Percent	100	100	100	100
Home	1	-	-	-
Physician's office	60	54	62	69
Hospital clinic[2]	23	27	23	17
Other and unknown	16	19	13	13

[Continued]

★ 1095 ★

Visits to Physicians and Dentists by Family Income, 1973

[Continued]

Subject	Total	Family income		
		Under $5,000	$5,000 to $9,999	$10,000 and over
Average number of physician visits per person:				
Total	4.5	5.1	4.1	4.6
Under 65 years	4.3	4.8	3.9	4.5
65 years and over	7.0	6.9	8.1	9.3
WHITE				
Total persons (thousands)	179,808[1]	26,121	44,141	97,265
Percent with one or more visits to:				
Physician	75	75	73	76
Dentist	51	34	42	60
Total physician visits (thousands)	914,208	154,765	218,643	489,209
Percent	100	100	100	100
Home	1	2	1	1
Physician's office	70	69	73	69
Hospital clinic[2]	9	11	9	9
Other and unknown	19	19	17	21
Average number of physician visits per person:				
Total	5.1	5.9	5.0	5.0
Under 65 years	4.9	5.6	4.8	5.0
65 years and over	6.5	6.5	6.4	7.0

Source: "Selected Characteristics of Population with One or More Physician or Dentist Visits, by Family Income: 1973," Current Population Reports, Special Studies, Series P-23, No. 54. *The Social and Economic Status of the Black Population in the United States, 1974*, 1975, p. 128. Primary source: U.S. Department of Health, Education, and Welfare, National Center for Health Statistics. *Notes:* The data presented in this table are from the Health Interview Survey conducted during 1973. The family income refers to the total of all income received by members of the family in the 12-month period ending with the week of interview. - Rounds to zero. 1. Includes persons who did not report family income. 2. Includes hospital emergency room.

★ 1096 ★

Health Care

Visits to Physicians and Dentists by Family Income, July 1966-June 1967

	Family income			
	$3,000 to $4,999		$7,000 to $9,999	
	Negro and other races	White	Negro and other races	White
Percent with one or more visits to –				
Physician	59.3	66.4	64.4	70.3
Dentist[1]	20.0	31.0	33.0	52.0
Percent of all visits to physicians made in –				
Physician's office	51.4	73.5	64.3	73.2
Hospital clinic	30.4	9.5	22.4	6.7
Other (mainly by telephone)	18.2	17.0	13.3	20.1

Source: "Percent of Population with One or More Physician or Dental Visits for Selected Income Groups, July 1966-June 1967," Current Population Reports, Special Studies, Series P-23, No. 29. *The Social and Economic Status of the Black Population in the United States, 1969,* 1969, p. 66. Primary source: U.S. Department of Health, Education, and Welfare. *Notes:* Physician's office visit includes prepaid insurance group; hospital clinic includes hospital emergency room; other includes home, company, health department, and unknown visits. 1. Dentist visits based on data for fiscal year July 1963-June 1964 (latest available) and for family income $2,000 to $3,999 and $7,000 to $9,999.

Health Support Services

★ 1097 ★

Private Funds: Julius Rosenwald Fund Expenditures for Black Health in the 1930s

Public Health Nurses	$97,332
Institutes for Physicians	1,013
National Negro Health Week	10,433
Health Education for Teachers	15,000
Tuberculosis, Studies and Demonstrations of Control Measures	74,820
Syphilis Control Demonstrations in Alabama, Georgia, Mississippi North Carolina, Tennessee and Virginia	72,883
Hospitals and Clinics	
a. Provident Hospital, Chicago	$130,614
b. Flint-Goodridge Hospital, New Orleans	4,575
c. Provident Hospital, Baltimore	24,629
d. Mercy Hospital and School for Nurses, Philadelphia	31,076
e. Knoxville Hospital, Knoxville, Tennessee	50,000
f. Charity Hospital, Savannah, Georgia	50,000
g. State Negro Sanitarium, Arkansas	8,000

[Continued]

★ 1097 ★

Private Funds: Julius Rosenwald Fund Expenditures for Black Health in the 1930s
[Continued]

h. Hampton Institute - Dixie Hospital and Hampton School of Nursing	99,045
i. St. Phillips Hospital, Richmond, Virginia	40,000
j. Good Samaritan Hospital, Charlotte, North Carolina	15,000
k. L. Richardson Memorial Hospital, Greensboro, North Carolina	17,000
l. St. Agnes Hospital, Raleigh, North Carolina	15,000
m. Spartanburg General Hopsital, Spartanburg, South Carolina	40,000
n. Tuomey Hospital, Sumter, South Carolina	25,000
o. Michael M. Shoemaker Center, Cincinnati	1,860
p. Harlem Birth Contral Clinic	10,000
	561,799
Consultation Service	24,227
	$857,507

Source: "Details of Expenditures for Negro Health," *Negro Year Book: An Annual Encyclopedia of the Negro, 1937-1938,* 1937, p. 190. Primary source: Reports of the Julius Rosenwald Fund.

Illness and Disease

★ 1098 ★

"Positive" Syphilis Tests among Black Persons, 1929-32

County	Number examined	Per cent positive
Macon, Ala.	3,363	35.0
Glynn, Ga.	5,674	26.9
Tipton, Tenn.	2,339	25.9
Bolivar, Miss.	2,304	23.6
Pitts, N.C.	10,198	11.8
Albemarle, Va.	3,253	7.1
Total	27,131	19.5

Source: "Rosenwald Serologic Survey—1929-32," *The Negro Handbook, 1944,* 1944, p. 187. Primary source: U.S. Public Health Services.

Income/Earnings

★ 1099 ★

Poverty: Racial Distribution of "Paupers in Almshouses" in 1910

RACIAL CLASS	PAUPERS IN ALMSHOUSES: 1910				DISTRIBUTION PERCENT: 1910		
	Number		Per 100,000 population of specified racial class		Paupers in almshouses		Total population
	Enumerated on January 1	Admitted during the year	Enumerated on January 1	Admitted during the year	Enumerated on January 1	Admitted during the year	
All classes	84,198	88,313	91.5	96.0	100.0	100.0	100.0
Negro	6,281	6,807	63.9	69.3	7.5	7.7	10.7
White	77,734	$1,135	95.1	99.3	92.3	91.8	88.9
Indian	74	130	27.9	48.9	0.1	0.1	0.3
Other	109	241	74.2	164.1	0.1	0.3	0.2

Source: [Untitled Table], *Negro Population, 1790-1915*, 1918, p. 454. Primary source: U.S. Bureau of the Census. *Negro Population, 1790-1915*. Washington, D.C.: Government Printing Office, 1918.

Mental Health

★ 1100 ★

Community Mental Health Centers: Personnel Categories and Percent Distribution in Federally-Funded Centers, 1975

Discipline	Total	White	Black	Spanish American	Asian American	American Indian	Other
Psychiatrists	100.00	81.15	2.79	6.85	7.10	0.0	2.11
Other Physicians	100.00	78.71	6.44	6.44	4.46	0.0	3.97
Psychologists (Master +)	100.00	93.28	3.60	1.82	.68	.21	.43
Other Psychologists	100.00	92.60	3.70	2.16	.93	0.0	.62
Social Workers (Master +)	100.00	86.06	9.06	2.79	1.52	.22	.35
Other Social Workers	100.00	83.50	12.76	3.41	.33	0.0	0.0
Nurses	100.00	88.0	8.38	2.07	1.16	.12	.27
LPN,LVN	100.00	70.99	20.49	5.80	1.85	.49	.37
Other Professionals	100.00	86.37	9.83	2.85	.65	.11	.18
Mental Health Workers	100.00	64.71	24.74	8.22	1.06	.90	.38
Physical Health	100.00	82.79	8.67	2.31	.58	1.16	.00
Administrative	100.00	87.66	7.88	3.01	1.05	.24	.16

[Continued]

★ 1100 ★

Community Mental Health Centers: Personnel Categories and Percent Distribution in Federally-Funded Centers, 1975
[Continued]

Discipline	Total	White	Black	Spanish American	Asian American	American Indian	Other
All Other (Clerical, Maintenance)	100.00	76.69	16.58	5.50	.70	.37	.15
TOTAL	100.0	80.27	13.23	4.56	1.23	.34	.37
TOTAL U.S. POPULATION		82.00	11.2	5.3		1.5	
NUMBER OF CENTERS = 321							

Source: "Percent Distribution of FTE Staff by Race/Ethnicity and Sex Within Disciplines: Federally-Funded CMHC's, February 1975," *Readings for Mental Health and Human Service Workers in the Black Community,*" 1980, pp. 10-11. Primary source: The Office of the Director Division of Biometry and Epidemiology National Institute of Mental Health.

Nutrition

★ 1101 ★

Relationships: Nutrient Intakes of Persons 1-74, by Income Status, 1971-72
[Preliminary. Covers persons aged 1-74 years. Based on preliminary findings of sample survey in the first Health and Nutrition Examination Survey (HANES). Caloric and protein standards take account of the weight of an individual.]

| NUTRIENTS | ALL PERSONS (1-74 years old) | | | PERSONS WITH INCOME-[1] | | | | | |
| | | | | Below low income level | | | Above low income level | | |
	Total	White	Negro	Total	White	Negro	Total	White	Negro
Calories, mean	2,042	2,072	1,810	1,787	1,846	1,681	2,080	2,095	1,905
Median	1,867	1,895	1,650	1,632	1,674	1,519	1,909	1,924	1,730
Protein (g), mean	81.04	82.48	70.05	68.98	71.79	64.15	82.68	83.35	74.40
Median	72.65	73.98	61.52	62.06	65.34	56.23	74.26	74.81	66.43
Calcium (mg), mean	862	892	646	765	841	637	877	898	651
As percent of standard	174	180	129	152	167	126	177	181	132
Median	717	746	564	634	689	556	735	755	572
Iron (mg), mean	12.10	12.28	10.69	10.54	10.89	9.91	12.31	12.39	11.31
As percent of standard	99	101	85	85	89	78	101	101	91
Median	10.70	10.85	9.35	9.16	9.59	8.39	10.94	10.98	10.16
Vitamin A (I.U.), mean	4,731	4,745	4,647	4,366	4,251	4,581	4,781	4,782	4,782
As percent of standard	148	148	149	145	141	152	149	148	151
Median	2,917	2,961	2,527	2,347	2,392	2,244	2,990	3,022	2,669
Vitamin C (mg), mean	83.91	85.22	73.18	65.79	61.70	72.37	86.61	87.52	74.35
As percent of standard	162	164	145	134	126	148	166	168	144
Median	57.90	59.46	45.01	36.33	34.09	41.07	61.47	62.77	46.92

Source: "Intake of Selected Nutrients, by Race and Income Levels: 1971-72," *Statistical Abstract of the United States, 1975,* p. 91. Primary source: U.S. National Center for Health Statistics, *Preliminary Findings of the First Health and Nutrition Examination Survey, United States, 1971- 1972: Dietary Intake and Biochemical Findings. Notes:* 1. Low income level as defined in U.S. Bureau of the Census, *Current Population Reports,* series P-60, No. 86.

Chapter 7
HOUSING

★ 1102 ★

Home Owners: Percent Change, 1920-1930

Section of United States	Number of homes occupied in 1930	Percentage owned in 1930	Percentage of increase between 1920 and 1930	Percentage of population increase during period
United States	2,803,756	23.9	23.4	13.6
New England	22,864	23.4	59.5	19.0
Middle Atlantic	243,371	15.6	98.4	75.4
East North Central	222,240	23.0	79.9	80.8
West North Central	87,853	31.0	25.2	19.1
South Atlantic	974,592	25.6	9.8	2.2
East South Central	653,847	21.8	19.7	5.3
West South Central	564,918	25.3	22.5	10.6
Mountain	8,743	35.8	43.7	-1.9[1]
Pacific	25,328	37.5	111.5	88.6

Source: "Percentage of Negro Home Owners in U.S. in 1930 and Percentage of Increase or Decrease Since 1920," Florence Murray, ed., *The Negro Handbook*, 1942, p. 182. Published by permission. Primary source: U.S. Bureau of the Census. *Note:* 1. Minus sign (-) denotes a decrease.

★ 1103 ★

Home Ownership

Home Owners: Types, by Region, 1930

Section, division and state	Number of homes (all tenures)	All owned homes
United States	2,803,756	669,645
The North	576,328	121,595
The South	2,193,357	535,433
The West	34,071	12,617
New England	22,864	5,355
Maine	259	129
New Hampshire	117	39
Vermont	135	48
Massachusetts	12,637	3,453
Rhode Island	2,542	599
Connecticut	7,174	1,087
Middle Atlantic	243,371	37,932
New York	95,621	7,920
New Jersey	48,636	11,329
Pennsylvania	99,114	19,683
East North Central	222,240	51,077
Ohio	75,709	17,928
Indiana	28,771	8,614
Illinois	78,737	15,321
Michigan	36,500	8,830
Wisconsin	2,523	384
West North Central	87,853	27,231
Minnesota	2,592	855
Iowa	4,571	1,918
Missouri	59,016	13,374
North Dakota	120	28
South Dakota	166	77
Nebraska	3,700	1,253
Kansas	17,688	9,726
South Atlantic	974,592	249,762
Delaware	7,682	2,017
Maryland	61,160	16,056
District of Columbia	29,995	7,316
Virginia	140,726	61,294
West Virginia	26,274	4,900
North Carolina	180,128	50,948
South Carolina	168,324	35,753
Georgia	249,942	41,318
Florida	110,361	30,160

[Continued]

★ 1103 ★

Home Owners: Types, by Region, 1930
[Continued]

Section, division and state	Number of homes (all tenures)	All owned homes
East South Central	653,847	142,608
Kentucky	60,672	21,398
Tennessee	120,402	33,655
Alabama	222,533	44,650
Mississippi	250,240	42,905
West South Central	564,918	143,063
Arkansas	123,009	27,722
Louisiana	190,876	39,457
Oklahoma	40,238	12,615
Texas	210,795	63,269
Mountain	8,743	3,131
Montana	458	169
Idaho	229	80
Wyoming	418	122
Colorado	3,538	1,503
New Mexico	799	298
Arizona	2,776	775
Utah	331	114
Nevada	194	70
Pacific	25,328	9,486
Washington	2,059	934
Oregon	674	269
California	22,595	8,283

Source: "Negro-Owned Homes-All Tenures," Florence Murray, ed., *The Negro Handbook*, 1942, p. 181. Published by permission. Primary source: U.S. Bureau of the Census, 1930.

★ 1104 ★

Home Ownership

Home Ownership and Families: Urban Communities: 2,500 or More: Characteristics, 1910

| City | Negro population 1910 | Number of homes of Negro families: 1910 | | | | | |
| | | Total | Owned | | | Rented | No report of ownership |
			Free	Encumbered	No encumbrance report		
Alabama							
Anniston	4,570	1,141	174	166	4	771	26
Bessemer	6,210	1,738	106	111	5	1,473	43
Birmingham	52,305	14,229	1,522	795	23	11,519	370
Dotham	3,483	675	96	94	-	466	19
Gadsden	3,435	714	119	24	1	533	37
Huntsville	3,309	970	303	58	9	585	15
Mobile	22,763	6,274	792	124	30	5,073	255
Montgomery	19,322	5,672	668	276	16	4,583	129
Selma	7,863	2,226	334	107	9	1,696	80
Talladega	2,793	670	277	28	7	310	48
Troy	2,543	658	122	58	4	467	7
Tuscaloosa	4,148	1,073	228	34	2	778	31
Union Springs	2,719	639	122	11	1	440	65
Arkansas							
Argenta	4,210	1,073	186	142	1	721	23
Fort Smith	4,456	1,034	200	103	4	682	45
Helena	5,596	1,526	105	15	67	1,250	89
Hot Springs	3,827	1,049	241	72	49	624	63
Little Rock	14,539	3,277	439	441	17	2,295	85
Marianna	2,991	546	304	65	-	167	10
Pine Bluff	6,124	1,551	310	54	41	1,093	53
Texarkana[1]	2,101	547	123	41	1	373	9
California							
Los Angeles	7,599	2,030	304	420	8	1,290	8
Oakland	3,055	712	89	119	2	501	1
Colorado							
Denver	5,426	1,380	159	115	5	1,082	19
Connecticut							
New Haven	3,561	898	39	46	-	812	1

[Continued]

★ 1104 ★

Home Ownership and Families: Urban Communities: 2,500 or More: Characteristics, 1910
[Continued]

City	Negro population 1910	Number of homes of Negro families: 1910					
		Total	Owned			Rented	No report of ownership
			Free	Encumbered	No encumbrance report		
Delaware							
Wilmington	9,081	2,136	100	117	14	1,780	125
District of Columbia							
Washington	94,446	19,246	1,294	747	31	16,437	737
Florida							
Gainesville	3,079	804	297	49	2	439	17
Jacksonville	29,293	7,276	977	281	56	5,552	410
Key West	5,515	1,376	122	25	84	1,087	58
Pensacola	10,214	2,778	383	234	19	2,033	109
Tallahassee	3,237	615	146	50	2	412	5
Tampa	8,951	2,378	212	113	2	2,012	39
Georgia							
Albany	4,812	1,391	160	26	6	1,094	106
Americus	4,574	1,270	444	7	2	810	7
Athens	6,316	1,676	322	109	5	1,200	40
Atlanta	51,902	13,620	1,267	481	18	11,502	352
Augusta	18,344	5,679	542	11	49	4,835	242
Brunswick	5,567	1,457	208	47	7	1,138	57
Columbus	7,644	2,156	211	12	2	1,856	75
Cordele	3,209	884	312	32	11	521	8
Dublin	2,769	690	162	87	7	409	25
Elberton	2,919	528	50	33	-	424	21
Griffin	3,425	867	199	48	4	593	23
Macon	18,150	5,419	678	102	81	4,326	232
Milledgeville	2,560	736	238	9	2	486	1
Rome	3,758	1,002	187	80	7	699	29
Savannah	33,246	9,530	430	152	43	8,459	446
Thomasville	3,789	1,065	338	108	4	587	28
Valdosta	3,844	975	155	104	9	682	25
Waycross	6,729	1,388	316	64	11	955	42
Illinois							
Cairo	5,434	1,517	163	61	5	1,191	97

[Continued]

★ 1104 ★

Home Ownership and Families: Urban Communities: 2,500 or More: Characteristics, 1910
[Continued]

City	Negro population 1910	Number of homes of Negro families: 1910					
		Total	Owned			Rented	No report of ownership
			Free	Encumbered	No encumbrance report		
Chicago	44,103	10,421	315	329	18	9,520	239
East St. Louis	5,882	1,547	81	117	4	1,292	53
Springfield	2,961	751	98	151	23	467	12
Indiana							
Evansville	6,266	1,560	100	68	4	1,388	-
Indianapolis	21,816	5,818	451	375	27	4,865	100
Terre Haute	2,503	703	55	132	10	485	21
Iowa							
Des Moines	2,930	767	113	76	34	542	-
Kansas							
Atchinson	2,618	621	243	55	35	251	37
Kansas City	9,286	2,676	630	388	18	1,590	50
Topeka	4,538	1,258	374	183	1	661	39
Kentucky							
Covington	2,899	813	36	42	-	719	16
Frankfort	2,851	579	119	25	1	434	-
Henderson	3,016	834	159	41	6	608	20
Hopkinsville	4,187	1,006	283	97	10	550	66
Lexington	11,011	3,157	553	89	2	2,484	29
Louisville	40,522	10,959	499	194	18	9,942	306
Owensboro	3,115	836	131	49	1	626	29
Pacucah	6,047	1,722	259	40	10	1,361	52
Winchester	2,688	747	296	45	19	337	50
Louisiana							
Alexanderia	5,854	1,288	185	44	5	999	55
Baton Rouge	7,899	1,985	288	54	14	1,566	63
Lafayette	2,792	598	200	38	13	336	11
Lake Charles	4,437	961	246	79	4	611	21
Monroe	5,320	1,533	137	87	10	1,269	30
New Iberia	3,480	789	220	56	-	499	14
New Orleans	89,262	21,880	1,854	490	87	18,313	1,136
Plaquemine	2,673	734	80	35	1	607	11

[Continued]

★ 1104 ★

Home Ownership and Families: Urban Communities: 2,500 or More: Characteristics, 1910
[Continued]

City	Negro population 1910	Number of homes of Negro families: 1910					
		Total	Owned			Rented	No report of ownership
			Free	Encumbered	No encumbrance report		
Shreveport	13,896	3,742	597	113	15	2,809	208
Maryland							
Annapolis	3,184	739	56	28	-	640	15
Baltimore	84,749	18,106	675	203	55	15,842	1,331
Massachusetts							
Boston	13,564	3,372	49	80	5	3,170	68
Cambridge	4,707	1,155	43	107	-	1,000	5
New Bedford	2,885	677	65	69	-	537	6
Michigan							
Detroit	5,741	1,383	127	110	1	1,094	51
Minnesota							
Minneapolis	2,592	646	70	48	2	477	49
St. Paul	3,144	748	106	73	1	534	34
Mississippi							
Brookhaven	2,732	606	89	70	-	432	15
Columbus	4,401	1,243	316	42	3	867	15
Greenville	6,010	2,002	413	131	10	1,396	52
Greenwood	3,062	821	94	60	-	635	32
Hattiesburg	4,357	1,080	184	92	6	749	49
Jackson	10,554	2,705	404	152	17	2,039	92
Laurel	3,103	758	112	64	4	550	28
Meridian	9,321	2,571	345	175	43	1,916	92
Natchez	6,700	2,041	236	58	2	1,708	37
Vicksburg	12,053	3,823	625	116	27	2,986	69
West Point	2,772	709	280	37	5	370	17
Yazoo City	4,154	1,115	152	108	-	808	47
Missouri							
Kansas City	23,566	6,204	235	329	10	5,244	386
St. Joseph	4,219	1,003	90	69	1	843	-
St. Louis	43,960	10,891	339	269	7	9,788	488

[Continued]

★ 1104 ★

Home Ownership and Families: Urban Communities: 2,500 or More: Characteristics, 1910
[Continued]

City	Negro population 1910	Number of homes of Negro families: 1910					
		Total	Owned			Rented	No report of ownership
			Free	Encumbered	No encumbrance report		
Nebraska							
Omaha	4,426	1,071	69	91	6	857	48
New Jersey							
Atlantic City	9,834	1,914	31	53	2	1,643	185
Camden	6,076	1,580	138	86	1	1,294	61
Jersey City	5,960	1,435	54	96	3	1,250	32
Newark	9,475	2,328	39	92	1	2,129	67
Trenton	2,581	483	13	20	1	429	20
New York							
New York City	91,709	22,452	218	324	3	21,351	556
Manhattan Borough	60,534	15,341	4	17	1	14,943	375
Bronx Borough	4,117	931	22	39	-	850	20
Queens Borough	3,198	726	65	86	2	550	23
Richmond Borough	1,152	255	26	17	-	204	8
North Carolina							
Asheville	5,359	1,247	244	79	10	878	36
Charlotte	11,752	3,167	349	187	27	2,483	121
Durham	6,869	1,570	171	92	6	1,259	42
Elizabeth City	3,977	886	146	155	18	513	54
Fayetteville	3,293	950	256	14	4	644	12
Goldsboro	2,521	665	94	5	-	549	17
Greensboro	5,710	1,383	229	98	4	1,019	33
Kinston	3,027	719	202	50	14	440	13
Newborn	5,649	1,395	437	46	1	886	25
Raleigh	7,372	1,777	331	75	17	1,344	10
Rocky Mount	3,069	760	142	53	-	552	13
Washington	3,072	757	196	17	3	526	15
Wilmington	12,107	3,048	508	114	195	2,127	104
Wilson	2,998	753	108	50	1	569	25
Winston	7,828	1,916	157	95	9	1,602	53
Ohio							
Cincinnati	19,639	5,415	161	127	6	5,009	112
Cleveland	8,448	2,225	100	139	3	1,950	33

[Continued]

★ 1104 ★

Home Ownership and Families: Urban Communities: 2,500 or More: Characteristics, 1910

[Continued]

City	Negro population 1910	Number of homes of Negro families: 1910					
		Total	Owned			Rented	No report of ownership
			Free	Encumbered	No encumbrance report		
Columbus	12,739	3,064	235	270	7	2,469	83
Dayton	4,842	1,324	75	221	6	986	36
Springfield	4,933	1,269	155	278	4	832	-
Oklahoma							
Guthrie	2,976	703	306	76	-	299	22
McAlester	2,997	498	105	35	6	334	18
Muskogee	7,831	1,707	419	115	8	1,072	93
Oklahoma City	6,546	1,235	169	115	12	808	131
Pennsylvania							
Chester	4,795	1,148	74	62	-	967	45
Harrisburg	4,535	1,025	74	72	1	836	42
Philadelphia	84,459	18,095	372	496	37	15,376	1,814
Pittsburgh	25,623	5,949	284	355	12	5,051	247
Rhode Island							
Providence	5,316	1,402	46	62	1	1,267	26
South Carolina							
Anderson	3,370	875	68	137	21	623	26
Charleston	31,056	9,370	694	87	55	7,836	698
Columbia	11,546	2,957	261	90	24	2,498	84
Florence	3,536	940	132	79	14	686	29
Georgetown	3,650	1,063	208	22	-	833	-
Greenville	6,319	1,712	198	87	-	1,387	40
Greenwood	2,943	593	161	68	4	353	7
Orangeburg	3,017	763	102	54	3	599	5
Spartanburg	6,873	1,712	262	166	3	1,248	31
Sumter	4,125	1,094	57	68	92	823	54
Tennessee							
Chattanooga	17,942	4,845	268	71	5	4,395	106
Clarksville	4,285	1,154	257	33	6	844	14
Jackson	5,719	1,538	250	30	15	1,206	37
Knoxville	7,638	1,834	248	68	8	1,462	48
Memphis	52,441	14,842	1,039	521	111	12,644	527

[Continued]

★ 1104 ★

Home Ownership and Families: Urban Communities: 2,500 or More: Characteristics, 1910
[Continued]

City	Negro population 1910	Number of homes of Negro families: 1910					
		Total	Owned			Rented	No report of ownership
			Free	Encumbered	No encumbrance report		
Nashville	36,523	9,979	1,461	557	25	7,853	83
Texas							
Austin	7,478	1,660	436	170	7	1,004	43
Beaumont	6,896	1,610	256	53	3	1,282	16
Corsicana	2,842	721	206	82	2	408	23
Dallas	18,024	4,256	435	159	7	3,481	174
Denison	2,799	721	205	118	3	380	15
Fort Worth	13,280	3,152	344	175	44	2,412	177
Galveston	8,036	2,023	131	35	3	1,752	102
Houston	23,929	5,890	809	350	24	4,504	203
Marshall	4,997	1,179	383	56	3	723	14
Palestine	3,554	896	213	127	2	518	36
Paris	3,131	793	204	33	2	539	15
San Antonio	10,716	2,402	404	184	34	1,700	80
Temple	2,814	582	64	76	1	388	53
Texarkana[1]	3,218	795	140	74	1	562	18
Tyler	2,954	714	199	29	14	443	29
Waco	6,067	1,288	232	63	29	887	77
Virginia							
Alexandria	4,188	1,072	229	26	2	729	86
Charlottesville	2,524	578	96	31	11	435	5
Danville	6,207	1,567	297	162	-	1,088	20
Lynchburg	9,466	2,294	486	126	3	1,641	38
Newport News	7,259	1,769	125	141	1	1,459	43
Norfolk	25,039	6,391	208	50	15	5,977	141
Petersburg	11,014	2,894	740	80	14	2,020	40
Portsmouth	11,617	2,948	256	165	2	2,472	53
Richmond	46,733	10,496	1,209	385	52	8,519	331
Roanoke	7,924	1,733	311	160	2	1,233	27
Suffolk	2,806	624	108	71	1	431	13

[Continued]

★ 1104 ★

Home Ownership and Families: Urban Communities: 2,500 or More: Characteristics, 1910
[Continued]

City	Negro population 1910	Number of homes of Negro families: 1910					
		Total	Owned			Rented	No report of ownership
			Free	Encumbered	No encumbrance report		
West Virginia							
Charleston	3,086	640	93	22	8	498	19

Source: "Home Ownership in Selected Urban Communities—Number of Homes Owned Free, Owned Encumbered, and Rented, by Negro Families in Urban Communities Having a Negro Population of 2,500 or More: 1910," U.S. Bureau of the Census, *Negro Population in the United States, 1790-1915*, p. 471. *Notes:* (-) Represents zero. 1. Total number of homes in Texarkana, Miller County, Arkansas, and Texarkana, Bowie County, Texas, 1,342; owned free, 263; owned mortgaged, 115; no encumbrance report, 2; rented; 935; no report of ownership, 27.

★ 1105 ★
Home Ownership

Homes Owned and Rented, 1890, 1900, 1910

Class of home and proprietorship	Homes of Negro families					
	Number			Percentage distribution		
	1910	1900	1890	1910	1900	1890
All homes	2,173,018	1,833,759	1,410,769	100.0	100.0	100.0
Owned	506,590	397,420	264,288	23.3	21.7	18.7
Rented	1,666,428	1,436,339	1,146,181	76.7	78.3	81.3
Farm homes	877,648	758,463	549,632	100.0	100.0	100.0
Owned	221,535	192,993	120,738	25.2	25.4	22.0
Rented	656,113	565,470	428,894	74.8	74.6	78.0
Other homes	1,295,370	1,075,296	861,137	100.0	100.0	100.0
Owned	285,055	204,427	143,550	22.0	19.0	16.7
Rented	1,010,315	870,869	717,887	78.0	81.0	83.3

Source: "Homes of Negro Families," U.S. Bureau of the Census, *Negro Population, 1790-1915*, p. 459.

★ 1106 ★

Home Ownership

Homes Owned and Rented: Geographic Area, 1890-I

Division and state	Number of homes of Negro families: 1890				
	Total	Owned			Rented
		Total	Free	Encumbered	
United States	1,410,769	261,288	234,747	29,541	1,146,481
Geographic divisions:					
New England	9,754	1,814	1,047	767	7,940
Middle Atlantic	44,158	7,915	4,761	3,154	36,243
East North Central	44,764	14,379	9,241	5,138	30,385
West North Central	44,261	15,372	10,819	4,553	28,889
South Atlantic	613,236	115,116	107,084	8,032	498,120
East South Central	399,065	60,232	55,643	4,589	338,833
West South Central	250,406	47,967	44,948	3,019	202,439
Mountain	2,255	635	519	116	1,620
Pacific	2,870	858	685	173	2,012
New England:					
Maine	254	99	71	28	155
New Hampshire	114	24	13	11	90
Vermont	176	42	32	10	134
Massachusetts	4,802	848	479	369	3,954
Rhode Island	1,759	254	152	102	1,505
Connecticut	2,649	547	300	247	2,102
Middle Atlantic:					
New York	14,586	2,119	1,259	860	12,467
New Jersey	9,509	2,222	1,289	933	7,287
Pennsylvania	20,063	3,574	2,213	1,361	16,489
East North Central:					
Ohio	18,821	6,276	4,097	2,179	12,545
Indiana	9,771	2,731	1,702	1,029	7,040
Illinois	12,014	3,621	2,471	1,150	8,393
Michigan	3,616	1,524	830	694	2,092
Wisconsin	542	227	141	86	315
West North Central:					
Minnesota	860	169	92	77	691
Iowa	2,166	765	497	268	1,401
Missouri	29,571	8,894	6,559	2,335	20,677
North Dakota	72	37	26	11	35
South Dakota	107	58	36	22	49
Nebraska	1,340	302	197	105	1,038
Kansas	10,145	5,147	3,412	1,735	4,998
South Atlantic:					
Delaware	5,193	1,264	794	470	3,929
Maryland	38,887	8,596	6,930	1,666	30,291

[Continued]

★ 1106 ★

Homes Owned and Rented: Geographic Area, 1890-I
[Continued]

Division and state	Number of homes of Negro families: 1890				
	Total	Owned			Rented
		Total	Free	Encumbered	
District of Columbia	14,299	2,132	1,766	366	12,167
Virginia	112,404	29,888	28,621	1,267	82,516
West Virginia	5,655	1,471	1,182	289	4,184
North Carolina	102,885	20,010	18,722	1,288	82,875
South Carolina	135,551	21,101	19,637	1,464	114,450
Georgia	165,037	20,005	19,203	802	145,032
Florida	33,325	10,649	10,229	420	22,676
East South Central:					
Kentucky	49,318	12,877	12,107	770	36,441
Tennessee	78,195	14,663	13,626	1,037	63,532
Alabama	132,311	15,736	14,701	1,035	116,575
Mississippi	139,241	16,956	15,209	1,747	122,285
West South Central:					
Arkansas	56,446	11,844	10,902	942	44,602
Louisiana	107,370	14,602	13,882	720	92,768
Oklahoma[2]	749	641	641	-	108
Texas	85,841	20,880	19,523	1,357	64,961
Mountain:					
Montana	222	53	40	13	169
Idaho	41	16	11	5	25
Wyoming	111	28	25	3	83
Colorado	1,216	296	211	85	920
New Mexico	394	168	161	7	226
Arizona	114	23	22	1	91
Utah	78	19	19	-	59
Nevada	79	32	20	2	47
Pacific:					
Washington	292	68	62	6	224
Oregon	171	74	56	18	97
California	2,407	716	567	149	1,691

Source: "Home Ownership, by Divisions and States: 1890—Number of Farm Homes and Other Homes Owned Free, Owned Encumbered, and Rented by Negro Families," U.S. Bureau of the Census, *Negro Population in the United States, 1790- 1915*, p. 470. *Note:* (-) Represents zero.

★ 1107 ★

Home Ownership

Homes Owned and Rented: Geographic Area, 1890-II

Division and state	Number of homes of Negro families: 1890									
	Farm homes					Other homes				
	Total	Owned			Rented	Total	Owned			Rented
		Total	Free	Encumbered			Total	Free	Encumbered	
United States	549,632	120,738	108,483	12,255	428,894	861,137	143,550	126,264	17,286	717,587
Geographic divisions:										
New England	357	220	146	74	137	9,397	1,594	901	693	7,803
Middle Atlantic	1,431	870	448	422	561	42,727	7,045	4,313	2,732	35,682
East North Central	5,795	3,187	1,873	1,314	2,608	38,969	11,192	7,368	3,824	27,777
West North Central	7,995	4,343	2,698	1,645	3,652	36,266	11,029	8,121	2,908	25,237
South Atlantic	218,003	53,261	49,601	3,660	164,742	395,233	61,855	57,483	4,372	333,378
East South Central	195,702	30,861	27,898	2,963	164,841	203,363	29,371	27,745	1,626	173,992
West South Central	119,976	27,709	25,588	2,121	92,267	130,430	20,258	19,360	898	110,172
Mountain	119	90	81	9	29	2,136	545	438	107	1,591
Pacific	254	197	150	47	57	2,616	661	535	126	1,955
New England:										
Maine	36	29	22	7	7	218	70	49	21	148
New Hampshire	8	6	3	3	2	106	18	10	8	88
Vermont	18	13	7	6	5	158	29	25	4	129
Massachusetts	108	75	50	25	33	4,694	773	429	344	3,921
Rhode Island	32	16	13	3	16	1,727	238	139	99	1,489
Connecticut	155	81	51	30	74	2,494	466	249	217	2,028
Middle Atlantic:										
New York	382	236	111	125	146	14,204	1,883	1,148	735	12,321
New Jersey	456	272	128	144	184	9,053	1,950	1,161	789	7,103
Pennsylvania	593	362	209	153	231	19,470	3,212	2,004	1,208	16,258
East North Central:										
Ohio	2,290	1,323	840	483	967	16,531	4,953	3,257	1,696	11,578
Indiana	1,083	528	315	213	555	8,088	2,203	1,387	816	6,485
Illinois	1,670	761	479	282	909	10,344	2,860	1,992	868	7,484
Michigan	674	507	211	296	167	2,942	1,017	619	398	1,925
Wisconsin	78	68	28	40	10	464	159	113	46	305
West North Central:										
Minnesota	28	20	9	11	8	832	149	83	66	683
Iowa	188	115	60	55	73	1,978	650	437	213	1,328
Missouri	5,478	2,745	1,812	933	2,733	24,093	6,149	4,747	1,402	17,944
North Dakota	23	20	14	6	3	49	17	12	5	32
South Dakota	22	18	10	8	4	85	40	26	14	45
Nebraska	114	67	40	27	47	1,226	235	157	78	991
Kansas	2,142	1,358	753	605	784	8,003	3,789	2,659	1,130	4,214
South Atlantic:										
Delaware	821	288	199	89	1,533	4,372	976	595	381	3,396
Maryland	4,958	2,150	1,691	459	2,808	33,929	6,446	5,239	1,207	27,483
District of Columbia	52	16	15	1	36	14,247	2,116	1,751	365	12,131
Virginia	31,839	13,678	13,097	581	18,161	80,565	16,210	15,524	686	64,355
West Virginia	846	489	436	53	357	4,809	982	746	236	3,827
North Carolina	40,061	10,494	9,670	824	29,567	62,824	9,516	9,052	464	53,308
South Carolina	63,738	13,075	12,048	1,027	50,663	71,813	8,026	7,589	437	63,787

[Continued]

917

★ 1107 ★

Homes Owned and Rented: Geographic Area, 1890-II

[Continued]

Division and state	Number of homes of Negro families: 1890									
	Farm homes					Other homes				
	Total	Owned			Rented	Total	Owned			Rented
		Total	Free	Encumbered			Total	Free	Encumbered	
Georgia	62,849	8,131	7,705	426	54,718	102,188	11,874	11,498	376	90,314
Florida	12,839	4,940	4,740	200	7,899	20,486	5,709	5,489	220	14,777
East South Central:										
Kentucky	10,153	4,110	3,870	240	6,043	39,165	8,767	8,237	530	30,398
Tennessee	27,860	6,378	5,951	427	21,482	50,335	8,285	7,675	610	42,050
Alabama	69,870	8,847	8,045	802	61,023	62,441	6,889	6,656	233	55,552
Mississippi	87,819	11,526	10,032	1,494	76,293	51,442	5,430	5,177	253	45,992
West South Central:										
Arkansas	33,486	8,004	7,319	685	25,482	22,960	3,840	3,583	257	19,120
Louisiana	38,061	6,685	6,257	428	31,376	69,309	7,917	7,625	292	61,392
Oklahoma[2]	531	507	507	-	24	218	134	134	-	84
Texas	47,898	12,513	11,505	1,008	35,385	37,943	8,367	8,018	349	29,576
Mountain:										
Montana	11	10	10	-	1	211	43	30	13	168
Idaho	6	5	2	3	1	35	11	9	2	24
Wyoming	4	2	1	1	2	107	26	24	2	81
Colorado	44	37	34	3	7	1,172	259	177	82	913
New Mexico	40	27	25	2	13	354	141	136	5	213
Arizona	5	4	4	-	1	109	19	18	1	90
Utah	6	4	4	-	2	72	15	15	-	57
Nevada	3	1	1	-	2	76	31	29	2	45
Pacific:										
Washington	14	11	11	-	3	278	57	51	6	221
Oregon	31	25	20	5	6	140	49	36	13	91
California	209	161	119	42	48	2,198	555	448	107	1,643

Source: "Home Ownership, by Divisions and States: 1890—Number of Farm Homes and Other Homes Owned Free, Owned Encumbered, and Rented by Negro Families," U.S. Bureau of the Census, *Negro Population in the United States, 1790- 1915,* p. 470. *Note:* (-) Represents zero.

★ 1108 ★

Home Ownership

Homes Owned and Rented: Increase, 1890-1910

Proprietorship	Increase in homes of negro families					
	All homes		Farm homes		Other homes	
	1900-1910	1890-1900	1900-1910	1890-1900	1900-1910	1890-1900
Total	339,259	422,990	119,185	208,831	220,074	214,159
Owned	109,170	133,132	28,542	72,255	80,628	60,877
Free	79,379	60,727	20,993	30,493	58,386	30,234

[Continued]

★ 1108 ★

Homes Owned and Rented: Increase, 1890-1910
[Continued]

| Proprietorship | Increase in homes of negro families | | | | | |
| | All homes | | Farm homes | | Other homes | |
	1900-1910	1890-1900	1900-1910	1890-1900	1900-1910	1890-1900
Encumbered	29,791	72,405	7,549	41,762	22,242	30,643
Rented	230,089	289,858	90,643	136,576	139,446	153,282

Source: "Increase in Homes of Negro Families," U.S. Bureau of the Census, *Negro Population in the United States, 1790-1915*, p. 460.

★ 1109 ★

Home Ownership

Homes Owned by Region, 1890-1910

| Section and census year | Homes of Negro families | | | | | |
| | Number | | | Percentage distribution | | |
	All homes	Farm homes	Other homes	All homes	Farm homes	Other homes
United States:						
1910	2,173,018	877,648	1,295,370	100.0	100.0	100.0
1900	1,833,759	758,463	1,075,296	100.0	100.0	100.0
1890	1,410,769	549,632	861,137	100.0	100.0	100.0
The South:						
1910	1,917,391	864,638	1,052,703	88.2	98.5	81.3
1900	1,637,024	743,521	893,503	89.3	98.0	83.1
1890	1,262,707	533,681	729,026	89.5	97.1	84.7
The North:						
1910	242,920	12,431	230,483	11.2	1.4	17.8
1900	189,770	14,580	175,190	10.3	1.9	16.3
1890	142,937	15,578	127,359	10.1	2.8	14.8
The West:						
1910	12,707	523	12,184	0.6	0.1	0.9
1900	6,965	362	6,603	0.4	0.0	0.6
1890	5,125	373	4,752	0.4	0.1	0.6

Source: "Homes of Negro Families," U.S. Bureau of the Census, *Negro Population in the United States, 1790-1915*, p. 460.

★ 1110 ★

Home Ownership

Homes Owned by Region: Percentages, 1890-1910

Section	Percentage owned of homes of Negro families								
	All homes			Farm homes			Other homes		
	1910	1900	1890	1910	1900	1890	1910	1900	1890
United States	23.3	21.7	18.7	10.2	10.5	8.6	13.1	11.1	10.2
The South	23.3	21.3	17.7	11.1	11.2	8.9	12.2	10.1	8.8
The North	23.0	24.3	27.6	3.2	4.7	6.0	19.8	19.6	21.6
The West	33.7	29.0	29.1	3.3	3.9	5.6	30.5	25.1	23.5

Source: "Percentage Owned of Homes of Negro Families," U.S. Bureau of the Census, *Negro Population in the United States, 1790-1915*, p. 461.

★ 1111 ★

Home Ownership

Homes Owned, Encumbered, Rented, 1890-1910, Part I

Section, division, and census year	Homes of Negro families All homes				
	Total	Owned			Rented
		Total	Free	Encumbered	
United States:					
1910	2,173,018	506,590	374,853	131,737	1,666,428
1900	1,833,759	397,420	295,474	101,946	1,436,339
1890	1,410,769	264,288	234,747	29,541	1,146,481
The South:					
1910	1,917,391	446,379	340,202	106,177	1,471,012
1900	1,637,024	349,296	267,160	82,136	1,287,728
1890	1,262,707	223,315	207,675	15,640	1,039,392
South Atlantic:					
1910	882,647	215,384	169,996	45,388	667,263
1900	761,105	169,910	133,147	36,763	591,195
1890	613,236	115,116	107,084	8,032	498,120
East South Central:					
1910	603,322	123,928	88,334	35,594	479,394
1900	527,908	97,779	71,495	26,284	430,129
1890	399,065	60,232	55,643	4,589	338,833
West South Central:					
1910	431,422	107,067	81,872	25,195	324,355
1900	348,011	81,607	62,518	19,089	266,404
1890	250,406	47,967	44,948	3,109	202,439

[Continued]

★ 1111 ★

Homes Owned, Encumbered, Rented, 1890-1910, Part I

[Continued]

Section, division, and census year	Homes of Negro families All homes				
	Total	Owned			Rented
		Total	Free	Encumbered	
The North:					
1910	242,920	55,926	32,061	23,865	186,994
1900	189,770	46,105	26,890	19,215	143,665
1890	142,937	39,480	25,868	13,612	103,457
The West:					
1910	12,707	4,285	2,590	1,695	8,422
1900	6,965	2,019	1,424	595	4,946
1890	5,125	1,493	1,204	289	3,632

Source: "Negro Homes, Farm and Other, Classified as Owned Free, Owned Encumbered, and Rented, by Sections and Southern Divisions: 1910, 1900, and 1890," U.S. Bureau of the Census, *Negro Population in the United States, 1790-1915*, p. 461.

★ 1112 ★

Home Ownership

Homes Owned, Encumbered, Rented, 1890-1910, Part II

Section, division, and census year	Homes of Negro families									
	Farm homes					Other homes				
	Total	Owned			Rented	Total	Owned			Rented
		Total	Free	Encumbered			Total	Free	Encumbered	
United States:										
1910	877,648	221,535	159,969	61,566	656,113	1,295,370	285,055	214,884	70,171	1,010,315
1900	758,463	192,993	138,976	54,017	565,170	1,075,296	204,427	156,498	47,929	870,869
1890	549,632	120,738	108,483	12,255	428,894	861,137	143,550	126,264	17,286	717,587
The South:										
1910	864,688	213,283	155,472	57,811	651,405	1,052,703	233,096	184,730	48,366	819,607
1900	743,521	183,817	133,731	50,086	559,704	893,503	165,479	133,429	32,050	728,024
1890	533,681	111,831	103,087	8,744	421,850	729,026	111,484	104,588	6,896	617,542
South Atlantic:										
1910	351,868	102,438	80,552	21,886	249,430	530,779	112,946	89,444	23,502	417,833
1900	293,512	86,794	67,582	19,212	206,718	467,593	83,116	65,565	17,551	384,477
1890	218,003	53,261	49,601	3,660	164,742	395,233	61,855	57,483	4,372	333,378
East South Central:										
1910	315,353	59,210	37,323	21,887	256,143	287,969	64,718	51,011	13,707	223,251
1900	273,753	51,136	33,481	17,655	222,617	254,155	46,643	38,014	8,629	207,512
1890	194,702	30,861	27,898	2,963	164,841	203,363	29,371	27,745	1,626	173,992
West South Central:										
1910	197,467	51,635	37,597	14,038	145,832	233,955	55,432	44,275	11,157	178,523
1900	176,256	45,887	32,668	13,219	130,369	171,755	35,720	29,850	5,870	136,035
1890	119,976	27,709	25,588	2,121	92,267	130,430	20,258	19,360	898	110,172
The North:										
1910	12,437	7,839	4,201	3,638	4,598	230,483	48,087	27,860	20,227	182,396
1900	14,580	8,004	5,028	3,876	5,676	175,190	37,201	21,862	15,339	137,989

[Continued]

★ 1112 ★

Homes Owned, Encumbered, Rented, 1890-1910, Part II
[Continued]

Section, division, and census year	Homes of Negro families									
	Farm homes					Other homes				
	Total	Owned			Rented	Total	Owned			Rented
		Total	Free	Encumbered			Total	Free	Encumbered	
1890	15,578	8,620	5,165	3,455	6,958	127,359	30,860	20,703	10,157	96,499
The West:										
1910	523	413	296	117	110	12,184	3,872	2,294	1,578	8,312
1900	362	272	217	55	90	6,603	1,747	1,207	540	4,856
1890	373	287	231	56	86	4,752	1,206	973	233	3,546

Source: "Negro Homes, Farm ad Other, Classified as Owned Free, Owned Encumbered, and Rented, by Sections and Southern Divisions: 1910, 1900, and 1890," U.S. Bureau of the Census, *Negro Population in the United States, 1790- 1915,* p. 461.

★ 1113 ★

Home Ownership

Homes Owned, Encumbered, Rented, and Farm – East North Central States, 1900 and 1910: Part I

Division, state and year	Negro population			Number of homes of Negro families						
				Total	Owned				Rented	No report of ownership
	Total	Rural	Urban		Total	Free	Encumbered	No encumbrance report		
East North Central:										
Ohio-										
1910	111,452	29,170	82,282	28,135	8,467	4,526	3,754	187	19,051	617
1900	96,901	31,915	64,986	22,420	6,927	3,677	3,032	218	14,589	904
Indiana-										
1910	60,320	11,895	48,425	15,302	4,036	2,284	1,656	96	10,990	976
1900	57,505	15,231	42,274	12,756	3,515	1,929	1,484	102	8,599	642
Illinois-										
1910	109,049	23,511	85,538	26,149	6,012	3,266	2,402	344	19,455	682
1900	85,078	24,085	60,993	19,240	4,479	2,539	1,730	210	13,810	951
Michigan-										
1910	17,115	4,959	12,156	4,391	1,932	1,040	874	18	2,382	77
1900	15,816	5,807	10,009	3,706	1,573	813	725	35	1,980	153
Wisconsin-										
1910	2,900	759	2,141	677	173	80	90	3	486	18
1900	2,542	683	1,859	616	167	96	63	8	425	24

Source: "Home Ownership by Divisions and States: 1910 and 1900—Number of Farm Homes and Other Homes Owned Free Owned Encumbered, and Rented by Negro Families," U.S. Bureau of the Census, *Negro Population in the United States, 1790-1915,* pp. 446-467.

★ 1114 ★

Home Ownership

Homes Owned, Encumbered, Rented, and Farm – East North Central States, 1900 and 1910: Part IIA

Division, state and year	Total	Farm homes				Rented	No report of ownership
		Owned					
		Total	Free	Encumbered	No encumbrance report		
East North Central:							
Ohio-							
1910	2,009	1,358	805	539	14	646	5
1900	2,174	1,379	785	562	32	770	25
Indiana-							
1910	824	478	246	231	1	343	3
1900	1,064	706	415	268	22	344	15
Illinois-							
1910	1,477	809	409	393	7	656	12
1900	1,569	834	472	332	30	719	16
Michigan-							
1910	640	505	227	275	3	135	-
1900	657	500	202	291	7	155	2
Wisconsin-							
1910	54	42	10	32	-	12	-
1900	60	45	21	23	1	14	1

Source: "Home Ownership by Divisions and States: 1910 and 1900—Number of Farm Homes and Other Homes Owned Free Owned Encumbered, and Rented by Negro Families," U.S. Bureau of the Census, *Negro Population in the United States, 1790-1915*, pp. 446-467.
Note: (-) Represents zero.

★ 1115 ★
Home Ownership

Homes Owned, Encumbered, Rented, and Farm – East North Central States, 1900 and 1910: Part IIB

| Division, state and year | Total | Other homes | | | | Rented | No report of ownership |
| | | Owned | | | | | |
		Total	Free	Encumbered	No encumbrance report		
East North Central:							
Ohio-							
1910	26,126	7,109	3,721	3,216	173	18,405	612
1900	20,246	5,548	2,892	2,470	186	13,819	879
Indiana-							
1910	14,478	3,558	2,038	1,425	96	10,647	273
1900	11,692	2,810	1,514	1,216	80	8,256	627
Illinois-							
1910	24,672	5,203	2,857	2,009	337	18,799	670
1900	17,671	3,645	2,067	1,398	180	13,091	935
Michigan-							
1910	3,751	1,427	813	599	15	2,247	77
1900	3,049	1,073	611	434	28	1,825	151
Wisconsin-							
1910	623	131	70	58	3	474	18
1900	556	122	75	40	7	411	23

Source: "Home Ownership by Divisions and States: 1910 and 1900—Number of Farm Homes and Other Homes Owned Free Owned Encumbered, and Rented by Negro Families," U.S. Bureau of the Census, *Negro Population in the United States, 1790-1915*, pp. 446-467.

★ 1116 ★
Home Ownership

Homes Owned, Encumbered, Rented, and Farm – East South Central States, 1900 and 1910: Part I

| Division, state, and year | Negro population | | | Number of homes of Negro families | | | | | | |
| | Total | Rural | Urban | Total | Owned | | | | Rented | No report of ownership |
					Total	Free	Encumbered	No report of ownership		
East South Central:										
Kentucky-										
1910	261,656	155,025	106,631	62,216	19,774	15,351	3,557	866	40,364	2,078
1900	284,706	184,561	100,145	60,311	17,906	13,248	3,374	1,284	39,154	3,251

[Continued]

★ 1116 ★

Homes Owned, Encumbered, Rented, and Farm – East South Central States, 1900 and 1910: Part I
[Continued]

Division, state, and year	Negro population			Number of homes of Negro families						
				Total	Owned				Rented	No report of ownership
	Total	Rural	Urban		Total	Free	Encumbered	No report of ownership		
Tennessee-										
1910	473,088	322,582	150,506	106,558	27,012	20,185	5,811	1,016	76,833	2,713
1900	480,243	349,099	131,144	96,427	21,023	15,141	3,679	2,203	69,911	5,493
Alabama-										
1910	908,282	751,679	156,603	206,884	33,941	22,729	10,105	1,107	164,024	8,919
1900	827,307	729,153	98,154	178,365	23,536	15,480	6,200	1,856	142,819	12,010
Mississippi-										
1910	1,009,487	914,130	95,357	227,664	38,564	23,319	14,033	1,223	182,015	7,085
1900	907,630	850,805	56,825	192,805	28,855	17,118	9,921	1,816	149,557	14,393

Source: "Home Ownership by Divisions and States: 1910 and 1900—Number of Farm Homes and Other Homes Owned Free Owned Encumbered, and Rented by Negro Families," U.S. Bureau of the Census, *Negro Population in the United States, 1790-1915*, pp. 468-469.

★ 1117 ★

Home Ownership

Homes Owned, Encumbered, Rented, and Farm – East South Central States, 1900 and 1910: Part IIA

Division, state, and year	Farm homes						
	Total	Owned				Rented	No report of ownership
		Total	Free	Encumbered	No emcumbrance report		
East South Central:							
Kentucky-							
1910	11,356	6,077	4,632	1,374	71	5,243	36
1900	11,985	5,915	4,451	1,179	285	5,927	143
Tennessee-							
1910	37,246	10,942	8,198	2,577	167	26,228	76
1900	35,325	9,819	7,358	1,827	634	25,046	460
Alabama-							
1910	107,698	17,227	10,434	6,379	414	90,218	251
1900	92,830	13,955	8,172	4,764	1,019	77,970	905

[Continued]

★ 1117 ★

Homes Owned, Encumbered, Rented, and Farm – East South Central States, 1900 and 1910: Part IIA
[Continued]

Division, state, and year	Total	Farm homes						
		Owned					Rented	No report of ownership
		Total	Free	Encumbered	No emcumbrance report			
Mississippi-								
1910	159,055	24,781	13,160	11,030	591		133,600	614
1900	133,613	20,939	11,086	8,612	1,214		111,461	1,213

Source: "Home Ownership by Divisions and States: 1910 and 1900—Number of Farm Homes and Other Homes Owned Free Owned Encumbered, and Rented by Negro Families," U.S. Bureau of the Census, *Negro Population in the United States, 1790-1915*, pp. 468-469.

★ 1118 ★

Home Ownership

Homes Owned, Encumbered, Rented, and Farm – East South Central States, 1900 and 1910: Part IIB

Division, state, and year	Total	Other homes						
		Owned					Rented	No report of ownership
		Total	Free	Encumbered	No emcumbrance report			
East South Central:								
Kentucky-								
1910	50,860	13,697	10,719	2,183	795		35,121	2,042
1900	48,326	11,991	8,797	2,195	999		33,227	3,106
Tennessee-								
1910	69,312	16,070	11,987	3,234	849		50,005	2,637
1900	61,102	11,204	7,783	1,852	1,569		44,865	5,033
Alabama-								
1910	99,188	16,714	12,295	3,726	693		73,806	8,668
1900	85,535	9,581	7,308	1,436	837		64,849	11,105
Mississippi-								
1910	68,609	13,783	10,159	2,992	632		48,355	6,471
1900	59,192	7,916	6,032	1,309	575		38,096	13,180

Source: "Home Ownership by Divisions and States: 1910 and 1900—Number of Farm Homes and Other Homes Owned Free Owned Encumbered, and Rented by Negro Families," U.S. Bureau of the Census, *Negro Population in the United States, 1790-1915*, pp. 468-469.

★ 1119 ★

Home Ownership

Homes Owned, Encumbered, Rented, and Farm – Geographic Divisions, 1900 and 1910: Part I

Division, state and year	Negro population			Number of homes of Negro families						
				Total	Owned				Rented	No report of ownership
	Total	Rural	Urban		Total	Free	Encumbered	No encumbrance report		
United States:										
1910	9,827,763	7,138,534	2,689,229	2,173,018	488,699	346,867	123,044	18,788	1,603,719	80,600
1900	8,833,994	6,828,022	2,005,972	1,863,759	373,450	255,156	89,900	28,394	1,335,276	125,033
Geographic divisions:										
New England-										
1910	66,306	5,429	60,877	15,214	2,615	1,201	1,371	43	12,302	297
1900	59,099	5,569	53,530	12,873	2,215	981	1,182	52	9,941	717
Middle Atlantic-										
1910	417,870	78,624	339,246	93,370	11,736	5,663	5,759	314	77,263	4,371
1900	325,921	78,152	247,769	65,965	8,779	4,183	4,265	331	53,576	3,610
East North Central-										
1910	300,836	70,294	230,542	74,654	20,620	11,196	8,776	648	52,364	1,670
1900	257,842	77,721	180,121	58,738	16,661	9,054	7,034	573	39,403	2,674
West North Central-										
1910	242,662	78,361	164,301	59,682	19,138	12,027	6,549	562	38,020	2,524
1900	237,909	98,546	139,363	52,194	16,386	10,524	5,231	631	33,263	2,545
South Atlantic-										
1910	4,112,488	3,202,968	909,520	882,647	208,247	157,711	42,147	8,389	641,368	33,032
1900	3,729,017	3,032,645	696,372	761,105	159,595	114,556	31,706	13,333	545,240	56,270
East South Central-										
1910	2,652,513	2,143,416	509,097	603,322	119,291	81,584	33,495	4,212	463,236	20,795
1900	2,499,886	2,113,618	386,268	527,908	91,320	60,987	23,174	7,159	401,441	35,147
West South Central-										
1910	1,984,426	1,548,588	435,838	431,422	102,911	75,045	23,345	4,521	311,047	17,464
1900	1,694,066	1,411,910	282,156	348,011	76,622	53,615	16,787	6,220	247,868	23,521
Mountain-										
1910	21,467	6,021	15,446	5,658	1,589	1,081	459	49	3,831	238
1900	15,590	5,756	9,834	3,547	801	539	210	52	2,440	306
Pacific-										
1910	29,195	4,833	24,362	7,049	2,552	1,359	1,143	50	4,288	209
1900	14,664	4,105	10,559	3,418	1,071	717	311	43	2,104	243

Source: "Home Ownership by Divisions and States: 1910 and 1900—Number of Farm Homes and Other Homes Owned Free Owned Encumbered, and Rented by Negro Families," U.S. Bureau of the Census, *Negro Population in the United States, 1790-1915*, pp. 446-467.

★ 1120 ★

Home Ownership

Homes Owned, Encumbered, Rented, and Farm – Geographic Divisions, 1900 and 1910: Part IIA

Division, state and year	Total	Owned				Rented	No report of ownership
		Total	Free	Encumbered	No encumbrance report		
United States:							
1910	877,648	220,698	156,450	60,167	4,081	653,768	3,182
1900	758,463	191,143	128,851	50,140	12,152	560,005	7,315
Geographic divisions:							
New England-							
1910	318	257	133	117	7	61	-
1900	296	225	120	100	5	71	-
Middle Atlantic-							
1910	1,392	865	436	407	22	514	13
1900	1,444	903	379	495	29	524	17
East North Central-							
1910	5,004	3,192	1,607	1,470	25	1,792	20
1900	5,524	3,463	1,895	1,476	92	2,002	59
West North Central-							
1910	5,723	3,472	1,853	1,571	48	2,199	52
1900	7,316	4,227	2,443	1,658	126	3,024	65
South Atlantic-							
1910	351,868	102,036	79,089	21,489	1,458	248,451	1,331
1900	293,512	86,009	62,725	17,831	5,453	204,848	2,655
East South Central-							
1910	315,353	59,027	36,424	21,360	1,243	255,349	977
1900	273,753	50,628	31,067	16,382	3,179	220,404	2,721
West South Central-							
1910	197,467	51,444	36,534	13,641	1,269	145,293	730
1900	176,256	45,421	30,015	12,146	3,260	129,043	1,792
Mountain-							
1910	233	178	134	40	4	53	2
1900	143	110	85	18	7	31	2

[Continued]

★ 1120 ★

Homes Owned, Encumbered, Rented, and Farm – Geographic Divisions, 1900 and 1910: Part IIA
[Continued]

Division, state and year	Farm homes						
	Total	Owned				Rented	No report of ownership
		Total	Free	Encumbered	No encumbrance report		
Pacific-							
1910	290	227	150	72	5	56	7
1900	219	157	122	34	1	58	4

Source: "Home Ownership by Divisions and States: 1910 and 1900—Number of Farm Homes and Other Homes Owned Free Owned Encumbered, and Rented by Negro Families," U.S. Bureau of the Census, *Negro Population in the United States, 1790-1915*, pp. 446-467. *Note:* (-) Represents zero. Adapted by the editors.

★ 1121 ★
Home Ownership

Homes Owned, Encumbered, Rented, and Farm – Geographic Divisions, 1900 and 1910: Part IIB

Division, state and year	Other homes						
	Total	Owned				Rented	No report of ownership
		Total	Free	Encumbered	No encumbrance report		
United States:							
1910	1,295,370	268,001	190,417	62,877	14,707	949,951	77,418
1900	1,075,296	182,307	126,305	39,760	16,242	775,271	117,718
Geographic divisions:							
New England-							
1910	14,896	2,358	1,068	1,254	36	12,241	297
1900	12,577	1,990	861	1,082	47	9,870	717
Middle Atlantic-							
1910	91,978	10,871	5,227	5,352	292	76,749	4,358
1900	64,521	7,876	3,804	3,770	302	53,052	3,593
East North Central-							
1910	69,650	17,428	9,499	7,306	623	50,572	1,650
1900	53,214	13,198	7,159	5,558	481	37,401	2,615
West North Central-							
1910	53,959	15,666	10,174	4,978	514	35,821	2,472
1900	44,878	12,159	8,081	3,573	505	30,239	2,480

[Continued]

★ 1121 ★

Homes Owned, Encumbered, Rented, and Farm – Geographic Divisions, 1900 and 1910: Part IIB
[Continued]

Division, state and year	Other homes						
	Total	Owned				Rented	No report of ownership
		Total	Free	Encumbered	No encumbrance report		
South Atlantic-							
1910	530,779	106,211	78,622	20,658	6,931	392,917	31,651
1900	467,593	73,586	51,831	13,875	7,880	340,392	53,615
East South Central-							
1910	287,969	60,264	45,160	12,135	2,969	207,887	19,818
1900	254,155	40,692	29,920	6,792	3,980	181,037	32,426
West South Central-							
1910	233,955	51,467	38,511	9,704	3,252	165,754	16,734
1900	171,755	31,201	23,600	4,641	2,960	118,825	21,729
Mountain-							
1910	5,425	1,411	947	419	45	3,778	236
1900	3,404	691	454	192	45	2,409	304
Pacific-							
1910	6,759	2,325	1,209	1,071	45	4,232	202
1900	3,109	914	595	277	42	2,046	239

Source: "Home Ownership by Divisions and States: 1910 and 1900—Number of Farm Homes and Other Homes Owned Free Owned Encumbered, and Rented by Negro Families," U.S. Bureau of the Census, *Negro Population in the United States, 1790-1915*, pp. 446-467. *Note:* Adapted by the editors.

★ 1122 ★
Home Ownership

Homes Owned, Encumbered, Rented, and Farm – Middle Atlantic States, 1900 and 1910: Part I

Division, state and year	Negro population			Number of homes of Negro families						
	Total	Rural	Urban	Total	Owned				Rented	No report of ownership
					Total	Free	Encumbered	No encumbrance report		
Middle Atlantic:										
New York-										
1910	134,191	16,705	117,486	31,434	2,437	1,224	1,164	49	28,070	927
1900	99,232	17,876	81,356	20,982	2,213	1,127	1,027	59	17,784	985
New Jersey-										
1910	89,760	24,333	65,427	19,825	3,682	1,683	1,917	82	15,406	737

[Continued]

★ 1122 ★

Homes Owned, Encumbered, Rented, and Farm – Middle Atlantic States, 1900 and 1910: Part I
[Continued]

Division, state and year	Negro population			Number of homes of Negro families							
					Owned						No report of ownership
	Total	Rural	Urban	Total	Total	Free	Encumbered	No encumbrance report	Rented	
1900	69,844	23,716	46,128	13,934	2,588	1,108	1,393	87	10,571	775
Pennsylvania-										
1910	193,919	37,586	156,333	42,111	5,617	2,756	2,678	183	33,787	2,707
1900	156,845	36,560	120,285	31,049	3,978	1,948	1,845	185	25,221	1,850

Source: "Home Ownership by Divisions and States: 1910 and 1900—Number of Farm Homes and Other Homes Owned Free Owned Encumbered, and Rented by Negro Families," U.S. Bureau of the Census, *Negro Population in the United States, 1790-1915,* pp. 446-467.

★ 1123 ★
Home Ownership

Homes Owned, Encumbered, Rented, and Farm – Middle Atlantic States, 1900 and 1910: Part IIA

Division, state and year	Farm homes						
	Total	Owned				Rented	No report of ownership
		Total	Free	Encumbered	No encumbrance report		
Middle Atlantic:							
New York-							
1910	311	210	99	105	6	100	1
1900	333	214	99	111	4	111	8
New Jersey-							
1910	489	289	142	139	8	194	6
1900	496	314	124	180	10	173	9
Pennsylvania-							
1910	592	366	195	163	8	220	6
1900	615	375	156	204	15	240	-

Source: "Home Ownership by Divisions and States: 1910 and 1900—Number of Farm Homes and Other Homes Owned Free Owned Encumbered, and Rented by Negro Families," U.S. Bureau of the Census, *Negro Population in the United States, 1790-1915,* pp. 446-467.
Note: (-) Represents zero.

★ 1124 ★
Home Ownership

Homes Owned, Encumbered, Rented, and Farm – Middle Atlantic States, 1900 and 1910: Part IIB

Division, state and year	Total	Other homes					Rented	No report of ownership
		Owned						
		Total	Free	Encumbered	No encumbrance report			
Middle Atlantic:								
New York-								
1910	31,123	2,227	1,125	1,059	43		27,970	925
1900	20,649	1,999	1,028	916	55		17,673	977
New Jersey-								
1910	19,336	3,393	1,541	1,778	74		15,212	731
1900	13,438	2,274	984	1,213	77		10,398	766
Pennsylvania-								
1910	41,519	5,251	2,561	2,515	175		33,567	2,701
1900	30,434	3,603	1,792	1,641	170		24,981	1,850

Source: "Home Ownership by Divisions and States: 1910 and 1900—Number of Farm Homes and Other Homes Owned Free Owned Encumbered, and Rented by Negro Families," U.S. Bureau of the Census, *Negro Population in the United States, 1790-1915*, pp. 446-467.

★ 1125 ★
Home Ownership

Homes Owned, Encumbered, Rented, and Farm – Mountain States, 1900 and 1910: Part I

Division, State and Year	Negro population			Number of homes of Negro families						
	Total	Rural	Urban	Total	Owned				Rented	No report of ownership
					Total	Free	Encumbered	No encumbrance report		
Mountain										
Montana										
1910	1,834	379	1,455	555	182	134	37	11	336	37
1900	1,523	592	931	393	75	56	17	2	280	38
Idaho										
1910	651	225	426	167	48	31	15	2	100	19
1900	293	222	71	81	36	26	7	3	39	6
Wyoming										
1910	2,235	1,194	1,041	375	69	48	21	-	288	18
1900	940	451	489	160	32	27	4	1	116	12
Colorado										
1910	11,453	2,094	9,359	3,079	849	533	294	22	2,141	89
1900	8,570	1,518	7,052	2,052	467	280	163	24	1,493	92
New Mexico										
1910	1,628	833	795	449	136	111	20	5	304	9
1900	1,610	1,029	581	381	69	51	5	13	265	47

[Continued]

★ 1125 ★

Homes Owned, Encumbered, Rented, and Farm – Mountain States, 1900 and 1910: Part I

[Continued]

Division, State and Year	Negro population			Number of homes of Negro families						
				Total	Owned				Rented	No report of ownership
	Total	Rural	Urban		Total	Free	Encumbered	No encumbrance report		
Arizona										
1910	2,009	699	1,310	583	179	122	50	7	376	28
1900	1,848	1,518	330	309	85	69	11	5	137	87
Utah										
1910	1,144	185	959	240	51	32	18	1	154	35
1900	672	329	343	119	19	16	2	1	85	15
Nevada										
1910	513	412	101	210	75	70	4	1	132	3
1900	134	97	37	52	18	14	1	3	25	9

Source: "Home Ownership by Divisions and States: 1910 and 1900—Number of Farm Homes and Other Homes Owned Free Owned Encumbered, and Rented by Negro Families." U.S. Bureau of the Census, *Negro Population in the United States, 1790-1915*, 1918, pp. 468-469.

★ 1126 ★

Home Ownership

Homes Owned, Encumbered, Rented, and Farm – Mountain States, 1900 and 1910: Part IIA

Division, State and Year	Farm homes						
	Total	Owned				Rented	No report of ownership
		Total	Free	Encumbered	No encumbrance report		
Mountain							
Montana							
1910	30	22	18	4	-	8	-
1900	24	16	9	6	1	6	2
Idaho							
1910	17	15	6	9	-	2	-
1900	9	9	7	1	1	-	-
Wyoming							
1910	18	16	10	6	-	2	-
1900	9	8	7	1	-	1	-
Colorado							
1910	88	57	40	17	-	29	2
1900	61	49	41	7	1	12	-
New Mexico							
1910	48	42	38	3	1	6	-
1900	26	9	5	2	2	7	-
Arizona							
1910	14	12	10	1	1	2	-
1900	10	9	7	-	2	1	-
Utah							
1910	12	9	8	-	1	3	-
1900	10	7	6	1	-	3	-

[Continued]

★ 1126 ★

Homes Owned, Encumbered, Rented, and Farm – Mountain States, 1900 and 1910: Part IIA
[Continued]

Division, State and Year	Farm homes						
	Total	Owned				Rented	No report of ownership
		Total	Free	Encumbered	No encumbrance report		
Nevada							
1910	6	5	4	-	1	1	-
1900	4	3	3	-	-	1	-

Source: "Home Ownership by Divisions and States: 1910 and 1900—Number of Farm Homes and Other Homes Owned Free Owned Encumbered, and Rented by Negro Families," U.S. Bureau of the Census. *Negro Population in the United States, 1790-1915,* pp. 468-469.

★ 1127 ★

Home Ownership

Homes Owned, Encumbered, Rented, and Farm – Mountain States, 1900 and 1910: Part IIB

Division, State and Year	Other homes						
	Total	Owned				Rented	No report of ownership
		Total	Free	Encumbered	No encumbrance report		
Mountain							
Montana							
1910	525	160	116	33	11	328	37
1900	369	59	47	11	1	274	36
Idaho							
1910	150	33	25	6	2	98	19
1900	72	27	19	6	2	39	6
Wyoming							
1910	357	53	38	15	-	286	18
1900	151	24	20	3	1	115	12
Colorado							
1910	2,991	792	493	277	22	2,112	87
1900	1,991	418	239	156	23	1,481	92
New Mexico							
1910	401	94	73	17	4	296	9
1900	365	60	46	3	11	258	47
Arizona							
1910	569	167	112	49	6	374	28
1900	299	76	62	11	3	136	87
Utah							
1910	228	42	24	18	-	151	35
1900	109	12	10	1	1	82	15

[Continued]

★ 1127 ★

Homes Owned, Encumbered, Rented, and Farm – Mountain States, 1900 and 1910: Part IIB

[Continued]

Division, State and Year	Total	Other homes						
		Owned					Rented	No report of ownership
		Total	Free	Encumbered	No encumbrance report			
Nevada								
1910	204	70	66	4	-		131	3
1900	48	15	11	1	3		24	9

Source: "Home Ownership by Divisions and States: 1910 and 1900—Number of Farm Homes and Other Homes Owned Free Owned Encumbered, and Rented by Negro Families," U.S. Bureau of the Census, *Negro Population in the United States, 1790-1915*, pp. 468-469.

★ 1128 ★

Home Ownership

Homes Owned, Encumbered, Rented, and Farm – New England States, 1900 and 1910: Part I

Division, state and year	Negro population			Number of homes of Negro families						
					Owned				Rented	No report of ownership
	Total	Rural	Urban	Total	Total	Free	Encumbered	No encumbrance report		
New England:										
Maine-										
1910	1,363	439	924	294	126	94	31	1	156	12
1900	1,319	401	918	292	121	80	32	9	156	15
New Hampshire-										
1910	564	208	356	121	37	18	18	1	80	4
1900	662	243	419	124	33	22	10	1	85	6
Vermont-										
1910	1,621	280	1,341	226	46	27	18	1	176	4
1900	826	382	444	154	49	24	23	2	97	8
Massachusetts-										
1910	38,055	2,812	35,243	8,705	1,412	599	799	14	7,136	157
1900	31,974	2,107	29,867	6,880	1,094	468	602	24	5,347	439
Rhode Island-										
1910	9,529	474	9,055	2,353	358	160	191	7	1,946	49
1900	9,092	669	8,423	2,120	319	132	178	9	1,684	117

[Continued]

★ 1128 ★

Homes Owned, Encumbered, Rented, and Farm — New England States, 1900 and 1910: Part I
[Continued]

Division, state and year	Negro population			Number of homes of Negro families						
	Total	Rural	Urban	Total	Owned				Rented	No report of ownership
					Total	Free	Encumbered	No encumbrance report		
Connecticut-										
1910	15,174	1,216	13,958	3,515	636	303	314	19	2,808	71
1900	15,226	1,767	13,459	3,303	599	255	337	7	2,572	132

Source: "Home Ownership by Divisions and States: 1910 and 1900—Number of Farm Homes and Other Homes Owned Free Owned Encumbered, and Rented by Negro Families," U.S. Bureau of the Census, *Negro Population in the United States, 1790-1915*, pp. 446-467.

★ 1129 ★

Home Ownership

Homes Owned, Encumbered, Rented, and Farm — New England States, 1900 and 1910: Part IIA

Division, state and year	Farm homes						
	Total	Owned				Rented	No report of ownership
		Total	Free	Encumbered	No encumbrance report		
New England:							
Maine-							
1910	29	26	19	7	-	3	-
1900	34	32	22	9	1	2	-
New Hampshire-							
1910	16	15	7	7	1	1	-
1900	13	8	5	2	1	5	-
Vermont-							
1910	22	17	7	10	-	5	-
1900	11	10	6	4	-	1	-
Massachusetts-							
1910	114	101	50	50	1	13	-
1900	91	72	37	33	2	19	-
Rhode Island-							
1910	38	26	16	10	-	12	-
1900	28	19	10	8	1	9	-

[Continued]

★ 1129 ★

Homes Owned, Encumbered, Rented, and Farm – New England States, 1900 and 1910: Part IIA

[Continued]

Division, state and year	Farm homes						
	Total	Owned				Rented	No report of ownership
		Total	Free	Encumbered	No encumbrance report		
Connecticut-							
1910	99	72	34	33	5	27	-
1900	119	84	40	44	-	35	-

Source: "Home Ownership by Divisions and States: 1910 and 1900—Number of Farm Homes and Other Homes Owned Free Owned Encumbered, and Rented by Negro Families," U.S. Bureau of the Census, *Negro Population in the United States, 1790-1915*, pp. 446-467.
Note: (-) Represents zero.

★ 1130 ★

Home Ownership

Homes Owned, Encumbered, Rented, and Farm – New England States, 1900 and 1910: Part IIB

Division, state and year	Other homes						
	Total	Owned				Rented	No report of ownership
		Total	Free	Encumbered	No encumbrance report		
New England:							
Maine-	265	100	75	24	1	153	12
1910	258	89	58	23	8	154	15
1900							
New Hampshire-							
1910	105	22	11	11	-	79	4
1900	111	25	17	8	-	80	6
Vermont-							
1910	204	29	20	8	1	171	4
1900	143	39	18	19	2	96	8
Massachusetts-							
1910	8,591	1,311	549	749	13	7,123	157
1900	6,789	1,022	431	569	22	5,328	439
Rhode Island-							
1910	2,315	332	144	181	7	1,934	49
1900	2,092	300	122	170	8	1,675	117

[Continued]

★ 1130 ★

Homes Owned, Encumbered, Rented, and Farm – New England States, 1900 and 1910: Part IIB
[Continued]

Division, state and year	Other homes						
	Total	Owned				Rented	No report of ownership
		Total	Free	Encumbered	No encumbrance report		
Connecticut-							
1910	3,416	564	269	281	14	2,781	71
1900	3,184	515	215	293	7	2,537	132

Source: "Home Ownership by Divisions and States: 1910 and 1900—Number of Farm Homes and Other Homes Owned Free Owned Encumbered, and Rented by Negro Families," U.S. Bureau of the Census, *Negro Population in the United States, 1790-1915*, pp. 446-467. *Note:* (-) Represents zero.

★ 1131 ★

Home Ownership

Homes Owned, Encumbered, Rented, and Farm – South Atlantic States, 1900 and 1910: Part I

Division, state, and year	Negro population			Number of homes of Negro families						
	Total	Rural	Urban	Total	Owned				Rented	No report of ownership
					Total	Free	Encumbered	No encumbrance report		
South Atlantic:										
Delaware-										
1910	31,181	20,024	11,157	6,476	1,501	884	543	74	4,669	306
1900	30,697	19,160	11,537	6,014	1,297	671	489	137	4,271	446
Maryland-										
1910	232,250	133,020	99,230	47,177	12,068	8,081	3,492	495	32,774	2,335
1900	235,064	141,215	93,849	45,310	10,401	6,784	2,763	854	30,826	4,083
District of Columbia-										
1910	94,446	-	94,446	19,246	2,072	1,294	747	31	16,437	737
1900	86,702	-	86,702	17,269	1,964	1,269	640	55	14,721	584
Virginia-										
1910	671,096	512,878	158,218	137,771	56,933	45,267	10,259	1,407	77,048	3,790
1900	660,722	535,923	124,799	128,530	46,268	34,234	9,054	2,980	75,895	6,367
West Virginia-										
1910	64,173	48,793	15,380	14,197	2,743	2,016	634	93	10,942	512
1900	43,499	34,738	8,761	8,248	1,983	1,383	433	167	5,888	377
North Carolina-										
1910	697,843	581,868	115,975	139,713	40,118	29,265	8,965	1,888	95,148	4,447
1900	624,469	548,300	76,169	122,208	29,019	20,247	6,129	2,643	85,681	7,508
South Carolina-										
1910	835,843	734,141	101,702	179,490	33,161	25,241	6,441	1,479	139,240	7,089

[Continued]

★ 1131 ★

Homes Owned, Encumbered, Rented, and Farm – South Atlantic States, 1900 and 1910: Part I

[Continued]

Division, state, and year	Negro population			Number of homes of Negro families						
				Total	Owned				Rented	No report of ownership
	Total	Rural	Urban		Total	Free	Encumbered	No encumbrance report		
1900	782,321	697,963	84,358	160,521	26,870	19,696	4,926	2,248	121,178	12,473
Georgia-										
1910	1,176,987	952,161	224,826	263,183	38,735	29,122	7,817	1,796	215,459	8,989
1900	1,034,813	873,752	161,061	221,254	26,636	19,123	4,988	2,525	174,251	20,367
Florida-										
1910	308,669	220,083	88,586	75,394	20,916	16,541	3,249	1,126	49,651	4,827
1900	230,730	181,594	49,136	51,751	15,157	11,149	2,284	1,724	32,529	4,065

Source: "Home Ownership by Divisions and States: 1910 and 1900—Number of Farm Homes and Other Homes Owned Free Owned Encumbered, and Rented by Negro Families," U.S. Bureau of the Census, *Negro Population in the United States, 1790-1915*, pp. 468-469. *Note:* (-) Represents zero.

★ 1132 ★

Home Ownership

Homes Owned, Encumbered, Rented, and Farm – South Atlantic States, 1900 and 1910: Part IIA

Division, state and year	Farm homes						
	Total	Owned				Rented	No report of ownership
		Total	Free	Encumbered	No encumbrance report		
South Atlantic:							
Delaware-							
1910	966	436	261	169	6	526	4
1900	827	336	181	124	31	481	10
Maryland-							
1910	6,653	4,091	2,710	1,357	24	2,536	26
1900	6,350	3,480	2,228	981	271	2,725	145
District of Columbia-							
1910	15	10	7	2	1	5	-
1900	18	9	6	3	-	9	-
Virginia-							
1910	48,410	32,528	26,972	5,420	136	15,793	89
1900	46,541	27,450	21,113	5,121	1,216	18,812	279
West Virginia-							
1910	674	523	456	66	1	150	1
1900	824	573	478	77	18	242	9

[Continued]

★ 1132 ★

Homes Owned, Encumbered, Rented, and Farm – South Atlantic States, 1900 and 1910: Part IIA

[Continued]

Division, state and year	Farm homes						
	Total	Owned				Rented	No report of ownership
		Total	Free	Encumbered	No encumbrance report		
North Carolina-							
1910	63,814	20,491	14,997	5,239	255	43,112	211
1900	55,356	16,952	11,909	4,108	935	38,099	305
South Carolina-							
1910	95,737	20,431	15,834	4,149	448	74,875	431
1900	88,014	18,874	13,743	3,671	1,460	66,499	641
Georgia-							
1910	120,822	16,191	11,854	3,883	454	104,053	578
1900	83,695	11,736	8,195	2,709	832	70,855	1,104
Florida-							
1910	14,777	7,335	5,996	1,204	133	7,401	41
1900	13,887	6,599	4,872	1,037	690	7,126	162

Source: "Home Ownership by Divisions and States: 1910 and 1900—Number of Farm Homes and Other Homes Owned Free Owned Encumbered, and Rented by Negro Families," U.S. Bureau of the Census, *Negro Population in the United States, 1790-1915*, pp. 448-467. *Note:* (-) Represents zero.

★ 1133 ★

Home Ownership

Homes Owned, Encumbered, Rented, and Farm – South Atlantic States, 1900 and 1910: Part IIB

Division, state and year	Other homes						
	Total	Owned				Rented	No report of ownership
		Total	Free	Encumbered	No encumbrance report		
South Atlantic:							
Delaware-							
1910	5,510	1,065	623	374	68	4,143	302
1900	5,187	961	490	365	106	3,790	436
Maryland-							
1910	40,524	7,977	5,371	2,135	471	30,238	2,309
1900	38,960	6,921	4,556	1,782	583	28,101	3,938

[Continued]

★ 1133 ★

Homes Owned, Encumbered, Rented, and Farm – South Atlantic States, 1900 and 1910: Part IIB

[Continued]

Division, state and year	Total	Other homes					Rented	No report of ownership
		Owned						
		Total	Free	Encumbered	No encumbrance report			
District of Columbia-								
1910	19,231	2,062	1,287	745	30		16,432	737
1900	17,251	1,955	1,263	637	55		14,712	584
Virginia-								
1910	89,361	24,405	18,295	4,889	1,271		61,255	3,701
1900	81,989	18,818	13,121	3,933	1,764		57,063	6,088
West Virginia-								
1910	75,899	19,627	14,268	3,726	1,633		52,036	4,236
1900	66,852	12,067	8,338	2,021	1,708		47,582	7,203
North Carolina-								
1910	83,753	12,730	9,407	2,292	1,031		64,365	6,658
1900	74,507	7,996	5,953	1,255	788		54,679	11,832
South Carolina-								
1910	142,361	22,544	17,268	3,934	1,342		111,406	8,411
1900	137,559	14,900	10,928	2,279	1,693		103,396	19,263
Georgia-								
1910	60,617	13,581	10,543	2,045	993		42,250	4,786
1900	37,864	8,558	6,277	1,247	1,034		25,403	3,903
Florida-								
1910	60,617	13,581	10,543	2,045	993		42,250	4,786
1900	37,864	8,558	6,277	1,247	1,034		25,403	3,903

Source: "Home Ownership by Divisions and States: 1910 and 1900—Number of Farm Homes and Other Homes Owned Free Owned Encumbered, and Rented by Negro Families," U.S. Bureau of the Census, *Negro Population in the United States, 1790-1915*, pp. 468-469. *Note:* (-) Represents zero.

★ 1134 ★

Home Ownership

Homes Owned, Encumbered, Rented, and Farm – West North Central States, 1900 and 1910: Part I

Division, state, and year	Negro population			Number of homes of Negro families						
				Total	Owned				Rented	No report of ownership
	Total	Rural	Urban		Total	Free	Encumbered	No encumbrance report		
West North Central:										
Minnesota-										
1910	7,084	566	6,518	1,685	416	247	168	6	1,169	100
1900	4,959	464	4,495	1,084	140	84	52	4	859	85
Iowa-										
1910	14,973	5,187	9,786	3,807	1,138	660	417	61	2,599	70
1900	12,693	4,596	8,097	2,915	900	521	353	26	1,892	123
Missouri-										
1910	157,452	52,990	104,462	38,134	10,130	6,148	3,668	314	26,208	1,798
1900	161,234	71,987	89,247	34,779	9,535	5,908	3,279	348	23,029	1,615
North Dakota-										
1910	617	211	306	146	52	32	16	4	75	19
1900	286	161	125	67	26	22	3	1	36	5
South Dakota-										
1910	817	405	412	215	97	57	39	1	100	18
1900	465	270	195	107	45	28	11	7	51	10
Nebraska-										
1910	7,689	1,088	6,621	1,885	454	275	170	9	1,337	94
1900	6,269	828	5,441	1,263	250	130	83	17	935	78
Kansas-										
1910	54,030	17,334	36,196	13,810	6,851	4,608	2,076	167	6,334	425
1900	52,003	20,240	31,763	11,979	5,489	3,811	1,450	228	5,861	629

Source: "Home Ownership by Divisions and States: 1910 and 1900—Number of Farm Homes and Other Homes Owned Free Owned Encumbered, and Rented by Negro Families," U.S. Bureau of the Census, *Negro Population in the United States, 1790-1915*, pp. 446-467.

★ 1135 ★

Home Ownership

Homes Owned, Encumbered, Rented, and Farm – West North Central States, 1900 and 1910: Part IIA

Division, state and year	Total	Farm homes					No report of ownership
		Owned				Rented	
		Total	Free	Encumbered	No encumbrance report		
West North Central:							
Minnesota-							
1910	42	24	16	8	-	16	2
1900	34	22	7	14	1	11	1
Iowa-							
1910	207	136	64	72	-	71	-
1900	197	116	58	58	-	78	3
Missouri-							
1910	3,734	2,156	1,092	1,031	33	1,562	16
1900	5,183	2,848	1,586	1,175	87	2,301	34
North Dakota-							
1910	28	23	12	11	-	5	-
1900	14	12	10	1	1	2	-
South Dakota-							
1910	71	59	36	23	-	10	2
1900	20	14	10	3	1	5	1
Nebraska-							
1910	100	82	64	18	-	26	1
1900	77	46	27	19	-	30	1
Kansas-							
1910	1,532	992	569	408	15	509	31
1900	1,791	1,169	745	388	36	597	25

Source: "Home Ownership by Divisions and States: 1910 and 1900—Number of Farm Homes and Other Homes Owned Free Owned Encumbered, and Rented by Negro Families," U.S. Bureau of the Census, *Negro Population in the United States, 1790-1915*, pp. 446-469.
Note: (-) Represents zero.

★ 1136 ★
Home Ownership

Homes Owned, Encumbered, Rented, and Farm – West North Central States, 1900 and 1910: Part IIB

Division, state and year	Total	Other homes				Rented	No report of ownership
		Owned					
		Total	Free	Encumbered	No encumbrance report		
West North Central:							
Minnesota-							
1910	1,643	392	231	155	6	1,153	98
1900	1,050	118	77	38	3	848	84
Iowa-							
1910	3,600	1,002	596	345	61	2,528	70
1900	2,718	784	463	295	26	1,814	120
Missouri-							
1910	34,400	7,974	5,056	2,637	281	24,644	1,782
1900	29,596	6,687	4,322	2,104	261	21,328	1,581
North Dakota-							
1910	118	29	20	5	4	70	19
1900	53	14	12	2	-	34	5
South Dakota-							
1910	144	38	21	16	1	90	16
1900	87	32	18	8	6	16	9
Nebraska-							
1910	1,776	372	211	152	9	1,311	98
1900	1,186	204	123	64	17	905	77
Kansas-							
1910	12,278	5,859	4,039	1,668	152	6,025	394
1900	10,188	4,320	3,066	1,062	192	5,264	604

Source: "Home Ownership by Divisions and States: 1910 and 1900—Number of Farm Homes and Other Homes Owned Free Owned Encumbered, and Rented by Negro Families," U.S. Bureau of the Census, *Negro Population in the United States, 1790-1915,* pp. 446-469.
Note: (-) Represents zero.

Home Ownership

Homes Owned, Encumbered, Rented, and Farm – West South Central States, 1900 and 1910: Part I

Division, state, and year	Negro population			Number of homes of Negro families						
				Total	Owned				Rented	No report of ownership
	Total	Rural	Urban		Total	Free	Encumbered	No encumbrance report		
West South Central:										
Arkansas-										
1910	442,891	383,744	59,147	97,787	24,018	15,908	6,879	1,231	69,202	4,567
1900	366,856	329,685	37,171	76,803	16,838	10,958	4,436	1,444	54,324	5,641
Louisiana-										
1910	713,874	553,029	160,845	159,350	27,237	20,795	5,195	1,247	125,926	6,187
1900	650,804	533,850	116,954	140,264	20,453	15,042	3,941	1,470	108,702	11,109
Oklahoma-										
1910	137,612	100,630	36,982	28,395	10,018	6,645	2,659	714	17,144	1,233
1900	55,684	46,982	8,702	11,256	6,039	4,409	490	1,140	4,939	548
Texas-										
1910	690,049	511,185	178,864	145,890	41,638	31,697	8,612	1,329	98,775	5,477
1900	620,722	501,393	119,329	119,418	33,292	23,206	7,920	2,166	79,903	6,223

Source: "Home Ownership by Divisions and States: 1910 and 1900—Number of Farm Homes and Other Homes Owned Free Owned Encumbered, and Rented by Negro Families," U.S. Bureau of the Census, *Negro Population in the United States, 1790-1915,* 1918, pp. 468-469.

Home Ownership

Homes Owned, Encumbered, Rented, and Farm – West South Central States, 1900 and 1910: Part IIA

Division, state, and year	Farm homes						No report of ownership
	Total	Owned				Rented	
		Total	Free	Encumbered	No emcumbrance report		
West South Central:							
Arkansas-							
1910	61,177	14,216	9,208	4,621	387	46,543	418
1900	47,547	11,713	7,481	3,477	755	34,944	890
Louisiana-							
1910	55,094	11,077	8,145	2,669	263	43,906	111
1900	57,639	9,577	6,495	2,510	572	47,649	413

[Continued]

★ 1138 ★

Homes Owned, Encumbered, Rented, and Farm – West South Central States, 1900 and 1910: Part IIA
[Continued]

Division, state, and year	Farm homes						
	Total	Owned				Rented	No report of ownership
		Total	Free	Encumbered	No emcumbrance report		
Oklahoma-							
1910	13,518	4,956	3,022	1,620	314	8,478	84
1900	6,735	4,005	2,870	314	821	2,604	126
Texas-							
1910	67,678	21,195	16,159	4,731	305	46,366	117
1900	64,335	20,126	13,169	5,845	1,112	43,846	363

Source: "Home Ownership by Divisions and States: 1910 and 1900—Number of Farm Homes and Other Homes Owned Free Owned Encumbered, and Rented by Negro Families," U.S. Bureau of the Census, *Negro Population in the United States, 1790-1915,* pp. 468-469.

★ 1139 ★

Home Ownership

Homes Owned, Encumbered, Rented, and Farm – West South Central States, 1900 and 1910: Part IIB

Division, state, and year	Other homes						
	Total	Owned				Rented	No report of ownership
		Total	Free	Encumbered	No emcumbrance report		
West South Central:							
Arkansas-							
1910	36,610	9,802	6,700	2,258	844	22,659	4,149
1900	29,256	5,125	3,477	959	689	19,380	4,751
Louisiana-							
1910	104,256	16,160	12,650	2,526	984	82,020	6,076
1900	82,625	10,876	8,547	1,431	808	61,053	10,696
Oklahoma-							
1910	14,877	5,062	3,623	1,039	400	8,666	1,149
1900	4,791	2,034	1,539	176	319	2,335	422
Texas-							
1910	78,212	20,443	15,538	3,881	1,024	52,409	5,360
1900	55,083	13,166	10,037	2,075	1,054	36,057	5,860

Source: "Home Ownership by Divisions and States: 1910 and 1900—Number of Farm Homes and Other Homes Owned Free Owned Encumbered, and Rented by Negro Families," U.S. Bureau of the Census, *Negro Population in the United States, 1790-1915,* pp. 468-469.

★ 1140 ★

Home Ownership

Homes Owned, Encumbered, Rented, and Farm – Pacific States, 1900 and 1910: Part I

Division, State and Year	Negro population			Number of homes of Negro families						
				Total	Owned				Rented	No report of ownership
	Total	Rural	Urban		Total	Free	Encumbered	No encumbrance report		
Pacific										
Washington										
1910	6,058	1,359	4,699	1,356	435	249	179	7	854	67
1900	2,514	908	1,606	566	161	140	19	2	356	49
Oregon										
1910	1,492	228	1,264	347	98	58	38	2	217	32
1900	1,105	227	878	191	49	32	7	10	120	22
California										
1910	21,645	3,246	18,399	5,346	2,019	1,052	926	41	3,217	110
1900	11,045	2,970	8,075	2,661	861	545	285	31	1,628	172

Source: "Home Ownership by Divisions and States: Owned Free Owned Encumbered, and Rented by Negro Families." U.S. Bureau of the Census. *Negro Population in the United States, 1790-1915,* pp. 468-469.

★ 1141 ★

Home Ownership

Homes Owned, Encumbered, Rented, and Farm – Pacific States, 1900 and 1910: Part IIA

Division, State and Year	Farm homes						
	Total	Owned				Rented	No report of ownership
		Total	Free	Encumbered	No encumbrance report		
Pacific							
Washington							
1910	87	71	49	19	3	16	-
1900	61	56	50	6	-	5	-
Oregon							
1910	30	23	19	4	-	7	-
1900	15	11	8	3	-	3	1
California							
1910	173	133	82	49	2	33	7
1900	143	90	64	25	1	50	3

Source: "Home Ownership by Divisions and States: 1910 and 1900—Number of Farm Homes and Other Homes Owned Free Owned Encumbered, and Rented by Negro Families," U.S. Bureau of the Census. *Negro Population in the United States, 1790-1915,* pp. 468-469.

★ 1142 ★

Home Ownership

Homes Owned, Encumbered, Rented, and Farm – Pacific States, 1900 and 1910: Part IIB

Division, State and Year	Total	Other homes					
		Owned				Rented	No report of ownership
		Total	Free	Encumbered	No encumbrance report		
Pacific							
Washington							
1910	1,259	364	200	160	4	838	67
1900	505	105	90	12	2	351	49
Oregon							
1910	317	75	39	34	2	210	32
1900	176	38	24	4	10	117	21
California							
1910	5,173	1,886	970	877	39	3,184	103
1900	2,518	771	481	260	30	1,578	169

Source: "Home Ownership by Divisions and States: 1910 and 1900—Number of Farm Homes and Other Homes Owned Free Owned Encumbered, and Rented by Negro Families," U.S. Bureau of the Census, *Negro Population in the United States, 1790-1915*, pp. 468-469.

★ 1143 ★

Home Ownership

Homes Ownership, 1890, 1900, 1910

Class of home	Homes of negro families					
	Number			Percentage distribution		
	1910	1900	1890	1910	1900	1890
All homes	2,173,018	1,833,759	1,410,769	100.0	100.0	100.0
Farm homes	877,648	758,463	549,632	40.4	41.4	39.0
Other homes	1,295,370	1,075,296	861,137	59.6	58.6	61.0

Source: "Homes of Negro Families," U.S. Bureau of the Census, *Negro Population in the United States, 1790-1915*, p. 459.

★ 1144 ★

Home Ownership

Inhabitants per Owned Home, 1890-1910

Division and state	Negro inhabitants per owned home and percentage owned of all homes: 1910, 1900, 1890					
	Negro inhabitants per owned home[1]			Percentage owned of Negro homes[1]		
	1910	1900	1890	1910	1900	1890
United States	20	24	28	22.5	20.4	18.7
Geographic divisions:						
New England	25	27	25	17.2	17.2	18.6
Middle Atlantic	36	37	28	12.6	13.3	17.9
East North Central	15	15	14	27.6	28.4	32.1
West North Central	13	15	15	32.1	31.4	34.7
South Atlantic	20	23	28	23.6	21.0	18.8
East South Central	22	27	35	19.8	17.3	15.1
West South Central	19	22	29	23.9	22.0	19.2
Mountain	14	19	20	28.1	22.6	28.2
Pacific	11	14	16	36.2	31.3	29.9
New England:						
Maine	11	11	12	42.9	41.4	39.0
New Hampshire	15	20	26	30.6	26.6	21.1
Vermont	35	17	22	20.4	31.8	23.9
Massachusetts	27	29	26	16.2	15.9	17.7
Rhode Island	27	28	29	15.2	15.0	14.4
Connecticut	24	25	22	18.1	18.1	20.6
Middle Atlantic:						
New York	55	45	33	7.8	10.5	14.5
New Jersey	24	27	21	18.6	18.6	23.4
Pennsylvania	35	39	30	13.3	12.8	17.5
East North Central:						
Ohio	13	14	14	30.1	30.9	33.3
Indiana	15	16	17	26.4	27.6	28.0
Illinois	18	19	16	23.0	23.3	30.1
Michigan	9	10	10	44.0	42.4	42.1
Wisconsin	17	15	11	25.6	27.1	41.9
West North Central:						
Minnesota	17	35	22	24.7	12.9	19.7
Iowa	13	14	14	29.9	30.9	35.3
Missouri	16	17	17	26.6	27.4	30.1
North Dakota	12	11	10	35.6	38.8	51.4
South Dakota	8	10	9	45.1	43.0	54.2
Nebraska	17	25	30	24.1	19.8	22.5
Kansas	8	9	10	49.9	45.8	50.7
South Atlantic:						
Delaware	21	24	22	23.2	21.6	24.3

[Continued]

★ 1144 ★

Inhabitants per Owned Home, 1890-1910
[Continued]

Division and state	Negro inhabitants per owned home and percentage owned of all homes: 1910, 1900, 1890					
	Negro inhabitants per owned home[1]			Percentage owned of Negro homes[1]		
	1910	1900	1890	1910	1900	1890
Maryland	19	23	25	25.6	23.0	22.1
District of Columbia	46	44	35	10.8	11.4	14.9
Virginia	12	14	21	41.3	36.0	26.8
West Virginia	23	22	22	19.3	24.0	26.0
North Carolina	17	22	28	28.7	23.7	19.4
South Carolina	25	29	33	18.5	16.7	15.6
Georgia	30	39	43	14.7	12.0	12.1
Florida	15	15	16	27.7	29.3	32.0
East South Central:						
Kentucky	13	16	21	31.8	29.7	26.1
Tennessee	18	23	29	25.3	21.8	18.8
Alabama	27	35	43	16.4	13.2	11.9
Mississippi	26	31	44	16.9	15.0	12.2
West South Central:						
Arkansas	18	22	26	24.6	21.9	21.0
Louisiana	26	32	38	17.1	14.6	13.6
Oklahoma	14	9	34	35.3	52.4	85.6
Texas	17	17	23	28.5	27.9	24.3
Mountain:						
Montana	10	20	28	32.8	19.1	23.9
Idaho	14	8	13	28.7	44.4	39.0
Wyoming	32	29	33	18.4	20.0	25.2
Colorado	13	18	21	27.6	22.8	24.3
New Mexico	12	23	12	30.3	18.1	42.6
Arizona	11	22	59	30.7	27.5	20.2
Utah	22	35	31	21.2	16.0	24.4
Nevada	7	7	8	35.7	34.0	40.5
Pacific:						
Washington	14	16	24	32.1	28.4	23.3
Oregon	15	23	16	28.2	25.7	43.3
California	10	13	16	37.8	32.4	29.7

Source: "Negro Inhabitants per Owned Home and Percentage Owned of All Homes: 1910, 1900, 1890," U.S. Bureau of the Census, *Negro Population in the United States, 1790-1915*, p. 462. *Notes:* 1. In 1890 homes for which no report of ownership was received were apportioned as owned or rented in proportion to homes for which reports of ownership were secured. No corresponding apportionment has been made for Negro homes, by states, for the years 1910 and 1900. Such an apportionment, if it had been made, would have reduced somewhat the population per owned home in 1920 and in 1900, and increased somewhat the percentage owned of Negro homes for these years.

★ 1145 ★

Home Ownership

Inhabitants per Owned Home: Geographic Area, 1910

Division and state	Negro inhabitants per owned home for the total population and for the aggregate population of selected urban communities, by divisions and states: 1910						
	Negro population 1910		Owned homes 1910		Negro inhabitants per owned home			
	Total	Cities having 2,500 negro inhabitants or more	Total	Cities having 2,500 negro inhabitants or more	Total		Cities having 2,500 Negro inhabitants or more: 1910
					1910	1900	
United States	9,827,763	2,031,691	488,699	77,005	20	26	26
Geographic divisions:							
New England	66,306	30,033	2,615	612	25	27	49
Middle Atlantic	417,870	245,047	11,736	3,014	36	37	81
East North Central	300,836	145,397	20,620	4,612	15	15	32
West North Central	242,662	101,309	19,138	3,967	13	15	26
South Atlantic	4,112,488	734,207	208,247	28,286	20	23	26
East South Central	2,652,513	405,566	119,291	19,330	22	27	21
West South Central	1,984,426	354,052	102,911	15,963	19	22	22
Mountain	21,467	5,426	1,589	279	14	19	19
Pacific	29,195	10,654	2,552	942	11	14	11
New England:							
Maine	1,363	-	126	-	11	11	-
New Hampshire	564	-	37	-	15	20	-
Vermont	1,621	-	46	-	35	17	-
Massachusetts	38,055	21,156	1,412	418	27	29	51
Rhode Island	9,529	5,316	358	109	27	28	49
Connecticut	15,174	3,561	636	85	24	25	42
Middle Atlantic:							
New York	134,191	91,709	2,437	545	55	45	168
New Jersey	89,760	33,926	3,682	630	24	27	54
Pennsylvania	193,919	119,412	5,617	1,839	35	39	65
East North Central:							
Ohio	111,452	50,601	8,467	1,787	13	14	28
Indiana	60,320	30,675	4,036	1,222	15	16	25
Illinois	109,049	58,380	6,012	1,365	18	19	43
Michigan	17,115	5,741	1,932	238	9	10	24
Wisconsin	2,900	-	173	-	17	15	-
West North Central:							
Minnesota	7,084	5,736	416	300	17	35	19
Iowa	14,973	2,930	1,138	225	13	14	13
Missouri	157,452	71,775	10,130	1,349	16	17	53
North Dakota	617	-	52	-	12	11	-
South Dakota	817	-	97	-	8	10	-

[Continued]

★ 1145 ★

Inhabitants per Owned Home: Geographic Area, 1910
[Continued]

Division and state	Negro inhabitants per owned home for the total population and for the aggregate population of selected urban communities, by divisions and states: 1910						
	Negro population 1910		Owned homes 1910		Negro inhabitants per owned home		
	Total	Cities having 2,500 negro inhabitants or more	Total	Cities having 2,500 negro inhabitants or more	Total		Cities having 2,500 Negro inhabitants or more: 1910
					1910	1900	
Nebraska	7,689	4,426	454	166	17	25	27
Kansas	54,030	16,442	6,851	1,927	8	9	9
South Atlantic:							
Delaware	31,181	9,081	1,501	231	21	24	39
Maryland	232,250	87,933	12,068	1,017	19	23	86
District of Columbia	94,446	94,446	2,072	2,072	46	44	46
Virginia	671,096	134,777	56,933	5,565	12	14	24
West Virginia	64,173	3,086	2,743	123	23	22	25
North Carolina	697,843	84,603	40,118	5,009	17	22	17
South Carolina	835,843	76,435	33,161	3,217	25	29	24
Georgia	1,176,987	183,557	38,735	7,908	30	39	23
Florida	308,669	60,289	20,916	3,054	15	15	20
East South Central:							
Kentucky	261,656	76,336	19,774	3,024	13	16	25
Tennessee	473,088	124,548	27,012	4,973	18	23	25
Alabama	998,282	135,463	33,941	6,860	27	35	20
Mississippi	1,009,487	69,219	38,564	4,473	26	31	15
West South Central:							
Arkansas	442,891	43,844	24,018	3,021	18	22	15
Louisiana	713,874	135,613	27,237	4,952	26	32	27
Oklahoma	137,612	20,350	10,018	1,366	14	9	15
Texas	690,049	154,245	41,638	6,624	17	17	23
Mountain:							
Montana	1,834	-	182	-	10	20	-
Idaho	651	-	48	-	14	8	-
Wyoming	2,235	-	69	-	32	29	-
Colorado	11,453	5,426	849	279	13	18	19
New Mexico	1,628	-	136	-	12	23	-
Arizona	2,009	-	179	-	11	22	-
Utah	1,144	-	51	-	22	35	-
Nevada	513	-	75	-	7	7	-
Pacific:							
Washington	6,058	-	435	-	14	16	-

[Continued]

★ 1145 ★

Inhabitants per Owned Home: Geographic Area, 1910

[Continued]

Division and state	Negro inhabitants per owned home for the total population and for the aggregate population of selected urban communities, by divisions and states: 1910						
	Negro population 1910		Owned homes 1910		Negro inhabitants per owned home		
	Total	Cities having 2,500 negro inhabitants or more	Total	Cities having 2,500 negro inhabitants or more	Total		Cities having 2,500 Negro inhabitants or more: 1910
					1910	1900	
Oregon	1,492	-	98	-	15	23	-
California	21,645	10,654	2,019	942	10	13	11

Source: "Negro Inhabitants per Owned Home for the Total Population and for the Aggregate Population of Selected Urban Communities, by Divisions and States: 1910," U.S. Bureau of the Census, *Negro Population in the United States, 1790-1915*, p. 463. *Note:* (-) Represents zero.

★ 1146 ★

Home Ownership

Non-Farm Homes Owned: Value 1930

Section of United States	All owned non-farm homes	Number of homes and their value				
		Under $1,000	$1,000 to $5,000	$5,000 to $10,000	$10,000 and over	Not reported
United States	480,324	188,795	227,634	41,947	9,862	12,086
New England	5,204	275	2,869	1,602	351	107
Maine	111	21	76	12	-	2
New Hampshire	35	2	29	3	-	1
Vermont	31	4	20	7	-	-
Massachusetts	3,381	164	1,854	1,074	213	77
Rhode Island	588	31	389	143	21	4
Connecticut	1,058	53	502	363	117	23
Middle Atlantic	37,210	2,104	18,752	11,885	3,651	818
New York	7,787	260	2,092	3,215	2,020	200
New Jersey	11,012	867	5,459	3,314	1,113	259
Pennsylvania	18,411	977	11,201	5,356	518	359
East North Central	48,887	6,607	28,744	10,013	2,491	1,032
Ohio	17,005	2,224	11,037	3,116	360	268
Indiana	8,317	1,317	5,921	765	97	217
Illinois	14,814	2,581	7,181	3,133	1,518	401
Michigan	8,415	455	4,407	2,918	401	134
Wisconsin	336	30	198	81	15	12

[Continued]

★ 1146 ★

Non-Farm Homes Owned: Value 1930
[Continued]

Section of United States	All owned non-farm homes	Number of homes and their value				
		Under $1,000	$1,000 to $5,000	$5,000 to $10,000	$10,000 and over	Not reported
West North Central	25,307	8,285	14,293	1,910	340	479
Minnesota	837	37	522	259	10	9
Iowa	1,840	411	1,352	55	2	20
Missouri	12,152	4,225	6,006	1,341	303	277
North Dakota	22	5	15	2	-	-
South Dakota	51	16	28	5	-	2
Nebraska	1,237	102	1,038	68	5	24
Kansas	9,168	3,489	15,332	180	20	147
South Atlantic	164,566	75,174	73,474	9,339	1,903	4,676
Delaware	1,607	568	868	113	6	52
Maryland	12,648	4,239	6,434	1,510	99	366
District of Columbia	7,314	47	2,201	3,684	139	243
Virginia	35,100	14,143	18,426	1,195	134	1,202
West Virginia	4,496	1,111	2,727	430	84	144
North Carolina	30,571	13,573	14,966	1,007	170	855
South Carolina	18,697	11,842	6,136	282	39	398
Georgia	29,988	17,077	11,584	545	96	686
Florida	24,145	12,574	10,132	573	136	730
East South Central	90,768	44,995	41,319	1,971	255	2,228
Kentucky	17,028	9,276	6,676	543	52	481
Tennessee	25,335	9,667	14,292	716	86	574
Alabama	28,068	12,642	14,193	559	76	598
Mississippi	20,337	13,410	6,158	153	41	575
West South Central	96,242	50,223	40,735	2,435	411	2,418
Arkansas	16,223	9,272	6,244	207	34	466
Louisiana	28,487	15,447	11,420	965	24	531
Oklahoma	9,115	5,007	3,561	259	49	239
Texas	42,417	20,497	19,530	1,004	204	1,182

Source: "Non-Farm Homes Owned by Negroes and their Value," Florence Murray, ed., *The Negro Handbook*, 1942, p. 182. Published by permission. Primary source: U.S. Bureau of the Census, 1930.

★ 1147 ★

Home Ownership

Owned Black Homes, 1890, 1900, 1910

Class of home and proprietorship	Owned negro homes					
	Number			Percentage distribution		
	1910	1900	1890	1910	1900	1890
All owned homes	506,590	397,420	264,288	100.0	100.0	100.0
Free	374,853	295,474	234,747	74.0	74.3	88.8
Encumbered	131,737	101,946	29,541	26.0	25.7	11.2
Owned farm homes	221,535	192,993	120,738	100.0	100.0	100.0
Free	159,969	138,976	108,483	72.2	72.0	89.8
Encumbered	61,566	54,017	12,255	27.8	28.0	10.2
Owned other homes	285,055	204,427	143,550	100.0	100.0	100.0
Free	214,884	156,498	126,264	75.4	76.6	88.0
Encumbered	70,171	47,929	17,286	24.6	23.4	12.0

Source: "Owned Negro Homes," U.S. Bureau of the Census, *Negro Population in the United States, 1790-1915*, p. 460.

★ 1148 ★

Home Ownership

Owned Homes of Families, 1900 and 1910: Increase by Division-I

Division and state	Owned homes or Negro families[1]					
	1910			1900		
	Total	Farm homes	Other homes	Total	Farm homes	Other homes
United States	488,699	220,698	288,001	373,450	191,143	182,307
Geographic divisions:						
New England	2,615	257	2,358	2,215	225	1,990
Middle Atlantic	11,736	865	10,871	8,779	903	7,876
East North Central	20,620	3,192	17,428	16,661	3,463	13,198
West North Central	19,138	3,472	15,666	16,386	4,227	12,159
South Atlantic	208,217	102,036	106,211	159,595	86,009	73,586
East South Central	119,291	59,027	60,264	91,320	50,628	40,692
West South Central	102,911	51,444	51,467	76,622	45,421	31,201
Mountain	1,589	178	1,411	801	110	691
Pacific	2,552	227	2,325	1,071	157	914

[Continued]

★ 1148 ★

Owned Homes of Families, 1900 and 1910: Increase by Division-I

[Continued]

Division and state	Owned homes or Negro families[1]					
	1910			1900		
	Total	Farm homes	Other homes	Total	Farm homes	Other homes
New England:						
Maine	126	26	100	121	32	89
New Hampshire	37	15	22	33	8	25
Vermont	46	17	29	49	19	39
Massachusetts	1,412	101	1,311	1,094	72	1,022
Rhode Island	358	26	332	319	19	300
Connecticut	636	72	564	599	84	515
Middle Atlantic:						
New York	2,437	210	2,227	2,213	214	1,999
New Jersey	3,682	289	3,393	2,588	314	2,274
Pennsylvania	5,617	366	5,251	3,978	375	3,603
East North Central:						
Ohio	8,467	1,358	7,109	6,927	1,379	5,548
Indiana	4,036	478	3,558	3,515	705	2,810
Illinois	6,012	809	5,203	4,479	834	3,645
Michigan	1,932	505	1,427	1,573	500	1,073
Wisconsin	173	42	131	167	45	122
West North Central:						
Minnesota	416	24	392	140	22	118
Iowa	1,138	136	1,002	990	116	784
Missouri	10,130	2,156	7,974	9,535	2,848	6,687
North Dakota	52	23	29	26	12	14
South Dakota	97	59	38	46	14	32
Nebraska	454	82	372	250	46	204
Kansas	6,851	992	5,859	5,489	1,169	4,320
South Atlantic:						
Delaware	1,501	436	1,065	1,297	336	961
Maryland	12,068	4,091	7,977	10,401	3,480	6,921
District of Columbia	2,072	10	2,062	1,964	9	1,955
Virginia	56,933	32,528	24,405	46,268	27,450	18,818
West Virginia	2,743	523	2,220	1,983	573	1,410
North Carolina	40,118	20,491	19,627	29,019	16,952	12,067
South Carolina	33,161	20,431	12,730	26,870	18,874	7,996
Georgia	38,735	16,191	22,544	26,636	11,736	14,900
Florida	20,916	7,335	13,581	15,157	6,599	8,558
East South Central:						
Kentucky	19,774	6,077	13,697	17,906	5,915	11,991
Tennessee	27,012	10,942	16,070	21,023	9,819	11,204

[Continued]

★ 1148 ★

Owned Homes of Families, 1900 and 1910: Increase by Division-I

[Continued]

| Division and state | Owned homes or Negro families[1] | | | | | |
| | 1910 | | | 1900 | | |
	Total	Farm homes	Other homes	Total	Farm homes	Other homes
Alabama	33,941	17,227	16,714	23,536	13,955	9,581
Mississippi	38,564	24,781	13,783	28,855	20,939	7,916
West South Central:						
Arkansas	24,018	14,216	9,802	16,838	11,713	5,125
Louisiana	27,237	11,077	16,160	20,453	9,577	10,876
Oklahoma[2]	10,018	4,956	5,062	6,039	4,005	2,034
Texas	41,638	21,195	20,443	33,292	20,126	13,166
Mountain:						
Montana	182	22	180	75	16	59
Idaho	48	15	33	36	9	27
Wyoming	69	16	53	32	8	24
Colorado	849	57	792	467	49	418
New Mexico	136	42	94	69	9	60
Arizona	179	12	167	85	9	76
Utah	51	9	42	19	7	12
Nevada	75	5	70	18	3	15
Pacific:						
Washington	435	71	364	161	56	105
Oregon	98	23	75	49	11	38
California	2,019	133	1,886	861	90	771

Source: "Owned Homes of Negro Families—Number, 1910 and 1900, and Increase, 1900-1910, by Division and States," U.S. Bureau of the Census, *Negro Population in the United States, 1790-1915*, p. 465. *Notes:* 1. Figures for 1900 represent private families only. 2. Includes population of Indian Territory for 1900.

★ 1149 ★

Home Ownership

Owned Homes of Families, 1900 and 1910: Increase by Division-II

Division and state	Owned homes or Negro families[1]							
	Increase: 1900-1910						Percent of all Negro homes	
	Number			Percent				
	Total	Farm homes	Other homes	Total	Farm homes	Other homes	1910	1900
United States	115,249	29,555	85,694	30.9	15.5	47.0	22.5	20.4
Geographic divisions:								
New England	400	32	368	18.1	14.2	18.5	17.2	17.2
Middle Atlantic	2,957	-38	2,995	33.7	-4.2	38.0	12.6	13.3

[Continued]

★ 1149 ★

Owned Homes of Families, 1900 and 1910: Increase by Division-II
[Continued]

Division and state	Owned homes or Negro families[1]							
	Increase: 1900-1910						Percent of	
	Number			Percent			all Negro homes	
	Total	Farm homes	Other homes	Total	Farm homes	Other homes	1910	1900
East North Central	3,959	-271	4,230	23.8	-7.8	32.1	27.6	28.4
West North Central	2,752	-755	3,507	16.8	-17.9	28.8	32.1	31.4
South Atlantic	48,652	16,027	32,625	30.5	18.6	44.3	23.6	21.0
East South Central	27,971	8,399	19,572	30.6	16.6	48.1	19.8	17.3
West South Central	26,289	6,023	20,266	34.3	13.3	65.0	23.9	22.0
Mountain	788	68	720	98.4	61.8	104.2	28.1	22.6
Pacific	1,481	70	1,411	138.3	44.6	154.4	36.2	31.3
New England:								
Maine	5	-6	11	4.1	-18.8	12.4	42.9	41.4
New Hampshire	4	7	-3	12.1	87.5	-12.0	30.6	26.6
Vermont	-3	7	-10	-6.1	70.0	-25.6	20.4	31.8
Massachusetts	318	29	289	29.1	40.3	28.3	16.2	15.9
Rhode Island	39	7	32	12.2	36.8	10.7	15.2	15.0
Connecticut	37	-12	49	6.2	-14.3	9.5	18.1	18.1
Middle Atlantic:								
New York	224	-4	228	10.1	-1.9	11.4	7.8	10.5
New Jersey	1,094	-25	1,119	42.3	-8.0	49.2	18.6	18.6
Pennsylvania	1,639	-9	1,648	41.2	-2.4	45.7	13.3	12.8
East North Central:								
Ohio	1,540	-21	1,561	22.2	-1.5	28.1	30.1	30.9
Indiana	521	-227	748	14.8	-32.2	26.6	26.4	27.6
Illinois	1,533	-25	1,558	34.2	-3.0	42.7	23.0	23.3
Michigan	359	5	354	22.8	1.0	33.0	44.0	42.4
Wisconsin	6	-3	9	3.6	-6.7	7.4	25.6	27.1
West North Central:								
Minnesota	276	2	274	197.1	9.1	232.2	24.7	12.9
Iowa	238	20	218	26.4	17.2	27.8	29.9	30.9
Missouri	595	-692	1,287	6.2	-24.3	19.2	26.6	27.4
North Dakota	26	11	15	100.0	91.7	107.1	35.6	38.8
South Dakota	51	45	6	110.9	321.4	18.8	45.1	43.0
Nebraska	204	36	168	81.6	78.3	82.4	24.1	19.8
Kansas	1,362	-177	1,539	24.8	15.1	35.6	49.6	45.8
South Atlantic:								
Delaware	204	100	104	15.7	29.8	10.8	23.2	21.6
Maryland	1,667	611	1,056	16.0	17.6	15.3	25.6	23.0
District of Columbia	108	1	107	5.5	-	5.4	10.8	11.4
Virginia	10,665	5,078	5,587	23.1	18.5	29.7	41.3	36.0
West Virginia	760	-50	810	38.3	-8.7	57.4	19.3	24.0

[Continued]

★ 1149 ★

Owned Homes of Families, 1900 and 1910: Increase by Division-II
[Continued]

Division and state	Owned homes or Negro families[1]							
	Increase: 1900-1910						Percent of	
	Number			Percent			all Negro homes	
	Total	Farm homes	Other homes	Total	Farm homes	Other homes	1910	1900
North Carolina	11,099	3,539	7,560	38.2	20.9	62.7	28.7	23.7
South Carolina	6,291	1,557	4,734	23.4	8.2	59.2	18.5	16.7
Georgia	12,099	4,455	7,644	45.4	38.0	51.3	14.7	12.0
Florida	5,759	736	5,023	38.0	11.2	58.7	27.7	29.3
East South Central:								
Kentucky	1,868	162	1,706	10.4	27.4	14.2	31.8	29.7
Tennessee	5,989	1,123	4,866	28.5	11.4	43.4	25.3	21.8
Alabama	10,405	3,272	7,133	44.2	23.4	74.4	16.4	13.2
Mississippi	9,709	3,842	5,867	33.6	18.4	74.1	16.9	15.0
West South Central:								
Arkansas	7,180	2,503	4,677	42.6	21.4	91.3	24.6	21.9
Louisiana	6,784	1,500	5,284	33.2	15.7	48.9	17.1	14.6
Oklahoma[2]	3,979	951	3,028	65.9	23.7	148.9	35.3	52.4
Texas	8,346	1,069	7,277	25.1	5.3	55.3	28.5	27.9
Mountain:								
Montana	107	6	101	142.7	37.5	171.2	32.8	19.1
Idaho	12	6	6	33.3	66.7	22.2	28.7	44.4
Wyoming	37	8	29	115.6	100.0	120.8	18.4	20.0
Colorado	382	8	374	81.8	16.3	89.5	27.6	22.8
New Mexico	67	33	34	97.1	366.7	56.7	30.3	18.1
Arizona	94	3	91	110.6	33.3	119.7	30.7	27.5
Utah	32	2	30	168.4	28.6	250.0	21.2	16.0
Nevada	57	2	55	316.7	66.7	366.7	35.7	34.6
Pacific:								
Washington	274	15	259	170.2	26.8	246.7	32.1	28.4
Oregon	49	12	37	100.0	109.1	974	28.2	25.7
California	1,158	43	1,115	134.5	47.8	144.6	37.8	32.4

Source: "Owned Homes of Negro Families—Number, 1910 and 1900, and Increase, 1900-1910, by Division and States," U.S. Bureau of the Census, *Negro Population in the United States, 1790-1915,* p. 465. *Notes:* (-) Represents zero. 1. Figures for 1900 represent private families only. 2. Includes population of Indian Territory for 1900.

★ 1150 ★

Home Ownership

Population and Homes, 1890-1910

Section	Negro population per owned home		
	1910	1900	1890
United States	19	22	28
The South	20	23	30
The North	18	19	18
The West	12	15	18

Source: "Negro Population per Owned Home." U.S. Bureau of the Census. *Negro Population in the United States, 1790-1915.* Washington, D.C.: Government Printing Office, 1918, p. 462.

Home Value

★ 1151 ★

Leading Black and Integrated Neighborhoods: Cost of Homes, 1974

The following is a list of some of the leading black and integrated neighborhoods in America. It is not meant to be conclusive, only indicative of the many neighborhoods and communities in which we now reside.

City	Neighborhood	Total population	Percent of blacks	Home value
Atlanta, Ga.	Cascade Heights	4,641	70%	$40,000-80,000
	Collier Heights	7,515	95%	$30,000-250,000
	Hunter Road	250	100%	$40,000-175,000
	Southwest	93,750	64%	$85,000-300,000
Baltimore, Md.	Ashburton	40,000	100%	$30,000-45,000
	Mount Washington	5,500	2.8%	$30,000-110,000
Baton Rouge, La.	Crestworth	791	100%	$40,000-80,000
Birmingham, Ala.	Briarmont	150	100%	$35,000-100,000
	North Smithfield	720	100%	$27,000-60,000
Cherry Hill, N.J.		64,000	5%	$45,000-200,000
Chicago, Ill.	Hyde Park	10,000	65%	$39,000-100,000
	Pill Hill	12,000	99%	$45,000-200,000
Cleveland, Ohio	Shaker Heights	36,306	14%	$40,000-90,000
Columbia, S.C.	Meadow Lake	1,320	100%	$33,000-65,000
	Highland Park	776	100%	$30,000-50,000
Dallas, Texas	Far North Dallas	89,906	3.2%	$75,000-up
	Wynnewood Hills	2,000	15%	$30,000-100,000
Denver, Colo.	East Denver	47,500	99%	$20,000-100,000
Detroit, Mich.	Palmer Woods	1,050	30%	$50,000-200,000
Englewood, N.J.		35,000	23%	$70,000-100,000
Gary, Ind.	Miller Area	14,000	30%	$15,000-40,000

[Continued]

★ 1151 ★

Leading Black and Integrated Neighborhoods: Cost of Homes, 1974
[Continued]

City	Neighborhood	Total population	Percent of blacks	Home value
Hampton, Va.	Glen Park	25,000	25%	$15,000-25,000
	Granger Court	125	100%	$40,000-80,000
Houston, Texas	Honey Circle	7,058	100%	$45,000-85,000
Kansas City, Mo.	Sheraton Estates	500	100%	$18,000-75,000
Los Angeles, Calif.	Baldwin Hills	23,982	90%	$50,000-150,000
	Ladera Heights	6,535	15%	$80,000- up
	View Park	6,500	70%	$50,000-250,000
New Orleans, La.	New Orleans East	44,550	65%	$36,000-150,000
	Sugar Hill	5,836	85%	$40,000-95,000
New York, N.Y.	Convent Avenue	2,088	99.2%	$20,000-65,000
	Striver's Row	1,060	100%	$25,000-65,000
Norfolk, Va.	Greenhill Farms	3,604	69.8%	$10,000-25,000
Oakland, Calif.	Oakland Hills	29,700	4.5%	$45,000-75,000
Pittsburgh, Pa.	Upper Hill	4,636	84.9%	$25,000-70,000
Richmond, Va.	Hungary Road Estates	360	99.6%	$30,000-100,000
San Francisco, Calif.	Ocean Mercedes Ingleside	40,000	9%	$45,000-50,000
St. Louis, Mo.	Black Jack	2,000	40%	$60,000-80,000
Teaneck, N.J.	North Teaneck	45,000	33.3%	$45,000- up
Washington	North Portal Estates	750	70%	$60,000-250,000

Source: Untitled table, *Black Enterprise* 4 (December 1974), p. 33. Published by permission.

Household Characteristics

★ 1152 ★

Households: Race, Marital Status, Sex, and Children, April 1947

Year, sex, marital status of head of number of children under 18 years old	Color of head	
	White	Nonwhite
Total	35,593,000	3,545,000
No own children under 18	19,120,000	2,119,000
1 or more own children	16,473,000	1,426,000
Male head	30,520,000	2,736,000
Marricd, wife present	28,164,000	2,381,000
No own children under 18	12,756,000	1,205,000
1 or more own children	15,408,000	1,176,000

[Continued]

★ 1152 ★

Households: Race, Marital Status, Sex, and Children, April 1947

[Continued]

Year, sex, marital status of head of number of children under 18 years old	Color of head	
	White	Nonwhite
Female head	5,073,000	809,000
No own children under 18	4,182,000	596,000
1 or more own children	891,000	213,000

Source: "Households by Color, Marital Status, and Sex, Number of Head's Own Children Under 18 Years Old, for the United States, April 1947," Florence Murray, ed., *The Negro Handbook, 1949,* p. 185. Published by permission. Primary source: U.S. Bureau of the Census.

★ 1153 ★

Household Characteristics

Households: Selected Characteristics, 1790 - 1957

Year	All households			Race of head			Sex of head		Median age of head
	Number	Median size[1]	Population per household	White	Negro	Other	Male	Female	
1957[2]	49,543,000	3.02	3.42	44,886,000	[3]	[3]	40,903,000	8,640,000	46.9
1950	42,857,335	3.05	3.52	38,429,035[4]	[3]	[3]	35,862,900[4]	6,388,515[4]	45.9[4]
1940	34,948,666	3.28	3.77	31,679,766	3,141,883	127,017	29,679,718	5,268,948	46.06
1930[5]	29,904,663	3.40	4.11	26,982,994	2,803,756	117,913	26,111,761	3,792,902	44.45[6]
1920	24,351,676	-	4.34	21,825,654	2,430,828	95,194	-	-	-
1910	20,255,555	-	4.54	[3]	2,173,018	[3]	-	-	-
1900	15,963,965	4.23	4.76	14,063,791	1,833,759	66,415	14,022,546	1,941,419	42.99
1890	12,690,152	4.48	4.93	11,255,169	1,410,769	24,214	10,857,249	1,832,903	42.55
1880	9,945,916	-	5.04	-	-	-	-	-	-
1870	7,579,363	-	5.09	-	-	-	-	-	-
1860[7]	5,210,934	-	5.28	-	-	-	-	-	-
1850[7]	3,598,240	-	5.55	-	-	-	-	-	-
1790	557,889	5.43	5.79	-	-	-	-	-	-

Source: "Selected Characteristics of Household: 1790 to 1957," U.S. Bureau of the Census. *Historical Statistics of the United States, Colonial Times to 1957,* p. 16. *Notes:* (-) Represents zero. 1. 1790 and 1940-1957 relate to households only but include lodgers and other non-relatives in addition to the head and his relatives; 1890 and 1900 include all persons whether related to the head or not, in both households and quasi-households; 1930 includes the household head and his relatives only. 2. Based on sample figures from Current Population Survey. 3. Not available. 4. Based on 20-percent sample of census returns. 5. Figures for race of head revised to include Mexicans as white. Mexicans were classified as non-white in the 1930 reports. 6. Based on white and negro households for which material status of head was reported. 7. Free population only.

Living Quarters

★ 1154 ★

Children Living in Institutions, 1960, 1970

Type of Institution or Quarters	1960 Rate	1970 Rate	1980 Number	1980 Rate
All Races/Ethnic Groups	670	572	260,425	408
Institutions	370	342	167,306	262
Mental Hospital	-	27	16,494	26
Nursing Home	-	3	5,614	9
Correctional Institution	-	1	10,803	17
Other Institutions	-	312	134,395	211
Group Quarters	300	231	93,119	146
Rooming or Boarding House[2]	147	73	11,887	19
Military Quarters[3]	66	36	21,979	34
College Dormitory	27	27	24,541	38
Other Group Quarters	60	94	34,712	54
Whites	599	497	173,866	226
Institutions	351	304	113,795	226
Mental Hospital	-	25	12,584	25
Correctional Institution	-	1	5,505	11
Other Institutions	-	276	91,696	182
Group Quarters	248	192	60,071	119
Rooming or Boarding House[2]	88	55	7,311	15
Military Quarters[3]	72	38	17,202	34
College Dormitory	28	29	17,451	35
Other Group Quarters	59	71	18,107	36
Blacks[4]	1,122	1,004	57,120	607
Institutions	490	560	40,252	428
Mental Hospital	-	41	3,133	33
Nursing Home	-	3	1,170	12
Correctional Institution	-	1	4,371	46
Other Institutions	-	516	31,578	336
Group Quarters	632	444	16,868	179
Rooming or Boarding House[2]	517	174	1,681	18
Military Quarters[3]	26	25	2,844	30
College Dormitory	23	20	3,579	38
Other Group Quarters	67	226	8,764	93
Hispanics	5	508	26,856	476
Institutions		270	13,531	240
Mental Hospital		16	935	17
Nursing Home		4	340	6
Correctional Institution		1	923	16
Other Institutions		250	11,333	201
Group Quarters		239	13,325	236
Rooming or Boarding House[2]		80	2,223	39
Military Quarters[3]		31	1,662	29

[Continued]

★ 1154 ★

Children Living in Institutions, 1960, 1970

[Continued]

Type of Institution or Quarters	1960 Rate	1970 Rate	1980 Number	1980 Rate
College Dormitory		18	2,148	38
Other Group Quarters		110	7,292	129

Source: "Number and Rate (per 1,000,000) of Children (Under Age 18) Living in Institutions or Group Quarters, 1960-1980," *U.S. Children and Their Families*, 1989, pp. 27-28. Primary source: Calculated from the following tables: 1960 U.S. Census of Population; Volume I, Characteristics of the Population; Part I, U.S. Summary; Table 182; 1970 U.S. Census of Population; Volume 1, Characteristics of the Population; Part 1, U.S. Summary; Section 2, Chapter D, Detailed Characteristics; Table 205; 1980 U.S. Census of Population; PC80-1-D1-A, U.S. Summary, Detailed Population Characteristics; Table 266. *Notes:* 1. In 1970, "Other institutions" include those in correctional facilities. 2. In 1960 and 1970, "Rooming or boarding house" included, among other categories, persons living in house units in which 6 or more unrelated persons were living together. In 1980, this definition was changed from "6 or more" or "10 or more." Had the same definition been applied in 1980, a larger proportion of children would have been classified as living in rooming houses. 3. In 1960 and 1970, "military quarters" comprises only males living in military quarters. The figures for 1980 includes females as well. This adds about 7 percent to the number of persons in military quarters in 1980. In 1970 and 1980 persons stationed on ships are included in "military quarters." In 1960 these are included in "other group quarters." 4. The figures for 1960 are for non-whites, rather than for blacks. The great majority of non-whites in the U.S. are black. 5. Not available.

Occupied Housing

★ 1155 ★

Distribution of Housing with Plumbing: 1940, 1960, and 1970

Area, type of residence, and year	Black[1] Total (thousands)	Black[1] With all plumbing facilities	Black[1] Lacking some or all plumbing facilities	White[2] Total (thousands)	White[2] With all plumbing facilities	White[2] Lacking some or all plumbing facilities
1940						
United States	3,293	19	74	31,561	55	38
Urban-Rural Residence						
Urban	1,728	35	58	18,868	75	18
Rural	1,565	2	93	12,693	27	69
Region						
South	2,408	9	86	7,870	37	58
North and West	886	48	44	23,691	62	32

[Continued]

★ 1155 ★

Distribution of Housing with Plumbing: 1940, 1960, and 1970

[Continued]

Area, type of residence, and year	Black[1]			White[2]		
	Total (thousands)	Percent of total		Total (thousands)	Percent of total	
		With all plumbing facilities	Lacking some or all plumbing facilities		With all plumbing facilities	Lacking some or all plumbing facilities
1960						
United States	5,144	56	27	47,880	87	10
Urban-Rural Residence						
Urban	3,978	68	19	34,342	93	5
Rural	1,165	14	54	13,538	72	23
Region						
South	2,756	38	39	12,747	80	16
North and West	2,388	76	14	35,133	90	8
1970						
United States	6,180	84	16	57,269	96	4
Urban-Rural Residence[3]						
Urban	5,209	92	8	42,358	98	2
Rural	965	39	61	14,912	89	11
Region						
South	3,110	71	29	16,148	93	7
North and West	3,070	96	4	41,122	96	4

Source: "Distribution of Occupied Housing Units by Availability of Plumbing Facilities, by Urban-Rural Residence and Region: 1940, 1960, and 1970," U.S. Department of Commerce, Bureau of the Census. *The Social and Economic Status of the Black Population in the United States: An Historical View, 1790-1978,* p. 139. Primary source: U.S. Department of Commerce, Bureau of the Census. *Notes:* Totals for 1940 include a small number not reporting on plumbing facilities and totals for 1960 include dilapidated occupied units, not shown separately. 1. Data for 1940 and 1960 include family heads of "other" races. 2. Data for 1970 include family heads of "other" races. Detail may not add to total because data are from different tabulations.

★ 1156 ★

Occupied Housing

Housing Units: Tenure and Population: 1900-1970

In thousands, except percent. Prior to 1960, excludes Alaska and Hawaii. Tenure allocated for housing units which did not report. Minus sign (-) denotes decrease.

Year, race, and residence	Occupied units[1]					Percent increase over preceding census		Population per occupied unit[2]
	Total	Owner occupied		Renter occupied		Total occupied units	Total population	
		Number	Percent	Number	Percent			
TOTAL								
1900	15,964	7,455	46.7	8,509	53.3	25.8	20.7	4.8
1910	20,256	9,301	45.9	10,954	54.1	26.9	21.0	4.5
1920	24,352	11,114	45.6	13,238	54.4	20.2	14.9	4.3
1930	29,905	14,280	47.8	15,624	52.2	22.8	16.1	4.1
1940	34,855	15,196	43.6	19,659	56.4	16.6	7.2	3.8
1950	42,826	23,560	55.0	19,266	45.0	22.9	14.5	3.4
1960	53,024	32,797	61.9	20,227	38.1	23.4	18.5	3.3
1970	63,450	39,885	62.9	23,565	37.1	19.7	13.3	3.1
RACE								
White								
1900	14,064	7,007	49.8	7,057	50.2	25.0	21.2	4.8
1910	(NA)	(NA)	(NA)	(NA)	(NA)	(NA)	22.3	(NA)
1920	21,826	10,511	48.2	11,315	51.8	(NA)	16.0	4.3
1930	26,983	13,544	50.2	13,439	49.8	23.6	16.3	4.1
1940	31,561	14,418	45.7	17,143	54.3	17.0	7.2	3.7
1950	39,044	22,241	57.0	16,803	43.0	23.7	14.1	3.3
1960	47,880	30,823	64.4	17,057	35.6	22.5	17.5	(NA)
1970	56,529	36,979	65.4	19,551	34.6	18.1	11.9	(NA)
Black and other								
1900	1,900	448	23.6	1,452	76.4	32.4	17.1	4.8
1910	(NA)	(NA)	(NA)	(NA)	(NA)	(NA)	11.5	(NA)
1920	2,526	603	23.9	1,923	76.1	(NA)	6.3	4.3
1930	2,922	737	25.2	2,185	74.8	15.7	14.7	4.3
1940	3,293	778	23.6	2,516	76.4	12.7	7.7	4.1
1950	3,783	1,319	34.9	2,464	65.1	14.9	17.1	3.9
1960	5,144	1,974	38.4	3,171	61.6	33.0	26.7	(NA)
1970	6,920	2,907	42.0	4,014	58.0	34.5	24.3	(NA)
RESIDENCE								
Nonfarm								
1900	10,274	3,790	36.9	6,484	63.1	29.7	(NA)	(NA)
1910	14,132	5,454	38.6	8,678	61.4	37.5	(NA)	(NA)
1920	17,600	7,189	40.8	10,411	59.2	24.5	(NA)	4.2
1930	23,300	10,721	46.0	12,579	54.0	32.4	25.0	4.0
1940	27,748	11,413	41.1	16,335	58.9	19.1	9.5	3.7
1950	37,105	19,802	53.4	17,304	46.6	33.7	25.8	3.3

[Continued]

★ 1156 ★

Housing Units: Tenure and Population: 1900-1970

[Continued]

Year, race, and residence	Occupied units[1]					Percent increase over preceding census		Population per occupied unit[2]
	Total	Owner occupied		Renter occupied		Total occupied units	Total population	
		Number	Percent	Number	Percent			
1960[3]	49,458	30,164	61.0	19,249	39.1	33.3	30.0	3.3
1970[3]	60,351	37,393	62.0	22,957	38.0	22.0	16.1	3.1
Farm[4]								
1900	5,690	3,665	64.4	2,025	35.6	19.4	(NA)	(NA)
1910	6,124	3,847	62.8	2,276	37.2	7.6	(NA)	(NA)
1920	6,751	3,925	58.1	2,827	41.9	10.2	(NA)	4.7
1930	6,605	3,560	53.9	3,045	46.1	-2.2	-4.6	4.6
1940	7,107	3,783	53.2	3,324	46.8	7.6	0.2	4.3
1950	5,721	3,758	65.7	1,963	34.3	-19.5	-23.7	4.0
1960[3]	3,566	2,633	73.8	933	26.2	-37.7	-41.7	3.8
1970[3]	3,095	2,492	80.5	603	19.5	-13.2	-21.2	3.4

Source: "Occupied Housing Units-Tenure, and Population Per Occupied Unit, by Race of Household Head and by Residence: 1900 to 1970," *The Ebony Handbook.* Chicago: Johnson Publishing Co., 1974, p. 348. Primary source: U.S. Bureau of the Census, "U.S. Census of Population and Housing: 1960" and "1970."
Notes: NA Not available. 1. Statistics on the number of occupied units are essentially comparable although identified by various terms—the term "family" applies to figures for 1930 and earlier; "occupied dwelling unit," 1940 and 1950; and "occupied housing unit," 1960 and 1970. For 1910 and 1920, includes the small number of quasi-families; 1900 and 1930 represent private families only. 2. From 1950 to 1970, population in occupied housing units was determined by dividing population units by number of occupied housing units. 3. Not comparable with data for earlier census because of a basic change in definition of farm residence. 4. For 1900 to 1920, excludes a small proportion of urban-farm families in addition to rural-farm.

★ 1157 ★

Occupied Housing

Housing with Plumbing, by Tenure and Region: 1975

Area and tenure	Black			White[1]		
	Total	With all plumbing facilities	Lacking some or all plumbing facilities	Total	With all plumbing facilities	Lacking some or all plumbing facilities
United States (thousands)	7,561	6,903	658	64,962	63,544	1,418
PERCENT DISTRIBUTION						
Tenure						
Total	100	91	9	100	98	2
Owner occupied	100	93	7	100	99	1
Renter occupied	100	90	10	100	96	4
Region						
Total	100	91	9	100	98	2
South	100	85	15	100	97	3
North and West	100	98	2	100	98	2

[Continued]

★ 1157 ★

Housing with Plumbing, by Tenure and Region: 1975
[Continued]

Area and tenure	Black			White[1]		
	Total	With all plumbing facilities	Lacking some or all plumbing facilities	Total	With all plumbing facilities	Lacking some or all plumbing facilities
Northeast	100	96	4	100	98	2
North Central	100	98	2	100	98	2
West	100	99	1	100	99	1

Source: "Availability of Plumbing Facilities of Occupied Housing Units, by Tenure and Region," U.S. Department of Commerce, Bureau of the Census. *The Social and Economic Status of the Black Population in the United States: An Historical View, 1790-1978*, p. 140. Primary source: U.S. Department of Commerce, Bureau of the Census. *Note:* 1. Includes family heads of "other" races.

★ 1158 ★

Occupied Housing

Persons Per Room in Occupied Housing: 1940, 1960, and 1970

Area, type of residence, and tenure	Black			White		
	1940[1]	1960[1]	1970	1940	1960	1970[1]
RESIDENCE						
Urban						
Owner occupied						
1.01 or more persons per room	20	17	14	9	7	5
1.51 or more persons per room	8	6	4	3	1	1
Renter occupied						
1.01 or more persons per room	34	29	20	18	11	8
1.51 or more persons per room	18	14	7	6	3	2
Rural						
Owner occupied						
1.01 or more persons per room	41	32	23	17	10	7
1.51 or more persons per room	26	17	9	8	3	2
Renter occupied						
1.01 or more persons per room	52	48	40	31	20	13
1.51 or more persons per room	33	31	22	16	7	4
REGION						
South						
Owner occupied						
1.01 or more persons per room	33	23	19	21	9	6

[Continued]

★ 1158 ★

Persons Per Room in Occupied Housing: 1940, 1960, and 1970

[Continued]

Area, type of residence, and tenure	Black			White		
	1940[1]	1960[1]	1970	1940	1960	1970[1]
1.51 or more persons per room	18	10	7	9	2	1
Renter occupied						
1.01 or more persons per room	47	40	29	36	19	11
1.51 or more persons per room	29	23	14	19	7	3
North and West						
Owner occupied						
1.01 or more persons per room	27	18	13	11	7	6
1.51 or more persons per room	18	7	3	4	1	1
Renter occupied						
1.01 or more persons per room	28	26	17	17	11	8
1.51 or more persons per room	13	11	5	6	3	2

Source: "Percent of Occupied Housing Units with Specific Number of Persons Per Room by Tenure, Urban-Rural Residence, and region: 1940, 1960, and 1970," U.S. Department of Commerce, Bureau of the Census. *The Social and Economic Status of the Black Population in the United States: An Historical View, 1790-1978*, p. 141. Primary source: U.S. Department of Commerce, Bureau of the Census. *Note:* 1. Includes family heads of "other" races.

★ 1159 ★

Occupied Housing

Tenure of Occupied Housing Units by Region: 1890-1970

Area and year	Black			White		
	Total (thousands)	Percent of total		Total (thousands)	Percent of total	
		Owner occupied	Renter occupied		Owner occupied	Renter occupied
SOUTH						
1890	1,263	18	82	2,494	53	47
1910[1]	1,917	23	77	2,200	64	36
1940	2,387	24	76	7,870	46	54
1960[2]	2,756	42	58	12,747	66	34
1970	3,110	47	53	16,047	68	32
NORTH AND WEST						
1890	148	28	72	8,761	51	49
1910[1]	256	24	76	15,409	47	53
1940	770	19	81	23,691	46	54

[Continued]

★ 1159 ★

Tenure of Occupied Housing Units by Region: 1890-1970
[Continued]

Area and year	Black			White		
	Total (thousands)	Percent of total		Total (thousands)	Percent of total	
		Owner occupied	Renter occupied		Owner occupied	Renter occupied
1960[2]	2,389	35	65	35,133	64	36
1970	3,070	36	64	40,482	64	36

Source: "Tenure of Occupied Housing Units, for Selected Years: 1890 to 1975," U.S. Department of Commerce, Bureau of the Census. *The Social and Economic Status of the Black Population in the United States: An Historical View, 1790-1978,* p. 138. Primary source: U.S. Department of Commerce, Bureau of the Census. *Notes:* 1. Data for White include family heads of "other" races. 2. Data for Black include family heads of "other" races.

★ 1160 ★
Occupied Housing

Tenure of Occupied Housing Units by Region: 1975

Numbers in thousands.

Tenure and race of family head	United States	South	North and West			
			Total	Northeast	North Central	West
BLACK						
Total occupied units	7,561	3,854	3,707	1,459	1,512	736
Owner occupied	3,309	1,875	1,434	423	708	303
Percent of total	44	49	39	29	47	41
Renter occupied	4,252	1,979	2,273	1,036	804	433
WHITE						
Total occupied units	63,860	19,084	44,776	14,858	17,755	12,163
Owner occupied	43,072	13,378	29,694	9,347	12,690	7,657
Percent of total	67	70	66	63	71	63
Renter occupied	20,788	5,706	15,082	5,511	5,065	4,506

Source: "Tenure of Occupied Housing Units, for Selected Years: 1890 to 1975," U.S. Department of Commerce, Bureau of the Census. *The Social and Economic Status of the Black Population in the United States: An Historical View, 1790-1978,* p. 137. Primary source: U.S. Department of Commerce, Bureau of the Census. *Notes:* Data shown in table are from the 1975 Annual Housing Survey conducted by the Bureau of the Census. The survey was sponsored by the U.S. Department of Housing and Urban Development.

★ 1161 ★

Occupied Housing

Tenure of Occupied Housing Units: 1890-1970

Numbers in thousands.

Year	Black			White		
	Total	Owner occupied	Renter occupied	Total	Owner occupied	Renter occupied
1890	1,411	264	1,146	11,255	5,794	5,462
1910[1]	2,173	507	1,666	17,609	8,577	9,031
1940	3,157	720	2,437	31,561	14,418	17,143
1960[2]	5,144	1,974	3,171	47,880	30,823	17,057
1970	6,180	2,568	3,612	56,529	36,979	19,551
PERCENT DISTRIBUTION						
1890	100	19	81	100	51	49
1910[1]	100	23	77	100	49	51
1940	100	23	77	100	46	54
1960[2]	100	38	62	100	64	36
1970	100	42	58	100	65	35

Source: "Tenure of Occupied Housing Units, for Selected Years: 1890 to 1975," U.S. Department of Commerce, Bureau of the Census. *The Social and Economic Status of the Black Population in the United States: An Historical View, 1790-1978,* p. 137. Primary source: U.S. Department of Commerce, Bureau of the Census. *Notes:* The first nationwide census of housing was taken in 1940. In 1940, 1960, and 1970, a housing (dwelling) unit was defined as the living quarters occupied or intended for occupancy by one household. Figures for 1890 and 1910 rest on the fairly close correspondence between the concept of occupied housing unit used in the housing censuses since 1940 and concepts used in previous censuses of population. The number of occupied housing units is closely comparable to the number of households shown in the family chapter. Since 1950, the number of occupied housing units has been identical by definition to the number of households. 1. Data for White include family heads of "other" races. 2. Data for Black include family heads of "other" races.

Public Housing Projects

★ 1162 ★

Federal Housing: Program and Construction Status, May 31, 1947

Program and construction status	Number of dwelling units		Estimated development cost of dwelling units available for Negroes ($000)
	Total active	Occupied by or programmed for Negroes	
All programs (excluding Veteran's Re-use Housing program and PWA and FSA project which have been sold, securities held for collection)	622,244	121,600	490,449
By status			
Under management	616,558	119,694	478,744
Under development[2]	5,686	1,906	11,705
By program			
Public War Housing (Lanham constructed)	376,947	51,902	156,044
Homes Conversion	38,961	2,290[3]	4,232[3]
Defense Homes Corporation	7,816	528	1,424
U.S. Housing Act Program (including PL-671 still in war use)	195,565	66,848	328,475
Subsistence Homestead and Greenbelt Towns	2,955	32	274

Source: "Public Housing Programmed for or Occupied by Negroes, by Type of Program and Construction Status of Dwelling Units, As of May 31, 1947," Florence Murray, ed., *The Negro Handbook, 1949*, p. 186. Published by permission. Primary source: U.S. Housing and Home Finance Agency. *Notes:* 1. Based on number of assigned units where definitely programmed for Negro tenants. For all other projects with 95 percent occupancy or more, based on number of occupied units and for projects with less than 95 percent occupancy, on proportion of total occupied units occupied by Negroes. 2. All U.S. Housing Act Program. 3. Data as of June 30, 1947; not available. for May 31, 1947.

★1163★
Public Housing Projects

Permanent Public Housing Projects, 1945 – General Field Office

Location	Project name	Total no. units in project	Est. no. of units occupied by Negro tenants[1]
District of Columbia			
Washington	Langston	274	
	James Creek Site	278	
	Douglass Dwellings	313	
	Stanton Road	300	
	Carrollsburg Dwellings	314	
	Kelly Miller Dwellings	169	
	Barry Farms Dwellings	442	
	Parkside Dwellings	373	
	Hillside	440	
Washington	Lucy Diggs Slowe Hall	322	
	George W. Carver Hall	206	
Maryland			
Cabin John	Seven Locks	120	20
St. Mary's County	Carver Heights	72	
	Carver Heights	120	
Virginia			
Alexandria	Parker Homes	110	
	Ramsey Homes	15	
Arlington	Paul Dunbar Homes	86	
	George Carver Homes	44	

Source: "Permanent Public Housing Projects Making Provision for Negro Tenants (As of July 31. 1945)," Jessie Parkhurst Guzman, ed., *Negro Year Book: A Review of Events Affecting Negro Life, 1941-1946*, p. 348.
Notes: 1. This column used only for projects partially occupied by Negro tenants.

★ 1164 ★
Public Housing Projects

Permanent Public Housing Projects, 1945 – Region I

Location	Project name	Total no. units in project	Est. no. of units occupied by Negro tenants[1]
Connecticut			
Bridgeport	Yellow Mill Village	1,239	88
	Marina Village	516	80
	Black Rock Village	176	16
	Success Park[2]	1,000	50
	Huntington Homes	250	18
	Lincoln Terrace	150	8
	Canaan Village	324	32
(Fairfield)	Knapps Highway	200	6
	Melville Avenue	200	4
(Stratford)	Stonybrook Gardens	400	42
East Hartford	Mayberry Village	500	1
Hartford	Nelton Court[2]	156	6
	Bellevue Square[2]	501	
	Charter Oak Terrace	1,000	1
(Manchester)	Orford Village	375	3
(Glastonbury)	Welles Village	200	1
(Rocky Hill)	Drum Hill Park	125	1
Middletown	Long River Village	190	15
New Britain	Mount Pleasant	340	4
	Ledgecrest	300	12
(Plainville)	East Mountain Terrace	200	3
New Haven	Elm Haven	487	326
	Farnam Courts	300	32
	West Hills	300	35
Norwalk	Washington Village	136	46
Stamford	Southfield Village	250	70
	Fairfield Court	148	4
Windsor Locks	Elm Plains	85	5
Maine			
Bangor	Fairmont Terrace	150	5
Portland	Sagamore Village	200	4
Massachusetts			
Ayer	Devencrest	300	42
Boston	Lenox Street	306	
	Orchard Park	774	93
	East Boston	414	1
Cambridge	Washington Park	324	1
	New Towne Court	294	3
Fall River	Sunset Hill	356	2
	Harbor Terrace	223	2
Hingham	Old Colony Village	78	2
New Bedford	Bay Village	200	95

[Continued]

★ 1164 ★

Permanent Public Housing Projects, 1945 – Region I

[Continued]

Location	Project name	Total no. units in project	Est. no. of units occupied by Negro tenants[1]
Springfield	Mallary Village	300	4
(Chicopee)	Curtis Terrace	250	8
New Hampshire			
Portsmouth	Wentworth	800	12
Rhode Island			
Newport	Tonomy Hill	538	17
Providence	Williams Homes	744	46

Source: "Permanent Public Housing Projects Making Provision for Negro Tenants (As of July 31. 1945)," Jessie Parkhurst Guzman, ed. *Negro Year Book: A Review of Events Affecting Negro Life, 1941-1946*, p. 342. *Notes:* 1. This column used only for projects partially occupied by Negro tenants. 2. Two projects.

★ 1165 ★

Public Housing Projects

Permanent Public Housing Projects, 1945 – Region II

Location	Project name	Total no. units in project	Est. no. of units occupied by Negro tenants[1]
Delaware			
Wilmington	Southbridge	180	
Maryland			
Annapolis	College Creek Terrace	108	
Baltimore	McCulloh Homes	434	
	Edgar Allen Poe Homes	298	
	Frederick Douglass Homes	393	
	Gilmor Homes	587	
	Somerset Court Homes	420	
	Lyon Homes	304	
	Cherry Hill Homes	600	
Frederick	Lincoln Apartments	50	
Havre de Grace	Concord Fields	500	3
New Jersey			
Asbury Park	Asbury Park Village	126	
Atlantic City	Stanley S. Holmes Village	277	
Beverly	Delacove Homes	71	24
Burlington	Dunbar Homes	90	40
Camden	Clement T. Branch Village	279	

[Continued]

★ 1165 ★

Permanent Public Housing Projects, 1945 – Region II

[Continued]

Location	Project name	Total no. units in project	Est. no. of units occupied by Negro tenants[1]
	Chelton Terrace	200	
Dover	Victory Gardens	300	1
Elizabeth	Pioneer Homes	495	72
Jersey City	Lafayette Gardens	490	1
	Marion Gardens	462	4
	Booker T. Washington Apts.	234	
	Hudson Gardens	224	2
	Holland Apartments	192	2
Long Beach	Garfield Court	128	36
	Grant Court	82	
Newark	Pennington Court	236	60
	James M. Baxter Terrace	614	408
	F.D. Roosevelt Homes	275	
	Felix Fuld Court	300	150
Paterson	Riverside Terrace	300	28
Trenton	Lincoln Homes	118	
	Prospect Homes	120	
New York			
Buffalo	Willert Park[2]	473	
Hempstead	Mitchell Gardens	200	4
Lackawanna	Baker Homes	271	9
	Albright Court	200	155
Mineville	Grover Hills	100	1
New York City	Williamsburg Houses	1,622	33
	Harlem River Houses	576	
	Red Hook Houses	2,545	146
	Queensbridge Houses	3,148	121
	Vladeck Houses	1,531	14
	South Jamaica Houses	448	340
	East River Houses	1,170	122
	Kingsborough Houses	1,166	552
	Clason Point Gardens	400	8
	Markham Houses	360	34
	Wallabout Houses	207	3
Syracuse	Pioneer Homes	678	52
Yonkers	Mulford Gardens	552	2
Pennsylvania			
Aliquippa	Griffith Heights	50	
	Mount Vernon	50	
Allentown	Hanover Acres	322	1
Beaver Falls	Harmony Dwellings	50	
Chester	Lamokin Village	350	

[Continued]

★ 1165 ★

Permanent Public Housing Projects, 1945 – Region II
[Continued]

Location	Project name	Total no. units in project	Est. no. of units occupied by Negro tenants[1]
	Fairground Homes	350	
Clairton	Blair Heights	148	
Coatsville	Carver Homes	100	
Duquesne	Cochrandale	83	
Erie	Lake City Dwellings	40	
Harrison Twp.	Sheldon Park	200	11
Johnstown	Prospect Homes	111	51
McKeesport	Harrison Village	50	
McKees Rocks	McKees Rocks Terrace	288	20
Midland	Midland Heights	280	12
Mifflin Twp.	River View Homes	450	73
	Monongahcla Heights	342	163
Moon Twp.	Mooncrest	400	32
North Braddock	North Braddock Heights	200	48
Philadelphia	Johnson Homes[2]	535	575
	Tasker Homes	1,000	100
	Allen Homes	1,324	1,300
Latrobe-Greensburg	Westmoreland Homestead	225	1
Pittsburgh	Addison Terrace	802	405
	Bedford Dwellings	420	405
	Wadsworth-Aliquippa	1,851	961
	Arlington Heights	660	108
	Allegheny Dwellings	282	60
	Broadhead Manor	448	46
	Glen Hazel Heights	999	212
Pulaski Twp.	Pulaski Homes	100	1
Rankin	Hawkins Village	182	48
Reading	Glenside Homes	400	8
Scott Twp.	Chartiers Terrace	200	47
Sharon-Farrell	Steel City Terrace	150	50
South Union Twp.	Grossland Place	40	
Van Port	Van Buren Homes	400	38
Washington Co.	Lincoln Terrace	46	
Wayne	Highland Homes	50	25

Source: "Permanent Public Housing Projects Making Provision for Negro Tenants (As of July 31. 1945)." Jessie Parkhurst Guzman, ed., *Negro Year Book: A Review of Events Affecting Negro Life, 1941-1946*, pp. 342-344. *Notes:* 1. This column used only for projects partially occupied by Negro tenants. 2. Two projects.

★ 1166 ★

Public Housing Projects

Permanent Public Housing Projects, 1945 – Region III

Location	Project name	Total no. units in project	Est. no. of units occupied by Negro tenants[1]
Illinois			
Cairo	Pyramid Courts	240	
Chicago	Ida B. Wells Homes	1,650	1,648
	Cabrini Homes	586	123
	Robert Brooks Homes	834	831
	Altgeld Gardens	1,500	1,413
	Wentworth Gardens	422	
	Ill-11208	250	232
	Jane Adams Houses[2]	1,027	43
Danville	Beecher Terrace	50	
Decatur	Longview Place	434	54
East St. Louis	Robinson Homes	144	
Madison Co.			
(Venice)	Jones Homes	37	
Peoria	Warner Homes	487	93
Quincy	Ball Homes	49	
Rockford	Central Terrace	150	34
Springfield	Hay Homes	599	147
Indiana			
Evansville	Lincoln Gardens	191	
Fort Wayne	Samuel Morris Homes	88	34
Gary	Delaney Community	305	
Indianapolis	Lockfield Gardens	748	
Muncie	Munsyana Homes	278	114
New Albany	Crystal Court	18	
Minnesota			
Minneapolis	Field Homes	464	119
Missouri			
St. Louis	Carr Square Village	658	
Nebraska			
Omaha	Southside Terrace Homes	522	65
	Fontenelle Homes	284	108
	Logan-Fontenelle Addition	272	103
Wisconsin			
Milwaukee	Parklawn	518	6

Source: "Permanent Public Housing Projects Making Provision for Negro Tenants (As of July 31, 1945)," Jessie Parkhurst Guzman, ed. *Negro Year Book: A Review of Events Affecting Negro Life, 1941-1946*, p. 344. *Notes:* 1. This column used only for projects partially occupied by Negro tenants. 2. Two projects.

★ 1167 ★
Public Housing Projects

Permanent Public Housing Projects, 1945 – Region IV

Location	Project name	Total no. units in project	Est. no. of units occupied by Negro tenants[1]
Alabama			
Birmingham	Southtown	480	
	Smithfield Courts	512	
Fairfield	Fairfield Courts	90	
Mobile	Orange Grove Homes	298	
Montgomery	Cleveland Courts	150	
	Paterson Courts	150	
Phenix City	Frederick Douglass Homes	206	
Florida			
Daytona Beach	Pine Haven[2]	167	
Ft. Lauderdale	Dixie Court	150	
Jacksonville	Blodgett Homes	708	
	Durkeeville	215	
Key West	Fort Village	84	
Lakeland	Lake Ridge Homes	160	
Miami	Liberty Square	243	
	Liberty Square Add.[2]	730	
Orlando	Griffin Park	250	
	Carver Court	160	
Pensacola	Attucks Court	120	
St. Petersburg	Jordan Park[2]	446	
Sarasota	Newtowne Heights	60	
Tampa	North Boulevard Homes	534	
	College Hill Homes	500	
West Palm Beach	Dunbar Village	246	
Georgia			
Albany	Hines Homes	56	
Athens	Broad Acres	126	
Atlanta	University Homes	675	
	John Hope Homes	606	
	Henry Grady Homes	616	
	John J. Eagan Homes	548	
	Alonzo F. Herndon Homes	520	
Augusta	Sunset Homes	168	
	Gilbert Manor	278	
Brunswick	McIntyre Courts	144	
Columbus	Booker T. Washington Apts.[2]	392	
	Williams Homes	160	
Decatur	Allen Wilson Terrace	200	
Macon	Tindall Heights	444	
Marietta	Fort Hill Homes	120	
Rome	Altoview	94	
Savannah	Fellwood Homes	176	

[Continued]

★ 1167 ★

Permanent Public Housing Projects, 1945 – Region IV
[Continued]

Location	Project name	Total no. units in project	Est. no. of units occupied by Negro tenants[1]
	Yamacraw Village	480	
Mississippi			
Biloxi	Bayou Augusta Homes	96	
Clarksdale	Magnolia Courts	120	
Hattiesburg	Robertson Place	120	
Laurel	Triangle Homes	125	
McComb City	Burglund Heights	76	
Meridian	Frank Berry Courts	113	
	George H. Reese Courts	97	
North Carolina			
Charlotte	Fairview Homes	452	
Fayetteville	Cape Fear Courts	56	
	Washington Square	75	
High Point	Daniel Brooks Homes	200	
Kinston	Mitchell Wooten Courts	142	
New Bern	Craven Terrace	253	
Raleigh	Chavis Heights	231	
Wilmington	Robert R. Taylor Homes	246	
	Hillcrest[2]	216	
South Carolina			
Charleston	Anson Borough Homes	162	
	Wragg Borough Homes	128	
	Cooper River Courts	137	
Columbia	University Terrace	122	74
	Allen Benedict Courts	244	
Spartanburg	Hartwell Homes	150	
	Spartanburg Defense Homes	10	
Tennessee			
Bristol	Johnson Court	68	
Chattanooga	College Hill	497	
Jackson	Merry Lane Courts	96	
Kingsport	Riverview	56	
Knoxville	College Homes	320	
	Austin Homes	200	
Memphis	William R. Foote Homes	900	
	LeMoyne Gardens[2]	842	
	Dixie Homes	636	
Nashville	Andrew Jackson Courts	398	
	John Napier Homes[2]	480	

[Continued]

★ 1167 ★

Permanent Public Housing Projects, 1945 – Region IV

[Continued]

Location	Project name	Total no. units in project	Est. no. of units occupied by Negro tenants[1]
Virginia Hopewell	Davisville	96	

Source: "Permanent Public Housing Projects Making Provision for Negro Tenants (As of July 31. 1945)," Jessie Parkhurst Guzman, ed, *Negro Year Book: A Review of Events Affecting Negro Life, 1941-1946*, pp. 344-346. *Notes:* 1. This column used only for projects partially occupied by Negro tenants. 2. Two projects.

★ 1168 ★

Public Housing Projects

Permanent Public Housing Projects, 1945 – Region V

Location	Project name	Total no. units in project	Est. no. of units occupied by Negro tenants[1]
Arkansas Little Rock	Tuxedo Park	100	
Colorado Denver	Platte Valley Homes	77	
Kansas Junction City	Pawnee Place	40	
Louisiana			
Alexandria	Carver Village	48	
East Baton Rouge	Clarksdale	50	
Lake Charles	Washington Courts	72	
New Orleans	Magnolia Street	723	
	Lafitte Avenue	896	
	Calliope Street	690	
	St. Bernard Avenue	744	
Texas			
Austin	Rosewood	130	
Corpus Christi	D.N. Leathers Center	122	
Dallas	Roseland Homes	650	
	Fraiser Courts	250	
El Paso	Tays Place	311	
Fort Worth	Butler Place	250	33
Galveston	Palm Terrace	228	
Houston	Cuney Homes	564	
	Kelly Courts	333	

[Continued]

★ 1168 ★

Permanent Public Housing Projects, 1945 – Region V

[Continued]

Location	Project name	Total no. units in project	Est. no. of units occupied by Negro tenants[1]
Pelly	Lincoln Courts	30	
San Antonio	Wheatley Courts	236	
	Lincoln Courts	342	
Texarkana	Stevens Courts	124	
Waco	Cain Homes	140	

Source: "Permanent Public Housing Projects Making Provision for Negro Tenants (As of July 31. 1945)," Jessie Parkhurst Guzman, ed., *Negro Year Book: A Review of Events Affecting Negro Life, 1941-1946*, p. 346. Notes: 1. This column used only for projects partially occupied by Negro tenants. 2. Two projects.

★ 1169 ★

Public Housing Projects

Permanent Public Housing Projects, 1945 – Region VI

Location	Project name	Total no. units in project	Est. no. of units occupied by Negro tenants[1]
Arizona			
Fort Huachuca	ARIZ-2011	30	
	ARIZ-2012	100	
Phoenix	Matthew Henson	150	
California			
Bakerfield	Adelante Vista	50	
Fresno	Sequoia Courts	60	
	Sierra Plaza	70	9
	Funston Place	150	10
Los Angeles	Cabrillo Homes	600	63
	Pueblo Del Rio	400	375
	Rancho San Pedro	285	44
	Aliso Village	802	173
	William Mead Homes	449	88
	Ramona Gardens	610	88
	Pico Gardens	260	40
	Rose Hill	100	2
	Hacienda Village	184	97
	Normont Terrace	400	2
	Channel Heights	600	88
Los Angeles County	Naravilla	504	50
Monterey (Ft. Ord)	CAL-4021	264	10
Oakland	Peralta Villa	396	186

[Continued]

★ 1169 ★

Permanent Public Housing Projects, 1945 – Region VI
[Continued]

Location	Project name	Total no. units in project	Est. no. of units occupied by Negro tenants[1]
Sacramento	Campbell Village	154	91
	New Helvetia	310	17
	Dos Rios	168	1
San Diego	Linda Vista	5,026	219
San Francisco	Westside Court	136	131
Vallejo	Mare Island	250	22

Source: "Permanent Public Housing Projects Making Provision for Negro Tenants (As of July 31. 1945)," Jessie ParkhurstGuzman, ed., *Negro Year Book: A Review of Events Affecting Negro Life, 1941-1946*, pp. 346-347. *Notes:* 1. This column used only for projects partially occupied by Negro tenants.

★ 1170 ★

Public Housing Projects

Permanent Public Housing Projects, 1945 – Region VII

Location	Project name	Total no. units in project	Est. no. of units occupied by Negro tenants[1]
Washington			
Seattle	Yesler Terrace	690	38
	Yesler Terrace Addition	178	6
	Ranier Vista[2]	622	32
	Holly Park[2]	1,000	42
	High Point[2]	1,300	13
Tacoma	Salishan[2]	1,600	186
	Lincoln Heights	400	1
Vancouver	McLaughlin Heights	4,406	196

Source: "Permanent Public Housing Projects Making Provision for Negro Tenants (As of July 31. 1945)," Jessie Parkhurst Guzman, ed., *Negro Year Book: A Review of Events Affecting Negro Life, 1941-1946*, p. 347. *Notes:* 1. This column used only for projects partially occupied by Negro tenants. 2. Two projects.

★ 1171 ★
Public Housing Projects

Permanent Public Housing Projects, 1945 – Region VIII

Location	Project name	Total no. units in project	Est. no. of units occupied by Negro tenants[1]
Kentucky			
Covington	Jacob Price Homes	163	
Lexington	Blue Grass-Aspendale Park	278	136
	Charlotte Courts	206	
Louisville	Beecher Terrace	808	
	College Park	125	
	Sheppard Square	423	
Madisonville	Rosenwald Homes	45	
Paducah	Abraham Lincoln Court	74	
Michigan			
Battle Creek	Prairie View Homes	250	22
Detroit	Brewster Homes[2]	941	
	Sojourner Truth Homes	200	
(Inkster)	Carver Homes[2]	698	
(Clinton Twp.)	Selfridge Homes	150	1
(Ypsilanti)	Park Ridge	100	
Ohio			
Akron	Elizabeth Park Homes	276	268
Cincinnati	Laurel Homes[2]	1,403	602
	Lincoln Court	1,015	993
(Lockland)	Valley Homes	350	
Cleveland	Carver Park	1,287	1,278
	Outhwaite Homes[2]	1,028	1,005
	Cedar Apartments	654	16
(Euclid)	Lake Shore Village	800	2
Columbus	Poindexter Village	426	
Dayton	Desoto Bass Courts[2]	510	
Hamilton	Bambo Harris Homes	141	51
Lorain	Fulton Homes	60	
(Elyria)	Riverside Homes	40	
Massillon	Walnut Hills	300	20
Portsmouth	G.W. Failey Square	135	112
Sandusky	Fairlawn Court	100	
Toledo	Branch Whitlock Homes[2]	376	
	Albertus Brown Homes	134	
	Port Lawrence Homes	195	178
Warren	Trumbull Homes	224	38
Youngstown	Westlake Terrace Homes	618	218
Zanesville	Coopermill Manor	324	22
West Virginia			
Charleston	Washington Manor	304	127
Huntington	Washington Square	80	

[Continued]

★ 1171 ★

Permanent Public Housing Projects, 1945 – Region VIII
[Continued]

Location	Project name	Total no. units in project	Est. no. of units occupied by Negro tenants[1]
Mount Hope	Stadium Terrace	70	20
Williamson	Williamson Terrace	38	

Source: "Permanent Public Housing Projects Making Provision for Negro Tenants (As of July 31. 1945)," Jessie Parkhurst Guzman, ed., *Negro Year Book: A Review of Events Affecting Negro Life, 1941-1946*, p. 347. Notes: 1. This column used only for projects partially occupied by Negro tenants. 2. Two projects.

★ 1172 ★

Public Housing Projects

Permanent Public Housing Projects, 1945 – Rural Projects

Location	Project name	Total no. units in project	Est. no. of units occupied by Negro tenants[1]
Arkansas			
Lonoke	East Ark. Reg. Hous. Auth	74	7
Georgia			
Thomas Co.	Ga. S.W. Assoc. Hous. Auth.	140	13
Mississippi			
Lee County	Miss. Reg. Hous. Auth. No. 1	186	21
	Miss. Reg. Hous. Auth. No. 2	30	3
South Carolina			
Darlington County	Darlington County Rural	71	17

Source: "Permanent Public Housing Projects Making Provision for Negro Tenants (As of July 31. 1945)," Jessie Parkhurst Guzman, ed., *Negro Year Book: A Review of Events Affecting Negro Life, 1941-1946*, p. 348. Notes: 1. This column used only for projects partially occupied by Negro tenants.

★ 1173 ★

Public Housing Projects

Public Housing Programs: Characteristics, 1945

Program and construction status	Number of dwelling units		Percent Negro	Estimated development cost of dwelling units available for Negroes ($000)
	Total	Occupied by or programmed for Negroes		
Low-rent and war housing				
All dwelling units	769,131	145,584	18.9	536,624
Dwelling units under management	730,730	139,459	19.1	507,730
Dwelling units under development	33,401	6,125	16.0	28,894
Under contract	19,168	2,925	15.3	15,328
Not under contract	19,233	3,200	16.6	13,566
Low-rent housing (excluding, PWA limited dividend projects)[2] Dwelling units under management	132,602	46,522	35.1	219,182
War housing, including projects built under U.S. Housing Act, and transferred to war use				
All dwelling units	636,529	99,062	15.6	317,442
Dwelling units under management	598,128	92,937	15.5	288,548
New construction	548,758	90,336	16.5	284,133
Conversion management	49,370[3]	2,601	5.3	4,415
Dwelling units under development	38,401	6,125	16.0	28,894
Under contract	19,168	2,925	15.3	15,328
Not under contract	19,233	3,200	16.6	13,566

Source: "Public Housing Programmed for or Occupied by Negroes, by Type of Program and Construction Status of Dwelling Units (as of July 31, 1945)," Jessie Parkhurst Guzman, ed., *Negro Year Book: A Review of Events Affecting Negro Life, 1941-1946*, 1947, p. 341. *Notes:* 1. Based on number of assigned units where definitely programmed for Negro tenants. For all other projects, with 95 percent occupancy or more, based on number of occupied units, and for projects with less than 95 percent occupancy, on proportion of total occupied units occupied by negroes. 2. All units under management. 3. Data as of June, not available for July.

Rural Housing

★ 1174 ★

Tenant-purchase Borrowers, 1943

Region and state	All borrowers 1943	White	Negro		Negro as percent of all tenants 1940
			Number	Percent	
United States	29,502	25,372	4,130	14	21
Four Southern Regions	21,196	17,271	3,925	19	35
Region IV	5,112	4,601	511	10	20
Kentucky	783	783	0	0	3
North Carolina	2,077	1,724	353	17	33
Tennessee	1,277	1,226	51	4	21
Virginia	670	563	107	16	27
West Virginia	305	304	1	-	1
Region V					
Alabama	7,484	5,736	1,721	33	43
Florida	2,423	1,817	606	25	42
Georgia	3,099	2,541	558	18	38
South Carolina	1,715	1,200	515	30	57
Region VI	5,406	4,000	1,406	26	58
Arkansas	1,770	959	811	15	40
Louisiana	1,142	834	308	27	54
Mississippi	2,494	1,646	848	34	71
Region VIII	3,194	2,097	287	9	13
Oklahoma	1,332	1,252	80	6	0
Texas	1,682	1,676	186	10	16

Source: "Tenant-purchase Borrowers, By Color, 1943," Jessie Parkhurst Guzman, ed., *Negro Year Book: A Review of Events Affecting Negro Life, 1941-1946,* 1947, p. 179. Primary source: United States Department of Agriculture, Farm Security Administration. Release No. 12, 1943. Family Progress Report. 16th Census of the U.S. Agriculture ch. III, Vol. III.

Tenure

★ 1175 ★

Dwelling Units: Metropolitan Districts, 1947

District	Total occupied	White occupied		Nonwhite occupied	
		Owner number	Tenant number	Owner number	Tenant number
New York City	2,662,875	636,525	1,814,400	25,650	186,300
Northeastern New Jersey	938,016	428,544	461,376	13,248	34,848
Chicago, IL	1,334,025	490,875	731,885	25,025	86,240
Philadelphia, PA	939,057	524,964	301,185	34,047	78,861
Washington, DC	343,440	117,448	157,940	18,444	49,608
Baltimore, MD	354,526	166,983	124,424	13,287	49,852
Detroit, MI	750,182	375,688	291,128	27,956	55,430
Atlanta, GA	136,899	56,334	40,139	10,414	30,012
Memphis, TN	111,383	35,836	30,287	14,880	30,380
Birmingham, AL	135,356	48,564	32,338	18,050	56,404
Norfolk, Portsmouth, Newport News, VA	133,292	42,723	53,251	11,469	25,850
Pittsburgh, PA	556,645	275,959	246,945	8,476	25,265
New Orleans	167,440	47,208	75,768	8,344	36,120
St. Louis, MO	461,846	200,508	194,348	14,784	52,206
Dallas, TX	144,276	73,040	50,028	7,920	13,288
San Antonio, TX	112,778	63,920	41,208	4,284	3,366
Columbus, OH	123,697	60,475	53,505	4,018	5,699
Tulsa, OK	64,848	35,889	22,806	2,856	3,297

Source: "Dwelling Units by Tenure and Color, by Percent of Total, for 19 Metropolitan Districts, 1947." Florence Murray, ed., *The Negro Handbook, 1949*, p. 185. Published, by permission. Primary source: U.S. Bureau of the Census.

★ 1176 ★

Tenure

Urban and Rural-Nonfarm Dwellings: by Race, 1947

Subject	Color of occupants	
	White number	Nonwhite number
Total	29,511,000	2,843,000
TENURE		
Owner-occupied	16,071,000	954,000
Tenant-occupied	13,440,000	1,889,000
REPAIR AND PLUMBING EQUIPMENT		
With private bath and private flush toilet	23,774,000	1,206,000

[Continued]

★ 1176 ★

Urban and Rural-Nonfarm Dwellings: by Race, 1947
[Continued]

Subject	Color of occupants	
	White number	Nonwhite number
No private bath or private flush toilet	5,737,000	1,637,000
In good condition or in need of minor repairs	27,810,000	2,134,000
With private bath and private flush toilet	23,145,000	1,104,000
No private bath or private flush toilet	4,665,000	1,030,000
In need of major repairs	1,701,000	709,000
With private bath and private flush toilet	629,000	102,000
No private bath or private flush toilet	1,072,000	607,000
CENTRAL HEATING		
With central heating	17,618,000	801,000
Without central heating	11,893,000	2,042,000
ELECTRIC LIGHTING		
With electric lighting	28,918,000	2,281,000
Without electric lighting	593,000	562,000
INSTALLED COOKING FACILITIES		
With installed cooking facilities	28,911,000	2,640,000
Without installed cooking facilities[1]	600,000	203,000
DESIGNATED FACILITIES		
Having all designated facilities[2]	23,523,000	1,177,000
Lacking one or more designated facilities	5,988,000	1,666,000
NUMBER OF ROOMS		
1 room	522,000	110,000
2 rooms	1,907,000	358,000
3 rooms	3,798,000	688,000
4 rooms	5,831,000	738,000
5 rooms	6,946,000	458,000
6 or more rooms	10,507,000	491,000
Median number of rooms	4.88	3.86
PERSONS PER ROOM		
0.50 or less	10,619,000	680,000
0.51 to 1.50	17,610,000	1,736,000
1.51 or more	1,282,000	427,000
MONTHLY RENT[3]		
Under $10	649,000	453,000
$10 or $19	2,384,000	654,000
$20 to $29	3,221,000	364,000
$30 to $39	3,207,000	235,000
$40 to $49	2,167,000	93,000

[Continued]

★ 1176 ★

Urban and Rural-Nonfarm Dwellings: by Race, 1947

[Continued]

Subject	Color of occupants	
	White number	Nonwhite number
$50 or more	1,812,000	90,000
Median monthly rent (dollars)	30.95	17.02

Source: "Characteristics of Urban and Rural-Nonfarm Ordinary Occupied Dwelling Units, by Color of Occupants, April 1947," Florence Murray, ed., *The Negro Handbook, 1949*, p. 184. Published by permission. Primary source: U.S. Bureau of the Census. *Notes:* 1. Includes dwelling units with shared cooking facilities. 2. Electric lighting and running water; flush toilet, bathtub or shower, and installed cooking facilities for exclusive use of unit's occupants. 3. Data are for tenant-occupied dwelling units only.

War Housing

★ 1177 ★

War Housing Units, 1941-1946

War locality	Units for Negroes	Total number of units
Portland-Vancouver	6,191	34,678
Detroit	5,619	13,270
San Francisco, San Pablo Bay	5,611	24,797
District of Columbia	5,176	26,730
San Francisco, East Bay	4,784	13,753
Norfolk-Portsmouth	4,320	18,309
Chicago	4,147	4,881
Los Angeles	3,825	20,938
Baltimore	3,359	11,421
Cleveland	3,209	6,031
San Francisco, West Bay	3,205	14,274

Source: "War Housing Units," Jessie Parkhurst Guzman, ed., *Negro Year Book: A Review of Events Affecting Negro Life, 1941-1946*, 1947, p. 341.

Chapter 8
INCOME, SPENDING, AND WEALTH

Income/Earnings

★ 1178 ★

Amount: Earnings and Other Income of Wage and Salary Workers, 1939

Wage or Salary Income and Receipt of Other Income in 1939	Number of Wage or Salary Workers			
	United States		The South	
	White	Nonwhite[1]	White	Nonwhite
Without other income	28,401,820	3,325,060	6,086,340	2,393,240
None	1,406,540	185,180	288,200	118,400
$1 to $999	15,280,020	2,993,760	3,843,080	2,270,620
$1,000 to $1,999	9,593,640	277,120	1,650,020	93,660
$2,000 to $4,999	3,044,540	21,960	504,140	6,760
$5,000 and over	197,560	1,020	29,800	420
Not reported	286,160	31,200	59,300	21,780
Median Wage or Salary income for persons with $1 or more	964	371	782	307
With other income	6,027,320	568,220	1,305,600	349,160
None	953,880	127,840	201,760	60,080
$1 to $999	2,410,560	351,120	584,360	238,000
$1,000 to $1,999	1,267,880	26,740	238,740	7,380
$2,000 to $4,999	655,500	3,180	135,260	1,040
$5,000 and over	157,220	300	29,140	200
Not Reported	510,280	59,040	116,340	42,460
Median Wage or Salary income for persons with $1 or more	893	318	774	245

Source: "Number of Persons who were Wage or Salary Workers (Except on Emergency Work) by Wage and Salary Income and Receipt of Other Income in 1939, for the United States and in the South," *The Negro Handbook, 1944*, 1944, p. 154. Primary source: Compiled from Statistics of the 1940 Census, Based on a 5 per cent sample. *Notes:* Statistics for persons for whom the receipt or nonreceipt of other income was not reported are combined with those persons with other income of $50 or more. 1. More than 95 per cent of the nonwhite population is Negro.

★ 1179 ★

Income/Earnings

Black Median Income in Low-Income Areas, 1970-1971

Subject	Low-income areas in--							
	Total urban areas[1]	New York	Chicago	Detroit	Philadelphia	Washington, D.C.	Los Angeles	Baltimore
INCOME								
Year-round full-time workers (thousands)	1,548	266	135	82	105	106	57	82
Median annual earnings:								
Male	$6,390	$6,448	$6,602	$7,895	$6,611	$6,650	$7,102	$6,207
Female	4,334	5,254	4,657	4,457	4,279	5,174	4,844	4,129

Source: "Characteristics of the Black Population in Selected Low-Income Areas," Current Population Reports, Special Studies, Series P-23, No. 42. *The Social and Economic Status of the Black Population in the United States, 1971,* 1972, p. 139. Primary source: U.S. Department of Commerce, Social and Economic Statistics Administration, Bureau of the Census. *Notes:* Statistics on low-income areas are based on information gathered in the Census Employment Survey (CES) conducted as part of the overall program of the 1970 Census of Population and Housing. 1. Includes selected low-income areas in 44 other cities, not shown separately.

★ 1180 ★

Income/Earnings

Blacks and Whites Below the Low-Income Level, 1959-1974

[Persons as of the following year]

Year	Number (thousands)			Percent below the low-income level[1]		
	Black and other races	Black	White	Black and other races	Black	White
1959	10,430	9,927	28,336	53.3	55.1	18.1
1960	11,542	(NA)	28,309	55.9	(NA)	17.8
1961	11,738	(NA)	27,890	56.1	(NA)	17.4
1962	11,953	(NA)	26,672	55.8	(NA)	16.4
1963	11,198	(NA)	25,238	51.0	(NA)	15.3
1964	11,098	(NA)	24,957	49.6	(NA)	14.9
1965	10,689	(NA)	22,496	47.1	(NA)	13.3
1966[2]	9,220	8,867	19,290	39.8	41.8	11.3
1967	8,786	8,486	18,983	37.2	39.3	11.0
1968	7,994	7,616	17,395	33.5	34.7	10.0
1969[3]	7,488	7,095	16,659	31.0	32.2	9.5
1970[3]	7,936	7,548	17,484	32.0	33.5	9.9
1971[3]	7,780	7,396	17,780	30.9	32.5	9.9
1972[3]	8,257	7,710	16,203	31.9	33.3	9.0

[Continued]

★ 1180 ★

Blacks and Whites Below the Low-Income Level, 1959-1974

[Continued]

Year	Number (thousands)			Percent below the low-income level[1]		
	Black and other races	Black	White	Black and other races	Black	White
1973[3]	7,831	7,388	15,142	29.6	31.4	8.4
1974[3]	7,970	7,467	16,290	29.5	31.4	8.9

Source: "Persons Below the Low-Income Level: 1959 to 1974," Current Population Reports, Special Studies, Series P-23, No. 54. *The Social and Economic Status of the Black Population in the United States, 1974,* 1975, p. 42. Primary source: U.S. Department of Commerce, Social and Economic Statistics Administration, Bureau of the Census. *Notes:* NA available. 1. The low-income threshold for a nonfarm family of four was $5,038 in 1974, $4,540 in 1973, and $2,973 in 1959. Families and unrelated individuals are classified as being above or below the low-income threshold, using the poverty index adopted by a Federal Interagency Committee in 1969. 2. Beginning with the March 1967 CPS, data based on revised methodology for processing income data. 3. Based on 1970 census population controls; therefore, not strictly comparable to data for earlier years.

★ 1181 ★

Income/Earnings

Female Median Income by Age, 1969

Age	Number with income (thousands)		Median income, 1969 (dollars)		Ratio, Negro to white median income
	Negro	White	Negro	White	
Total	1,718	13,541	$4,126	$5,182	80
14 to 19 years	24	333	(B)	3,423	(B)
20 to 24 years	217	1,996	3,926	4,714	83
25 to 34 years	452	2,294	4,439	5,496	81
35 to 44 years	450	2,644	4,556	5,314	86
45 to 54 years	359	3,452	3,818	5,423	70
55 to 64 years	192	2,386	3,701	5,283	70
65 years and over	24	436	(B)	4,841	(B)

Source: "Median Income of Female Year-Round Full-Time Workers, by Age: 1969," Current Population Reports, Special Studies, Series P-23, No. 38. *The Social and Economic Status of the Black Population in the United States, 1970,* 1970, p. 124. Primary source: U.S. Department of Commerce, Bureau of the Census. *Note:* B Base less than 75,000.

★ 1182 ★

Income/Earnings

Median Earnings by Occupational Groups, 1973

[Persons as of the following year]

Occupation	Men		Women		Ratio: Black to white	
	Black	White	Black	White	Men	Women
ALL WORKERS						
Total, with earnings	$5,785	$9,046	$3,030	$3,299	0.64	0.92
Professional, technical, and kindred workers	9,668	13,142	7,543	6,790	0.74	1.11
Managers and administrators, except farm	9,394	13,831	8,021	5,605	0.68	1.43
Farmers and farm managers	(B)	5,590	(B)	1,408	(B)	(B)
Clerical and kindred workers	8,007	8,905	4,170	4,409	0.90	0.95
Sales workers	4,270	8,952	1,405	1,637	0.48	0.86
Craft and kindred workers	7,346	10,111	4,446	4,357	0.73	1.02
Operatives, including transport workers	6,539	7,985	3,629	3,618	0.82	1.00
Private household workers	(B)	(B)	1,072	364	(B)	2.95
Service workers, except private household	4,562	4,609	2,773	1,663	0.99	1.67
Farm laborers and supervisors	855	1,384	370	463	0.62	0.80
Laborers, except farm	4,052	3,146	(B)	1,938	1.29	(B)
YEAR-ROUND FULL-TIME WORKERS						
Total, with earnings	7,880	11,516	5,487	6,434	0.68	0.85
Professional, technical, and kindred workers	10,682	14,455	9,015	9,076	0.74	0.99
Managers and administrators, except farm	11,498	14,662	(B)	7,602	0.78	(B)
Farmers and farm managers	(B)	6,824	(B)	(B)	(B)	(B)
Clerical and kindred managers	9,241	10,811	6,522	6,462	0.85	1.01
Sales workers	(B)	12,415	(B)	4,632	(B)	(B)
Craft and kindred workers	8,857	11,387	(B)	6,224	0.78	(B)
Operatives, including transport workers	7,830	9,782	4,824	5,449	0.80	0.89
Private household workers	(B)	(B)	2,232	1,827	(B)	1.22
Service workers, except private household	6,397	8,618	4,595	4,577	0.74	1.00
Farm laborers and supervisors	(B)	5,104	(B)	(B)	(B)	(B)
Laborers, except farm	6,554	8,423	(B)	4,722	0.78	(B)

Source: "Median Earnings in 1973 of Civilians 14 Years Old and Over, by Occupation of Longest Job, Work Experience, and Sex," Current Population Reports, Special Studies, Series P-23, No. 54. *The Social and Economic Status of the Black Population in the United States, 1974,* 1975, p. 80. Primary source: U.S. Department of Commerce, Social and Economic Statistics Administration, Bureau of the Census. *Note:* B Base too small for figure to be shown.

★ 1183 ★

Income/Earnings

Median Income of 25- to 54-Year-Old Men by Level of Education, 1968 and 1969

Years of School Completed	Median Income 1968		Negro Income as a percent of white	Median income 1969		Negro Income as a percent of white
	Negro	White		Negro	White	
Elementary:						
Total	$3,900	$5,844	67	[1]	[1]	[1]
Less than 8	3,558	5,131	69	$3,922	$5,509	71
8 years	4,499	6,452	70	4,472	7,018	64
High school:						
Total	5,580	7,852	71	[1]	[1]	[1]
1 to 3 years	5,255	7,229	73	5,327	7,812	68
4 years	5,801	8,154	71	6,192	8,829	70
College:						
1 to 3 years	7,481[2]	10,149[2]	74	7,427	9,831	76
4 years or more	---	---	---	8,669	12,354	70

Source: Adapted by the editors from "Median Income of Men 25 to 54 Years Old, by Educational Attainment, 1968," Current Population Reports, Special Studies, Series P-23, No. 29. *The Social and Economic Status of the Black Population in the United States, 1969,* 1972, p. 21; and Current Population Reports, Special Studies, Series P-23, No. 38. *The Social and Economic Status of the Black Population in the United States, 1970,* 1970, p. 34. Primary source: U.S. Department of Commerce, Social and Economic Statistics Administration, Bureau of the Census. *Notes:* 1. Not reported for 1969. 2. Reported as "1 or more years" in 1968.

★ 1184 ★

Income/Earnings

Median Income of Females 25 and over by Level of Education, 1969

Years of school completed	Women 25 years and over, 1970 (thousands)		Median income, 1969 (dollars)	
	Negro	White	Negro	White
Total, 25 years and over	4,397	33,402	$2,078	$2,513
Elementary:				
Less than 8 years	1,261	4,028	1,195	1,303
8 years	496	4,447	1,320	1,688
High school:				
1 to 3 years	1,075	5,562	2,268	2,355
4 years	1,054	12,673	3,257	3,234
College:				
1 to 3 years	285	3,395	4,247	3,427
4 years or more	226	3,296	6,747	5,707

[Continued]

★ 1184 ★

Median Income of Females 25 and over by Level of Education, 1969
[Continued]

Years of school completed	Women 25 years and over, 1970 (thousands)		Median income, 1969 (dollars)	
	Negro	White	Negro	White
Increase (amount) in median income: College 4 years or more over elementary 8 years	(X)	(X)	5,427	4,019
College 4 years or more over high school 4 years	(X)	(X)	3,485	2,473

Source: "Median Income of Women 25 Years Old and Over, by Educational Attainment: 1969," Current Population Reports, Special Studies, Series P- 23, No. 38. *The Social and Economic Status of the Black Population in the United States, 1970*, 1970, p. 125. Primary source: U.S. Department of Commerce, Bureau of the Census. *Note:* X Not applicable.

★ 1185 ★

Income/Earnings

Median Income of Full- and Part-Time Workers in 1973
[Persons 14 years old and over as of following year]

Work experience	Men			Women		
	Black	White	Ratio: Black to white	Black	White	Ratio: Black to white
Worked at full-time job	$6,630	$10,184	0.65	$4,107	$4,967	0.83
50 to 52 weeks	7,880	11,516	0.68	5,487	6,434	0.85
40 to 49 weeks	5,744	7,799	0.74	4,017	4,409	0.91
27 to 39 weeks	4,935	5,578	0.83	2,855	3,222	0.89
14 to 26 weeks	2,186	2,919	0.75	1,656	1,979	0.84
1 to 13 weeks	584	956	0.61	478	593	0.81
Worked at part-time job	782	1,092	0.72	802	981	0.82
50 to 52 weeks	2,134	1,962	1.09	1,479	2,108	0.70
40 to 49 weeks	(B)	2,140	(B)	1,699	1,778	0.96
27 to 39 weeks	(B)	1,555	(B0	1,345	1,391	0.97
14 to 26 weeks	719	931	0.77	657	789	0.83
1 to 13 weeks	306	353	0.87	303	319	0.95

Source: "Median Earnings of Persons with Work Experience in 1973, by Sex," Current Population Reports, Special Studies, Series P-23, No. 54. *The Social and Economic Status of the Black Population in the United States, 1974*, 1975, p. 81. Primary source: U.S. Department of Commerce, Social and Economic Statistics Administration, Bureau of the Census. *Note:* B Base too small for figure to be shown.

Income/Earnings

Median Income of Year-Round Workers, 1970-1974
[In current dollars]

Subject	Men		Women	
	Total	Year-round full-time workers	Total	Year-round full-time workers
BLACK				
1970	$4,157	$6,435	$2,063	$4,536
1971	4,316	6,771	2,145	5,092
1972	4,733	7,373	2,444	5,280
1973	5,113	7,953	2,548	5,595
1974				
United States	5,370	8,705	2,806	6,371
South	4,306	7,411	2,193	5,440
North and West	6,874	10,491	3,643	7,402
WHITE				
1970	$7,011	$9,447	$2,266	$5,536
1971	7,237	9,902	2,448	5,767
1972	7,814	10,918	2,616	6,172
1973	8,453	11,800	2,823	6,598
1974				
United States	8,794	12,434	3,133	7,021
South	7,988	11,508	2,952	6,393
North and West	9,161	12,782	3,207	7,330
RATIO: BLACK TO WHITE				
1970	0.59	0.68	0.91	0.82
1971	0.60	0.68	0.88	0.88
1972	0.61	0.68	0.93	0.86
1973	0.61	0.67	0.90	0.85

Source: "Median Income, 1970 to 1974, of Persons 14 Years Old and Over, by Sex, Work Experience, and Region," Current Population Reports, Special Studies, Series P-23, No. 54. *The Social and Economic Status of the Black Population in the United States, 1974,* 1975, p. 28. Primary source: U.S. Department of Commerce, Social and Economic Statistics Administration, Bureau of the Census.

★ 1187 ★

Income/Earnings

Money Earned: Median Individual Income in 1974 Dollars, 1947-1974

[Prior to 1960, excludes Alaska and Hawaii.]

YEAR	ALL RACES Unrelated individuals	WHITE Unrelated individuals	NEGRO AND OTHER RACES Unrelated individuals	NEGRO AND OTHER RACES COMPARED WITH WHITE	
				Ratio[1] Unrelated individuals	Absolute difference in medians Unrelated individuals
1947	$2,164	$2,285	$1,647	0.72	-$638
1950	2,141	2,284	1,674	0.73	-610
1955	2,424	2,582	1,722	0.67	-860
1960	2,864	3,097	1,772	0.57	-1,325
1965	3,365	3,510	2,562	0.73	-948
1970	3,984	4,169	2,849	0.68	-1,320
1972	4,151	4,334	3,219	0.74	-1,115
1973	4,588	4,738	3,541	0.75	-1,197
1974	4,439	4,636	3,149	0.68	-1,487

Source: "Median Income in Constant (1974) Dollars of Families and Individuals, by Race: 1947 to 1974," *Statistical Abstract of the United States, 1975,* p. 391. Primary source: U.S. Bureau of the Census, *Current Population Reports,* series P-60, No. 101 and earlier issues. *Notes:* 1. Ratios may differ from those calculated from current dollar distributions because of interpolation differences introduced in the derivation of constant dollar distribution.

★ 1188 ★

Income/Earnings

Money Earned: Median income of Wage/Salary Workers, 1939-1974

[In current dollars]

Subject	Black and other races		White	Ratio:	
	Total	Black		Black and other races to White	Black to White
ALL PERSONS WITH WAGE OR SALARY INCOME					
Men					
1939[1]	$460	(NA)	$1,112	0.41	(NA)
1947	1,279	(NA)	2,357	0.54	(NA)
1953	2,233	(NA)	3,760	0.59	(NA)
1959	2,844	(NA)	4,902	0.58	(NA)
1964	3,426	(NA)	5,853	0.59	(NA)
1969	5,237	$5,130	7,859	0.67	0.65
1974	7,617	7,407	10,745	0.71	0.69

[Continued]

★ 1188 ★

Money Earned: Median income of Wage/Salary Workers, 1939-1974
[Continued]

Subject	Black and other races		White	Ratio: Black and other races to White	Ratio: Black to White
	Total	Black			
Women					
1939[1]	$246	(NA)	$676	0.36	(NA)
1947	432	(NA)	1,269	0.34	(NA)
1953	994	(NA)	2,049	0.49	(NA)
1959	1,289	(NA)	2,422	0.53	(NA)
1964	1,652	(NA)	2,841	0.58	(NA)
1969	2,884	$2,808	3,640	0.79	0.77
1974	4,751	4,607	4,863	0.98	0.95
YEAR-ROUND FULL-TIME WORKERS					
WITH WAGE OR SALARY INCOME					
Men					
1939	$639	(NA)	$1,419	0.45	(NA)
1959	3,339	(NA)	5,456	0.61	(NA)
1964	4,285	(NA)	6,497	0.66	(NA)
1969	6,158	$5,982	8,876	0.69	0.67
1974	9,082	8,703	12,343	0.74	0.71
Women					
1939	$327	(NA)	$863	0.38	(NA)
1959	2,196	(NA)	3,306	0.66	(NA)
1964	2,674	(NA)	3,859	0.69	(NA)
1969	4,231	$4,102	5,168	0.82	0.79
1974	6,611	6,445	7,025	0.94	0.92

Source: "Median Wage or Salary Income of Wage and Salary Workers for Selected Years: 1939 to 1974," *The Social and Economic Status of the Black Population in the United States: An Historical View, 1790-1978,* 1979, p. 48. Primary source: U.S. Department of Commerce, Bureau of the Census. *Notes:* NA Not available. Data for 1939 are based on the 1940 decennial census; all other data are based on Current Population Surveys. Data on year-round full-time workers with wage or salary income have only been tabulated in the Current Population Survey on an intermittent basis. 1. Excludes public emergency workers but includes members of the Armed Forces.

★ 1189 ★

Income/Earnings

Money Earned: Minority Median Household Per Capita Income in Relation to Majority Per Capita Income, 1959, 1969, and 1975

	Raw Measure			Social Indicator Values (Ratios of raw measures to the majority population)		
	1959	1969	1975	1959	1969	1975
For All Households						
Amer. Ind./Alask. Nat.	$467	$1122	$2453	.32	.43	.57[1]
Blacks	680	1303	2263	.46	.50	.52
Mexican Americans	742	1334	2130	.50	.51	.49
Japanese Americans	1680	3184	6105	1.14	1.22	1.41
Chinese Americans	1416	2449	3867	.96	.94	.89
Philipino Americans	1145	2208	3897	.78	.85	.90
Puerto Ricans	869	1362	2153	.59	.52	.50
Majority	1472	2601	4333	1.00	1.00	1.00
For Female-Headed Households						
Amer. Ind./Alask. Nat.	378	711	1310	.26	.27	.30
Blacks	399	783	1310	.27	.30	.30
Mexican Americans	428	808	1228	.29	.31	.28
Japanese Americans	1168	2051	2341	.79	.79	.54
Chinese Americans	1309	2163	1778	.89	.83	.41
Philipino Americans	569	999	2333	.39	.38	.54
Puerto Ricans	716	759	1252	.49	.29	.29
Majority	1099	1658	2563	.75	.64	.59

Source: "Median Household Per Capita Income," *Social Indicators of Equality for Minorities and Women*, 1978, p. 50. Primary source: U.S. Commission on Civil Rights. *Social Indicators of Equality for Minorities and Women*. Washington, D.C.: 1978. *Notes:* 1. This can be interpreted as follows: "In 1975 members of American Indian and Alaskan Native headed households had a median household per capital income that was 57 percent as much as the median for members of majority-headed households."

★ 1190 ★

Income/Earnings

Money Earned: Original and Adjusted Minority Mean Earnings in Relation to Majority Male Earnings, 1959, 1969, and 1975

	Original means			Original Ratios (group/majority males)			Adjusted Means (group/majority males)			Earnings Ratios for Adjusted Means		
	1959	1969	1975	1959	1969	1975	1959	1969	1975	1959	1969	1975
Males												
Amer. Ind./Alask. Nat.	$2878	$5623	$8302	.54	.62	.73[2]	$3926	$7097	$10575	.73	.78	.92[3]
Blacks	2808	5434	7470	.52	.59	.65	3793	6885	9741	.71	.75	.85
Mexican Americans	3412	5852	7456	.64	.64	.65	4527	7219	9414	.84	.79	.82
Japanese Americans	5142	9159	12615	.96	1.00	1.10	4490	8363	9999	.84	.91	.88
Chinese Americans	4771	8001	10339	.89	.87	.90	4465	7430	8817	.83	.81	.77
Philipino Americans	3603	6852	11366	.67	.75	.99	3707	7550	11874	.69	.82	1.04
Puerto Ricans	3200	5839	8269	.60	.64	.72	4654	7776	11233	.87	.85	.98
Majority	5369	9150	11427	1.00	1.00	1.00	5369	9150	11427	1.00	1.00	1.00

[Continued]

★ 1190 ★

Money Earned: Original and Adjusted Minority Mean Earnings in Relation to Majority Male Earnings, 1959, 1969, and 1975

[Continued]

	Original means			Original Ratios (group/majority males)			Adjusted Means (group/majority males)			Earnings Ratios for Adjusted Means		
	1959	1969	1975	1959	1969	1975	1959	1969	1975	1959	1969	1975
Females												
Amer. Ind./Alask. Nat.	$1924	$3378	$3958	.36	.37	.35	$2824	$4683	$6136	.53	.51	.54
Blacks	1566	3383	4918	.29	.37	.43	2502	4707	6973	.47	.51	.61
Mexican Americans	1790	3030	3527	.33	.33	.31	2572	4298	5525	.48	.47	.48
Japanese Americans	2550	4618	5881	.48	.50	.51	2911	5303	6670	.54	.58	.58
Chinese Americans	2639	4366	6759	.49	.48	.59	3163	5348	7960	.59	.58	.70
Philipino Americans	2268	4499	6784	.42	.49	.59	2862	4996	6712	.53	.55	.59
Puerto Ricans	2244	4071	4714	.42	.44	.41	2958	5060	6468	.55	.55	.57
Majority	2686	4072	5122	.50	.44	.45	3039	4958	6568	.57	.54	.57

Source: "Adjusted Mean Earnings for Those with Earnings," *Social Indicators of Equality for Minorities and Women*, 1978, p. 54. Primary source: U.S. Commission on Civil Rights. *Social Indicators of Equality for Minorities and Women*. Washington, D.C.: 1978. *Notes:* 1. The adjusted technique substitutes the majority male mean values in a regression equation for the following variables: occupational prestige, age, education, weeks worked, hours worked last week, and the average income in the State of residence. 2. This can be interpreted as follows: "In 1975, American Indian and Alaskan Native males earned, on the average, 73 percent of the majority male average earnings." 3. This can be interpreted as follows: "In 1975, American Indian and Alaskan Native males with the same characteristics as majority males (in terms of occupational prestige, age, education, weeks worked, hours worked last week, and State of residence) could be expected to earn 92 percent of the amount that majority males earned."

★ 1191 ★

Income/Earnings

Money Earned: Percent Distribution of Individual Income in 1974 Dollars, 1970-1974 - I

[Prior to 1960, excludes Alaska and Hawaii.]

ITEM AND INCOME LEVEL	WHITE						
	1950	1955	1960	1965	1970	1973	1974
UNRELATED INDIVIDUALS							
Under $1,500	39.0	34.5	28.8	21.7	15.3	11.1	9.2
$1,500-$2,999	18.2	20.5	20.7	23.3	23.7	21.4	23.6
$3,000-$4,999	17.3	16.2	15.2	15.8	17.4	20.3	20.3
$5,000-$6,999	14.4	13.7	13.2	11.8	12.0	13.4	13.7
$7,000-$9,999	8.1	9.8	13.7	13.4	13.6	13.6	14.2
$10,000-$14,999	3.1[1]	4.0	6.5	9.7	11.6	12.6	12.5
$15,000 and over	3.1[1]	1.4	1.9	4.3	6.4	7.6	6.4

Source: "Money Income—Percent Distribution of Families and Individuals, by Income Level and Race, in Constant (1974) Dollars: 1950 to 1974," *Statistical Abstract of the United States, 1975*, p. 390. Primary source: U.S. Bureau of the Census, *Current Populaton Reports*, series P-60, No. 101. *Note:* 1. Data includes income levels from $10,000 and over.

★ 1192 ★

Income/Earnings

Money Earned: Percent Distribution of Individual Income in 1974 Dollars, 1970-1974 - II

[Prior to 1960, excludes Alaska and Hawaii.]

ITEM AND INCOME LEVEL	NEGRO AND OTHER RACES						
	1950	1955	1960	1965	1970	1973	1974
UNRELATED INDIVIDUALS							
Under $1,500	49.3	47.0	44.7	30.6	26.3	20.2	16.6
$1,500-$2,999	20.6	22.6	19.8	24.6	25.7	24.2	31.4
$3,000-$4,999	17.8	18.7	15.8	16.8	17.1	16.9	15.6
$5,000-$6,999	7.9	7.6	8.4	10.9	11.0	11.4	13.1
$7,000-$9,999	3.4	3.5	8.6	11.4	11.2	13.3	12.4
$10,000-$14,999	1.1[1]	0.4	2.1	4.9	7.5	9.8	7.6
$15,000 and over	1.1[1]	0.2	0.7	0.7	1.2	4.1	3.2

Source: "Money Income—Percent Distribution of Families and Individuals, by Income Level and Race, in Constant (1974) Dollars: 1950 to 1974," *Statistical Abstract of the United States, 1975*, p. 390. Primary source: U.S. Bureau of the Census, *Current Population Reports*, series P-60, No. 101. *Note:* 1. Data includes income levels from $10,000 and over.

★ 1193 ★

Income/Earnings

Money Earned: Percent Distribution of Individual Income in Constant 1968 Dollars, 1950-1968

[Prior to 1960, excludes Alaska and Hawaii.]

ITEM AND INCOME LEVEL	WHITE					NEGRO AND OTHER RACES				
	1950	1955	1960	1965	1968	1950	1955	1960	1965	1968
Unrelated individuals	100.0	100.0	100.0	100.0	100.0	100.0	100.0	100.0	100.0	100.0
Under $1,500	48.4	44.0	38.6	32.6	27.2	59.0	57.2	55.2	42.8	39.5
$1,500-$2,999	19.0	21.4	21.2	23.5	23.3	21.5	24.4	19.9	24.3	22.9
$3,000-$4,999	21.7	19.6	18.3	16.8	19.1	15.2	14.3	13.8	15.8	17.8
$5,000-$6,999	7.6	9.2	13.0	12.7	12.2	3.1	3.1	8.2	10.9	10.7
$7,000-$9,999	2.1	4.1	6.2	9.3	10.6	1.2	0.7	2.1	5.3	7.1
$10,000 and over	1.2	1.6	2.4	5.1	7.5	-	0.1	0.8	1.0	2.0
Median income	$1,613	$1,830	$2,187	$2,478	$2,952	$1,190	$1,264	$1,332	$1,847	$1,999
Ratio, Negro and other to white	(X)	(X)	(X)	(X)	(X)	0.74	0.69	0.61	0.75	0.68

Source: "Money Income—Percent Distribution of Families and Unrelated Individuals, by Income Level and Race, in Constant (1968) Dollars: 1950 to 1968," *Statistical Abstract of the United States, 1970*, p. 322. Primary source: Dept. of Commerce, Bureau of the Census; *Current Population Reports*, Series P-20, and unpublished data. *Note:* - Represents zero. X Not applicable.

★ 1194 ★
Income/Earnings
Money Earned: Percent Distribution of Individual Income, by Region, 1966

INCOME LEVEL	FAMILIES							UNRELATED INDIVIDUALS		
	All races	United States		North and West		South		All races	White	Negro
		White	Negro	White	Negro	White	Negro			
Under $1,000	3.0	2.6	7.6	1.9	3.2	4.1	11.3	23.6	22.4	31.3
$1,000 to $1,999	6.1	5.2	14.5	4.1	7.4	8.1	20.6	24.7	24.5	27.4
$2,000 to $2,999	7.4	6.6	15.2	5.9	11.6	8.3	18.3	12.6	12.4	12.2
$3,000 to $3,999	7.8	7.2	14.5	6.6	13.3	8.6	15.6	9.2	9.3	8.4
$4,000 to $4,999	8.0	7.8	10.7	7.1	11.4	9.4	10.2	8.0	8.0	7.2
$5,000 to $5,999	9.3	9.4	9.2	9.1	11.1	10.1	7.5	7.0	7.1	5.9
$6,000 to $6,999	9.3	9.5	6.9	9.5	8.6	9.6	5.4	4.9	5.1	3.5
$7,000 to $9,999	24.1	25.3	13.1	26.2	20.0	22.6	7.2	6.9	7.4	3.1
$10,000 and over	24.9	26.6	8.3	29.3	13.3	19.1	4.0	3.3	3.7	0.9
Median income	$6,882	$7,170	$3,874	$7,546	$5,278	$6,141	$2,988	$2,110	$2,199	$1,555
Percent with income less than $3,000	16.5	14.4	37.3	11.9	22.2	20.5	50.2	60.9	59.3	71.0

Source: "Money Income—Percent Distribution of Families and Unrelated Individuals, by 1965 Income Levels, by Race and Region: 1966," *Statistical Abstract of the United States, 1967*, p. 335. Primary source: Dept. of Commerce, Bureau of the Census; *Current Population Reports*, Series P-20, forthcoming issue, series P-60, No. 51.

★ 1195 ★
Income/Earnings
People in Poverty and People Receiving Assistance, 1968
[In millions]

	Negro and other races	White
Total population	24.5	175.6
Below poverty level	8.0	17.4
Percent of total population	33	10
Receiving welfare	3.8	5.6
Percent of total population	16	3

Source: "Number and Percent of Persons Below the Poverty Level and of Persons Receiving Welfare, 1968," Current Population Reports, Special Studies, Series P-23, No. 29. *The Social and Economic Status of the Black Population in the United States, 1969*, 1969, p. 26. Primary source: U.S. Department of Commerce, Bureau of the Census; U.S. Department of Health, Education, and Welfare.

★ 1196 ★

Income/Earnings

Poverty: Geographical Distribution of "Paupers" in 1910

SECTION AND DIVISION	PAUPERS IN ALMSHOUSES: 1910			
	Enumerated on January 1		Admitted during the year	
	Negro	White	Negro	White
United States	6,281	77,734	6,807	81,135
The South	4,286	9,281	4,338	8,737
South Atlantic	2,578	5,122	2,971	4,969
East South Central	1,356	2,908	967	2,148
West South Central	352	1,251	400	1,650
The North	1,914	61,425	2,180	58,107
New England	178	11,703	246	14,459
Middle Atlantic	678	23,081	848	23,057
East North Central	716	20,626	822	16,277
West North Central	342	6,015	264	4,314
The West	81	7,028	289	14,291
Mountain	19	1,620	83	3,375
Pacific	62	5,408	206	10,916

Source: [Untitled Table], *Negro Population, 1790-1915*, 1918, p. 455. Primary source: U.S. Bureau of the Census. *Negro Population, 1790-1915.* Washington, D.C.: Government Printing Office, 1918.

★ 1197 ★

Income/Earnings

Poverty: Individuals Below Poverty Level and Income Deficit in 1975 Dollars, by Gender, 1970-1973

[Number in thousands; deficit in millions of 1973 dollars, except percent.]

FAMILY STATUS AND RACE	NUMBER BELOW LOW INCOME LEVEL					AGGREGATE INCOME DEFICIT (1973 dollars)				
	1959	1964	1970	1972	1973	1959	1964	1970	1972	1973
All persons	39,490	36,055	25,420	24,460	22,973	20,838	17,864	13,241	12,781	11,975
Percent	100.0	100.0	100.0	100.0	100.0	100.0	100.0	100.0	100.0	100.0
Unrelated individuals	12.5	14.3	20.0	20.0	20.3	28.2	30.1	35.4	36.7	36.4
Male	3.9	4.1	5.6	5.8	6.5	8.7	8.9	11.4	11.9	12.9
Female	8.5	10.2	14.4	14.2	13.8	19.5	21.2	24.0	24.8	23.5
White, total	28,484	24,957	17,484	16,203	15,142	14,953	12,724	9,416	8,934	8,224
Percent	100.0	100.0	100.0	100.0	100.0	100.0	100.0	100.0	100.0	100.0
Unrelated individuals	14.2	17.0	23.8	24.3	24.6	31.9	34.3	39.7	41.4	40.9
Male	4.1	4.4	6.2	6.3	7.2	9.0	9.2	11.9	12.2	13.0
Female	10.1	12.6	17.6	18.0	17.4	22.9	25.1	27.8	29.2	27.8
Negro and other	11,006	11,098	7,936	8,257	7,831	5,882	5,138	3,825	3,851	3,754
Percent	100.0	100.0	100.0	100.0	100.0	100.0	100.0	100.0	100.0	100.0
Unrelated individuals	8.1	8.1	11.7	11.5	12.1	18.9	19.7	24.9	25.9	26.7

[Continued]

★ 1197 ★

Poverty: Individuals Below Poverty Level and Income Deficit in 1975 Dollars, by Gender, 1970-1973
[Continued]

FAMILY STATUS AND RACE	NUMBER BELOW LOW INCOME LEVEL					AGGREGATE INCOME DEFICIT (1973 dollars)				
	1959	1964	1970	1972	1973	1959	1964	1970	1972	1973
Male	3.6	3.3	4.4	4.7	5.2	8.1	8.1	10.2	11.4	12.6
Female	4.5	4.9	7.3	6.8	6.9	10.8	11.6	14.7	14.5	14.1

Source: "Persons Below Low Income Level and Aggregate Income Deficit, by Race of Head and Family Status: 1959 to 1973," *Statistical Abstract of the United States, 1975,* p. 402. Primary source: U.S. Bureau of the Census, *Current Population Reports,* series P-60, No. 98 and earlier issues, and unpublished data.

★ 1198 ★
Income/Earnings

Poverty: Individuals Below Poverty Level, by Work Experience, 1968
[Number in thousands.]

CHARACTERISTIC	NUMBER OF POOR HOUSEHOLDS				INCIDENCE OF POVERTY[1]			
	Total	White	Negro and other races		Total	White	Negro and other races	
			Total	Negro			Total	Negro
UNRELATED INDIVIDUALS[3]								
Total[2]	4,694	3,849	845	777	34.0	32.2	45.7	46.3
Worked in 1968, total	1,494	1,109	385	360	17.7	15.5	30.0	30.8
At full-time jobs	857	638	219	202	12.4	10.8	21.5	21.7
50-52 weeks	384	263	120	115	7.7	6.2	16.6	17.2
At part-time jobs	637	471	167	158	41.4	37.0	63.3	66.1
Did not work in 1968	3,196	2,737	460	417	60.4	57.9	81.6	82.4

Source: "Families and Unrelated Individuals with Income Below Poverty Level, by Race and Work Experience of Head: 1968," *Statistical Abstract of the United States, 1970,* p. 330. Primary source: Dept. of Commerce, Bureau of the Census, *Current Population Reports,* series P-60, No. 68, and unpublished data. *Notes:* 1. Poor households as percent of total households in specified group. 2. Includes members of the Armed Forces, not shown separately by work experience. 3. 14 years old and over.

★ 1199 ★
Income/Earnings

Poverty: Individuals and Families Below Poverty Level, 1970-1974

FAMILY STATUS, RACE, AND SEX OF HEAD	NUMBER BELOW LOW INCOME LEVEL (millions)						PERCENT BELOW LOW INCOME LEVEL					
	1959	1965	1969	1970	1973	1974	1959	1965	1969	1970	1973	1974
All persons	39.5	33.2	24.1	25.4	23.0	24.3	22.4	17.3	12.1	12.6	11.1	11.6
In families	34.6	28.4	19.2	20.3	18.3	19.4	20.8	15.8	10.4	10.9	9.7	10.2
Head	8.3	6.7	5.0	5.3	4.8	5.1	18.5	13.9	9.7	10.1	8.8	9.2
Related children under 18 yr.	17.2	14.4	9.5	10.2	9.5	10.2	26.9	20.7	13.8	14.9	14.2	15.5
Other family members	9.0	7.2	4.7	4.8	4.0	4.1	15.9	11.8	7.2	7.4	5.9	6.0
Unrelated individuals	4.9	4.8	5.0	5.1	4.7	4.8	46.1	39.8	34.0	32.9	25.6	25.5
White	28.5	22.5	16.7	17.5	15.1	16.3	18.1	13.3	9.5	9.9	8.4	8.9
In families	24.4	18.5	12.6	13.3	11.4	12.5	16.5	11.7	7.8	8.1	6.9	7.5
Head	6.2	4.8	3.6	3.7	3.2	3.5	15.2	11.1	7.7	8.0	6.6	7.0
Related children under 18 yr.	11.4	8.6	5.7	6.1	5.5	6.2	20.6	14.4	9.7	10.5	9.7	11.2
Other family members	6.9	5.1	3.4	3.5	2.7	2.9	13.3	9.2	5.8	5.9	4.5	4.7
Unrelated individuals	4.0	4.0	4.0	4.2	3.7	3.8	44.1	38.1	32.1	3.8	23.7	23.2
Negro	(NA)	(NA)	7.1	7.5	7.7	7.5	(NA)	(NA)	32.2	33.5	31.4	31.4
In families	(NA)	(NA)	6.2	6.7	6.8	6.5	(NA)	(NA)	30.9	32.2	30.8	30.3
Head	(NA)	(NA)	1.4	1.5	1.5	1.5	(NA)	(NA)	27.9	29.5	28.1	27.8

[Continued]

★ 1199 ★

Poverty: Individuals and Families Below Poverty Level, 1970-1974

[Continued]

FAMILY STATUS, RACE, AND SEX OF HEAD	NUMBER BELOW LOW INCOME LEVEL (millions)						PERCENT BELOW LOW INCOME LEVEL					
	1959	1965	1969	1970	1973	1974	1959	1965	1969	1970	1973	1974
Related children under 18 yr.	(NA)	(NA)	3.7	3.9	4.0	3.8	(NA)	(NA)	39.6	41.5	40.6	40.7
Other family members	(NA)	(NA)	1.2	1.3	1.3	1.2	(NA)	(NA)	20.0	20.5	18.7	17.6
Unrelated individuals	(NA)	(NA)	.9	.9	.9	1.0	(NA)	(NA)	46.7	48.3	37.9	41.0

Source: "Persons Below Low Income Level by Family Status, and Race and Sex of Head: 1959 to 1974," *Statistical Abstract of the United States, 1975*, p. 399. Primary source: U.S. Bureau of the Census, *Current Population Reports*, series P-60, No. 98 and earlier issues. *Note:* NA Not available.

★ 1200 ★

Income/Earnings

Poverty: Individuals and Families Below Poverty Level, by Residence Area, 1969 and 1973

[Numbers in thousands.]

ITEM	PERSONS BELOW LOW INCOME LEVEL						PERCENT BELOW LOW INCOME LEVEL					
	All races		White		Negro		All races		White		Negro	
	1969	1973	1969	1973	1969	1973	1969	1973	1969	1973	1969	1973
Metropolitan areas	13,084	13,759	8,804	8,452	4,005	4,998	9.5	9.7	7.4	6.9	24.5	28.2
In families	9,909	10,778	6,275	6,154	3,421	4,408	7.8	8.4	5.7	5.6	23.0	27.7
Head	2,611	2,838	1,782	1,723	782	1,057	7.4	7.6	5.7	5.3	21.2	25.4
Related children[1]	5,199	5,889	2,966	3,115	2,128	2,667	11.0	13.1	7.5	8.4	31.4	37.9
Other family members	2,099	2,050	1,527	1,317	511	684	4.7	4.5	3.9	3.3	11.6	14.5
Unrelated individuals	3,174	2,981	2,529	2,298	584	591	29.7	22.3	27.8	20.3	40.8	32.8
Inside central cities	7,993	8,594	4,765	4,305	3,076	4,062	12.7	14.0	9.7	9.3	24.3	29.6
In families	6,166	6,750	3,384	2,997	2,664	3,599	10.8	12.5	7.6	7.4	23.1	29.4
Head	1,609	1,753	955	851	623	860	9.8	10.9	7.2	6.8	21.4	26.7
Related children[1]	3,322	3,816	1,617	1,550	1,659	2,189	16.4	20.4	11.0	12.1	31.9	40.0
Other family members	1,234	1,181	812	597	383	549	6.1	6.2	4.9	3.9	11.1	15.5
Unrelated individuals	1,827	1,844	1,382	1,308	411	463	29.5	24.0	27.8	21.7	37.1	31.9
Outside central cities	5,091	5,165	4,038	4,147	930	936	6.8	6.4	5.8	5.5	25.4	23.4
In families	3,744	4,028	2,891	3,157	757	809	5.3	5.4	4.4	4.5	22.7	22.2
Head	1,002	1,086	827	872	159	197	5.3	5.1	4.6	4.3	20.1	21.1
Related children[1]	1,877	2,073	1,350	1,565	469	477	7.0	7.8	5.4	6.4	29.9	30.6
Other family members	865	869	715	720	129	135	3.6	3.2	3.1	2.8	13.1	11.6
Unrelated individuals	1,347	1,137	1,147	990	173	127	29.9	20.0	27.9	18.8	53.5	36.5
Nonmetropolitan areas	11,063	9,214	7,855	6,690	3,089	2,390	17.9	14.0	14.1	11.2	54.3	41.1
In families	9,266	7,521	6,348	5,258	2,824	2,152	16.0	12.3	12.1	9.5	53.2	39.6
Head	2,397	1,990	1,793	1,496	584	470	14.8	11.2	12.0	9.2	49.0	36.5
Related children[1]	4,301	3,564	2,700	2,348	1,549	1,156	19.9	16.6	14.2	12.4	61.4	48.6
Other family members	2,568	1,968	1,855	1,414	691	527	12.8	9.1	10.1	7.1	43.5	29.8
Unrelated individuals	1,797	1,692	1,507	1,432	265	238	45.7	34.6	43.2	32.1	68.5	62.2

Source: "Persons Below Low Income Level by Residence, Race, and Family Status: 1969 and 1973," *Statistical Abstract of the United States, 1975*, p. 402. Primary source: U.S. Bureau of the Census, *Current Population Reports*, series P-60, No. 98 and earlier issues, and unpublished data. *Note:* 1. Under 18 years.

★ 1201 ★

Income/Earnings

Poverty: Minority Family and Individual Poverty Rates in Relation to Majority Rates, 1969 and 1975

	Raw Measure[1]		Social Indicator Values (Ratios of raw measures to the majority population)	
	1969	1975	1969	1975
Families and Unrelated Individuals				
Amer. Ind./Alask. Nat.	36	26	2.73	2.89[2]
Blacks	33	28	2.50	3.11
Mexican Americans	28	24	2.12	2.67
Japanese Americans	12	7	0.91	0.78
Chinese Americans	16	17	1.21	1.89
Philipino Americans	19	6	1.44	0.67
Puerto Ricans	28	32	2.12	3.56
Majority	13	9	1.00	1.00
Female-Headed Families and Female Unrelated individuals				
Amer. Ind./Alask. Nat.	54	49	4.09	5.44[3]
Blacks	53	46	4.01	5.11
Mexican Americans	53	46	4.02	5.11
Japanese Americans	32	22	2.42	2.44
Chinese Americans	29	19	20	11
Philipino Americans	39	20	2.95	2.22
Puerto Ricans	52	49	3.94	5.44
Majority	28	22	2.12	2.44

Source: "Poverty Rates," *Social Indicators of Equality for Minorities and Women*, 1978, p. 62. Primary source: U.S. Commission on Civil Rights. *Social Indicators of Equality for Minorities and Women.* Washington, D.C.: 1978. *Notes:* 1. The percent of families and unrelated individuals that are below the poverty line. 2. This can be interpreted as follows: "In 1975 American Indian and Alaskan Native-headed families were 2.89 times as likely to be living in poverty as majority-headed families." 3. This can be interpreted as follows: "In 1975 American Indian and Alaskan Native female-headed families were 5.44 times as likely to be living in poverty as all majority-headed families."

★ 1202 ★

Income/Earnings

Poverty: Poverty Status of People 65 and Over, 1959-1974

[Number in thousands.]

FAMILY STATUS AND RACE	NUMBER BELOW LOW INCOME LEVEL					PERCENT BELOW LOW INCOME LEVEL				
	1959	1970	1972	1973	1974	1959	1970	1972	1973	1974
Persons, 65 and older	5,481	4,793	3,738	3,354	3,308	35.2	24.6	18.6	16.3	15.7
White	4,744	4,011	3,072	2,698	2,642	33.1	22.6	16.8	14.4	13.8
Negro	711	735	640	620	626	62.5	47.7	39.9	37.1	36.4

Source: "Selected Characteristics of Persons 60 and 65 Years Old and Over, Below Low Income Level: 1959 to 1974," *Statistical Abstract of the United States, 1975*, p. 403. Primary source: U.S. Bureau of the Census, *Current Population Reports*, series P-60, No. 95 and 98.

★ 1203 ★

Income/Earnings

Poverty: Poverty Status of People in Metropolitan Areas, 1973

[In thousands, except percent.]

INCOME STATUS	IN POVERTY AREAS			NOT IN POVERTY AREAS			POVERTY AREA AS PERCENT OF TOTAL AREA		
	Metropolitan areas	Inside central cities	Outside central cities	Metropolitan areas	Inside central cities	Outside central cities	Metropolitan areas	Inside central cities	Outside central cities
Below low income level, as races	5,391	4,363	1,029	8,368	4,231	4,136	30.1	32.4	22.9
White	1,973	1,303	670	6,479	3,002	3,477	22.5	23.5	20.8
Negro	3,355	2,998	357	1,643	1,064	579	37.7	39.0	29.6
Above low income level, as races	12,545	9,087	3,457	115,491	43,845	71,646	69.9	67.6	77.1
White	6,786	4,232	2,554	106,400	37,855	68,545	77.5	76.5	79.2
Negro	5,549	4,697	852	7,153	4,942	2,212	62.3	61.0	70.5

Source: "Persons in Metropolitan Areas by Poverty Area Residence: 1973," *Statistical Abstract of the United States, 1975*, p. 403. Primary source: U.S. Bureau of the Census, *Current Population Reports*, series P-60, No. 95 and 98.

★ 1204 ★

Income/Earnings

Poverty: Racial Distribution of "Paupers in Almshouses," by Gender, 1910

RACIAL CLASS	PAUPERS IN ALMSHOUSES: 1910				MALES TO 1000 FEMALES: 1910		
	Enumerated on January 1		Admitted during the year		Paupers in almshouses		Total population
					Enumerated on January 1	Admitted during the year	
	Male	Female	Male	Female			
All classes	57,049	27,149	67,195	21,118	2,101	3,182	1,060
Negro	3,763	2,518	4,612	2,195	1,494	2,101	989
White	54,149	24,585	62,262	18,873	2,162	3,299	1,066
Indian	41	33	95	35	[1]	[1]	1,035
Other	96	13	226	15	[1]	[1]	9,608

Source: [Untitled Table], *Negro Population, 1790-1915*, 1918, p. 455. Primary source: U.S. Bureau of the Census. *Negro Population, 1790-1915*. Washington, D.C.: Government Printing Office, 1918. *Note:* 1. Ratio not shown, the number of females being less than 100.

★ 1205 ★
Income/Earnings

Poverty: The Age Group and Residence Area of People in Poverty, 1959 and 1968

[**Persons in millions**. Excludes inmates of institutions, Armed Forces living in barracks, and unrelated individuals under 14 years old.]

| YEAR, AGE, AND RATE | NUMBER BELOW POVERTY LEVEL | | | | | PERCENT BELOW POVERTY LEVEL | | | | |
| | United States | Metropolitan areas | | | Outside metropolitan areas | United States | Metropolitan areas | | | Outside metropolitan areas |
		Total	Central cities	Suburban rings			Total	Central cities	Suburban rings	
1959										
All races	38.8	17.0	10.4	6.6	21.7	22.0	15.3	18.3	12.2	33.2
Under 25 years	20.0	8.8	5.4	3.4	11.2	25.3	18.1	22.5	13.9	36.8
25-64 years	13.3	5.8	3.5	2.2	7.5	16.2	10.8	12.7	8.8	26.3
65 years and over	5.5	2.5	1.5	0.9	3.0	35.2	26.9	28.2	25.1	47.0
White	28.3	11.8	6.5	5.3	16.5	18.1	12.0	13.8	10.4	28.2
Under 25 years	13.7	5.6	3.0	2.6	8.1	20.0	13.4	15.9	11.3	30.4
25-64 years	9.9	4.0	2.2	1.8	5.8	13.4	8.4	9.5	7.5	22.4
65 years and over	4.7	2.2	1.3	0.9	2.6	33.1	25.5	26.4	24.3	43.9
Negro	9.9	5.0	3.8	1.2	4.9	55.1	42.8	40.8	50.9	77.7
Under 25 years	6.0	3.0	2.3	0.7	2.9	63.7	52.2	50.0	60.6	82.4
25-64 years	3.2	1.7	1.3	0.4	1.6	43.3	32.0	30.4	38.9	69.4
65 years and over	0.7	0.3	0.2	0.1	0.4	62.5	46.5	45.8	49.6	81.6
1968										
All races	25.4	12.9	7.8	5.1	12.5	12.8	10.0	13.4	7.3	18.0
Under 25 years	13.1	6.7	4.1	2.6	6.4	14.3	11.4	16.0	7.9	19.5
25-64 years	7.6	3.8	2.2	1.5	3.9	8.7	6.5	8.5	4.9	13.0
65 years and over	4.6	2.4	1.4	0.9	2.3	25.0	20.5	22.3	18.3	32.3
White	17.4	8.5	4.4	4.1	8.9	10.0	7.6	9.8	6.2	14.2
Under 25 years	8.0	3.9	2.0	1.9	4.1	10.2	7.9	10.6	6.2	14.3
25-64 years	5.4	2.5	1.3	1.3	2.9	6.9	5.0	6.1	4.2	10.5
65 years and over	3.9	2.0	1.2	0.9	1.9	23.1	19.3	20.9	17.4	29.3
Negro	7.6	4.1	3.2	0.9	3.5	34.7	26.6	26.2	28.3	54.6
Under 25 years	4.9	2.7	2.1	0.6	2.2	39.7	31.5	31.1	33.2	58.6
25-64 years	2.1	1.2	0.9	0.2	0.9	25.2	18.6	18.5	18.9	45.0
65 years and over	0.7	0.3	0.2	0.1	0.4	47.7	36.2	34.1	44.4	64.3

Source: "Persons Below Poverty Level, by Metropolitan-Nonmetropolitan Residence, by Age and Race: 1959 and 1968," *Statistical Abstract of the United States, 1970,* p. 329. Primary source: Dept. of Commerce, Bureau of the Census, *Current Population Reports,* series P-60, No. 68, and unpublished data.

★ 1206 ★

Income/Earnings

Poverty: "Paupers" in Relation to Population of Same Race in 1910

SECTION AND DIVISION	PAUPERS IN ALMSHOUSES PER 100,000 POPULATION OF SAME RACE AND NATIVITY: 1910					
	Enumerated on January 1			Admitted during the year		
	Negro	White		Negro	White	
		Native	Foreign born		Native	Foreign born
United States	63.9	64.7	248.2	69.3	67.9	249.9
The South	49.9	40.5	160.3	49.6	35.6	185.5
South Atlantic	62.7	56.8	228.5	72.2	52.0	263.3
East South Central	51.1	46.5	267.1	36.5	33.4	124.3
West South Central	17.7	15.2	76.8	20.2	17.4	135.9
The North	186.3	76.2	248.9	212.1	72.4	229.6
New England	268.5	127.7	314.5	371.0	159.7	380.4
Middle Atlantic	162.3	80.6	242.7	202.9	84.6	227.9
East North Central	238.0	81.6	273.5	273.2	64.1	209.3
West North Central	140.9	37.0	147.0	108.9	25.4	104.0
The West	159.9	61.3	291.4	570.4	153.3	462.7
Mountain	88.5	39.0	181.0	386.6	92.4	306.7
Pacific	212.4	76.0	347.4	705.6	193.5	541.9

Source: [Untitled Table], *Negro Population, 1790-1915,* 1918, p. 455. Primary source: U.S. Bureau of the Census. *Negro Population, 1790-1915.* Washington, D.C.: Government Printing Office, 1918.

★ 1207 ★

Income/Earnings

Regional Median Income, 1968

	Median income of Negro workers		Ratio: Female to male income	
	Male	Female	Negro	White
All wage and salary workers[1]	$4,733	$2,454	.52	.48
Year-round full-time workers[2]	5,370	3,561	.66	.58
Northeast	5,900	3,945	.67	.61
North Central	6,856	4,096	.60	.55

[Continued]

★ 1207 ★

Regional Median Income, 1968
[Continued]

	Median income of Negro workers		Ratio: Female to male income	
	Male	Female	Negro	White
South	4,167	2,884	.69	.59
West	7,517	4,547	.60	.59

Source: "Median Income of Negro Male and Female Workers, by Region, 1968," Current Population Reports, Special Studies, Series P-23, No. 29. *The Social and Economic Status of the Black Population in the United States, 1969,* 1969, p. 20. Primary source: U.S. Department of Commerce, Bureau of the Census. *Notes:* 1. With wage and salary income, including full and part-time workers. 2. Refers to total income.

★ 1208 ★

Income/Earnings

Relationships: Minority Average Annual Age Increment in Earnings in Relation to Majority Male Increment, 1959, 1969, and 1975

	Raw Measure[1]			Social Indicator Values (Ratios of raw measure to the majority male population)		
	1959	1969	1975	1959	1969	1975
Males						
Amer. Ind./Alask. Nat.	$74.40	$145.60	$320.15	.58	.60	.85[2]
Blacks	60.00	108.90	185.30	.46	.45	.49
Mexican Americans	84.20	136.00	147.40	.65	.56	.39
Japanese Americans	157.50	272.20	536.85	1.22	1.12	1.43
Chinese Americans	156.50	306.50	459.45	1.21	1.26	1.22
Philipino Americans	69.00	251.80	283.30	.53	1.03	.75
Puerto Ricans	41.20	83.80	97.95	.32	.34	.26
Majority	129.20	243.80	375.75	1.00	1.00	1.00
Females						
Amer. Ind./Alask. Nat.	-19.10	0.20	81.30	-.15	.00	.22
Blacks	4.30	4.80	29.95	.03	.02	.08
Mexican Americans	9.80	10.10	5.55	.08	.04	.02
Japanese Americans	-39.00	79.40	-11.00	-.30	.33	-.03
Chinese Americans	-20.20	40.20	41.70	-1.6	.16	.11
Philipino Americans	-10.00	-6.30	8.35	-.08	-.03	.02
Puerto Ricans	-9.20	-6.60	-20.00	-.07	-.03	-.05
Majority	18.00	22.20	57.55	.14	.09	.15

Source: "Earnings Mobility," *Social Indicators of Equality for Minorities and Women,* 1978, p. 58. Primary source: U.S. Commission on Civil Rights. *Social Indicators of Equality for Minorities and Women.* Washington, D.C.: 1978. *Notes:* 1. The average annual increment in earnings by single years of age for full-time workers ages 20 to 44. 2. This can be interpreted as follows: "In 1975 American Indian and Alaskan Native males' average earnings increment by age was 85 percent as much as the earnings increment for majority males."

★ 1209 ★

Income/Earnings

"Big-City" Black Income in Relation to Black Percent of Population, 1969

[Cities ranked by percent black population in 1970]

Selected cities	Per capita income of persons	Families		Median income of unrelated individuals	Per capita income-- percent black of all persons	Median income-- percent black of all families
		Median income	Percent with 10,000 and over			
Black Population 50 Percent or More						
Washington, D.C.	$2,734	$8,488	40	$3,918	71	89
Newark, N.J.	2,077	6,742	27	3,348	83	87
Atlanta, Ga.	1,909	6,451	25	1,838	60	77
Black Population 40 to 50 Percent						
Baltimore, Md.	2,056	7,289	31	2,456	71	83
New Orleans, La.	1,458	4,745	15	1,601	54	64
Detroit, Mich.	2,534	8,645	40	3,059	79	86
Birmingham, Ala.	1,522	5,184	15	1,561	59	67
Richmond, Va.	1,881	6,179	22	1,942	59	71
St. Louis, Mo.	1,912	6,534	25	2,093	69	80
Black Population 30 to 40 Percent						
Memphis, Tenn.	1,438	5,177	16	1,567	51	60
Cleveland, Ohio	2,255	7,617	34	2,547	79	84
Oakland, Calif.	2,365	7,700	35	2,658	65	80
Philadelphia, Pa.	2,243	7,379	32	2,705	74	79
Chicago, Ill.	2,321	7,883	36	3,179	68	77
Black Population Under 30 percent						
Cincinnati, Ohio	1,979	6,504	24	1,925	63	73
Houston, Tex.	1,812	6,392	21	2,048	53	65
Dallas, Tex.	1,828	6,311	23	2,239	49	63
Jacksonville, Fla.	1,502	5,122	15	1,571	53	59
Kansas City, Mo.	2,090	7,247	30	2,376	62	73
New York, N.Y.	2,402	7,150	30	3,449	64	74
Columbus, Ohio	2,293	7,556	34	2,320	74	78
Pittsburgh, Pa.	1,993	6,097	22	1,948	64	69
Indianapolis, Ind.	2,210	7,849	35	2,789	63	73
Los Angeles, Calif.	2,435	7,200	31	3,109	61	68
Boston, Mass.	2,054	6,346	25	3,035	66	70
Milwaukee, Wis.	1,974	7,491	32	2,943	62	73

Source: "Income of Black Persons, Families, and Unrelated Individuals in 1969 for Cities with 100,000 or More Blacks," Current Population Reports, Special Studies, Series P-23, No. 42. *The Social and Economic Status of the Black Population in the United States, 1971,* 1972, p. 131. Primary source: U.S. Department of Commerce, Social and Economic Statistics Administration, Bureau of the Census.

Money Earned

★ 1210 ★

Salaries: Average Hourly, Daily, and Weekly Wage Rates for Farm Workers in 1945

Area, race, and sex	Cash wages earned May 20-26, 1945 (on reporting farm)			Time Worked May 20-26, 1945 (on reporting farm)		
	Hourly	Daily	Weekly	Hours per day	Days per week	Hours per week
	Dollars	Dollars	Dollars	Number	Number	Number
United States						
White	.41	4.00	19.80	9.8	4.9	48
Nonwhite	.28	2.70	10.60	9.7	3.9	38
Male	.38	3.70	18.20	9.8	4.9	48
Female	.33	3.00	10.20	9.1	3.4	31
Northeast						
White	.38	3.60	21.60	9.7	5.9	57
Nonwhite	.65	5.70	27.70	8.7	4.9	42
Male	.39	3.80	22.20	9.7	5.9	57
Female	.59	4.90	22.30	8.3	4.6	38
North Central						
White	.30	3.20	18.10	10.7	5.6	60
Nonwhite	.27	2.90	12.00	10.5	4.2	44
Male	.30	2.80	18.40	10.8	5.6	61
Female	.28	2.40	10.30	8.4	4.4	36
South						
White	.66	2.80	11.10	9.6	3.9	38
Nonwhite	.23	2.30	8.60	9.7	3.8	37
Male	.27	2.70	11.10	9.7	4.2	40
Female	.21	2.00	5.80	9.4	2.9	28
West						
White	.30	6.10	33.70	9.2	5.5	51
Nonwhite	.70	6.60	35.70	9.3	5.4	51

[Continued]

★ 1210 ★

Salaries: Average Hourly, Daily, and Weekly Wage Rates for Farm Workers in 1945
[Continued]

Area, race, and sex	Cash wages earned May 20-26, 1945 (on reporting farm)			Time Worked May 20-26, 1945 (on reporting farm)		
	Hourly	Daily	Weekly	Hours per day	Days per week	Hours per week
Male	.66	6.10	34.00	9.3	5.5	51
Female	.72	6.20	32.40	8.7	5.2	45

Source: "Average Hourly, Daily, and Weekly Cash Wages, Average Hours and Days Worked during Week for Hired Farm Workers, by Race and Sex, United States and Major Regions, May, 1945," *Negro Year Book: A Review of Events Affecting Negro Life, 1941-1946,* 1947, p. 162. Primary source: Survey of wages and wage rates in agriculture, report number 7. February 1946, Washington, D.C. *Notes:* Excludes approximately 87,000 custom workers since the hire of machinery, equipment or workstock was included in their reported cash wages.

★ 1211 ★

Money Earned

Salaries: Extension Worker Salaries in Southern States in 1950

States	County Agent Negro	County Agent White	Asst. Agents White	Home Agents Negro	Home Agents White	Asst. Agents White
Alabama	$2,752	$5,011	$3,683	$2,288	$3,560	$3,009
Arkansas	4,713	4,259	3,050	2,563	3,602	2,687
Delaware	-	-	-	3,300	3,500	-
Florida	2,604	4,368	3,669	2,604	3,533	3,087
Georgia	2,298	3,508	2,950	2,049	2,821	2,446
Kentucky	2,860	4,254	3,262	2,808	3,605	2,950
Louisiana	2,980	4,879	3,455	2,668	3,973	2,722
Maryland	3,214	5,197	3,422	2,973	3,825	3,100
Mississippi	2,782	4,333	3,366	2,327	3,557	2,758
Missouri	-	-	-	2,477	3,059	-
North Carolina	3,732	5,202	3,841	3,221	3,910	3,071
Oklahoma	2,943	4,436	3,466	2,547	3,737	2,967
South Carolina	2,791	4,297	3,263	2,323	3,067	2,445
Tennessee	2,745	4,046	3,403	2,510	3,300	2,935
Texas	3,079	4,481	3,427	2,684	3,842	3,312
Virginia	3,152	4,401	3,100	2,951	3,784	2,744
West Virginia	(no report)				(no report)	

Source: "Average Annual Salaries of Extension Workers in South by States and Race, October 1950," *1952 Negro Year Book: A Review of Events Affecting Negro Life,* 1952, p. 107. Primary source: USDA Extension Service Report on Average Annual Salaries, No. 1033 (10-50). *Note:* White County and Home Agents have assistants; Negro Agents do not.

★ 1212 ★

Money Earned

Salaries: Median Income in Selected Cities in 1949

Area	White	Nonwhite	Amount White Greater than Nonwhite	Per cent Nonwhite of White
Atlanta, Ga.	$3,208	$1,343	$1,865	42.0
Birmingham, Ala.	3,285	1,552	1,733	47.2
Memphis, Tenn.	3,085	1,348	1,737	44.0
Nashville, Tenn.	2,811	1,214	1,597	43.1
New Orleans, La.	2,968	1,423	1,545	48.0
Norfolk-Portsmouth, Va.	2,842	1,230	1,612	43.2
Richmond, Va.	3,466	1,495	1,971	43.1
Washington, D.C.	3,592	2,152	1,440	60.0

Source: "Median Income by Color of Families and Individuals in Selected Standard Metropolitan Areas, 1949,: *1952 Negro Year Book: A Review of Events Affecting Negro Life,* 1952, p. 130. Primary source: U.S. Bureau of the Census, Preliminary Reports, Series PC-5, 1950.

Wealth

★ 1213 ★

Organizations: Wealth of Black Fraternal Organizations, c. 1913

"Secret societies among Negroes may be roughly divided into two classes: the old line societies, such as Masons, the Odd Fellows, and the Knights of Pythias, and the benevolent secret societies; such as the True Reformers, the Grand United Order of Galilean Fishermen and the National Order of Mosaic Templars. Large sums of money have come into the treasuries of the various secret organizations. The United Brothers of Friendship of Texas have over $40,000 in their treasury; in two cities of the State the Grand Lodge owns over $200,000 worth of property, which brings in a revenue of $800 per month...The Knights of Pythias have collected over $1,000,000 for endowment. There is over $40,000 in the Grand Lodge treasury...It is estimated that the Masons have about $1,000,000 worth of property; the Odd Fellows, $2,000,000; and the Pythians, $1,500,000. It is probable that altogether the Negro secret societies in the United States own between $9,000,000 and $10,000,000 Worth of property."

Source: "Fraternal Organizations," *Negro Year Book and Annual Encyclopedia of the Negro,* 1913, p. 273. Primary source: Work, Monroe N. (Ed.), *Negro Year Book and Annual Encyclopedia of the Negro.* Tuskegee Institute, Ala.: Negro Year Book Co., 1913.

★ 1214 ★
Wealth

Property: Black Accumulations Early in the 20th Century

The United States Census reports show that from 1900 to 1910 there was a phenomenal increase in the Agricultural wealth of the Negroes in the South. The value of the domestic animals which they owned increased from $85,216,337 to $177,278,785 or 107 per cent; poultry from $3,788,792 to $5,113,756 or 35 per cent; implements and machinery from $18,586,225 to $36,861,418 or 98 per cent; land and buildings from $69,636,420 to $273,501,665 or 293 per cent. From 1900 to 1910 the total value of farm property owned by the colored farmers of the South increased from $177,404,688 to $492,898,218 or 177 per cent.

The total wealth of the Negroes is estimated to be about $700,000.00. It is estimated that the Negroes are adding each year to their wealth, from $20,000,000 to $30,000,000. They now own about 20,000,000 acres of land or 31,000 square miles, an area almost equal to that of Vermont. New Hampshire, Massachusetts, Connecticut and Rhode Island. It is estimated that Negroes now own 220,000 farms, and 500,000 homes. In 1900 they owned 187,799 farms and 373,450 homes. In Arkansas, Georgia, North Carolina and Virginia, the amount of property owned by Negroes is reported. They own in Arkansas $20,000,000 worth of property; in Georgia $34,022,379 worth; in North Carolina, $28,602,280; in Virginia, their real estate holdings are assessed at $19,488,577. In Georgia, the Negroes own 1,639,919 acres of land; in Virginia, they own 1,517,500 acres. According to a recent investigation, the Negroes of Pennsylvania own about $20,000,000 worth of property. Negroes now own and operate 64 banks, 100 insurance companies 300 drug stores, and over 20,000 dry goods and grocery stores, and other industrial enterprises.

Source: "Amount of Property Owned," *Negro Year Book and Annual Encyclopedia of the Negro*, 1912, p. 180. Primary source: United States Census, 1900 and 1910.

Chapter 9
LABOR AND EMPLOYMENT

Employees and Employment

★ 1215 ★

Actors in Broadway and Off-Broadway Shows: 1960-61-1964-65

	1964-65	1963-64	1962-63	1961-62	1960-61
Employed					
Bdwy.	74	168	51	123	126
Off-Bdwy.	32	116	26	50	29
Shows employing blacks					
Bdwy.	22	24	21	14	18
Off-Bdwy.	20	27	12	20	9
Shows with integrated casts					
Bdwy.	15	16	13	10	8
Off-Bdwy.	11	11	7	11	4

Source: Untitled table, *The Ebony Handbook.* Chicago: Johnson Publishing Co., 1974, p. 443. Published by permission.

★ 1216 ★

Employees and Employment

Aerospace Industry: Employed Persons by Race, Gender, and Region, 21 Companies, 140 Establishments, 1963

Region	All employees			Male			Female		
	Total	Negro	Percent Negro	Total	Negro	Percent Negro	Total	Negro	Percent Negro
Northeast	147,395	3,598	2.4	128,764	3,258	2.5	18,631	340	1.8
New England	69,823	1,048	1.5	60,094	975	1.6	9,729	73	0.8
Middle Atlantic	77,572	2,550	3.3	68,670	2,283	3.3	8,902	267	3.0
South	60,175	1,095	1.8	52,152	945	1.8	8,023	150	1.9
Southeast	29,314	506	1.7	25,224	394	1.6	4,090	112	2.7
Southwest	30,861	589	1.9	26,928	551	2.0	3,933	38	1.0
Midwest	87,858	3,310	3.8	77,566	3,015	3.9	10,292	295	2.9
West Coast	352,547	10,284	2.9	284,025	8,293	2.9	68,522	1,991	2.9
Southern California	234,144	8,303	3.5	184,679	6,660	3.6	49,465	1,643	3.3
Other West Coast	118,403	1,981	1.7	99,346	1,633	1.6	19,057	348	1.8
Total United States	647,975	18,287	2.8	542,507	15,511	2.9	105,468	2,776	2.6

Source: "Aerospace Industry Employment by Race, Sex, and Region, 21 Companies, 140 Establishments, 1963," Herbert R. Northrup, *The Negro in the Aerospace Industry*, p. 32. Primary source: Data supplied to Plans for Progress. *Notes:* Geographic definitions are as follows: New England: Maine, Vermont, New Hampshire, Massachusetts, Connecticut, and Rhode Island; Middle Atlantic: New York, Pennsylvania, New Jersey, Maryland, and Delaware; Southeast: Virginia, West Virginia, North Carolina, South Carolina, Georgia, Florida, Alabama, Mississippi, Louisiana, Tennessee, and Kentucky; Southwest: Texas, Oklahoma, New Mexico, and Arizona; West Coast: Washington, Oregon, California, Idaho, and Nevada; Midwest: All Midwest and Rocky Mountain States. Actual plants only in Colorado and Midwest except for small military installations.

★ 1217 ★

Employees and Employment

Aerospace Industry: Employed Persons for Seven SMSA's, by Race, 1950, 1960

Standard Metropolitan Statistical Area	1960			1950		
	All employees	Negroes	Percent Negro	All employees	Negroes	Percent Negro
Los Angeles-Long Beach	153,337	6,283	4.1	70,209	1,183	1.7
Seattle, Washington	50,276	967	1.9	16,274	152	0.9
New York	37,826	1,558	4.1	19,643	358	1.8
Wichita, Kansas	26,254	520	2.0	11,681	97	0.8
Fort Worth, Texas	22,690	342	1.5	15,028	237	1.6
St. Louis, Mo.-Ill.	20,366	874	4.3	5,165	103	2.0
Philadelphia, Pa.-N.J.	4,221	136	3.2	2,366	67	2.8

Source: "Total Employed Persons, Aircraft and Parts Manufacturing Industry for Seven Standard Metropolitan Statistical Areas, by Race 1950 and 1960," Herbert R. Northrup, *The Negro in the Aerospace Industry*, p. 28. Primary source: U.S. *Census of Population*: 1950, Vol. II, *Characteristics of the Population*, State volumes, Table 83; 1960, PC(1)D, *Detailed Characteristics*, State volumes, Table 129.

★ 1218 ★

Employees and Employment

Aerospace Industry: Total Employees for Selected States, by Race, 1940-1960

State	1960			1950			1940		
	All employees	Negroes	Percent Negro	All employees	Negroes	Percent Negro	All employees	Negroes	Percent Negro
California	182,826	6,665	3.6	82,534	1,301	1.6	37,719	10	[1]
Connecticut	57,743	782	1.4	18,234	120	0.7	10,817	3	[1]
Washington	54,118	1,034	1.9	17,254	155	0.9	5,449	-	-
New York	51,415	1,681	3.3	26,513	378	1.4	13,791	18	0.1
Ohio	49,500	2,023	4.1	16,078	682	4.2	4,299	14	0.3
Texas	40,178	838	2.1	23,116	339	1.5	118	4	3.4
Kansas	32,141	547	1.7	12,960	104	0.8	1,582	-	-
Missouri	22,841	861	3.8	5,979	104	1.7	806	8	1.0
New Jersey	22,452	523	2.3	15,762	211	1.3	10,993	11	0.1
Indiana	21,425	477	2.2	9,545	209	2.2	2,835	7	0.2
Georgia	12,973	814	6.3	66	7	10.6	11	-	-
Pennsylvania	11,921	158	1.3	4,917	61	1.2	3,773	19	0.5
Massachusetts	11,252	110	1.0	2,540	8	0.3	-	-	-
Oklahoma	6,346	108	1.7	818	24	2.9	137	-	-
Florida	3,833	107	2.8	209	5	2.4	54	-	-

Source: "Total Employed Persons, Aircraft and Parts Manufacturing Industry for Selected States, by Race, 1940-1960," Herbert R. Northrup, *The Negro in the Aerospace Industry*, p. 26. Primary source: U.S. *Census of Population*: 1940, Vol. III, *The Labor Force*, parts 2- 5, Table 18; 1950, Vol. II, *Characteristics of the Population*, State volumes, Table 83; 1960, PC(1)D, *Detailed Characteristics*, State volumes, Table 129. *Note:* 1. Less than 0.05 percent.

★ 1219 ★

Employees and Employment

Business Employing 200 or More, 1910

Jewelry	206
Ice dealers	208
Saw and Planning Mill Proprietors	219
Wholesale Merchants and Dealers	241
Dry goods, Fancy goods and Notions	280
Manufacturers and Proprietors of clothing factories	310
Livery stable keepers	323
Buyers and shippers of grain , live stock, etc.	357
Candy and Confectionery	384
Proprietors of Transfer Companies	632
Saloon Keepers	652
Drugs and Medicines	695
General Stores	736
Produce and Provisions	756
Real Estate Dealers	762
Junk Dealers	794

[Continued]

★ 1219 ★

Business Employing 200 or More, 1910
[Continued]

Billiard and Pool Room Keepers	875
Undertakers	953
Hotel keepers and managers	973
Coal and Wood Dealers	1,155
Butchers and Meat Dealers	2,957
Builders and Contractors	3,107
Hucksters and Peddlers	3,434
Groceries	5,550
Restaurant, Cafe, and Lunch Room keepers	6,369

Source: "Business Enterprises in Which 200 or More Negroes Are Engaged," Monroe N. Work, ed., *Negro Year Book: An Annual Encyclopedia of the Negro, 1916- 1917*, p. 298.

★ 1220 ★

Employees and Employment

Chemical Industry: Employed Persons by Race and Selected States, 1940-1960

State	1940[1]			1950			1960		
	Total employees	Negroes		Total employees	Negroes		Total employees	Negroes	
		Number	Percent		Number	Percent		Number	Percent
New Jersey	51,740	1,307	2.5	74,891	3,413	4.6	93,084	4,867	5.2
New York	58,307	832	1.4	77,212	3,322	4.3	85,653	4,569	5.3
Illinois	30,309	1,272	4.2	45,404	3,793	8.4	57,620	4,289	7.4
Pennsylvania	31,260	933	3.0	42,778	2,112	4.9	59,011	2,636	4.5
Tennessee	17,701	2,681	15.1	33,509	3,548	10.6	43,378	2,625	6.1
Ohio	27,175	900	3.3	39,952	2,290	5.7	56,267	2,578	4.6
Texas	9,375	1,754	18.7	29,141	3,559	12.2	46,970	2,782	5.9
California	17,920	113	0.6	30,139	990	3.3	45,143	1,377	3.1
Michigan	19,050	170	0.9	30,577	557	1.8	40,909	849	2.1
Virginia	20,617	3,234	15.7	28,908	3,735	12.9	31,982	2,705	8.5
Delaware	9,266	230	2.5	14,533	625	4.3	21,096	764	3.6
West Virginia	15,166	84	0.6	21,739	267	1.2	25,566	232	0.9
Missouri	11,000	390	3.5	15,757	965	6.1	21,675	1,178	5.4
Indiana	8,390	328	3.9	17,447	838	4.8	24,747	1,125	4.5
South Carolina	4,274	2,967	69.4	5,015	2,082	41.5	12,571	1,807	14.4

Source: "Chemicals and Allied Products Industry, Total Employed Persons by Race, Selected States, 1940-1960," William Howard Quay, Jr., *The Negro in the Chemical Industry*, p. 26. Primary source: *U.S. Census of Population*: 1940, Vol. III, *The Labor Force*, Parts 2- 5, Table 18; 1950, Vol. II, *Characteristics of the Population*, Parts 2-54, Table 83; 1960, PC(1) D, *Detailed Characteristics*, State Volumes, Table 29. *Note:* 1. Industry: "Rayon and Allied" and "Other Chemical and Allied."

★ 1221 ★

Employees and Employment

Chemical Industry: Percent Black Employment by Gender and Region, 1964-1968

Region	All employees			Male			Female		
	1964	1966	1968	1964	1966	1968	1964	1966	1968
Northeast	3.9	4.1	4.8	4.3	4.5	5.1	1.8	2.3	3.6
New England	3.4	3.7	4.3	3.9	4.1	4.6	0.6	0.9	2.6
Middle Atlantic	3.9	4.2	4.8	4.4	4.6	5.1	1.9	2.4	3.7
South	6.0	6.3	7.3	6.6	6.8	7.4	2.0	3.6	6.9
Southeast	6.2	6.6	7.7	7.0	7.1	7.8	2.1	3.8	7.2
Southwest	4.9	5.2	5.4	5.1	5.4	5.6	0.6	1.4	2.4
Midwest	3.8	3.9	5.3	4.1	4.2	4.9	1.8	2.3	7.0
north Central	3.8	3.8	5.2	4.0	4.0	4.9	2.0	2.4	7.0
Other Midwest	3.9	4.4	5.4	4.3	4.8	5.0	1.5	1.9	6.7
West Coast	3.5	3.7	4.7	3.1	3.4	4.3	5.9	6.1	6.8
Total United States	4.7	5.0	6.0	5.2	5.4	6.0	1.9	2.9	5.6

Source: "Chemical Industry, Percent Negro Employment by Sex and Region, 1964- 1968," William Howard Quay, Jr., *The Negro in the Chemical Industry*, p. 46. Primary source: Appendix Tables A-1-A-33. *Notes:* Geographic definitions are as follows: New England: Connecticut, Maine, Massachusetts, New Hampshire, Rhode Island, and Vermont; Middle Atlantic: Delaware, Maryland, New Jersey, New York, and Pennsylvania; Southeast: Alabama, Florida, Georgia, Kentucky, Louisiana, Mississippi, North Carolina, South Carolina, Tennessee, Virginia, and West Virginia; Southwest: Arizona, New Mexico, Oklahoma, and Texas; North Central: Illinois, Indiana, Michigan, Ohio, and Wisconsin; Other Midwest: Iowa, Kansas, Minnesota, Missouri, Nebraska, North Dakota, Rocky Mountain States, and South Dakota; West Coast: California, Idaho, Nevada, Oregon, and Washington.

★ 1222 ★

Employees and Employment

Chemical Industry: Percent Black Employment by Size of Establishment and Region, 1964-1968

Region	Large establishments (over 2,500 employees in 1966)			Small establishments (500-700 employees in 1966)		
	1964	1966	1968	1964	1966	1968
Southeast	6.1	6.1	7.2	27.8	26.7	27.0
	5.8	7.1	8.7	22.4	20.4	23.8
	7.2	9.4	16.5	13.1	13.0	13.8
	1.7	3.7	4.4	0.2	0.2	0.5
	0.8	0.8	1.3	17.5	18.2	17.8
				0.2	0.6	1.2
Southwest	0.3	0.4	1.0	0.5	0.6	1.2
				7.3	6.3	7.5
Middle Atlantic	1.8	2.2	2.4	11.0	12.0	13.1
	4.8	4.5	5.1	6.6	10.2	11.9
	3.4	3.1	3.0	1.7	1.7	1.8
	0.3	0.4	0.9	1.4	1.9	4.3
				7.9	2.1	2.8

[Continued]

★ 1222 ★

Chemical Industry: Percent Black Employment by Size of Establishment and Region, 1964-1968

[Continued]

Region	Large establishments (over 2,500 employees in 1966)			Small establishments (500-700 employees in 1966)		
	1964	1966	1968	1964	1966	1968
				0.9	0.2	2.3
				1.2	2.4	2.0
				0.2	0.8	1.8
North Central	0.1	0.2	0.3	0.2	0.1	0.2
				1.5	1.8	4.3
				27.0	29.1	29.7
				1.0	2.6	2.5
				2.2	2.7	4.3
				2.7	3.2	3.2
				7.4	0.9	2.1
				6.2	5.6	8.9
				1.6	2.4	3.2
				-	0.8	1.1
Other Midwest	2.8	2.8	3.7	1.8	1.4	6.0
				4.6	2.9	4.3
West Coast		none		1.3	1.2	3.1
Total	2.6	3.0	3.8	6.5	6.1	7.0

Source: "Chemical Industry, Percent Negro Employment by Size of Establishment and Region, 1964-1968," William Howard Quay, Jr., *The Negro in the Chemical Industry*, p. 61. Primary source: Data in author's possession.

★ 1223 ★

Employees and Employment

Clerical, Sales, and Other Employees: (Males), 1940

Occupation	Total	White	Negro	Per cent Negro
Bookkeepers, Accountants, etc.	447,606	445,934	907	0.2
Mail Carriers	119,246	113,542	5,642	4.7
Stenographers, Typists & Sec'ys	68,805	68,187	467	0.7
Telegraph Operators	31,554	31,515	35	0.1
Insurance Agents & Brokers	226,061	221,130	4,744	2.1
Real Estate Agents & Brokers	100,856	99,716	1,086	1.1
Shipping & Receiving Clerks	200,669	195,579	4,915	2.4
Other Clerical & Kindred Workers	1,256,689	1,238,241	16,470	1.3

Source: "Employed Clerical, Sales and Kindred Workers (Male) in Selected Commercial Occupations by Race—1940," Jessie Parkhurst Guzman, ed., *Negro Year Book: A Review of Events Affecting Negro Life, 1941-1946*, p. 143.

★ 1224 ★

Employees and Employment

Employment Status of Persons in Selected Cities of 100,000 – March 24-30, 1940

City	Population		Percent in labor force		Per cent employed (except on public emergency work)		Employed on public emergency work		Seeking work	
	Total	Non-white	White	Non-white	White	Non-white	White	Non-white	White	Non-white
Atlanta	243,454	81,759	57.8	66.8	89.8	83.6	30	3.7	7.2	12.8
Baltimore	691,204	126,798	54.5	62.5	91.4	83.5	1.0	4.4	7.5	12.1
Birmingham	209,525	82,702	52.7	58.9	88.4	78.4	3.5	5.2	8.0	16.4
Chattanooga	99,292	28,070	55.5	61.3	89.5	84.1	3.5	4.4	6.9	11.5
Chicago	2,775,496	222,113	57.6	56.3	86.7	64.5	2.7	16.2	10.6	19.4
Cincinnati	372,262	43,903	53.0	57.0	89.1	63.3	2.6	14.7	8.3	22.0
Cleveland	718,155	65,475	55.9	53.9	81.9	58.7	5.9	22.7	12.2	18.6
Dallas	240,137	40,555	58.1	71.4	89.5	80.6	2.4	3.6	8.1	15.8
Detroit	1,283,145	116,531	56.9	58.0	87.3	67.8	2.6	15.6	10.1	16.6
Houston	308,518	68,966	55.3	68.1	91.1	87.4	1.8	1.7	7.1	10.8
Indianapolis	314,968	40,296	54.4	58.0	89.7	68.3	2.8	10.9	7.5	20.9
Jacksonville	136,110	48,219	55.0	65.1	87.9	79.4	5.4	6.5	6.6	14.1
Kansas City, Mo.	331,928	34,922	57.0	65.2	86.3	66.7	4.6	14.1	9.1	19.1
Los Angeles	1,269,397	78,892	54.1	62.2	86.2	80.4	2.4	5.1	11.4	14.5
Louisville	254,174	37,996	54.2	60.8	87.9	77.0	1.6	5.3	10.5	17.7
Memphis	236,094	96,751	53.9	63.4	90.6	80.2	2.7	4.6	6.7	15.3
Miami	143,531	29,447	54.1	77.3	90.6	87.7	0.9	0.4	8.5	11.9
Nashville	132,078	37,728	54.7	63.6	88.0	83.3	3.4	2.3	8.5	14.4
Newark, N.J.	347,060	34,907	57.4	58.7	82.4	64.9	2.8	13.6	14.8	21.5
New Orleans	393,600	114,080	53.4	58.9	84.2	72.9	5.5	11.5	10.3	15.6
New York	6,092,372	381,463	56.7	64.5	82.6	72.9	2.4	7.6	15.0	19.5
Norfolk	116,569	35,795	54.0	65.0	93.1	83.5	2.4	5.4	4.5	11.1
Philadelphia	1,556,110	191,752	55.9	59.6	82.9	64.6	2.0	5.8	15.2	29.6
Pittsburgh	535,035	49,331	52.9	52.5	80.1	58.4	3.6	12.1	16.3	29.5
Richmond	157,815	47,390	57.6	67.2	90.6	82.8	2.0	2.4	7.4	14.8
St. Louis	671,571	86,777	56.8	56.7	87.2	69.1	2.6	11.1	10.2	19.8
Washington	552,543	149,559	60.5	65.4	93.3	82.6	1.3	5.9	5.4	11.4

Source: "Employment Status of Persons 14 Years Old and Over by Color, in Cities of 100,000 Inhabitants or More, for Selected Cities: March 24-30, 1940," Florence Murray, ed., *The Negro Handbook*, 1942, p. 148. Primary source: 1940 Census.

★ 1225 ★

Employees and Employment

Federal Employees: Officers, Clerks, and Others, 1913

	No.	Salary
Diplomatic and Consular Service	16	$38,410
Departmental Service, Washington, D.C.:		
State	26	19,360
Treasury	926	588,801
War	176	130,380
Navy	74	52,610
Post Office	187	118,173
Interior	593	358,112
Justice	43	26,640
Agriculture	164	89,816
Commerce and Labor	139	94,800

[Continued]

★ 1225 ★

Federal Employees: Officers, Clerks, and Others, 1913
[Continued]

	No.	Salary
Washington Navy Yard	189	94,000
Government Printing Office	364	228,454
Interstate Commerce Commission	41	22,080
United State Capitol	115	73,100
Library of Congress	46	24,920
Washington, D.C., City Post Office	171	174,600
District of Columbia Government, including unskilled laborers	2,413	1,479,000
Miscellaneous	194	104,114
Departmental Service at large:		
State (Diplomatic and Consular)	16	38,410
Treasury	1,082	743,373
War	2,342	1,075,320
Post Office	3,599	2,807,134
Interior	31	25,738
Agriculture	102	53,217
Commerce and Labor	64	42,612
United States Army, Officers	11	29,295
United States Army, enlisted men	4,416	1,133,766
United States Navy Yards and stations	2,146	1,210,070
Miscellaneous, including unclassified	775	581,515
Total	22,440	$12,456,760

Source: "Number of Colored Officers, Clerks and Other Employees in the Service of the United States Government," Monroe N. Work, ed., *Negro Year Book: An Annual Encyclopedia of the Negro,* p. 101.

★ 1226 ★

Employees and Employment

Furniture Industry: Employment by Race and Gender, 1900-1960

	All employees			Male			Female		
	Total	Negro	Percent Negro	Total	Negro	Percent Negro	Total	Negro	Percent Negro
1900[1]	23,078	456	2.0	21,842	456	2.1	1,236	-	-
1910[2]	160,271	4,254	2.7	152,382	4,090	2.7	7,889	164	2.1
1920[2,3]	90,989	4,164	4.6	81,506	3,520	4.3	9,483	644	6.8
1930[2]	268,098	7,934	3.0	246,610	7,324	3.0	21,488	610	2.8
1940	225,675	8,123	3.6	2.4,411	7,518	3.7	21,264	605	2.8

[Continued]

★ 1226 ★

Furniture Industry: Employment by Race and Gender, 1900-1960
[Continued]

	All employees			Male			Female		
	Total	Negro	Percent Negro	Total	Negro	Percent Negro	Total	Negro	Percent Negro
1950	330,243	20,116	6.1	278,874	16,748	6.2	51,369	3,368	6.6
1960	376,694	27,938	7.4	311,556	23,569	7.6	65,138	4,279	6.6

Source: "Furniture Industry, Total Employment by Race and Sex, United States, 1900-1960," William E. Fulmer, *The Negro in the Furniture Industry*, p. 49. Primary source: *U.S. Census of Population* 1900: *Special Reports, Occupations*, Table 1 and *Negroes in the United States*, Table 26; 1910: Volume IV, *Occupation Statistics*, Table VI; 1920: Volume IV, *Occupations*, Table 5; 1930: Volume V, *General Report on Occupations*, Table 2; 1940: Volume III, *The Labor Force*, Part I, Table 76; 1950: Volume II, *Characteristics of the Population*, Part I, Table 133; 1960: *U.S. Summary*, PC (1)1D, Table 213. *Notes:* 1. Furniture manufactory employees. 2. Furniture factories. 3. Laborers and operatives only.

★ 1227 ★

Employees and Employment

Furniture Industry: Major Job Categories by Race and Gender, United States, 1910

	All employees			Male			Female		
	Total	Negro	Percent Negro	Total	Negro	Percent Negro	Total	Negro	Percent Negro
Supervisors[1]	10,082	61	0.6	9,895	60	0.6	187	1	0.5
Office and clerical[2]	4,700	29	0.6	3,276	26	0.8	1,424	3	0.2
Cabinetmakers	32,280	270	0.8	32,272	269	0.8	8	1	12.5
Caners and seaters	2,610	370	14.2	1,712	279	16.3	898	91	10.1
Laborers	23,571	1,376	5.8	23,055	1,365	5.9	516	11	2.1
Repairers	1,070	176	16.4	1,036	171	16.5	34	5	14.7
Teamsters	2,019	183	9.1	2,019	183	9.1	-	-	-
Upholsterers	17,555	797	4.5	16,487	772	4.7	1,068	25	2.3
Painters	5,485	91	1.7	5,337	90	1.7	148	1	0.7
Finishers	8,270	87	1.1	8,169	86	1.1	101	1	1.0
Packers and wrappers	2,820	101	3.6	2,566	99	3.9	254	2	0.8
Other	49,809	713	1.4	46,558	690	1.5	3,251	23	0.7
Total	160,271	4,254	2.7	152,382	4,090	2.7	7,889	164	2.1

Source: "Furniture Industry, Major Job Categories by Race and Sex, United States," William E. Fulmer, *The Negro in the Furniture Industry*, p. 52. Primary source: U.S. Bureau of the Census, *Negro Population: 1790-1915*, Table 22. *Notes:* 1. Includes "Manufacturers and Proprietors," "Officials," "Managers and Superintendents," and "Foremen and Overseers." 2. Includes "Clerk (general)," "Clerk (shipping)," "Messenger, Errand and office Boys," and "Stenographers and Typewriters."

★ 1228 ★

Employees and Employment

Furniture Industry: Manufacturing Employees and Cabinetmakers, by Region, 1900

	Furniture manufactory employees		Cabinetmakers	
	Total Negroes	Percent of U.S. total	Total Negroes	Percent of U.S. total
New England	13	2.8	5	1.5
Southern North Atlantic	30	6.6	22	6.4
North Atlantic Division	43	9.4	27	7.9
Northern South Atlantic	35	7.7	51	15.0
Southern South Atlantic	205	45.0	107	31.5
South Atlantic Division	240	52.7	158	46.5
Eastern North Central	20	4.4	17	5.0
Western North Central	15	3.3	9	2.7
North Central Division	35	7.7	26	7.7
Eastern South Central	101	22.1	68	20.0
Western South Central	35	7.7	61	17.9
South Central Division	136	29.8	129	37.9
Rocky Mountain	-	-	-	-
Basin & Plateau	-	-	-	-
Pacific	2	04	-	-
Western Division	2	0.4	-	-
United States	456	100.0	340	100.0

Source: "Furniture Industry, Regional Location of Negro Furniture Manufacturing Employees and Cabinetmakers, 1900," William E. Fulmer, *The Negro in the Furniture Industry*, p. 50. Primary source: *U.S. Census of Population, 1900: Negroes in the United States*, Table 26.

★ 1229 ★

Employees and Employment

Furniture Industry: Percent Black Employment by Job Category and Region, 1964-1970 - I

Region	Total					White collar				
	1964	1966	1967	1969	1970	1964	1966	1967	1969	1970
New England	2.6	1.2	2.2	1.1	-	0.3	0.1	1.2	0.3	-
Middle Atlantic	6.1	6.9	8.5	10.4	7.9	1.6	1.7	2.0	3.3	3.3
South	6.9	16.2	18.0	19.6	19.5	0.5	0.8	1.1	1.5	1.7
Midwest	6.2	7.1	7.0	6.1	6.6	0.5	07	1.1	1.1	1.3
West (Pacific)	8.1	10.0	9.5	7.8	-	1.1	1.7	2.0	1.3	-
United States	6.4	11.5	12.7	13.4	13.2	0.8	1.0	1.2	1.6	1.7

Source: "Furniture Industry, Percent negro Employment by Job Category, United States Regions, 1964-1970," William E. Fulmer, *The Negro in the Furniture Industry*, p. 84. Primary source: Tables 22, 28, 29, 33, 38, and 43.

★ 1230 ★

Employees and Employment

Furniture Industry: Percent Black Employment by Job Category and Region, 1964-1970 - II

Region	Blue collar				
	1964	1966	1967	1969	1970
New England	3.4	1.5	2.4	1.3	-
Middle Atlantic	7.5	8.5	10.1	12.3	9.1
South	8.1	18.5	20.7	22.6	22.5
Midwest	8.5	8.9	8.6	7.7	8.4
West (Pacific)	10.1	12.4	11.5	9.5	-
United States	8.0	13.8	15.1	16.1	15.9

Source: "Furniture Industry, Percent negro Employment by Job Category, United States Regions, 1964-1970," William E. Fulmer, *The Negro in the Furniture Industry*, p. 84. Primary source: Tables 22, 28, 29, 33, 38, and 43.

★ 1231 ★

Employees and Employment

Furniture Industry: Percent Black Employment by Job Category in Ten Major Employment States, 1966-1970

	Total				White collar				Blue collar			
	1966	1967	1969	1970	1966	1967	1969	1970	1966	1967	1969	1970
North Carolina	11.6	13.4	15.1	14.4	0.7	0.7	1.2	1.6	13.1	15.2	17.1	16.4
California	10.0	11.0	9.7	8.9	1.7	2.2	1.5	1.9	12.4	13.5	12.1	10.8
New York	4.0	5.7	7.3	7.7	1.7	1.7	2.9	3.4	4.7	6.9	8.7	9.1
Pennsylvania	5.2	6.2	10.0	6.4	1.0	0.3	2.0	1.7	6.5	7.3	11.7	7.5
Illinois	16.3	16.5	15.6	16.1	1.4	1.8	2.1	2.1	21.7	21.4	22.5	23.4
Virginia	19.0	20.9	23.5	25.2	0.7	0.7	1.0	1.4	22.1	24.2	27.2	28.9
Indiana	1.4	1.7	2.5	1.7	0.1	0.2	0.5	0.3	1.6	2.0	2.9	2.0
Tennessee	15.1	14.1	13.9	14.4	1.3	1.6	1.8	1.9	17.2	16.1	15.9	16.8
Michigan	7.1	5.0	5.7	5.7	0.6	0.5	0.8	1.1	8.9	6.3	7.3	7.3
Ohio	6.7	7.8	6.4	6.6	0.8	2.3	1.3	1.6	9.1	9.7	8.2	8.3
United States	11.5	12.7	13.4	13.2	1.0	1.2	1.6	1.7	13.8	15.1	16.1	15.9

Source: "Furniture Industry, Percent negro Employment by Job Category, Ten Major Employment States, 1966-1970," William E. Fulmer, *The Negro in the Furniture Industry*, p. 85. Primary source: Appendix tables A-2 to A-5 and A-29 to A-68.

★ 1232 ★

Employees and Employment

Furniture Industry: Percent Black Employment by State and Job Category, the South, 1964-1970

State[1]	Total				White collar				Blue collar			
	1964	1967	1969	1970	1966	1967	1969	1970	1964	1967	1969	1970
Alabama	19.4	23.6	30.9	30.8	1.0	0.4	0.4	1.2	23.4	27.3	34.8	34.9
Arkansas	11.3	8.8	4.2	11.2	0.3	0.3	0.1	0.6	12.9	10.0	5.0	12.9
Florida	13.3	15.7	17.4	17.5	0.6	2.5	1.0	1.6	15.5	18.0	20.1	20.6
Georgia	26.7	25.8	28.8	34.4	0.7	1.0	0.9	2.3	30.4	29.9	35.1	39.2
Kentucky	3.2	4.7	3.1	4.5	0.3	0.7	0.5	0.7	3.7	5.4	3.6	5.1
Mississippi	34.0	37.8	40.3	34.4	2.3	2.7	4.1	2.7	39.3	43.5	46.4	40.6
North Carolina	11.6	13.4	15.1	14.4	0.7	0.7	1.2	1.6	13.1	15.2	17.1	16.4
South Carolina	47.7	40.3	53.8	54.2	1.2	0.8	1.5	3.1	51.8	46.3	60.7	62.6
Tennessee	15.1	14.1	13.9	14.4	1.3	1.6	1.8	1.9	17.2	16.1	15.9	16.8
Texas	9.1	11.7	17.0	16.4	0.3	1.1	1.8	1.2	10.9	13.8	20.2	19.7
Virginia	19.0	20.9	23.5	25.2	0.7	0.7	1.0	1.4	22.1	24.2	27.2	28.9

Source: "Furniture Industry, Percent Negro Employment by State and Job Category," William E. Fulmer, *The Negro in the Furniture Industry*, p. 96. Primary source: 1966: U.S. Equal Employment Opportunity Commission, *Job Patterns for Minorities and Women in Private Industry, 1966*, Report No. 1 (Washington: The Commission, 1968), Part II; 1967: U.S. Equal Employment Opportunity Commission, *Job Patterns for Minorities and Women in Private Industry, 1967*, Report No. 2 (Washington: The Commission, 1970), Vol. I; 1969: U.S. Equal Employment Opportunity Commission; 1970: U.S. Equal Employment Opportunity Commission. *Notes:* 1. Louisiana, Maryland, and Oklahoma have been eliminated due to the small number of reporting units. .

★ 1233 ★

Employees and Employment

Furniture Industry: Total Employment by Race and Gender, by Region, 1940-1960

	All employees			Male			Female		
	Total	Negro	Percent Negro	Total	Negro	Percent Negro	Total	Negro	Percent Negro
				Northeast					
1940	61,154	1,006	1.6	54,755	959	1.8	6,399	47	0.7
1950	86,201	3,378	3.9	73,324	2,929	4.0	12,877	449	3.5
1960	89,252	5,279	5.9	73,795	4,480	6.1	15,457	799	5.2
				North Central					
1940	84,005	918	1.1	74,564	754	1.0	9,441	164	1.7
1950	115,744	3,861	3.3	95,132	2,974	3.1	20,612	887	4.3
1960	107,272	5,170	4.8	85,637	4,211	4.9	21,635	959	4.4
				South					
1940	61,750	6,133	9.9	57,953	5,747	9.9	3,797	386	10.2
1950	96,577	12,100	12.5	83,601	10,171	12.2	12,976	1,929	14.9
1960	138,313	16,092	11.6	117,277	13,742	11.7	21,036	2,350	11.2

[Continued]

★ 1233 ★

Furniture Industry: Total Employment by Race and Gender, by Region, 1940-1960

[Continued]

	All employees			Male			Female		
	Total	Negro	Percent Negro	Total	Negro	Percent Negro	Total	Negro	Percent Negro
West									
1940	18,766	66	0.4	17,139	58	0.3	1,627	8	0.5
1950	31,721	777	2.4	26,817	674	2.5	4,904	103	2.1
1960	41,857	1,397	3.3	34,847	1,226	3.5	7,010	171	2.4

Source: "Furniture Industry, Total Employment by Race, Sex, and Region: 1940- 1960," William E. Fulmer, *The Negro in the Furniture Industry*, p. 59. Primary source: *U.S. Census of Population* 1940: Vol. III, *The Labor Force, Part 1*, Table 77; 1950: Vol. II, *Characteristics of the Population, Part 1*, Table 161; 1960: *U.S. Summary*, PC(1)1D, Table 260.

★ 1234 ★

Employees and Employment

General Merchandise Industry, Employment by Race and Gender, Twelve Cities, 1940, 1950, and 1960

Year	All employees			Male			Female		
	Total	Negro[1]	Percent Negro	Total	Negro[1]	Percent Negro	Total	Negro[1]	Percent Negro
1940[2]	197,675	6,108	3.1	78,162	4,418	5.7	119,513	1,690	1.4
1950	362,817	19,623	5.4	122,736	8,908	7.3	240,081	10,715	4.5
1960	473,267	41,181	8.7	157,785	16,141	10.2	315,482	25,040	7.9

Source: "General Merchandise Industry, Including Department Stores: Employment by Race and Sex in Twelve Cities, 1940, 1950, and 1960," Charles R. Perry, *The Negro in the Department Store Industry*, p. 34. Primary source: *U.S. Census of Population*: 1940, Vol. III, *The Labor Force*, Parts 2- 5, Selected States, Table 17; 1950, Vol. II, *Characteristics of the Population*, State Volumes, Table 83; 1960, PC (1) D, *Detailed Characteristics*, State Volumes, Table 129. *Notes:* The twelve cities are Atlanta, Baltimore, Chicago, Detroit, Houston, Los Angeles-Long Beach, New York, Philadelphia, Pittsburgh, San Francisco- Oakland, St. Louis, and Washington, D.C. Cities are listed in Table 1. San Francisco omitted in 1940. 1. Nonwhite in 1940. 2. Does not include limited price variety stores.

★ 1235 ★

Employees and Employment

General Merchandise Industry, Employment by Race and Gender, United States, 1940, 1950, and 1960

	All employees			Male			Female		
	Total	Negro	Percent Negro	Total	Negro	Percent Negro	Total	Negro	Percent Negro
1940	802,640	17,472	2.2	318,173	12,988	4.1	484,467	4,484	0.9
1950	1,138,775	41,908	3.7	370,775	21,018	5.7	768,000	20,890	2.7
1960	1,581,797	78,411	5.0	498,061	34,885	7.0	1,083,736	43,526	4.0

Source: "General Merchandise Industry, Including Department Stores: Employment by Race and Sex, United States, 1940, 1950, and 1960," Charles R. Perry, *The Negro in the Department Store Industry*, p. 33. Primary source: *U.S. Census of Population*: 1940, Vol. III, *The Labor Force*, Part 1, United States Summary, Table 76; 1950, Vol. II, *Characteristics of the Population*, Part 1, United states Summary, Table 133; 1960, PC (1) 1D, United States Summary, *Detailed Characteristics*, Table 213.

★ 1236 ★

Employees and Employment

General Merchandise Industry: Employment by Gender and Occupational Group in Twelve Metropolitan Areas, 1966, 1967, 1969

Occupational group	All employees			Male			Female		
	1966[1]	1967	1969	1966	1967	1969	1966	1967	1969
Officials and managers	2.4	2.8	4.2	2.1	2.7	3.9	2.9	2.9	4.8
Professionals	1.2	2.1	3.2	1.2	2.3	3.0	1.1	1.7	3.5
Technicians	3.9	4.4	8.2	3.3	4.6	8.0	5.2	3.9	8.6
Sales workers	5.8	6.1	7.6	4.8	5.5	6.7	6.1	6.3	7.9
Office and clerical	15.1	15.2	13.6	12.0	13.3	15.3	15.6	15.5	13.3
Total white collar	7.7	8.3	8.7	4.8	5.5	6.9	9.3	9.4	9.4
Craftsmen	9.3	8.6	8.7	7.4	7.0	8.2	18.8	15.2	11.2
Operatives	22.8	23.7	21.2	20.2	21.5	21.4	26.6	27.6	20.8
Laborers	28.3	28.3	29.1	28.3	26.4	26.7	28.4	30.8	32.8
Service workers	36.2	34.1	33.0	43.5	39.8	40.2	30.1	29.3	27.1
Total blue collar	26.1	26.8	25.8	26.7	25.5	25.7	28.2	28.6	26.1
Total	12.3	12.9	12.4	14.1	13.8	13.9	12.4	12.5	11.7

Source: "General Merchandise Industry, Including Department Stores: Employment by Sex and Occupational Group, Twelve Metropolitan Areas, 1966, 1967, and 1969," Charles R. Perry, *The Negro in the Department Store Industry*, p. 57. Primary source: Appendix Tables A-4—A-6. *Notes:* 1. Twelve metropolitan areas used in total white collar, blue collar, and total. Individual occupational groups based on ten metropolitan areas, excluding Pittsburgh and San Francisco. Cities are Atlanta, Baltimore, Chicago, Detroit, Houston, Los Angeles-Long Beach, New York, St. Louis, and Washington, D.C.

★ 1237 ★

Employees and Employment

General Merchandise Industry: Employment by Gender and Occupational Group, United States, 1966, 1967, 1969

Occupational group	All employees			Male			Female		
	1966	1967	1969	1966	1967	1969	1966	1967	1969
Officials and managers	1.4	1.7	2.4	1.3	1.6	2.3	1.5	1.8	2.7
Professionals	1.5	1.9	2.6	1.6	2.0	2.6	1.3	1.9	2.7
Technicians	3.0	3.5	5.1	2.7	3.5	5.1	3.5	3.5	5.2
Sales workers	3.3	3.6	4.7	2.8	3.3	4.4	3.4	3.6	4.8
Office and clerical	7.4	8.2	7.4	8.8	9.9	10.3	7.3	8.0	7.0
Total white collar	4.0	4.5	5.0	2.9	3.4	4.2	4.4	4.8	5.3
Craftsmen	5.6	5.7	6.3	4.3	4.7	5.4	12.1	10.6	10.4
Operatives	14.8	16.1	14.9	14.5	15.3	15.8	15.3	17.6	13.2
Laborers	19.1	21.2	21.0	18.8	20.1	20.3	19.7	23.1	22.3
Service workers	26.2	25.2	24.1	34.5	32.8	30.4	19.9	19.7	19.2
Total blue collar	19.1	19.4	18.5	19.6	19.5	19.0	18.4	19.3	17.8
Total	7.4	7.8	7.8	9.5	9.7	9.7	6.4	6.9	6.9

Source: "General Merchandise Industry, Including Department Stores: Employment by Sex and Occupational Group, United States, 1966, 1967, and 1969," Charles R. Perry, *The Negro in the Department Store Industry*, p. 56. Primary source: Appendix Tables A-1—A-3.

★ 1238 ★

Employees and Employment

General Merchandise Industry: Employment by Race and Gender, United States and Twelve Metropolitan Areas, 1966, 1967, 1969

Year	All employees			Male			Female		
	Total	Negro	Percent Negro	Total	Negro	Percent Negro	Total	Negro	Percent Negro
United States									
1966	1,456,624	108,024	7.4	484,856	45,939	9.5	971,768	62,085	6.4
1967	1,619,729	126,653	7.8	539,709	52,115	9.7	1,080,020	74,538	6.9
1969	1,553,610	121,381	7.8	521,843	50,540	9.7	1,031,767	70,841	6.9
Twelve metropolitan areas									
1966[1]	487,538	59,774	12.3	n.a.	n.a.	n.a.	n.a.	n.a.	n.a.
1967	562,699	72,868	12.9	193,471	26,755	13.8	369,228	46,113	12.5
1969	505,344	62,806	12.4	173,069	24,011	13.9	332,275	38,795	11.7

Source: "General Merchandise Industry, Including Department Stores: Employment by Race and Sex, United States and Twelve Metropolitan Areas, 1966, 1967, and 1969," Charles R. Perry, *The Negro in the Department Store Industry*, p. 453. Primary source: Appendix Tables A-1—A-6. *Notes:* The cities are Atlanta, Baltimore, Chicago, Detroit, Houston, Los Angeles-Long Beach, New York, Philadelphia, Pittsburgh, san Francisco- Oakland, St. Louis, and Washington, D.C. 1. Including Pittsburgh and san Francisco-Oakland.

★ 1239 ★

Employees and Employment

General Merchandise Industry: Employment by Race, Gender, and Region, Twelve Cities, 1940, 1950, and 1960

Region	All employees			Male			Female		
	Total	Negro[1]	Percent Negro	Total	Negro[1]	Percent Negro	Total	Negro[1]	Percent Negro
Northeast									
1940[2]	88,402	2,132	2.4	37,171	1,645	4.4	51,231	487	1.0
1950	143,981	7,958	5.5	52,762	3,752	7.1	91,219	4,206	4.6
1960	172,350	16,239	9.4	60,020	6,807	11.3	112,330	9,432	8.4
Border									
1940[2]	25,045	1,792	7.2	9,395	1,353	14.4	15,650	439	2.8
1950	43,339	3,987	9.2	13,389	1,995	14.9	29,950	1,992	6.7
1960	50,377	5,974	11.9	14,373	2,583	18.0	36,004	3,391	9.4
South									
1940[2]	6,511	644	9.9	2,325	492	21.2	4,186	152	3.6
1950	16,484	1,440	8.7	5,270	853	16.2	11,214	587	5.2
1960	27,177	3,150	11.6	9,444	1,773	18.8	17,733	1,377	7.8
Midwest									
1940[2]	63,747	1,091	1.7	24,297	607	2.5	39,450	484	1.2
1950	97,585	4,636	4.8	32,498	1,529	4.7	65,087	3,107	4.8
1960	128,869	12,222	9.5	44,163	3,482	7.9	84,706	8,740	10.3
West									
1940[2]	13,970	449	3.2	4,974	321	6.5	8,996	128	1.4
1950	61,428	1,602	2.6	18,817	779	4.1	42,611	823	1.9
1960	94,494	3,596	3.8	29,785	1,496	5.0	64,709	2,100	3.2

Source: "General Merchandise Industry, Including Department Stores: Employment by Race and Sex in Twelve Cities, 1940, 1950, and 1960," Charles R. Perry, *The Negro in the Department Store Industry*, p. 41. Primary source: *U.S. Census of Population*: 1940, Vol. III, *The Labor Force*, Parts 2- 5, Selected States, Table 17; 1950, Vol. II, *Characteristics of the Population*, State Volumes, Table 83; 1960, PC (1) D, *Detailed Characteristics*, State Volumes, Table 129. *Notes:* 1. Nonwhite in 1940. 2. Does not include limited price variety stores.

★ 1240 ★

Employees and Employment

Longshore Industry: Employment Distribution, Region and Selected States, 1970

State	Total	Percent	Negro	Percent
Total United States	42,349	100.0	15,326	100.0
Northeast (4)	12,530	29.6	2,606	17.0
South Atlantic (5)	5,886	13.9	4,325	28.2
South Central (3)	8,508	20.1	5,018	32.7
North Central (2)	978	2.3	434	2.8
West (1)	6,276	14.8	1,636	10.7

Source: "Longshore Industry, Total and Negro Employment for the United States and Selected States, 1970," Lester Rubin, *The Negro in the Longshore Industry*, p. 44. Published by permission. Primary source: *U.S. Census of Population: 1970*, PC(1)- D, *Detailed Characteristics*, U.S. Summary, Table 223, State Volumes, Table 171. *Note:* Figures for employed males only.

★ 1241 ★

Employees and Employment

Longshore Industry: Employment by Race, United States and Selected States, 1940-1960

State	1940			1950			1960		
	Total	Negro	Percent Negro	Total	Negro	Percent Negro	Total	Negro	Percent Negro
Total United States	63,241	20,279	32.1	62,003	21,197	34.2	55,479	19,129	34.5
Total eight states	20,418	15,759	77.2	17,964	13,279	73.9	16,912	12,223	72.3
Alabama	1,272	1,173	92.2	1,112	1,036	93.2	1,080	1,027	95.1
Florida	2,845	2,645	93.0	1,658	1,434	86.5	1,543	1,272	82.4
Georgia	1,353	1,308	96.7	687	657	95.6	787	744	94.5
Louisiana	3,874	2,719	70.2	4,870	3,734	76.7	4,722	3,561	75.4
Maryland	3,358	2,016	60.0	3,445	2,314	67.2	2,117	1,248	59.0
South Carolina	748	729	97.5	504	479	95.0	607	583	96.0
Texas	4,393	2,790	63.5	4,044	2,142	53.0	4,615	2,517	54.5
Virginia	2,575	2,379	92.4	1,644	1,483	90.2	1,441	1,271	88.2
New York	16,242	1,509	9.3	18,105	2,643	14.6	13,638	2,014	14.8
New Jersey	3,816	463	12.1	3,839	509	13.3	3,524	421	11.9
Pennsylvania	3,273	1,342	41.0	3,152	1,502	47.7	2,156	1,120	51.9
Massachusetts	2,221	172	7.7	1,611	86	5.3	1,322	41	3.1
California	6,865	83	1.2	8,481	2,032	24.0	7,869	1,820	23.1

Source: "Longshore Industry, Total and Negro Employment by Race for United States and Selected States, 1940-1960," Lester Rubin, *The Negro in the Longshore Industry*, p. 42. Published by permission. Primary source: *U.S. Census of Population*: 1940, Vol. III, *The Labor Force*, Part 1, U.S. Summary, Table 62; Part 2, Table 13, State Volumes, Parts 2-5, Table 13; 1950, Vol. II, *Characteristics of the Population*, Part 1, U.S. Summary, Table 128, State Volumes, Table 77; 1960, Vol. I, *Characteristics of the Population*, Part 1, U.S. Summary, Table 205, State Volumes, Table 122. *Note:* Figures for employed males only.

★ 1242 ★

Employees and Employment

Longshore Industry: Employment for United States and Selected States

State	Total	Negro	Percent Negro
Total United States	42,349	15,326	36.2
Total eight states	14,394	9,343	64.9
Alabama	752	652	86.7
Florida	1,570	1,155	73.6
Georgia	672	564	83.9
Louisiana	3,644	2,499	68.6
Maryland	1,756	980	55.8
South Carol	547	524	95.8
Texas	4,112	1,867	45.4
Virginia	1,341	1,102	82.2
New York	7,175	1,098	15.3
New Jersey	2,955	661	22.4
Pennsylvania	1,634	843	51.6
Massachusetts	766	4	0.5
California	6,276	1,636	26.1

Source: "Longshore Industry, Total and Negro Employment for the United States and Selected States, 1970," Lester Rubin, *The Negro in the Longshore Industry*, p. 44. Published by permission. Primary source: *U.S. Census of Population: 1970*, PC(1)- D, *Detailed Characteristics*, U.S. Summary, Table 223, State Volumes, Table 171. *Note:* Figures for employed males only.

★ 1243 ★

Employees and Employment

Longshore Industry: United States and Selected States, 1910-1930

State	1910			1920			1930		
	Total	Negro	Percent Negro	Total	Negro	Percent Negro	Total	Negro	Percent Negro
Total United States	62,813	16,379	26.1	85,605	27,206	31.8	73,944	25,434	34.4
Total eight states	16,390	12,084	73.7	22,419	17,519	78.1	20,800	16,775[1]	80.6
Alabama	888	715	80.5	1,117	1,010	90.4	1,443	1,383	95.8
Florida	1,709	1,530	89.5	1,470	1,312	89.3	2,028	1,882	92.8
Georgia	1,762	1,683	95.5	1,799	1,680	93.4	1,608	1,554	96.6
Louisiana	2,654	1,588	59.8	4,390	2,862	65.2	5,322	3,953	74.3
Maryland	2,975	1,933	65.0	4,349	3,179	73.1	3,400	2,334	68.6
South Carolina	560	513	91.6	762	733	96.2	963	n.a.	-
Texas	2,386	843	35.3	3,601	2,052	57.0	3,926	2,739	69.8
Virginia	3,456	3,279	94.9	4,931	4,691	95.1	3,073	2,930	95.3
New York	18,545	1,119	6.0	37,526	5,429	14.5	22,119	3,357	15.2
New Jersey	4,984	136	2.7	4,977	383	7.7	4,477	542	12.1
Pennsylvania	3,522	1,428	40.5	4,224	2,409	57.0	4,345	2,252	51.8

[Continued]

★ 1243 ★

Longshore Industry: United States and Selected States, 1910-1930

[Continued]

State	1910			1920			1930		
	Total	Negro	Percent Negro	Total	Negro	Percent Negro	Total	Negro	Percent Negro
Massachusetts	3,341	154	4.6	2,843	275	9.7	3,049	255	8.4
California	2,593	38	1.5	3,728	44	1.2	6,346	91	1.4

Source: "Longshore Industry, Total and Negro Employment for United States and Selected States, 1910-1930," Lester Rubin, *The Negro in the Longshore Industry*, p. 41. Published by permission. Primary source: *U.S. Census of Population*: 1910, Vol. IV, *Occupational Statistics*, Tables 6, 7; 1920, Vol. IV, *Occupations*, Table 1, pp. 875-10323, Table 6, p. 386, Table 10, p. 427; 1930, Vol. IV, *Occupations by States*, Tables 4, 11, 13. *Notes:* Figures for employed males only. 1. Seven states only.

★ 1244 ★

Employees and Employment

Proprietors, Managers, and Officials (Males), 1940

Commercial Field	Total	White	Negro	Per cent Negro
Wholesale Trade	227,334	222,779	3,589	1.6
Manufacturing	402,506	401,366	841	0.2
Transportation and Communication	134,232	133,343	818	0.6
Eating & Drinking Places	200,519	191,402	6,410	3.2
Retail Trades (except eating and drinking places)	1,242,323	1,225,551	13,467	1.1
Finance, Insurance, Real Estate	174,668	173,647	907	0.5
Construction	113,898	112,532	1,339	1.2
Postmaster and Misc. Governmental Officials	198,377	197,541	693	0.3

Source: "Employed Proprietors, Managers, and Officials (Male) in Selected Commercial Fields by Race—1940," Jessie Parkhurst Guzman, ed., *Negro Year Book: A Review of Events Affecting Negro Life, 1941-1946*, p. 143.

★ 1245 ★

Employees and Employment

Retail Food Industry Employees by Race and Gender, United States, 1940, 1950, 1960

Year	All employees			Male			Female		
	Total	Negro	Percent Negro	Total	Negro	Percent Negro	Total	Negro	Percent Negro
1940	1,489,303	53,483	3.6	1,206,548	47,157	3.9	282,755	6,326	2.2
1950	1,719,403	74,190	4.3	,238,605	55,056	4.4	480,798	19,134	4.0
1960	1,691,982	77,014	4.6	1,121,656	55,568	5.0	570,326	21,446	3.8

Source: "Retail Food Industry, Employment by Race and Sex, United States, 1940, 1950, and 1960," Gordon Bloom and F. Marion Fletcher, *The Negro in the Supermarket Industry*, p. 44. Primary source: *U.S. Census of Population*: 1940, Vol. III, *The Labor Force*, Part 1, U.S. Summary, Table 76; 1950, Vol. II, *Characteristics of the Population*, Part 1, U.S. summary, Table 133; 1960, PC (2) 7F, *Industrial Characteristics*, Table 3. *Notes:* Tables 10-13 are based on the census definition "Food and dairy product stores and milk retailing." This is more inclusive than the SIC 541-543 groups shown in tables 4 and 7.

★ 1246 ★

Employees and Employment

Retail Food Industry: Employees by Race, Sex and Regions, 1940, 1950, 1960

Region	All employees			Male			Female		
	Total	Negro	Percent Negro	Total	Negro	Percent Negro	Total	Negro	Percent Negro
Northeast									
1940	508,101	6,710	1.3	424,007	6,017	1.4	84,094	693	0.8
1950	515,834	11,488	2.2	398,214	9,306	2.3	117,620	2,182	1.9
1960	458,689	13,846	3.0	319,030	10,256	3.2	139,659	3,590	2.6
South									
1940	366,533	39,981	10.9	303,187	35,530	11.7	63,346	4,361	6.9
1950	491,927	48,568	9.9	354,178	35,944	10.1	137,749	12,624	9.2
1960	512,180	46,460	9.1	346,005	34,333	9.9	166,175	12,127	7.3
Midwest									
1940	451,555	6,379	1.4	349,703	5,194	1.5	101,852	1,185	1.2
1950	501,508	12,086	2.4	335,503	8,266	2.5	166,005	3,820	2.3
1960	477,672	14,167	3.0	294,507	9,627	3.3	183,165	4,540	2.5
West									
1940	163,114	503	0.3	129,651	416	0.3	33,463	87	0.3

[Continued]

★ 1246 ★

Retail Food Industry: Employees by Race, Sex and Regions, 1940, 1950, 1960

[Continued]

Region	All employees			Male			Female		
	Total	Negro	Percent Negro	Total	Negro	Percent Negro	Total	Negro	Percent Negro
1950	210,134	2,048	1.0	150,710	1,540	1.0	59,424	508	0.9
1960	241,147	3,082	1.3	163,049	2,295	1.4	78,098	787	1.0

Source: "Retail Food Industry, Employment by Race and Sex, Four Regions, 1940, 1950, and 1960," Gordon Bloom and F. Marion Fletcher, *The Negro in the Supermarket Industry*, p. 47. Primary source: *U.S. Census of Population*: 1940, Vol. III, *The Labor Force*, Part 1, U.S. Summary, Table 77; 1950, Vol. II, *Characteristics of the Population*, Part 1, U.S. summary, Table 161; 1960, PC (1) 1D, *United States Summary*, Table 260.

★ 1247 ★

Employees and Employment

Textile Industries as Major Employers, 1910 and 1920

	1910	1920
Lace and Embroidery Mills	165	252
Silk Mills	560	605
Woolen Mills	343	661
Dyeing, Finishing and Printing Mills	645	836
Knitting Mills	816	1,991
Cotton Mills	7,216	16,465
Other Textile Mills	555	3,924

Source: "Textile Industries Employing the Largest Number of Negroes, 1910 and 1920," Monroe N. Work, ed., *Negro Year Book: An Annual Encyclopedia of the Negro, 1925-26*, p. 364.

★ 1248 ★

Employees and Employment

Urban Transit Industry: Employment and the Population in Selected SMSA's, 1950 and 1960

SMSA	Year	Negro employment in transit	Negro population	Participation rate[1]
Atlanta	1950	153	165,591	0.09
	1960	169	230,737	0.07
Boston	1950	109	51,568	0.21
	1960	116	77,753	0.15
Chicago	1950	1,300	586,598	0.22
	1960	3,053	889,961	0.34

[Continued]

★ 1248 ★

Urban Transit Industry: Employment and the Population in Selected SMSA's, 1950 and 1960

[Continued]

SMSA	Year	Negro employment in transit	Negro population	Participation rate[1]
Cincinnati	1950	114	95,059	0.12
	1960	93	127,713	0.07
Cleveland	1950	744	152,118	0.49
	1960	792	257,258	0.31
Detroit	1950	1,399	357,800	0.39
	1960	1,339	558,792	0.24
Houston	1950	215	149,286	0.14
	1960	182	246,118	0.07
Los Angeles-Long Beach	1950	594	218,770	0.27
	1960	799	464,112	0.17
New Orleans	1950	151	199,527	0.08
	1960	175	267,303	0.07
New York	1950	5,730	820,227	0.70
	1960	8,086	1,224,590	0.66
Philadelphia	1950	941	480,075	0.20
	1960	1,019	670,939	0.15
Pittsburgh	1950	125	136,285	0.09
	1960	104	160,845	0.06
St. Louis	1950	248	215,436	0.12
	1960	433	294,715	0.15
San Francisco	1950	494	147,223	0.34
	1960	716	237,428	0.30
Washington, D.C.	1950	598	337,757	0.18
	1960	578	485,117	0.12

Source: "Urban Transit Industry, Negro Employment Relative to Negro Population, Selected Standard Metropolitan Statistical Areas, 1950 and 1960," Philip W. Jeffress, *The Negro in the Transit Industry*, p. 68. Primary source: *U.S. Census of Population*: 1950: Vol. II, *Characteristics of the Population*, State Volumes, Tables 34 and 83; 1960: PC (1) 1D, *Detailed Characteristics*, State Volumes, Tables 96 and 127. *Note:* 1. Negro employment in transit as a percentage of the Negro population.

★ 1249 ★

Employees and Employment

Urban Transit Industry: Employment by Race and Gender, Four Regions, 1940-1960

Region	Year	All employees			Male			Female		
		Total	Negro	Percent Negro	Total	Negro	Percent Negro	Total	Negro	Percent Negro
Northeast	1940	79,187	1,961	2.5	75,884	1,897	2.5	3,303	64	1.9
	1950	118,312	7,349	6.2	110,551	6,943	6.3	7,761	406	5.2
	1960	102,121	10,040	9.8	94,275	9,344	9.9	7,846	696	8.9
North Central	1940	64,194	966	1.5	61,611	926	1.5	2,583	40	1.5

[Continued]

★ 1249 ★

Urban Transit Industry: Employment by Race and Gender, Four Regions, 1940-1960

[Continued]

Region	Year	All employees			Male			Female		
		Total	Negro	Percent Negro	Total	Negro	Percent Negro	Total	Negro	Percent Negro
	1950	89,400	4,701	5.3	82,690	4,370	5.3	6,710	331	4.9
	1960	68,000	6,474	9.5	60,585	6,162	10.2	7,415	312	4.2
South	1940	35,373	2,891	8.2	33,857	2,775	8.2	1,516	116	7.7
	1950	78,586	7,447	9.5	70,990	6,531	9.2	7,596	916	12.1
	1940	81,053	12,959	16.0	70,270	11,414	16.2	10,783	1,545	14.3
West	1940	23,916	283	1.2	23,011	248	1.2	905	35	3.9
	1950	37,667	1,339	3.6	33,761	1,215	3.6	3,906	124	3.2
	1960	37,314	1,848	5.0	31,061	1,741	5.6	6,253	107	1.7

Source: "Urban Transit Industry, Employment by Race and Sex, Four Regions, 1940- 1960," Philip W. Jeffress, *The Negro in the Transit Industry,* p. 50. Primary source: *U.S. Census of Population*: 1940: Vol. III, *The Labor Force,* Table 77; 1950: Vol. II, *Characteristics of the Population,* Part 1, U.S. Summary, Table 161; 1960: PC(1) 1D, U.S. *Summary,* Detailed Characteristics, Table 260.

★ 1250 ★

Employees and Employment

Urban Transit Industry: Employment by Race and Gender, Selected SMSA's, 1950 and 1960

SMSA	Year	All employees			Male			Female			Percent Negro in SMSA	Percent Negro employed in all industries in SMSA
		Total	Negro	Percent Negro	Total	Negro	Percent Negro	Total	Negro	Percent Negro		
Atlanta	1950	1,612	153	9.5	1,493	141	9.4	119	12	10.1	24.6	25.4
	1960	1,783	169	9.5	1,640	154	9.4	143	15	10.5	22.7	21.4
Boston	1950	10,279	109	1.1	9,496	104	1.1	783	5	0.6	2.2	2.2
	1960	7,344	116	1.6	6,904	116	1.7	440	-	-	3.0	2.9
Chicago	1950	24,931	1,300	5.2	23,499	1,247	5.3	1,432	53	3.7	10.7	9.6
	1960	16,863	3,053	18.1	15,715	2,955	18.8	1,148	98	8.5	14.3	11.8
Cincinnati	1950	2,952	114	3.9	2,768	93	3.4	184	21	11.4	10.5	9.6
	1960	1,871	93	5.0	1,756	77	4.4	115	16	13.9	11.9	10.9
Cleveland	1950	5,520	744	13.5	5,002	662	13.2	518	82	15.8	10.4	9.6
	1960	3,916	792	20.2	3,479	749	21.5	437	43	9.8	14.3	12.6
Detroit	1950	8,465	1,399	16.5	7,897	1,375	17.4	568	24	4.2	11.9	10.6
	1960	4,862	1,339	27.5	4,210	1,308	31.1	652	31	4.8	14.8	12.8
Houston	1950	2,237	215	9.6	2,080	206	9.9	157	9	5.7	18.5	19.9
	1960	2,197	182	8.3	1,464	140	9.6	733	42	5.7	19.8	19.2
Los Angeles-Long Beach	1950	9,262	594	6.4	8,392	521	6.2	870	73	8.4	5.0	5.2
	1960	8,509	799	9.4	7,147	744	10.4	1,362	55	4.0	6.9	6.4
New Orleans	1950	2,265	151	6.7	2,083	113	5.4	182	38	20.9	29.1	27.0
	1960	2,182	175	8.0	2,067	149	7.2	115	26	22.6	30.8	26.9
New York[1]	1950	47,775	5,730	12.0	45,571	5,398	11.8	2,204	332	15.1	8.6	8.8
	1960	46,419	8,086	17.4	44,238	7,516	17.0	2,181	570	26.1	11.4	11.5
Philadelphia	1950	14,967	941	6.3	13,466	904	6.7	1,501	37	2.5	13.1	11.9
	1960	10,553	1,019	9.7	9,451	956	10.1	1,102	63	5.7	15.4	14.6
Pittsburgh	1950	5,985	125	2.1	5,636	119	2.1	349	6	1.7	6.2	5.3
	1960	3,786	104	2.7	3,530	101	2.9	256	3	1.2	6.7	5.7
St. Louis	1950	4,722	248	5.3	4,471	241	5.4	251	7	2.8	12.8	11.2
	1960	3,501	433	12.4	3,207	413	12.9	294	20	6.8	14.3	11.8

[Continued]

★ 1250 ★

Urban Transit Industry: Employment by Race and Gender, Selected SMSA's, 1950 and 1960
[Continued]

SMSA	Year	All employees			Male			Female			Percent Negro in SMSA	Percent Negro employed in all industries in SMSA
		Total	Negro	Percent Negro	Total	Negro	Percent Negro	Total	Negro	Percent Negro		
San Francisco	1950	7,375	494	6.7	6,593	471	7.1	782	23	2.9	6.6	5.8
	1960	6,000	716	11.9	5,091	687	13.5	909	29	3.2	8.5	7.0
Washington, D.C.	1950	6,117	598	9.8	5,755	567	9.9	362	31	8.6	23.1	24.1
	1960	5,362	578	10.8	4,693	487	10.4	669	91	13.6	24.4	24.5

Source: "Urban Transit Industry, Employment by Race and Sex, Selected Standard Metropolitan Statistical Areas, 1950 and 1960," Philip W. Jeffress, *The Negro in the Transit Industry,* pp. 56-57. Primary source: *U.S. Census of Population*: 1950: Vol. II, *Characteristics of the Population*, State Volumes, Tables 34 and 83; 1960: PC (1) 1D, *Detailed Characteristics*, State Volumes, Tables 96 and 129. *Notes:* Data include interurban bus line employment. 1. New York portion of New York-Northeastern New Jersey SMSA.

★ 1251 ★
Employees and Employment

Urban Transit Industry: Employment by Race and Gender, Southern and Border States, 1940

State	All employees			Male			Female		
	Total	Negro	Percent Negro	Total	Negro	Percent Negro	Total	Negro	Percent Negro
Alabama	1,632	184	11.3	1,562	174	11.1	70	10	14.3
Arkansas	1,012	97	9.6	963	95	9.9	49	2	4.1
Florida	2,045	243	11.9	1,938	230	11.9	107	13	12.1
Georgia	1,894	177	9.3	1,799	165	9.2	95	12	12.6
Kentucky	2,345	114	4.9	2,231	109	4.9	114	5	4.4
Louisiana	2,340	171	7.3	2,266	166	7.3	74	5	6.8
Maryland	4,049	153	3.8	3,888	146	3.8	161	7	4.3
Mississippi	772	89	11.5	720	85	11.8	52	4	7.7
Missouri	6,998	197	2.8	6,727	193	2.9	271	4	1.5
North Carolina	1,807	234	12.9	1,728	230	13.3	79	4	5.1
Oklahoma	1,529	106	6.9	1,459	102	7.0	70	4	5.7
South Carolina	563	66	11.7	531	64	12.1	32	2	6.2
Tennessee	2,581	327	12.7	2,474	318	12.9	107	9	8.4
Texas	5,408	365	6.7	5,219	350	6.7	189	15	7.9
Virginia	2,868	237	8.3	2,744	225	8.2	124	12	9.7
Total	37,843	2,760	7.3	36,249	2,652	7.3	1,594	108	6.8

Source: "Urban Transit Industry, Employment by Race and Sex, Southern and Border States, 1940," Philip W. Jeffress, *The Negro in the Transit Industry,* p. 42. Primary source: *U.S. Census of Population*: 1940: Vol. III, *The Labor Force*, Parts 2-5, Table 18.

Employment and Training

★ 1252 ★

Civilian Conservation Core Activities, 1940

300,000 youths have served in the CCC since its establishment.

30,000 youths and war veterans were actively participating in the total enrollment.

$700,000 was allotted each month to parents and dependents at home.

12,000 have completed courses in first-aid.

2,000 project assistants, leaders, and assistant leaders were employed.

600 cooks were employed in CCC kitchens.

151 college graduates were serving as educational directors.

400 typists were assigned to the headquarters of the camps.

6 chaplains of the U.S. Army Reserve Corps directed the religious activities in the camps, aided by ministers of nearby communities.

15,000 enrollees have been taught to read and write.

27,000 have regularly attended academic, vocational and job training classes offered in the camps during leisure hours. (Howard University, Wilberforce University, Tuskegee Institute, Hampton Institute, Florida A.& M. College, Tennessee A.&I. State College and some other colleges have granted fellowships and scholarships to CCC enrollees.)

2 colored camp commanders were on active duty.

1 colored camp superintendent and three graduate engineers were in charge of the and project at Gettysburg National Military Park.

Source: "Statistics on Negro CCC Activities (As of May 1940)," Florence Murray, ed., *The Negro Handbook,* 1942, p. 159.

★ 1253 ★

Employment and Training

Civilian Conservation Core: Characteristics, 1940

The creation of the Civilian Conservation Corps in the spring of 1933 set in motion a program for the conservation of human and natural resources in the United States. Utilizing the services of the War Department, the Department of the Interior and Agriculture, the Veterans' Administration and conservation and welfare agencies in every State, the CCC has, for nine years, been operating a chain of outdoor camps in forests, parks and on farm lands, as well as the public domain.

A constant stream of unmarried, unemployed young men between the ages of 17 and 23 have entered these camps, working for periods of from six months to two years and receiving vocational and other training.

The CCC operated as an independent agency from April, 1933, through June 30, 1939, when it became a part of the Federal Security Agency.

During the first six months that the Corps was in operation, about 1500 CCC camps were set up in the national parks, forests and on farms. At its peak strength in the late summer of 1935, a total of 2,652 camps were in operation, of which about 265, or ten per cent, were for colored youth only. In some of the Northern areas, a few Negroes were enrolled in camps with white youths.

Records show that 2,450,000 young men, war veterans, Indians and territorials, had been enrolled for CCC work since the conservation plan was begun up to 1941. Of this number, about 300,000 were colored.

In May, 1940, 151 all-colored and racially mixed camps were distributed throughout 43 States. A total of 83 all-colored camps were located in 12 Southern States; while the remaining 68 were distributed throughout 30 Eastern and Northern States, with 3 in California.

As of May, 1940, there were approximately 40 colored CCC companies in soil conservation projects. More than 100 companies were carrying on reforestation and forest protection work, recreational development, levee and drainage projects, mosquito control, fish and game conservation and flood control work.

Source: Florence Murray, ed. *The Negro Handbook,* 1942, p. 159.

Federal Security Agencies

★ 1254 ★

U.S. Employment Service Division: Placements, 1940

Social Security Board region and State	Total placements	Black placements	Social Security Board region and state	Total placements	Black placements
Total	3,782,984	756,880	South Carolina	39,034	24,149
Region I:			Tennessee	65,945	30,277
Connecticut	67,691	3,452	Region VIII:		
Maine	23,021	70	Iowa	78,383	665
Massachusetts	52,849	678	Minnesota	71,922	168
New Hampshire	23,290	114	Nebraska	33,908	458
Rhode Island	11,031	112	North Dakota	41,432	93
Vermont	12,118	36	South Dakota	17,823	101
Region II:			Region IX:		
New York	339,935	41,177	Arkansas	71,365	18,636
Region III:			Kansas	51,876	3,321
Delaware	14,144	7,709	Missouri	96,876	11,376
New Jersey	120,397	27,281	Oklahoma	57,237	12,979
Pennsylvania	155,004	11,788	Region X:		
Region IV:			Louisiana	60,839	37,231
District of Columbia	48,092	29,786	New Mexico	20,051	792
Maryland	48,945	17,621	Texas	371,018	125,821
North Carolina	97,419	50,910	Region XI:		
Virginia	70,906	41,280	Arizona	30,951	9,759
West Virginia	33,975	6,856	Colorado	61,718	13,693
Region V:			Idaho	30,828	89
Kentucky	33,906	7,364	Montana	21,450	204
Michigan	133,407	6,709	Utah	18,612	95
Ohio	183,510	23,818	Wyoming	13,312	333
Region VI:			Region XII:		
Illinois	166,367	15,513	California	264,423	16,543
Indiana	98,407	8,004	Nevada	12,977	164
Wisconsin	81,770	539	Oregon	63,358	
Region VII:			Washington	89,117	877
Alabama	50,099	26,132	Territories:		
Florida	67,101	27,299	Alaska	6,650	485
Georgia	96,222	57,019	Hawaii	10,903	8,522
Mississippi	51,370	28,570			

Source: "Comparison of Total and Colored Placements by States, January-December 1940," Florence Murray, ed., *The Negro Handbook*, 1942, p. 164. Primary source: Research and Statistics, Bureau of Employment Security, Social Security Board.

Federal Works Agencies

★ 1255 ★

National Defense Vocational Training Project, March 1941

On March 26, 1941, a survey of an eight-month period indicated 8,113 Negro WPA trainees during the period.

	Number
Enrolled in training classes	3,732
Known to have obtained other employment	792
Voluntarily separated, reason unknown	484
Reemployed on other WPA projects	2,005
All other	1,100
Total	8,113

Source: "National Defense Vocational Training Project," Florence Murray, ed., *The Negro Handbook*, 1942, p. 161.

★ 1256 ★

Federal Works Agencies

WPA Employment: Distribution, 1941

On April 30, 1941, the 236,636 certified Negro workers assigned to WPA projects were 16.3 per cent of the total. The median age of these workers was 41.14. Male workers numbered 197,439; female 39,197. These workers were 43.3 per cent of the workers in Louisiana, 42.9 per cent in South Carolina, 34.2 per cent in Delaware, 32.4 per cent in Maryland, and 30.8 per cent in Alabama. They were 22.6 per cent in Illinois, 22.1 per cent in Ohio, 19.5 per cent in Michigan, and 16.8 per cent in Pennsylvania. They were 68.9 per cent in the District of Columbia, where 958 of the 5,503 Negro workers were female, and 22 per cent in New York City. On April 2, 1941, there were 95,576 Negro workers employed in eleven Southern States; 24.5 per cent of the total workers. A year ago (1940), they numbered 100,234 but were only 22.9 per cent of the total.

State	Number	Percent of state total
Alabama	10,048	29.1
Arkansas	5,589	17.2
Florida	6,803	25.4
Georgia	9,444	27.2
Louisiana	11,874	40.8
Mississippi	7,856	24.8
North Carolina	11,056	28.8
South Carolina	11,182	40.0
Tennessee	3,328	10.7

[Continued]

★ 1256 ★

WPA Employment: Distribution, 1941
[Continued]

State	Number	Percent of state total
Texas	14,217	16.8
Virginia	4,179	22.4

Source: "Work Projects Administration, Project Employment," Florence Murray, ed., *The Negro Handbook*, 1942, p. 161.

★ 1257 ★
Federal Works Agencies

WPA Workers in Southern States: Type of Employment, 1935-1941

Most of the WPA workers in Southern states, 79,620, were employed on construction and operation type projects—highways, roads and streets, public buildings, recreational facilities, public utilities, airports and airways, conservation, sanitation and other. Some 14,843 were employed on community service programs—education, recreation, sewing, and other. A total of 743 were on national defense training projects, and 370 assigned to the supply fund. Thirty-seven were supervisory employees, 659 classified as professional and technical, 2,569 skilled, 6,205 intermediate, and the balance unskilled.

Source: "Work Projects Administration," Florence Murray, ed., *The Negro Handbook*, 1942, p. 161.

★ 1258 ★
Federal Works Agencies

Works Project Administration Classes and Activities, January 1941

In January, 1941, there were 266,551 Negro participants in WPA classes and related activities, 19 per cent of the total.

	Number
Adult education classes (literacy, radio, aeronautics, commercial)	182,868
Nursery schools	7,075
Handicapped and institutionalized instruction	2,176
Isolated persons' instruction	3,475
Workers' service, adult education	5,772
Art instruction, children and adults	17,397
Music instruction classes	47,788

Source: "WPA Classes and Related Activities," Florence Murray, ed., *The Negro Handbook*, 1942, p. 161.

★ 1259 ★
Federal Works Agencies

Works Project Administration Workers in Southern States, April 1941

State	Number	Percent of state total
Alabama	10,048	29.1
Arkansas	5,589	17.2
Florida	6,803	25.4
Georgia	9,444	27.2
Louisiana	11,874	40.8
Mississippi	7,856	24.8
North Carolina	11,056	28.8
South Carolina	11,182	40.0
Tennessee	3,328	10.7
Texas	14,217	16.8
Virginia	4,179	22.4

Source: "Negro WPA Workers in Southern States, April 1941," Florence Murray, ed., *The Negro Handbook*, 1942, p. 161.

★ 1260 ★
Federal Works Agencies

Works Projects Administration Workers, 1936-1942

Year	Range	Negro workers	Per cent of total
1936	High	400,000	13.0
1937	Low	225,000	16.0
1938	High	450,000	12.0
1939	Average	350,000	14.0
1940	Average	250,000	15.0
1941	Average	225,000	17.0
1942	Low	71,000	20.0

Source: Untitled table, Florence Murray, ed., *The Negro Handbook*, 1944, p.209.

Labor Force

★ 1261 ★

Civilian Labor Force: 1890-1970

Numbers in thousands.

| Year and race | All persons | Civilian labor force | | Employed | Unemployed | Not in labor force |
| | | Total | | | | |
		Number	Percent of all persons			
ALL RACES						
1890	47,414	23,318	49.2	(NA)	(NA)	24,095
1900	57,950	29,073	50.2	(NA)	(NA)	28,877
1910[1]	71,580	38,167	53.3	(NA)	(NA)	33,413
1920	82,739	41,614	50.3	(NA)	(NA)	41,125
1930	98,723	48,830	49.5	(NA)	(NA)	49,893
1940	101,458	52,705	51.9	45,070	7,635	48,447
1950	112,801	59,304	52.6	56,449	2,854	52,472
1960	126,277	68,144	54.0	64,639	3,505	56,399
1970	141,087	80,051	56.7	76,554	3,497	59,038
BLACK						
1890	5,329	3,073	57.7	(NA)	(NA)	2,256
1900	6,416	3,992	62.2	(NA)	(NA)	2,423
1910[1]	7,318	5,193	71.0	(NA)	(NA)	2,125
1920	8,053	4,824	59.9	(NA)	(NA)	3,229
1930	9,293	5,504	59.2	(NA)	(NA)	3,789
1940[2]	9,780	5,680	58.1	4,728	952	4,092
1950	10,509	5,847	55.6	5,388	459	4,600
1960	12,088	6,689	55.3	6,099	590	5,281
1970	14,015	7,912	56.5	7,361	550	5,923
WHITE						
1890	41,931	19,542	46.6	(NA)	(NA)	22,389
1900	51,251	24,913	48.6	(NA)	(NA)	26,338
1910[1]	63,934	32,774	51.3	(NA)	(NA)	31,160
1920	74,360	36,616	49.2	(NA)	(NA)	37,744
1930	87,981	42,584	48.4	(NA)	(NA)	45,396
1940	91,678	47,052	51.3	40,369	6,683	44,355
1950	101,670	53,178	52.3	50,804	2,374	47,553

[Continued]

★ 1261 ★

Civilian Labor Force: 1890-1970
[Continued]

Year and race	All persons	Civilian labor force				Not in labor force
		Total		Employed	Unemployed	
		Number	Percent of all persons			
1960	113,123	60,885	53.8	58,010	2,875	50,645
1970	125,367	71,177	56.8	68,283	2,895	52,413

Source: "Persons by Civilian Labor Force Status: 1890 to 1970," U.S. department of Commerce, Bureau of the Census, *The Social and Economic Status of the Black Population in the United States: An Historical View, 1790-1978*, p. 64. Primary source: U.S. Department of Commerce, Bureau of the Census. *Notes:* NA Not available. Data for 1960 and 1970 are from two different sources, decennial censuses and Current Population Surveys, therefore figures may vary from table to table. Data from the 1890 to 1930 censuses refer to gainful workers. The concept "gainful worker" included all persons who usually followed a gainful occupation, although they may not have been employed at the time the census was taken. It did not include women doing housework in their own home without wages and having no other employment, nor children working in the home at general household work, chores, or at odd times at other work. Data from the 1940 to 1970 censuses refer to the civilian labor force. The category "civilian labor force" includes employed and unemployed persons. In this table, data are based on decennial censuses. Data for 1890 to 1930 are for persons 10 years old and over; 1940 to 1960, for persons 14 years old and over; and 1970 for persons 16 years old and over. 1. In the 1910 census an unusually large number of children were classified as gainful workers because of an unique instruction given to the enumerators. 2. The reader should exercise caution when interpreting the 1940 census data which include persons of "other" races and therefore, may reflect an overstatement of the labor force and employment levels of the Black population.

★ 1262 ★
Labor Force

Classes of the Population in Occupations, 1900-1920

Class of Population	1920			1910			1900		
	Both Sexes	Male	Female	Both Sexes	Male	Female	Both Sexes	Male	Female
All Classes	50.3	78.2	21.1	53.3	81.3	23.4	50.2	80.0	18.8
Native White – Native Parentage	46.6	75.1	17.2	48.4	78.5	17.1	45.8	77.3	13.0
Native White – Foreign or Mixed Parentage	49.7	75.2	24.8	50.4	76.5	24.6	48.5	75.4	21.7
Foreign-Born White	57.4	89.3	18.4	60.3	90.0	21.7	57.3	89.7	19.1
Negro	59.9	81.1	38.9	71.0	87.4	54.7	62.2	84.1	40.7
Indian, Chinese, Japanese, all other	53.4	75.4	13.7	61.1	80.8	17.6	59.2	80.0	14.2

Source: "Number of Negroes in Each Main Class of Occupations," Monroe N. Work, ed., *Negro Year Book: An Annual Encyclopedia of the Negro, 1925-26*, p. 362.

★ 1263 ★

Labor Force

Distribution of Black Male Labor Force by Age and Education, 1940-1970

Age and years of school	1940	1950	1960	1970
25-34				
0-11 yrs.	95.9	92.1	93.1	89.0
12-15	95.6	86.0	93.8	94.0
16+	96.7	89.6[1]	95.5	91.3
35-44				
0-11 yrs.	95.3	94.6	92.5	89.4
12-15	95.6	93.4	95.7	93.6
16+	96.9	95.6[1]	98.0	97.4
45-54				
0-11 yrs.	92.2	91.9	89.6	84.3
12-15	94.4	91.1	92.6	92.2
16+	94.8	95.1	96.6	95.7
55-64				
0-11 yrs.	87.5	82.6	76.6	72.2
12-15	95.3	80.7[1]	87.1	81.0
16+	89.1	92.9[1]	88.1	92.0
Total				
0-11 yrs.	93.8	91.4	88.8	83.6
12-15	95.7	88.5	93.7	92.6
16+	95.8	93.2	95.8	94.2

Source: "Black Male Civilian Labor Force Participation Rates by Age and Education," *The Economic Progress of Black Men in America*, p. 29. Primary source: Census of Population, 1940-1980, Public Use Sample. *Note:* 1. Less than 100 observations per cell.

★ 1264 ★

Labor Force

Distribution of Black Male Labor Force by Sector and Age, 1940-1970

	1940	1950	1960	1970
Agriculture				
25-34	32.5	16.6	8.2	4.0
35-44	29.3	17.3	9.0	4.4
45-54	36.0	19.7	12.2	5.9
55-64	48.2	27.2	15.7	9.8
Total	37.6	21.0	12.0	5.8
Private nonagriculture				
24-34	61.8	73.0	78.0	78.9
35-44	63.7	73.8	76.4	75.9
45-54	57.1	71.9	75.9	74.0
55-64	45.4	66.1	74.3	73.9

[Continued]

★ 1264 ★

Distribution of Black Male Labor Force by Sector and Age, 1940-1970

[Continued]

	1940	1950	1960	1970
Total	56.5	70.9	76.1	75.8
Government				
25-34	5.7	10.4	13.8	17.1
35-44	7.0	8.9	14.6	19.7
45-54	6.9	8.4	11.9	20.1
55-64	6.5	6.7	10.0	16.4
Total	5.9	8.1	11.9	18.4

Source: "Distribution of Black Male Labor Force by Sector and Age," *The Economic Progress of Black Men in America*, p. 84. Primary source: Census of Population, 1940-1980; Public Use Sample.

★ 1265 ★

Labor Force

Employment Status of Persons 16 and Over: 1954-1975

Number in thousands. Annual averages. Minus sign (-) denotes decrease.

Year	Black and other races			White		
	Civilian labor force	Employed	Unemployed	Civilian labor force	Employed	Unemployed
1954	6,824	6,150	674	56,817	53,957	2,860
1955	6,942	6,341	601	58,082	55,834	2,248
1956	7,127	6,535	592	59,427	57,265	2,162
1957	7,188	6,619	569	59,741	57,452	2,289
1958	7,347	6,422	925	60,293	56,614	3,679
1959	7,418	6,624	794	60,953	58,005	2,947
1960	7,714	6,927	787	61,913	58,850	3,063
1961	7,802	6,832	970	62,654	58,912	3,742
1962	7,863	7,004	859	62,750	59,698	3,052
1963	8,004	7,140	864	63,830	60,622	3,208
1964	8,169	7,383	786	64,921	61,822	2,999
1965	8,319	7,643	676	66,136	63,445	2,691
1966	8,496	7,875	621	67,274	65,019	2,253
1967	8,648	8,011	638	68,699	66,361	2,338
1968	8,760	8,169	590	69,977	67,751	2,226
1969	8,954	8,384	570	71,779	69,518	2,261
1970	9,197	8,445	752	73,518	70,182	3,337
1971	9,322	8,403	919	74,790	70,716	4,074
1972	9,584	8,628	956	76,958	73,074	3,884
1973	10,025	9,131	894	78,689	75,278	3,411
1974	10,334	9,316	1,018	80,678	76,620	4,057
1975	10,529	9,070	1,459	82,084	75,713	6,371

[Continued]

★ 1265 ★

Employment Status of Persons 16 and Over: 1954-1975

[Continued]

Year	Black and other races			White		
	Civilian labor force	Employed	Unemployed	Civilian labor force	Employed	Unemployed
Change:						
1954-1965						
Number	1,495	1,493	2	9,319	9,488	-169
Percent	21.9	24.3	0.3	16.4	17.6	-5.9
1965-1970						
Number	878	802	76	7,382	6,737	646
Percent	10.6	10.5	11.2	11.2	10.6	24.0
1970-1975[1]						
Number	1,112	405	487	8,436	5,401	2,904
Percent	12.1	4.8	64.8	11.5	7.7	87.0

Source: "Employment Status of Persons 16 Years Old and Over: 1954 to 1975," U.S. Department of Commerce, Bureau of the Census, *The Social and Economic Status of the Black Population in the United States: An Historical View, 1790-1978,* p. 68. Primary source: U.S. Department of Labor, Bureau of the Labor Statistics. *Notes:* The information on employment and unemployment is obtained from the Current Population Survey (a monthly sample survey of households). All persons 16 years of age and over are classified as employed, unemployed, or not in the labor force for the calendar week containing the 12th of the month. The unemployed are persons who did not work or have a job during the survey week, and who had looked for work within the past 4 weeks, and were currently available for work. Also included are those waiting to be called back to a job from which they had been laid off or waiting to report to a new job. The sum of the employed and the unemployed constitutes the civilian labor force. The change 1970 to 1975, was computed taking into account these population control adjustments. 1. Beginning in 1972, data based on 1970 census population controls; therefore, not strictly comparable with data for earlier years. Census population control adjustments were introduced in January 1972 and March 1973. The 1972 adjustment raised the employment level for Whites by about 255,000 and that for Black and other races by about 45,000. The March 1973 adjustment lowered the employment level for Whites by about 150,000, while Black and other races levels were raised by about 210,000. Unemployment levels (and rates) were not significantly affected in either year.

★ 1266 ★

Labor Force

Gainful Workers 10 Years Old and Over by Gender, 1910, 1920, 1930

Sex and census year	Population		Persons 10 years old and over gainfully occupied		
	Total	10 years old and over	Number	Percent of total population	Percent of population 10 years old and over
Total					
1930	11,891,143	9,292,556	5,503,535	46.3	59.2
1920	10,463,131	8,053,225	4,824,151	46.1	59.9
1910	9,827,763	7,317,922	5,192,535	52.8	71.0
Male					
1930	5,855,669	4,564,690	3,662,893	62.6	80.2

[Continued]

★ 1266 ★

Gainful Workers 10 Years Old and Over by Gender, 1910, 1920, 1930
[Continued]

Sex and census year	Population		Persons 10 years old and over gainfully occupied		
	Total	10 years old and over	Number	Percent of total population	Percent of population 10 years old and over
1920	5,209,436	4,009,462	3,252,862	62.4	81.1
1910	4,885,881	3,637,386	3,178,554	65.1	87.4
Female					
1930	6,035,474	4,727,866	1,840,642	30.5	38.9
1920	5,253,695	4,043,763	1,571,289	29.9	38.9
1910	4,941,882	3,680,536	2,013,981	40.8	54.7

Source: "Number and Proportion of Negroes Gainfully Occupied, by Sex, for the United States: 1910 to 1930," U.S. Bureau of the Census, *Negroes in the United States*, 1920-1932, p. 288.

★ 1267 ★
Labor Force

Gainful Workers 10 Years Old and Over by Gender, Age, Sections, Divisions, States, 1930: Part I A

Section, division, and state	10 years old and over			10 to 17 years		18 and 19 years		20 to 24 years	
	Total	Male	Female	Male	Female	Male	Female	Male	Female
United States	5,503,535	3,662,893	1,840,642	299,903	171,726	190,823	113,542	517,707	299,103
The North	1,228,670	829,353	399,317	14,541	9,959	25,615	18,844	101,507	63,304
The South	4,210,163	2,790,120	1,420,043	284,839	161,526	164,088	94,094	411,952	233,337
The West	64,702	43,420	21,282	523	241	1,120	604	4,248	2,462
New England	45,129	29,686	15,443	641	477	933	776	3,038	2,030
Maine	510	363	147	3	3	7	4	27	14
New Hampshire	493	421	72	6	3	10	3	57	10
Vermont	247	194	53	3	3	9	6	21	6
Massachusetts	24,666	16,187	8,479	309	214	468	387	1,544	1,055
Rhode Island	4,693	3,023	1,670	75	74	106	102	295	176
Connecticut	14,520	9,498	5,022	245	180	333	274	1,094	769
Middle Atlantic	560,738	360,329	200,409	6,132	5,490	11,850	10,491	47,016	34,132
New York	239,305	143,554	95,751	1,764	1,822	4,415	4,666	19,851	16,934
New Jersey	107,114	68,487	38,627	1,705	1,525	2,472	2,063	9,236	6,238
Pennsylvania	214,319	148,288	66,031	2,663	2,143	4,963	3,762	17,929	10,960
East North Central	457,245	325,016	132,229	4,818	2,700	9,197	5,571	39,141	20,257
Ohio	145,379	104,982	40,397	1,725	864	3,101	1,870	12,583	5,994
Indiana	53,332	38,683	14,649	641	358	1,183	589	4,451	1,996

[Continued]

★ 1267 ★

Gainful Workers 10 Years Old and Over by Gender, Age, Sections, Divisions, States, 1930: Part I A

[Continued]

Section, division, and state	10 years old and over			10 to 17 years		18 and 19 years		20 to 24 years	
	Total	Male	Female	Male	Female	Male	Female	Male	Female
Illinois	171,073	115,236	55,837	1,777	1,056	3,241	2,178	13,750	8,751
Michigan	82,249	62,089	20,160	647	405	1,561	882	7,872	3,336
Wisconsin	5,212	4,026	1,186	28	17	111	52	485	180
West North Central	165,558	114,322	51,236	2,950	1,292	3,635	2,006	12,312	6,885
Minnesota	4,809	3,562	1,247	46	25	86	43	271	151
Iowa	7,931	5,927	2,004	132	54	173	90	607	255
Missouri	114,825	77,530	37,295	2,206	1,003	2,567	1,458	8,557	5,131
North Dakota	219	175	44	3	-	3	-	7	12
South Dakota	308	241	67	8	-	11	4	21	10
Nebraska	7,179	4,910	2,269	91	39	125	83	458	256
Kansas	30,287	21,977	8,310	464	171	670	328	2,391	1,070
South Atlantic	1,951,791	1,275,378	676,413	135,841	72,615	83,383	47,582	191,400	114,604
Delaware	15,887	11,172	4,715	401	197	468	222	1,474	661
Maryland	136,014	91,537	44,477	4,286	2,104	4,416	2,396	13,088	7,010
District of Columbia	73,122	41,811	31,311	857	649	1,525	1,299	5,827	4,770
Virginia	258,066	181,064	77,002	13,374	5,210	11,294	4,962	24,925	12,313
West Virginia	47,207	38,547	8,660	877	276	1,342	390	4,846	1,328
North Carolina	365,544	245,479	120,065	29,031	14,918	17,680	9,528	40,459	22,902
South Carolina	343,476	213,167	130,309	35,625	22,372	17,142	11,140	32,549	21,535
Georgia	494,384	311,550	182,834	41,642	21,599	22,607	13,334	47,652	31,006
Florida	218,091	141,051	77,040	9,748	5,290	6,909	4,311	20,580	13,079
East South Central	1,250,026	816,059	433,967	95,106	59,008	44,096	28,033	117,171	68,023
Kentucky	106,572	73,098	33,474	3,048	1,008	3,056	1,268	8,639	4,030
Tennessee	222,693	147,237	75,456	10,588	5,388	8,052	4,248	20,745	12,044
Alabama	432,349	279,829	152,520	36,018	22,522	15,558	10,550	41,427	24,758
Mississippi	488,412	315,895	172,517	45,452	30,090	17,430	11,967	46,360	27,191
West South Central	1,008,346	698,683	309,663	53,892	29,903	36,609	18,479	103,381	50,710
Arkansas	201,948	147,538	54,410	12,763	6,871	7,463	3,410	21,215	8,346
Louisiana	345,389	233,907	111,482	20,133	12,193	12,681	6,902	34,594	17,781
Oklahoma	71,254	51,578	19,676	2,304	742	2,429	974	7,417	3,664
Texas	389,755	265,660	124,095	18,692	10,097	14,036	7,193	40,155	20,919
Mountain	16,204	11,741	4,463	192	78	358	130	1,288	448
Montana	695	528	167	2	1	14	3	33	10
Idaho	368	305	63	6	1	10	3	22	4
Wyoming	696	536	160	7	2	11	2	43	13
Colorado	6,220	3,991	2,229	64	39	98	69	340	226
New Mexico	1,355	1,012	343	29	12	42	7	105	49
Arizona	5,986	4,705	1,281	83	21	173	41	703	128
Utah	550	428	122	1	2	8	2	28	14
Nevada	334	236	98	-	-	2	3	14	4

[Continued]

★ 1267 ★

Gainful Workers 10 Years Old and Over by Gender, Age, Sections, Divisions, States, 1930: Part I A

[Continued]

Section, division, and state	10 years old and over			10 to 17 years		18 and 19 years		20 to 24 years	
	Total	Male	Female	Male	Female	Male	Female	Male	Female
Pacific	48,498	31,679	16,819	331	163	762	474	2,960	2,014
Washington	3,672	2,761	911	29	16	57	30	196	100
Oregon	1,331	948	383	9	7	14	8	66	40
California	43,495	27,970	15,525	293	140	691	436	2,698	1,874

Source: "Negro Gainful Workers 10 Years Old and Over, by Sex, and Age, by Sections, Divisions, and States: 1930," U.S. Bureau of the Census, *Negroes in the United States, 1920-1930*, p. 335.

★ 1268 ★
Labor Force

Gainful Workers 10 Years Old and Over by Gender, Age, Sections, Divisions, States, 1930: Part I B

Section, division, and state	25 to 29 years		30 to 34 years		35 to 39 years	
	Male	Female	Male	Female	Male	Female
United States	483,423	267,688	403,804	210,157	418,037	219,586
The North	133,351	70,824	125,817	58,693	124,608	57,312
The South	344,856	193,738	272,228	148,395	287,067	158,775
The West	5,216	3,126	5,759	3,069	6,362	3,499
New England	3,654	1,984	3,885	1,891	4,071	2,002
Maine	35	23	32	15	47	18
New Hampshire	39	4	62	6	60	10
Vermont	23	-	20	5	22	6
Massachusetts	1,758	1,063	2,106	1,045	2,256	1,122
Rhode Island	346	157	331	184	375	179
Connecticut	1,453	737	1,334	636	1,311	667
Middle Atlantic	61,969	36,902	57,096	29,163	54,358	27,911
New York	27,135	19,158	24,373	14,568	22,381	13,668
New Jersey	10,805	6,348	9,793	5,199	9,520	5,103
Pennsylvania	24,029	11,396	22,930	9,396	22,457	9,140
East North Central	53,235	24,299	50,657	20,744	50,805	20,190
Ohio	16,196	6,903	15,536	6,009	16,316	6,162
Indiana	5,475	2,171	5,414	2,042	5,494	2,122
Illinois	19,025	10,771	17,752	8,907	17,940	8,546
Michigan	11,834	4,220	11,310	3,574	10,411	3,164
Wisconsin	705	234	645	212	644	196
West North Central	14,493	7,639	14,179	6,895	15,374	7,209
Minnesota	346	128	435	166	509	181
Iowa	652	229	675	252	736	278

[Continued]

★ 1268 ★

Gainful Workers 10 Years Old and Over by Gender, Age, Sections, Divisions, States, 1930: Part I B

[Continued]

Section, division, and state	25 to 29 years		30 to 34 years		35 to 39 years	
	Male	Female	Male	Female	Male	Female
Missouri	10,134	5,780	9,645	5,127	10,551	5,278
North Dakota	18	6	15	4	23	5
South Dakota	29	8	32	7	22	6
Nebraska	660	342	634	296	721	386
Kansas	2,654	1,146	2,743	1,043	2,812	1,075
South Atlantic	153,742	92,180	122,324	70,463	130,062	75,796
Delaware	1,416	655	1,243	545	1,412	598
Maryland	12,682	6,365	10,917	5,453	11,107	5,630
District of Columbia	6,653	5,092	5,647	4,158	5,598	4,242
Virginia	19,632	9,870	17,028	8,201	19,443	9,263
West Virginia	5,801	1,370	5,601	1,182	5,810	1,226
North Carolina	30,446	17,053	23,087	11,855	22,833	11,825
South Carolina	21,282	14,820	16,506	11,110	19,080	12,786
Georgia	35,023	23,866	26,208	18,061	28,172	20,198
Florida	20,807	13,089	16,087	9,898	16,607	10,028
East South Central	98,584	55,464	75,535	42,460	79,281	46,171
Kentucky	8,239	4,018	7,752	3,838	8,789	4,248
Tennessee	18,481	10,720	15,250	8,512	16,135	9,113
Alabama	34,090	19,182	24,171	14,298	24,957	15,631
Mississippi	37,774	21,544	28,362	15,812	29,400	17,179
West South Central	92,530	46,094	74,369	35,472	77,724	36,808
Arkansas	17,950	7,053	14,124	5,549	14,973	5,990
Louisiana	30,923	15,828	23,915	12,044	26,340	13,020
Oklahoma	7,102	3,450	5,861	2,674	5,839	2,548
Texas	36,555	19,763	30,469	15,205	30,572	15,250
Mountain	1,327	612	1,445	617	1,691	690
Montana	44	24	48	18	60	22
Idaho	22	5	27	11	48	8
Wyoming	43	11	67	22	84	20
Colorado	394	281	436	270	534	311
New Mexico	116	46	107	48	130	58
Arizona	648	221	685	219	745	236
Utah	42	13	48	16	60	20
Nevada	18	11	27	13	30	15
Pacific	3,889	2,514	4,314	2,452	4,671	2,809
Washington	233	73	273	108	317	115
Oregon	91	37	105	41	140	59
California	3,565	2,404	3,936	2,303	4,214	2,635

Source: "Negro Gainful Workers 10 Years Old and Over, by Sex, and Age, by Sections, Divisions, and States: 1930," U.S. Bureau of the Census, *Negroes in the United States, 1920-1930*, p. 335.

★ 1269 ★

Labor Force

Gainful Workers 10 Years Old and Over by Gender, Age, Sections, Divisions, States, 1930: Part II

A

Section, division, and state	40 to 44 years		45 to 49 years		50 to 54 years		55 to 59 years		60 to 64 years	
	Male	Female	Male	Female	Male	Female	Male	Female	Male	Female
United States	329,762	166,355	314,200	144,011	268,330	103,328	166,770	57,173	123,515	41,711
The North	93,534	40,789	79,029	32,903	56,052	21,246	33,524	11,735	20,051	6,772
The South	230,584	123,043	230,104	108,837	208,417	80,490	130,826	44,544	101,959	34,448
The West	5,644	2,523	5,067	2,266	3,861	1,592	2,420	894	1,505	491
New England	3,414	1,741	3,318	1,531	2,600	1,200	1,723	738	1,144	524
Maine	36	15	54	15	27	16	23	10	26	7
New Hampshire	53	10	65	5	32	12	20	5	6	-
Vermont	17	4	23	8	19	4	13	4	9	3
Massachusetts	1,914	976	1,960	880	1,538	702	1,031	432	626	298
Rhode Island	346	179	353	182	285	154	206	103	144	85
Connecticut	1,048	557	863	441	699	312	430	184	333	131
Middle Atlantic	39,466	19,655	32,291	15,586	22,649	9,885	12,918	5,298	7,393	2,961
New York	15,662	9,369	11,925	6,990	7,611	4,187	4,075	2,127	2,231	1,114
New Jersey	7,173	3,869	6,305	3,251	4,890	2,251	2,969	1,279	1,800	716
Pennsylvania	16,631	6,417	14,061	5,345	10,148	3,347	5,874	1,892	3,362	1,131
East North Central	37,247	13,629	30,946	10,717	21,173	6,636	12,587	3,582	7,273	1,959
Ohio	12,060	4,244	10,321	3,406	7,186	2,262	4,344	1,246	2,658	713
Indiana	4,400	1,651	3,765	1,406	3,089	1,015	2,030	593	1,196	335
Illinois	13,410	5,772	11,339	4,511	7,622	2,614	4,411	1,370	2,512	715
Michigan	6,872	1,848	5,158	1,319	3,022	702	1,650	342	846	178
Wisconsin	505	114	363	75	254	43	152	31	61	18
West North Central	13,407	5,764	12,474	5,074	9,630	3,525	6,296	2,117	4,241	1,328
Minnesota	480	158	463	165	375	100	259	66	146	30
Iowa	652	245	676	198	568	158	419	110	284	69
Missouri	9,108	4,097	8,448	3,572	6,231	2,443	3,971	1,407	2,723	937
North Dakota	22	6	26	5	25	4	14	1	8	1
South Dakota	26	12	25	7	22	6	14	4	10	2
Nebraska	628	297	606	233	443	156	225	94	156	33
Kansas	2,491	949	2,230	894	1,966	658	1,394	435	914	25
South Atlantic	106,328	59,194	96,912	51,574	96,156	38,311	58,348	20,447	45,698	15,739
Delaware	1,115	446	1,009	441	957	380	599	220	467	153
Maryland	8,944	4,446	8,045	3,887	6,638	2,853	4,169	1,625	3,068	1,147
District of Columbia	4,306	3,296	4,051	3,023	3,203	2,131	1,803	1,154	1,109	714
Virginia	17,423	7,344	17,026	6,875	14,686	5,081	9,790	2,839	7,092	2,276
West Virginia	4,641	958	3,811	740	2,490	562	1,539	252	872	172
North Carolina	18,473	9,244	17,053	8,042	17,056	6,137	11,220	3,403	7,686	2,425
South Carolina	16,457	10,467	14,922	9,153	13,408	6,780	8,479	3,758	8,519	3,056
Georgia	21,505	15,708	18,257	13,679	28,180	10,629	14,830	5,335	12,856	4,448
Florida	13,464	7,285	12,738	5,734	9,538	3,758	5,919	1,861	4,029	1,348

[Continued]

★ 1269 ★

Gainful Workers 10 Years Old and Over by Gender, Age, Sections, Divisions, States, 1930: Part II

A

[Continued]

Section, division, and state	40 to 44 years		45 to 49 years		50 to 54 years		55 to 59 years		60 to 64 years	
	Male	Female	Male	Female	Male	Female	Male	Female	Male	Female
East South Central	62,451	36,259	68,998	33,504	63,211	25,606	40,619	14,547	31,748	11,535
Kentucky	7,535	3,775	7,349	3,637	6,480	2,812	4,295	1,763	3,212	1,358
Tennessee	12,359	7,011	11,057	6,134	13,656	5,115	8,125	2,805	5,658	2,023
Alabama	18,847	12,378	29,452	11,556	19,747	8,393	12,658	4,631	10,278	3,885
Mississippi	23,710	13,095	21,140	12,177	23,328	9,286	15,541	5,348	12,600	4,269
West South Central	61,805	27,590	64,194	23,759	49,050	16,573	31,859	9,550	24,513	7,174
Arkansas	12,035	4,865	15,266	4,345	11,902	3,446	7,822	1,838	5,501	1,346
Louisiana	21,307	9,792	20,894	8,768	15,741	6,134	10,684	3,641	7,609	2,551
Oklahoma	4,724	1,891	4,445	1,527	4,447	936	2,959	598	1,794	314
Texas	23,739	11,042	23,589	9,119	16,960	6,057	10,394	3,473	9,609	2,963
Mountain	1,422	521	1,339	487	1,052	376	634	228	484	116
Montana	66	20	61	18	67	20	49	13	40	7
Idaho	48	11	37	7	28	6	16	5	19	1
Wyoming	65	28	64	28	66	14	30	10	31	5
Colorado	487	253	519	270	414	219	271	133	204	60
New Mexico	119	35	107	28	117	24	49	19	49	9
Arizona	550	143	452	109	274	76	172	33	111	26
Utah	52	15	63	15	60	7	29	9	16	4
Nevada	35	16	36	12	26	10	18	6	14	4
Pacific	4,222	2,002	3,728	1,779	2,809	1,216	1,786	666	1,021	375
Washington	360	107	370	123	356	93	253	64	134	45
Oregon	142	52	125	51	98	38	80	25	32	11
California	3,720	1,843	3,233	1,605	2,355	1,085	1,453	577	855	319

Source: "Negro Gainful Workers 10 Years Old and Over, by Sex, and Age, by Sections, Divisions, and States: 1930," U.S. Bureau of the Census, *Negroes in the United States, 1920-1930*, p. 336.

★ 1270 ★

Labor Force

Gainful Workers 10 Years Old and Over by Gender, Age, Sections, Divisions, States, 1930: Part II B

Section, division, and state	65 to 69 years		70 to 74 years		75 years and over		Unknown	
	Male	Female	Male	Female	Male	Female	Male	Female
United States	72,646	23,513	38,786	11,328	30,228	8,278	4,959	3,143
The North	11,346	3,577	5,343	1,501	3,539	982	1,496	871
The South	60,433	19,643	33,015	9,719	26,424	7,235	3,328	2,219
The West	867	293	428	108	265	61	135	53
New England	684	292	313	128	228	96	40	33

[Continued]

★ 1270 ★

Gainful Workers 10 Years Old and Over by Gender, Age, Sections, Divisions, States, 1930: Part II B
[Continued]

Section, division, and state	65 to 69 years		70 to 74 years		75 years and over		Unknown	
	Male	Female	Male	Female	Male	Female	Male	Female
Maine	18	2	9	3	18	1	1	1
New Hampshire	6	1	3	-	1	2	1	1
Vermont	6	2	4	2	5	-	-	-
Massachusetts	378	162	171	64	105	56	23	23
Rhode Island	89	49	40	27	30	16	2	3
Connecticut	187	76	86	32	69	21	13	5
Middle Atlantic	3,828	1,563	1,759	588	1,011	353	593	431
New York	1,125	604	480	206	300	129	226	209
New Jersey	927	417	473	165	266	94	153	109
Pennsylvania	1,776	542	806	217	445	130	214	113
East North Central	4,143	959	1,927	416	1,220	266	647	304
Ohio	1,522	363	747	173	495	112	192	76
Indiana	785	177	405	84	229	52	126	58
Illinois	1,339	325	577	131	363	80	178	110
Michigan	457	89	181	25	125	19	143	57
Wisconsin	40	5	17	3	8	3	8	3
West North Central	2,691	763	1,344	369	1,080	267	216	103
Minnesota	97	24	28	5	15	4	6	1
Iowa	196	35	79	18	61	9	17	4
Missouri	1,680	523	854	269	699	186	156	84
North Dakota	5	-	4	-	2	-	-	-
South Dakota	9	-	6	1	3	-	3	-
Nebraska	86	30	29	14	41	9	7	1
Kansas	618	151	344	62	259	59	27	13
South Atlantic	27,104	9,030	15,034	4,404	11,193	3,088	1,853	1,386
Delaware	318	120	165	42	115	33	13	2
Maryland	1,955	682	1,064	335	683	201	475	343
District of Columbia	648	386	281	136	153	98	150	163
Virginia	4,526	1,387	2,691	742	1,993	527	141	112
West Virginia	492	91	221	56	135	31	69	26
North Carolina	4,872	1,384	2,934	640	2,311	467	338	242
South Carolina	4,735	1,804	2,584	828	1,779	576	100	124
Georgia	7,185	2,491	3,966	1,302	3,112	940	355	238
Florida	2,373	685	1,128	323	912	215	212	136
East South Central	19,062	6,668	10,601	3,495	8,797	2,691	799	503
Kentucky	2,264	853	1,400	450	947	356	93	60
Tennessee	3,476	1,135	1,866	593	1,524	450	265	165
Alabama	6,064	2,352	3,403	1,230	2,875	981	284	173
Mississippi	7,258	2,328	3,932	1,222	3,451	904	157	105

[Continued]

★ 1270 ★

Gainful Workers 10 Years Old and Over by Gender, Age, Sections, Divisions, States, 1930: Part II B

[Continued]

Section, division, and state	65 to 69 years		70 to 74 years		75 years and over		Unknown	
	Male	Female	Male	Female	Male	Female	Male	Female
West South Central	14,267	3,945	7,380	1,820	6,434	1,456	676	330
Arkansas	3,206	718	1,784	345	1,446	246	88	42
Louisiana	4,545	1,495	2,319	706	2,062	561	160	65
Oklahoma	1,113	202	567	66	517	65	60	25
Texas	5,403	1,529	2,710	703	2,409	584	368	198
Mountain	254	95	141	37	90	17	24	11
Montana	20	6	16	3	7	2	1	-
Idaho	11	1	3	-	8	-	-	-
Wyoming	12	3	6	2	4	-	3	-
Colorado	125	59	63	26	35	11	7	2
New Mexico	16	5	13	1	13	-	-	2
Arizona	49	16	32	2	15	4	13	6
Utah	14	2	4	3	3	-	-	-
Nevada	7	3	4	-	5	-	-	1
Pacific	613	198	187	71	175	44	111	42
Washington	101	19	45	7	25	9	12	2
Oregon	24	11	9	2	9	-	4	1
California	488	168	233	62	141	35	95	39

Source: "Negro Gainful Workers 10 Years Old and Over, by Sex, and Age, by Sections, Divisions, and States: 1930," U.S. Bureau of the Census, *Negroes in the United States, 1920-1930*, p. 336.

★ 1271 ★

Labor Force

Gainful Workers 10 Years Old and Over by Race, Nativity, Gender, and Sections, 1920 and 1930

Class of population	Total			Male			Female			Percent distribution of gainfully occupied		
	Total number	Gainfully occupied		Total number	Gainfully occupied		Total number	Gainfully occupied		Total	Male	Female
		Number	Percent		Number	Percent		Number	Percent			
						The South						
1930	29,168,784	14,310,217	49.1	14,624,017	11,147,292	76.2	14,544,767	3,162,925	21.7	100.0	100.0	100.0
Negro	7,194,750	4,210,163	58.5	3,506,598	2,790,120	79.6	3,688,152	1,420,043	38.5	29.4	25.0	44.9
Native white	20,864,225	9,521,762	45.6	10,515,369	7,864,076	74.8	10,348,856	1,657,686	16.0	66.5	70.5	52.4
Foreign-born white	527,946	300,195	56.9	298,860	260,006	87.0	229,086	40,189	17.5	2.1	2.3	1.3
Other races[1]	581,863	278,097	47.8	303,190	233,090	76.9	278,673	45,007	16.2	1.9	2.1	1.4
1920	24,930,212	12,367,091	49.6	12,631,002	9,753,727	77.2	12,299,210	2,613,364	21.2	100.0	100.0	100.0
Negro	6,733,428	3,969,144	58.9	3,320,344	2,654,917	80.0	3,413,084	1,314,227	38.5	32.1	27.2	50.3
Native white	17,326,889	7,903,995	45.6	8,809,398	6,664,304	75.6	8,517,491	1,239,691	14.6	63.9	68.3	47.4
Foreign-born white	812,649	472,208	58.1	470,172	415,191	88.3	342,477	57,017	16.6	3.8	4.3	2.2
Other races[1]	57,246	21,744	38.0	31,088	19,315	62.1	26,158	2,429	9.3	.2	.2	.1
						The North						
1930	59,722,192	29,549,871	49.5	30,155,263	22,961,102	76.1	29,566,929	6,588,769	22.3	100.0	100.0	100.0
Negro	1,994,085	1,228,670	61.6	1,005,003	829,353	82.5	989,082	399,317	40.4	4.2	3.6	6.1
Native white	46,302,661	21,943,512	47.4	23,078,577	16,755,601	72.6	23,224,084	5,187,911	22.3	74.3	73.0	78.7
Foreign-born white	11,256,622	6,279,199	55.8	5,958,416	5,283,750	88.7	5,298,206	995,449	18.8	21.2	23.0	15.1

[Continued]

★ 1271 ★

Gainful Workers 10 Years Old and Over by Race, Nativity, Gender, and Sections, 1920 and 1930
[Continued]

Class of population	Total			Male			Female			Percent distribution of gainfully occupied		
	Total number	Gainfully occupied		Total number	Gainfully occupied		Total number	Gainfully occupied		Total	Male	Female
		Number	Percent		Number	Percent		Number	Percent			
Other races[1]	168,824	98,490	58.3	113,267	92,398	81.6	55,557	6,092	11.0	.3	.4	.1
1920	50,632,869	25,578,453	50.5	25,780,163	20,253,565	78.6	24,852,706	5,324,888	21.4	100.0	100.0	100.0
Negro	1,250,708	807,343	64.6	649,154	561,774	86.5	601,554	245,569	40.8	3.2	2.8	4.6
Native white	38,074,208	18,326,750	48.1	19,003,721	14,215,814	74.8	19,070,487	4,110,936	21.6	71.6	70.2	77.2
Foreign-born white	11,238,397	6,408,617	57.0	6,081,256	5,442,379	89.5	5,157,141	966,238	18.7	25.1	26.9	18.1
Other races[1]	69,556	35,743	51.4	46,032	33,598	73.0	23,524	2,145	9.1	.1	.2	[2]

The West

Class of population	Total number	Number	Percent	Total number	Number	Percent	Total number	Number	Percent	Total	Male	Female
1930	9,832,071	4,969,832	50.5	5,170,518	3,969,410	76.8	4,661,553	1,000,422	21.5	100.0	100.0	100.0
Negro	103,721	64,702	62.4	53,089	43,420	81.8	50,632	21,282	42.0	1.3	1.1	2.1
Native white	7,596,853	3,708,096	48.8	3,881,955	2,892,185	74.5	3,714,898	815,911	22.0	74.6	72.9	81.6
Foreign-born white	1,432,360	831,733	58.1	820,947	711,315	86.6	611,413	120,418	19.7	16.7	17.9	12.0
Other races[1]	699,137	365,301	52.3	414,527	322,490	77.8	284,610	42,811	15.0	7.4	8.1	4.3
1920	7,176,234	3,668,704	51.1	3,878,804	3,057,445	78.8	3,297,430	611,259	18.5	100.0	100.0	100.0
Negro	69,089	47,664	69.0	39,964	36,171	90.5	29,125	11,493	39.5	1.3	1.2	1.9
Native white	5,460,766	2,638,718	48.3	2,837,926	2,145,562	75.6	2,622,840	493,156	18.8	71.9	70.2	80.7
Foreign-born white	1,446,840	865,365	59.8	868,263	770,427	88.7	578,577	95,208	16.5	23.6	25.2	15.6
Other races[1]	199,539	116,687	58.5	132,651	105,285	79.4	66,888	11,402	17.0	3.2	3.4	1.9

Source: "Number and Proportion of Persons 10 Years Old and Over Gainfully Occupied, by Color, Nativity, and Sex, by Sections: 1930 and 1920," U.S. Bureau of the Census, *Negroes in the United States, 1920-32*, p. 289. *Notes:* 1. Comprises Mexicans, Indians, Chinese, Japanese, Filipinos, Hindus, Koreans, Hawaiians, etc., in 1930. In 1920 Mexicans were included for the most part in the white population. 2. Less than 1/10 of 1 percent.

★ 1272 ★
Labor Force

Gainful Workers 10 Years Old and Over by Race, Nativity, and Gender, 1910, 1920, 1930

Class of population	Total			Male			Female			Percent distribution of gainfully occupied		
	Total number	Gainfully occupied		Total number	Gainfully occupied		Total number	Gainfully occupied		Total	Male	Female
		Number	Percent		Number	Percent		Number	Percent			
1930	98,723,047	48,829,920	49.5	49,949,798	38,077,804	76.2	48,773,249	10,752,116	22.0	100.0	100.0	100.0
Negro	9,292,556	5,503,535	59.2	4,564,690	3,662,893	80.2	4,727,866	1,840,642	38.9	11.3	9.6	17.1
Native white	74,763,739	35,173,370	47.0	37,475,901	27,511,862	73.4	37,287,838	7,661,508	20.5	72.0	72.3	71.3
Foreign-born white	13,216,928	7,411,127	56.1	7,078,223	6,255,071	88.4	6,138,705	1,156,056	18.8	15.2	16.4	10.8
Other races	1,449,824	741,888	51.2	830,984	647,978	78.0	618,840	93,910	15.2	1.5	1.7	.9
Mexican[1]	1,002,241	498,765	49.8	547,863	431,677	78.8	454,378	67,088	14.8	1.0	1.1	.6
Indian	238,981	98,148	41.1	123,469	80,306	65.0	115,512	17,842	15.4	.2	.2	.2
Chinese	63,392	47,106	74.3	53,650	45,547	84.9	9,742	1,559	16.0	.1	.1	-
Japanese	97,273	54,230	55.8	60,580	47,489	78.4	36,693	6,741	18.4	.1	.1	.1
Filipino	42,964	39,615	92.2	41,128	39,073	95.0	1,836	542	29.5	.1	.1	-
All other	4,973	4,024	80.9	4,294	3,886	90.5	679	138	20.3	-	-	-
1920	82,739,315	41,614,248	50.3	42,289,969	33,064,737	78.2	40,449,346	8,549,511	21.1	100.0	100.0	100.0
Negro	8,053,225	4,824,151	59.9	4,009,462	3,252,862	81.1	4,043,763	1,571,289	38.9	11.6	9.8	18.4
Native white[1]	60,861,863	28,869,463	47.4	30,651,045	23,025,680	75.1	30,210,818	5,843,783	19.3	69.4	69.6	68.4
Foreign-born white[1]	13,497,886	7,746,460	57.4	7,419,691	6,627,997	89.3	6,078,195	1,118,463	18.4	18.6	20.0	13.1
Other races	326,341	174,174	53.4	209,771	158,198	75.4	116,570	15,976	13.7	.4	.5	.2
Indian	176,925	63,326	35.8	91,546	53,478	58.4	85,379	9,848	11.5	.2	.2	.1
Chinese	56,230	45,614	81.1	51,041	44,882	87.9	5,189	732	14.1	.1	.1	-
Japanese	84,238	57,903	68.7	58,806	52,614	89.5	25,432	5,289	20.8	.1	.2	.1
All other	8,948	7,331	81.9	8,378	7,224	86.2	570	107	18.8	-	-	-
1910	71,580,270	38,167,336	53.3	37,027,558	30,091,564	81.3	34,552,712	8,075,772	23.4	100.0	100.0	100.0
Negro	7,317,922	5,192,535	71.0	3,637,386	3,178,554	87.4	3,680,536	2,013,981	54.7	13.6	16.6	24.9
Native white[1]	50,989,341	24,962,554	49.0	25,843,033	20,141,636	77.9	25,146,308	4,820,918	19.2	65.4	66.9	59.7
Foreign-born white[1]	12,944,529	7,811,502	60.3	7,321,196	6,588,711	90.0	5,623,333	1,222,791	21.7	20.5	21.9	15.1

[Continued]

★ 1272 ★

Gainful Workers 10 Years Old and Over by Race, Nativity, and Gender, 1910, 1920, 1930

[Continued]

Class of population	Total			Male			Female			Percent distribution of gainfully occupied		
	Total number	Gainfully occupied		Total number	Gainfully occupied		Total number	Gainfully occupied		Total	Male	Female
		Number	Percent		Number	Percent		Number	Percent			
Other races	328,478	200,745	61.1	225,943	182,663	80.8	102,535	18,082	17.6	.5	.6	.2
Indian	188,758	73,916	39.2	96,582	59,206	61.3	92,176	14,710	16.0	.2	.2	.2
Chinese	68,924	] 123,811	90.6	65,479	120,460[2]	95.4[2]	3,445	3,351[2]	32.5[2]	.3[2]	.4[2]	-
Japanese	67,661			60,809	120,460[2]	95.4[2]	6,852	3,351[2]	32.5[2]	.3[2]	.4[2]	-
All other	3,135	3,018	96.3	3,073	2,997	97.5	62	21	-	-	-	-

Source: "Number and Proportion of Persons 10 Years Old and Over Gainfully Occupied, by Color, Nativity, and Sex, for the United States: 1930, 1920, and 1910," U.S. Bureau of the Census, *Negroes in the United States, 1920- 1932*, p. 288. *Notes:* 1. In 1920 and in 1910 Mexicans were included for the most part in the white population. 2. Data includes Chinese and Japanese.

★ 1273 ★

Labor Force

Gainful Workers 10 Years Old and Over by Race, Nativity, and Occupation, 1910, 1920, 1930 - I

General division of occupations	Total		Negro		Native white		Foreign-born white	
	Number	Percent distribution	Number	Percent distribution	Number	Percent distribution	Number	Percent distribution
1930								
All occupations	48,829,920	100.0	5,503,535	100.0	35,173,370	100.0	7,411,127	100.0
Agriculture	10,471,998	21.4	1,987,839	36.1	7,518,519	21.4	673,662	9.1
Forestry and fishing	250,469	.5	31,732	.6	167,077	.5	44,846	.6
Extraction of minerals	984,323	2.0	74,972	1.4	658,267	1.9	232,121	3.1
Manufacturing and mechanical industries	14,110,652	28.9	1,024,656	18.6	9,663,796	27.5	3,265,381	44.1
Transportation and communication	3,843,147	7.9	397,645	7.2	2,876,682	8.2	488,303	6.6
Trade	6,081,467	12.5	183,809	3.3	4,835,498	13.7	1,012,605	13.7
Public service (not elsewhere classified)	856,205	1.8	50,203	.9	678,578	1.9	120,775	1.6
Professional service	3,253,884	6.7	135,925	2.5	2,775,453	7.9	328,745	4.4
Domestic and personal service	4,952,451	10.1	1,576,205	28.6	2,327,821	6.6	940,904	12.7
Clerical occupations	4,025,324	8.2	40,549	.7	3,671,679	10.4	303,785	4.1
1920								
All occupations	41,614,248	100.0	4,824,151	100.0	28,869,463	100.0	7,746,460	100.0
Agriculture	10,665,812	25.6	2,133,135	44.2	7,595,135	26.3	865,752	11.2
Forestry and fishing	270,214	.6	31,375	.7	168,438	.6	65,802	.8
Extraction of minerals	1,090,223	2.6	73,229	1.5	637,934	2.2	377,138	4.9
Manufacturing and mechanical industries	12,831,879	30.8	901,181	18.7	8,274,144	28.7	3,633,914	46.9
Transportation and communication	3,096,829	7.4	312,538	6.5	2,227,024	7.7	549,269	7.1
Trade	4,257,684	10.2	141,119	2.9	3,240,479	11.2	862,365	11.1
Public service (not elsewhere classified)	738,525	1.8	50,436	1.0	560,231	1.9	125,723	1.6
Professional service	2,171,251	5.2	81,771	1.7	1,847,442	6.4	238,875	3.1
Domestic and personal service	3,379,995	8.1	1,063,008	22.0	1,510,796	5.2	762,280	9.8
Clerical occupations	3,111,836	7.5	36,359	.8	2,807,901	9.7	265,342	3.4
1910								
All occupations	38,167,336	100.0	5,192,535	100.0	24,962,554	100.0	7,811,502	100.0
Agriculture	12,388,309	32.5	2,834,969	54.6	8,433,130	33.8	1,039,760	13.3
Forestry and fishing	241,806	.6	33,776	.7	146,719	.6	57,137	.7
Extraction of minerals	965,169	2.5	61,129	1.2	438,448	1.8	463,036	5.9
Manufacturing and mechanical industries	10,656,545	27.9	655,906	12.6	6,582,277	26.4	3,389,379	43.4
Transportation and communication	2,665,269	7.0	256,098	4.9	1,703,338	6.8	694,215	8.9
Trade	3,633,265	9.5	119,775	2.3	2,725,426	10.9	774,575	9.9
Public service (not elsewhere classified)	431,442	1.1	22,229	.4	310,323	1.2	97,969	1.3

[Continued]

★ 1273 ★

Gainful Workers 10 Years Old and Over by Race, Nativity, and Occupation, 1910, 1920, 1930 - I

[Continued]

General division of occupations	Total		Negro		Native white		Foreign-born white	
	Number	Percent distribution	Number	Percent distribution	Number	Percent distribution	Number	Percent distribution
Professional service	1,711,275	4.5	68,350	1.3	1,434,560	5.7	205,550	2.6
Domestic and personal service	3,755,798	9.8	1,121,251	21.6	1,661,140	6.7	919,022	11.8
Clerical occupations	1,718,458	4.5	19,052	.4	1,527,193	6.1	170,859	2.2

Source: "Gainful Workers 10 Years Old and Over, by Color, Nativity, and General Divisions of Occupations: 1930, 1920, and 1910," U.S. Bureau of the Census, *Negroes in the United States, 1920-1932,* p. 290.

★ 1274 ★

Labor Force

Gainful Workers 10 Years Old and Over by Race, Nativity, and Occupation, 1910, 1920, 1930 - II

General division of occupations	Other races[1]		Percent of total			
	Number	Percent distribution	Negro	Native white	Foreign-born white	Other races
1930						
All occupations	741,888	100.0	11.3	72.0	15.2	1.5
Agriculture	291,978	39.4	19.0	71.8	6.4	2.8
Forestry and fishing	6,814	.9	12.7	66.7	17.9	2.7
Extraction of minerals	18,963	2.6	7.6	66.9	23.6	1.9
Manufacturing and mechanical industries	156,819	21.1	7.3	68.5	23.1	1.1
Transportation and communication	80,517	10.9	10.3	74.9	12.7	2.1
Trade	49,555	6.7	3.0	79.5	16.7	.8
Public service (not elsewhere classified)	6,649	.9	5.9	79.3	14.1	.8
Professional service	13,761	1.9	4.2	85.3	10.1	.4
Domestic and personal service	107,521	14.5	31.8	47.0	19.0	2.2
Clerical occupations	9,311	1.3	1.0	91.2	7.5	.2
1920						
All occupations	174,174	100.0	11.6	69.4	18.6	.4
Agriculture	71,851	41.3	20.0	71.2	8.1	.7
Forestry and fishing	4,599	2.6	11.6	62.3	24.4	1.7
Extraction of minerals	1,922	1.1	6.7	58.5	34.6	.2
Manufacturing and mechanical industries	22,640	13.0	7.0	64.5	28.3	.2
Transportation and communication	7,998	4.6	10.1	71.9	17.7	.3
Trade	13,721	7.9	3.3	76.1	20.3	.3
Public service (not elsewhere classified)	2,135	1.2	6.8	75.9	17.0	.3
Professional service	3,163	1.8	3.8	85.1	11.0	.1
Domestic and personal service	43,911	25.2	31.4	44.7	22.6	1.3
Clerical occupations	2,234	1.3	1.2	90.2	8.5	.1

[Continued]

★ 1274 ★

Gainful Workers 10 Years Old and Over by Race, Nativity, and Occupation, 1910, 1920, 1930 - II

[Continued]

General division of occupations	Other races[1]		Percent of total			
	Number	Percent distribution	Negro	Native white	Foreign-born white	Other races
1910						
All occupations	200,745	100.0	13.6	65.4	20.5	.5
Agriculture	80,450	40.1	22.9	68.1	8.4	.6
Forestry and fishing	4,174	2.1	14.0	60.7	23.6	1.7
Extraction of minerals	2,556	1.3	6.3	45.4	48.0	.3
Manufacturing and mechanical industries	28,983	14.4	6.2	61.8	31.8	.3
Transportation and communication	11,618	5.8	9.6	63.9	26.0	.4
Trade	13,489	6.7	3.3	75.0	21.3	.4
Public service (not elsewhere classified)	921	.5	5.2	71.9	22.7	.2
Professional service	2,815	1.4	4.0	83.8	12.0	.2
Domestic and personal service	54,385	27.1	29.9	44.2	24.5	1.4
Clerical occupations	1,354	.7	1.1	88.9	9.9	.1

Source: "Gainful Workers 10 Years Old and Over, by Color, Nativity, and General Divisions of Occupations: 1930, 1920, and 1910," U.S. Bureau of the Census, *Negroes in the United States, 1920-1932,* p. 290. *Notes:* 1. Comprises Mexicans, Indians, Chinese, Japanese, Filipinos, Hindus, Koreans, Hawaiians, etc. In 1920 and 1910 Mexicans were included for the most part in the white population.

★ 1275 ★

Labor Force

Gainful Workers 10 Years Old and Over by Race, Nativity, and Occupation, 1930 - I

Percent not shown where less than 1/10 of 1 percent.

General division of occupations	Total		Negro		Native white		Foreign-born white	
	Number	Percent distribution	Number	Percent distribution	Number	Percent distribution	Number	Percent distribution
Total								
All occupations	48,829,920	100.0	5,503,535	100.0	35,173,370	100.0	7,411,127	100.0
Agriculture	10,471,998	21.4	1,987,839	36.1	7,518,519	21.4	673,662	9.1
Forestry and fishing	250,469	.5	31,732	.6	167,077	.5	44,846	.6
Extraction of minerals	984,323	2.0	74,972	1.4	658,267	1.9	232,121	3.1
Manufacturing and mechanical industries	14,110,652	28.9	1,024,656	18.6	9,663,796	27.5	3,265,381	44.1
Transportation and communication	3,843,147	7.9	397,645	7.2	2,876,682	8.2	488,303	6.6
Trade	6,081,467	12.5	183,809	3.3	4,835,498	13.7	1,012,605	13.7
Public service (not elsewhere classified)	856,205	1.8	50,203	.9	678,578	1.9	120,775	1.6
Professional service	3,253,884	6.7	135,925	2.5	2,775,453	7.9	328,745	4.4
Domestic and personal service	4,952,451	10.1	1,576,205	28.6	2,327,821	6.6	940,904	12.7
Clerical occupations	4,025,324	8.2	40,549	.7	3,671,679	10.4	303,785	4.1
Male								
All occupations	38,077,804	100.0	3,662,893	100.0	27,511,862	100.0	6,255,071	100.0
Agriculture	9,562,059	25.1	1,492,555	40.7	7,151,291	26.0	647,249	10.3
Forestry and fishing	250,140	.7	31,652	.9	166,883	.6	44,837	.7
Extraction of minerals	983,564	2.6	74,919	2.0	657,654	2.4	232,042	3.7
Manufacturing and mechanical industries	12,224,345	32.1	923,586	25.2	8,212,540	29.9	2,951,751	47.2
Transportation and communication	3,561,943	9.4	395,437	10.8	2,610,354	9.5	476,095	7.6

[Continued]

★ 1275 ★

Gainful Workers 10 Years Old and Over by Race, Nativity, and Occupation, 1930 - I
[Continued]

General division of occupations	Total		Negro		Native white		Foreign-born white	
	Number	Percent distribution	Number	Percent distribution	Number	Percent distribution	Number	Percent distribution
Trade	5,118,787	13.4	169,241	4.6	4,004,558	14.6	903,042	14.4
Public service (not elsewhere classified)	838,622	2.2	49,273	1.3	662,974	2.4	119,795	1.9
Professional service	1,727,650	4.5	72,898	2.0	1,419,063	5.2	225,397	3.6
Domestic and personal service	1,772,200	4.7	423,645	11.6	813,780	3.0	465,465	7.4
Clerical occupations	2,038,494	5.4	29,687	.8	1,812,765	6.6	189,398	3.0
Female								
All occupations	10,752,116	100.0	1,840,642	100.0	7,661,508	100.0	1,156,056	100.0
Agriculture	909,939	8.5	495,284	26.9	367,228	4.8	26,413	2.3
Forestry and fishing	329	-	80	-	194	-	9	-
Extraction of minerals	759	-	53	-	613	-	79	-
Manufacturing and mechanical industries	1,886,307	17.5	101,070	5.5	1,451,256	18.9	313,630	27.1
Transportation and communication	281,204	2.6	2,208	.1	266,328	3.5	12,208	1.1
Trade	962,680	9.0	14,568	.8	830,940	10.8	109,563	9.5
Public service (not elsewhere classified)	17,583	.2	930	.1	15,604	.2	980	.1
Professional service	1,526,234	14.2	63,027	3.4	1,356,390	17.7	103,348	8.9
Domestic and personal service	3,180,251	29.6	1,152,560	62.6	1,514,041	19.8	475,439	41.4
Clerical occupations	1,986,830	18.5	10,862	.6	1,858,914	24.3	114,387	9.9

Source: "Gainful Workers 10 Years Old and Over, by Color, Nativity, and General Divisions of Occupations for the United States: 1930," U.S. Bureau of the Census, *Negroes in the United States, 1920-1932*, p. 290.

★ 1276 ★

Labor Force

Gainful Workers 10 Years Old and Over by Race, Nativity, and Occupation, 1930 - II

Percent not shown where less than 1/10 of 1 percent.

General division of occupations	Other races[1]		Percent of total			
	Number	Percent distribution	Negro	Native white	Foreign-born white	Other races[1]
Total						
All occupations	741,888	100.0	11.3	79.0	15.2	1.5
Agriculture	291,978	39.4	19.0	71.8	6.4	2.8
Forestry and fishing	6,814	.9	12.7	66.7	17.9	2.7
Extraction of minerals	18,963	2.6	7.6	66.9	23.6	1.9
Manufacturing and mechanical industries	156,819	21.1	7.3	68.5	23.1	1.1
Transportation and communication	80,517	10.9	10.3	74.9	12.7	2.1
Trade	49,555	6.7	3.0	79.5	16.7	.8
Public service (not elsewhere classified)	6,649	.9	5.9	79.3	14.1	.8
Professional service	13,761	1.9	4.2	85.3	10.1	.4
Domestic and personal service	107,521	14.5	31.8	47.0	19.0	2.2
Clerical occupations	9,311	1.3	1.0	91.2	7.5	.2
Male						
All occupations	647,978	100.0	9.6	72.3	16.4	1.7

[Continued]

★ 1276 ★

Gainful Workers 10 Years Old and Over by Race, Nativity, and Occupation, 1930 - II

[Continued]

General division of occupations	Other races[1]		Percent of total			
	Number	Percent distribution	Negro	Native white	Foreign-born white	Other races[1]
Agriculture	270,964	41.8	15.6	74.8	6.8	2.8
Forestry and fishing	6,768	1.0	12.7	66.7	17.9	2.7
Extraction of minerals	18,949	2.9	7.6	66.9	23.6	1.9
Manufacturing and mechanical industries	136,468	21.1	7.6	67.2	24.1	1.1
Transportation and communication	80,057	12.4	11.1	73.3	13.4	2.2
Trade	41,946	6.5	3.3	78.2	17.6	.8
Public service (not elsewhere classified)	6,580	1.0	5.9	79.1	14.3	.8
Professional service	10,292	1.6	4.2	82.1	13.0	.6
Domestic and personal service	69,310	10.7	23.9	45.9	26.3	3.9
Clerical occupations	6,644	1.0	1.5	88.9	9.3	.3
Female						
All occupations	93,910	100.0	17.1	71.3	10.8	.3
Agriculture	21,014	22.5	54.4	40.4	2.9	2.9
Forestry and fishing	46	-	24.3	59.0	2.7	14.0
Extraction of minerals	14	-	7.0	80.8	10.4	1.8
Manufacturing and mechanical industries	20,351	21.7	5.4	76.9	16.6	1.1
Transportation and communication	460	.5	.8	94.7	4.3	.2
Trade	7,609	8.1	1.5	86.3	11.4	.8
Public service (not elsewhere classified)	69	.1	5.3	88.7	5.6	.4
Professional service	3,4698	3.7	4.1	88.9	6.8	.2
Domestic and personal service	38,211	40.7	36.2	47.6	14.9	1.2
Clerical occupations	2,667	2.8	.5	93.6	5.8	.1

Source: "Gainful Workers 10 Years Old and Over, by Color, Nativity, and General Divisions of Occupations for the United States: 1930," U.S. Bureau of the Census, *Negroes in the United States, 1920-1932,* p. 290. *Notes:* 1. Comprises Mexicans, Indians, Chinese, Japanese, Filipinos, Hindus, Koreans, Hawaiians, etc.

★ 1277 ★

Labor Force

Gainful Workers 10 Years Old and Over by Race, Nativity, and Sections, 1930 - I

Percent not shown where less than 1/10 of 1 percent.

General division of occupations	Total		Negro		Native white		Foreign-born white	
	Number	Percent distribution	Number	Percent distribution	Number	Percent distribution	Number	Percent distribution
				United States				
All occupations	48,829,920	100.0	5,503,535	100.0	35,173,370	100.0	7,411,127	100.0
Agriculture	10,471,998	21.4	1,987,839	36.1	7,518,519	21.4	673,662	9.1
Forestry and fishing	250,469	.5	31,732	.6	167,077	.5	44,846	.6
Extraction of minerals	984,323	2.0	74,972	1.4	658,267	1.9	232,121	3.1
Manufacturing and mechanical industries	14,110,652	28.9	1,024,656	18.6	9,663,796	27.5	3,265,381	44.1
Transportation and communication	3,843,147	7.9	397,645	7.2	2,876,682	8.2	488,303	6.6
Trade	6,081,467	12.5	183,809	3.3	4,835,498	13.7	1,012,605	13.7

[Continued]

★ 1277 ★

Gainful Workers 10 Years Old and Over by Race, Nativity, and Sections, 1930 - I

[Continued]

General division of occupations	Total		Negro		Native white		Foreign-born white	
	Number	Percent distribution	Number	Percent distribution	Number	Percent distribution	Number	Percent distribution
Public service (not elsewhere classified)	856,205	1.8	50,203	.9	678,578	1.9	120,775	1.6
Professional service	3,253,884	6.7	135,925	2.5	2,775,453	7.9	328,745	4.4
Domestic and personal service	4,952,451	10.1	1,576,205	28.6	2,327,821	6.6	940,904	12.7
Clerical occupations	4,025,324	8.2	40,549	.7	3,671,679	10.4	303,785	4.1
The North								
All occupations	29,549,871	100.0	1,228,670	100.0	21,943,512	100.0	6,279,199	100.0
Agriculture	3,943,198	13.3	38,816	3.2	3,415,620	15.6	475,150	7.6
Forestry and fishing	72,355	.2	478	1	50,906	.2	19,672	.3
Extraction of minerals	516,593	1.7	14,364	1.2	319,621	1.5	182,006	2.9
Manufacturing and mechanical industries	10,065,768	34.1	375,083	30.5	6,730,939	30.7	2,928,430	46.6
Transportation and communication	2,478,876	8.4	130,711	10.6	1,916,761	8.7	414,639	6.6
Trade	3,982,800	13.5	64,159	5.2	3,074,609	14.0	839,963	13.4
Public service (not elsewhere classified)	526,523	1.8	18,319	1.5	406,249	1.9	100,796	1.6
Professional service	2,104,244	7.1	36,551	3.0	1,803,300	8.2	261,878	4.2
Domestic and personal service	2,926,899	9.9	524,989	42.7	1,573,954	7.2	801,696	12.8
Clerical occupations	2,933,383	9.9	25,200	2.1	2,051,553	12.1	254,969	4.1
The South								
All occupations	14,310,217	100.0	4,210,163	100.0	9,521,762	100.0	300,195	100.0
Agriculture	5,581,438	39.0	1,945,210	46.2	3,462,362	36.4	40,130	13.4
Forestry and fishing	102,152	.7	31,155	.7	67,886	.7	1,624	.5
Extraction of minerals	339,266	2.4	60,025	1.4	257,065	2.7	18,626	6.2
Manufacturing and mechanical industries	2,858,258	20.0	639,844	15.2	2,077,400	21.8	88,867	29.6
Transportation and communication	944,863	6.6	261,069	6.2	644,032	6.8	14,886	5.0
Trade	1,355,153	9.5	117,062	2.8	1,154,027	12.1	63,922	21.3
Public service (not elsewhere classified)	221,148	1.5	28,860	.7	182,821	1.9	6,631	2.2
Professional service	728,564	5.1	96,832	2.3	605,708	6.4	21,385	7.1
Domestic and personal service	1,503,305	10.5	1,015,776	24.1	423,850	4.5	32,541	10.8
Clerical occupations	676,070	4.7	14,330	.3	646,611	6.8	11,583	3.9
The West								
All occupations	4,969,832	100.0	64,702	100.0	3,708,096	100.0	831,733	100.0
Agriculture	947,362	19.1	3,813	5.9	640,537	17.3	158,382	19.0
Forestry and fishing	75,962	1.5	99	.2	48,285	1.3	23,550	2.8
Extraction of minerals	128,464	2.6	583	.9	81,581	2.2	31,489	3.8
Manufacturing and mechanical industries	1,187,286	23.9	9,729	15.0	855,457	23.1	248,084	29.8
Transportation and communication	419,516	8.4	5,865	9.1	315,889	8.5	58,778	7.1
Trade	743,514	15.0	2,588	4.0	606,862	16.4	108,720	13.1
Public service (not elsewhere classified)	108,534	2.2	3,024	4.7	89,508	2.4	13,348	1.6
Professional service	421,076	8.5	2,542	3.9	366,445	9.9	45,482	5.5
Domestic and personal service	522,247	10.5	35,440	54.8	330,017	8.9	106,667	12.8
Clerical occupations	415,871	8.4	1,019	1.6	373,515	10.1	37,233	4.5

Source: "Gainful Workers 10 Years Old and Over, by Color, and Nativity, by Sections: 1930," U.S. Bureau of the Census, *Negroes in the United States, 1920-1932*, p. 291.
Note: 1. Less than 1/10 of 1 percent.

★ 1278 ★
Labor Force

Gainful Workers 10 Years Old and Over by Race, Nativity, and Sections, 1930 - II

Percent not shown where less than 1/10 of 1 percent.

General division of occupations	Other races[1]		Percent of total			
	Number	Percent distribution	Negro	Native white	Foreignborn white	Other races[1]
United States						
All occupations	741,888	100.0	11.3	72.0	15.2	1.5
Agriculture	291,978	39.4	19.0	71.8	6.4	2.8
Forestry and fishing	6,814	.9	12.7	66.7	17.9	2.7
Extraction of minerals	18,963	2.6	7.6	66.9	23.6	1.9
Manufacturing and mechanical industries	156,819	21.1	7.3	68.5	23.1	1.1
Transportation and communication	80,517	10.9	10.3	74.9	12.7	2.1
Trade	49,555	6.7	3.0	79.5	16.7	.8
Public service (not elsewhere classified)	6,649	.9	5.9	79.3	14.1	.8
Professional service	13,761	1.9	4.2	85.3	10.1	.4
Domestic and personal service	107,521	14.5	31.8	47.0	19.0	2.2
Clerical occupations	9,311	1.3	1.0	91.2	7.5	.2
The North						
All occupations	98,490	100.0	4.2	74.3	21.2	0.3
Agriculture	13,612	13.8	1.0	86.6	12.0	.3
Forestry and fishing	1,299	1.3	.7	70.4	27.2	1.8
Extraction of minerals	602	.6	2.8	61.9	35.2	.1
Manufacturing and mechanical industries	30,656	31.1	3.7	66.9	29.1	.3
Transportation and communication	16,657	16.9	5.3	77.3	16.7	.7
Trade	4,069	4.1	1.6	77.2	21.1	.1
Public service (not elsewhere classified)	1,159	1.2	3.5	77.2	19.1	.2
Professional service	2,515	2.6	1.7	85.7	12.4	.1
Domestic and personal service	26,260	26.7	17.9	53.8	27.4	.9
Clerical occupations	1,661	1.7	.9	90.4	8.7	.1
The South						
All occupations	278,097	100.0	29.4	66.5	2.1	1.9
Agriculture	133,736	48.1	34.9	62.0	.7	2.4
Forestry and fishing	1,487	.5	30.5	66.5	1.6	1.5
Extraction of minerals	3,550	1.3	17.7	75.8	5.5	1.0
Manufacturing and mechanical industries	52,147	18.8	22.4	72.7	3.1	1.8
Transportation and communication	24,876	8.9	27.6	68.2	1.6	2.6
Trade	20,142	7.2	8.6	85.2	4.7	1.5
Public service (not elsewhere classified)	2,836	1.0	13.1	82.7	3.0	1.3
Professional service	4,639	1.7	13.3	83.1	2.9	.6
Domestic and personal service	31,138	11.2	67.6	28.2	2.2	2.1
Clerical occupations	3,546	1.3	2.1	95.6	1.7	.5
The West						
All occupations	365,301	1.3	1.3	74.6	16.7	7.4

[Continued]

★ 1278 ★

Gainful Workers 10 Years Old and Over by Race, Nativity, and Sections, 1930 - II

[Continued]

General division of occupations	Other races[1]		Percent of total			
	Number	Percent distribution	Negro	Native white	Foreignborn white	Other races[1]
Agriculture	144,630	39.6	.4	67.6	16.7	15.3
Forestry and fishing	4,028	1.1	.1	63.6	31.0	5.3
Extraction of minerals	14,811	4.1	.5	63.5	24.5	11.5
Manufacturing and mechanical industries	74,016	20.3	.8	72.1	20.9	6.2
Transportation and communication	38,984	10.7	1.4	75.3	14.0	9.3
Trade	25,344	6.9	.3	81.6	14.6	3.4
Public service (not elsewhere classified)	2,654	.7	2.8	82.5	12.3	2.4
Professional service	2,654	.7	2.8	82.5	12.3	2.4
Domestic and personal service	50,123	13.7	6.8	63.2	20.4	9.6
Clerical occupations	4,104	1.1	.2	89.8	9.0	1.0

Source: "Gainful Workers 10 Years Old and Over, by Color, and Nativity, by Sections: 1930," U.S. Bureau of the Census, *Negroes in the United States, 1920-1932*, p. 291. *Notes:* 1. Comprises Mexicans, Indians, Chinese, Japanese, Filipinos, Hindus, Koreans, Hawaiians, etc.

★ 1279 ★

Labor Force

Labor Force Distribution by Race and Sex, 1910

Sex and racial class	Total	Gainfully employed			Not gainfully employed
		Total	In agriculture, forestry, and animal husbandry	In other employment	
			Number		
Both sexes					
All classes	71,580,270	38,167,336	12,659,082	25,508,254	33,412,934
Negro	7,317,922	5,192,535	2,893,375	2,299,160	2,125,387
White	63,933,870	32,774,056	9,681,069	23,092,987	31,159,814
Other	328,478	200,745	84,638	116,107	127,733
Male					
All classes	37,027,558	30,091,564	10,851,581	19,239,983	6,935,994
Negro	3,637,386	3,178,554	1,842,238	1,336,316	458,832
White	33,164,229	26,730,347	8,929,937	17,800,410	6,433,882
Other	225,943	182,663	79,406	103,257	43,280
Female					
All classes	34,552,712	8,075,772	1,807,501	6,268,271	26,476,940
Negro	3,680,536	2,013,981	1,051,137	962,844	1,666,555
White	30,769,641	6,043,709	751,132	5,292,577	24,725,932
Other	102,535	18,082	5,232	12,850	84,453

[Continued]

★ 1279 ★

Labor Force Distribution by Race and Sex, 1910
[Continued]

Sex and racial class	Total	Gainfully employed			Not gainfully employed
		Total	In agriculture, forestry, and animal husbandry	In other employment	
Percentage distribution by sex					
Both sexes					
All classes	100.0	100.0	100.0	100.0	100.0
Negro	100.0	100.0	100.0	100.0	100.0
White	100.0	100.0	100.0	100.0	100.0
Other	100.0	100.0	100.0	100.0	100.0
Male					
All classes	51.7	78.8	85.7	75.4	20.8
Negro	49.7	61.2	63.7	58.1	21.6
White	51.9	81.6	92.2	77.1	20.6
Other	68.8	91.0	93.8	88.9	33.9
Female					
All classes	48.3	21.2	14.3	24.6	79.2
Negro	50.3	38.8	36.3	41.9	78.4
White	48.1	18.4	7.8	22.9	79.4
Other	31.2	9.0	6.2	11.1	66.1
Percentage distribution by racial class					
Both sexes					
All classes	100.0	100.0	100.0	100.0	100.0
Negro	10.2	13.6	22.9	9.0	6.4
White	89.3	85.9	76.5	90.5	93.3
Other	0.5	0.5	0.7	0.5	0.4
Male					
All classes	100.0	100.0	100.0	100.0	100.0
Negro	9.8	10.6	17.0	6.9	6.6
White	89.6	88.8	82.3	92.5	92.8
Other	0.6	0.6	0.7	0.5	0.6
Female					
All classes	100.0	100.0	100.0	100.0	100.0
Negro	10.6	24.9	58.2	15.4	6.3
White	89.1	74.8	41.6	84.4	93.4
Other	0.3	0.2	0.3	0.2	0.3
Percentage distribution by occupational group					
Both sexes					
All classes	100.0	100.0	100.0	100.0	100.0
Negro	100.0	71.0	39.5	31.4	29.0
White	100.0	51.3	15.1	36.1	48.7
Other	100.0	61.1	25.8	35.3	38.9

[Continued]

★ 1279 ★

Labor Force Distribution by Race and Sex, 1910
[Continued]

Sex and racial class	Total	Gainfully employed			Not gainfully employed
		Total	In agriculture, forestry, and animal husbandry	In other employment	
Male					
All classes	100.0	81.3	29.3	52.0	18.7
Negro	100.0	87.4	50.6	36.7	12.6
White	100.0	80.6	26.9	53.7	19.4
Other	100.0	80.8	35.1	45.7	19.2
Female					
All classes	100.0	23.4	5.2	18.1	76.6
Negro	100.0	54.7	28.6	26.2	45.3
White	100.0	19.6	2.4	17.2	80.4
Other	100.0	17.6	5.1	12.5	82.4

Source: "Negro Population 10 Years of Age and Over: 1910," U.S. Bureau of the Census, *Negro Population, 1790-1915*, p. 503. *Note:* Includes age unknown.

★ 1280 ★
Labor Force

Labor Force Distribution, 1910

Sex and section	Total	Gainfully employed			Not gainfully employed
		Total	In agriculture, forestry, and animal husbandry	In other employment	
			Number		
Both sexes					
United States	7,317,922	5,192,535	2,893,375	2,299,160	2,125,387
The South	6,408,539	4,592,353	2,845,163	1,747,190	1,816,186
The North and West	909,383	600,182	48,212	551,970	309,201
Male					
United States	3,637,386	3,178,554	1,842,238	1,336,316	458,832
The South	3,174,163	2,781,233	1,795,610	985,623	392,930
The North and West	463,223	397,321	46,628	350,693	65,902
Female					
United States	3,680,536	2,013,981	1,051,137	962,844	1,666,555
The South	3,234,376	1,811,120	1,049,553	761,567	1,423,256
The North and West	446,160	202,861	1,584	201,277	243,299

[Continued]

★ 1280 ★

Labor Force Distribution, 1910
[Continued]

Sex and section	Total	Gainfully employed			Not gainfully employed
		Total	In agriculture, forestry, and animal husbandry	In other employment	
Percentage distribution by section					
Both sexes					
United States	100.0	100.0	100.0	100.0	100.0
The South	87.6	88.4	98.3	76.0	85.5
The North and West	12.4	11.6	1.7	24.0	14.5
Male					
United States	100.0	100.0	100.0	100.0	100.0
The South	87.3	87.5	97.5	73.8	85.6
The North and West	12.7	12.5	2.5	26.2	14.4
Female					
United States	100.0	100.0	100.0	100.0	100.0
The South	87.9	89.9	99.8	79.1	85.4
The North and West	12.1	10.1	0.2	20.9	14.6
Percentage distribution by sex					
Both sexes					
United States	100.0	100.0	100.0	100.0	100.0
The South	100.0	100.0	100.0	100.0	100.0
The North and West	100.0	100.0	100.0	100.0	100.0
Male					
United States	49.7	61.2	63.7	58.1	21.6
The South	49.5	60.6	63.1	56.4	21.6
The North and West	50.9	66.2	96.7	63.5	21.3
Female					
United States	50.3	38.8	36.3	41.9	78.4
The South	50.5	39.4	36.9	43.6	78.4
The North and West	49.1	33.8	3.3	36.5	78.7
Percentage distribution by occupational group					
Both sexes					
United States	100.0	71.0	39.5	31.4	29.0
The South	100.0	71.7	44.4	27.3	28.3
The North and West	100.0	66.0	5.3	60.7	34.0
Male					
United States	100.0	87.4	50.6	36.7	12.6
The South	100.0	87.6	56.6	31.1	12.4
The North and West	100.0	85.8	10.1	75.7	14.2
Female					
United States	100.0	54.7	28.6	26.2	45.3

[Continued]

★ 1280 ★

Labor Force Distribution, 1910
[Continued]

Sex and section	Total	Gainfully employed			Not gainfully employed
		Total	In agriculture, forestry, and animal husbandry	In other employment	
The South	100.0	56.0	32.4	23.5	44.0
The North and West	100.0	45.5	0.4	45.1	54.5

Source: "Negro Population 10 Years of Age and Over: 1910," U.S. Bureau of the Census, *Negro Population, 1790-1915*, p. 503.

★ 1281 ★

Labor Force

Labor Force Distribution – March 24-30, 1940

Labor force, NYA Employment status	Total	Percent of distribution	Non-white		White	
			Number	Percent of distribution	Number	Percent of distribution
Total in the labor force	52,840,762	100.0	5,637,047	100.0	47,203,715	100.0
Male	39,994,197	75.7	3,787,439	67.2	36,206,758	76.7
Female	12,846,565	24.3	1,849,608	32.8	10,996,957	23.3
Employed (except on public emergency work)[1]	45,350,430	85.8	4,699,485	83.4	40,650,945	86.1
Male	34,201,490	64.7	3,118,642	55.3	31,082,848	65.8
Female	11,148,940	21.1	1,580,843	28.0	9,568,097	20.3
On public emergency work (WPA, NYA, CCC)[2]	2,380,062	4.5	320,434	5.7	2,059,628	4.4
Male	1,947,975	3.7	261,737	4.6	1,686,238	3.6
Female	432,087	0.8	58,697	1.0	373,390	0.8
Seeking work[3]	5,110,270	9.7	617,128	10.9	4,493,142	9.5
Male	3,844,732	7.3	407,060	7.2	3,437,672	7.3

Source: "Number and Percent Distribution of Non-White and White Persons 14 Years of Age and Over in the Labor Force, by Sex, for the United States: March 24-30, 1940," Florence Murray, ed., *The Negro Handbook*, 1942, p. 147. *Notes:* 1. Persons who, at any time during the week of March 24-30, 1940, worked for pay or profit (except on public emergency work) or assisted without pay in a family enterprise; or who, during that week, had jobs (except on public emergency work), businesses, or professional enterprises at which they did not work because of vacation, industrial dispute, bad weather, temporary illness, or a layoff not exceeding four weeks with instructions to return by a specified date. 2. The number of persons reported in the census as on public emergency work (WPA, NYA, and CCC) was considerably less than the number indicated by the records of the various emergency work agencies. Of those classified erroneously in the census, it is probable that a majority were returned as employed in private or non-emergency government work. 3. Persons seeking work during the week of March 24-30, 1940, who were not working on private or non-emergency government work, nor on public emergency work.

★ 1282 ★

Labor Force

Labor Force Participation Rates, by Age and Gender: 1948, 1960, 1970, 1975

Annual averages.

Age and sex	Black and other races				White			
	1948	1960	1970	1975	1948	1960	1970	1975
MEN								
Total, 16 years old and over	87	83	77	72	87	83	80	79
16 and 17 years	60	46	35	30	51	46	49	52
18 and 19 years	78	71	62	58	76	69	67	73
20 to 24 years	86	90	84	78	84	88	83	86
25 to 34 years	95	96	94	91	96	98	97	96
35 to 44 years	97	96	93	90	98	98	97	96
45 to 54 years	95	92	88	85	96	96	95	93
55 to 64 years	89	83	79	69	90	87	83	77
65 years and over	50	31	27	21	47	33	27	22
WOMEN								
Total, 16 years old and over	46	48	50	49	31	37	43	46
16 and 17 years	29	22	24	27	32	30	37	43
18 and 19 years	41	44	45	45	54	52	55	60
20 to 24 years	47	49	58	56	45	46	58	65
25 to 34 years	51	50	58	61	31	34	43	54
35 to 44 years	53	60	60	62	35	42	50	55
45 to 54 years	51	61	60	57	33	49	54	54
55 to 64 years	38	47	47	44	23	36	43	41
65 years and over	18	13	12	11	9	11	10	8

Source: "Civilian Labor Force Participation Rates by Age and Sex: 1948, 1960, 1970, and 1975," U.S. Department of Commerce, Bureau of the Census, *The Social and Economic Status of the Black Population in the United States: An Historical View, 1790-1978,* p. 67. Primary source: U.S. Department of Labor, Bureau of Labor Statistics.

★ 1283 ★

Labor Force

Labor Force Participation Rates, by Educational Level: 1965, 1970, 1975

Years of school completed and sex	Black and other races			White		
	1965	1970	1975[1]	1965	1970	1975[1]
MEN						
Total, 18 years old and over	82	79	70	83	82	78
Elementary: 8 years or less	74	69	55	68	64	56
High school: 1 to 3 years	87	86	63	86	83	69

[Continued]

★ 1283 ★

Labor Force Participation Rates, by Educational Level: 1965, 1970, 1975

[Continued]

Years of school completed and sex	Black and other races			White		
	1965	1970	1975[1]	1965	1970	1975[1]
4 years	90	89	85	92	90	88
College: 1 or more years	88	80	82	86	86	86
WOMEN						
Total, 18 years old and over	49	51	49	38	43	46
Elementary: 8 years or less	38	35	30	26	25	23
High school: 1 to 3 years	49	51	40	36	39	39
4 years	60	63	61	44	49	52
College: 1 or more years	69	68	67	47	52	57

Source: "Labor Participation Rates of the Rates of the Population 18 Years Old and Over by Years of School Completed and Sex: March of 1965, 1970, and 1975," U.S. Department of Commerce, Bureau of the Census, *The Social and Economic Status of the Black Population in the United States: An Historical View, 1790-1978,* p. 67. Primary source: U.S. Department of Labor, Bureau of Labor Statistics. *Notes:* Data first became available by race in 1965. 1. Data are for persons 16 years old and over.

★ 1284 ★

Labor Force

Labor Force Status of Women 15 to 49 Years Old by Age and Presence of Children, 1971

Age and race	Percent in labor force			
	Single women	Women ever married		
		Total	With own children under 5 years old	Without own children 5 years old
Negro				
15 to 49 years	39	59	47	66
15 to 24 years	33	51	44	64
25 to 29 years	64	58	46	74
30 to 49 years	60	62	49	65
White				
15 to 49 years	50	46	28	56
15 to 24 years	45	46	31	67
25 to 29 years	82	39	27	62
30 to 49 years	78	48	26	53

Source: Labor Force Status of Women 15 to 49 Years Old, by Age of Women and Presence of Young Children: 1971," U.S. Bureau of the Census, *The Social and Economic Status of the Black Population in the United States, 1970,* p. 112. Primary source: U.S. Department of Commerce, Social and Economic Statistics Administration, Bureau of the Census.

★ 1285 ★

Labor Force

Labor Force and Employment, by Industry, 1800-1960 - I

[In thousands of persons 10 years old and over]

Year	Labor force			Employment			
	Total	Free	Slave	Agriculture	Fishing	Mining	Construction
1960	74,060	-	-	5,970	45	709	3,640
1950	65,470	-	-	7,870	77	901	3,029
1940	56,290	-	-	9,575	60	925	1,876
1930	48,830	-	-	10,560	73	1,009	1,988
1920	41,610	-	-	10,790	53	1,180	1,233
1910	37,480	-	-	11,770	68	1,068	1,949
1900	29,070	-	-	11,680	69	637	1,665
1890	23,320	-	-	9,960	60	440	1,510
1880	17,390	-	-	8,920	41	280	900
1870	12,930	-	-	6,790	28	180	780
1860	11,110	8,770	2,340	5,880	31	176	520
1850	8,250	6,280	1,970	4,520	30	102	410
1840	5,660	4,180	1,480	3,570	24	32	290
1830	4,200	3,020	1,180	2,965	15	22	-
1820	3,135	2,185	950	2,470	14	13	-
1810	2,330	1,590	740	1,950	6	11	-
1800	1,900	1,370	530	1,400	5	10	-

Source: "Labor Force and Employment, by Industry: 1800 to 1960," U.S. Bureau of the Census, *Historical Statistics of the United States: Colonial Times to 1970, Part I.* Bicentennial Edition, p. 139.

★ 1286 ★

Labor Force

Labor Force and Employment, by Industry, 1800-1960 - II

[In thousands of persons 10 years old and over]

Year	Employment							
		Manufacturing			Transport		Service	
	Total persons engaged	Cotton textile wage earners	Primary iron and steel wage earners	Trade	Ocean vessels	Railway	Teachers	Domestics
1960	17,145	300	530	14,051	135	883	1,850	2,489
1950	15,648	350	550	12,152	130	1,373	1,270	1,995
1940	11,309	400	485	9,328	150	1,160	1,086	2,300
1930	9,884	372	375	8,122	160	1,659	1,044	2,270
1920	11,190	450	460	5,845	205	2,236	752	1,660
1910	8,332	370	306	5,320	150	1,855	595	2,090
1900	5,895	303	222	3,970	105	1,040	436	1,800
1890	4,390	222	149	2,960	120	750	350	1,580
1880	3,290	175	130	1,930	125	416	230	1,130
1870	2,470	135	78	1,310	135	160	170	1,000

[Continued]

★ 1286 ★

Labor Force and Employment, by Industry, 1800-1960 - II
[Continued]

| Year | Total persons engaged | Manufacturing | | Trade | Transport | | Service | |
		Cotton textile wage earners	Primary iron and steel wage earners		Ocean vessels	Railway	Teachers	Domestics
1860	1,530	122	43	890	145	80	115	600
1850	1,200	92	35	530	135	20	80	350
1840	500	72	24	350	95	7	45	240
1830	(NA)	55	20	-	70	-	30	160
1820	(NA)	12	5	-	50	-	20	110
1810	75	10	5	-	60	-	12	70
1800	-	1	1	-	40	-	5	40

Source: "Labor Force and Employment, by Industry: 1900 to 1960," U.S. Bureau of the Census, *Historical Statistics of the United States: Colonial Times to 1970, Part I*, Bicentennial Edition, p. 139. *Note:* NA Not available.

★ 1287 ★

Labor Force

Labor Force in Agricultural and Other Pursuits – 1890, 1900, 1910

| Occupational group | Negro population 10 years of age and over[1] | | | | | |
| | Male | | | Female | | |
	1910	1900	1890	1910	1900	1890
			Number			
Total	3,637,386	3,181,650	2,646,171	3,680,536	3,233,931	2,682,801
Gainfully employed	3,178,554	2,675,497	2,101,379	2,013,981	1,316,840	971,785
In agricultural pursuits	1,830,424	1,561,153	1,300,658	1,051,030	582,001	427,667
In other pursuits	1,348,130	1,114,344	800,821	962,951	734,839	544,118
Not gainfully employed	458,832	506,153	544,792	1,666,555	1,917,091	1,711,016
			Percentage distribution by occupational group			
Total	100.0	100.0	100.0	100.0	100.0	100.0
Gainfully employed	87.4	84.1	79.4	54.7	40.7	36.2
In agricultural pursuits	50.3	49.1	49.2	28.6	18.0	15.9
In other pursuits	37.1	35.0	30.3	26.2	22.7	20.3
Not gainfully employed	12.6	15.9	20.6	45.3	59.3	63.8

Source: "Gainfully Employed in Agricultural and Other Pursuits, and Not Gainfully Employed—Number and Percentage of Negro Males and Females: 1910, 1900, and 1890," U.S. Bureau of the Census, *Negro Population, 1790-1915*, p. 504. *Note:* 1. Includes age unknown.

★ 1288 ★
Labor Force

Labor Force in Agriculture, Forestry, and Animal Husbandry: by Class of Worker, 1910

| Class of worker | Gainfully Employed in Agriculture, Forestry, and Animal Husbandry: 1910 | | | | | |
| | All classes | | Negro | | White | |
	Male	Female	Male	Female	Male	Female
Number						
Total	10,851,581	1,807,501	1,842,238	1,051,137	8,929,937	751,132
Farm	10,074,199	1,779,314	1,757,509	1,047,130	8,261,291	728,052
Other	777,382	28,187	84,729	4,007	668,646	23,080
Operator	5,872,005	273,149	803,801	79,932	5,042,485	192,036
Farm	5,606,789	257,703	798,397	79,308	4,788,967	177,468
Other	265,216	15,446	5,404	624	253,518	14,568
Foreman	48,338	7,776	1,690	285	46,286	7,466
Farm	34,017	7,504	1,277	269	32,524	7,210
Other	14,321	272	413	16	13,762	256
Laborer	4,931,238	1,526,576	1,036,747	970,920	3,841,166	551,630
Farm	4,433,393	1,514,107	957,835	967,553	3,439,800	543,374
Other	497,845	12,469	78,912	3,367	401,366	8,256
Percentage distribution by class of worker						
Total	100.0	100.0	100.0	100.0	100.0	100.0
Farm	100.0	100.0	100.0	100.0	100.0	100.0
Other	100.0	100.0	100.0	100.0	100.0	100.0
Operator	54.1	15.1	43.6	7.6	56.5	25.6
Farm	55.7	14.5	45.4	7.6	58.0	24.4
Other	34.1	54.8	6.4	15.6	37.9	63.1
Foreman	0.4	0.4	0.1	[1]	0.5	1.0
Farm	0.3	0.4	0.1	[1]	0.4	1.0
Other	1.8	1.0	0.5	0.4	2.1	1.1
Laborer	45.4	84.5	56.3	92.4	43.0	73.4
Farm	44.0	85.1	54.5	92.4	41.6	74.6
Other	64.0	44.2	93.1	84.0	60.0	35.8
Percentage distribution by racial class						
Total	100.0	100.0	100.0	100.0	100.0	100.0
Farm	100.0	100.0	17.7	58.9	82.0	40.9
Other	100.0	100.0	10.9	14.2	86.0	81.9
Operator	100.0	100.0	13.7	29.3	85.9	70.3
Farm	100.0	100.0	14.2	30.8	85.4	68.9
Other	100.0	100.0	2.0	4.0	95.6	94.3
Foreman	100.0	100.0	3.5	3.7	95.8	96.0
Farm	100.0	100.0	3.8	3.6	95.6	96.1
Other	100.0	100.0	2.9	5.9	96.1	94.1
Laborer	100.0	100.0	21.0	63.6	77.9	36.1
Farm	100.0	100.0	21.6	63.9	77.6	35.9
Other	100.0	100.0	15.9	27.0	80.6	66.2

Source: "Gainfully Employed in Agriculture, Forestry, and Animal Husbandry: 1910," U.S. Bureau of the Census, *Negro Population, 1790-1915,* p. 506. *Note:* 1. Less than one-tenth of 1 per cent.

★ 1289 ★
Labor Force

Labor Force in Agriculture, Forestry, and Animal Husbandry: by Farm, 1910

Class of farm	Gainfully employed in agriculture, forestry, and animal husbandry: 1910						
	Total	Negro		White	Other	Percentage distribution by class of farm	
		Number	Per cent			Negro	White
Male							
Total	10,851,581	1,842,238	17.0	8,929,937	79,406	100.0	100.0
General farm	10,074,199	1,757,509	17.4	8,261,291	55,399	95.4	92.5
Turpentine farm	28,647	24,345	85.0	4,289	13	1.3	1
Garden	152,541	15,857	10.4	129,976	6,708	0.9	1.5
Dairy farm	92,478	2,490	2.7	89,784	204	0.1	1.0
Orchard	61,259	1,925	3.1	53,771	5,563	0.1	1
Nursery	14,486	989	6.8	12,987	510	0.1	0.1
Greenhouse	25,109	829	3.3	24,130	150	1	0.3
Cranberry bog	1,754	446	25.4	1,297	11	1	1
Vineyard	2,659	20	0.8	2,315	324	1	1
Other	398,449	37,828	9.5	350,097	10,524	2.1	3.9
Female							
Total	1,807,501	1,051,137	58.2	751,132	5,232	100.0	100.0
General farm	1,779,314	1,047,130	58.9	728,052	4,132	99.6	96.9
Turpentine farm	320	285	89.1	34	1	1	1
Garden	9,423	2,492	26.4	6,759	172	0.2	0.9
Dairy farm	5,438	454	8.3	4,973	11	1	0.7
Orchard	3,347	281	8.4	2,823	243	1	0.4
Nursery	421	125	29.7	292	4	1	1
Greenhouse	2,032	62	3.1	1,965	5	1	0.3
Cranberry bog	86	13	15.1	73	-	1	1
Vineyard	159	-	-	156	3	-	1
Other	6,961	295	4.2	6,005	661	1	0.8

Source: "Gainfully Employed in Agriculture, Forestry, and Animal Husbandry: 1910," U.S. Bureau of the Census, *Negro Population, 1790-1915,* p. 505. *Note:* 1. Less than one-tenth of one per cent.

★ 1290 ★
Labor Force

Labor Force in Agriculture, Forestry, and Animal Husbandry: by Farm and Worker, 1910

| Class of farm and of worker | Gainfully Employed in Agriculture, Forestry, and Animal Husbandry: 1910 | | | | | |
| | Male | | | Female | | |
	All classes	Negro	White	All classes	Negro	White
Total	10,851,581	1,842,238	8,929,937	1,807,501	1,051,137	751,132
Operator	5,872,005	803,801	5,042,485	273,149	79,932	192,036
Foreman	48,338	1,690	46,286	7,776	285	7,466
Laborer	4,931,238	1,036,747	3,841,166	1,526,576	970,920	551,630
Farm	10,074,199	1,757,509	8,261,291	1,779,314	1,047,130	728,052
Operator	5,606,789	798,397	4,788,967	257,703	79,308	177,468
Foreman	34,017	1,277	32,524	7,504	269	7,210
Laborer	4,433,393	957,835	3,439,800	1,514,107	967,553	543,374
Turpentine farm	28,647	24,345	4,289	320	285	34
Operator	508	112	396	3	1	2
Foreman	898	146	751	1	-	1
Laborer	27,241	24,087	3,142	316	284	31
Garden	152,541	15,857	129,976	9,423	2,492	6,759
Operator	75,481	4,009	69,534	4,413	457	3,918
Foreman	887	57	794	68	11	57
Laborer	76,173	11,791	59,648	4,942	2,024	2,784
Dairy farm	92,478	2,490	89,784	5,438	454	4,973
Operator	59,240	174	59,009	2,576	34	2,540
Foreman	1,001	14	985	85	1	84
Laborer	32,237	2,302	29,790	2,777	419	2,349
Orchard	61,259	1,925	53,771	3,347	281	2,823
Operator	39,702	280	38,272	2,179	26	2,140
Foreman	1,750	40	1,651	52	1	51
Laborer	19,807	1,605	13,848	1,116	254	632
Nursery	14,486	989	12,987	421	125	292
Operator	2,931	20	2,825	79	5	73
Foreman	682	4	673	33	3	30
Laborer	10,873	965	9,489	309	117	189
Greenhouse	25,109	829	24,130	2,032	62	1,965
Operator	7,977	96	7,829	1,051	20	1,029
Foreman	336	4	329	20	-	20
Laborer	16,796	729	15,972	961	42	916
Cranberry bog	1,754	446	1,297	86	13	73
Operator	306	2	299	18	1	17
Foreman	132	1	131	-	-	-
Laborer	1,316	443	867	68	12	56
Vineyard	2,659	20	2,315	159	-	156
Operator	1,247	1	1,225	79	-	78
Foreman	123	-	115	2	-	2
Laborer	1,289	19	975	78	-	76
Other	398,449	37,828	350,097	6,961	295	6,005
Operator[1]	77,824	710	74,129	5,048	80	4,771

[Continued]

★ 1290 ★

Labor Force in Agriculture, Forestry, and Animal Husbandry: by Farm and Worker, 1910
[Continued]

Class of farm and of worker	Gainfully Employed in Agriculture, Forestry, and Animal Husbandry: 1910					
	Male			Female		
	All classes	Negro	White	All classes	Negro	White
Foreman[2]	8,512	147	8,333	11	-	11
Laborer[3]	312,113	36,971	267,635	1,902	215	1,223

Source: "Gainfully Employed in Agriculture, Forestry, and Animal Husbandry: 1910," U.S. Bureau of the Census, *Negro Population, 1790-1915,* p. 505. *Notes:* 1. Includes foresters, forestry owners and managers, apiarists, poultry raisers, stock raisers, and landscape gardeners. 2. Includes forestry foremen and stock farm foremen. 3. Includes corn shellers, grain thrashers, wood sawyers, etc.; ditchers; hay and straw balers; irrigators and ditch tenders; choppers and cutters in lumber camps; inspectors and surveyors; log drivers; sawyers; scalers; teamsters; woodchoppers and tie cutters; fishermen and oystermen; poultry yard laborers; stock herders, drovers, and feeders; gardeners employed by steam railroads; and not specified pursuits.

★ 1291 ★
Labor Force

Laborers in Agriculture, Forestry, and Animal Husbandry: by Class of Laborer, 1910

Class of laborer	Both sexes		Male		Female	
	Negro	White	Negro	White	Negro	White
Number						
Total	2,007,667	4,392,796	1,036,747	3,841,166	970,920	551,630
Farm	1,925,388	3,983,174	957,835	3,439,800	967,553	543,374
Home farm	1,145,353	2,157,872	441,203	1,687,461	704,150	470,411
Working out	780,035	1,825,302	516,632	1,752,339	263,403	72,963
Other	82,279	409,622	78,912	401,366	3,367	8,256
Percentage distribution by sex						
Total	100.0	100.0	51.6	87.4	48.4	12.6
Farm	100.0	100.0	49.7	86.4	50.3	13.6
Home farm	100.0	100.0	38.5	78.2	61.5	21.8
Working out	100.0	100.0	66.2	96.0	33.8	4.0
Other	100.0	100.0	95.9	98.0	4.1	2.0
Percentage distribution by class of labor						
Total	100.0	100.0	100.0	100.0	100.0	100.0
Farm	95.9	90.7	92.4	89.6	99.7	98.5
Home farm	57.0	49.1	42.6	43.9	72.5	85.3
Working out	38.9	41.6	49.8	45.6	27.1	13.2
Other	4.1	9.3	7.6	10.4	0.3	1.5

Source: "Laborers Employed in Agriculture, Forestry, and Animal Husbandry: 1910," U.S. Bureau of the Census, *Negro Population, 1790-1915,* p. 506.

★ 1292 ★

Labor Force

Level of Education of Men Who Are Earners by Region and Race, 1940-1970

Characteristic	1940	1950	1960	1970
Total U.S.				
White	9.03	9.85	10.65	11.65
Black	5.78	6.58	7.80	9.35
Difference[1]	3.25	3.27	2.85	2.31
South				
White	8.71	9.37	10.13	11.22
Black	5.13	5.88	6.91	8.53
Difference[1]	3.58	3.49	3.22	2.69
Non-South				
White	9.15	10.6	10.83	11.80
Black	7.31	7.98	8.94	10.20
Difference[1]	1.84	2.08	1.89	1.60

Source: "Mean Years of School of Male Wage Earners Ages 25-64 by Region and Race," *The Economic Progress of Black Men in America*, p. 55. Primary source: Census of Population, 1940-1980; Public Use Sample. *Note:* 1. White mean schooling minus black mean schooling.

★ 1293 ★

Labor Force

Major Industry of Employed Persons: 1940, 1960, and 1970

Numbers in thousands.

Industry and year	All races	Black	Percent Black of all races
1940			
Total employed	45,166	4,479	10
Percent	100	100	(X)
Agriculture, forestry, and fisheries	19	33	18
Construction	5	3	7
Manufacturing	23	12	5
Wholesale and retail trade	17	8	5
Personal services	9	29	32
Professional and related services	7	4	5
Public administration	4	1	3
Other industries	15	9	6
Industry not reported	2	1	9
1960			
Total employed	64,639	6,099	9

[Continued]

★ 1293 ★

Major Industry of Employed Persons: 1940, 1960, and 1970
[Continued]

Industry and year	All races	Black	Percent Black of all races
Percent	100	100	(X)
Agriculture, forestry, and fisheries	7	9	13
Construction	6	5	9
Manufacturing	27	19	7
Wholesale and retail trade	18	12	6
Personal services	6	22	34
Professional and related services	12	11	9
Public administration	5	5	9
Other industries	15	10	6
Industry not reported	4	7	17
1970			
Total employed	77,309	7,420	10
Percent	100	100	(X)
Agriculture, forestry, and fisheries	3	3	8
Construction	5	4	8
Manufacturing	24	22	9
Wholesale and retail trade	19	12	6
Personal services	4	11	26
Professional and related services	17	18	10
Public administration	5	6	11
Other industries	16	12	7
Industry not reported	6	12	19

Source: "Major Industry of Employed Persons 14 Years Old and Over by Region: 1940, 1960, and 1970," U.S. Department of Commerce, Bureau of the Census, *The Social and Economic Status of the Black Population in the United States: An Historical View, 1790-1978*, p. 77. Primary source: U.S. Department of Commerce, Bureau of the Census. *Notes:* - Rounds to zero. Occupation and industry statistics for the census years 1940, 1960, and 1970 are not strictly comparable. However, adjustments have been made in the 1960 data to achieve as close comparability with the 1970 classification systems as possible. Since these adjustments sometimes involved estimates, the reader should exercise caution in interpreting small changes between the two census. In the figures for persons 14 years old and over, the "not reported" cases for 1970 are treated according to the 1960 presentation; that is, the cases allocated to major groups in 1970 are removed from those groups and combined into a separate "not reported" category. The table reflects these adjustments which have been made *only* at the national level.

★ 1294 ★

Labor Force

Male Labor Force Participation Rates by Race and Age, 1940-1970

Race and age	1940	1950	1960	1970
Whites				
25-34	97.2	94.6	96.7	95.8
35-44	96.8	97.0	97.2	96.5
45-54	94.0	94.2	95.1	94.2
55-59	89.6	87.7	89.7	88.5
60-64	80.9	80.0	80.0	74.9
Total	94.4	93.6	94.3	92.8
Difference in participation				
(White minus black):				
25-34	1.2	3.6	3.3	4.4
35-44	1.5	2.5	3.9	5.3
45-54	1.7	2.3	5.0	7.8
55-59	-1.2	4.2	6.8	9.0
60-64	-2.9	5.8	10.0	8.3
Total	0.5	2.4	4.4	6.1

Source: "Male Civilian Labor Force Participation Rates by Race and Age," *The Economic Progress of Black Men in America*, p. 28. Primary source: Census of Population, 1940-1980; Public Use Sample.

★ 1295 ★

Labor Force

Male Unemployment by Race, Education, and Region, 1940-1970

Characteristic	1940	1950	1960	1970
Black				
Less than 12 years				
Non-South	17.0	10.3	10.7	5.7
South	7.1	4.6	6.8	3.9
12 years or more				
Non-South	12.6	5.6	5.9	3.8
South	5.0	3.3	3.9	2.4
Total	9.6	6.4	7.8	4.2
White				
Less than 12 years				
Non-South	9.5	4.7	5.5	4.2
South	5.9	3.0	4.9	2.8
12 years or more				
Non-South	5.2	2.3	2.1	2.0
South	3.3	1.6	1.6	1.3
Total	7.6	3.4	3.7	2.6

[Continued]

★ 1295 ★

Male Unemployment by Race, Education, and Region, 1940-1970

[Continued]

Characteristic	1940	1950	1960	1970
Difference (black minus white)				
Less than 12 years				
Non-South	7.5	5.6	5.2	1.5
South	1.2	1.6	1.9	1.1
12 years or more				
Non-South	7.4	3.3	3.8	1.8
South	1.7	1.7	2.3	1.1
Total	2.0	3.0	4.1	1.6
Ratio (black divided by white)				
Less than 12 years				
Non-South	1.8	2.2	1.9	1.4
South	1.2	1.5	1.4	1.4
12 years or more				
Non-South	2.4	2.4	2.8	1.9
South	1.5	2.1	2.4	1.8
Total	1.3	1.8	2.1	1.6

Source: "Male Unemployment by Race, Education, and Region," *The Economic Progress of Black Men in America*, p. 44. Primary source: Census of Population, 1940-1980; Public Use Sample. *Note:* Ages 25-64.

★ 1296 ★

Labor Force

Male and Female Workers by Median Income and Region, 1970

Numbers in thousands.

Subject	Number of Negro workers, 1971		Median income of Negro workers, 1970		Ratio: Female to male median income	
	Male	Female	Male	Female	Negro	White
All wage and salary workers[1]	3,859	3,066	$5,370	$3,200	60	47
Year-round full-time workers[2]	2,878	1,786	6,435	70	59	
Northeast	570	411	7,430	5,519	74	60
North Central	600	396	7,859	4,859	62	57
South	1,488	835	5,241	3,723	71	57
West	219	144	8,751	5,495	63	61

Source: "Negro Male and Female Workers, by Median Income in 1970, by Region," U.S. Bureau of the Census, *The Social and Economic Status of the Black Population in the United States, 1970*, p. 37. Primary source: U.S. Department of Commerce, Social and Economic Statistics Administration, Bureau of the Census. *Notes:* 1. With wage and salary income, including full- and part-time workers. 2. Refers to total with income.

★ 1297 ★

Labor Force

Occupational Changes in Manufacturing and Mechanical Industries, 1920 to 1930

Data for 1920 have been made comparable with those for 1930 by excluding those occupations which were classified in "Manufacturing and mechanical industries" group in 1920 but transferred to other groups in 1930; similarly, certain occupations classified in other groups in 1920 but included in the "Manufacturing and mechanical industries" in 1930 have been included in 1920 data.

[Percent not shown where base is less than 100.]

Occupation	1930	1920	Increase or decrease (-)	
			Number	Percent
Manufacturing and mechanical industries	1,024,656	901,181[1]	123,475	13.7
Apprentices to building and hand trades	643	1,267	-624	-49.3
Apprentices, other (except to building and hand trades)	448	1,052[2]	-604	-57.4
Bakers	4,527	3,164	1,363	43.1
Blacksmiths, forgemen, and hammermen	5,682	8,886	-3,204	-36.1
Boilermakers	1,030	1,398	-368	-26.3
Brick and stone masons and tile layers	11,701	10,609	1,092	10.3
Builders and building contractors	2,570	1,454	1,116	76.8
Cabinetmakers	479	456	23	5.0
Carpenters	32,413	34,243	-1,830	-5.3
Compositors, linotypers and typesetters	2,101	1,540	561	36.4
Coopers	1,849	2,191	-342	-15.6
Dressmakers and seamstresses (not in factory)	20,439	26,973	-6,534	-24.2
Dyers	510	298	212	71.1
Electricians	1,913	1,342	571	42.5
Electrotypers, stereotypers, and lithographers	48	78	-30	-
Engineers (stationary), cranemen, hoistmen, etc.	5,236	6,353	-1,117	-17.6
Engravers	29	45	-16	-
Filers, grinders, buffers, and polishers (metal)	1,607	936	671	71.7
Firemen (except locomotive and fire department)	18,265	23,153	-4,888	-21.1
Foremen and overseers (manufacturing)	2,653	3,444[3]	-791	-23.0
Furnace men, smelter men, heaters, puddlers, etc.	3,091	3,236	-145	-4.5
Glass blowers	34	45	-11	-
Jewelers, watchmakers, goldsmiths, and silversmiths	275	524	-249	-47.5
Loom fixers	9	29	-20	-
Machinists, millwrights, and toolmakers	8,218	10,286	-2,068	-20.1
Managers and officials (manufacturing)	337	177	160	90.4
Manufacturers	1,046	401[4]	645	160.8
Mechanics (not otherwise specified)	26,710	[5]	-	-
Millers (grain, flour, feed, etc.)	240	367	-127	-34.6
Milliners and millinery dealers	451	590	-139	-23.6
Molders, founders, and casters (metal)	8,346	6,634	1,712	25.8
Oilers of machinery	1,073	1,027	46	4.5
Painters, glaziers, varnishers, enamelers, etc.	18,293	9,432	8,861	93.9
Paper hangers	2,154	954	1,200	125.8
Pattern and model makers	54	48	6	-
Piano and organ tuners	80	77	3	-

[Continued]

★ 1297 ★

Occupational Changes in Manufacturing and Mechanical Industries, 1920 to 1930
[Continued]

Occupation	1930	1920	Increase or decrease (-)	
			Number	Percent
Plasterers and cement finishers	13,465	7,082	6,383	90.1
Plumbers and gas and steam fitters	4,729	3,516	1,213	34.5
Pressmen and plate printers (printing)	189	101	88	87.1
Rollers and roll hands (metal)	1,224	736	488	66.3
Roofers an slaters	1,044	609	435	71.4
Sawyers	3,449	2,755	694	25.2
Shoemakers and cobblers (not in factory)	4,150	4,707	-557	-11.8
Skilled occupations (not elsewhere classified)	149	161	-12	-7.5
Stonecutters	328	280	48	17.1
Structural iron workers (building)	348	196	152	77.6
Tailors and tailoresses	7,505	6,892	613	8.9
Tinsmiths and coppersmiths	887	970	-83	-8.6
Upholsterers	915	648	267	41.2
Operatives (not otherwise specified)				
Building industry	685	345	340	98.6
Chemical and allied industries	4,368	3,155	1,213	38.4
Cigar and tobacco factories	20,721	19,849	872	4.4
Clay, glass, and stone industries	3,516	3,551	-35	-1.0
Clothing industries	22,216	13,888	8,328	60.0
Food and allied industries	17,834	16,515	1,319	8.0
Iron and steel, machinery, and vehicle industries	23,922	23,616	306	1.3
Metal industries (except iron and steel)	1,241	1,234	7	.6
Leather industries	2,004	2,907	-903	-31.1
Lumber and furniture industries	10,241	9,598	643	6.7
Paper, printing, and allied industries	2,866	2,704	162	6.0
Textile industries	7,238	7,687	-449	-5.8
Miscellaneous manufacturing industries	18,066 ⎫ 20,148	11,765	58.4	
Not specified industries and services	13,847 ⎭			
Laborers (not otherwise specified)				
Building, general, and not specified laborers	224,136	148,051	76,085	51.4
Chemical and allied industries	37,724	27,706	10,018	36.2
Cigar and tobacco factories	12,254	21,334	-9,080	-42.6
Clay, glass, and stone industries	22,399	18,753	3,646	19.4
Clothing industries	1,809	1,407	402	28.6
Food and allied industries	26,760	29,316	-2,556	-8.7
Iron and steel, machinery, and vehicle industries	107,739	105,641	2,098	2.0
Metal industries (except iron and steel)	5,293	3,996	1,297	32.5
Leather industries	2,705	3,391	-686	-20.2
Lumber and furniture industries	112,056	106,276	5,780	5.4
Paper, printing, and allied industries	6,276	4,318	1,958	45.3

[Continued]

★ 1297 ★

Occupational Changes in Manufacturing and Mechanical Industries, 1920 to 1930
[Continued]

Occupation	1930	1920	Increase or decrease (-)	
			Number	Percent
Textile industries	15,022	17,047	-2,025	-11.9
Miscellaneous manufacturing industries	78,782	88,096[6]	-9,314	-10.6

Source: "Occupational Gains and Losses Made by Negroes in the Manufacturing and Mechanical Divisions, for the United States: 1920 to 1930," U.S. Bureau of the Census, *Negroes in the United States, 1920-1932*, p. 292. *Notes:* 1. Includes 9,290 Negroes omitted in detail because not comparable with 1930. 2. Excludes "architects', designers', and draftsmen's apprentices." 3. Includes "Farm foremen, turpentine farms." 4. Includes "Farmers, turpentine farms." 5. Comparable figures for 1920 not available. 6. Includes "Farm laborers (turpentine farms)."

★ 1298 ★

Labor Force

Occupations in Pittsburgh Industrial Concerns, 1916-1917

Name of Concern	No. of Negroes employed at present	No. employed to 1916	Per cent doing unskilled labor
Carnegie Steel Co. (all plants)	4,000	1,500	95
Jones and Laughlin	1,500	400	100
Westinghouse Elec. and Mfg. Co.	900	25	90
Harbinson and Walker	250	50	80
National Tube Co. (all plants)	250	100	100
Pressed Steel Car Co.	25	25	50
Pgh. Forge and Iron	75	-	100
Moorehead Brothers	200	200	75
Am. Steel and Wire	25	25	100
Clinton Iron and Steel	25	25	75
Oliver Iron and Steel	50	-	100
Carbon Steel Co.	200	50	75
Crucible Steel Co.	400	150	90
A.M. Byers Co.	200	-	60
Lockhart Steel Co.	160	-	95
Mesta Machine Co.	50	-	100
Marshall Foundry Co.	15	-	-

Source: "Occupations Negroes, Pittsburgh Industrial Concerns, 1916-1917," Monroe N. Work, ed., *Negro Year Book: An Annual Encyclopedia of the Negro, 1918- 1919*, p. 340. Primary source: Epstein, "The Negro Migrant in Pittsburgh."

★ 1299 ★
Labor Force

Occupations of Persons Employed, by Gender: 1940, 1960, and 1970

Occupation and sex	All races			Black			White		
	1940	1960	1970	1940	1960	1970	1940	1960	1970
BOTH SEXES									
Total employed (thousands)	45,166	64,639	77,309	4,479	6,097	7,420	40,495	58,010	68,972
Percent	100	100	100	100	100	100	100	100	100
White-collar workers	32	41	46	6	13	24	35	44	48
Professional, technical, and kindred workers	7	11	14	3	5	8	8	11	15
Managers and administrators, except farm	8	9	8	1	2	2	9	9	9
Sales, clerical, and kindred workers	17	21	24	2	7	14	18	23	25
Blue-collar workers	36	37	33	28	38	37	37	36	33
Craft and kindred workers	11	14	13	3	6	8	12	15	14
Operatives, including transport	18	18	16	10	19	21	19	17	16
Laborers, except farm	7	5	4	14	13	8	6	4	4
Farm workers	18	6	3	32	8	3	17	6	3
Farmers and farm managers	11	4	2	15	3	-	11	4	2
Farm laborers and supervisors	7	2	1	17	5	2	6	2	1
Service workers	12	12	12	34	32	25	10	9	10
Private household workers	5	3	1	22	15	7	3	1	1
Other service workers	8	9	10	12	17	18	7	8	10
Occupation not reported	1	5	6	1	8	12	1	5	6
MEN									
Total employed (thousands)	34,028	43,467	48,139	2,937	3,642	4,091	30,932	39,462	43,501
Percent	100	100	100	100	100	100	100	100	100
White-collar workers	28	35	38	5	11	17	30	37	40
Professional, technical, and kindred workers	6	10	14	2	3	5	6	11	14
Managers and administrators, except farm	10	11	11	1	2	3	11	12	11
Sales, clerical, and kindred workers	13	14	14	2	6	9	13	14	14
Blue-collar workers	41	46	44	38	54	53	42	45	43
Craft and kindred workers	15	20	20	4	10	13	16	21	20
Operatives, including transport	18	19	18	13	23	26	19	18	17
Laborers, except farm	9	7	6	21	21	14	8	6	5
Farm workers	23	8	4	41	11	4	21	8	4
Farmers and farm managers	15	5	3	21	4	1	14	6	3
Farm laborers and supervisors	8	3	2	20	7	3	7	2	1
Service workers	7	7	8	15	15	14	6	6	7
Private household workers	-	-	-	3	1	-	-	-	-
Other service workers	6	6	8	12	14	14	6	6	7

[Continued]

★ 1299 ★

Occupations of Persons Employed, by Gender: 1940, 1960, and 1970
[Continued]

Occupation and sex	All races			Black			White		
	1940	1960	1970	1940	1960	1970	1940	1960	1970
Occupation not reported	1	5	6	1	8	12	1	4	5
WOMEN									
Total employed (thousands)	11,138	21,172	29,170	1,542	2,455	3,329	9,564	18,549	25,471
Percent	100	100	100	100	100	100	100	100	100
White-collar workers	45	54	58	6	17	32	52	59	61
Professional, technical, and kindred workers	13	13	15	4	7	10	15	13	15
Managers and administrators, except farm	4	4	3	1	1	1	4	4	4
Sales, clerical, and kindred workers	28	37	40	1	9	21	33	41	42
Blue-collar workers	20	17	16	7	14	17	22	18	16
Craft and kindred workers	1	1	2	-	1	1	1	1	2
Operatives, including transport	18	15	13	6	12	14	20	15	13
Laborers, except farm	1	1	1	1	1	1	1	1	1
Farm workers	4	2	1	16	3	1	2	1	1
Farmers and farm managers	1	1	-	3	1	-	1	1	-
Farm laborers and supervisors	3	1	-	13	3	1	1	1	-
Service workers	29	22	19	70	57	38	22	17	16
Private household workers	18	8	4	60	36	15	11	4	2
Other service workers	11	14	15	10	21	23	11	13	14
Occupation not reported	1	6	7	1	8	12	1	5	6

Source: "Occupation of Employed Persons 14 Years Old and Over by Sex: 1940, 1960, and 1970," U.S. Department of Commerce, Bureau of the Census, *The Social and Economic Status of the Black Population in the United States: An Historical View, 1790-1978*, p. 74. Primary source: U.S. Department of Commerce, Bureau of the Census. *Notes:* - Rounds to zero. Occupation and industry statistics for the census years 1940, 1960, and 1970 are not strictly comparable. However, adjustments have been made in the 1960 data to achieve as close comparability with the 1970 classification systems as possible. Since these adjustments sometimes involved estimates, the reader should exercise caution in interpreting small changes between the two census. In the figures for persons 14 years old and over, the "not reported" cases for 1970 are treated according to the 1960 presentation; that is, the cases allocated to major groups in 1970 are removed from those groups and combined into a separate "not reported" category. The table reflects these adjustments which have been made *only* at the national level.

★ 1300 ★
Labor Force

Occupations of Persons Employed, by Region: 1890, 1910, 1930

Area and occupation	1890	1910	1930
SOUTH			
Total, gainful workers (thousands)	2,746	4,592	4,210
Percent	100	100	100
Agriculture, forestry, and fishing[1]	62	62	47
Manufacturing and mechanical	5	9	15
Transportation and communications[2]	4	4	6
Domestic and personal service	28	18	24
Other occupations[3]	1	7	8
NORTH AND WEST			
Total, gainful workers (thousands)	327	600	1,293
Percent	100	100	100
Agriculture, forestry, and fishing[1]	16	8	3
Manufacturing and mechanical	9	20	30
Transportation and communications[2]	9	9	11
Domestic and personal service	63	48	43
Other occupations[3]	2	16	13

Source: "Occupation of the Gainfully Employed Population 10 Years Old and Over by Region: 1890, 1910, and 1930," U.S. Department of Commerce, Bureau of the Census, *The Social and Economic Status of the Black Population in the United States: An Historical View, 1790-1978,* p. 73. Primary source: U.S. Department of Commerce, Bureau of the Census. *Notes:* Occupational statistics for the census years 1890, 1910, and 1930 are not strictly comparable due to changes in definition. 1. Includes the occupation "mining" for 1890. 2. Includes the occupation "trade" for 1890. 3. Includes the occupation "professional service" for 1890. Includes the following occupations for 1910 and 1930—extraction of minerals, trade, public service, and clerical occupations.

Labor Force

Occupations of Persons Employed, by Region: 1940, 1960, and 1970

Numbers in thousands.

Area and occupation	All races			Black			Percent Black of all races		
	1940	1960	1970[1]	1940	1960	1970[1]	1940	1960	1970[1]
UNITED STATES									
Total employed	45,166	64,639	77,309	4,479	6,097	7,420	10	9	10
Percent	100	100	100	100	100	100	100	100	100
White-collar workers	32	41	46	6	13	24	2	3	5
Professional, technical, and kindred workers	7	11	14	3	5	8	4	4	5
Managers and administrators, except farm	8	9	8	1	2	2	1	2	3
Sales, clerical, and kindred workers	17	21	24	2	7	14	1	3	6
Blue-collar workers	36	37	33	28	38	37	8	10	11
Craft and kindred workers	11	14	13	3	6	8	3	4	6
Operatives, including transport	18	18	16	10	19	21	6	10	12
Laborers, except farm	7	5	4	14	13	8	21	24	19
Farm workers	18	6	3	32	8	3	18	13	8
Farmers and farm managers	11	4	2	15	3	-	13	7	2
Farm laborers and supervisors	7	2	1	17	5	2	25	22	17
Service workers	12	12	12	34	32	25	27	26	20
Private household workers	5	3	1	22	15	7	48	53	48
Other service workers	8	9	10	12	17	18	15	18	16
Occupation not reported	1	5	6	1	8	12	7	16	19
SOUTH									
Total employed	13,778	18,616	22,797	3,571	3,537	3,799	26	19	17
Percent	100	100	100	100	100	100	(X)	(X)	(X)
White-collar workers	24	38	45	4	10	20	5	5	7
Professional, technical, and kindred workers	6	10	14	2	5	8	11	9	9
Managers and administrators, except farm	7	8	8	1	1	2	3	3	4
Sales, clerical, and kindred workers	12	19	23	1	4	11	2	4	8
Blue-collar workers	30	36	38	25	36	43	22	19	19
Craft and kindred workers	8	13	14	2	6	9	8	8	10
Operatives, including transport	15	18	18	9	16	23	16	17	21
Laborers, except farm	7	6	5	14	15	11	49	48	37
Farm workers	31	9	4	40	14	5	33	30	23
Farmers and farm managers	19	5	2	18	5	1	26	18	8
Farm laborers and supervisors	12	4	2	21	9	4	45	47	39
Service workers	13	13	13	30	35	31	59	52	40
Private household workers	7	4	3	21	18	12	82	79	76

[Continued]

★ 1301 ★

Occupations of Persons Employed, by Region: 1940, 1960, and 1970

[Continued]

Area and occupation	All races			Black			Percent Black of all races		
	1940	1960	1970[1]	1940	1960	1970[1]	1940	1960	1970[1]
Other service workers	6	8	11	9	16	20	35	38	31
Occupation not reported	1	5	(X)	1	6	(X)	20	23	(X)
NORTH AND WEST									
Total employed	31,388	46,024	53,756	908	2,560	3,562	3	6	7
Percent	100	100	100	100	100	100	(X)	(X)	(X)
White-collar workers	36	43	49	10	18	33	1	2	4
Professional, technical, and kindred workers	8	12	15	3	5	9	1	2	4
Managers and administrators, except farm	9	8	8	2	2	3	1	1	2
Sales, clerical, and kindred workers	19	23	26	5	12	22	1	3	6
Blue-collar workers	39	37	35	36	41	41	3	6	8
Craft and kindred workers	12	14	14	5	8	9	1	3	5
Operatives, including transport	20	19	17	16	22	24	2	7	9
Laborers, except farm	7	4	4	15	11	7	7	13	11
Farm workers	13	5	3	3	1	1	1	1	1
Farmers and farm managers	8	3	2	1	-	-	-	-	1
Farm laborers and supervisors	4	2	1	2	1	-	1	2	3
Service workers	12	10	13	50	29	25	12	15	13
Private household workers	4	2	1	27	10	5	21	29	30
Other service workers	8	9	12	24	18	20	8	12	12
Occupation not reported	1	5	(X)	1	12	(X)	2	13	(X)

Source: "Occupation of Employed Persons 14 Years Old and Over by Region: 1940, 1960, and 1970," U.S. Department of Commerce, Bureau of the Census, *The Social and Economic Status of the Black Population in the United States: An Historical View, 1790-1978*, p. 75. Primary source: U.S. Department of Commerce, Bureau of the Census. *Notes:* - Rounds to zero. X = not applicable. Occupation and industry statistics for the census years 1940, 1960, and 1970 are not strictly comparable. However, adjustments have been made in the 1960 data to achieve as close comparability with the 1970 classification systems as possible. Since these adjustments sometimes involved estimates, the reader should exercise caution in interpreting small changes between the two census. In the figures for persons 14 years old and over, the "not reported" cases for 1970 are treated according to the 1960 presentation; that is, the cases allocated to major groups in 1970 are removed from those groups and combined into a separate "not reported" category. The table reflects these adjustments which have been made *only* at the national level. 1. Regional data are for persons 16 years old and over.

★ 1302 ★

Labor Force

Occupations of Persons Employed: 1890, 1910, 1930

Occupation and sex	Black			White		
	1890	1910	1930	1890	1910	1930
BOTH SEXES						
Total, gainful workers (thousands)	3,073	5,193	5,504	19,542	32,774	42,584
Percent	100	100	100	100	100	100
Agriculture, forestry, and fishing[1]	57	55	37	37	30	20
Manufacturing and mechanical	6	13	19	25	30	30
Transportation and communications[2]	5	5	7	16	7	8
Domestic and personal service	31	22	29	17	8	8
Other occupations[3]	1	6	9	5	25	34
MALE						
Total, gainful workers (thousands)	2,101	3,179	3,663	16,603	26,730	33,767
Percent	100	100	100	100	100	100
Agriculture, forestry, and fishing[1]	63	57	42	42	33	24
Manufacturing and mechanical	7	18	25	24	31	33
Transportation and communications[2]	7	8	11	18	9	9
Domestic and personal service	22	8	12	13	3	4
Other occupations[3]	1	8	10	4	24	30
FEMALE						
Total, gainful workers (thousands)	972	2,014	1,841	2,939	6,044	8,818
Percent	100	100	100	100	100	100
Agriculture, forestry, and fishing[1]	44	52	27	9	12	4
Manufacturing and mechanical	3	3	5	34	29	20
Transportation and communications[2]	-	-	-	8	2	3
Domestic and personal service	52	42	63	39	28	23
Other occupations[3]	1	2	5	10	29	50

Source: "Occupation of the Gainfully Employed Population 10 Years Old and Over by Sex: 1890, 1910, and 1930," U.S. Department of Commerce, Bureau of the Census, *The Social and Economic Status of the Black Population in the United States: AN Historical View, 1790-1978*, p. 72. Primary source: U.S. Department of Commerce, Bureau of the Census. *Notes:* - Represents or rounds to zero. Occupational statistics for the census years 1890, 1910, and 1930 are not strictly comparable due to changes in definition. 1. Includes the occupation "mining" for 1890. 2. Includes the occupation "trade" for 1890. 3. Includes the occupation "professional service" for 1890. Includes the following occupations for 1910 and 1930—extraction of minerals, trade, public service, professional service, and clerical occupations.

★ 1303 ★

Labor Force

Occupations of the Employed, 1900 – 1920

Occupation	1920	1910	1900	Per Cent Negroes Each Main Class Occupation		
				1920	1910	1900
Agricultural Pursuits	2,178,888	2,893,674	2,143,176	44.4	55.7	53.7
Professional Service	80,183	69,929	41,324	1.7	1.3	1.0
Domestic and Personal Service	1,064,590	1,099,715	1,324,160	22.7	21.2	33.2
Trade and Transportation	540,451	425,043	209,154	11.2	8.2	5.2
Manuf. and Mechan. Pursuits	960,039	704,174	275,149	19.9	13.6	6.9

Source: "Number of Negroes in Each Main Class of Occupations," Monroe N. Work, ed., *Negro Year Book: An Annual Encyclopedia of the Negro, 1925-26*, p. 362.

★ 1304 ★

Labor Force

Percent Employed in Main Classes of Occupations, 1890-1920

	1890	1900	1910	1920
Agricultural Pursuits	21.7	20.6	23.1	19.9
Professional Service	3.6	3.7	3.8	3.7
Domestic and Personal Service	22.6	23.6	20.5	31.2
Trade and Transportation	4.3	4.4	5.5	4.8
Manufacturing and Mechanical Pursuits	3.6	3.9	6.5	6.9

Source: "Per Cent of Negroes of Total Persons in Each of the Main Classes of Occupations in 1890, 1900, 1910, and 1920," Monroe N. Work, ed., *Negro Year Book: An Annual Encyclopedia of the Negro, 1925-26*, p. 362.

★ 1305 ★

Labor Force

Percent Population Gainfully Employed, 1900 – 1920

	1920	1910	1900
Per Cent of Total Population	50.3	53.3	50.2
Per Cent of All Males	78.2	81.3	80.0
Per Cent of All Females	21.1	23.4	18.8
Per Cent of All Negroes	59.9	71.0	62.2

[Continued]

★ 1305 ★

Percent Population Gainfully Employed, 1900 – 1920
[Continued]

	1920	1910	1900
Per Cent of All Negro Males	81.1	87.4	84.1
Per Cent of All Negro Females	38.9	54.7	40.7

Source: "Percent Population 10 Years of Age and Over in Gainful Occupation," Monroe N. Work, ed., *Negro Year Book: An Annual Encyclopedia of the Negro, 1925-26,* p. 362.

★ 1306 ★
Labor Force

Percent of Persons in Labor Force, by Region and Gender: 1910-1970

Area, sex, and race	1910	1930	1940[1]	1960	1970
BLACK					
Both sexes					
United States	71	59	58	55	56
South	72	59	59	54	55
North and West	66	62	57	57	58
Male					
United States	87	80	80	70	67
South	88	80	81	68	65
North and West	86	82	77	73	69
Female					
United States	55	39	38	42	47
South	56	39	37	41	47
North and West	45	40	39	44	48
WHITE					
Both sexes					
United States	51	48	52	54	57
South	51	46	50	51	55
North and West	51	49	52	55	58
Male					
United States	81	76	79	75	74
South	83	75	80	72	71
North and West	80	76	79	77	76

[Continued]

★ 1306 ★

Percent of Persons in Labor Force, by Region and Gender: 1910-1970

[Continued]

Area, sex, and race	1910	1930	1940[1]	1960	1970
Female					
United States	20	20	24	34	41
South	17	16	21	32	39
North and West	20	22	25	34	41

Source: "Percent of Persons in the Civilian Labor Force, by Region and Sex for Selected Years: 1910 to 1970," U.S. Department of Commerce, Bureau of the Census, *The Social and Economic Status of the Black Population in the United States: An Historical View, 1790-1978,* p. 65. Primary source: U.S. Department of Commerce, Bureau of the Census. *Notes:* Data for 1910 and 1930 are for persons 10 years old and over; 1940 and 1960, for persons 14 years old and over; and 1970 for persons 16 years old and over. 1. Data are for the total labor force (including Armed Forces) and are not strictly comparable to other census years.

★ 1307 ★

Labor Force

Percent of Population Employed, by Age and Gender: 1890 and 1930

Age and sex	Black		White	
	1890[1]	1930	1890	1930
MALE				
Total, 10 years old and over	80	80	77	76
10 to 14 years	30	17	8	3
15 to 19 years	73	65	56	46
20 to 24 years	94	94	92	89
25 to 34 years	97	97	97	97
35 to 44 years	98	97	98	98
45 to 54 years	98	97	96	96
55 to 64 years	97	94	92	90
65 years and over	88	75	72	57
Age unknown	83	70	74	57
FEMALE				
Total, 10 years old and over	36	39	14	20
10 to 14 years	20	10	3	1
15 to 19 years	43	30	25	26
20 to 24 years	47	46	28	42
25 to 34 years	37	47	15	26
35 to 44 years	37	48	10	20
45 to 54 years	38	46	10	18
55 to 64 years	37	41	10	15

[Continued]

★ 1307 ★

Percent of Population Employed, by Age and Gender: 1890 and 1930

[Continued]

Age and sex	Black		White	
	1890[1]	1930	1890	1930
65 years and over	26	24	7	7
Age unknown	41	47	26	29

Source: "Percent of Population Gainfully Employed by Age and Sex: 1890 and 1930," U.S. Department of Commerce, Bureau of the Census, *The Social and Economic Status of the Black Population in the United States: An Historical View, 1790-1978*, p. 65. Primary source: U.S. Department of Commerce, Bureau of the Census. *Note:* 1. Data include persons of "other" races.

★ 1308 ★

Labor Force

Professional Service Groups: Persons Employed, 1910

Occupation	Negro	White	Population per person in specified professional service group	
			Negro	White
Total, professional service	67,245	1,593,791	146	51
Actors	1,279	26,877	7,684	3,041
Architects	59	16,549	166,572	4,939
Artists, sculptors, and teachers of art	329	33,698	29,872	2,425
Authors, editors, and reporters	247	38,370	39,789	2,130
Authors	27	4,334	363,991	18,858
Editors and reporters	220	34,036	44,672	2,401
Chemists, assayers, and metallurgists	123	16,133	79,901	5,066
Civil and mining engineers and surveyors	237	58,687	41,467	1,393
Civil engineers and surveyors	217	51,786	45,289	1,578
Mining engineers	20	6,901	491,388	11,843
Clergymen	17,495	100,315	562	815
College presidents and professors	242	15,419	40,611	5,361
Dentists	478	39,476	20,560	2,070
Designers, draftsmen, and inventors	96	47,338	102,373	1,727
Designers	30	11,755	327,592	6,953
Draftsmen	47	33,257	209,101	2,458
Inventors	19	2,326	517,251	35,138
Lawyers, judges, and justices	798	113,801	12,315	718
Musicians and teachers of music	5,606	133,605	1,753	612
Photographers	404	31,267	24,326	2,614
Physicians and surgeons	3,077	147,741	3,194	553
Showmen	1,066	18,846	9,219	4,337
Teachers	29,485	569,289	333	144
Teachers (athletics, dancing, etc.)	53	3,875	185,429	21,092
Teachers (school)	29,432	565,414	334	145
Trained nurses	2,433	79,844	4,039	1,024

[Continued]

★ 1308 ★

Professional Service Groups: Persons Employed, 1910

[Continued]

Occupation	Negro	White	Population per person in specified professional service group	
			Negro	White
Veterinary surgeons	122	11,524	80,555	7,092
Other professional pursuits	150	15,306	65,518	5,340
Semiprofessional pursuits	2,144	62,518	4,584	1,307
Abstractors, notaries, and justices of peace	117	7,311	83,998	11,179
Fortune tellers, hypnotists, spiritualists, etc.	100	1,482	98,278	55,150
Healers (except physicians and surgeons)	332	6,428	29,602	12,715
Keepers of charitable and penal institutions	124	7,358	79,256	11,108
Officials of lodges, societies, etc.	279	7,887	35,225	10,363
Religious and charity workers	501	15,408	19,616	5,305
Theatrical owners, managers, and officials	93	11,209	105,675	7,292
Other occupations	598	5,435	16,434	15,038
Attendants and helpers (professional service)	1,375	17,188	7,147	4,755

Source: "Persons in Specified Professional Service Groups: 1910," U.S. Bureau of the Census. *Negro Population, 1790-1915*, p. 510.

★ 1309 ★

Labor Force

Trades in Which Black Have Made Large Gains, 1890-1900

Trade	Number		Per Cent of Gain
	1890	1900	
Miners	15,809	36,568	132.0
Masons	9,647	14,387	49.0
Dressmakers	7,479	12,572	65.3
Iron and Steel Workers	5,790	12,327	112.7
Stationary Engineers	6,326	10,277	62.4

Source: "Trades in Which Negroes Have Made Large Gains," Monroe N. Work, ed., *Negro Year Book: An Annual Encyclopedia of the Negro*, p. 204.

★ 1310 ★
Labor Force

Unemployment Rates by Duration of Unemployment: 1947-1975

Annual averages.

Duration of unemployment and race	1957	1960	1965	1970[1]	1975[1]
ALL RACES					
Total with unemployment (thousands)	2,936	3,931	3,456	4,088	7,830
Percent	100	100	100	100	100
1 to 4 weeks	81	76	78	84	68
15 weeks or more	19	24	22	16	32
27 weeks or more	8	12	10	6	15
BLACK AND OTHER RACES					
Total with unemployment (thousands)	584	802	702	752	1,459
Percent	100	100	100	100	100
1 to 4 weeks	78	70	75	84	67
15 weeks or more	22	30	25	17	33
27 weeks or more	10	15	13	6	16
WHITE					
Total with unemployment (thousands)	2,352	3,129	2,754	3,337	6,371
Percent	100	100	100	100	100
1 to 4 weeks	82	77	79	84	69
15 weeks or more	18	23	21	16	31
27 weeks or more	8	11	10	6	15
BLACK AND OTHER RACES AS A PERCENT OF ALL RACES					
Total with unemployment	20	20	20	18	19
1 to 4 weeks	19	19	20	18	18
15 weeks or more	23	25	23	19	20
27 weeks or more	24	26	25	20	20

Source: "Unemployment Rates for Persons 14 Years Old and Over by Duration of Unemployment for Selected Years: 1957 to 1975," U.S. Department of Commerce, Bureau of the Census, *The Social and Economic Status of the Black Population in the United States: An Historical View, 1790-1978*, p. 71. Primary source: U.S. Department of Labor, Bureau of the Labor Statistics. *Note:* 1. Data are for persons 16 years old and over.

★ 1311 ★

Labor Force

Unemployment Rates, by Gender and Age: 1954-1975

Annual averages.

Sex, age, and race	1954	1960	1965	1970	1974	1975
BLACK AND OTHER RACES						
Total, 16 years and over	9.9	10.2	8.1	8.2	9.9	13.9
Both sexes, 16 to 19 years	16.5	24.4	26.2	29.1	32.9	36.9
Men, 20 years and over	9.9	9.6	6.0	5.6	6.8	11.7
Women, 20 years and over	8.5	8.3	7.4	6.9	8.4	11.5
WHITE						
Total, 16 years and over	5.0	4.9	4.1	4.5	5.0	7.8
Both sexes, 16 to 19 years	12.1	13.4	13.4	13.5	14.0	17.9
Men, 20 years and over	4.4	4.2	2.9	3.2	3.5	6.2
Women, 20 years and over	5.1	4.6	4.0	4.4	5.0	7.5
RATIO: BLACK AND OTHER RACES TO WHITE						
Total, 16 years and over	2.0	2.1	2.0	1.8	2.0	1.8
Both sexes, 16 to 19 years	1.4	1.8	2.0	2.2	2.4	2.1
Men, 20 years and over	2.3	2.3	2.1	1.8	1.9	1.9
Women, 20 years and over	1.7	1.8	1.9	1.6	1.7	1.5

Source: "Unemployment Rates, by Sex and Age, for Selected Years:1954 to 1975," U.S. Department of Commerce, Bureau of the Census, *The Social and Economic Status of the Black Population in the United States: An Historical View, 1790-1978,* p. 70. Primary source: U.S. Department of Labor, Bureau of the Labor Statistics.

★ 1312 ★

Labor Force

Unemployment Rates, for Married Men with Spouse Present: 1962-1975

Annual averages.

Year	Unemployment rate		Ratio: Black and other races to White
	Black and other races	White	
1962	7.9	3.1	2.5
1963	6.8	3.0	2.3
1964	5.3	2.5	2.1
1965	4.3	2.1	2.0
1966	3.6	1.7	2.1
1967	3.2	1.7	1.9

[Continued]

★ 1312 ★

Unemployment Rates, for Married Men with Spouse Present: 1962-1975

[Continued]

Year	Unemployment rate		Ratio: Black and other races to White
	Black and other races	White	
1968	2.9	1.5	1.9
1969	2.5	1.4	1.8
1970	3.9	2.4	1.6
1971	5.0	3.0	1.7
1972	4.5	2.6	1.7
1973	3.8	2.1	1.8
1974	4.3	2.5	1.7
1975	8.3	4.8	1.7

Source: "Unemployment Rates for Married Men, With Spouse Present: 1962 to 1975," U.S. Department of Commerce, Bureau of the Census, *The Social and Economic Status of the Black Population in the United States: An Historical View, 1790-1978,* p. 70. Primary source: U.S. Department of Labor, Bureau of the Labor Statistics. *Notes:* Data for 1962 to 1965 are for persons 14 years old and over; data for 1966 to 1975 are for persons 16 years old and over.

★ 1313 ★

Labor Force

Unemployment Rates: 1948-1975

Annual averages.

Year	Unemployment rate		Ratio: Black and other races to White
	Black and other races	White	
1948	5.9	3.5	1.7
1949	8.9	5.6	1.6
1950	9.0	4.9	1.8
1951	5.3	3.1	1.7
1952	5.4	2.8	1.9
1953	4.5	2.7	1.7
1954	9.9	5.0	2.0
1955	8.7	3.9	2.2
1956	8.3	3.6	2.3
1957	7.9	3.8	2.1
1958	12.6	6.1	2.1
1959	10.7	4.8	2.2
1960	10.2	4.9	2.1
1961	12.4	6.0	2.1
1962	10.9	4.9	2.2
1963	10.8	5.0	2.2
1964	9.6	4.6	2.1
1965	8.1	4.1	2.0
1966	7.3	3.3	2.2

[Continued]

★ 1313 ★

Unemployment Rates: 1948-1975
[Continued]

Year	Unemployment rate		Ratio: Black and other races to White
	Black and other races	White	
1967	7.4	3.4	2.2
1968	6.7	3.2	2.1
1969	6.4	3.1	2.1
1970	8.2	4.5	1.8
1971	9.9	5.4	1.8
1972	10.0	5.0	2.0
1973	8.9	4.3	2.1
1974	9.9	5.0	2.0
1975	13.9	7.8	1.8

Source: "Unemployment Rates for Persons 16 Years Old and Over: 1948 to 1975," U.S. Department of Commerce, Bureau of the Census, *The Social and Economic Status of the Black Population in the United States: An Historical View, 1790-1978*, p. 69. Primary source: U.S. Department of Labor, Bureau of the Labor Statistics. *Notes:* The unemployment rate is the percent of the civilian labor force that is unemployed.

★ 1314 ★

Labor Force

Women Employed in New York, 1910

Industry	Factories	Colored Women Workers
Needle Trades	121	892
Toys	10	194
Buttons	9	120
Candy	4	196
Leather Goods	9	96
Marabou	5	66
Paper Boxes and Bags	10	58
Millinery	6	30
Flowers and Feathers	6	17
Miscellaneous	37	516
Total	127	2,185

Source: "Untitled Table, Monroe N. Work, ed., *Negro Year Book: An Annual Encyclopedia of the Negro, 1918-1919*, p. 341. Primary source: Schwartz, Jackson, Bowles and others, "A New Day for the Colored Women Worker.".

★ 1315 ★
Labor Force

Women in Domestic Service Occupations, 1940

Black Women Engaged in Domestic Service Occupations

In 1940, there were 917,942 black women engaged in domestic service occupations, according to the Federal Census of Occupations. These workers were distributed as follows:

- Northeastern States—132,745
- North Central States—73,915
- Southern States—696,042
- Western States—15,240

In the Southern States, black women composed 81 per cent of the total number of women found in this occupational category. In the Northeast, they were 26.2 per cent; in the North Central, 15.9 per cent; and in the West, 10.8 per cent. Black women accounted for 46.6 per cent of all women engaged in domestic service in 1940, the percentage having increased 10 per cent since 1930.

Source: "Negro Women in Domestic Service Occupation," Jessie Parkhurst Guzman, ed., *Negro Year Book: A Review of Events Affecting Negro Life, 1941-1946*, p. 139. Primary source: Federal Census of Occupations, 1940.

★ 1316 ★
Labor Force

Women: 5,000 or More in Occupations, 1910

Laborers (Manufacturing and Mechanical Pursuits	6,159
Trade (Wholesale and Retail)	7,304
Char Women and Cleaners	6,962
Waitresses	7,377
Boarding and Lodging Housekeepers	9,183
Housekeepers	9,911
Ladies' Maids	10,239
Laundresses (In Laundries)	10,371
Cigar and Tobacco Factory Workers	10,746
Chamber Maids	14,071
Nurses (Not trained)	17,874
Seamstresses	18,216
Dressmakers	20,061
Teachers	22,528
Farmers	79,308
Servants	184,889
Cooks	205,584
Farm Laborers (Working Out)	263,403

[Continued]

★ 1316 ★

Women: 5,000 or More in Occupations, 1910
[Continued]

Laundresses (not in laundries)	361,551
Farm Laborers (Home Farm)	704,150

Source: "Occupations in Which in 1910 There Were at Least 5,000 Negro Women," Monroe N. Work, ed., *Negro Year Book: An Annual Encyclopedia of the Negro, 1918-1919*, p. 340.

Labor Unions

★ 1317 ★

AFL Unions, 1944

AFL Unions	Negro members
Hodcarriers & Common Laborers	55,000
Hotel & Restaurant Employees, etc.	35,000-40,000
Building Service Employees	35,000
Maintenance of Way Employees, Bro. of	25,000
Meat Cutters & Butcher Workmen	25,000
Railway Clerks & Freighthandlers	12,000
Teamsters, Chauffeurs, etc.	15,000
Boilermakers & Iron Shipbuilders (Jan. 1944)	14,000
Laundry Workers International Union	12,000
Longshoremen's Association, International	10,000
Garment Workers, International Ladies	10,000
Tobacco Workers International Union	9,100
Porters, Bro. of Sleeping Car	8,500
Musicians, American Federation of	4,500
Carmen of America, Bro. Railway	4,500
Carpenters & Joiners, United Bro. of	3,000
Bricklayers, Masons & Plasterers	3,000
Printing Pressmen, International	3,000
Cement, Lime & Gypsum Workers	3,000
Pulp, Sulphite & Paper Mill Workers	2,000
Painters of America, Bro. of	1,500
Cigarmakers International Union	500
Brick and Clay Workers, etc.	500
Glass Worker, Amer. Flint	400

[Continued]

★ 1317 ★

AFL Unions, 1944
[Continued]

AFL Unions	Negro members
Other Unions	
United Mine Workers (now affiliated with AFL)	50,000

Source: Untitled Table, Jessie Parkhurst Guzman, ed., *Negro Year Book: A Review of Events Affecting Negro Life, 1941-1946*, p. 147. Primary source: Labor Research Association, *Labor Fact Book*, No. 7, pp. 73-77.

★ 1318 ★

Labor Unions

CIO Unions, 1944

CIO Unions	Negro members
Steelworkers of America, United	95,000
Automobile, Aircraft, Agricultural Implement Workers of America	90,000
Marine and Shipbuilding Workers of America, Industrial Union of	40,000
Electrical, Radio & Machine Workers of America, United	40,000
Packinghouse Workers of America, United	22,500
Mine, Mill & Smelter Workers, International Union of	20,000
Clothing Workers of America, Amalgamated	15,000
Federal Workers of America, United	10,000
Fur & Leather Workers Union, International	8,000-10,000
Transport Service Employees of America, United	10,000
Maritime Union of America, National	8,500
Textile Workers Union of America	6,500
Flood, Tobacco, Agricultural & Allied Workers Union of America	6,000
Longshoremen's & Warehousemen's Union, International	13,000
Retail, Wholesale & Department Store Employees of America	6,000
Furniture Workers of America, United	6,000
Woodworkers of America, international	3,000
Transport Workers Union of America	3,000
Farm Equipment & Metal Workers of America, United	3,000
State, County & Municipal Workers of America	2,800
Playthings, Jewelry & Novelty Workers Union	2,500

Source: Untitled Table, Jessie Parkhurst Guzman, ed., *Negro Year Book: A Review of Events Affecting Negro Life, 1941-1946*, p. 146. Primary source: Labor Research Association, *Labor Fact Book*, No. 7, pp. 73-74.

★ 1319 ★

Labor Unions

Labor Union Membership, 1930-1945

One of the most significant developments of the period, 1941-1945, was the movement of Negroes into the labor movement. It was reliably estimated that 1,250,000 Negroes were enrolled in labor unions at peak war production. The importance of this change may best be recognized by comparing this figure with estimates of other authorities in this field. Dr. Ira DeA. Reid[1] estimated the total Negro union membership at 110,000 in 1930. By 1935, the number of Negroes in the labor movement was estimated to be 180,000. In 1940, the number of Negro union members was estimated at 600,000. Thus the war years brought an increase of some 650,000 Negroes in the labor movement, while the total membership in labor unions increased from 8,500,000 in 1940 to 14,000,000 in 1945.

Source: "Negroes in the Labor Movement," Jessie Parkhurst Guzman, ed., *Negro Year Book: A Review of Events Affecting Negro Life, 1941-1946*, p. 146. Primary source: *Labor Fact Book*, No. 7—Labor Research Association, pp. 73-74. *Note:* 1. "Negro Membership in American Labor Unions."—Ira DeA. Reid.

★ 1320 ★

Labor Unions

Members by Race, Philadelphia Longshore Locals, 1970

	Local	Total	Negro	Percent Negro
Longshoremen	1291	2,200	1,430	65.0
Carloaders	1332	650	585	90.0
Cleaners and carpenters	1566	185	92	49.7
Clerks and checkers	1242	507	11	2.2
Timekeepers	1242-1	30	-	-

Source: "Longshore Industry, Estimated Negro Membership in Philadelphia Longshore Locals, 1970," Lester Rubin, *The Negro in the Longshore Industry*, p. 76. Published by permission.

★ 1321 ★

Labor Unions

Members by Race, Texas International Longshoremen's Association Locals, 1972

Location	Local	Jurisdiction	Approximate membership	Race Negro	Race White	Mexican-American
Houston	1351	Clerk and Checker	n.a.		X	
Houston	872	Deep sea	1,100	X		
Houston	1273	Deep sea	1,005		X	
Houston	1231	Coastwise	Merged with 1273[1]		X	
Houston	1271	Coastwise	Merged with 872[1]	X		
Houston	1330	Warehouse	180		X	
Houston	1331	Warehouse	175	X		
Houston	1525	Warehouse	200	X		
Houston	1581	Warehouse	150			X
Port Arthur	440	Deep sea and Warehouse	60	X		
Port Arthur	1029	Deep sea	64		X	
Port Arthur	1175	Deep sea	105	X		
Beaumont	325	Deep sea	77	X		
Beaumont	1306	Deep sea	75	X		
Beaumont	1610	Deep sea	96		X	
Orange	341	Deep sea	20		X	
Orange	814	Deep sea	42	X		
Freeport	1723	Deep sea	20		X	
Freeport	1818	Deep sea	50	X		
Galveston	307	Deep sea	200		X	
Galveston	329	Deep sea	180	X		
Galveston	851	Deep sea	400	X		
Galveston	1576	Deep sea	140			X
Brownsville	1367	Deep sea	48		X	
Brownsville	1368	Deep sea	45	X		
Brownsville	1372	Coastwise	n.a.		X	
Texas City	636	Deep sea	n.a.		X	
Texas City	991	Deep sea	n.a.	X		
Texas City	1405	Warehouse	n.a.		X	
Texas City	1406	Warehouse	n.a.	X		
Corpus Christi	1224	Deep sea	73		X	
Corpus Christi	1225	Deep sea	75	X		
Corpus Christi	1241	Coastwise	Merged with 1225[2]	X		
Corpus Christi	1245	Coastwise	Merged with 1224[2]		X	
Corpus Christi	1280	Warehouse	15		X	
Corpus Christi	1281	Warehouse	16	X		

[Continued]

★ 1321 ★

Members by Race, Texas International Longshoremen's Association Locals, 1972
[Continued]

Location	Local	Jurisdiction	Approximate membership	Race Negro	Race White	Mexican-American
Port Lavaca	1758	Deep sea	18	X		
Port Lavaca	1763	Deep sea	25		X	

Source: "Longshore Industry, Approximate Membership by Race, Texas International Longshoremen's Association Locals," Lester Rubin, *The Negro in the Longshore Industry*, p. 129. Published by permission. Primary source: Pre-trial brief for Plaintiff, *United States V. International Longshoremen's Ass'n*, Civil Action No. 69-B-3 (S.D. Tex. 1970), Appendix pp. 2-30. Post-trial brief for Plaintiff, *United States V. International Longshoremen's Ass'n*, Civil Action No. 69-B-3 (S.D. Tex. 1970), Appendix pp. 15-32. *Notes:* 1. Prior to merger in late 1968, Local 1271 had 86 blacks and Local 1231 had 60 whites. 2. Date of merger and approximate membership unknown.

Occupations

★ 1322 ★

Aerospace Industry: Occupational Distribution by Race and Gender, 1960

Occupation	All employees Total	Nonwhite	Percent nonwhite	Male Total	Nonwhite	Percent nonwhite	Female Total	Nonwhite	Percent nonwhite
Managers, officials, and proprietors	19215	22	0.1	18,238	22	0.1	977	-	-
Professional, technical, and kindred workers	143,933	2,816	2.0	137,560	2,715	2.0	6,373	101	1.6
Clerical and kindred workers	108,742	1,501	1.4	48,370	1,030	2.1	60,372	471	0.8
Sales workers	3,030	-	-	2,971	-	-	59	-	-
Craftsmen, foremen, and kindred workers	167,173	4,338	2.6	162,775	4,217	2.6	4,398	121	2.8
Operatives and kindred workers	175,461	10,731	6.1	148,193	8,993	6.1	27,268	1,738	6.4
Laborers	5,219	981	18.8	5,038	961	19.1	181	20	11.0
Service workers	10,855	2,395	22.1	9,314	2,055	22.1	1,541	340	22.1
Occupation not reported	10,762	675	6.3	9,221	574	6.2	1,541	101	6.6
Total	644,390	23,459	3.6	541,680	20,567	3.8	102,710	2,892	2.8

Source: "Total Employed Persons, Aircraft and Parts Manufacturing Industry, Occupational Distribution by Race and Sex, 1960," Herbert R. Northrup, *The Negro in the Aerospace Industry*, p. 25. Primary source: U.S. *Census of Population 1960*, PC(2) 7A, *Occupational Characteristics*, Table 36.

★ 1323 ★

Occupations

Air Transport Industry: Black Employment by Sex and Occupational Group, 1964, 1966, 1968

Occupational group	All Employees			Male			Female		
	1964	1966	1968	1964	1966	1968	1964	1966	1968
Officials and managers	0.2	0.3	0.6	0.2	0.3	0.6	0.3	0.3	0.6
Professionals	0.1	0.2	0.3	0.1	0.2	0.3	0.6	0.3	0.8
Technicians	0.2	0.5	0.5	0.2	0.5	0.5	-	0.7	1.1
Sales workers	1.3	2.3	3.3	1.1	1.8	2.6	1.5	2.7	3.8
Office and clerical	1.9	2.4	3.7	2.5	3.3	4.5	1.4	1.7	3.2
Total white collar	1.0	1.5	2.2	0.8	1.1	1.5	1.4	2.2	3.4
Craftsmen	1.3	1.7	2.3	1.3	1.7	2.3	-	-	2.1
Operatives	11.0	10.2	10.6	10.8	10.1	10.5	32.4[1]	28.8[1]	20.9[1]
Laborers	27.1	33.7	25.9	27.6	33.4	25.2	12.6[1]	39.7[1]	45.7[1]
Service workers	15.5	12.7	11.7	33.6	32.2	32.8	2.6	2.6	2.8
Total blue collar	7.8	8.1	8.3	8.5	9.0	9.5	3.1	3.4	3.5
Total	3.9	4.3	4.8	4.6	4.9	5.3	1.8	2.5	3.4

Source: "Air Transport Industry, Percent Negro Employment by Sex and Occupational Group, United States, 1964, 1966, and 1968," Northrup, Thieblot, and Chernish, *The Negro in the Air Transport Industry*, p. 42. Published by permission. *Notes:* Data for 1964 cover 8 companies; data for 1966 and 1968 cover 12 companies. 1. Very small numbers involved.

★ 1324 ★

Occupations

Air Transport Industry: Distribution of Employees by Race and Occupational Group, 1964, 1966, 1968

Occupational group	1964		1966		1968	
	Total employees	Negro employees	Total employees	Negro employees	Total employees	Negro employees
Officials and managers	8.1	0.5	7.8	0.6	7.4	0.9
Professionals	13.8	0.4	14.8	0.6	15.0	0.9
Technicians	2.0	0.1	1.9	0.2	2.2	0.3
Sales workers	16.0	5.4	17.2	9.3	18.1	12.4
Officer and clerical	17.6	8.7	15.8	9.0	14.6	11.3
Total white collar	57.5	15.1	57.5	19.7	57.3	25.8
Craftsmen	22.2	7.6	19.7	7.8	19.1	9.3
Operatives	8.6	24.3	10.0	23.9	9.2	20.2
Laborers	2.2	15.0	2.2	17.0	3.2	17.2
Service workers	9.5	38.0	10.6	31.6	11.2	27.5

[Continued]

★ 1324 ★

Air Transport Industry: Distribution of Employees by Race and Occupational Group, 1964, 1966, 1968

[Continued]

Occupational group	1964		1966		1968	
	Total employees	Negro employees	Total employees	Negro employees	Total employees	Negro employees
Total blue collar	42.5	84.9	42.5	80.3	42.7	74.2
Total	100.0	100.0	100.0	100.0	100.0	100.0

Source: "Air Transport Industry, Percentage Distribution of Employees by Race and Occupational Group, United States, 1964, 1966, and 1968," Northrup, Thieblot, and Chernish, *The Negro in the Air Transport Industry*, p. 43. Published by permission. *Notes:* Data for 1964 cover 8 companies; data for 1966 and 1968 cover 12 companies.

★ 1325 ★

Occupations

Air Transport Industry: Employment by Race and Gender United States, 1940, 1950, 1960

	All employees			Male			Female		
	Total	Negro	Percent Negro	Total	Negro	Percent Negro	Total	Negro	Percent Negro
1940	23,175	760	3.3	20,878	729	3.5	2,297	31	1.3
1950	98,241	3,993	4.1	78,977	3,576	4.5	19,264	417	2.2
1960	198,139	9,096	4.6	154,863	8,201	5.3	43,276	895	2.1

Source: "Air Transport Industry, Employment by Race and Sex, United States, 1940, 1950, and 1960," Herbert R. Northrup at. al., *The Negro in the Air Transport Industry*, p. 29. Published by permission. Primary source: U.S. *Census of Population*: 1940, Vol. III, *The Labor Force*, Part 1, Table 76; 1950, Vol. II, *Characteristics of the Population*, Table 133; 1960, PC(1) 1D, *U.S. Summary*, Table 213.

★ 1326 ★

Occupations

Air Transport Industry: Employment by Race and Gender in Four Regions, 1940, 1950, 1960

Region	All employees			Male			Female		
	Total	Negro	Percent Negro	Total	Negro	Percent Negro	Total	Negro	Percent Negro
Northeast									
1940	6,484	152	2.3	5,793	137	2.4	691	15	2.2
1950	23,738	697	2.9	18,977	633	3.3	4,761	64	1.3
1960	48,090	2,123	4.4	36,582	1,834	5.0	11,508	289	2.5
North Central									
1940	5,751	144	2.5	4,947	140	2.8	8.4	4	0.5

[Continued]

★ 1326 ★

Air Transport Industry: Employment by Race and Gender in Four Regions, 1940, 1950, 1960
[Continued]

Region	All employees			Male			Female		
	Total	Negro	Percent Negro	Total	Negro	Percent Negro	Total	Negro	Percent Negro
1950	22,531	695	3.1	17,617	592	3.4	4,914	103	2.1
1960	38,202	1,612	4.2	28,443	1,426	5.0	9,759	186	1.9
South									
1940	6,214	393	6.3	5,788	381	6.6	426	12	2.8
1950	31,976	2,133	6.7	26,367	1,922	7.3	5,609	211	3.8
1960	64,160	3,915	6.1	52,519	3,593	6.8	11,641	322	2.8
West									
1940	4,726	71	1.5	4,350	71	1.6	376	-	-
1950	19,996	468	2.3	16,016	429	2.7	3,980	39	1.0
1960	47,687	1,446	3.0	37,319	1,348	3.6	10,368	98	0.9

Source: "Air Transport Industry, Employment by Race and Sex, Four Regions, 1940, 1950, and 1960," Northrup, Thiebolt, and Chernish, *The Negro in the Air Transport Industry*, p. 31. Published by permission.

★ 1327 ★

Occupations

Airline Pilots on Six Major Carriers by Race, May 1969

Carrier	Total pilots	Negro pilots	Percent Negro
American	3,300	10	0.3
Eastern	3,300	6	0.2
Delta	1,596	2	0.1
Pan American	3,600	6	0.2
Trans World	4,099	16	0.4
United	5,800	11[1]	0.2
Total industry	33,000	85[2]	0.3

Source: "Air Transport Industry, Employment of Pilots by Race, Six Carriers, May 1969," Northrup, Thiebolt, and Chernish, *The Negro in the Air Transport Industry*, p. 70. Published by permission. Primary source: Company interviews and *Chicago Tribune*, May 18, 1969. *Notes:* 1. Includes three flight instructors. 2. Authors' estimate.

★ 1328 ★

Occupations

Aviators Licensed, 1940

Classification	Number of listed aviators				
	1940	1939	1937	1936	1935
Total	269	125	103	69	47
Commercial	7	4	...	...	...
Limited Commercial[1]	2	4	4	3	4
Transport[2]	...	...	3	2	2
Private	102	23	17	10	9
Amateur[2]	...	...	3	6	4
Solo[1]	18	12	...	...	1
Student	140	82	76	48	27

Source: "Licensed Civil Aviators." Florence Murray, ed., *The Negro Handbook*, 1942, p. 82. *Notes:* 1. Solo and limited commercial licenses no longer issued, but holders of these classifications may renew licenses until May 1, 1941 and May 1, 1942, respectively. 2. Transport and amateur licenses have not been issued since Nov. 1, 1937.

★ 1329 ★

Occupations

Black Airline Pilots, 1974

Airline company	No. black pilots
Allegheny Airlines	1
American Airlines	11
Delta Airlines	13
Eastern Airlines	25
Flying Tiger Lane	2
New York Airways	1
North Central Airlines	1
Pan American World Airway	3
Piedmont Airlines	1
Southern Airways	1
Trans World Airlines	11
United Air Lines	6
Western airlines	6
Total	82

Source: Black Enterprise 4 (April 1974), pp. 19, 22, 23. Compiled by the editors.

★ 1330 ★

Occupations

Chemical Industry: Percent Black Employment by Gender and Occupation, Middle Atlantic, 1964-1968

Occupational group	All employees			Male			Female		
	1964	1966	1968	1964	1966	1968	1964	1966	1968
Officials and managers	0.2	0.3	0.5	0.2	0.3	0.5	0.5	1.0	1.8
Professionals	0.5	0.6	1.0	0.4	0.5	0.9	0.7	1.8	3.2
Technicians	1.4	1.7	2.3	1.4	1.7	2.2	1.4	2.1	3.1
Sales workers	0.5	0.4	0.8	0.5	0.5	0.8	-	-	-
Office and clerical	1.9	2.3	3.8	3.4	3.3	4.9	1.3	1.9	3.3
Total white collar	1.0	1.2	1.9	0.9	1.0	1.4	1.3	1.9	3.3
Craftsmen (skilled)	4.1	4.0	4.7	4.1	4.1	4.7	-	-	2.4
Operatives (semiskilled)	6.6	7.1	8.7	7.5	7.9	10.0	1.7	1.9	2.3
Laborers	15.5	15.7	13.3	17.2	17.5	15.1	4.0	4.8	5.9
Service Workers	18.3	16.6	19.5	18.0	16.1	18.5	20.0	19.9	24.8
Total blue collar	7.4	7.4	8.5	7.7	7.8	9.0	3.8	4.0	4.8
Total	3.9	4.2	4.8	4.4	4.6	5.1	1.9	2.4	3.7

Source: "Chemical Industry, Percent Negro Employment by Sex and Occupational Group, Middle Atlantic Region, 1964-1968," William Howard Quay, Jr., *The Negro in the Chemical Industry*, p. 51. Primary source: Appendix Tables A-10-A-12. *Note:* For regional definitions, see Table 21, p. 46.

★ 1331 ★

Occupations

Chemical Industry: Percent Black Employment by Gender and Occupation, Midwest Region, 1964-1968

Occupational group	All employees			Male			Female		
	1964	1966	1968	1964	1966	1968	1964	1966	1968
Officials and managers	0.3	0.3	0.7	0.3	0.3	0.7	-	-	1.7
Professionals	0.4	0.6	1.0	0.4	0.6	1.0	0.4	2.0	2.7
Technicians	1.2	1.7	3.2	1.3	1.7	2.9	0.7	1.6	4.9
Sales workers	0.1	0.2	0.8	0.1	0.2	0.8	-	0.7	0.7
Office and clerical	1.1	1.7	2.8	1.3	1.6	2.3	1.0	1.7	3.1
Total white collar	0.7	0.9	1.7	0.6	0.7	1.3	1.0	1.6	3.2
Craftsmen (skilled)	1.5	1.7	3.3	1.5	1.7	2.8	-	5.0	18.4
Operatives (semiskilled)	6.8	6.8	8.7	7.2	7.2	8.0	3.1	3.3	13.0
Laborers	13.1	11.4	11.8	14.5	13.5	13.1	4.2	2.4	8.1
Service Workers	16.3	18.3	17.0	17.0	18.9	17.2	10.1	12.8	16.3

[Continued]

★ 1331 ★

Chemical Industry: Percent Black Employment by Gender and Occupation, Midwest Region, 1964-1968
[Continued]

Occupational group	All employees			Male			Female		
	1964	1966	1968	1964	1966	1968	1964	1966	1968
Total blue collar	6.4	6.4	8.1	6.7	6.7	7.5	3.8	3.7	12.3
Total	3.8	3.9	5.3	4.1	4.2	4.9	1.8	2.3	7.0

Source: "Chemical Industry, Percent Negro Employment by Sex and Occupational Group, Midwest Region, 1964-1968," William Howard Quay, Jr., *The Negro in the Chemical Industry*, p. 57. Primary source: Appendix Tables A-22-A-24. *Note:* For regional definitions, see Table 21, p. 46.

★ 1332 ★

Occupations

Chemical Industry: Percent Black Employment by Gender and Occupation, New England, 1964-1968

Occupational group	All employees			Male			Female		
	1964	1966	1968	1964	1966	1968	1964	1966	1968
Officials and managers	0.3	0.3	0.3	0.3	0.3	0.3	-	-	-
Professionals	0.7	0.7	0.6	0.5	0.6	0.5	2.7	3.0	1.4
Technicians	3.5	3.6	4.3	4.2	4.2	4.6	-	0.8	2.1
Sales workers	-	-	-	-	-	-	-	-	-
Office and clerical	0.7	1.1	1.8	0.8	1.8	0.8	0.7	0.9	2.2
Total white collar	1.0	1.2	1.4	1.0	1.2	1.2	0.7	1.0	2.1
Craftsmen (skilled)	4.2	5.2	4.9	4.2	5.2	4.9	-	-	-
Operatives (semiskilled)	5.3	5.6	7.4	5.7	6.0	7.5	0.5	0.5	5.0
Laborers	5.1	5.5	5.8	5.4	5.9	5.7	-	-	7.6
Service Workers	128	11.7	16.2	14.0	12.8	17.6	-	-	-
Total blue collar	5.3	5.8	6.8	5.5	6.1	6.9	0.3	0.3	5.3
Total	3.4	3.7	4.3	3.9	4.1	4.6	0.6	0.9	2.6

Source: "Chemical Industry, Percent Negro Employment by Sex and Occupational Group, New England Region, 1964-1968," William Howard Quay, Jr., *The Negro in the Chemical Industry*, p. 50. Primary source: Appendix Tables A-7-A-9. *Note:* For regional definitions, see Table 21, p. 46.

★ 1333 ★

Occupations

Chemical Industry: Percent Black Employment by Gender and Occupation, North Central Region, 1964-1968

Occupational group	All employees			Male			Female		
	1964	1966	1968	1964	1966	1968	1964	1966	1968
Officials and managers	0.1	0.1	0.6	0.1	0.2	0.6	-	-	2.1
Professionals	0.5	0.7	1.2	0.5	0.6	1.1	0.6	2.5	3.2
Technicians	1.4	1.9	3.3	1.5	1.8	3.0	0.8	2.1	4.9
Sales workers	0.1	0.3	0.9	0.1	0.2	0.9	-	0.7	0.7
Office and clerical	1.2	1.6	2.8	1.1	1.2	2.3	1.2	1.8	3.0
Total white collar	0.7	0.9	1.7	0.6	0.7	1.3	1.1	1.8	3.2
Craftsmen (skilled)	1.5	1.7	2.2	1.5	1.7	2.2	-	-	-
Operatives (semiskilled)	7.0	6.9	8.7	7.5	7.3	7.9	3.2	3.5	13.6
Laborers	10.9	9.3	12.7	12.1	11.0	13.9	4.1	2.8	9.3
Service Workers	11.6	13.4	12.6	12.2	13.8	12.3	5.8	8.2	14.1
Total blue collar	6.1	6.0	7.9	6.3	6.3	7.2	3.6	3.5	12.4
Total	3.8	3.8	5.2	4.0	4.0	4.9	2.0	2.4	7.0

Source: "Chemical Industry, Percent Negro Employment by Sex and Occupational Group, North Central Region, 1964-1968," William Howard Quay, Jr., *The Negro in the Chemical Industry*, p. 57. Primary source: Appendix Tables A-25-A-28. *Note:* For regional definitions, see Table 21, p. 46.

★ 1334 ★

Occupations

Chemical Industry: Percent Black Employment by Gender and Occupation, Northeast, 1964-1968

Occupational group	All employees			Male			Female		
	1964	1966	1968	1964	1966	1968	1964	1966	1968
Officials and managers	0.2	0.3	0.5	0.2	0.3	0.6	0.4	0.9	1.8
Professionals	0.5	0.6	1.0	0.5	0.5	0.9	0.9	1.9	3.1
Technicians	1.5	1.9	2.5	1.6	1.9	2.4	1.3	2.0	3.1
Sales workers	0.4	0.4	0.7	0.4	0.4	0.8	-	-	-
Office and clerical	1.9	2.3	3.7	3.2	3.2	4.7	1.3	1.9	3.3
Total white collar	1.0	1.2	1.9	0.9	1.0	1.4	1.2	1.8	3.2
Craftsmen (skilled)	4.1	4.1	4.7	4.1	4.1	4.7	-	-	2.2
Operatives (semiskilled)	6.5	6.9	8.6	7.3	7.7	9.8	1.6	1.8	2.3
Laborers	13.4	14.1	12.2	14.7	15.6	13.5	3.5	4.4	6.1
Service Workers	17.9	16.3	19.3	17.6	15.9	18.4	19.2	18.9	24.0

[Continued]

★ 1334 ★

Chemical Industry: Percent Black Employment by Gender and Occupation, Northeast, 1964-1968
[Continued]

Occupational group	All employees			Male			Female		
	1964	1966	1968	1964	1966	1968	1964	1966	1968
Total blue collar	7.1	7.3	8.3	7.5	7.6	8.8	3.6	3.8	4.8
Total	3.9	4.1	4.8	4.3	4.5	5.1	1.8	2.3	3.6

Source: "Chemical Industry, Percent Negro Employment by Sex and Occupational Group, Northeast Region, 1964-1968," William Howard Quay, Jr., *The Negro in the Chemical Industry*, p. 50. Primary source: Appendix Tables A-4-A-6. *Note:* For regional definitions, see Table 21, p. 46.

★ 1335 ★

Occupations

Chemical Industry: Percent Black Employment by Gender and Occupation, South Region, 1964-1968

Occupational group	All employees			Male			Female		
	1964	1966	1968	1964	1966	1968	1964	1966	1968
Officials and managers	0.1	0.1	0.3	0.1	0.1	0.3	-	-	-
Professionals	0.1	0.2	0.4	0.1	0.2	0.4	0.8	2.9	3.8
Technicians	0.7	1.0	2.0	0.7	1.0	1.8	0.1	1.0	3.1
Sales workers	-	-	0.4	-	-	0.4	-	-	-
Office and clerical	0.6	1.1	2.3	1.0	1.6	2.6	0.4	0.9	2.2
Total white collar	0.3	0.5	1.0	0.3	0.4	0.8	0.4	0.9	2.3
Craftsmen (skilled)	0.9	1.3	2.0	0.9	1.3	2.0	[1]	1.0	3.0
Operatives (semiskilled)	7.9	8.5	11.0	9.2	9.7	11.6	3.1	4.6	9.1
Laborers	44.7	46.9	41.5	46.5	48.7	43.5	2.2	11.6	13.6
Service Workers	34.6	33.4	32.4	34.9	33.4	32.2	29.8	32.6	36.4
Total blue collar	8.7	9.1	10.2	9.6	9.7	10.3	2.9	5.2	9.4
Total	6.0	6.3	7.3	6.6	6.8	7.4	2.0	3.6	6.9

Source: "Chemical Industry, Percent Negro Employment by Sex and Occupational Group, South Region, 1964-1968," William Howard Quay, Jr., *The Negro in the Chemical Industry*, p. 54. Primary source: Appendix Tables A-13-A-15. *Notes:* For regional definitions, see Table 21, p. 46. 1. Less than 0.05 percent.

★ 1336 ★

Occupations

Chemical Industry: Percent Black Employment by Gender and Occupation, Southeast Region, 1964-1968

Occupational group	All employees			Male			Female		
	1964	1966	1968	1964	1966	1968	1964	1966	1968
Officials and managers	0.1	0.1	0.3	0.1	0.1	0.3	-	-	-
Professionals	0.1	0.2	0.5	0.1	0.2	0.4	1.0	3.3	4.3
Technicians	0.7	1.0	2.0	0.8	1.1	1.8	0.1	1.0	3.2
Sales workers	-	-	0.3	-	-	0.3	-	-	-
Office and clerical	0.6	1.1	2.4	1.0	1.6	2.8	0.3	0.7	2.1
Total white collar	0.3	0.5	1.1	0.3	0.5	0.8	0.3	0.8	2.3
Craftsmen (skilled)	1.0	1.5	2.3	1.1	1.5	2.3	[1]	1.0	3.1
Operatives (semiskilled)	8.2	8.7	11.4	9.7	10.2	12.3	3.1	4.6	9.1
Laborers	40.9	42.4	36.7	42.9	44.3	38.7	2.2	11.6	13.6
Service Workers	37.0	35.6	34.5	37.4	35.6	34.3	31.9	34.8	37.7
Total blue collar	8.9	9.3	10.5	10.0	10.0	10.7	2.9	5.2	9.5
Total	6.2	6.6	7.7	7.0	7.1	7.8	2.1	3.8	7.2

Source: "Chemical Industry, Percent Negro Employment by Sex and Occupational Group, Southeast Region, 1964-1968," William Howard Quay, Jr., *The Negro in the Chemical Industry*, p. 54. Primary source: Appendix Tables A-16-A-18. *Notes:* For regional definitions, see Table 21, p. 46. 1. Less than 0.05 percent.

★ 1337 ★

Occupations

Chemical Industry: Percent Black Employment by Gender and Occupation, Southwest Region, 1964-1968

Occupational group	All employees			Male			Female		
	1964	1966	1968	1964	1966	1968	1964	1966	1968
Officials and managers	0.1	0.2	0.2	0.1	0.2	0.2	-	-	-
Professionals	[1]	0.1	0.3	[1]	0.1	0.3	-	-	-
Technicians	0.3	0.8	1.8	0.3	0.7	1.7	-	1.0	2.7
Sales workers	-	-	0.7	-	-	0.7	-	-	-
Office and clerical	0.8	1.5	2.1	1.0	1.3	1.6	0.7	1.6	2.4
Total white collar	0.3	0.5	0.9	0.2	0.4	0.7	0.6	1.5	2.4
Craftsmen (skilled)	0.3	0.5	1.1	0.3	0.5	1.1	-	-	-
Operatives (semiskilled)	6.1	6.4	7.5	6.1	6.4	7.5	-	-	-
Laborers	65.0	69.8	67.8	65.0	69.8	67.8	-	-	-
Service Workers	22.8	22.6	21.9	23.3	23.0	22.0	-	-	12.5

[Continued]

★ 1337 ★

Chemical Industry: Percent Black Employment by Gender and Occupation, Southwest Region, 1964-1968

[Continued]

Occupational group	All employees			Male			Female		
	1964	1966	1968	1964	1966	1968	1964	1966	1968
Total blue collar	7.7	8.1	8.1	7.7	8.2	8.1	-	-	2.9
Total	4.9	5.2	5.4	5.1	5.4	5.6	0.6	1.4	2.4

Source: "Chemical Industry, Percent Negro Employment by Sex and Occupational Group, Southwest Region, 1964-1968," William Howard Quay, Jr., *The Negro in the Chemical Industry*, p. 55. Primary source: Appendix Tables A-19-A-21. *Notes:* For regional definitions, see Table 21, p. 46. 1. Less than 0.05 percent.

★ 1338 ★

Occupations

Chemical Industry: Percent Blacks Employed by Occupational Group and Gender, 1964-1968

Occupational group	All employees			Male			Female		
	1964	1966	1968	1964	1966	1968	1964	1966	1968
Officials and managers	0.2	0.2	0.4	0.2	0.2	0.4	0.2	0.4	1.1
Professionals	0.4	0.5	0.8	0.3	0.4	0.7	0.9	2.1	3.1
Technicians	1.2	1.5	2.5	1.2	1.5	2.3	0.8	1.5	3.5
Sales workers	0.3	0.3	0.7	0.3	0.3	0.7	-	0.4	0.5
Office and clerical	1.4	1.8	3.2	2.1	2.4	3.5	1.0	1.6	3.0
Total white collar	0.7	0.9	1.6	0.6	0.8	1.2	1.0	1.6	3.0
Craftsmen (skilled)	1.9	2.2	2.9	1.9	2.2	2.8	[1]	1.2	12.7
Operatives (semiskilled)	7.2	7.6	9.9	8.1	8.4	10.3	2.9	3.9	8.3
Laborers	25.5	25.8	22.4	27.7	28.5	25.2	3.6	5.6	8.5
Service workers	23.4	22.9	23.0	24.0	23.2	23.0	18.9	20.4	22.9
Total blue collar	7.7	8.0	9.2	8.2	8.3	9.2	3.4	4.7	9.1
Total	4.7	5.0	6.0	5.2	5.4	6.0	1.9	2.9	5.6

Source: "Chemical Industry, Percent Negro Employment by Occupational Group and Sex, Total United States, 1964-1968," William Howard Quay, Jr., *The Negro in the Chemical Industry*, p. 34. Primary source: Tables A-1-A-3. *Note:* 1. Less than 0.05 percent.

★ 1339 ★

Occupations

Distribution of Employees by Industry, 1910 and 1920

	1910	1920
Chemical and Allied Industries	10,870	19,739
Clay, Glass and Stone Industries	28,519	22,349
Clothing Industries	11,692	15,295
Extraction of Minerals	62,755	73,229
Food and Kindred Industries	17,894	43,512
Iron and Steel Industries	41,739	129,257
Lumber and Furniture Industries	126,018	115,874
Metal Industries (except iron and steel)	2,861	5,230
Paper and Pulp Industries	1,455	3,771
Printing and Book Binding	4,058	4,649
Textile Industries	11,333	24,734
Miscellaneous Industries	87,388	109,041
Total	406,582	566,680

Source: "Distribution of Negroes in the Industries 1910 and 1920," Monroe N. Work, ed., *Negro Year Book: An Annual Encyclopedia of the Negro, 1925-26*, p. 363.

★ 1340 ★

Occupations

Employed Persons in Specific Occupations: by Sex, 1910: Part I, Agricultural

Occupation	Total	Male	Female
Negro population 10 years of age and over	7,317,922	3,637,386	3,680,536
All occupations	5,192,535	3,178,554	2,013,981
Agriculture, forestry, and animal husbandry	2,893,375	1,842,238	1,051,137
Dairy farmers	208	174	34
Dairy farm laborers	2,721	2,302	419
Farmers[1]	877,818	798,509	79,309
Farm laborers	1,949,759	981,922	967,837
Farm laborers (home farm)	1,145,353	441,203	704,150
Farm laborers (working out)	780,035	516,632	263,403
Turpentine farm laborers	24,371	24,087	284
Farm, dairy farm, garden, orchard, etc., foremen	1,828	1,543	285
Dairy farm foremen	15	14	1
Farm foremen[2]	1,692	1,423	269
Garden and greenhouse foremen	72	61	11
Orchard, nursery, etc., foremen	49	45	4
Fishermen and oystermen	8,268	8,160	108
Foresters	17	17	-

[Continued]

★ 1340 ★

Employed Persons in Specific Occupations: by Sex, 1910: Part I, Agricultural
[Continued]

Occupation	Total	Male	Female
Gardeners, florists, fruit growers, and nurserymen	5,147	4,638	509
Florists	116	96	20
Fruit growers and nurserymen	335	303	32
Gardeners	4,466	4,009	457
Landscape gardeners	230	230	-
Garden, greenhouse, orchard, and nursery laborers	18,011	15,562	2,449
Cranberry bog laborers	455	443	12
Garden laborers	13,825	11,801	2,024
Greenhouse laborers	771	729	42
Orchard and nursery laborers	2,960	2,589	371
Lumbermen, raftsmen, and woodchoppers	25,296	25,262	34
Foremen and overseerers	111	111	-
Lumbermen and raftsmen	14,021	14,005	16
Teamsters and haulers	2,465	2,465	-
Woodchoppers and tie cutters	8,699	8,681	18
Owners and managers of log and timber camps	195	195	-
Stock herders, drovers, and feeders	1,387	1,366	21
Stock raisers	202	187	15
Other agricultural and animal husbandry pursuits	2,518	2,401	117
Apiarists	24	23	1
Corn shellers, hay balers, grain thrashers, etc.	96	96	-
Ditchers	1,751	1,751	-
Poultry raisers and poultry yard laborers	368	261	107
Other and not specified pursuits	279	270	9

Source: "Negroes 10 Years of Age and Over Engaged in Specific Occupation: by Sex: 1910." U.S. Bureau of the Census. *Negro Population 1790-1915.* Washington, D.C.: Government Printing Office, 1918, p. 523. Adapted by the Editors. *Notes:* 1. Includes turpentine farmers. 2. Includes turpentine farm foremen.

★ 1341 ★
Occupations

Employed Persons in Specific Occupations: by Sex, 1910: Part II, The Extraction of Minerals

Occupation	Total	Male	Female
Extraction of minerals	61,129	61,048	81
Foremen, overseerers, and inspectors	200	200	-
Foremen and overseerers	190	190	-
Inspectors	10	10	-
Operators, officials, and managers	146	146	-
Managers	17	17	-
Officials	3	3	-
Operators	126	126	-

[Continued]

★ 1341 ★

Employed Persons in Specific Occupations: by Sex, 1910: Part II, The Extraction of Minerals
[Continued]

Occupation	Total	Male	Female
Coal mine operatives	39,567	39,530	37
Copper mine operatives	272	272	-
Gold and silver mine operatives	286	284	2
Iron mine operatives	5,235	5,226	9
Operatives in other and not specified mines	5,067	5,052	15
Lead and zinc mine operatives	259	259	-
All other mine operatives	4,808	4,793	15
Quarry operatives	9,953	9,938	15
Oil, gas, and salt well operatives	403	400	3
Oil and gas well operatives	215	214	1
Salt well and works operatives	188	186	2

Source: "Negroes 10 Years of Age and Over Engaged in Specific Occupation: by Sex: 1910." U.S. Bureau of the Census. *Negro Population 1790-1915.* Washington, D.C.: Government Printing Office, 1918, p. 523. Adapted by the Editors.

★ 1342 ★

Occupations

Employed Persons in Specific Occupations: by Sex, 1910: Part III, Manufacturing and Industries

Occupation	Total	Male	Female
Manufacturing and mechanical industries	631,377	563,410	67,967
Apprentices	1,854	1,596	258
Apprentices to building and hand trades	853	852	1
Dressmakers' and milliners' apprentices	225	-	225
Other apprentices	776	744	32
Bakers	2,125	1,928	197
Blacksmiths, forgemen, and hammermen	9,837	9,834	3
Blacksmiths	9,730	9,727	3
Forgemen, hammermen, and welders	107	107	-
Boiler makers	475	475	-
Brick and stone masons	12,403	12,401	2
Builders and building contractors	3,293	3,272	21
Butchers and dressers (slaughterhouse)	1,099	1,099	-
Cabinetmakers	293	292	1
Carpenters	30,468	30,464	4
Compositors, linotypers, and typesetters	1,141	990	151
Coopers	2,305	2,304	1
Dressmakers and seamstresses (not in factory)	38,216	68	38,148
Dyers	255	236	19
Electricians and electrical engineers	703	703	-
Electrotypers, stereotypers, and lithographers	41	40	1

[Continued]

★ 1342 ★

Employed Persons in Specific Occupations: by Sex, 1910: Part III, Manufacturing and Industries
[Continued]

Occupation	Total	Male	Female
Electrotypers and sterotypers	21	21	-
Lithographers	20	19	1
Engineers (mechanical)	55	55	-
Engineers (stationary)	4,802	4,802	-
Engravers	33	29	4
Filers, grinders, buffers, and polishers (metal)	441	434	7
Buffers and polishers	219	213	6
Filers	111	111	-
Grinders	111	110	1
Firemen (except locomotive and fire department)	14,927	14,927	-
Foremen and overseerers (manufacturing)	1,596	1,548	48
Furnacemen, smeltermen, heaters, pourers, etc.	3,206	3,203	3
Furnacemen and smeltermen	2,675	2,672	3
Heaters	136	136	-
Ladlers and pourers	53	53	-
Puddlers	342	342	-
Glass blowers	42	41	1
Jewelers, watchmaakers, goldsmiths, and silversmiths	157	153	4
Goldsmiths and silversmiths	37	36	1
Jewelers and lapidarics (factory)	19	18	1
Jewelers and watchmakers (not in factory)	101	99	2
Laborers (not otherwise specified)			
Building and hand trades	172,548	166,374	6,174
General and not specified laborers	157,657	151,494	6,163
Helpers in building and hand trades	14,891	14,880	11
Chemical industries	9,130	9,044	86
Fertilizer factories	7,002	6,934	68
Paint factories	126	126	-
Powder, cartridge, fireworks, etc., factories	71	67	4
Other chemical factories	1,931	1,917	14
Clay, glass, and stone industries	22,523	22,357	166
Brick, tile, and terra-cotta factories	15,891	15,792	99
Glass factories	1,704	1,666	38
Lime, cement, and gypsum factories	3,850	3,828	22
Marble and stone yards	737	731	6
Potteries	341	340	1
Iron and steel industries	31,307	31,112	195
Automobile factories	183	180	3
Blast furnaces and mills[1]	13,601	13,519	82
Car and railroad shops	3,664	3,645	19
Wagon and carriage factories	861	855	6
Other iron and steel works	12,998	12,913	85
Other metal industries	826	814	12
Brass mills	115	114	1
Copper factories	92	91	1
Lead and zinc factories	315	315	-

[Continued]

★ 1342 ★

Employed Persons in Specific Occupations: by Sex, 1910: Part III, Manufacturing and Industries
[Continued]

Occupation	Total	Male	Female
Tinware and enamel-ware factories	236	228	8
Other metal factories	68	66	2
Lumber and furniture factories	98,054	97,115	939
Furniture, piano, and organ factories	1,462	1,449	13
Saw and planing mills[3]	91,887	91,181	706
Other woodworking factories	4,705	4,485	220
Textile industries	5,871	5,284	587
Cotton mills	4,663	4,256	407
Silk mills	125	67	58
Woolen and worsted mills	148	129	19
Other textile mills	935	832	103
Other industries	55,895	51,321	4,574
Charcoal and coke works	2,903	2,895	8
Cigar and tobacco factories	8,173	5,768	2,405
Clothing industries	405	357	48
Electric light and power plants	1,143	1,138	5
Electrical supply factories	145	145	-
Food industries			
Bakeries	400	375	25
Butter and cheese factories	88	87	1
Fish curing and packing	271	228	43
Flour and grain mills	1,098	1,088	10
Fruit and vegetable canning, etc.	178	133	45
Slaughter and packing houses	3,080	2,963	117
Sugar factories and refineries	592	584	8
Other food factories	1,963	1,392	571
Gas works	1,671	1,668	3
Liquor and beverage industries	1,384	1,355	29
Oil refineries	905	901	4
Paper and pulp mills	805	772	33
Printing and publishing	689	663	26
Rubber factories	93	92	1
Shoe factories	178	171	7
Tanneries	1,529	1,498	31
Turpentine distilleries	5,719	5,670	49
Other factories	22,483	21,378	1,105
Loom fixers	8	8	-
Machinists, millwrights, and toolmakers	3,323	3,322	1
Machinists and millwrights	3,296	3,296	-
Toolmakers and diesetters and sinkers	27	26	1
Managers and superintendents (manufacturing)	227	218	9
Manufacturers and officials	1,760	1,708	52
Manufacturers	1,727	1,677	50
Officials	33	31	2
Mechanics (not otherwise specified)	752	752	-
Gunsmiths, locksmiths, and bellhangers	38	38	-

[Continued]

★ 1342 ★

Employed Persons in Specific Occupations: by Sex, 1910: Part III, Manufacturing and Industries
[Continued]

Occupation	Total	Male	Female
Wheelwrights	90	90	-
Other mechanics	624	624	-
Millers (grain, flour, feed, etc.)	383	382	1
Milliners and millinery dealers	991	38	953
Molders, founders, and casters (metal)	2,221	2,221	-
Brass molders, founders, and casters	55	55	-
Iron molders, founders, and casters	2,156	2,156	-
Other molders, founders, and casters	10	10	-
Oilers of machinery	416	416	-
Painters, glaziers, varnishers, enamelers, etc.	8,927	8,915	12
Enamelers, laquerers, and japanners	24	24	-
Painters, glaziers, and varnishers (building)	8,040	8,035	5
Painters, glaziers, and varnishers (factory)	863	856	7
Paper hangers	968	954	14
Pattern and model makers	53	50	3
Plasterers	6,175	6,175	-
Plumbers and gas and steam fitters	2,285	2,285	-
Pressmen (printing)	136	132	4
Rollers and rollhands (metal)	322	322	-
Roofers and slaters	613	613	-
Sawyers	3,152	3,151	1
Semiskilled operatives (not otherwise specified)			
Chemical industries	764	722	42
Paint factories	69	68	1
Powder, cartridge, fireworks, etc., factories	20	20	-
Other chemical factories	675	634	41
Cigar and tobacco factories	16,306	8,039	8,267
Clay, glass, and stone industries	2,544	2,489	55
Brick, tile, and terra-cotta factories	1,057	1,048	9
Glass factories	561	524	37
Lime, cement, and gypsum factories	496	494	2
Marble and stone yards	341	336	5
Potteries	89	87	2
Clothing industries	2,910	2,389	521
Hat factories (felt)	64	59	5
Suit, coat, cloak, and overall factories	2,231	1,998	233
Other clothing factories	615	332	283
Food industries	3,803	2,391	1,412
Bakeries	147	124	23
Butter and cheese factories	29	24	5
Candy factories	480	387	93
Flour and grain mills	240	230	10
Fruit and vegetable canning, etc.	131	52	79
Slaughter and packing houses	391	343	48
Other food factories	2,385	1,231	1,154
Harness and saddle industries	277	270	7

[Continued]

★ 1342 ★

Employed Persons in Specific Occupations: by Sex, 1910: Part III, Manufacturing and Industries
[Continued]

Occupation	Total	Male	Female
Iron and steel industries	6,094	5,983	111
Automobile factories	62	58	4
Blast furnaces and mills[1]	1,813	1,804	9
Car and railroad shops[2]	663	656	7
Wagon and carriage factories	202	194	8
Other iron and steel works	3,354	3,271	83
Other metal industries	300	258	42
Brass mills	83	79	4
Clock and watch factories	10	9	1
Gold and silver and jewelry factories	37	27	10
Lead and zinc factories	11	11	-
Tinware and enamel-ware factories	133	107	26
Other metal factories	26	25	1
Liquor and beverage industries	471	453	18
Breweries	67	65	2
Distilleries	65	61	4
Other liquor and beverage factories	339	327	12
Lumber and furniture industries	11,941	11,473	468
Furniture, piano, and organ factories	1,212	1,094	118
Saw and planing mills[3]	9,322	9,201	121
Other woodworking factories	1,407	1,178	229
Paper and pulp mills	203	163	40
Printing and publishing	491	313	178
Shoe factories	2,485	2,318	167
Tanneries	596	591	5
Textile industries			
Beamers, warpers, and slashers	25	13	12
Cotton mills	13	10	3
Silk mills	8	-	8
Woolen and worsted mills	1	1	-
Other textile mills	3	2	1
Bobbin boys, doffers, and carriers	62	48	14
Cotton mills	48	39	9
Silk mills	1	1	-
Woolen and worsted mills	4	3	1
Other textile mills	9	5	4
Carders, combers, and lappers	140	123	17
Cotton mills	101	88	13
Silk mills	-	-	-
Woolen and worsted mills	7	7	-
Other textile mills	32	28	4
Drawers, rovers, and twisters	113	74	39
Cotton mills	81	59	22
Silk mills	11	2	9
Woolen and worsted mills	4	-	4
Other textile mills	17	13	4

[Continued]

★ 1342 ★

Employed Persons in Specific Occupations: by Sex, 1910: Part III, Manufacturing and Industries
[Continued]

Occupation	Total	Male	Female
Spinners	169	73	96
Cotton mills	110	43	67
Silk mills	9	1	8
Woolen and worsted mills	15	10	5
Other textile mills	35	19	16
Weavers	339	162	177
Cotton mills	83	53	30
Silk mills	75	2	73
Woolen and worsted mills	14	4	10
Other textile mills	167	103	64
Winders, reelers, and spoolers	150	35	115
Cotton mills	44	12	32
Silk mills	80	6	74
Woolen and worsted mills	3	-	3
Other textile mills	23	17	6
Other occupations	2,500	1,566	934
Cotton mills	1,030	744	286
Silk mills	195	60	135
Woolen and worsted mills	88	69	19
Other textile mills	1,187	693	494
Other industries	6,969	6,101	868
Electrical supply factories	42	39	3
Paper-box factories	49	30	19
Rubber factories	85	77	8
Other factories	6,793	5,955	838
Sewers and sewing-machine operators (factory)[4]	1,924	679	1,245
Shoemakers and cobblers (not in factory)	3,739	3,695	44
Skilled occupations (not otherwise specified)	113	113	-
Annealers and temperers (metal)	20	20	-
Piano and organ tuners	50	50	-
Wood carvers	14	14	-
Other skilled occupations	29	29	-
Stonecutters	500	500	-
Structural-iron workers (building)	80	80	-
Tailors and tailoresses	5,043	4,652	391
Tinsmiths and coppersmiths	884	883	1
Coppersmiths	15	15	-
Tinsmiths	869	868	1
Upholsterers	809	784	25

Source: "Negroes 10 Years of Age and Over Engaged in Specific Occupation: by Sex: 1910." U.S. Bureau of the Census. *Negro Population 1790-1915.* Washington, D.C.: Government Printing Office, 1918, p. 523-524. Adapted by the Editors. *Notes:* 1. Includes tin-plate mills. 2. Includes car repairers for street and steam railroads. 3. Includes wooden-box factories. 4. Includes sewers and sewing-machine operators in all factories except shoe and harness factories, and sack sewers in cement, sugar, and grain mills.

★ 1343 ★
Occupations

Employed Persons in Specific Occupations: by Sex, 1910: Part IV, Transportation

Occupation	Total	Male	Female
Transportation[1]	255,969	254,683	1,286
Water transportation (selected occupations)			
Boatmen, canalmen, and lock keepers	260	260	-
Captains, masters, mates, and pilots	465	465	-
Longshoremen and stevedores	16,405	16,379	26
Sailors and deck hands	6,508	6,503	5
Road and street transportation (selected occupations)			
Carriage and hack drivers	7,878	7,871	7
Chauffeurs	4,676	4,674	2
Draymen, teamsters, and expressmen[2]	50,711	50,689	22
Foremen of livery and transfer companies	426	426	-
Garage keepers and managers	33	33	-
Hostlers and stable hands	12,967	12,965	2
Livery-stable keepers and managers	403	395	8
Proprietors and managers of transfer companies	651	636	15
Railroad transportation (selected occupations)			
Baggagemen and freight agents	242	242	-
Baggagemen	225	225	-
Freight agents	17	17	-
Boiler washers and engine hostlers	1,328	1,328	-
Brakemen	4,719	4,719	-
Conductors (steam railroad)	120	120	-
Conductors (street railroad)	44	44	-
Foremen and overseerers	987	982	5
Laborers	90,560	89,721	839
Steam railroad	87,188	86,380	808
Street railroad	3,372	3,341	31
Locomotive engineers	355	355	-
Locomotive firemen	5,188	5,188	-
Motormen	108	108	-
Officials and superintendents	39	39	-
Steam railroad	37	37	-
Street railroad	2	2	-
Switchmen, flagmen, and yardmen	2,471	2,469	2
Switchmen and flagmen (steam railroad)	2,127	2,125	2
Switchmen and flagmen (street railroad)	33	33	-
Yardmen (steam railroad)	311	311	-
Ticket and station agents	50	44	6
Express, post, telegraph, and telephone (selected occupations)			
Agents (express companies)	12	12	-
Express messengers and railway mail clerks	796	796	-
Express messengers	94	94	-
Railway mail clerks	702	702	-
Mail carriers	2,781	2,756	25

[Continued]

★ 1343 ★

Employed Persons in Specific Occupations: by Sex, 1910: Part IV, Transportation
[Continued]

Occupation	Total	Male	Female
Telegraph and telephone linemen	488	488	-
Telegraph messengers	263	262	1
Telegraph operators	73	57	16
Telephone operators	289	197	92
Other transportation pursuits			
Foremen and overseerers (not otherwise specified)	246	246	-
Road and street building and repairing	97	97	-
Telegraph and telephone companies	5	5	-
Water transportation	137	137	-
Other transportation	7	7	-
Inspectors	190	186	4
Steam railroad	178	175	3
Street railroad	6	6	-
Other transportation	6	5	1
Laborers (not otherwise specified)	40,626	40,489	137
Road and street building and repairing	33,914	33,914	-
Street cleaning	1,009	1,009	-
Other transportation	5,703	5,566	137
Proprietors, officials, and managers (not otherwise specified)	59	59	-
Telegraph and telephone companies	5	5	-
Other transportation	54	54	-
Other occupations (semiskilled)	2,552	2,480	72
Steam railroad	2,007	1,960	47
Street railroad	123	120	3
Other transportation	422	400	22

Source: "Negroes 10 Years of Age and Over Engaged in Specific Occupation: by Sex: 1910." U.S. Bureau of the Census. Negro Population 1790-1915. Washington, D.C.: Government Printing Office, 1918, p. 524. Adapted by the Editors. Notes: 1. Does not include the 15,116 porters, the 2,396 waiters, and the 2,943 cooks employed by steam railroads: or the 1,247 porters, the 650 waiters, and the 1,537 cooks employed by other transportation companies. 2. Teamsters in agriculture, forestry, and the extraction of minerals are classified with the other workers in those industries, respectively, and drivers for bakeries and laundries are classified with deliverymen in trade.

★ 1344 ★

Occupations

Employed Persons in Specific Occupations: by Sex, 1910: Part V, Clerical

Occupation	Total	Male	Female
Clerical occupations	19,336	16,204	3,132
Agents, canvassers, and collectors	997	782	215
Agents	264	226	38

[Continued]

★ 1344 ★

Employed Persons in Specific Occupations: by Sex, 1910: Part V, Clerical

[Continued]

Occupation	Total	Male	Female
Canvassers	284	166	118
Collectors	449	390	59
Bookkeepers, cashiers, and accountants	1,675	766	909
Clerks (except clerks in stores)	7,030	6,077	953
Shipping clerks	1,010	996	14
Other clerks	6,020	5,081	939
Messenger, bundle, and office boys[1]	8,553	8,262	291
Bundle and cash boys and girls	105	88	17
Messenger, errand, and office boys	8,448	8,174	274
Stenographers and typewriters	1,081	317	764

Source: "Negroes 10 Years of Age and Over Engaged in Specific Occupation: by Sex: 1910." U.S. Bureau of the Census. *Negro Population 1790-1915.* Washington, D.C.: Government Printing Office, 1918, p. 525. Adapted by the Editors. *Note:* 1. Except telegraph and telephone messengers.

★ 1345 ★

Occupations

Employed Persons in Specific Occupations: by Sex, 1910: Part VI, Trades

Occupation	Total	Male	Female
Trade	119,491	112,464	7,027
Bankers, brokers, and money lenders	336	309	27
Bankers and bank officials	135	122	13
Commercial brokers and commission men	76	71	5
Loan brokers and loan company officials	11	11	-
Pawnbrokers	19	18	1
Stockbrokers	36	32	4
Brokers not specified and promoters	59	55	4
Clerks in stores[1]	3,497	2,582	915
Commercial travelers	332	286	46
Decorators, drapers, and window dressers	46	42	4
Deliverymen	31,196	31,168	28
Bakeries and laundries	659	657	2
Stores	30,537	30,511	26
Floorwalkers, foremen, and overseerers	318	309	9
Floorwalkers and foremen in stores	267	258	9
Foremen in warehouses, stockyards, etc.	51	51	-
Inspectors, gaugers, and samplers	890	874	16
Insurance agents and officials	1,833	1,520	313
Insurance agents	1,728	1,419	309
Officials of insurance companies	105	101	4
Laborers in coal and lumber yards, warehouses, etc.	12,772	12,711	61

[Continued]

★ 1345 ★

Employed Persons in Specific Occupations: by Sex, 1910: Part VI, Trades
[Continued]

Occupation	Total	Male	Female
Coal yards	3,708	3,705	3
Elevators	625	624	1
Lumberyards	6,205	6,201	4
Stockyards	531	531	-
Warehouses	1,703	1,650	53
Laborers, porters, and helpers in stores	37,576	36,906	670
Newsboys	1,221	1,207	14
Proprietors, officials, and managers (not otherwise specified)	205	119	86
Employment office keepers	148	85	83
Proprietors, etc., elevators	8	8	-
Proprietors, etc., warehouses	23	23	-
Other proprietors, officials, and managers	26	23	3
Real-estate agents and officials	762	717	45
Retail dealers	20,653	17,659	2,994
Salesmen and saleswomen	5,178	3,680	1,498
Auctioneers	14	14	-
Demonstrators	45	21	24
Sales agents	420	251	169
Salesmen and saleswomen (stores)	4,699	3,394	1,305
Undertakers	953	907	46
Wholesale dealers, importers, and exporters	241	229	12
Other pursuits (unskilled)	1,482	1,239	243
Fruit graders and packers	348	168	180
Meat cutters	225	224	1
Other occupations	909	847	62

Source: "Negroes 10 Years of Age and Over Engaged in Specific Occupation: by Sex: 1910." U.S. Bureau of the Census. *Negro Population 1790-1915*. Washington, D.C.: Government Printing Office, 1918, p. 525. Adapted by the Editors. *Notes:* 1. Many of the "clerks" in stores evidently are "salesmen and saleswomen".

★ 1346 ★

Occupations

Employed Persons in Specific Occupations: by Sex, 1910: Part VII, Public Service

Occupation	Total	Male	Female
Public service (not elsewhere classified)	22,382	22,033	349
Firemen (fire department)	321	321	-
Guards, watchmen, and doorkeepers	3,544	3,541	3
Laborers (public service)	13,005	12,767	238
Garbage men and scavengers	1,100	1,100	-
Other laborers	11,905	11,667	238

[Continued]

★ 1346 ★

Employed Persons in Specific Occupations: by Sex, 1910:
Part VII, Public Service
[Continued]

Occupation	Total	Male	Female
Marshals, sheriffs, detectives, etc.	246	235	11
Detectives	72	70	2
Marshals and constables	121	121	-
Probation and truant officers	16	7	9
Sheriffs	37	37	-
Officials and inspectors (city and county)	251	227	24
Officials and inspectors (city)	182	172	10
Officials and inspectors (county)	69	55	14
Officials and inspectors (state and United States)	426	369	57
Officials and inspectors (state)	33	30	3
Officials and inspectors (United States)	393	339	54
Policemen	576	576	-
Soldiers, sailors, and marines[1]	3,734	3,734	-
Other pursuits	279	263	16
Life-savers	12	12	-
Lighthouse keepers	36	34	2
Other occupations	231	217	14

Source: "Negroes 10 Years of Age and Over Engaged in Specific Occupation: by Sex: 1910." U.S. Bureau of the Census. *Negro Population 1790-1915*. Washington, D.C.: Government Printing Office, 1918, p. 525. Adapted by the Editors. *Notes:* 1. Includes only those resident in continental United States at the date of the enumeration.

★ 1347 ★

Occupations

Employed Persons in Specific Occupations: by Sex, 1910:
Part VIII, Professional Service

Occupation	Total	Male	Female
Professional service	67,245	37,600	29,645
Actors	1,279	750	529
Architects	59	56	3
Artists, sculptors, and teachers of art	329	201	128
Authors, editors, and reporters	247	219	28
Authors	27	19	8
Editors and reporters	220	200	20
Chemists, assayers, and metallurgists	123	119	4
Civil and mining engineers and surveyors	237	237	-
Civil engineers and surveyors	217	217	-
Mining engineers	20	20	-
Clergymen	17,495	17,427	68
College presidents and professors	242	169	73
Dentists	478	452	26
Designers, draftsmen, and inventors	96	92	4

[Continued]

★ 1347 ★

Employed Persons in Specific Occupations: by Sex, 1910: Part VIII, Professional Service
[Continued]

Occupation	Total	Male	Female
Designers	30	29	1
Draftsmen	47	45	2
Inventors	19	18	1
Lawyers, judges, and justices	798	796	2
Musicians and teachers of music	5,606	3,259	2,347
Photographers	404	363	41
Physicians and surgeons	3,077	2,744	333
Showmen	1,066	1,006	60
Teachers	29,485	7,035	22,450
Teachers (athletics, dancing, etc.)	53	44	9
Teachers (school)	29,432	6,991	22,441
Trained nurses	2,433	275	2,158
Veterinary surgeons	122	122	-
Other professional pursuits	150	94	56
Semiprofessional pursuits	2,144	1,389	755
Abstractors, notaries, and justices of peace	117	96	21
Fortune tellers, hypnotists, spiritualists, etc.	100	29	71
Healers (except physicians and surgeons)	332	141	191
Keepers of charitable and penal institutions	124	87	37
Officials of lodges, societies, etc.	279	183	96
Religious and charity workers	501	169	332
Theatrical owners, managers, and officials	93	91	2
Other occupations	598	593	5
Attendants and helpers (professional service)	1,375	795	580

Source: "Negroes 10 Years of Age and Over Engaged in Specific Occupation: by Sex: 1910." U.S. Bureau of the Census. *Negro Population 1790-1915*. Washington, D.C.: Government Printing Office, 1918, p. 525. Adapted by the Editors.

★ 1348 ★

Occupations

Employed Persons in Specific Occupations: by Sex, 1910: Part IX, Domestic and Personal Service

Occupation	Total	Male	Female
Domestic and personal service	1,122,231	268,874	853,357
Barbers, hairdressers, and manicurists	23,228	19,446	3,782
Bartenders	2,666	2,661	5
Billiard room, dance hall, skating rink, etc., keepers	1,011	926	85
Billiard and pool room keepers	875	866	9
Dance hall, skating rink, etc., keepers	136	60	76
Boarding and lodging house keepers	10,601	1,418	9,183
Bootblacks	3,850	3,842	8

[Continued]

★ 1348 ★

Employed Persons in Specific Occupations: by Sex, 1910: Part IX, Domestic and Personal Service

[Continued]

Occupation	Total	Male	Female
Charwomen and cleaners	8,614	1,618	7,026
Elevator tenders	6,278	6,276	2
Hotel keepers and managers	973	620	353
Housekeepers and stewards	11,624	1,603	10,021
Janitors and sextons	24,871	22,419	2,452
Laborers (domestic and personal service)	11,087	10,380	707
Launderers and laundresses (not in laundry)	368,124	6,573	361,551
Laundry operatives[2]	14,146	1,950	12,196
Laundry owners, officials, and managers[2]	210	164	46
Midwives and nurses (not trained)	20,536	1,028	19,508
Midwives	1,634	-	1,634
Nurses (not trained)	18,902	1,028	17,874
Porters (except in stores)[1]	51,538	51,520	18
Restaurant, cafe, and lunch-room keepers	6,369	3,635	2,734
Saloon keepers	652	636	16
Servants	507,693	92,277	415,416
Bell boys, chore boys, etc.	8,212	7,934	278
Chambermaids	14,082	11	14,071
Coachmen and footmen	7,679	7,679	-
Cooks	238,392	32,453	205,939
Other servants	239,328	44,200	195,128
Waiters	43,098	35,664	7,434
Other pursuits	5,032	4,218	814
Bathhouse keepers and attendants	798	358	440
Cemetery keepers	216	212	4
Cleaners and renovators (clothing, etc.)	3,744	3,385	359
Umbrella menders and scissors grinders	30	28	2
Other occupations	244	235	9

Source: "Negroes 10 Years of Age and Over Engaged in Specific Occupation: by Sex: 1910." U.S. Bureau of the Census. *Negro Population 1790-1915*. Washington, D.C.: Government Printing Office, 1918, p. 525. Adapted by the Editors. *Notes:* 1. Includes only those resident in continental United States at the date of enumeration. 2. Some owners of hand laundries are included with "laundry operatives."

★ 1349 ★

Occupations

Employees in Agricultural Pursuits by Occupational Class, 1910

Occupational class	Number			Increase[1]	
	1910	1900	1890	1900-1910	1890-1900
	Male				
Total	1,830,424	1,561,153	1,300,658	269,271	260,495
Farmers, planters, and overseers	799,923	686,157	541,300	113,766	144,857
Agricultural laborers	973,695	834,438	729,197	139,257	105,241

[Continued]

★ 1349 ★

Employees in Agricultural Pursuits by Occupational Class, 1910

[Continued]

Occupational class	Number			Increase[1]	
	1910	1900	1890	1900-1910	1890-1900
Dairymen	2,302	403	485	1,899	-82
Gardeners, florists, nurserymen, etc.	4,663	2,288	5,182	2,375	-2,894
Stock raisers, herders, and drovers	2,110	1,289	1,300	821	-11
Lumbermen and raftsmen	14,293	6,203	3,738	8,090	2,465
Woodchoppers	8,707	9,656	7,661	-949	1,995
Turpentine farmers and laborers	24,345	20,509		3,836	
Other agricultural pursuits	386	210	11,795	176	8,924
Female					
Total	1,051,030	582,001	427,667	469,029	154,334
Farmers, planters, and overseers	79,677	71,665	49,366	8,012	22,299
Agricultural laborers	970,060	509,687	377,531	460,373	132,156
Dairywomen	419	134	181	285	-47
Gardeners, florists, etc.	508	168	306	340	-138
Other agricultural pursuits	366	347	283	19	64

Source: "Negroes 10 Years of Age and Over Gainfully Employed in Agricultural Pursuits," U.S. Bureau of the Census, Negro Population, 1790-1915, p. 507. Note: 1. A minus sign (-) denotes decrease.

★ 1350 ★

Occupations

Employees in the Air Transport Industry by Gender and Occupational Group, 1966-1969

Occupational group	All employees				Male				Female			
	1966	1967	1968	1969	1966	1967	1968	1969	1966	1967	1968	1969
Officials and managers	0.4	0.4	0.6	0.8	0.4	0.4	0.6	0.8	0.2	0.3	0.6	0.8
Professionals	0.2	0.2	0.3	0.4	0.2	0.2	0.3	0.3	0.3	0.5	0.8	1.4
Technicians	0.9	0.9	0.5	1.3	1.0	0.9	0.5	1.2	0.6	0.8	1.1	1.4
Sales workers	1.4	2.2	3.3	3.9	1.1	1.6	2.6	2.9	1.7	2.7	3.8	4.6
Office and clerical	2.0	2.5	3.7	3.7	2.7	3.3	4.5	4.7	1.4	1.9	3.2	2.9
Total white collar	1.1	1.5	2.2	2.4	1.0	1.1	1.5	1.7	1.4	2.2	3.4	3.7
Craftsmen	2.2	2.5	2.3	2.6	2.2	2.5	2.3	2.6	0.4	2.2	2.1	4.4
Operatives	9.3	9.3	10.6	12.1	9.2	9.2	10.5	12.0	13.6[1]	13.0[1]	20.9[1]	20.2[1]
Laborers	30.1	24.8	25.9	34.2	29.3	24.2	25.2	31.9	51.8[1]	40.3[1]	45.7[1]	68.6[1]
Service workers	14.3	13.5	11.7	11.2	30.3	29.7	32.8	27.2	2.5	2.6	2.8	2.8
Total blue collar	8.0	8.5	8.3	9.2	8.7	9.3	9.5	10.2	3.4	3.5	3.5	4.8
Total	4.3	4.6	4.8	5.4	5.0	5.3	5.3	6.0	1.9	2.5	3.4	4.0

Source: "Air Transport Industry, Percentage Negro Employment by Sex and Occupational Group," Northrup, Thieblot, and Chernish, The Negro in the Air Transport Industry, p. 70. Published by permission. Note: 1. Very small members involved.

★ 1351 ★

Occupations

Employment in Corporations, 1974 - I

	Overall percentage	Officials & managers	Professionals	Technicians	Sales workers	Office & clerical workers	Craftsmen	Operatives	Laborers	Service workers
Aetna Life & Casualty	9.1	0.9	2.5	7.5	6.9	13.4	11.3	23.6	55.6	13.6
American Airlines	11.4	5.6	1.5	4.4	10.7	14.4	7.3	23.3		23.3
American Can	14.2[1]	3.4[1]	4.3[1]	5.7[1]	5.7[1]	9.1[1]	9.9[1]	18.0[1]	26.0[1]	29.0[1]
American Motors	12.5[1]	5.1[1]	1.7[1]	1.6[1]		7.1[1]	6.1[1]	16[1]	14[1]	11[1]
American Telephone & Telegraph	11.1	4.3	3.1	7.4	5.4	17.1	6.3	25.2		30.9
Avon Products	14.5[1]					14.7[1]				
Bank of America	24.6[1]	9.9[1,2]	9.9[1,2]			89.1[1]				
Bankers Trust	26	9	12.5	0	14	33	11	38		24
Bendix	7.4	2.0	2.0	5.5	0.05	10.0	4.3	9.1	15.4	23.2
Bethlehem Steel	14.2	4.1	1.2	2.7	0.3	6.4	9.6	18.8	31.9	19.7
Brown & Williamson Tobacco	30.3	8.2	5.9	14.3	13.1	14	8.1	39	40.4	48.2
Chase Manhattan Bank	24	6	11	26	11	32	5	19		26
Citizens & Southern National Bank	20.2	5.4	3.2	17.9	1.2	25.6	0.1	46.8		98
Connecticut General Insurance	9.6	3.0	7.9	12.5	3.5	14.2	2.2	18.2		44.6
Consolidated Edison of N.Y.	14.3	4.7	4.4	6.4		22.2	14.5	22.0	18.4	25.6
Delta Air Lines	12.2	1.2	0.6	0.5	11.1	10.6	7.1	3.7	58.5	9.5
Eastern Airlines	7.8	2.4	1.2	2.4	8.7	5.2	2.1	17.9		77.3
First National City Bank	16.9	4.3	10.5	11.8	10.5	23.9		13.7		10.2
First Pennsylvania Bank	20.3	8.6								
Ford Motor	19.6[1,3]	5.6[1,3]	5.7[1,3]	9.1[1,3]		14.0[1,3]	7.7[1,3]	29.6[1,3]	29.5[1,3]	31.7[1,3]
General Foods	17.1[1]	5.0[1]	7.3[1]	12.6[1]	9.1[1]	9.9[1]	8.0[1]	24.9[1]	29.0[1]	36.6[1]
General Motors	14.9[3]	5.2[3]	3.6[3]	6.8[3]	4.2[3]	12.1[3]	5.3[3]	19.7[3]	29.1[3]	23.6[3]
Goodyear Tire & Rubber	9.2	3.0	1.7	5.3	3.1	5.8	6.5	13.7	19.2	16.2
Greyhound	17.5	11	2	18.7	17	15	9.8	32	19.2	16.2

Source: "Employment in Corporations," *Black Enterprise* 5 (June 1975), pp. 28-29. Published by permission. *Notes:* 1. All minority employees. 2. Combined figure for "Official and Managers" and "professionals". 3. For end of 1973.

★ 1352 ★

Occupations

Employment in Corporations, 1974 - II

	Overall percentage	Officials & managers	Professionals	Technicians	Sales workers	Office & clerical workers	Craftsmen	Operatives	Laborers	Service workers
Grumman Aerospace	6.1	2.2	2	4.4		6.4	8.2	11.7	15.7	2.8
Gulf Oil	8.0	0.8	2.55	5.7	3.2	11.0	5.8	16.45	27.1	28.1
Honeywell	5.3	1.3	2.4	5.8	5.5	7.1	3.1	9.7	8.3	9.8
Kraftco	12.9[1]	2.2[1]	7.0[1]	7.2[1]	6.7[1]	10.8[1]	13.4[1]	16.6[1]	17.1[1]	23[1]
Liggett Group	29.2	2.2	4.0	6.5	5.3	8.8	2.6	28.7	86.5	86.5
Metropolitan Life Insurance	14[1]	4.2[1]	6.4[1]	18.5[1]	7.6[1]	23.8[1]	18.8[1]	36.2[1]		51.2[1]
Montgomery Ward	8.6[2]	2.9[2]	4.2[2]	6.9[2]	5.6[2]	7.8[2]	6.0[2]	17.0[2]	25.1[2]	22.1[2]
Mutual Life Insurance	6.2	0.8	3.0	4.5	5.8	9.6				0.2
National Homes	8.6	2.8	6	3	2.1	1.8	6	17.2	12.2	4.3
Owens-Illinois	14.9	1.8	2.5	6.7	2.9	6.7	5.3	15.8	15.5	28.2
J.C. Penny	5.8	2.9	3.8	11.8	3.8	6.8	5.4	10.8	32.5	13.2
Pitney Bowes	9	2	3	3	3	16	8[3]	8[3]	47	12
Prudential Insurance	7.8[2]	1.4[2]	3.4[4]	6.1[4]	3.4[4]	15.5[2]	3.6[4]	9.0[4]		11.0[4]
Ralston Purina	10.7	4.0	2.4	7.7	2.9	7.6	3.8	18.5	22.6	9.2
Scott Paper	12.5[5]	3.3[5]	4.8[5]	6.6[5]	8.3[5]	9.3[5]	4.5[5]	16.5[5]	22.9[5]	34.9[5]
Sears, Roebuck	11.1	3.8	3.7	6.5	9.4	9.6	6.4	18.5	21.3	32.1
Shell Oil	7.8	1.4	3.0	5.9	5.3	15.1	5.1	15.3	18.8	26.9
Southern Pacific Transportation	7.5	2.1	1.2	3.9	0.4	7.4	3.3	6.0	23.7	57.1
Standard Oil (Indiana)	12.0	2.1	4.8	8.5	2.0	21.6	8.4	21.4	27.3	30.7
Trans World Airlines	7.4	3.8	0.4	3.7	12.3	7.2	2.6	13.7	29.4	11.6
United Airlines	7.8	4.0	1.0	4.3	7.0	7.1	2.6	15.3	42.1	10.85

[Continued]

★ 1352 ★

Employment in Corporations, 1974 - II
[Continued]

	Overall percentage	Officials & managers	Professionals	Technicians	Sales workers	Office & clerical workers	Craftsmen	Operatives	Laborers	Service workers
Western Electric	15.1[1]	2.8[1]	3.9[1]	8.0[1]		13.4[1]	6.3[1]	23.7[1]		27.0[1]
Xerox	16.1	6.7	9.0	13.8	11.9	16.1	23.4	30.9	34.1	33.2

Source: "Employment in Corporations," *Black Enterprise* 5 (June 1975), pp. 28-29. Published by permission. *Notes:* 1. All minority employees. 2. Not comparable with figures published by *Black Enterprise* a year ago, which covered all minority and female employees. 3. Combined figure for "Official and Managers" and "professionals". 4. For end of 1973. 5. All minority employees, described by company as "approximately 90% black."

★ 1353 ★
Occupations

Employment on Five Major Airline Carriers by Race, Gender and Occupational Group, 1968

Occupational group	All employees			Male			Female		
	Total	Negro	Percent Negro	Total	Negro	Percent Negro	Total	Negro	Percent Negro
Officials and managers	12,425	79	0.6	11,648	73	0.6	777	6	0.8
Professionals	25,958	83	0.3	25,156	76	0.3	802	7	0.9
Technicians	4,180	22	0.5	3,896	20	0.5	284	2	0.7
Sales workers	29,250	1,118	3.8	11,653	345	3.0	17,597	773	4.4
Office and clerical	27,188	1,054	3.9	12,232	540	4.4	14,956	514	3.4
Total white collar	99,001	2,356	2.4	64,585	1,054	1.6	34,416	1,302	3.8
Craftsmen	32,508	798	2.5	32,399	795	2.5	109	3	2.8
Operatives	14,527	1,900	13.1	14,414	1,862	12.9	113	38	33.6
Laborers	5,025	1,002	19.9	4,876	969	19.9	149	33	22.1
Service workers	16,178	2,123	13.1	4,580	1,751	38.2	11,598	372	3.2
Total blue collar	68,238	5,823	8.5	56,269	5,377	9.6	11,969	446	3.7
Total	167,239	8,179	4.9	120,854	6,431	5.3	46,385	1,748	3.8

Source: "Air Transport Industry, Employment by Race, Sex, and Occupational Group, Seven Regional Carriers, 1968," Northrup, Thieblot, and Chernish, *The Negro in the Air Transport Industry*, p. 88. Published by permission. Primary source: Data in authors' possession. *Note:* Carriers are American, Eastern, Pan American, Trans World, and United.

★ 1354 ★

Occupations

Employment on Seven Regional Airline Carriers by Race, Gender and Occupational Group, 1968

Occupational group	All employees			Male			Female		
	Total	Negro	Percent Negro	Total	Negro	Percent Negro	Total	Negro	Percent Negro
Officials and managers	3,873	15	0.4	3,641	15	0.4	232	-	-
Professionals	7,286	11	0.2	7,155	11	0.2	131	-	-
Technicians	751	5	0.7	684	3	0.4	67	2	3.0
Sales workers	10,651	201	1.9	4,331	64	1.5	6,320	137	2.2
Office and clerical	5,094	146	2.9	1,496	74	4.9	3,598	72	2.0
Total white collar	27,655	378	1.4	17,307	167	1.0	10,348	211	2.0
Craftsmen	9,715	187	1.9	9,681	187	1.9	34	-	-
Operatives	5,799	247	4.3	5,725	246	4.3	74	1	1.4
Laborers	2,043	826	40.4	1,949	748	38.4	94	78	83.0
Service workers	8,637	791	9.2	2,857	685	24.0	5,780	106	1.8
Total blue collar	26,194	2,051	7.8	20,212	1,866	9.2	5,982	185	3.1
Total	53,849	2,429	4.5	37,519	2,033	5.4	16,330	396	2.4

Source: "Air Transport Industry, Employment by Race, Sex, and Occupational Group, Seven Regional Carriers, 1968," Northrup, Thieblot, and Chernish, *The Negro in the Air Transport Industry*, p. 89. Published by permission. Primary source: Data in authors' possession. *Notes:* Carriers are Braniff, Continental, Delta, National, Northeast, Northwest, Western.

★ 1355 ★

Occupations

Farmers, Planters, Overseerer and Other farm Workers: Geographical Area, 1900 and 1910

Division and state	Negro population 10 years of age and over gainfully employed											
	Male						Female					
	Farmers, planters, and overseerers[1]		Farm laborers, home farm		Farm laborers, working out		Farmers, planters, and overseerers[1]		Farm laborers, home farm		Farm laborers, working out	
	1910	1900	1910	1900	1910	1900	1910	1900	1910	1900	1910	1900
United States	799,923	686,157	441,203	363,528	516,632	465,980	79,677	71,665	704,150	323,295	263,403	185,931
Geographic divisions												
New England	264	234	58	36	1,139	1,457	14	18	7	-	20	6
Middle Atlantic	1,133	1,289	377	320	8,940	8,177	46	53	20	7	161	53
East North Central	4,375	5,059	1,234	1,883	6,708	5,319	198	265	107	28	228	47
West North Central	5,310	6,935	1,579	2,608	8,198	7,996	255	386	87	78	189	75
South Atlantic	317,039	259,087	183,470	148,708	242,806	214,763	26,831	25,028	274,891	126,072	129,744	82,753
East South Central	288,503	248,616	158,858	130,928	124,624	130,254	34,430	29,397	282,070	134,873	71,985	63,269
West South Central	182,851	164,652	95,554	78,971	123,457	97,653	17,873	16,493	146,954	62,236	61,060	39,723
Mountain	220	116	31	15	296	97	13	10	8	-	5	-
Pacific	228	169	42	59	464	264	17	15	6	1	11	5
New England												
Maine	35	21	7	3	38	20	2	4	-	-	2	-
New Hampshire	21	11	2	-	43	29	2	1	-	-	1	-
Vermont	23	12	8	1	47	67	2	1	-	-	-	1
Massachusetts	73	70	15	12	346	479	7	5	7	-	8	-
Rhode Island	30	29	4	2	217	271	1	3	-	-	-	1

[Continued]

★ 1355 ★

Farmers, Planters, Overseerer and Other farm Workers: Geographical Area, 1900 and 1910

[Continued]

Division and state	Negro population 10 years of age and over gainfully employed											
	Male						Female					
	Farmers, planters, and overseerers[1]		Farm laborers, home farm		Farm laborers, working out		Farmers, planters, and overseerers[1]		Farm laborers, home farm		Farm laborers, working out	
	1910	1900	1910	1900	1910	1900	1910	1900	1910	1900	1910	1900
Connecticut	82	91	22	18	448	591	-	4	-	-	9	4
Middle Atlantic												
New York	267	320	69	68	1,820	1,842	16	16	9	1	25	13
New Jersey	404	472	177	125	3,901	3,638	9	16	8	2	62	27
Pennsylvania	462	497	131	127	3,219	2,697	21	21	3	4	74	13
East North Central												
Ohio	1,636	1,945	405	720	2,727	2,082	72	115	18	7	43	11
Indiana	721	950	246	329	1,458	1,232	25	48	9	5	11	7
Illinois	1,330	1,467	436	625	1,965	1,562	66	70	62	15	164	25
Michigan	587	639	131	188	487	404	29	29	12	1	8	2
Wisconsin	101	58	16	21	71	39	6	3	6	-	2	2
West North Central												
Minnesota	61	33	12	6	63	33	2	2	2	-	6	-
Iowa	195	194	58	54	135	203	12	8	5	2	11	2
Missouri	3,506	4,852	1,060	2,029	6,862	6,493	155	294	69	69	150	67
North Dakota	37	11	6	3	40	15	9	1	2	-	1	2
South Dakota	60	19	3	-	30	15	6	1	-	-	-	-
Nebraska	92	70	10	17	67	47	5	8	-	1	-	-
Kansas	1,359	1,756	430	499	1,001	1,190	66	72	9	6	21	4
South Atlantic												
Delaware	803	788	455	359	3,562	2,746	18	25	107	14	113	24
Maryland	5,106	5,178	2,531	2,790	19,658	17,848	178	263	582	189	1,099	327
District of Columbia	11	38	3	4	162	217	2	-	2	1	4	-
Virginia	39,113	37,470	18,229	17,228	42,266	35,161	3,450	3,726	10,816	3,467	6,418	4,739
West Virginia	581	694	245	270	1,390	1,061	41	44	27	-	45	6
North Carolina	58,767	49,540	37,479	30,683	40,366	36,382	4,295	4,261	55,090	21,030	24,816	15,674
South Carolina	86,534	75,752	55,596	45,917	52,759	49,274	9,083	9,014	100,029	53,305	45,115	31,682
Georgia	113,687	77,606	62,720	45,707	68,343	64,900	8,499	6,025	98,404	43,029	45,243	27,354
Florida	12,437	12,021	6,212	5,750	14,300	7,174	1,265	1,670	9,834	5,037	6,891	2,947
East South Central												
Kentucky	11,074	11,261	4,257	5,376	19,654	19,890	451	598	599	299	474	282
Tennessee	35,394	32,503	18,925	17,338	22,256	23,034	2,348	2,382	24,861	9,600	4,190	4,281
Alabama	95,581	82,878	58,152	49,275	42,761	44,541	13,118	12,077	102,838	56,343	35,803	30,201
Mississippi	146,454	121,974	77,524	58,939	39,953	42,789	18,513	14,340	153,772	68,631	31,518	28,505
West South Central												
Arkansas	57,728	44,796	28,855	20,849	19,956	20,602	5,601	4,852	49,511	15,931	13,570	9,551
Louisiana	48,814	53,133	23,808	27,329	59,916	47,738	5,346	5,332	37,327	31,160	28,906	22,069
Oklahoma	13,007	6,236[2]	6,330	2,568	6,399	2,199	742	535[2]	6,043	474	1,262	196
Texas	63,302	60,487	36,561	28,225	37,186	27,114	6,184	5,774	54,073	14,671	17,322	7,907
Mountain												
Montana	28	21	5	2	38	19	1	3	3	-	1	-
Idaho	25	9	1	2	18	7	1	-	1	-	-	-
Wyoming	15	5	3	-	17	16	-	1	-	-	-	-
Colorado	91	47	11	5	128	27	5	5	1	-	2	-
New Mexico	37	12	8	2	42	10	4	1	3	-	1	-
Arizona	5	8	1	-	24	5	-	-	-	-	-	-
Utah	14	10	2	4	17	6	-	-	-	-	-	-
Nevada	5	4	-	-	12	7	2	-	-	-	1	-

[Continued]

★ 1355 ★

Farmers, Planters, Overseerer and Other farm Workers: Geographical Area, 1900 and 1910
[Continued]

Division and state	Negro population 10 years of age and over gainfully employed											
	Male						Female					
	Farmers, planters, and overseerers[1]		Farm laborers, home farm		Farm laborers, working out		Farmers, planters, and overseerers[1]		Farm laborers, home farm		Farm laborers, working out	
	1910	1900	1910	1900	1910	1900	1910	1900	1910	1900	1910	1900
Pacific												
Washington	77	43	12	19	97	21	5	2	3	-	6	1
Oregon	32	16	14	5	23	15	4	1	-	-	3	1
California	119	110	16	35	344	228	8	12	3	1	2	3

Source: "Negro Farmers, Planters, and Overseerers: Farm Laborers, Home Farm; and Farm Laborers, Working Out, by Divisions and States: 1910 and 1900." U.S. Bureau of the Census. *Negro Population, 1790-1915.* Washington, D.C.: Government Printing Office, 1918, p. 528. *Notes:* 1. Includes farmers, dairy farmers, cranberry growers, dairy farm foremen and managers, farm and plantation foremen and managers, cranberry bog foremen and managers, and poultry raisers. 2. Includes Indian Territory.

★ 1356 ★

Occupations

Free Blacks: Occupations in Two States and Two Cities, 1850

Occupation	Connecticut			Louisiana			New York City			New Orleans		
	Total	Blacks	Mulattoes	Total	Blacks	Mulattoes	Total	Blacks	Mulattoes	Total	Blacks	Mulattoes
Total	1,973	1,572	401	2,809	492	2,317	3,337	2,617	720	1,792	329	1,463
Apprentices	1	-	1	11	1	10	2	2	-	4	-	4
Architects	-	-	-	1	-	1	-	-	-	1	-	1
Bakers	-	-	-	4	-	4	4	3	1	1	-	1
Barbers	39	18	21	46	6	40	122	80	42	41	6	35
Barkeepers	1	1	-	2	-	2	3	2	1	2	-	2
Basket makers	10	8	2	-	-	-	-	-	-	-	-	-
Blacksmiths	12	8	4	26	6	20	1	-	1	15	4	11
Boarding-house keepers	5	4	1	18	1	17	21	15	6	18	1	17
Boatmen	5	4	1	39	7	32	28	25	3	37	5	32
Bookbinders	-	-	-	4	-	4	-	-	-	4	-	4
Brickmakers	1	1	-	3	-	3	-	-	-	2	-	2
Brokers	-	-	-	9	1	8	-	-	-	9	1	8
Butchers	-	-	-	25	1	24	33	30	3	18	1	17
Cabinetmakers	-	-	-	24	3	21	-	-	-	19	2	17
Capitalists	-	-	-	4	-	4	-	-	-	4	-	4
Carriage makers	2	1	1	-	-	-	-	-	-	-	-	-
Carmen	13	8	5	39	19	20	39	28	11	39	19	20
Carpenters	4	3	1	521	74	447	12	10	2	355	56	299
Cigar makers	-	-	-	169	14	155	8	6	2	156	13	143
Clerks	4	1	3	63	-	63	7	3	4	61	-	61
Clothiers	1	1	-	1	1	-	-	-	-	-	-	-
Collectors	-	-	-	2	-	2	-	-	-	2	-	2
Colliers	5	3	2	-	-	-	-	-	-	-	-	-
Coachmen	16	9	7	12	5	7	107	96	11	10	4	6
Confectioners	-	-	-	-	-	-	2	2	-	-	-	-
Cooks	34	24	10	37	18	19	95	78	17	25	7	18
Coopers	2	2	-	55	18	37	7	7	-	43	17	26
Daguerreotypists	1	1	-	-	-	-	-	-	-	-	-	-
Doctors	-	-	-	6	1	5	9	7	2	4	-	4
Druggists	-	-	-	-	-	-	3	1	2	-	-	-
Dyers	3	2	1	-	-	-	-	-	-	-	-	-

[Continued]

★ 1356 ★

Free Blacks: Occupations in Two States and Two Cities, 1850
[Continued]

Occupation	Connecticut			Louisiana			New York City			New Orleans		
	Total	Blacks	Mulattoes	Total	Blacks	Mulattoes	Total	Blacks	Mulattoes	Total	Blacks	Mulattoes
Engineers	-	-	-	4	-	4	-	-	-	1	-	1
Farmers	146	122	24	158	10	148	24	12	12	-	-	-
Gardeners	5	4	1	13	6	7	7	5	2	9	4	5
Gunsmiths	2	2	-	4	-	4	1	1	-	4	-	4
Hatters	-	-	-	-	-	-	2	2	-	-	-	-
Hostlers	10	9	1	3	-	3	11	10	1	3	-	3
Hunters	-	-	-	9	5	4	-	-	-	7	4	3
Ink makers	-	-	-	-	-	-	5	5	-	-	-	-
Jewelers	-	-	-	5	-	5	3	2	1	5	-	5
Laborers	1,108	914	194	411	139	272	1,144	957	187	179	71	108
Lawyers	-	-	-	-	-	-	4	4	-	-	-	-
Lithographers	-	-	-	1	-	1	-	-	-	1	-	1
Mariners	316	262	54	22	2	20	434	316	118	10	1	9
Market men	-	-	-	32	8	24	15	13	2	25	6	19
Masons	1	1	-	325	68	257	-	-	-	278	65	213
Mechanics (generally)	4	4	-	58	7	51	2	1	1	52	6	46
Merchants	2	1	1	77	8	69	3	2	1	64	6	58
Ministers	12	9	3	1	-	1	21	12	9	1	-	1
Musicians	5	3	2	4	-	4	24	17	7	4	-	4
Music teachers	-	-	-	1	-	1	-	-	-	1	-	1
Overseers	-	-	-	25	3	22	-	-	-	11	1	10
Painters	2	1	1	30	4	26	4	3	1	28	4	24
Peddlers	1	1	-	9	2	7	-	-	-	9	2	7
Pilots	-	-	-	2	-	2	-	-	-	2	-	2
Planters	-	-	-	244	23	221	-	-	-	2	-	2
Powder makers	2	2	-	-	-	-	-	-	-	-	-	-
Printers	1	-	1	-	-	-	4	2	2	-	-	-
Sailmakers	1	1	-	6	1	5	-	-	-	2	-	2
Servants	108	83	25	4	2	2	808	612	196	-	-	-
Sextons	1	1	-	1	-	1	12	9	3	1	-	1
Ship carpenters	1	1	-	6	2	4	-	-	-	6	2	4
Shoemakers	41	28	13	99	18	81	23	18	5	92	16	76
Stevedores	-	-	-	7	1	6	-	-	-	7	1	6
Stewards	4	3	1	11	2	9	44	34	10	9	-	9
Students	1	1	-	7	-	7	1	1	-	7	-	7
Tailors	9	2	7	86	3	83	23	18	5	82	3	79
Tanners	1	1	-	-	-	-	-	-	-	-	-	-
Teachers	-	-	-	15	1	14	8	6	2	12	-	12
Upholsterers	-	-	-	8	1	7	-	-	-	8	1	7
Other occupations	30	17	13	-	-	-	207	160	47	-	-	-

Source: "Occupations of Free Colored Males 15 Years of Age and Over in Two States and in Two Cities: 1850." U.S. Bureau of the Census. *Negro Population in the United States, 1790-1915.* Washington, D.C.: Government Printing Office, 1918, p. 511.

★ 1357 ★
Occupations

Furniture Industry: Occupational Distribution of Employees, United States, 1964-1970

Occupational group	All employees					Negro employees				
	1964	1966	1967	1969	1970	1964	1966	1967	1969	1970
Officials and managers	5.3	6.0	5.9	6.4	6.9	0.3	0.3	0.3	0.5	0.7
Professionals	1.7	1.2	0.9	1.0	1.2	0.1	0.1	0.1	[1]	0.1
Technicians	2.0	1.1	1.2	1.4	1.5	0.1	0.1	0.1	0.2	0.2
Sales workers	3.4	2.0	1.9	2.1	2.0	-	[1]	[1]	[1]	[1]
Office and clerical workers	10.3	7.6	7.2	7.4	7.4	2.2	1.0	1.2	1.4	1.4
Total white collar	22.7	17.9	17.1	18.3	19.0	2.7	1.5	1.7	2.1	2.4
Craftsmen	14.1	18.0	17.8	17.4	17.8	8.8	9.4	9.9	11.5	12.1
Operatives	38.4	40.2	40.7	38.8	39.6	56.0	44.2	44.5	45.4	46.6
Laborers	23.1	22.4	22.9	23.9	22.0	26.6	41.7	41.0	38.1	36.2
Service workers	1.7	1.5	1.5	1.6	1.6	5.9	3.2	2.9	2.9	2.7
Total blue collar	77.3	82.1	82.9	81.7	81.0	97.3	98.5	98.3	97.9	97.5
Total	100.0	100.0	100.0	100.0	100.0	100.0	100.0	100.0	100.0	100.0

Source: "Furniture Industry, Occupational Distribution of Negroes and All Employees, by Percent, United States, 1964-1970," William E. Fulmer, *The Negro in the Furniture Industry*, p. 70. Primary source: Appendix Tables A-1 to A-5. *Note:* 1. Less than 0.05 percent.

★ 1358 ★
Occupations

Furniture Industry: Percent Black Employed by Gender and Occupation, United States, 1964-1970 - I

Occupational group	All employees				
	1964	1966	1967	1969	1970
Officials and managers	0.4	0.5	0.7	1.1	1.4
Professionals	0.3	0.6	0.7	0.5	0.7
Technicians	0.5	0.9	1.2	1.5	1.6
Sales workers	-	[1]	0.1	0.3	0.3
Office and clerical workers	1.4	1.6	2.0	2.5	2.5
Total white collar	0.8	1.0	1.2	1.6	1.7
Craftsmen	4.0	6.1	7.0	8.9	8.9
Operatives	9.3	12.7	13.9	15.7	15.5
Laborers	7.3	21.4	22.8	21.4	21.8
Service workers	22.5	24.3	24.2	24.6	23.0

[Continued]

★ 1358 ★

Furniture Industry: Percent Black Employed by Gender and Occupation, United States, 1964-1970 - I
[Continued]

Occupational group	All employees				
	1964	1966	1967	1969	1970
Total blue collar	8.0	13.8	15.1	16.1	15.9
Total	6.4	11.5	12.7	13.4	13.2

Source: "Furniture Industry, Percent Negro Employed by Sex and Occupational Group, United States, 1964-1970," William E. Fulmer, *The Negro in the Furniture Industry*, p. 66. Primary source: Appendix Tables A-1 to A-5. *Notes:* 1964: 105 establishments; 1966: 978 establishments; 1967: 1,092 establishments; 1969: 1,139 establishments; 1970: 1,170 establishments. 1. Less than 0.05 percent.

★ 1359 ★

Occupations

Furniture Industry: Percent Black Employed by Gender and Occupation, United States, 1964-1970 - II

	Male					Female				
	1964	1966	1967	1969	1970	1964	1966	1967	1969	1970
Officials and managers	0.3	0.5	0.7	1.1	1.4	2.1	0.4	0.6	1.7	2.4
Professionals	0.3	0.7	0.7	0.4	0.6	-	-	0.6	1.5	1.6
Technicians	0.5	0.9	1.2	1.5	1.6	-	0.6	1.2	1.4	2.0
Sales workers	-	1	0.1	0.2	0.2	-	-	-	1.6	1.9
Office and clerical workers	2.0	3.0	4.0	4.1	4.2	1.1	1.1	1.4	2.0	2.0
Total white collar	0.6	0.9	1.2	1.4	1.5	1.0	1.1	1.3	1.9	2.0
Craftsmen	3.9	6.1	7.1	8.6	8.6	6.1	5.3	6.5	10.5	11.4
Operatives	9.3	12.9	14.2	15.6	15.3	9.6	11.5	12.7	16.1	16.2
Laborers	7.5	21.8	22.8	22.5	22.5	6.7	20.3	22.8	19.1	20.5
Service workers	21.7	23.5	23.8	23.5	22.0	29.2	33.3	28.7	32.4	31.6
Total blue collar	7.9	13.8	14.8	15.8	15.4	8.6	14.0	15.9	16.9	17.4
Total	6.6	11.9	12.9	13.5	13.0	5.4	10.1	12.1	13.3	13.8

Source: "Furniture Industry, Percent Negro Employed by Sex and Occupational Group, United States, 1964-1970," William E. Fulmer, *The Negro in the Furniture Industry*, p. 66. Primary source: Appendix Tables A-1 to A-5. *Notes:* 1964: 105 establishments; 1966: 978 establishments; 1967: 1,092 establishments; 1969: 1,139 establishments; 1970: 1,170 establishments. 1. Less than 0.05 percent.

★ 1360 ★

Occupations

Furniture Industry: Percent Black Employment by Gender and Occupation, the Midwest, 1964-1970 - I

Occupational group	All employees					Male				
	1964	1966	1967	1969	1970	1964	1966	1967	1969	1970
Officials and managers	0.4	0.4	0.5	0.9	1.4	0.3	0.4	0.5	0.9	1.3
Professionals	0.4	0.6	0.3	0.2	0.5	0.4	0.7	0.3	0.2	0.6
Technicians	0.3	1.1	1.0	1.2	1.0	0.3	1.0	1.0	1.2	1.0
Sales workers	-	-	-	0.2	0.1	-	-	-	0.1	0.1
Office and clerical workers	0.8	1.2	1.8	1.7	1.7	1.5	1.9	2.5	2.3	2.3
Total white collar	0.5	0.7	1.1	1.1	1.3	0.5	0.7	0.8	0.9	1.1
Craftsmen	4.4	4.9	7.6	6.9	8.6	4.3	4.7	7.5	6.3	7.3
Operatives	8.4	9.7	7.8	6.8	7.4	8.2	9.9	8.0	6.7	7.5
Laborers	11.7	10.5	11.0	9.7	10.0	10.1	11.5	12.1	10.8	10.1
Service workers	18.5	8.0	11.4	10.3	11.0	17.0	7.7	11.6	10.5	10.6
Total blue collar	8.5	8.9	8.6	7.7	8.4	8.0	9.1	8.9	7.7	8.1
Total	6.2	7.1	7.0	6.1	6.6	6.1	7.5	7.3	6.2	6.5

Source: "Furniture Industry, Percent Negro Employment by Sex and Occupational Group, Midwest, 1964-1970," William E. Fulmer, *The Negro in the Furniture Industry*, p. 109. Primary source: Appendix Tables A-20 to A-24.

★ 1361 ★

Occupations

Furniture Industry: Percent Black Employment by Gender and Occupation, the Midwest, 1964-1970 - II

Occupational group	Female				
	1964	1966	1967	1969	1970
Officials and managers	4.3	0.3	0.7	0.6	4.7
Professionals	-	-	-	-	-
Technicians	-	2.1	2.0	2.0	0.9
Sales workers	-	-	-	1.8	-
Office and clerical workers	0.4	0.8	1.6	1.5	1.5
Total white collar	0.4	0.8	1.5	1.5	1.5
Craftsmen	6.0	6.4	8.3	11.3	17.4
Operatives	9.1	8.7	7.3	7.1	7.2
Laborers	20.8	7.0	8.7	8.0	9.9
Service workers	27.0	11.1	10.5	8.9	13.8
Total blue collar	12.1	7.9	7.9	7.8	9.2
Total	6.5	5.5	6.1	6.1	6.9

Source: "Furniture Industry, Percent Negro Employment by Sex and Occupational Group, Midwest, 1964-1970," William E. Fulmer, *The Negro in the Furniture Industry*, p. 109. Primary source: Appendix Tables A-20 to A-24.

★ 1362 ★

Occupations

Furniture Industry: Percent Black Employment by Gender and Occupation, the South, 1964-1970 - I

Occupational group	All employees					Male				
	1964	1966	1967	1969	1970	1964	1966	1967	1969	1970
Officials and managers	0.3	0.4	0.6	1.2	1.4	0.3	0.4	0.6	1.2	1.4
Professionals	-	0.1	0.2	0.3	0.4	-	0.1	0.1	0.2	0.3
Technicians	-	0.1	1.3	1.4	1.6	-	0.1	1.4	1.4	1.4
Sales workers	-	0.1	0.1	0.3	0.3	-	0.1	0.1	0.2	0.2
Office and clerical workers	1.0	1.5	1.8	2.2	2.5	2.9	4.2	5.1	5.7	6.8
Total white collar	0.5	0.8	1.1	1.5	1.7	0.5	1.0	1.3	1.6	1.8
Craftsmen	2.8	7.6	8.0	10.3	10.5	3.0	7.9	8.3	10.2	10.2
Operatives	11.8	16.6	19.1	22.6	23.0	12.5	16.6	19.1	22.3	22.3
Laborers	5.8	28.8	31.5	30.6	31.1	6.3	29.5	30.9	31.7	32.6
Service workers	30.9	39.7	37.3	38.2	33.0	29.0	38.5	36.2	35.6	31.4
Total blue collar	8.1	18.5	20.7	22.6	22.5	8.5	18.4	19.9	22.0	21.6
Total	6.9	16.2	18.0	19.6	19.5	7.6	16.6	17.8	19.5	19.0

Source: "Furniture Industry, Percent Negro Employment by Sex and Occupational Group, South, 1964-1970," William E. Fulmer, *The Negro in the Furniture Industry*, p. 98. Primary source: Appendix Tables A-10 to A-14.

★ 1363 ★

Occupations

Furniture Industry: Percent Black Employment by Gender and Occupation, the South, 1964-1970 - II

Occupational group	Female				
	1964	1966	1967	1969	1970
Officials and managers	-	0.5	0.5	1.5	1.1
Professionals	-	-	1.5	1.0	1.2
Technicians	-	-	-	0.8	3.6
Sales workers	-	-	-	1.6	1.6
Office and clerical workers	0.3	0.6	0.6	1.2	1.3
Total white collar	0.3	0.6	0.6	1.2	1.3
Craftsmen	-	5.2	5.7	10.9	12.2
Operatives	6.0	17.1	19.0	23.4	24.9
Laborers	2.8	26.1	33.3	28.4	28.7
Service workers	72.7	52.7	51.2	60.8	45.9
Total blue collar	4.3	19.2	23.7	24.4	25.0
Total	3.0	14.5	18.9	20.1	20.8

Source: "Furniture Industry, Percent Negro Employment by Sex and Occupational Group, South, 1964-1970," William E. Fulmer, *The Negro in the Furniture Industry*, p. 98. Primary source: Appendix Tables A-10 to A-14.

★ 1364 ★

Occupations

Furniture Industry: Percent Black Employment by Gender and Occupation, the West, 1964-1969

Occupational group	All employees				Male				Female			
	1964	1966	1967	1969	1964	1966	0967	1969	1964	1966	1967	1969
Officials and managers	-	1.6	1.7	1.5	-	1.6	1.7	1.6	-	-	-	-
Professionals	-	-	4.2	1.0	-	-	4.5	1.1	-	-	-	-
Technicians	10.0	4.8	6.1	3.7	10.3	5.2	5.1	4.2	-	-	25.0	-
Sales workers	-	-	-	0.2	-	-	-	0.2	-	-	-	-
Office and clerical workers	1.3	2.3	2.4	1.3	1.0	4.5	5.2	1.8	1.4	1.4	1.1	1.2
Total white collar	1.1	1.7	2.0	1.3	1.0	2.0	2.4	1.4	1.3	1.2	1.1	1.0
Craftsmen	3.8	6.6	6.2	6.0	3.8	6.8	6.4	5.6	3.7	5.9	5.2	8.5
Operatives	11.4	11.1	14.7	10.8	11.0	12.1	16.5	11.8	13.2	7.1	7.3	5.9
Laborers	5.4	21.9	9.8	10.3	5.9	25.4	11.3	11.8	-	3.9	3.3	6.1
Service workers	41.0	20.3	14.5	12.7	51.6	21.7	14.2	12.4	-	-	25.0	14.3
Total blue collar	10.1	12.4	11.5	9.5	9.9	13.9	12.8	10.2	11.0	6.1	5.8	6.4

Source: "Furniture Industry, Percent Negro Employment by Sex and Occupational Group, West, 1964-1969," William E. Fulmer, *The Negro in the Furniture Industry*, p. 109. Primary source: .

★ 1365 ★

Occupations

Furniture Industry: Percent Black Employment by Gender and Occupational Group, Middle Atlantic, 1964-1969 - I

Occupational group	All employees					Male				
	1964	1966	1967	1969	1970	1964	1966	1967	1969	1970
Officials and managers	0.5	0.9	1.0	1.7	1.9	0.5	0.9	0.9	1.6	1.8
Professionals	1.1	1.1	1.5	1.7	1.7	1.2	1.1	1.7	1.2	1.5
Technicians	-	0.9	1.2	2.1	2.9	-	0.9	1.2	2.2	3.1
Sales workers	-	-	0.1	0.4	0.5	-	-	0.1	0.2	0.3
Office and clerical workers	2.9	2.9	3.4	5.8	5.7	2.9	3.3	4.7	6.0	5.0
Total white collar	1.6	1.7	2.0	3.3	3.3	1.0	1.3	1.6	2.1	2.1
Craftsmen	5.6	3.4	4.2	9.2	6.3	5.0	3.2	3.8	9.1	6.3
Operatives	8.4	9.1	10.8	12.8	9.0	7.8	9.4	11.2	12.1	9.7
Laborers	6.8	12.1	14.0	14.8	11.6	8.7	11.9	15.5	17.1	12.2
Service workers	12.2	8.7	7.8	7.1	11.2	11.3	8.6	8.1	7.2	11.7
Total blue collar	7.5	8.5	10.1	12.3	9.1	7.4	8.4	10.4	12.4	9.6
Total	6.1	6.9	8.5	10.4	7.9	6.2	7.0	9.0	10.5	8.2

Source: "Furniture Industry, Percent Negro Employment by Sex and Occupational Group, Middle Atlantic States," William E. Fulmer, *The Negro in the Furniture Industry*, p. 90. Primary source: Appendix Tables A-10 to A-14.

★ 1366 ★

Occupations

Furniture Industry: Percent Black Employment by Gender and Occupational Group, Middle Atlantic, 1964-1969 - II

Occupational group	Female				
	1964	1966	1967	1969	1970
Officials and managers	-	1.5	1.4	4.9	3.9
Professionals	-	-	-	8.0	2.9
Technicians	-	-	-	2.0	-
Sales workers	-	-	-	2.2	2.9
Office and clerical workers	2.8	2.7	2.9	5.7	6.0
Total white collar	2.7	2.6	2.7	5.5	5.6
Craftsmen	11.9	6.3	9.1	10.9	6.8
Operatives	11.9	7.8	9.0	15.3	6.5
Laborers	0.3	12.8	7.3	6.4	9.9
Service workers	21.4	9.5	2.8	5.9	4.9
Total blue collar	8.2	9.1	8.5	12.1	7.6
Total	5.8	6.5	6.5	9.9	7.0

Source: "Furniture Industry, Percent Negro Employment by Sex and Occupational Group, Middle Atlantic States," William E. Fulmer, *The Negro in the Furniture Industry*, p. 90. Primary source: Appendix Tables A-10 to A-14.

★ 1367 ★

Occupations

Furniture Industry: Percent Black Employment by Gender and Occupational Group, New England, 1964-1969

Occupational group	All employees				Male				Female			
	1964	1966	1967	1969	1964	1966	1967	1969	1964	1966	1967	1969
Officials and managers	-	-	0.5	0.2	-	-	0.5	0.2	-	-	-	-
Professionals	-	-	-	-	-	-	-	-	-	-	-	-
Technicians	-	-	-	1.0	-	-	-	1.1	-	-	-	-
Service workers	-	0.8	-	-	-	0.8	-	-	-	-	-	-
Office and clerical workers	0.7	-	2.5	0.5	1.8	-	-	-	-	-	3.0	0.6
Total white collar	0.3	0.1	1.2	0.3	0.4	0.2	0.3	0.2	-	-	2.7	0.5
Craftsmen	1.4	0.4	2.3	0.9	1.4	0.5	2.4	1.0	-	-	1.4	0.6
Operatives	4.8	1.1	2.2	0.9	4.3	1.2	2.0	0.7	7.7	0.5	2.8	1.4
Laborers	4.1	3.0	2.8	2.0	4.3	3.3	2.9	1.6	-	2.4	2.5	3.1
Service workers	-	-	7.1	0.8	-	-	7.1	-	-	-	-	7.7

[Continued]

★ 1367 ★

Furniture Industry: Percent Black Employment by Gender and Occupational Group, New England, 1964-1969
[Continued]

Occupational group	All employees				Male				Female			
	1964	1966	1967	1969	1964	1966	1967	1969	1964	1966	1967	1969
Total blue collar	3.4	1.5	2.4	1.3	3.1	1.6	2.4	1.0	5.9	1.3	2.5	2.1
Total	2.6	1.2	2.2	1.1	2.6	1.3	2.1	0.9	2.7	0.9	2.6	1.6

Source: "Furniture Industry, Percent Negro Employment by Sex and Occupational Group, New England," William E. Fulmer, *The Negro in the Furniture Industry*, p. 88. Primary source: Appendix Tables A-6 to A-9.

★ 1368 ★
Occupations

Labor Force: Farmers, Planters, and Overseers: by Region, 1900 and 1910

Section	Negro farmers, planters, and overseers per 1,000 farm laborers working out			
	Male		Female	
	1910	1900	1910	1900
United States	1,548	1,473	302	385
The South	1,606	1,519	301	382
The North	444	589	1	1
The West	1	1	1	1

Source: "Negro Farmers, Planters, and Overseers Per 1,000 Farm Laborers Working Out," U.S. Bureau of the Census, *Negro Population, 1790-1915*, p. 508. *Note:* 1. Number of farm laborers working out, less than 1,000.

★ 1369 ★
Occupations

Labor Force: Region, Occupational Class and Year, 1900 and 1910

Occupational class and year	Negro population 10 years of age and over gainfully employed						
	United States	The South				The North	The West
		Total	South Atlantic division	East South Central division	West South Central division		
Male							
Number							
Farmers, planters, and overseers[1]							
1910	799,923	788,393	317,039	288,503	182,851	11,082	448

[Continued]

★ 1369 ★

Labor Force: Region, Occupational Class and Year, 1900 and 1910
[Continued]

Occupational class and year	Negro population 10 years of age and over gainfully employed						
	United States	The South				The North	The West
		Total	South Atlantic division	East South Central division	West South Central division		
1900	686,157	672,355	259,087	248,616	164,652	13,517	285
Farm laborers, home farm							
1910	441,203	437,882	183,470	158,858	95,554	3,248	73
1900	363,528	358,607	148,708	130,928	78,971	4,847	74
Farm laborers, working out							
1910	516,632	490,887	242,806	124,624	123,457	24,985	760
1900	465,980	442,670	214,763	130,254	97,653	22,949	361
Increase: 1900-1910[2]							
Farmers, planters, and overseers	113,766	116,038	57,952	39,887	18,199	-2,435	163
Farm laborers, home farm	77,675	79,275	34,762	27,930	16,583	-1,599	-1
Farm laborers, working out	50,652	48,217	28,043	-5,630	25,804	2,036	399
				Female			
Number							
Farmers, planters, and overseers[1]							
1910	79,677	79,134	26,831	34,430	17,873	513	30
1900	71,665	70,918	25,028	29,397	16,493	722	25
Farm laborers, home farm							
1910	704,150	703,915	274,891	282,070	146,954	221	14
1900	323,295	323,181	126,072	134,873	62,236	113	1
Farm laborers, working out							
1910	263,403	262,789	129,744	71,985	61,060	598	16
1900	185,931	185,745	82,753	63,269	39,723	181	5
Increase: 1900-1910[2]							
Farmers, planters, and overseers	8,012	8,216	1,803	5,033	1,380	-209	5
Farm laborers, home farm	380,855	380,734	148,819	147,197	84,718	108	13
Farm laborers, working out	77,472	77,044	46,991	8,716	21,337	417	11

Source: "Negro Population 10 Years of Age and Over Gainfully," U.S. Bureau of the Census, *Negro Population, 1790-1915*, p. 508. *Notes:* 1. Includes farmers, dairy farmers, cranberry growers, dairy farm foremen and managers, farm and plantation foremen and managers, cranberry bog foremen and managers, and poultry raisers. 2. A minus sign (-) denotes decrease.

★ 1370 ★

Occupations

Longshore Industry: Percent Distribution of Employees by Region and Selected States, 1910-1970

	Total United States	Region				
		Northeast (4)	South Atlantic (5)	South Central (3)	North Central (2)	West (1)
1910						
Total	62,813	30,392	10,462	5,928	2,239	2,593
Percent	100.0	48.4	16.7	9.4	3.6	4.1
Negro	16,379	2,837	8,938	3,146	229	38
Percent	100.0	17.3	54.6	19.2	1.4	0.2
1920						
Total	85,605	49,570	13,311	9,108	n.a.	3,728
Percent	100.0	57.9	15.5	10.6	-	4.4
Negro	27,206	8,496	11,595	5,924	n.a.	44
Percent	100.0	31.2	42.6	21.8	-	0.2
1930						
Total	73,944	33,990	11,072	10,691	705	6,346
Percent	100.0	46.0	15.0	14.5	1.0	8.6
Negro	25,434	6,406	8,700	8,075	n.a.	91
Percent	100.0	25.2	34.2	31.7	-	0.4
1940						
Total	63,241	25,552	10,879	9,539	1,443	6,865
Percent	100.0	40.4	17.2	15.1	2.3	10.9
Negro	20,279	3,486	9,077	6,682	104	83
Percent	100.0	17.2	44.8	33.0	0.5	0.4
1950						
Total	62,003	26,707	7,938	10,026	1,080	8,481
Percent	100.0	43.1	12.8	16.2	1.7	13.7
Negro	21,197	4,740	6,367	6,912	170	2,032
Percent	100.0	22.4	30.0	32.6	0.8	9.6
1960						
Total	55,479	20,640	6,495	10,417	939	7,869
Percent	100.0	37.2	11.7	18.8	1.7	14.2
Negro	19,129	3,596	5,118	7,105	385	1,820
Percent	100.0	18.8	26.8	37.1	2.0	9.5
1970						
Total	42,349	12,530	5,886	8,508	978	6,276
Percent	100.0	29.6	13.9	20.1	2.3	14.8
Negro	15,326	2,606	4,325	5,018	434	1,636
Percent	100.0	17.0	28.2	32.7	2.8	10.7

Source: "Longshore Industry, Percent Distribution of Total and Negro Employment by Region, Selected States, 1910-1970," Lester Rubin, *The Negro in the Longshore Industry*, p. 38. Published by permission. *Notes:* Totals do not equal sum of entries due to the exclusion of all but 15 states.

★ 1371 ★
Occupations

Males and Females in Occupations: by State, 1910

Division and state	Negroes 10 Years of age and over: 1910					
	Male			Female		
	Total number	Engaged in gainful occupations		Total number	Engaged in gainful occupations	
		Number	Percent		Number	Percent
United States	3,637,386	3,178,564	87.4	3,680,536	2,013,981	54.7
Geographic divisions:						
New England	27,389	23,607	86.2	27,932	13,899	49.8
Middle Atlantic	171,008	148,638	86.9	180,538	94,457	52.3
East North Central	133,614	113,526	85.0	120,931	46,813	38.7
West North Central	106,567	89,765	84.2	97,074	39,148	40.3
South Atlantic	1,470,297	1,280,335	87.1	1,516,639	828,451	54.6
East South Central	970,921	866,089	89.2	989,977	604,003	61.0
West South Central	732,945	634,809	86.6	727,760	378,666	52.0
Mountain	10,461	9,125	87.2	8,294	3,735	45.0
Pacific	14,184	12,660	89.3	11,391	4,809	42.2
New England						
Maine	610	591	96.9	556	206	37.1
New Hampshire	247	239	96.8	233	128	54.9
Vermont	1,089	1,022	93.8	357	123	34.5
Massachusetts	15,629	13,488	86.3	16,089	8,026	49.9
Rhode Island	3,839	3,347	87.2	4,074	2,059	50.5
Connecticut	5,975	4,920	82.3	6,623	3,357	50.7
Middle Atlantic						
New York	55,170	49,205	89.2	60,673	34,782	57.3
New Jersey	36,191	30,918	85.4	38,386	20,004	52.1
Pennsylvania	79,647	68,515	86.0	81,479	39,671	48.7
East North Central						
Ohio	49,297	41,243	83.7	44,613	17,593	39.4
Indiana	26,258	21,932	83.5	24,392	9,534	39.1
Illinois	49,031	42,624	86.9	43,897	17,105	39.0
Michigan	7,727	6,511	84.3	6,830	2,133	31.2
Wisconsin	1,301	1,216	93.5	1,199	448	37.4
West North Central						
Minnesota	3,835	3,479	90.7	2,531	923	36.5
Iowa	6,813	5,843	85.8	5,567	1,781	32.0
Missouri	68,113	57,984	85.1	64,272	28,796	44.8
North Dakota	348	309	88.8	198	86	43.4
South Dakota	404	337	83.4	293	91	31.1
Nebraska	3,751	3,366	89.7	2,974	1,175	39.5
Kansas	23,303	18,447	79.2	21,239	6,296	29.6
South Atlantic						
Delaware	12,886	10,512	81.6	11,891	5,313	44.7
Maryland	89,335	75,495	84.5	91,119	45,231	49.6
District of Columbia	35,540	28,937	81.4	44,424	26,699	60.1
Virginia	243,957	205,093	84.1	252,461	102,729	40.7
West Virginia	30,058	26,527	88.3	20,867	6,360	30.5
North Carolina	236,640	209,373	88.5	253,755	141,391	55.7

[Continued]

★ 1371 ★

Males and Females in Occupations: by State, 1910
[Continued]

Division and state	Negroes 10 Years of age and over: 1910					
	Male			Female		
	Total number	Engaged in gainful occupations		Total number	Engaged in gainful occupations	
		Number	Percent		Number	Percent
South Carolina	282,305	250,443	88.7	301,759	201,623	66.8
Georgia	415,552	366,612	88.2	430,643	248,924	57.8
Florida	124,024	107,343	86.6	109,720	50,181	45.7
East South Central						
Kentucky	105,770	89,018	84.2	104,258	46,510	44.6
Tennessee	177,698	154,155	86.8	182,965	92,220	50.4
Alabama	325,655	295,019	90.6	336,701	214,533	63.7
Mississippi	361,798	327,897	90.6	366,053	250,740	68.5
West South Central						
Arkansas	165,880	148,088	89.3	161,129	93,248	57.9
Louisiana	259,937	222,284	85.5	265,513	128,512	48.4
Oklahoma	53,686	44,793	83.4	47,471	17,659	37.2
Texas	253,442	219,644	86.7	253,647	139,247	54.9
Mountain						
Montana	963	819	85.0	670	312	46.6
Idaho	364	335	92.0	214	106	49.5
Wyoming	1,442	1,390	96.4	582	283	48.6
Colorado	5,154	4,385	85.1	4,836	2,132	44.1
New Mexico	766	672	87.7	578	247	42.7
Arizona	892	743	83.3	799	402	50.3
Utah	634	555	87.5	392	135	34.4
Nevada	246	226	91.9	223	118	52.9
Pacific						
Washington	3,473	3,103	89.3	2,044	776	38.0
Oregon	838	810	96.7	521	230	44.1
California	9,873	8,747	88.6	8,826	3,803	43.1

Source: "Negro Males and Females 10 Years of Age and Over Engaged in Gainful Occupations, by Divisions and States: 1910."
U.S. Bureau of the Census. *Negro Population, 1790-1915.* Washington, D.C.: Government Printing Office, 1918, p. 512.

★ 1372 ★

Occupations

Men and Women Employed in Agriculture, Forestry, and Animal Husbandry: by States, 1910: Part 1

Occupation	United States			Alabama		Arizona	
	Both sexes	Male	Female	Male	Female	Male	Female
Agriculture, forestry, and animal husbandry	2,893,375	1,842,238	1,051,137	201,852	152,054	65	1
Agriculture	2,857,618	1,806,767	1,050,851	199,897	152,042	43	1
Dairy farms							
Farmers	208	174	34	5	-	-	-
Foremen	15	14	1	-	-	-	-
Laborers	2,721	2,302	419	141	63	-	-
Farms[1]							
Farmers	877,818	798,509	79,309	95,500	13,096	5	-
Foremen	1,692	1,423	269	86	19	-	-
Laborers							
Home farm	1,145,353	441,203	704,150	58,152	102,838	1	-
Working out	780,035	516,632	263,403	42,761	35,803	24	-
Turpentine farms	24,371	24,087	284	2,034	24	-	-
Gardens and greenhouses							
Florists	116	96	20	1	2	-	-
Gardeners	4,466	4,009	457	151	46	3	-
Foremen	72	61	11	1	-	-	-
Laborers							
Gardens	13,825	11,801	2,024	715	96	3	-
Greenhouses	771	729	42	35	1	-	-
Orchards, nurseries, etc.							
Fruit growers and nurserymen	335	303	32	7	-	-	1
Foremen	49	45	4	3	-	-	-
Laborers	2,960	2,589	371	190	54	-	-
Other pursuits							
Corn shellers, hay balers, thrashers, etc.	96	96	-	1	-	-	-
Cranberry bog laborers	455	443	12	-	-	-	-
Ditchers	1,751	1,751	-	77	-	-	-
Landscape gardeners	230	230	-	27	-	-	-
Not specified	279	270	9	10	-	7	-
Forestry	25,508	25,474	34	1,774	1	1	-
Foresters	17	17	-	-	-	-	-
Log and timber camps and lumbering							
Owners and managers of camps	195	195	-	24	-	-	-
Foremen and overseerers	111	111	-	3	-	-	-
Lumbermen and raftsmen	14,021	14,005	16	1,028	1	-	-
Teamsters and haulers	2,465	2,465	-	288	-	-	-
Woodchoppers and tie cutters	8,699	8,681	18	431	-	1	-
Animal husbandry	10,249	9,997	252	181	11	21	-
Apiarists	24	23	1	1	1	-	-
Fishermen and oystermen	8,268	8,160	108	126	4	-	-
Poultry raisers and poultry yard laborers	368	261	107	5	4	-	-

[Continued]

★ 1372 ★

Men and Women Employed in Agriculture, Forestry, and Animal Husbandry: by States, 1910: Part 1

[Continued]

Occupation	United States			Alabama		Arizona	
	Both sexes	Male	Female	Male	Female	Male	Female
Stock herders, drovers, and feeders	1,387	1,366	21	47	2	16	-
Stock raisers	202	187	15	2	-	5	-

Source: "Negro Males and females 10 Years of Age and Gainfully Employed in Agriculture, Forestry, and Animal Husbandry, by States 1910." U.S. Bureau of the Census. *Negro Population, 1790-1915.* Washington, D.C.: Government Printing Office, 1918, p. 513. Adapted by the Editors. *Note:* 1. Includes turpentine farms.

★ 1373 ★

Occupations

Men and Women Employed in Agriculture, Forestry, and Animal Husbandry: by States, 1910: Part 2

Occupation	Arkansas		California		Colorado	
	Male	Female	Male	Female	Male	Female
Agriculture, forestry, and animal husbandry	108,709	68,790	768	21	262	8
Agriculture	107,069	68,777	694	19	250	7
Dairy farms						
Farmers	6	3	3	-	2	-
Foremen	-	-	-	-	-	-
Laborers	36	17	15	-	1	-
Farms[1]						
Farmers	57,669	5,568	109	6	87	4
Foremen	52	26	5	1	1	-
Laborers						
Home farm	28,855	49,511	16	3	11	1
Working out	19,956	13,570	344	2	128	2
Turpentine farms	-	-	-	-	-	-
Gardens and greenhouses						
Florists	-	-	-	-	-	-
Gardeners	86	19	12	-	3	-
Foremen	10	7	-	-	-	-
Laborers						
Gardens	289	49	133	5	11	-
Greenhouses	10	1	2	-	-	-
Orchards, nurseries, etc.						
Fruit growers and nurserymen	5	1	15	1	3	-
Foremen	-	-	1	1	-	-
Laborers	40	5	36	-	1	-
Other pursuits						
Corn shellers, hay balers, thrashers, etc.	3	-	-	-	-	-
Cranberry bog laborers	-	-	-	-	-	-
Ditchers	36	-	1	-	-	-
Landscape gardeners	1	-	2	-	2	-

[Continued]

★ 1373 ★

Men and Women Employed in Agriculture, Forestry, and Animal Husbandry: by States, 1910: Part 2
[Continued]

Occupation	Arkansas		California		Colorado	
	Male	Female	Male	Female	Male	Female
Not specified	15	-	-	-	-	-
Forestry	1,478	4	14	-	-	-
Foresters	1	-	-	-	-	-
Log and timber camps and lumbering						
Owners and managers of camps	8	-	-	-	-	-
Foremen and overseerers	1	-	-	-	-	-
Lumbermen and raftsmen	917	4	3	-	-	-
Teamsters and haulers	109	-	1	-	-	-
Woodchoppers and tie cutters	442	-	10	-	-	-
Animal husbandry	162	9	60	2	12	1
Apiarists	2	-	-	-	-	-
Fishermen and oystermen	135	3	10	-	-	-
Poultry raisers and poultry yard laborers	4	4	3	1	1	1
Stock herders, drovers, and feeders	21	-	30	-	7	-
Stock raisers	-	2	17	1	4	-

Source: "Negro Males and females 10 Years of Age and Gainfully Employed in Agriculture, Forestry, and Animal Husbandry, by States 1910." U.S. Bureau of the Census. *Negro Population, 1790-1915.* Washington, D.C.: Government Printing Office, 1918, p. 513. Adapted by the Editors. *Note:* 1. Includes turpentine farms.

★ 1374 ★

Occupations

Men and Women Employed in Agriculture, Forestry, and Animal Husbandry: by States, 1910: Part 3

Occupation	Connecticut		Delaware		District of Columbia	
	Male	Female	Male	Female	Male	Female
Agriculture, forestry, and animal husbandry	704	12	5,092	253	387	16
Agriculture	673	11	5,048	253	368	16
Dairy farms						
Farmers	2	-	-	-	2	-
Foremen	1	-	-	-	-	-
Laborers	23	-	17	-	14	-
Farms[1]						
Farmers	68	-	794	18	7	2
Foremen	9	-	9	-	2	-
Laborers						
Home farm	22	-	455	107	3	2
Working out	448	9	3,562	113	162	4
Turpentine farms	-	-	-	-	-	-

[Continued]

★ 1374 ★

Men and Women Employed in Agriculture, Forestry, and Animal Husbandry: by States, 1910: Part 3

[Continued]

Occupation	Connecticut		Delaware		District of Columbia	
	Male	Female	Male	Female	Male	Female
Gardens and greenhouses						
Florists	-	-	-	-	6	-
Gardeners	8	-	103	3	9	5
Foremen	-	-	-	-	-	-
Laborers						
Gardens	78	1	70	6	104	2
Greenhouses	4	1	6	5	48	1
Orchards, nurseries, etc.						
Fruit growers and nurserymen	1	-	14	-	1	-
Foremen	-	-	-	-	-	-
Laborers	4	-	14	1	4	-
Other pursuits						
Corn shellers, hay balers, thrashers, etc.	-	-	-	-	-	-
Cranberry bog laborers	-	-	-	-	-	-
Ditchers	-	-	3	-	1	-
Landscape gardeners	4	-	1	-	5	-
Not specified	1	-	-	-	-	-
Forestry	14	-	18	-	4	-
Foresters	-	-	-	-	-	-
Log and timber camps and lumbering						
Owners and managers of camps	-	-	-	-	-	-
Foremen and overseerers	-	-	-	-	-	-
Lumbermen and raftsmen	7	-	13	-	-	-
Teamsters and haulers	5	-	-	-	-	-
Woodchoppers and tie cutters	2	-	5	-	4	-
Animal husbandry	17	1	26	-	15	-
Apiarists	-	-	-	-	-	-
Fishermen and oystermen	14	1	23	-	13	-
Poultry raisers and poultry yard laborers	2	-	-	-	-	-
Stock herders, drovers, and feeders	1	-	3	-	2	-
Stock raisers	-	-	-	-	-	-

Source: "Negro Males and females 10 Years of Age and Gainfully Employed in Agriculture, Forestry, and Animal Husbandry, by States 1910."
U.S. Bureau of the Census. *Negro Population, 1790-1915*. Washington, D.C.: Government Printing Office, 1918, p. 513. Adapted by the editors.
Note: 1. Includes turpentine farms.

★ 1375 ★
Occupations

Men and Women Employed in Agriculture, Forestry, and Animal Husbandry: by States, 1910: Part 4

Occupation	Florida		Georgia		Idaho		Illinois	
	Male	Female	Male	Female	Male	Female	Male	Female
Agriculture, forestry, and animal husbandry	52,348	18,349	258,573	152,513	51	2	4,117	326
Agriculture	47,953	18,330	254,814	152,495	46	2	3,972	323
Dairy farms								
Farmers	6	1	3	4	-	-	2	-
Foremen	-	-	2	-	-	-	-	-
Laborers	67	40	216	74	-	-	16	-
Farms[1]								
Farmers	12,425	1,258	113,655	18,471	24	1	1,311	65
Foremen	110	5	137	25	1	-	15	1
Laborers								
Home farm	6,212	9,834	62,720	98,404	1	1	436	62
Working out	14,300	6,891	68,343	45,243	18	-	1,965	164
Turpentine farms	12,088	137	7,900	96	-	-	-	-
Gardens and greenhouses								
Florists	3	-	7	2	-	-	2	1
Gardeners	408	35	172	28	-	-	90	6
Foremen	2	-	16	-	-	-	-	-
Laborers								
Gardens	914	98	1,141	57	2	-	91	20
Greenhouses	37	1	58	1	-	-	16	-
Orchards, nurseries, etc.								
Fruit growers and nurserymen	136	4	4	2	-	-	7	-
Foremen	24	-	4	-	-	-	1	-
Laborers	996	21	284	88	-	-	11	4
Other pursuits								
Corn shellers, hay balers, thrashers, etc.	1	-	-	-	-	-	2	-
Cranberry bog laborers	-	-	-	-	-	-	-	-
Ditchers	79	-	130	-	-	-	3	-
Landscape gardeners	2	-	11	-	-	-	2	-
Not specified	143	5	11	-	-	-	2	-
Forestry	3,626	9	2,272	6	3	-	93	-
Foresters	2	-	2	-	-	-	-	-
Log and timber camps and lumbering								
Owners and managers of camps	28	-	20	-	-	-	-	-
Foremen and overseers	14	-	12	-	-	-	-	-
Lumbermen and raftsmen	1,468	3	778	-	2	-	22	-
Teamsters and haulers	337	-	245	-	-	-	6	-
Woodchoppers and tie cutters	1,777	6	2,215	6	1	-	65	-
Animal husbandry	769	10	487	12	2	-	52	3
Apiarists	5	-	-	-	-	-	1	-
Fishermen and oystermen	727	7	455	10	-	-	20	2
Poultry raisers and poultry yard laborers	15	1	8	2	-	-	13	-

[Continued]

★ 1375 ★

Men and Women Employed in Agriculture, Forestry, and Animal Husbandry: by States, 1910: Part 4

[Continued]

Occupation	Florida		Georgia		Idaho		Illinois	
	Male	Female	Male	Female	Male	Female	Male	Female
Stock herders, drovers, and feeders	12	-	22	-	1	-	13	-
Stock raisers	10	2	2	-	1	-	5	1

Source: "Negro Males and females 10 Years of Age and Gainfully Employed in Agriculture, Forestry, and Animal Husbandry, by States 1910." U.S. Bureau of the Census. *Negro Population, 1790-1915.* Washington, D.C.: Government Printing Office, 1918, p. 513. *Note:* 1. Includes turpentine farms.

★ 1376 ★

Occupations

Men and Women Employed in Agriculture, Forestry, and Animal Husbandry: by States, 1910: Part 5

Occupation	Indiana		Iowa		Kansas	
	Male	Female	Male	Female	Male	Female
Agriculture, forestry, and animal husbandry	2,595	49	475	35	3,109	123
Agriculture	2,550	47	434	30	3,064	114
Dairy farms						
Farmers	1	-	2	-	1	-
Foremen	-	-	1	-	-	-
Laborers	26	-	-	-	8	-
Farms[1]						
Farmers	710	23	188	12	1,349	64
Foremen	9	1	3	-	8	-
Laborers						
Home farm	246	9	58	5	430	9
Working out	1,458	11	135	11	1,001	21
Turpentine farms	-	-	-	-	-	-
Gardens and greenhouses						
Florists	1	-	1	-	-	-
Gardeners	35	-	12	2	118	10
Foremen	-	-	-	-	1	-
Laborers						
Gardens	36	1	17	-	69	6
Greenhouses	9	2	1	-	2	-
Orchards, nurseries, etc.						
Fruit growers and nurserymen	2	-	3	-	9	3
Foremen	-	-	-	-	-	-
Laborers	5	-	-	-	57	1
Other pursuits						
Corn shellers, hay balers, thrashers, etc.	3	-	-	-	-	-
Cranberry bog laborers	-	-	-	-	-	-
Ditchers	9	-	13	-	6	-
Landscape gardeners	-	-	-	-	5	-

[Continued]

★ 1376 ★

Men and Women Employed in Agriculture, Forestry, and Animal Husbandry: by States, 1910: Part 5

[Continued]

Occupation	Indiana		Iowa		Kansas	
	Male	Female	Male	Female	Male	Female
Not specified	-	-	-	-	-	-
Forestry	19	-	2	-	3	-
Foresters	-	-	-	-	1	-
Log and timber camps and lumbering						
Owners and managers of camps	-	-	-	-	-	-
Foremen and overseerers	-	-	-	-	-	-
Lumbermen and raftsmen	3	-	1	-	-	-
Teamsters and haulers	3	-	-	-	-	-
Woodchoppers and tie cutters	13	-	1	-	2	-
Animal husbandry	26	2	39	5	42	9
Apiarists	-	-	-	-	-	-
Fishermen and oystermen	4	-	5	-	9	-
Poultry raisers and poultry yard laborers	14	2	31	4	7	8
Stock herders, drovers, and feeders	7	-	2	-	16	1
Stock raisers	1	-	1	1	10	-

Source: "Negro Males and females 10 Years of Age and Gainfully Employed in Agriculture, Forestry, and Animal Husbandry, by States 1910." U.S. Bureau of the Census. *Negro Population, 1790-1915.* Washington, D.C.: Government Printing Office, 1918, p. 514. Adapted by the editors. *Note:* 1. Includes turpentine farms.

★ 1377 ★

Occupations

Men and Women Employed in Agriculture, Forestry, and Animal Husbandry: by States, 1910: Part 6

Occupation	Massachusetts		Michigan		Minnesota		Mississippi	
	Male	Female	Male	Female	Male	Female	Male	Female
Agriculture, forestry, and animal husbandry	1,115	42	1,334	52	151	10	268,570	204,024
Agriculture	1,053	42	1,286	50	143	10	265,921	204,014
Dairy farms								
Farmers	1	1	1	1	-	-	3	5
Foremen	-	-	-	-	-	-	2	-
Laborers	16	-	2	-	-	-	117	47
Farms[1]								
Farmers	66	4	580	25	60	1	146,309	18,484
Foremen	2	1	5	2	1	1	146	22
Laborers								
Home farm	15	7	131	12	12	2	77,524	153,772
Working out	346	8	487	8	63	6	39,953	31,518
Turpentine farms	-	-	-	-	-	-	784	8

[Continued]

★ 1377 ★

Men and Women Employed in Agriculture, Forestry, and Animal Husbandry: by States, 1910: Part 6

[Continued]

Occupation	Massachusetts		Michigan		Minnesota		Mississippi	
	Male	Female	Male	Female	Male	Female	Male	Female
Gardens and greenhouses								
Florists	7	1	-	-	-	-	5	1
Gardeners	14	-	28	1	4	-	171	50
Foremen	-	-	-	-	-	-	-	2
Laborers								
Gardens	133	4	22	-	2	-	696	90
Greenhouses	7	-	1	1	-	-	22	2
Orchards, nurseries, etc.								
Fruit growers and nurserymen	2	1	11	-	1	-	3	-
Foremen	-	-	-	-	-	-	1	-
Laborers	19	2	8	-	-	-	34	13
Other pursuits								
Corn shellers, hay balers, thrashers, etc.	-	-	3	-	-	-	-	-
Cranberry bog laborers	423	12	-	-	-	-	-	-
Ditchers	-	-	7	-	-	-	147	-
Landscape gardeners	2	-	-	-	-	-	-	-
Not specified	-	1	-	-	-	-	4	-
Forestry	8	-	40	-	7	-	2,457	2
Foresters	4	-	-	-	-	-	-	-
Log and timber camps and lumbering								
Owners and managers of camps	-	-	2	-	2	-	17	-
Foremen and overseerers	-	-	-	-	-	-	8	-
Lumbermen and raftsmen	3	-	32	-	3	-	1,497	1
Teamsters and haulers	-	-	5	-	1	-	438	-
Woodchoppers and tie cutters	1	-	1	-	1	-	497	1
Animal husbandry	54	-	8	2	1	-	192	8
Apiarists	-	-	-	-	-	-	3	-
Fishermen and oystermen	49	-	4	-	-	-	140	3
Poultry raisers and poultry yard laborers	4	-	1	2	1	-	7	3
Stock herders, drovers, and feeders	1	-	2	-	-	-	41	2
Stock raisers	-	-	1	-	-	-	1	-

Source: "Negro Males and females 10 Years of Age and Gainfully Employed in Agriculture, Forestry, and Animal Husbandry, by States 1910." U.S. Bureau of the Census. *Negro Population, 1790-1915.* Washington, D.C.: Government Printing Office, 1918, p. 514. Adapted by the Editors. *Note:* 1. Includes turpentine farms.

★ 1378 ★

Occupations

Men and Women Employed in Agriculture, Forestry, and Animal Husbandry: by States, 1910: Part 7

Occupation	Kentucky		Louisiana		Maine		Maryland	
	Male	Female	Male	Female	Male	Female	Male	Female
Agriculture, forestry, and animal husbandry	35,989	1,548	140,015	71,858	119	5	31,444	2,103
Agriculture	35,637	1,541	135,162	71,844	84	4	29,072	2,084
Dairy farms								
Farmers	4	-	13	2	1	-	7	-
Foremen	-	-	-	1	-	-	-	-
Laborers	82	4	194	38	1	-	218	11
Farms[1]								
Farmers	11,039	444	48,645	5,333	34	2	5,040	173
Foremen	31	4	157	8	-	-	57	2
Laborers								
Home farm	4,257	599	23,808	37,327	7	-	2,531	582
Working out	19,654	474	59,916	28,906	38	2	19,658	1,099
Turpentine farms	-	-	713	-	-	-	-	-
Gardens and greenhouses								
Florists	5	-	12	-	-	-	4	-
Gardeners	118	7	339	31	-	-	470	20
Foremen	1	-	1	-	-	-	3	-
Laborers								
Gardens	366	5	630	143	3	-	844	132
Greenhouses	29	-	63	13	-	-	41	1
Orchards, nurseries, etc.								
Fruit growers and nurserymen	2	2	16	-	-	-	6	2
Foremen	-	-	1	1	-	-	1	-
Laborers	15	2	97	41	-	-	163	62
Other pursuits								
Corn shellers, hay balers, thrashers, etc.	6	-	2	-	-	-	4	-
Cranberry bog laborers	-	-	-	-	-	-	-	-
Ditchers	24	-	530	-	-	-	24	-
Landscape gardeners	4	-	5	-	-	-	1	-
Not specified	-	-	20	-	-	-	-	-
Forestry	79	-	4,386	4	9	-	249	3
Foresters	1	-	-	-	-	-	-	-
Log and timber camps and lumbering								
Owners and managers of camps	1	-	13	-	1	-	-	-
Foremen and overseerers	-	-	37	-	-	-	-	-
Lumbermen and raftsmen	28	-	2,801	3	7	-	93	1
Teamsters and haulers	21	-	272	-	-	-	34	-
Woodchoppers and tie cutters	28	-	1,263	1	1	-	122	2
Animal husbandry	273	7	467	10	26	1	2,123	16
Apiarists	1	-	1	-	-	-	-	-
Fishermen and oystermen	12	-	409	5	26	1	2,074	13
Poultry raisers and poultry yard laborers	10	6	4	2	-	-	18	3

[Continued]

★ 1378 ★

Men and Women Employed in Agriculture, Forestry, and Animal Husbandry: by States, 1910: Part 7

[Continued]

Occupation	Kentucky		Louisiana		Maine		Maryland	
	Male	Female	Male	Female	Male	Female	Male	Female
Stock herders, drovers, and feeders	244	1	46	2	-	-	30	-
Stock raisers	6	-	7	1	-	-	1	-

Source: "Negro Males and females 10 Years of Age and Gainfully Employed in Agriculture, Forestry, and Animal Husbandry, by States 1910." U.S. Bureau of the Census. *Negro Population, 1790-1915.* Washington, D.C.: Government Printing Office, 1918, p. 514. Adapted by the editors. *Note:* 1. Includes turpentine farms.

★ 1379 ★

Occupations

Men and Women Employed in Agriculture, Forestry, and Animal Husbandry: by States, 1910: Part 8

Occupation	Missouri		Montana		Nebraska		Nevada	
	Male	Female	Male	Female	Male	Female	Male	Female
Agriculture, forestry, and animal husbandry	11,893	394	96	5	206	5	24	3
Agriculture	11,722	389	73	5	187	5	18	3
Dairy farms								
Farmers	3	1	-	-	-	-	-	-
Foremen	-	-	-	-	-	-	-	-
Laborers	28	-	-	-	2	-	-	-
Farms[1]								
Farmers	3,487	146	28	1	91	5	5	2
Foremen	14	7	-	-	1	-	-	-
Laborers								
Home farm	1,060	69	5	3	10	-	-	-
Working out	6,862	150	38	1	67	-	12	1
Turpentine farms	-	-	-	-	-	-	-	-
Gardens and greenhouses								
Florists	1	1	-	-	-	-	-	-
Gardeners	98	7	-	-	2	-	-	-
Foremen	-	-	-	-	-	-	-	-
Laborers								
Gardens	107	3	2	-	6	-	1	-
Greenhouses	25	3	-	-	-	-	-	-
Orchards, nurseries, etc.								
Fruit growers and nurserymen	5	2	-	-	2	-	-	-
Foremen	1	-	-	-	-	-	-	-
Laborers	9	-	-	-	3	-	-	-
Other pursuits								
Corn shellers, hay balers, thrashers, etc.	4	-	-	-	-	-	-	-
Cranberry bog laborers	-	-	-	-	-	-	-	-
Ditchers	8	-	-	-	3	-	-	-
Landscape gardeners	10	-	-	-	-	-	-	-

[Continued]

★ 1379 ★

Men and Women Employed in Agriculture, Forestry, and Animal Husbandry: by States, 1910: Part 8

[Continued]

Occupation	Missouri		Montana		Nebraska		Nevada	
	Male	Female	Male	Female	Male	Female	Male	Female
Not specified	-	-	-	-	-	-	-	-
Forestry	98	-	13	-	-	-	-	-
Foresters	-	-	-	-	-	-	-	-
Log and timber camps and lumbering								
Owners and managers of camps	-	-	-	-	-	-	-	-
Foremen and overseerers	1	-	-	-	-	-	-	-
Lumbermen and raftsmen	27	-	-	-	-	-	-	-
Teamsters and haulers	10	-	-	-	-	-	-	-
Woodchoppers and tie cutters	60	-	13	-	-	-	-	-
Animal husbandry	73	5	10	-	19	-	6	-
Apiarists	-	-	-	-	-	-	-	-
Fishermen and oystermen	11	-	-	-	1	-	-	-
Poultry raisers and poultry yard laborers	22	4	-	-	6	-	-	-
Stock herders, drovers, and feeders	38	-	9	-	9	-	6	-
Stock raisers	2	1	1	-	3	-	-	-

Source: "Negro Males and females 10 Years of Age and Gainfully Employed in Agriculture, Forestry, and Animal Husbandry, by States 1910." U.S. Bureau of the Census. *Negro Population, 1790-1915.* Washington, D.C.: Government Printing Office, 1918, p. 514. Adapted by the editors. *Note:* 1. Includes turpentine farms.

★ 1380 ★

Occupations

Men and Women Employed in Agriculture, Forestry, and Animal Husbandry: by States, 1910: Part 9

Occupation	New Hampshire		New Jersey		New Mexico		New York	
	Male	Female	Male	Female	Male	Female	Male	Female
Agriculture, forestry, and animal husbandry	76	3	5,414	96	124	8	2,805	65
Agriculture	68	3	5,304	95	93	8	2,711	65
Dairy farms								
Farmers	-	-	-	-	-	-	24	-
Foremen	-	-	1	-	-	-	1	-
Laborers	2	-	29	-	-	-	88	4
Farms[1]								
Farmers	19	2	378	9	35	4	230	15
Foremen	1	-	20	-	2	-	12	1
Laborers								
Home farm	2	-	177	8	8	3	69	9
Working out	43	1	3,901	62	42	1	1,820	25
Turpentine farms	-	-	-	-	-	-	-	-

[Continued]

★ 1380 ★

Men and Women Employed in Agriculture, Forestry, and Animal Husbandry: by States, 1910: Part 9
[Continued]

Occupation	New Hampshire		New Jersey		New Mexico		New York	
	Male	Female	Male	Female	Male	Female	Male	Female
Gardens and greenhouses								
Florists	-	-	9	-	-	-	2	-
Gardeners	-	-	59	8	2	-	22	-
Foremen	-	-	1	-	-	-	-	-
Laborers								
Gardens	1	-	610	8	3	-	367	9
Greenhouses	-	-	16	-	-	-	31	2
Orchards, nurseries, etc.								
Fruit growers and nurserymen	-	-	3	-	-	-	3	-
Foremen	-	-	1	-	-	-	2	-
Laborers	-	-	36	-	-	-	23	-
Other pursuits								
Corn shellers, hay balers, thrashers, etc.	-	-	27	-	-	-	1	-
Cranberry bog laborers	-	-	20	-	-	-	-	-
Ditchers	-	-	5	-	-	-	1	-
Landscape gardeners	-	-	9	-	-	-	14	-
Not specified	-	-	2	-	1	-	1	-
Forestry	6	-	12	-	4	-	16	-
Foresters	-	-	1	-	-	-	-	-
Log and timber camps and lumbering								
Owners and managers of camps	-	-	-	-	-	-	1	-
Foremen and overseerers	-	-	1	-	-	-	-	-
Lumbermen and raftsmen	4	-	6	-	1	-	9	-
Teamsters and haulers	-	-	-	-	-	-	-	-
Woodchoppers and tie cutters	2	-	4	-	3	-	6	-
Animal husbandry	2	-	98	1	27	-	78	-
Apiarists	-	-	-	-	-	-	1	-
Fishermen and oystermen	-	-	70	1	-	-	59	-
Poultry raisers and poultry yard laborers	1	-	9	-	-	-	5	-
Stock herders, drovers, and feeders	1	-	18	-	21	-	10	-
Stock raisers	-	-	1	-	6	-	3	-

Source: "Negro Males and females 10 Years of Age and Gainfully Employed in Agriculture, Forestry, and Animal Husbandry, by States 1910." U.S. Bureau of the Census. *Negro Population, 1790-1915.* Washington, D.C.: Government Printing Office, 1918, p. 515. Adapted by the Editors. *Note:* 1. Includes turpentine farms.

★ 1381 ★
Occupations

Men and Women Employed in Agriculture, Forestry, and Animal Husbandry: by States, 1910: Part 10

Occupation	North Carolina		North Dakota		Ohio	
	Male	Female	Male	Female	Male	Female
Agriculture, forestry, and animal husbandry	142,028	84,494	83	12	5,226	142
Agriculture	137,902	84,470	83	12	5,162	142
Dairy farms						
Farmers	10	-	-	-	5	-
Foremen	3	-	-	-	-	-
Laborers	106	18	-	-	22	-
Farms[1]						
Farmers	58,681	4,264	37	9	1,620	64
Foremen	80	27	-	-	9	8
Laborers						
Home farm	37,479	55,090	6	2	405	18
Working out	40,366	24,816	40	1	2,727	43
Turpentine farms	61	2	-	-	-	-
Gardens and greenhouses						
Florists	3	1	-	-	2	-
Gardeners	142	20	-	-	106	4
Foremen	6	1	-	-	-	-
Laborers						
Gardens	553	203	-	-	128	1
Greenhouses	16	-	-	-	46	-
Orchards, nurseries, etc.						
Fruit growers and nurserymen	2	1	-	-	4	1
Foremen	-	1	-	-	-	-
Laborers	90	26	-	-	36	3
Other pursuits						
Corn shellers, hay balers, thrashers, etc.	1	-	-	-	15	-
Cranberry bog laborers	-	-	-	-	-	-
Ditchers	288	-	-	-	32	-
Landscape gardeners	9	-	-	-	4	-
Not specified	6	-	-	-	1	-
Forestry	3,465	1	-	-	27	-
Foresters	1	-	-	-	-	-
Log and timber camps and lumbering						
Owners and managers of camps	36	-	-	-	1	-
Foremen and overseerers	14	-	-	-	-	-
Lumbermen and raftsmen	2,815	-	-	-	5	-
Teamsters and haulers	266	-	-	-	8	-
Woodchoppers and tie cutters	333	1	-	-	13	-
Animal husbandry	661	23	-	-	37	-
Apiarists	2	-	-	-	-	-
Fishermen and oystermen	634	18	-	-	2	-
Poultry raisers and poultry yard laborers	3	5	-	-	8	-

[Continued]

★ 1381 ★

Men and Women Employed in Agriculture, Forestry, and Animal Husbandry: by States, 1910: Part 10
[Continued]

Occupation	North Carolina		North Dakota		Ohio	
	Male	Female	Male	Female	Male	Female
Stock herders, drovers, and feeders	20	-	-	-	24	-
Stock raisers	2	-	-	-	3	-

Source: "Negro Males and females 10 Years of Age and Gainfully Employed in Agriculture, Forestry, and Animal Husbandry, by States 1910." U.S. Bureau of the Census. *Negro Population, 1790-1915*. Washington, D.C.: Government Printing Office, 1918, p. 515. Adapted by the editors. *Note:* 1. Includes turpentine farms.

★ 1382 ★

Occupations

Men and Women Employed in Agriculture, Forestry, and Animal Husbandry: by States, 1910: Part 11

Occupation	Oklahoma		Oregon		Pennsylvania		Rhode Island	
	Male	Female	Male	Female	Male	Female	Male	Female
Agriculture, forestry, and animal husbandry	26,191	8,068	97	8	4,606	113	337	2
Agriculture	25,927	8,064	79	8	4,502	113	301	-
Dairy farms								
Farmers	1	-	-	-	4	-	-	-
Foremen	-	-	-	-	-	-	-	-
Laborers	7	2	1	-	58	-	8	-
Farms[1]								
Farmers	12,991	723	31	4	425	21	27	-
Foremen	14	15	-	-	30	-	2	-
Laborers								
Home farm	6,330	6,043	14	-	131	3	4	-
Working out	6,399	1,262	23	3	3,219	74	217	-
Turpentine farms	-	-	-	-	-	-	-	-
Gardens and greenhouses								
Florists	2	1	-	-	9	-	-	-
Gardeners	69	13	-	-	42	2	2	-
Foremen	-	-	-	-	3	-	-	-
Laborers								
Gardens	73	4	5	1	369	8	37	-
Greenhouses	4	-	-	-	70	-	2	-
Orchards, nurseries, etc.								
Fruit growers and nurserymen	5	-	1	-	3	1	-	-
Foremen	1	-	1	-	-	1	1	-
Laborers	3	1	2	-	44	3	-	-
Other pursuits								
Corn shellers, hay balers, thrashers, etc.	1	-	-	-	9	-	-	-
Cranberry bog laborers	-	-	-	-	-	-	-	-
Ditchers	23	-	-	-	5	-	-	-

[Continued]

★ 1382 ★

Men and Women Employed in Agriculture, Forestry, and Animal Husbandry: by States, 1910: Part 11

[Continued]

Occupation	Oklahoma		Oregon		Pennsylvania		Rhode Island	
	Male	Female	Male	Female	Male	Female	Male	Female
Landscape gardeners	-	-	-	-	79	-	1	-
Not specified	4	-	1	-	2	-	-	-
Forestry	212	-	7	-	60	-	1	-
Foresters	-	-	-	-	1	-	-	-
Log and timber camps and lumbering								
Owners and managers of camps	-	-	1	-	-	-	-	-
Foremen and overseerers	-	-	-	-	-	-	-	-
Lumbermen and raftsmen	105	-	4	-	46	-	-	-
Teamsters and haulers	3	-	1	-	5	-	-	-
Woodchoppers and tie cutters	104	-	1	-	8	-	1	-
Animal husbandry	52	4	11	-	44	-	35	2
Apiarists	-	-	-	-	-	-	-	-
Fishermen and oystermen	5	-	-	-	6	-	35	1
Poultry raisers and poultry yard laborers	1	4	1	-	15	-	-	1
Stock herders, drovers, and feeders	32	-	6	-	20	-	-	-
Stock raisers	14	-	4	-	3	-	-	-

Source: "Negro Males and females 10 Years of Age and Gainfully Employed in Agriculture, Forestry, and Animal Husbandry, by States 1910." U.S. Bureau of the Census. *Negro Population, 1790-1915.* Washington, D.C.: Government Printing Office, 1918, p. 515. Adapted by the Editors. *Note:* 1. Includes turpentine farms.

★ 1383 ★

Occupations

Men and Women Employed in Agriculture, Forestry, and Animal Husbandry: by States, 1910: Part 12

Occupation	South Carolina		South Dakota		Tennessee	
	Male	Female	Male	Female	Male	Female
Agriculture, forestry, and animal husbandry	197,431	154,499	105	7	78,276	31,572
Agriculture	196,079	154,480	96	6	77,709	31,554
Dairy farms						
Farmers	3	3	-	1	15	6
Foremen	1	-	-	-	1	-
Laborers	75	29	-	-	192	25
Farms[1]						
Farmers	86,375	9,055	60	5	35,338	2,332
Foremen	159	18	-	-	38	7
Laborers						
Home farm	55,596	100,029	3	-	18,925	24,861
Working out	52,759	45,115	30	-	22,256	4,190
Turpentine farms	325	2	-	-	-	-

[Continued]

★ 1383 ★

Men and Women Employed in Agriculture, Forestry, and Animal Husbandry: by States, 1910: Part 12

[Continued]

Occupation	South Carolina		South Dakota		Tennessee	
	Male	Female	Male	Female	Male	Female
Gardens and greenhouses						
Florists	3	1	-	-	2	2
Gardeners	74	16	1	-	232	25
Foremen	4	1	-	-	1	-
Laborers						
Gardens	553	183	-	-	513	94
Greenhouses	12	1	-	-	35	3
Orchards, nurseries, etc.						
Fruit growers and nurserymen	-	3	-	-	10	-
Foremen	-	-	-	-	-	-
Laborers	30	24	-	-	102	9
Other pursuits						
Corn shellers, hay balers, thrashers, etc.	-	-	-	-	2	-
Cranberry bog laborers	-	-	-	-	-	-
Ditchers	108	-	2	-	24	-
Landscape gardeners	-	-	-	-	18	-
Not specified	2	-	-	-	5	-
Forestry	920	2	1	-	453	-
Foresters	2	-	-	-	-	-
Log and timber camps and lumbering						
Owners and managers of camps	9	-	-	-	5	-
Foremen and overseerers	7	-	-	-	1	-
Lumbermen and raftsmen	669	2	-	-	185	-
Teamsters and haulers	76	-	1	-	114	-
Woodchoppers and tie cutters	157	-	-	-	148	-
Animal husbandry	432	17	8	1	114	18
Apiarists	-	-	-	-	1	-
Fishermen and oystermen	397	6	-	-	35	1
Poultry raisers and poultry yard laborers	6	10	-	-	16	14
Stock herders, drovers, and feeders	27	1	3	-	57	2
Stock raisers	2	-	5	1	5	1

Source: "Negro Males and females 10 Years of Age and Gainfully Employed in Agriculture, Forestry, and Animal Husbandry, by States 1910." U.S. Bureau of the Census. *Negro Population, 1790-1915*. Washington, D.C.: Government Printing Office, 1918, p. 515. Adapted by the Editors. *Note:* 1. Includes turpentine farms.

★ 1384 ★

Occupations

Men and Women Employed in Agriculture, Forestry, and Animal Husbandry: by States, 1910: Part 13

Occupation	Texas		Utah	Vermont		Virginia	
	Male	Female	Male	Male	Female	Male	Female
Agriculture, forestry, and animal husbandry	140,189	77,743	53	87	2	106,184	21,551
Agriculture	138,292	77,723	35	83	2	102,358	21,499
Dairy farms							
Farmers	12	-	-	1	-	26	5
Foremen	1	-	-	-	-	-	-
Laborers	138	23	-	3	-	328	21
Farms[1]							
Farmers	63,222	6,137	14	22	2	38,953	3,407
Foremen	63	41	-	-	-	130	24
Laborers							
Home farm	36,561	54,073	2	8	-	18,229	10,816
Working out	37,186	17,322	17	47	-	42,266	6,418
Turpentine farms	182	15	-	-	-	-	-
Gardens and greenhouses							
Florists	4	-	-	-	-	5	7
Gardeners	231	32	-	-	-	556	65
Foremen	-	-	-	-	-	11	-
Laborers							
Gardens	467	62	1	1	-	1,565	732
Greenhouses	31	2	-	-	-	49	1
Orchards, nurseries, etc.							
Fruit growers and nurserymen	1	4	-	-	-	10	2
Foremen	-	-	-	-	-	1	-
Laborers	127	10	1	1	-	83	1
Other pursuits							
Corn shellers, hay balers, thrashers, etc.	8	-	-	-	-	3	-
Cranberry bog laborers	-	-	-	-	-	-	-
Ditchers	30	-	-	-	-	130	-
Landscape gardeners	3	-	-	-	-	7	-
Not specified	25	2	-	-	-	6	-
Forestry	1,368	2	-	4	-	1,182	-
Foresters	-	-	-	-	-	-	-
Log and timber camps and lumbering							
Owners and managers of camps	17	-	-	-	-	8	-
Foremen and overseerers	5	-	-	-	-	4	-
Lumbermen and raftsmen	677	1	-	4	-	688	-
Teamsters and haulers	99	-	-	-	-	114	-
Woodchoppers and tie cutters	570	1	-	-	-	368	-
Animal husbandry	529	18	18	-	-	2,644	52
Apiarists	5	-	-	-	-	-	-
Fishermen and oystermen	73	1	-	-	-	2,571	31
Poultry raisers and poultry yard laborers	6	8	-	-	-	11	18

[Continued]

★ 1384 ★

Men and Women Employed in Agriculture, Forestry, and Animal Husbandry: by States, 1910: Part 13

[Continued]

Occupation	Texas		Utah	Vermont		Virginia	
	Male	Female	Male	Male	Female	Male	Female
Stock herders, drovers, and feeders	399	7	17	-	-	56	2
Stock raisers	46	2	1	-	-	6	1

Source: "Negro Males and females 10 Years of Age and Gainfully Employed in Agriculture, Forestry, and Animal Husbandry, by States 1910." U.S. Bureau of the Census. *Negro Population, 1790-1915.* Washington, D.C.: Government Printing Office, 1918, p. 516. Adapted by the Editors. *Note:* 1. Includes turpentine farms.

★ 1385 ★

Occupations

Men and Women Employed in Agriculture, Forestry, and Animal Husbandry: by States, 1910: Part 14

Occupation	Washington		West Virginia		Wisconsin		Wyoming	
	Male	Female	Male	Female	Male	Female	Male	Female
Agriculture, forestry, and animal husbandry	260	17	2,332	118	207	15	64	1
Agriculture	210	16	2,307	118	198	15	35	-
Dairy farms								
Farmers	-	-	1	-	3	1	-	-
Foremen	-	-	-	-	-	-	-	-
Laborers	1	-	3	2	1	1	-	-
Farms[1]								
Farmers	75	4	578	39	98	5	15	-
Foremen	-	1	2	2	-	-	-	-
Laborers								
Home farm	12	3	245	27	16	6	3	-
Working out	97	6	1,390	45	71	2	17	-
Turpentine farms	-	-	-	-	-	-	-	-
Gardens and greenhouses								
Florists	-	-	-	-	-	-	-	-
Gardeners	2	-	12	2	3	-	-	-
Foremen	-	-	-	-	-	-	-	-
Laborers								
Gardens	12	-	54	1	4	-	-	-
Greenhouses	-	-	1	-	-	-	-	-
Orchards, nurseries, etc.								
Fruit growers and nurserymen	2	1	4	-	-	-	-	-
Foremen	1	-	-	-	-	-	-	-
Laborers	5	-	15	-	1	-	-	-
Other pursuits								
Corn shellers, hay balers, thrashers, etc.	-	-	-	-	-	-	-	-
Cranberry bog laborers	-	-	-	-	-	-	-	-
Ditchers	1	-	1	-	-	-	-	-

[Continued]

★ 1385 ★

Men and Women Employed in Agriculture, Forestry, and Animal Husbandry: by States, 1910: Part 14

[Continued]

Occupation	Washington		West Virginia		Wisconsin		Wyoming	
	Male	Female	Male	Female	Male	Female	Male	Female
Landscape gardeners	1	-	1	-	-	-	-	-
Not specified	-	1	-	-	1	-	-	-
Forestry	42	-	20	-	5	-	2	-
Foresters	1	-	-	-	-	-	-	-
Log and timber camps and lumbering								
Owners and managers of camps	-	-	1	-	-	-	-	-
Foremen and overseerers	1	-	1	-	1	-	-	-
Lumbermen and raftsmen	36	-	14	-	4	-	-	-
Teamsters and haulers	-	-	2	-	-	-	1	-
Woodchoppers and tie cutters	4	-	2	-	-	-	1	-
Animal husbandry	8	1	5	-	4	-	27	1
Apiarists	-	-	-	-	-	-	-	-
Fishermen and oystermen	2	-	2	-	2	-	-	-
Poultry raisers and poultry yard laborers	2	-	1	-	-	-	-	-
Stock herders, drovers, and feeders	3	-	2	-	2	-	22	1
Stock raisers	1	1	-	-	-	-	5	-

Source: "Negro Males and females 10 Years of Age and Gainfully Employed in Agriculture, Forestry, and Animal Husbandry, by States 1910." U.S. Bureau of the Census. *Negro Population, 1790-1915.* Washington, D.C.: Government Printing Office, 1918, p. 516. Adapted by the Editors. *Note:* 1. Includes turpentine farms.

★ 1386 ★

Occupations

Nonwhite Workers in Selected War Industries, July 1942 and July 1943

Industry	Percentage of nonwhite workers	
	July 1942	July 1943
Agricultural Machinery and Tractors	1.9	4.2
Aircraft	2.9	4.6
Aluminum & Magnesium Products	7.1	12.6
Aluminum (Except for small arms)	5.2	7.6
Bituminous Coal Mining		12.9
Blast furnaces, Steel Workers, and Rolling Mills	9.8	11.9
Communication Equipment and Related Products	0.7	3.8
Electrical Equipment for Industrial Use	1.0	1.9
Engines and Turbines	1.9	3.1
Explosives	3.3	5.1
Firearms (caliber .60 and under)	] 0.7	4.1
Fireworks and Pyrotechnics		
General Industrial Machinery	1.6	3.5

[Continued]

★ 1386 ★

Nonwhite Workers in Selected War Industries, July 1942 and July 1943

[Continued]

Industry	Percentage of nonwhite workers	
	July 1942	July 1943
Guns	3.4	4.8
Iron and Steel Foundry Products	18.6	24.7
Metal Working Machinery	1.0	1.7
Ordnance Accessories, not elsewhere classified	1.4	4.2
Plastic Materials	-	5.9
Primary Smelting and Refining of Nonferrous Metals and Alloys	8.7	9.7
Rolling, Drawing and Alloying of Nonferrous Metals (except Aluminum)	4.6	7.4
Scientific Instruments	0.9	2.2
Shipbuilding	5.7	9.4
Small Arms Ammunition	7.2	5.4
Tanks	2.2	6.4
Tires and Inner Tubes	3.3	5.7

Source: "Proportion of Nonwhite Workers in Selected War Industries, July, 1942 and July 1943," Florence Murray, ed., *The Negro Handbook*, 1944, p. 200.

★ 1387 ★

Occupations

Occupations: Manufacturing and Mechanical Industries, 1910 and 1920

Occupation	Number
Blacksmiths	9,047
Boilermakers	1,420
Brickmasons	10,736
Carpenters and Cabinet Makers	34,916
Cigar and Tobacco Workers	19,849
Clay, Glass and Stone Industries	3,596
Clothing Industries	13,888
Coopers	2,252
Dressmakers	27,160
Electricians	1,411
Engineers (Locomotive)	111
Engineers (Stationary)	6,353
Firemen (Locomotive)	6,505
Firemen (Stationary Engines)	23,135
Harness and Saddle Industries	255
Food Industries	
Bakers	3,887

[Continued]

★ 1387 ★

Occupations: Manufacturing and Mechanical Industries, 1910 and 1920
[Continued]

Occupation	Number
Butter, Cheese and Condensed Milk Factories	190
Candy Factories	1,405
Fish Curing and Packing	3,191
Flour and Grain Mill	871
Fruit and Vegetable Canning, etc.	494
Slaughter and Packing Houses	7,558
Sugar Factories and Refineries	161
Other Food Factories	1,570
Iron, Steel and Other Metal Industries	60,307
Jewelry and Engraving	601
Lumber and Furniture Industries	9,598
Managerial Work	
Builders and Building Contractors	1,454
Foremen and Overseers (Manufacturing)	3,287
Managers and Superintendents	163
Manufacturers and Officials	354
Milliners	607
Painters, Glaziers and Varnishers	9,512
Paper and Pulp Mills	845
Plasters and Paper Hangers	8,125
Plumbers, Gas and Steam Fitters	3,599
Printers and Engravers	3,405
Shoe Factories	1,306
Shoemakers and Cobblers (Not in Factories)	4,707
Stone Cutters	280
Upholsterers	648
Tailors	6,892
Tanneries	971
Textile Industries	
Carpet Mills	191
Cotton Mills	3,649
Knitting Mills	1,034
Lace and Embroidery Mills	227
Silk Mills	328
Textile Dyeing, Finishing and Printing Mills	3
Woolen & Worsted Mills	322
Other Textile Mills	1,631
Tinsmiths, Coppersmiths and Roofers	1,651
Other Industries	26,271
Total	332,249

Source: "Number Negroes, 1920 in Skilled and Semi-Skilled Occupations in Manufacturing and Mechanical Industries," Monroe N. Work, ed., *Negro Year Book: An Annual Encyclopedia of the Negro, 1925-26*, p. 363.

★ 1388 ★
Occupations

Occupations: Manufacturing and Mechanical Industries, 1930

Occupation	Number	Percentage of increase or decrease since 1920
Total	1,024,655	-13.7
Apprentices to building trades	643	-49.3
Apprentices, other	448	-57.4
Bakers	4,527	43.1
Blacksmiths, forgemen and hammermen	5,682	-36.1
Boilermakers	1,030	-26.3
Brick and stone masons and tile layers	11,701	10.3
Builders and building contractors	2,570	76.8
Cabinetmakers	479	5.0
Carpenters	32,413	-5.3
Compositors, linotypers, and typesetters	2,101	36.4
Coopers	1,849	-15.6
Dressmakers and seamstresses (not in factory)	20,439	-24.2
Dyers	510	71.1
Electricians	1,913	42.5
Electrotypers, stereotypers, and lithographers	48	-
Engineers (stationary), cranemen, hoistmen	5,236	-17.6
Engravers	29	-
Filers, grinders, buffers, and polishers of metal	1,607	71.7
Firemen (except locomotive and fire department)	18,265	-21.1
Foremen and overseerers (manufacturing)	2,653	-23.0
Furnace men, smelter men, heaters, puddlers, etc.	3,091	-4.5
Glass blowers	34	-
Jewelers, watchmakers, goldsmiths, and silversmiths	275	-47.5
Loom fixers	9	-
Machinists, millwrights and toolmakers	8,218	-20.1
Managers and officials (manufacturing)	337	90.4
Manufacturers	1,046	160.8
Mechanics (not otherwise specified)	26,710	-
Millers (grain, flour, feed, etc.)	240	34.6
Milliners and millinery dealers	451	-23.6
Moulders, founders, casters (metal)	8,346	25.8
Oilers of machinery	1,073	4.5
Painters, glaziers, varnishers, enamelers, etc.	18,293	93.9
Paper hangers	2,154	125.8
Pattern and model makers	54	-
Piano and organ tuners	80	-
Plaster and cement finishers	13,465	90.1
Plumbers and gas and steam fitters	4,729	34.5
Pressmen and plate printers	189	87.1
Rollers and roll hands (metal)	1,224	66.3
Roofers and slaters	1,044	71.4
Sawyers	3,449	25.2

[Continued]

★ 1388 ★

Occupations: Manufacturing and Mechanical Industries, 1930

[Continued]

Occupation	Number	Percentage of increase or decrease since 1920
Shoemakers and cobblers (not in factory)	4,150	-11.8
Skilled occupations (not elsewhere classified)	149	-7.5
Stonecutters	328	17.1
Structural iron workers	348	77.6
Tailors and tailoresses	7,505	8.9
Tinsmiths and coppersmiths	887	-8.6
Upholsters	915	41.2
Operatives not otherwise specified:		
Building industry	685	98.6
Chemical and allied industries	4,368	38.4
Cigar and tobacco factories	20,721	4.4
Clay, glass and stone industries	3,516	-1.0
Clothing industries	22,216	60.0
Food and allied industries	17,834	8.0
Iron and steel, machinery, and vehicle industries	23,922	1.3
Metal industries (except iron and steel)	1,241	.6
Leather industries	2,004	-31.1
Lumber and furniture industries	10,241	6.7
Paper, printing and allied industries	2,866	2,704
Textile industries	7,238	-5.8
Not specified industries and services	18,066	58.4
Laborers (not otherwise specified)	13,847	-
Building, general, and not specified laborers	224,136	51.4
Chemical and allied industries	37,724	36.2
Cigar and tobacco factories	12,254	-42.6
Clay, glass, and stone industries	22,399	19.4
Clothing industries	1,809	28.6
Food and allied industries	26,760	-8.7
Iron and steel, machinery, and vehicle industries	107,739	2.0
Metal industries (except in iron and steel)	5,293	32.5
Leather industries	2,705	-20.2
Lumber and furniture industries	112,056	5.4
Paper, printing and allied industries	6,276	45.3
Textile industries	15,022	-11.9
Miscellaneous manufacturing industries	78,782	-10.6

Source: "Occupations of Negroes in the Manufacturing and Mechanical Industries: 1930 Census," Florence Murray, ed., *The Negro Handbook*, 1942, p. 142. Primary source: 1930 Census. *Note:* 1940 Census figures have not been released.

★ 1389 ★

Occupations

Pennsylvania Railroad: Black Employees by Occupation, September 1942

Occupation	Number of employees
Shop crafts	2,160
Boilermakers	18
Carmen	40
Electricians	5
Helpers, all shop crafts	350
Machinists	14
Other shop craft occupations	75
Maintenance of Way and Structures	6,257
Helpers	12
Plumbers	2
Track foremen and assistants	29
Trackmen (laborers)	6,214
Dining car service	3,147
Chefs and cooks	549
Waiters, dishwashers, and kitchen help	2,598
Station service employees	2,952
Baggagemen	317
Freight truckers	2,012
Porters	623
Miscellaneous	1,639
General laborers inc. station	380
Janitors and cleaners	437
Watchmen	209
Other occupations	613
Total	16,155

Source: "Railroad Industry, Negro Employees by Occupation, Pennsylvania Railroad, September 1942," Howard W. Risher, *The Negro in the Railroad Industry*, p. 67. Published by permission. Primary source: "Occupational Status of Negro Railroad Employees," *Monthly Labor Review*, Vol. 56 (March 1943), p. 485.

★ 1390 ★

Occupations

Percent Employees in Main Occupations, 1890, 1900

	1890	1900
Agricultural pursuits	21.7	20.6
Professional service	3.6	3.7
Domestic and personal service	22.6	23.6
Trade and transportation	4.3	4.4
Manufacturing and mechanical pursuits	3.6	3.9

Source: "Per Cent of Negroes of Total Persons in Each of the Main Classes of Occupations in 1890 and 1900," Monroe N. Work, ed., *Negro Year Book and Annual Encyclopedia of the Negro, 1912,* p. 163.

★ 1391 ★

Occupations

Principal Occupations by Gender, 1910

Occupation	Number	Percent
	Occupations of males	
Total breadwinners	3,178,554	100.0
Farm laborers	981,922	30.9
Farmers	798,509	25.1
Laborers, building trades	166,374	5.2
Laborers, sawmills	91,181	2.9
Laborers, railroads	86,380	2.7
Porters, not in stores	51,471	1.6
Draymen and teamsters	50,689	1.6
Coal-mine operatives	39,530	1.2
Laborers, in stores	36,906	1.2
Waiters	35,664	1.1
Laborers, road building	33,914	1.1
Cooks	32,453	1.0
Deliverymen, stores	30,511	1.0
Carpenters	30,464	1.0
Janitors and sextons	22,419	.7
Barbers and hairdressers	19,446	.6
Retail dealers	17,659	.6
Clergymen	17,427	.5
Longshoremen, stevedores	16,379	.5
Laborers, brick factories	15,792	.5
Firemen, stationary	14,927	.5
Lumbermen and raftsmen	14,005	.4
Laborers, blast furnaces	13,519	.4
Hostlers, stable hands	12,965	.4
Laborers, public service	12,767	.4

[Continued]

★ 1391 ★

Principal Occupations by Gender, 1910
[Continued]

Occupation	Number	Percent
Brick and stone masons	12,401	.4
Garden laborers	11,801	0.4
Laborers, domestic	10,380	.3
Blacksmiths	9,835	-
Painters and glaziers	8,915	-
Messenger boys	8,262	-
Coachmen and footmen	7,679	-
Elevator tenders	6,276	-
Plasterers	6,175	-
Clerks, not in stores	6,077	-
Firemen, locomotive	5,188	-
Engineers, stationary	4,802	-
Brakemen, locomotive	4,719	-
Chauffeurs	4,674	-
Tailors	4,652	-
Soldiers and sailors	3,734	-
Shoemakers	3,695	-
Restaurant keepers	3,635	-
Cleaners, clothing	3,385	-
Builders	3,272	-
Furnace and smelter men	3,203	-
Sawyers	3,151	-
Mail carriers	2,756	-
Physicians and surgeons	2,744	-
Clerks in stores	2,582	-
Plumbers, steamfitters	2,285	-
All other occupations	385,211	12.11

Occupations of females

Occupation	Number	Percent
Total breadwinners	2,013,981	100.0
Farm laborers	967,837	48.1
Laundresses not in laundry	361,551	17.9
Cooks	205,939	10.2
Farmers	79,309	3.9
Dressmakers and seamstresses	38,148	1.9
School-teachers	22,441	1.1
Nurses (not trained)	17,874	.9
Chambermaids	14,071	.7
Laundry operatives	12,196	
Housekeepers	10,021	.5
Boarding-house keepers	9,183	-
Cigar and tobacco workers	8,267	-
Waiters	7,434	-
Charwomen and cleaners	7,026	-
Building trades	6,174	-
Hairdressers	3,782	-

[Continued]

★ 1391 ★

Principal Occupations by Gender, 1910

[Continued]

Occupation	Number	Percent
Retail dealers	2,994	-
Restaurant keepers	2,734	-
Musicians and teachers	2,347	-
Trained nurses	2,158	-
All other occupations	232,495	11.54

Source: "Principal Occupations of Negroes—1910," U.S. Bureau of Education. *Negro Education: A Study of the Private and Higher Schools for Colored People in the United States, Vol. I*, p. 84.

★ 1392 ★

Occupations

Protective Service Workers, 1964 and 1970

Annual averages. Numbers in thousands.

Protective service workers	1964	1970
Total	884	968
Negro and other races	47	76
Percent of total	5.0	8.0
White	837	892
Policemen and detectives		
Total	329	370
Negro and other races	14	28
Percent of total	4.0	8.0
White	315	342

Source: "Employment of Persons as Protective Service Workers: 1964 and 1970," U.S. Bureau of the Census, *The Social and Economic Status of the Black Population in the United States, 1970*, p. 104. Primary source: U.S. Department of Labor, Bureau of Labor Statistics.

★ 1393 ★

Occupations

Railroad Industry: Employment by Race and Railroad Districts, 1950-1960

District	1940			1950			1960		
	Total	Negro	Percent Negro	Total	Negro	Percent Negro	Total	Negro	Percent Negro
United States	1,135,019	96,315	8.5	1,386,961	143,497	10.3	941,214	77,194	8.2
Male	1,099,361	95,064	8.6	1,314,208	137,769	10.5	888,911	74,072	8.3
Female	35,658	1,251	3.5	72,753	5,728	7.9	52,303	3,122	6.0
Eastern district	613,241	35,027	5.7	724,213	60,563	8.4	480,758	35,398	7.4
Southern district	137,801	36,272	26.3	166,046	43,121	26.0	107,454	20,312	18.9
Western district	383,977	25,016	6.5	496,702	39,813	8.0	351,542	21,451	6.1

Source: "Railroad Industry, Percentage Distribution of Employment by Race and Railroad Districts, United States, 1940-1960," Howard W. Risher, *The Negro in the Railroad Industry*, p. 73. Published by permission. Primary source: U.S. *Census of Population*: 1940, Vol. III, *The Labor Force*, Tables 76 and 18; 1950, Vol. II, *Characteristics of the Population*, Tables 133 and 83; 1960, Vol. II, *Characteristics of the Population*, Tables 213 and 129. *Notes:* The districts are not strictly comparable with those shown elsewhere. States of Michigan and Illinois were included in the Eastern District; Louisiana in the Western District.

★ 1394 ★

Occupations

Railroad Industry: Employment by Race, Gender, and Occupational Group, Southern Region, 1940

Occupational group	Male			Female		
	Total	Nonwhite	Percent nonwhite	Total	Nonwhite	Percent nonwhite
Officials and managers	19,866	21	0.1	85	1	1.2
Professional, semiprofessional and kindred	2,064	2	0.1	42	1	2.4
Clerical, sales and kindred	49,626	738	1.5	6,775	8	0.1
Craftsmen	85,264	4,279	5.0	150	10	6.7
Operatives	48,383	8,254	17.1	187	55	29.4
Laborers	69,016	38,750	56.1	364	249	68.4
Service workers	16,109	10,127	62.9	598	310	51.8
Occupation not reported	914	186		19	6	
Total	291,242	62,357[1]	21.4	8,220	640[2]	7.8

Source: "Railroad Industry, Employment by Color, Sex, and Occupational Group, Southern Region, 1940," Howard W. Risher, *The Negro in the Railroad Industry*, p. 58. Published by permission. Primary source: U.S. *Census of Population, 1940*, Vol. III, *The Labor Force*, Part I, Table 82. *Notes:* 1. Includes 90 men other than Negroes. 2. Includes 1 female other than Negro.

★ 1395 ★

Occupations

Railroad Industry: Employment by Race, Sex, and Occupational Group, 19 Large Companies, 1968

	All employees			Male			Female		
	Total	Negro	Percent Negro	Total	Negro	Percent Negro	Total	Negro	Percent Negro
Officials and managers	22,013	45	0.2	21,928	45	0.2	85	-	-
Professionals	5,776	17	0.3	5,679	17	0.3	97	-	-
Technicians	6,376	32	0.5	6,275	32	0.5	101	-	-
Sales workers	5,975	12	0.2	5,805	11	0.2	170	1	0.6
Office and clerical	99,878	1,853	1.9	75,183	1,372	1.8	24,695	481	1.9
Total white collar	140,018	1,959	1.4	114,870	1,477	1.3	25,148	482	1.9
Craftsmen	177,453	4,593	2.6	177,329	4,577	2.6	124	16	12.9
Operatives	105,645	5,806	5.5	105,392	5,755	5.5	253	51	20.2
Laborers	58,035	18,509	31.9	56,661	17,730	31.3	1,374	779	56.7
Service workers	13,328	6,250	46.9	12,677	6,074	47.9	651	176	27.0
Total blue collar	354,461	35,158	9.9	352,059	34,136	9.7	2,402	1,022	42.5
Total	494,479	37,117	7.5	466,929	35,613	7.6	27,550	1,504	5.5

Source: "Railroad Industry, Employment by Race, Sex, and Occupational Group, 19 Large Companies, 1968," Howard W. Risher, *The Negro in the Railroad Industry*, p. 184. Published by permission. Data in author's possession. *Note:* Companies with 10,000 or more employees.

★ 1396 ★

Occupations

Railroad Industry: Employment by Race, Sex, and Occupational Group, 1966-1969 - I

	1966		1967		1968		1969	
	Total	Negro	Total	Negro	Total	Negro	Total	Negro
Officials and managers	4.5	0.1	4.6	0.1	4.7	0.1	5.0	0.3
Professionals	1.0	[1]	1.1	[1]	1.2	0.1	1.2	0.1
Technicians	1.2	[1]	1.2	0.1	1.3	0.1	1.3	0.1
Sales workers	1.1	[1]	1.0	[1]	1.2	[1]	1.1	0.2
Office and clerical	18.9	2.4	19.3	3.4	20.2	5.0	19.2	6.3
Total white collar	26.7	2.5	27.2	3.6	28.6	5.3	27.8	7.0
Craftsmen	33.1	9.1	33.3	9.8	35.4	12.0	34.0	12.9
Operatives	22.9	14.8	22.5	15.5	21.3	15.3	23.1	16.8
Laborers	14.2	54.2	13.9	52.3	12.1	51.1	12.8	49.0
Service workers	3.1	19.4	3.1	18.8	2.6	16.3	2.3	14.3

[Continued]

★ 1396 ★

Railroad Industry: Employment by Race, Sex, and Occupational Group, 1966-1969 - I

[Continued]

	1966		1967		1968		1969	
	Total	Negro	Total	Negro	Total	Negro	Total	Negro
Total blue collar	73.3	97.5	72.8	96.4	71.4	94.7	72.2	93.0
Total	100.0	100.0	100.0	100.0	100.0	100.0	100.0	100.0

Source: "Railroad Industry, Percentage Distribution of Employment by Race and Occupational Group, United States, 1966-1969," Howard W. Risher, *The Negro in the Railroad Industry*, p. 95. Published by permission. *Notes:* 1968 is Field Sample and therefore is not strictly comparable with other years. 1. Less than 0.05 percent.

★ 1397 ★

Occupations

Railroad Industry: Employment by Race, Sex, and Occupational Group, 1966-1969 - II

Occupational group	Male			Female		
	Total	Nonwhite	Percent nonwhite	Total	Nonwhite	Percent nonwhite
Officials and managers	79,847	372	0.5	627	-	-
Professional, technical, and kindred workers	16,629	62	0.4	1,100	61	5.5
Sales workers	1,906	20	1.0	20	-	-
Clerical and kindred workers	160,750	4,361	2.7	42,427	364	0.9
Craftsmen, foremen, and kindred workers	269,756	5,614	2.1	537	-	-
Operatives and kindred workers	198,252	10,680	5.4	944	121	12.8
Laborers	119,460	34,560	28.9	2,762	1,520	55.0
Service workers	35,142	18,958	53.9	2,574	995	38.7
Occupations not reported	11,020	1,865	16.9	675	40	5.9

Source: "Railroad Industry, Percentage Distribution of Employment by Race and Occupational Group, United States, 1966-1969," Howard W. Risher, *The Negro in the Railroad Industry*, p. 95. Published by permission. Primary source: U.S. Census of Population, 1960, PC(2) 7A *Occupational Characteristics*, Table 36. *Note:* Negroes were 96.3 percent of the nonwhite employment.

★ 1398 ★

Occupations

Retail Food Industry: Employees by Race and Sex: Three Occupations, 1940, 1950, 1960

Occupation	Year	All employees			Male			Female		
		Total	Percent Negro	Negro	Total	Percent Negro	Negro	Total	Percent Negro	Negro
Managers, officials, and proprietors										
Salaried	1950	98,400	2.0	1,920	85,890	1.5	1,290	12,510	5.0	630
	1960	104,286	1.3	1,336	94,849	1.0	955	9,437	4.0	381
Self-employed	1950	379,560	3.8	14,520	309,150	2.8	8,640	70,410	8.4	5,880

[Continued]

★ 1398 ★

Retail Food Industry: Employees by Race and Sex: Three Occupations, 1940, 1950, 1960
[Continued]

Occupation	Year	All employees			Male			Female		
		Total	Percent Negro	Negro	Total	Percent Negro	Negro	Total	Percent Negro	Negro
Meat cutters[1]	1960	218,903	8,740	4.0	175,393	5,238	3.0	43,510	3,502	8.0
	1950	167,700	6,420	3.8	164,010	6,300	3.8	3,690	120	3.3
	1960	180,302	7,391	4.1	174,955	6,724	3.8	5,347	667	12.5
Sales clerks	1960	499,936	17,976	3.6	270,788	9,812	3.6	229,148	8,164	3.6

Source: "Retail Food Industry, Employment by Race and Sex, Four Regions, 1940, 1950, and 1960," Gordon Bloom and F. Marion Fletcher, *The Negro in the Supermarket Industry*, p. 49. Primary source: *U.S. Census of Population*: 1950, Vol. VI, *Occupational Characteristics*, Table 3; 1960, PC (2) 7A, *Occupational Characteristics*, Table 3. *Note:* 1. Meat cutters include about 13 percent non-food store employment.

★ 1399 ★

Occupations

Shipbuilding Industry: Employment by Race, Gender, and Occupation in Fourteen Largest Shipyards, 1969

Occupational group	All employees			Male			Female		
	Total	Negro	Percent Negro	Total	Negro	Percent Negro	Total	Negro	Percent Negro
Officials and managers	8,435	277	3.3	8,392	277	3.3	43	-	-
Professionals	7,679	90	1.2	7,556	88	1.2	123	2	1.6
Technicians	4,899	171	3.5	4,705	160	3.4	194	11	5.7
Sales workers	36	-	-	36	-	-	-	-	-
Office and clerical	6,363	419	6.6	3,473	266	7.7	2,890	153	5.3
Total white collar	27,412	957	3.5	24,162	791	3.3	3,250	166	5.1
Craftsmen	45,018	6,916	15.4	45,003	6,913	15.4	15	3	20.0
Operatives	15,919	5,621	35.3	15,861	5,618	35.4	58	3	5.2
Laborers	4,232	2,103	49.7	4,231	2,102	49.7	1	1	100.0
Service workers	957	277	28.9	919	255	27.7	38	22	57.9
Total blue collar	66,126	14,917	22.6	66,014	14,888	22.6	112	29	25.9
Total	93,538	15,874	17.0	90,176	15,679	17.4	3,362	195	5.8

Source: "Shipbuilding Industry, Employment by Race, Sex, and Occupational Group, 14 Largest Shipyards," Philip W. Jeffress, *The Negro in the Transit Industry*, p. 83. Primary source: Data in author's possession.

★ 1400 ★

Occupations

Shipbuilding Industry: Percent Black Employees by Occupation and Gender, United States, 1964, 1966, and 1968

Occupational group	All employees			Male			Female		
	1964	1966	1968	1964	1966	1968	1964	1966	1968
Officials and managers	0.9	1.0	2.2	0.9	1.0	2.2	-	-	-
Professionals	0.1	0.2	0.9	0.1	0.2	0.9	2.1	4.8	1.5
Technicians	1.8	1.4	2.9	1.8	1.2	2.8	2.4	5.7	5.3
Sales workers	-	-	-	-	-	-	-	-	-
Office and clerical	2.5	2.9	5.5	2.6	3.1	7.2	2.4	2.6	3.8
Total white collar	1.3	1.4	2.8	1.1	1.2	2.6	2.4	2.8	3.7
Craftsmen	10.2	10.2	12.9	10.2	10.2	12.9	-	-	6.4
Operatives	27.7	24.1	30.4	27.7	24.2	30.5	-	-	1.9
Laborers	57.2	51.1	47.8	57.2	51.1	47.8	-	-	-
Service workers	13.1	21.9	25.1	12.1	20.7	24.2	52.7	49.2	41.8
Total blue collar	17.0	16.6	19.2	17.0	16.6	19.2	37.7	28.7	19.3
Total	13.2	13.2	14.9	13.5	13.5	15.3	3.5	3.7	4.4

Source: "Shipbuilding Industry,Percent Negro Employment by Occupational Group and Sex, United States, 1964, 1966, and 1968," Philip W. Jeffress, *The Negro in the Transit Industry*, p. 72. Primary source: Tables A-1 to A-3.

★ 1401 ★

Occupations

Supermarket Industry: Employees by Chain Companies and Independents, 1966, 1967, 1969, 1970

Year	All employees			White collar			Blue collar		
	Total	Negro	Percent Negro	Total	Negro	Percent Negro	Total	Negro	Percent Negro
1966	583,997	29,149	5.0	92,461	1,249	1.4	491,536	27,900	5.7
1967	755,345	41,697	5.5	568,803	23,561	4.1	186,542	18,136	9.7
1969	731,048	47,295	6.5	558,167	27,773	5.0	172,881	19,522	11.3
1970	731,865	51,905	7.1	555,483	28,135	5.1	176,382	23,770	13.5

Source: "Supermarket Industry: Total and Negro Employment by Major Occupational Group Chain Companies and Large Independents, United States. 1966, 1967, 1969, and 1970," Gordon Bloom and F. Marion Fletcher, *The Negro in the Supermarket Industry*, p. 55. Primary source: Employment figures vary to some degree because of reporting differences.

★ 1402 ★

Occupations

Supermarket Industry: Employment by Race and Gender in Five Regions, 1966, 1967, 1969

Region	All employees			Male			Female		
	Total	Negro	Percent Negro	Total	Negro	Percent Negro	Total	Negro	Percent Negro
New England									
1966	40,592	707	1.7	25,912	481	1.9	14,680	226	1.5
1967	47,110	883	1.9	30,447	600	2.0	16,663	283	1.7
1969	48,713	958	2.0	30,315	672	2.2	18,398	286	1.6
Middle Atlantic									
1966	95,396	4,897	5.1	65,488	3,141	4.8	29,908	1,756	5.9
1967	141,422	6,349	4.5	93,558	4,051	4.3	47,864	2,298	4.8
1969	150,569	8,237	5.5	96,988	5,205	5.4	53,581	3,032	5.7
South									
1966	161,185	13,369	8.3	117,402	11,636	9.9	43,783	1,733	4.0
1967	222,265	21,047	9.5	159,853	17,389	10.9	62,412	3,658	5.9
1969	202,627	20,094	9.9	141,647	15,961	11.3	60,980	4,133	6.8
Midwest									
1966	161,294	6,535	4.1	105,741	4,565	4.3	55,553	1,970	3.5
1967	211,723	9,458	4.5	138,328	6,618	4.8	73,395	2,840	3.9
1969	224,731	14,110	6.3	143,657	9,611	6.7	81,074	4,499	5.5
West									
1966	119,526	3,604	3.0	88,821	2,973	3.3	30,705	631	2.1
1967	127,741	3,940	3.1	92,991	3,144	3.4	34,750	796	2.3
1969	95,938	3,479	3.6	68,667	2,723	4.0	27,271	756	2.8

Source: "Supermarket Industry: Employment by Race and Sex, Five Regions, 1966, 1967, and 1969," Gordon Bloom and F. Marion Fletcher, *The Negro in the Supermarket Industry*, p. 102. *Notes:* Variations in total employment are due to variations in reporting completeness during the three reporting periods. It is felt that the latest data, 1969, most accurately reflect food store employment within the definition of companies with 100 or more employees, although one major company's data are missing in 1969.

★ 1403 ★

Occupations

Supermarket Industry: Percent Employed by Sex and Occupational Group in Chain and Independent Companies, 1967, 1969, 1970

Occupational group	All employees			Male			Female		
	1967	1969	1970	1967	1969	1970	1967	1969	1970
Officials and managers	1.2	2.0	2.4	1.1	1.9	2.3	2.1	3.8	4.1
Professionals	5.7	3.4	3.1	5.0	3.3	2.8	13.0	4.9	5.2
Technicians	6.9	7.6	4.5	6.6	7.2	5.2	7.6	8.5	2.7
Sales workers	4.7	5.4	5.5	5.2	5.9	5.9	3.8	4.8	4.9
Office and clerical	3.8	5.2	5.4	6.0	6.6	7.8	2.9	4.6	4.7
Total white collar	4.1	5.0	5.1	4.4	5.1	5.2	3.7	4.7	4.8
Craftsmen	3.4	4.3	6.2	3.4	4.3	6.2	4.3	4.4	4.8
Operatives	10.2	13.4	13.9	12.4	16.1	15.6	5.2	7.4	9.1
Laborers	11.5	13.9	18.3	12.7	14.6	18.8	5.9	10.4	16.3
Service workers	14.9	13.5	15.7	17.7	15.7	16.4	9.5	8.4	14.5
Total blue collar	9.7	11.3	13.5	10.6	12.2	13.9	6.6	8.1	12.1
Total	5.5	6.5	7.1	6.1	7.1	7.7	4.2	5.2	5.9

Source: "Supermarket Industry: Percent Negro Employment by Sex and Occupational Group, Chain Companies and Large Independents, United States. 1967, 1969, and 1970," Gordon Bloom and F. Marion Fletcher, *The Negro in the Supermarket Industry*, p. 68. Primary source: Employment figures vary to some degree because of reporting differences.

★ 1404 ★

Occupations

Supermarket Industry: Training Courses for Store Employees, Supermarket Institute and Members, 1955-1970

Employee group	Percentages of companies			
	1955	1959	1967	1970
Checkers	25	30	36	41
Baggers	13	18	21	28
Store managers	16	16	25	28
Meat personnel	13	17	26	27
Produce personnel	19	17	22	23
Grocery clerks	14	14	18	19
Store manager candidates	n.a.	15	18	16
Any training course	32	37	43	51

Source: "Supermarket Industry: Formal Training Courses for Store Employees, Supermarket Institute Members, Selected Years, 1955-1970," Gordon Bloom and F. Marion Fletcher, *The Negro in the Supermarket Industry*, p. 74. Primary source: Reprinted from *The Super Market Industry Speaks, 1970*, p. 29, by permission of the Super Market Institute.

★ 1405 ★

Occupations

Urban Transit and Related Industries: Employment Characteristics for the U.S., 1966

Occupational group	All employees			Male			Female		
	Total	Negro	Percent Negro	Total	Negro	Percent Negro	Total	Negro	Percent Negro
Officials and managers	5,753	101	1.8	5,654	101	1.8	99	-	-
Professionals	571	14	2.5	554	14	2.5	17	-	-
Technicians	1,251	44	3.5	1,223	42	3.4	28	2	7.1
Sales workers	7,499	725	9.7	6,131	613	10.0	1,368	112	8.2
Office and clerical	9,867	347	3.5	5,180	176	3.4	4,687	171	3.6
Total white collar	24,941	1,231	4.9	18,742	946	5.0	6,199	285	4.6
Craftsmen	21,630	1,122	5.2	21,518	1,118	5.2	112	4	3.6
Operatives	59,317	11,870	20.0	58,258	11,766	20.2	1,059	104	9.8
Laborers	5,626	2,129	37.8	5,346	1,978	37.0	280	151	53.9
Service workers	10,646	3,013	28.3	10,199	2,859	28.0	447	154	34.5
Total blue collar	97,219	18,134	18.7	95,321	17,721	18.6	1,898	413	21.8
Total	122,160	19,365	15.9	114,063	18,667	16.4	8,097	698	8.6

Source: "Urban Transit and Related Industries (SIC 41), Employment by Race, Sex, and Occupational Group, United States," Philip W. Jeffress, *The Negro in the Transit Industry*, p. 62. Primary source: U.S. Equal Employment Opportunity Commission, *Job Patterns for Minorities and Women in Private Industry, 1966*, Report No. 1 (Washington: The Commission, 1968), Part II.

★ 1406 ★

Occupations

Women Employees in the Air Transport Industry by Occupational Group: 12 Companies, 1968

Occupational group	Total United States	Northeast	New England	Middle Atlantic	North Central	East North Central	West	West Coast	South	South Border
Officials and managers	0.6	0.7	-	0.8	1.1	1.4	0.9	1.0	-	-
Professionals	0.8	1.4	-	1.5	-	-	1.3	1.4	-	-
Technicians	1.1	1.5	-	1.6	-	-	4.3	5.4	-	-
Sales workers	3.8	5.2	2.5	5.9	5.8	6.7	2.8	2.9	2.0	4.2
Office and clerical	3.2	4.5	1.1	4.8	2.6	2.0	4.2	4.4	0.7	2.5
Total white collar	3.4	4.7	2.0	5.1	4.1	4.6	3.3	3.5	1.5	3.7
Craftsmen	2.1	-	-	-	-	-	5.6[1]	6.2[2]	-	-
Operatives	20.9	37.8	-	37.8	18.6	50.0	12.9	14.3	16.7	-
Laborers	45.7	9.1[3]	-	10.0[4]	40.8	48.8	6.7	90.3	-	-
Service workers	2.8	3.7	1.4	4.1	3.5	5.8	2.2	2.3	1.9	3.1

[Continued]

★ 1406 ★

Women Employees in the Air Transport Industry by Occupational Group: 12 Companies, 1968

[Continued]

Occupational group	Total United States	Northeast	New England	Middle Atlantic	North Central	East North Central	West	West Coast	South	South Border
Total blue collar	3.5	4.1	1.4	4.5	4.3	7.4	2.3	2.4	4.9	3.1
Total	3.4	4.5	1.9	4.9	4.1	5.1	2.8	3.0	2.2	3.6

Source: "Air Transport Industry, Percent Negro Female Employment by Occupational Group, 12 Companies, United States and Regions, 1968," Northrup, Thieblot, and Chernish, *The Negro in the Air Transport Industry*, p. 85. Published by permission. Primary source: Appendix tables of 1968 data. *Notes:* Southern Border includes Delaware, Washington, D.C., Maryland, and northern Virginia. 1. Three of 54. 2. Three of 48. 3. One of 11. 4. One of 10.

★ 1407 ★

Occupations

Women Gainfully Employed: by State, 1910: Part 1

	United States	Alabama	Arizona	Arkansas	California	Colorado	Connecticut	Delaware	District of Columbia	Florida	Georgia	Idaho
Total, 10 years of age and over	3,680,536	336,701	799	161,129	8,826	4,836	6,623	11,891	44,424	109,720	430,643	214
Gainfully employed	2,013,981	214,533	402	93,248	3,803	2,132	3,357	5,313	26,699	50,181	218,924	106
Agriculture, forestry, and animal husbandry	1,051,137	152,054	1	68,790	21	8	12	253	16	18,349	152,513	2
Agriculture	1,050,851	152,042	1	68,777	19	7	11	253	16	18,330	152,495	2
Forestry	34	1	-	4	-	-	-	-	-	9	6	-
Animal husbandry	252	11	-	9	2	1	1	-	-	10	12	-
Barbers, hairdressers, and manicurists	3,782	68	8	68	95	47	6	13	168	45	80	1
Charwomen and cleaners	7,026	280	3	94	54	11	42	45	457	155	570	-
Dealers, retail	2,994	223	1	99	19	4	5	12	114	122	600	-
Dressmakers and seamstresses, not in factory	38,148	2,316	13	1,073	212	86	164	91	1,805	1,995	3,540	5
Housekeepers and stewardesses	10,021	343	12	323	123	60	115	114	181	228	470	2
Janitresses and sextons	2,452	76	2	30	36	20	6	13	87	17	112	-
Keepers of boarding and lodging houses	9,183	587	11	527	101	74	30	27	96	467	437	2
Keepers of restaurants, cafes, and lunch rooms	2,734	149	5	88	35	26	6	7	86	139	296	-
Laborers, cigar and tobacco factories	2,405	-	-	-	-	-	-	-	-	69	2	-
Laborers, general, and not specified, in manufactures	6,163	301	3	203	31	18	14	42	55	224	661	3
Laundresses not in laundries	361,551	27,667	130	9,464	734	589	1,056	1,459	7,754	14,312	43,862	19
Midwives and nurses, not trained	19,508	1,875	4	468	91	27	47	48	391	711	2,893	1
Musicians and teachers of music	2,347	100	1	62	30	19	17	6	77	75	128	-
Nurses, trained	2,158	139	-	37	18	3	12	6	91	118	337	1
Operatives, in laundries	12,196	631	16	281	128	20	60	38	494	763	1,503	1
Operatives, semiskilled, in cigar and tobacco factories	8,267	2	-	-	2	-	1	-	2	690	15	-
Servants	415,416	24,823	179	10,080	1,763	1,000	1,564	2,937	13,062	9,795	35,628	59
Teachers, school	22,441	1,616	1	883	16	23	14	91	574	721	2,837	2
Waitresses	7,434	153	3	91	60	19	73	44	382	263	245	2
All other occupations	26,618	1,130	9	587	234	78	113	67	807	923	2,195	6

Source: "Negro Females 10 Years of Age and Over Gainfully Employed: by States: 1910." U.S. Bureau of the Census. *Negro Population, 1790-1915.* Washington, D.C.: Government Printing Office, 1918, p. 521. Adapted by the Editors.

★ 1408 ★

Occupations

Women Gainfully Employed: by State, 1910: Part 2

	Illinois	Indiana	Iowa	Kansas	Kentucky	Louisiana	Maine	Maryland	Massachusetts	Michigan	Minnesota	Mississippi
Total, 10 years of age and over	43,897	24,392	5,567	21,239	104,258	265,513	556	91,119	16,089	6,830	2,531	366,053
Gainfully employed	17,105	9,534	1,781	6,296	46,510	128,512	206	45,231	8,026	2,133	923	250,740
Agriculture, forestry, and animal husbandry	326	49	35	123	1,548	71,858	5	2,103	42	52	10	204,024
Agriculture	323	47	30	114	1,541	71,844	4	2,084	42	50	10	204,014
Forestry	-	-	-	-	-	4	-	3	-	-	-	2
Animal husbandry	3	2	5	9	7	10	1	16	-	2	-	8
Barbers, hairdressers, and manicurists	423	147	37	53	118	105	2	70	80	83	25	51
Charwomen and cleaners	189	93	32	61	137	208	6	394	205	29	8	333
Dealers, retail	44	23	4	27	60	171	-	112	17	4	6	183
Dressmakers and seamstresses, not in factory	1,163	388	96	244	1,167	2,740	8	1,208	493	125	79	1,843
Housekeepers and stewardesses	371	274	66	188	275	439	11	415	200	62	44	319
Janitresses and sextons	89	50	20	19	119	50	1	107	46	18	5	33
Keepers of boarding and lodging houses	475	161	55	84	275	566	-	122	185	65	50	548
Keepers of restaurants, cafes, and lunch rooms	108	54	18	53	102	120	1	85	15	15	2	136
Laborers, cigar and tobacco factories	-	11	-	-	240	4	-	4	-	-	-	-
Laborers, general, and not specified in manufactures	104	60	42	72	144	358	-	269	22	22	9	421
Laundresses not in laundries	4,935	3,260	498	2,342	18,964	21,184	25	14,667	1,842	398	85	17,913
Midwives and nurses, not trained	129	72	21	52	653	1,179	7	669	94	22	14	1,126
Musicians and teachers of music	174	40	14	43	68	89	1	59	61	25	14	60
Nurses, trained	49	14	2	12	79	99	-	40	28	8	2	90
Operatives, in laundries	293	118	13	124	301	528	3	579	159	19	19	532
Operatives, semiskilled, in cigar and tobacco factories	4	97	-	-	1,410	89	-	97	1	3	1	-
Servants	6,848	4,105	688	2,341	18,886	26,574	108	21,463	3,653	995	409	20,265
Teachers, school	217	167	29	172	1,006	965	5	566	43	19	13	1,872
Waitresses	186	44	21	46	131	130	3	736	135	42	33	123
All other occupations	978	307	90	240	827	1,055	20	1,466	705	127	95	868

Source: "Negro Females 10 Years of Age and Over Gainfully Employed: by States: 1910." U.S. Bureau of the Census. *Negro Population, 1790-1915.* Washington,D.C.: Government Printing Office, 1918, p. 521. Adapted by the Editors.

★ 1409 ★

Occupations

Women Gainfully Employed: by State, 1910: Part 3

	Missouri	Montana	Nebraska	Nevada	New Hampshire	New Jersey	New Mexico
Total, 10 years of age and over	64,272	670	2,974	223	233	38,386	578
Gainfully employed	28,796	312	1,175	118	128	20,004	247
Agriculture, forestry, and animal husbandry	394	5	5	3	3	96	8
Agriculture	389	5	5	3	3	95	8
Forestry	-	-	-	-	-	-	-
Animal husbandry	5	-	-	-	-	1	-
Barbers, hairdressers, and manicurists	268	4	30	1	-	89	3
Charwomen and cleaners	194	5	16	2	1	211	1
Dealers, retail	54	1	3	-	1	54	1
Dressmakers and seamstresses, not in factory	729	21	54	4	6	726	5
Housekeepers and stewardesses	364	13	40	2	7	366	7
Janitresses and sextons	153	5	7	-	1	53	-
Keepers of boarding and lodging houses	493	20	35	2	1	207	6

[Continued]

★ 1409 ★

Women Gainfully Employed: by State, 1910: Part 3
[Continued]

	Missouri	Montana	Nebraska	Nevada	New Hampshire	New Jersey	New Mexico
Keepers of restaurants, cafes, and lunch rooms	90	5	11	2	-	29	-
Laborers, cigar and tobacco factories	8	-	-	-	-	-	-
Laborers, general, and not specified	147	14	11	3	-	70	1
Laundresses, not in laundry	12,980	48	253	31	17	5,496	64
Midwives and nurses, not trained	174	3	8	2	4	172	5
Musicians and teachers of music	96	5	6	2	-	77	-
Nurses, trained	26	2	4	-	-	23	-
Operatives, in laundries	425	2	30	7	1	180	1
Operatives, semiskilled, in cigar and tobacco factories	28	-	-	-	-	1	-
Servants	10,660	138	572	51	76	10,776	137
Teachers, school	612	-	3	1	-	137	2
Waitresses	243	3	27	3	2	848	2
All other occupations	658	18	60	2	8	393	4

Source: "Negro Females 10 Years of Age and Over Gainfully Employed: by States: 1910." U.S. Bureau of the Census. *Negro Population, 1790-1915.* Washington,D.C.: Government Printing Office, 1918, p. 522. Adapted by the Editors.

★ 1410 ★

Occupations

Women Gainfully Employed: by State, 1910: Part 4

	New York	North Carolina	North Dakota	Ohio	Oklahoma	Oregon
Total, 10 years of age and over	60,673	253,755	198	44,613	47,471	521
Gainfully employed	34,782	141,391	86	17,593	17,659	230
Agriculture, forestry, and animal husbandry	65	84,494	12	142	8,068	8
Agriculture	65	84,470	12	142	8,064	8
Forestry	-	1	-	-	-	-
Animal husbandry	-	23	-	-	4	-
Barbers, hairdressers, and manicurists	344	36	-	320	33	9
Charwomen and cleaners	418	331	-	258	44	2
Dealers, retail	49	115	1	48	45	3
Dressmakers and seamstresses, not in factory	2,285	1,635	2	944	381	17
Housekeepers and stewardesses	622	306	2	445	236	13
Janitresses and sextons	456	44	1	113	7	2
Keepers of boarding and lodging houses	261	216	7	404	224	11
Keepers of restaurants, cafes, and lunch rooms	93	88	3	82	49	-
Laborers, cigar and tobacco factories	-	229	-	3	-	-
Laborers, general, and not specified	94	573	-	124	95	-

[Continued]

★ 1410 ★

Women Gainfully Employed: by State, 1910: Part 4

[Continued]

	New York	North Carolina	North Dakota	Ohio	Oklahoma	Oregon
Laundresses, not in laundry	7,151	22,070	7	5,623	3,425	16
Midwives and nurses, not trained	411	1,395	1	149	47	13
Musicians and teachers of music	201	65	2	125	36	1
Nurses, trained	129	115	1	26	13	2
Operatives, in laundries	736	586	1	131	89	8
Operatives, semiskilled, in cigar and tobacco factories	22	2,045	-	100	-	-
Servants	18,907	23,279	33	7,486	3,860	93
Teachers, school	121	1,735	3	217	627	4
Waitresses	914	137	2	126	66	6
All other occupations	1,503	1,897	8	727	314	22

Source: "Negro Females 10 Years of Age and Over Gainfully Employed: by States: 1910." U.S. Bureau of the Census. *Negro Population, 1790-1915.* Washington,D.C.: Government Printing Office, 1918, p. 522. Adapted by the Editors.

★ 1411 ★

Occupations

Women Gainfully Employed: by State, 1910: Part 5

Occupation	Pennsylvania	Rhode Island	South Carolina	South Dakota	Tennessee	Texas	Utah
Total, 10 years of age and over	81,479	4,074	301,759	293	182,965	253,647	392
Gainfully employed	39,671	2,059	201,623	91	92,220	139,247	135
Agriculture, forestry, and animal husbandry	113	2	154,499	7	31,572	77,743	-
Agriculture	113	-	154,480	6	31,554	77,723	-
Forestry	-	-	2	-	-	2	-
Animal husbandry	-	2	17	1	18	18	-
Barbers, hairdressers, and manicurists	309	11	21	2	133	178	8
Charwomen and cleaners	689	30	336	6	192	196	1
Dealers, retail	89	1	189	1	130	103	-
Dressmakers and seamstresses, not in factory	1,673	157	2,376	-	2,097	1,933	11
Housekeepers and stewardesses	906	52	311	4	387	472	3
Janitresses and sextons	256	5	21	1	103	70	2
Keepers of boarding and lodging houses	448	11	141	6	520	693	12
Keepers of restaurants, cafes, and lunch rooms	91	8	148	4	139	134	3
Laborers, cigar and tobacco factories	1	-	11	-	232	13	-
Laborers, general, and not specified in manufactures	222	14	491	-	184	426	1
Laundresses, not in laundries	7,189	666	19,523	12	25,950	28,070	4
Midwives and nurses, not trained	338	30	1,418	4	1,385	878	5
Musicians and teachers of music	150	14	40	1	110	150	1
Nurses, trained	65	6	116	-	151	64	-

[Continued]

★ 1411 ★

Women Gainfully Employed: by State, 1910: Part 5
[Continued]

Occupation	Pennsylvania	Rhode Island	South Carolina	South Dakota	Tennessee	Texas	Utah
Operatives, in laundries	356	26	295	1	988	815	2
Operatives, semiskilled, in cigar and tobacco factories	152	-	50	-	222	18	-
Servants	24,289	840	18,997	33	24,940	24,152	74
Teachers, school	244	8	1,560	3	1,369	1,846	-
Waitresses	987	43	162	3	156	290	2
All other occupations	1,104	135	918	3	1,260	1,003	6

Source: "Negro Females 10 Years of Age and Over Gainfully Employed: by States: 1910." U.S. Bureau of the Census. *Negro Population, 1790-1915.* Washington, D.C.: Government Printing Office, 1918, p. 522. Adapted by the Editors.

★ 1412 ★

Occupations

Women Gainfully Employed: by State, 1910: Part 6

	Vermont	Virginia	Washington	West Virginia	Wisconsin	Wyoming
Total, 10 years of age and over	357	252,461	2,044	20,867	1,199	582
Gainfully employed	123	102,729	776	6,360	448	283
Agriculture, forestry, and animal husbandry	2	21,551	17	118	15	1
Agriculture	2	21,499	16	118	15	-
Forestry	-	-	-	-	-	-
Animal husbandry	-	52	1	-	-	1
Barbers, hairdressers, and manicurists	-	99	27	50	12	2
Charwomen and cleaners	1	643	9	29	4	1
Dealers, retail	-	240	2	10	4	-
Dressmakers and seamstresses, not in factory	5	1,957	55	182	29	10
Housekeepers and stewardesses	7	626	42	126	18	9
Janitresses and sextons	1	165	4	23	2	1
Keepers of boarding and lodging houses	1	268	45	184	14	8
Keepers of restaurants, cafes, and lunch rooms	1	173	3	29	2	1
Laborers, cigar and tobacco factories	-	1,578	-	-	-	-
Laborers, general, and not specified, in manufactures	-	561	7	37	10	-
Laundresses, not in laundries	13	27,723	105	1,857	42	57
Midwives and nurses, not trained	5	2,294	30	133	6	4
Musicians and teachers of music	1	77	5	12	3	4
Nurses, trained	-	211	1	16	1	1
Operatives in laundries	-	821	9	52	3	8
Operatives, semiskilled, in cigar and tobacco factories	-	3,215	-	-	-	-

[Continued]

★ 1412 ★

Women Gainfully Employed: by State, 1910: Part 6
[Continued]

	Vermont	Virginia	Washington	West Virginia	Wisconsin	Wyoming
Servants	79	34,931	295	3,114	222	157
Teachers, school	1	1,861	14	209	8	3
Waitresses	2	355	26	48	7	9
All other occupations	4	3,380	80	131	46	7

Source: "Negro Females 10 Years of Age and Over Gainfully Employed: by States: 1910." U.S. Bureau of the Census. *Negro Population, 1790-1915*. Washington, D.C.: Government Printing Office, 1918, p. 522. Adapted by the Editors.

★ 1413 ★

Occupations

Women: Distribution in Occupations, 1910 and 1920

	1910	1920
Agriculture	1,051,137	612,261
Professional Service	30,071	39,127
Domestic and Personal Service	852,812	790,631
Trade and Transportation	11,521	23,950
Manufacturing and Mechanical Pursuits	68,440	105,320
Total	2,013,981	1,571,289

Source: "Distribution Negro Females in Gainful Occupations: 1910 and 1920," Monroe N. Work, ed., *Negro Year Book: An Annual Encyclopedia of the Negro, 1925-26*, p. 364.

★ 1414 ★

Occupations

Women: Distribution in Same Occupations: 1910 and 1920

	1910	1920
Musicians and Teachers of Music	2,347	2,150
Iron, Steel and other Metal Industries	349	2,208
Elevator Tenders and Managers	1	3,073
Nurses, Trained	2,158	3,199
Business (Storekeepers, etc.)	3,200	3,440
Restaurant, Cafe and Lunchroom Keepers	2,734	3,455
Lumber and Furniture Industries	1,456	4,066
Janitresses	2,124	5,448
Ladies' Maids	10,239	5,488
Clerks in Stores, etc.	2,898	5,932

[Continued]

★ 1414 ★

Women: Distribution in Same Occupations: 1910 and 1920

[Continued]

	1910	1920
Laborers, General	6,159	6,968
Char Women and Cleaners	6,962	7,183
Textile Industries	2,234	7,257
Food Industries	6,347	7,724
Clothing Industries	2,003	7,861
Bookkeepers, Stenographers, etc.	2,941	8,301
Boarding and Lodging House Keepers	9,183	9,536
Chamber Maids	14,071	10,443
Hairdressers and Manicurists	3,782	12,660
Housekeepers	9,911	13,250
Nurses (Not Trained)	17,874	13,888
Waitresses	7,377	14,155
Laundresses (In Laundries)	10,371	21,084
Cigar and Tobacco Factory Workers	10,746	21,829
Dressmakers and Seamstresses	38,277	26,961
Teachers	22,528	29,244
Farmers	79,308	79,893
Farm Laborers (Working Out)	263,403	162,443
Cooks	205,584	168,710
Other Servants	184,889	216,376
Laundresses (Not in Laundries)	361,551	283,557
Farm Laborers (Home Farm)	704,150	364,878
Total	1,997,207	1,532,620

Source: "Occupations in Which in 1920 There Were at Least 2,000 Negro Women and Number of Negro Women in These Same Occupations in 1910," Monroe N. Work, ed., *Negro Year Book: An Annual Encyclopedia of the Negro, 1925-26*, p. 364.

Placement

★ 1415 ★

Male Job Seekers by Occupations, 1941

Occupational Group	Total	Non-white	
		Number	% of total
All occupations	2,991,642	370,258	12.4
Professional and managerial	116,128	4,933	4.2
Clerical and sales	245,184	6,113	2.5
Service	229,233	68,689	30.0
Agricultural, fishery, and forestry	272,786	37,777	13.8
Skilled	671,086	26,515	4.0

[Continued]

★ 1415 ★

Male Job Seekers by Occupations, 1941

[Continued]

Occupational Group	Total	Non-white Number	Non-white % of total
Semiskilled	614,347	56,007	9.1
Unskilled	758,219	162,126	21.3
Unassigned[1]	84,659	8,098	9.6

Source: "Male Job Seekers Registered in the Public Employment Offices, by Occupational Group, by Color, April 1941," Florence Muray, ed. *The Negro Handbook,* 1942, p. 89. *Notes:* 1. Includes unemployables, recent students, persons without work experience, and unspecified.

★ 1416 ★

Placement

Placement of Job Seekers, 1941

Month	Selected skilled and semi-skilled occupations[1] (I)	Twenty selected defense industries[2] (II)	All industries (III)	Con-struction (IV)	Manu-facturing (V)	Service (VI)	All other (VII)
Total	215,427	221,600	2,676,976	565,600	539,355	881,380	690,641
Non-white	4,443	7,382	534,350	128,274	35,432	288,146	82,498
Percent non-white	2.1	3.3	20.0	22.7	6.6	32.7	11.9
1940							
October	16,856	27,647	407,494	82,354	74,818	129,269	121,053
Non-white	287	1,503	78,685	16,077	5,665	40,611	16,332
Percent non-white	1.7	5.4	19.3	19.5	7.6	31.4	13.9
November	16,575	25,615	364,799	80,554	73,458	113,518	97,269
Non-white	415	758	73,363	20,440	5,593	34,787	12,543
Percent non-white	2.5	3.0	20.1	25.4	7.6	30.6	12.9
December	14,183	26,126	377,697	82,336	68,866	114,639	111,856
Non-white	432	1,063	69,527	19,331	5,209	35,004	9,983
Percent non-white	3.0	4.1	18.4	23.5	7.6	30.5	8.9
1941							
January	44,606[3]	30,743	363,163	93,182	69,993	124,447	75,541
Non-white	880	935	76,593	21,662	3,954	41,055	9,922
Percent non-white	2.0	3.0	21.1	23.2	5.6	33.0	13.1
February	44,546	31,278	344,335	88,096	72,647	111,434	72,158
Non-white	933	984	70,779	19,484	4,083	37,444	9,768
Percent non-white	2.1	3.1	20.6	22.1	5.6	33.6	13.5
March	39,305	37,085	376,308	68,849	84,411	127,061	95,987
Non-white	741	1,054	76,556	16,501	4,821	43,277	11,937
Percent non-white	1.9	2.8	20.3	24.0	5.7	34.1	12.4
April	39,256	43,106	443,180	70,229	95,162	161,012	116,777

[Continued]

★ 1416 ★

Placement of Job Seekers, 1941
[Continued]

Month	Selected skilled and semi-skilled occupations[1] (I)	Twenty selected defense industries[2] (II)	All industries (III)	Con-struction (IV)	Manu-facturing (V)	Service (VI)	All other (VII)
Non-white	755	1,085	88,847	14,779	6,107	55,968	11,993
Percent non-white	1.9	2.5	20.0	21.0	6.4	34.8	10.3

Source: "Placements of Job Seekers," Florence Murray, ed., *The Negro Handbook*, 1942, p. 89. *Notes:* 1. These occupations include most of the occupations important to defense production, but some of these placements were made in industries other than the "twenty selected industries" in column II. For a list of the twenty industries see table II in the source. 2. The quarterly totals here would differ slightly from those in Table II, which were preliminary. 3. The number of skilled and semi-skilled occupations was considerably increased in January and a few professional and technical occupations were added. This, in part, explains the great increase in placements beginning in January.

★ 1417 ★
Placement

Placement of Males in Defense Industries: Selected Months, 1940-1941

Industry	All male placements		
	Total	Non-white	
		Number	% of total
Total	154,673	6,151	4.0
Aircraft and parts	27,651	68	.2
Automobiles and automobile equipment	10,889	272	2.5
Clocks and watches	677	0	0
Electrical machinery	13,100	75	.6
Hardwood distillation, charcoal, and naval stores	158	21	13.3
industrial chemicals	10,322	1,218	11.8
Industrial rubber goods	515	2	.4
Iron and steel and their products	30,103	1,472	4.9
Lighting fixtures	944	30	3.2
Machinery (except electrical)	29,674	624	2.1
Miscellaneous chemical products	1,665	89	5.3
Motorcycles, bicycles and parts	100	2	2.0
Nonferrous metals not elsewhere classified	5,982	112	1.9
Petroleum refining	4,998	482	9.6
Primary alloying, and rolling and drawing of nonferrous metals (except aluminum)	1,672	19	1.1
Professional and scientific instruments, photographic apparatus and optical goods	1,409	26	1.8
Railroad equipment	2,795	100	3.5
Ship and boat building and repairing	10,674	1,500	14.1

[Continued]

★ 1417 ★

Placement of Males in Defense Industries: Selected Months, 1940-1941

[Continued]

Industry	All male placements		
	Total	Non-white	
		Number	% of total
Surgical, medical, and dental instruments, equipment, and supplies	759	22	2.9
Tires and inner tubes	586	17	2.9

Source: "Placements of Males by Public Employment Offices in 20 Major Defense Industries, October 1940 through March 1941," Florence Murray, ed., *The Negro Handbook*, 1942, p. 88.

★ 1418 ★

Placement

Placement of Workers Important to National Defense: Select Months, 1940-1941

Selected Defense Occupations	October-December 1940			January-March 1941		
	Total	Non-white[2]	Percent Non-white	Total	Non-white[2]	Percent Non-white
Aircraft	2,269	1	.05	8,769	13	.1
Building construction	13,121	722	5.5	69,637	2,061	3.0
Electrical equipment	1,716	18	1.0	1,066	5	.5
Metal trades[3]	24,524	231	.9	34,834	245	.7
Optical goods	101	1	1.0	213[4]	1	.5
Shipbuilding	759	39	5.1	1,499	25	1.7

Source: "Placements of Workers in Selected Essential Skilled and Semiskilled Occupations Important to National Defense, by Color, October-December 1940 and January-March 1941," Florence Murray, ed., *The Negro Handbook*, 1942, p. 87. Primary source: Division of Research and Statistics, Bureau of Employment Security. *Notes:* 1. The two quarters are not comparable, since a considerable number of occupations were added beginning in January. 2. Nearly all "non-white" placements are Negro placements. 3. Includes "foundry and forging, machine shop and machine tool, metal processing and forming." 4. Includes instruments, watches and clocks.

Unemployment

★ 1419 ★

Male Unemployment Rates by Race, Age, and Region, 1940-1970

Characteristic	1940	1950	1960	1970
Black				
Less than 12 years				
Non-South	17.0	10.3	10.7	5.7
South	7.1	4.6	6.8	3.9
12 years or more				
Non-South	12.6	5.6	5.9	3.8
South	5.0	3.3	3.9	2.4
Total	9.6	6.4	7.8	4.2
White				
Less than 12 years				
Non-South	9.5	4.7	5.5	4.2
South	5.9	3.0	4.9	2.8
12 years or more				
Non-South	5.2	2.3	2.1	2.0
South	3.3	1.6	1.6	1.3
Total	7.6	3.4	3.7	2.6
Difference (black minus white)				
Less than 12 years				
Non-South	7.5	5.6	5.2	1.5
South	1.2	1.6	1.9	1.1
12 years or more				
Non-South	7.4	3.3	3.8	1.8
South	1.7	1.7	2.3	1.1
Total	2.0	3.0	4.1	1.6
Ratio (black divided by white)				
Less than 12 years				
Non-South	1.8	2.2	1.9	1.4
South	1.2	1.5	1.4	1.4
12 years or more				
Non-South	2.4	2.4	2.8	1.9
South	1.5	2.1	2.4	1.8
Total	1.3	1.8	2.1	1.6

Source: "Male Unemployment by Race, Education, and Region," *The Economic Progress of Black Men in America*, p. 44. Primary source: Census of Population, 1940-1980; Public Use Sample. *Note:* Ages 25-64.

★ 1420 ★

Unemployment

Unemployment Rates and Ratios for Male Workers by Race and Age, 1955-1975

Characteristic	1955	1965	1975
18-19 years			
Black	12.9	20.2	32.9
White	10.4	11.4	17.2
Black/White ratios	1.2	1.5	1.9
20-24 years			
Black	12.4	9.3	22.9
White	7.0	5.9	13.2
Black/White ratios	1.8	1.3	1.7
25-34 years			
Black	8.6	6.2	11.9
White	2.7	2.6	6.3
Black/White ratios	3.2	2.2	1.9
35-44 years			
Black	8.2	6.2	11.9
White	2.7	2.6	36.3
Black/White ratios	3.2	2.0	1.9
45-54 years			
Black	6.4	5.1	9.0
White	2.9	2.3	4.4
Black/White ratios	2.2	2.2	2.2
55-64 years			
Black	9.0	5.4	6.1
White	3.9	3.1	4.1
Black/White ratio	2.3	1.7	1.5

Source: "Unemployment Rates and Unemployment Ratios 1955-1983 for Male Workers by Race," *Equality and Excellence: The Educational Status of Black Americans,* 1985, p. 7. Primary source: *Employment and Training Report of the President,* 1982; *Employment and Earning,* Bureau of Labor Statistics, November 1983.

★ 1421 ★

Unemployment

Unemployment Rates and Ratios for Women Workers by Race and Age, 1955-1975

Characteristic	1955	1965	1975
18-19 years			
Black	21.4	27.8	38.3
White	7.7	13.4	16.1
Black/White ratios	2.8	2.1	2.4
20-24 years			
Black	13.0	13.7	22.5
White	5.1	6.3	11.2
Black/White ratios	2.5	2.1	2.0
25-34 years			
Black	10.2	8.2	12.9
White	4.3	4.8	8.5
Black/White ratios	2.4	1.8	1.5
35-44 years			
Black	5.5	7.6	8.6
White	3.8	4.1	6.6
Black/White ratios	1.4	1.9	1.3
45-54 years			
Black	5.2	4.4	6.7
White	3.4	3.0	5.8
Black/White ratios	1.4	1.5	1.2
55-64 years			
Black	5.5	3.9	5.3
White	2.2	2.7	5.1
Black/White ratio	2.5	1.4	1.0

Source: "Unemployment Rates and Unemployment Ratios 1955-1983 for Female Workers by Race," *Equality and Excellence: The Educational Status of Black Americans*, 1985, p. 7. Primary source: *Employment and Training Report of the President*, 1982; *Employment and Earning*, Bureau of Labor Statistics, November 1983.

War and Non-War Industries

★ 1422 ★

Employees: Distribution, 1940

Unemployment Among Blacks Almost Disappears During World War II

Almost 1,000,000 blacks were added to the work force between 1940 and 1944, the Bureau of Labor Statistics reported in January, 1945. The number of employed men increased from 2,900,000 to 3,200,000, and the number of employed women increased from 1,500,000 to 2,100,000. During the same period, 700,000 blacks had been inducted into the Armed Forces. By the middle of 1945, the number of blacks in the Armed Forces had reached a million, and inductions were continuing although at a reduced rate. Unemployment among blacks almost disappeared, although there was ample evidence of under-employment in several sections of the nation, particularly in the agricultural South.

Source: "Workers in War and Non-War Industries," Jessie Parkhurst Guzman, ed., *Negro Year Book: A Review of Events Affecting Negro Life, 1941-1946*, p. 136. Primary source: Bureau of Labor Statistics.

★ 1423 ★

War and Non-War Industries

Employment: Manufacturing and Mechanical Industries, 1940

	Total labor force	Non-white[1]	Per cent
All manufacturing	16,500,000	1,256,000	7.6
Munitions	9,500,000	693,000	7.3
All other manufacturing	7,000,000	563,000	8.0

Source: "The Manufacturing and Mechanical Industries," Jessie Parkhurst Guzman, ed., *Negro Year Book: A Review of Events Affecting Negro Life, 1941-1946*, p. 136. Primary source: Bureau of Labor Statistics, Division of Review and Analysis. *Notes:* 1. The term "non-white" includes all workers not classified as white. Negroes constitute approximately 96 per cent of the total.

★ 1424 ★

War and Non-War Industries

Employment: Munitions Industries, 1940

Industry	Total	Negro	Per cent
Aircraft	2,100,000	116,000	5.5
Shipbuilding	1,700,000	192,000	11.3
Ordnance and Communications Equipment	1,900,000	122,000	6.4
Basic Metals and Rubber	1,000,000	103,000	10.3
Other Munitions and Metallic non-Munitions	2,800,000	160,000	5.7
Totals	9,500,000	693,000	7.3

Source: "The Manufacturing and Mechanical Industries," Jessie Parkhurst Guzman, ed., *Negro Year Book: A Review of Events Affecting Negro Life, 1941-1946*, p. 136. Primary source: Bureau of Labor Statistic, Division of Review and Analysis.

★ 1425 ★

War and Non-War Industries

Employment: Selected Manufacturing Industries, 1940

Industry	Total	Negro	Per cent
Lumber and Furniture	900,000	108,000	12.0
Stone, Clay and Glass	400,000	24,000	6.0
Textile, Apparel & Leather	2,400,000	94,000	3.9
Food and Tobacco	1,500,000	219,000	14.6
Paper and Printing	900,000	73,000	8.1
Other Manufacturing	900,000	45,000	5.0
Totals	7,000,000	563,000	8.0

Source: "The Manufacturing and Mechanical Industries," Jessie Parkhurst Guzman, ed., *Negro Year Book: A Review of Events Affecting Negro Life, 1941-1946*, p. 137. Primary source: Bureau of Labor Statistics, Division of Review and Analysis.